For Reference

Not to be taken from this room

Encyclopedia of the

NORTH AMERICAN COLONIES

Encyclopedia of the

NORTH AMERICAN COLONIES

EDITOR IN CHIEF
Jacob Ernest Cooke, *Lafayette College*

ASSOCIATE EDITORS
W. J. Eccles, *University of Toronto*
Ramón A. Gutiérrez, *University of California, San Diego*
Milton M. Klein, *University of Tennessee*
Gloria Lund Main, *University of Colorado*
Jackson Turner Main, *University of Colorado*
Alden Vaughan, *Columbia University*

SPECIAL CONSULTANTS
Mathé Allain, *University of Southwestern Louisiana*
Carl A. Brasseaux, *University of Southwestern Louisiana*
Charles T. Gehring, *New Netherland Project*
William C. Sturtevant, *Smithsonian Institution*

Volume II

CHARLES SCRIBNER'S SONS / NEW YORK
MAXWELL MACMILLAN CANADA / TORONTO
MAXWELL MACMILLAN INTERNATIONAL / NEW YORK   OXFORD   SINGAPORE   SYDNEY

Charles Scribner's Sons
Macmillan Publishing Company
866 Third Avenue
New York, NY 10022

Maxwell Macmillan Canada, Inc.
1200 Eglinton Avenue East
Suite 200
Don Mills, Ontario M3C 3N1

Library of Congress Cataloging-in-Publication Data

Encyclopedia of the North American colonies/ editor in chief, Jacob Ernest Cooke; associate
editors, W. J. Eccles . . . [et al.]; special consultants, Mathé Allain . . . [et al].
   p cm.
   Includes bibliographical references and index.
   ISBN 0-684-19269-1 (set: alk. paper)
   1. Europe--Colonies--America--History--Encyclopedias. 2. North America--History--
Encyclopedias. I. Cooke, Jacob Ernest, 1924–
   E45.E53 1993
   940′.03--dc20

93-7609
CIP

ISBN 0-684-19269-1 Set
ISBN 0-684-19609-3 Volume 1
ISBN 0-684-19610-7 Volume 2
ISBN 0-684-19611-5 Volume 3

3 4 5 6 7 8 9 10

Printed in the United States of America

CONTENTS

Volume II

CONTENTS

CONTENTS

CONTENTS

LIST OF MAPS

Volume I

Volume II

Volume III

CONTENTS

Encyclopedia of the

NORTH
AMERICAN
COLONIES

VI

LABOR SYSTEMS

HIRED LABOR
BOUND LABOR
THE SLAVE TRADE
SLAVERY

HIRED LABOR

THE NEED TO SECURE a permanent labor force was a critical problem in colonial North America from the outset. Colonization itself was labor intensive. Land had to be cleared, crops planted, and shelters constructed. All had to be done relatively quickly. Anticipating the need for extra hands, the Virginia Company sent over indentured servants. When possible, migrants to New England brought their servants with them. William Penn promised land in Pennsylvania not only to those who came as servants but also to the individuals who paid the passage of such servants and benefited from their labor. French laborers and craftsmen, reluctant to migrate, were persuaded by high wages and the promise of passage home or free land at the end of three years of service. Spaniards exacted needed labor from the local Indian population in the form of tribute.

The purpose of this essay is to consider hired labor in the rich and often ambiguous contexts of the colonial period. Broadly defined, a hired worker is one who works for others for a wage, whether in cash, in kind, or for some other form of compensation, such as maintenance. Most persons worked for others at some time, and wages, although frequently computed in the local currency, were apt to be paid in kind or service or simply used as credit in bookkeeping arrangements.

Findings on labor practices reflect the disparate national goals of the British, French, Span-

ish, and Dutch colonizers and settlers and the distinctive regional opportunities they encountered. The unit of production in British America was the individual household with the immediate family of the landholder at its center. In New France and the Spanish Borderlands, landholders filled a similar role but shared their position as organizers of production with heads of missions, trading stations, and military posts. The Dutch came to trade. Their settlements grew up around the trading posts established along the Hudson, Delaware, and Connecticut rivers. Labor needs of various colonial groups were met in a number of ways: by unpaid family labor, hired (wage) labor, contract (indentured) labor, forced labor, and slave labor. An overview reveals that almost all, if not all, regions in colonial America provide examples of the various types of labor. What is more, changes in broad economic, social, or demographic conditions as well as personal preferences and family priorities caused adjustments in the equation of demand and supply that resulted in shifts over time in the mix of labor types employed, sometimes within relatively small geographic areas.

In general, British plantation owners in the South turned ultimately to slavery; northern landholders developed efficient methods for retaining and utilizing wage labor. The French initially imported wage laborers under contracts that paid the passage home at the end of a stated period. The Spaniards harnessed the labor of the large Indian population. However, these broad statements conceal the complexity of relationships involved and the ingenuity and strategies necessary to reconcile labor needs with dreams of independence, family self-sufficiency, and upward mobility. Similarly unrevealed is the role of various economic factors including disruptions to international trade and the frequent shortage of cash.

Appreciation of the role of wage labor in the British colonies of the North increased greatly in the 1980s. In large part this can be attributed to the better overall understanding of the colonial period resulting from the community studies of the 1960s and 1970s. Previously, the study of the British colonies of the North lacked a unifying theme because their significance was underestimated. The gradual emergence of a permanent wage labor force in the rural North during the eighteenth century went unnoticed for the most part. It was generally assumed that the families of rural householders were able to meet most of their labor demands individually or collectively through the family or community and that the few who needed additional labor purchased slaves or servants. Hired rural labor was approached almost exclusively as a life-course phenomenon, as a means by which young persons could acquire the capital necessary for upward mobility.

The notable exception to this minimization of hired labor was the attention to the problems of the work force that developed in the port cities. Visible in the second half of the eighteenth century because of sheer numbers and obvious poverty, these workers have stood almost exclusively for wage labor in colonial historiography.

Work on the economic and social development of New England and the Middle Atlantic region in the eighteenth century by historians such as Winifred B. Rothenberg (New England labor markets) and Thomas Main Doerflinger (consumer markets in the Philadelphia hinterland) refutes assertions minimizing the labor demands of landholders in the rural North. Contributing to the increasing awareness of hired labor is the fact that American and European scholars have taken a second look at the industrial revolution and concluded that it was actually a process—a process of transformation from an agricultural to an industrial economy. Indus-

trialization began in the countryside and was associated with seasonal underemployment and cottage industry. It was not an import but had native roots, and industrialization can be traced in both the New England and middle colonies. This makes possible the broad social and economic comparisons over time important in overcoming the particularism of the community study. Wage labor can be placed in a context comparable with that of slave labor.

Wage workers appeared in numerous guises, as the following three examples indicate:

(1) In French Canada, New Spain, and British America, as well as in Britain and Europe, poor or orphaned children and young adults, working for room, board, and "clothing befitting their station," contributed substantially to the local labor force.

(2) Throughout North America local authorities regularly called upon adult males to work on the roads and to build bridges or even grist mills. When wages were paid for such service, they usually came from public revenues. The fines imposed on those who neither appeared for work nor sent a substitute reflected not only the value of labor withheld but also the inconvenience caused by their noncompliance.

(3) Labor itself could be used as a medium of exchange. Landholders repaid neighborliness with neighborliness, exhibiting community spirit. But the fact that they kept regular records on these exchanges suggests that an intense drive for competency (family well-being) within a cash poor economy lurked just below the surface.

To appreciate the full extent of the need for labor, it is necessary to look not only at the use of slave, forced, indentured, and wage labor but also at the strategies whereby landholders achieved their ends less directly. Tenancy, leasing, and sharecropping offered colonists a means of capturing the labor of others or a means by which to acquire the capital necessary for upward mobility. That is, it was an attractive alternative to using wage or bound labor.

Tenancy underlies the manorial arrangements common in the Dutch settlements of the fertile Hudson Valley. Large landlords subdivided their holdings and leased the land to wheat farmers willing to invest in improvements. The land was brought into production at no cost to the owner, and the farmer was spared the need to purchase. These commercially oriented landowners demanded their rents in "merchantable" wheat and frequently insisted that they be given the right to purchase surplus grain at the going rate. Since labor was scarce and wages high, the bargaining power of the farmers was strong, and the arrangements generally remained equitable.

Students of Essex County, Massachusetts, have broadened the issue of labor in colonial America by pointing out that landholders frequently chose to rent out part of their lands rather than to struggle with the problems of securing and supervising a larger labor force. The rental approach highlights a number of points of interest. First, it responded to the worker's desire for independence in the workplace. Tenants under the terms offered were working for themselves. Second, it points up the presence of commercial agriculture and market involvement. Ideally, renters had to be able to pay a rent and yet provide a competency for their families. Owners demanded a rent that allowed a return on capital. Third, it was a solution to the problem of scarce labor that was adopted frequently in areas of colonial North America where, because of the nature of the market crops, little was to be gained by economies of scale. Fourth, it fit the family strategy of the landholders. In a sense, to rent out land for which the owner had no immediate use but for which he or she anticipated a need, perhaps to set up a child, to raise capital, or to expand production, was to bank it at interest. Farm improvements deteriorated rapidly if not used and used carefully. Leases spelled out the agricultural practices to be followed, and in doing so they provided for the proper maintenance and even improvement of the farm. The land could be held without loss until such time as the owner or heirs needed it.

Cattle ranchers in some sections of the western Spanish Borderlands, an area extending from Texas to California, adopted a contrasting strategy for meeting the heavy labor demands of cattle ranching. To retain the openness of the range and secure the labor necessary to maintaining the extensive irrigation systems, ranchers with little capital requested that their lands be granted under a communal arrangement.

Groups of families, sometimes fifty or more—persons of Spanish, Indian, African, and mixed descent—banded together in a common effort. Families received individual titles to land for a home and garden plot, but pasture, woodlands, and farmlands were held as common land. Common responsibilities included the clearing of irrigation ditches.

WAGES

A general review of wage labor in colonial North America suggests that wage laborers weighed their opportunities carefully and were responsive to labor markets. The ebb and flow of indentured servants in response to conditions at home and in the area of destination is a prime example. Information about wages and prices within the English world circulated efficiently. A shift in wages and opportunities either at home or in the colonies influenced migration patterns. A lack of information led to indifference. The reluctance of French laborers to migrate to Canada has been attributed in part to the failure of immigrants to send back enthusiastic letters describing the opportunities for upward mobility.

However, the labor issue was double-edged. It was not merely a problem of obtaining laborers through immigration or natural increase; retaining laborers was also important. This could be done in a variety of ways depending on the labor force, as for example by withholding inheritance, by contracts, and by manipulating wages. In seventeenth-century Andover, Massachusetts, for instance, fathers were apt to possess title to the lands on which they settled their sons. By so doing they maintained their authority over their heirs and kept them at home during the years when the younger men might have chosen to sell and seek their fortunes elsewhere.

Wages provided an efficient mechanism for fostering a stable labor market and for retaining a labor force. In places where a wage labor system worked successfully, moderately high wages attracted workers by providing the opportunity to save and eventually attain upward mobility. Of course, if the saving could be accomplished in too short a period, the labor force would be depleted. In a few situations where a captive pool of potential labor existed, a solution (from the viewpoint of employers) was to combine a wage with a company store credit arrangement.

HIRED LABOR

Debt peonage created by freely offered credit lines could provide a stranglehold on the labor of those with limited opportunities. Debts bound wage-earning Indians of the borderlands to their Spanish employers. As was true for some Englishmen involved in maritime labor, indebtedness effectively placed the whaling Indians of Nantucket in a position where they had no choice but to sign on for one more season at the oars.

The seventeenth-century colonial governments experimented with wage and price regulations in an effort to establish social control over the free labor force. In New England and Virginia, central authorities and later town officials established ceilings on wages and penalties for employers who offered excessive wages. The governing body on Long Island set maximum wages to be paid Indians engaged in whaling. In various areas over the century, elaborate codes specifying wages by skill and task developed but were allowed to die out in the eighteenth century except during wars or rapid inflation. On the one hand, the English in the West Indies determined minimum wages and maintenance standards to assure a continued supply of white labor; on the other hand, in the French Caribbean laws set maximum wage scales. Little effort was made in the colonies of the British mainland to regulate wages by law in the eighteenth century. Comparative analysis shows that hiring practices were similar to those common to eighteenth-century England. Laborers living at home, smallholders, and artisans hired for the day or for a short period usually were taken on to perform specific tasks: for instance, to help in the field at harvest, build new stairs, assist masons, or make bricks. Generally wages were set by custom, task, and level of skill with an additional sum if the workers did not require room and board; that is, if they "found for themselves."

Laborers who lived in the household or cottages of their employers were hired by the month, the season, or the year at customary wages reflecting seasonal labor demands. Harvest wages were highest, winter wages were lowest, and common wages fell somewhere in between. Included in labor agreements with these wage workers were numerous fringe benefits, varying from case to case, that increase the problems of comparative analysis. Did the workers have the right to gather wood, or did they pay

by the cord, and if the latter, at what rate? Was washing included in the agreement or was it extra? Did the harvest wage include rum? Who provided feed for the farmer's horse when it was rented by the worker to plow his garden plot? The account books of the eighteenth century indicate that wages were often adjusted within such arrangements.

Changes in wage rates often are useful indicators of new methods of production or economic swings. An increase in wages paid for haying in the second half of the eighteenth century marked the growing importance of that crop as stock was more frequently stall fed. The labor market was competitive. For example, since artisans were a potential source of labor during harvest, rising wages for carpenters caused farmers to raise wages offered harvest hands. At the same time, an increase in these builders' wages signaled economic expansion.

Wives and daughters of wage workers must be included in any count of the wage labor force. Their contributions to family incomes were often essential to either upward mobility or family security. For the most part, married women engaged in cottage-type industries within their homes at piece rates and only occasionally worked outside the home by the day. Single women hired as domestics or dairymaids "came to live."

Wages of live-in servants (male or female) usually included room and board. Wages for domestics were generally quoted at a weekly rate, and days missed (not worked) were deducted accordingly. Variation of wage rates within the same household indicated differences in tasks, skills, and ages. The earnings, for instance, of housekeepers reflected their greater responsibilities and status within the household. Women with special skills (tailors, spinners, weavers, midwives, and nurses) went from home to home. They stayed only until a household's needs were met, as did men of similar skill.

The extent to which women worked in the fields is a matter of debate. Women who were dependent on wages or wives and daughters in New England households that relied primarily on family labor probably did work both indoors and outdoors. Account books provide evidence that in areas such as southeastern Pennsylvania, where wages were commonly paid for work in the harvest fields, women were paid the same wages as men for comparable work. Women working in the fields at the wages offered boys were perhaps doing the same type of work as were boys.

The labor of minors was extremely important throughout North America. Children and young adults, still in their minority, provided a substantial labor pool. Some were sons and daughters of local laborers and some were children of landholders. In addition children were sent from France to Canada and from Europe and Britain to the British colonies to be bound out as servants until of age. Most children in this period, regardless of family income, spent time in the household of someone other than their parents. Children of the prosperous were apt to serve an apprenticeship and to pay for the privilege. Others, particularly those bound out at a very young age (orphans or children of the very poor), received only room, board, and clothing. Although youths in their teens at times worked for wages, these were apt to be paid to the parent, particularly in the case of children of poor widows. In periods of prosperity, families usually permitted daughters to retain some of their earnings to use as a dowry.

A REGIONAL APPROACH
TO THE BRITISH COLONIES

British settlers looked first to bound servants as a labor supplement, indentured servitude being particularly appropriate as a source of labor to settlements with abundant, affordable land ready to accommodate the newly freed. The success of the institution can be measured to some extent by the flow of servants into an area and in the subsequent growth rate of this population by natural increase. Ideally, individuals who completed their servitude by working for a number of years as hired hands, tenants, or sharecroppers accumulated the capital necessary to establish their own farms. They married, occasionally hired out to earn additional income, and raised a family capable of contributing to the welfare of the community. For many early colonists, servitude represented the first step toward land ownership, wage labor the second, and tenancy the third before the status of landholder was attained.

The transition from bound servant to wage laborer can be tacitly recognized by examining the following regional descriptions of wage labor in the agricultural economies of the colonial period: (1) southeastern Pennsylvania, which had a clearly articulated use of wage labor; (2) the Chesapeake and other slave societies, which represented the transition from servitude to slave labor; and (3) New England—a region in which scholars still debate the role and extent of wage labor. After considering the role of hired labor in the rural economies of British America, this essay turns to wage labor in urban areas and then to labor in New France and the Spanish Borderlands, with their somewhat different problems and approaches.

Southeastern Pennsylvania

The landed in the Philadelphia hinterland purchased slaves and indentured servants but also made extensive use of servants in husbandry and cottagers in the English manner. Unmarried or widowed workers were hired for a number of months or for the year and lived in the homes of the landholders. Generally the servant of this type was the colonial equivalent of the British servant in husbandry. The more distinctive group of workers were the cottagers, the married but landless laborers and artisans referred to on Pennsylvania tax lists as inmates. As defined by usage, inmates were nonlandholding heads of households (married men, widows, and widowers). In England at the time, similar workers were referred to as cottagers. The two terms will be used interchangeably in this essay. Some were laborers and some were highly skilled artisans, but all were dependent on wages and the landholders for living space. Through the colonial period many cottagers supplemented their wages by engaging in home manufacture.

In 1740 the names of eleven cottagers appeared on the tax lists for Chester County, the county that is frequently used as a model for the Philadelphia hinterland. By 1760 approximately one out of every five householders was a cottager. Their increase in numbers paralleled the rise in land prices and the landholders' need for a large but flexible work force to meet the seasonal labor demands of wheat, the primary staple for export. Underemployed agricultural labor provided an incipient manufacturing labor force ready to take advantage of the rising prosperity of the 1730s; the combination of prosperity and underemployed labor offered incentives for diversification of agriculture and for the further development of biooccupational production. Farmers, both landowners and laborers, combined farming with the production of various goods and articles for local markets. Commercial wheat farming, as a household operation, set a floor as well as a ceiling on farm size. Farm size was carefully maintained during the eighteenth century at what was considered for a given farm a market-viable unit. For landholders the issue was not only to obtain a labor force but to retain one without reducing farm sizes, which would reduce profits and flexibility. Wheat farming required a large labor force during the planting and harvesting seasons but a much smaller one during most of the year. Agricultural diversification and cottage industry led to year-round employment for all involved.

Cottagers met the needs of the landed and the landless. The landholders gained a work force by offering a cottage at a low rent that was to be paid by work at wages set according to the seasonal demands. Cottagers, unable to buy or rent land in an area where most good land was already in private hands, bargained labor for housing. They agreed to work whenever needed at the daily rate for that job in return for a cottage, a small plot of land for a garden, and, perhaps, the right to run a pig and to rent pasture for a cow. The cottagers were assured of at least part-time work at customary seasonal rates. When not needed they were free to work by the day for others, to engage in cottage industry, or to follow their trade—weaving, shoemaking, or spinning, for example. They could marry and establish households. The flexibility of the arrangement was well suited to the uncertainties of the expanding economy of the eighteenth century.

As agricultural essayist John Bordley pointed out in *Essays and Notes on Husbandry and Rural Affairs* (Philadelphia, 1801), a cottager added not one laborer to the household but a family of workers: a man, woman, and a number of children. Bordley estimated that a cottager family (a hired man, woman, and their children) would probably be more productive than a comparable family of slaves with little possibility of

upward mobility through work. Furthermore, since cottagers and servants were paid only for days or hours worked, purchased their own clothing, and, in the case of the cottagers, even paid a modest rent, the cost of labor to the householder would be substantially less than if slave laborers were purchased and maintained. That he wrote this particular essay to recommend the cottager system to the farmers of southeastern Pennsylvania as a replacement for slave labor reveals how unaware even contemporaries were of the sizable wage labor force, and how far more conscious they were of the relatively small non-free labor force (slaves and indentured servants). Bordley's readers quickly pointed out to him that cottagers and live-in servants such as he described had long provided labor in the area.

In 1775 approximately 25 percent of householders were cottagers, moving between field and shop, supporting their families by wage labor. They stood at the foot of the tenurial ladder, but the possibility of climbing it seemed good. Their labor agreements continued to work to their advantage as well as to that of the landholders through the eighteenth century. Early in the nineteenth century, the union of agriculture and manufacture that had provided many with year-round work would slip apart as both agriculture and manufacture came to demand year-round wage commitment. In the process of transition from an agricultural to an industrial economy, the role of the wage-earning cottagers was a significant one.

The Chesapeake and Other Slave Societies

Slave societies in the Chesapeake and elsewhere provide examples of colonies where wage labor, although experimented with, was relatively insignificant in the long run. The present survey can only touch on the complex issues that determined this outcome. Indentured servitude remained the major source of labor in the Chesapeake through the seventeenth century. The supply of indentured (bound) servants remained relatively steady as long as those who survived seasoning could readily move into the landholding class, which was the case to about 1660. The flow declined steadily over the next thirty or forty years as opportunities for upward mobility through servitude began to dry up. The anticipated native-born labor force was slow to materialize in the region because of demographic conditions that plagued servant populations in the southern colonies: late age of marriage, high mortality rates, and imbalanced sex ratios. (Until late in the seventeenth century in the Chesapeake there were more than three men for every two women.) Moreover, even if a free labor force had shown early signs of natural increase, it seems likely that with land prices rising, a substantial number would have moved on to take advantage of the better opportunities available elsewhere.

Falling prices, coupled with assurance of regular supply, made slave labor an attractive and economically competitive alternative. In 1690 servants still outnumbered slaves, but by 1704 the situation was reversed; slaves had become the dominant labor force and were to continue in that role. Indentured servants did not disappear from the Chesapeake. They continued to be purchased to fill certain supervisory positions or to perform craft functions. But a dwindling number of servants was able in the eighteenth century to rise through tenancy to the status of landholder. Our knowledge of individual responses to declining opportunities remains spotty at best. Undoubtedly some moved on and some made do, but they spread the word that the future for servants was no longer as promising there as it had been.

The search for wage laborers in the southern colonies and those of the West Indies reveals patterns similar to those of the Chesapeake. For example, during the last decades of the seventeenth century and the first decades of the eighteenth, Montserrat, one of the Leeward Islands, shifted from a tobacco economy dependent on indentured servants to a sugar economy relying on slave labor. Studies show that only a small number of men and women survived servitude. Those who did found themselves locked into poverty. Given high food and clothing prices, restrictive land policies, fines, taxes, and skewed sex ratios that meant few men could marry and establish families, wages or profits to be earned as tenants or sharecroppers were inadequate. Incentives for servitude vanished. A slave market offered the planters a viable alternative. Wage laborers, when possible, left in hopes of finding better opportunities elsewhere. With few exceptions wage labor and indentured servitude were significant in the long run primarily in the colonies north of the Mason-Dixon line and in the larger towns to the south.

New England

In seventeenth-century New England, a rural labor market could barely be said to exist. The need for laborers that developed quickly in the Chesapeake and Pennsylvania was directly related to significant markets for tobacco in the first case and wheat in the second. But within the Atlantic trading community, there was little demand for crops suited to the New England soil and climate. Without a staple for export, the New England farmer had fewer incentives for buying or hiring additional laborers, had less capital to spend on consumer goods, and had less to offer indentured servants than did landholders in the other regions. The agricultural sector of the economy expanded slowly through the seventeenth century. In an effort to decrease the export-poor region's dependence on imported cloth, the Massachusetts Court passed a law in the mid seventeenth century ordering every family to provide at least one spinner to spin for thirty weeks per year at the rate of three pounds of wool per week. The law proved impractical, and the effort was abandoned.

Given an acute shortage of cash and credit resulting from an imbalance of imports and exports, the development of community interdependence and of a barter economy at the local level is not surprising, nor is the stress on self-sufficiency. However, during the first half of the twentieth century historians projected the economic problems of the seventeenth century and their social consequences upon the eighteenth century. They ignored the developments in agriculture and manufacture, in labor and capital, that led to industrialization in the nineteenth century. Building primarily on seventeenth-century literary sources stressing the importance of the family and community within New England society and concentrating on eastern Massachusetts, historians have portrayed the rural landholder as a self-sufficient, subsistence farmer whose family produced practically everything it consumed: food, clothing, household goods, and farm implements. New England historians writing in the late twentieth century have been righting the balance, restoring a sense of the changes taking place over time in terms of markets, labor, and mentalité.

Historians now think of self-sufficiency in relative terms. Seventeenth-century families probably produced more of what they consumed than did those of a later period, but data suggest that farmers made a conscious effort to produce a surplus to exchange for those goods they could not produce. Although community studies are not constructed in ways that yield estimates of the size and importance of wage labor in rural New England as a whole, the records for individual towns clearly attest to the presence of a wage labor force.

Records of hired labor in seventeenth-century Springfield, Massachusetts, a town unique for the period in its manipulation of wage labor, are particularly pertinent because they illustrate the threat of dependence that the New Englanders associated with wage labor and a cash market. In any given year, John Pynchon, son of the town's founder and by the 1650s one of the most important figures in western Massachusetts, employed half the population of Springfield for a month or longer. He managed to secure and control this labor force by placing most of the community in a patron-client relationship, a relationship of dependence. Pynchon dominated local politics, owned from 20 percent to 40 percent of the town's resources, and mediated access to world markets. Immigrants advanced through opportunities controlled by Pynchon. Even after they had established themselves as landed members of the community their interests remained secondary to his.

Community studies proved too particular to alter the long-held perceptions of historians. And Springfield was exceptional, if not unique. However, the records and methodology appropriate for such studies are also useful for testing broad social constructs, such as self-sufficiency. An analysis of probate inventories and another of the 1771 tax valuations for some forty-two Massachusetts towns reveal that few farm families had the tools and raw materials necessary for self-sufficiency. Furthermore, the study found that the produce of most farms in Massachusetts in that year did not meet levels estimated as necessary for the subsistence of a family of average size.

As in the case of the middle colonies and the Chesapeake, the analysis of account books has also provided new insights into the workings of the New England economy. The books reveal that eighteenth-century farmers not only employed day laborers but also offered live-in wage laborers monthly and seasonal contracts. Careful study of the accounts indicates market embeddedness and linkages between communities. They provide persuasive evidence of growing price uniformity in New England, which shows that the region was becoming integrated into a single market. New England agricultural wages moved more and more systematically in coordination with New York City prices, indicating that New England agriculture was progressively a regional export market within an even larger area.

Such findings have caused historians to modify long-standing views on hired labor and the New England community. Historians since the 1980s have viewed self-sufficiency as an ideal state in which the needs of the family were met by combining home and market production, with surplus paying for items not produced by the household. Communities rather than families were self-sufficient units. Through a series of nonmonetary exchanges based on use values, community needs were satisfied.

The networking of families involved in textile manufacture illustrates the communal exchange. Since few households had the raw materials and tools necessary for manufacturing the clothing required by a family, production was not organized on an individual basis but as a community. Some households kept sheep or grew flax; they or others prepared the fiber for spinning. From spinners the yarn was passed to weavers and then to fullers. The finished fabric was distributed and made into clothing by wives, daughters, or tailors. Labor and its product in various stages were exchanged within an elaborate network, well-delineated by local custom and understood by the women of the community, as diaries such as that of Martha Ballard testify. When data from diaries are combined with information from account books, similarities between the pre-revolutionary economies of New England, Pennsylvania, and the Chesapeake become evident and an integrated overview emerges.

A new definition of the colonial mentalité stresses "competency" or "comfortable independence" as opposed to self-sufficiency. Rejecting the familiar concept of self-sufficiency as a nostalgic romantic notion, historians are beginning to see the marketplace as a liberating factor. However, comfortable independence is, as is self-sufficiency, relative. Expectations vary from one person to another and tend to increase over the life cycle. To achieve competency requires constant attention; it provides the motivation for day-to-day efforts. The level of competency sought is directly related to family needs and to emotional rewards to be gained from further accumulation. Moreover, the notion of competency is linked to the concept of a "moral economy," in which it is assumed that those householders dependent on wages will receive a living wage and that prices and rents will be fair.

Urban Areas

Inequality in the port cities of Philadelphia, New York, and Boston increased rapidly following the Seven Years' War (1754–1763). Devastating poverty in these urban areas resulting from unemployment and low wages belied the promises of economic independence and competency. Between 1756 and 1774 the percentage of landless taxables in Philadelphia more than doubled. Historians find that the increase in poverty there was due to economic factors, not to demographic change. The rising level of international trade forced many of the smaller merchants out of business while elevating a limited number. Workers were powerless in this situation. Increased imports reduced the markets of local craftsmen; the substantial immigration of unskilled workers lowered wage rates; certain economies of scale accompanied the shift to larger ships, reducing jobs for seamen. In short, work was scarce and the heaviest hit were "the lower sort," families completely dependent on wages. The wages paid unskilled and semiskilled workers were too low to cover the minimum cost of food, fuel, rent, and clothing. Family survival was difficult, and facilities for poor relief were inadequate.

Conditions were similar in New York. In the third quarter of the century, the population doubled and the poverty rate increased fourfold. The almshouse was overcrowded, and out-relief revenues were strained by the number of families and individuals unable to find work and too poor to survive without public assistance.

Not only did poverty became a problem in Boston earlier than in the other two cities, but the last decades of the colonial period witnessed comparable hardship to that of New York and Philadelphia. The already high level of unemployment was exacerbated by an influx of landless workers from the countryside who had no claim to city support. Hundreds of families (men, women, and children) willing to work could not find employment at survival wages. The careful analysis of public records, particularly those records dealing directly with the problems of the poor, undertaken in the 1970s and 1980s, have not only increased the visibility of the poor but have led to a greater understanding of, and sympathy for, their plight.

NEW FRANCE

Labor for hire was for the most part in short supply in the French settlements until late in the colonial period. Neither land policy nor markets were such as to create a substantial wage labor force. To induce laborers and artisans to cross the Atlantic and work for even a brief term, usually three years, it was necessary to promise a prepaid return passage as well as high wages and a cash advance to seal the bargain. Individuals who chose to stay were given free land. Yet while workers from Britain and Germany compared notes to determine which of the British colonies was the "best poor man's country," French migrants saw their time in Canada as just an interlude that they hoped would advance their careers at home. As a group the French were reluctant exiles. In spite of the fact that land was free, only about a third of the workers remained in Canada after their term of service was over. More would have left if the authorities had not made it extremely difficult for them to claim their promised return passage.

As it became clear that the French population had little enthusiasm for settlement in Canada, the government took a more active role. The Crown made money available to pay for passage to Canada. After 1715 ships were forbidden to sail without a given number of emigrants aboard, although this regulation was often ignored. An attempt was made to have a stipulated number of able workmen aboard, but shipmasters generally were able to avoid this requirement. And so the labor problem remained.

The French reluctance to emigrate can be explained in a number of ways. As a people they were deeply attached to their lands, their families, and the Catholic church. Their country was not overpopulated. Reports from the colonists were not enthusiastic; letters did not urge friends to take advantage of the promises of free land. Instead reports from the New World stressed the dangers of the wilderness, the uncivilized life style, the poor wine, and the atrocities committed by the Indians. The problems of marketing farm produce and grain made farming far less attractive than it might have been, given the fertility of the free land. There was little incentive for the single man to choose it over the more romantic and profitable life of the fur trader. The case of New France eloquently testifies to the importance of cultural, social, and similar intangibles in determining migration patterns.

In the seventeenth century, the critical factor in the failure of the French government to turn the contract workers who did come to New France into settlers seems to have been the unbalanced sex ratio. Most of the immigrants were males. Those with wives left them behind, to be returned to as soon as the contracts expired. Those without wives either adopted the Indian way of life or awaited the day when they could return, marry, and raise a family. A decision to send women and girls from the orphanages was an important step forward in the process of colonization. Population increase in New France in the period between 1681 and 1765 and the gradual growth of a free labor force were the result of natural increase resulting from the importation of prospective brides. Once married, men and women established partnerships, and the free land was brought under cultivation. Farmers began to produce for wider markets. Sons and daughters of French settlers provided a population to fill the increasing demand for hired labor.

THE SPANISH BORDERLANDS

The lands over which the Spanish held sway and that are now part of the United States stretched from Florida across the Gulf of Mexico to Texas, across New Mexico, Colorado, Arizona, and up the Pacific Coast to San Francisco Bay. A survey of the economy of the area late in the colonial period reveals a complex picture of coexisting labor systems rooted in some two hundred years of conquest, settlement, and experiment: slavery, coercion, debt peonage, and wage labor. Conquered Indians were enslaved. However, for the most part Indian enslavement ended in the first half of the sixteenth century. Enslavement was followed by the institution of the *encomienda,* followed by the *repartimiento;* the latter, finally, was gradually replaced by free wage labor.

Military officers and government officials were rewarded for service with a formal grant of *encomienda,* in which a designated group of Indians and the necessary land to use them profitably was entrusted to their charge. The Indians accompanying the land were obligated to give service as well as tribute in kind. Technically, the Indians were not enslaved: they were drafted and coerced for tasks as needed. Although there was considerable overlapping of labor institutions throughout much of the period of conquest and early settlement, the *encomienda* was the accepted practice. Its imposition may have been eased by the fact that the payment of tribute by commoners to chieftains was customary among Indians of the area. As the holder of an *encomienda,* a single Spaniard might control more than a dozen communities and thousands of laborers and tribute payers. The institution depended for its success on the existence of a substantial Indian population. However, early in the sixteenth century that population was severely reduced by disease, including epidemics of measles, smallpox, and typhoid. As a result of depopulation, competition for labor in the Spanish Borderlands became particularly intense from the middle of the sixteenth century to the middle of the seventeenth. African slaves were imported to relieve the labor shortage from depopulation.

Encomienda was replaced by *repartimiento.* As before, Indians were apportioned among employers and jobs. However, an effort was made to encourage free Indian labor. Under *repartimiento* the Indians were once again offered neither wages nor credit advances, but landowners were to employ Indians only when there was work to be done that was in accord with the interest of the Spanish Crown. An essential difference between the *encomienda* and *repartimiento* was the replacement of the notion of personal service from the Indian to the holder of the *encomienda* with an assertion of the rights of the Crown over both landholders and Indians. *Repartimiento* assured the landed of a supply of laborers at peak times, primarily during planting and harvest, and allowed them to avoid the responsibility of supporting workers during the dead times of the year when they were not needed.

As more land was settled and markets developed, the labor supply failed to keep up with demand. Competition for workers increased and landholders began to circumvent the governmental restrictions. Indian craftsmen began to compete directly with the Spanish. Landholders tried to increase their labor forces by negotiating free labor contracts with individual Indians. They relied on debt peonage to bind their worker force to the plantation, or hacienda. Debts were to be repaid in labor.

Although draft labor was originally used in the silver mines of New Mexico in the sixteenth century, from the seventeenth century on wage labor was the rule. Throughout the colonial period, miners were the highest paid wage laborers in the borderlands. In addition, a number of mines offered workers a *pepena* (an allotment of ore from the mine). A steady worker could increase his wages from two to threefold in this way. The tribute assessments collected from ordinary laborers provided subsistence for these elite workers.

The succession of institutions governing Indian labor (*encomienda, repartimiento*, wage labor, and debt peonage) can be read as sequential responses to demographic change. When the Indian population was large, Indians worked under grants of *encomienda;* with subsequent depopulation more controlled exploitation through *repartimiento* was adopted. A continuing decline in population and an increased need for workers led to wage labor and debt peonage. Similarly the shift to ranching as opposed to labor-intensive farming reflected demographic change.

CONCLUSION

Generally, throughout colonial America where productive enterprises were linked to markets, free wage labor came to predominate. The South and the island colonies are the exceptions. Studies of labor in Pennsylvania show a growing dependence on wage labor and the development of distinctive labor contracts designed to accommodate the labor needs of the landed and the aspirations of the free but landless workers. Since the 1980s analysis of levels of slavery, production, labor markets, wealth distribution, and similar factors in New England in the pre-revolutionary period suggest that hired labor was more common there than had been thought and that similarities between the labor force in New England and Pennsylvania were greater than expected. The evidence of factory production at the end of the eighteenth and in the early nineteenth century north of the Mason-Dixon line indicates that, however much specific patterns and arrangements within the framework of wage labor between workers and employers differed, the labor force necessary to industrialization had come into being in both New England and the middle colonies. Few cases better illustrate the link between markets and wage labor in colonial America than that of the Spanish mines where, in spite of high costs, wage labor was employed almost from the start.

BIBLIOGRAPHY

Adams, Donald R., Jr. "Prices and Wages in Maryland, 1750–1850." *Journal of Economic History* 46, no. 3 (1986):625–645.
Bauer, Arnold J. "Rural Workers in Spanish America: Problems of Peonage and Oppression." *Hispanic American Historical Review* 59, no. 1 (1979):34–63.
Berleant-Schiller, Riva. "Free Labor and the Economy in Seventeenth-Century Montserrat." *William and Mary Quarterly,* 3rd ser., 46, no. 3 (1989):539–564.
Bidwell, Percy W. "The Agricultural Revolution in New England." *American Historical Review* 26, no. 4 (1921):683–702.
Carr, Lois Green, Philip D. Morgan, and Jean B. Russo. *Colonial Chesapeake Society.* Chapel Hill, N.C., 1988.

Clark, Christopher. *The Roots of Rural Capitalism: Western Massachusetts, 1780–1860.* Ithaca, N.Y., 1990.

Daniels, Bruce C. *The Connecticut Town: Growth and Development, 1635–1790.* Middletown, Conn., 1979.

Deeds, Susan M. "Rural Work in Nueva Vizcaya: Forms of Labor Coercion on the Periphery." *Hispanic American Historical Review* 69, no. 3 (1989):425–449.

Doerflinger, Thomas M. "Farmers and Dry Goods in the Philadelphia Market Area, 1750–1800." In *The Economy of Early America: The Revolutionary Period, 1763–1790,* edited by Ronald Hoffman, John J. McCusker, and Russell R. Menard. Charlottesville, Va., 1988.

Dunn, Richard S. "Servants and Slaves: The Recruitment and Employment of Labor." In *Colonial British America: Essays in the New History of the Early Modern Era,* edited by Jack P. Greene and J. R. Pole. Baltimore, Md., 1984.

Earle, Carville, and Ronald Hoffman. "The Foundation of the Modern Economy: Agriculture and the Costs of Labor in the United States and England, 1800–60." *American Historical Review* 85, no. 5 (1980):1055–1094.

Eccles, W. J. *The Canadian Frontier, 1534–1760.* New York, 1969; rev. ed. Albuquerque, N.Mex., 1983.

Gibson, Charles. *Spain in America.* New York, 1966.

Gongora, Mario. *Studies in the Colonial History of Spanish America.* Translated by Richard Southern. Cambridge Latin American Studies, no. 20. Cambridge, England, 1975.

Greven, Philip J., Jr. *Four Generations: Population, Land, and Family in Colonial Andover, Massachusetts.* Ithaca, N.Y., 1970.

Hall, Thomas D. *Social Change in the Southwest, 1350–1880.* Lawrence, Kans., 1989.

Henretta, James A. "Families and Farms: *Mentalité* in Pre-Industrial America." *William and Mary Quarterly,* 3rd ser., 35, no. 1 (1978):3–32.

Innes, Stephen. *Labor in a New Land: Economy and Society in Seventeenth-Century Springfield.* Princeton, N.J., 1983.

———, ed. *Work and Labor in Early America.* Chapel Hill, N.C., 1988.

Jensen, Joan M. *Loosening the Bonds: Mid-Atlantic Farm Women, 1750–1850.* New Haven, Conn., 1986.

Kim, Sung Bok. *Landlord and Tenant in Colonial New York: Manorial Society, 1664–1775.* Chapel Hill, N.C., 1978.

Kulikoff, Allan. "The Transition to Capitalism in Rural America." *William and Mary Quarterly,* 3rd ser., 46, no. 1 (1989):120–144.

Lemon, James T. *The Best Poor Man's Country: A Geographical Study of Early Southeastern Pennsylvania.* Baltimore, Md., 1972.

Loehr, Rodney C. "Self-Sufficiency on the Farm." *Agricultural History* 26, no. 2 (1952):37–41.

Loveman, Brian. "Critique of Arnold J. Bauer's 'Rural Workers in Spanish America: Problems of Peonage and Oppression.'" *Hispanic American Historical Review* 59, no. 3 (1979):478–485.

McCusker, John J., and Russell R. Menard. *The Economy of British America, 1607–1789.* Chapel Hill, N.C., 1985; rev. ed. 1991.

Main, Jackson Turner. *Social Structure of Revolutionary America.* Princeton, N.J., 1965.

———. *Society and Economy in Colonial Connecticut.* Princeton, N.J., 1985.

Menard, Russell R. "From Servant to Freeholder: Status Mobility and Property Accumulation in Seventeenth-Century Maryland." *William and Mary Quarterly,* 3rd ser., 30, no. 1 (1973):37–64.

Merrill, Michael. "Cash Is Good to Eat: Self-Sufficiency and Exchange in the Rural Economy of the United States." *Radical History Review* 3, no. 1 (1977):42–71.

Merwick, Donna. *Possessing Albany, 1630–1710: The Dutch and English Experiences.* Cambridge, England, 1990.

Moogk, Peter N. "Reluctant Exiles: Emigrants from France in Canada Before 1760." *William and Mary Quarterly,* 3rd ser., 46, no. 3 (1989):463–505.

Morris, Richard B. *Government and Labor in Early America.* New York, 1946.

Nash, Gary B. "Urban Wealth and Poverty in Pre-Revolutionary America." *Journal of Interdisciplinary History* 4 (1976):545–584.

Pruitt, Bettye Hobbs. "Self-Sufficiency and the Agricultural Economy of Eighteenth-Century Massachusetts." *William and Mary Quarterly,* 3rd ser., 41, no. 3 (1984):333–364.

Riley, James D. "Crown Law and Rural Labor in New Spain: The Status of *Gañanes* during the Eighteenth Century." *Hispanic American Historical Review* 64, no. 2 (1984):259–285.

Rothenberg, Winifred B. *From Market Places to a Market Economy: The Transformation of Rural Massachusetts, 1750–1850.* Chicago, 1992.

———. "The Market and Massachusetts Farmers: Reply." *Journal of Economic History.* 43 (1983):479–480. See the Weiss "Comment" below.

Salinger, Sharon V. "Artisans, Journeymen, and the Transformation of Labor in Late Eighteenth-Century Philadelphia." *William and Mary Quarterly,* 3rd ser., 40, no. 1 (1983):62–84.

Shammas, Carole. "How Self-Sufficient Was Early America?" *Journal of Interdisciplinary History* 13, no. 2 (1978):247–272.

Smith, Billy G. *The "Lower Sort": Philadelphia's Laboring People, 1750–1800.* Ithaca, N.Y., 1990.

14

Steinfeld, Robert J. *The Invention of Free Labor: The Employment Relation in English and American Law and Culture, 1350–1870.* Chapel Hill, N.C., 1991.

Thomas, David Hurst, ed. *Columbian Consequences.* Vol. 1, *Archeological and Historical Perspectives on the Spanish Borderlands West.* Vol. 2, *Archeological and Historical Perspectives on the Spanish Borderlands East.* Washington, D.C., 1989–1990.

U.S. Department of Agriculture. *History of Wages in the United States from Colonial Times to 1928.* Bureau of Labor Statistics Bulletin No. 604. Washington, D.C., 1934. Includes Supplement, 1929–1933.

Vickers, Daniel. "Competency and Competition: Economic Culture in Early America." *William and Mary Quarterly,* 3rd ser., 47, no. 1 (1990):3–29.

Walett, Francis G., ed., *Diary of Ebenezer Parkman, 1719–1755.* Worcester, Mass., 1974.

Weber, David J. *Foreigners in Their Native Land: Historical Roots of the Mexican Americans.* Albuquerque, N.Mex., 1973.

———. *New Spain's Far Northern Frontier: Essays on Spain in the American West, 1540–1821.* Albuquerque, N.Mex., 1979.

Weiss, Rona S. "The Market and Massachusetts Farmers, 1750–1850: Comment." *Journal of Economic History* 43, no. 2 (1983):475–478. See Rothenberg "Reply" above.

Lucy Simler

SEE ALSO **Bound Labor; Crafts; Free Blacks; Rural Life;** and **Urban Life;** and various essays in ECONOMIC LIFE.

BOUND LABOR

THE BRITISH AND DUTCH COLONIES

BOUND LABOR WAS ubiquitous in colonial America. It came with the first settlers and was still thriving as the American Revolution began. Many of the first Roanoke colonists were Sir Walter Raleigh's servants. Military-style work gangs composed of contract laborers were central to the Jamestown settlement. The first recorded black slaves to reach British America arrived in Bermuda in 1616. The original colonists of Barbados included servants belonging to Sir William Courteen, and a dozen indentured servants arrived on the *Mayflower*. On the eve of the American Revolution, Dr. Andrew Turnbull brought fourteen hundred Italian, Greek, and Minorcan servants, bound to lengthy terms, to his New Smyrna settlement in East Florida, where they were subjected to a fearful labor discipline; a year before the Declaration of Independence, George Washington bought a group of servants and marched them to his twenty-thousand-acre (8,000-hectare) tract on the Great Kanawha River in Ohio; and in 1783 George Salmon, a prominent Maryland merchant, even arranged for the resumption of the convict trade to his newly independent state.

Directly or indirectly bound labor touched everyone. It encompassed the lowly and occa-sionally the famous: Shetlander John Harrower, who sold himself for four years of bonded servi-tude and died in Virginia before his term was out; Sarah Gambrell, a teenage servant in Mid-dlesex County, Virginia, beaten to death by the mistress of the house in which she boarded; statesman and scientist Benjamin Franklin, ap-prenticed at the age of twelve to learn the print-er's trade in Boston; and Colonel Henry Morgan, lieutenant governor of Jamaica, who arrived in Barbados in the 1640s as an indentured servant. Bound labor embraced all ethnic and racial groups: the Indian debtor bound as a servant to work at least two years on a Nantucket whaling boat; the Dutch servant who signed on for three or four years with the West India Company in New Netherland; the German family that arrived in Pennsylvania and bound its eldest son to help pay off the costs of transportation; the Irish Catholic soldier captured in Oliver Cromwell's campaigns and shipped as a prisoner of war to Montserrat; and the African slave brought involuntarily to work on tobacco quarters in the Chesapeake, rice plantations in low-country South Carolina and Georgia, and sugar estates in the Caribbean.

The omnipresence of bound labor is as evi-dent in the aggregate as in individual stories. Scholarship in the 1980s revised upward the number of bound laborers brought to the British-American colonies. The best estimate of British migration to the seventeenth-century Chesa-peake puts the number at 123,000, of whom at least 90,000 were servants. In the same century, about 200,000 British immigrants, of whom perhaps 150,000 were servants, arrived in the British West Indies. In his excellent study of the British convict trade, A. Roger Ekirch calculates that Britain banished about 50,000 people to its American colonies between 1718 and 1775. Another 100,000 or so servants reached American shores from Britain, primarily from Ireland and Scotland, during the first three quarters of the eighteenth century. If German redemptioners always entered servitude at the rate they did in 1771–1773, then about 50,000 became servants between 1700 and 1775. Finally, David Richardson provides the most authoritative study of the eighteenth-century British slave trade and calculates that 1,705,000 slaves were delivered to the British-American colonies between 1698 and 1779.

Combining these new estimates with older ones, it is possible to arrive at an approximation of the overall labor recruitment of the British-American colonies. From this perspective British America was unquestionably the land of the unfree rather than the free, for the vast majority of immigrants to the mainland and islands came either as servants for a limited term or slaves for life. Between 1580 and 1775, colonial British America imported about 500,000 white bound laborers—approximately two-thirds of all whites who reached the colonies—and about 1,980,000 African slaves. In other words nine out of ten of the 2,730,000 persons who arrived in the British-American colonies were bound laborers. Moreover British America was clearly the land of the permanently unfree rather than the temporarily unfree: the ratio among unfree immigrants was four to one. From the standpoint of seventeenth- and eighteenth-century immigration, British America was an extension of Africa rather than of Europe.

TYPES OF BOUND LABOR

Bound labor took three main forms in the colonies: apprenticeship, servitude, and slavery. Apprenticeship had the highest status, for the apprentice could usually expect vocational training in exchange for his labor and could not be sold.

Unlike the other two modes of coerced labor, it was not designed to secure overseas labor. Slavery had the lowest status, for it demanded service for life, was hereditary, and reduced the laborer to the status of chattel who could be bought and sold at will. Unlike apprenticeship and servitude, slavery was not a contractual arrangement, except between buyers and sellers; the institution essentially rested on force, and although masters provided food and clothing in return for the slaves' labor, it was a minimal subsistence. Servitude was a form of contract labor, like apprenticeship, but was less prestigious. A servant's labor—in effect, the servant—could be sold from master to master during the period of service; furthermore, the purchaser could employ the servant in any type of work. Servitude was therefore akin to apprenticeship in its contractual nature but was like slavery in its alienable character and labor demands.

The two major categories of contract labor embraced a number of distinct subcategories. Apprenticeship, for example, varied according to the originator and purpose of the contract. On the one hand, parents apprenticed their child to a family they knew in order to secure training in a trade or profession, perhaps even paying a fee to the master for the privilege. On the other hand, a local governmental agency apprenticed orphans or children of paupers in order to relieve the community of the burden of taking care of them. The educational purpose in the latter arrangement was often muted or absent altogether.

Servitude was even more elastic. Its most common form in the colonies was indentured servitude. Unable or unwilling to pay the costs of migration, an indentured servant entered into a contract with a merchant or ship captain, who paid the costs of transportation in exchange for full-time service for a period of years, commonly from four to five. The indentured servant was transported to an agreed destination, where his contract was sold to a colonist, who provided the servant with food, lodging, and clothing during the time the servant worked for him and with "freedom dues" at the expiration of the contract. A small minority of indentees, usually experienced tradesmen, were able to negotiate contracts for specific employment, where they were provided salaries or cash payments in addition to maintenance. Another group of servants—usually young and unskilled, and in some areas estimated to have formed about half of all the seventeenth-century immigrants—arrived without an indenture. They served by the "custom of the country," which usually meant longer terms than experienced by indentured servants. Yet another group of servants arrived without an indenture, but they generally fared better than the "customary" servants. They were redemptioners, allowed a specific length of time upon their arrival in America to raise the unpaid portion of the costs of their transportation. Only if they failed did they or members of their family become indentees whose length of service was determined in part by the amount owed. Other individuals might enter servitude to pay off a debt; still more because they had been made prisoners of war; and yet others as convicts who had to work off their commuted death sentences by seven- or fourteen-year terms. Servitude was a remarkably broad category.

To some degree all three major forms of bound labor, and some of the subgroups, had precise origins in the Old World. Apprenticeship was directly rooted in the English experience, where it had two basic aims: to provide skilled labor and to relieve the community of the burden of supporting orphaned or other dependent children. The system was put on a legal basis in the Statute of Artificers of 1563, which imposed a minimum of seven years of service for all persons entering an industrial calling. Servitude was also widespread in England. In a typical early modern English village, three out of every four males between the ages of fifteen and nineteen years had left home and were in service of some kind. "Servants in husbandry" lived and worked in the households of their masters on annual contracts. Overall, at any point in the seventeenth century, about one in eight of the total population was in service and around half of all the people in England were, or had been, servants. Slavery—or its closest English equivalent, villenage—had virtually disappeared in sixteenth-century England. However, while villenage was almost extinct, it survived in common law, providing a constant reminder of a sharply differing alternative to personal liberty.

Furthermore, Englishmen and Scotsmen occasionally proposed versions of involuntary servitude for their own poor that approximated slavery. In 1547, for example, a parliamentary statute provided that vagabonds should be branded on the chest and made a "slave" for two years; should the slave run away, he was to be adjudged a slave "for ever." The act was soon repealed, but schemes to enslave the poor continued to entice thinkers such as Andrew Fletcher of Saltoun in the seventeenth century and Frances Hutcheson in the eighteenth. Finally, Englishmen could hardly be unaware of the slavery practiced in Mediterranean Europe and Africa.

All three forms of labor underwent modifications and adaptations in their transit to the New World. Most obviously, there was a wholesale expansion of slavery in the colonial world. Furthermore, it was a notably rigorous form of slavery because of its extreme degree of economic rationalization—the single-minded exploitation of labor for profit—and the extent to which racial ideologies were developed as a means of controlling the enslaved. Servitude also became more extensive and more onerous in the New than in the Old World. Perhaps two-thirds of all the white immigrants to British America were indentured servants, and in many regions of the New World the early labor force was overwhelmingly composed of servants. Their ordinary term of service was not a year, as in England, but several years because of the size of the debt incurred in their transportation. Since they were under contract for a number of years, a master might buy and sell a servant "like a damnd slave," as one Virginia servant put it. Finally, because of the availability of cheap land, New World masters had little reason to treat their servants well in order to obtain a renewal of their services at the expiration of their terms. Instead the masters became primarily interested in extracting a full quota of work from them. If slavery and servitude flowered in the New World, apprenticeship withered. Guilds and the restrictive craft environment they fostered failed to take root in the colonies; the practice of importing already trained adult immigrants further weakened apprenticeship; and the ease with which a colonist could enter a craft, trade, or even profession led to scaled-down apprenticeships.

BOUND LABOR: BRITISH AND DUTCH

WHY BOUND LABOR?

The attractiveness of bound labor—particularly servitude and slavery—in the New World is often explained by the low labor-land ratio. Employers throughout the Americas lamented the scarcity of labor and, because free labor was in short supply, they also complained of its expense even when available. Furthermore, since land was cheap, workers who earned high wages could establish themselves as independent farmers, thereby continously depleting the pool of free workers. The availability of land and scarcity of labor, therefore, constituted a powerful inducement to recruit bound labor. Nevertheless, cheap land and scarce labor were not in themselves sufficient to explain a resort to bound labor, because neither servitude nor slavery took deep root in all regions of the New World—most notably New England, the mid Atlantic regions in British America, and New France. In other words cheap land tended to produce either a population of owner-occupier farms or an aristocracy and slaves. Which system gained the upper hand depended on other factors.

The extent to which a region produced commodities that were in demand—a bonanza crop—is crucial in explaining the rise of bound labor. A lucrative staple created a pressing need for large amounts of labor and generated a rapid growth of capital that could purchase bound labor. Moreover certain crops—most notably, sugar—lent themselves to large aggregations of labor on plantations. Plantation crops had a number of features that encouraged bound labor: they demanded a great deal of continous labor to grow, thereby lowering the cost of bound labor by increasing productivity; they necessitated a high ratio of workers to land, which reduced supervision costs; they facilitated substantial returns to scale; they allowed the division of the production process into a series of simple and easily monitored tasks that were best performed in gangs, a system of labor to which free laborers were loath to submit; they required a level of work commitment and submission to discipline that free workers were reluctant to provide; and they provided employment for women and children. For all these reasons, a vibrant export sector and plantation agriculture combined to facilitate a dependence on bound labor. Where these factors were absent, free labor tended to prevail. Thus in New England, the lack of a staple and the marginal productivity of the land discouraged a heavy expenditure in bound labor; rather, the farmers' offspring provided an inexpensive, efficient, and available alternative. Only in more commercialized pockets within the New England region—the ranching and dairying Narragansett country of Rhode Island, for instance—did farmers invest in bound labor in plantation-like fashion.

Differences in the supply of free workers, indentured servants, and slaves were also important in the mix of any colony's work force. The availability of free wageworkers from Europe was always limited, except at high-wage levels, but freedmen and sons who did not yet have sufficient capital to establish farms eventually became available as free laborers. Indeed in the northern and middle colonies of North America, where natural increase occurred early and rapidly, the pool of free workers eventually became quite large. The supply of indentured servants depended in large part on their economic opportunities at home and the comparative advantages of various colonial regions. The supply of African slaves was the most elastic, but substantial costs of procurement and transport kept prices beyond the means of many colonial purchasers. The composition of the work force depended in part on changes in supply.

CHANGES IN THE LABOR FORCE OVER TIME AND ACROSS SPACE

Whatever explains the precise nature of a colony's work force, three broad changes occurred in the overall composition of Anglo-America's bound laborers. First, in the early years of many colonies, English servants were a primary source of labor, and certainly of bound labor. To be sure, indentured servants were most important in the early development of those regions that produced staple crops for export. Thus in the seventeenth century, the Caribbean and Chesapeake regions received the vast majority—about 90 percent—of England's servants. But servants were not insignificant even in New England; in fact they were more common among the earliest settlers in Massachusetts than in the towns and villages they left behind. About one in five of the immigrants on three ships arriving in New England in 1637 were servants, as compared to one in eight in their homeland. In commercial pockets of New England—Springfield, Massachusetts, and Bristol, Rhode Island, for instance—servants were an important part of the labor force through the seventeenth century. The peak decade of seventeenth-century English emigration, however, was the 1650s. Largely because of improved conditions at home, the supply of English servants began to decline in the second half of the century.

As the supply of servants ebbed, the supply of slaves swelled. The second major change, then, saw African slaves supplant servants in some regions and become more widely available in others. This transformation occurred first and most intensively in the West Indies, followed somewhat later in the Chesapeake. Even where slaves did not take the place of servants, they became a more visible presence. Of course slavery was vastly more pervasive on the islands than on the mainland and on plantations rather than farms, but it was ubiquitous. Slavery was not a peculiar institution in British America. In New England the number of black slaves increased slowly but steadily from 1,000 in 1690 to 6,000 in 1720 to 15,000 on the eve of the American Revolution. In the mid Atlantic region the black population was larger and grew more quickly—from 6,000 in 1710 to 16,500 in 1740 to 35,000 in 1770. Eighteenth-century New York City was the second largest urban center of slavery in colonial British America.

Although Africa rather than England became the primary source of bound labor from the 1680s onward, Europe remained a significant supplier of servants to America. The eighteenth-century servant trade, however, was more complex than its seventeenth-century predecessor, not just socially but also geographically. Eighteenth-century servants were generally more skilled than their seventeenth-century counterparts (except for the burgeoning convict trade), because with slaves having assumed much of the field labor, pressures for unskilled Englishmen to leave their homeland became less intense. Colonial demand was now concentrated in the managerial, craft, and service sectors. Furthermore eighteenth-century servants now came less from

southern England than from Scotland, Ireland, the Palatinate, and the Swiss principalities. The final change, therefore, in the recruitment of bonded labor was the development of a more varied and skilled servant influx.

Just as the composition of Anglo-America's labor force changed over time, variations across space were also important. There was not one colonial American bound labor system, but many. In highly diverse work environments, Anglo-Americans developed different methods of supplying their labor needs and different combinations of free and unfree labor. The watchwords everywhere were flexibility and fluidity as masters experimented with different products, responded to changing market demands, and calculated the costs and output of alternative sources of labor. A quick sketch of the composition of labor in four regions—the West Indies, the lower South, the Chesapeake, and the mid Atlantic—will suggest the complexity and range of possibilities in bound labor systems.

Of all British-American regions, the West Indies relied most heavily on bound labor and shifted most quickly from servitude to slavery. Barbados was the pioneer, and thus merits particular study, but the Leeward Islands and Jamaica followed its lead. Before 1640 Barbados was primarily a mixed farming economy. Its cash crops—first tobacco, then cotton and indigo—were not particularly successful, although each required progressively more capitalization and labor. However, the supply of indentured servants met the colony's needs, and by 1640 the island held about fourteen thousand whites and only a few hundred slaves. In the 1640s the sugar revolution greatly intensified labor requirements, and the white population more than doubled. A majority of the whites on the island were servants, and Barbados at mid century possessed—with thirty thousand whites—the largest white population of any British-American colony.

Largely because of the rigors of sugar planting, Barbadian servitude, Hilary Beckles argues, resembled chattel slavery more than traditional English servitude. As knowledge of the harshness of life in Barbados filtered back to Britain, young Englishmen became increasingly reluctant to risk a stint on the island. As a result voluntary servants bound for the West Indies received considerably shorter terms than those bound for the mainland as compensation for traveling to a less desirable destination; and from the late 1640s onward, the catchment for Barbadian servants widened to include a variety of involuntary servants—vagrants and beggars, political prisoners, and convicts. Not even these new sources satisfied the voracious labor demands of sugar planters, and increasingly they turned to African slaves. By 1650 thirteen thousand slaves resided on the island. The numbers doubled over the next decade as the white population began to decline. In 1660 blacks outnumbered whites. By then, slave labor possessed a clear price and marginal cost advantage over servant labor, primarily because of changed supply prices. Servants continued to fill skilled and managerial positions for another few decades, but poor whites began to leave the island and slaves became its mainstay.

The lower South, as befits a region settled by many former Barbadians, turned to slavery more quickly than any other on the mainland. Although the early labor force of low-country South Carolina was notably polyglot, consisting of free and indentured white workers, local Indian slaves, and black slaves brought from the West Indies—quite appropriate for a provisioning, lumbering, and ranching economy—half of its population was unfree by the beginning of the eighteenth century, when slaves outnumbered servants by seventeen to one. As the colony began to export significant amounts of naval stores and its newly discovered plantation staple, rice, the effects on the labor supply were dramatic. As early as 1710, servants had almost disappeared from the work force and slaves formed almost 60 percent of the population. Indian slaves were actually the most rapidly growing group, comprising a quarter of all slaves. As their supply dwindled from disease and white fears of alienating powerful Indian groups, South Carolina planters soon came to depend almost totally on Africans and the descendants of Africans for both their unskilled and skilled labor. Other parts of the lower South at first rejected South Carolina's example, but low-country Georgians and East Floridians soon came to agree with Henry Laurens, a prominent Carolinian merchant–planter, that "negroes are the most useful servants" in "southern climes."

Planters in the Chesapeake region discovered their staple crop, tobacco, in the late 1610s. For almost three-quarters of a century, they relied primarily on an indentured servant labor force to grow it. Tobacco neither generated as much profit nor demanded as much labor as rice or sugar. Servants sufficed because they cost less than slaves and their supply grew, peaking between 1650 and 1680. This high point in servant immigration to the Chesapeake was no accident: by 1650 the West Indies' bad reputation was well-known and the tobacco coast became the most attractive destination for servants, while by 1680 emigration from England had slackened, economic opportunities for freedmen were deteriorating in the Chesapeake, and the emergence of Pennsylvania, and to a lesser extent the Carolinas, siphoned migrants away from the Chesapeake. As servants became scarce, their price in the Chesapeake increased, indicating that the region's planters still preferred white to black laborers. Desperate for labor, Chesapeake planters bought more white women and Irish men than in the past.

But the supply of white laborers was insufficient to meet demand, so planters turned reluctantly to African slaves. Coincidentally slave prices were falling because of depressed sugar markets, and slaves became more available. In time Chesapeake planters became enthusiastic about slaves, who they soon learned could be worked harder and maintained more cheaply than servants. Consequently slaves gradually replaced servants in the Chesapeake labor force. However, during the eighteenth century many Chesapeake planters faced diminishing returns from tobacco; in some areas they stopped growing tobacco almost entirely, and everywhere grains became a significant part of the agricultural mix.

Moreover new sources of labor became available as the region's large white population began to grow by natural increase, forty thousand convicts poured into the region from 1718 to 1775, and British servants aimed predominantly for Maryland in the late colonial years. As a result many planters maintained economic flexibility by combining different types of workers—not just slaves but also white servants, both native- and foreign-born, and convicts. Many planters employed apprentices and hired workers on contracts, live-in servants, and local debt servants who worked either by task, share, or long-term contract alongside their slaves.

In some respects parts of the eighteenth-century Chesapeake began to approximate the labor system of the mid Atlantic region. The middle colonies had always been a mixed farming region, and bound labor was from the first a vital part of its labor market. Slaves and servants manned farms, tended livestock, and loaded and unloaded ships in New Netherland. Research since the mid 1970s has focused on Pennsylvania, the leading colony of the region. In the first half of the eighteenth century, servitude was primarily a rural institution. In early Chester County, for instance, landowners relied heavily on live-in servants, hired by the week, month, or year, to grow their grains, raise their livestock, and assist in their rural industries. However, from the 1740s onward land became more expensive, market activity intensified, and the number of landless laborers increased. Servitude declined and all but disappeared by the end of the century. Wage labor became the norm in the Pennsylvania countryside. As demand for servants and slaves slackened in the countryside, it increased in the towns and cities of the region. Urban merchants and artisans put servants and slaves to work as domestics, clerks, sailors, stevedores, cartmen, and craftsmen. In 1729 a third of Philadelphia's work force was comprised of servants and slaves, with the figure rising to almost 40 percent in the early 1750s. By mid century, in other words, unfree laborers had become more important for urban than for rural masters. The unfree proportion of the city's labor force then declined to about 13 percent on the eve of the American Revolution as urban masters, like their rural cousins, discovered that, with a surplus of workers, wage labor was cheaper than bound labor.

TYPES OF WORK

Just as the composition of a labor force changed from region to region, and within regions, so the kinds of work performed by bound laborers varied enormously. Masters employed their bound laborers in almost every conceivable task, from brute field labor to technically exacting crafts, in towns and in the countryside, on small farms and on huge plantations, in shops and in homes. Bound labor knew no limits; it penetrated every economic activity. To make sense of this bewildering variety, it will be best to analyze the differences according to crop or economic activity, size of work unit, mode of labor organization, level of skill, and degree of urbanization.

Economic Activities

Sugar was the crop that shaped the lives of most bound laborers in British America. It was universally recognized as the most taxing staple. It devoured thousands of British indentured servants before they learned to stay away from the islands and then did the same to millions of African slaves. Two-thirds of all the slaves carried to the New World ended up on sugar plantations. It is possible to grow sugar with free labor, but one might be forgiven for thinking otherwise in the early modern New World. "Not one of the Caribbean islands," Barbara L. Solow declares, "succeeded in establishing a viable society on the basis of free labor; they flourished under slavery." Slaves worked longer hours in cultivating sugar than any other agricultural staple; they toiled at three of the most exhausting operations—cane holing, manuring, and harvesting—known to man; processing occurred in a factory-like environment and at a frightening pace; and sugar slaves suffered such fearsome morbidity and mortality rates that not until the early nineteenth century did a single sugar island even begin to show evidence of a self-reproducing slave population. The spoils that this carnage produced were immense. Sugar alone provided 60 percent of British America's exports to Britain before the revolution and a fifth of all British imports; by the third quarter of the eighteenth century, three-quarters of New England's exports were destined for Caribbean sugar plantations.

After sugar, tobacco was the second largest employer of bound labor, but the requirements of its cultivation were quite different. If sugar was almost unthinkable without bound labor, the same could not be said of tobacco. As tobacco cultivation spread around the globe in the late sixteenth and seventeenth centuries—whether in England, the Netherlands, or India—it was nearly everywhere the product of the small farmer or peasant. Likewise throughout the history of the Chesapeake region, many family farmers grew the crop without the assistance of bound labor. In mid-nineteenth-century Piedmont Virginia, for example, tobacco was as much a free-labor as a slave-labor crop. One historian has even suggested that tobacco was intrinsically a free man's crop because it required much decision making and was not easily entrusted to bound laborers working by routine. What this overlooks, however, is the long cultivation schedule required by tobacco that rendered feasible a significant—although never massive—investment in coerced labor. Tobacco required consistently applied labor, not the crests and troughs of sugar cultivation. Its cultivation moved with slow and measured tread, not at the breakneck and killing speed of sugar. Since tobacco had to be cultivated with care, planters divided their bound laborers into small groups in order that their performance could be closely monitored. Slaves cultivating tobacco in the Chesapeake were the first self-reproducing enslaved population in plantation America.

Although tobacco had the reputation of a free man's crop, the consensus in low-country South Carolina and Georgia was that there was no raising of rice without slaves. One of the reasons for this close association was the length and laboriousness of the rice production schedule, which lasted from twelve to fourteen months. Among the world's cereals, rice holds the record for the manhandling it requires. The rice cycle was the most arduous, unhealthy, and prolonged of all mainland staples. The reclamation of river swamp, requiring large embankments, long canals and irrigation ditches, and imposing sluice gates, was a massive undertaking. Slaves dug about five thousand cubic yards (5,500 cubic meters) of swamp for every acre of ricefield as they constructed its banks, canals, ditches, and drains. The worst came last, however, for pounding by hand to remove the grain's outer husk and inner film—an operation that began in early December and could extend into February—cost the lives of many slaves annually. Low-country South Carolina slaves did not become self-reproducing until the 1760s—and then only marginally.

At first glance wheat and other small grains, with their extremely uneven and rather low labor demands, seem ideal free-labor crops. They required two intense but short periods of labor—at planting and harvesting—but then could be left largely alone. A farmer might well consider it rational to hire laborers for these occasions and thus be free of their maintenance costs. Indeed many New England and mid Atlantic farmers acted in exactly this fashion. Nevertheless the ownership of bound labor was certainly possible in grain farming. There were considerable economies of scale in wheat production, most obviously during the harvest but also in other operations such as ground preparation and threshing. The wheat harvest also demanded intense physical exertion; it was amenable to the harsh driving of gang labor. Moreover efficient grain farming required plowing, which in turn demanded draft animals, manuring, and fodder production. Attending to these activities were ways to fill up the agricultural year and keep bound laborers fully occupied. And everywhere—most notably in the late colonial Chesapeake and mid Atlantic regions—some grain farmers, usually those with quite large amounts of land, employed bound labor.

Although various staples dominated the working lives of bound laborers, it would be a mistake to overlook the other activities—often common to all work units—in which they engaged. Food production, for example, was important almost everywhere. Caribbean sugar plantations were somewhat of an exception, but even they devoted increasing time to foodstuffs as the eighteenth century proceeded, either by encouraging their slaves to grow food crops on their own time or by devoting some portion of estate labor to the task. On many plantations slaves spent as much time growing subsistence crops as they did staples. Increasingly, masters sought to employ their bound laborers year-round. Slack periods were filled with an array of tasks: repairing equipment; building roads; opening new fields; and so on. In many areas masters searched for secondary crops or crafts to complement the seasonality of their primary staple. In late colonial South Carolina, rice planters integrated indigo into their agricultural repertoire; in parts of the Chesapeake, tobacco planters added wheat to their cultivation cycles; many small planters and penkeepers, or livestock farmers, in Jamaica hired out their slaves as jobbing gangs or combined staple production with ranching.

Bound labor was also significant in more specialized kinds of economic activity. Bound and, particularly, slave labor was important to ranching and dairying in the Narragansett region of Rhode Island, the cowpens of low-country South Carolina, and the livestock pens of upland regions in Jamaica. Although monthly wage work was common in the maritime world, bound labor was also pervasive: most crews included at least one or two apprentices; procurers of seamen called "crimps" and professional kidnappers called "spirits" sold the services of many an indebted sailor and then received the sailor's advance pay; Indian debt peons were bound for up to two years at a time to work on whaling boats; many slaves and servants worked as dockers, stevedores, and fishermen in British-American ports. Servants and slaves produced much of the naval stores and cut much of the lumber of British America. Each North Carolina turpentine worker had a "district" of about four thousand trees and a weekly quota; small groups of ten or so slaves cut mahogany on a seasonal basis in Belize; and many bound laborers on farms and plantations alike cut firewood and sawed planks during the winter months.

Industries also sought bound labor. The manufacture of iron, Bernard Bailyn notes, constituted "probably the largest labor-consuming industry in America." On the eve of the American Revolution, over 250 ironworks, dotted about the mid-Atlantic and Chesapeake regions, produced about one-seventh of the world's iron supply. These ironworks employed about thirty thousand workers, a majority of whom were bound laborers. Indeed masters of ironworks have left us some of the most detailed calculations on the costs and benefits of free and unfree labor—and most preferred the latter. Most slaves toiled at unskilled jobs, including mining, carting, and woodcutting. Over half the work force produced charcoal. In some works slaves filled the skilled posts of foundryman and forgeman. Skilled German ironworkers were also in particular demand: in 1714 forty-two German ironworkers and their families bound themselves for three years to labor in Germanna in the Virginia backcountry. Shipbuilding was another labor-consuming industry; the colonies built about a third of all British-owned vessels. Construction in general recruited thousands of indentured servants, slaves, and convicts in colonial America.

Size of the Work Unit

The size of work unit was closely connected to the type of economic activity. Although sugar plantations could vary greatly in size, they were consistently larger than all other types of rural holdings. Indeed sugar planters created, as Robert Fogel has observed, the "largest privately owned enterprises of the age." In 1750 the average Jamaican sugar plantation numbered 140 slaves. Tobacco planters, on the other hand, rarely possessed large numbers of slaves, and even when they did, they dispersed them on small quarters. During the eighteenth century, the median size of tobacco plantations remained below twenty slaves. Rice, coffee, and cotton tended to be grown on estates that fell somewhere between the size of sugar and tobacco plantations. Other commodities—naval stores, cattle, and small grains—were generally produced on small units, although large livestock pens and wheat plantations did exist. On the eve of the revolution, between thirty and fifty slaves worked at most forges and furnaces in the Chesapeake region—far larger than the average tobacco plantation.

Whether large or small, plantation or farm, the size of a unit had important consequences for bound laborers. On small units, the master often worked directly alongside his bound laborers; on large units the master might not know his laborers. In some Caribbean islands more than half the slaves, all resident on large estates, belonged to absentees resident in London; some wealthy rice planters retreated to Charleston, a barrier island, or even Rhode Island for the summer; almost all tobacco planters, by contrast, stayed all year on their small plantations. The division of labor had to be fluid on small units, while rigid managerial hierarchies were possible on large estates. Planters with few bound laborers could not afford the luxury of an artisan, but specialization was feasible on large estates. For slaves, family life was generally less stable on small units than on large ones—the rapid turnover and large number of divided households were inimical to slave life. On the other hand, slaves on small plantations—especially in areas of dense concentrations of blacks—tended to marry earlier than their counterparts on isolated, large plantations because they were less confined in their choice of mates and could marry off the plantation.

Masters organized their bound labor force in three main ways. Provided the master had at least a handful of laborers and the economic activity was appropriate, the preferred method was ganging—a term almost synonymous with bound labor because of the degree of coercion it entailed. Under the gang system, bound laborers worked in unison, the pace set by one or two key laborers. They generally labored in carefully defined groups, often segregated by age and sex, under direct and close supervision. They toiled from sunup to sundown, and on occasion well into the night. Regimentation and discipline were the defining characteristics of ganging. Indeed Robert Fogel credits planters, and particularly sugar planters, with pioneering the development of a new labor discipline—the organization of laborers into highly coordinated and precisely functioning gangs. Planters spoke of "driving" their slaves; they employed military, machine-like, even orchestral metaphors to suggest their aims. Sugar was the archetypal gang labor crop. Dividing the labor force into two or three—by the late eighteenth century, five or six—gangs, the sugar planter emphasized the abilities of his "first row" men to set the pace for the other workers and of his superintendents to monitor their progress.

Tobacco planters also ganged their bound laborers, but Chesapeake gangs were tiny, almost never divided into teams, and were far less regimented than their Caribbean counterparts. Hard driving was counterproductive, for the tobacco plant was delicate and easily damaged by rough handling. On diversified Chesapeake plantations, gang labor was almost a misnomer. Squads or small groups of slaves had to perform a variety of functions; and while there might have been one slave setting the tempo of the work, there were often so few slaves in a group that the notion of their being driven was often inappropriate.

A second method was tasking. The size of the unit did not dictate the utility of tasking, and almost any economic activity—or at least some operations in any activity—could be tasked. Under the task system, slaves were assigned a certain amount of work for the day or perhaps week, upon the completion of which their time was their own. Tasking was common on rice plantations in the low-country of South Carolina and Georgia, on long-staple cotton estates both on the mainland and in the islands, in timber or naval stores production in Belize and North Carolina, on coffee estates in the Caribbean, and in a variety of miscellaneous crops, crafts, and industrial activities throughout British America. Tasking became more widely adopted over time and even began invading sugar regimes. Sugar planters, for example, experimented with tasking in cane holing. Many masters favored the system because of its precise measurement of output, reduced costs of supervision, and incentives to complete work quickly. Bound laborers enjoyed the latitude to apportion their day, even when their labors were not lessened. The self-regulated nature of the labor and the absence of direct supervision were the distinguishing characteristics of tasking.

Where the master had only one or two bound laborers, the question of whether to task or gang was moot. Moreover certain types of workers—fishermen, domestics, watchmen, and various tradesmen—could not be subjected to either system. The slaves essentially worked a full day, usually on their own, with no clear measurement of their output possible. Similarly in certain economic activities—most notably, farming—the bound laborer worked at a multitude of jobs even in a single day; neither tasking nor ganging was appropriate. This third way of working might be termed traditional jobwork—the laborer toiled until the job was done.

Skills Required

Different crops produced different magnitudes and repertoires of skilled labor. Some commodities required a near army of skilled workers; others hardly any. Sugar estates were literally factories in the field; consequently, a battery of specialists was necessary to process the crop. A typical sugar estate boasted coopers, carpenters,

26

masons, boilers, and distillers. Nearly one-fifth of the slaves residing on sugar plantations had occupations other than that of field hand.

Tobacco was almost the complete antithesis of sugar. It required little in the way of processing—little more than a shed to hang up the leaves. Even by the 1730s and 1740s, most slave men and almost all slave women worked in the fields. Over time, however, tobacco's low and uneven returns encouraged the region's planters, particularly the wealthiest ones, to hedge their bets by diversifying into crafts and engaging in import replacement. Consequently, skilled work opened up for some slaves. Such labor was available to far fewer slaves on tobacco than sugar estates, but the range of skills was greater, reflecting the region's growing commitment to diversification. On the eve of the revolution, many large plantations in the Chesapeake boasted shoemakers, tanners, curriers, blacksmiths, tailors, masons, millers, spinners, and weavers. The proportion and range of skills among slaves on rice plantations fell somewhere between the extremes of those found on tobacco and sugar estates.

The population beyond the plantation also had a direct bearing on the skills present within the plantation. As slaves replaced servants in Barbadian sugar fields during the third quarter of the seventeenth century, the still-numerous white freedmen on the island assumed many of the craft and managerial posts. Slaves would soon compete for these posts, leading many whites to emigrate, but for a time free labor was crucial to the sugar estates of Barbados. Free labor was also important in another part of the plantation world. In tobacco- and wheat-producing Talbot County, Maryland, between 1690 and 1760 over eight hundred free craftsmen found employment. Their presence helps explain the absence of skilled workers among bound laborers. Here, too, slaves would become effective competitors of white artisans over time. In another part of British America, the relationship between free and unfree labor was more complementary than competitive. The development of milling, tanning, distilling, ironworking, tavernkeeping, coopering, smithing, and wagonmaking in the mid-Atlantic region, particularly after 1750, helps explain why slavery grew more quickly in parts of rural Pennsylvania than in

Philadelphia. The free craftsmen who were making their way in the Pennsylvania countryside were able to afford the odd worker who could be put to year-round labor.

The Urban Environment

Although the boundaries between town and countryside in British America were not rigid, a distinctively urban form of bound labor emerged. Where slavery was marginal in British America—in colonies like Belize, the Bahamas, Massachussetts, and Pennsylvania—it was often concentrated in towns or cities. Slavery grew more rapidly and became more prevalent in Philadelphia, for example, than in the surrounding countryside—at least before 1750. In full-fledged slave societies, by contrast, only a small proportion of slaves lived in cities.

But in either case, bound labor in towns assumed similar configurations. First, towns in general contained more women than men, and female bound labor was in particular demand because of the pressing need for domestics, washerwomen, seamstresses, and marketwomen. Second, the latitude of urban slavery was best revealed in the system of "self-hire," as it was known, where slaves were allowed to find their own employers and pay their owners a stipulated sum either weekly or monthly. Third, openings for skilled labor seem to have been at least twice as great in towns as in the countryside. In eighteenth-century Philadelphia, for instance, over 40 percent of the city's slaves worked for artisans, mariners, and owners of ropewalks, shipyards, breweries, tanneries, and brickyards. Finally, apprenticeship seems to have been primarily an urban institution in British America.

THE LABOR FORCE

The Structure of the Labor Force

The structure of the bound labor force of colonial America rested on three major foundations: unending but varied demand; highly variegated sources of foreign supply; and extreme contrasts in the rates of natural increase and decrease of local populations. The combination of these forces—ever changing, both temporally and spatially—shaped the salient characteristics of any region's bound labor system. An analysis by class, sex, age, and ethnicity will uncover some of the key structural features of servitude and slavery in British America.

The social origins of foreign bound laborers is better known for the English than for other ethnic groups. Once viewed as rogues, whores, and vagabonds, and later as predominantly middle class, seventeenth-century indentured servants represented a broad cross-section of the lower levels of English society. Unindentured servants—about a half of all servants in some regions—were probably less skilled and of lower social origins than indentured servants. A majority of English emigrant laborers in the seventeenth century, therefore, appear to have had low status and little training. Most were laborers or servants in husbandry. It is also possible that the proportion of servants of low social status increased in the late seventeenth and early eighteenth centuries. From about the 1720s onward, however, the social composition of British servants became more varied. The English servant stream was still drawn predominantly from the working classes but included more artisans and craftsmen. On the eve of the revolution, artisans formed about half of all English indentured servants, including many from the most highly skilled crafts. British convicts, by contrast, were more comparable to the seventeenth-century servants. They were largely the working poor. Although some convicts were craftsmen, the majority held either unskilled or low-skilled occupations.

In the early part of the eighteenth century, German immigrants seem to have been predominantly farmers and to a lesser extent building craftsmen; by the end of the eighteenth century, they were predominantly retail and industrial tradesmen. Little is known about the social origins of African slaves, although the major techniques of enslavement—wars, kidnapping, indebtedness, and judicial procedures—suggest that most came from the ranks of the poor and defenseless.

Perhaps the most striking characteristic of immigrant bound laborers was the preponderance of males. But there were significant variations, particularly over time and by ethnic group. The English consistently exhibited the most im-

balanced sex ratios. In the seventeenth century, English servants were about 90 percent male before 1650 and 77 percent after 1650. Women probably became more numerous in the second half of the century because they were more aggressively recruited as the number of men declined, because they continued to be mobile within England and thus willing to migrate, and because demand increased for their services both as potential wives and as subsistence workers. In the eighteenth century, the proportion of men among English servants rose once more, to as high as 90 percent male among servants and 82 percent male among convicts. The number of English women might have declined due to a decreased need for them as wives and subsistence workers and an increased need in the eighteenth century for the skills offered by men. Other European servant groups comprised far more women: German redemptioners were 63 percent male, and Scottish servants were 60 percent male. Similarly, African slave shipments were usually from 60 to 70 percent male, although some regions, most notably the Bight of Biafra, exported even lower proportions of men—in many cases, roughly equal numbers of men and women. Women also usually outnumbered men among Indian slaves. In general, then, immigrant slaves had more balanced sex ratios than immigrant servants.

The effects of male majorities and their decline—and the many variations in this general trend—were profound. As Richard Dunn has pointed out, many early-seventeenth-century servant men must have been sex-starved. Finding wives once they were freed was also a problem. The pressures on servant women in the seventeenth-century Chesapeake are captured in the revelation that half of them bore bastard children or were pregnant at marriage. Moreover, labor-starved planters put some white servant women to work at the hoe, although with a certain ambivalence about the types of work proper for them. Planters had no such reservations concerning slave women. Once slaves predominated in the labor force, white women servants all but disappeared from the fields, while every able-bodied slave woman performed regular field labor. As progressively more slave men occupied skilled positions, the burden of field work fell disproportionately on slave women. In many parts of British America, a larger proportion of enslaved women than enslaved men worked as field hands by the late eighteenth century. One of the few advantages that slaves enjoyed over English servants was the greater availability of mates.

Bound laborers were predominantly youthful, but there were significant variations over time and by ethnic group. In general about two-thirds of the males and four-fifths of the females among English immigrant servants were in the fifteen to twenty-four age bracket. Few English servants below the age of fourteen migrated to America. Other European immigrant servant populations had much higher proportions of children and youths because they included far more families: one in four German redemptioners were below fifteen, while one in six Scottish servants were aged one to fourteen.

The age structure of slave shipments are difficult to compare with that of servants, because merchants were imprecise about what they meant by boy and girl. Much was guesswork, but most commonly they appear to have calculated boys as between the ages of ten and fifteen and girls as from ten to fourteen. Sometimes the proportion of boys and girls on a slave shipment was negligible, while at other times, quite considerable. In general the proportion increased over time and on average was about 10–15 percent early in the eighteenth century, rising to 20–25 percent later in the century. From certain regions along the African coast—most notably Sierra Leone, the Bight of Biafra, and west-central Africa—boys and girls regularly comprised one-third of the slave shipments. Immigrant slaves were, therefore, clearly younger than immigrant English servants and not that much older than immigrant German servants.

The age structure of the bound labor force, originally a function of immigration, assumed different shape under American conditions. In the Chesapeake considerable numbers of young children—landless orphans, bastards, and the indigent—were added to the servant population. Most girls served between six and twelve years; boys served even longer. Many native-born children of lower-income families entered service or apprenticeship around the age of twelve to fourteen, much like their British counterparts. As might be expected, slaves endured longer working lives. Some slave children entered the labor force—taken into a master's house to be groomed as a domestic, for example—at age four. By age seven many slave children were already working in some capacity; the process was usually complete by age twelve. A major difference between white and black labor patterns was the much later entry into craftwork for the latter. Few slave men were tradesmen in their late teens and early twenties. Apparently as slaves aged and their productivity in field work declined, masters shifted them into trades. Masters shaped age structures in other ways. On frontiers—whether in the islands or in the backcountry of mainland slave societies—masters sought especially young slaves, those who would be most useful in establishing plantations, who were often cheaper, and who were less familiar with customary work routines.

The bound labor force of colonial America, like the population itself, was ethnically heterogeneous. The Catholic Irish were particularly numerous among the mid-seventeenth-century servants who arrived in the Caribbean. They even formed a majority on Montserrat. English masters feared the Irish, relations between the two were often tense, and on occasion the Irish rebelled. The shift from a predominantly English to a predominantly German and Scotch-Irish servant influx has been pointed to as a major reason for the rise of a more impersonal, less benign form of indentured servitude in Pennsylvania. Planters distinguished among various African nations on the basis of their strength, resistance to disease, willingness to work, and ability to reproduce. In part such notions were shallow stereotypes, but these ideas also drew on the planters' experiences directing slave labor. The above-average height of certain African ethnic groups, for instance, seems to explain why they were especially valued.

WORKERS AS ACTIVE AGENTS

In many ways bound workers responded to their servitude in similar ways. They used many of the same methods to resist exploitation by their masters. They feigned ignorance, shirked work, injured animals, ran away, and as a last resort, confronted their superiors directly and violently.

At the same time, there were obvious differences in the responses of slaves and servants, the most critical, of course, stemming from the fact that slaves served for life while servants had fixed terms. Viewing slaves and servants as active agents rather than passive victims can highlight some of these similarities and differences.

Many bound laborers of all stripes resorted to flight to escape their bondage. Benjamin Franklin hardly labored under harsh conditions, working as an apprentice printer to his brother in Boston, but at age seventeen, four years before his term expired, he decided to renege on his contract by seeking independence and the main chance in Philadelphia. The fluidity of crafts, the size of the British-American Empire, and its many different political jurisdictions must have encouraged many an apprentice to imitate Franklin and flee their master. If the flight of bound laborers was commonplace, servants and convicts (and possibly apprentices, though no statistics are available) ran away at much greater rates than slaves. In 1682 perhaps 7.5 percent of the two hundred or so white servants of Middlesex County, Virginia, ran away. Among servants indentured in Pennsylvania in 1745, about 10 percent fled over the next five years; from 1770 to 1775, 3 percent of the eight thousand or so servants and redemptioners in Pennsylvania ran away per year. In Maryland in 1755, about 2 percent of the nineteen hundred adult convicts ran off, and at least 9 percent of the twelve thousand convicts who arrived in Maryland between 1746 and 1775 escaped their bondage.

The rates for slaves were much lower. For most of the eighteenth century, only one or two out of every hundred slaves in Virginia ran away in a ten-year period. On the islands and even in South Carolina the rates were higher, but even in Jamaica—where mountains were nearby and blacks heavily outnumbered whites—only about 1–2 percent of the slaves ran away each year. Clearly it was much easier for servants and convicts to mix with the general population or get aboard a ship, as Franklin did, than for slaves.

For similar reasons slaves, as Edmund Morgan notes with reference to colonial Virginia, proved "less dangerous" than servants. Servants became restive freemen who in 1676 fomented Bacon's Rebellion, the largest rebellion in colo-

nial British America; by contrast, "no white person was killed in a slave rebellion in colonial Virginia." Slaves, Morgan observes, "had none of the rising expectations that have so often prompted rebellion in human history. They were not armed and did not have to be armed. They were without hope and did not have to be given hope." Crime rates seem to point to the same conclusion. In the late seventeenth century, Middlesex County court in Virginia registered twenty-four misdeeds per one thousand servants a year; in the early eighteenth century, slaves stood before the court at an annual rate of only 3.5 appearances per one thousand slaves. Yet as Darrett and Anita Rutman, who compiled these figures, point out, part of the reason for this difference was simply that planters, rather than courts, became the slaves' judge and jury. Slaves were not more placid than servants, but masters wielded far more force over their black than their white labor. In other parts of British America, where slave population was greater relative to free people than in Virginia, slaves had somewhat more success in resisting masters. Major slave rebellions occurred frequently in Jamaica and at least once in South Carolina.

Bound laborers also sought ways to limit exploitation without resorting to violence or escape. They malingered, broke tools, feigned illness, or sometimes simply refused to work. Although the master was always the final arbiter, bound laborers were not powerless. They helped establish customary expectations about the pace of labor, the length of the work day, standard rations, and much else. But a key difference in the degree of influence that could be exerted by slaves and servants was that the former had no recourse other than the master, whereas servants could appeal to the law. Servants were able to sue their masters in county court; they sometimes won their cases, even though courts were composed of masters.

Most obviously of all, servants became free and slaves generally did not. True, a servant had to survive long enough to become free, and many did not. In the seventeenth-century Chesapeake, only about half of the arriving servants survived to freedom. The proportion was probably even lower in the islands. True also, many servants had their terms extended because they committed a transgression. Nevertheless, if servants could complete their term of servitude, opportunity then beckoned. The degree to which servants made good on these opportunities varied greatly. In the pre-sugar eras of various British-American islands, a few ex-servants gained access to land and rather more worked as artisans, but opportunities severely diminished once the sugar boom began. The chances that an ex-servant would acquire land and a responsible social and political position in the Chesapeake were quite high to about 1660 and then declined. Former servants could always emigrate when opportunities severely contracted; in Barbados emigration began in earnest during the 1660s, in the Chesapeake about two decades later. Pennsylvania was the best poor man's country in the eighteenth century. A majority of German redemptioners, arriving in Pennsylvania, established themselves as smallholders and artisans, and a handful even became highly influential merchants and traders. Opportunities for slaves, by contrast, were almost nonexistent. Although a few acquired freedom in colonial British America, the vast majority did not. Slaves had to take consolation in their families, their access to small amounts of property, their music, and religion.

The story of bound labor in colonial America points up the central contradiction of American history. America provided unprecedented opportunities for some, predicated on the unprecedented exploitation of others. The source of the contradiction's two sides was essentially the same. Cheap land allowed many to own land, but particularly where plantation agriculture was possible, led many others into bondage. What liberated some coerced others. Slaves were the most conspicuous and tragic victims, but they were also the most extreme examples of the coercion of labor so prevalent in early America. Liberation and exploitation were the reverse sides of the same coin.

BIBLIOGRAPHY

General Works

Bailyn, Bernard. *Voyagers to the West: A Passage in the Peopling of America on the Eve of the Revolution.* New York, 1986.
Dunn, Richard S. "Servants and Slaves: The Recruitment and Employment of Labor." In *Colonial British America: Essays in the New History of the Early Modern Era,* edited by Jack P. Greene and J. R. Pole. Baltimore, Md., 1984.
Galenson, David W. "Labor Market Behavior in Colonial America: Servitude, Slavery, and Free Labor." In *Markets in History: Economic Studies of the Past,* edited by David W. Galenson. New York, 1989.
Innes, Stephen, ed. *Work and Labor in Early America.* Chapel Hill, N.C., 1988.
McCusker, John J., and Russell R. Menard. *The Economy of British America, 1607–1789.* Chapel Hill, N.C., 1985.
Morris, Richard B. *Government and Labor in Early America.* New York 1946, 2nd ed., 1981.

Recruitment

Altman, Ida, and James Horn, eds. *"To Make America": European Emigration in the Early Modern Period.* Berkeley, Calif., 1991.
Emmer, P. C., ed. *Colonialism and Migration: Indentured Labor Before and After Slavery.* Dordrecht, The Netherlands, 1986.
Fogleman, Aaron. "Migration to the Thirteen British North American Colonies, 1700–1775: New Estimates." *Journal of Interdisciplinary History* 22, no. 4 (1992):691–709.
Gemery, Henry A. "Emigration from the British Isles to the New World, 1630–1700: Inferences from Colonial Populations." *Research in Economic History* 5 (1980):179–231.
———. "European Emigration to North America, 1700–1820: Numbers and Quasi-Numbers." *Perspectives in American History* n.s. 1 (1984):283–342.
Grubb, Farley. "The Incidence of Servitude in Trans-Atlantic Migration." *Explorations in Economic History* 22, no. 3 (1985):316–339.
Richardson, David. "The Eighteenth-Century British Slave Trade: Estimates of its Volume and Coastal Distributions in Africa." *Research in Economic History* 12 (1989):151–195.

Servants, Convicts, and Apprentices

Ekirch, A. Roger. *Bound for America: The Transportation of British Convicts to the Colonies, 1718–1775.* New York, 1987.
Galenson, David W. *White Servitude in Colonial America: An Economic Analysis.* Cambridge, England, 1981.
Rorabaugh, William J. *The Craft Apprentice from Franklin to the Machine Age in America.* New York, 1986.
Smith, Abbot Emerson. *Colonists in Bondage: White Servitude and Convict Labor in America, 1607–1776.* Chapel Hill, N.C., 1947.
Towner, Lawrence W. "The Indentures of Boston's

Poor Apprentices: 1734–1805." Colonial Society of Massachusetts, *Publications* 43 (1966):417–468.

Slaves

Berlin, Ira, and Philip D. Morgan, eds. *Cultivation and Culture: Labor and the Shaping of Slave Life in the Americas.* Charlottesville, Va., 1993.

Dunn, Richard S. *Sugar and Slaves: The Rise of the Planter Class in the English West Indies, 1624–1713.* Chapel Hill, N.C., 1972.

Fogel, Robert William. *Without Consent or Contract: The Rise and Fall of American Slavery.* New York, 1989.

Lauber, Almon Wheeler. *Indian Slavery in Colonial Times Within the Present Limits of the United States.* Columbia University Studies in History, Economics, and Public Law, 54, no. 3. New York, 1913.

Solow, Barbara L., ed. *Slavery and the Rise of the Atlantic System.* Cambridge, England, 1991.

Ward, J. R. *British West Indian Slavery, 1750–1834: The Process of Amelioration.* Oxford, 1988.

Wood, Peter H. *Black Majority: Negroes in Colonial South Carolina from 1670 Through the Stono Rebellion.* New York, 1974.

Local Studies

Beckles, Hilary McD. *White Servitude and Black Slavery in Barbados, 1627–1715.* Knoxville, Tenn., 1989.

Carr, Lois Green, Philip D. Morgan, and Jean B. Russo, eds. *Colonial Chesapeake Society.* Chapel Hill, N.C., 1988.

Daniels, Christine. "Alternative Workers in a Slave Economy: Kent County, Maryland, 1650–1810." Ph.D. diss., The Johns Hopkins University, 1990.

Innes, Stephen. *Labor in a New Land: Economy and Society in Seventeenth-Century Springfield.* Princeton, N.J., 1983.

Kulikoff, Allan. *Tobacco and Slaves: The Development of Southern Cultures in the Chesapeake, 1680–1800.* Chapel Hill, N.C., 1986.

Main, Gloria L. *Tobacco Colony: Life in Early Maryland, 1650–1720.* Princeton, N.J., 1982.

Morgan, Edmund S. *American Slavery, American Freedom: The Ordeal of Colonial Virginia.* New York, 1975.

Rink, Oliver A. *Holland on the Hudson: An Economic and Social History of Dutch New York.* Ithaca, N.Y., 1986.

Rutman, Darrett B., and Anita H. Rutman. *A Place in Time: Middlesex County, Virginia, 1650–1750.* New York, 1984.

Sainsbury, John A. "Indian Labor in Early Rhode Island." *New England Quarterly* 48, no. 3 (1975): 378–393.

Salinger, Sharon V. *"To Serve Well and Faithfully": Labor and Indentured Servants in Pennsylvania, 1682–1800.* New York, 1987.

Siebert, Wilbur H. "Slavery and White Servitude in East Florida, 1726 to 1776." *Florida Historical Society Quarterly* 10, no. 1 (1931):3–23.

Vickers, Daniel. "The First Whalemen of Nantucket." *William and Mary Quarterly*, 3rd ser., 40, no. 4 (1983):560–583.

Philip D. Morgan

SEE ALSO **Farming, Planting, and Ranching; Interracial Societies;** and **Trade and Commerce;** and various essays in THE SOCIAL FABRIC.

THE FRENCH COLONIES

INDENTURED SERVICE in France's North American Empire was superficially the same as contract labor in British North America: workers recruited in Europe were transported to the Americas to serve a colonial master for a set number of years. The French system, however, operated with very different assumptions, and it was a less reliable source of settlers than the French troops stationed in the colonies.

Temporary servitude in the colonies is regarded by modern scholars as a way by which the poor obtained transportation to the Americas, where they intended to make a new home. It undoubtedly assisted the mass migration of potential colonists to British North America. In France it was not seen as assisted migration nor was settlement abroad the ambition of contract workers. Labor abroad was regarded as a temporary expediency without any commitment to the place of work. French indenturing seems to have evolved from the hiring of fishermen and sailors for one sea voyage. It was assumed that the workers would return home and most did so. There was no special term for colonial contract workers; they were called *engagés*, which applied to all hirelings.

RESISTANCE TO
OVERSEAS RESETTLEMENT

Migrant workers were males as were almost all the indentured servants going to the French colonies. Family migration to New France was rare. The Société de Montréal recruited some families in 1649, and John Law's Compagnie de la Louisiane (1717–1720), popularly known as the Louisiana Company, sought families for the southern colony. Individuals or families seldom accepted redemption contracts that were explicitly a form of assisted emigration. Why the peoples of France were so resistant to overseas resettlement can only be guessed at; the semiliterate *gens du peuple* (common people) never explained their reluctance to go to the colonies or their unwillingness, once there, to stay.

Work in a colony was not seen as repayment for the transatlantic passage; it was labor worthy of remuneration, and all French colonial *engagés* were paid a salary. Contracts made in the first half of the seventeenth century also promised workers from France a prepaid passage back to the homeland—a clear acknowledgement that they were migrant workers rather than immigrants. In the 1700s skilled specialists could still demand this right from an employer. Symptomatic of the migrant-worker outlook of *engagés*, was the fact that two-thirds of those who came to the Saint Lawrence Valley settlements in the 1600s returned to France once their term of service had expired. The danger of Iroquois attacks and the shortage of European females in New France offset the attraction of fertile land and fewer taxes. Acadia had a better retention rate whereas survivors of the twenty-five hundred *engagés* sent to Louisiana in 1718–1720 fled back to France. Surviving private letters show that permanent resettlement overseas was not accepted as a solution to hardship at home. Absentees were enjoined to come home, and no writer in France enquired about the prospects for an emigrant coming from Europe.

The total number of workers indentured in France for the American colonies did not exceed thirty-five thousand. La Rochelle, which was the principal port of embarkation for the Americas in Louis XIV's reign, sent seventy-three hundred *engagés* to the New World. Most went to the French West Indies, particularly Saint-Domingue (Haiti); only eleven hundred were destined for New France. The flow of indentured workers out of Nantes from 1632 to 1732 was even more lopsided: a mere eighteen out of six thousand *engagés* departed for New France and Louisiana. Bayonne, by contrast, sent more workers to North America than to the French Caribbean islands. Dieppe, Granville, and Saint-Malo shared in this traffic, but Bordeaux was the heir to La Rochelle during Louis XV's reign, dispatching sixty-five hundred workers to the Americas in the period 1698 to 1771. The number of contract laborers was shrinking in the 1700s, and the flow to New France nearly ceased.

The declining number of recruits for North America occurred when colonial life was more secure, and there were now marriageable European women in the overseas territories. Those facts were not communicated to potential emigrants. The farming and laboring population in France, which would have benefited most from emigration to the Americas, knew nothing about the advantages of life there. Printed propaganda to stimulate emigration was rare: tracts and posters were printed to encourage enlistment for service in seventeenth-century Cayenne and for eighteenth-century Louisiana. This was but a faint echo of the vigorous campaign to promote colonies in contemporary England.

As a consequence, the lower classes of France relied on hearsay for their information about the Americas. What they heard was unfavorable. Canada's cold winters were legendary. Tales of how the Iroquois tortured and killed enemy captives blended with a popular conviction that colonies were a dumping ground for the social outcasts of France. Petty criminals were dispatched to Canada and Louisiana in the early 1700s, but they were outnumbered by respectable, voluntary migrants. Nonetheless, people in France remained convinced that the American colonies were populated by prostitutes and criminals; Abbé Antoine François Prévost's popular novel *Histoire du Chevalier des Grieux et de Manon Lescaut* (1731) proceeded from that assumption.

Given the reluctance of people in France to immigrate to the American colonies, recruiters of indentured servants had to offer benefits that would have astounded bond workers in the British colonies. In addition to receiving a salary, *engagés* were usually not required to serve more than three years, whereas workers in the English possessions served from four to seven years without pay. Workers were assured of food, shelter, and some clothing; their pay—impressive by French standards—was often a credit against which they could obtain goods, such as liquor or personal articles, from their employer. Colonial *engagés* were ill fed, poorly clothed, and given arduous tasks, such as land clearing. In 1681 Governor Louis de Buade de Frontenac of New France described an indentured worker as "a man obliged to go everywhere and to do whatever his master commanded, like a slave."

Employers were likely to be members of the colonial gentry, merchants, or religious orders, socially far above their *engagés*. Those signing a direct, personal contract with a colonial employer fared better than unskilled men hired in groups for resale to people in the colonies. In the mid 1600s, when there was a good market for land clearers in Canada and the West Indies, merchant-shipowners enrolled hundreds of young men whose contracts were sold to colonials. From 1662 to 1673 the French Crown subsidized transportation of mass levies of the unskilled to New France. The consolation was that the workers' purgatory rarely extended beyond three years.

During the eighteenth century New France *engagés* working as domestic servants were replaced by young orphans and children of the poor who were bound out until age eighteen or twenty-one. Parents placed their children in domestic service with only a promise of maintenance and clothing as the child's reward. These young servants were a cheap replacement for imported workers. The growing range of craftsmen in the colony also permitted colonials to call on the artisans' skills as they needed them, without taking on the long-term risk of an *engagé* from France, who might prove to be incompetent, sickly, or debauched. In 1682 the Séminaire de Quebec's proctor had recommended employment of colonial laborers "even if they are more costly . . . since one is often deceived in those who are sent from France." African slaves replaced European bond servants as agricultural laborers in the West Indies and Louisiana. New France was largely populated by self-employed

farmers, fishermen, and craftsmen, and the disappearance of French indentured workers there was unrelated to slavery. Domestic sources of skilled and unskilled workers filled the void.

By the late 1600s the Canadian labor market was more selective and did not offer recruiters profits like those made in the 1650s. Speculative hiring of *engagés* for North America declined, and it might have faded away, had not laws passed in 1714 and in later years required each ship bound for New France to carry a small quota of indentured workers, proportionate to the vessel's tonnage. Such a requirement had been in force since 1699 for ships going to the West Indies. In practice, two to four craftsmen were to be carried on each vessel going to the colonies. Although frequently evaded, the laws did sustain a small flow of workers to New France; because the quantity of ships going to the West Indies was greater, the number of *engagés* arriving there was larger. By this time, the Canadian population was growing more by reproduction than through immigration, and there were three discharged soldiers for every former *engagé* among the new settlers. Indentured servitude was important in the settlement of the French colonies during the 1600s, but it was a secondary source of European immigrants in the eighteenth century.

BIBLIOGRAPHY

Allain, Mathé. "French Emigration Policies, 1699–1715." In *Proceedings of the Fourth Meeting of the French Colonial History Society,* edited by Alf Andrew Heggoy and James J. Cooke. Washington, D.C., 1979.

Brasseaux, Carl. "The Image of Louisiana and the Failure of Voluntary French Emigration, 1683–1731." In *Proceedings of the Fourth Meeting of the French Colonial History Society,* edited by Alf Andrew Heggoy and James J. Cooke. Washington, D.C., 1979.

Conrad, Glenn. "Emigration Forcée: French Attempts to Populate Louisiana, 1716–1720." In *Proceedings of the Fourth Meeting of the French Colonial History Society,* edited by Alf Andrew Heggoy and James J. Cooke. Washington, D.C., 1979.

Debien, Gabriel. "Les Engagés pour les Antilles (1634–1715)." *Revue d'histoire des colonies* 38 (1951):7–122.

Giraud, Marcel. *Histoire de la Louisiane française.* 4 vols to date. Paris, 1953–.

Moogk, Peter. "Manon Lescaut's Countrymen: Emigration from France to North America before 1763." In *Proceedings of the Fifteenth Meeting of the French Colonial Historical Society,* edited by Patricia Galloway. Lanham, Md., 1992.

———. "Reluctant Exiles: Emigrants from France in Canada before 1760." *William and Mary Quarterly,* 3rd ser., 46, no. 3 (July 1989):463–505.

Peter N. Moogk

SEE ALSO **Internal Migration; Interracial Societies; Repeopling the Land;** and **Trade and Commerce.**

THE SPANISH BORDERLANDS

BOUND LABOR CAN REFER to a variety of labor relations such as chattel slavery, serfdom, debt peonage, indentured labor, and penal labor. All these existed in the Spanish Empire and most were found at one time or another in the borderlands. They differed considerably throughout the Spanish colonies over time, by region, and with local conditions. Labor relations in the borderlands, however, were even more variable than in central areas of the Spanish colonies.

This article begins with some brief definitions, then turns to general discussions of slavery and feudalism—the latter a term often inappropriately associated with bound labor—and their relevance to debates about the roles of both in social change. Once the definitional issues have been clarified, the various forms of bound labor in the borderlands are described in greater detail.

DEFINITIONS OF BOUND LABOR

The following definitions of bound labor are the most widely accepted but are not universal. Un-der chattel slavery—the most extreme form of bound labor—humans are bought and sold like animals or machines; they have no social rights and they are, as the sociologist Orlando Patterson has stated, "socially dead." Slavery in the pre–Civil War United States South is the most familiar example of chattel slavery. Under serfdom laborers, typically called peasants, are required to live on the land of the landowner, typically a noble, to pay him a portion of all they produce, to work on the landowner's lands, and to perform other services. Such estates were overwhelmingly run by men, although on rare occasion a widow was in charge. Throughout the world, and in the Spanish Empire, serf systems are notoriously patriarchal. Debt peonage differs from the preceding two forms in that some action of the debtor, or an accident he or she experienced, caused that person to incur a debt to another. To repay the debt, the debtor agrees to work for the lender until the debt is repaid. This is bound labor—the debtor is legally obligated to pay the debt by labor and could be punished for leaving before repayment. An indentured servant is an individual who agrees in a legal document to work for another for a specified period in return for some favor, typically a loan of money for passage to a work site. Indentured servitude differs from debt peonage in that a definite term of labor is specified in the contract.

As described these seem to be distinct forms of bound labor. In practice, however, they overlapped considerably, with many gray areas. This is one source of confusion in terminology. From the perspective of the bound laborer, differences in these forms were frequently more theoretical than real. He or she was trapped in a situation of having little or no freedom of action. An indenture of fifteen years under harsh frontier conditions might be difficult to distinguish from a life as a chattel slave. Debt peonage could become a lifelong trap, since new debts were often incurred, making full repayment an ever receding possibility. What linked these variations was that the bound laborer was legally required to perform certain types of work and was not free to choose the type of work or the circumstances under which it had to be performed.

Two issues arise in regard to bound labor. One is the meanings and varieties of slavery. The other is that all forms of bound labor, except slavery, are frequently associated with feudalism, another term with many definitions.

Slavery

Several aspects of slavery in the Spanish Borderlands merit explication. First, chattel slavery was not the most common form of bound labor in the Spanish colonies. There were, of course, regional and temporal exceptions. Other forms, such as debt peonage and forced labor, especially for captives taken in wars with Indians, were more familiar. Second, the New Laws of the Indies, promulgated in 1542 and reaffirmed in 1680, declared Indians to be human; thus they were worthy of salvation and were not legitimate objects of enslavement. Third, the rapidly declining numbers of indigenous populations that followed Spanish contact made large-scale enslavement or even enserfment of Indians impractical in many areas because too few survived. Fourth, nomadic Indians, as opposed to sedentary agricultural Indians such as the Incas or Aztecs, were difficult to enslave because they knew little of agriculture and were unaccustomed to sedentary life. Still, enslavement of Indians did occur.

Because such enslavement was illegal, various subterfuges were used to accomplish this end. The most common was "punishment" for defeat in a "just war." According to Spanish law, when explorers claimed territory in the name of the king, people indigenous to that area became vassals of the monarch. Resistance to Spanish rule was interpreted as rebellion, provoking a "just war"; hence, enslavement of prisoners taken captive was legitimate punishment for the crime of treason. Such wars were easy to provoke when there was a good market for slaves.

A second technique for enslavement of Indians derived from indigenous customs and from the conditions of continual frontier warfare. Indians captured in wars with other Indian groups were often held as "slaves" and forced to work. Such "slaves," or war captives, were typically children or fertile females who performed customary tasks of nomadic life: tanning hides, preparing food, grinding grains, and so forth. In practice this amounted to forced adoption into the capturing group because these slaves did the same type of work as other members of the group. But there was little specialized work that could be relegated to slaves, nor were group

members available to be the constant overseers that forced labor requires.

When there was no need for captives, they could be killed or traded for desirable goods such as food, metal tools, guns, or horses. Sometimes slaves served the purpose of conspicuous consumption, either by demonstrating the valor of their possessor in having obtained them, or on occasion more literally by being eaten. However, cannibalism was a rare and generally symbolic act, reports of which were considerably exaggerated because cannibalism could be used as an excuse for waging a "just war." In times and places where labor was scarce, captives might be sold for money. There is evidence that the taking and trading of captives predated European contact. However, it is clear that the trade in captives spread and intensified under European influence.

Captives could be rescued or ransomed by Spaniards. They would be taken into Spanish custody for their own protection and benefit. Civilizing them required that they learn to work and obey, thus repaying the cost of their own ransom. In practice this amounted to slavery. The major points with respect to this form of bound labor are its extreme variability and the widely divergent views of Indians and Spaniards about how captives should be treated.

Thus war captive slavery was a highly varied social practice that ranged from chattel slavery to coerced adoption and acculturation. It is useful to distinguish between war captive slavery and chattel slavery because the capture, transportation, and sale of large numbers of Spanish Borderland Indians was extremely rare—in contrast to the African slave trade. Still, it must be noted that in some instances Indians were held as chattel slaves. Virtually all debates over the existence of chattel slavery for Indians in the borderlands hinge on definitions of terms rather than on disagreements about day-to-day social practices.

Bound Labor and Feudalism

Bound labor is often associated with serfdom and feudalism. At one extreme the latter two terms are labels for what is asserted to be a unique form of social relations found only in medieval Western Europe. At the other extreme, they are labels for any form of agricultural labor in which workers are not perfectly free to change jobs at will.

The association of bound labor with feudalism is unfortunate because it conjures up confusing connotations such as "backward," "traditional," or "stagnant." Entangled in this confusion are debates about whether feudal relations are always a legacy of medieval Western European traditions, or a product of continuing and historical social processes. This debate cannot be settled here, but readers should be aware that it affects the way some scholars interpret and report bound labor in the Spanish colonies, especially in the borderlands, and sparks scholarly interest in the region because its history has some bearing on this debate.

The debate centers on the origins of bound labor. One view holds that such labor relations are always an indication of "backwardness," or an incomplete transition to capitalist labor relations characterized by free wage labor. The other opinion counters that capitalist trade relations, under certain specific conditions and in specific areas, do not promote free wage labor but rather various forms of bound labor. Thus the first interpretation sees bound labor as a sign of a failed transition to capitalism, while the second sees bound labor as a product of a peculiar kind of transition to capitalism.

The second interpretation merits further explanation. Typically, there are three conditions necessary for the spread of bound labor within a system of capitalist trade relations: a potential class of large landholders, a labor shortage, and labor-intensive technology. Landownership need not be concentrated initially, but its potential must exist. Thus concentration can arise through market relations or from a tradition in which a small elite holds most of the land rights. Similarly, a labor shortage can arise in two ways. Either there are simply too few people to do the necessary agricultural work or too many people have other options for making a living. The latter can include migration, industrial alternatives, or the availability of new land for colonization as small private holdings. Where twentieth-century technology is not present, agriculture is always labor-intensive. However, labor intensity varies with the types of products grown and with even small changes in technology.

Under conditions of economic growth and increasing trade, demand for agricultural (and other) products grows, which allows those who already hold land to enlarge their profits and to obtain more land. This, in turn, creates a demand for more agricultural laborers. Depending on a variety of local conditions, potential laborers might have other opportunities that would magnify the relative shortage of labor. While increased trade contributes to greater prosperity and availability of capital, it is typically not enough to raise wages sufficiently to attract workers from other activities. In these circumstances, landholders try to coerce labor, typically through political or economic means. If, as often occurs, population growth accompanies increased trade and prosperity, there may be a labor surplus. In such cases wages can be lowered, and some workers may be willing to accept bound labor in order to guarantee work.

Because preindustrial agriculture was typically risky and variable in its results, there were always some producers who did better than others in any given year. Those who had done well could lend money, seeds, land, or other capital to those who had fared less well, entrapping them in debt peonage. If one group had recently conquered another, the conquered group could be forced into, and restricted to, agricultural labor. This could be done by forcing conquered peoples to give up other occupations and take up agriculture or by barring them from settlement of unused lands. If the indigenous population still lived in communal subsistence communities, it could be compelled to work either directly through force or indirectly through tribute or tax obligations. These techniques lowered labor costs because the maintenance cost of labor was transferred to the indigenous community, which was outside the capitalist economy, so that its maintenance was not a production cost. Coercion, tribute, or taxation was frequently used when there were extreme social differences—typically, but not exclusively, racial or ethnic differences. Racist ideologies that presupposed the inferiority of conquered people often rationalized such treatment. Within limits, at times when trade increased, the pressure to bind labor to agriculture increased. The process led to the seemingly contradictory association of increasingly capitalistic relations and an increasing frequency of bound labor.

Various combinations of these conditions obtained at different times and places throughout the Spanish Empire. In particular, as capitalist trade relations began to penetrate the colonies during the late-eighteenth-century Bourbon reforms, some kinds of bound labor developed as wage labor also grew. A variety of specific local conditions determined whether bound or free wage labor was more common.

This, however, is not the end of the issue. The connotations of "backwardness," interpreted as "inferior," have colored scholarly attitudes toward the Spanish colonies and the states that arose from them. Responses to the term "feudal" and its associations have been similarly affected.

Specifically the connotations of feudalism recall the "black legend," which attributes to Spanish explorers and settlers a dark or evil tradition of cruelty that was supposedly replaced by "progressive" Americans who came to own and control much of northern New Spain in the nineteenth century. After Mexico opened its borders to foreign trade in 1821, comments on the "feudal" nature of New Mexican society appeared in the writings of American travelers. These remarks were used to justify the conquest of Northern Mexico in the name of "progress" and Manifest Destiny during the Mexican–American War (1846–1848). The term was later used to degrade former Mexican citizens who had become Americans by virtue of having been conquered. The malicious use of the term "feudal" to justify conquest, racist attitudes, and discriminatory behavior toward people of Hispanic ancestry has led some scholars to go to great lengths not only to avoid using the term but also to argue that there never were "feudal," or more accurately, feudal-like relations in the Spanish colonies, especially in the borderlands.

This understandable but unfortunate reaction has confused the study of forms of bound labor in the Spanish colonies, and especially in the borderlands. A reasonable compromise would seem to include accepting that peculiar conditions could give rise to such forms of labor relations as bound labor, which appear to be feudal-like, but rejecting uncritical conclusions about the origins or relationship of bound labor to economic or social backwardness. It is more useful to examine what actually happened and, where possible, to discover the history and changes in the forms of labor relations. That is the next task of this article.

BOUND LABOR IN THE BORDERLANDS

All forms of bound labor—indentured servitude, penal labor, slavery, debt peonage, and livestock sharecropping (*partido*)—existed at a given time or place in the borderlands. The western borderlands—the *Provincias Internas* (internal provinces), which made up approximately the areas now covered by south-central and west Texas, New Mexico, Arizona, and California in the United States, and Tamaulipas, Nuevo León, Coahuila, Chihuahua, Sonora, Sinaloa, and Baja California in Mexico—seem to have had both the largest variety and the greatest extent of bound labor. This could be an artifact of closer scrutiny of that region by scholars, but more probably reflects a greater intensity of Spanish occupation and colonization. Consequently, much of what follows focuses on New Mexico and contiguous regions since they held the bulk of Spanish population in the borderlands.

The eastern borderlands—approximately the areas now covered by Florida, southern Alabama, southern Mississippi, and at times much of Georgia, parts of the Carolinas, Louisiana, and southeastern Texas—are more problematic, primarily because ownership of these areas changed hands several times among European countries and the United States. In the early sixteenth century, several Spanish officials authorized or led slaving expeditions to Florida—including those of Ponce de León and the more successful Lucas Vasquez de Ayllón. Captive Indians were shipped to various West Indies locations. In Florida, Indians were compelled to work on the construction of the fort at Saint Augustine. Some of the early settlements also employed convict labor. Enslaved Indians were also forced to do agricultural work. Indians living in and around Spanish settlements in Florida were required to wear insignia indicating whether they were slave or free.

Throughout the region that is now the southeastern United States, the British seem to have enslaved Indians more intensively than the Spaniards did. The British, in particular, shifted gradually from directly capturing slaves to buying them through Indian middlemen. European occupation intensified indigenous slaveholding patterns, especially among those groups that practiced agriculture. The local and regional trade in Indian slaves peaked in the late seventeenth and early eighteenth centuries. At times this included trade in illegally captured Indians over officially closed borders between British- and Spanish-held territories. Hence official records are extremely rare. Thereafter slaves imported from Africa replaced Indian slaves for the familiar reasons: the Africans were more amenable to farming semitropical crops, they had a much higher immunity to European diseases, they were less likely to escape or rebel, and they were easier to identify.

The eastern borderlands were distinctive in that Indian slaves in this region were often used in agricultural production, for clearing and fencing land, tilling crops, and so on. There is also some evidence of male African slaves breeding with female Indian slaves. Chattel slavery was more common in the eastern borderlands during the first two centuries of colonial occupation because of the greater presence of agricultural Indians, lesser danger from nomadic raiders, and the practice of more intensive forms of agriculture by European settlers in the eastern than in the western borderlands.

A significant number of slaves, Indian and African, went to Florida when it reverted from British to Spanish control in 1783. Some moved on with their owners, others were sold, and some stayed on in Florida. Because a census was taken at this time, more detailed information is available.

Compulsory Labor

The first settlers and explorers of the Americas were granted *encomiendas,* which gave them the right to collect tribute from Indians who lived on the land covered by the grant. An *encomendero* (recipient of the *encomienda*) also could compel labor from Indians living on his *encomienda.* While at times such compulsory labor was technically illegal, it was a common means of collecting tribute; in return the *encomendero* was responsible for the defense and administration of the territory. A combination of abuses by *encomenderos,* rapid population losses among Indians, and the Crown's desire to prevent the formation of an hereditary aristocracy in the Americas led to an abolition of the *encomienda* system with the promulgation of the New Laws of the Indies in 1542. Like many other such changes, this regulation

was honored in the breach. Still, the granting of *encomiendas* declined rapidly in the seventeeth century. Frontier areas were granted exceptions; there *encomiendas* were dispensed as short-term (from one to three generations) enticements and rewards to those who colonized new areas. Several grants were awarded to the founders of New Mexico, Texas, and Florida.

In more central areas, like the core of New Spain, the *encomienda* was replaced by the *repartimiento,* under which Indians within the granted territory owed the *repartimiento* holder a fixed amount of paid labor per year. *Repartimiento* regulations were often abused, leading to the virtual enserfment of Indians. Even in the frontier areas, and especially the northern borderlands, the *repartimiento* eventually replaced the *encomienda.* In some borderland areas such as New Mexico, *repartimientos* lasted longer than in central areas like the regions around Mexico City and Guanajuato; in some cases it survived through Mexican independence (1821). In the *Provincias Internas, repartimiento* relations lasted into the Bourbon reform era in the late eighteenth century. Abuses were less extreme in the *Provincias Internas* because there were fewer Indians and because nomadic Indians were not amenable to labor levies.

At first glance, the early *encomenderos* would seem to fit the description of a landholding elite in a feudal system, but landownership patterns in much of the borderlands, including New Mexico, more often took the form of smallholdings than of large estates. Furthermore, conquered nomads were not easily converted to agricultural workers. Thus, while the potential for formation of an elite class existed, the actual process did not go very far.

Still, excesses in both the *encomienda* and *repartimiento* were contributing factors to Indian revolts in many parts of the borderlands during the seventeenth century. Indians who were required to perform *repartimiento* labor registered many complaints: One, demands were seen as excessive; two, *repartimiento* labor took them away from necessary labor at home, undermining their livelihoods; and three, many indigenous women were sexually molested by Spaniards while performing their labor duties. Besides outright lust, these molestations were incited by the relative shortage of Spanish women on the frontier.

These and other abuses, such as attempts by the church to suppress Native religions, created resentments that exploded in New Mexico's Pueblo Revolt in 1680. Several sedentary, agricultural Pueblo Indian groups united to oust the Spaniards from New Mexico in the first successful Indian expulsion of Europeans from Spanish America.

Spain decided to reconquer New Mexico for several reasons. First, Spanish pride was wounded by defeat at the hands of Indians. Second, the Spanish administration wanted to maintain its claim on the territory, both for its own sake and to preempt potential claims by European rivals. Third, New Mexico served as a buffer that protected the highly profitable silver mines farther south from European rivals and nomadic raiders. Finally, the church had an interest in the souls of Christianized Indians left behind without priests to minister to their spiritual needs.

When Diego de Vargas reconquered and recolonized New Mexico in 1693, a few new *encomiendas* were granted but never actually operationalized. The resumption of incessant fighting with nomadic Indians forced Spaniards and Pueblo groups into an uneasy alliance. This, along with the experience of the revolt, tempered Spanish attempts to collect tribute or to enforce labor obligations on the Pueblo Indians. However, other sources of labor were available, chiefly captives or ransomed Indians obtained from nomadic groups.

There is considerable debate about Indian labor in California. Some historians argue that Indian labor on the California missions during the late eighteenth and early nineteenth centuries constituted a form of compulsory labor that bore marks of both the *repartimiento* and debt peonage. While the argument is largely definitional, it is clear that Indians were made to work on mission lands as part of the conversion process. There was a great deal of temporal and regional variation in the practices employed, but it is clear that Indian labor at missions was rarely performed without some form of compulsion.

Indian Slaves

In warfare among nomadic groups, prisoners—typically women and children—were taken as captives. As discussed above, nomads could not easily use chattel slaves in their indigenous economies. Consequently, being captured was more akin to forced adoption. As contact and warfare with Spaniards increased, nomadic groups learned that these prisoners were one item for which Spaniards would trade valuable goods such as horses, metal, or occasionally guns. Such captives, known as *Indios de rescate* (bartered Indians), could be enslaved in order to "civilize," that is, Hispanicize and Christianize, them—supposedly "for their own good."

As the demand for horses, guns, and metal among nomadic Indians increased, so did the incentives for intertribal warfare to supply captives to trade for these goods. Spaniards encouraged friendly groups to raid their Indian enemies for captives. Thus constant warfare and a desire for trade goods provided a ready supply of captured Indians to Spaniards. "Just wars" were another source of captives. Many punitive raids in the borderlands against nomadic Indians were in fact thinly disguised slave raids. While common throughout the borderlands, these practices abated in the eastern borderlands in the first half of the eighteenth century but lasted through the colonial era, Mexican independence, and on into the American era in the western borderlands. The continuing value of captives on the frontier undermined leaders' incentive to pursue permanently peaceful relations with and among nomadic groups.

In the western borderlands, captive or ransomed Indians either became domestic servants or were sold to work in the silver mines farther south or even in the Yucatan or Havana. In the eastern borderlands, captives were used in local agricultural production or sold in the West Indies. Trade in captives was officially discouraged because captives, especially men, were very hard to control. They escaped frequently and on their way home wreaked revenge on any available Spaniard. What's more, the men were not particularly suited for work in mines or agricultural drudge labor. However, at times when labor was especially scarce, such disabilities were ignored and trade in slaves became lively. Because slave trading was officially illegal, a regular and successful trade in slaves required considerable demand as an incentive and bribery as a facilitator. Several governors in the borderlands were brought to trial and punished for trading in In-

40

dian slaves. The imperial administration was less concerned with slavery itself than it was with the constant warfare that slave trading and raiding engendered; these conflicts magnified administrative costs in terms of soldiers and their supplies.

Because enslavement of Indians was illegal, captives were often referred to by a variety of euphemisms. Consequently, the extent of Indian slavery has been difficult to assess.

The use of slaves as domestic servants was much more common in the borderlands than in central areas. This form of slavery was less visible to official scrutiny and could be easily disguised as a form of adoption. The latter tendency has caused some historians to interpret Indian slavery as relatively benign; in fact it could be quite brutal. There are numerous instances of captive Indians complaining to officials about abuses, although the protests seldom effected any relief.

The use of captives as domestic servants led to a strong preference for women and children over adult men. In eighteenth-century New Mexico, a young woman often brought double the price of an adult male for several reasons: men were more troublesome and more likely to try to escape than women, while children offered hardly any resistance at all. Women not only worked as servants, performing "female" tasks such as food preparation, cooking, plastering, and housekeeping, but also served as concubines and, albeit rarely, as wives in regions with insufficient Spanish women. Children of such unions, unless there was an official marriage, were also slaves (although there was some regional variation in this), so that sexual relations with female slaves satisfied the carnal desires of a slave owner and increased his wealth. Also, because of the relatively high infant mortality typical of agrarian societies, female slaves were useful in populating the area. This contribution has been given too little attention until recently.

The symbolic importance of owning slaves cannot be ignored. For Spaniards with pretensions to nobility, or even with actual titles, having slaves constituted a public validation of status and high social honor. Slaves were sometimes part of a dowry not only to help a bride in her new household but also to validate her standing as the daughter of an important family.

Spaniards in Bound Labor: Debt Peonage

The penetration of capitalist relations and the increased prosperity that accompanied the imposition of the Bourbon reforms in the latter part of the eighteenth century led to many changes. Due to the peculiar conditions on the frontier, the growth of bound labor, especially debt peonage, sometimes accompanied the expansion of wage labor. This process began in the 1760s and continued until after the U.S. Civil War (1860–1865), with significant variations in degree between localities and with reversals in some. These changes were most evident in the western borderlands, especially New Mexico. The eastern borderlands were far less populated, changed hands several times, and have been studied less thoroughly than the western borderlands.

The Bourbon reforms led to relative frontier peace and accelerated trade. This prosperity facilitated population growth. During peaceful times villagers could sell their land and colonize new areas; during less peaceful times, this option was more dangerous. Population growth put greater ecological pressure on the region and swelled the demand for land. Large tracts of land were sold throughout the region, but the prices were such that the landless could not afford to buy, while the wealthy could easily do so. These conditions contributed to increasing concentration of land ownership and a concomitantly higher proportion of the population owning no land.

The increase in the landless population is a major factor in the seemingly contradictory simultaneous growth of both wage and bound labor. On the one hand, landless people had to work for their subsistence; as long as the economy was growing, there was adequate employment. On the other hand, when there was a downturn or an individual family fell on hard times, they were candidates for debt peonage.

The plunge into debt peonage could be initiated by any reversal of fortune: an illness, an expensive marriage, a bad crop, heavy losses in a raid by hostile nomadic Indians, and so on. Droughts in the late 1770s in New Mexico forced many families to sell children into domestic service. A reversal in fortune might spur a colonist to approach another, better-off settler for a loan. The loan might be made on the condition that the borrower work it off in the form of service to the lender. Once such an agreement had been struck, it became difficult for the borrower to extract himself from service. Generally the agreement gave the lender veto power over other employment for the debtor and included a small, but typically insufficient, allotment of food for the debtor and his family. This often pushed him to borrow more, which meant going further in debt.

The extent of debt peonage is difficult to assess because in many cases formal contracts were either never drawn up or not preserved. In census records the presence of multiple family households without obvious kinship ties is a reasonable indicator that there was a debt peonage relationship. Research indicates that debt peonage began to increase very late in the eighteenth century, continued to do so through Mexican independence (1821) and beyond, and then decreased. One aim of the Bourbon reforms was to reverse the late-eighteenth-century trend of growing debt peonage. Several royal decrees issued between 1805 and 1820 were aimed at redistributing land and wealth. It is important that the incidence of debt peonage has not yet been thoroughly investigated, so these changes could be artifacts of data collection rather than actual changes. It is clear, however, that debt peonage was a common form of servile or bound labor throughout the western borderlands in the late colonial era.

Livestock Sharecropping: The *Partido* System

Partido can refer to a district or territorial division or to a shares agreement between an owner and a contractor to raise crops or livestock for a fixed percentage of the yield. The latter meaning refers to another form of bound labor, one that was available to landless persons for making a living. The shareholder was known as a *partidario*.

In the late eighteenth and early nineteenth centuries, such contracts amounted to the rental of a herd of livestock, typically sheep. As with debt peonage, this seems to have been a western borderland practice. However this, too, may be an artifact of the greater intensity of research for that area rather than a valid depiction of the regional differences within the borderlands as a whole. The *partidario* received the animals from their owner for a fixed number of years

and was responsible for the maintenance of the herd. Depending on the terms of the contract, this might include losses due to weather or Indian raids. Each year the *partidario* had to augment the number of animals and the amount of wool. Any surplus beyond that remained with the *partidario*.

In theory this was a way for a landless person to build up his own flock; in practice it was another form of bound labor. The *partidario* had to care for the herd until he could return the original investment. If weather, disease, or Indian raids reduced the herd, he became trapped—either as a permanent herder, unable to gain economic independence, or as a debt peon—in order to repay the losses. The *partido* system was a ready avenue to increased wealth for landowners and herd owners, since nearly all the risks were passed on to the *partidario*, with initial profits returned to the owner.

The role of Indian warfare in both debt peonage and *partido* formation was important in the western borderlands, especially in New Mexico. When there was relative peace, new lands were available to found new villages, to spread livestock herds, and to replace land sold to clear old debts. This encouraged the spread of settlement in new areas. In New Mexico this led to sporadic expansion eastward onto the Plains from the Rio Grande Valley, beginning in the late eighteenth century and continuing through the Mexican era (1821–1848). This, of course, meant encroachment into Indian land, albeit land that was not used intensively by indigenous nomadic hunters living there. Under these conditions there was more pressure on wealthier landowners to ensure a labor supply through either increased wages or greater efforts to bind labor to the land.

When Indian raiding increased, movement onto the Plains became hazardous and less effort was needed to control the labor supply. Wages could be lower, and the terms of *partido* and debt contracts could be stricter. This tendency was mitigated to some extent by the need to encourage colonization of new lands to provide goods for trade and to feed the growing population. If the need for new lands was sufficiently high, incentives in the form of improved terms of *partido* could result. Thus the effects of population growth, ecological pressure on the land, and intensity of Indian raiding were closely intertwined.

Because of the competing tendencies of these processes, frontier labor relations were highly changeable, both temporally and regionally. As a result, conclusions about labor relations remain tentative, and their variability remains both a puzzle to scholars and an inducement to further research. Future investigation of borderland labor relations offers insights into continuing debates about the processes of social change.

SUMMARY

While there was some similarity in the forms of bound labor found in the borderlands to that found in feudal Europe, their origins were quite different. European feudalism was an outgrowth of isolation and the absence of money; borderland "feudalism" was the result of increasing trade, dependence on imports, and various local conditions. Hence, the "feudal-like" appearance of some regions of the borderlands was not due to stagnation or isolation but rather to their increasing incorporation into an expanding capitalist economy. These contradictory appearances and the continual social change in the borderlands since the first Spaniards set foot there make the study of bound labor a fascinating topic.

BIBLIOGRAPHY

Chirot, Daniel. "The Growth of the Market and Servile Labor Systems in Agriculture." *Journal of Social History* 8, no. 2 (1975):67–80. An excellent overview and summary of the arguments about how advancing capitalist relations can create bound or servile labor.

Dunkle, John R. "Population Change as an Element in the Historical Geography of St. Augustine." *Florida Historical Quarterly* 37, no. 1 (1958):3–32. The best single account of the population history of Florida. Summarizes much of the data on slavery.

Frank, Andre Gunder. *Capitalism and Underdevelopment in Latin America: Historical Studies of Chile and Brazil.* New York, 1967; rev. ed. 1969.

———. *Latin America: Underdevelopment or Revolution.* New York, 1969. These two works by Frank contain detailed discussions about how capitalist relations

created feudal-like conditions in Latin America.

Greenleaf, Richard E. "Land and Water in Mexico and New Mexico, 1700–1821." *New Mexico Historical Review* 47, no. 2 (1972):85–112. This article contains detailed information about conditions during the era of the Bourbon reforms.

Gutiérrez, Ramón A. *When Jesus Came, the Corn Mothers Went Away: Marriage, Sexuality, and Power in New Mexico, 1500–1846.* Stanford, Calif., 1991. A path-breaking analysis that uses marriage data to explore traditional questions about class, ethnicity, and gender, this study helps to redress the severe neglect of these topics.

Hall, Thomas D. *Social Change in the Southwest, 1350–1880.* Lawrence, Kans., 1989. A sociological analysis of ethnic and social change in the region focusing on Indian-European relations. As with most sociological works, it argues an explicit theoretical position.

Hurtado, Albert L. *Indian Survival on the California Frontier.* New Haven, Conn., 1988. An excellent study of California Indian relations, with a wealth of detailed information on forms of bound labor to which Indians were subjected by Spaniards, Mexicans, and Americans.

Macleod, Murdo J. "Aspects of the Internal Economy of Colonial Spanish America: Labour; Taxation; Distribution and Exchange." In *The Cambridge History of Latin America*, vol. 2, edited by Leslie Bethell. Cambridge, Mass., 1984. An excellent overview of internal conditions and variations in the late colonial era.

Patterson, Orlando. *Slavery and Social Death: A Comparative Study.* Cambridge, Mass., 1982. A thoughtful and thorough study of slavery by a noted sociologist.

Ríos-Bustamante, Antonio. "A Contribution to the Historiography of the Greater Mexican North in the Eighteenth Century." *Aztlan* 7, no. 3 (1976): 347–356.

———. "New Mexico in the Eighteenth Century: Life, Labor, and Trade in La Villa de San Felipe de Albuquerque, 1706–1790." *Aztlan* 7, no. 3 (1976):357–389. These articles by Ríos-Bustamante provide a close look at eighteenth-century New Mexican social conditions and their relation to conditions throughout the *Provincias Internas*.

Simpson, Lesley Byrd. *The Encomienda in New Spain: The Beginning of Spanish Mexico.* Berkeley, Calif., 1950. The classic discussion of *encomiendas*.

Stoddard, Ellwyn R., Richard L. Nostrand, and Jonathan P. West. *The Borderlands Sourcebook: A Guide to the Literature on Northern Mexico and the American Southwest.* Norman, Okla., 1983. An excellent collection of articles on the borderlands.

Thomas, David Hurst, ed. *Columbian Consequences.* Vol. 1, *Archaeological and Historical Perspectives on the Spanish Borderlands West*; vol. 2, *Archaeological and Historical Perspectives on the Spanish Borderlands East*; and vol. 3, *The Spanish Borderlands in Pan-American Perspective.* Washington, D.C., 1989–1991. An outstanding collection of current research on the borderlands.

Weber, David J. " 'Scare More Than Apes': Historical Roots of Anglo-American Stereotypes of Mexicans." In *New Spain's Far Northern Frontier: Essays on Spain in the American West, 1540–1821*, edited by David J. Weber. Albuquerque, N.Mex., 1979. Also appears in David J. Weber, *Myth and History of the Hispanic Southwest: Essays by David J. Weber* (Albuquerque, N.Mex., 1988). This essay discusses the roots of prejudice against Hispanic peoples in both past and present.

Wright, James Leitch, Jr. *The Only Land They Knew: The Tragic Story of the American Indians in the Old South.* New York, 1981. An excellent account of Indians in the southeastern United States. Chapter 6 stands out for its discussion of slavery.

Zeleny, Carolyn. *Relations Between the Spanish-Americans and Anglo-Americans in New Mexico: A Study of Conflict and Accommodation in a Dual-Ethnic Situation.* New York, 1974. A slightly revised version of a 1944 dissertation, with a great deal of information on social conditions in New Mexico.

Thomas D. Hall

SEE ALSO **Detribalized and Manumitted Indians** and **Indian-Colonist Contact.**

THE SLAVE TRADE

THE NORTH AMERICAN colonies remained peripheral markets for the European slaving industries in the Atlantic, which, in the years before about 1800, delivered 90 percent or more of their captives to the West Indies, Brazil, and the mainland colonies of Spain. From the point of view of the English colonists in North America, access to imported African captives became vital only for about a century, between 1670 and 1775, in the Chesapeake and in South Carolina. Only the merchants of Rhode Island committed themselves significantly to the Africa voyage as a commercial strategy during that period. The French in Canada, the Dutch in New Netherland, and the Spaniards and French in the lower Mississippi Valley bought slaves from their countrymen and from English smugglers, but only in smaller numbers, and they seldom set out to obtain African labor on their own accounts.

ORIGINS OF SLAVING
IN THE ATLANTIC

Atlantic slaving arose from an older Slavic, Mediterranean, and North African trade in captives that long antedated Columbus's voyage to "the Indies." The maritime slave trade is conventionally dated to a Portuguese raid on the desert coasts of northwestern Africa in 1444. Columbus himself has been reported to have gained experi-

ence as a mariner on Portuguese voyages along West African coasts during the 1470s. Portuguese sailors had worked their way south around western Africa mainly in search of gold but had returned to Lisbon also with one thousand to two thousand slaves per year before American markets attracted the bulk of this trade westward after about 1520. This initial European phase of the trade set the focus of European merchants' economic strategies in the Atlantic on precious metals, an undertone that persisted much later in the trade in slaves to the Americas.

The fifteenth century also saw the emergence of a second recurrent pattern in slaving, in which overseas traders lacking capital and commercial connections in Europe sought indirect access through slaving to the primary flows of gold—and later silver—to Europe. Portuguese renegades who settled along the rivers of far western Africa, the source of nearly all African captives bought before the 1520s, became suppliers of slaves and African commodities to their seagoing countrymen. Others married African women of the aristocratic and merchant families of the mainland and developed slave-worked enterprises on the eastern Atlantic islands—Madeira, the Cape Verdes, and especially São Tomé, a small island in the Gulf of Guinea. They supported these estates and workshops with slave-trading networks linking the islands to the mainland. Such colonials made São Tomé a major producer of slave-grown sugar between about 1520 and 1570, with the financial and commercial support of merchants from Italy.

São Tomé sugar supported a turn toward systematic slave exporting from west-central Africa, around the mouth of the Zaire River and for several hundred miles to the south. Typical of many later colonial planters, the sugar growers of São Tomé were in persistent debt to the European merchants, mostly Genoese, who financed the high costs of establishing plantations. They therefore used the nearby African mainland as a source of labor they could acquire without expending specie, or commodities valuable in terms of gold or silver. These they saved to send to Europe to satisfy their creditors. This pattern of indebted planters, and independent colonial ventures to acquire slaves in Africa, became a fundamental characteristic of less prosperous overseas fringes of the Atlantic economy throughout much of the colonial era.

The Spanish Antilles became a secondary destination to which Iberian merchants and their Italian backers began to direct slaves beginning in the 1510s, though never in quantities comparable with the slaves kept on São Tomé or, later, sent to Brazil or to the mainland colonies. In early sixteenth-century Puerto Rico, Hispaniola (Santo Domingo), and Cuba, as elsewhere in the Americas, the Europeans looked first to local Indians as laborers on mines and plantations. On his second voyage Columbus declared all the adult Indians of Hispaniola slaves and sent several hundred of them to Spain, adding them to the inflow of captive labor. Supported by a decree of 1512 authorizing the enslavement of captives taken in a "just war" in defense of the Catholic faith against heathens, other Spaniards systematically raided the Caribbean islands, the Mexican coast, Florida, and the southeastern regions of North America for Indian slaves during most of the sixteenth century.

The search for slaves may have attracted Juan Ponce de León, Lucas Vásquez de Ayllon, and Pánfilo de Narváez, the Spanish conquerors of Florida, to the mainland as much as any other objective throughout the 1520s. Hernando de Soto was reported to have seized thousands of Indians in his marches through the southern mainland from 1539 to 1542. For American planters or miners, Indian slaves possessed the same advantage that Africans held for Portuguese in Africa or on São Tomé: extremely low acquisition cost, usually no more than that of kidnapping or seizure in wars. African slaves were much more costly, arriving in the New World burdened with the expenses of transatlantic transport and heavy losses to mortality. They also required payment in specie or in commodities worth specie in Europe. Only the most prosperous sectors of the American economies could afford them. However, as would happen elsewhere, European diseases soon reduced circum-Caribbean Indian populations below the numbers of hands the Europeans required.

On the mainland, Spanish conquests outside the main reservoirs of Indian labor among the Aztecs in central Mexico and the Incas of highland Peru turned repeatedly to slave raiding, particularly where discoveries of silver or gold created demand for labor in the first generation of plundering conquistadores, before Spanish civil authority reigned. The early years in Central America, where the conquerors found numerous Maya, were particularly brutal. The Spaniards captured Indians by the thousands from the 1520s to the 1540s, putting most to work panning for gold in the streams of the region. They dispatched others as slaves to Hispaniola and Cuba, and by the late 1530s sent many south to Panama and Peru.

The Crown prohibited enslavement of conquered Indians in 1542 and replaced slavery with other methods of extracting labor service in the regions firmly within its jurisdiction, mainly central Mexico, Peru, and Central America. Raiding continued to be tolerated elsewhere in the name of "just wars" against the enemies of Christianity. A frontier of such slaving formed in northern Mexico as early as the 1530s and then advanced north to the headwaters of the Rio Grande River in present-day New Mexico by about 1600. Many of the captives taken there were sent south to the Valley of Mexico and, later, to the colony's silver mines and coastal plantations. Each slaving raid provoked Indian resistance, and Indian counterattacks in turn justified further assaults on the enemies of Christendom. In a cascade of spreading violence, Indians armed themselves with guns and horses and took up slave raiding among their neighbors. The latter in turn formed new and stronger communities to protect themselves or fled the fighting to spread disruption to still more remote regions. Raiding by Spaniards declined and was replaced with purchases of the captives seized by Indian trading partners.

Enslaved Africans arrived in Spain's New World colonies beginning in 1518. They first supplemented Indians in the brief flurry of gold mining on Hispaniola, Cuba, and other islands in the Caribbean. Sporadic attempts to follow the rapid exhaustion of these deposits with production of sugar in imitation of São Tomé attracted some four hundred to five hundred Africans annually in the first half of the sixteenth century. They were at first drawn mostly from the Old World trade in Iberia. When conquest of the Aztecs in Mexico and of the Incas in Peru had turned Spain's attention to the mainland in the 1520s and 1530s, the importation of African slaves to the islands declined.

As diseases reduced Indian populations by as much as 90 percent during the following century, the Spanish commercial and administrative cities, especially Mexico City and Lima, became the primary markets for African slaves. Mines and sugar, cacao, and other plantations in lowland areas supplemented the demand. After about 1550, discovery of silver in northern Mexico and in Upper Peru generated commercial expansion and a demand for new labor. The wealth in precious metals supported inflows of Africans for urban domestic service and for year-round duties on mines and plantations. The Crown accorded its Indian subjects limited protection from Spanish miners and landowners, effectively restricting the Indians' obligations to seasonal service. Indian slaves from the northern borderlands went mostly to mining camps and plantations rather than to the cities. The numbers of enslaved Africans imported rose steadily to around two thousand per year by 1600 and reached twice to three times that number in the seventeenth century.

To stimulate the supply of African slaves, as well as to regulate the maritime trade in the interests of the monarchy, starting in 1518 the Crown issued contracts, known as *asientos de negros* (or more briefly, the *asiento*), that authorized the transport of slaves directly from Africa and set conditions under which shippers could land them in Spanish America. Merchants holding the *asiento* in effect gained royal permission to buy, with the slaves, silver in the New World, and so these licenses became coveted prizes among favorites of the court. The *asientistas* typically subcontracted operation of the slaving voyages to merchants, usually foreigners. The Italians, who had backed the planters of São Tomé and other Portuguese trading along African coasts, delivered the first slaves under the *asiento*. The Portuguese themselves became the principal subcontractors once they developed mainland sources of captives from the Senegal River to the Angolan coast south of the Zaire River mouth after about 1550. The shippers also smuggled actively, to obtain as much silver as they could.

The Portuguese thus developed the first large-scale transatlantic commerce in slaves during the middle of the sixteenth century to buy silver in Spain's American colonies. They were, as a result, well positioned to develop their sources of captives in Africa and to extend their deliveries of slaves in the Americas in the 1570s and 1580s. A sharp drought in west-central Africa during those decades provoked wars inland from the Bay of Luanda, in Angola, where São Tomé planters had been taking many of their slaves. Starvation and political disruption among the Africans created numerous refugees and captives, whom Portuguese military adventurers, searching fruitlessly for rumored mountains of silver in the valley of the Kwanza River, purchased very cheaply as slaves. The union of the Portuguese and Spanish monarchies after 1580 under Philip II confirmed these slavers' legal access to the silver of Spain's American colonies. Merchants then went to Luanda for captives to sell in Mexico and Peru, and the Portuguese in the interior turned the conflicts attending the environmental disaster into systematic hunts for slaves. As the Portuguese established military control over Luanda and its environs, they also laid the bases for Lisbon's colony of Angola—from that time on, a major source of slaves for the Americas. The search for silver proved illusory in Angola, but the slaves coming from the Angolan wars of conquest were as good as "black gold," since they earned specie in Spanish America.

With a maritime slaving industry of substantial proportions financed by Spanish silver, Portuguese merchants found themselves positioned to deliver slaves to Brazil at affordable prices. Since the 1530s Portugal had sought, with little success, to derive revenues from a series of small settlements, held privately as captaincies by Portuguese subjects, strung along South America's Atlantic coast south from the equator to Spain's claim of sovereignty over the Plata estuary. For labor they had relied heavily on enslaved Indians, often hunted in the backlands beyond the inland settlement at São Paulo. Settlers at Olinda in the captaincy of Pernambuco and later around the Bay of All Saints (or Bahia) had established sugar plantations on the model of São Tomé but had experienced difficulty in controlling local Indians as workers in the cane fields. These Indian slaves fled into the woods and, in the 1560s, suffered heavily from outbreaks of smallpox and measles. The decline in their numbers forced the Brazilian planters to look to the Atlantic trade for labor, no matter how expensive the slaves delivered from Africa.

At the same time, Portuguese merchants of Sephardic Jewish background fled the Spanish Inquisition to the Low Countries. There, backed by Dutch investors, they made available the credit necessary to finance importation of expensive African slaves in Brazil. They sold slaves against the security of the coming harvest, hoping thereby to secure control of the semirefined *muscovado* sugar that the slaves would produce and to earn profits from transporting casks of it to Europe, completing the refining process there and selling the final product. Brazilian demand and Dutch finance thus attracted a portion of the slaves then coming out of Angola in growing numbers and at low prices away from the Spanish Main and toward Pernambuco and Bahia. By the 1580s the majority of slaves growing sugar in Brazil were Africans. By around 1600 Pernambuco and Bahia in northeastern Brazil had become the largest sugar colonies in the world and were importing four thousand to five thousand individuals each year, only somewhat fewer than the Spanish trade at the time. This extension of the maritime trade in African slaves to northeastern Brazil forcefully demonstrated the recurrent tendency of slavers active in supplying one labor-short region of the Atlantic to spread slaves also to other areas at low prices that, in effect, subsidized the costs of starting new colonial agricultural sectors. São Tomé had supported Portugal's entry into the competition for Spain's *asiento,* as the *asiento* had supported the trade to Brazil. Similarly, later, the English trade to the West Indies would allow deliveries of slaves to North American colonies that tobacco and rice planters there would otherwise have hesitated to afford.

At the start of the seventeenth century, on the eve of English settlement in North America, Portugal controlled the key components of the maturing Atlantic commerce in slaves, African as well as Indian. It did so with important financial contributions from the Netherlands in its major Brazilian sector and only under license to the colonies of Spain. From a few hundred slaves each year delivered to Europe and the Atlantic islands, the trade had grown to approach ten thousand captives delivered annually to American ports ranging from Cuba to Buenos Aires. Ships sailing under the Spanish *asiento* in the early sixteenth century had brought Africans primarily from the Cape Verde Islands, which served as entrepôt for Portuguese traders resident on the adjacent mainland, or from Upper Guinea. As the Portuguese intensified their search for captives in the 1580s and 1590s, they had moved directly into the rivers of these coasts. Angola, which had developed at midcentury to supply São Tomé, grew rapidly during the widespread distress there at the end of the century and became the main African supply area of the early seventeenth century. At first, European merchants, principally the Genoese, had confined themselves to financing the trade and to transporting slaves back to Europe, and had left slaving to Portuguese settled in Africa. The silver of Spanish America had attracted European merchants to Angola, and the high value of sugar and the fiscal backing of the Dutch had extended their interest to Brazil.

The planters of northeastern Brazil, indebted to their Dutch backers and to the Portuguese slavers who brought them Africans from Angola, Guinea, and Cape Verde, achieved only a precarious prosperity in the following thirty years. They devoted much of the land near the coast to sugar in order to cover the high costs of the African slaves they bought, and so they displaced ancillary, but necessary, elements of cane production elsewhere. Cattle for beef and for animal power and transport on the planta-

Table 1 Volume of the Atlantic Slave Trade, 1450–1650

| | Destination (numbers of slaves) | | |
| | | Atlantic | |
Period	Europe	Islands	São Tomé
1451–1475	12,500	2,500	—
1476–1500	12,500	5,000	1,000
1501–1525	12,500	5,000	25,000
1526–1550	7,500	5,000	18,800
1551–1575	2,500	5,000	18,800
1575–1600	1,300	2,500	12,500
1601–1625	300	—	12,500
1626–1650	300	—	6,300

| | Destination (numbers of slaves) | | |
| | Spanish | | British |
Period	America	Brazil	Caribbean
1451–1475	—	—	—
1476–1500	—	—	—
1501–1525	—	—	—
1526–1550	12,500	—	—
1551–1575	25,000	10,000	—
1575–1600	56,000	40,000	—
1601–1625	148,800	100,000	—
1626–1650	111,600	100,000	20,700

| | Destination (numbers of slaves) | | |
| | French | North | |
Period	Caribbean	America	Total
1451–1475	—	—	15,000
1476–1500	—	—	18,500
1501–1525	—	—	42,500
1526–1550	—	—	43,800
1551–1575	—	—	61,300
1575–1600	—	—	112,300
1601–1625	—	200	261,800
1626–1650	2,500	1,200	242,600

Source: William D. Phillips, *Slavery from Roman Times*, p. 193.

tions were brought from the dry interior, where livestock raising thrived. The slaves on the plantations ate mostly manioc, or cassava, in addition to fish from local waters. Bahian and Pernambucan planters fed their slaves manioc flour from around Guanabara Bay, where the city of Rio de Janeiro now stands.

Portuguese settlers at Guanabara Bay, unable to match the established colonies of the Northeast in growing sugar, cultivated manioc with the labor of enslaved Indians, whom they bought from frontier settlers living inland at São Paulo. These Paulistas, known also as *bandeirantes* from the banners (*bandeiras*) of the leaders they followed, raided and traded for slaves among Indian populations far to the west. This southern Brazilian trade in Indian slaves was characteristic, as elsewhere, of regions marginal to the prosperous export sectors of the American economies, and was stimulated by the success of sugar that enabled the planters of Bahia and Pernambuco to afford slaves from Africa. The Paulistas' trade in Indian slaves endured until the end of the seventeenth century, when discoveries of gold and diamonds in adjoining mountainous regions drew large numbers of enslaved Africans to southern Brazil through merchants seeking precious minerals.

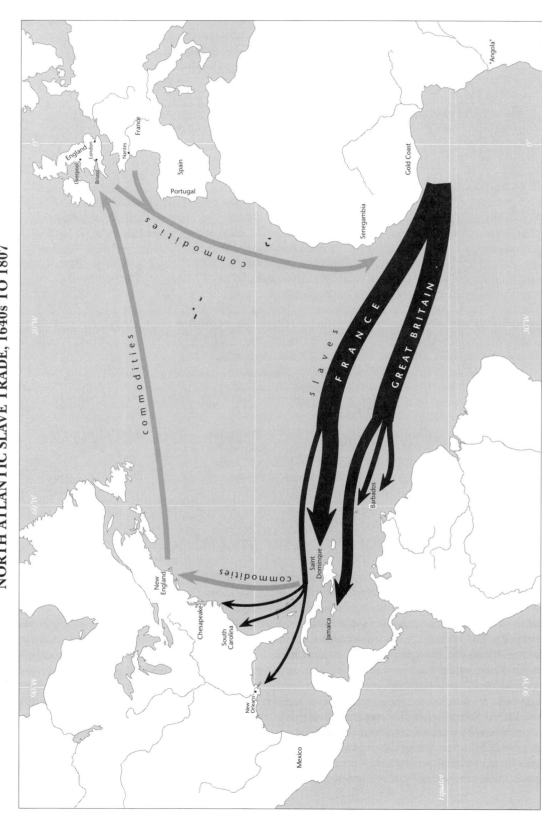

NORTH ATLANTIC SLAVE TRADE, 1640s TO 1807

DUTCH DEVELOPMENT
OF THE ATLANTIC TRADE
IN THE SEVENTEENTH CENTURY

The European nations active in the African trade in the seventeenth century organized large trading companies of merchant "adventurers" to spread the substantial risks of investing large amounts of capital in Africa and America. The companies also lowered their risks by claiming monopoly rights in the Atlantic trade and within the colonial territories controlled by the sponsoring governments. These companies mustered the capital necessary to expand slaving into regions where the trade had not previously reached on a significant scale.

The Dutch had been pioneers in mercantile trading firms overseas since their creation of the Dutch East India Company in 1602. They were the first to apply the company strategy to the Atlantic trade in slaves, though only gradually. In the course of the struggle mounted by the United Provinces against Spain, and later against England, over control of the western ocean between the 1620s and the 1670s, the Dutch launched a sister company, the Dutch West India Company, in 1621. Merchants in Amsterdam interested in American sugar had reliable access to supplies of *muscovado* through the Brazilian connections of the Sephardic Jews resident in the Low Countries, and they had built up a substantial sugar-processing capacity in Holland. Dutch shipping, backed by the financial strength of home merchants, therefore went to fetch Brazilian sugar directly in the early seventeenth century, obtaining as much as half to three-quarters of each harvest. Few independent Dutch voyages to Africa had to resort to slaving. Private Dutch traders there, like other Europe-based investors, originally focused on gold and so established their first trading stations on the Gold Coast, where the Portuguese had been buying the metal at their fortress at Mîna (or Elmina, "the mine") for many years.

Dutch captains sought booty as much as trading partners, and so Dutch West India Company captains regularly attacked Portuguese ships carrying slaves and sailing under the Spanish flag during the years when the Dual Monarchy linked the Portuguese to Spain. Privateering supplemented the company's rather peripheral commercial interests in salt and other American commodities during its earlier years. The first slaves reported to have reached an English colony in North America, twenty individuals bought from a passing "dutch man of warre" at Point Comfort, near Jamestown, in 1619, very likely arrived on a Dutch privateer en route to New Netherland, where the company had established a trading post in 1613. Their arrival preceded Dutch commercial commitments to slaving, made in the 1640s. The official historian of the company estimated that through the 1620s its captains took fewer than two hundred slaves each year from the Portuguese.

Since the Dutch West India Company had no position in African slaving, which the Portuguese controlled, it depended in part on harassing the Spanish silver fleets in the Caribbean and occasionally on seizure and enslavement of Indians in northern South America during the 1620s, especially in the forests that later became Suriname. These Indians the company delivered mostly to support its struggling labor-short colonies in the Caribbean: Saint Croix, Saba, Saint Martin, Saint Eustatius, and other islands, especially Curaçao. In these islands, as in Brazil fifty years earlier, settlers bought captured Indians because they were too poor to purchase slaves from European suppliers who had paid goods to acquire them in Africa and had to cover the costs of transatlantic transport.

The character of the company's activities in Africa changed from buying gold, ivory, and such other commodities as dyewoods after it took possession of the Portuguese sugar plantations in northeastern Brazil in 1630, renaming Bahia and Pernambuco the colony of New Holland. The company thereby not only took direct control of their countrymen's investments in Portuguese sugar but also acquired the Brazilian plantations' needs for African slaves. A Dutch fleet from Brazil crossed the Atlantic to capture Portugal's Mina fortress in 1638, adding purchases of slaves to the gold available there, and a second fleet took São Tomé and Luanda, in Angola, in 1641, the year after Spanish authority there under the Dual Monarchy came to an end. The Dutch West India Company thus took possession of Portugal's main source of slaves and entered the slave trade in the Atlantic during the 1640s, not long after other Dutch were settling at New

Netherland and in the Hudson River valley in North America, claiming extensive tracts of land and committing themselves to import the labor necessary to work them. The company was in serious financial straits by this time and had lost its monopoly on Brazilian sugar to Dutch traders unaffiliated with it. Its engagement in slaving thus reflected in part its weakness in other, less risky, commercial spheres, and it came to depend on its remaining privileged access to the African trade. As a result, for a few years in the 1640s, the Dutch dominated the trade, though at levels somewhat lower than the Portuguese had attained, averaging around twenty-five hundred slaves per year. Of greater consequence in the longer term was the fact that the company forced the withdrawal of peninsular Portuguese from the trade in slaves.

The Portuguese in Brazil regrouped to expel the Dutch from the northeastern sugar colonies in a series of wars lasting from 1645 to 1654. A Brazilian fleet from Rio de Janeiro restored Angola to the control of Portugal in 1648. Brazilians thereafter dominated slaving in the southern Atlantic. Dutch interests in sugar had shifted away from Brazil and toward English islands in the Caribbean, particularly Barbados, in the later 1640s, perhaps as a hedge against the prospect of losing their colony in Brazil. Financiers and refiners in the Netherlands provided the capital to invest in land then held by small English farmers raising tobacco, indigo, and cotton on Barbados, mostly with the labor of indentured servants from the British Isles. Few of them possessed enough capital to consolidate landholdings on a scale capable of supporting sugar or to acquire the costly roller mills, boiling facilities, and other technology essential to sugar production. Fewer still had the cash to purchase slaves direct from Africa. In spite of the pervasive mercantilist restrictions on trade that characterized the century, Dutch planters with experience in Pernambuco arrived on the island. Company slavers delivered Africans, providing the credit that allowed them and the English settlers to consolidate large plantations and carrying the semi-refined sugar back to Amsterdam. Others started the sugar industry on the French islands of Guadeloupe and Martinique. The Dutch interest in Barbadian sugar created an opening for traders in England to enter the trade in slaves in significant numbers for the first time, and the French joined in supplying slaves to their islands not long after.

New Netherland, in North America, remained a backwater of the Dutch trade in slaves, unable to compete against the wealthier labor markets in the sugar colonies of Brazil and the Caribbean, not to mention the attractions of silver in the Spanish colonies. Small numbers of Africans reached the Hudson on ships returning to Europe from the West Indies, but only two full cargoes of slaves direct from Africa are known to have reached there, one in 1654, and the other in 1664, just before the English captured the colony. So insignificant was New Netherland to the company as a market for slaves that it surrendered its precious monopoly on them there in 1652. The West Indies Company thereafter devoted its attention to the slave-trading depot that it had developed on Curaçao. Until 1662 the island served largely as a base for smuggling slaves to the Spanish mainland colonies, after that year it was a base for supplying slaves to the Genoese merchants who held the *asiento* of that period, and eventually for obtaining the Spanish slave-delivery contract for themselves in 1667. The two thousand or more slaves that the company delivered to the Spaniards, and increasingly to Suriname and other Dutch colonies in the Guianas, came largely from west-central Africa north of the mouth of the Zaire River, a part of the coast known as Loango. During the 1670s the Dutch had a great deal to do with extending slaving to the Loango Coast; it would become a major supplier of labor to all European slaving nations throughout the eighteenth century. In the Caribbean, the Dutch were the dominant suppliers of slaves to the island possessions of all the European nations for two decades after midcentury.

BEGINNINGS OF THE ENGLISH TRADE: THE ROYAL AFRICAN COMPANY

English captains entered the Atlantic slave trade to sell captive Africans to the developing sugar plantations of Barbados. Once the English had developed the shipping capability to supply slaves to Barbados, they extended their delivery system to other islands in the West Indies and also to the mainland colonies around the Chesapeake and in New York. The introduction of slaves to Barbados converted the island from thousands of small ten-acre (4-hectare) farms, worked mostly by indentured English, to a much smaller number of large, slave-worked plantations. As of 1640, there had been approximately 52,000 English settlers in the West Indies, compared with 22,000 in all the settlements in New England. By 1659 only 259 planters controlled about half of the land area in Barbados, and by 1680 that number had fallen to 175. The island's slave population grew from about 6,000 in 1643 to 20,000 in 1655 and to 38,782 in 1680. By that year fewer than 2,000 indentured servants remained. Consolidation of the large plantations forced English farmers in the islands to emigrate in search of land, and some of them, together with their slaves, went to South Carolina.

This "sugar revolution" spread quickly to the English Leeward Islands—Saint Kitts, Nevis, Antigua, Montserrat—and to Jamaica. The French occupied the western end of the formerly Spanish island of Santo Domingo, calling their colony there Saint-Domingue. By 1700 the French and English had joined the Dutch as major slaving powers and together had delivered some 450,000 Africans to the Caribbean area, nearly all of them laboring in the cane fields of growing numbers of large plantations. The English may have been carrying as many as 10,000 slaves each year by 1700, and these numbers increased decade by decade throughout the 1700s, to more than 30,000 per year, except in times of war on the high seas. The French were delivering slaves at something less than half the English levels of trade by the 1710s, increased their trade in rough proportion to that of the English throughout the century, and approached the English totals in the 1780s, when slavers of each nation may have brought some 30,000 Africans to the Americas each year.

In Africa, the increased West Indian demand for captives caused captains from France and England to develop new parts of the coast as suppliers of slaves. The Portuguese retained control of Angola, the main sources of slaves in west-central Africa, preventing the northern Europeans from open slaving south of the Zaire River mouth. The Gold Coast, the area around the Portuguese (subsequently Dutch) "castle" at Mina, began to export slaves as well as gold after the 1670s. The French led the movement east from there along the coast, taking the captives who gave the region its European name, the Slave Coast. The English then leapfrogged to the delta of the Niger River, still farther east, and entered the rivers and creeks beyond in search of captives. Increasing numbers of French and English ships joined the Dutch along the Loango Coast north of the Zaire. These regions became the principal African sources of slaves destined for the Caribbean and North America throughout the eighteenth century, although Senegambia and Upper Guinea in far western Africa contributed smaller numbers to the trade as well.

The organization of the English trade followed patterns set earlier in Spain, Portugal, and the Netherlands: wealthy investors close to the centers of power tended to combine in large trading companies with commercial privileges, to concentrate on the specie-yielding forms of African and American trade, and in the longer run to limit their participation in slaving itself to licensing and financing. Operation of the ships that carried the slaves was left to others: the Brazilians within the Portuguese sphere, and the Dutch West India Company in the Netherlands. The first English to venture out to Africa, like the Dutch, had sought gold and other commodities, not slaves.

An early African Company was in place from 1588, with stations on the Gambia River and near the Niger delta in the Bight of Benin. Its successors supplemented Dutch deliveries of slaves to meet the growing demand in Barbados in the 1640s. Given new charters after the Restoration, in 1660 and 1663, the highly aristocratic Company of Royal Adventurers into Africa received monopoly trading rights to the West African coast and began to challenge Dutch slavers in African waters as part of the generally aggressive posture of the English toward their commercial rivals across the Channel. The Company of Royal Adventurers served as much as an instrument of royal political strategy as an active commercial firm, and consequently it both incurred damages from Dutch counterattacks and bore the heavy expenses of maintaining permanent trading posts on the African coast.

Encumbered by these costs and losses, it was unable to deliver more than a fraction of the slaves needed by English sugar planters in the Caribbean.

Unauthorized private merchants, known in official circles as "interlopers," intruded on the company's monopoly of the African trade to meet the planters' demands for slaves almost at once. By 1669 the company acknowledged its inability to compete and began selling licenses to the interlopers to buy slaves within the area of its protected rights. Established London merchants organized a new Royal African Company in 1672 and set about developing the commercial opportunities of the African trade, including slaves, whom they transported to the Americas in quantities three times greater than had their predecessors. Still, the Royal African Company never delivered as many as ten thousand slaves in a year, against a demand that some estimated at more than twice that number. Its capital was encumbered by expensive obligations to maintain the coastal fortresses, or "castles," that it had inherited from its predecessors and—typical of the slave trade throughout the Americas— by growing debt owed to it by planters. The company frequently sold its slaves on credit, leaving them with planters to tend a new crop of cane and accepting delayed payment in the form of a pledge of the harvest.

The implicit emphasis of the illiquid company's strategy then shifted to methods of raising cash to maintain its commercial operations. By 1689 it had entered into an agreement with the Spanish holder of the current *asiento* that, it was hoped, would bring returns, as usual in the Spanish trade, in silver. During the 1690s the company endured scathing criticism from planters in the West Indies, unable to obtain the labor they wanted and resentful at the rising prices they had to pay, and from merchant competitors in England unable to penetrate its monopoly. The company effectively opened the trade to these private merchants in 1698, in return for a 10 percent duty paid to it to maintain the forts on the African coast. It later contracted to supply as many as three thousand slaves per year to yet another English company formed to obtain the Spanish *asiento* in 1713, the South Sea Company. Nonetheless, the English trade had fallen definitively into the hands of private merchants,

at first illegally, then legally through payment of the 10 percent duty, and finally—after 1712— without further legal impediment. It was they who carried English slaving to its heights later in the eighteenth century, always focused on Jamaica, the largest of England's sugar islands by far, and the other plantations of the Caribbean.

THE ENGLISH TRADE OF THE EIGHTEENTH CENTURY

The entry into the Atlantic slave trade by the English free traders was part of the massive growth in English merchant shipping in the second half of the seventeenth century, as England fought successfully to overcome the superiority of the Dutch on the high seas. In the decade after the Ten Per Cent Act (1698), the free traders delivered slaves to the West Indies at three times the rate of the Royal African Company. Most of these slavers came not from London, the seat of finance and official privilege, but from the outports of the west of England. Bristol surged to the forefront of English slaving in the first three decades of the eighteenth century, propelled by the strength of a local woolen industry, copper and brass manufacturers, distilleries using West Indian sugar to manufacture spirits for sale in Africa, and merchants with experience and good connections in the Caribbean. Viewed in terms of the broader patterns of English trade, Bristol lay outside the main currents of commerce with the Continent and so had to content itself, however prosperously, with the risky and slow voyage to Africa, across the Atlantic to America, and then back to England. Such a triangular passage normally lasted twelve months and more.

Bristol merchants concentrated on delivering slaves to the North American colonies, especially to Virginia for tobacco; they dominated the trade to the York River until about 1740 and then in the upper James. It is likely that they served the Chesapeake as a second-best alternative to the more attractive trade in Caribbean sugar, on which the Royal African Company concentrated. Slavers from Bristol were briefly important in South Carolina in the 1720s, but the rice and indigo of this southern colony were destined for continental markets controlled by merchants elsewhere in England. In the broader sweep of English economic development in the eighteenth century, Bristol gained its greatest prominence in the early, often rough, years of the trade, based on local manufacturers and maritime experience. It fell behind as the greater industrial and commercial strength of Liverpool and London came to the fore in the mature years of high-volume slaving after mid century.

Liverpool became the largest slaving port in the Atlantic during the second half of the eighteenth century. Like Bristol, it entered slaving through earlier contacts in the Americas, where in the late seventeenth century its merchants had bought sugar in the Caribbean and tobacco in the Chesapeake through resident factors who remained in close touch with their customers and secured advance payment in produce in anticipation of the arrival of a ship. By the 1720s Liverpool had fifteen to twenty-five ships in the trade each year, mostly selling local manufactures and reexported Asian textiles. By the 1740s the city had passed Bristol as Britain's major slaving port, and it dominated the trade from then on. Although the slaving sector of Liverpool's maritime trade contributed importantly to the considerable growth and prosperity of the city, it never amounted to more than about 10 percent of the total. Prominent citizens led the way to Africa, but few of them risked their fortunes, or even the fortunes of a specific voyage, on slaving. They spread their investments over many branches of commerce and took shares in African voyages with three or four associates. Clearly, the delays and hazards of slaving deterred even the most prosperous.

Liverpool's ships grew large and specialized as volume rose, with capacities rated between one hundred and two hundred tons and often carrying three hundred to four hundred slaves and more. Vessels of such great volume strained the sources of supply in Africa, so those leaving Liverpool during its mature years as a slaving port tended to frequent the highly organized markets of the Niger Delta and the Loango Coast. They also found it difficult to sell large cargoes in many American markets, and so in the New World they concentrated on Britain's

largest sugar island, Jamaica, and, late in the trade, on French Saint-Domingue, which had developed similarly a large appetite for slaves. It was Liverpool that brought Britain's slave trade to its peak in the 1780s and 1790s. The much smaller North American colonies did not remain a principal object of the attention of Liverpool slavers.

London, the commercial and financial capital of Britain, involved itself in the slave trade mostly indirectly and, after the 1720s, to a lesser degree than Bristol and Liverpool. Londoners had backed the failures of the Royal African Company and its predecessors, and private traders from London outnumbered competitors from outports Bristol and Liverpool until 1730. Thereafter London merchants concentrated their involvement in financing purchases of slaves by planters in the West Indies, accepting bills of exchange (promissory notes secured against future sugar harvests) payable through the City. They thus guaranteed receipts to the less well capitalized slavers of western England and supplied the credit that underwrote the massive expansion of British sugar in the West Indies after that date. London avoided the risks and delays of selling slaves in the Americas but gained the valuable sugar that they cut, boiled, and packed. Bristol and Liverpool merchants returning from the Caribbean had to content themselves with commercial paper and leave the core profits of the entire trade—the transport, refining, and resale of the *muscovado*—to London. London merchants returned to the slave trade in modest numbers after 1750.

London investors handled insurance for the slave trade, refined most of the sugar reaching the British Isles, and supplied the Asian textiles on which Bristol and Liverpool merchants depended for successful trade in Africa. They also invested in the tobacco trade from the Chesapeake, becoming shippers and creditors who backed much of the expansion in Virginia tobacco early in the eighteenth century. Virginia planters fell badly into debt to London in the 1730s and at other times when tobacco prices declined, which prompted them to sell their tobacco directly to a wave of traders from Glasgow who followed the tobacco frontier into the hinterland from the 1720s on. Beyond the vital credit that London merchants and bankers contributed to the slaving of their countrymen, Londoners supported the sale of slaves to buy silver in the Spanish colonies. After gold and diamonds in Minas Gerais, not far from São Paulo and inland from Rio de Janeiro, drew tens of thousands of slaves from Angola to southern Brazil beginning in the 1710s, they supported slaving through Lisbon merchants. London's financial strength thus stimulated slaving from one end of the Americas to the other.

Londoners who remained active in the transport of the slaves were smaller specialists who evidently were not connected to the sugar merchants, financiers, and insurers dominant in the City's West Indian trade. These slavers found themselves displaced from Barbados and Jamaica by specialized Bristol, and then Liverpool, merchants by the 1720s and 1730s. With their smaller vessels they remained dominant longer in the minor markets of North America, principally South Carolina. They lost out by the 1720s in the Chesapeake, owing to the control that the Bristol and Liverpool merchants gained over the region's exports of tobacco.

The three axial points of the commerce in slaves—Europe, Africa, and the Americas—led to description of it as a "triangular trade." Although there was generally a movement of manufactured goods from Europe to Africa, of slaves across the Atlantic to the Americas, and of sugar from the West Indies to Britain, fewer and fewer ships completed all three legs after London became the trade's principal financier. Nearly all vessels setting out to Africa picked up slaves in exchange for the goods they delivered to the coast and then continued west to the New World. But not many could afford to linger in the sugar islands until the planters had processed the next harvest for shipment. The availability of payment in bills of exchange drawn on London merchants made it unnecessary for them to do so. Some of these ships, faced with returning to England in ballast, continued north to the North American colonies, in search of return cargoes. These vessels sometimes carried partial or even full cargoes of slaves that they had not sold advantageously in the West Indies. Two-thirds or more of the sugar moved directly in London ships, in an out-and-back shuttle trade between Britain and the Caribbean.

From the perspective of the English slave trade as a whole, North America remained a minor appendage of the larger and more influential interests in Spanish silver, indirectly in Brazilian gold through Portugal, and in the sterling profits available from the transport, processing, and sale of refined sugar. The lesser carriers, from Bristol and London, favored the mainland colonies as large and specialized Liverpool slavers displaced them from markets in the West Indies. However, ships from Liverpool became prominent everywhere after mid century. The larger vessels concentrated on the main markets in Jamaica and elsewhere in the Caribbean, continuing on to South Carolina and the Chesapeake mostly in special circumstances and often with partial cargoes of slaves.

THE CHESAPEAKE AND CAROLINA

The landing of twenty enslaved Africans at Jamestown in 1619 led to a systematic trade in slaves only very gradually. In the early seventeenth century, England had no significant possessions in the West Indies, and hence no market for Indian slaves comparable with that lying behind Spanish slaving in Florida a century earlier. No organized trade in Indian captives developed in the Chesapeake region, though captives were occasionally taken and held. Nonetheless, the tobacco planters of Virginia took occasional Powhatan captured in war as bond servants and kept a few as slaves in the towns, but the colony was too weak to risk the violence and retaliation that could result from systematic resort to local slaving. The feebleness of the Virginia colony also meant that its demand for labor did not exceed its capacity to attract indentured servants from England, Scotland, and Ireland for labor in the tobacco fields. Greater prosperity in the 1650s and 1660s may have brought more Indians as slaves into the colony, and the frontier wars of that period probably involved more regular seizures of captives for enslavement, even if they were nominally held as indentured servants, converted to Christianity, and trained in English culture as justification. The interest of the English in enslaved Indians in Virginia, as else-

56

where, centered on women and children, whom they found easier to control than men and whom they employed as domestic servants.

The supply of indentured labor to the Chesapeake dwindled in the 1660s as wages rose in England, alternative opportunities for settlement opened in the middle colonies, and the chances of moving through servitude into the landholding classes in Maryland and Virginia dropped. Beyond turning to raiding for Indian slaves, the Chesapeake began to look to Africa for labor, buying a few hundred slaves annually, mostly from the intercolonial trade between the Chesapeake and the West Indies.

In the aftermath of Bacon's Rebellion (1676), which awakened the wealthy of the Virginia colony to the restiveness of a growing class of landless former servants among them, Virginia planters began to buy Africans in larger numbers from English slavers and from captains of small colonial vessels returning from carrying North American foodstuffs and naval stores to the West Indies. Unable to obtain specie in return for these products from West Indian planters already heavily indebted to merchants in London, they accepted by-products of the sugar islands' principal business: molasses, rum, and slaves not wanted on the plantations.

At about the same time, in 1670, a number of small English farmers, driven from Barbados by the island's conversion to large, slave-worked sugar plantations, settled on the southern mainland coast at the estuary of the Ashley and Cooper rivers in search of new lands. Lacking capital to invest in the development of export agriculture, settlers at the town of Charleston traded for deerskins with the Indians of the region. Slaves taken in wars against coastal Indians appeared almost at once among the colony's exports to the West Indies. Conflict between England and Spain sparked Queen Anne's War (1702–1713), and the Indians allied with both sides—the Spaniards in Florida, the English in Carolina—seized and sold thousands of captives as slaves. With depletion of the coastal deer populations after 1710, this exchange developed almost at once into a systematic commerce in slaves to offset the rising costs of carrying skins from distant locations inland. The English bought them from Indian trading partners, whose hunt-

ing they had financed with credit in trade goods and whose debts they could no longer collect in deerskins. They then armed the Indians, particularly the Yamassee, to take up raiding among their neighbors farther in the interior. The raids of the Yamassee extended hundreds of miles to the south and west, into Spanish Florida, the Gulf Coast, and French Louisiana.

By the early eighteenth century, Charleston merchants had handled more than ten thousand captive Indians, sending them as slaves to other English colonies in the Chesapeake and around the Caribbean. The Indian slave trade of the southern mainland thus supplemented the African trade during the years of greatest planter demand in excess of the still-limited ability of English slavers to supply labor from Africa between 1680 and about 1720. The South Carolina colony's reliance on enslaving and selling Indians ended with the Yamassee War of 1715–1717. Traders had begun seizing Yamassee women and children in satisfaction of the debts owed, and the Yamassee and several allies attacked the English settlements, threatening them seriously before suffering defeat. The rice growers of the coastal lowlands then began to buy Africans from the large number of English slavers delivering labor to the Caribbean.

At the same time, planters in the Chesapeake had turned to buying African slaves. In addition to rising wages in England and a consequent decline in the numbers of English willing to indenture themselves as servants in the New World, the rush of slaves available in the Caribbean owing to the creation of the Royal African Company and the growth of sugar production there, and sharp increases in European demand for Virginia tobacco contributed to the extension of English slaving to Virginia beginning about the 1680s. London ships brought six hundred to one thousand slaves each year between 1699 and 1718. Virginians needed slaves after the disruptions of trade during the European wars settled by the Treaty of Utrecht (1713), in order to increase production of tobacco. They added greater (though still modest) numbers of slaves to their commodity trade with the Caribbean, bought Indians from slavers in South Carolina (including some of the prisoners taken in the Yamassee War), and sent eight vessels of their

57

own to Africa between 1718 and 1726, just as Carolinians turned definitively to buying slaves from Africa. These tactics raised the numbers of slaves imported to two thousand in some years.

In this period, most Africans reaching Virginia came still from the West Indies, in a continuation of the established pattern of selling local produce to obtain labor needed in the tobacco-growing sectors of the Chesapeake economy. Landowners in the less prosperous counties of the region entered the West Indian trade in foodstuffs and naval stores, taking some of their returns in slaves, whom they then sold to the increasingly wealthy tobacco-planting elite. Like planters everywhere in the New World, when faced with the high costs of establishing a new export sector and committed to selling all their crops to cover debts to merchants from Europe, they displaced the provisioning sectors of the economy from the commodity-exporting core and used secondary exports and by-products of their main cash-earning commodities to barter for provisions and labor within the region. Virginians here duplicated the strategies of Brazilians in the sugar captaincies of the Northeast, of Spaniards resorting to Indian slaving, and of their English countrymen in Charleston.

Bristol slavers came to the Chesapeake in the 1720s and were followed by the ships from Liverpool, as the latter came to dominate slaving in all of England's American colonies during the 1730s and 1740s. The vast majority (over 90 percent) of these slaves came from Africa, more than half of them from the Gold Coast, though sometimes they were on ships that had the West Indies as their primary destination and had then continued to the Chesapeake with unsold slaves. They usually arrived during the spring and summer months, when Chesapeake demand for labor rose and when the new slaves would have several months of mild weather in which to adjust before facing the rigors of a winter in a temperate latitude. Annual imports of slaves rose well above two thousand, and in one year (1752) approached four thousand individuals. This peak followed Britain's loss of access to the mainland Spanish markets in 1750, and may thus have represented a temporary diversion of slaves no longer salable in the West Indies. A few Norfolk merchants lacking tobacco to sell in England sent ships to the West Indies that returned with modest numbers of slaves to supply the lower James River region. Elsewhere, earnings from tobacco allowed planters to buy up to 90 percent of their slaves from large English ships arriving from Africa.

As the fortunes of tobacco waned after mid century, the high levels of imports of the 1730s and 1740s declined. The distinctive ability of Chesapeake slaves to reproduce themselves had manifested itself by the 1730s, increasingly saving planters the scarce cash that they would otherwise have had to pay to buy labor from abroad. Though Norfolk's low-cost regional trade in slaves tended to fare better than its increasingly costly British counterpart, the extra hands reared in the slave quarters of Virginia's plantations were available for sale to lesser landowners, thus initiating a trend toward disposing of unneeded laborers that later matured to become the large interstate trade in slaves that supplied the labor for the nineteenth-century growth of cotton cultivation in the South. The Seven Years' War (1756–1763) reduced imports of costly slaves from Africa to a few hundred each year. In 1777 Virginia planters with large numbers of locally born laborers on their hand, facing the British blockade of maritime trade during the Revolutionary War and sharply reduced demand for their tobacco, and seeking to reduce their indebtedness, banned further entries of new slaves.

South Carolina settlers had brought African slaves with them from Barbados, and some of the English proprietors of the colony had interests in the Royal African Company. They did not, however, begin importing Africans as slaves in substantial numbers until the first decade of the eighteenth century, when planters began to develop rice as a plantation crop in the coastal lowlands. After the Yamassee War, between 1717 and 1775 over ninety thousand slaves passed through the hands of Charleston merchants, an average of about thirteen hundred each year, about 86 percent of them direct from Africa, particularly Senegambia and the Windward Coast. The first wave of Africans brought to develop rice in the lowlands peaked at around twenty-five hundred arrivals each year in the 1730s but receded sharply after the Stono Rebellion of 1739 brought a reaction against dangerous new Africans and a new import duty against continued deliveries of them. Though the volume of imports dropped in the 1740s, the spread of indigo cultivation through the higher elevations of the interior after 1748 restored the colony's demand for African labor, and South Carolina continued to import two thousand to three thousand slaves each year through the 1750s and 1760s, long after imports from Africa had dropped to insignificant levels in the Chesapeake.

In South Carolina—unlike Virginia, where Norfolk had only modest prominence as a seaport—Charleston emerged as a significant regional commercial entrepôt for the trade in African slaves. Merchants there acted as commission agents for English slavers and supplied not only the indigo growers of the Carolina upcountry but also the rice-growing planters of North Carolina from the 1730s to the 1760s. They also sold to buyers in Georgia after that colony's early ban against slaves fell to its rice-growing planters' demands for slaves in 1750. As in other North American markets, London ships opened the trade but then yielded to competitors from Bristol as volume grew. Liverpool merchants arrived in force during the Seven Years' War in 1758. After 1766, the Liverpool ships began to take slaves directly from Africa to Savannah, and half a dozen Georgia vessels sailed directly to the Guinea Coast to bring back slaves to meet the heavy demand of that decade. Charleston merchants sent ships of their own to Africa only occasionally, especially in the first decade of the eighteenth century, when Carolina could not yet compete with markets in the West Indies for the attention of the Royal African Company. Much of the trade during its most robust years in the 1750s was owing to the efforts of the merchant Henry Laurens, a man well connected in England and having sufficient credit to finance his customers' purchases of the slaves he sold.

THE FRENCH AND SPANISH TRADE TO THE LOWER MISSISSIPPI

The French entered the Atlantic slave trade in the seventeenth century through a monopoly company similar to the English Royal African Company. The Compagnie des Indes Occiden-

tales (1664) was chartered to develop France's Caribbean possessions, then only the islands of Martinique and Guadeloupe, through heavily regulated colonial trade focused on the sugar estates started there by the Dutch. The company failed to meet the planters' demand for slaves, and other companies and private merchants joined it to manage as many as three thousand slaves a year to the French Antilles—including the large island of Saint-Domingue—early in the eighteenth century. Company directors were diverted by the lure of the *asiento* until 1713, the year of the Treaty of Utrecht, in which the English South Sea Company won the Spanish slaving contract from them. Private merchants, led by those from Nantes, at once dispatched ships to Africa to fill the unmet needs of the sugar planters on the French islands. After 1730, Bordeaux, like London in the British trade, became the main French port financing and supplying the Antilles and importing their sugar. And Nantes, having no other entrée to the wealth of the islands, concentrated on Africa and supplied slaves to earn its share of colonial commerce. Together with a dozen smaller ports, Nantes took the French slave trade to its heights late in the eighteenth century, always delivering the majority of captive Africans to Saint-Domingue.

The French slave trade extended intermittently to the small French settlements in the lower Mississippi Valley. The arrival of Robert Cavalier, sieur de La Salle, from the north in 1682 led to establishment of a French colony on the Gulf Coast in 1699, and construction at New Orleans got under way in 1718. The colonists met their needs for labor during the first decades of the eighteenth century by enslaving Indians, many of them war captives taken by Choctaw, Mississippi, and other western groups allied with the French and locked in conflict with Creek and Chickasaw, who traded with the English in South Carolina. Until the end of the eighteenth century, a significant minority of the domestics in the towns of Louisiana, including many female concubines, were of Indian origin. Consolidation of French authority upriver led to war against the Natchez in the 1720s, the seizure of numerous captives, and export of a thousand of them to the Caribbean islands.

A trading company established in France in 1717 for the development of Louisiana (the Compagnie de l'Occident) failed to provide indentured servants to meet the labor needs of the colony and merged in 1719 with the Compagnie des Indes Orientales. Like nearly all its predecessors, it was unable to compete with private merchants as a supplier of African slaves to the rapidly growing sugar plantations of Saint-Domingue, and so it concentrated its deliveries of enslaved Africans in its protected market in Louisiana, sending over thirteen hundred in 1721 and several hundred annually during the following decade. However, Louisiana remained a remote and very minor destination for French slavers, owing to their inability to meet the much greater demands of the rich sugar islands in the Caribbean. The slaves who reached Louisiana—seldom more than several hundred in a given year, and only about twenty-eight thousand in all, perhaps 8 percent of the French trade before 1763—came mostly from Senegambia.

Spain reacquired Louisiana in 1763 as part of the settlement of the Seven Years' War. Sugar production and imports of slaves had begun, belatedly, to increase in Cuba under British occupation during the war. With the return of peace, Britain opened several West Indian ports to Spanish buyers in order to maintain the markets in Spain's colonies, but no imports to Louisiana were permitted. However, the English in West Florida had access to the east bank of the Mississippi River and presumably smuggled slaves across the river to the Spanish in this period. In 1773 a new *asiento* liberalized the ancient restrictions on commerce within the empire, allowing trade in slaves within the Caribbean, but the outbreak of the American Revolution in 1776 turned the Spaniards to French sources of slaves. It was during this period of largely illegal trade that imports of slaves into Louisiana increased, a step to establishing the lower Mississippi as a significant producer of sugar early in the nineteenth century.

SLAVERS FROM THE MIDDLE COLONIES AND NEW ENGLAND

The middle colonies—Pennsylvania, New Jersey, and New York—were markets too small to attract the great English ships carrying 250 to 350 Africans, so local merchants there tended to handle the more modest numbers of slaves they required. New York, as the major mercantile center of the northern colonies, had opportunities less risky than the African trade to pursue its fortunes. Its merchants consequently seldom became involved in slaving other than for the needs of the colony. Still, New York traders were large enough to risk ventures of their own, direct to Africa, from the late seventeenth century on. At that time they favored the remote Indian Ocean island of Madagascar, perhaps because of contacts there inherited from the Netherlands East India Company, which regularly bought Madagascar slaves for delivery to the Cape Colony in South Africa. However, the monopoly held by the English East India Company prohibited England's colonial subjects from trading beyond the Cape, except for the years from 1716 to 1721, when New York merchants brought a number of slaves from the Indian Ocean. They turned to the African trade in greater numbers after about 1748, averaging five or six voyages, and several hundred slaves, per year until 1775. New Jersey became a significant market for these New York slavers because lower duties there made the colony a center for smuggling slaves to its faster-growing neighbors, New York and Pennsylvania.

Philadelphians imported only a few slaves from the West Indies between the founding of the Pennsylvania colony in 1681 and the outbreak of the Seven Years' War in 1756. General merchants there doing business with the West Indies, like their counterparts elsewhere in the mainland colonies, found it expedient from time to time to include small numbers of slaves along with the goods they brought from the islands. Then British conscription of indentured servants and the wartime disruption of the usual supplies of immigrants left a sudden unmet demand for labor. Between 1760 and 1772 a small number of Philadelphia merchants defied the Quaker antipathy to slavery in the colony and sent a dozen ships directly to Africa. These returned with 100 to 160 or 170 slaves each, often unloading their cargoes on the New Jersey side of the Delaware to avoid the Pennsylvania duty on imported Africans.

In New England, with family farms and hence little demand for African labor, the slave trade paradoxically reached levels higher than in any other of the North American colonies. The reasons for the relative prominence of New England slavers lay partly in the maritime orientation of the region's economy but more importantly in the difficulties that Massachusetts and Rhode Island experienced in paying for the manufactures and other imports that their consuming free populations bought from England. Without the plantation staples in demand in Europe—sugar, tobacco, rice, indigo—they found the bills and specie they needed to cover persistent trade deficits with the mother country by selling the fish, beef, barrel staves, and other products of their seas, fields, and forests to the West Indies. There they purchased molasses that the sugar planters drained off the *muscovado* they prepared for shipment back to London. This inexpensive by-product of the centerpiece of England's slave-based economy was carried back to New England, where it was distilled into a harsh rum of very high proof.

Shippers carried casks of the concentrated spirits directly to West Africa, where they found a strong demand for their cargoes among the English and other slavers on the coast. They then filled their ships with slaves, recrossed the Atlantic to the Caribbean, and sold their captive cargoes for bills good in London and for more molasses to complete the cycle. To the varying extent to which these captains sold their slaves in the Caribbean, this circuit of New England products for West Indian molasses, distilled to rum in New England, rum to Africa for slaves, and slaves across the middle passage to the Caribbean for more molasses constituted one of the few full triangles plied by any of the slavers in the Atlantic. Its contribution to the overall balance of the colonies' payments with the mother country was small but—undoubtedly for those who participated in it—significant. It was primarily a way of disposing of surpluses of molasses bought for the consumption of New Englanders and for North American distribution in the coastal trade. Rum was virtually the only product, other than tobacco, that North Americans could deliver less expensively to Africa than could England. This triangle could function by delivering slaves to Virginia and Maryland, rather than to

West Indian sources of sugar, because its volume was so small relative to total Yankee imports of molasses and exports of rum. Sales of slaves in the Chesapeake added tobacco, also in demand in Africa, to the cargoes that New England slavers had to sell there.

Bostonians first acquired slaves in the seventeenth century as part of their large direct trade with the West Indies, as did their counterparts in the Chesapeake. They, however, had the resources and experience to mount ventures to the African coast at least as early as the 1680s, where they joined other interlopers in violating the monopoly of the Royal African Company. Representatives of the city's large and energetic merchant fleet then joined slavers from Carolina in exploiting the opportunities to buy slaves in Africa granted by the Ten Per Cent Act of 1698, since the company neglected all the North American colonies other than the Chesapeake in order to obtain the high prices then available in the West Indies for slaves. Not many attempted to compete with London ships in the West Indies and instead delivered their captives to the Chesapeake, where demand was increasing rapidly. Few brought many slaves back to Massachusetts. Although vessels from Boston, and also Salem, continued to return from Africa with slaves for the remainder of the century, Massachusetts merchants had too many other, less difficult commercial opportunities to devote more than a very minor portion of their trading to slaves.

Not so well placed were the merchants and distillers of Newport, Rhode Island, and they accordingly concentrated their shipping ventures on the rum-slave-molasses triangle to a degree that made them the leading slave carriers in the North American colonies and their home port one of the five leading entrepôts of the mainland. Weak participants in the West Indian trade compared even with their brethren in Massachusetts, they further tended to concentrate on foreign sugar islands, helping to meet labor demands there in excess of what the slavers of the mother countries, particularly France, were able to deliver. The town of Newport led the way to Africa, followed by Bristol and, later, by Providence. Rhode Island ships usually set sail in the summer or early fall, intending to arrive on the West African coast after the rainy season had ended and to acquire their slave cargoes during the fall hurricane season in the Caribbean. In Africa, at least before 1775, the Rhode Islanders favored the Gold Coast, where they could exchange their cargoes of rum, sugar, and tobacco with British merchants bringing the other goods necessary to buy slaves from African suppliers, or—optimally—sell their rum for gold. Their inability to muster the whole range of metalwares, textiles, firearms, beads, and shells demanded by Africans made it difficult for them to trade independently in less organized markets elsewhere on the coast, though they expanded after 1750 to Senegambia and northern Upper Guinea. British ships found them an inexpensive, direct supplementary source of the American products they required.

The Rhode Islanders aimed to deliver slaves to Barbados, Jamaica, or the French colony of Saint-Domingue from January on, or occasionally to continue to North American markets in the spring. Until the 1750s they tended to correspond with England through merchants in Boston, but thereafter they began to build commercial contacts with the southern colonies through New York and Philadelphia. However, before the revolution they did not attempt to compete with the English suppliers of the largest continental markets in Carolina and the Chesapeake. The Rhode Islanders' ships were small, averaging only a hundred slaves or so per voyage, in comparison with the three hundred to four hundred-slave cargoes of the English vessels of the time. They mounted perhaps ten to fifteen voyages per year from 1723 through about 1740 and then dropped back to five or so in the 1740s during King George's War (the War of the Austrian Succession, 1743–1748). Rhode Islanders returned to the African trade during the early 1750s, sending twelve or thirteen ships annually; they shied away during the Seven Years' War (1756–1763), then returned in greater force until 1775, with twenty or more ships in the trade in most years. During the years before the revolution they carried nearly sixty thousand slaves, up to twenty-five hundred per year at their peak.

Rhode Island slavers contributed less than 1 percent of the total trade in the Caribbean, only a slightly greater proportion of the English trade, and an insignificant part of the much smaller trade of the North American colonies. They were dominant suppliers only of the minor local market in Rhode Island. Slaving constituted a major commitment for only a few families, principally the Malbones and Vernons of Newport. Other large merchants participated from time to time, as a minor part of their diversified trading strategies. The contribution of Rhode Island's slave trade to the growth of the New England economy was marginal; Africa never accounted for more than 5 percent of the region's overseas trade in the colonial period, although it was a part of the much more significant commerce in commodities with the slave plantations of the West Indies.

THE MIDDLE PASSAGE

The ocean voyage from Africa to North America, known generally as "the middle passage" between the African homeland and slavery in the New World, was among the lengthiest in the Atlantic trade, owing to the greater sailing distance from Africa to the mainland than to the Caribbean. A few highly edited, personal accounts survive, one by Ayuba Suleiman Diallo, taken from Senegambia to Maryland in 1731, and another by Olaudah Equiano, taken from the Niger Delta region of Africa to Barbados and then Virginia in 1756. A small sample of voyages from 1804 to 1807 shows that Rhode Island slavers leaving the Senegambian region took thirty-nine days, on the average, to reach Charleston; those from the Upper Guinea (modern Sierra Leone) coast, fifty-six days; and those from the Gold Coast, seventy days. Presumably colonial slavers crossed in similar times. During the voyage slaves huddled amid indescribable filth in the cramped deck of the ship and dreaded their fates at the hands of mysterious masters whom they often believed were cannibals. The numbers of deaths from disease, malnutrition, and mistreatment probably resembled the rates that prevailed generally throughout the trade, falling from more than 20 percent, on average, in the seventeenth century to around 10 percent by the end of the colonial period, although few reports record the specific experience of slaves coming to North America.

Table 2 Summary Imports of Slaves in North America

Decade	Estimated Annual Imports (1)	Total Atlantic Trade (2)	Percent (3)
1731–1740	4,050	52,230	8
1741–1750	5,850	53,620	11
1751–1760	4,190	52,900	8
1761–1770	4,380	73,040	6
1771–1780	3,300	63,500	5
1781–1790	1,770	88,770	2
1791–1800	7,660	76,350	10
1801–1805	11,800	36,910	16

(1) Imports for 1731–1760 from James Rawley, *Transatlantic Slave Trade*, p. 324.
(2) Overall volume, Paul E. Lovejoy, "The Volume of the Atlantic Slave Trade," p. 485.
(3) Percentages, James Rawley, *Transatlantic Slave Trade*, p. 328.

SLAVE TRADING AFTER THE REVOLUTION

The deterioration in relations between the North American colonies and Great Britain after Parliament passed the Coercive Acts of 1774 brought a suspension of trade in slaves with the mainland's main suppliers, the English. American ships did not risk seizure by the powerful English navy during the period. The Virginia legislature had earlier attempted to restrict, or tax, imports of slaves, at a time of substantial indebtedness to England and with the slaves in the hands of the planters growing in numbers through reproduction. Disputes over the authority of the colonies to levy these import duties had contributed to the tensions leading to the Declaration of Independence in 1776 and then to war. Northern colonies had much earlier prohibited the entry of slaves, and the Continental Congress adopted a continent-wide formal boycott in 1776. Privateering and the distractions of war virtually eliminated slaving until 1783 and the return of peace.

It was the Rhode Islanders who took advantage of independence in the new United States to deliver slaves in larger numbers than ever before and to extend North American slave markets to the Caribbean, principally Cuba in the 1780s. British slavers labored under new restrictions on the numbers of slaves they could carry, enacted in 1788, and the unregulated American ships became more competitive in the larger At-

lantic trade. Most of the states remained closed to imports of Africans, except for South Carolina between 1803 and 1807. American shipping was, of course, excluded from British sugar islands. However, the French Antilles remained open until the largest eighteenth-century French producer, Saint-Domingue, was consumed by the Haitian revolution of 1791 and then occupied by British forces (1793). It dropped entirely out of the picture as a market for slaves. Cuba and the remainder of Spanish America, isolated by the European wars and open since 1789 to free trading in slaves, then became the major customers of the North American slavers.

Rhode Island traders sent no more than ten ventures per year to Africa in the 1780s but raised their average commitment to slaving above twenty ships from 1792 through 1807, rising to thirty-two in 1795 and thirty-eight in 1799 and as many as fifty-one ships as markets anticipated the end of slave importing in 1807. Cuba took about half of these slaves; South Carolina, starting to add cotton to its rice and indigo, received a sixth; and Georgia, emerging as an importer of African labor, twelfth. The French Caribbean islands of Martinique and Guadeloupe also took a twelfth.

Charleston became a significant investor in the slave trade during the 1790s and especially during the last years of the trade, from 1803 to 1807, in part through connections with merchants in Rhode Island. Louisiana, long left without French or Spanish sources of slaves, became a significant target for these slavers upon its acquisition by the United States in 1803, and thousands of slaves from numerous sources entered before formal abolition of the trade in 1807. Much of the feverish demand for slaves between 1803 and 1807 arose from anticipation of the trade's end.

The federal slave trade statute of 1807 prohibited the importation of slaves into the United States after 1 January 1808. It was the culmination of more than thirty years of opposition to the trade, dating back to the Quaker-sponsored measure adopted by the Continental Congress in 1774 and followed by a largely unenforceable prohibition of 1794. Few slaves entered the United States after 1807, owing in part to the internal trade that sprang up from the Chesapeake to supply the growing demand of cotton planters in the South and sugar estate owners in Louisiana. But North American slavers were far from inactive: Rhode Islanders certainly continued to supply Cuba in the 1810s, probably under legal cover of Spanish ownership of the ventures. By the 1820s an entirely new generation of slavers based in New York, Baltimore, Norfolk, New Orleans, and elsewhere had joined the rush to supply slaves to the fast-growing plantations of that Spanish island.

OVERALL VOLUME AND PATTERNS

Overall, the Africans brought to the North American colonies constituted only a small percentage of overall Atlantic slaving, some six hundred thousand persons over the entire course of the trade (1619–1807), perhaps two-thirds of them during the colonial period. The best estimates of the overall volume run to a few hundred slaves entering all the ports of North America each year in the seventeenth century, mostly in the Chesapeake after 1670, supplemented by similar numbers of Indians, principally in South Carolina. The numbers of Africans rose to a little more than one thousand slaves annually in the first three decades of the eighteenth century. The trade then increased to four to six times that level for the middle of the century, through 1775.

BIBLIOGRAPHY

Coughtry, Jay. *The Notorious Triangle: Rhode Island and the African Slave Trade, 1700–1807.* Philadelphia, 1981. The fullest study of Rhode Island slaving.

Craton, Michael. *Sinews of Empire: A Short History of British Slavery.* New York, 1974. Introductory overview of British slavery in the Caribbean.

Cuello, José. "The Persistence of Indian Slavery and Encomienda in Northeastern and Colonial Mexico, 1577–1723." *Journal of Social History* 21, no. 4 (1988):683–700. Shows the persistence of slave raiding on the northern Mexican frontier as a means of profiting from hunter-gatherer Indian populations unable to provide tribute in commodities.

Curtin, Philip D. *The Atlantic Slave Trade: A Census.* Madison, Wis., 1969. Still the best synthesis.

———. *Economic Change in Precolonial Africa: Senegambia in the Era of the Slave Trade.* Madison, Wis., 1975. Thorough overview of slaving and slavery in far western Africa in the seventeenth and eighteenth centuries.

———, ed. *Africa Remembered: Narratives by West Africans from the Era of the Slave Trade.* Madison, Wis., 1968. Collection of narratives by slaves, including those of Ayuba and Equiano.

Davies, Kenneth Gordon. *The Royal African Company.* London, 1957. Classic interpretation of the company phase of English slaving in the late seventeenth century.

Deyle, Steven. " 'By Farr the Most Profitable Trade': Slave Trading in British Colonial North America." *Slavery and Abolition* 10, no. 2 (1989):107–125. The most current (though brief) survey at the time the present article was written.

Galenson, David. *Traders, Planters, and Slaves: Market Behavior in Early English America.* New York, 1986. Close review of the records of the Royal African Company's trade in slaves to Barbados.

Galloway, J. H. *The Sugar Cane Industry: An Historical Geography from Its Origins to 1914.* New York, 1989. Now the survey of choice for the history of sugar. For an interpretation, see also Mintz.

Goslinga, Cornelis C. *The Dutch in the Caribbean and on the Wild Coast, 1580–1680.* Gainesville, Fla., 1971. Authoritative on the Dutch West India Company and its slaving among Indians and in Africa.

Grinde, Donald, Jr. "Native American Slavery in the Southern Colonies," *The Indian Historian* 10, no. 2 (1977):38–42. The Carolina Indian slave trade.

Gutiérrez, Ramón A. *When Jesus Came, the Corn Mothers Went Away: Marriage, Sexuality, and Power in New Mexico, 1550–1846.* Stanford, Calif., 1991. For Spanish and Indian slaving in New Mexico after 1680.

Kiple, Kenneth F. *The Caribbean Slave: A Biological History*. New York, 1984. Best review of the nutritional and epidemiological aspects of the slave trade.

Klein, Herbert S. *African Slavery in Latin America and the Caribbean*. New York, 1986. Introductory survey of the history of slavery in the Americas.

———. *The Middle Passage: Comparative Studies in the Atlantic Slave Trade*. Princeton, N.J., 1978. Quantitative studies on selected sectors.

Littlefield, Daniel C. *Rice and Slaves: Ethnicity and the Slave Trade in Colonial South Carolina*. Baton Rouge, La., 1981. The basic study on slaves imported into South Carolina.

———. "The Slave Trade to Colonial South Carolina: A Profile." *South Carolina Historical Magazine* 91, no. 2 (1990):68–98. An update based on Colonial Office naval lists. See Minchinton for Virginia.

Lockhart, James, and Stuart B. Schwartz. *Early Latin America: A History of Colonial Spanish America and Brazil*. New York, 1983. A balanced interpretation of the colonial history, including slavery, of Portugal and Spain in the Americas.

Lovejoy, Paul E. "The Volume of the Atlantic Slave Trade: A Synthesis." *Journal of African History* 23, no. 4 (1982):473–501.

Manning, Patrick. *Slavery and African Life: Occidental, Oriental, and African Slave Trades*. New York, 1990. Demographic survey of the effects of the slave trade in Africa: Atlantic, trans-Saharan, and Indian Ocean.

Miller, Joseph C. *Slavery: A Worldwide Bibliography, 1900–1982*. White Plains, N.Y., 1985. With annual supplements, by collaborators, in *Slavery and Abolition* (since 1983). Comprehensive current bibliographies.

———. *Way of Death: Merchant Capitalism and the Angolan Slave Trade, 1730–1830*. Madison, Wis., 1988. The Portuguese and Brazilian slave trade in the southern Atlantic.

Minchinton, Walter E., Celia King, and Peter Waite, eds. *Virginia Slave-Trade Statistics, 1698–1775*. Richmond, Va., 1984. Comprehensive statistics on the entry of slaves into Virginia.

Mintz, Sidney W. *Sweetness and Power: The Place of Sugar in Modern History*. New York, 1985. Anthropological interpretation of the place of sugar in the history of industrializing Europe.

Palmer, Colin. *Human Cargoes: The British Slave Trade to Spanish America, 1700–1739*. Urbana, Ill., 1981. The South Sea Company *asiento*.

Phillips, William D. *Slavery from Roman Times to the Early Transatlantic Trade*. Minneapolis, Minn., 1985. Summary of medieval European and Muslim slavery and the sixteenth-century Atlantic trade. Solid European and early Atlantic background.

Postma, Johannes Menne. *The Dutch in the Atlantic Slave Trade, 1600–1815*. New York, 1990. Most comprehensive study of the Dutch trade in slaves from Africa. See also Goslinga.

Rawley, James A. *The Transatlantic Slave Trade: A History*. New York, 1981. Reviews the trade, country by country and port by port, for England and North America; the most complete treatment of the trade of the continental colonies and the role of London.

Reynolds, Edward. *Stand the Storm: A History of the Atlantic Slave Trade*. New York, 1985. Evocative and thorough overview of the Middle Passage.

Richardson, David. *Bristol, Africa, and the Eighteenth-Century Slave Trade to America*, 2 vols. Gloucester, England, 1986–1987. Detailed summary of the slaving records from a major English slaving port, the most thorough for any slaving center there.

———. "The British Slave Trade to Colonial South Carolina." *Slavery and Abolition* 12, no. 3 (1991):125–172. Integrates detailed research on distinctive characteristics of slaving at Charleston into broad patterns of eighteenth-century British commerce in the Atlantic. Highly recommended.

Saunders, A. C. de C. M. *A Social History of Black Slaves and Freedmen in Portugal, 1441–1555*. New York, 1982. Includes a survey of the Iberian trade in this era.

Schwartz, Stuart B. *Sugar Plantations in the Formation of Brazilian Society: Bahia, 1550–1835*. New York, 1985. Comprehensive and authoritative on plantation slavery in northeastern Brazil.

Sharp, William F. *Slavery on the Spanish Frontier: The Colombian Chocó, 1680–1810*. Norman, Okla., 1976. The principal example of Spanish use of Africans as slaves in mining (in Colombia, for gold).

Sherman, William L. *Forced Native Labor in Sixteenth-Century Central America*. Norman, Okla., 1979. Includes the history of Spanish slaving in Central America to the 1540s.

Stein, Robert Louis. *The French Slave Trade in the Eighteenth Century: An Old Regime Business*. Madison, Wis., 1979. Basic survey of the French trade.

———. *The French Sugar Business in the Eighteenth Century*. Baton Rouge, La., 1988. The economy of the French Antilles, slaving, and the slave trade.

Usner, Daniel H., Jr. *Indians, Settlers, and Slaves in a Frontier Exchange Economy: The Lower Mississippi Valley Before 1783*. Chapel Hill, N.C., 1992. Probing social history of French and Spanish Louisiana, though more on Indian slaving than on imports of Africans.

Vila Vilar, Enriqueta. *Hispanoamérica y el comercio de esclavos*. Seville, Spain, 1977. The history of the Spanish *asiento*.

Westbury, Susan. "Analysing a Regional Slave Trade: The West Indies and Virginia, 1698–1715." *Slavery and Abolition* 7, no. 3 (1986):241–256. The Norfolk slavers in the period of rising slave imports into Virginia.

Joseph C. Miller

SEE ALSO **African-American Culture; Slave Resistance; Slavery;** and **Trade and Commerce.**

SLAVERY

THE BRITISH COLONIES

WHEN AND WHY did slavery begin in the British colonies of North America and the Caribbean? For the better part of a century, historians of the United States spun out an engrossing if somewhat mystifying tale of slavery gradually evolving out of the labor institutions of the Chesapeake Bay region. The adaptation of slavery on the mainland was, indeed, quite gradual during the years from 1619 to 1660, but the English colonists in the Chesapeake all came from the same mother country as the English who settled several islands in the West Indies and adopted slavery rapidly and decisively during the same years. And Englishmen, whether in Virginia or Barbados, were but imitating the Spaniards, who had introduced African-American slavery in the New World during the lifetime of Christopher Columbus. Therefore it must be emphasized that whether British colonists settled in the Caribbean or on the mainland, they neither invented nor reinvented slavery, any more than they originated the idea of planting colonies in the Americas.

ATLANTIC SLAVERY BEFORE BRITISH COLONIZATION

Though late and, in their earliest years quite inept, the British eventually became the greatest colonizers the world has ever known. By the time they began the colonies that were destined to survive and eventually flourish—Virginia in 1607, Bermuda in 1612, Plymouth in 1620, Barbados in 1624, and so on—the basic trades and products of the new Atlantic economy had all appeared; and Africans, whether free, bound by various terms of service, or enslaved for life, were scattered among the principal Atlantic seaports of Europe as well as in the flourishing Spanish and Portuguese colonies. Because slavery had become so general a feature of Atlantic life before 1600, it may be worth considering, for a moment, why several generations of Americans regarded it as a late and anomalous development.

The Founding Fathers persuaded themselves that they had created a *novus ordo seclorum* ("new world order"). Frederick Jackson Turner persuaded most American historians that, having sprung up along the American frontier, where society recomposed itself from its simplest elements, U.S. institutions were fundamentally different from those of Europe. Within a climate of opinion that emphasized American exceptionalism, the legend grew that even the forms of slavery present in the colonies at the time of the American Revolution were of local and peculiar origin, that slavery had not existed in any of the colonies when they were first founded.

Such thinking mistook adaptation for origins. Slavery, like a number of other social, economic, religious, and intellectual practices, took on increasingly distinctive provincial characteristics as the colonies of British America matured. But African-American slavery was part, and a crucially important part, of the origins and development of an Atlantic economy involving four continents. Over more than four centuries, from approximately 1450 to 1870, Europeans, most often with the active and profitable cooperation of African merchants, removed from ten to twelve million people from Africa.

This colossal transfer of people began in a small way as a by-product of the Portuguese program of exploration and commercial expansion directed by Prince Henry the Navigator. But during the latter part of the fifteenth century, the Portuguese demanded slaves by the hundreds, and then by the thousands, partly to supply labor for their own commercial empire and that of neighboring Spain, and especially to work on the sugar plantations developing in islands off the coast of Africa, such as the Cape Verde Islands and São Tomé, and in more distant Atlantic island groups such as the Canaries, the Madeiras, and the Azores. Practical considerations, reinforced by the papally negotiated Treaty of Tordesillas (1494), made the Portuguese slave traders to the extraordinary new Spanish Empire of the sixteenth century as well as to their own profitable plantations. The treaty divided the globe in half: all the Americas except Brazil (no European knew, in 1494, that South America existed, let alone that it extended so far eastward) constituted Spain's hemisphere for empire and commerce; all of Africa and Asia except the Philippines (also unknown to Europe before the voyage of Ferdinand Magellan) "belonged" to Portugal.

By the seventeenth century, Spain and Portugal had carried African slaves all over the world. They could be found as agricultural laborers on Caribbean islands, as gold miners in Mexico, as domestic servants in any commercial cities in touch with the Atlantic (and not merely the Portuguese and Spanish cities), as field hands and mill workers in the sugar-growing Atlantic islands, and as sailors on the seven seas. Africans appeared frequently in London and other English and Scottish ports during the long reign of Elizabeth I. The bold English sailor and trader, John Hawkins, made at least one successful triangular voyage, capturing black slaves in Africa

and selling them, in violation of Spain's navigation acts, to Spanish planters in the New World.

If slavery had disappeared in most parts of Europe by the Middle Ages, it had nevertheless persisted on the southern and eastern borders of that small but rising portion of the world. Since the Dark Ages, the Mediterranean had been the center of European trade as well as an arena for conflict with the world of Islam. Muslims regularly enslaved Christians, and Christians regularly enslaved Muslims. Black Africans often appeared for sale as slaves on all shores of the Mediterranean, typically brought from south of the Sahara in the caravans of Arab traders. But white Europeans enslaved by the Tartars and shipped from the Black Sea, not black Africans from south of the Sahara, were the most numerous slaves of the Mediterranean world during Europe's so-called Age of Discovery. For that reason we have the word "slave," a variant spelling of Slav, originally referring to a race of people but eventually connoting only a status. It may be useful, and add perspective to the history of the world, to realize that slaves were originally white people.

The Spanish introduced enslaved Africans to their then new Caribbean colonies as early as 1502; by 1517 the Spanish had signed their first contract with Portuguese merchants to provide a regular supply of African slaves for the New World. Here was a pattern that would eventually repeat itself in all the New World colonies: the native inhabitants of the Caribbean islands retreated, fought, or sickened and died, just as had a primitive white, but non-European, aboriginal population in the Canaries. Spain had no large surplus population of workers to entice or draft for service in the Americas, but it did have gold and silver with which to buy laborers, and Africans were available. Spain continued to purchase Africans throughout the sixteenth century, but the trade, though steady and often requiring more ships, sailors, and trading goods than Portugal could supply, remained small in comparison with later centuries. Eventually the Dutch, the French, and the English received the lucrative contract, known as the *asiento,* to supply thousands of slaves to the Spanish Empire each year.

Several factors contributed to the enormous growth of the slave trade in the seventeenth and eighteenth centuries. The greatest was the sugar industry, spread to Atlantic islands by the Spanish and Portuguese and introduced in desultory fashion in the Caribbean by the Spanish. During the Thirty Years' War, the Dutch undertook to replace Portugal in the African slave trade. Furthermore a number of Dutchmen invaded Brazil and launched a sugar industry there. Gifted with commercial skill and industrial ingenuity, the Dutch failed to produce adequate numbers of migrants and pioneers. Though they had become the most important traders in the Atlantic by the end of the Thirty Years' War, the attempt by the Dutch to conquer and develop Brazil failed chiefly for want of numbers; similarly their struggling colony of New Netherland had insufficient force to resist the duke of York's invasion in 1664. To the African slave trade, however, they brought larger and sturdier ships, a wider variety of trading goods, and the practice of setting up their own fortified trading posts such as Elmina along the West African coast, where they gathered slaves continuously to guarantee their ships full cargoes without costly delays.

Aware of the profits being made by the Dutch and Portuguese in the slave trade and in marketing sugar, the English, beginning in the 1640s, and then the French plunged deeply into both sugar planting in the Caribbean and slave trading between Africa and the Americas. By the later seventeenth and early eighteenth centuries, different groups of English had established most of the colonies of North America and the Caribbean. But it is only with hindsight that we see the importance of those once-struggling and remote settlements.

Sustained growth in population and prosperity came even to North American colonies only after the British Empire had assumed a preeminent position in the African slave trade and an important one in the production and marketing of sugar. In 1700 the population of all the British colonies of North America, excluding the Native Americans over whom the British claimed a shadowy sovereignty, was probably not much more than 250,000—a rather feeble establishment, considering that it was spread from Hudson's Bay to South Carolina. A hundred years later, the United States and Canada had a population well over five million, an astonish-

ing rate of growth exceeding even Benjamin Franklin's calculation that the population of North America was doubling every twenty-five years. Boom times in the British colonies coincided with the peak years of the slave trade.

In studying slavery in colonial times, however, it is necessary to note that there was nothing peculiar about the institution, whether one was English, French, Spanish, Dutch, or of any other commercial nation. African slaves were everywhere. Even colonies where they were relatively scarce, such as Massachusetts, relied as early as the middle of the seventeenth century for their prosperity on trade with colonies where blacks made up a majority of the population.

UNDERSTANDING SLAVERY IN A HIERARCHY

Before detailing the role that slavery and the slave trade played in the development of particular regions, a few more general observations may help to establish historical perspective. If slavery in some absolute sense had disappeared in most of Europe by 1600, freedom as it is generally understood in the world today was hardly known. Wherever one encountered advanced and complex civilizations with highly differentiated economic functions, one also encountered hierarchies of rule, preferment, and privilege. Government was the province of small, exclusive, and usually hereditary castes. Custom and some sense of justice may have protected most people from the grossest forms of exploitation, but custom also bound them to a certain status in society as well as a certain space. The majority were servants, or peasants, or tenants, or laborers and took orders from their superiors.

One may see the seeds of egalitarian democracy in such documents as the Mayflower Compact or, for that matter, in certain passages of the Old and New Testaments. The English Revolution of the 1640s produced a radical group, the Levellers, that anticipated in some respects the egalitarian ideas of the nineteenth and twentieth centuries. But the common sense of mankind was still that kings and notables should rule the state, and that those whom God favored would, like Job or Solomon, own numerous and loyal servants.

Religion as commonly practiced indeed taught that masters should be kind to servants. Reciprocally, and with far more support from civil authority, it also insisted that servants should serve fully and faithfully. Rare were those who said, as Abraham Lincoln did in the morning years of American democracy, that they preferred to be neither master nor servant. Old habits die hard; the Founding Fathers, justly famous for creating a free republic, were for the most part reluctant to extend freedom to their own slaves. Indeed the plantation system, based on slave labor, expanded even more rapidly in North America after the Declaration of Independence than it had before. Slavery did not seem out of place in the largely hierarchical world of colonial America.

There were voices raised against the patent injustices of slavery across the colonial centuries; indeed, when slavery and the slave trade reached their peak of extent and prosperity, a vocal, persistent, and ultimately successful abolitionist movement began in the very commercial centers that were benefiting most from the products of slave labor. But abolitionists were at first a tiny minority; slavery was generally and widely accepted as an appropriate form of that inequality that seemed the basis of all civilization to our ancestors. Africans and Native Americans themselves owned, bought, and sold slaves (though without the racial prejudices that came to characterize British slavery), and Africans who had somehow managed to become free in the colonies sometimes became slaveholders there. Even Voltaire, progressive and liberal in most things, invested in and profited from the slave trade. Benjamin Franklin wrote against African-American slavery at the end of his life, but earlier he had owned slaves himself and promoted their sale, as well as the recovery of runaways, in his *Pennsylvania Gazette.* The devout and brilliant theologian and preacher Jonathan Edwards owned two slaves, a man and woman, who labored to maintain his establishment at the Manse in Northampton, Massachusetts. Abolitionism, not slavery, is the novelty that needs explaining. The proper question to ask of history, as David Brion Davis instructed us twenty-five years ago, is: Why did the most advanced moral and political thinkers suddenly discover, late in the eighteenth century, that slavery was wrong?

Of course slavery was right only under certain circumstances. English men and women might be bond servants for a year, or several years at a time. When the English served indentures in the New World, they had no more rights than minor children—for the term of their service. And labor contracts could be bought and sold. But unless convicted of a crime, no subject of the Crown could be a bond servant for life, nor, by an agreeable extension, could the subjects of other Christian rulers. The English, like the Portuguese, Spanish, French, and Dutch, at first allowed themselves to enslave Native Americans and Africans because they were heathen as well as foreign. By the end of the colonial period neither language, nor strange customs, nor heathenish religion could serve as justification. By that time hundreds of thousands of African-descended Americans were speaking fluent English and living, so far as their circumstances permitted, very much the same as their European-descended masters. Thousands of them learned and professed the creeds of Christianity and, again so far as circumstances permitted, worshipped regularly in the churches of the European-descended. By that time slavery had switched from a cultural to a racial basis; the African American might speak the same language, profess the same religion, and do the same work as his master and might be honest and upstanding in all transactions, yet remain a slave for life, as would his children and grandchildren.

Many serious scholars see the evolution of African-American slavery as proof that some deep-seated racial prejudice existed at the very dawn of the European expansion and colonization that begat the Atlantic slave trade. Others see the emergence of racial justifications for slavery as a rationalization to protect economic advantages and civil security against the egalitarian doctrines of the late eighteenth century. Isolated instances of seeming racial prejudice may be found from the Renaissance onward, but so can affirmations of the African's humanity. Kings and princes sometimes bought or hired Africans for their retinues because of their gift for decorative and courtly ritual. The lecherous Moor imagined by Don Quixote no doubt existed in popular imaginations, but so did the Moor imagined by Shakespeare as Othello. Never mind that Othello murdered his wife; he was clearly a tragic, noble figure, more admirable in his overall character than such white tragic protagonists as Lear or Macbeth. Renaissance painters often placed black servants in the backgrounds of their scenes and portraits but increasingly, after 1500, those who painted the Epiphany—and thousands did so—portrayed a black Balthazar who was regal, handsome, and decidedly subsaharan in his African features. It must be remembered that the three kings represented wisdom as well as nobility. In a later, racist United States, no such dignified iconography of Africans would appear until after the Civil War.

Though all the British colonies had slave codes, and many regularly practiced punishments long since denounced as cruel and inhuman, the fact remains that there was altogether less prejudice against Africans as such in the colonial period than there was during the era of antebellum slavery, Reconstruction, and the period that immediately followed. Except South Carolina, no mainland colony had laws against blacks learning to read and write, and the idea that African males particularly threatened white women found hardly any echo in the colonies. On the other hand, colonies generally passed laws prohibiting interracial marriages, and planters often protested against the efforts of ministers and other devout persons to instruct, baptize, and otherwise elevate blacks so that they might, in some respects, be considered equal to their masters. It should also be noted that the British ceased enslaving American Indians at about the same time—the eighteenth century— that African slaves were becoming the principal workers on mainland plantations.

This is not to portray slavery as practiced in colonial times in rosy, nostalgic terms but rather to affirm that Africans had not yet been singled out among the peoples of the world as particularly degraded or wanting in intellect or moral feeling. Or if they were, little distinction was made, in a hierarchical society, between them and others of the "lower orders," whatever their race or place of origin. Because they did put slavery on a racial basis, virtually all white colonists were racists to some degree, but not nearly to the degree that most white Americans were a hundred years after the Declaration of Independence. Racism itself is not a simple affect,

but rather a complex of ethnic and emotional attitudes, varying with time and place, even in the same mind and soul.

On hearing some radical revolutionaries argue in favor of emancipating blacks, Landon Carter, that unattractive example of Virginia's ruling elite, confided to his diary, that blacks were "devils" and freeing them would be setting devils free. One may search that diary from beginning to end, however, and find almost nothing but complaints about acquaintances, relatives, servants black and white, or mankind in general; yet one character appeared now and again over the years, a black man named Jack Lubbar, whom Carter admired more than anyone besides himself. Indeed, Carter found fault with Jack Lubbar only once: assigned as overseer over fellow blacks, Lubbar proved a poor disciplinarian. But otherwise the atrabilious Landon Carter had nothing but praise for old Jack. At tasks he was a skillful, tireless, and inventive worker, and when he completed all the tasks his master assigned, he cleverly invented new ways in which to enrich his master's plantation. When Jack Lubbar died at a very advanced age, Landon Carter poured onto the pages of his diary unqualified praise for his good life and sorrow at his loss. Yet it never occurred to the planter that exceptionally good (from his point of view) blacks needed to figure in his estimate of the race. In a warp of logic to which wealthy slaveholding planters seemed all but universally prone, Carter believed that the people on whom he depended for his very existence were, on the whole, immoral and incompetent—"devils" for short.

Evidences of respect and affection between white and black, master and slave, abound in the historic documents that survive from the colonial era. So, of course do evidences of conflict, cruelty, rebellion, escape, and punishment. But any extensive survey of colonial records demonstrates that the worst conflicts and rebellions on the mainland were between rival groups of whites or between whites and Native Americans; the criminal records and notices indicate that white indentured servants and especially convict servants were a more disruptive and unruly group than blacks. Although there are many unresolved debates concerning every aspect of the history of slavery, today almost no one doubts that it was a good deal for the slaveholders or a bad one for the slaves. Throughout the history of emancipation, the slaveholders who voluntarily advocated the liberation of their "property" were rare indeed.

THE SIGNIFICANCE OF WEST INDIAN SLAVERY

The records of Bermuda disclose an African there as early as 1616; better known but largely misunderstood is the appearance of a small shipment of blacks in Virginia in 1619. What happened there will be treated in detail later on, but for now it must be affirmed that there was nothing particularly unusual about one or a few blacks showing up in any of the colonies of the Americas after the European invasion of the New World began. The transformation of the West Indies in the middle years of the seventeenth century, however, brought British subjects into slaveholding and slavetrading in a large way. From 1640 to the British outlawing of the international slave trade in 1807, the sugar-producing British West Indies were among the most valuable economic units in the empire. Besides bringing great wealth to England, they contributed more than any part of the world to the rapid growth of the North American colonies, half of whose trade centered in the Caribbean until the end of the Napoleonic Wars.

English settlements began in the Caribbean in the mid 1620s. Most were in the archipelago known as the Lesser Antilles, forming the Caribbean's eastern boundary. The prevailing trade winds blow from east to west in their latitude, and in the age of sail, European ships passed by the Lesser Antilles when entering the Caribbean but sailed out of the area far to the north through the Straits of Florida on their return passage. Spain, her colonizing resources stretched to the limit, had never settled the Lesser Antilles nor even placed outposts there. Barbados, the island that first attracted thousands of English, lies well to the east of even the easternmost Antilles. The Spanish tolerated their recent enemies swarming in Barbados and fanning out to other tiny islands, as they tolerated the new settlements from Virginia northward,

for these settlements seemed too remote to threaten Spanish trade or territory.

There was an exception: in 1629 a hardy band of English Puritans settled a small island in the eastern Caribbean near the coast of Central America. Piously naming it Providence Island, they proceeded to plunder nearby Spanish commerce and settlements. Seriously annoyed, the Spanish overran Providence Island in 1641, but not before these piratical Puritans had stolen thousands of their slaves, keeping some to work their island plantations and selling others in the fledgling colonies to the east. In its brief and lurid history, Providence Island illustrates the first method of collecting slaves practiced by English in the New World: stealing them from mature and well-stocked Spanish plantations or looting them along with other valuable cargo from Spanish ships. The legacy of piracy, started by the English in the Caribbean, lasted over two centuries.

The earliest profits realized by settlers in Barbados came from cutting dyewoods; experimenting with various crops, they grew more tobacco than anything else in the 1630s, but by 1640 many planters had begun switching to sugar. Twenty years later the conversion was nearly complete. From a maximum of approximately eight thousand freeholds, Barbados, undergoing an economic transformation, settled into about eight hundred sugar plantations. Though the white population continued to grow in the 1640s, the population of enslaved Africans grew far more rapidly: in 1650 there were approximately thirty thousand whites and thirteen thousand blacks; by 1700 whites had declined to something over fifteen thousand while blacks numbered more than fifty thousand.

A similar process went on, somewhat more slowly, in the nearby Lesser Antilles. Dutch traders frequently visited the British colonies of the New World during the English Civil War, interregnum, and Protectorate; Dutch activity among British overseas possessions was, in fact, the immediate cause for the new Navigation Act of 1651 and the Anglo-Dutch War of 1652–1654. However hostile the merchants of England may have been toward Dutch interlopers, English colonists welcomed them and, in the plantation colonies, bought slaves and sugar-refining equipment from them and happily traded their tobacco and sugar for eventual marketing in Europe. These Dutch activities led some historians to believe that the Dutch largely financed the initial development of the British colonial sugar industry. Detailed research, however, has indicated that English merchants, whether imitating the Dutch or not, appear to have advanced most of the credit required for capitalizing the sugar plantations.

However troubled conditions may have been in England during the 1640s and 1650s, knowledgeable Englishmen realized that their new Caribbean empire offered treasure greater than gold with its new-found ability to produce sugar by the thousands of tons. One reason for the political neglect of the mainland colonies during the rest of the seventeenth century and the first half of the eighteenth century was that they were far less important to the newly rising prosperity of the metropolis than the tropical islands. Recognizing the value of Caribbean real estate, the Lord High Protector Oliver Cromwell dispatched Admiral William Penn and General Robert Venables to conquer Jamaica, in the very heart of the Caribbean, which they accomplished in 1655. This time the Spanish could not dislodge the English, still prone to plunder and piracy, and as the century advanced Jamaica—many times larger than Barbados—became England's foremost producer of sugar. Trade, often illegal in the eyes of Spanish officials, replaced plundering as the chief neighborly activity. With the signing of the Treaty of Utrecht in 1713, some of the trade even became legal, including a contract for the British to supply the Spanish with up to four thousand blacks each year. Legal or not, trade with the far-flung colonies of Spain seems to have gone on continually, with North American colonists actively engaged in it.

Sugar and Demographics

The replacement of white labor by black in the Lesser Antilles is worth noting, for it anticipated a process strikingly observable in the Chesapeake colonies a few years later. In the earliest years of Barbados, Saint Kitt's, Antigua, and other islands, the white servant who signed an indenture and agreed to work for a term of years had some hope of becoming an independent farmer in the islands afterwards. But land quickly ran out, and those who owned it quickly gained a reputation for working servants very hard, and feeding, clothing, and sheltering them very poorly. Furthermore men and women raised in England died off rapidly in the tropics. The islands, having deflected would-be planters and indentured servants from Virginia in the 1630s, offered declining opportunities for ambitious young Englishmen and so attracted decreasing numbers of white servants after the 1640s. Tobacco prices collapsed in the 1630s; thereafter tobacco planters, wherever located, required skill, luck, and the strictest economy to show a profit.

Sugar proved far more profitable; its profits opened sources of credit, allowing rapid expansion. Given a choice between black and white labor, sugar planters might, on gaining additional experience, have preferred blacks anyway. Owners were under no obligation to release them after a short term of years, and the Africans proved somewhat more resistant to the diseases endemic in the islands, now peopled by a mixture of Native Americans, Africans, and Europeans, than either of the other groups. But after 1650 or so, West Indian planters really had no choice between white and black labor; by that time Virginia and Maryland did not exactly enjoy good reputations in the outports of England either, but men and women selling themselves for a period of years were almost unanimous in refusing to take service in the tropics.

The displacement of white by black labor in the Caribbean would shortly be repeated in those parts of Virginia, Maryland, and North Carolina where commercial tobacco growing was most concentrated. But the Chesapeake area had a huge hinterland. If the choicest land along the coast or near the banks of the major rivers was taken up, the poor could move to the fringes of settlement either to the west or in the less accessible areas between the rivers. In the Caribbean available land quickly dwindled. The result was that the sugar islands became demographically and socially quite different from the mainland colonies. By 1780, 90 percent or more of the island peoples were black, most of them slaves. In rounded numbers there were 48,000 whites and 489,000 blacks.

Unlike tobacco or cotton, sugar could not be produced competitively on small holdings. Sugarcane has no tolerance for frost and takes at least a year to mature. Once ready for harvest, it must be cut and crushed rapidly; only after its sap has been boiled down does one have a syrup that will keep without spoiling. Labor on sugar plantations was heavy and continuous; sugar planters generally preferred buying the strongest young men in the Caribbean slave markets. Until the end of the slave trade, men so outnumbered women as to make the population incapable of reproducing itself on all but a few of the tropical islands.

The size and wealth of sugar plantations, combined with the limited social and educational opportunities of the islands, resulted in many plantation owners returning to England to settle and raise their families. They left the management of their plantations in the hands of men—usually young, poor, and ambitious—who tried to earn enough money to buy land or go into business for themselves. This often meant that profits which the absentee owner expected for himself found their way into the pockets of his agent.

The custom developed of such managers living openly with black or mulatto women, without the blessings of church or state. But whereas law and custom in the mainland colonies dictated that the children of slave women should have the same status as their mothers, the white men of the islands often freed the children of their slave concubines. The sugar planting society lasted for almost two hundred years, during which time concubinage became an established custom in the islands. It produced an important class of free people of mixed race. Typically these enlarged the essential managerial class, but some especially enterprising mulattoes became merchants, planters, and slaveholders. However wealthy or educated they became, however, mulattoes were never accepted in the top level of island society, nor did they hold official positions. In cases of slave insurrections, however, they characteristically sided with the white minority.

No two British sugar islands were exactly alike, and Jamaica, much larger than the rest and located in the center of the Caribbean, had several distinctive qualities. One of these was its free black population, the Maroons, in the central mountains. All the British colonies were familiar with runaways; their apprehension and return was a constant problem from Massachusetts to Georgia. But only in Jamaica did a group of runaways manage to find a means to defy all pursuit and recapture. The Maroons eventually became sufficiently organized so as to work out a modus vivendi with the white government of Jamaica, helping suppress brigandage and return runaways in exchange for being left alone.

Broadly speaking, however, the slave system of the British West Indies required a steady supply of fresh Africans. As we have seen, planters predominantly bought males, preferring to pay for strong young adults rather than raise slaves from infancy. Sugar took precedence over foodstuffs, which made the islands a large and dependable market for the grain, flour, salt fish, and timber produced on the mainland. Whatever the price of slaves in Africa, the West Indies could always purchase slaves for substantially less than North Americans, because they were closer to the source and paid correspondingly less. With respect to provisions, the situation was exactly reversed. Almost always food cost less on the mainland than in the islands. Small wonder, then, that North American planters, once slavery was well established, encouraged the proliferation of their African populations while West Indians did not.

The islands did not have a surplus of slaves to sell to the mainland. For many years textbooks in American history stated that African slaves, before being imported into North America, underwent a few years of seasoning in the West Indies. This notion seems to have derived from a misunderstanding of an observation made by a British lieutenant governor of Virginia concerning where Virginians had bought their slaves before 1700. His reply was that slave ships of the Royal African Company specially steered toward Virginia after 1670 but that before then Virginians had imported their slaves from Barbados. But this did not mean that the slaves so purchased had been long-term residents of Barbados. Because of its size and location, Barbados was the entrepôt of the Lesser Antilles; just as ships from Africa brought slaves to Barbados, ships from the mainland bringing provisions purchased slaves there and carried them northward. The North American ships were normally quite small, and their consignments of blacks very small indeed: often but one or two, and rarely more than ten.

Because of the great difference in sex ratios, and perhaps because of less healthy working conditions, the islands of the Caribbean absorbed more than a third of all Africans brought to the Americas. That includes, of course, sugar-producing colonies with far more acreage and therefore far larger populations than the British West Indies. By 1760 the French almost equaled the British both as slave traders and sugar producers, their largest plantations being in the western third of Hispaniola (Haiti). When Haiti became independent in the 1790s as a result of the only successful slave revolt in Caribbean history, the Spanish—the first colonists to introduce sugar in the New World—finally turned in a serious way to modern methods of producing and marketing sugar on the previously undeveloped island of Cuba, the largest of Caribbean islands. Since the early nineteenth century, only Brazil has been in Cuba's class as a producer of cane sugar in the Americas.

The West Indies suffered from military operations and shortages during the War for American Independence, but subsequently expanded into the Bahamas and Trinidad. They annexed another profitable sugar colony, Trinidad, in 1798. Parliament's outlawing of the African slave trade in 1807, however, halted the expansion of Britain's tropical plantations and even contributed to the decline of existing colonies that had depended on fresh Africans to maintain their labor force. Thereafter, the Caribbean islands became increasingly less important in an otherwise expanding British imperial economy. On the other hand, most sugar plantations continued to operate profitably, and many planters adopted meaningful improvements—for instance, excusing pregnant women from work in the cane fields. The male and female population tended to balance, and Barbados actually began gaining rather than losing black population. Abolitionists argued that slavery was inefficient as well as unjust. That it was unjust and often cruel is beyond dispute, but Caribbean slavery was not only efficient, it was clearly gaining in efficiency in the early years of the nineteenth century until Parliament passed its act of general emancipation in 1833.

SLAVERY IN THE COLONIAL CHESAPEAKE

Even books published within the last few years still contain the slightly mistaken facts and largely mistaken interpretations set down almost a hundred years ago concerning the origins of slavery in Virginia. The mistaken view may be summarized as follows: in 1619 a Dutch ship unexpectedly arrived at Jamestown and left twenty blacks, who were treated as indentured servants because the Virginians had not yet invented slavery.

The surviving source for this story, a letter from John Rolfe to the Virginia Company in London, in fact says the Dutch ship had an English pilot, "Mr. Marmaduke," and had been cruising in the Caribbean "in consort" with an English ship, *Treasurer,* that had long been engaged in traffic between London, Bermuda, and Virginia. The unnamed Dutch ship stopped not at Jamestown but at Point Comfort, and left not twenty but "twenty and odd Negroes." The location is important, for Point Comfort, right on Chesapeake Bay rather than upstream at Jamestown, was the private plantation of Abraham Piersey, merchant representative of the Virginia Company, who became the wealthiest man in Virginia while the Virginia Company went broke. Cruising in the Caribbean was a euphemism for piratical raids on Spaniards, of which that earnest monarch, James I of England, sternly disapproved. So the sale of the blacks was a shady transaction, best carried out well away from the public view of Jamestown. Six years later, in the census of 1625, seven blacks still lived at Point Comfort. *Treasurer,* after parting company with the unnamed Dutch ship in 1619, put in at Bermuda and there sold sixteen blacks.

The grounds for calling these blacks indentured servants are conjectural. James C. Ballagh argued that slavery could not exist without positive statutory law to define it. So also argued William Murray, Baron Mansfield in the famous Somerset case of 1772, and the argument has a certain lucidity for an age of professional lawyers and elaborate, systematic legal codes. But blacks were held as slaves in Britain both before and even after the Somerset case until the growing abolitionist movement turned public opinion entirely against the practice. More to the point here is that European enslavement of Africans began everywhere in the New World before slaveholders became legislators and passed legal codes to define and protect their human property.

Changes in the meanings of words contributed to the confusion. Before 1656 no black Virginian was described as a slave in the records that survive, but during the first half of the seventeenth century the word "servant" had either its present meaning or its original meaning of slave, after the Latin *servus,* from which it derives. A careful study of the early court records of Virginia suggests that many blacks lived out their lives with the planters who first acquired them; even though by 1640 the word "slave" had yet to appear in the records, several Africans had been designated as "servants for life."

Among the several hundred blacks who lived in Virginia before 1660, a few were clearly free, including the patriarch and planter Anthony Johnson on the Eastern Shore. A case involving Johnson dragged on for several terms of court; Johnson claimed that one of his own black servants was "bound for life," whereas a nearby white planter testified that the servant had been bound only for a limited term. There could be no question then that everyone involved understood the distinction between slavery and indentured servitude! The case was first decided against Johnson, but later, when it appeared that the white man who had testified for Johnson's servant was in fact keeping him as his own, the court reversed its decision and an African slave was restored to his original African owner. African-Virginians, whether slaves, indentured servants, or free, did not constitute more than from 2 percent to 5 percent of the population before Bacon's Rebellion of 1676 and were certainly not the backbone of the laboring force in the early tobacco culture of the region.

The distinguished colonial historian Edmund S. Morgan argued in his book, *American Slavery, American Freedom,* that Virginia planters made a conscious decision to purchase black slaves after Bacon's Rebellion. According to this theory, the widespread and destructive behavior of white servants and former servants caused planters to seek workers who could be kept in a permanent state of subordination. Whatever

the merits of this thesis, certain facts stand forth as fairly clear regarding the last third of the seventeenth century. The short-term effects of the second and third Anglo-Dutch Wars, reinforced by bad weather and Indian troubles, made life miserable and denizens irritable in the Chesapeake, especially in the 1670s. Many difficulties seemed to contribute to the civil war in Virginia, including the bold and daring personality of young Nathaniel Bacon. The proportion of blacks in the colony was gradually increasing before the rebellion; on the other hand, there was no sharp turning away from the importation of white servants afterward. The position taken here is that Bacon's Rebellion, though revealing much about the tensions in early Virginia society, was not especially caused by the labor system of the colony—there were approximately thirty-five thousand Virginians then, of whom two thousand were African—and that the very gradual shift from white to black labor resulted from developments mainly external to Virginia. In 1700 the estimated total population of Virginia and Maryland together was about ninety-eight thousand, of whom twelve thousand were black. The transition from white to black labor was already well under way.

The emerging British commercial empire was slowly but surely establishing itself in the African trade from the creation of the Royal African Company in 1672 (an earlier company had faltered). When Parliament rescinded the company's monopoly in 1698, it was, in effect, recognizing the impossibility of preventing private traders from purchasing slaves along the western shores of Africa. In legalizing private traders, Parliament required them to pay a 10-percent duty to the company, which maintained fortified posts in Africa, allegedly for the benefit of all British traders. This requirement seems to have been ignored more often than not. In any case the trade grew steadily if unevenly, especially through the long series of international wars that continued with little surcease from 1689 until 1713. These wars, in which France was Britain's principal enemy, proved harder on the Netherlands and its commercial empire than any of the three Anglo-Dutch Wars had been, in spite of the fact that England's King William III was also stadtholder of the Netherlands. British colonists everywhere were buying more African slaves, and more of them from British traders. The trade continued to center in the West Indies, but now in Jamaica, which had replaced Barbados as the most populous and prosperous of Britain's tropical isles. Occasionally large slave ships came directly to the Chesapeake and lingered for weeks in the broad tidal rivers, especially the James and York, retailing slaves for tobacco or bills of exchange drawn on London merchants.

The same years that saw Britain become preeminent in the African slave trade also saw the creation and rapid growth of new mainland colonies. Unemployed or poorly employed men and women who might have tried their fortune as indentured servants in the Chesapeake before the restoration of Charles II increasingly found work in New York, New Jersey, and especially Pennsylvania (founded in 1682) more to their liking. Furthermore the Chesapeake colonies kept growing: having almost reached a population of one hundred thousand in 1700, they doubled that before 1730 and exceeded half a million by 1760. Although the population of England, Scotland, and Ireland also grew rapidly in the eighteenth century, it came nowhere near this pace. Even had prospective indentured servants no place to go but Virginia and Maryland, there would not have been enough of them to keep up with the rapidly expanding tobacco culture. Conditions, then, were favorable for the growth of slavery there.

The importation of blacks into the Chesapeake was, compared with the hothouse growth of the West Indies earlier or of South Carolina later, rather slow and steady. With British customs officers keeping presumably accurate records, one sees that the trade grew almost every year in the first half of the eighteenth century until it peaked in the late 1740s; after that importations declined steeply. The number of white servants imported actually increased again in the 1760s, reflecting hard times in the British Isles, while slave importations continued to sink through 1773. They then ceased altogether as a result of nonimportation agreements, followed by the dislocations of the War for Independence. Finally legislation against further importations meant that there were virtually no more new

Africans entering the Chesapeake during or after the War for Independence.

Quite apart from the interference with normal trade occasioned by the War for Independence, the politically astute planters of Virginia had increasingly come to desire an end to importation of Africans anyway. Since the 1720s the African-American population in the Chesapeake had actually been increasing more rapidly by natural means than by importation—this is especially remarkable considering that the greatest importations were yet to come. By 1770 the ruling elite of Virginia could be said to need no further slaves, not because they believed their economy in decline, but because their bond servants increased as rapidly as they desired. All things being equal, an African American born and bred in the Chesapeake, fluent in English, and accustomed to plantation business, was inherently more valuable and commanded a higher price than a newly imported African. Therefore the poorer sort of planters and men just entering the business of planting were likely to purchase Africans. If the price of new Africans was to fall, the price of country-born slaves would fall proportionally. Therefore the elite was protecting the value of its own property.

But besides this, the established planters of the Chesapeake hoped to limit the rate at which tobacco production increased; since the 1630s their most persistent and insoluble problem had been overproduction, with its inevitable bad effect on prices. Another reason for ending the slave trade, difficult to weigh in importance, but unquestionably present, was an underlying determination to maintain a white majority. Virginia and Maryland had suffered no major slave rebellions during the colonial era, but their planters were in touch with a larger Atlantic world in which such rebellions were frequent and bloody.

Finally one should mention that the first stirrings of an organized antislavery movement occurred during the same years as the American Revolution. That movement will be discussed in some detail at the end of this essay; here it may be pointed out that antislavery sentiments, though never adopted by a majority or even a large minority of planters in the Chesapeake, were still treated with respect, especially by the ruling classes. The movement did have some adherents in Virginia, especially but by no means exclusively among Quakers. Those who were convinced that slavery was wrong added their weight to the less idealistic slaveholders who wished to end the slave trade largely to protect their own positions.

The typical images we have of American slavery were drawn chiefly in the years just before the Civil War. Cotton was king, and slavery seemed especially centered in a belt of southern states running westward from South Carolina and Georgia into Texas. Yet as late as 1790 Virginia, Maryland, and the booming frontier area that would become the state of Kentucky in 1792 had over four hundred thousand black slaves, well over half the total in the entire United States. North Carolina, much of which resembled Virginia in its tobacco culture, stood next in total slaves. South Carolina and Georgia were late getting started, with permanent settlement in the former beginning around 1670 and in the latter not until 1732. Georgia's late start was also slow, because the proprietors originally insisted that no slaves should be admitted. Furthermore, although British armies operated in Virginia and North Carolina during the final, southern campaign of the Revolutionary War, they began their campaign and occupied the most territory in South Carolina and Georgia, carrying away many slaves in the process. Students of U.S. history do not usually see the long-term perspective: slavery existed in British North America and the United States for almost two hundred and fifty years; only during the last fifty did cotton arise to become the most important crop produced by black labor. To be sure, it attained a significance in the world economy never reached by tobacco. Nevertheless, Virginia continued to have the largest black population of any state right down to the end of the Civil War.

Demographics, Work, and Mobility

It has already been pointed out that the Chesapeake colonies, unlike those in the West Indies, were supplying their demand for African labor more by natural increase than by importation before 1730. That point now requires considerable discussion, for the Chesapeake slave system was strikingly different from any found in the tropics. Although no one has satisfactory evidence as to how so many African women came to be in the Chesapeake, we know that something like parity between men and women had been attained in the early eighteenth century. The high birth rate itself indicates this, and probate records, with their inventories of slaves, prove it. Even though virtually all seventeenth-century records that distinguish sex indicate that Virginia planters imported twice as many males as females, the women seem to have survived and to have reproduced in sufficient number to achieve balance.

Chesapeake planters came to value black women very highly. They served from age six or so as nursemaids and as household, garden, and dairy help. When full grown, they worked in the tobacco fields along with the men. Though black women sometimes ran away, engaged in petty theft, and were even suspected of poisoning their masters, they were, generally speaking, far less likely to disturb the peace and prosperity of white planters than were black males—or white indentured males. Furthermore, the white planters of Virginia were convinced, and in this they were almost certainly correct, that having wives and children increased the likelihood that black males would neither run away nor foment rebellion. Many a recalcitrant and belligerent African reined in his resentment and settled down to his tasks, not as a result of whipping, but on being convinced that further disobedience would place him in chains on a one-way trip by sea to South Carolina or the West Indies, removed from his family. This was the colonial version of the dreaded antebellum punishment in the upper South of being "sold down the river." As the value of slaves was almost always rising, and because both custom and law in the Chesapeake dictated that all the children of slave mothers should also be slaves, regardless of the status of their fathers, a healthy young slave woman was usually the best investment a planter could make.

Two valuable works have supplied us with extremely important insights into the nature of Chesapeake plantations. Robert E. and B. Katherine Brown, in *Virginia, 1706–1776,* were the first historians to study comprehensively the probate records of eighteenth-century Virginia and thereby establish the distribution of property in the colony. They found that more than half the blacks of colonial Virginia lived in groups that numbered ten or less, including children. The most numerous owners of slaves were those that owned but one or two. Gerald Mullin, in *Flight and Rebellion* demonstrated that even the wealthiest of Virginia planters—the Carters, Byrds, Harrisons, and such propertied patriots as George Washington and Thomas Jefferson—typically owned a series of small plantations, often scattered among several counties. The Virginia tobacco plantation almost never had more than thirty-five resident blacks, and very often had far fewer. None of the crops produced in the Chesapeake benefited particularly from economies of scale; the small farmer without slaves could produce tobacco quite as good in quality, and with about as much efficiency, as the greatest aristocratic planter—who was, during much of his long life, Robert "King" Carter.

There were, to be sure, areas in Virginia where blacks outnumbered whites, but in nothing like the ratio in South Carolina or in the sugar islands. The most distinctive feature of Chesapeake slavery was its relative economic democracy. The most distinctive feature of the African American in the colonial Chesapeake was that he or she was most often country-born—that is, native to North America rather than Africa—and lived an entire life span among a mixture of white and black people. The largest Chesapeake plantations had their rows of slave cabins, but nothing like the African villages one encountered on rice, indigo, and sugar plantations farther south. Furthermore, although distinctions have often been made between house servants and field servants, task assignments on most Virginia plantations were more a function of age and ability than lifelong status. Thus boys, before acquiring the muscles of grown men, were likely to share household and garden tasks with girls of the same approximate age. Because much of the work with tobacco required more dexterity than sheer strength, women—as we have already noted—worked in the fields along with men, especially during the busiest seasons. Men who survived to old age drew tasks that required experience and skill rather than strength and suppleness; thus they might give up felling trees and digging ditches in favor of caring for livestock.

Whether the Chesapeake planter owned no slaves, a few, or many, he faced the problem that his main cash crop, tobacco, had to be of good quality but could not be counted on to bring a high price. To make a profit he had to produce in quantity, and even then it was essential to keep production costs as low as possible. The best way for the planter to do this was to produce as many necessities as possible on his own acres. After a few years of neglecting food crops in favor of tobacco in the earliest years of the colony, Virginians learned—rather brutally after tobacco prices collapsed around 1630—that they must be self-sufficient with respect to food; thereafter they would almost always produce a surplus of corn and other foodstuffs. George Washington, a farsighted planter whose thousands of acres were for the most part not of the finest quality, gave up growing tobacco altogether in the 1760s, preferring to specialize in wheat and other exportable provisions for the dependable West Indian market. Generally speaking most planters continued to grow tobacco for export, but for their own consumption they produced a plenitude of garden vegetables, fruits—especially apples and peaches—poultry, cattle, sheep, and swine.

If Chesapeake farms often looked ill kempt, the reason was not, as foreign visitors sometimes charged, that the people were lazy or their "servants" incompetent. At almost any time in the colonial era, most farms in the rapidly growing provinces were relatively new and rather poor. Planters had to clear land, raise their own crops and livestock, tend their own buildings, and generally see to an endless round of duties. Their cash crop was certainly not easy to raise: tobacco as grown in colonial times was a demanding, labor-intensive crop. Plants had to be started in seedbeds and then transplanted to hills. Each plant required pruning and topping; otherwise the good leaves for smoking would not develop. The surest way to keep pests from destroying the plants was to remove them by hand. Finally leaves required careful curing in tobacco sheds, a slow process, before they could be packed for export in huge wooden barrels, commonly called hogsheads and weighing as much as half a ton. Small wonder that planters acquired as many African-American slaves as their resources permitted and that these slaves, while mainly engaged as agricultural laborers, specializing in producing tobacco, were also required to be as handy as possible in a highly diversified agriculture.

Thousands also became skilled artisans. Most of Virginia and North Carolina, and even much of Maryland, remained covered with forest during the colonial era. This was somewhat less true of Maryland, because that colony lacked the vast west that its neighbors lying immediately to the South enjoyed. But throughout the tobacco-growing Chesapeake region, masters and slaves labored incessantly to convert trees into houses, "Negro cabins," tobacco sheds, hogsheads, wagons, barrels, and firewood. Again, visitors from more "civilized" parts of the world observed that fields in the region rarely had fences around them, but they probably did not know the reason. Adjusting to their environment, planters depended to a large degree on pork rather than beef for their diet; self-reliant hogs, free of confinement, foraged for themselves and saved their overworked owners the effort of feeding them.

Besides working as lumberjacks, sawyers, carpenters, and coopers, African Americans were blacksmiths, teamsters, and watermen. They rowed and poled small craft up and down the rivers of Virginia and served as crew—sometimes as skippers—on the larger boats that sailed across Chesapeake Bay or, later in the colonial period, ventured to the Caribbean. Female slaves, besides helping in all but the heaviest outdoor tasks, worked endlessly at spinning and weaving, dairying, and all the other household tasks that went along with eighteenth-century rural life.

Slave auctions supplied one of the most memorable features of the plantation regime— so much so that inheritance, the more normal pattern of slave transmission, has been, by comparison, overlooked. Of course Chesapeake planters always purchased newly arrived Africans from the traders who visited the region or the agents who handled their human cargoes. But once a planter acquired a slave, he was not disposed to sell him or her. Planters acquired slaves in the first instance to do work that would increase their wealth. But in the Chesapeake, they were only in rare instances absentees, and only the wealthiest of them owned more than one parcel of land. By the eighteenth century, white as well as black women were about as nu-

merous as men, and the practice of early marriage predominated—women marrying on the average in their late teens and men in their early twenties. The Chesapeake planter, always needing more land because tobacco rapidly depleted the soil, also needed more land to bequeath to his children. He also needed more slaves to work his land, and then more slaves for the land he gave his children. To the extent his resources permitted, the Chesapeake planter presented equal or almost equal estates to each of his sons and a dowry of land and slaves to his daughters. Because white as well as black Virginians were prolific—early marriage and abundant resources winning out, demographically speaking, over endemic diseases—more than half the Virginia-born African Americans could expect to move at least once in their lifetime even if they were not sold. In many cases an African American who grew up with "young massa" or "young missus" would leave the old home for a new one with him or her. Such moves usually meant departing with some relatives but separating from others. After American independence migrating planters might take their slaves to Kentucky or, later, to Arkansas or Mississippi—"far from the old folks at home." But in the colonial era such relocations were often within visiting distance of the original home. In this respect, certainly, colonial slavery was less wrenching for the African American than antebellum slavery.

A glance at any map of the early United States will show that the free states occupied far less territory than those states where slavery was the predominant labor system. The plantation societies of British North America—later the United States—were explosively expansive.

Much has been written in the last quarter of the twentieth century about the formation of community with regard to ethnic groups, and especially African Americans. In some cases the mere existence of people living close to one another has led to deductive assumptions for which evidence is, to say the least, sketchy. Mechal Sobel has argued imaginatively that the Chesapeake pattern of settlement produced such continuous interactions between white owners and black slaves as to cause a near-complete interpenetration of the Anglo-Virginian and African-American cultures. The position taken here is more cautious: there are classes of people who are together for long stretches of time, and are certainly engaged in common enterprises, who yet remain culturally quite distinct; social classes are human inventions but are so widespread as to seem almost natural among human beings, existing as they do in virtually every traditional civilization.

Rich or poor, white Virginians set themselves apart by marriage and social customs from their African-American servants; even when they worshiped in the same church, the servants sat or stood together in their own balcony or section. If the planter was too poor to build a separate cabin for his servants, they had a basement or a lean-to to themselves. To the extent that their white masters permitted—and often beyond the limits permitted by law—blacks sought each other for sociability. Nevertheless the close and lifelong association of Chesapeake blacks with their masters and their masters' families led to different patterns of assimilation and socialization than one found in colonial South Carolina or later in the great cotton plantations of the Old Southwest. The Chesapeake African American had the wide experience of white culture we usually associate with slaves in or near urban centers. There is also considerable evidence that, despite laws to the contrary, Chesapeake blacks moved about with considerable freedom, so long as they gave prior attention to the tasks their masters set them and stayed out of trouble.

SLAVERY IN THE NORTHERN COLONIES

Slavery and slave trading were present in many northern colonies before the first permanent English settlement in South Carolina (1670) or Georgia (1732). The permanent settlements of New Netherland—as opposed to trading posts—began around 1624. The Dutch, beginning to engage seriously in the slave trade, introduced Africans almost immediately.

Whites in Pennsylvania, New Jersey, New York, and New England seem to have been no different from those of the plantation provinces in their racial attitudes, their willingness to exploit Africans in any profitable way, the stringency of their slave codes, their severity toward free blacks, and their reluctance (with a few distinguished exceptions, of which the emerging South also had its share) to include blacks in the fellowship of their churches.

After 1640 the rapid development of trade between New England and the islands of the West Indies led to the purchase of slaves on an occasional basis by skippers who brought them back to Massachusetts, Connecticut, and Rhode Island or sold them at intermediate points, usually in the Chesapeake. New Jersey and New York grew rapidly after the expulsion of the Dutch in 1664; they too became involved in the West Indian trade. Pennsylvania and Delaware, settled by the English beginning in 1682 and included with Pennsylvania in the Penn proprietorship, were soon also engaged in a regular and profitable trade with the West Indies. Gary Nash points out that an enterprising merchant in Philadelphia imported 150 Africans as early as 1684 and had no difficulty selling them in just a few days.

Incomplete records prove that several hundred ships brought over four thousand blacks to New York City alone during the colonial period. Only a few of these ships were from Africa; the rest were engaged in trade with the West Indies and brought on average fewer than ten blacks per cargo. A long-lived legend in textbooks of American history concerning a triangle trade connecting New England, Africa, and the American South is largely untrue. Over 90 percent of the slaves brought to North America came in large English slave ships, mostly out of London and, later, Liverpool. A few North Americans, especially in Rhode Island, tried the direct trade with Africa, though most significantly in the years immediately following independence.

There is very little to distinguish the climate of the lower Delaware River valley and Delaware Bay from the neighboring province of Maryland; tobacco grew just as well in the one region as the other. Back when they consisted only of small Dutch and Swedish settlements, tiny Delaware and the southern part of New Jersey supplemented white servants with African Americans at about the same time the Chesapeake colonies did; to put it differently, these areas were not, by our usual definitions, northern at all, but economically were the northern edge of Chesapeake society. Delaware, indeed, remained a slave state (though most of its blacks had become free) until

1865. Farther to the north, there were prosperous farmers in the lower Hudson and Connecticut River valleys, on Long Island, and around Narragansett Bay who owned African-American laborers. These were all regions that specialized in market agriculture; the farmers who owned slaves were those who owned farms large enough to keep a crew busy the year-round and do so profitably enough to pay the cost of their purchase and maintenance.

Otherwise, however, northern slavery was predominantly an urban institution. The same labor shortage throughout colonial North America that caused southern planters to turn to Africans caused the wealthier sort in the northern seaports to buy Africans to work as household servants, help around their docks and warehouses, or serve as teamsters and sailors. To be sure indentured English servants were preferable to new Africans, because they understood the language, laws, and routines of the colonies. But English servants of the desired quality became very scarce in the early eighteenth century; the demand, in classic economic terms, grew much more rapidly than the supply. Some prosperous farmers and merchants, especially in Pennsylvania, then bought up the contracts of German-speaking redemptioners. But whatever their other virtues, these European immigrants were no more likely to understand English than new Africans and could be bound to service only for a few years. Indeed it may well be the case that many moderately prosperous citizens in Pennsylvania, New York, and other northern colonies regularly purchased redemptioners not because they made better servants, but because they cost less than Africans.

The urban slaves of the North were even more likely than their cousins of the Chesapeake to be engaged in every variety of skilled trade. When one looks at colonial estimates of population or the federal census of 1790, the proportion of African Americans in each province seems rather small north and east of Delaware. But most blacks lived in rather small areas of those provinces; there were always enough in Boston, Providence, Newport, New York, and Philadelphia to form a self-conscious community. By contrast—and this was an important difference in the forming sections—the more isolated farming communities of Pennsylvania, New York, and

New England usually had no African-American residents whatsoever; comparable communities in Virginia and the Carolinas always had at least a few.

At the end of the colonial era, African Americans were approximately 2.4 percent of population of New England colonies and 6 percent in New York, Pennsylvania, New Jersey, and Delaware. But it must be emphasized again that they were by no means distributed equally through these provinces but rather concentrated in commercial areas.

SOUTH CAROLINA AND GEORGIA: THE DEEP SOUTH

Cotton was a minor but significant cash crop in the British West Indies during the colonial era; it was not a staple crop in South Carolina until after the winning of independence. South Carolina struggled in its early years from 1670 to 1700 in a way somewhat reminiscent of Virginia and took far longer than Virginia to find a major crop. Among the earliest British settlers there were several who held slaves; although African Americans were still a small proportion of the laboring force in the Chesapeake during the 1670s and 1680s, they were, as we have seen, already the majority in Barbados and rapidly becoming so in other Caribbean colonies. The same concentration of land into large sugar plantations that drove the demand for African labor radically reduced the opportunities for free white Englishmen in the West Indies. South Carolina became a new home for thousands who had lived on the islands; some brought slaves with them, while others sought to own slaves as soon as they could afford them.

The economic history of colonial South Carolina may be divided conveniently into three parts. The earliest, roughly from 1670 to 1700, found the early settlers prospering more from trading with the Indians than from raising any cash crop. After the usual early difficulties, settlers grew enough corn and other crops to sustain themselves, and some grew tobacco. Early Carolinians raised hogs, cattle, and grain and cut timber for sale in the West Indies, knowing such commodities were always in demand where sugar tended to crowd out other crops. For several years they enjoyed a brisk trade in hides and furs—most profitably in deerskins. In a shameful trade now largely forgotten, these pioneers of South Carolina bought captive Native Americans from friendly tribes and then either set them to work or sold them as slaves to the West Indies. Nor were the South Carolinians unique in this; the English settlers of New England and the Chesapeake also enslaved Indians taken as prisoners of war in the seventeenth century. Indians themselves bought and sold slaves of all races; some, notably the Creek and Cherokee, would eventually imitate Europeans in applying the labor of African-American slaves to the cultivation of their staple crops.

The colony still lacked a staple, though almost everything grown in the West Indies had been tried within the first years of settlement. The second phase of Carolina agriculture began late in the 1690s, when someone finally succeeded in growing rice of good quality and in quantity enough to export. Rice then transformed South Carolina much as sugar had transformed Barbados; once the planters had mastered the art of growing rice, it proved reasonably dependable from season to season, and so did its market. Requiring alternate flooding and draining of paddies, rice could not be grown economically on small estates. A rice plantation had to be large and required many hands. Black labor was increasingly available during the rise of the rice industry (from 1700 to 1750 and beyond), while free European labor was both scarce and likely to perish in the semitropical lowlands, where Africans were far more resistant to malaria than Europeans. The growth of slavery along with rice planting was virtually inevitable. Certain Africans already having proved themselves expert in the care of cattle, South Carolina planters now sought slaves from those parts of Africa that cultivated rice; to a considerable degree Africans helped introduce and perfect the great cash crop of colonial South Carolina.

South Carolina, which from 1670 to 1700 had grown only from a few hundred to approximately sixty-eight hundred settlers, now began a modest boom. By 1740 the population had grown to approximately fifty-nine thousand; over half were enslaved Africans. A significant if temporary boost to this growth came after 1705, when Parliament voted a subsidy for naval

stores. The abundance of pine in the region held great promise for producing pitch, tar, turpentine, and ship timbers, and encouraged by the subsidy, many Carolinians turned to their manufacture. Again they relied very largely on slave labor.

The 1740s saw South Carolina succeed in establishing another staple crop, the blue-dye-producing indigo. The earliest settlers had known about indigo, for it grew extensively in the West Indies, but before Eliza Lucas Pinckney perfected its processing, no one had succeeded in producing dyestuff of sufficient quality to sell in England. There were many advantages in having a second staple. Indigo was likely to be most valuable when rice was least marketable, typically during times of war. Furthermore, even within the rice belt of South Carolina, much of the land was unsuitable for the hydraulic engineering that rice required; that same land was fine for indigo. Both crops were labor intensive, but they required the maximum amount of labor at different seasons. Indigo was like sugar in one important respect: if the plant was not processed immediately after picking, it would spoil. Planters had to invest in boiling vats and other equipment in addition to land and slaves. Indigo, like rice, required large-scale establishments.

The history of Georgia has its own fascination, not only for its idealistic and philanthropic beginnings under the warrior and humanitarian, General James Oglethorpe, but also when followed into the times of Cherokee removal, the era of the cotton kingdom, and the War for Southern Independence. The story of slavery in colonial Georgia is, however, briefly told. As a part of the humanitarian social engineering of the Georgia Trustees, slavery and alcoholic beverages were forbidden as incompatible with the rehabilitation of criminals and other social outcasts sent there. As a humanitarian enterprise the colony largely failed. In 1752 the Crown replaced the trustees, and it subsequently opened the valuable coastal lands of the province to eager settlers from South Carolina. Because rice fields could be irrigated only along streams influenced by the rise and fall of tides, South Carolina had run out of suitable land. Between 1752 and the outbreak of the American War of Independence, the tidewater region of Georgia developed rapidly, duplicating the Carolina tidewater; from

1751 to 1773 the colony's black population increased from about five hundred to around fifteen thousand.

The African-American culture that developed in South Carolina and Georgia combined West Indian and Chesapeake features. In the low country especially, blacks greatly outnumbered whites and lived in villages on extensive rice and indigo plantations. The owners preferred, if they could afford it, to maintain their families in Charleston, with its presumably healthier climate and desirable social amenities. Compared with the Chesapeake, there was proportionally less interaction among white and black, fewer small plantations in which white master and black servant worked side by side, and as in the West Indies, a greater presence of the African born. South Carolina and Georgia were the only two states that imported Africans in as many as the thousands between 1783 and 1808, when Congress passed and President Jefferson signed a law declaring the importation of foreign slaves illegal.

And what of North Carolina, that legendary "valley of humility" between proud Virginia and South Carolina? Migrants from Virginia began settling there in the 1650s, developing tobacco culture and gradually adopting slave labor in the Chesapeake fashion. After South Carolina became a distinct province, the southeastern portion of North Carolina became rather more like its southern neighbor than the Chesapeake. More than South Carolina, and unlike Virginia, North Carolina carried on a successful naval stores industry in the colonial era, applying the labor of blacks to the extensive pine forests that divide the North Carolina tidewater and Piedmont.

WHY SLAVERY FLOURISHED

As detailed above, the British Empire had some minor connections with African-American slavery from its earliest beginnings, became deeply involved in slavery in the West Indies from around 1640 onward, and competed with great success in the slave trade itself from around 1670 until Parliament outlawed that trade in 1807. At the time of the American Revolution, slavery was established in practice and in law in every American colony of the British Empire, including recently conquered Canada. The British and the French participated in the African-Atlantic slave trade and exploited slave labor in their colonies in emulation of the older overseas commercial-colonial empires, especially those of Portugal, Spain, and the Netherlands. The Atlantic slave trade peaked in the years 1760 to 1810, though by then the British share was beginning to decline. The British—along with their recently liberated colonies of North America—had quit entirely by the latter date, save only for outlaws who usually delivered slaves to the relatively new sugar frontiers of Cuba and Brazil.

There should be no mystery about why slavery flourished in the colonial era. An expanding Europe needed laborers by the millions to extract the wealth of the Americas and found excellent laborers for sale in West Africa. The record of economic growth in all of the colonies that depended on slave labor proves the profitability if not the humanity of the slave labor system.

Besides accomplishing the tasks set by their masters in colonial slave societies, many African Americans also worked on their own time to raise extra crops, poultry, and hogs, catch fish, or hunt game. Technically they could not own property, but custom generally permitted these extracurricular economic activities; on the whole they benefited the planters by increasing the overall supply of food and lowering costs. If the very extensive descriptions of runaway slaves are a fair indication, colonial blacks often owned tools, musical instruments, and several articles of clothing. The new world of abundant goods, partly created by their industry, brought them the simple luxuries of the colonial poor: molasses, tobacco, and rum. Their artistic impulses and creativity brought them much more in the form of storytelling, dance, and song.

With local legislatures writing laws and societies of radically different composition developing their own customs, it is quite amazing how similar slave codes were from Jamaica to the Carolinas, the Chesapeake, and even New England. Massachusetts, not Virginia, was the first mainland English colony legally and explicitly to affirm the institution of slavery in her 1641 Body of Liberties. Elaborate slave codes were more a product of the eighteenth than the seventeenth century; Virginia produced hers in 1705, rationalizing and regularizing half a century's piecemeal legislation. Slaves were everywhere expected at all times to be both submissive and dutiful. They were not to wander from their plantations without permission. They were not to strike any white people nor testify against them in courts of law. They were not to own or bear arms except under close regulation. They could be sold at the pleasure of their owners and bequeathed to heirs or surrendered to creditors, much as any other property. Massachusetts passed a law in 1705 establishing marriages between slaves, but marriages between black and white were illegal. Elsewhere only custom, not law, protected slave marriages, and it did so quite imperfectly.

The value of bond servants resided in the work they accomplished; therefore imprisonment for crime was against the interest of slaveholders. Indeed death, maiming, whipping, or other painful and humiliating punishments were the rule for most crimes before the era of the American Revolution, and certainly for slaves. It is significant, however, that "cruel and unusual punishments" continued for African-American slaves long after an otherwise enlightened nation prohibited them for white people. White men and women convicted (wrongly) of witchcraft in Salem Village died by hanging; African men convicted (wrongly) of arson in New York City burned at the stake in 1741.

Two of the three most widely discussed slave rebellions in U.S. history never took place. Both Gabriel's Rebellion in Virginia (1800) and Denmark Vesey's in South Carolina (1822) were betrayed before they started; only Nat Turner's in Virginia (1831) was a true insurrection. By contrast there were several armed clashes between blacks and whites in colonial times, of which the largest was the Stono Rebellion in South Carolina in 1739.

Provincial legislatures passed laws preventing slaves from holding meetings for any purpose whatever and otherwise tried to remove the occasion of plots and conspiracies. A few laws were designed to protect slaves from sadistic or murderous masters; there were even a few cases where notorious offenders were hanged for murdering slaves. But most planters were reluctant to prosecute their neighbors or even inquire too closely into how they disciplined their slaves. Because blacks were generally barred from testifying against whites and because slaveholders ran the courts, most criminal acts by white people against black went unpunished.

Laws barring manumission or surrounding it with stringent requirements testified to two quite different concerns: the public, as represented in colonial assemblies, regarded free blacks as a nuisance and, in colonies with large populations of slaves, as a potential source of subversion or rebellion; the assemblies feared additionally that some owners would free elderly or incapacitated slaves who were no longer useful to them, in effect making them public charges.

A few African Americans became celebrities during the colonial and revolutionary eras. One such was Phillis Wheatley, a devout poet in Massachusetts; another, in the same colony, was the patriot-martyr Crispus Attucks, shot dead in the Boston Massacre of 1770. Many black field preachers appeared in the train of the Great Awakening. The evangelical witness Gustavus Vassa, also known by his African name, Oloudah Equiano, was known to the devout on both sides of the Atlantic; Jupiter Hammon of New York was also notable for his piety.

Broadly speaking, however, the Christian churches of the British colonies did little, outside of Massachusetts, to soften the rigors of chattel slavery for African Americans. Unable in most colonies even to supply ministers, buildings, schools, and seminaries to keep up with burgeoning populations, the churches failed in their self-appointed tasks almost as badly with free whites as with enslaved blacks. But precisely because the churches did so little for blacks and so often hedged what they did do with hypocritical pseudo-Christian instruction concerning obedience, historians have, with some notable exceptions, failed to notice that the British colonial experience in large measure produced the American, European, and ultimately worldwide antislavery movement. However much the Europeans, and especially the British, extended and expanded the enslavement of fellow humans, they certainly did not invent slavery. A few of them did, on the other hand, formulate the idea that slavery is itself a crime, that the enslaving of innocent human beings must everywhere be wrong.

The insight was not peculiar to Englishmen. Bishop Bartolomé de Las Casas argued it at the imperial court of Spain in the early years of European expansion; 250 years later the radical Girondist, Brissot de Warville, organized Les Amis des Noirs and urged emancipation in all the colonies of Europe, beginning with the French. Antislavery statements were issued in 1680 by Morgan Godwyn, former minister in Virginia; in 1689 by the pietistic settlers of Germantown, Pennsylvania; and in 1700 from Judge Samuel Sewall in Boston, Massachusetts. English and colonial antislavery voices, scattered at first, became more and more numerous until the Quakers of Pennsylvania, urged on by John Woolman, Anthony Benezet, and others, established manumission as a moral duty for members of their society in the 1760s.

Concern for the immortal souls and temporal condition of African slaves had been present in the missionary wing of the Church of England ever since the Reverend Thomas Bray founded the Society for the Propagation of the Gospel (SPG) in 1701. The Reverend John Wesley, sometime missionary to Georgia under SPG auspices, eventually tried to persuade his fellow Methodists that slavery was a sin; ultimately, after his death and several short-term setbacks, antislavery sentiment prevailed. Many American Presbyterians turned antislavery, including the celebrated Dr. Benjamin Rush of Philadelphia and Reverend David Rice in Virginia. A few political leaders, including the young Alexander Hamilton and Gouverneur Morris, denounced slavery and called for emancipation.

Eric A. Williams, the brilliant historian from Trinidad—later the Prime Minister of Trinidad and Tobago—made two remarkable generalizations about British colonial slavery in his widely read and often reprinted *Capitalism and Slavery*. The first was that the industrial revolution in England was possible only because of the surplus value resulting from the profits of the Atlantic slave trade. The second was that the British Parliament outlawed the trade only after it had ceased to be profitable and outlawed slavery throughout the empire only after those colonies that depended on slave labor had become insignificant.

On the latter point Williams was immediately challenged and eventually refuted. Both slavery and the slave trade were highly profitable—in some respects more profitable than ever—when Britain and the United States outlawed the trade in 1807 and 1808. As Seymour Drescher has demonstrated in *Econocide*, the end of a virtually unlimited source of African labor

was itself the cause of decline in existing British sugar colonies and effectively prevented the development of new ones. Cuba and Brazil became the world's leaders in sugar production during the first half of the nineteenth century precisely because they continued to import African labor.

It is also untrue, narrowly speaking, that the trade with Africa itself produced profits enough to capitalize Britain's industrial economy. But Eric Williams's first point, if modified somewhat, is both true and important: the system of slave labor—virtually the whole labor system in the West Indies, most of it in the lowlands of South Carolina and Georgia and half of it in the Chesapeake—made possible a rapid economic development where, without African labor, there would have been slow development or none at all. On the eve of the American Revolution, the West Indies trade absorbed almost half the exports of Britain's northern colonies. So even though slave labor was relatively unimportant in the middle and New England colonies, slave labor elsewhere was very important for them.

One might imagine, counterfactually, a more innocent colonial history in which no Africans were dragged in chains to the Americas or set to hard labor on behalf of white masters. No such history could have produced thirteen colonies populous and wealthy enough to fight and win their independence between 1776 and 1783. In history as it actually happened, the odious slave trade and the long-discredited system of slavery were essential elements in the prosperity of the British Atlantic Empire.

BIBLIOGRAPHY

General Works

Craton, Michael. *Sinews of Empire: A Short History of British Slavery.* Garden City, N.Y., 1974.
Curtin, Philip D. *The Atlantic Slave Trade: A Census.* Madison, Wis., 1969.
———. *The Rise and Fall of the Plantation Complex: Essays in Atlantic History.* Cambridge, England, 1990.
Davis, David Brion. *The Problem of Slavery in Western Culture.* Ithaca, N.Y., 1966.
———. *Slavery and Human Progress.* New York, 1984.
Drescher, Seymour. *Econocide: British Slavery in the Era of Abolition.* Pittsburgh, Pa., 1977.
Finkelman, Paul, ed. *Articles on American Slavery 3: Colonial Southern Slavery.* New York, 1989.

Frey, Silvia R., *Water from the Rock: Black Resistance in a Revolutionary Age.* Princeton, N.J., 1991.

Galenson, David W. *Traders, Planters, and Slaves: Market Behavior in Early English America.* Cambridge, England, 1986.

Jordan, Winthrop D. *White Over Black: American Attitudes Toward the Negro, 1550–1812.* Chapel Hill, N.C., 1968.

McCusker, John J., and Russell R. Menard. *The Economy of British America, 1607–1789.* Chapel Hill, N.C., 1985.

Williams, Eric A. *Capitalism and Slavery.* Chapel Hill, N.C., 1944.

Wood, Peter H. " 'I Did the Best I Could for My Day': The Study of Early Black History During the Second Reconstruction, 1960 to 1976." *William and Mary Quarterly,* 3rd ser., 35, no. 2 (1978):185–225. Note that the entire issue containing this article is devoted to colonial British slavery.

The West Indies

Dunn, Richard S. *Sugar and Slaves: The Rise of the Planter Class in the English West Indies, 1624–1713.* Chapel Hill, N.C., 1972.

Goveia, Elsa V. *Slave Society in the British Leeward Islands at the End of the Eighteenth Century.* New Haven, Conn., 1965.

Hamshere, Cyril. *The British in the Caribbean.* London, 1972.

Patterson, Orlando. *The Sociology of Slavery: An Analysis of the Origins, Development, and Structure of Negro Slave Society in Jamaica.* London, 1967.

Sheridan, Richard B. *Sugar and Slavery: An Economic History of the British West Indies, 1623–1775.* Baltimore, Md., 1974.

Ward, J. R. *British West Indian Slavery, 1750–1834: The Process of Amelioration.* Oxford, 1988.

The Mainland Colonies

Brown, Robert E., and B. Katherine Brown. *Virginia, 1705–1786: Democracy or Aristocracy?* East Lansing, Mich., 1964.

Greene, Lorenzo J. *The Negro in Colonial New England, 1620–1776.* New York, 1942.

Kulikoff, Allan. *Tobacco and Slaves: The Development of Southern Cultures in the Chesapeake, 1680–1800.* Chapel Hill, N.C., 1986.

Littlefield, Daniel C. *Rice and Slaves: Ethnicity and the Slave Trade in Colonial South Carolina.* Baton Rouge, La., 1981.

Main, Gloria L. *Tobacco Colony: Life in Early Maryland, 1650–1720.* Princeton, N.J., 1982.

McManus, Edgar J. *Black Bondage in the North.* Syracuse, N.Y., 1973.

————. *A History of Negro Slavery in New York.* Syracuse, N.Y., 1966.

Morgan, Edmund S. *American Slavery, American Freedom: The Ordeal of Colonial Virginia.* New York, 1975.

Mullin, Gerald W. *Flight and Rebellion: Slave Resistance in Eighteenth-Century Virginia.* New York, 1972.

Nash, Gary B. *Forging Freedom: The Formation of Philadelphia's Black Community, 1720–1840.* Cambridge, Mass., 1988.

Sobel, Mechal. *The World They Made Together: Black and White Values in Eighteenth-Century Virginia.* Princeton, N.J., 1987.

Winks, Robin. *The Blacks in Canada: A History.* New Haven, Conn., 1971.

Wood, Betty. *Slavery in Colonial Georgia, 1730–1775.* Athens, Ga., 1984.

Wood, Peter H. *Black Majority: Negroes in Colonial South Carolina from 1670 Through the Stono Rebellion.* New York, 1974.

Robert McColley

SEE ALSO **Farming, Planting, and Ranching; Marriage;** and **The Slave Trade;** and various essays in RACIAL INTERACTION; and the map accompanying **The Slave Trade.**

THE DUTCH COLONY

SLAVERY IN NEW NETHERLAND developed under the auspices of the Dutch West India Company (WIC), a commercial organization whose major profits flowed from the slave trade. From the company's viewpoint, the establishment of slavery in New Netherland was of little consequence, since the market for slaves in the colony was small. Seen from the perspective of New York's (and New Jersey's) subsequent history, however, the institutionalization of slavery in the Dutch colony was a fateful step. The precedent of holding human beings as slaves in perpetuity, however softened by pragmatism, set the stage for the subjugation of African peoples in centuries to come.

THE DUTCH SLAVE TRADE

Granted a monopoly of the Dutch slave trade at its founding in 1621, the WIC shipped slaves from bases on the West African coast such as Elmina to eager purchasers in the Dutch colony of Brazil. After Brazil was recaptured by the Portuguese in 1654, the Dutch slave trade was directed toward new markets. Curaçao, an island off the coast of Venezuela captured from the Spanish in 1634, became an entrepôt for the Dutch slave trade, which was now concentrated on supplying slaves to the Spanish and English colonies. Though the directors made some efforts to stimulate the demand for slaves in New Netherland after 1654, the major thrust of the WIC's slave trade was focused elsewhere.

Slaves arrived in New Netherland starting in the 1620s, many of them captives seized from Spanish and Portuguese ships. Their numbers increased slowly and haphazardly until the reorientation of the company's slave trade after 1654 made slaves more readily available. During the last five years of Dutch rule, slave ships arrived in New Amsterdam by way of Curaçao with some degree of regularity. Because of the premium placed on physical strength in New Netherland's labor-scarce economy, men outnumbered women among the slaves imported to the colony. Yet New Netherland buyers could not compete for African workers in their prime and therefore received a disproportionate share of older slaves who were castoffs from the West Indies.

The majority of enslaved Africans were held in New Amsterdam, but slaves were found as well in other parts of the colony including Beverswyck, the patroonship of Rensselaerswyck, the Long Island towns, and the settlements on the Delaware River. By the end of the period of Dutch rule, New Netherland's slave population probably numbered about five hundred.

Any European settler in New Netherland with sufficient cash could purchase a slave, since slave ownership was not restricted to any economic or ethnic group. New Netherlanders also participated in the slave trade to some extent. Several New Amsterdam merchants invested in small-scale slave trading ventures, importing slaves from the West Indies and selling them locally or to buyers in the British mainland colonies.

Slavery flourished in New Netherland primarily because of the shortage of labor, but the fact that the clergy of the Dutch Reformed church failed to raise a voice against the enslavement and exploitation of human beings from Africa undoubtedly soothed any scruples that may have arisen. Nonetheless, the church took an interest in Christianizing New Netherland's African population. New Amsterdam church records reveal that black couples were married in the church and had their children baptized there.

GROWTH OF SLAVERY IN NEW NETHERLAND

Initially, most of the colony's slaves belonged to the WIC and were used in clearing land, performing agricultural labor, and constructing and repairing Fort Amsterdam. Slaves worked in groups under the supervision of an overseer. The company provided them with housing and medical care.

In light of the inadequate supply of indentured servants in New Netherland, local officials of the WIC at times consented to lease out slaves to individual colonists for specifically defined periods of time. Before the 1650s private ownership of slaves was rare, but by the time the English conquered the colony in 1664, it was not uncommon. Individual owners employed slaves as farm hands, heavy laborers, skilled workers, and domestic servants.

FLEXIBLE STATUS OF AFRICAN SLAVES

Though slavery was well entrenched in New Netherland, it was never codified in law. As a result the status of Africans forced into slavery was flexible to a degree unknown in the colony under English rule. The WIC inaugurated the practice of manumitting slaves who had served the company well and giving them plots of land on the perimeter of the New Amsterdam settlement. The company's grant of freedom, however, included certain conditions. Former slaves had to remain ready to work for the company when asked, but now they would receive a fair wage for their labor. They were also required to pay a yearly tribute to the company consisting of thirty *schepels* of grain and a fat hog. Although still subject to the demands of the West India Company, the people of African ancestry who held the status alternatively called "half-free-dom" or "half-slavery" were allowed to live in family units on their own farms, independent of European control. Other slaves were granted their freedom outright.

At the time of the English conquest, there were approximately seventy-five free blacks in New Amsterdam. These men, women, and children who formed the city's first African-American community enjoyed a significant measure of control over their lives and served to inspire the slaves with whom they came in contact.

BIBLIOGRAPHY

Boogaart, Ernst van den. "The Servant Migration to New Netherland, 1624–1664." In *Colonialism and Migration: Indentured Labour Before and After Slavery*, edited by P. C. Emmer. Dordrecht, The Netherlands, 1986.

Christoph, Peter R. "The Freedmen of New Amsterdam." In *A Beautiful and Fruitful Place; Selected Rensselaerswijck Seminar Papers*, edited by Nancy Anne McClure Zeller. Albany, N.Y., 1991.

Goodfriend, Joyce D. "Burghers and Blacks: The Evolution of a Slave Society at New Amsterdam." *New York History* 59, no. 2 (1978):125–144.

Kobrin, David. *The Black Minority in Early New York.* Albany, N.Y., 1971.

McManus, Edgar J. *A History of Negro Slavery in New York.* Syracuse, N.Y., 1966.

Postma, Johannes Menne. *The Dutch in the Atlantic Slave Trade, 1600–1815.* Cambridge, England, 1990.

Joyce D. Goodfriend

SEE ALSO **Farming, Planting, and Ranching; Marriage;** and **The Slave Trade;** and various essays in RACIAL INTERACTION; and the map accompanying **The Slave Trade.**

THE FRENCH COLONIES

THE CHARACTER OF SLAVERY in the French colonies of North America varied according to the demographic and economic conditions in particular regions. The colonies of Canada and Louisiana evolved under divergent circumstances, and the Illinois country—although technically part of the latter province—produced a third variation in the life of French North America's slave population. As in most other North American colonies, slavery began in New France at a slow and random pace. African slaves trickled into the Saint Lawrence Valley over the late seventeenth century, while American Indians who were captured from the western interior became Canada's majority of enslaved laborers throughout its colonial era. French colonization of the Mississippi Valley also mixed Indian with African slaves, but a surge of slave shipments from the Senegal Valley of West Africa during the 1720s quickly transformed Louisiana slavery into a predominantly black experience. Black slaves reached the Illinois country through Louisiana, but their relatively small number and the kind of production that occupied them made their bondage somewhat different from the plantation slavery under which most African Americans lived in the lower Mississippi Valley.

NEW FRANCE

The colony of New France quickly became a market for Indians captured in the west. Indian allies of the French sold their captives, taken from enemy nations, to Canadian merchants who resold them to the settlers. Many of these captives were Pawnee, so *panis* became the generic name for all Indian slaves. African slaves reached Canada in scattered numbers and, like their Indian counterparts, worked as household servants and field workers for wealthier settlers. The ethnic diversity of this slave population and the vague boundaries between free and unfree labor generated some objection to the establishment of slavery in New France. But in 1709 Intendant Jacques Raudot issued an ordinance that firmly legalized ownership of Indian and black slaves. By the 1760s Canada's slave population reached some three thousand Indians and one thousand blacks, mostly living in or near Montreal. Because of their vulnerability to diseases, slaves in New France suffered a high mortality rate. The average age of death for *panis* was eighteen and for blacks twenty-five.

LOUISIANA

French Louisiana acquired Indian slaves mostly from nearby enemy tribes, especially the Chitimacha, although some *panis* did reach the colony from the upper Mississippi Valley. Louisiana's first several black slaves arrived on the Gulf coast during the first decade of the eighteenth century as plunder captured by French officers from the English West Indies. But not until the Compagnie de l'Occident (later the Compagnie des Indes) assumed responsibility over Louisiana in 1717 did regular shipments of African slaves begin reaching the lower Mississippi Valley. Under the company's management through the 1720s, some seven thousand blacks were transported directly from West Africa to Louisiana. Nearly half of them perished en route or shortly after arriving. As in Canada, the Code Noir was adopted as the legal framework of slavery in Louisiana. These regulations imposed restrictions on slaves, Indian and African alike, and responsibilities on slaveholders. Slaves were supposed to be converted to Catholicism and to be protected from abusive masters. The weak administration of colonial affairs and the fluidity of socioeconomic relations in early Louisiana, however, militated against full enforcement of the Code Noir.

Bondage of Indians was not officially prohibited in Louisiana until Spanish acquisition, but a convergence of factors shared with other North American colonies slowed down the rate of Indian enslavement significantly. The decimation of Indians by disease, the desire to secure stable trade relations with neighboring tribes, the availability of African slaves, and the ease with which Indian captives could abscond all contributed to a declining number of Indian slaves in the lower Mississippi Valley after the 1720s. Conflicts with the Natchez and Chickasaw nations produced hundreds of Indian slaves, but most were shipped away from the region to the West Indies. Also influencing the process was the tendency in both custom and law to classify slaves automatically as "Negro" or "mulatto." Liaisons between Indian and African-American slaves produced children who were ascribed with increasing regularity to Negro or mulatto identities. A portion of Indians was also assimilated into the free segment of colonial society, as the offspring of Indian slave women and freemen grew up as free people of color or as whites. By 1732 Louisiana contained fewer than one hundred Indian slaves amid a colonial population of some four thousand black slaves and two thousand settlers.

A high percentage of Louisiana slaves lived on large indigo and tobacco plantations along the Mississippi River. Nevertheless, African Americans participated widely in the colonial economy of the lower Mississippi Valley. Slaves were employed as skilled artisans, boatmen, household servants, and, in some urgent circumstances, soldiers. They worked in the wetland forests as lumbermen and herdsmen and even served as traders and interpreters in the Indians' deerskin commerce with the colony. These and other activities allowed some degree of flexibility and mobility within the otherwise tightening grip of slavery. Many slaves even managed to earn or purchase their freedom under these frontier conditions. Meanwhile, the relatively large number of African Americans in French Louisiana facilitated the deep contribution of slaves to the evolution of a Creole culture.

THE ILLINOIS COUNTRY

Along the upper reaches of the Mississippi River, slaves remained a minority within colonial districts like Arkansas and Illinois. Their labor was nonetheless important to agricultural, mineral, and fur-trade activities. By the mid eighteenth century, the Illinois settlements numbered nearly 800 settlers, 450 black slaves, and 150 Indian slaves. Situated on the peripheries of both Canada and Louisiana, officials and slaveowners in the upper Mississippi Valley administered slave laws more erratically. As in Louisiana, interaction between blacks and Indians endured in fluid, and sometimes volatile, forms. Small-scale farming and tightly knit households, on the other hand, minimized the cultural and social autonomy of slaves in Illinois as well as in Canada.

BIBLIOGRAPHY

Allain, Mathé. "Slave Policies in French Louisiana." *Louisiana History* 21, no. 2 (1980):127–137.

Arnold, Morris S. *Colonial Arkansas, 1686–1804: A Social and Cultural History.* Fayetteville, Ark., 1991.

Brasseaux, Carl A. "The Administration of Slave Regulations in French Louisiana, 1724–1766." *Louisiana History* 21, no. 2 (1980):139–158.

Briggs, Winstanley. "Slavery in French Colonial Illinois." *Chicago History* 18, no. 4 (1989–1990):66–81.

Ekberg, Carl J. *Colonial Ste. Genevieve: An Adventure on the Mississippi Frontier.* Gerald, Mo., 1985.

Giraud, Marcel. *A History of French Louisiana.* Vol. 5, *The Company of the Indies, 1723–1731.* Translated by Brian Pearce. Baton Rouge, La., 1991.

Hall, Gwendolyn Midlo. *Africans in Colonial Louisiana: The Development of Afro-Creole Culture in the Eighteenth Century.* Baton Rouge, La., 1992.

Trudel, Marcel. *L'Esclavage au Canada français: Histoire et conditions de l'esclavage.* Quebec, 1960.

Usner, Daniel H., Jr. "From African Captivity to American Slavery: The Introduction of Black Laborers to Colonial Louisiana." *Louisiana History* 20, no. 1 (1979):25–48.

————. *Indians, Settlers, and Slaves in a Frontier Exchange Economy: The Lower Mississippi Valley Before 1783.* Chapel Hill, N.C., 1992.

Winks, Robin W. *The Blacks in Canada: A History.* New Haven, Conn., 1971.

Daniel H. Usner, Jr.

SEE ALSO **Farming, Planting, and Ranching; Marriage;** and **The Slave Trade;** and various essays in RACIAL INTERACTION; and the map accompanying **The Slave Trade.**

THE SPANISH BORDERLANDS

ABORIGINAL SLAVERY

SLAVERY AMONG THE NATIVE PEOPLES of the Spanish Borderlands during precontact times is poorly understood. Some authorities suggest that the institution was unknown prior to its introduction by Old World peoples, but most accept that it was practiced in some form. A few even postulate a slave trade from the region to the more complex civilizations of central Mexico.

There is sufficient evidence of warfare to indicate that at the very least there were captives taken into societies at all levels of complexity. The fate of captives is not well described. Many were killed, but some survived under circumstances that varied from tribe to tribe. Most descriptions derive from postcontact times.

Among the Natchez, perhaps the most rigidly ranked society in the Southeast, captives had to participate in dancing and were later given to families who had lost members in war. Women captives were used as slaves, but men might be chosen as husbands by Natchez widows or tortured and killed. Whether the man's status as captive spouse would be equivalent to slavery has not been investigated, but among many cultures adoption did become a form of enslavement. In the southeastern chiefdoms through which Hernando de Soto traveled between 1539 and 1542, slavery included the mutilation of captives' feet to prevent escape.

On the Texas coast tribes had extremely simple sociopolitical institutions. Their first contacts with Europeans were with survivors of shipwrecks whom they kept as slaves, but whether this was an opportunistic response to a novel situation or an application of a traditional practice is unclear.

The first contacts of the Pueblo peoples of the Southwest with exploring expeditions in the early 1540s led to the trading or giving of captives from other tribes to Spanish soldiers. Again, it is not obvious from the surviving accounts whether this trading had antecedents in the native cultures, but it is clear that captives among the Pueblo lacked sufficient status to forbid their exchange when an offer was made.

Information on the treatment of captives in other areas derives from sources so late that the influence of Old World customs must be suspected. The data do suggest that some form of slavery existed in most cultures prior to the arrival of Europeans.

SPANISH SLAVERY

Slavery had had a long history on the Iberian Peninsula by the time of the discovery of the New World, having begun at least as early as Roman times and probably long before. Christian theology essentially recognized all people as human beings. While it did not forbid slavery, by defining the condition of slavery as a misfortune suffered by a person otherwise deserving, it placed restraint on masters and on officials responsible for laws governing the treatment of slaves. An early legal code that protected slaves and that gave them some rights was the *Siete partidas*, instituted by Alfonso X (the Wise) in the mid thirteenth century. Most notable, perhaps, were the many ways in which a slave might gain freedom. The portion of the *Siete partidas* dealing with involuntary servitude was applied in the New World primarily in the regulation of the owners of black slaves, while the Laws of the Indies governed the enslavement of Indians.

These differences have geographical as well as racial significance. The eastern colonies of Florida and Louisiana were under the administration of Havana, and most slaves were of African origin. The other colonies were a part of the viceroyalty of New Spain, with Mexico City as the capital. As frontier bastions, they neighbored the lands of many free tribes with which warfare was frequent. Slavery in these colonies was based largely on the right to reduce those taken in just war to servitude. The few black slaves seem not to have passed on their condition to descendants, a trend shared with the rest of Mexico, where manumission was frequent.

By law Indian slavery was very strictly limited, and it possessed feudalistic institutions such as the *encomidenda* (a grant to an individual Spaniard of tribute from a specific Indian Pueblo) and *repartimiento* (a grant of a right to require labor for pay from an Indian Pueblo). These institutions imposed conditions more akin to serfdom than slavery, being the usual methods of harnessing the labor of conquered tribes. Simple religious obligation was employed at the missions. In time, debt peonage and wage labor came to replace the institutions that had originated in the Middle Ages, but Indian slavery continued as before. While there were repeated prohibitions on enslaving Native Americans—at least

ten from 1530 to 1553 alone, including the New Laws—the exceptions provided ways to evade the spirit and often the letter of the law. Perhaps the most important difference between black and Indian slavery was that black slavery was hereditary through the female line, while Indian slavery was not passed on to offspring.

European forms of slavery were introduced into the New World with the earliest contacts. Slaves were present on many of the expeditions of exploration, conquest, and colonization. Large-scale slavery was imposed on Indians in the Caribbean very early, and Indian slaves were exported to Spain. The Crown reacted in an erratic fashion. Queen Isabella forbade the enslavement of her vassals, but the wealth of the Indies, which was demanded of the colonizers, could not be extracted without slavery. Fray Bartolomé de las Casas, a conquistador and an *encomendero* (holder of an *encomienda*), was conscience-stricken by what he observed and became the foremost of several defenders of the Indians.

The servitude debated in Spain was the *encomienda,* but in the Caribbean the differences between this feudal institution and actual slavery seem not to have been great, especially as the numbers of local Indians declined and Indians from elsewhere were taken from their homes to work among the settlers. Indeed, the most critical difference between slavery and serfdom is perhaps the separation of the slave from the support of his friends and kin. Reforms in the *encomienda* system gradually brought it more in line with European concepts of vassalage, one motivating factor being the imperative to convert the Indians to Christianity.

Even as the distinction between slavery and the *encomienda* was being made more explicit, Las Casas suggested that both white and black slaves be imported to the New World to replace Indian laborers. He was later to regret this proposal, for the use of black slaves ultimately became the solution to a shortage of Indians in the tropics.

The justification of the enslavement of Indians taken in war permitted the capture of Indians who practiced cannibalism. While justifications for slave raids were often little more than legal fictions and those who abused the restrictions too openly were sometimes arrested, war for no reason other than to take slaves was a continuing problem on frontiers where unconquered Indians were near at hand. In addition, the economics of Spanish slavery soon spread to neighboring Indian peoples who found slaves valuable for trade with the whites and as much needed labor in their own economies. A tribe that became a supplier of captives could also feel less threat that it would be itself raided for slaves.

Florida

Florida, as the name was applied in Spanish, encompassed all of the southeastern part of the present United States. Prior to settlement, slave raids were made in the area to supply labor for the islands. Exploration soon introduced European slavery to the area. The travels of Hernando de Soto in the mid sixteenth century depended in large part on Indian captives as interpreters and as porters. De Soto once sent twenty Indian women to his wife in Cuba. He also took leading Indians as hostages and sometimes local chiefs, intent on securing his friendship, provided men as bearers and women for other services. When De Soto died, his property, including his slaves, was sold at auction. When the remnants of the force finally embarked to return to country controlled by Spain, due to lack of space aboard vessels built for the return voyage some five hundred captives were abandoned on the bank of the Mississippi, far from their homes; another one hundred slaves, belonging to the more favored officers, were taken away. Whether the experiences of local chiefs with Spanish slavery in situations such as these influenced local practices cannot be ascertained from available data, although the Spanish custom of branding slaves was adopted at an early date and applied to Spanish as well as Indian captives.

There were probably few black slaves in Florida in the sixteenth century. In 1621 there were thirty-six blacks on the government payroll who apparently were not slaves. Indians were brought to Saint Augustine as laborers as early as about 1638. By 1676 as many as three hundred Indian men were brought annually to work, few of them surviving to return home. By 1684 white raiders from the Carolinas were attacking the Spanish missions for Native American captives to sell to the English colonists. This continued into the early eighteenth century. The British pressure was such that thousands of Indians were carried off and the missions abandoned.

By the eighteenth century Florida's most conspicuous involvement in the slave complex was as a refuge for black and Indian slaves fleeing the British colonies. While liberty for black fugitives was never certain in the early years, in 1738 the governor established a settlement for black freedmen, Pueblo de la Gracia Real de Santa Teresa de Mose. This new Spanish policy was publicized, resulting in an increase in slaves taking flight from the north. There were over four hundred blacks (both free and slave) living in the Saint Augustine area in 1746. Some had been purchased by Spanish owners from their British masters and were kept by the Spanish families on the condition that they receive religious instruction. In 1756 the blacks at Santa Teresa were allowed to organize a military company, and when England acquired Florida in 1763, the eighty-seven free blacks left for Cuba along with the rest of the population. Over three hundred slaves, presumably most of them blacks, were also taken to Cuba.

During the period of British rule the black slave population of Florida increased dramatically. When Spain returned in 1784, one of the governor's early concerns was to determine which blacks were born free, which were freedmen, and which were the property of English settlers. Owners were required to register their slaves and to produce proof of their claims. Most British subjects left, taking their slaves with them. In 1782–1783, there had been 11,285 blacks in East Florida. In 1785, only 275 were counted in a general census, 70 of them belonging to Spanish masters. Census data of the 1780s and 1790s reveal an interesting pattern of ownership. Many families had one slave and some had from two to four. A small number held from five to eleven slaves. Plantations with large numbers of slaves did not exist under Spanish rule. The number of female slaves was greater than the number of black women, suggesting that a number of Indian women served in Spanish households.

In the Saint Augustine area in 1797, there were 102 free mulattoes and blacks and 483 slaves. A census dating from about 1810–1812 reveals similar numbers and provides age distributions. The black population was predominantly in the sixteen–to–twenty-five-year age range, with very few over the age of forty. A final census in 1815 revealed that the population of married slaves was very low. Throughout this second Spanish period in East Florida, the slave population was consistently less than one-third of the total population. There were also slaves in West Florida. The Spanish residents were reported to treat their slaves kindly there. A number of Anglo-American settlers in West Florida also held black slaves.

Despite the greater slave population, Florida again became a haven for escaped slaves from the former English colonies to the north. Those who did not tarry among the Indians were frequently granted their freedom in the Spanish settlements, whether at Saint Augustine or at Pensacola. Not until 1790 did the Spanish government agree to return fugitives. Acquisition by the United States through the Adams-Onis Treaty of 1819 ended Spanish control.

Louisiana

Spain held Louisiana from 1762 to 1800. The colony was much larger than the present state, but the greater part of the European population was in the south. French settlers had already established plantations, and there were both urban and rural black slaves. French law regulated slavery with the *Code Noir* (Black Laws), a legal code which the second Spanish governor, Alejandro O'Reilly, extended under the new regime. He outlawed the sale of Indian slaves and reported to the king on Indian slavery, apparently hoping to outlaw it entirely, but his major concern was with the large African-American slave population.

The plantation economy of the southern part of Louisiana resulted in a larger slave population than elsewhere, up to about half of the total non-Indian population, and in some of the rural areas perhaps reaching as high as two-thirds or more. Black slaves were held in the interior areas such as at Natchitoches, although probably in smaller numbers. Treatment of slaves under plantation conditions generally was not as good as in smaller-scale slaveholdings. Spanish efforts for better treatment of slaves brought complaints that leniency would show weakness and lead to revolts.

The unrest caused by the French Revolution swept through the Caribbean and reached the Mississippi delta. Slave revolts in the French Antilles drove refugees to Louisiana in 1791. News of slave successes, new ideas of liberty, and the unrest of Frenchmen under Spanish rule were

sufficient to stir fears of black revolt. A plot discovered in that same year led to arrests. The owners of the blacks objected to any punishment that would cause them economic loss, and the conspirators escaped prosecution. Francisco Luis Héctor, Baron de Carondelet, then governor, in 1792 prohibited the importation of slaves from the French Caribbean colonies. He also ordered better treatment of slaves. News of the abolition of slavery in the French colonies in 1794 did nothing to quell the fears of the settlers.

New rumors of an insurrection surfaced in the spring of 1795. On the basis of slaves' reports, a number of suspected plotters were apprehended. By mid May, over sixty suspects had been arrested. A special prosecutor who spoke French was appointed to investigate and to try the accused. Testimony was taken and severe sentences were handed down: execution for some twenty-three to twenty-six blacks, hard labor and *presidio* duty for others, and exile for several blacks and one white man. The heads of some of those who were hanged were displayed, to dissuade others who might think about revolt. At least one black suspect was acquitted.

New regulations were drafted by Carondelet to forestall further trouble: a census of slaves, a request for contributions to repay owners for losses suffered, a revised policy for treatment of slaves, and an offer of reward to any slave reporting a conspiracy. Limits on gatherings of blacks were also made as was a ban on the importation of slaves (first for blacks from the French islands and, in 1796, of any blacks). The ban was not lifted until 1799.

Another plot was discovered on the German Coast in the western part of Louisiana in the spring of 1796 and was quickly put down. Slave revolts were not unique to the period of Spanish rule nor were they the consequence of Spanish protection of the rights of slaves. Perhaps the most immediate factor was congregation of large numbers of slaves on the estates of planters, making organization of united action by the slaves an easier response to their misery.

Texas

After brief contact with Álvar Núñez Cabeza de Vaca and his companions during their enslavement by Indians from 1528–1536 on the coast, the Indians of Texas remained undisturbed by whites until the frontier in Mexico moved northward into areas from which slavers could profitably attack them. The villages at the junction of the Conchos River with the Rio Grande suffered attacks by the late 1570s or early 1580s. Captives were taken to serve as laborers in the mines of Coahuila, Nuevo León, and Nueva Vizcaya. Raids from the mining areas continued well into the seventeenth century. In the 1640s in Nuevo León the distribution of captives was sometimes by auction, the proceeds after reservation of the royal fifth for the king being divided among the soldiers. In 1673 some Texas tribes were reported to have Spanish children as captives.

In the 1660s and 1670s the Crown ordered that Indians from the northern frontiers who had been enslaved should be freed and those responsible should be punished. These orders provoked a defense of the practice from the governor of Nueva Vizcaya, who asserted that the captives were guilty of unprovoked raids against the Spanish and the friendly Indians.

Following the establishment of missions in the San Antonio region in the early eighteenth century, the question of keeping Indian captives was again addressed. In 1731 Governor Fernando Pérez de Almazán complained that unless the settlers were rewarded with captives, they were unwilling to join the troops on campaign. In the following decade, there are records of the distribution of captive Apache. One reason for allowing the sale of captives by allied tribes was that the eighteenth-century customs of the Caddoan-speaking tribes dictated that many war captives be tortured, killed, and perhaps eaten. As the value of slaves increased, captives were frequently kept as slaves or sold to settlers and traders (French and English as well as Spanish). In Texas in the 1750s, the purchase of these captives was cited as a way to protect Christian captives, or those baptized in the Catholic church, but it also helped to justify buying non-Christians.

In 1759 the Apache who had accompanied a Spanish campaign disposed of ninety-seven Yoyuane they had taken by selling them to settlers at San Antonio. The return of captives to their kin, especially when they were relatives of chiefs, frequently figured in efforts to establish peace. Repatriation offers came from both sides. A notable instance was the return of a Spanish

soldier named Treviño whose bravery had been so admired by the Taovayas that they spared his life in 1765.

In 1772 a detachment of soldiers from San Antonio helping a priest collect potential converts from near the mouth of the Rio Grande, brought back Indians from a free-living band which subsisted by producing salt for nearby settlers. Some settlers had recently stolen children from the band, including children of one of the women who had been gathered up for the mission. The settlers had taken the children to sell in Nuevo León. The governor of Texas wrote to the viceroy, complaining of the enslavement of these children. The viceroy ordered the governors of Texas and Nuevo Santander, where the kidnapping had taken place, to arrest the kidnappers. While the governor of Nuevo Santander condemned the capture of Indians for sale, he also protested that priests were engaged in similarly unjust work when they forced Indians into the missions and cited an order from a former viceroy that priests limit their efforts to their mission locales. Officials in Nuevo Santander reported that incursions from Texas had caused unrest among the local Indians, who feared being removed from their homes, and that two settlers had been killed as a result.

It may be that slaveholding was not common in Texas and that the priests there were able to secure most Indian captives for the missions. If census records are accurate, the slave population of Texas was quite small. The 1779 census listed 20 slaves in a population of 3,803. These were probably all black slaves. By 1791 the Apache were trading horses, mules, and Spanish captives to more easterly tribes for arms and ammunition.

Secularization of the Texas missions began in 1793. Whether the captives' descendants and the former mission Indians formed a distinct class in Texas society is not clear, but they were absorbed into the Hispanic population. The remaining slave population was made up primarily of blacks traded from Louisiana to the more easterly settlements of Bucareli and Nacogdoches.

New Mexico

The first black to visit New Mexico was the slave Estebanico. Sent to help guide Fray Marcos de

Niza, he was killed at Háwikuh, a Zuni village, in 1539.

Subsequent expeditions of exploration brought slaves into the area and obtained others while there. The captives from eastern tribes that Francisco Vásquez de Coronado found at the pueblo of Pecos led him into fruitless wanderings on the Great Plains, but it was the taking of captives from among the Pueblo people that aroused antagonisms which contributed to the decision to return to Mexico. One of the captives given to Coronado at Pecos was executed when it was learned that he had deliberately taken them astray, but most of the local Indians were released when the expedition left, so as to prevent one pretext under which the natives might injure the missionaries who remained behind.

Members of the expedition led by Antonio de Espejo (1582–1583) traded for captives from the Hopi. By the time of colonization, the Pueblo had acquired some knowledge of Spanish customs in this regard, but we know little of how they dealt with captives prior to contact.

Juan de Oñate brought the first colonists to New Mexico in 1598. Members of his entourage included both black and Indian servants, a few explicitly described as slaves. In 1598 the Indian pueblo of Acoma defied Spanish authority and suffered defeat in 1599 as a result. Some five hundred survivors were taken captive to the pueblo of Santo Domingo, where a trial was held. All Acoma over twelve years of age were sentenced to twenty years of personal servitude; the men over twenty-five also had one foot amputated. The elderly disabled were entrusted to the care of neighboring Apachean people. Girls under twelve were given to the father commissionary of the missions and the boys to the sergeant major, for distribution to individuals or monasteries to be raised as Christians. Sixty to seventy of the girls were taken to Mexico City to become nuns. After sentencing, the adults were distributed to the members of the army for use as slaves during the period of their sentences, but most later escaped.

The free tribes that surrounded the colony soon became the major source of slaves, both for local use and for sale in the south to mine owners and as gifts to officials whom local gentry wished to obligate. In the seventeenth century, the demand for captives appears to have been steady, for there were few other sources of wealth. Apachean tribes suffered the most, but the Ute were also subject to attack.

Mutual raiding was frequent. Governors seldom lacked provocation to justify campaigns. The subsequent relatiation provided the rationale for the next campaign. Authorities are divided in assigning blame for the initiation of warfare, but the commercial motivation of slaving can certainly be noted as an obstacle to peace. Governors frequently paid the king more for appointment to office than they would receive in salary. They then found few legitimate opportunities to profit from their position in the poverty-stricken colony.

The Pueblo Revolt of 1680 drove the settlers south to El Paso. During the siege of Santa Fe, the Indians had called for the release of captives, including all Apaches and even Mexican Indians. Governor Antonio de Otermín refused, and many slaves were taken on the retreat. During the revolt, the Indians took and kept captives. Several Spanish women remained among the Pueblo. At least two Navajo clans claim origin from Spanish girls captured during this period.

Spanish retaliation was initially limited to forays against the Pueblo people. Otermín's incursion in the fall of 1681 saved the people of Isleta, who had not joined the revolt, from attack by the other Pueblo with the intention of enslaving their women and children and delivering them to the Apaches in order to ensure good relations. On the other hand, there was at least one raid on an Apache camp for captives by the Spanish exiles at El Paso. Later thrusts into Pueblo country resulted in prisoners destined for slavery, often sold to serve the ten years that was punishment for rebellion. Part of the proceeds were used to pay the costs of the wars.

When Governor Diego de Vargas retook Santa Fe at the end of 1693, four hundred of the defeated Tanos were sentenced to ten years of servitude. Women and children were captured when Vargas's forces defeated Pueblo rebels on a mesa near Jémez, but he later returned them to the Jémez men who had allied themselves with the Spaniards, and restored most of the other captives as well.

The revolt of 1696 led to further fighting and the taking of Pueblo captives who were distributed among the settlers, but soon captives from the free tribes were once again to be the source of slaves. The earliest reports were of Pawnee and Jumano captives sold in New Mexico by Navajos. By 1703 Jicarilla Apache also were trading captives to the colonists, receiving two or three horses for a child.

Wars with the Apacheans recurred throughout the first decade of the eighteenth century. The sources are silent on the numbers of captives taken, but the records in New Mexico reveal baptisms of sixty-six Navajo and Apache plus a few Pawnee, Jumano, and Hopi. Others identified merely as Indian increase what was obviously a significant addition to the labor pool of the colony.

Some of those baptized were children of Pueblo women and Apachean fathers. The mothers were returned to their home pueblos, where they and their children joined the Pueblo population, but others were truly captives and became servants in the households of their captors. Some had been purchased from tribes that had taken them in wars with more distant peoples, and they also were destined to be raised as slaves within Spanish society.

A typically New Mexican *casta* (class) became established as a result of the incorporation of these people into the society. Made up of captives and their descendants, and including other Indians living in the settlements (such as Pueblo people who had left their towns, often due to expulsion by the Pueblo officials), they were collectively called *genízaros*. The name is thought to derive either from the Turkish word *yenicheri* (new troops), which was applied to infantry made up of captives, or from the Spanish *género* (children of different nations). Their numbers and specific ethnic origins fluctuated according to the wars fought, the vulnerability of the various tribes to raiding, and the availability of captives through trade. An interesting correlation shows a positive statistical association between increases in Spanish deaths caused by enemy tribes and increases in the baptisms of captives. Which was cause and which was effect is not always clear, but an effective feedback relationship developed in which each group could convincingly be labeled the victim of the other. The stimulus of a market for captives among the Spanish, the strongest economic power in the region, cannot be ignored, however.

Slaves became a status symbol in New Mexican society as well as a source of wealth, at times even functioning as a medium of exchange in an economy chronically short of specie. Indian children were used to pay debts and to make purchases. Indian female servants became traditional wedding gifts to brides, a practice so institutionalized that a standing joke was the observation that they frequently became pregnant at about the same time as their mistresses. Euphemistic terms came into use to avoid their identification as slaves. A captive was called a *pieza* (piece), a term used originally for game bagged by hunters, while *chusma* (galley slave, in this region without ships) referred to the women and children of enemy Indians. *Criado*, which implies upbringing and derives from the verb *criar* (to raise), referring to the raising of children or livestock, today means "servant."

The terms used by the priests when they recorded the baptisms of captives give some insight into their status. About a third were listed as adopted, and the implication that they should be treated as well as stepchildren is strong. Captives purchased by their ultimate owners were said to have been "ransomed" or "redeemed," at least when the seller had been a non-Christian Indian. Very rarely was the term "slave" used. Whatever the rationale, however, they were people forcibly removed from their kin and natal societies and incorporated into a foreign society at the lowest social status, treated initially as commodities. Baptismal entries frequently describe them as being "in the power of" the owners.

Whether slaves were taken in war or purchased from the free tribes, there were institutional safeguards that afforded them some protection. Captives were subject to only a limited period of servitude under Spanish law, varying from ten to twenty years. As the custom became integrated into a frontier society, this seems to have been translated into a folk usage that encouraged manumission at the time of marriage, if not before. Few were able to establish legal matrimonial unions, however, and there is reason to suspect that slave status often developed into debt peonage when child captives reached maturity.

The owners were expected to treat the captives well and to see that they were converted to Christianity. Pueblo Indians, being regarded as imperfectly converted, were not allowed to keep captives due to the risk that they would not bring them up as good Christians, although the Pueblo were sometimes allowed to keep children obtained in other ways. Education beyond catechism appears to have been limited to speaking Spanish, often poorly, and training as maids, weavers, herders, and other duties categorized as drudgery by the upper class. Baptism provided godparents who had spiritual responsibilities toward the captive. In about one in eight cases, the owners were the godparents, but fictive kin obligations usually were extended to others in Spanish society, frequently relatives of the owners. Priests, by their attitudes and admonitions at the time of baptism, gave moral support to the requirement of good treatment and a Christian education. Since priests often held captives, they gave sanction to the custom, but they also set examples of how slaves should be treated.

Slaves could be inherited, but their status did not extend to their children, who were free unless burdened by debt. Slaves were found in most upper-class and many middle-class families, but in small numbers, a single captive being most usual. Thus, they did not live under conditions that would encourage formation of a class consciousness conducive to unified action. The free *genízaros*, on the other hand, tended to come together in the larger towns or to be settled in less desirable places, particularly at frontier locations subject to attack by enemies. Their reputation as warriors led to their filling a role similar to that of the *yenicheri*, from whom their name presumably derived. The other attributes by which they were stereotyped were less complimentary, for they were considered likely to be vagabonds, gamblers, liars, and thieves. While priests who served *genízaro* communities often wrote of them in more kindly terms, the one virtue that all conceded them, their bravery, was also one that led to their being assigned the most precarious lands. Several *genízaro* communities did not survive Indian wars, but a few still exist.

Most free tribes tended to market their captives to the settlers, having limited need for labor themselves. This was not true of the Navajos, who had developed a pastoral economy having many parallels with the Spanish livestock industry. Whether due to similar economic demands

or the influence of the Spanish example, the Navajo slave complex came to share many characteristics with that of the settlers, but it lacked the rigidity that the Hispanic class structure imposed. The life of a slave in Navajo society was more precarious, with some risk of death, but there were also more opportunities to rise in status. Some tribes, such as the Comanche and Chiricahua Apache, as their numbers dwindled through war and disease, supplemented their population with captives in an effort to perpetuate their existence.

The beginnings of the *genízaro* class lie in the reconquest and the wars of the first decades of the eighteenth century. It is unfortunate that the baptismal records identify by tribe as few as 10 percent of the captives taken, making a study of the ethnic origins dependent on a sample that is not selected on a basis that ensures representative figures. For the second decade of the century, the baptismal records identify twenty-six Apache, three Navajo, five Ute, four Pawnee, and two Jumano. Captives sold outside of New Mexico—for instance, at the mining town of Parral in Nueva Vizcaya (modern Chihuahua)—were usually not baptized in New Mexico, although in 1714 Governor Juan Ignacio Flores Mogollón did order that all captive Apaches should be baptized prior to being sent away, in order to protect their souls in case of death on the journey (this was already done with black slaves sent to Mexico). Over four hundred captives were taken during the 1710s. Some were later judged to have been taken illegally, but by then many had been sold at Parral, most had died of smallpox, and the rest had been baptized, which prevented their return to a non-Christian people. The governor claimed that those sold had been the king's fifth, but the records showed that he and his brother kept the proceeds. He was ordered to pay for the return to New Mexico of those taken to Parral.

There were, in addition, the poorly documented sales of captives at the trade fairs held at Taos and Pecos. The Comanche advance onto the Great Plains was already beginning to devastate the Plains Apache. The Comanche were doubtless the suppliers of most of the captives from Plains tribes; they also were peddling Apache women to the French settlers who were moving ever closer on the east.

98

By the 1740s captives found to be poorly treated were settled on the frontier at Valencia and Tomé and entrusted to the care of a missionary. There were soon over fifty families brought together at three places, an indication of active enforcement of the law. Litigation arising from these orders revealed, among other facts, that captives were sometimes purchased by *genízaros* and that even following baptism a captive might be sold repeatedly.

Governor Tomás Vélez Cachupín had to deal with the treatment of captives a number of times in the 1760s. One case involved the sale of a Comanche woman whom he had specified should be held ready to return to her people if that should be necessary. Twice he removed *genízaro* women from their owners due to bad treatment. Female slaves were to serve only within households, where they would not be as exposed to molestation. One of the two women who complained had, in fact, become pregnant while working alone outside the house. The other case involved a woman so badly used that she had been ready to hang herself until a priest intervened on her behalf.

Baptisms in the 1700s included high proportions of Plains people, but by the first decade of the nineteenth century the shift from Plains captives to those from farther west was decisive. Numic speakers, primarily Paiute, made up by far the bulk of new slaves, with 163 baptisms from those tribes recorded, a trend that would continue through the 1810s. Mexican independence (1821) and the Santa Fe trade would soon alter, but not extinguish, the trade in captives, a trade that would last until the effects of the Emancipation Proclamation were felt after the Civil War.

Arizona

In Spanish times, the extreme northern part of Sonora included what is now southern Arizona, after missions were established among various Piman-speaking people toward the end of the seventeenth century, soon to be followed by military and civilian settlers. A trade in Indian captives was not long in developing on this new frontier. It was in many ways similar to that in New Mexico, there even being a special term for the captives: *nixoras*. This name apparently derives from the Maricopa language, where it was used to designate female captives given to old men who no longer had to fear the supernatural danger felt to be inherent in contact with foreigners. The name came to be used in Sonoran Spanish in much the same sense as was *genízaro* in New Mexico, although it was not passed on to the *nixoras'* descendants.

The lives of captives were much like those of Indian slaves in New Mexico. They were captured in war, often by other Indians who sold them, directly or indirectly, to the settlers. Many seem to have been taken by the ancestral groups of the modern Maricopas and traded by them to the Gila River Pimas, who then sold them to the Spanish. They were baptized in the settlements and kept in involuntary servitude. In theory they were entitled to emancipation after ten years of service or when they married. They were often traded to settlers in the interior, where escape would be more difficult. The trade was justified as a means of saving the lives of prisoners who would otherwise be executed by their captors and as a way of Christianizing the captives.

Since it was somewhat less remote than New Mexico, administration of legal requirements was more rigorous on the Arizona frontier. In the late eighteenth century it was required that captives taken in wars with the free tribes be sent south, and many were transported from Nueva Vizcaya. Many of the campaigns mounted from Sonora were carried out in conjunction with those from Nueva Vizcaya, and it is probable that their captives were included with those taken by the troops of Nueva Vizcaya. It is notable that during the 1780s Sonoran contingents reported unusually high proportions of women and children among those killed in engagements with the Apache. In four attacks in 1784, troops from the Tucson *presidio* killed fifteen warriors and fourteen women and children. In five campaign encounters in 1788, of 111 Apache killed, at least 55 were noncombatants. Payment for the heads and ears of Apaches and the expectation that captives would not be sold or kept as slaves may well account for these proportions, giving an ironic reality to the justification often argued that enslaving Indians saved their lives.

Indians purchased from tribal captors appear to have made up the majority of those held by settlers in northern Sonora. The proportion of captives to the total population of the Hispanic community served by the priest at San Xavier del Bac reached a high of 20 percent in 1801, compared with 5 percent to 7 percent in a sample of communities in Nueva Vizcaya and New Mexico.

As in other provinces, the practice of enslaving Indians continued beyond the colonial period, up to the Civil War.

California

As elsewhere, slavery existed among at least some of the California tribes. It was most prominent in the north, where the class structure so dramatically a part of the social life of the Northwest Coast tribes extended into the less complex, more southern cultures of the Yurok, Hupa, Tolowa, Wiyot, and Karok, who practiced debt slavery. Enslavement of captives was more widespread, and was known to the Shasta, the Juaneño, and probably many other tribes. The northern tribes also suffered raids by the Modoc, who were seeking captives to sell in the Native trade center at The Dalles.

Involuntary servitude that can be classed as slavery apparently existed in Spanish society in two forms. While Native tribes congregated in missions by missionaries in their home territories should be considered conquered people exploited for the growth of Christianity. In California even more than in Texas the practice of coercively bringing Indians from more distant tribes into the missions was a form of servitude that falls within most definitions of slavery. Whereas in Texas the Native population was so demoralized by the surrounding pressures of the expanding Spanish, Apache, and Comanche presence that they frequently sought refuge in the missions and outright capture was the exception, in California expeditions to capture Indians destined for conversion in the missions became increasingly common and were the norm after 1800. Emancipation came with the secularization of the missions. In fairness it must be noted that most Catholic scholars deny that life in the missions was a form of slavery and that the issue is still disputed.

Where converts were forcibly brought from more distant tribes, the conditions for slavery set forth by Orlando Patterson in his *Slavery and Social Death: A Comparative Study* (1982) were very nearly approximated, if not met fully. Whether the status of such converts was slavery is an open question, with highly politicized positions sometimes taken by activists supporting Indian causes on one side and by proponents of traditional mission history on the other. It is noteworthy that the interpretation of these Indians' condition in public history programs often falls into a paradigm shared with similar interpretations by apologists for black slavery. On the other hand, missions in established Indian communities, much like those in New Mexico, were dealing with peoples on their home ground who had organized social units that were able to protect the interests of their members sufficiently, so that they cannot be considered to have been reduced to slavery, however much they may have been exploited by government or religious authorities.

Personal servitude of the kind experienced by the original *genízaros* and by the *nixoras* very probably existed as well, but study of the practice in California has thus far been eclipsed by the clash between those who would romanticize the missions and those who would condemn them.

SUMMARY

Most tribal peoples kept captives under conditions approximating slavery as known elsewhere. Under Spanish law slavery was governed by two systems of law, one for Native Americans and the other for blacks. With one or two exceptions, slaveholding was a small-scale activity in which manumission was not difficult.

Economic pressures on high officials fostered exploitation of captives in the early years of empire. Ways of manipulating the law then evolved into folk customs that integrated the practice into colonial society. The effects were felt not only among the colonists, but in their relations with neighboring tribes and in the tribal societies as well.

BIBLIOGRAPHY

Brugge, David M. *Navajos in the Catholic Church Records of New Mexico, 1694–1875*. Window Rock, Ariz., 1968; Tsalie, Ariz., 2nd ed., 1985. Slavery in Navajo and New Mexican Hispanic societies.

Dobyns, Henry F. *Spanish Colonial Tucson: A Demographic History.* Tucson, Ariz., 1976.

Dobyns, Henry F., Paul H. Ezell, Alden W. Jones, and Greta S. Ezell. "What Were Nixoras?" *Southwestern Journal of Anthropology* 16, no. 2 (Summer 1960):230–258.

Dunkle, John R. "Population Change as an Element in the Historical Geography of St. Augustine." *Florida Historical Quarterly* 37, no. 1 (July 1958):3–32.

Gutiérrez, Ramón A. *When Jesus Came, the Corn Mothers Went Away: Marriage, Sexuality, and Power in New Mexico, 1500–1846.* Stanford, Calif., 1991. Slavery in New Mexican Hispanic society.

Holmes, Jack D. L. "The Abortive Slave Revolt at Pointe Coupée, Louisiana, 1795." *Louisiana History* 11, no. 4 (Fall 1970):341–362.

Horvath, Steven Michael Jr. "The Social and Political Organization of the Genízaros of Plaza de Nuestro Señora de Los Dolores de Belén, New Mexico, 1740–1812." Ph.D. diss., Brown University, 1979.

John, Elizabeth A. H. *Storms Brewed in Other Men's Worlds: The Confrontation of Indians, Spanish, and French in the Southwest, 1540–1795.* College Station, Tex., 1975; repr. Lincoln, Neb., 1981. Detailed account of white-Indian relations.

Kroeber, Alfred L. *Handbook of the Indians of California.* Washington, 1925; repr. New York, 1976. Basic source on aboriginal customs.

Navarro García, Luis. *Don José de Gálvez y la comandancia general de las provincias internas del norte de Nueva España.* Seville, Spain, 1964. An administrative history.

Patterson, Orlando. *Slavery and Social Death: A Comparative Study.* Cambridge, Mass., 1982. Important source on slavery.

Siebert, Wilbur H. "Slavery in East Florida, 1776–1785." *Florida Historical Quarterly* 10, no. 3 (January 1932):139–161.

Tjarks, Alicia Vidaurreta. "Comparative Demographic Analysis of Texas, 1777–1793." In David J. Weber, ed., *New Spain's Northern Frontier: Essay on Spain in the American West, 1540–1821.* Albuquerque, N.Mex., 1979.

Washburn, Wilcomb E., ed. *History of Indian-White Relations,* vol. 4 of *Handbook of North American Indians.* Washington, D.C., 1988. Includes chapters on policies and slavery.

Wright, James Leitch, Jr. *The Only Land They Knew: The Tragic Story of the American Indians in the Old South.* New York, 1981. Includes chapters on slavery.

Zavala, Silvio. *Los esclavos indios en Nueva España.* Mexico City, 1968. Basic historical account and a comprehensive overview.

David M. Brugge

SEE ALSO **Farming, Planting, and Ranching; Marriage;** and **The Slave Trade;** and various essays in RACIAL INTERACTION; and the map accompanying **The Slave Trade.**

VII

RACIAL INTERACTION

INDIAN-COLONIST CONTACT

BRITISH, FRENCH, AND DUTCH COLONIES

THE SIXTEENTH CENTURY

INDIAN PEOPLE HAD been living in eastern North America for thousands of years when Giovanni da Verrazano, Jacques Cartier, and other mariners recorded the first contacts between these natives and Europeans in the early sixteenth century. Written records of the period are generally fragmentary and ridden with cultural biases, leaving modern scholars with relatively little knowledge of the lives of these people. Transmitting views of the past essential for cultural survival, most oral traditions preserve a record of how events are remembered rather than a chronicle of actual occurrences. Archaeological deposits and artifacts preserved in museums and private collections presently provide the only direct tangible evidence of Indian life in eastern America during the first century of contact. Struggling to understand such remains, scholars use ethnographic field data gathered from Indian informants and the fuller documentary record produced during subsequent centuries of colonization to interpret and explain events associated with historic contact in the region.

No matter where or how its members lived, each Native community in eastern North America maintained its own distinct language, culture, history, and sense of identity. All also participated to one extent or another in a complex and dynamic system of often interlocking networks that both joined and separated individuals, families, and communities throughout the region. Native people adjusted to seasonal and social constraints and opportunities by forming coalitions through marriage, treaty, and trade, or they acclimated themselves by dissolving existing relationships through amicable separation or war. Historically chronicled rites, such as the Iroquois Condolence Ceremony and the central Algonquian Calumet Dance, probably perpetuated or built upon traditional intercultural rituals regulating contact with people from other communities.

While at first regarding Europeans as far different from themselves, Indian people long accustomed to dealing with strangers soon came to regard those who followed simply as more colorful and exotic than most visitors traveling to their towns. Along the coast Indian people were eager to have firsthand looks at European strangers and their unusual possessions; the Indians exchanged furs, food, and favors for metal objects, glass beads, and other goods with sailors sailing offshore or landing at the Gulf of Saint Lawrence, Boston Harbor, Chesapeake Bay, Pamlico Sound, Charleston Harbor, and other places to repair vessels, dry fish, or take on fresh water and supplies. Many of these objects, such as iron axes and latten spoons worn suspended from the neck as ornaments, soon were put to uses unintended by their creators. Others found their way into graves as equipment for the deceased or as contributions to spirits who had departed this world before such goods became available.

In the north few visitors stayed more than several days or weeks. Farther south Spanish, French, and English colonists attempted to establish permanent outposts. Some of these settlements, like the French Huguenot colony of Fort Caroline established in Florida in 1564, the Spanish Franciscan mission of Ajacan built along Virginia's James River in 1570, and Sir Walter Raleigh's enterprise at Roanoke in 1585, quickly failed. Others, like the Spanish fortress built at Saint Augustine in 1565 and the mission of Santa Elena built one year later at Guale along the South Carolina coast, were more successful.

Farther inland Indian people struggled to come to terms with more aggressive intruders. To the north Saint Lawrence Iroquoians living in what is today Quebec City tried to coexist with the Frenchman Jacques Cartier as he attempted to establish permanent settlements in their country in 1534 and 1542. At the same time, Native people in the south were forced to supply, flee, or fight against rapacious columns of Spanish conquistadores, led by men like Hernando de Soto, intent upon finding gold and slaves. Later on Native people destroyed outposts established in their homelands by Juan Pardo and other Spaniards from Saint Augustine seeking to exert imperial authority over the region and its inhabitants.

Analyzing available demographic data, Henry F. Dobyns and scholars inspired by his work believe that whole regions were devastated or depopulated when European intruders like de Soto and Pardo directly and indirectly spread smallpox, measles, influenza, and other "virgin soil epidemics" to Indian communities possessing neither natural immunities nor effective remedies. Numerous archaeological and archival sources preserve evidence suggesting episodes of migrations and disappearances of entire societies. Saint Lawrence Iroquoians last seen by French visitors in 1543, for example, had entirely disappeared by the time Samuel de Champlain recorded the next chronicled French visit to Canada in 1603.

To the south archaeological discoveries of unprecedentedly larger and more densely settled towns support archival and oral sources indicating that Iroquois people gathering together for protection and security formed their League of Five Nations sometime during the sixteenth century. At the same time farther south, in and around Lancaster County, Pennsylvania, villages and pottery associated with Shenks Ferry people disappeared, while people making the distinctive Schultz Incised wares associated with historic Susquehannock culture moved south along the Susquehanna River away from the Iroquois heartland towards increasingly important trading entrepôts along Chesapeake Bay. Cherokees, Chickasaws, Choctaws, and Creeks visited by French and English explorers during the following century did not know who had made the now-abandoned overgrown mounds; these mounds represented the only visible remains of the many imposing Mississippian towns chronicled by de Soto's men and other sixteenth-century Spanish intruders. Although most investigators see the effects of European intrusion in these sixteenth-century disappearances and dispersions, the exact role of contact remains unclear and in need of further study.

THE SEVENTEENTH CENTURY

Indian people throughout the Atlantic Coast encountered increasing numbers of English, French, and Dutch visitors sailing to their shores during the first decades of the seventeenth century. To the north Montagnais-Naskapi, Micmac, and other Algonquian-speaking people met Frenchmen in search of furs and trade routes to the Orient. Discovering that the rapids at La Chine barred the way to China, French explorers traveling to the region like Samuel de Champlain obtained Indian permission to establish small trading posts and Catholic missions at what they came to call New France in the Saint Lawrence Valley and Acadia, Canada's present-day maritime provinces, and eastern Maine.

Both Canadian Algonquians and the Iroquoian-speaking Hurons, Neutrals, and Petuns living farther west found that these new French visitors did not commit the same mistakes made earlier by Cartier and his contemporaries. Most appreciated the fact that these Frenchmen generally treated them with tact and respect. They welcomed young French boys sent to their communities to learn their languages and customs. They did not take offense when Sulpician, Recollet, and Franciscan priests hung aloof while most other Frenchmen mingled freely in their towns. Unlike the Spanish, whose soldiers often forcibly herded Indian people into their missions, these French priests only ministered to those willing to come to their small bark chapels. Many Indians appreciated French willingness to help them in times of need. Priests ministered to their sick while soldiers protected Indian people fleeing from attack. Frenchmen also occasionally accompanied war parties to support their friends and learn more about the land and its people. During one of these excursions in 1609, Champlain and two of his soldiers used their guns to help a force of Montagnais, Huron, and Algonquian warriors defeat a sizable Mohawk war party on the banks of the lake that today bears his name. Securing the French alliance with Canadian Algonquians, this incident also cast a long shadow affecting subsequent relations with the Mohawks and the other members of the Iroquois confederacy.

Indian people living from Newfoundland south to the Carolinas met other Western European voyagers searching for the same things that the French sought. Those along the coast from Delaware Bay to Massachusetts met and traded with Englishmen in Dutch employ like Henry Hudson and Dutch navigators like Cornelis May and Adriaen Block between 1609 and 1615. Shortly thereafter they allowed the Dutch to establish small trading posts along navigable portions of the Delaware, Hudson, and Connecticut rivers. Sharing French avidity for trade and commerce, Dutch merchants traveled widely through the region speaking an Algonquian-Dutch trade jargon that developed there.

Swedish colonists established small trading posts near Delaware Indian towns along the lower Delaware River in 1638. Unlike the Dutch, who officially prohibited sales of firearms to most Indian people, Swedes began trading guns and ammunition to Delawares and Susquehannocks coming to their posts. Most Indians found that Dutch and Swedish settlers generally conducted themselves much like their French visitors. Like the French, a large number of these settlers adopted many aspects of Indian dress and tech-

nology after moving to the frontiers of New Sweden or New Netherland. Unlike the French, settlers in both places showed little interest in converting Indians to Christianity.

Leaders of Indian communities near Dutch and Swedish trading posts managed to establish alliances with their powerful new neighbors. In the north Mahicans and then Mohawks formed particularly close ties with Dutch officials eager to maintain a peaceful and lucrative trade at Fort Orange in today's Albany, New York. Farther south Susquehannock chiefs concluded advantageous trade agreements for goods and guns with Swedish administrators after defeating Delaware Indian rivals. Concluding similar agreements with the Dutch conquerors of New Sweden in 1655, Susquehannocks struggled to dominate regional trade. To the south Susquehannock traders labored to control trade along Chesapeake Bay with English colonists in Virginia, established in 1607, and in Maryland, established at Saint Mary's City in 1634. Dominating the trade along the upper Susquehanna West Branch to the Allegheny and the domain of the Neutral Indians, the Susquehannock warriors also disputed Iroquois access to the vital trapping and trading grounds in the Great Lakes and the Ohio River valleys.

Susquehannocks and other powerful Indian nations living beyond the borders of coastal towns also were able to take advantage of Dutch and Swedish policies that denied firearms to most Delaware Indians living near their settlements. Armed with flintlock muskets that soon became indispensable in regional warfare, these interior nations were able to extort tribute from less well-armed communities in the form of trade goods and the highly valued blue and white cylindrical wampum shell beads produced by coastal Indian people.

Although many Englishmen sought to emulate Dutch, Swedish, and French examples, most Indian people soon found that voyagers from the British Isles often tended to act more like raiders than visitors. Englishmen often made unreasonable demands, frequently entered homes while their occupants were elsewhere, stole food supplies and other possessions, plundered graves, and on occasion kidnapped Indians for sale into slavery across the ocean. What was worse, unlike the other Europeans, the English soon showed every sign of establishing permanent colonies of settlers on their lands. Alarmed, Indian people from Maine and Massachusetts Bay south to Virginia soon began to regard their English visitors as invaders.

These fears soon were realized as thousands of English men, women, and children started flooding onto Indian land at places these newcomers began to call New England and Virginia. Chastened by English incursions into their villages and devastated by epidemics striking their towns in 1616–1619 and again during the early 1630s, Indian people throughout New England encouraged leaders like Wampanoag chief Massasoit, Narragansett chief sachem Canonicus, and Mohegan chief Uncas to establish amicable relations with their new English neighbors. Farther south in Virginia, Powhatan leaders in the midst of their own expansion program sought accommodation with Englishmen moving in and around Jamestown in 1607 as the Powhatans struggled to increase their sphere of influence while administering often-restive subject people.

Although they came from different cultures and saw things from different perspectives, there were few misunderstandings between Native people and the English about their conflicting aims. Native people soon came to understand that the English wanted their lands and labor as well as their furs. English people, for their part, quickly realized that Indians would not freely give up either their land or their freedom. The many hundreds of marks of Indian people affixed to European treaties, deeds, and other documents mutely attest to Native efforts to arrive at some sort of diplomatic modus vivendi with the aggressive newcomers. The English to the north tried to bring some sense of order to their relations with Indians. Enacting laws meant peacefully to regulate relations with Indian people, New England settlers began using trade goods and wampum beads to pay Indians for their land, labor, and pelts. Farther south Virginians tried to overawe the Powhatans and their neighbors into submission.

In the end both efforts failed. Unwilling to give up control of their lands and lives, Indian people began to fight against their would-be English overlords. In the north Pequot people seeking to extend their own sphere of influence among the region's Indian people were driven into war with New Englanders in 1637. Devas-

tated that year by an English attack that destroyed one of their main fortified towns and killed nearly all of its from three hundred to seven hundred occupants, the Pequots subsequently were dispersed, defeated, and subjugated by New England soldiers aided by Mohawk, Narragansett, and Mohegan allies. In Virginia, Powhatan people tried to stop English expansion into their lands in a series of three desultory wars. Beginning in 1610 and ending in 1646, these wars ended with the total defeat and subjugation of the Powhatan people. Hundreds of Indian people captured in wars with the English were sold into slavery. Survivors wishing to remain on ancestral lands were forced to accept Virginian authority and give up the best of their remaining lands. Those refusing to live under these conditions, including many Weanocks who moved south beyond the limits of Virginia settlements, had to move elsewhere.

Relations between coastal Algonquian Indian people and colonists in New Netherland also worsened during these years. Like their Delaware relatives to the south, Munsees living near the heart of the expanding Dutch settlements along the lower Hudson River found themselves pressed between aggressive coastal colonists on one side and powerfully domineering interior Indian nations on the other. Living far from fur-rich lands, most Munsees were denied access to inland sources of supply by Mahican and Mohawk competitors. Unable to secure firearms and devastated by epidemics repeatedly striking their towns during the 1630s and 1640s, most Munsees were unable to resist either Mahican and Mohawk tribute demands or Dutch attempts to extort what they called taxes in the form of corn and other commodities.

A series of unresolved murders, assaults, and thefts increased tensions between the Munsees and their Dutch neighbors. Open war finally broke out when a Dutch detachment sent to inquire into the theft of hogs on Staten Island instead attacked an unsuspecting Indian town during the early summer of 1640. The war that followed, known today as Governor Kieft's War after Willem Kieft, the Dutch administrator believed to have instigated the struggle, became the first of a series of conflicts pitting Indian people against colonists and each other. Although a formal treaty brokered by Mohawk diplomats formally ended the war on 30 August 1645, hostilities again flared when Munsee warriors, evidently angered by the murder of an Indian woman picking peaches, attacked Dutch settlements around New Amsterdam with Swedish encouragement while Dutch troops were away reducing New Sweden during the fall of 1655. Known as the Peach War, this conflict dragged on fitfully for two years until most of the several hundred settlers captured during the fighting were ransomed by Dutch officials. One year later another series of conflicts, known as the Esopus Wars, broke out between Indian people and settlers moving to their lands in the mid Hudson Valley. Like the earlier conflicts, these wars were marked by unprovoked attacks, abortive truces, and periodic massacres. Although the Dutch concluded a peace agreement with Esopus leaders during the spring of 1664, fighting in the area did not finally come to an end until Englishmen signed conclusive peace treaties with all Indians in the province after seizing control of the province from the Dutch during the following fall.

Armed conflict was not restricted to the coastal colonies. In the north the Iroquois confederacy waged implacable war against Canadian Indians, their French allies, and other Indian people living on their frontiers. The league's Mohawk, Cayuga, Onondaga, Oneida, and Seneca warriors fought to protect their communities, expand their commerce, avenge loved ones lost in warfare and epidemics, seize plunder, take prisoners to restore their dwindling strength resulting from war casualties and epidemics, and earn reputations for skill and bravery on the battlefield. Iroquois nations pursuing these goals methodically struck out against neighboring tribes throughout the middle decades of the century.

In the north Mohawk warriors using firearms obtained from their Dutch allies and other Iroquois war parties constantly assaulted Montagnais and Algonquian communities, waylaid travelers journeying to French trading posts, and fought a protracted series of wars against Mahican and New England Algonquian Indian people. At the same time, Senecas and their allies fought against and ultimately dispersed Huron, Neutral, and Petun competitors to the north, destroyed their Erie, Monongahela, and Massawomeck enemies to the west, and defeated Sus-

quehannock rivals to the south after a drawn out struggle that dragged on for nearly three decades.

Many of these people turned to the French for help. Despite constant pledges of assistance, all found that they could not rely on the French for protection. Inadequately supplied themselves and few in number, the French were forced to temporarily give New France up to English invaders between 1629 and 1632. Although Jesuit priests establishing their first missions among the Hurons in 1634 also tried to help their Native hosts as best they could, French policies restricting trade of firearms to Indians accepting the Catholic faith limited their effectiveness. Outgunned and ravaged by epidemic disease, the Hurons—divided into rival factions of converts to Christianity and nonconverts— were finally defeated and dispersed by the Iroquois in 1649.

Thousands of people died in these and other wars raging through the east during the first half of the seventeenth century. Thousands more were killed by epidemics ravaging the region. Lacking antibiotics and unaware of the microscopic agents causing epidemic contagion, Indians and colonists alike appealed for spiritual help during plague years. Often sheltering themselves behind fortification walls, both peoples also struggled to counter human threats through negotiation and compromise. Failing in such efforts, most ultimately tried to drive away or extirpate enemies. Acadian frontier settlements along the Maine coast, such as French Pentagoet and English Pemaquid, were repeatedly sacked and finally abandoned. Colonists refusing to abandon places like New Sweden and New Netherland were, for their part, forced to endure repeated conquests by European rivals.

Entire Indian nations were destroyed or dispersed. Some people, like the Pequots, were all but destroyed by European enemies. Others, like the inhabitants of Huronia forced from their homes by Seneca war parties in 1649, were devastated by Indian rivals. Responses to such devastation often were complex. Some Hurons, for example, moved further westward to new towns on the Upper Great Lakes where they became known as Wyandots. Other Huron people relocated themselves in Catholic mission communities like Lorette that were closer to the settlements of their French allies. Still others, like those Hurons permitted to establish a community of their own at Gandougarae in Seneca country, did their best to build new lives among their conquerors.

European immigrants transported by the thousands to North America more than made up for colonial losses. Indian people, for their part, adopted captives and did their best to assimilate people willing to live among them. Individuals and entire communities were adopted into existing clans or formed into new lineages. Research conducted by William A. Starna and Ralph Watkins also indicates that Iroquois people enslaved many adopted captives. Slavery among Iroquois and other eastern American Indian people, though, was something far different than the more familiar chattel slavery of the antebellum South. While slaves often were treated as second-class citizens, they were not regarded as commodities nor was their status considered hereditary.

In these and other ways, Indian people throughout eastern America struggled to adjust to a changing and unprecedentedly violent world as they approached mid century. Seeking stability in an era of upheaval, people everywhere looked for physical security and spiritual guidance. Settlers using Old World tools and weapons adapted native hunting, fishing, and planting practices to feed their families and make their livings. Indian people put new European imports like firearms, metal tools, ceramics, glassware, cloth and woolen textiles, and glass beads to old uses. Although they did not abandon still-useful traditional skills like archery, for example, people living near traders gradually replaced stone arrowheads with new ones made out of cut metal. Aboriginal potters increasingly began using new copper, iron, and brass kettles and European earthenwares. Woven textile shirts, coats, and blankets and glass beads supplanted but did not replace tanned skin clothing and shell beads.

Growing numbers of Indian people also accepted the teachings of Christian missionaries during these years. Hundreds of northern Algonquian Indian people periodically visited Catholic missions established at Tadoussac, Trois-Rivières, and other locales along the lower Saint Lawrence. Others were visited by priests traveling to their camps. Hurons, Neutrals, and

Petuns attended services and accepted instruction at missions established in and around their towns. Iroquois people, by contrast, at first ejected Jesuit priests trying to establish missions in their towns. Farther south Catholic priests worked among thousands of Indians living in mission communities along the Carolina coast at Guale and other locales along the Spanish frontier while Franciscan missionaries accompanying English Catholics settling Maryland built new missions among the Piscataway Indians along the Potomac River in 1634.

Indian people on Martha's Vineyard and Nantucket began listening to sermons preached by Puritan Thomas Mayhew, Jr., shortly after his father obtained patents authorizing settlement on both islands in 1641. Five years later other Indian people living around the burgeoning English colonies at Massachusetts Bay and Plymouth began to welcome the Puritan minister John Eliot into their homes. Local Native people instructed Eliot in their language and helped him and his assistants gain entry to their towns. Several of these people subsequently moved to the first permanent Puritan praying Indian town established at Natick in 1651. These first converts ultimately were followed by several thousand other Indian people settling in thirteen additional praying towns scattered around the periphery of the Massachusetts Bay and Plymouth colonies by 1674.

Although scant data are available on the subject, all but the most enthusiastic proselytes probably incorporated Christian beliefs and ritual into their traditional religious observances. In so doing they tried to assimilate the Christian god into their already-existing pantheon of spiritual helpers. Horrified by strangely persistent and lethal new forms of war and disease or excited by possibilities opened by contact with a wider world than any known by their ancestors, Indian people attempted to avail themselves of all possible sources of spiritual and material assistance.

Native religious leaders promising protection against new European diseases and guns also arose during these years. Although much has been written about the Shawnee Prophet Tenskwatawa and other late-eighteenth-century Indian spiritual leaders, little presently is known about their seventeenth-century antecedents.

One, a Powhatan spiritual leader named Nemmattew who helped Opechancanough organize an assault against Virginian colonists in 1622, claimed that English musket balls could not harm him. He was shot just before the attack was to begin, and his body was buried secretly by companions anxious to preserve belief in his powers.

Indian people called on the familiar powers of spoken words as they struggled to come to grips with the strange new force of written words used by newcomers. Appreciation of the power of small written marks, accompanied by gift exchanges, to end wars or take land could not have eluded people long accustomed to making and sealing contracts with memorable speeches and exchanges of wampum beads and other gifts. Indian people participated in paper-signing rituals with growing frequency during the second half of the seventeenth century as increasing numbers of European immigrants landed at established colonial ports like Boston and New Amsterdam and new ones like Charleston, South Carolina (established in 1670), and Philadelphia, Pennsylvania (founded in 1683). Pressing inland from the Atlantic Coast, they pushed the frontiers of Indian territories inexorably westward.

This vast movement was not the majestic westward sweep of frontier expansion celebrated by later chroniclers. In the far north, most Indian people continued to have to put up only with the brief visits of passing fur traders, itinerant missionaries, and the odd explorer or adventurer. Unlike other Indian people tied to their towns and fields, northern hunters and gatherers were able easily to avoid or move away from places harboring epidemic contagion. In the same way, they were able to take what they wanted of European technology and ignore the rest. Continually working as trappers or periodically employed by the French as scouts, soldiers, and laborers, they took their pay in the form of arms and ammunition, iron knives and axes, brass and copper kettles, cloth and woolen textiles, glass beads, and other easily transportable, durable goods. They also continued to accept gifts of similar goods offered by Catholic missionaries and colonial administrators cultivating their goodwill and support. Traveling widely, northern Algonquian Indian people came to use these goods as a species of currency throughout the north country during these years.

In the east Montagnais-Naskapi, Algonquian, Micmac, and Abenaki people continued to visit Catholic missions as they traded with and fought for themselves and their French allies. Abenaki people living along the Acadian frontier in Maine, for example, traveled to French trading posts and missions to the north as they traded with Plymouth and Massachusetts Bay colonists operating small posts like Cushnoc (established in Augusta, Maine, sometime around 1628) in their territories. Unable to peacefully discourage English colonists from establishing more substantial settlements at the sites of their favorite coastal camps, Abenaki people and their French allies separately and collectively drove them from the region in the course of the series of wars that ravaged the entire region during the last quarter of the seventeenth century.

Far to the west, Crees doing business with Hudson Bay Company traders setting up shop in their country after 1670 continued to serve as primary suppliers of furs. So did other Algonquian-speaking people, generally referred to collectively as Ojibwas and Ottawas, living along the upper Great Lakes. Ojibwa and Ottawa people welcomed refugees fleeing from Iroquois attacks as the Ojibwa and Ottawa moved southeastward along the major trade routes connecting the north country with the major European entrepôts at French Montreal and English Albany. Ojibwa people moving into Huronia and other abandoned portions of Ontario successfully stopped Iroquois colonists attempting to move north of Lakes Ontario and Erie during the 1660s and 1670s.

The defeats in Ontario were nothing more than minor setbacks to otherwise successful Iroquois people living within the walls of their prosperous wooden castles. Seneca and other western Iroquois people continued to raid and trade with Indian people to the north and west and their French allies. Farther east Mohawk people anxious to assure an unrestrained flow of trade goods maintained close relations with their nearby Dutch suppliers at Fort Orange. In 1664 they quickly established a similar relationship with Englishmen who had seized the Dutch province and renamed the place Albany. This special relationship grew into a vast system of alliances later known as the Covenant Chain that spread to include the English from New England to Virginia, the Indians from Massachusetts, and the Iroquois and their clients. The Mohawks labored to use it to secure prosperity and protection for themselves while asserting Iroquois dominance over neighboring tribes.

The Mohawks soon had need to call upon the support of their English allies. Unwilling to join the other four Iroquois nations in a peace accord with the French in 1665, the Mohawks were forced to abandon and burn their towns in front of a large raiding party marching south from Montreal in 1666. Signing a new treaty with the French in 1667, they rebuilt their towns and joined their Iroquois confederates in renewed attempts to neutralize the threat presented by their Susquehannock rivals to the south.

Both peoples suffered dreadful losses in the war that followed. Finally weakened by nearly incessant Iroquois attacks, the Susquehannocks abandoned their main fortress on the banks of the lower Susquehanna River in 1674 and moved south to the Potomac River at the insistence of Maryland authorities. One year later they found themselves besieged by settlers led by a Virginia planter named Nathaniel Bacon, who was revolting against provincial authorities. Escaping from their encircled fort after most of their chiefs were treacherously murdered by settlers during a parley, the Susquehannocks soon were dispersed and scattered. Some moved back to the Susquehanna Valley for a time. Both they and most other Susquehannock people were forced to settle among their erstwhile Iroquois rivals. Others less willing to live under Iroquois control moved farther away among more distant Indian nations.

Mohawks accepting Susquehannocks into their recently rebuilt towns took advantage of another war to settle accounts with old enemies to the east. In 1675 southern New England Indian people who were unwilling to relocate to praying towns or live on diminishing plots of land, and who were surrounded by settlers cutting down the forest and driving away the game, began attacking colonists. The ensuing conflict, known as King Philip's War after the Wampanoag chief thought by settlers to have instigated it, soon spread across the region. In the north Abenakis in Maine drove English settlers and traders from their lands. Farther south Wampanoags and their allies withdrawing to more se-

cure strongholds to the west along the Connecticut River successfully defeated several English detachments sent to destroy them. They had less luck against subsequent attacks from the settlers' Mohawk allies. Forced eastward King Philip's followers were joined by formerly neutral Narragansetts who had survived an English strike on their own town in Rhode Island. Starving and cut off from all sources of supply, they were relentlessly hunted down by now-experienced English soldiers aided by praying Indians and others allying themselves with the victorious settlers.

By 1676 King Philip was dead and other prominent leaders were either killed, captured, or in hiding. The war forever broke the power of the New England tribes. Like the Pequots before them, captives were executed or sold into slavery. Those refusing to submit moved elsewhere. Many moved north and east, where the Abenakis continued to carry on the struggle. Others took up New York governor Edmund Andros's invitation to relocate to a new community at Schaghticoke, twenty or so miles north of Albany. The several hundred Schaghticoke residents subsequently guarded New York's vulnerable northern border as they smuggled goods and information across the frontier separating New France from British America.

Coastal Algonquian people refusing to abandon their homes in Massachusetts, Rhode Island, and Connecticut gradually were forced to sell most of their remaining lands and move onto small reservations under provincial supervision during the years following the end of King Philip's War. Many settled at Natick, Mashpee, and the few other praying towns remaining after the war. Others were compelled to submit to overseers appointed by town or provincial authorities to supervise the lives of Indians living in places like the Narragansett Reservation in North Kingstown, Rhode Island, and the Western Pequot Reservation at Mashantucket in eastern Connecticut.

Munsee and Delaware people living in the former Dutch colony of New Netherland gradually submitted to Iroquois domination as New York, East and West Jersey, and Pennsylvania settlers purchased ever larger portions of their remaining lands. Along the coast many people belonging to Shinnecock, Montauk, and other

Long Island Indian communities found employment as whalers or offshore fishermen. Other coastal Algonquian people took jobs as laborers or servants in households of European neighbors. Still others sold homemade baskets, brooms, and medicinal preparations door-to-door through the backcountry.

The number of such itinerant peddlers grew as Indian people unable to wrest livings from relatively unproductive sandy barrenlands, swampy wetlands, and stony uplands not yet sold to settlers or speculators became nomads in their own homelands. Their numbers continued to dwindle as those not carried off by the still-unrelenting epidemics contemplated relocation to new towns far away from settlers along the Susquehanna and Allegheny River valleys. Those moving west often found marriage partners among new neighbors from other tribes. Finding increasingly fewer marriage partners available in their shrinking communities, those staying on ancestral lands gradually were compelled to take spouses from other tribes or marry non-Indians.

Indian people living around Chesapeake Bay also tried to live quietly among their non-Indian neighbors during these years. Like Native inhabitants in New England, most of these people moved onto small reservations or settled on lands unwanted by colonists. Farther south Indian people living along the Carolina and Georgia coast had to adjust to new English colonists establishing their first settlement at Charleston, South Carolina, in 1670. Yamassees moving eastward near Catawba and other coastal tribes competed with inland Creeks and Chickasaws to supply deerskins and Indian slaves demanded by Carolina traders. Adding guns and ammunition to the usual inventory, Charleston merchants furthered the interests of empire as well as commerce by encouraging clients to capture Native people allied with their Spanish enemies. Yamassees and other coastal people raiding the Georgia coast forced the Spanish to abandon their Guale missions by 1684. Farther inland Creek warriors raided nearby Spanish missions at Apalachee, while Chickasaws attacked Choctaws and other lower Mississippi Valley Indian nations in search of slaves to sell at the Charleston markets. These attacks devastated Indian communities throughout the region. French officials arranging a truce between the Chickasaws and Choctaws in 1702, for example, estimated that Chickasaws had killed eighteen hundred Choctaws and carried off another five hundred as slaves while losing eight hundred of their own people since the commencement of the Charleston trade.

Chickasaws joined other English Indian clients throughout the East in pledging to support their allies when fighting between France and England spread from Europe to America in 1689. In what was known in America as King William's War, thousands of Indian people would die or be driven from their homes before the contending empires made peace among themselves with the Treaty of Ryswick in 1697. In the north Abenakis assisted by Acadian "Capitaine des Sauvages" Jean-Vincent de Saint-Castin, who lived among them and married the daughter of the influential Indian leader Madockawando, drove the English from Pemaquid and other posts reoccupied after King Philip's War. Other Abenakis moved to a new mission built by the French on the upper Kennebec River at Norridgewock after Massachusetts troops burned their main community farther downriver at Taghkanik in 1692.

In the Ohio Valley, Shawnees supporting the French were driven from their homes and dispersed by Iroquois warriors. Scattering throughout the east, some Shawnees fled farther west to French settlements in Illinois country while others abandoned the French altogether and sought asylum among the English along the Pennsylvania and Carolina frontiers. The Iroquois confederacy itself was devastated by the war. Some Iroquois nations, like the Senecas, who had to burn all of their towns in front of an invading French army in 1687, were already reeling from grievous blows when the war started. By the time it ended, nearly all of their towns lay in smoking ruins, burned like the Seneca towns to prevent their capture by the French enemy. The Iroquois collectively lost from one-third to one-half of their population during the war. Some of these people were killed or captured in the fighting. Others died when returning warriors brought smallpox home with them in 1691. Most, however, had simply fled north among friends and relatives living in French Catholic missions along the Saint Lawrence Valley.

Although most of these people and others displaced by the war longed to return home after the Europeans stopped fighting one another, few were willing to make the journey until they made their own separate peaces with their enemies. Although the diplomats in Europe had forgotten to mention their Indian allies in the treaty ending a European war that had spilled over onto American soil, this made little difference to Indian people, who had gone to war for reasons of their own. Rather than make peace on European terms, war-weary Indian people saw the end of King William's War as an opportunity to conclude lasting agreements on the basis of their own needs and interests among themselves and their colonial neighbors.

THE EIGHTEENTH CENTURY

One by one Indian diplomats seeking peace negotiated treaties with each other and Europeans as the new century began. Iroquois leaders did not forget that their British Covenant Chain allies, who had urged them into the recent fighting, had been unable to do more than care for those of their people fleeing to them as French troops and their Indian allies rampaged freely through their country. At Montreal in 1701, Iroquois diplomats courteously but firmly declined to hold fast to the Covenant Chain and declared their intention to remain neutral in future wars involving France. In so doing they ushered in what scholars today call the golden age of Iroquois diplomacy.

Realizing that they could not keep individuals or entire communities from pursuing their own courses of action, Iroquois leaders struggled to assure that their league remained neutral in all disputes involving foreign Indians and Europeans. In more dangerous times like Queen Anne's War, fought between France and England from 1702 to 1713, Iroquois diplomats asserting official neutrality struggled to maintain the balance of power by alternately threatening to enter the conflict on one side or another. At peace with both sides, neither the Iroquois nor their Indian allies saw any reason not to carry the illicit trade between Montreal and Albany that continued unabated during and after the con-

flict. And so long as the league did not formally go to war, individuals like the three Mohawk leaders and their Covenant Chain ally Etowacom, the Schaghticoke chief, felt free to go to England to help drum up support for an invasion of Canada in 1710.

Lasting for more than half a century, this official peace policy allowed Iroquois people time and again to play foreign Indian and European rivals off against one another. Turning their attention to trade and diplomacy, Iroquois people took full advantage of their neutral status. Iroquois diplomats continued to solicit and accept gifts from French and British officials anxious to secure their friendship and support. Iroquois traders free to travel widely throughout the region brought unprecedented wealth home to their families and friends. Others, eager to win glory, plunder, and slaves on the battlefield, continued to follow the warrior's path south through Appalachian Mountain valleys to the towns of their Cherokee, Catawba, and other southern Indian enemies. Taking advantage of almost untrammeled access to European and Indian markets, Iroquois people abandoned most traditional crafts almost entirely in favor of European imports. Neither they nor other Indians gave up their traditional arts or subsistence systems, however. Women continued to supervise the planting and harvesting of corn, beans, squash, and other crops while weaving beads or sewing glass beads and silk strips into traditional motifs and designs. Men, for their part, continued most of their traditional pursuits.

No longer feeling compelled to live within the cramped confines of wooden fortresses that had in any event become with changes in warfare smoky deathtraps, most Iroquois people moved to spacious homesteads spread out along the river valleys running through their heartland. Other Iroquois people chose to move north among kinsfolk who had become Catholic converts in Canada. Still others moved south to new towns like Tioga (present Athens, Pennsylvania) and Ochquaga (near Binghamton in south central New York). These and other towns were built to accommodate displaced coastal Indian refugees invited to settle along the upper Susquehanna Valley by Mohawk and Oneida leaders anxious to secure their exposed southern frontiers from colonial expansion.

Ever growing numbers of coastal Indian people moved to these settlements during the early decades of the century. Some of them, like many Delawares, Munsees, and Mahicans, were voluntary immigrants tired of living among increasingly intolerant and insensitive settlers who were no longer interested in making accommodations with Indians. A few of these immigrants, like those Delawares swindled out of their lands along the Delaware River by Pennsylvania proprietors under color of a 1737 agreement known as the Walking Purchase, came less willingly. Others, like the hundreds of Tuscaroras moving to Iroquoia between 1713 and 1722, were refugees forcibly driven from their homes by armed colonists intent upon their destruction or removal.

Wars continued to ravage other areas of the East while the Iroquois enjoyed their half century of peace. In the north Abenaki and other Indian people living along the Maine coast repeatedly fought off Massachusetts settlers moving onto their lands. Unable to avoid involvement in Queen Anne's War, Abenaki warriors ravaged British communities while armies of settlers aided by Indian allies burned Norridgewock and other towns. Several years later another conflict, known as Lovewell's or Dummer's War, broke out in 1722. Fighting in this local struggle began when colonists refused to abandon recently established settlements built in disputed territory. Again devastating coastal towns, Abenakis—who were skilled in managing sailing vessels—ranged along the Maine coast in a flotilla of twenty-two shallops captured from colonial ports until a Massachusetts fleet sank them. Another Massachusetts army attacked and burned the rebuilt Norridgewock community in 1724. Exhausted by the inconclusive struggle, both sides made an uneasy peace in 1727.

Farther south violence continually flared up as Indians struggled with Europeans and each other for supremacy and survival. In 1702 during Queen Anne's War, a force of Indians and Charleston settlers led by James Moore destroyed most of the remaining Spanish Guale and Timucuan missions between South Carolina and Saint Augustine. In 1703 Moore led another army, consisting of one thousand Yamassee and Creek Indians and fifty settlers, on an expedition that destroyed nearly every mission and fortified *pre-sidio* along the northern Florida frontier. Hundreds of Indian people were killed while hundreds of others were carried off as slaves.

No longer fearful of Spanish attack, enterprising Carolinians sensing business opportunities in the hinterland pressed toward Creek, Choctaw, and Cherokee towns. Many were plunged into debt by traders offering credit to Indian people increasingly unable to find sufficient numbers of deerskins or slaves. Many also were angered by settlers moving onto their lands, concerned by growing alcohol abuse among their people, and outraged by thefts, assaults, and rapes committed by traders. Fearful of being enslaved themselves for debt and incensed by particularly provocative incidents, Indian people throughout the region went to war against the British. In 1711 war broke out between the Tuscaroras and North Carolina settlers. Calling on Moore's son, South Carolina troops, again aided by their Yamassee and Creek allies, devastated the Tuscarora towns, killed hundreds of Tuscarora people, and took hundreds of captives. Those unwilling to submit to the Carolinians were forced to abandon their lands and flee north to Iroquois country, where they became the sixth nation around 1722.

In 1715 Yamassee, Creek, and Choctaw people long allied to the British had had enough. Killing unwelcome traders and agents in their towns, they soon launched assaults against frontier towns built on their eastern borders. Although the war at first went well for the Indians, South Carolina officials exploiting ancient animosities managed to turn the Cherokees against the Creeks and their allies. Caught between the Cherokees on one side and the Carolinians on the other, most Yamassees subsequently fled to the Creeks, who concluded a peace treaty surrendering Yamassee territory to the British in 1717. Frequently encouraged by British agents eager to buy captives enslaved in wars and to keep powerful inland nations divided against one another, Creek and Cherokee people continued to fight each other for many years thereafter.

Farther west Miamis living in the Ohio Valley, Illinois people, and Chickasaws, Choctaws, Natchez, and other Mississippi Valley people found their lands invaded by French troops marching south from New France and north from new outposts built at Biloxi and Mobile

Bay. French explorers Jacques Marquette, Louis Joliet, René-Robert Cavelier de La Salle, and Henri de Tonti had traveled westward to Indian communities in what the French came to call Louisiana during the 1670s and 1680s. Following in their footsteps, French administrators worked to encircle and contain their British rivals by erecting a string of forts stretching from the Saint Lawrence to the mouth of the Mississippi.

In the north most Indian people living near outposts established at Detroit, Michilimackinac, Ouiatenon, and Kaskaskia managed to live peaceably with their new French neighbors. Those unwilling to accept such incursions into their territory, like the Fox Indians who fought against the French and their Indian allies from 1712 until driven from their lands in 1731, ultimately were forced to make peace with their new neighbors or move away. Other communities asserting the right to make their own friends also were suppressed. In 1752, for example, a French and Indian party destroyed a Miami community in Ohio led by the influential leader Memeskia (called La Demoiselle by the French and Old Britain by the British); the community had been welcoming English traders to the town since signing a separate treaty with Pennsylvanians four years earlier at the close of a conflict between France and England known as King George's War (1744–1748).

Farther south French colonists were soon embroiled in a series of wars with other people who resented the invasion of their lands. In 1724 Natchez people, the last recorded Indian people preserving the highly stratified ancient Mississippi way of life, failed to eject French colonists settling on their lands. Five years later Natchez warriors aided by Chickasaw allies destroyed French Fort Rosalie and temporarily drove the French from their territory. Returning one year later, French troops aided by Choctaw allies destroyed the Natchez, sold survivors into slavery in Santo Domingo, and initiated a series of wars with the Chickasaws that did not end until the French were forced to surrender their North American colonies to Spain (1762) and Britain (1763).

At peace or at war, Indian people struggled to accommodate change on their own terms. By 1750 Native people living east of the Mississippi River used European tools and weapons almost exclusively. Those living close to European settlements or moving to missions also began tending apple, cherry, or peach trees and raising small numbers of chickens, pigs, and cattle. Increasing numbers of Indian people interested in becoming literate or learning new industrial skills visited new missions established in Appalachian Mountain valleys during the second quarter of the century. Foremost among these in the north were those of the Moravians, who worked among displaced Mahicans, Munsees, and Delawares in New York and Pennsylvania, and of the New Light Presbyterian missionaries inspired by the Great Awakening. Among the latter was John Sergeant, who established the Stockbridge settlement in the Berkshire Mountains of Massachusetts in 1736 as a refuge for dispossessed New England Algonquian people.

Although Indian people throughout the East had grown accustomed to woven textiles, milled sugar, refined white flour, coffee, tea, and alcohol, none had yet become dependent upon settlers for food and clothing, except during times of emergency. And although Indian people knew that colonists had occupied nearly all coastal lands within the space of a hundred years, they were also aware of the fact that only a few hundred non-Indian settlers had yet managed to establish themselves on Indian lands to the west of the Appalachians. No longer relying on French or British promises that their lands would not be invaded, Indian people began to look to one another for the support and strength they would need to hold the settlers back behind the mountain wall.

Coming to regard the British as the greater threat, most Indian people sided with the French as both empires drifted toward their final confrontation during the 1750s. Throughout the east Indian warriors launched assaults that hurled British American settlers back toward the Atlantic Coast. In the north Delaware and Shawnee warriors anxious to avenge the loss of lands and loved ones devastated the New York and Pennsylvania frontier. Farther south Cherokees and Creeks made up their differences and struck out against Carolina and Georgia colonists. Successful for a time, they soon found that the French could not supply them with sufficient ammunition and provisions to carry on the struggle. Devastated by British counterattacks, discouraged by British victories over their French opponents, and listening—albeit skeptically—to British promises to dismantle their forts and leave their lands in peace once the fighting ended, the tribes began to negotiate treaties with their adversaries. Turning on their former French allies, Delawares and Shawnees hastened the final French defeat in North America in 1760.

Threatened as never before by now-united colonists no longer easily divided by diplomatic maneuvers, the Indians waited for the British to honor their promises. Although they did manage to halt colonial expansion into Indian country, British authorities refused to give up the old French forts. Indian people were united to an unprecedented degree, galvanized by Native prophets promising victory to all who would fight against the British; in 1763 they attacked and captured every British outpost in the Midwest except Detroit, Niagara, and Fort Pitt. Known as Pontiac's War after the Ottawa war chief thought by the British to have been the guiding genius behind the Indian effort, the conflict finally ended when Sir William Johnson, an influential New York trader with close ties to the Mohawks who had been appointed the Crown's agent to all northern tribes in 1756, met with the assembled chiefs at Fort Niagara in 1765. Promising to prevent future expansion into their territories, he drew a line separating their country from the coastal colonies that was later ratified by the Six Nations and other Indians at the Treaty of Fort Stanwix in 1768.

However, good intentions and a thin line of forts manned by troops largely unwilling to restrain their own people were insufficient; they could not keep the millions of settlers crowding along the coast from spilling over the paper line onto Indian lands west of the Appalachians. The number of murders and assaults grew as long-standing rules of conduct regulating intercultural relations suddenly broke down. Rioters embittered by years of frontier warfare, like the Susquehanna Valley Paxton Boys, murdered the few Indians unlucky enough to fall into their hands and drove away the rest. Although in New Jersey Governor William Franklin saw to it that

two of the three men convicted for raping and killing two local Indian women were hanged, other murderers, both Indian and non-Indian, escaped retribution.

Nearly every Indian man, woman, and child not willing to submit to colonial authority was forced to move west of the Appalachians as Britain and her estranged colonies drifted toward war during the early 1770s. People belonging to a few communities, such as the Stockbridge mission town in Massachusetts, some Oneidas, and the Catawbas of South Carolina, sided with the Americans when the war broke out in 1775. Nearly every other Indian nation either tried to remain neutral or joined the British against the rebels. No matter what position they took or who they fought for, all Indian communities were devastated by war's end. Left out of a peace treaty signed in Europe, many fought on for their lands until soldiers of the young American republic finally defeated the last eastern Indian coalition by killing its political leader, Tecumseh, and discrediting its spiritual leader, Tecumseh's brother Tenskwatawa, the Shawnee Prophet, during the War of 1812.

BIBLIOGRAPHY

Axtell, James. *The Invasion Within: The Contest of Cultures in Colonial North America.* New York, 1985.

Cronon, William. *Changes in the Land: Indians, Colonists, and the Ecology of New England.* New York, 1983.

Crosby, Alfred W., Jr. *The Columbian Exchange: Biological and Cultural Consequences of 1492.* Westport, Conn., 1972.

Dobyns, Henry F. *Their Number Become Thinned: Native American Population Dynamics in Eastern North America.* Knoxville, Tenn., 1983.

Downes, Randolph C. *Council Fires on the Upper Ohio: A Narrative of Indian Affairs in the Upper Ohio Valley Until 1775.* Pittsburgh, Pa., 1940.

Fitzhugh, William W., ed. *Cultures in Contact: The Impact of European Contacts on Native Cultural Institutions in Eastern North America, A.D. 1000–1800.* Washington, D.C., 1985.

Grumet, Robert S. *Historic Contact: Early Relations Between Indian People and Colonists in Northeastern North America, 1524–1783.* Philadelphia, Pa., 1992.

Harris, Robert Cole, and Geoffrey Matthews, editor and cartographer. *Historical Atlas of Canada.* Vol. 1. Toronto, Ontario, 1966.

Helm, June, ed. *Handbook of North American Indians.* Vol. 6, *Subarctic.* Washington, D.C., 1981.

Hudson, Charles M. *The Southeastern Indians.* Knoxville, Tenn., 1976.

Jennings, Francis. *The Ambiguous Iroquois Empire: The Covenant Chain Confederation of Indian Tribes with English Colonies from its Beginning to the Lancaster Treaty of 1744.* New York, 1984.

———. *Empire of Fortune: Crowns, Colonies, and Tribes in the Seven Years' War in America.* New York, 1988.

———. *The Invasion of America: Indians, Colonialism, and the Cant of Conquest.* Chapel Hill, N.C., 1975.

Leacock, Eleanor Burke, and Nancy Oestreich Lurie, eds. *North American Indians in Historical Perspective.* New York, 1971.

Mooney, James. *The Siouan Tribes of the East.* Bureau of American Ethnology Bulletin no. 22. Washington, D.C., 1894.

Morgan, Lewis Henry. *League of the Ho-De-No-Sau-Nee.* Rochester, N.Y., 1851; rev. ed., 2 vols., 1904.

Silver, Timothy. *A New Face on the Countryside: Indians, Colonists, and Slaves in South Atlantic Forests, 1500–1800.* New York, 1990.

Swanton, John R. *The Indians of the Southeastern United States.* Bureau of American Ethnology Bulletin no. 137. Washington, D.C., 1946.

Tanner, Helen Hornbeck. *Atlas of Great Lakes Indian History.* Norman, Okla., 1987.

Trelease, Allen W. *Indian Affairs in Colonial New York: The Seventeenth Century.* Ithaca, N.Y., 1960.

Trigger, Bruce T. *The Children Aataentsic: A History of the Huron People to 1660.* 2 vols. Montreal and Quebec, 1976.

———, ed. *Handbook of North American Indians.* Vol. 15, *Northeast.* Washington, D.C., 1978.

Trudel, Marcel. *Histoire de la Nouvelle-France.* Vol. 1, *Les vaines tentatives, 1524–1603.* Montreal, 1963. Vol. 2, *Le comptoir, 1604–1627.* Montreal, 1966.

Vaughan, Alden T., gen. ed. *Early American Indian Documents: Treaties and Laws, 1607–1789.* 8 vols. to date. Washington, D.C., 1979–.

Washburn, Wilcomb E., ed. *Handbook of North American Indians.* Vol. 4, *History of Indian-White Relations.* Washington, D.C., 1988.

White, Richard. *The Middle Ground: Indians, Empires, and Republics in the Great Lakes Region, 1650–1815.* Cambridge, England, and New York, 1991.

Robert S. Grumet

SEE ALSO **Ecological Consequences of Economic Development; The First Americans; The Fur Trade; Interracial Societies; Medical Practice, Health and Disease;** and **Native American Religions;** the maps accompanying **The First Americans.**

THE SPANISH BORDERLANDS

FOR ALMOST THREE HUNDRED years, from the first Spanish *entradas* into the Spanish Borderlands in the early sixteenth century to the independence of Mexico from the mother country in 1821, Spaniards and Native Americans led each other in a complex dance of war, peace, enslavement, trade, evangelization, enmity, and alliance. It is not easy to categorize cultural and social relations on a vast frontier of thousands of miles with dozens, even hundreds of Indian groups over the course of three centuries. On one side of the frontier were the Spaniards, and those grouped along with them: Africans, mestizos, and mulattoes. On the other side were Native Americans, the many disparate Indian tribes, bands, and groups of the borderlands. In between the two ethnic and cultural worlds lay the frontier, not a geographical division, or as one famous historian, Frederick Jackson Turner, termed it, "the meeting point between savagery and civilization," but a complex zone of racial, cultural, social, religious, and political interaction.

The Spanish Borderlands stretched from the coast of Baja California in the west to the swampy marshes of Florida in the east, from the mines of Zacatecas in the south to the Great Salt Lake in the land of the Ute in the far north. It included wild hunters and gatherers known generically as *chichimecas* (a Nahuatl word meaning "sons of dogs"), semisedentary river valley dwellers, nomadic buffalo hunters on the Great Plains, and fortress-dwelling agriculturalists in the Rio Grande Valley. With such a great variety of aboriginal societies, the frontier between European and Indian was, in the words of the ethnohistorian Jack Forbes, "an instance of dynamic interaction between human beings" involving acculturation, assimilation, miscegenation, conquest, and colonization but also voluntary and forced conversion to Christianity, and coerced as well as willing exchange of labor and goods between Spaniard and Indian. If one ceases to regard the Spanish-Indian frontier as any sort of absolute line or division and begins to consider it as a meeting point between wholly disparate cultures, then one begins to comprehend the complex nature of European-Native interactions.

The aim of the Spanish in the borderlands was conquest, conversion, assimilation, and inclusion of the Native peoples into their empire. They sought, in short, to make of the Indians peaceful Christian subjects of the Spanish monarch. The goal of the Indians, everywhere, was resistance to such incorporation into European political, economic, and religious patterns of life when possible. Resistance was both violent and pacific in nature. Indians proved remarkably successful at acculturation (the transfer of cultural traits from one ethnic group to another) on their own terms, which in practice meant an eager acceptance of European cultural artifacts, including horses, cattle, iron implements, cloth, weapons, and European foodstuffs, and customarily a rejection, where possible, of European cultural concepts, especially the Christian religion. Where Europeans controlled Indians politically and socially (especially in the mission villages of the Californias and the Sierra Madre Occidental), a syncretic and hybrid culture and religion, indicative of a partial acceptance of European social norms, developed. In areas where Spanish political control was less secure or absent (as in the pueblos of New Mexico and the vast plains of the northern *apachería*, as the plains to the east of New Mexico were known), acculturation was usually on Indian terms.

After the conquest of the Aztec Empire in 1519–1521, the Spanish moved cautiously and slowly northward into the vast realm north of the Valley of Mexico. The Aztec Empire had been a highly centralized, political and social entity. After destroying its military and religious hierarchy, the Spaniards were able to control large numbers of Native peoples, ruling through Native elites (the *caciques,* or chieftains) and adapting Native institutions for tribute collection and labor to their own use. They also made extensive use of troops from Tlaxcala, a small autonomous Indian city-state which had sided with the Spaniards against the Aztec Empire. However, with more-or-less complete political control over the people of central Mexico, conversion of the Native peoples to Christianity and their integration into the Spanish Empire as subjects was a slow and laborious process that took the better part of several centuries to complete. Indians in central Mexico were to rule themselves in their own communities (from which, in theory, all non-Indians were rigorously excluded), paying tribute to the Spanish monarchies as a reflection of their relationship to the Crown. They were given in *encomiendas* (the word comes from the Spanish *encomendar,* to commend or entrust) to Spaniards, with the obligation to pay tribute and provide labor and personal service to their new masters. They had rights and privileges, carefully defined and legally enumerated (and often completely ignored), just as they had duties and obligations. They were, in short, theoretically integrated into European society and acculturated to European political, religious, social, and cultural norms.

North of central Mexico lies a vast arid and semi-arid landscape, with agricultural land limited to river valleys, which were occupied by sedentary and semisedentary *ranchería* peoples. The Spaniards were partly successful in controlling these *ranchería* dwellers, although the various revolts of Indian communities (the Tepehuane in 1616, the Tarahumara in 1648, 1650, 1652, and 1690, the Yaqui in 1740, and the Pueblo tribes in 1680, among others), show that Spanish control was often very shaky. In most cases the secular and religious authorities had to come to a modus vivendi with the Indians in order to maintain peace. When the Spanish moved northward, they also encountered a large number of disparate nomadic tribes and bands of hunters and gatherers, from the *chichimecas* of the Zacatecas region to the Apache and Comanche of the northern deserts and the many bands of the vast Texas plains loosely termed *norteños.* The Spanish were never able to control these nomads; indeed, a long series of military struggles, beginning with the first chichimec war in 1540 and continuing throughout the entire colonial period, only emphasized the feeble grip the Spaniards had on their overextended northern empire.

MISSION, *PRESIDIO, ESTANCIA*

The Spanish frontier in northern Mexico differed greatly from both its Anglo-American and its French counterparts in North America. There were few hardy mountain men, or *coureurs de bois* (woods runners) roaming the wilderness far ahead of the advancing urban frontier. The Spanish frontier was settled largely by government fiat, by persons authorized by the Crown to settle and populate. Three institutions played a crucial role in Spanish-Indian frontier relations: the mission, the *presidio,* and the cattle *estancia.*

The Franciscans and Jesuits were the most important missionary orders to work in the borderlands. Sometimes alone, at other times accompanied by small groups of soldiers (often the cause of European-Native friction), the missionaries established churches or chapels far in advance of European civilian penetration of the frontier. These places of worship were nuclei for the ingathering of Indians into missionary villages, not only to be baptized and ministered to by the friars, but also to be "civilized," to be taught European methods of farming, weaving, metalworking, carpentry, masonry, and a hundred other crafts. Thus the missions were the focus of Spanish attempts to acculturize the natives, a process which they intended to be a one-way process.

The *presidio,* or fort, was another vital element of frontier life. The *presidios* were the nuclei of settlement in the borderlands; soldiers usually accompanied and guarded the missionaries during their attempts to convert natives. *Presidio* soldiers were usually recruited from among the castes of the frontier.

Finally, the cattle *estancia,* or ranch, was an economic institution that often followed in the wake of the missionaries and soldiers. Vast areas of the borderlands were arid or semi-arid, unsuitable for farming. Livestock ranching could make use of these lands, and enormous stretches

of northern Mexico were turned into ranges for *ganado mayor* (cattle) and *menor* (sheep). In some areas of the borderlands, Indians were hired as *vaqueros,* or cowboys; more often mestizos and mulattoes tended the herds. This livestock was the target of a great deal of raiding by nomadic tribes, from the Chichimeca of the Zacateca area to the Comanche and Apache of the northern plains.

FLORIDA

Florida, which was colonized first, was settled entirely for strategic reasons. The failure of numerous expeditions to the mainland (Juan Ponce de León in 1513, Pánfilo de Narváez in 1527, and Hernando de Soto in 1538), the hostility of the natives (due entirely to their brutal treatment at the hands of the conquistadores), and the martyrdom of several Dominicans in 1545 seemed to rule out any chance of permanent Spanish presence in Florida. The attempt by Tristán de Luna to establish a settlement in 1559 in Pensacola Bay was quickly wrecked by a hurricane.

But Florida guarded the straits used by treasure ships bearing gold and silver back to Spain. When French Huguenots began a settlement on the northern coast of Florida, the Spanish reacted with amazing speed. An expedition under Pedro Menéndez de Avilés quickly took the French fort, massacred its soldiers, and established a permanent settlement at Saint Augustine in 1565.

Jesuit missionaries arrived in Florida in 1566, the Franciscans in 1573. The latter order established a chain of missions, many administered from Spanish military outposts, from Parris Island, South Carolina, to the Gulf Coast of the Florida peninsula. The natives belonged to the Calusa and Tequesta tribal areas in the south, and to the Tocobaga, Timuca, and Apalachee cultures further north. By the mid seventeenth century the Franciscans claimed thirty-eight mission villages (*doctrinas*) and twenty-six thousand Christianized natives. Still, European-Indian relations followed patterns familiar in other borderland regions. Catholic displacement of Native cultural and religious practices and authorities caused resentment and revolt (the Guales of south Georgia rebelled in 1597, the Timuca and Apalache of Florida in 1656). Secular and religious authorities argued over jurisdiction and what amounted to economic exploitation of the Indians. Many were enslaved by the Spaniards and sent to the Caribbean as labor. Epidemic disease brought by the Europeans drastically reduced Indian populations.

Like other Native tribes in the Southwest, the Indians of Florida were caught up in European politics. Florida was necessary as a buffer against English intrusion from the north and French incursion from the west (Louisiana). English settlers from Charleston armed the Yamassee and Creek Indians; together these groups destroyed the Georgia missions and pushed the Spanish back on the defensive. Many Guale mission towns renounced their allegiance to Spain and joined with the English and their allies. The English had virtually no interest in Christianizing the natives; the Indians had chafed under the iron rule of the friars, who were no less strict than their other borderland brethren. In 1763 Florida was ceded by Spain to England as part of the price she paid for losing Havana in the Seven Years' War. A wholesale exodus of Spaniards from Florida towns took place, and with the departure of the Spanish the remnants of the Christian Indian communities were evacuated to Cuba and Mexico.

NORTHWESTERN NEW SPAIN

Regular missionaries accompanied most of the early *entradas* (expeditions) into the borderlands, but their impact upon Indian tribes there was minimal. A Franciscan priest and two lay brothers remained behind in New Mexico after Francisco Vásquez de Coronado abandoned his quest for Cíbola in 1542. None were ever heard from again, and they were presumably martyred by hostile Indians. The Jesuits arrived in New Spain in the 1570s full of zeal for converting Indians to the Christian faith. By 1600 they had established a network of missions among the Tepehuan Indians in the southern Sierra Madre Mountains as far north as the borders of present-day Chihuahua. They then planned their advance further north into the Sierras Madres, into the lands of the Tarahumara Indians. At the same time, Franciscans were at work to the east of the Sierras in the country of the Conchos, north of Santa Barbara (near present-day Parral), where silver had been discovered. In 1598 Franciscan missionaries accompanied Juan de Oñate's settlement expedition into New Mexico, a bold leap many hundreds of miles to the north of the limits of Spanish settlement and a radical departure from the slow and steady pace of frontier colonization.

Missionary friars aimed everywhere in New Spain at the "reduction" of the Indians, that is, their concentration into communities centered around a church. Many of the *ranchería* peoples were accustomed to living in widely scattered dwellings, and many also moved from their fields in the summer to canyon areas in the winter. The missionaries sought not only to replace the Indians' religious beliefs with their own, but also to reorganize their economic, social, family, and community life. Although such reduction was generally not as drastic or harsh as the *congregación* (congregation) carried out by Viceroy Francisco de Toledo in Peru, it nevertheless struck at the heart of Indian life and was a source of friction between priest and Indian.

Another source of conflict lay in the basic act of conversion itself. Opposition to the friars was generally interpreted as sorcery or witchcraft, and in fact a great deal of such animosity was generated by the *hechiceros*, or shamans, of the Indian tribes, who quite naturally resisted the wholesale replacement of their beliefs by an alien and exclusive creed brought by outsiders. The missionaries naturally regarded all Native religious practices as idolatry and black magic, and all its practitioners as agents of the devil. For example, in 1616 the Tepehuane revolted; hundreds of Spaniards (including friars) and at least a thousand Indians were killed in the fighting, which lasted two years. It was essentially a religious crusade, in which a Native religious leader prophesied that the Spaniards would be driven out of the land, never to return. (A pattern of millenarian revolts, from Taqui Ongoy in Peru in 1565 to the Ghost Dance of the Sioux in 1890, punctuated the steady erosion of Native American religious beliefs by Christianity.) Several Spanish military expeditions from Durango were necessary before the revolt was crushed and the Jesuits could resume their missionary efforts.

This pattern of rebellion and reconquest became a familiar one in the Spanish Borderlands.

The steady influx of Spanish settlers into the north usually undid the work of the missionaries. Silver strikes at Parral drew Spanish and mixed-caste miners into the area. The need for labor led to the enslavement of Indians; since any Indians who did not accept Christianity were legitimate targets of slavers, a vicious cycle of raiding began, one which invariably led to Indian revolt and Spanish military response. Although by the 1640s the Jesuits had established a number of prosperous missionary communities among the Tarahumara, Spanish labor abuses, apostate Indians, and the effects of raiding by unconverted Indian groups led to an uprising among the Tarahumara in 1648. But this time it was clear that divisions among the Indians themselves hampered effective military action. The missionaries' efforts had not been unavailing; several communities refused to join the revolt. Some men prominent among the Tarahumara joined the rebels; others stood by the missionaries and refused to act against the Spanish. Thus even in the short span of several decades, the missionaries had made inroads into Native culture and religious beliefs.

Parts of the Tarahumara nation revolted again in 1652 and 1690; in each case disaffected Indians in areas not yet missionized resisted not only the Jesuits, but also encroachments upon their lands by Spanish settlers and miners who followed in the wake of the priests. After each revolt Spanish troops restored the rule of the padres, while haciendas and ranches took Indian land and labor. On the other side of the Sierra, in the river valleys of the Sonora coast, the Mayo and Yaqui nations waited the coming of the Spaniards. After initially defeating Spanish troops under Captain Diego de Hurdaide in 1609, the Yaqui relented and asked that Jesuit missionaries be sent to forge a peace with the Europeans. By 1619 nearly thirty thousand Yaqui had been baptized. No settlers or miners entered the lands between the Mayo and Yaqui rivers. Epidemics in mid century killed many Indians, but no serious trouble developed until mining activity at Alamos and in Sonora brought the usual flood of Spanish miners and ranchers. (Ranching activity customarily sprang up to support mining with wood, hides, mules, and food.)

In 1740 the Mayo and Yaqui revolted. In this instance one Juan Ignacio Muni developed a hatred of the missionaries, probably brought on by the whipping of a relative administered at the behest of a Jesuit priest. The missionaries frequently resorted to corporal punishment (usually carried out by an Indian or mulatto subordinate) to enforce orthodoxy and their decrees.

Rumors of maltreatment at the hands of Spanish priests spread, and an Indian, Juan Calixto, led a revolt. A lieutenant of a Mayo town was murdered, suggesting that the grievances of the Indians had much to do with the leaders the Spaniards appointed in place of traditional Native authorities. With the battle cry, "Long live the king! Long live the blessed Virgin Mary! Down with bad government!" the Yaqui, Mayo, and Lower Pima initially drove all Spaniards out of the territory. By the time Spanish troops destroyed the Indian armies, more than a thousand Spaniards and five times as many Indians had been killed. Every mine and hacienda in the Mayo and Yaqui lands had been abandoned, all the missionaries had been forced to flee, and large numbers of horses and cattle had been stolen. Peace was restored, but the rebuilding of fruitful social, economic, and religious relations was a long time in coming.

The Spanish missionaries themselves complained vociferously of the ephemeral nature of the non-Indian residents on the Sonoran frontier. In 1723, when the non-Indians of Sonora could hardly have numbered more than a few thousand, one Jesuit wrote that the largest segment of that population was made up of "coyotes [a person of mixed black and Indian blood], mulattoes, and other scum of the earth, who wandered like vagabonds in the province, without any other occupation than stealing, gambling, seducing women, sowing discord, and other evils." He bitterly condemned the Spanish justices, who did little or nothing to prevent people from roaming the countryside, allegedly in search of precious metals. There were numerous parties, he wrote, miners in name only, who had neither mines nor means to sustain themselves. Thirty years later a civil inspector reiterated the same chorus of complaints. Among the Indians there lived, he wrote, "vicious men of bad habits, thieves, gamblers, dissolute and lost men, who with their bad customs, laziness, mistakes, and vices, could spoil and pervert the salvation, growth, and peace of the Indians." Spanish law forbade the residence of such men, be they Spanish, mestizo, or mulatto, in Indian towns. But just as these laws were ignored in the metropolitan core areas of New Spain, they were unenforceable on the frontier.

By the mid eighteenth century, many Indian towns in Sonora had "sister" communities nearby, settlements of mestizos and mulattoes; many land and water disputes ensued between Indian towns and these settlements. In 1772 another padre wrote that the two main reasons for Sonora's deplorable state were the invasions of the enemy Indians (Apache) and the vagabond nature of the non-Indian population. "The Spanish traders, mulattoes, blacks, and all castes have entered, and enter Sonora with the sole aim of using for themselves the first mines and placers that they find, until they find in another part a better one," he wrote. According to him, the moment that one silver strike was played out and another found, all abandoned their dwellings and rushed to the new bonanza. "This is the reason that there is not in all the province of Sonora a proper and formal population of Spaniards," he asserted.

The two principal economic enterprises on the frontier were mining and ranching. Mining especially was a transient activity; the mining centers were the focus of such diverse social and ethnic groups that they formed the centers of racial mixing among Spaniards, Indians, and blacks. They were also the focus of the innumerable clerical complaints against the civil population. Padre Juan Nentvig, in his description of the province of Sonora in 1764, complained that the mission Indians of Sonora left their villages and sought work with Spaniards in their *rancherías* and mines: "There they found such instructors that in two hours they learnt everything necessary to the irremediable ruin of body and soul." Padre Daniel Januske was of the opinion that the Opata, for example, were naturally a very docile people, of good inclinations, but that they were upset by the bad examples and counsel furnished them by the *coyotes,* mulattoes, and other *vecinos* (Spaniards), which necessitated "unceasing vigilance and zeal on the part of the padres."

A good example of what the missionaries feared was a story related by another cleric, Padre Reyes; he told how a wandering peddler arrived at a town near Cucurpe Mission, to swap glass beads, ribbons, horns, and bells to the Indians in exchange for earthenware jugs of mescal, a liquor which the Indians distilled from the agave cactus. The Indians' padre told his charges that the viceroy, governor, and justices had forbidden them to manufacture mescal. When the peddler learned of the regular's interference, he "ordered [the Indians] to come together and preached to them a sermon." He told them that they were fools to believe all that the padre had told them; they were free to do whatever they wished, and could not be prohibited from making mescal. The Spaniards, he declared, wanted to make them all slaves and deprive them of their liberty. A vagabond problem of immense proportion was developing in the borderlands, fueled by racial intolerance, the lack of a developed economy, and perpetual warfare between Europeans and natives.

The missionaries, many of them European born and contemptuous of Americans, especially Americans of mixed race, had their own agenda: they desired the strict segregation of their charges from all outside influences. Ironically the haciendas, ranches, and missions of Sonora found a ready market for the agricultural goods produced on Jesuit haciendas, most notably in support of the mining sector of the province. Thus the missionaries' bitter and constant complaints about the transient nature of the mining sector and its itinerant population reflected their own dependence upon this activity for the economic well-being of their mission communities.

The banishment of the Jesuits in 1767 brought to an end an era of missionary activity. The Franciscans, who took over from the Jesuits, were unable to sustain the missions as viable religious and economic institutions. Steady encroachment upon Indian lands by Spaniards and other non-Indians brought increasing acculturation to European patterns of life. The end of Spanish colonial rule brought new pressures to bear upon communities that were less and less Indian, and more and more Mexican by both decree (the Mexican government abolished all legal distinctions of caste) and by mode of living.

NEW MEXICO

New Mexico represented a distinctly different Spanish frontier society. Largely due to the absence of precious metals, New Mexico was a province of small farmers and ranchers. Because Spanish political and military power was less secure, Indian communities preserved a greater degree of cultural and religious autonomy than those on the west coast of New Spain. New Mexico also differed as a colonial enterprise in that it was a planned effort on the part of the Spanish authorities, in contrast to the unsystematic infiltration of miners and settlers into the Sinaloa and Sonora river valleys. Civil and religious authority was established simultaneously when Juan de Oñate was awarded a contract for New Mexico's colonization.

What Oñate found was a large number of agricultural villages whose inhabitants lived in compact houses of two or three stories. Some groups had built their villages on top of cliffs or mesas, attesting to intermittent warfare among themselves and with the nomadic peoples from the east, the Apache. The Pueblo Indians, as they came to be called, lived in individual villages politically and linguistically distinct from one another; the major divisions were the Piro, Southern and Northern Tiwa, Tewa, Towa, Tano, and Kere. Altogether the Rio Grande villages had a population of some forty thousand inhabitants. Farther to the west lived the Zuni, and to the northwest the Hopi.

In contrast to Coronado's bloody and imperialist legacy of fifty years previously, Oñate's establishment of Spanish rule in the valley was bloodless. Everywhere he went he obtained agreement of obedience or submission to Spanish rule. For example, at one Kere village Oñate met with a number of *caciques*, who were said to represent more than thirty villages. Oñate, at a general meeting, explained that he was an emissary of the king of Spain, offered the Indians protection from their enemies, and explained the ritual of baptism. When he had concluded, the chieftains knelt at his feet, kissed his hand and that of the Spanish friar who accompanied him, and gave what the Spaniards believed was a pledge of allegiance to the Spanish monarch. What the Indians believed had transpired was probably quite different. But by 1599 all the villages in the valley had submitted themselves to the Spaniards.

Spanish zeal for the enterprise of New Mexico soon faded as the harvest of both gold and souls proved to be meager. But the Crown would not allow New Mexico to be abandoned because of its missionary potential. It was sustained as a lonely outpost colony, far to the north of Spanish silver and ranching settlements, with thousands of square miles of enemy-infested wilderness between New Spain's northern frontier and its northernmost colony. By 1630 there were fifty Franciscans working in twenty-five missions in New Mexico.

The mid seventeenth century was not a period of prosperity or growth for New Mexico. Antagonistic relations between the Spanish civil and religious authorities sapped energies that could have enhanced, rather than diminished, the development of the colony. The governor and the friars quarreled, and the Indians took advantage of these disputes to forge autonomy for themselves in their pueblos. One cause of the quarrels was the manner in which various governors required Indians to labor for them, to gather hides, salt, and other foodstuffs, and to deliver textiles to them for resale. The missionaries argued that their own economic enterprises (which they naturally claimed were established for the ultimate benefit of the Indians themselves) were disrupted. The civil authorities charged that the friars were exploiting the Indians for their own gain.

The missionaries were frequently at odds with their charges. As in the Yaqui lands, when the friars needed to enforce their rule in the mission villages, they generally resorted to corporal punishment, usually administered by a *mayordomo,* quite often a mulatto or mestizo whose arbitrary enforcement of authority was much resented by the Indians. One *coyote* at Acoma compelled his Indians to supply him weekly with sheep, lard, beans, and tortillas. It was not only persons of mixed race who caused such friction; in 1695 the Pima revolted against the Christianized Opata, whom the friars had put in charge of their missionary communities.

The friars were not tolerant of religious or social deviation. Their goal necessitated the eradication of Native religious practices, the elimination of the influence of traditional Native leaders, and the imposition of rigid monogamy on a people whose sexual and marital mores were decidedly at variance with Spanish ideas of "normalcy." Indians who had customarily gone about nude were forced to cover themselves. Whippings were meted out to Indians for offenses such as failure to attend religious services, sexual immorality (as defined by the missionaries), and participating in traditional ceremonial dances. The missionaries were themselves not immune to human temptation; one Franciscan lamented in 1671 that "all the pueblos are full of friars' children." Indeed, one case of abuse of natives by the friars was so flagrant as to require the intervention of higher ecclesiastical authority.

In 1655 several Hopi Indian leaders appeared before a clerical custodian to denounce their priest. It seemed that an Indian from Oraibi pueblo had been caught in an act of idolatry. Before the entire pueblo, the friar beat the backslider so severely that he was "bathed in blood." After a second beating inside the church, the missionary applied burning turpentine to the unfortunate man, who died soon after. The Hopi testified that other boys and girls guilty of "immoral conduct" had been beaten and tarred with hot turpentine. The friar had also demanded that the natives weave cotton and woolen cloth or suffer more beatings. The friar admitted to corporal punishment of men and women for idolatry and sexual offenses, but defended his actions on religious and moral grounds. For once, justice prevailed, and the missionary was removed from his post and remanded to a convent.

Gradually the friars began to realize that the Indians' conversion, as so often was the case throughout New Spain, had only been skin-deep. Indians, sometimes encouraged by Spanish governors seeking to strike at the missionaries' authority, continued to dance their masked kachina ceremonies, offer prayer sticks, strew ritual cornmeal, and meet in their underground kivas to undergo ritual purification ceremonies. Indeed, the need of the natives to hold onto their traditional rituals deepened as the faith which the Christians brought failed to deliver good harvests or fruitful hunts. Pueblo religion served definite material and social ends; if the new faith was no more successful than the old in guaranteeing

material and spiritual rewards, what advantage had been gained in submitting to Spanish rule?

In 1661 the Franciscans decreed that no more kachina dances were to be held, and all "idolatrous" materials were to be destroyed. Kivas were raided, and some sixteen hundred masks and many prayer feathers were confiscated and destroyed. In 1675 Governor Juan Francisco de Treviño, rather than fight with the friars, supported them in their efforts to stamp out "heresy" in the pueblos; forty-seven Indian leaders from many villages were accused of witchcraft or idolatry, and were whipped and imprisoned.

In 1680 Pueblo resentment of what has been termed "Franciscan theocracy" boiled over in a widespread revolt. The years leading up to 1680 had been years of drought and famine, as well as a period marked by Apache and Navajo attacks of unprecedented fury. One pueblo, that of the Tewa, had openly defied the Franciscans and resumed dancing the ceremonial dances which the friars had prohibited, calling on their old gods to return to them and destroy their occupiers.

One Popé, a ceremonial leader from San Juan Pueblo who had been chastised by the friars in their campaign, joined with another leader, Catiti of Santo Domingo Pueblo, in plotting an uprising. For once the scattered and disunited Pueblo villages managed to unite to expel their occupiers. A force of Indians besieged Santa Fe, while outlying Spanish settlements were sacked. Of 33 missionaries in the province, 21 were killed, along with 401 colonists. Some two thousand Spaniards were allowed to evacuate New Mexico; they pulled back to El Paso del Norte on the lower Rio Grande. There they remained for twelve years.

But once the Spaniards had been expelled, Indian unity collapsed. No alternative political structure came into existence, not even to deal with an anticipated Spanish military response. The Indians quarreled among themselves. Some purists wanted to destroy every vestige of European influence, even to the extent of tearing out by their roots the fruit trees the missionaries had brought. The Spanish tongue was forbidden; wives taken in matrimony with Christian ceremony might be abandoned if so desired. Indians should plant only maize and beans, the crops cultivated before the Europeans came. But most Indians refused to abandon the new crops, foodstuffs, cattle, horses, iron implements, and other cultural artifacts that the Spanish had brought into their lands. As a result of Indian disunity, when the Spanish reentered the Pueblo lands in the 1690s, they were able to retake Indian towns piecemeal; no united resistance was formed against Spanish reoccupation.

The Spanish were shocked upon returning at the extent to which their churches had been vandalized and their holy images desecrated by the natives during their absence. It demonstrated to the Europeans how much the forcible imposition of their religion and the iron rule of the friars had been resented. The Spaniards also found that not all non-Pueblos had remained true; upon retaking some villages, Governor Antonio Otermín described Indian rebels fleeing into the mountains; with them were "many mestizos, mulattoes, and people who speak Spanish [who] have followed them, and who can manage firearms as well as any Spaniard. These persons incited them to disobedience and boldness in excess of their natural iniquity."

The eighteenth century was a quiet one for New Mexico as far as the Pueblo Indians were concerned. Their population declined, while that of the Spaniards, mestizos, mulattoes, and non-Pueblo Indians grew. Conflict among the Europeans and Apache and Comanche raiders intensified, with the Pueblo Indians suffering depredations from the nomads and forced to rely on the Spanish for their defense. Still the Spaniards trod lightly in New Mexico in the wake of the great revolt of 1680. The friars never reestablished real control over the Indians. Native religious ceremonies moved underground into the kivas, while aboveground the natives practiced a form of syncretic Catholicism. After 1767 the missions were secularized, and for all practical purposes the missionization of the Pueblos came to an end.

Both in New Mexico and on the western slopes of the Sierra Madre, the same pattern of Indian-European contact resulted in both relative acculturation of the Indians to European patterns of life and absolute population decline. In both areas civil authorities or settlers exploited the natives economically, forcing labor or tribute from them; the missionaries not only repeated this exploitation but added to it a deliberate program of eradicating Native religious practices and customs. At the same time, epidemic diseases brought by the Europeans caused Indian populations to decline, and warfare among Europeans, nomadic raiders, and Indians like the Seris of Sonora, who resisted missionization, sapped the demographic and military strength of Native communities. While the missionaries brought agricultural implements, techniques, seeds, fruits, cattle, and sheep to the Indians, they altered Native agricultural patterns by congregating the Indians in mission villages and disrupting, for example, the customary *ranchería* practice of moving households between planting seasons. The manufactured implements of the Europeans tended to displace Native handicrafts. The friars replaced traditional Native leaders with their own appointed men, often placing over them mestizos and mulattoes who abused their authority and their Native charges.

Interaction between Indians and civilians seems to have produced other deleterious results as well. While in some areas Indians were forced to labor on Spanish farms and mines, in many places Indians willingly deserted their villages to work for the Europeans for relatively high wages, especially in silver mines in the Sierras. This added to the economic and social disruption of Indian life. Indians who flocked to the mining centers, learned Spanish, dressed in European clothing, and adopted European diet and manners were halfway to becoming mestizos, culturally if not biologically. Vagabonds and runaways formed a sort of floating population between Native and European societies. Comprised of detribalized Indians, blacks, mestizos, mulattoes, and poor Spaniards, this population of *gente baja*, or "underclass," was a prime cause of concern to both civilian and military authorities.

What arose to replace traditional Indian structures was a hybridized society. The European settlers adopted Indian crops and foodstuffs, even as the natives expanded their agriculture to include European crops and adopted animal husbandry as an occupation. (The advantages of wool as a covering were immediately apparent.) Genetic intermingling began very early, as a shortage of Spanish women resulted in the rise of mestizos and other castes. The net result of European-Indian acculturation was a continual weakening of Indian political authority, a dislocation of Indian economic and agricultural patterns, and a diminution of Native cultural and religious values.

TEXAS

Farther east in Texas, aboriginal society's structure (or lack thereof) resulted in different European settlement patterns and Indian-Spanish interaction. The Spaniards moved north out of the Valley of Mexico in search of precious metals; they settled Texas later, primarily in order to safeguard the silver that they found at Zacatecas, Parral, and other frontier mining areas. Always in the minds of the Spanish government in Mexico City there lurked a vague and indeterminate threat of French incursions from either Canada (New France) or the Gulf Coast.

Rumors of Frenchmen among Indians far to the east of New Mexico brought alarmed responses from the Spanish in 1695. While these particular rumors were false, French traders were in fact voyaging down the Mississippi, using its many tributaries to promote their exchange of manufactured goods for furs. In this process they introduced metal goods, horses, and weapons into a world of small, stable farming villages, causing changes that far preceded their actual presence.

One vital part in the equation of change was firearms and ammunition. The Spanish forbade giving or selling guns to Indians; the French supplied certain tribes with muskets, tipping the balance of power in the Mississippi Valley irretrievably toward those nations armed with that weapon. This trade also caused an increase in the taking of captives by the Indians; these unfortunates were then exchanged for more French goods. Tribes with muskets put pressure on Indian groups unarmed with modern weaponry; these nations were then obliged to migrate, entering the traditional hunting grounds of other bands. A ripple effect reached across the borderlands in the late seventeenth and early eighteenth centuries as nations like the Osage pressured the Comanche, who moved south and west into Apache territories. The Apache were then obliged to migrate, causing an increase in raiding activities as far west as New Mexico and south-

wards deep into the borderlands. (Apache routinely raided as far south as Parral and Saltillo.)

In 1683 a chief of the Juamos asked for missionaries to be sent to his people. Although contact was brief and ephemeral, Franciscan friars saw Texas Indians as ripe subjects for evangelization. Spanish *entradas* were made in order to check on the whereabouts of reported Frenchmen. (All the expeditions found were the ruins of Sieur de La Salle's colony, between the Brazos and Trinity rivers in Texas.) In 1691 Texas was created as a frontier province, and a governor was named. In the intervening years a few missions had been established among Indians on the Neches River. But Texas was abandoned in 1693 as an economizing measure; the few Spaniards living there were pulled back to the more prosperous frontier in Coahuila and Nuevo León. The missionaries had ultimately failed as well. Caddo Indians repeatedly warned Franciscans to leave their missions or be killed; finally in October 1693, the friars admitted failure among the natives, buried their sacred objects, set fire to their mission, and abandoned their efforts at conversion. On the way back to Monclova, four of the ten soldiers accompanying the Franciscans deserted to go back and live among the Indians.

But the Spaniards remained aware that the French were still active among the Indians in Texas. When a party of Frenchmen showed up at San Juan Bautista on the Río Grande in 1714 in an attempt to open trade relations with the Spaniards, the reaction in Mexico City was quick and forceful. Texas was to be reoccupied, missions were to be established among the Texas Indians, and *presidios* and cities were to be built to keep French (and ultimately English) interlopers at bay. Within ten years there were ten missions and four *presidios* erected in Texas. San Antonio de Béjar was the capital of the province, and also a mission and fort. A *presidio* was built at Nacogdoches, facing a small French outpost at Natchitoches; other *presidios* watched the coast at Bahía del Espíritu Santo and Apache and Comanche activities at San Sabá.

But in Texas, Spanish-Indian relations were even more complicated and frustrating than in Sonora or New Mexico. Missionary work among nomadic hunters proved mostly futile. Relations of alliance and enmity between Comanche,

Apache, and numerous bands collectively called *norteños* made for an Indian policy of byzantine complexity. There were many subtribes of the Apache: Faraone, Jicarilla, Carlana, Cuartelejo, Lipan, and Mescalero among others. Peace made with one group did not necessarily halt raiding by others. Virtually all Apache were enemies of the Comanche. By the eighteenth century all of the tribes were mobile, thanks to the introduction of horses among the Plains nations. A combination of Spanish military action, persistent missionary zeal, and disease had always conquered Indians in the rest of the borderlands, but in Texas the Spanish were on the defensive throughout the eighteenth century.

In 1758 two thousand warriors from among the Teja, Bidai, Tonkawa, and other nations killed the missionaries at San Sabá and burned the mission to the ground; they then besieged the *presidio* soldiers in their fort, taunting them and displaying firearms. Small numbers of Spaniards had always overawed huge numbers of Native Americans throughout North and South America with their armor, horses, and muskets; to be confronted by their own technology in the hands of thousands of mobile warriors was a rude shock. A year after the siege at San Sabá, a Spanish punitive expedition (reinforced with friendly Apache) attempted to extract revenge for the slain friars. One battle went favorably: 55 Yojuane were killed and 149 captured. But when the Spaniards closed in on the Taovaya camp on the Red River, they were in for another unpleasant surprise: inside a fortified and moated palisade, Indians fired muskets and even raised a French flag over the stockade; the Spanish retreated. The Indians had learned how to play the Spaniards and French off against one another to their advantage. It was not until the Spanish decided in 1778 to back the Comanche against the Apache that any strategic plan for pacifying the frontier was formulated. Even then the numerous Indian groups frustrated any grand design for winning the Indians of the far northern borderlands to a Europeanized and Christianized life. Spanish successes in Coahuila, Nuevo León, Chihuahua, and Sonora were not repeated in New Mexico or Texas.

Life in colonial Texas was drab and dangerous. Economic activity was confined to small-scale farming and ranching. San Antonio de Béxar, San Saba, Nacogdoches, and a few other small towns were the focus of Spanish settlement. There, Spaniards, mestizos, mulattoes, detribalized Indians, Native auxiliaries from other areas, and other *castas* formed a diverse multiethnic society, in which the lines between European and Native American were blurred.

The proximity of territory inhabited by nomadic tribes that were often on antagonistic terms with the Spanish was a powerful inducement to cross over culturally from the European to the aboriginal world, and many became transculturites. One Miguel Menchaca, who had previously been refused enlistment as a presidial soldier, fled from San Antonio de Béxar in 1781 and was captured by Comanche. Two years later a shepherd tending his flock near the town was astonished when a Comanche warrior armed with a bow and arrow approached him and spoke to him; the Indian was the missing Menchaca! The governor of San Antonio rounded up all his soldiers, but was unable to apprehend the renegade. In another case, Antonio Treviño, a presidial soldier, was escorting Apache buffalo hunters (in an attempt to keep peace between Apache and Comanche) when he was attacked and wounded by Taovaya Indians. He fought so fiercely that the Indians spared his life and made him their guest, rather than their prisoner. He spent six months among the Taovaya, and was returned to Mission Nacogdoches in east Texas dressed in a breechclout. Treviño afterwards functioned as a translator and emmisary to the *norteños* on the frontier.

Still other Spaniards, mestizos, and mulattoes went over willingly to the Indians, or collaborated with them. Two Texas *vaqueros* assisted Tonkawa Indians in stealing horses from the Lipan Apache. When the Lipan caught the pair, they took them to the governor of Texas for justice. Because the two nearly wrecked the precarious peace, he gave them each one hundred lashes, in the presence of as many Lipan Apache as could be assembled in San Antonio. Many presidial soldiers deserted, either living among the Indians or heading for French territory in Louisiana. Many mulattoes, occupying the lowest rung of the Spanish social ladder and the victims of open prejudice and discrimination, were attracted to the open frontier and its freedom, preferring to live among the Indians rather than among neighbors who scorned them. Acculturation on the frontier worked in both directions;

while Indians adapted to European material society, many in Spanish society found the freedoms of Native society alluring enough to become transculturites.

THE IMPACT OF ACCULTURATION

Throughout the vast areas of the Spanish Borderlands, Indians and Spaniards confronted one another with radically different objectives. The overall aim of the Spanish was simple: to transform the Indians into *gente decente;* that is, good Christians who lived in a civilized polity, in an urban community, contributing to the economic welfare of the Spanish Empire and of the Crown by paying tribute and taxes. This objective was not an unrealistic one in the environs of the Valley of Mexico, where the Indians had in fact lived in similar economic and political structures prior to the invasion of the Europeans. Nor was it completely unrealistic in many areas of the borderlands: in the northwest, in New Mexico, and in the Californias, Indians lived in permanent or semipermanent communities and were agriculturalists. But among nomadic hunters and gatherers in the territories of the borderlands, it was a vain hope. Once the Indians had become mobile by acquiring horses (through theft, trade, or rounding up wild strays), they were impossible to congregate for the task of conversion. Without conversion, voluntary or forced, the process of "civilization" as the Spanish defined it was impossible.

In all areas of the borderlands, Indians were eager to accept the material goods that the Europeans had brought with them to the New World: horses for transportation; sheep for wool; and cattle, chickens, and pigs for meat. They appreciated the olive and fruit trees the missionaries transported from Spain. They valued highly iron pots, knives, and metal implements of all kinds, as well as muskets and ammunition, although the latter two items were not always obtainable. These things changed Indian patterns of life. Tribes formerly on foot became mobile, and the buffalo-hunting bands of the Great Plains flourished for a few hundred years. Nomads sought to trade with the Spanish in their communities; the annual trade fair at Taos, New Mexico, brought Comanche, Ute, Apache, and other tribes to a degree into the economic marketplace

of the borderlands. (Unfortunately, one of the most commonly traded commodities at that fair were captives, either Spaniards or Christianized natives; once the Indians learned that the Spanish always ransomed such unfortunates, they deliberately stepped up their kidnapping of such people.) In matters of trade and war, Indians were nothing if not adaptable; in New Mexico Spaniards encountered bands riding horses, wearing leather armor, and carrying muskets and even, in one case, a bugle, all taken on raids. In eastern Texas they found to their horror evidence that renegade Frenchmen were teaching the Indians to make gunpowder.

But nearly everywhere Indian-Spanish acculturation was limited to the material. Natives usually rejected Christianity as incomprehensible or irrelevant to their worldview; where the missionaries made a foothold, they invariably learned that a sort of syncretic faith had arisen in which the Indians had added Christian beliefs and divinities to their own deities and cosmological universe. Missionaries who insisted too intolerantly on the exclusivity of their faith over that of their charges were rebuffed. And except in rare cases, the Indians resented the tutelage of the friars and, even more fiercely, that of the Indians of other tribes or persons of mixed blood whom the missionaries placed over them.

The interaction of European and Native American created an enormous stirring and intermixing of peoples throughout the borderlands. The destruction, through war or disease, of bands or tribal groups gave rise to new associations, even "supertribes," that arose from the amalgamation of disparate groups. The union of Europeans, blacks, and Indians gave rise to new peoples: mestizos, mulattoes, *coyotes, lobos,* and many other persons of mixed blood. These people often found themselves with no fixed place in the social order, and accordingly, many became outcasts, vagabonds, and renegades, existing between aboriginal and European society with no place in either.

Thousands of Indians ran away from their missionary communities to become vagabonds, to work in Spanish mining and ranching establishments, and to join gangs of Apache and outcasts from European society. Others became translators, guides, and spies for the Spanish; Opata served as auxiliaries in many campaigns against the Apache. Whole communities of detribalized Indians, the *genízaros* of New Mexico, who were baptized and lived near Spanish towns, worked as stockmen or laborers for the Europeans and served as soldiers against the Comanche. (*Genízaros* is Spanish for janissaries, the famed Christian warriors of the Ottoman Empire.)

A vast and tragic traffic in human beings developed, as Spaniards enslaved first *chichimecas*, then Tepehuan and Tarahumara apostates, then Seri, and above all, Apache. Shipped to the mines in northern Mexico, to the *obrajes*, or woolen mills, of central Mexico, or even to the islands of the Caribbean, this traffic drained the nomadic bands and small communities of needed population. In retaliation the Indians kidnapped Europeans, especially women and children, converting the children to Indian ways and so reinforcing their bands. Later they resorted to such abductions in the certainty that the Spaniards would ransom back their people in exchange for goods.

Above all the result of interaction between Indians and Spaniards in the borderlands was continual change. War, trade, evangelization, miscegenation, and most important, disease, wrenched Indian societies out of their customary economic, political, and social patterns and forced them into new ones. Some tribes derived a new lease on life from these changes and flourished as new and hybrid societies for a limited period of time. But most were diminished in population, religious faith, economic independence, and cultural autonomy. Acculturation was a two-way street; the Spaniards themselves were forced to adapt to their new frontier. But technology, immunity from disease, material resources, and inherent belief in their own cultural superiority were on their side. The Indians of the borderlands were either exterminated, segregated, or absorbed culturally and genetically into the mestizo societies that arose in both Mexico and the United States. But the survival of traditions among groups such as the Yaqui, the many Apache nations, and the Pueblo Indians demonstrates that Indian-Spanish cultural contact did not result in a complete victory for the Europeans. That survival testifies to the strength of enduring culture among Native Americans in the borderlands.

BIBLIOGRAPHY

Alessio Robles, Vito. *Coahuila y Texas en la época colonial.* Mexico City, 1983. A massive history, based on primary Spanish archival sources, of the settlement of Coahuila and Texas. Especially good on mission establishment and land and labor institutions on the frontier, a much-neglected subject in borderland studies.

Bannon, John Francis. *The Spanish Borderlands Frontier, 1513–1821.* New York, 1970. To date the only synthesis of all of borderland history, from the conquistadores to the end of the colonial period. Mainly chronological, it has been superseded by the many ethnohistorical works that have appeared since its publication; it remains, however, a basic tool for borderland history.

Bolton, Herbert E. "The Mission As a Frontier Institution in the Spanish-American Colonies." *American Historical Review* 23, no. 1 (1917):42–61. A pioneering essay, in which Bolton, the father of borderland studies at the University of California at Berkeley, emphasizes the crucial importance of the mission as a frontier institution. Bolton, a deeply romantic historian, admired the Spanish missionaries and is much less critical of their role in acculturation than later historians.

———. *Texas in the Middle Eighteenth Century.* Berkeley, Calif., 1915. A well-documented work on the establishment of Spanish colonization in Texas.

Cuello, José. "Beyond the 'Borderlands' Is the North of Colonial Mexico: A Latin-Americanist Perspective to the Study of the Mexican North and the United States Southwest." In *Proceedings of the Pacific Coast Council on Latin American Studies,* edited by Kristyna P. Damaree. San Diego, Calif., 1982. A controversial revisionist paper in which Cuello argues that United States historians have "colonized" borderland history and that it should be reclaimed by Latin Americanists. A provocative and thoughtful essay.

Deeds, Susan M. "Rural Work in Nueva Vizcaya: Forms of Labor Coercion on the Periphery." *Hispanic American Historical Review* 69, no. 3 (1989): 425–449. Deeds examines slavery and the labor institutions of *encomienda* and *repartimiento* in the frontier economy. An insightful look into a much-neglected area.

Dunne, Peter Masten. *Pioneer Black Robes on the West Coast.* Berkeley, Calif., 1940. A moving, if somewhat biased (Dunne was a Jesuit), examination of the missionary work of the Jesuits in northwestern New Spain.

Forbes, Jack D. *Apache, Navaho, and Spaniard.* Norman, Okla., 1960. A biting examination of the interaction of Spaniards and Indians in New Mexico. Forbes leaves little doubt that the Spanish acted like cruel, greedy barbarians in their conquest of the Pueblo Indians.

Gannon, Michael V. *The Cross in the Sand: The Early Catholic Church in Florida, 1513–1870.* Gainesville, Fla., 1965. Standard reference work on Spanish missionization in Florida.

Griffen, William B. *Culture Change and Shifting Populations in Central Northern Mexico.* Anthropological Papers of the University of Arizona, no. 13. Tucson, Ariz., 1969. A superb ethnohistorical examination of acculturation among the Indians of the central northern borderlands, an area usually slighted for study of other areas such as Sonora, New Mexico, and Texas.

Gutiérrez, Ramón A. *When Jesus Came, the Corn Mothers Went Away: Marriage, Sexuality, and Power in New Mexico, 1500–1846.* Stanford, Calif., 1991. A daring, if unorthodox, examination of gender, marriage, and power within New Mexican society. Excellent overview of missionary-Indian relations and the Pueblo Revolt of 1680.

Hackett, Charles W. *Historical Documents Relating to New Mexico, Nueva Vizcaya, and Approaches Thereto, to 1773.* 3 vols. Washington, D.C., 1923–1937. A massive, three-volume accumulation of Spanish primary documents on New Mexico and other borderland provinces. Particularly illuminating on the Pueblo Revolt of 1680 and the warfare between the Spaniards and the Apache.

Hann, John H. *Apalachee: The Land Between the Rivers.* Gainesville, Fla., 1988. Excellent ethnohistorical study of the Florida Indian experience.

Hu-DeHart, Evelyn. *Missionaries, Miners, and Indians: Spanish Contact with the Yaqui Nation of Northwestern New Spain, 1533–1820.* Tucson, Ariz., 1981. This book is the standard work on Spanish interaction with the Yaqui nation of Sonora.

Jackson, Robert H. "Demographic Change in Northwestern New Spain." *The Americas* 41, no. 4 (1985):462–479. Jackson has written widely on the depopulation that disease caused among Indians in both the northwestern borderlands and the Californias. This article discusses not only demographic loss but the changes that those losses caused in Indian society.

John, Elizabeth A. H. *Storms Brewed in Other Men's Worlds: The Confrontation of Indians, Spanish, and French in the Southwest, 1540–1794.* College Station, Tex., 1975. A massive, exhaustively documented, and sweeping work on the southwestern Indians of New Mexico and Texas and their relations with each other and the European powers that invaded their lands. A superb work of investigation and

writing, John's work is simply one of the best histories of war and peace in the borderlands available.

Jones, Oakah L. *Los Paisanos: Spanish Settlers on the Northern Frontier of New Spain.* Norman, Okla., 1979. Jones, a noted borderland scholar, examines the economic and social roots of Spanish life in frontier society.

Kessel, John. *Friars, Soldiers, and Reformers: Hispanic America and the Sonora Mission Frontier, 1767–1856.* Tucson, Ariz., 1976. Kessel has written a number of works on the missionaries and Indians of the Arizona frontier. His work is particularly readable and sympathetic to Native Americans.

Mirafuentes Galván, José Luis. *Movimientos de resistencia y rebeliones indígenas en el norte de México, 1680–1821.* Mexico City, 1975. A number of important primary documents on Indian rebellions, along with a good synthesis on resistance movements.

Morrisey, Richard J. "The Northward Expansion of Cattle Ranching in New Spain, 1550–1600." *Agricultural History* 25, no. 3 (1951):115–121. A little-known but excellent article on the crucial role of cattle ranching in the settlement of the borderlands.

Navarro García, Luis. *Sonora y Sinaloa en el siglo XVII.* Seville, Spain, 1967. Navarro García's work on Sonora and Sinaloa, written from primary archival sources, is the standard history of the conquest and settlement of the two provinces.

Nentvig, Juan. *Rudo Ensayo: A Description of Sonora and Arizona in 1764.* Edited and translated by Alberto Francisco Pradeau and Robert R. Rasmussen. Tucson, Ariz., 1980. Nentvig, a Jesuit father, traveled throughout Sonora and left a detailed description of the people and land of the province. A crucial primary source, not only for its wealth of geographic and ethnographic material, but also because it illuminates the attitudes and prejudices of the European missionaries toward the Indians.

Pffeferkorn, Ignaz. *Sonora: A Description of the Province.* Edited and translated by Theodore E. Treutline. Albuquerque, N.Mex., 1949. Another primary document on the Sonoran frontier as seen by a missionary.

Powell, Philip Wayne. "The Chichimecas: Scourge of the Silver Frontier in Sixteenth-Century Mexico." *Hispanic American Historical Review* 25, no. 3 (1945):315–338. Powell has written several books on the first war between nomadic Indian raiders and Spaniards. The Spaniards learned lessons in their war against the Chichimeca that they were to use over and over again against the Apache in the following centuries.

Radding de Murieta, Cynthia. "La minería en la economía colonial de Sonora." *Revista universitaria de Sonora* 2 (1977):4–10. An extremely important paper that explores the mining town as the center of economic, cultural, and racial contact between Spaniard and Indian.

Spicer, Edward H. *Cycles of Conquest: The Impact of Spain, Mexico, and the United States on the Indians of the Southwest, 1533–1960.* Tucson, Ariz., 1962. One of the finest ethnohistorical works written on the cultural changes that the Indians of the Southwest underwent over the course of several centuries. Excellent on the Tarahumara, Yaqui, and Pueblo peoples and their struggle to survive in the face of war, disease, and forced conversion.

Stern, Peter. "The White Indians of the Borderlands." *Journal of the Southwest* 33, no. 3 (1991):262–281. An examination of the phenomenon of transculturation among Spanish, mestizo, and mulatto captives.

Thomas, Alfred Barnaby. *The Plains Indians and New Mexico, 1752–1778.* Albuquerque, N.Mex., 1940. Thomas authored a number of pioneering works on the Spanish conquest of the Southwest; particularly important is his use of translated primary documents, which are reproduced in his work.

Weber, David J. "John Francis Bannon and the Historiography of the Spanish Borderlands: Retrospect and Prospect." *Journal of the Southwest* 29, no. 4 (1987):331–363.

———. "Turner, the Boltonians, and the Borderlands." *American Historical Review* 91, no. 1 (1986):66–81. Weber (who is writing a synthesis of borderland history that should update Bannon with more recent ethnohistoric work) discusses both the enormous historiography of the borderlands and the many controversies that have attended the various schools of research on the frontier. Together the two bibliographies cited here are the best guides available on the literature of borderland history.

Worcester, Donald. "The Spread of Spanish Horses in the Southwest, 1700–1800." *New Mexico Historical Review* 20 (1945):1–13. Worcester was one of the first historians to examine the tremendous impact of the spread of the horse on Indian society. He also laid to rest the myth that a few horses left behind by Coronado multiplied to furnish the enormous herds of the American Great Plains.

Peter A. Stern

SEE ALSO **Detribalized and Manumitted Indians; The First Americans; The Fur Trade; Interracial Societies;** and **Medical Practice, Health and Disease;** the maps accompanying **The First Americans.**

132

MISSION COMMUNITIES

IT IS GENERALLY ACCEPTED by archaeologists and anthropologists that human beings were living in the Western Hemisphere at least thirty thousand years ago. They may have arrived on foot much earlier than that, but during the Fourth Pleistocene enough tundra was exposed to form a land bridge across the Bering Straits. Game animals and their hunters easily made their way from Siberia to the Americas. These people gradually populated the entire hemisphere and created a wide variety of cultural patterns. At the time of contact with Europeans, there were approximately 2,000 separate Native civilizations flourishing in the New World, with at least 350 of them in the area that would become the United States.

When Christopher Columbus encountered some of these indigenous groups in 1492, he referred to them as "los Indios" in the belief that he had reached the Asian subcontinent. Further exploration disproved that idea, but the name for Native Americans remained. Explorers and conquerors generally viewed Indians as an exploitable resource, cheap labor for mines and plantations with few personal rights. After much debate about the humanity and intellectual capacity of Indians, Pope Paul III issued *Sublimis Deus* in 1537, a bull affirming the spiritual equality of all people and supporting the missionary efforts of those who sought to bring natives into the Catholic church. Evangelical work had actually begun shortly after first contact, most of it

conducted by Franciscans, and numerous mission stations had already been established in Mexico and Central America. The pope's declaration simply made it easier for missionaries to pursue their efforts amid the brutalities of warfare and the *encomienda* system of extracting tribute and labor from Native Americans.

THE SPANISH BORDERLANDS

In 1513 Juan Ponce de Léon charted the coast of territory north of Cuba; eight years later he died during an attempt to settle on the western coast of Florida. In 1528 Pánfilo de Narváez led a similar expedition, and it, too, failed. A Franciscan who accompanied this colonizing force was Juan Suárez, one of the first of twelve friars to enter Mexico, but he perished along with most of his fellow passengers in a shipwreck near the mouth of the Mississippi River. Among the few survivors was Alvar Núñez Cabeza de Vaca, and his subsequent wanderings in northern Mexico had a direct bearing on mission activity in what eventually became the U.S. Southwest.

But the Florida mainland still held promise and, spurred by the presence of unwanted French Huguenots, Spanish authorities established Saint Augustine in 1565. This first permanent settlement within the future United States also contained the first Catholic parish and served as a base for missions into the interior.

133

Farther north, Spanish Jesuits tried between 1566 and 1571 to plant missions among natives in Georgia, South Carolina, and Virginia; all of them, however, ended in death and ruin. Franciscan ventures in Florida fared considerably better, especially among the Timucuan and Apalachee tribes. In 1595 missionary work began in earnest with the arrival of Juan de Silva. Some friars, such as Francisco Pareja, mastered local dialects and succeeded in influencing Native practices. By 1606 converts had grown to two thousand, enough to warrant a visit from the bishop of Santiago de Cuba to preside over their confirmation.

Three decades later the estimated number of Christianized Indians was ten times that number, but things declined rapidly after reaching that apogee. One reason for decline was that Florida was never self-sustaining and had to be supplied from the outside. Another was that several tribes like the Guales and Westoes had always been hostile to Spanish presence, and their attacks hastened the end of many evangelical stations. Incursions from English colonists to the north also contributed to their collapse. Missionary work in the borderlands ended here but flourished much better a thousand miles (1,600 kilometers) west of the Florida Peninsula.

Early Incursions into the Southwest

In 1536 Cabeza de Vaca and three companions arrived in Mexico City after an eight-year trek through northern Mexico. Their mere arrival after so many years startled everyone, but their tales of reportedly rich Indian cities revived dreams of wealth for the taking. Three years later a Franciscan, Marcos de Niza, led a small party, including a black servant named Estevanico, to locate the fabled cities. Estevanico knew the Rio Grande Valley because he had accompanied Cabeza de Vaca in his prior travels. But upon returning to territory inhabited by Zuni Indians, Estevanico was unexpectedly slain, and de Niza investigated no further. He returned instead to the capital in 1539 and, without evidence, confirmed rumors of wealthy civilizations on the northern edges of New Spain.

In 1540 Francisco Vásquez de Coronado received permission to explore lands that later became Arizona and New Mexico. There he made contact with various Pueblo tribes, earning the resentment of some by commandeering their food and houses for winter quarters, and then he scoured the area in search of precious metals. He went as far west as the Grand Canyon and as far east as central Kansas, all to no avail. Three Franciscans went with him: Juan de Padilla, Juan de la Cruz, and Luis de Ubeda. After Coronado admitted failure and returned home, these three stayed behind. Later reports disclosed that Padilla and his co-workers were killed very shortly thereafter at their tiny missions in Kansas and the Texas panhandle. No one replaced these evangelical pioneers, but they are often mentioned as protomartyrs of the missionary movement in the borderlands.

Reducing the Pueblos

After Coronado's failure several other explorations—sanctioned and unsanctioned—were attempted, with little result. Finally in 1598 an aristocrat named Juan de Oñate received royal permission to colonize land along the Rio Grande north of present-day El Paso. Early that year he led four hundred colonists, including twelve Franciscans under Alonso Martínez, to that region to engage in ranching and to provide the local Pueblo Indians with the benefits of Christian culture. The Indians had probably lived there for millennia in permanent, independent towns, back to the time of their forebears, the cliff-dwelling Anasazis. They spoke a variety of dialects in the Keresan and Tanoan language families. More than one hundred towns with names like Acoma and Isleta, Nambe and Taos, boasted large fields of maize, beans, and squash that supported an estimated population of over eighty thousand people. The inhabitants had a stable economy, elaborate social structures, and a sophisticated religion. Their peaceable way of life and adequate physical comforts, together with their intricate theology and diversified liturgical practices, placed them far above neighboring tribes and made their civilization superior to most other North American civilizations as well.

But Spaniards did not appreciate the virtues of Pueblo civilization. They had already made up their minds about Indian cultures as a whole and viewed them all with undiscriminating disdain. This was equally true of the Franciscans. Accustomed to cooperating closely with government officials, the Franciscans chose to represent Christianity as complementary to Spanish civilization and sought to bring both to the Indians (in contrast with the Jesuits, who will be discussed below). As emissaries of Iberian culture, the friars, too, looked down upon technologically underdeveloped societies, and their attitude toward Native religions was also decidedly negative. As soon as Franciscans saw pagan images and evidence of human sacrifice in Mexico in the 1520s, they formed the unalterable conviction that all Indian religions were idolatrous and benighted. They saw nothing whatever to admire in Native faiths and believed that the first step toward saving souls was to crush earlier beliefs and fill the vacuum with proper faith. Church and state worked closely together, conducting a unified program to "reduce" the Indians to "correct" standards of behavior based on acceptable ideological foundations.

So the Pueblos were confronted by outsiders who wanted to change their political orientation by making them subjects to the Spanish king, to save their souls by making them members of the Roman Catholic church, and to Hispanicize their culture. At first things went well, primarily because Pueblos were trained from childhood to be cooperative and adaptable to the predominant social pressures. After an exceptionally bloody confrontation at Acoma, leaders in most towns expressed polite interest in Christianity and acquiesced in baptism at the hands of visiting friars. Some colonists became discouraged in the early years and wanted to abandon their venture, but by 1609 it was officially decided that New Mexico would remain a component of the Spanish Empire. In 1610 colonists built Santa Fe to serve as headquarters for secular government, and in the same year Franciscans established their base of operations at a pueblo named Santo Domingo.

Franciscan Missionary Techniques. Mission territory comprised some eighty-seven thousand square miles (223,000 square kilometers). The friars divided into seven districts and tried to spread their meager personnel over the entire area. This approach had significant implications for the way in which missionary work was conducted. Even though the Crown subsidized missions, providing for more than sixty missionaries

annually, there were hardly ever as many as forty present at any one time. In order for the short-handed staff to reach the greatest possible number of towns, preachers traveled from one place to another, returning to a given site at intervals but unable to spend enough time anywhere to maintain continuous relationships.

If the term "mission communities" implies a group of people with a resident priest who maintains a core of believers and augments it through further conversions, then such communities did not exist in New Mexico during the seventeenth century. Instead of groups centered around a permanent missionary as its nucleus, precontact Indian communities persisted in a state of semiautonomy. The friars linked them arbitrarily into circuits, assigned various itineraries for traveling preachers to follow, and in this manner provided for New Mexico's spiritual needs as best they could.

It was Franciscan policy that no individual could stay in one assignment for very long. Most missionaries came up from Mexico City, preached on circuits for a few years, and returned. Very few remained as long as ten years, and a decade's service on the upper reaches of the Rio Grande was the exception rather than the rule. Short-term duties and constant rotation of personnel were ways to ensure that Franciscans would not become inordinately fond of any single place or people. This policy may have been good for the missionaries' virtue, but it also ensured that Native understanding of Christian beliefs and behavior would remain superficial. A visiting friar could hardly get to know the people in a town, let alone earn their trust, through sporadic contacts over the course of a few years.

Franciscan mission technique had the additional deficiency of ignoring local languages. Missionaries did not stay in one place long enough to learn how to use any dialect effectively. The single exception was Jerónimo de Zárate Salmerón who mastered the Jemez dialect and wrote several books in it. There is no evidence that the friars tried consistently to translate scripture, prayers, catechism, or creeds into any of the Pueblo tongues. Instead the local population was expected to learn Spanish, and of course those who attended church were expected to use the appropriate Latin terminology. This linguistic subtheme is consistent with the overall attitude that Spaniards held regarding Indian ways; namely, that they would have to abandon traditional patterns and adopt European usages if they hoped to improve themselves.

Pueblo Religion and Christianity. Despite these impediments to conversion, some natives did accept Christianity rather enthusiastically. It is impossible to tabulate numbers with much accuracy, but there were enclaves of Pueblo Christians in the some two-dozen Native towns that had survived conquest. Alonso de Benavides was custodian of New Mexican missions from 1625 to 1629. In memoirs written several years later, he claimed that some thirty-four thousand Indians had become faithful members of the church. His estimate is undoubtedly too high, but the number of baptized converts was probably well into the thousands of people.

For most Pueblo Indians, however, Christianity was tangential to their lives. An indication of this was their placement of churches. When there were enough converts to warrant building a place of worship, townspeople (sometimes under levy) constructed a church of suitable size. But these sanctuaries were always placed outside the village proper. Pueblo towns consisted of from two- to three-story apartment dwellings made of mud-glazed stone with no windows or doors (the entrance was in the ceiling), built to form a hollow rectangle that served as the town plaza. In this plaza were sunken ceremonial chambers called kivas, in which sacred rituals were performed to give meaning and purpose to everyday life. Churches were never built in a plaza. The plazas were at the center of Pueblo life, while the churches were obtrusions that did not fit the Native scheme of things but could be tolerated if kept sufficiently distant from what really counted.

Pueblos based their pre-contact values and activities on the conviction that all derived from guidelines that had been given to them by the gods, known collectively as kachinas. The gods had led them up several levels from the underworld to a place of emergence called *shipapu*. At the *shipapu* the people were taught how to hunt, plant crops, build houses, and organize their social life. All patterns for coping with affairs on earth were divinely inspired; adhering

to them was a sacred obligation required by benevolent kachinas—especially Iatiku, the chief female deity—who had human welfare uppermost in their minds. Pueblos joined voluntary associations to preserve divine teachings and to perform ritual obligations. Leaders of these associations were priests with a solemn responsibility to ensure that traditional lore remain unchanged and that liturgical performance give proper orientation to the prosaic tasks of survival.

Kivas were the central area for Pueblo holy work. We know very little about what actually took place in those chambers, which were usually built underground. But they were unmistakably churches in the Native scheme of things, and the crucial ritual activities performed there generated an energy and direction for all that happened thereafter. Various voluntary associations corresponded to the many different tasks necessary for community existence: planting, irrigating, and harvesting, for example. Accomplishing work for the community meant recalling the kachinas' original teachings, and this the members of associations did in the kiva. When they emerged from their underground devotions, members wore masks and colorful regalia that depicted their gods. Symbolically, the human actors actually became kachinas in the eyes of community onlookers, representing tangible divine presence as they danced in the plaza with elaborate and colorful costumes. Townspeople observed the dances, recalled the kachinas who instructed them on coping with life on earth, and then went out to perform the physical labor necessary to fulfill divine instructions at the most mundane level.

It is clear that there were several common denominators underlying both Pueblo religion and Spanish Christianity. Both perspectives accepted the notion of divine power beyond human control directing worldly affairs. Each operated with the firm conviction that obedience to providential sanctions in this ordered world brought reward, while lack of compliance entailed dire consequences. Each religion was familiar with priesthoods, special rituals, symbolic regalia, and sacred vessels for worship, all of them associated with sanctuaries set aside exclusively for holy purposes. Both sides understood the importance of a religious calendar that regulated community life through an annual cycle. Even the Christian sacrament of baptism had a parallel in Pueblo ritual bathing, done most often as initiation into a voluntary association and involving head-washing and name-giving ceremonies.

Spanish missionaries either were blind to these similarities or chose to ignore them because differences between the religious systems struck them as more important. Perhaps most fundamental was the difference between polytheism on one side and monotheism on the other. The Judeo-Christian tradition was steeped in opposition to idolatry, and Pueblo religions seemed rife with it. Furthermore, the Pueblos' gods and goddesses came from the underworld rather than from heaven above, which to the missionaries was antithetical to the proper cosmological orientation. Pueblos viewed human nature differently, too. The Christian perspective taught by Spaniards held that everyone was tainted by sin and therefore in need of supernatural grace to rescue their souls from this perilous condition. Lacking salvation, people would suffer the agonies of eternal damnation. Pueblos did not think individuals were depraved or incapable of pleasing the gods of their own volition. They anticipated no hell and therefore did not especially welcome the proffered means of avoiding it.

Because of these observed incompatibilities and their many preconceived judgments regarding Native religions, the friars did not stress shared religious beliefs or practices. They chose, rather, to condemn Pueblo religion, and they felt they had a divine mandate to eliminate—by force if necessary—those aspects of Native faith that offended the one true God. They insisted that voluntary associations be forbidden to perform their pagan rituals in kivas and that the ceremonial chambers themselves be filled with rubble. They confiscated masks and all other dance materials, plus whatever additional liturgical paraphernalia they could lay their hands on, and burned it all. Whenever they discovered members of voluntary associations surreptitiously using new kivas or making new masks, they demanded that Indian leaders be whipped and fined for disobedience to evangelical regulations. The only way to deal with paganism and idolatry was, they thought, to root it out and destroy every vestige that reminded natives of what had flourished before the missionaries arrived.

The demands of the friars were not executed with the same zeal with which they were made. Actual compliance with missionary policy depended on the secular arm of the Spanish presence, and several governors and military leaders were indifferent, even hostile, to the friars and their overbearing requirements. Some civil servants helped carry out the Franciscans' evangelical warfare, but many did not. Nonenforcement frustrated the preachers, especially since they thought that Spain's decision of 1609 to remain in New Mexico had given them paramount authority there. New kivas, masks, and dances appeared to the degree that secular administrators defied the church's campaign against precontact worship patterns. But on the whole, during the seventeenth century the Pueblos were gradually deprived of their traditional religious practices and increasingly forced to conform outwardly to Christian beliefs.

The Pueblo Revolt of 1680. Repressive tactics were bound to create some ill feeling, but the habitually self-effacing Pueblos rarely expressed open discontent. When some did, the result was usually an isolated incident protesting local conditions. In 1639, for instance, Taos Indians killed two soldiers and a friar and destroyed the town's church before escaping reprisal by fleeing into the mountains. In several towns, including Jemez, there were protests in the form of mass meetings and threats of violence during the 1640s against the imprisonment and flogging of Native religious leaders. The Spanish government responded by hanging twenty-nine Pueblo priests and jailing many more. In 1650 several Tewa and Keres towns plotted to rid themselves of colonial domination, but authorities forestalled the incipient insurrection, hanging nine conspirators while sentencing many others to hard labor. On the whole, though, these symptoms of unrest seemed controllable, and the overall tendency of forced conformity appeared successful in barring natives from their preferred customs.

New circumstances, however, led to escalating discontent. Missionaries had long assured Pueblos that certain earthly blessings—particularly prosperity, health, and protection from enemies—would attend their acceptance of Spanish rule and Christian supervision. Between 1665 and 1672, however, New Mexico experienced a prolonged drought. As crops failed repeatedly, natives began to question the promise that the god of Christianity could sustain agricultural efforts. In 1671 a pestilence carried off many inhabitants, and the survivors wondered if the friars' deity was any better at controlling disease than at providing good weather. In 1672 marginal hunter-gatherer groups such as Apaches and Navajos, who were even more desperate than the farmers in the pueblos, began attacking towns in the Rio Grande Valley for foodstuffs. It seemed clear to the Pueblos that the king's promise of protection was as illusory as the other supposed advantages of conversion. Famine, disease, and mounting war casualties convinced most Pueblos that they had erred in accepting the outsiders' religion alongside their own. It was, they believed, necessary for them to return to the ways of the kachinas and, before it was too late, to restore the ritual patterns of their forebears.

Ironically, while Pueblos were embracing precontact religion in growing numbers, the ecclesiastical and secular wings of Spanish authority were reaching an unprecedented degree of accord. Juan Francisco de Treviño arrived in the early 1670s as the new governor and placed his office wholeheartedly at the disposal of missionary policy. More and more Pueblos rallied to their old faith in hopes of rectifying present circumstances, while Treviño acted on the clergy's demand that idolatry be destroyed once and for all. In 1675 the governor arrested forty-seven Native leaders on a variety of charges. One detainee committed suicide in prison; three others were hanged. The authorities bowed to popular protests by releasing the others after beating them severely. Among those released was a Tewa priest named Popé from the town of San Juan. He moved to remote Taos and there constructed an elaborate plan for unprecedented intertribal cooperation, the better to resist further foreign oppression.

In August 1680 the Spanish colonists were attacked by a unique alliance of Pueblos from all of the towns. Within a few days, the settlers were seeking safety in Santa Fe. However, the Pueblos overwhelmed the garrison there and hounded refugees as they fled southward toward El Paso. Native warriors were content to keep the outsiders moving along, wishing them good riddance instead of death. Out of 2,347 Spanish inhabitants only 401, or 17 percent of them, were killed. But there was a decidedly anticlerical aspect to the revolt. Out of the thirty-three missionaries there at the time, a total of twenty-one, or 64 percent, were killed. Angry Indians burned churches and destroyed records of baptisms, marriages, and burials while also razing all the statuary and altars they could find. Natives wanted every Spanish colonist out of their land, true enough, but they viewed missionaries as the central cause of their sufferings. This coordinated uprising expressed a determination to reject Christianity because it posed a direct threat to the Pueblos' integrated religion and culture. They hoped that after the revolt they could return to Native ways and cleave to the kachinas' perennial wisdom.

The Aftermath of the Revolt. Such was not to be. The inter-Pueblo coalition began to disintegrate as soon as the Spaniards had fled because their departure removed the need for further cooperation. Spanish authorities persisted over the next decade in trying to regain their troublesome jurisdiction and to redress insults to their honor. By 1696 government troops had succeeded in retaking all of the lost territory and in extinguishing the last sparks of revolt. While doing so they slaughtered natives in much higher numbers than the casualties sustained by the Spanish in 1680. The Native population, always declining under colonial influence, fell drastically during the years of reconquest. By 1700 there were no more than fourteen thousand Pueblos in the land close to *shipapu*.

After 1700 missions in New Mexico took on a different character. For one thing, investigators blamed missionary tactics for most of the earlier difficulties, and so Spanish authorities never allowed the friars to have as much power as they once had. For another, many of the surviving Pueblos fled the Rio Grande Valley to live among the Hopis in Arizona, beyond reach of the missionaries. Those who remained in their traditional homeland found other ways to resist Spanish domination. With the decrease of the missionaries' authority, it was possible for the Pueblos to accept foreign control over secular matters while simultaneously keeping the private sphere of religious sensibilities to themselves and preventing Christianity from making serious inroads into it. With their bifurcated frame of mind, known as compartmentalization, Pueblos were able to cooperate outwardly with dominant social patterns while maintaining the integrity of their ancient society. Their languages, kinship systems, and voluntary associations remained intact. Since 1700 they have occasionally added unobtrusive elements of Christianity to their traditional belief system without altering its solid, precontact core.

The Franciscans did not return to New Mexico in the same numbers as were there prior to expulsion, and after 1700 their activities shifted focus, too. Possibly having learned from earlier mistakes and wielding reduced authority, they evangelized less aggressively and relied more upon persuasion than repression to bring natives into the fold. In this post-revolt environment, missionary efforts proceeded no further than Native preferences allowed. The results were syncretistic amalgams of beliefs and behavior, creative blends of traditional ways with European trappings. In the meantime, as the eighteenth century progressed, Franciscans gravitated toward parish work in white settlements. By the time Mexico became an independent republic in 1821, friars had settled down alongside regular clergy as ministers to an overwhelmingly Hispanic population.

Missions in Early Texas

Missionary activities to the east of El Paso, in a vast land eventually named after the Tejas Indians, began in 1675 with the work of Juan Larios at a small settlement called San Ysidro. In ventures closer to the Mississippi River that mixed religion with political maneuvers against the French, Damian Massanet led six friars in ineffectual attempts to convert natives near the Neches River between 1690 and 1693. A more promising effort began in 1718, when a military and civilian contingent established San Antonio de Béjar in south central Texas. A Franciscan named Antonio de San Buenaventura Olivares worked near the *presidio* and founded a mission called San Antonio de Valero—later known as the Alamo. In 1720 friar Antonio Margil founded the mission of San José y San Miguel de Aguayo, just a few miles away, though not

without heated opposition from Olivares. There were numerous other activities in the borderlands north of Coahuila province throughout the eighteenth century. One notable effort centered on the mission of San Sabá and efforts to convert Apaches and Comanches. Work among those fiercely independent peoples was particularly frustrating and dangerous, especially in 1758 when a bloody uprising virtually destroyed the community and its personnel. Subsequent efforts among them were never very successful. Texas missions as a whole experienced repeated misfortunes and reverses. Their story contains many episodes of heroic faith and gallant deeds, but they produced few lasting results among the people who had called it home long before the Spanish arrived.

Kino in Pimería Alta

West of El Paso were lands drained by the Gila and Colorado rivers, known as Pimería Alta. Some Franciscans preached in the area among the Moqui Indians, but the New Mexican disaster of 1680 caused a general missionary withdrawal that included abandoning this region. In 1687 Eusebio Francisco Kino was one of three new missionaries reentering the Pimería Alta, and for the next quarter century he made considerable progress in establishing mission communities there. Kino was vaguely aware of conditions in the area, having served as head missionary in the Atondo expedition to Lower California between 1683 and 1685. The province of Sonora and lands northward were much more promising, and he pursued opportunities there with both zeal and tact. Most of the gains made in that area were due to this singularly gifted individual.

Kino did not look down on Indians, nor did he believe their ways of life and religions were utterly worthless. He approached them with soft words and a friendly manner, often giving small presents of dried fruit or trinkets to smooth initial contacts. In this, Kino's attitude differed markedly from that of most Franciscan missionaries. He belonged to the Society of Jesus, and this institutional affiliation might help to explain his different perspective, though an element of personal choice probably figured in the equation as well. Unlike those—including the Franciscans—who believed that original sin deprived humanity of all virtue, the Jesuits generally thought that residual capabilities survived despite a state of sin. People like Kino proceeded on the theory that they could appeal successfully to human beings on a rational basis, instead of simply denouncing them, because they retained some worthwhile notions of divinity. Their mistaken ideas needed modification, of course, to bring them into line with Christian truth, but at least some common denominators existed upon which to build better religious understanding. So the Jesuit missionary approach during the seventeenth century was often much more positive and gentle than the concurrent Franciscan one.

The first mission founded in the community was named Nuestra Señora de los Dolores, and served as headquarters for Kino and his two companions as they crisscrossed Sonora. The people there were mostly Pimas, with Papagos to the north of them. Both of these tribes probably descended from the ancient Hohokam, who had flourished alongside the Anasazi, ancestors to the Pueblos. These sedentary, farming natives were generally peaceful, and many of the estimated thirty thousand population responded favorably to the Jesuits' patient ministrations. Converts gathered into enclaves of their own, and Kino eventually established more than twenty of them in such river valleys as San Miguel, Magdelena, Altar, Sonóita, Santa Cruz, and San Pedro. In addition to salvation, he introduced material benefits including wheat and other European cereal grains with which neophytes could enhance their diet. More important, he introduced cattle and other livestock. The twenty Christian settlements became ranches capable not only of feeding themselves but also of providing beef to outlying mission stations as well.

Over the years Kino traveled thousands of miles on horse and mule back, personally baptizing an estimated forty-five hundred Pimas. By his own admission he could have baptized many more, but he insisted on careful preparatory instruction and on catechizing instead of using the easy sacramental approach in order to inflate the statistics. In addition to his own direct efforts, Kino wisely utilized Christian Indians to win additional converts among their own people.

Total efforts of all missionaries in the region during his lifetime resulted in thirty thousand people baptized into the church. Communities of these Christians were almost as self-sufficient spiritually as they were economically. While Jesuits visited them regularly, Native lay leaders under missionary tutelage provided spiritual counsel on a continuous basis. Raids conducted by marauding Apache and Yuma (or Quechan) warriors were a danger for the missionaries, but nevertheless Kino made his rounds and conducted at least forty trips through the countryside. Reports of his work convinced European cartographers that Lower California was not an island but a peninsula. He planned to build a road around the head of the Gulf of California, but it was left to a later generation of missionaries to accomplish this.

In 1700 Kino participated in founding San Xavier del Bac in what later became Arizona. In addition to that venerable mission, he and three associates established San Gabriel de Guevavi and San Cayetano de Tumacácori. Finally in 1711 this soul of enterprise and foresight, also known as "the apostle of Sonora and Arizona," died of natural causes, and his missions fell into disrepair through neglect. During the early 1730s, two Jesuits named Ignacio Xavier Keller and Jacob Sedelmayr made the only effort to revive Kino's work, but it was ultimately ineffectual.

In 1767 all Jesuits were expelled from Spanish territories as a result of high-level decisions by papal and royal authorities. All missions reverted to Franciscan supervision. The most notable individual in the last phase of mission history was Francisco Garcés, who was based at San Xavier del Bac. He built a church at Tucson, a new *presidio* established near San Xavier del Bac in 1776, and persevered in efforts to spread gospel teachings among surrounding natives. In 1781 his name was added to the lengthening list of martyr missionaries when he fell victim to the warlike Yumas.

Serra and the California Missionaries

Northwest of Tucson the fruitful lands of California beckoned, but the Spanish did not explore the region seriously until Russian traders began probing down the Pacific coast. However, when Gaspar de Portolá led an expedition into Upper California in 1769, a seasoned Franciscan missionary of remarkable fortitude and skill accompanied him. Junípero Serra first gained fame as a professor of philosophy and a pulpit orator in Spain. Then he added nearly two decades of missionary and college administration experience in central Mexico. When the Jesuits were expelled in 1767, he was named to supervise Eusebio Kino's old mission field in Sonora and Arizona. This widely experienced and capable president of missions was on hand when Portolá proposed to open a new section of the borderlands around the head of the Gulf of California. Few could anticipate at the time how deeply and durably Serra's contributions would affect the culture of this northernmost of Spain's territories.

The indigenous peoples of California were quite diverse, with very different ways of life. The many different groups scattered across that vast territory spoke six distinct languages and scores of separate dialects. Most of those influenced by Serra's missions spoke some version of Chumash or Penutian, the former group occupying the southern part of the region while the latter was located in pockets farther north. The Indian groups employed simple methods to exploit a bounteous environment. Most of them were hunter gatherers, and they roamed freely in the mild climate, going wherever the chase or seasonal wild plants led them. Simple methods of utilizing rich resources made for easy living, and few groups (except for some Chumash) thought it necessary to reside at regular town sites or to develop advanced handicrafts. Perhaps it was the ease of subsistence, together with the small size of most tribes, that made California Indians generally peaceable and serene. Whatever the reasons, there were very few hostile outbursts by natives in mission communities in this part of the borderlands.

The way Franciscans pursued their evangelical work in the eighteenth century was noticeably different from the techniques employed a hundred years earlier. Having developed a more sophisticated perspective and having learned that repressive measures yielded rebellion rather than obedience, the missionaries of Serra's generation treated natives gently and with patience. They still uncritically linked Christianity with Spanish culture but no longer tried to force the amalgam on reluctant subjects. They also continued to depend on the military for protection.

Serra and his colleagues explored new areas to establish additional missions, but they were always accompanied by a handful of soldiers, and every mission had its small garrison. This dependency often caused more strife than it prevented when the soldiers became unruly, and Franciscans clashed with their secular countrymen much more frequently than they did with the tractable natives.

The first two missionaries under Serra's supervision to reach Upper California did so by sea in April 1769. The main contingent, including Serra and other friars, traveled overland and arrived by midyear. Later in 1769 they founded the mission of San Diego, the first of nine established during Serra's lifetime. The following year he founded San Carlos Borromeo much farther north on Monterey Bay, choosing this second mission settlement as his headquarters. Franciscans, with Serra to guide them, subsequently founded San Antonio (1771), San Gabriel (1771), San Luis Obispo (1772), San Francisco de Assisi (1776), San Juan Capistrano (1776), Santa Clara (1777), and San Buenaventura (1782). As president of missions, Serra proved to be an effective administrator as well as a zealous spiritual shepherd. He inspected mission communities often, and his frequent visits maintained discipline among the clergy while mitigating feelings of isolation and neglect. Serra traveled thousands of miles by ship and on horseback; it is only pious legend that he journeyed everywhere on foot. During the fifteen crowning years of his life that he spent in California, Serra personally baptized an estimated six thousand people as a mark of their salvation.

Mission communities sought to provide for both the spiritual and temporal welfare of Native converts. There were usually two friars at each mission, and they offered religious instruction to enhance their charges' understanding of basic Christian doctrines and moral precepts. In addition they taught the Indians how to improve their standard of living by means of permanent dwellings, agriculture, and ranching. Missionaries also helped Christian Indians to acquire simple skills in weaving, carpentry, masonry, and blacksmithing. Cattle, grain, and manufactured products kindled as much interest as new religious teachings; ideas and material goods formed a mutually supporting whole that benefited natives while subtly eroding their former customs.

The earliest buildings in California mission communities were no better than the crude structures found in any frontier settlement. Most were simple cabins with dirt floors and thatch or sod roofs. In time these were replaced by adobe buildings with stone floors and tile roofs. Typical mission sites featured a rectangular enclosure that contained a church, a convent, dormitories, a school, storerooms, and workshops. Miles of surrounding countryside contained the orchards, gardens, fields, and livestock that fed and clothed local inhabitants. Daily life consisted of prayers, meals, work for adults either in the fields or at simple industries, and school for children. This satisfying round of duties gave mission communities a stability and tranquil regularity that prolonged Native survival while transforming them through the dissemination of European religion and technology.

Not everything European was necessarily beneficial, and one of the worst consequences for natives of European domination was racial-ethnic prejudice. In California the attitude of contempt for Indians was confined to civil and military personnel, but it was nonetheless virulent. Brutalities extending to murder and rape were commonplace among the soldiery, especially between 1770 and 1774, when Pedro Fages succeeded Portolá as military commander. Serra defended the natives' civil rights wherever he could, and when remonstrations with local authorities proved ineffectual, he traveled to Mexico City in 1773 to lay his demands for justice before the viceroy. That heroic effort gained some protection for the Indians by placing them exclusively under the friars' care, but missionary efforts were frequently impeded by conflicts and disputes between friars and secular authorities over mistreatment of the Indians.

Eighteenth-century Franciscans, in contrast to their seventeenth-century predecessors, were the champions of, rather than the chief offenders against, Native rights. Their efforts to protect the Indians' human rights strengthened Christian faith. Their failures to prevent abuse of Native Americans by other Spaniards allowed arrogant Europeans to deplete further the Indian population and doom Native cultures to eventual oblivion.

In 1784 Serra, "the apostle of California," died at San Carlos, Monterey-Carmel, after seventy years of notable accomplishments. His successor as head of missions was Fermín Francisco de Lasuén, who for the next eighteen years built on the solid foundations already in place. Special papal permission had been granted for the Franciscan supervisor to confirm natives as full members of the church. Serra had confirmed fifty-three hundred under this unique dispensation, and Lasuén confirmed another nine thousand during his administration. He also added nine more mission communities to the chain extending along the coast and inland. They were Santa Barbara (1786), Purísima Concepción (1787), Santa Cruz (1791), Soledad (1791), San José (1797), San Juan Bautista (1797), San Miguel (1797), San Fernando (1797), and San Luis Rey (1798). Three more mission communities were built in the nineteenth century, making a total of twenty-one erected within little more than fifty years. These last were Santa Inés (1804), San Rafael (1817), and San Francisco Solano (1823), located six hundred miles (960 kilometers) north of the original mission at San Diego.

The missions could take credit for some considerable successes. An estimated thirty thousand Indians were converted at that time in California. There were also significant material advances that made daily life more comfortable. At their peak, the mission communities collectively owned 230,000 cattle, 268,000 sheep, 8,300 goats, and 3,400 swine. In their most prosperous years, the mission farms yielded 125,000 bushels of grain together with a wealth of produce from vineyards and orchards. But in spite of this, the Indian population continued to dwindle even during the most prosperous years, primarily because of diseases.

By the early nineteenth century, Spain was fading quickly as an international power. One consequence was that missions received less financial aid. When an independent Mexican government demanded in 1834 that all missions be secularized—which involved the seizure of almost all mission land—the Franciscan enterprises were reduced to little more than architectural artifacts. Meanwhile, the real heart of the missions—the Native peoples themselves—had succumbed to disease and cultural despair due to perennial harassment at the hands of white people.

BORDERLAND MISSION COMMUNITIES

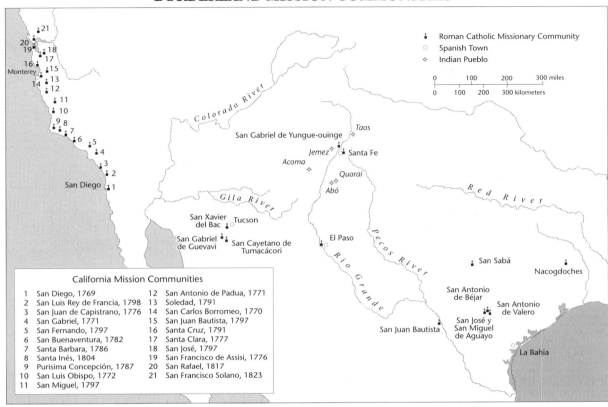

- ◉ Roman Catholic Missionary Community
- ○ Spanish Town
- ◇ Indian Pueblo

0 ___ 100 ___ 200 ___ 300 miles
0 ___ 100 ___ 200 ___ 300 kilometers

Colorado River

San Gabriel de Yungue-ouinge

Taos

Jemez ◇   Santa Fe

Acoma ◇

Quarai ◇

Abó ◇

San Diego

Gila River

San Xavier del Bac   Tucson

San Gabriel de Guevavi   San Cayetano de Tumacácori

El Paso

Rio Grande

Pecos River

Red River

San Sabá

Nacogdoches

San Antonio de Béjar

San Antonio de Valero

San José y San Miguel de Aguayo

San Juan Bautista

La Bahia

Monterey

21
20
19   18
16   17
14   15
13
12
11
10
9 8
7
6
5
4
3
2
1

California Mission Communities

1	San Diego, 1769	12	San Antonio de Padua, 1771
2	San Luis Rey de Francia, 1798	13	Soledad, 1791
3	San Juan de Capistrano, 1776	14	San Carlos Borromeo, 1770
4	San Gabriel, 1771	15	San Juan Bautista, 1797
5	San Fernando, 1797	16	Santa Cruz, 1791
6	San Buenaventura, 1782	17	Santa Clara, 1777
7	Santa Barbara, 1786	18	San José, 1797
8	Santa Inés, 1804	19	San Francisco de Assisi, 1776
9	Purisima Concepción, 1787	20	San Rafael, 1817
10	San Luis Obispo, 1772	21	San Francisco Solano, 1823
11	San Miguel, 1797		

MISSIONS IN NEW FRANCE

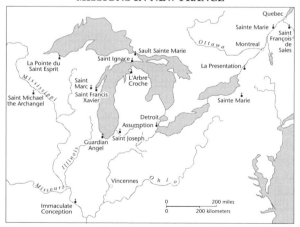

Quebec

Sainte Marie

Saint François de Sales

Ottawa

Montreal

Sault Sainte Marie

Saint Ignace

La Pointe du Saint Esprit

L'Arbre Croche

La Presentation

Mississippi

Saint Marc

Saint Francis Xavier

Saint Michael the Archangel

Detroit
Assumption

Sainte Marie

Guardian Angel

Saint Joseph

Illinois

Vincennes

Ohio

Missouri

Immaculate Conception

0 ___ 200 miles
0 ___ 200 kilometers

NEW ENGLAND MISSION COMMUNITIES, CIRCA 1670

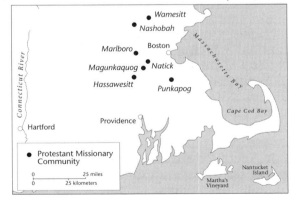

Wamesitt

Nashobah

Marlboro   Boston

Magunkaquog   *Natick*

Hassawesitt   *Punkapog*

Connecticut River

Massachusetts Bay

Cape Cod Bay

Hartford

Providence

Nantucket Island

Martha's Vineyard

- ● Protestant Missionary Community

0 ___ 25 miles
0 ___ 25 kilometers

THE FRENCH COLONIES

As early as 1504, Breton fishermen plied the cod rich waters off Acadia (Nova Scotia) and Newfoundland. But the first French explorer of any note was Jacques Cartier, who in 1534, 1535, and 1541 charted the northern Atlantic coastline and the Saint Lawrence River. Support for further exploration declined because of disruptions in Europe. It decreased still further after it became clear that New France contained no mineral wealth to rival Spanish possessions to the south. In 1603 Samuel de Champlain, recognizing the value of Canada's fish, fur, and timber, reinitiated French enterprise in the New World. In 1608 he built the first permanent trading post, Quebec City. Whenever Champlain made treaties or trade agreements with natives, he included a codicil providing for missionary contact with the Indians. This genuinely pious gesture introduced Christianity to the various Laurentian tribal groups and had a particularly significant impact in a large confederacy known as the Hurons.

Jesuit Missionary Principles

The first missionaries in New France were a reform branch of the Franciscan order called Récollets. In 1615 four friars, Joseph Le Caron, Denys Jamet, Jean Dolbeau, and Pacifique Duplessis, devoted themselves to the Algonquian-speaking Indians in the lower Saint Lawrence Valley. Some of them also accompanied Champlain on his journeys to the Great Lakes, scattering the first evangelical seeds among the Hurons in the winter of 1615–1616 and again in 1623–1624. Franciscan missionary policy depended heavily on European colonization, and since the French trading companies did not encourage permanent settlers, it was soon apparent that laborers from another monastic order would be needed to pursue matters successfully. So a new era began in 1625 when three Jesuit volunteers, Charles Lalemant, Jean de Brébeuf, and Ennemond Massé, arrived in Quebec. Brébeuf lived alone with the Hurons from 1626 to 1629. Squabbles between British and French forces interrupted missionary work during the next few years, but Brébeuf and several others returned in 1634 to spend the rest of their lives among the Hurons.

There they hoped to pattern their work on what their confreres had accomplished in Paraguay. In that South American country, Jesuits had produced a model missionary colony that not only converted natives to Christian beliefs and morality but also preserved essentials of their precontact civilization. The key to achieving religious change within cultural continuity was independence from other forms of European influence. Jesuits had always acted on the assumption that some good remained in pagan thought and society; they sought merely to improve indigenous concepts through exposure to Christian beliefs. They used precontact religions as a preliminary basis for discussing faith and then tried gradually to develop ideas about God and morality based on Judeo-Christian Scriptures. Native languages and symbols were retained, so that Indian versions of Christianity expressed Catholicism through indigenous forms. Jesuits did not tie gospel teachings to European customs or to the military, political, and economic designs of any particular Old World regime—they refused to act as representatives of any state. They lived among the Native peoples, and they often sought to guard natives from being contaminated by association with other Europeans. Their bold spiritual independence, and not infrequent physical courage, made French Jesuit mission communities quite different from the Spanish Franciscan ones discussed above.

The Jesuits and the Huron Indians

The relatively primitive Laurentian Indians, comprising many Algonquian tribes, were at a relatively primitive stage; but the Iroquoian-speaking Hurons of southern Canada (later Ontario province) enjoyed a much more complex culture with advanced material accomplishments. They cultivated large fields of maize, beans, and squash, supplementing those staples with hunting and fishing in the many lakes that dotted their territory. Semipermanent town sites featured log palisades for protection against raids and had room for dozens of longhouses within their walls. All townspeople who identified with a particular clan, through matrilineal descent, lived in the same longhouse. These structures were often fifty yards (45 meters) long, made of poles and beams and covered with thatch or overlapping sheets of bark. The most valued individual achievements in this society were restricted to males, with the most prestigious areas being warfare and trading. Political organization on the local level was fairly democratic, with everyone allowed to speak at town council fires. Beyond this Hurons were distinguished by having risen above tribalism to form a large confederacy that preserved peace among separate tribes as a means to enhance their mercantile success—a success made possible in the first instance by their central location between nonfarming Algonquians to the north and agricultural peoples to the south.

Having reached Huronia in 1626, the Jesuits were tolerated there as an element of Champlain's trading alliances. For their own part, Brébeuf and his colleagues were determined to be as unobtrusive as they could, living as much as possible according to local ways of doing things. They spent years learning the Native dialects, never insisting that Christian concepts were best confined to the French language. Jesuits dressed in European clothing, usually cassocks and boots, but they ate the same fare as the Hurons, disciplining themselves to overcome European tastes in order to share whatever was provided from the clans' cooking fires. Unlike Spanish Franciscans, these "blackrobes" were prepared to spend the rest of their lives among the same people. During the sixteen years of Jesuit missionary work among the Hurons, only five priests left the region because of some deficiency in health or resolution. Nineteen of the twenty-four sent there remained until they died at their posts or were forced out. Their apostolate began at villages like Ihonatiria and Ossossané and had developed enough positive response by 1639 to warrant building Sainte-Marie, a special compound and headquarters for more extensive mission work.

Evangelical efforts won converts for many reasons. Some natives thought Christian baptism could, like a talisman, protect them against illness; others saw church membership as providing an insider's advantage when trading in Quebec or Montreal. Most important, Jesuits stressed in quiet conversation how easily one could cross the bridge from indigenous concepts to Christian ones. Hurons already believed in divine power derived from sources above, principally associated with the sky, and their beliefs were compatible with European ideas of heaven. A significant deity named Aataentsic was a female entity with a ready counterpart in the Virgin Mary. Her son, Iouskeha, formed an obvious parallel to Jesus. Both religions understood that supernatural forces permeated everyday affairs and that it was important to interact harmoniously with them. Both had a keen sense that ritual and personal morality were sanctioned by a divine being or beings. In each, spiritual guidance was accessible through fasts and vigils that prepared one for meaningful religious experience. Personal encounters with divine power were a common bond between these two forms of religious consciousness.

Jesuits succeeded in making friends and winning converts by what they did not do as much as by what they did. They were not, as indicated above, overly fastidious regarding Native foods and language. While it made daily life somewhat capricious, missionaries did not decry as superstition the Huron practice of placing an inordinate emphasis on the importance of dreams. Instead they took advantage of it. As soon as someone dreamed of suffering the torments of hell—which was facilitated by vivid depictions on triptychs—the evangelists suggested that the need to convert was the meaning behind such a dream. Hurons brought captives home after raids into enemy territory. There they tortured the captives at leisure and, after ritual execution, consumed their bodies. Jesuits did not immediately denounce this occasional cannibalism or insist that it be stopped. They refused, however, to partake of such meals and tried to mitigate the practice through patient persuasion. They also tried to reduce the high frequency of divorce, but again through modest words geared to realistic goals.

Mission communities among Hurons did not consist of separate villages. Converts shared the same logistics and way of life as those who preferred precontact gods and rituals. Fifteen years after Brébeuf began serious evangelical labors in Huronia, some three thousand people had been baptized. Blackrobe priests gave the converts more attention in the form of liturgical leadership and Christian nurture, but they continued to follow Native practices in subsistence, dress, housing, trade, and warfare. They did, however, begin separating themselves physically from nonconverts, forming enclaves within the villages. As this separation gradually deepened, it made Huronia vulnerable to invasion.

In fact a shocking and unprecedented invasion did occur in 1648. That year the Iroquois League, another confederacy with a similar culture that was scattered across the Finger Lakes district of New York, inaugurated an unaccountably prolonged invasion of Huronia. These two intertribal leagues had been bitter enemies for centuries, but in the winter of 1648–1649 the Iroquois pursued a campaign of unprecedented conquest and devastation. Brébeuf and Gabriel Lalemant were executed at a town called Taenhatentaron in March 1649 while the remaining twenty Jesuits, lay assistants, and all surviving Hurons sought refuge on an island known as Gahoendoe (later Christian Island) in Georgian Bay of Lake Huron. About three thousand of the demoralized refugees sought baptism while in flight from the implacable Iroquois. But by 1650 the Huron confederacy was broken, with most of its members either killed or scattered. The mission to the Hurons was reluctantly declared to be at an end. The Jesuits and their straggling flock retreated to Quebec and in 1697 succeeded in establishing a Christian town named Jeune Lorette. This Canadian settlement was all that remained of the Christian community that the Jesuits had hoped to erect among the canny and capable Hurons.

When news of Brébeuf's and Lalemant's deaths reached other Jesuits, they celebrated Masses of thanksgiving, not mournful requiems. It had always been their practice to rejoice whenever a member of the order achieved martyrdom while serving the cause of missions. A similar Mass had been sung in 1646 when word came that Isaac Jogues had fallen at the hands of Iroquois warriors. His experiences up to that point illustrate both the zeal with which missionaries pursued their work and the extent to which they helped explore the farther reaches of New France.

The Jesuits and the Iroquois

After living among the Hurons from 1636 to 1641, Jogues volunteered to accompany a group of western Indians known as Ojibwas (or Chippewas) on a return voyage home. He and Charles Raymbault traveled with the natives along customary waterways to reach Ojibwa country in

what later became Michigan and Wisconsin. At the junction of Lakes Superior and Huron they named the rapids Sault Sainte Marie. The two blackrobes wintered in Native quarters but traveled to Quebec in the summer of 1642 for supplies and medical care. Jogues recruited two lay assistants and in August set out for western lands again. But the party was seized by Mohawks, one of the five tribes of the Iroquois confederacy, who routinely ambushed traders hazarding trips to Quebec. Thus it was as captives that Jesuits first entered the future state of New York.

The Iroquois treated prisoners the same way the Hurons did, and Jogues and his helpers were tortured and mutilated in the traditional manner. One of them, René Goupil, died from such treatment, but Jogues was spared execution and made to perform menial labor. Even under such precarious conditions, he managed to baptize over fifty sick and dying children. When the Mohawks visited Fort Orange (Albany) in the spring of 1643, Jogues was ransomed and helped to escape by the resident Dutch Reformed minister. Upon his return to France he was lionized, and his popularity induced many others to volunteer for missions in the New World.

In 1644 Jogues returned to Canada. The following year it seemed possible that French officials might reach a peace agreement with the troublesome Mohawks. Jogues helped the two sides reconcile their differences and immediately asked for permission to enter Iroquois lands after the treaty was signed. Peace was fragile if not illusory. Finally in October 1646 Jogues was summarily killed by those who thought he was responsible for recent sickness and poor harvests.

During the next decade several other priests under Claude Dablon tried to revive missions among the Iroquois, but their efforts, too, were a failure. The logic of the situation was simple and irreversible: the Iroquois hated the Hurons and anyone allied with them; because of French-Huron trading pacts, the Iroquois developed an abiding hostility to the French; and since Catholicism was introduced through French missionaries, the Iroquois League firmly disdained it. Any Christian influences on the Iroquois came from the Dutch and English Protestants who were their Hudson River trading partners.

Not all Laurentian endeavors ended as disastrously as the one in Huronia. By the late 1600s, several groups of Iroquoian-speaking natives had gathered in communities near French population centers. Christian Mohawks settled at Sault Saint-Louis in the 1680s, and other Iroquois converts gathered at La Presention mission near present-day Ogdensburg. This community's most famous resident was probably an Indian girl, Catherine Tekakwitha, who embodied Catholic piety in colonial New France. A mission community for Algonquians and Nipissing was established by Sulpician fathers quite close to Montreal, and its successful growth required its transfer to Oka near the mouth of the Ottawa River. In Maine and eastern Canada, tribes of the Abnaki suffered increasingly from rapacious and land hungry New Englanders. Many converts to French Catholicism moved to the Saint Lawrence Valley for greater protection and the freedom to practice their faith.

One of their particularly successful settlements was Saint-Francois de Sales, led during its heyday by Jacques Bigot, S.J., and located near the falls of the Chaudière River. Such communities survived over the years and transmitted Christian ideas to successive generations. In the 1830s Pierre Jean DeSmet received Blackfoot Indians in his Saint Louis office. These Native Americans had traveled from Idaho to Missouri in search of Jesuits because "Iroquois Indians" had told them that blackrobe missionaries could be trusted. Those "Iroquois" were probably products of the Laurentian communities who, in their travels west for the Hudson's Bay Company, had spread their faith into the Rockies.

Missions to the Western Indians

Meanwhile, missions to the Ojibwas and lesser tribes were not abandoned. In 1660 René Ménard made his way along the southern shore of Lake Superior to Keweenaw Bay. There he established a small community for Christian Indians, and when spring came the next year he set out to reach a similar camp to the southwest in Wisconsin. He apparently lost his way and was never heard from again. But the pioneering examples of Jogues and Ménard led in 1664 to the appointment of another explorer-evangelist for the western region, this one a truly effective missionary whose career spanned the next quarter of a century. Claude Jean Allouez arrived at Sault Sainte Marie in September 1665 with

seven years of missionary experience already to his credit. He pushed on to the western end of Lake Superior and erected a bark chapel on the shore of Chequamegon Bay, naming his first mission station La Pointe du Saint Esprit.

Natives frequented La Pointe because fish were plentiful there. Some of the better-known tribes that frequented the area were the Miamis, Menominees, Winnebagoes, and Dakotas (or Santee Sioux). Most of them were Algonquian-speaking groups with a hunting and gathering economy. La Pointe was a crossroads for dozens of tribes and smaller groupings as they traveled for food, trade, or a change of scene. Allouez took advantage of every opportunity to preach to these various groups. In time a small number of converts began to settle permanently around the chapel, forming an intertribal community of Christian Indians.

In 1668 a new director of missions, Claude Dablon, sent Allouez to new work at Green Bay on Lake Michigan. The following year Jacques Marquette succeeded his fellow blackrobe at La Pointe. Between 1669 and 1671 Marquette continued the ministry that Allouez had inaugurated so successfully. But difficulties lay ahead in the form of warlike Dakotas. This loose coalition of tribes was as much a scourge to Indians of the Midwest as the Iroquois were to those farther east. After many threats and intrigues, the Jesuits and their flock decided to abandon La Pointe and move to a place of greater safety. They finally chose Michilimackinac Island in the straits between lakes Michigan and Huron. Marquette established the mission community of Saint Ignace there, and it flourished much as before with a larger population that was happy to have escaped the rapacious Dakotas.

Using Saint Ignace as headquarters, Marquette approached other tribes such as the Potawatomis, the Sac-Foxes, and the Illinois. He also accompanied Louis Jolliet in 1673 on an expedition that proved the Mississippi River flowed south to the Gulf of Mexico instead of west to the Pacific Ocean. In those travels he was so impressed with Illinois tribesmen and their pleas that he set up a mission among them. In November 1674 he settled at the village of Kaskaskia and named his new station Immaculate Conception. Though his health had been precarious since the Jolliet expedition, Marquette lived with his charges during the winter months. Shortly after Easter in 1675, he set out for Saint Ignace but died before reaching it.

Meanwhile, Allouez had remained active around Green Bay and in 1673 laid the foundations of Saint Francis Xavier mission near present-day De Pere, Wisconsin. He was ordered south to take over Marquette's work among the Illinois, first visiting Immaculate Conception in 1677. During the last eleven years of his life, Allouez divided his time between the mission community at Kaskaskia and at a community named Saint Joseph in southwestern Michigan, which he established among the Miamis. By the time of his death in 1689, he had traveled thousands of wilderness miles and contacted at least twenty different Indian tribes. He composed a prayer book in the Illinoian dialect and reportedly baptized some ten thousand natives. Jacques Gravier succeeded him, and a steady stream of Jesuits supplied mission communities of Christian Indians. The death of Sébastien Louis Meurin in 1777 finally ended the long line of black-robe evangelists who served in the northern French colonies.

The Louisiana Territory

By that time the French presence in western lands was largely clustered around forts established in a chain along the Great Lakes and the Mississippi River to contain British expansion. Catholic priests established mission communities at such posts as Detroit, Vincennes, and Saint Louis, but there were only a few farther to the south. There, too, they proved to be sporadic, temporary, and ultimately ineffectual.

In early exploration Jolliet and Marquette had descended the Mississippi only as far as the mouth of the Arkansas River. In 1682 Robert Cavelier Sieur de La Salle led a party to the great river's mouth and claimed the whole drainage system for the king of France. Capitals for Louisiana emerged at Mobile (1711–1719), Biloxi (1719–1722), and, finally, New Orleans (from 1722). Missionary activities faced many difficulties there, perhaps the least of which came from Native American peoples.

Priests and friars in Louisiana came from several religious orders because many of the early political, military, and economic sponsors of the missions were suspicious of the Jesuits and their independent ways. Franciscans were present, as were Capuchins, a strict reformed branch within the larger order, together with Carmelites and some Jesuits. In the early 1700s, French officials established fairly amicable relations with principal tribes in the area, including the Chickasaws and Choctaws, as well as some lesser ones like the Alibamu, the Natchez, and the Yazoo. Most of these groups were Muskogean-speaking farmers with a sophisticated cultural heritage going back fifteen centuries to mound-building days. But mission communities never flourished among any of these tribes. Louisiana languished economically, and this forced the clergy to seek means for their own survival before they could turn to supporting Native converts. Many of them were reduced to serving as chaplains to whites on large land concessions.

The more debilitating problem by far lay in decades of wrangling over ecclesiastical jurisdiction in a three-way dispute involving the bishop of Quebec, the Congregation de Propaganda Fide in Rome, and the Society for Foreign Missions. Each claimed special authority for policy and appointments, and each faction spoiled, or at least enervated, the efforts of others. No mission community of any note was established in this sprawling territory, except perhaps for that among the Natchez that was built near Fort Rosalie on the banks of the Mississippi. In 1729 the Natchez destroyed the fort, killing nearly three hundred French men, women, and children as well as the recently arrived Jesuit priest, Paul du Poisson. With conflict among religious authorities continuing, missionary activity yielded only modest gains up to 1769, when the first Spanish governor arrived to assume control over recently ceded Louisiana.

THE ENGLISH COLONIES

Early on there were a few English Catholic attempts to evangelize Native Americans, but these accomplished little because of Protestant interference. After his father's death in 1632, Cecilius Calvert, the second Lord Baltimore, carried out the former's plans to create a New World refuge for fellow Catholics in the colony of Maryland. The first group of settlers, which left England in 1633, included Jesuit priest Andrew White.

Landing in 1634 on the shores of Chesapeake Bay, White celebrated the first Eucharist in the colony of Maryland. It was necessary to meet the needs of white settlers first, but by 1639 White was living among the Patuxents, and shortly thereafter he moved to the much friendlier Piscataway tribe. Within five years he saw the beginnings of a Christian way of life emerge, and he promoted this embryonic development with a catechism in the local dialect. A grammar and dictionary followed. But success raised suspicions among Protestants in nearby Virginia, and in 1645 White was arrested and sent back to England in chains. Though he was acquitted of Protestant charges of treason, his mission communities lay in ruins with no successor to pursue the work.

The Seventeenth-Century

Farther to the north, primarily around Massachusetts and Narragansett bays, English Protestant settlers inaugurated colonial enterprises of another sort. They were greeted by Algonquian-speaking peoples—possibly as many as one hundred fifty thousand strong in southeastern New England—comprised of tribes known as Massachusets, Wampanoags, Narragansetts, and Nipmuks. These natives were seminomadic, living parts of each year in villages with extensive cultivated fields but moving seasonally to exploit what the region afforded in game, fish, and wild plants. Easily constructed family lodges (wigwams), made of poles and thatch or bark, were admirably suited to this peripatetic way of life. Political organization was generally confined to small bands, each led by a sachem who "ruled" through advice and persuasion rather than by hereditary right or force. Native spirituality was highly individualistic, rooted in private visions and personal prayers as well as a degree of shared ceremonialism. All in all, these groups consisted of sturdy and independent people who had developed a superbly adept way of life long before the Europeans' arrived on their shores.

English Protestants conducted far less mission activity than Spanish Franciscans or French Jesuits in the seventeenth century. The whites who claimed New England were mostly Puritans, the name given the reformist, low-church Anglicans who first arrived in 1630. One of the reasons they gave for coming to America was to convert the natives, but very few clergymen actually made any effort in that direction. Among the first was Thomas Mayhew, Jr., who lived on Martha's Vineyard and in 1642 began to converse with Indians in their own language about religious matters. Five generations of the family followed his example on that island and on nearby Nantucket. More well known because longer lived was John Eliot, minister of the church at Roxbury, near Boston, who in 1646 began preaching to Massachuset groups in their Native tongue. He compiled a grammar and dictionary for his own use and for the Indians whom he taught to read. After translating many tracts and edifying books into the Native dialect, Eliot translated the entire Bible into Algonquian and had his work printed in 1663. In 1669 his helpful *Indian Primer* appeared; its purpose was to start young minds on the road to intellectual as well as spiritual enrichment. This typically Puritan emphasis on literacy and doctrinal cognizance placed heavy demands on nonliterate natives.

The cultural transformation of the "red Puritans" went well beyond conversion. Converts settled down in permanent town sites that welcomed only Christian inhabitants. They fenced their land, used domesticated animals, and sold surplus food in a capitalist marketplace. These genuine mission communities eventually numbered fourteen, with Natick as their model, and they formed an arc some twenty-five miles (40 kilometers) from Boston. Under clerical guidance resident converts, known as "Praying Indians," drew up laws to regulate personal and corporate morality. In addition to proscribing murder, theft, and adultery, they also prescribed standards for hygiene, dress, and Sabbath observance. For almost thirty years, the Praying Indian towns represented—from the Puritan perspective—an ideal model of cultural transformation in which natives accustomed to oral traditions, the chase, and a permissive society dedicated themselves to the pursuit of literacy, fenced in their real estate, and accepted the rigors of Puritan virtue.

However, all hopes for successful missionary communities among New England Indians ended in 1675 when warfare broke out between Wampanoag natives and white colonists. Increasing tensions, fed by conflicts over property rights and the universally applicable standards of

English law, finally reached a flashpoint, and disgruntled Indians from many tribes rallied around a sachem named Metacomet, known as King Philip to the colonists. Most Praying Indians were not implicated in these hostilities; indeed many volunteered to fight alongside their white coreligionists. But war hysteria unleashed pent-up fears of all Indians—even baptized ones who read their Bibles in church on Sundays. Eliot's converts were unjustly accused of complicity with the enemy, summoned from their peaceful communities, and herded into what amounted to concentration camps. There, many died from exposure or malnutrition during the winter of 1675–1676.

When King Philip's War ended with the death of its leader, Praying Indians had been scattered and reduced in number to such an extent that they could not resume living at their town sites. Mission communities were thus victimized by the indiscriminate anti-Indian prejudice that war brought to the surface. A small remnant of believers retained their group identity on Cape Cod, but most of Eliot's converts cannot be traced after 1676. By 1700 most aspects of aboriginal culture along the seacoast had been crushed along with Native lives in King Philip's War. In the end Puritan efforts to save the Indians produced few tangible results of a beneficial nature.

The Eighteenth Century
In many colonies outside New England, the Anglican Church—which the Puritans abandoned soon after arriving in America in favor of their own Congregational churches—had a strong presence. During the early eighteenth century, representatives of the Church of England pursued missionary work in the middle and especially the southern colonies. In 1701 Thomas Bray, colonial commissary for the bishop of London, founded the Society for the Propagation of the Gospel in Foreign Parts (SPG), hoping that the organization would subsidize evangelism among Native Americans and the increasing number of African slaves. Bray envisioned sending priests to establish missionary communities in borderland areas where Indians still lived on the edges of white civilization. He hoped ministers in such outposts would change Native beliefs and values in accordance with British work hab-

its, commerce, and political loyalty. But intentions did not translate into actions. For example an early SPG missionary, Samuel Thomas, was sent to the Carolinas in 1702 expressly to work with the Yamasee tribe; within a short time, however, he settled into a comfortable white parish, scarcely ever making an effort to discharge his original mandate.

A total of 309 SPG appointees worked at locations up and down the Atlantic coast during the 1700s. Instead of living among Indians, the missionaries only visited them sporadically. Those who tried to fulfill the SPG's stated purpose usually contented themselves with teaching young natives in schools that emphasized the English language, British manners, and the niceties of Anglican worship. One exception was John Stuart, who in 1770 began his labors among the Mohawk Indians in New York. He tried to make young Iroquois literate in their own tongue, but this fledgling project was brought to an end by the revolutionary war. Stuart helped keep the Iroquois League loyal to the Crown during the war, an illustration of how SPG agents everywhere were at least as effective in serving the British government as in furthering ecclesiastical interests. As for winning significant numbers of converts among Native American peoples, perhaps the best that can be said about SPG missionaries is that they contributed little to the steady decline of Indian civilizations in English colonial jurisdictions.

In 1743 a Congregationalist minister named Eleazar Wheelock developed a new approach to missions at an academy, called Moor's Charity School, near his church in Lebanon, Connecticut. That year he decided to admit Indians to his already flourishing preparatory school in order to train Native youths for evangelical work among their respective tribes. These Native apostles would be more welcome at their natal homes than would white emissaries, he theorized, and they could more easily employ local idioms to facilitate conversions. During the next quarter century, nearly fifty Indian students were introduced to academic discipline for varying lengths of time. Wheelock hoped to produce among his graduates, mostly Algonquians but a few Iroquois, too, a full spectrum of scholars and farmers, schoolmistresses and housewives, who would spread Christianity to Indian settlements without depending on white preachers. Few natives actually graduated, and even fewer accepted missionary assignments. Among that handful none were accepted at home because they had acculturated too much and were regarded as representatives of white society. Most of them drifted back to the margins of English colonial life.

The one notable exception to this general failure was Samson Occom, a full-blooded Mohegan. Occom mastered the regimen that required him to be industrious as well as studious. He learned to be up early and decently dressed for morning prayers, to do chores on the farm, and to use tools in the shop. He studied Greek, Latin, and Hebrew in addition to English. Severe eyestrain induced by these latter rigors did not stop him. Poor health prevented his attending college, but Occom persevered as he pursued a ministerial career. The Congregationalists delayed accepting his candidacy, so in 1747 he sought and obtained a Presbyterian license to preach. Within two years he had settled at Montauk, Long Island, and began serving the natives there, who made up one of the oldest Indian Presbyterian churches in the British colonies.

In 1759 Occom became a fully ordained Presbyterian minister as he continued to preach regularly and taught school as well. Between 1761 and 1763, he made three lengthy visits to the Oneidas, an Iroquois tribe adjacent to the Mohawks. In 1766 he traveled to England to solicit funds for Wheelock's mission school. Over the course of two years there he received great acclaim as an example of what gospel teachings could do to make Native Americans both pious and learned. He also collected substantial sums that Wheelock later applied to a new enterprise, Dartmouth College. Occom felt betrayed as Wheelock virtually abandoned his missionary activity. Occom continued his work with Native groups, but he no longer resided with any single mission community; rather, he itinerated among scattered gatherings in Connecticut. There he ministered as best he could to dwindling numbers who lived in increasing despair as whites crowded the natives out of their ancestral lands.

As early as 1773 a group of young Indians in New England decided to move west, but the revolution postponed action on that decision. By 1784, however, a major exodus was under way, and Occom led the first contingent of parishioners to a site named Brothertown in Oneida territory. Occom based his evangelical work there while riding a circuit through large segments of New York and preaching six or seven times a week. We do not know how many baptisms Occom performed or how many church members he served. But his labor in two cultures and travels on two continents are an outstanding example of missionary dedication embodied in a Native American who took the gospel seriously.

There was a counterpart to the SPG in the Society in Scotland for Propagating Christian Knowledge (SSPCK). Beginning in 1744 David Brainerd toured much of New Jersey and eastern Pennsylvania as an SSPCK evangelist. He worked primarily with Delaware Indians by preaching through a recent convert named Moses Tattamy, and he established a notable missionary community at Crossweeksung near Trenton. There he baptized twenty-five believers and in 1746 celebrated their first Lord's Supper. These displaced natives led a marginal existence, peddling homemade wares to prosperous white neighbors. Decimated by disease and impoverished by whiskey traders, they clung to Brainerd as a possible way out of their misery. But the doleful missionary was frequently absent, and in 1747 he died at the home of Jonathan Edwards in Northampton, Massachusetts. The famous theologian memorialized Brainerd by publishing his journal, thereby popularizing the cause of missions and probably, by promoting Brainerd's work when other individual's achievements were not known, giving the young evangelist more credit than he deserved.

David's younger brother, John, held the Jersey mission community together and augmented its numbers over the next thirty years. In 1748 he received an SSPCK commission to serve as pastor to Christian Delawares, advising them on secular as well as spiritual matters in order to protect what remained of Native culture. By 1758 he saw the wisdom of accepting offers from the colonial legislature to buy all remaining Indian land claims and of establishing a reservation where they could live undisturbed. John Brainerd was superintendent, minister, and guardian of this reservation, named Brotherton and situated in the pine barrens of Burlington County (not to be confused with Brothertown in Oneida territory). At its peak Brotherton had a population of three hundred people, but by 1774 deaths and departures had reduced that figure to less than sixty, of whom scarcely a dozen were qualified to receive communion. Brainerd visited the Brotherton mission until he died in 1781. By 1801 surviving Jersey Delawares sold their reservation, moved to New York, and joined other tribes in a sequence of further removals to the Great Lakes and then beyond the Mississippi River.

Another missionary working in the middle colonies was Samuel Kirkland, who spent most of his life among the Oneidas in New York near Brothertown. In 1765 he began living with the Senecas, westernmost of the Iroquois tribes, but the following year he moved to the more centrally located Oneidas. Kirkland lived in longhouses, learned to speak Iroquoian, and shared most other aspects of the indigenous way of life. He refused gifts of land and used much of his SSPCK salary to buy supplies for his adopted kinsmen. He was determined not to intrude too much on Oneida culture, and over the years this policy won a considerable number of converts. Still, he urged some accommodation to white practices and thus persuaded natives to build a meetinghouse, a sawmill, and a blacksmith shop. He also introduced diversified farming and draft animals to help Christian Indians cope with the more complex material culture that was slowly engulfing them. However, Kirkland's gains came to grief because most of the Iroquois supported Britain during the revolution, and in the 1780s vindictive Americans pushed remaining tribesmen—Christian as well as non-Christian—into Canada.

The Plight of Native Americans After the Revolution

The revolution ended the colonial period and so crippled many of the missions begun with English personnel and financing. The revolution inaugurated a new era, one of political independence in which Indians were perceived differently. During the colonial era, European powers often tried to use Native Americans as pawns in larger maneuverings for power and influence. Yet because they saw Indians as useful, Europeans had to grant tribesmen a modicum of respect. However, once the United States came into existence, its citizens looked westward and saw Indi-

ans as unwelcome occupants of land that belonged to the new nation.

Respect virtually disappeared, and the indigenous peoples were depicted as obstacles in the path of advancing American civilization. Missionaries in the early national period tried to teach Indians how to maintain their integrity within this new context. As matters turned out, however, the only real choices were assimilation to white culture or staying ahead of territorial expansion until there was no place left to go.

BIBLIOGRAPHY

Documents

Benavides, Alonso de. *Fray Alonso de Benavides' Revised Memorial of 1634,* edited by Frederick W. Hodge, George P. Hammond, and Agapito Rey. Albuquerque, N.Mex., 1945.

Ellis, John Tracy, ed. *Documents of American Catholic History.* 3 vols. Wilmington, Del., 1987.

Serra, Junípero. *Writings of Junípero Serra,* edited by Antonine Tibesar. Academy of American Franciscan History. Documentary Series, vols. 4–7. Washington, D.C., 1955–1966.

Thwaites, Reuben G., ed. *The Jesuit Relations and Allied Documents.* 73 vols. Cleveland, Ohio, 1896–1901.

Biographies

Blodgett, Harold. *Samson Occom.* Hanover, N.H., 1935.

Bolton, Herbert E. *Rim of Christendom: A Biography of Eusebio Francisco Kino, Pacific Coast Pioneer.* New York, 1936.

Brainerd, Thomas. *The Life of John Brainerd: The Brother of David Brainerd, and His Successor As Missionary to the Indians of New Jersey.* Philadelphia, 1865.

Donnelly, Joseph P. *Jacques Marquette, S.J., 1637–1675.* Chicago, 1968.

———. *Jean de Brébeuf, 1593–1649.* Chicago, 1975.

Geiger, Maynard J. *The Life and Times of Fray Junípero Serra, or the Man Who Never Turned Back, 1713–1784: A Biography.* 2 vols. Washington, D.C., 1959.

Hare, Lloyd C. M. *Thomas Mayhew: Patriarch to the Indians, 1593–1682.* New York, 1932.

Lothrop, Samuel K. *Life of Samuel Kirkland, Missionary to the Indians.* Boston, 1848.

McCallum, James D. *Eleazar Wheelock: Founder of Dartmouth College.* Hanover, N.H., 1939.

Talbot, Francis. *Saint Among the Hurons: The Life of Jean de Brébeuf.* New York, 1949.

_____. *Saint Among Savages: The Life of Isaac Jogues.* New York, 1935.

Winslow, Ola E. *John Eliot: "Apostle to the Indians."* Boston, 1968.

Wynbeek, David. *David Brainerd, Beloved Yankee.* Grand Rapids, Mich., 1961.

Anthropological Studies

Dozier, Edward P. *The Pueblo Indians of North America.* New York, 1970.

Heidenreich, Conrad. *Huronia: A History and Geography of the Huron Indians, 1600–1650.* Toronto, Ontario, 1971.

Hudson, Charles. *The Southeastern Indians.* Knoxville, Tenn., 1976.

Jennings, Jesse D., and Edward Nordbeck, eds. *Prehistoric Man in the New World.* Chicago, 1964.

Kraft, Herbert C. *The Lenape: Archaeology, History, and Ethnography.* Newark, N.J., 1986.

Leacock, Eleanor B., and Nancy O. Lurie, eds. *North American Indians in Historical Perspective.* New York, 1971.

Martin, Paul S., George I. Quimby, and Donald Collier, eds. *Indians Before Columbus: Twenty Thousand Years of North American History Revealed by Archaeology.* Chicago, 1947.

Ortiz, Alfonso. *The Tewa World: Space, Time, Being, and Becoming in a Pueblo Society.* Chicago, 1969.

Parsons, Elsie C. *Pueblo Indian Religion.* 2 vols. Chicago, 1939.

Salisbury, Neal. *Manitou and Providence: Indians, Europeans, and the Making of New England, 1500–1643.* New York, 1982.

Trigger, Bruce G. *The Children of Aataentsic: A History of the Huron People to 1660.* 2 vols. Montreal, 1976.

Weslager, Clinton A. *The Delaware Indians: A History.* New Brunswick, N.J., 1972.

Cultural Studies

Axtel, James. *After Columbus: Essays in the Ethnohistory of Colonial North America.* New York, 1988.

_____. *The Invasion Within: The Contest of Cultures in Colonial North America.* New York, 1986.

Bailey, Alfred G. *The Conflict of European and Eastern Algonkian Cultures, 1504–1700: A Study in Canadian Civilization.* Sackville, New Brunswick, 1937; rev. ed. 1969.

Bowden, Henry Warner. *American Indians and Christian Missions: Studies in Cultural Conflict.* Chicago, 1981.

Crane, Verner. *The Southern Frontier, 1670–1732.* Durham, N.C., 1928; rev. ed. 1956.

Hammond, George P. *Don Juan de Oñate and the Founding of New Mexico.* Santa Fe, N.Mex., 1927.

Jacobs, Wilbur R. *Dispossessing the American Indian: Indians and Whites on the Colonial Frontier.* New York, 1972.

Jaenen, Cornelius J. *Friend and Foe: Aspects of French-Amerindian Cultural Contact in the Sixteenth and Seventeenth Centuries.* Toronto, Ontario, 1976.

Jennings, Francis. *The Invasion of America: Indians, Colonialism, and the Cant of Conquest.* New York, 1975.

Leach, Douglas E. *Flintlock and Tomahawk: New England in King Philip's War.* New York, 1958.

Peckham, Howard., and Charles Gibson, eds. *Attitudes of Colonial Powers Toward the American Indian.* Salt Lake City, Utah, 1969.

Smith, James M., ed. *Seventeenth-Century America: Essays in Colonial History.* Chapel Hill, 1959.

Spicer, Edward H. *Cycles of Conquest: The Impact of Spain, Mexico, and the United States on the Indians of the Southwest, 1533–1960.* Tucson, Ariz., 1962.

Thomas, David H., ed. *Columbian Consequences.* Vol. 1, *Archaeological and Historical Perspectives on the Spanish Borderlands West.* Washington, D.C., 1989, and Vol. 2, *Archaeological and Historical Perspectives on the Spanish Borderlands East.* Washington, D.C., 1989.

Vaughan, Alden T. *New England Frontier: Puritans and Indians, 1620–1675.* Boston, 1965.

Wright, Louis B. *The Atlantic Frontier: Colonial American Civilization, 1607–1763.* New York, 1947.

_____. *Gold, Glory, and the Gospel: The Adventurous Lives and Times of the Renaissance Explorers.* New York, 1970.

_____. *Religion and Empire: The Alliance Between Piety and Commerce in English Expansion, 1558–1625.* Chapel Hill, N.C., 1943.

Spanish Missions

Castañeda, Carlos E. *Our Catholic Heritage in Texas, 1519–1936.* 7 vols. Austin, Tex., 1936–1958.

Ellis, John T. *Catholics in Colonial America.* Baltimore, Md., 1965.

Engelhardt, Zephyrin. *The Missions and Missionaries of California.* 4 vols. San Francisco, 1908–1915.

Geiger, Maynard J. *The Franciscan Conquest of Florida, 1573–1618.* Washington, D.C., 1937.

Gutiérrez, Ramón A. *When Jesus Came, the Corn Mothers Went Away: Marriage, Sexuality, and Power in New Mexico, 1500–1846.* Stanford, Calif., 1991.

Lewis, Clifford M., and Albert J. Loomie. *The Spanish Jesuit Mission in Virginia, 1570–1572.* Chapel Hill, N.C., 1953.

Shea, John G. *History of the Catholic Missions Among the Indian Tribes of the United States, 1529–1854.* New York, 1854.

French Missions

Campbell, Thomas J. *Pioneer Priests of North America, 1642–1710.* 3 vols. New York, 1908–1911.

Delanglez, Jean. *The French Jesuits in Lower Louisiana, 1700–1763.* The Catholic University of America. Studies in American Church History, vol. 21. Washington, D.C., 1935.

Ellis, John T. *Catholics in Colonial America.* Baltimore, Md., 1965.

Grant, John W. *Moon of Wintertime: Missionaries and the Indians of Canada in Encounter Since 1534.* Toronto, Ontario, 1984.

Kennedy, John H. *Jesuit and Savage in New France.* New Haven, Conn., 1950.

Shea, John G. *History of the Catholic Missions Among the Indian Tribes of the United States, 1529–1854.* New York, 1854.

English Missions

Calam, John. *Parsons and Pedagogues: The S. P. G. Adventure in American Education.* New York, 1971.

Ellis, John T. *Catholics in Colonial America.* Baltimore, Md., 1965.

Shea, John G. *History of the Catholic Missions Among the Indian Tribes of the United States, 1529–1854.* New York, 1854.

Szasz, Margaret C. *Indian Education in the American Colonies, 1607–1783.* Albuquerque, N. Mex., 1988.

Henry Warner Bowden

SEE ALSO **Detribalized and Manumitted Indians; The French Settlements; Indian-Colonist Conflicts and Alliances, The Spanish Borderlands; Settlements in the Spanish Borderlands;** and **Theories of Education;** and various essays in THE ARTS and RELIGION.

DETRIBALIZED AND MANUMITTED INDIANS

A VARIED AND VOLUMINOUS historical literature exists on the plight of whites captured and pressed into domestic servitude by America's Indians. These captivity narratives have fascinated lay readers and scholars for several centuries. The travails captives endured as they were assimilated into Native American societies or silently resisted are gripping stories. For some readers the narratives offered a fantastical escape to a land of savages devoid of the hierarchical structures of colonial society. For others, the savagery of the Indians depicted in the narratives served to justify whatever military action was necessary to annihilate the foe. But whatever the textual politics of specific captivity narratives, whatever the experiences of the white men, women, and children forced to serve Indian masters, the enslavement of whites by Native Americans is fairly well known.

What we know much less about is the mirror image, the stories of the Indians who were detribalized—torn from their natal worlds and incorporated into French, English, and Spanish colonial society as slaves. Obviously such an experience was not unique or unfamiliar in the indigenous world. Indians in pre-Columbian America had waged war against their enemies since time immemorial and expected from vanquishment the spoils of slavery. If one surveys the cultural geography of North America, one

finds from time to time words in the indigenous lexicon that referred to such slaves.

For many years, for example, anthropologists and ethnohistorians believed that the word *Nixoras* signified a tribal group in southern Arizona. On closer examination it became clear that *Nixoras* was not a tribe but a word of Maricopa origin that was used quite widely in the Pimería Alta (modern Arizona) to refer to individuals pressed into slavery through conquest or to Indian slaves purchased from other tribes. In colonial America it was not uncommon for Indian slaves to pass into European hands through purchase, as gifts, or through war. Since these persons did not speak or write the language of their European masters, and infrequently became literate, their experiences are very little known.

In most regions where the incorporation of such indigenous slaves into colonial society is recorded, the phenomenon is of limited dimensions; the slaves are few in number and never formed a significant portion of the regional population. Slavery in colonial New Mexico stands out as the exception. As one of the oldest and most densely populated of Spain's outposts in what became the United States, this kingdom developed a heavy reliance on Indian servitude. By 1800 perhaps as much as one-third of the population originally had entered the colony as slaves. These Native American slaves, referred to generically as *genízaros*, by 1750 were deemed a distinct ethnic group in Spanish society. This essay focuses on New Mexico's *genízaros*. We will explore how they were detribalized and pressed into slavery, how they gained their freedom, and the forms of identity they forged in relationship to genteel society in New Mexico.

INDIAN SLAVERY IN COLONIAL NEW MEXICO

Theoretically, Indian slavery had been outlawed in all of Spain's possessions with the 1542 publication of the New Laws, a prohibition reiterated in the 1680 *Recompilation of the Laws of the Indies*. But on the remote margins of Spain's empire—in places such as Chile, the Amazon, and New Mexico—Indian slavery was tolerated as a way of compensating the colonizers of these regions. Accordingly, Native Americans who refused to submit to Spanish rule and who resisted the word of God, could be captured as slaves in "just war" and kept in bondage for ten to twenty years. This was the justification New Mexico's Governor Juan de Oñate invoked in 1599–1600 when he razed Acoma and the Tompiro pueblos and enslaved their inhabitants.

Spanish raids into Indian territory, ostensibly to punish heathen insubordination but in reality to capture slaves, became a common occurrence throughout the colonial period. At the beginning of the eighteenth century, however, as the level of nomadic Indian depredations on New Mexico's settlements intensified, the number of "just wars" against the Apaches and other enemy tribes increased; as a result, scores of men, women, and particularly children were brought into Spanish towns enslaved as prisoners of war. In New Mexico these slaves became known as *genízaros* (from the Turkish *yeni*, "new," and *cheri*, "troops"). Like the janissaries of the Ottoman Empire, whence the term derives, *genízaros* were slaves, primarily children, who had been seized for use as shock troops, the first line of assault against enemy Indian tribes in war.

Throughout the colonial period, New Mexico's Spanish residents characterized the constant state of war they waged as simple retaliation and punishment of the *indios bárbaros* (barbarous Indians). But a simple tally of the booty colonists seized in these raids unmasks their true intent. In mineral-poor New Mexico slaving was one of the few ways of obtaining domestic service and chattels that could be exchanged for luxury goods. Slaves "are the kingdom's gold and silver and the richest treasure," claimed one friar in 1761. They were a medium of exchange and pieces of easily convertible wealth. "I owe Felipe Saíz, a resident of Parral, a few pesos, which I agreed to pay with a little Indian girl," stated a 1718 will. Don Joseph Reaño paid for his purchases in Chihuahua in 1761 with *inditos* (little Indians), as did others.

One index of the extent of this warfare and its effects on New Mexican society can be gained through a comparison of the burial records of Hispanos killed during Native American raids and the baptismal records of nomadic Indians. Since captives were always baptized before their incorporation into a Christian home, such baptisms are a fair index of the levels of Indian enslavement. Admittedly, baptismal records underestimate the true levels of slave hunting in New Mexico because slaves bound for labor elsewhere were infrequently christened.

Between 1700 and 1820, 584 Spanish residents were killed by nomadic Indians and 2,708 nomadic Indians were baptized. An analysis of these numbers indicates that there was a strong positive statistical association between the number of white settlers killed by nomadic Indians and the number of nomadic Indian baptisms. The strength of this statistical relationship grew over time. As the number of Indian captives rose, so did the number of Spanish deaths.

In addition to slaves captured by the Spaniards in war, throughout the eighteenth and early nineteenth centuries New Mexico's slave population was augmented by the purchase of Indian slaves from the Apaches and Comanches, captives these tribes had seized from each other and their enemies. Beginning in the early 1700s, the Apache and Comanche regularly entered Pecos, Taos, and Picuris pueblos to trade meat, hides, and captives for Pueblo blankets, pottery, corn, and turquoise. The Spanish colonists encouraged this trade, offering the Native Americans manufactured products, agricultural implements, and horses in exchange for slaves.

The Christians justified the purchase of these *indios de rescate* (bartered Indian captives) because they had been enslaved through intertribal warfare. Governor Vélez Cachupín encouraged the trade in 1752, fearing that if it were curtailed, endless bloodshed would result. The Indians would kill their captives rather than allowing them to be "ransomed" by the Spanish and "redeemed" through baptism. The 1680 *Recompilation of the Laws of the Indies* stated that such ransomed Indians incurred a debt that had to be repaid to their master through work for an unspecified period. Masters were to treat their captives well and to Hispanicize and Christianize them. The Crown repeatedly ordered that these captives not be "marketed as slaves," but no one paid these decrees much heed, asserted Fray Pedro Serrano in 1761.

Between 1700 and 1820, 2,708 nomadic Indians were baptized and placed in New Mexican households. Approximately two out of every five were identified explicitly as slaves "in the power of," "in the dominion of," or "a captive of" a particular person. Ethnically the largest group were Navajo, representing 37.5 percent of the total. Apache followed at 24 percent, Ute at 16 percent, and Comanche at 5 percent.

One out of every eight of these newly baptized Indians was identified as an *indio de rescate*, a slave purchased at the Native American trade fairs. Baptism made spiritual salvation possible for such slaves, and it was to this that friars alluded when they occasionally penned in the baptismal registers that an Indian had been "redeemed" from the gentiles (unbaptized Indians). Thirty-three percent were referred to as "adopted," an expression of the officiating friar's hope that the master/slave relation would be a quasi-filial one. One out of every five was listed as a *criado* (servant; from the verb *criar*, "to rear"). New Mexicans skirted the laws against Indian slavery, writes historian Marc Simmons, and often avoided the term slaves, employing instead the euphemism of *criado*. Fray Juan Agustín Morfi wrote in 1776 that these Indian slaves were "called genízaros; they are Comanche and Apache captives obtained as children and reared (*criados*) among us." Over time, the words *genízaro* and *criado* were used interchangeably to refer to all detribalized Indians residing in Spanish towns. Indeed, the residents of Abiquiu referred to themselves as *genízaros criados* in 1820.

During the course of the eighteenth century the *genízaro* slave population of New Mexico's towns was swelled by out-migrants from Pueblo Indian villages. These were predominantly marginalized Pueblo Indians who had been shunned by their kinsmen, were exiled from their towns because of some transgression, or who simply thought life in Hispanic towns was more appealing. In Spanish society these "fallen" Pueblo Indians fared poorly. Displaced and caught between two cultures, they entered Hispano households as domestic slaves and generally were referred to as *genízaros*.

The expulsion of "fallen" Pueblo Indians from their own villages was largely the by-product of Spanish labor demands. Though tribute payment had ceased with the abolition of the *encomienda* after New Mexico's reconquest in 1693, the settlers continued to demand labor and raw materials from the Pueblo Indians. The entry of Pueblo women into Spanish towns to perform such labor became a perfect occasion for their sexual abuse. Many were raped while performing their weekly labor, complained the governors of fourteen pueblos in 1707. "When Indian women enter Santa Fe to mill wheat and spin wool they return to their pueblos deflowered and crying over their dishonor or pregnant," attested Fray Pedro Serrano in 1761. When Pueblo men discovered the defilement of their wives or daughters, they banished them from the pueblo, observed Fray Carlos Delgado in 1750. These victims of Spanish sexual abuse were permanently stigmatized as outcasts. The only options such marginalized women had were to become servants in Spanish households or to join a nomadic tribe.

If somehow a woman concealed her disgrace but later gave birth to a fair-skinned child or one that displayed visible signs of mixed ancestry, the child was abandoned on the doorstep of the local mission. The baptismal registers record these babies as *hijos de la iglesia* (children of the church). *Hijos de la iglesia* were baptized and placed in Christian homes, and subsequently referred to as *criados* or fosterlings. Approximately one out of every ten persons living in Spanish towns during the eighteenth century declared that they had been "children of the church."

The number of *genízaros* one finds in eighteenth-century New Mexico greatly depends on who is included in the category. If one counts only persons explicitly identified as *genízaros* on census records, the number is a small fraction of the total population. There were, for example, 677 *genízaros* in 1765. If one takes as a whole the nomadic slaves who entered Spanish New Mexico as "intruders" and the Pueblo outcasts who became members of Spanish households as "extruders" from their Native villages, then the number of *genízaros* is more substantial, reaching perhaps as high as one-third of all persons residing in Spanish towns. Taking this proportion, by 1800, *genízaros* may have numbered as many as 7,000 individuals out of a total Spanish population of 19,276.

THE TREATMENT OF DETRIBALIZED INDIANS

In colonial New Mexico bondage was a household institution and its meaning, particularly to *genízaros*, was found at the interpersonal level. Before slaves entered a Hispano household, they were stripped of their former name, baptized, and given Christian names. Marc Simmons in *Little Lion of the Southwest* quotes Manuel A. Chávez who, in the early 1800s, wrote that "on arriving home [after a slaving expedition] the first thing to do was to take the children to the priest to baptize them and give them a name. They would naturally take your name."

Kinship was the dominant mode of affiliation in colonial New Mexico; everyone was enmeshed in its web. Lacking genealogical ties to the community, slaves entered their owner's household as part of his or her symbolic capital by which eminence in the community was known. The enmeshment of Indian servitude in the language of kinship has led some historians to conclude erroneously that the treatment of Indian slaves was "benevolent." This claim is based primarily on declarations before the courts in which slaves spoke of their masters and mistresses as "father" and "mother," and were referred to by them as "son" and "daughter."

The use of filial and kinship terms to refer to detribalized Indians in legal documents tells us little about the nature of slavery or whether it was benevolent. Rather, they were statements concerning authority relationships within the household, particularly of a father's right to rule over wife, children, and thralls. The Crown tolerated slavery in New Mexico as a way of "civilizing" the Indians. When slave owners came before the courts to answer to charges of slave mistreatment, it was in their interest to portray slave relations as governed by the same rules that regulated the family. Fathers were ideally loving, stern, and guiding. To have said otherwise would have been to expose oneself to the loss of mastership over another.

The language of ownership used in court documents to refer to slaves is more frequent and more revealing than the fictive kinship terminology. To Don Francisco Guerrero, Santa Fe's chief constable, the escapee from the town's guardhouse in 1757 was "the *genízaro* Indian servant of Doña Feliciana Coco." "Manuela, the servant of Isabel Chávez," complained of mistreatment in 1763. And the words with which "the boy servant of Francisco Apodaca" was returned to his owner after a flaying for petty larceny revealed his legal status. The youth was entrusted to Apodaca in 1765 "with total power over his person." In each of these instances, and in many others like them, the Spanish preposition *de*, denoting ownership and possession, was used to refer to the slaves. As persons who had no honor, slaves had social and legal personalities primarily through their masters.

Within New Mexican households the treatment of *genízaros* ran the gamut from kindly neglect to utter sadism. To be a slave or *criado* in a Hispano household was to be a marginal and stigmatized person. This was evident in the types of duties *genízaros* performed, such as emptying chamber pots and clipping the master's toenails. Both inside the household and outside of it, *genízaros* were addressed as children, in the second-person Spanish informal and personal *tu* (you), but had to address their masters and local citizens with the formal *usted*. In Indian society growing older brought increasing respect, but not for New Mexico's slaves. Many of them were permanently infantilized, even by the master's children.

That detribalized *genízaros* lacked genealogical ties to the Spanish community and had been torn violently from their communities was humiliation enough in a society that prided itself on ancestry. Some masters compounded the hurt by refusing to allow their slaves to marry, to establish families, or to retain their progeny. When slave women bore children while in captivity, the children were sometimes sold or given to others as gifts.

The only picture of ideal treatment of *genízaros* in New Mexico is a rather late one, offered by Pedro León, an Indian trader from Abiquiu, as he stood accused of illegal slave trafficking in 1852. Begging clemency of the court, and thus coloring what he had to say about slavery, León stated:

[Slaves] are adopted into the family of those who get them, are baptized and remain [and are] trusted as one of the family—The head of the house standing as Godfather—The Prefect has the right to free them whenever maltreated—The Indian has a right to choose a guardian—Women are freed whenever married—say from 14 to 16—Men ditto from 18 to 20—At the death of Godfather never sold—always freed—The Godfathers provide husbands and wives for them the same as their children—When the Godfather dies they are free—As soon as they are baptized they cannot be sold any more. . . . It would be contrary to the laws of the Church. (Ramón A. Gutiérrez. *When Jesus Came*, p. 184)

In some households *genízaros* undoubtedly were treated as warmly as León suggests. For when a slave was obtained in infancy, close emotional attachments developed with the master. Slaves, after all, resided in the same house with their owner; they served the master and his children; they ate the same food the female servants prepared for everyone else; and they slept in their master's house, sometimes in his bed for his pleasure and frequently at his feet. Some slave women even offered their breasts to the master's children, suckling them with their milk.

The sheer proximity between slave and master, the slaves' outsider status and their lack of honor, regularly made them scapegoats. Frustrations precipitated by a poor harvest, by the low price one's livestock brought at market, by a wife's infidelities, or by an affront to one's honor, could be, and often were, vented on slaves. Trivial insubordination or impertinences, whether real or imagined, were paid for by slaves with beatings that not infrequently ended in death.

Native American slavery was illegal but tolerated in New Mexico, said Governor Vélez Cachupín in 1752, "so that they [captives] can be instructed in Our Holy Catholic Faith and made cognizant of the Divine Precepts, so that they may win their own salvation in honor and glory of God, our Lord." Slavery "civilized" Indians by giving them the requisites of culture: clothes, life in a European-style home, and knowledge of the one true God. At the baptismal font every friar reminded owners that these were things they had to provide their slaves. Slaves silently endured assaults, humiliations, and cruelties but were quick to seek legal redress when deprived of these minimal needs. A good master was supposed to clothe them, house them, and teach them how to pray.

New Mexico's settlers valued female slaves more highly than males and paid twice as much to acquire them. At the 1776 Taos fair, girls between the ages of twelve and twenty sold for two horses and some trifles—roughly 60 to 80 pesos—while men in the same age group cost half as much. A preference for female slaves is easy to understand. In a province where only one out of every three children born was likely to reach the age of twenty, female slaves were essential for their ability to bear children and to perform the basic household chores that guaranteed food and shelter.

Male slaves, particularly those between the ages of fifteen and thirty, were a troublesome lot and posed serious threats to the tranquillity of the province. These men were brought before the civil courts for apostasy, for not knowing or respecting their state in society, for failing to respect the property of others, and for their unbridled lust. Throughout the eighteenth century male slaves escaped as soon and as often as possible from the households into which they had been pressed. The authorities always were distressed when Indian slaves fled "from the kingdom or dismembered themselves from Christianity" because, as one apostate, Pedro de la Cruz, put it in 1747, "I will return within a short time with the Comanches and will expel the Spaniards by the hairs." For this reason the number of male slaves in the province was kept low. That is why they fetched a lower price at market than females. Indian captives regularly were marched south to work in the Parral silver mines. Some went on to plantations in Veracruz, and after 1800 many were shipped to Havana and to the Yucatán.

REPRESENTATIONS OF THE *GENÍZARO*

The presence in Spanish towns and villages of significant numbers of *genízaro* slaves and *criados* who had no genealogical ties to the Hispano community, who were dishonored by their status as thralls, and who were deemed socially dead amid men and women of honor generated negative stereotypes of what it meant to be a *genízaro*. Indeed, much of what was considered Spanish culture on the New Mexican frontier gained its meaning in opposition to and as an exaggeration of what it meant to be a *genízaro* or detribalized slave. It was by contrasting themselves with *genízaros* that Spaniards, aristocrats, and landed peasants alike, defined themselves and their honor.

Genízaros were first and foremost prisoners of war captured by the Spanish or, as Fray Atanasio Domínguez put it in 1776, "ransomed from the pagans by our people, [they] are then emancipated to work out their account." Because Spaniards "only as a last resort . . . serve themselves," said Domínguez, *genízaros* "are servants among our people." Writing in 1778 on the state of affairs in New Mexico, Fray Juan Agustín de Morfi said that *genízaros* were

captive Comanches, Apaches, etc., who were taken as youngsters and raised among us. . . . Since they are the offspring of enemy tribes, the natives of this province, who bear long grudges, never admit them to their pueblos. Thus [*genízaros*] are forced to live among Spaniards, without lands, or other means to subsist . . . they desire sites for villages but fail to obtain any, either because no one wants to provide them or because most lands have been occupied . . . on account of their poverty, which leaves them afoot and without arms . . . they bewail their neglect and they live like animals. (Ramón A. Gutiérrez. *When Jesus Came,* p. 189)

Domínguez observed that New Mexico's residents spoke Castilian of various sorts. The European-origin Spaniards spoke "with courtly polish," the landed peasants spoke "simply and

naturally among themselves," and the *genízaros* did "not wholly understand it [Spanish] or speak it without twisting it somewhat." Domínguez offered several assessments of the *genízaro* character. They were "weak, gamblers, liars, cheats, and petty thieves" and comprised "examples of what happens when idleness becomes the den of evils." Belén's *genízaros* had no way of supporting themselves, he added, and lived by their luck: "Only they and God know whether they have managed to get their hands on what belongs to their neighbors."

The caricatures Domínguez and Morfi drew, portrayed the *genízaros* as Indians of pagan ancestry who owned no land, lacked the means to earn a subsistence, owned no horses, carried no firearms, lived like animals, spoke a twisted form of Spanish, and were characterized by their depraved habits. Salvador Martínez, a Spaniard from Albuquerque, summarized the popular stereotype of the *genízaros* when he complained in the early 1800s that those living in the vicinity of Belén "were fugitives from their masters, odious people, vagabonds, gamblers, and thieves without the political or economic organization of a Republic."

These stereotypes remained ingrained in the popular memory, for to this day, mischievous and unruly children are taunted with the saying, "Genízaro! Genízaro! Puro indio de rescate" (Genízaro! Genízaro! Pure bartered Indian). When New Mexicans say today, "No seas genízaro" (Don't be a genízaro), they mean "Don't be a liar." Frances Swadesh discovered that in northern New Mexico, when someone was referred to as a *genízaro*, it meant crude, low-class, or *"indiado"* (Indian-like). In the 1950s Florence Hawley Ellis was told similar things about Belén's *genízaros* by the settlers who lived across the river in Tomé. Belén's *genízaros* were "semi-slave, low class and without ability."

If Indianness, slave and former slave pagan origin, dishonor, crude character, bad habits, and distorted language defined the *genízaros,* a list of antonyms defined what it was to be a Spaniard. The differences between aristocrats and landed peasants were of degree rather than of kind. Spaniards, whatever their estate, were men of honor in comparison with the vanquished Indians. Even the lowliest Spaniard felt a sense of honor around slaves. Landed peasants shared

160

fully in the benefits of a timocratic culture because, unlike *genízaro* slaves, they were long-time members of the Christian community and as such had been given land by the king. Landowners were *vecinos* or citizens with full voting rights in town councils (*cabildos*). By owning land, Spaniards could earn their own subsistence and were not dependent on others for their livelihood, as were slaves. Spaniards owned horses and firearms, and spoke Castilian well.

When men of honor said that *genízaros* "lived like animals," they meant that they dressed poorly or scantily and showed little modesty or restraint in their sexual comportment. Because slave women bore illegitimate children, failed to establish stable unions, were frequently sexually assaulted, and reputedly licentious, to be a Spanish woman, regardless of one's class, was to be concerned for one's sexual purity and reputation, to guard one's virginity, to marry, and to be continent in matrimony. Finally, men of honor were men of their word; their word carried force and was as binding as a modern contract. Conversely *genízaros* and former slaves were considered liars and cheats.

By the 1770s *genízaros* were perceived as a distinct and dangerous ethnic group. Spanish society viewed them as marginalized and degraded because of their slave and former slave status. They spoke a distinctive (broken) form of Spanish. Fray Carlos Delgado observed that *genízaros* practiced marriage class endogamy, taking "women of their own status and nature." They also "lived in great unity *como si fueran una nación,*" as if they were a nation.

TOWARD CULTURAL AUTONOMY

Over time, the number of manumitted slaves residing in Spanish towns increased, and as it did, various attempts to congregate these former slaves into their own villages were undertaken. *Genízaros* were resettled on the margins of the kingdom at Belén in 1740, at Abiquiu and Ojo Caliente in 1754, and at San Miguel del Vado in 1794. Aside from ridding Santa Fe, Albuquerque, and Santa Cruz of former slaves who were deemed unruly, the authorities hoped that by strategically locating *genízaro* villages as buffers along nomadic Indian raiding routes, the impact of Indian depredations on Spanish towns would be softened. Thus Belén guarded the southern approach to the Rio Grande Valley; Analco, the *genízaro* suburb of Santa Fe, protected the town's eastern approach; Abiquiu and Ojo Caliente, the northwest approach to Santa Cruz; and San Miguel, the northeast access route to Santa Cruz and Santa Fe.

With the emancipation and movement of *genízaros* onto the frontier, they finally had an independent space in which to express their own identity. Some *genízaros* abandoned their Christian baptismal names for what appear to be indigenous ones. Antonio Jiménez called himself Cuasipe. Miguel Reaño was Tasago. Juana, the Apache slave of Diego Velásquez, was Guisachi. *Genízaros* also began to take active roles in the defense of the kingdom. Fray Carlos Delgado reported in 1744 that the *genízaros* at Belén were obliged to "go out and explore the country in pursuit of the enemy, which they do with great bravery and zeal." They were "great soldiers, very warlike and the ones most feared by our enemies," wrote Fray Agustín Morfi in 1782. When Governor Pedro Fermín de Mendinueta gave chase to a band of Apaches in 1777, he dispatched fifty-five *genízaros* in their pursuit.

For their services as soldiers, scouts, and interpreters during the second half of the eighteenth century, *genízaros* solicited and were given special distinctions. Manuel Antonio, a *genízaro*, received a *presidio* post in 1768. Others must similarly have been honored, for when the authorities in Tomé had to use force to arrest Marcos Sánchez for maltreating his concubine in 1793, he vigorously protested: "I am a genízaro unworthy of such base treatment."

In 1790 a general census of the kingdom of New Mexico was undertaken. Therein a sizable number of *genízaros* were listed as artisans: blacksmiths, silversmiths, masons, carders, spinners, and weavers. One out of every five *genízaro* former slaves had acquired land and was listed in the household census as a farmer. Nevertheless, the majority of *genízaros* were employed as day laborers, field hands, and domestic servants. As the development of export-oriented agriculture and livestock production progressed during the first half of the nineteenth century, many *genízaros* were emancipated, only to have no other option than a debt peonage relationship with their former master. Fray Juan Agustín Morfi summarized the predicament of such *genízaros* well when he wrote in 1776 that "without land, without livestock, without any other manner of subsisting than with their bows and arrows . . . they [*genízaros*] have surrendered themselves into wage labor and suffer all sorts of tyrannies." By the time of Mexican independence in 1821, the plight of many of the emancipated Indians in New Mexican society was very similar to that of poor landless peasants. They remained marginal to the affairs of the kingdom, but as their independent towns developed, they did manage to enjoy a modicum of cultural autonomy.

BIBLIOGRAPHY

Adams, Eleanor B., and Fray Angélico Chávez, eds. and trans. *The Missions of New Mexico, 1776: A Description by Fray Atanasio Domínguez.* Albuquerque, N.Mex., 1975.

Bailey, Lynn Robinson. *Indian Slave Trade in the Southwest.* Los Angeles, 1966.

Brugge, David M. *Navajos in the Catholic Church Records of New Mexico, 1694–1875.* Window Rock, Ariz., 1968.

———. "Some Plains Indians in the Church Records of New Mexico." *Plains Anthropologist* 10 (October 1965):181–189.

Chávez, Fray Angélico. "Genízaros." In *Handbook of North American Indians,* vol. 9. Washington, D.C., 1979.

Cook, Will. *Comanche Captives.* New York, 1960.

Dozier, Edward. *The Pueblo Indians of North America.* New York, 1970.

Gutiérrez, Ramón A. *When Jesus Came, the Corn Mothers Went Away: Marriage, Sexuality, and Power in New Mexico, 1500–1846.* Stanford, Calif., 1991.

Hackett, Charles W., ed. and trans. *Historical Documents Relating to New Mexico, Nueva Vizcaya, and Approaches Thereto, 1773,* vol. 3. Washington, D.C., 1937.

Horvath, Steven M. "The Social and Political Organization of the Genízaros of Plaza de Nuestra Señora de los Dolores de Belén, New Mexico, 1740–1812." Ph.D. diss., Brown University, 1979.

McNitt, Frank. *The Indian Traders.* Norman, Okla., 1962.

Malouf, Carling, and A. Arline Malouf. "The Effects of Spanish Slavery on the Indians of the Intermountain West." *Southwestern Journal of Anthropology* 1, no. 3 (1945):378–391.

Simmons, Marc. *Little Lion of the Southwest.* Chicago, 1973.

———, ed. and trans. *Father Juan Agustín Morfi's Account of Disorders in New Mexico, 1778.* Isleta Pueblo, N.Mex., 1977.

Snow, William J. "Utah Indians and the Spanish Slave Trade." *Utah Historical Quarterly* 2, no. 3 (July 1929):67–75.

Swadesh, Frances Leon. *Los Primeros Pobladores: Hispanic Americans of the Ute Frontier.* Notre Dame, Ind., 1974.

Zavala, Silvio. *Los esclavos indios en Nueva España.* Mexico City, 1967.

Ramón A. Gutiérrez*

SEE ALSO **Indian-Colonist Contact; Interracial Societies, The Spanish Borderlands;** and **Settlements in the Spanish Borderlands.**

* Portions of this essay appeared in the author's work *When Jesus Came, the Corn Mothers Went Away,* published by Stanford University Press in 1991.

INTERRACIAL SOCIETIES

THE SPANISH BORDERLANDS

THE "DISCOVERY" OF THE CARIBBEAN by Christopher Columbus and his compatriots in 1492 began a massive process of cultural mixing, of exchanges, and of population movements that inextricably tied the Old World to the New. Quickly a whole series of syncretisms developed in culture, in language, and in worldviews that today stand as emblems of what is distinctively Spanish American. Of all the legacies that Spanish colonialism bequeathed to America, one of the most enduring was the extensive biological mixing that occurred when peoples of European, African, and American Indian origin produced offspring together. In Spanish America this process of racial mixture was known as *mestizaje,* a phenomenon that has dominated the national character and consciousness of those states created in areas of dense pre-Columbian indigenous populations.

The history of interracial societies in the Spanish Borderlands—the ways in which peoples and cultures mixed on the margins of empire, thereby producing hybrid societies—is best understood not by geographic units and boundaries but by examining the discourses that were dominant at specific times surrounding the concept of race and how those discourses reflected behavior. So ordered, the history of interracial societies in Spain's borderlands in North America falls roughly into three periods, each characterized by a particular theme. In the first period, from 1538 to 1770, the issue of race was totally subsumed within the discourse of conquest that described and justified why one group dominated another. In the second period, from roughly 1770 to 1800, a distinct concept of race emerged to describe the anxieties over racial mixing that gripped elite thought and legal discourse. In the third period, from 1800 to 1821, discussions about race and racial categories virtually disappeared and were replaced by concerns over class, citizenship, and property rights.

This essay will examine each of these periods and the dominant discourse of the time, fully cognizant that neither the dates nor the discourses identified are perfectly clear or discrete entities. There was a great deal of overlap in the social conversations about race that occurred at every time and place. In California, for example, active colonization did not begin until 1769, precisely the moment when anxieties over racial mixing were being articulated most vociferously in what are today the states of New Mexico, Texas, and Arizona. Thus what one finds in the historical sources on California in the period 1769–1800 are several discourses about race expressed simultaneously.

DISCOURSES OF CONQUEST, 1538–1770

From the earliest days of the conquest and colonization of New Spain's far north, the soldiers, settlers, and friars who went there envisioned the societies they were creating as composed of two groups: conquerors and conquered. The various indigenous groups they encountered on the frontier were said to be vanquished heathens engulfed in satanic darkness. Had the Christians not arrived, they self-righteously explained, the natives might never have heard the word of the One True God or known of either the celestial kingdom that awaited believers or the pain and suffering that would befall those who heard the word and did not heed it.

The "us-them" distinction the conquistadors drew between themselves and the natives they conquered, though primarily religious, was thoroughly imbued with notions of race and nationality. The conquerors were Christians, Spaniards, "civilized," and white—and thereby men of honor and distinction. The vanquished Indians were everything their victors were not—heathens, Amerindians, "uncivilized," dark—and therefore dishonored.

Much of the terminology that the conquerors in the Spanish Borderlands used during this initial period was drawn from the religious crusades that the Christian kingdoms of the Iberian Peninsula waged against the forces of Islam during the Reconquest (711–1492). Explaining how the habits of warfare forged over centuries died slowly, Francisco López de Gómara, one of the chroniclers of Mexico's conquest, wrote in 1523 that since the Christians had long fought infidels, "the conquest of the Indies began when that of the Moors was over." Thus, despite the fact that there were few, if any, Moors in the Spanish Borderlands, it was not uncommon for the colonists there to refer to the Indians as Moors. The Indians were described as carrying "Moorish bows" (bows and arrows). They were accused of worshiping the devil in "mosques" (ceremonial chambers). And according to one Santa Fe resident, Joseph de Armijo, who suffered from insomnia, his sleeplessness in 1749 was due to a fear that "the Moors might attack unexpectedly."

Like Muslims and Jews residing in conquered territory during the Iberian reconquest who were forced to convert to Christianity, Native New World converts became known as New Christians and were differentiated from the born standard-bearers of the faith, the Old Christians, to whom all honor and distinction flowed. Don Joseph Romo de Vera and Doña Angela Valdez, residents of the kingdom of New Mexico, expressed this sense of distinction when they boasted in 1745, "Our families are Old Christian Spaniards, descendants of such, and pure of taint with the bad races—Moors, Jews, and those newly admitted to the flock of Holy Mother Church."

The conquerors of the Spanish Borderlands frequently spoke of themselves as being *gente de razón*, literally "people of reason," rational beings. This category, too, was born of religious preoccupations. The legal distinction was concocted by the Holy Office of the Inquisition to protect Indians from prosecution for ideas contrary to the faith. The Indians were considered *gente sin razón*, "people lacking reason," irrational persons. As children who lacked the rational faculties to understand religious dogmas, they could not be punished by the Inquisition for acts that might otherwise be judged heretical. Since *gente de razón* were ethnically Spanish and *gente sin razón* were Amerindians, the distinction between rationality and irrationality became one of the many ways in which the conquerors differentiated themselves from those they had conquered.

Of course, as was the case on the Islamic frontier, Spain's monarchs bestowed all the honors and privileges of Castilian noblemen upon the notables of the conquest and their descendants for showing prowess and courage in forcing the infidel Indians to submit. The honor of the men so ennobled was based on their power and might, on their titles of nobility, and on the large tracts of land they were given. The wealth they accumulated from those Indians entrusted to their Christian care in *encomienda* (a grant of entitlement to Indian tribute, often forcibly extracted in the form of labor, foodstuff, or cloth) also contributed to this honor. The conquistadors deluded themselves and their progeny, believing that their social preeminence had a metaphysical basis and was rooted in their racial purity and gentle births, on their religion and Christian names, and on their personal elegance and pomp. But in reality, their honor, their fame, and their glory rested on the backs of Indians who were dishonored and treated as disgraced because of their vanquishment.

To assure that the privileges of the Spanish lords of the land were protected and perpetuated over time, whenever a person stood before the law, be it civil or ecclesiastical, one of the first things recorded was the person's *calidad* (social status). The *Primer diccionario general etimológico de la lengua española* (1789?) defined *calidad* as "the various qualities that constitute the essence of a person or thing; that which constitutes the status of a person, his nature, his age and other circumstances and conditions." *Calidad* and *nobleza* (nobility) were synonyms, the dictionary stated. Both referred to the character of a person deemed privileged by the state. "*Calidad* evaluates the person solely . . . in relation to his rights and privileges; *nobleza,* in relation to the honor and virtue which is assumed to accompany it."

When a person's *calidad* was requested in a legal proceeding, the response was usually the individual's age, sex, place of residence, race, legitimacy or illegitimacy of birth, civic status (whether a landowner or not), occupation, or any combination of these. The type and severity of punishment one received was based on this information. Spaniards, by virtue of their honor, could not be publicly flogged. For erring Indians and half-breeds, the whip was the only sure teacher.

Examination of the *calidad* labels recorded in legal documents between 1598 and 1846 reveals that social standing generally was defined by citizenship, occupation, race, and nationality. Between 1598 and 1759, the period when the definition of social personhood was deeply enmeshed in the religious discourse of conquest, the vast majority of individuals—approximately eight out of ten—were categorized by their civic standing. They were listed as *vecinos* (landowners with full citizenship rights in the community), as *residentes* (residents of a particular place), or as *naturales* (natives). Occasionally, in this period, social status was equated with occupation. This was true primarily of soldiers, who enjoyed special legal privileges (*fueros*), and slaves and *criados* (domestic servants), who lacked full community membership.

Race was very infrequently mentioned as the basis of a person's status before 1760. By saying that race was infrequently mentioned, I do not mean to imply that racial preoccupations did not exist. Clearly, they did. But in the period when the conquest structure of domination was being established in every region from Florida to California, the racial divisions and boundaries were also clearly cultural, and for that reason, I suspect, were unspoken matters of fact. For whatever the realities of biology or the nature of an identity rooted in one of Spain's or New Spain's many regions, on the Spanish Borderlands one was simply a Spaniard, an Indian, or an African slave; there was little concern initially about intermediate hues and fine distinctions.

DISCOURSES OF RACIAL ANXIETY, 1770–1800

Throughout New Spain, the major demographic trend of the eighteenth century was the rapid growth of a population of mixed racial ancestry, born of the exploitative and illicit sexual relationships that occurred between Spaniards and their subject Indians and African domestic slaves. The numerical increase of such groups fueled the racial fears of the nobility, who expressed concern that biological mixing with inferiors would pollute their bloodlines and ultimately lead to the loss of their honor and social standing.

The growth of a large mixed-blood population for whom the original ascribed status categories of the conquest were meaningless was a cause for alarm throughout the elite of the Spanish Borderlands. Widespread racial passing and the increasing importance of achieved status garnered through hard work and economic enterprise—anathema to the aristocracy—had begun to erode the primacy of the nobility in local affairs. Between 1760 and 1800, precisely when the Spanish Borderlands experienced increased levels of immigration, population growth, and economic activity as a result of the Bourbon reform policies to develop and safeguard the northern frontier, the nobility attempted to reassert its dominance. As social bonds were loosened and the status hierarchies of the conquest began to crumble under the weight of economic development and social mobility, the nobility turned to race to buttress its waning power.

165

During these years of rapid social change, an intense preoccupation with racial categories, categories that were often physically indistinguishable from each other, dominated civil and ecclesiastical discourse. The language of racial purity, increasingly a fiction as the population expanded and intermixed, became the imaginary basis on which the nobility asserted its claim to preeminence. And thus, whereas before 1760 the equation of *calidad* with race was quite infrequent in legal dockets, after 1760, and until the beginning of the nineteenth century, race became the dominant way that literate elites defined social status.

Spaniards suddenly were differentiated by national origin as *español europeo* (European Spaniard), *español* (Spaniard), and *español mexicano* (Mexican Spaniard). Indians were referred to simply as *indios,* and occasionally as Indians of a particular nation, nation being synonymous with language group (for instance, *indio de la nación tegua,* a Tewa-speaking Indian). An Indian who spoke Spanish, was referred to as an *indio ladino.* Persons of African origin were identified as *negros* (blacks) and as slave or free. Broader still, without specifying the nature or extent of racial mixture, was the category *color quebrado,* literally "broken color" or half-breed.

An elaborate racial lexicon classified the issue of interracial unions and liaisons. A Spanish father and an Amerindian mother engendered a *mestizo.* A Spaniard and a black woman begot a *mulato.* A *mestizo* and a Spanish woman produced a *castizo,* and so on. In New Spain a precise legal term was assigned to every degree of racial mixture, even if it could not be detected in physical appearance. Individuals of mixed racial ancestry were called *castas,* and the hierarchical legal relationship of one *casta* to another became known as the *régimen de castas* (society of castes).

The Chilean sociologist Alejandro Lipschutz referred to this racial system as a "pigmentocracy," because honor, status, and prestige were judged by skin color and phenotype. The whiter one's skin, the greater one's claim to the honor and precedence Spaniards expected and received. The darker a person's skin, the closer one was presumed to be to the physical labor of slaves and tributary Indians, and the closer the visual association with the disgrace of the conquered. In Spain families guarded their *lim-pieza de sangre* (blood purity) through avoidance of Moors and Jews. In the Spanish Borderlands, families of aristocratic pretension feared that their bloodlines might be metaphysically polluted by Indians, *mulatos,* and, as one man put it, "castes which are held or reputed as despicable."

The temporal frequency and distribution of these racial categories posed some rather complex interpretative problems. Sometimes a racial classification was the result of a person's declaration; at other times it was the subjective assessment of, say, a census taker. Priests and bureaucrats gave race differing amounts of significance and thus could classify the same person quite differently. The use of certain racial categories fluctuated enormously over time and from place to place. Aside from their legal definitions, we have little information concerning what racial classifications may or may not have meant in the routine of daily life. The racial hues recognized in law and practice often remained fixed for a century or so, even though the meanings attached to them changed, as did the people who were classified. One only has to look at the word *mulato* to see this.

According to Professor John Nitti of the University of Wisconsin's Medieval Spanish Dictionary Project, the word *mulato* initially meant a racial mixture of any sort. Offsprings of Spaniards and Moors were known as *mulatos* in medieval Iberia, as were later mixtures of blacks and Indians, and of Frenchmen and Indians in the New World. By the mid eighteenth century *mulato* specifically meant a mixture of black and white.

To demonstrate how complex racial labels are to interpret, take the use of the word *mulato,* which appeared in New Mexican church records, though there is no clear evidence that the individuals classed as such had any black African ancestry. From 1700 to 1744 Fathers Junco and Maulanda listed all the baptisms at Cañada de Cochiti as *indios.* After 1744 the same priests listed all Spanish baptisms as *mulatos. Mulato* in New Mexico simply meant an individual of mixed Spanish-Indian ancestry. Father Prada of Abiquiu gave the word this meaning in 1802 when he referred to his parishioners as "indios mulatos."

Don Pedro Bautista Pino, New Mexico's representative to the 1812 Cortes at Cádiz, Spain, reported to that assembly, "In New Mexico there has never been known any caste of people of African origin. My province is probably the only one in Spanish America to enjoy such distinction." Don Pedro, though patently wrong, advanced the claim to validate a myth he wished to perpetuate: that those men who had become members of the nobility by virtue of Indian wars had preserved their honor and racial purity over the centuries. Had Don Pedro or others bothered to investigate the matter, they would have discovered that several blacks had settled the borderlands. Sebastián Rodríguez, "a Black from San Pablo de Luanda" in Angola, was Don Diego de Vargas's drummer during the 1692 reconquest of the Kingdom of New Mexico. Francisco Rico, "a native Black from the Congo," was married in Santa Fe in 1697, as was Dominga de la Concepción, "a black slave," in 1705. The number of blacks in the Spanish Borderlands was never very large—5 percent of the population at most—except in Spanish Florida, where black slaves from the British colonies were attracted by the prospect of freedom under the Spanish.

Even within the limits imposed by law, the racial labels recorded in civil and ecclesiastical documents were perhaps as precise as frontier conditions, marked by social fluidity, permitted. There was no direct correspondence, except perhaps at the extreme ends of the classification scale, between race and actual physical color. A 1677 roster of colonists bound for northern New Spain listed several as Spaniards, though they had very different appearances. The *españoles* Juan Blanco and José López were described as having "fair skin," while José Cortez, Phelipe López García, and José de Alvarado had "dark complexions." Gaspar Luís and Juan González were listed as *mestizos*, yet in appearance they were identical to most of the *españoles*: they were "dark."

In 1766 Juan Sandoval was "by appearance of white racial status." Julián Vigil's racial status was "*mestizo*, according to reputation." Joseph Baca was appointed militia lieutenant at Ojo Caliente in 1766 because "he is known as a white man." Racial categories (*español, mestizo, mulato*) were sometimes used interchangeably with descriptions of physical color such as *blanco, pardo, prieto* (white, dark, blackish), though the latter

had no real definition in law. Comments that a person "appeared to be," "was reputed to be," or "was known to be" of a certain race indicate the degree to which miscegenation and passing existed on this remote fringe of northern New Spain, and complicated the system of racial classifications.

The nobility and landed peasantry on New Spain's borderlands thought that persons of mixed racial ancestry were despicable because they were presumed to be of illegitimate birth. Indeed, many of them were of illegitimate birth. Throughout the eighteenth century, high levels of illegitimacy occurred in Hispanic settlements because of the sexual exploitation of female slaves and domestic servants.

One friar complained in the 1730s that it was not uncommon for slave owners to boast that "fornicating with servants is good." Fray Joseph Manuel de Equía y Leronbe wondered whether it was not total hypocrisy for him to "free the Indians from their heathen existence," only to enslave them with the stigma of illegitimacy.

In New Mexico, where the levels of illegitimacy are well known, the baptismal registers bore the friar out. Between 1693 and 1848, 176 infants were recorded as born to Indian slaves and baptized. Of these, 144 (82 percent) were illegitimate. Similar results can be found in heredity declarations at the time of marriage. Of the 7,128 persons who declared their birth status in these same years, 3,349 said that they were illegitimate (approximately 25 percent of all persons officially married). Admittedly, such declarations underrepresent the true level of illegitimacy. Individuals could, and often did, lie about their ancestry because illegitimacy was a mark of dishonor.

One has only to examine the sexual history of an Indian slave named Melchora Martín to see how the generative capacities of thralls reproduced the labor force and swelled the ranks of the illegitimate. Melchora's story begins in 1731, when Manuel Martín married Elena Roybal and established a household near the Spanish New Mexican settlement of San Juan. Shortly after his marriage, Martín purchased an Indian slave; three years later she bore a child, named Melchora. Melchora was reared in Martín's home and some time about 1761 gave birth to an illegitimate baby girl, "father unknown." Manuel Martín may have impregnated Melchora; she would not say, though did not hesitate to name the fathers of her other children.

Around 1770 María Martín, Manuel's legitimate daughter, married Salvador García. Melchora and her daughter were given to the newlyweds as a wedding present. In the García household Melchora bore two more illegitimate children, a daughter and a son. Joseph Antonio García, Salvador García's brother, fathered the daughter. Joseph Lujan, the bastard servant of San Juan's chief constable, Don Manuel Parejas, fathered Melchora's son.

María Martín fell ill and died, and when Salvador García remarried, Manuel Martín demanded Melchora's return. A few days after Melchora and her children were reinstated in Martín's home, Juan Sandoval asked for her hand in marriage. Melchora wanted to marry Juan, with whom she had become intimate while both were servants of Salvador García. Sandoval's father opposed the marriage, and shortly thereafter Melchora bore her fourth illegitimate child.

Manuel Martín was furious that Juan Sandoval had broken his promise of marriage to Melchora and ordered his former son-in-law, Salvador, to rid himself of Sandoval's services. Julián Vigil became Salvador García's new servant, and hardly a year later Melchora gave birth again: the father, Julián Vigil. Manuel Martín was so angry with Melchora over this last birth that he beat her severely. In 1766 Melchora sought succor from the ecclesiastical judge, and the complaint she launched against her master for mistreatment brought this story to light. Manuel Martín admitted that he had repeatedly chastised Melchora, but "because of her perverse untamable inclination the whippings were not enough to contain or to correct her." Melchora was placed in a good Christian home "so that she can be subjected and contained." Her children were left in Manuel Martín's custody, and one can only wonder whether he was able to keep them from falling prey to the same misfortunes that characterized their mother's life.

Church and state officials saw concubinage as the standard form of interracial sexual relations. Consequently, persons of mixed origin were automatically presumed to be illegitimate. The Spanish legal theorist Juan de Solorzano Pereira, writing on *mestizos* and *mulatos,* noted that "generally they are born in adultery and other ugly and illicit unions, because there are few Spaniards of honor who marry Indians or Negroes. This defect of their birth makes them infamous to which are added the stain of different color and other vices." For Solorzano, illegitimacy, racial mixture, and infamy were synonymous. The first edition of the *Diccionario de la Academia española* (1737) reached a similar conclusion. *Raza* (race) meant "caste or racial status of origin. When speaking of persons, it usually means illegitimacy. Also, stain or dishonor of the lineage."

Signs of mixed ancestry were often associated with illegitimate birth and, by implication, with illicit sexual unions. The racially mixed progeny that resulted from concubinage and adultery ultimately led to the blurring of phenotypic characteristics in the population and, particularly after the 1760s, this necessitated a stricter racial classification of the population. Without such categories, the aristocracy's claims of racial purity and honor had no significance.

DISCOURSES OF CLASS, CITIZENSHIP, AND PROPERTY, 1800–1821

As the eighteenth century ended and the nineteenth began, specifications of race vanished from official documents almost as rapidly as they had appeared. Whereas between 1760 and 1799 almost 80 percent of all individuals were classified by race, beginning in 1800 the proportion of racial status labels declined both in absolute terms and in relationship to the identification of persons by civic standing, nationality, or "no mentions." Also of importance was the progressive polarization of racial labels between 1760 and 1800 into just two: *español* and *indio.* The intermediate hues of race, which were so important between 1760 and 1799, by 1800 had begun to disappear from the records.

With Mexican Independence in 1821 racial distinctions were legally abolished. This fact largely explains why race disappeared from legal documents. My suspicion is that in popular behavior, various racial idioms continued in use. I say this primarily because to this day, it is not uncommon throughout the Southwest to hear persons of mixed descent call themselves, or be called by others, *coyotes,* which means "mixed-blood." We know quite well from the experiences in other western Atlantic societies that during the height of the Enlightenment, when ideas about social equality were broadly disseminated, the notion that "all men are created equal" required the definition of marginal, stigmatized, and subordinate groups as nonpersons. Zoomorphic labels—dog, fox, lobo, coyote, and so on—became terms of social location and derision in popular speech that still remain.

In the Spanish colonial documents from the borderlands after 1821 individuals were increasingly classified by their nationality as *mexicanos* (Mexicans). This occurred simultaneously with the increasing use of the label *ciudadano* (citizen).

The social mobility created by the economic measures of the Bourbon reforms shattered the isolation of the Spanish Borderland frontier and quickly eroded the forms of ascribed status on which conquest society had been established. As achieved status became more important in establishing a person's place in society, it was increasingly irrelevant, except to members of the nobility, whether one was of pure or impure blood, whether one was an Old or New Christian, and whether one was white or not. Society changed as a result of economic development, immigration, and massive racial mixing. As it did, one's value and social standing were determined more by wealth and income. If one had money, land, or political power, one had or could purchase full citizenship before the law. By 1830 social class was what mattered most on the borderlands.

THE CHANGING CONCEPT OF RACE

In the long sweep, from 1538 to 1846, a person's social standing, *calidad*, was always a complex set of interlocking values and forms of identity. In the conquest phase, it was power and might that counted most in dominating Indians and Africans. During the second half of the eighteenth century, race became an easy way to reassert the power of the conquest nobility because the society was in a rapid flux. And by the beginning of the nineteenth century, citizenship, class, and power determined standing. The essential point here is that the concept of race was never static. It constantly changed as the distribution of the means and instruments of production changed hands, from one generation to the next.

BIBLIOGRAPHY

Cocker, William S. "Religious Censuses of Pensacola, 1796–1801." *Florida Historical Quarterly* 61, no. 1 (1982):54–63.

Corbett, Theodore G. "Migration to a Spanish Imperial Frontier in the Seventeenth and Eighteenth Centuries: St. Augustine." *Hispanic American Historical Review* 54, no. 3 (1974):414–430.

Deagan, Kathleen A. "*Mestizaje* in Colonial St. Augustine." *Ethnohistory* 20, no. 1 (1973):55–65.

Dobyns, Henry F. *Spanish Colonial Tucson: A Demographic History.* Tucson, Ariz., 1976.

Gutiérrez, Ramón A. *When Jesus Came, the Corn Mothers Went Away: Marriage, Sexuality, and Power in New Mexico, 1500–1846.* Stanford, Calif., 1991.

Jones, Oakah L. *Los Paisanos: Spanish Settlers on the Northern Frontier of New Spain.* Norman, Okla., 1979.

Lipschütz, Alejandro. *El indoamericanismo y el problema racial en las Américas.* Santiago, Chile, 1944.

Morner, Magnus. *Race Mixture in the History of Latin America.* Boston, 1967.

Olmsted, Virginia Langham, comp. *Spanish and Mexican Censuses of New Mexico, 1750–1830.* Albuquerque, N.Mex., 1981.

Solórzano Pereira, Juan de. *Política Indiana.* Madrid, 1776.

Tjarks, Alicia V. "Comparative Demographic Analysis of Texas, 1777–1793." *Southwestern Historical Quarterly* 77, no. 3 (1974):291–338.

Ramón A. Gutiérrez

SEE ALSO **Indian-Colonist Contact; Interracial Societies; Mission Communities;** and **Settlements in the Spanish Borderlands.**

THE FRENCH COLONIES

Canada

MISCEGENATION, OR *métissage,* eventually gave rise to a "people in between," but the mixed racial

Métis (a term not found in the early literature and documents) initially were amalgamated either into Native American or colonial society. The American Indians accepted adopted Europeans as full-fledged kin. The colonists were quite aware of mixed origins, but life-style and culture, rather than ancestry, determined admissibility into the French colonial community. Racial biases appeared only as the colonial society matured. Cornelius de Pauw employed the term Métis in his *Recherches philosophiques sur les Américains* (1768–1769), stating categorically that they were superior to the Native inhabitants but inferior to Europeans.

EMERGENCE OF RACIAL BIAS

Racial prejudice, such as that exhibited in De Pauw's writings, resulted in the 1768 expulsion of mixed-blood militia officers. Julien Raymond in *Observations sur l'origine et le progrès du préjugé des colons blancs* (1791) traced the rise of contemporary French racial prejudice (as distinct from earlier ethnocentrism) in the Antilles and Louisiana to the early eighteenth century when relatively few numbers of French women and children immigrated to the New World.

These immigrants brought with them many enlightenment ideas and scientific theories, including views affecting popular attitudes toward *métissage*. The prevailing categorization of races with distinct characters, temperaments, and mentalities relegated Native Americans to the status of inferiors. While humanity's alleged natural condition was whiteness, groups could lose this characteristic through environmental factors and degeneracy. Some races were thus closer to animals than to men in the chain of being; physical characteristics reflected moral qualities.

These concepts fueled the debate on the consequences of racial mixing. De Pauw argued that, like plants and animals that degenerated in an alien environment, humans and their institutions experienced *dégénérescence* if detached from the higher racial orders. But Charles Augustin Vandermonde in *Essai sur la manière de perfectionner l'espèce humaine* (1756) stressed the "necessity to cross the human races in order to prevent them from degenerating." To have "children of handsome and strong constitution," he

observed, one should "seek a union with foreign women."

Many colonists agreed that such unions strengthened trade relations, cemented military alliances, and opened doors to missionary work. Two factors also contributed to the practice. Most encounters occurred in the hinterland, far from the social controls of the European settlements; women enjoyed undisputed custody of children because little importance was attached to paternal rights. Together, these factors permitted four distinct forms of *métissage:* sanctified unions, or sacramental marriages; customary unions *à la façon de pays*, which might eventually be regularized "before the church" or terminated if the European partner returned to the Laurentian settlements; "concubinage" or cohabitation, especially with domestics or slaves; and casual encounters or sexual promiscuity.

OFFICIAL RESPONSES TO *MÉTISSAGE*

It is widely assumed that, unlike the British, the French encouraged *métissage* in their colonies. The combination of Champlain's assimilationist policy, Article XVII of the charter of the Company of New France (1627), Jesuit and officialdom's promotion of interracial marriages in the 1660s to populate a colony that attracted few immigrants, and the permissive statements emanating from the Crown regarding the conversion and assimilation of Native Americans gave rise to the tradition of official approbation and encouragement of the practice.

Canon law forbade the marriage of Catholics with pagans, but as early as 1648 missionaries asked for dispensations from Rome in order to regularize illicit unions between French fur traders and Native American women. Such unions persisted throughout the French regime, despite the clergy's efforts to combat "disorders" and "concubinage." As early as 1639 missionaries had started gathering natives on *réductions*, or reserves, near French settlements, to promote their conversion and acculturation. By 1685 Governor Denonville opined that the integrationist objectives were not being achieved; instead, "they communicate very much to us all they have that is the very worst, and they take on likewise all that is evil and vicious in us."

In 1699 Pierre Le Moyne d'Iberville asked royal permission "to allow the French who will settle in this country to marry Indian girls." Louis XIV's response, often cited as an encapsulization of official policy throughout the period, was that he saw "no inconvenience in this, provided they be Christians," his intention being that colonial officials should apply themselves to "prevent debauchery and all disorderly conduct" and "protect the missionaries" in their evangelical work.

The following year La Mothe Cadillac, in planning the founding of Detroit, informed the Crown that the settlement would be composed of Europeans and natives so that they could intermarry and "form one people," echoing Champlain's phrase almost a century earlier. It would be absolutely essential, Cadillac asserted, "to allow the soldiers and Canadians to marry the savage maidens when they have been instructed in religion and know the French language." These marriages were necessary to consolidate the proposed military base, trading post, and mission station with an agricultural support base at an important communications hub. But Cadillac made two unsubstantiated claims—that Native women preferred Frenchmen to their own people as mates and that the children of such unions would speak French and live in the European fashion. Contrary to Cadillac's claim, "as experience shows daily in Canada" there were more examples of Frenchmen "going native" than of gallicized natives.

More convincing was his argument that "marriages of this kind will strengthen the friendship of these tribes, as the alliances of the Romans perpetuated peace with the Sabines through the intervention of the women whom the former had taken from the latter." This allusion might invite thoughts of forcible integration and reinforce the image of the subjugation of a barbaric people. In a belated effort to rally the clergy's support, Cadillac suggested that his plan would assist evangelization so that "the deplorable sacrifices which they offer to Baal" would be eradicated. But the missionaries responded that his plan would result in a decline of civilized standards, in a demoralization of both parties in contact, and in uninhibited trafficking of brandy—all of which would undermine missionary efforts.

Quebec's governor, the marquis de Vaudreuil, agreed with the Jesuits and sought direction from Versailles. He ordered Cadillac, as commandant at Fort Pontchartrain, to prevent soldiers and habitants "from having scandalous intercourse with native women, and to permit no Frenchman whatever, soldier or otherwise, to marry them until such time as we have received orders from the court on this matter." The royal dispatch of July 1709, while recognizing "the great utility of marriages" as proposed by Cadillac, upheld the governor's position but urged him to reexamine the need for prohibition. Vaudreuil replied that he was persuaded that "one must never mix bad blood with good," that in Canada all the French who had contracted such marriages were "licentious, lazy, and insufferably independent," and that the children of these unions were "as lazy as the natives themselves." The king approved Vaudreuil's prohibitionary order on 17 July 1711.

There matters stood for several decades in the interior country, as officers exercised control over their soldiers while the missionaries did what they felt was necessary to stabilize family life and root out immorality. This long-enduring policy would eventually be complemented by a notable decision in Louisiana jurisprudence and by royal reprimands against two religious orders condoning *métissage*. Following a dispute over the inheritance rights of the Native wife and Métis child of a French settler in the Illinois country, the Superior Council of Louisiana, which had acquired jurisdiction over the area, issued an edict in October 1735 requiring state approval of mixed marriages. Meanwhile the Crown informed the directors of the Seminary of Foreign Missions in Paris that the missionaries had been too lax in permitting such unions, which were "dishonorable for the nation" and tended to lead to social unrest because "the children thus begotten are more libertine than the savages themselves." The Jesuit missionaries made their views known in France too, asserting that they were attempting to regularize conjugal arrangements in New France because there would inevitably be a Métis population. The Jesuits believed it important that the distinct Métis settlements appearing near the forts and posts be respectable and acceptable elements in the community.

The secular authorities, unlike the clergy, placed obstacles in the way of intermarriage. In 1749 Canadian interim governor La Galissonière informed Bishop Pontbriand that marriages of Frenchmen to Native women were "pernicious for the state and at least useless so far as concerns religion." He therefore anticipated no difficulty in procuring a royal prohibition such as had been issued in Louisiana. However, La Galissonière favored a more "natural course of events" whereby the bishop would order the missionary clergy to "perform the fewest possible such marriages and especially never to perform any without the very express consent of the commandants of the place." Two years later, the marquis de Vaudreuil instructed the newly assigned Illinois commandant to prevent these marriages because they were "shameful and of dangerous consequences because of the familiarity that they encourage between the natives and the French and because of the bad race that they produce." This was not what Anglo-Americans imagined to be the French point of view, nor what most historians have believed.

Were the prohibition orders carried out? Governor Duquesne associated "dissoluteness with native women" with running the woods. Consequently, in 1755 he ordered post commanders to send offenders back to Quebec for trial. At Louisbourg an ensign who married a Métisse against his commanding officer's wishes had his marriage annulled and was sent back to France in disgrace, along with the priest who had performed the ceremony. The case may have been exceptional, but the punishment was exemplary.

THE MÉTIS IN NEW FRANCE

No reliable statistics or estimates of the number of Métis in the colony during the French regime exist. *Métissage* occurred in different circumstances: parish registers indicate that there were a few such unions, and at Lorette, for example, francisation had become so acceptable that several men had taken French wives. Such unions existed on other reserves, most often with English captives but also with foundlings and orphans whom colonists had left to be reared there. A large number of Métis children born out of wedlock lived at Detroit and Michilimackinac.

The Swedish botanist Peter Kalm observed during his 1749 visit to the colony that "the Indian blood in Canada is very much mixed with European blood, and a large number of the Indians now living owe their origin to Europe." Numerous Métis could be found at Forts Frontenac, Niagara, Duquesne, Chartres, Kaministiquia, and Michipicoten. By the 1730s Métis were so numerous in the Lake Superior region that they formed their own villages and came to regard themselves as a "new nation" occupying a social niche between the French and Native tribes. In Cahokia, Kaskaskia, Saint Philippe, Prairie du Rocher, and Sainte Geneviève they constituted a visible element in the population. Not surprisingly, eyewitnesses reported that the voyageurs in the Mississippi and Missouri countries had a marked preference for Native women over their own compatriots.

Métissage was not confined to the western frontiers. The greatest degree of racial admixture was reported in Acadia, and leading families such as the Denys, d'Entremonts, and Saint-Castins were proud of their Native American ancestry. The Acadians who relocated at Louisbourg were reported in 1756 to be "a mixed breed, that is to say, most of them proceed from marriages or concubinage of the savage women with the first settlers." The abbé Pierre Maillard believed that there was so much intermarriage between Micmac and Malecite that soon "it will be impossible to distinguish them apart."

By contrast "domiciled natives" on reserves were most affected by *métissage* in the Saint Lawrence Valley settlements. In the upper country of the Great Lakes basin and the Illinois region the mixed-blood population was sufficiently numerous and visible to constitute a third element.

EXPLANATIONS OF *MÉTISSAGE*

Historical interpretations of this social phenomenon have been confused by three major factors. First, the promotion of *métissage* during the early "heroic age" of the colony, before the introduction of royal government in 1663, has mistakenly been supposed to have continued until 1760. Second, clerical-nationalist historians like Lionel Groulx have abhorred any suggestion that a pure and select French stock, which formed the embryonic French-Canadian nation, should have been contaminated through *métissage*. Finally, historians have postulated that the advantages that the French enjoyed over their rivals in the fur trade and military alliances were based on their promotion of intermarriage.

The French were not unanimous in their approval of such relations—at least at the elitist and official level. Miscegenation might be good for trade and war, but administrators deemed it detrimental to colonial social development, particularly to the civilizing mission and the perpetuation of a French racial stock in the New World. At the beginning of the seventeenth century New France seemed to have embarked on state-subsidized *métissage,* but by the beginning of the eighteenth century it was permissible but not necessarily recommended. By the end of the French regime *métissage* was by and large suspect and out of favor—when not outrightly denounced. This hardening of attitudes was consonant with the anticolonialism of the *philosophes.*

BIBLIOGRAPHY

Giraud, Marcel. *The Métis in the Canadian West.* Lincoln, Nebr., 1986.

Jaenen, Cornelius J. *Friend and Foe: Aspects of French-Amerindian Cultural Contact in the Sixteenth and Seventeenth Centuries.* New York, 1976.

———. "Miscegenation in Eighteenth Century New France." In *New Dimensions in Ethnohistory,* edited by Barry Gough and Laird Christie. Ottawa, Ontario, 1991.

Pagliaro, Harold E., ed. *Racism in the Eighteenth Century.* Cleveland, Ohio, 1973.

Peterson, Jacqueline. "Prelude to Red River: A Social Portrait of the Great Lakes Métis." *Ethnohistory* 25 (1978):41–67.

Peterson, Jacqueline, and Jennifer S. H. Brown, eds. *New Peoples: Being and Becoming Métis in North America.* Lincoln, Nebr., 1985.

Upton, Leslie F. S. *Micmacs and Colonists: Indian-White Relations in the Maritimes, 1763–1867.* Vancouver, British Columbia, 1979.

Cornelius J. Jaenen

SEE ALSO **Indian-Colonist Contact; Interracial Societies; and Mission Communities.**

Louisiana

FRENCH LOUISIANA, like other North American colonies, from the beginning comprised a racially diverse society. From the first penetration of Europeans into what would become the French colony of Louisiana, Spanish and French explorers encountered the Native populations. The resulting racial mix became more complex with the importation of African slaves as the colony developed under French administration.

Throughout most of the French period (1682–1763) Louisiana remained a colonial backwater, struggling and poor. The administrative programs that governed its early settlement and development reflected the concern for order and unity that preoccupied France in the eighteenth century. But it would take more than idealistic colonial theory, more than the indignant remonstrances of colonial governors and Catholic missionary priests, to regulate human personal and sexual relationships in the hot, humid, insect- and hurricane-plagued, poverty-stricken, racially diverse settlement and to create a rationally ordered new society. A population composed initially of Indians, soldiers, woodsmen, vagabonds, deserters, and criminals and prostitutes exiled from France attempted to live with later immigrating farmers, artisans, tradesmen, and free and enslaved blacks, all coming to Louisiana for different, often incompatible, reasons. The law, the church, and the colony's governing officers argued for cultural unity, Christian piety, moral rectitude, and family stability according to European standards. Frontier conditions in a harsh wilderness determined a far different reality.

RELATIONS WITH INDIANS

While Indian slavery was never successful in Louisiana, experiments with it persisted throughout the French period and had a defining impact on relations between Indians and whites. The French enslaved the Indians almost immediately, often with the cooperation of rival Indian tribes that did not hesitate to sell or barter their captured enemies to the French. Indian slavery proved to be frustratingly unsatisfactory—the Indians simply disappeared into the woods. Moreover, it hampered administrative efforts to stabilize relationships with tribal allies, and the colonists constantly complained of the difficulties of getting the Indians to work. There were consequently never very many Indian slaves in the colony—the 1726 census reported 229, and the 1737 census listed only 240. Conflict between the Indian and the French populations remained intense, especially after the Natchez uprising in 1729, and a harmonious interracial mix was rare, despite the number of both legal and extralegal liaisons that created a stream of criticism in the administrative correspondence.

Complaints about French concubinage with Indian women began almost immediately after the establishment of the first small, struggling fort at Mobile Bay. After cession of the colony to Antoine Crozat in 1712, despite efforts to attract a more stable population, the constant contact between the Canadian woodsmen and adventurers and the Native Americans, whose mores seemed debauched and promiscuous to the French officials, undermined efforts to impose a homogeneous order.

Most of these liaisons between white men and Indian women were domineering and exploitive, although a few were committed, even legal, marriages. Some French-Indian marriages indicate the adaptation of Indian wives to French social and legal practices, as well as the more commonly assumed French or Canadian assimilation of Indian ways. More frequently, interracial French-Indian liaisons meant a brutal experience for Indian women. Among the earliest preserved documents are accounts of cruel treatment of Indians, as illustrated by the example of one young Indian slave who was so severely beaten she nearly died of her injuries. Even after the importation of French women as prospective brides for the bachelor settlers, many French men preferred the freer, illicit unions with Indian concubines. Because both civil and church authorities disapproved of miscegenation, the children born of these unions faced difficult lives, rejected by both Indian and French, if indeed they survived at all. One early church report on the conduct of the French in Louisiana notes that many of these babies were strangled. Undoubtedly many also succumbed to the diseases that ravaged the starving colony.

Early census records for Louisiana indicate that the number of individuals of mixed Indian and European backgrounds remained quite small. They made up a marginal group living on the fringes of colonial society, where they mingled with racially mixed mulattos to form a small population of triracial heritage. Little is known of this outcast and silent population, living in the shadowy penumbra of French administrative reach.

DOMINANCE OF WHITE OVER BLACK

The intransigent behavior of the early voyageurs and woodsmen and the unsuitability of later immigrants—many of them forced, involuntary exiles—for the necessary hard agricultural work retarded the hoped-for development of a stable, homesteading society. Unable to meet the demand for labor and facing the failure of Indian slavery, the colonists imported black slaves into Louisiana as early as 1712. Not every black colonist came as a slave; listed among the early passengers are the names of several free black women. In the 1720s a steady flow of slaves augmented a growing black population. Two thousand arrived in Louisiana before 1721, but early-eighteenth-century census records indicate that only 680 survived for very long after reaching the colony. Conditions on the voyages decimated slave ranks during the transoceanic journey, and disease, harsh treatment, and despair killed many of those who survived the voyage. By 1731 slightly over 2,500 black slaves served 5,000 white settlers, with the slave population growing to 4,581 by 1737 and 5,499 by the end of the French period. Most slaveholdings were small, seldom numbering over five or six, which meant that close interaction between blacks and whites influenced the experiences and the cultural behaviors of both. Some slaves were assigned to merchant craftsmen and learned skills through short-term apprenticeships, leading ultimately to the existence of a class of skilled black artisans and craftsmen in the colony. Economic and demographic conditions made interracial relationships flexible and unpredictable and ensured the interpenetration of cultural values, but the paternalism of French society permeating the legal codes maintained the dominance of white over black.

The *Code Noir* issued by the Crown in 1685 and reissued in 1724, along with later ordinances promulgated in Louisiana, regulated the patriarchal interracial society nurtured under the policies of absolutist France. Less harsh in its provisions than is commonly thought, the code required masters to govern slaves paternally and to provide religious education and proper material care. It permitted slaves to sue owners who failed to provide adequate clothing and food and prohibited slaveowners from physically abusing, torturing, mutilating, or killing their slaves, allowing them to chain slaves or beat them only in extraordinary cases. Violations of the code could be prosecuted, although they seldom were and only if the abuses were so severe as to offend even other white slaveowners who usually brought the suits to court, as few slaves knew how to exploit the legal system to their advantage.

Although the original code permitted interracial marriages, the 1724 code forbade them, not in order to preserve racial purity, an indifferent concern in eighteenth-century France, where numerous interracial marriages occurred, but in the interest of preserving order. The colonial administration feared interracial liaisons out of the conviction that they divided loyalties and encouraged insurrection. Louisiana's biracial and even triracial population posed unprecedented challenges to colonial administrators.

Freed blacks enjoyed all the rights of native-born French but faced formidable economic challenges and could be reduced to slavery for failing to pay their debts, for immoral behavior, or for inciting or supporting slave rebellion. As the population of slaves grew to surpass the number of white settlers, slaveowners feared the influence of free blacks on discontented slaves. Whites saw free blacks as an antagonistic and threatening community within the white population with more sympathy for black slaves than for the established white order. Slave regulations were tightened in the 1750s; subsequent records reveal a hardening of attitudes toward blacks, both slave and free.

Frontier conditions made the Black Code difficult to enforce, and the provisions forbidding slave abuse and requiring education were frequently violated. Because of the helplessness of blacks within the institution of slavery, slaves endured great emotional and physical stresses; surviving records document incidents of shockingly cruel treatment of slaves. Runaways were a serious problem, and punishment was harsh.

One brutish overseer was charged with causing frequent miscarriages among slave women by his violent beatings. He was particularly vindictive to those who rejected his sexual advances and was harshly criticized for the long hours he required and the terrible rations he provided—one meal of rotten beans a day.

The presence of black women in intimate relationships within white households and the availability of black women unable to resist the demands of white owners resulted in a small but significant mulatto population during the French period. Miscegenation did not, however, constitute a major problem in the French regime. Although black-white sexual liaisons occasionally resulted in the emancipation of racially mixed children, this occurred infrequently. One woman who was granted her child's freedom after her owner's death was denied the legality of the manumission, and the child remained enslaved to the administrative officer entrusted with freeing her. At best, the children born of black-white unions survived in relatively small numbers. Nonetheless, the often inaccurate census records indicate that this racially mixed group, however small the number, formed the foundation of the Creoles (Louisiana-born) of color who would emerge as a significant ethnic element in Louisiana after 1763.

French Louisiana's racial diversity provided a cultural heterogeneity that by the end of the French period had created a new and unique synthesis. Although racial and ethnic boundaries remained largely distinct throughout the French administration, the foundation for later and larger racially mixed societies had been firmly established under French colonial policy and goals.

BIBLIOGRAPHY

Allain, Mathé. "Slave Policies in French Louisiana." *Louisiana History* 21, no. 2 (1980):127–137.

Brasseaux, Carl A. "The Administration of Slave Regulations in French Louisiana." *Louisiana History* 21, no. 2 (1980):139–158.

Everett, Donald. "Free People of Color in Colonial Louisiana." *Louisiana History* 7, no. 1 (1966):5–20.

McCoy, Shelby. "Negroes and Mulattoes in Eighteenth-Century France." *Journal of Negro History* 30, no. 3 (1945):276–292.

O'Neill, Charles E. *Church and State in French Colonial*

Louisiana: Policy and Politics to 1732. New Haven, Conn., 1966.

Taylor, Joe Gray. *Negro Slavery in Louisiana.* Baton Rouge, La., 1963.

Usner, Daniel H., Jr. "From African Captivity to American Slavery: The Introduction of Black Laborers to Colonial Louisiana." *Louisiana History* 20, no. 1 (1979):25–48.

Vaughan Burdin Baker

SEE ALSO **British Settlements, The Lower South; Free Blacks, Indian-Colonist Contact; and Interracial Societies.**

THE BRITISH COLONIES

IN 1735 AN IMMIGRANT German scholar named Christian Priber sold most of his worldly possessions and headed for Cherokee territory on the southeastern frontier. Priber learned the Cherokee anguage and adopted Cherokee customs and dress. He also taught the tribal leaders how best to protect themselves from the European colonists. He spoke of the need to trust no one nation and to trade with numerous European powers. In addition, he instructed the Cherokee in the fundamentals of weights and measures to shield them from dishonest traders. Becaause of recent abuses they had suffered at the hands of the English, the Cherokee considered Priber "a great beloved man," and he quickly won their support for his plans. Priber had abandoned his former life because he was sick of the hopeless corruption of European society, and he dreamed of establishing a new community in British North America based on Plato's *Republic* and on radical political and social philosophies of the time. In Priber's new society all property was to be held in common; there would be no class distinctions, and no laws. Women were to be treated as equals with men. Most important, Priber's community was to be open to all, a haven for oppressed people everywhere: refugees from other tribes, escaped fugitives or debtors, runaway servants or slaves. Discrimination based on wealth, sex,

color, or race would not be tolerated. Priber appropriately named his new utopian republic the "Kingdom of Paradise."

When knowledge of Priber's plans reached officials in South Carolina, they quickly took steps to stop him. For the British, such a man and such a community were dangerous. They assumed he was working for the French or some other European power and was trying to cause trouble on their western border. They could not allow any disruption of the relationship then existing between white settlers and their Indian neighbors and correctly feared that Priber was trying to destroy the British trade monopoly with the Cherokee. Even more disturbing for the South Carolinians was the steady stream of runaway slaves that headed for asylum in Priber's new republic. No crack in the solidifying slave system could be tolerated. Accordingly, in 1739 South Carolina officials ordered Priber's arrest and made numerous attempts to apprehend him, but the Cherokee defended him. Eventually, in 1743, Priber was captured by Creek Indians while fleeing to the French and was imprisoned in Georgia, where he soon died.

These energetic efforts by British officials reveal the type of society that British authorities and probably most colonists wanted America to be. Native Americans, poor whites, and African slaves simply could not live together as equals— at least not openly. To do so would challenge fundamental assumptions about race, class, and social order. From the beginning of European settlement, efforts were made to keep the various races apart. While there was a certain amount of informal interracial cooperation at first, due to the demands of settlement, by the eighteenth century evolving "white" notions of racial categories and barriers between the different races had grown more rigid.

SOLIDIFYING SOCIAL BARRIERS

British North America was always a racially diverse place, and in many ways the entire region could be considered an interracial society. Interracial contact occurred immediately as European settlers encountered the Native Americans and drew upon their guidance and support for survival. Yet the British colonists soon passed laws restricting contact between the two races and eventually tried to enslave Indians. The picture became even more complex and discriminatory with the importation of Africans, which began in the second decade of British settlement and increased rapidly in the late seventeenth century. Initially, the British colonists drew upon African expertise in areas such as agriculture and architecture, but as the number of Africans increased, a system of slavery became more firmly entrenched and laws increasingly kept the races socially separate. By the early eighteenth century, most British colonies had codified their laws of slavery and regulated other aspects of interracial relations, including (usually by prohibiting) intermarriage.

Thus, while British North America was always racially diverse, it was never truly integrated. This does not mean that non-Europeans did not participate in either the formal or the informal politics of their own communities, nor that only Europeans contributed to the emerging American culture. It also does not mean that Native Americans, Europeans, and Africans never lived and worked together as equals. Throughout the colonial period there was always some intermingling of races, especially on the fringes of the European-controlled areas. Even within some European-dominated communities, Indians, whites, and blacks frequently worked in the same fields, drank in the same taverns, and shared the same beds, although in the last instance such activities were seldom openly acknowledged.

INTERRACIAL SOCIETIES OUTSIDE BRITISH SETTLEMENTS

A mixing of the races also occurred outside the British settlements. It is impossible to estimate precisely the number of Europeans and Africans who fled the colonies for a new life within the various Indian nations. Many of these refugees had initially been captured by the Indians and later decided to remain with them; others joined Indian communities of their own free will. And often whites and blacks together sought shelter within Native society, especially in the seventeenth century when indentured servants and slaves frequently worked on the same farm or plantation. The fates of these escapees is usually impossible to determine. Many died from the elements, and others were returned or even put

to death by their intended protectors. Nevertheless, many whites and blacks did meld into Indian society. Such individuals often made useful contributions to their new nations, frequently serving as interpreters in negotiations between Indians and white settlers, bringing needed skills, including knowledge of European technology and customs, and simply replenishing depleting populations. Still, while Native American life changed with the inclusion of its new white and black members, it was not truly interracial in that the groups did not contribute equally to the culture. In order to remain within their adopted communities, the newcomers had to embrace almost entirely the culture of the Native Americans.

Some truly interracial societies were founded by Africans, Europeans, and Indians outside of British settlements and separate from the Native American tribes. Because such communities could never be openly acknowledged and because the individuals involved were usually either fugitives or exiles from the dominant culture, the interracial societies existed beyond the reach of colonial law. These outlaw communities, whose inhabitants were often called maroons, existed either in secret or in places that were almost impossible to find.

EMERGENCE OF MAROON COMMUNITIES

Maroon communities emerged in all areas of the Western Hemisphere that practiced plantation slavery, especially during each colony's formative period, when the slave system and ruling structure were less established. Most maroon enclaves were small and their existence brief, but some, such as Palmares in Brazil, had up to twenty thousand people and lasted a century. There was almost constant maroon activity in Jamaica, but most groups were much smaller and more fluid in composition.

While maroon communities were present in British North America from the earliest days of settlement until the institution's demise in the nineteenth century, most were much smaller and of shorter duration than their Caribbean and Latin American counterparts. In several ways, conditions for maroon communities were less favorable in British North America than in these other areas. One factor was North America's relatively small slave force, which could be more effectively policed. Important, too, was eastern North America's paucity of mountains, forests, swamps, and other rugged terrain in which maroons could seek sanctuary. Finally, the political instability that encouraged maroon communities in other regions was largely absent in North America.

Although never as prominent in British North America as in other slave societies, maroon activity did affect most British mainland colonies, especially in the South and especially in the eighteenth century, when the African slave trade took on greater importance. African-born slaves predominated in maroon societies, partly because newly arrived Africans tended to run away in groups and, unlike American-born slaves who often fled alone, usually ran toward the backcountry rather than toward urban centers. Most runaways were young, unskilled, and male. Because so many of the maroons were African-born, the cultural characteristics of the maroon communities were strongly African. Rather than re-creating African society, however, maroon communities mixed African, European, and Native American cultures, for individuals from all American races could usually be found there. Runaway indentured servants and other poor whites, as well as American Indians—especially escaped Indian slaves and survivors of recently decimated tribes—often found their way into maroon communities.

Most maroon societies were resourceful. They relied on agriculture and on raising livestock, as well as on hunting and fishing. Sometimes they traded with nearby planters and townspeople or raided neighboring plantations for food and supplies. Occasionally they degenerated into genuine outlaw camps, preying on anyone of any race in order to survive.

Maroon societies were present in British North America almost from the beginning, and by the mid seventeenth century, small maroon groups were active in many parts of Virginia. In an effort to thwart such enclaves, the Virginia House of Burgesses in 1661 passed a law against white and black servants running away together; a law of 1672 rewarded the killing of such outlaws. In 1691 a group of fugitives in Rappahannock County committed several depredations, including the theft of some guns. In 1729 a small maroon settlement in the Blue Ridge Mountains was captured by a strong body of armed white men who had feared what would result with the acquisition of guns, ammunition, and farm tools by the maroon settlement. Afterwards, the militia went into training, according to Lieutenant Governor William Gooch, to "prevent this for the future."

One of the most common destinations for whites and blacks fleeing Virginia authorities was the backcountry of North Carolina. The isolated settlements and subsistence economy in the colony made escape easy, especially in the seventeenth and early eighteenth centuries before a plantation society became firmly established. The North Carolina legislature even encouraged such settlement—unwittingly, no doubt—by passing a law that made the colony a sanctuary for debtors from other colonies; local governments generally accepted both black and white fugitives. In part this generous policy grew out of the fugitive status of many early North Carolina leaders, but it also reflected the absence of the entrenched slave system and strong master class that would characterize the eighteenth century. Thus, in many ways early North Carolina itself became an informal maroon community in the sense that many of its settlers were refugees from British society; for the most part, Europeans, Africans, and Native Americans coexisted peacefully.

The Dismal Swamp Settlements
The largest and most authentic maroon enclave in British North America was located in the Great Dismal Swamp, which straddles the Virginia–North Carolina border. Although its population fluctuated, estimates of the number of inhabitants reached as high as two thousand. Unlike most other maroon settlements, which were often temporary, those that developed in the Dismal Swamp formed a true community. Lasting over one hundred fifty years, they enjoyed a stable core of inhabitants, including numerous women and children, and social institutions permitting the establishment and continuation of families and the forging of political alliances. They also saw the growth of a spiritual activity combining religious and magical beliefs.

Like the regions of the Caribbean and Latin America that nurtured large maroon societies, the Dismal Swamp had the necessary conditions for an outlaw community to exist. First, the geography of the region was ideal for both protection and survival. The swamp was so large that entire villages could remain hidden: in the eighteenth century, roughly two thousand square miles (5,200 square kilometers), about the size of Delaware. The region was also a jungle and unapproachable to outsiders; one needed a guide to explore it safely. But, contrary to its name, the swamp provided a bountiful existence for those who learned to live there. The water was fresh and brimmed with fish; numerous islands offered opportunities for habitation and agriculture; the area was alive with game. And because the swamp spills over into both Virginia and North Carolina, its boundaries and legal jurisdiction remained in dispute and its interior was largely ignored by authorities from both colonies. Yet the Dismal Swamp was near enough to plantation societies for those who wanted to escape from them to do so, and its proximity made it convenient, too, for those living in the swamp to plunder food, supplies, and cattle or seek revenge on the outside world.

In the seventeenth century, the swamp's few inhabitants were mostly Native Americans who were remnants from the small nations that had been quickly destroyed by the English or refugees from slavery in the British colonies. In addition, there were some fugitive white indentured servants and a few runaway African slaves, although the black population remained small until the eighteenth century. After the Tuscarora War (1711–1713), an influx of defeated Tuscarora and white North Carolinians who had supported them made the swamp a true maroon community. As the refuge grew in numbers and strength, the number of individual runaways heading toward the swamp also increased.

Within the Dismal Swamp the races tended to cluster in separate settlements, although there was much intermingling. Over the course of time, each group took its turn at influencing the overall structure of the society. At first, the Tuscarora provided political and social leadership, because they had come from a relatively stable society and were numerically predominant. By the 1730s Native Americans, Europe-

ans, and Africans were probably of equal strength within the maroon, and Europeans had become the main faction. By the mid eighteenth century, Africans predominated. The changing human composition of the Dismal Swamp largely reflected the shift in bound labor patterns within the British colonies, and each settlement mirrored the source of its residents. By the end of the colonial period, Africans dominated the communities in the northern and middle parts of the swamp, while Europeans and Native Americans were more prevalent in the south.

Although there were some cultural differences between the various settlements within the Dismal Swamp, there were also great similarities. Most important, all residents were fugitives from British society and shared an active hostility to it. In addition, there was a blending of cultures. As early as the beginning of the eighteenth century, outsiders reported that a new culture was emerging in the Dismal Swamp. The environment probably did more than anything to shape this new maroon culture, but it is also true that the various groups needed to cooperate and work together for their security and survival. There is no record of discord among the various races, and much intermarrying occurred between them.

One of the most prominent features of this maroon community was its steady confrontation with the outside world. Maroon residents frequently raided neighboring plantations for food and supplies. British officials made numerous efforts to destroy the maroons but were always unsuccessful. Damage to nearby plantations reached a peak during the American Revolution, when many maroons joined Lord Dunmore's Army, and, after his retreat, continued to attack the Americans, seize supplies, and entice slaves to run away. Following the war, the Dismal Swamp remained a prominent, and troublesome, maroon community until the abolition of slavery in the mid nineteenth century.

Communities Along the Southeastern Frontier

While the Dismal Swamp was the largest maroon community in British North America, others existed along the southeastern frontier. When South Carolina was being settled in the late seventeenth century, many of its white and black fugitives, like their counterparts from Virginia, fled to the North Carolina backcountry. By the eighteenth century, most fugitives headed west or south. Uncertain of the treatment they would receive from Native Americans, a majority chose Spanish Florida as their destination. This was especially true for Africans who had been promised their freedom by Spain if they left British America. Florida was well-suited for maroon activity: sparsely settled, it had adequate natural resources and was politically unstable. Not surprisingly, its maroon community became the largest in what would become the United States.

In addition to maroon activity in Spanish Florida, there were numerous other small communities along the rivers and swamps of South Carolina and Georgia. In 1711 maroons who had been terrorizing the southern parishes of South Carolina were tracked down and killed. Twenty-two years later that colony's assembly offered a £20 reward for the capture of anyone associated with a certain maroon settlement along the Congaree River (£10 if the person were killed). During the 1760s and 1770s the number of maroons in South Carolina and Georgia greatly increased, mainly because of the expansion of the African slave trade into that region. The confusion of the Revolutionary War years contributed to the formation of maroon outposts. At one of the largest, roughly three hundred people enjoyed an autonomous community along the Savannah River until they were uprooted in a bloody fight in 1786.

In addition to these more traditional refugee communities, by the mid eighteenth century a large number of people were living outside British society along the far reaches of the southeastern frontier. Some had fled from South Carolina, but others were fugitives from Virginia and North Carolina. Many were outright bandits who lived in organized gangs and committed acts of theft and violence, while others lived in small settlements scattered across the countryside. Either way, most of them lived in multiracial communities. One 1767 petition referred to the backwoods inhabitants as "Persons of all Countries Complexions and Characters"—not surprising for a society of fugitive poor whites, runaway black slaves, and displaced American Indians.

Much like seventeenth century North Carolina, the original settlers of the South Carolina backcountry were in many ways a maroon people. They lived in multiracial communities that had developed their own unique culture, based in part on the demands of the environment but also on contributions of its peoples. In addition, most had rejected British society and actively fought against it. The Regulator Movement of the 1760s and 1770s, which called on the legislature to provide orderly government in the backcountry, was largely a response to the lawless activities of these people. And like other maroons during the revolution, the frontier settlers continued their resistance by supporting the Loyalist cause and engaging in what has often been recognized as the war's most bitter fighting.

Still, despite these limited successes, maroons in the lower South failed to form large, relatively stable communities like those in the Dismal Swamp and in other slave-based regions. This was partly because the terrain was not as isolated, partly because the local Native populations were too politically and militarily strong, and partly because of efforts by colonial officials who sought to divide and rule. South Carolina and Georgia authorities did not want any "unnatural alliances" to form between their African slaves and the local Native American population, so they deliberately tried to foment fear and hostility between the two groups and passed numerous laws to keep the races apart. While laws of this nature existed from the beginning of the eighteenth century, as the African population rose the number and strength of such laws increased. By mid century whites were prohibited from bringing their African slaves into Indian territory under any pretext, and most treaties with Indian tribes offered substantial rewards for the return of fugitive slaves. Of course, these laws were not totally successful, and cooperation from the tribes varied over place and time. Sometimes blacks were enslaved by the larger Indian tribes, particularly the Creek and Cherokee. Nevertheless, the efforts of colonial officials did generate enough distrust between the two groups to keep relations between them ambivalent.

White South Carolinians needed to pursue this policy because they were greatly outnumbered by their African and Native American neighbors. In the mid eighteenth century, approximately twenty-five thousand whites, forty thousand black slaves, and sixty thousand American Indians lived in South Carolina. One colonial official guessed that "nothing can be more alarming to Carolinians than the idea of an attack from Indians and Negroes." Whites feared the other two groups would unite and destroy them in open revolt; they also feared the growth of maroon communities, knowing full well the destruction such refugees had caused elsewhere. One of their most common responses was to use Indian allies to help destroy maroon communities.

Maroons thus posed a threat to British society in many ways. First, they presented a physical challenge in the form of constant guerrilla warfare. Maroons killed slave owners, stole slaves, and inflicted great property damage. They also increased the likelihood of open slave revolt. Their presence, moreover, was an embarrassment to white society. Maroons expressed the slaves' hatred for the system and demonstrated that members found leaving "civilization" preferable to living in it. This action was implicitly subversive to notions of white supremacy and directly contradicted white slave owners' interpretations of both the institution of slavery and African-American preferences.

Just as slave owners had to destroy maroon communities because the settlements were a threat and a contradiction to the values of white colonial society, colonial officials in British North America could not allow a truly interracial society to develop. By the eighteenth century changes in demography had altered the social context of race in America. Native Americans were no longer needed for white survival and, despite numerous and mostly unsuccessful efforts to incorporate them into British society, were increasingly categorized with blacks and other outsiders to that society. The rapid rise in the black population resulting from the upsurge in the African slave trade in the late seventeenth and early eighteenth centuries increasingly solidified an institution of slavery based on race. The result was a forced separation of the races and a growing need to prevent threats to that system. Consequently, British officials did everything in their power to prevent frontier maroon societies or any true interracial community like that proposed by Christian Priber from forming. They could not allow anything resembling Paradise to exist.

BIBLIOGRAPHY

Axtell, James. *The Invasion Within: The Contest of Cultures in Colonial North America.* New York, 1985. Describes the interaction and struggle between English, French, and Indian cultures in colonial North America.

Braund, Kathryn E. Holland. "The Creek Indians, Blacks, and Slavery." *Journal of Southern History* 57, no. 4 (1991):601–636.

Genovese, Eugene D. *From Rebellion to Revolution: Afro-American Slave Revolts in the Making of the New World.* New York, 1979. Discusses the role maroon communities played in Western Hemisphere slave societies.

Klein, Rachel N. *Unification of a Slave State: The Rise of the Planter Class in the South Carolina Backcountry, 1760–1808.* Chapel Hill, N.C., 1990. Looks at the various groups living in the South Carolina backcountry.

Kulikoff, Allan. *Tobacco and Slaves: The Development of Southern Cultures in the Chesapeake, 1680–1800.* Chapel Hill, N.C., 1986. Examines the changing social relations between whites and blacks in the eighteenth-century Chesapeake.

Leaming, Hugo Prosper. "Hidden Americans: Maroons of Virginia and the Carolinas." Ph.D. diss., University of Illinois at Chicago Circle, 1979.

Mellon, Knox, Jr. "Christian Priber's Cherokee 'Kingdom of Paradise'." *Georgia Historical Quarterly* 57, no. 3 (1973):319–331.

Mullin, Gerald W. *Flight and Rebellion: Slave Resistance in Eighteenth-Century Virginia.* New York, 1972.

Nash, Gary B. *Red, White and Black: The Peoples of Early America.* 2nd ed. Englewood Cliffs, N.J., 1982.

Perdue, Theda. *Slavery and the Evolution of Cherokee Society, 1540–1866.* Knoxville, Tenn., 1979.

Price, Richard, ed. *Maroon Societies: Rebel Slave Communities in the Americas.* Garden City, N.Y., 1973. This collection of articles examines maroon activity in all of the Americas and contains an essay by Herbert Aptheker that explores maroon communities in the United States.

Willis, William S. "Divide and Rule: Red, White, and Black in the Southeast." *Journal of Negro History* 48, no. 3 (1963):157–176.

Wood, Peter H. *Black Majority: Negroes in Colonial South Carolina from 1670 through the Stono Rebellion.* New York, 1974.

Wright, J. Leitch, Jr. *The Only Land They Knew: The Tragic Story of the American Indians in the Old South.* New York, 1981. Looks at the interaction between Indians, Europeans, and Africans in the colonial South.

Steven Deyle

SEE ALSO **African-American Culture; Free Blacks; Indian-Colonist Contact; Mission Communities;** and **Slave Resistance.**

THE DUTCH COLONY

INTERRACIAL MATING IN NEW NETHERLAND is difficult to document. Physical appearances can be misleading, and such matters are not always recorded in writing. There are, however, documented examples of mating between Native Americans and whites and between African Americans and whites as well as general statements about mating between blacks and Indians. Aside from these isolated examples, at least one racially mixed group of people can be traced back to Dutch New Netherland. Contrary to legends about this group being a society of refugees and outlaws, the historical evidence indicates that during the colonial period they were an integral part of the Dutch-American regional culture.

THE INDIANS AND THE DUTCH

The documentary record contains contradictory statements about the chastity of Indian women. In 1644 the Dutch Reformed minister Johannes Megapolensis wrote about the Mohawk, "The women are exceedingly addicted to whoring; they will lie with a man for the value of one, two, or three shillings, and our Dutchmen run after them very much." In 1655 Adriaen van der Donck wrote, "To be unchaste during wedlock is held to be very disgraceful among them [Indian women]." However he also noted, "When their women are young, free, and unmarried, they act as they please, but they are always mercenary in their conduct, and deem it disgraceful to be otherwise; neither is the fruit of illicit connections despised."

Jasper Danckaerts, a member of a small, Protestant religious sect known as the Labadists,

and who traveled through the middle colonies in 1679–1680, blamed the Dutch for corrupting the Indians. He wrote that fornication and adultery were "not as common before the arrival of the Europeans as was thought." That which occurred after the Europeans arrived, he believed, "must be attributed mostly to the Europeans, especially if you have any knowledge about what goes on in the countryside and what used to go on was much worse. It is certain that the Indians have imitated them because just as the Europeans have done when they have no or few women, so they have done."

There are documented examples of such mating between Native Americans and the Dutch. In February 1660, during the Esopus Indian war, the Dutch attempted to ransom the son of Evert Pels, who had been captured by Indians at Wiltwyck (Kingston). But the Indians refused, saying that "the boy has a wife there and the wife is with child, who will not let him go and he will not leave her."

Hilletie van Olinda, who was an interpreter between the Native Americans and Europeans during the 1690s, was the daughter of a Dutch father and a Mohawk mother. She lived among the Mohawk until she converted to Christianity. Ostracized by the Indians because she was a Christian, she was taken in by a female Dutch trader, who raised her. As an adult Hilletie married a Dutchman from Schenectady.

THE INDIANS AND BLACKS

Mating between Native Americans and blacks is more difficult to document. In 1722 Governor Alexander Spotswood of Virginia accused the Iroquois in New York of harboring escaped slaves from Virginia. The Iroquois replied, "You have told us that there are Negroes among us. According to the best of our knowledge we know not there is one among any of the Six Nations." In 1748 the Swedish naturalist Peter Kalm stated that in general when Indians "saw these black people for the first time, they thought they were a real breed of devils, . . . but since that time, they have entertained less disagreeable notions of the negroes, for at present many live among them, and they even sometimes intermarry, as

I myself have seen." Yet in 1765, when Sir William Johnson called for the Delaware Indians to return escaped slaves, the Delaware said that any African Americans among the Indians "are with their uncles, the Six Nations, and therefore cannot be considered in captivity." Nevertheless they agreed to return any "English prisoners, deserters, Frenchmen, and Negroes" and "never to screen, protect or encourage any such persons in the future."

THE CREATION OF A NEW TRIBAL ENTITY

There emerged in the Dutch-settled regions in the nineteenth century a number of isolated groups that claimed or were said to have Indian and white or Indian, white, and African-American ancestry. In New York State there are the Van Guilders in Rensselaer County; the Bushwackers or Pondshiners in Columbia County; and the Honies, Slaughters, Clappers, and "Arabs" in Schoharie County. In Delaware there are the Moors and Nanticokes, and on the border between New York and New Jersey are the Ramapo Mountain People, formerly known as the Jackson Whites. Little or no research has been done on the New York State groups. While the Moor and Nanticoke are located today on the Atlantic Coast of the Delmarva Peninsula, their historic ties were more with the English settlement on the Chesapeake Bay than with the short-lived Dutch settlements in northern Delaware. Most of these names are considered by the people themselves to be derogatory.

According to legend the Ramapo Mountain People were descended from escaped slaves, Tuscarora Indians migrating from North Carolina to the province of New York, Hessian deserters during the American Revolution, and black and white prostitutes brought to New York by a man named Jackson for the British soldiers stationed there. The prostitutes were referred to as either Jackson's blacks or Jackson's whites, and hence the name Jackson Whites.

Genealogical evidence, however, indicates that their ancestors were free blacks. One of them was the son of a Dutch army captain named Johan de Fries and a black woman named Swartinne (the feminine form of the Dutch word zwart, meaning "black"), who was probably one of his slaves. The mulatto son, named John De Vries, inherited free status and property from his father. He became one of several free blacks living on the outskirts of New York in the 1670s. They were culturally Dutch, having Dutch names, speaking a dialect of the Dutch language, and attending the Dutch Reformed church.

In 1687 several of these Dutch free blacks bought shares in the Tappan Patent in the Hackensack Valley, making them some of the earliest free black landowners in America. Around 1800 they moved farther inland to the Ramapo Mountains. However they maintained an oral tradition of Indian ancestry, perhaps as a way of distinguishing themselves from other blacks who were slaves. In 1979 the New Jersey state legislature designated them as the Ramapough Indians, thereby recognizing a new tribal entity.

BIBLIOGRAPHY

Berry, Brewton. *Almost White*. New York, 1963. A survey of racially mixed communities throughout the eastern United States. Mentions the Van Guilders, the Bushwackers, the Honies, the Slaughters, the Clappers, and the Arabs.

Cohen, David Steven. *The Ramapo Mountain People*. New Brunswick, N.J., 1974. A study of the history and folklore of the people once known as the Jackson Whites but today known as the Ramapough Indians. Argues that they are the descendants of free blacks who were culturally Dutch.

Trelease, Allen W. *Indian Affairs in Colonial New York: The Seventeenth Century*. Ithaca, N.Y., 1960. Recounts relations between the Dutch and the Indians, including some documentation of intermarriage.

Weslager, Clinton A. *Delaware's Forgotten Folk: The Story of the Moors and Nanticokes*. Philadelphia, 1943. Analyzes various theories of the origin of two racially mixed groups in Delaware.

David Steven Cohen

SEE ALSO **Free Blacks** and **Indian-Colonist Contact.**

2

FREE BLACKS

FREE PEOPLE OF African descent—alternately called free people of color, free Negroes, or free blacks—composed only a tiny fragment of the population in colonial North America, but their significance greatly outweighed their numbers. Far more than with the more numerous slave population, the changing status and circumstances of black free people presaged the development of race relations in North America. The lives of free blacks also served as a harbinger of the status of all black people when slavery ended. Often the laws, attitudes, and institutions that victimized free blacks during the slave years—far more than the laws, attitudes, and institutions that victimized slaves—became the dominant mode of racial oppression ensnaring all black people when slavery ended. In a like manner, the free blacks' experience during slave times profoundly influenced the pattern of post-emancipation black life. Drawing on their experience in freedom, free people of African descent moved into leadership positions in the post-emancipation world and played a disproportionately large role in shaping African-American life throughout North America.

Whereas the role of free people of African descent in the post-emancipation world was uniformly important, their pre-emancipation history was anything but uniform. In some places, at some times, black free people enjoyed near legal equality, economic prosperity, and a measure of social recognition. In other places, at

other times, however, they faced brutal opposition that not only constrained their legal rights but also threatened their very existence.

Generally, three circumstances shaped the history of free black people in colonial America: first, the nature of European settlement; second, the demographic balance of white and black, free and slave; and third, the degree of commitment to chattel bondage and plantation production.

EUROPEAN SETTLERS AND ADVENTURERS

Europeans came to the New World as settlers and adventurers. Settlers brought their wives, children, and trappings of life in Europe in an effort to remake the New World in their own image. Adventurers—almost always men—sallied forth to make their fortunes and return to their European homelands, hopefully richer for their efforts. They left their families and cultural moorings in Europe and, for the most part, viewed their American experience as transient. Without wives or families, adventurers joined with enslaved women of color—African, African-American, and Native American—in the New World. Such relationships were often short-lived affairs founded upon power and violence. But just as often, white men and black women found love and affection in their unions, transforming fleeting encounters into stable and permanent matches. Such relationships were marriages in everything but name, and the mixed-race progeny of these unions were illicit only in the eyes of the law.

The men who participated in these relations were frequently loath to consign their loved ones—especially their own posterity—to chattel bondage, and they commonly freed them, often finding ingenious subterfuges to evade restrictive manumission laws. Moreover, the absence of European and European-American families—particularly wives with claims of exclusive rights to the legitimacy of their lineage—allowed adventurers, as opposed to settlers, to recognize their black mistresses and their mixed-race children and provide for their future as free people. Sometimes such provision took the form of land and other valuable property. More often European and European-American fathers elevated their children by training them in a trade or patronizing their petty enterprises. In such circumstances the free descendants of mixed racial unions might suffer galling discrimination, but they had a recognized place in colonial society and the resources to protect it.

Such was the case of colonial Louisiana, North America's preeminent adventurer society. Louisiana's peculiar demography—in which white men outnumbered white women and black women outnumbered black men—encouraged white men and black women to join together in a variety of matches, licit and illicit. During the eighteenth century, white men—often of high standing—lived "almost publicly with colored concubines" and, according to one churchman, "[did] not blush" when they carried their mixed-race descendants "to be recorded in the parochial registries as their *natural children*." Numerous masters freed their slave wives and mistresses and the children they bore for reasons of love and affection. Under French and later Spanish rule, more than half of the voluntary manumissions were children, and three-quarters of these were of mixed racial origins. Most of the adults were women. Similarly inspired manumissions, creating free black populations of a like sort, could be found in lesser degrees in other parts of colonial North America wherever European and European-American men pioneered alone and slave women of African descent were readily available.

THE BLACK AND WHITE DEMOGRAPHIC BALANCE

The demographic balance between whites and blacks, free and slave also shaped the history of free people of African descent in colonial North America. Outnumbered by their slaves, slave owners needed allies to assure their dominance. In most North American slave societies, those allies came from the white nonslaveholding population, which furnished soldiers and slave catchers.

In the absence of a white nonslaveholding class, planters were forced to turn to black men to protect them. Sometimes they assigned such duty to slaves. More often, however, slaveholders called upon free black men, frequently their own mixed-race sons, for protection. Playing off the slaveholders' vulnerability to foreign invasion and domestic insurrection, free African and African-American men gained special standing fighting the white man's battles—sometimes figuratively, often literally. As soldiers in behalf of transplanted Europeans, free blacks not only tamed interlopers but also disciplined plantation slaves and captured runaways. Service in the white man's cause enabled free black soldiers, however grossly discriminated against, to inch up the social ladder, taking their families with them.

Free black men entered into military service wherever Europeans and European-Americans felt threatened. They were most fully organized in Florida and Louisiana, where Spanish and French colonists employed free black and occasionally slave soldiers in regularly organized militia units. Spanish authorities in Saint Augustine established a black militia as early as 1687, employing runaway slaves from the English settlements in South Carolina. Welcoming these fugitives from their enemy, Spanish officials instructed them in the Catholic faith, allowed them to be baptized and married within the church, and then sent them against their former enslavers in raids on the English settlements at Port Royal and Edisto. Black militiamen later fought against the English and their Indian allies in the Yamasee War and protected Florida against retaliatory raids. In the late 1730s, Spanish officials stationed the black fighting force at Gracia Real de Santa Teresa de Mose, a fortified free black settlement some two miles (3.2 kilometers) north of Saint Augustine. Mose became the center of free black life in colonial Florida until its destruction in 1740. Thereafter black free people were more fully integrated into town life in Saint Augustine. They intermarried among themselves and with Native Americans and slaves, worked as craftsmen, sailors, and laborers, purchased property, and enjoyed a modicum of prosperity and respectability. During the 1750s the settlement at Mose was revived, and it once again became a center of free black life in Spanish Florida.

French authorities in Louisiana first employed black soldiers in quelling an African-Indian revolt in 1729. Thereafter officials incorporated black men into Louisiana's defense force and called upon them whenever Indian confederations, European colonial rivals, or slave insurrectionists jeopardized the safety of the colony. On each such occasion—be it the Chickasaw War of the 1730s, the Choctaw War of the 1740s, or the threatened English invasion of the 1750s—French officials mobilized black men, free and slave, with slaves offered freedom in exchange for military service. By 1739 at least 270 black men were under arms in Louisiana, including some 50 free blacks. In 1770, when Spain took effective control of Louisiana, the militia included over three hundred free black men.

The black militia played an even larger role in Spanish Louisiana than it had under the French. Spain gained control of the colony as part of the settlement of the Seven Years' War in 1763. Finding themselves surrounded by hostile French planters, Spanish authorities embraced free people of African descent as an ally against internal as well as external foes and recommissioned Louisiana's colored militia, adopting the division between *pardo* (or light-skinned) and *moreno* (or dark-skinned) units present elsewhere in Spanish America. They clad the black militiamen in colorful uniforms and granted them *fuero militar* rights, thereby exempting black militiamen from civil prosecution, certain taxes, and licensing fees—no mean privileges for free black men in a society based upon racial slavery.

The black militia thrived under Spanish rule, becoming an integral part of the colony's defense force. When they were not fighting foreign enemies, free black militiamen were employed by Spanish officials to maintain the levees that protected New Orleans and the great riverfront plantations, extinguish fires within the city limits, and hunt fugitive slaves. As the value of the free black militia to Spain increased, so did the size and status of the class from which the militia sprang.

The Spanish regularly established free black militias in the Caribbean and South America and found it easy to extend the practice to the North American mainland. English colonists had little experience creating free black fighting forces, and since most British mainland settlements had white majorities, they had little need to rely upon black men to defend them against external and internal foes. However, when English colonists felt themselves endangered, they too armed black men to fight their battles. To bolster colonial defenses, South Carolina officials not only drafted slaves in time of war but also regularly enlisted them in the militia. Between the settlement of the Carolinas and the conclusion of the Yamasee War almost fifty years later, black soldiers helped fend off every military threat to the colony. But the dangers facing English settlers in the Carolinas never required slaveholders to reward their slave soldiers with freedom or to create a permanent free black fighting force. Nonetheless English colonists were not averse to such a policy when they felt endangered. In 1765 Georgia colonists, threatened by hostile Spaniards and Indians and desperately in need of able-bodied men, encouraged free black immigrants to settle in the colony and offered free people of mixed racial origins all the rights of "any person born of British parents" except voting and sitting in the colonial legislature.

Their military experience allowed free black men to enlarge their numbers and improve their place within colonial society. Black militiamen did this by using their pay and bounties to secure freedom for their families and by employing connections with white officers and imperial bureaucrats to advance their fortunes. Militia service thus enabled free black men to secure a modest place in a society otherwise hostile to their very being.

The same demographic realities that propelled free black men into the ranks of colonial militias also enlarged opportunities for free black men and women to practice skilled trades and open small businesses. In societies with white majorities, white nonslaveholders monopolized such positions, often securing employment for their sons as plantation overseers and for their wives and daughters as midwives, seamstresses, and plantation tutors. Where there were few such white people, black free people eagerly moved into these interstitial roles. As skilled workers, shopkeepers, tradesmen, and market women—occasionally even as overseers and midwives—free black men and women gained a modest prosperity. They accumulated wealth enough to elevate their economic standing and increase their numbers by buying freedom for their kin and neighbors.

Free people of African descent thus stood midway between white free people and black slaves. Their middling position frequently had a somatic embodiment in their tawny color, an economic embodiment in their interstitial occupations as artisans and tradesmen, and a legal embodiment in statutes that elevated them above slaves but denied them many of the rights enjoyed by free people of European descent. The middle ground, however, covered a large terrain. While black free people tried to raise themselves to the equal of free whites, they had to fend off enemies who tried to equate them with slaves. The success of black free people depended in large measure on the ever-changing European and European-American commitment to slavery and plantation production, which shaped and reshaped the free blacks' history.

COMMITMENT TO PLANTATION PRODUCTION

Where and when the commitment to chattel bondage remained weak and plantation production was undeveloped, slaves generally exited bondage with relative ease and the free black population grew, sometimes rapidly. Under such circumstances, free people of African descent purchased land, held servants, and occasionally attained minor offices. Like transplanted Europeans, they accumulated property, sued their neighbors, and passed their estates on to their children. While liable to enslavement and subject to rank discrimination, many black free people did well.

The history of the Johnson clan of Virginia is a case in point. Anthony Johnson landed in chains as "Antonio the Negro" around 1621, when the tobacco boom had just begun and there were yet few slaves in Virginia. During the next thirty years, Johnson somehow wriggled out of servitude, changed his name, married, began to farm on his own, and in 1651 earned a 250-acre (100-hectare) headright. When his eastern shore plantation burned to the ground within a year, Johnson petitioned the county court and was awarded a special reduction of his taxes. Johnson's son, John, did even better than his father, receiving a patent for 550 acres (220 hectares), and a brother, Richard, owned a 100-acre (40 hectare) estate. Like other men of substance, the Johnsons farmed independently, held servants, and left their heirs sizable estates. As established members of their community, they enjoyed the rights of citizens and frequently employed the law to protect themselves and advance their interests. When a servant claiming his freedom fled Anthony Johnson's plantation and found refuge with a nearby white planter, Johnson took his neighbor to court and won the return of his servant along with damages against the white man.

Landed independence not only afforded free people of African descent like the Johnsons near legal equality, but also allowed them a wide range of cultural expression; and while black free people stood on a par with white people of equal rank, they nonetheless understood they were different and openly celebrated those differences. Although his father had Anglicized the family name, John Johnson called his own estate "Angola."

Similar success stories could be told of free black men and women in other places where slavery remained a marginal institution. In such circumstances Africans and their descendants propelled themselves into positions of modest privilege and authority. In eighteenth-century French Louisiana, Samba, a Bambara who had been enslaved and transported to the New World for leading a revolt against the French in Africa, employed his knowledge of French and various African tongues to gain his freedom and a position as an interpreter before the Superior Council, the colony's highest judicial body. Later he became an overseer on one of the largest plantations in Louisiana. Louis Congo, another African slave who arrived in Louisiana early in the eighteenth century, followed a slightly different route to freedom. Playing upon the colony's need for an executioner, Congo assumed that grisly duty in return for his liberty and permission to live with his wife (although she was not freed, as he demanded) on land of his own choosing.

Samba and Louis Congo were not alone. A handful of the first African arrivals in eighteenth-century Louisiana followed Samba and Louis Congo out of bondage. Some gained the respect and affection of their owners and won their freedom for some extraordinary deed or years of faithful service. Once free they helped others out of bondage. Several free black men purchased their wives by indenturing themselves into long years of labor. Although the French *Code Noir* required manumitted slaves to defer to their former masters, punished black free people more severely than free white people, and barred racial intermarriage, free people of African descent in Louisiana enjoyed many of the same legal rights as other free people, and they did not hesitate to exercise them. During the 1720s free blacks successfully petitioned French authorities for the removal of a special head tax and sued white colonists for transgressions on their rights.

The status of African and African-American people in colonial New Netherland, another colony where the commitment to chattel bondage and plantation production remained weak, suggests how the absence of a well-developed slave system dedicated to the production of commodities for export widened the avenue to freedom. The diverse needs of the Dutch mercantile economy in New Amsterdam induced the Dutch West India Company, the largest slaveholder in the colony, to allow its slaves to live and work on their own in return for a stipulated amount of labor and an annual tribute. "Half-freedom," as this system came to be known, expanded the opportunities of black people and allowed them to develop strong communal institutions. Half-free men and women took surnames—generally reflecting their African origins, status, or color—collected wages, had access to the courts, served in the militia, and registered their marriages and baptized their children in the Dutch Reformed church. They witnessed the baptism of each others' children, rarely calling upon Europeans and European-Americans—owners or not—to serve in this capacity, which suggests close family ties among the blacks. Upon occasion established black families legally adopted orphaned black children.

The most successful black men and women translated half-freedom into full legal freedom. They purchased land in New Amsterdam and the Dutch settlements in the city's hinterland. In 1659 the town of Southampton granted "Peeter the Neigro" three acres (about 1 hectare), and somewhat later John Neiger, who had "set himself up a house in the street" of Easthampton, was given "for his own use a little quantity of land about the house for him to make a yard or garden." Twenty years later a visitor to lower Manhattan observed that the residents were "formerly slaves of the [Dutch West India] company but in consequence of the frequent changes and conquests of the country, they have obtained their freedom, and settled themselves down where they thought proper and thus on this road, where they have ground enough to live on with their families." Half-free men and women of African descent not only enjoyed many of the rights of free people of European descent, but they also shared their responsibilities. Like other residents of New Netherland, half-free blacks attended the militia, paid taxes, and were sued by their neighbors.

Black people in New Netherland tried to expand half-freedom into the full measure. When the Dutch West India Company refused to make the privileges associated with half-freedom hereditary, half-free blacks protested, demanding that they be allowed to pass their rights on to their children. Failing that, black residents of New Netherland pressed officials to elevate their children's status in other ways. Some, hearing rumors that baptism meant freedom, tried to gain church membership. A Dutch prelate complained that black people "wanted nothing else than to deliver their children from bodily slavery, without striving for piety and Christian virtues." Even after the conquering English abolished "half-freedom" and instituted a more rigorous system of racial servitude, slaves in what had become New York continued to employ the leverage gained by their prominent role in the city's economy to set standards of treatment well above those in the plantation colonies and, occasionally, to gain full legal freedom.

The absence of a firm commitment to chattel bondage in colonial North America enabled many free black men to compete successfully for that scarcest of all New World commodities: the affection of white women. Bastardy lists indicate that white servant women ignored the strictures against what white lawmakers later termed "shameful" and "unnatural" acts and joined together with those of their own condition regardless of color. Other fragmentary evidence from various parts of seventeenth-century Virginia and Maryland affirm that approximately one-quarter to one-third of the bastard children born to white women were of mixed racial origins. Although most of the relationships that produced these children were between indentured servants, successful, property-owning white and black men and women also intermarried. On Virginia's Eastern Shore Francis Payne, a free black man, married a white woman who later married a white man after Payne's death. William Greensted, a white attorney who represented Elizabeth Key, a woman of mixed racial origins, in her successful suit for her freedom, later married her. In 1691, when the General Assembly finally ruled against the practice, some propertied white Virginians found the legislation novel and obnoxious enough to muster a protest.

Thus, viewed from the perspective of Anthony Johnson, Louis Congo, and Peeter the Neigro, some black people gained their freedom and enjoyed a modicum of economic success and social recognition. Until slavery became a central institution in American life, it was no anomaly in colonial North America for free people of African descent to share and fulfill the same ideals and aspirations as free people of European descent.

Elsewhere on the edges of the North American continent—in New England, Canada, and the Southwest—some black men and women also gained their freedom via manumission, successful flight, self purchase, or free birth. In such areas, where chattel bondage was of minor economic importance, a few black men and women slipped through the web of enslavement entirely. A minority of a minority residing on the margins of the mainland's great slave societies, these free people of African descent lived in stark isolation. That isolation propelled them into relations with Indians, outcast Europeans, and other marginal peoples. Although generally impoverished and

without standing, their singular presence sometimes allowed such black men and women to participate as near equals in their society, often mediating—as interpreters, for example—between the dominant and subordinate classes. Generally, however, their unusual existence was little appreciated, and they were lumped with the most despised of the lower orders.

THE ENTRENCHMENT OF SLAVERY AND THE DEGRADATION OF BLACK FREEDOM

As the commitment to slavery deepened, the status and circumstances of free people of African descent changed dramatically. Slaveholders, consolidating their position atop colonial society, equated African origins with chattel bondage: white people were free or eventually would be; black people were slave or certainly should be. From this perspective free people of African descent were a literal contradiction in terms. Their very presence—demonstrating that black people could be free, earn an independent livelihood, care for their children, and improve themselves—encouraged slaves to conceive of what their owners hoped would be inconceivable. Thus, by definition free people of African descent were rebels, as dangerous as the most militant slave insurrectionist. They could not be tolerated. The rise of slavery and the degradation of black free people were part of the same process.

As slavery grew, planter-controlled legislatures set about recasting the status of black free people to meet the standards implicit in the slaveholders' equation of race with bondage. Lawmakers systematically limited the access of African and African-American slaves to freedom by restricting or prohibiting manumission and self-purchase. In many colonies legislators enslaved for long periods—well into adulthood—the mixed-race children of free white women by black men. That done, colonial legislatures circumscribed the rights of black people who had secured their liberty. Legislators and judges filled colonial statute books with regulations distinguishing between the rights of free blacks and those of whites, depriving free people of African descent of the most elementary liberties.

In Virginia, for example, free blacks lost the right to employ white indentured servants, hold office, serve in the militia, and vote. They were required to pay special taxes and might be fined or imprisoned for striking a white person, no matter what the cause. In the colony where the Johnson family once stood on a par with other freeholders, white planters petitioned for the removal of all free people of African descent. Indeed, rumors that black free people would be enslaved sent the remnants of the Johnson clan fleeing from Virginia. In its absence, white neighbors seized the Johnsons' property. Where free black men and women had once resided as substantial propertyholders, they encountered difficulty maintaining their presence.

The law made it difficult for persons of African descent to escape bondage and improve their social and economic status. Slowly the character and circumstance of free black people began to change. In the century before the revolution, both the proportion of black people enjoying freedom and the status of free blacks slipped in most of colonial North America. Free people of African descent became, more and more, economically impoverished and socially marginal; they rarely owned property or participated in the institutions of the larger society. The success of the slaveholders' policy of delegitimization and isolation could be seen nowhere so clearly as in the growing number of black free people who spent a portion of their lives—often the most productive part—in servitude.

Falling prey to numerous legal snares—bastardy laws, tax forfeitures, and debt—free blacks found themselves working and living alongside slaves. Whereas in the early years of settlement, free blacks had frequently intermarried with whites to create a mulatto caste, in the eighteenth century they generally joined together with slaves, darkening the free black population. The close connection—social and somatic—between free and slave black people made it easy for slaveholding planters to treat them as one. Unscrupulous planters and traders sold black free people into permanent servitude simply by removing them beyond the reach of evidence that they were free, thereby demonstrating the disdain in which they held the freedom of people of African descent. Those black men and women who maintained their freedom could scarcely hope for the opportunities an earlier generation of black free people had routinely enjoyed.

The transformation of free black life that accompanied the deepening commitment to slavery operated mercilessly to fulfill the slaveholders' presumption that black people were (or should be) slaves. Throughout colonial North America, lawmakers limited the growth of the free black population by restricting manumission and enacting a panoply of prohibitions and restrictions that confined free people of African descent to the lowest ranks of free society and denied them almost every privilege colonial Americans identified with freedom. By the time of the American Revolution, most colonies proscribed black free persons from voting, holding office, attending the militia, serving on a jury, or testifying against a white person. Often they punished free black persons more severely than white ones for various crimes, especially involving slaves, and taxed them more heavily—for example, subjecting free black women, but not white women, to a tithe on the presumption that free black women working in the field were more productive than the white women who did not.

A DIVIDED WORLD

Striving toward full freedom while pushed toward slavery, free people of African descent lived in a divided world and their loyalties were equally fragmented. Sometimes free black people identified with European and European-American colonists and their institutions, currying favors from powerful white men and women—often their kin—and imitating the standards of European and European-American communities by converting to Christianity and adopting the cultural trappings—language, clothing, and deportment—that white people equated with civilization. To a degree colonial leaders—slaveholders first among them—encouraged free people of African descent to do so, as the policy favoring light-skinned free people over dark-skinned ones suggests. But whereas black free people who adopted the white man's ways generally benefited, those benefits could never be translated into equality. Black free persons might be given a place in colonial society, but that place fell well short of what colonials—white and black—understood as freedom.

Frustrated in their quest for equal standing, free people of African descent often identified with slaves, with whom they lived, worked, and played, intermarrying and joining together in dance, song, and prayer that reached back to Africa. Colonial leaders—slaveholders first among them—discouraged such relations, sometimes denying black free people the right to marry slaves or even meet with them. Yet by excluding free blacks from all but the most marginal role in colonial society, slaveholders pushed them into just such relationships with slaves, creating their own worst nightmare: a revolutionary union of all black people, free and slave.

In time, free people of African descent began to develop an interest and a culture of their own, apart from both whites—slaveholders and nonslaveholders—and from slaves. This culture was clearly formed by the years following the American Revolution. Yet even as a unique free black identity emerged, it was complicated by divisions within free black society itself: by color—black and brown; by generation—African and Creole; by geography—urban and rural; by work—skilled and unskilled; and by wealth—rich, middling, and poor. The distance between successful, light-skinned free people of color—some of whom climbed into the slaveholding class—and the impoverished black people who stood just a step away from chattel bondage could be as great as that dividing planters and white nonslaveholders. Such intragroup divisions intersected and crossed each other, complicating lives of free people of African descent and their relationships with both white free people and black slaves.

Like the free blacks' numbers, status, and circumstances, their identity thus changed over time. On the eve of the American Revolution, even after more than 150 years of settlement, the status of black free people had not been fully determined. In the 1770s, when the avenues to freedom seemed all but shut in the English seaboard colonies, Spanish officials in Louisiana and Florida expanded them greatly, encouraging manumission and self-purchase and allowing the free black population to grow rapidly. Even within the English colonies, the free blacks' status continued to differ from place to place, and the law left large areas in which black free people enjoyed legal equality with free white people—perhaps because free blacks were so few in number, perhaps because they performed functions powerful slaveholders found useful. For example, Virginia barred free black men from holding office, but no other colony did. South Carolina and Virginia sought to ensure white dominance by whipping blacks, "free or bond," who dared raise a hand to strike a white person, but they remained alone in that action.

Perhaps the racial strictures placed on suffrage best reveal the patchwork nature of colonial regulations of free people of African descent. Early in the eighteenth century, South Carolina (1715), North Carolina (1715), and Virginia (1723) barred free black men from the polls. But by 1761, when Georgia finally joined the ranks of those who excluded black voters, North Carolina had lifted its ban. In short, the legal restrictions black free people faced were a jumble whose haphazard construction reflected the refusal, inability, or disinclination of colonial legislatures to fix the free blacks' status.

As the colonial period drew to a close, free people of African descent continued to suffer grievous discrimination, but differences within the colonial world suggest an openness to change that would disappear in the nineteenth century. The age of revolutions—the American, French, and Haitian—would see a radical transformation of free black life throughout mainland North America. No one would play a larger role in this transformation than the free people of color themselves.

BIBLIOGRAPHY

Berlin, Ira. *Slaves Without Masters: The Free Negro in the Antebellum South.* New York, 1974.

Billings, Warren M. "The Case of Fernando and Elizabeth Key: A Note on the Status of Blacks in the Seventeenth Century." *William and Mary Quarterly,* 3rd ser., 30, no. 3 (1973):467–474.

Breen, T. H., and Stephen Innes. *"Myne Owne Ground": Race and Freedom on Virginia's Eastern Shore, 1640–1676.* New York, 1980.

Cohen, David W., and Jack P. Greene, eds. *Neither Free Nor Slave: The Freedman of African Descent in the Slave Societies of the New World*. Baltimore, Md., 1972.

Deal, Douglas. "A Constricted World: Free Blacks on Virginia's Eastern Shore, 1680–1750." In *Colonial Chesapeake Society,* edited by Lois Green Carr, Philip D. Morgan, and Jean B. Russo. Chapel Hill, N.C., 1988.

Everett, Donald E. "Free Persons of Color in Colonial Louisiana." *Louisiana History* 7, no. 1 (1966):21–50.

Foner, Laura. "The Free People of Color in Louisiana and St. Domingue: A Comparative Portrait of Two Three-Caste Slave Societies." *Journal of Social History* 3, no. 7 (1970):406–430.

Goodfriend, Joyce D. "Burghers and Blacks: The Evolution of a Slave Society at New Amsterdam." *New York History* 59, no. 2 (1978):125–144.

Greene, Lorenzo J. *The Negro in Colonial New England, 1620–1776*. New York, 1942.

Hanger, Kimberly S. "Avenues to Freedom Open to New Orleans' Black Population, 1769–1779." *Louisiana History* 31, no. 3 (1990):237–264.

Ingersoll, Thomas N. "Free Blacks in a Slave Society: New Orleans, 1718–1812." *William and Mary Quarterly,* 3rd ser., 48, no. 2 (1991):173–200.

Jordan, Winthrop D. "American Chiaroscuro: The Status and Definition of Mulattoes in the British Colonies." *William and Mary Quarterly,* 3rd ser., 19, no. 2 (1962):183–200.

———. *White Over Black: American Attitudes Toward the Negro, 1550–1812*. Chapel Hill, N.C., 1968.

Kimmel, Ross M. "Free Blacks in Seventeenth-Century Maryland." *Maryland Magazine of History* 71, no. 1 (1976):19–25.

Landers, Jane. "Gracia Real de Santa Teresa de Mose: A Free Black Town in Spanish Colonial Florida." *American Historical Review* 95, no. 1 (1990):9–30.

Love, Edgar F. "Legal Restrictions on Afro-Indian Relations in Colonial Mexico." *Journal of Negro History* 55, no. 2 (1970):131–139.

McConnell, Roland C. *Negro Troops of Antebellum Louisiana: A History of the Battalion of Free Men of Color*. Baton Rouge, La., 1968.

McManus, Edgar J. *Black Bondage in the North*. Syracuse, N.Y., 1973.

Morgan, Edmund S. *American Slavery, American Freedom: The Ordeal of Colonial Virginia*. New York, 1975.

Nash, Gary B. *Forging Freedom: The Formation of Philadelphia's Black Community, 1720–1840*. Cambridge, Mass., 1988.

Nicholls, Michael L. "Passing Through This Troublesome World: Free Blacks in the Early Southside." *Virginia Magazine of History and Biography* 92, no. 1 (1984):50–70.

Porter, Dorothy, comp. *Early Negro Writings, 1760–1837*. Boston, 1971.

Riley, Carroll L. "Blacks in the Early Southwest." *Ethnohistory* 19, no. 3 (1972):247–260.

Rippy, J. "The Negro and the Spanish Pioneer in the New World." *Journal of Negro History* 6, no. 2 (1921):183–189. (1921):183–189.

Russell, John H. *The Free Negro in Virginia, 1619–1865*. Baltimore, Md., 1913; repr. 1969.

Sterkx, Herbert E. *The Free Negro in Ante-Bellum Louisiana, 1724–1860*. Rutherford, N.J., 1972.

Wright, James M. *The Free Negro in Maryland, 1634–1860*. Baltimore, Md., 1921.

Ira Berlin

See also **African-American Culture; Artisans; Farming, Planting, and Ranching; Hired Labor; Interracial Societies;** and **The Slave Trade.**

193

AFRICAN-AMERICAN CULTURE

THE LINES BETWEEN RACE AND CULTURE have never been finely drawn in African-American studies. In general when we talk of African-American research we mean scholarship about people with ancestors from sub-Saharan Africa. But in terms of ways of living, the African-American legacy is far broader, since it has come to be shared by people of different racial and ethnic backgrounds. In that sense to be American is to be partly African American.

INTRODUCTION

The great collision of cultures that began with the invasion and settlement of the Americas and the Atlantic slave trade resulted in an intermingling of African, European, and Native American customs; the result was a new mode of life in the colonies. Africans were especially affected because slavery forced cultural compromise upon them. Still there was much from their old lives they retained and much from the new they were willing to adopt.

The first African Americans were only enslaved physically; mentally and spiritually they retained a certain independence despite a variety of external oppressions. Whether the political control of a colony was held by the Spanish, French, Dutch, or English, African Americans still had enough autonomy and cultural leverage to influence the development of new American ways of life.

For generations the historical profession's obsession with political power at the expense of cultural history inhibited our understanding of African culture and its importance. Getting at the truth was all the more difficult because African-American studies were inconveniently bounded as far as the historical profession normally divided things. They were defined neither by particular disciplines nor by particular colonial systems. Aggravating the problem was a scarcity of evidence, since black slaves left few written records and white observers were rarely interested in African-American life. We know far more about African-American culture in the nineteenth century, when the African component was probably more diluted, simply because there is so much more evidence about it.

Scholars interested in the African-American heritage have had to reconstruct a context for their work by backtracking across the Atlantic to the cultural traditions of literally hundreds of African societies. Then came immersion in the colonial systems of Spain, France, Holland, and England, which set the political rules of colonial life. Native American peoples had to be examined for their interactions with African Americans. Then the various blendings between source cultures—African, European, and Native American—along with Creole cultures, including the African-American cultures of the Caribbean, Latin America, and Brazil, had to be considered. It was, and remains, a daunting task.

195

But since scholars fortunately share what they learn, insights from one region have often illuminated material from another so that the full importance of African-American culture in shaping the Americas is becoming ever more apparent.

HISTORICAL OVERVIEW

The first Africans who arrived in North America were *ladinos,* Africans acculturated in the ways of Spain, who acted as servants, soldiers, and scouts with the Spanish campaigns of the early sixteenth century.

The most famous was the dark-skinned Moroccan Estevanico, who landed in Florida as a servant of the ill-fated Panfilo de Narvaez expedition of 1528. When that venture was destroyed by disease and Indian resistance, Estevanico and three other survivors escaped across the lower Gulf Coast and reached Mexico City after an eight-year journey. Because their survival had depended so much on Estevanico's skills as a healer, linguist, and diplomat to the native peoples, the fantastic stories he reported hearing about a land of gold in the interior of North America were taken seriously. Therefore, Estevanico was sent in 1539 to guide Father Marcos de Niza to the seven cities of Cibola.

Perhaps the recently looted riches of Mexico and Peru inspired Estevanico's plans to explore deep into the desert-like North American interior, but it is also likely that the achievements of the conquistadors blended in his imagination with contemporaneous North African tales about the fabled wealth of the African Sudan. Within forty years of the Cibola expedition, similar but far better equipped Moroccan ventures were sent southward across the Sahara to conquer the golden lands of the African interior. Thus it may well be that from the dreams of Europe and Africa swirling together arose one of the first golden visions of America's future.

But despite these first Afro-Spanish ventures, it was the arrival of Africans in British North America at the beginning of the seventeenth century that established the first African-American culture in the region that would later become part of the United States. During the seventeenth century, most African immigrants to the area came in small groups of slaves by way of the West Indies, where some had already experienced bondage and become partially African Americanized. By the early eighteenth century, however, shiploads of new slaves were far more commonly carried directly from coastal West and Central Africa. When the dislocations of the American Revolution temporarily halted forced African immigration as the colonial period ended, about a fifth of the North American colonial population was African or African American, and the burgeoning African-American culture influenced not only the blacks but also a large number of the whites as well.

FACTORS SHAPING THE RATE OF CULTURAL TRANSFORMATION

African-American culture developed in a process of give and take. How much of Africa remained and how much a new slave was willing to adopt from European America depended on a variety of factors: age, class status in Africa, isolation from countrymen, and the degree of interaction with whites. In the same way, how much a white American was influenced by African culture likewise depended on class and interaction with blacks, with members of the white elite and indentured servant classes being the most affected.

Few Africans over thirty-five were shipped to the Americas, in part because older men and women found learning new ways difficult; they were extremely reluctant to change. As the Reverend James Falconer explained from Virginia in 1724, those slaves had no sooner "grown up before they are carried from their own country . . . are never being able either to speak or understand our language perfectly." Older slaves were simply unwilling to forget their African lives; thus the London-based *Gentleman's Magazine* cautioned in 1764, "No Negro should be bought old; such are always sullen and unteachable, and frequently put an end to their lives."

Younger slaves were much more adaptable; they learned the new language with ease, such as the boy advertised in the *Boston Newsletter* in 1759 as "about twelve months from the coast of Guinney, speaks good English." Children's natural curiosity made younger slaves willing pupils of the new European-American culture. Olaudah Equiano, who had been shipped from Africa as a child, explained that once he learned English and got over the crushing isolation common to those sold away from their shipmates, "I now not only felt myself quite easy with these new countrymen, but relished their society and manners."

Class status also affected a new slave's interest in adopting the new culture. Virginia's Hugh Jones explained in 1724 that "those Negroes make the best slaves that have been slaves in their own country; for they that have been kings and great men are generally lazy, haughty, and obstinate; whereas the others are sharper, better humored, and more laborious." Nobles knew little about agriculture and like other rich men were not strong enough to be of much use to New World planters in positions of hard labor. Elite Africans resented their new circumstances far more than did commoners or former slaves, who were used to hard work and low status, but African nobles retained the respect of their fellows and so did very well as foremen and house slaves.

As important as age or class in the acceptance of new ways and conditions was the degree of separation from other Africans and the kind of work the new slaves undertook. African Americans such as those in South Carolina, who worked in the fields in labor gangs away from most whites, remained relatively traditional in their habits, while skilled black workers in urban settings or those in white household service assimilated more quickly.

LANGUAGE

Upon arrival Africans from literally hundreds of societies were mixed together with little attention paid to their national origins, so that few new slaves found themselves near enough countrymen to continue speaking their old languages, except on special occasions. Although many Africans could understand at least one other African language, communication in America called for learning and compromise, especially since the commands of the master class, which had to be obeyed, were given in a European tongue. Newcomers quickly moved from simple improvised sign language to stumbling attempts to master the language they needed to communicate with to be understood by whites and blacks alike.

For the building blocks of the new African-American speech there was the basic working vocabulary of their European-American masters.

Adoption of that vocabulary was enforced not only by the demands of slavery but also by the necessity of avoiding what Virginia Governor Alexander Spotswood called in 1710 "that Babel of Languages" spoken by the first-generation Africans. Grammatically, however, most new slaves designed their syntax around familiar African patterns. The resultant mixture of a European vocabulary with an eclectic blending of grammars and pronunciations made intraslave communication often unintelligible to masters, who blamed the problem on African stupidity. As the Virginia House of Burgesses complained in 1699, "The variety and Strangeness of their languages, and the weakness and Shallowness of their minds renders it in a manner impossible to attain any Progress in their Conversion."

Of course from the African perspective this conclusion was blatant nonsense, as the Mendi-born Ka-le pointed out to John Adams: "Some people say Mendi people crazy dolts because we no talk American language. Americans no talk Mendi. American people crazy dolts?" During the colonial era, many African Americans spoke a European tongue such as French, Spanish, Portuguese, or Dutch in addition to English and several African languages; almost all were able to be understood in both the black and white forms of their master's tongue. In that sense African Americans were usually more cosmopolitan than the elite who owned them.

By the early 1700s in the lowland rice plantations of South Carolina, the African-born majority—which was relatively isolated from both whites and the highly assimilated urban blacks of Charleston—had created a Creole language (later known as Gullah) that had significant retentions of African vocabulary. But where black slaves were relatively few, as in the New England colonies, African immigrants, and especially the younger ones, quickly adopted more European-American patterns of talking.

In general African Americans reshaped the languages of their masters and old homelands into what was recognized as an African-American mode of speech. While neighboring whites could usually understand and even parody what was being said, the African-American pattern was spoken mainly by blacks. And so the shift from African to African-American speech was not simply a matter of assimilation; black English was also a form of self-identification that had begun in cultural compromise but was maintained as a marker of ethnic consciousness.

Because of the importance of the African-American population in the lower colonies, African-American speech soon began transforming the language of the southern master class into a colonial variant that was strongly African-American. Visiting Europeans complained that white colonials were learning the "drawling, dissonant gibberish" of their slaves.

Some whites began to suspect that living among so many blacks was corrupting; thus, Du Pratz Le Page admonished his Louisiana countrymen in 1758: "Never . . . suffer [black slaves] to come near your children, who . . . can learn nothing good from them, either as to morals, education, or language." But the warnings did little good as American wealth continued to be built on slave labor.

A proper display of status required elite whites in the southern colonies, and to a lesser degree elsewhere, to surround themselves with African-American body servants, with the richest commonly using black nurses as constant attendants to their children. Little wonder then that by 1773, when New Englander Josiah Quincy visited the southern colonies, he noticed what he called "a Negroish kind of accent, pronunciation and dialect" appearing in the speech of the region's white children. He also noted that among white adults, women were "vastly infected" by what he called the same "disorder."

MARRIAGE, FAMILY STRUCTURES, AND MANNERS

One of the greatest sacrifices that faced the new black Americans was the loss of the extended family structures that had organized most social relationships in Africa. The first African Americans had to make marriage choices without the traditional guidance and protection of kinsmen symbolized in bridewealth payments. At first African-American premarital sexual standards seem to have been shaped by those of the European laboring classes who worked alongside them and by customs brought from African societies, especially those that permitted relative sexual freedom before marriage. Pregnancy was not uncommon among couples getting married, but outwardly, at least, those who were able to find

spouses seemed to settle into European-American-style, monogamous, nuclear families that traced inheritance bilaterally through the lines of both parents. In contrast African families were generally polygamous and traced ancestry only through one parent's line. The results were larger families and closer kinship connections within Africa, since cousins were related to precisely the same set of ancestors.

As the product of two cultural influences, African-American marriages were not exactly like European-American ones. Whereas marriage was a sacrament for Christians, it was a social contract in Africa, and the greater openness of African-American marriages to voluntary dissolution reflected that. On the other hand, involuntary separations caused by the sale of spouses by slaveholders were a different matter, and they seriously eroded the stability of African-American marriages. The combination of willing and unwilling separations created a variety of African-American marriage relationships that even white observers recognized as different from their own. As the Reverend John Bartow of New York complained in 1725, "[The blacks] will not or cannot live up to the Christian covenant in one notorious instant at least, viz., matrimony, for they marry after their heathen way and divorce and take others as often as they please."

In Africa much of a man's prestige came from his ability to support several wives and a large family. Because there was a surplus of black males in colonial America, only a few African newcomers continued to maintain several wives; of those African-American men who married, most entered monogamous unions, although some men seem to have additionally entered into supporting relationships with other women and children outside of their legal families.

From the female perspective, African women were reluctant to adopt uncritically a Christian monogamy that not only lacked the protections of African marriage, such as the right of a wife's family to consult with her husband's kin over any mistreatment, but also gave husbands complete economic control over their assets. Since in slavery basic subsistence was the responsibility of the master, not the husband, black women had the economic independence to avoid or withdraw from bad relationships (except forced relationships with their masters).

The result was a looser system of alliances that often looked immoral to white Americans, who recorded only the formal unions they blessed.

As best they could within the constraints of the monogamy required of them, African Americans tried to rebuild the cohesive institutions of extended families. Colonial naming choices underscored the importance of kinship as black children were often named after recently deceased relatives. This practice was common enough among whites, but among blacks such naming also had connections to African beliefs in rebirth. African immigrants also tried to replace missing kinsmen with shipmates of the middle passage, and their children honored such relationships with the terms "uncle" and "aunty." Many African Americans also treated the blacks and whites who lived with them in the slaveholding unit as a kind of artificial kin, and the nexus between them was far more than economic.

Family relationships lay at the heart of the African system of manners. The old, who were nearer to the ancestors, were especially honored, and African Americans maintained this respect for age. Unlike white Americans, who for the most part came from the middle and lower classes, colonial African-American communities typically had members who came from royalty, nobility, and the elite classes of Africa. These men and women were honored by their peers, and even whites usually acknowledged the great personal dignity among the serving members of their households, although they were often made uncomfortable by it. Slaveholder manners were deeply shaped by the sensibilities of the African-American nurses who raised the children of the white elite.

RELIGION

If Africans organized society around kinship, their social relationships were also infused and enlivened with religion. Although some of the new slaves were Muslims, most were polytheists who were open to useful new deities. In Africa religion and family combined in rites designed to honor and propitiate ancestral spirits, who had the power to both harm and reward their living kinsmen. Because these spirits resided in Africa, most Africans in the colonies expected to return to their native lands after death. Their children, whose families were American, soon transferred this idea of a spiritual African homeland into their own conception of heaven, which outwardly seemed Christian but was in fact a blending of African and European-American ideas, a hereafter where deceased kin would gather and oppression would end.

Early funerals remained African in style, with emotional displays of grief often followed after the burial by music, dancing, and joy that the deceased had gone to a better place. In eighteenth-century Virginia, a delayed African-style second funeral was customary. Over the years black funerals throughout the colonies became more Christian in content, but at the same time white funerals in the South become more African American in their emotionalism and their conception of heaven as a joyous home hereafter.

Belief in protective charms to guard against sickness and injury remained strong, even if knowledge of the African "medicine" that had energized such amulets in the homelands was fading away. Since charms were also common among the whites, no one complained of the devilishness of these small fetishes. Similarly, African-inspired beliefs in fortune-telling, the divination of lost objects or stolen goods, and the influence of evil spirits or ghosts continued since they, too, were similar to European-American folk beliefs. One of the most interesting crossovers in this regard was the transformation of a West African divination technique using cowrie shells into a gambling game called paw paw played by both blacks and whites in colonial seaports.

Oddly enough, given witchcraft fears that were common to European and African cultures, heathen Africans and African Americans were rarely accused by white Christians of witchcraft. In part this followed from a European misunderstanding of the terminology of black witchcraft. Visiting New York in 1748, Peter Kalm described black conjure, or what we would now call hoodoo, as "poisoning": "The negroes commonly employ it on such of their brethren as behave well toward whites, are beloved by their masters, and separate, as it were, from their countrymen, or do not like to converse with them." Whites took such "poisoning" literally although they also knew, as did the blacks, that it worked far more effectively on African-American believers than on European Americans.

African Americans continued the African tradition of interpreting untimely or unexplained misfortune and illness as the result of unnatural human intervention, the evil product of another's magical work. In fact, as belief in the ancestral spirits declined, fear of antisocial human magic seems to have increased. Formal specialists in protective or harmful magic like those who practiced in Africa were rarely permitted in Christian North America, but the general African worldview about misfortune was maintained in folk beliefs about "roots" or hoodoo, as such magic would later be called. And informally many African Americans became noted practitioners of the magical arts.

Nonetheless with the spirits and old gods weakened by distance, the divinity who had the most power in the New World was clearly the god of the Christians. African polytheists considered it realism rather than heresy to recognize this fact. Nonetheless in the colonial era only a small assimilated minority became formally Christian—in good part because whites judged the legitimacy of black conversion by European-American standards; but the whites' vision of Christianity seemed too self-serving to African Americans. Why was there so much white preaching about lying, drinking, theft, fornication, and obedience when the central spiritual message the blacks heard was the good news that the oppressed were God's chosen people?

Even when African Americans adopted a veneer of European Christianity, they reinterpreted it in harmony with African beliefs. Sin, which was not important in Africa, was downplayed; the Devil became more of a trickster in line with African deities, and spiritual possession—not knowledge of the holy book—became the mark of the initiate. Services without improvisational singing were hardly worthy of the name for African Americans, even though European traditions precluded holy drumming and dancing as too heathenish.

The powerful need to express religion through joyful emotional responses, shouting, and bodily agitation was so strong among the early black worshipers that it helped shape the Great Awakening. The shift by white preachers away from cold lectures and toward hot emotionalism occurred in good part because of the energizing effect that black religious behavior had on their preaching style. But only in the South,

where the African-American population predominated, would both white and black Protestantism retain this emphasis. For while blacks were being converted, they were likewise converting. Southern Protestantism was becoming more African American.

MUSIC AND DANCE

White ministers quickly recognized that they could increase black attendance at services by encouraging singing. Having a soloist line out the hymns to the answering congregation paralleled the call-and-response style that infused most African and African-American music. In Virginia the Reverend Samuel Davies described the artistry that resulted as "a torrent of sacred harmony, enough to bear away the whole congregation to heaven."

Actually most African-American singing was secular rather than religious. Black work songs daily carried across the fields and waters of colonial America, and on moonlit evenings and holidays songs of relaxation and saturnalia could also be heard. Since most black melodies featured improvisational lyrics, the trials of slavery received a variety of artistic renderings. But in the colonial period, most of the songs dealing with slavery were not sorrow songs but satires based on African precedents of musically commenting on and ridiculing improper behavior. As Nicholas Cresswell reported from Maryland in 1774, African-American tunes were a "very droll music indeed. In their songs they generally related the usage they have received from their masters or mistresses in a very satirical style and manner." This tradition of aggressive musical criticism was ubiquitous among blacks in the Americas and went on to influence a wide variety of later American music.

Instrumentally African Americans combined African and European-American traditions. African-style banjos, tambourines, drums, and rattles joined European-style fiddles, flutes, and horns (all of which had their own African versions). Drumming quickly became less important than in Africa because whites generally discouraged it, while European tunes and styles of playing were rapidly adopted. African-American fiddle players played for both black and white dances and sometimes called the figures. In the colonial period, most black fiddlers were described as "natural musicians" by the whites—who did not recognize that musicians who had been taught to play in Africa or by African-American instructors were formally trained. Doubtless they arranged the European tunes they played into a more African-American style. The blending of traditions that resulted was the beginning of a new African-American music that was the first truly great post-Columbian American art.

On free days and holidays, the sounds of banjo and fiddle would draw blacks together with magnetic force. Because the drums so common in West Africa were often not permitted, dancers and spectators clapped their hands, beat their thighs, and stomped their feet to give the beat. The ethnic dances of Africa, which the first generation demonstrated on holidays, were quickly blended into more generalized African-American styles; some featured the shuffling, counterclockwise circles of African religious dances, while others focused on rings—into and out of which dancers moved as spirit and energy took them. Often the dances reached a frenzy of bizarre movements and stylized postures.

Unlike European-American dancers, who usually followed set patterns and kept back and pelvis straight, African-American dancers were extremely loose-limbed and improvised their performances in response to the shouted encouragement of their audiences. The dancers' well-oiled pelvic movements sometimes scandalized whites who, like the observer of a Pinkster dance in New York, considered them "most lewd and indecent." Nonetheless, sprightly African-American jigs were often featured during colonial white dances, and black dancing contests of the era created a new form, tap-dancing, with the dancers supplying their own drum rhythm by dancing on a board. As early as the colonial era, African-American dance was becoming the primary shaping influence in American dance.

VERBAL ARTS

Like their African forebears, African Americans used folktales for educational purposes as well as entertainment. Where African traditions had blamed the slave trade on white cannibalism and black greed, African Americans more commonly told stories of kidnapping to emphasize to the black and white children who heard their tales that in moral truth enslavement was based upon the theft of human labor. The majority of African-American stories, however, were humorous and satirical. Just as in Africa, aggressive satire—not sorrow—was the predominant reaction to social oppression. Blacks were especially noted for their ability to speak metaphorically, which made their commentary on white masters less dangerous to them than might first appear.

Benjamin Franklin recorded a typical African-American witticism that, as he noted, was widely repeated: "Boccarorra (meaning White men) make de black man workee, make de Horse workee, make de Ox workee, make ebery ting workee; only de Hog. He, de hog, no workee; he eat, he drink, he walk about, he go to sleep when he please, he libb like a Gentleman." This observation could be enjoyed by colonials of both races, but the basic point was clearly African American in perspective. So was that of a popular African-American anecdote telling of an old white gentleman who called his faithful slave to tell him that he would honor his service by allowing the black servant to be buried in the family vault. "'Ah! Massa,' returned Cato, 'me no like dat. Ten pounds would be better to Cato. Me no care where me be buried; besides, Massa, suppose we be buried together, and de devil come looking for Massa, in de dark, he might take away poor Negro man in mistake.'" These two examples symbolize the colonial African American's ability to assess critically the white man's inflated claims about the European American's contribution to an American ethic of hard work and Christian morality.

APPEARANCE AND KINESICS

Nominally African Americans adopted European-American clothing styles, since white masters handed out the cheap clothes their slaves wore; moreover masters did not permit blacks to appear in African attire except in certain rare holiday situations. Yet black Americans still expressed their own ideas about work attire. When season and climate permitted, African-American children wore little clothing except for a loose shift or trousers, not just because their masters were stingy but because black parents thought more would be both uncomfortable and falsely modest. Away from white eyes in the coastal low country, black field-workers of both sexes often worked stripped to the waist during the summer, much as they would have in Africa, and their habit of going barefoot in warm weather reflected their own traditional sense of comfort.

For rare dressier occasions African Americans loved European-American higher fashions, which had long been imported to the African coast as part of the luxury trade. During holidays when blacks had personal autonomy, they pulled out all the stops, mixing and matching the best European-style garments they could obtain. The assortments often looked as odd to white observers as the imported ensembles worn by the African coastal elite for the simple reason that Africans and African Americans shared many ideas about style quite different from European standards. Clothing is an important indicator of self-image, and it is therefore important to note that throughout the colonies, blacks were reported during holidays to be "very fond of dress." They often chose bold, contrasting colors worn in eye-catching combinations set off with a variety of colored ribbons and appliqué. On these occasions African Americans often dressed so grandly that whites commonly complained it was unseemly for slaves to look so much better than their owners.

In dress as in language, African-American style was like, but not the same as, European-American style. African Americans were not simply assimilating. Their style of dress, which was developing in the colonial era, reflected their particular values.

Both African-American men and women commonly tied kerchiefs on their heads (it was a working style for men, but women used head-kerchiefs as a dress style as well), and what jewelry they wore, especially their large hoop earrings, was also African in fashion. Interestingly enough, the typical "West Indian" male style that featured a tied headkerchief and hoop earring became the stereotypical garb of the pirate crews that roamed the Atlantic seas from Caribbean ports. Whites in the crews adopted African-American dress as readily as they patterned their sea chanties after African-American call-and-response work songs.

African Americans did not maintain scarification patterns that had been both a form of body art and a marker of status and ethnicity in Africa, but they did continue some of the traditional hairstyles. Most hair was cut short, but braiding women's and girls' hair into African-based patterns was common. Plaits held in place by ties were found on both sexes. Odd styles achieved by shaping and cutting hair into forms such as gentlemen's wigs were especially ingenious, if less common, and represented a freer, more improvisational style of hair design than was common among the era's whites.

In the southern colonies, black women continued to carry heavy loads balanced on their heads as their ancestors had, giving them an unusually erect posture and graceful carriage. General African standards of beauty considered a full figure to be more attractive in a woman than a slender one, and African-American women seem to have maintained this ideal. Men set themselves off by adopting individual and distinctive walking styles, probably patterned at first after those typical of African chiefs, wrestlers, and master dancers. Such forms of what today might be termed styling out were added to the looser and slower movements that typified first-generation Africans from the tropics; the result was an African-American kinesics, a language of moving the human body that soon came to typify the southern region as a whole and which probably influenced the developing American pattern.

Africans bathed far more frequently than Europeans and took much better care of their teeth as well. And although African Americans tried to maintain their cleanliness once they were settled in the colonies, it often became impossible inland from the coast and in the more northern colonies. The use of chew sticks to clean the teeth and gums also seems to have fallen out of use after the first generation.

FOLK CRAFTS AND COOKING

The great wood-carving traditions of coastal West Africa did not transfer to the North

American colonies. Religiously based ancestral figures quickly disappeared, although African Americans sometimes created clay figures to honor their old gods. Wood-carving skills were put to use in secular work on spoons, drums, chairs, canes, and the like. But the African artistry was in the religious vision, not the ability to shape wood. In the southern colonies, African Americans continued to make low-fired coiled and molded earthenware pottery and clay pipes reminiscent of Africa, and they often drank from carved gourds just as they would have in their homelands. But for the most part, the craft skills of African Americans served the wider economy and were performed with European-American tools and techniques. Other African influences like the style of weaving grass baskets probably survived, but the record of physical artifacts is much stronger for the nineteenth century than for the colonial era.

Throughout the colonies blacks were considered the best chefs. At first this is surprising since African cooking is relatively simple, and few African dishes crossed into American cuisine. African Americans generally preferred to eat communally from bowls rather than from individual plates like their masters, but among white Americans the display and serving of food, even when cooked by slaves, continued along traditional European lines.

Nonetheless African-American influence did make itself felt in the general adoption of certain foods relished in West Africa but little appreciated in Britain or Ireland. Okra, black-eyed peas, collard greens, yams, sorghum, benne seed, peanuts, roasted ears of corn, and watermelon all became staples of African-American and southern colonial cooking. Pepper pots, hoe cakes (called johnny cakes in New England), and gumbo likewise became standard regional dishes. In the southern colonies, cutting meats into small portions for frying began replacing the roasting initially preferred by white Americans. Still it was not exotic foods or novel dishes that gave black cooks in the colonial era their superior reputation; it was their wider knowledge of seasonings, the greater zest they put into the culinary arts.

WORK PATTERNS AND ENTREPRENEURSHIP

Africans brought not only their physical labor to America; they also carried with them knowledge about how to work effectively. African familiarity with rice agriculture, for example, helped create the first successful money crop for South Carolina. Africans knew how to clear swamps in preparation for rice growing and how to make the necessary drains from hollowed out tree trunks. Just as in West Africa, Carolina rice production depended upon slash-and-burn clearing and gang labor to prepare the land, heel and foot methods of planting the seed, communal task work to tend it, fanner baskets for winnowing the harvest, and mortars and pestles to husk the grain.

White Americans selected the plow as their farming implement of choice, but African Americans favored the hoe, a shorter version of which had been ubiquitous in Africa. Hoes protected tropical soils from rapid oxidation and fostered the communal labor preferred by Africans and African Americans.

While white colonials soon gave up village residence patterns to move out on the land, African Americans stayed together whenever possible; this was generally true whether the men and women involved were free northerners or southern bondsmen. There was more to the development of a quarters mentality than white prejudice or the slave owners' need to control labor. A basic African and African-American value was involved in communal living.

African-American housing structures also reflected continuity with Africa. Much early black housing was constructed by black craftsmen on a ten- to twelve-foot (approximately 3- to 4-meter) African pattern rather than the more common sixteen-foot (approximatly 5-meter) European-American standard. Moreover, African-American craftsmen working under white masters used African precedents and African-American preferences to influence southern housing in general by radically lightening frames, adding roof coverings as structural elements, joining buildings dogtrot style, separating kitchens from the main house, and expanding the shading of front porches.

African skills were especially useful in developing the colonial frontier. Black knowledge about cattle keeping, canoe making, hunting, and fishing contributed to the general American store of pioneer lore. Blacks were especially knowledgeable about herbal medicines and experimented with the flora of the new land to develop useful medications. Horticultural skills from African tradition led African-American gardeners to commingle plants of different heights within rows so as to improve resistance to insects, drought, and nutrient depletion.

In many of these areas of pioneering skills, traditional African techniques had close Native American parallels. Africans were probably quicker to adopt Indian ideas than were most European Americans, and in canoe making, fishing techniques, pottery, and herbal medicines, African-American culture combined African with Native American as well as European-American techniques. In the colonial southeast, African techniques and plants were likewise adopted by the Indians.

In their homelands many Africans, and especially African women, used the herbs they gathered and the surpluses from their fields to sell and trade in local weekly markets. In the colonial era this interest in business and market culture was maintained, even though whites generally disapproved and attempted to inhibit black enterprise. In New England the church tried to repress Sabbath markets because they attracted more blacks than did the church, whereas in the Carolinas, African-American entrepreneurship was distrusted because slaves could too easily sell their master's goods along with their own. Throughout the colonies white businessmen used the racial inequalities of the legal system to reduce the competition from free black enterprise; however, colonial African Americans maintained a strong entrepreneurial spirit that only generations of slavery and agricultural labor would crush.

MEDICINE

The great strength of early African-American medicine was its holistic approach. It was not enough to treat the physical symptoms of an illness; sociological and psychological manifestations had to be considered as well. This followed from African religious beliefs that illness was most often the unnatural result of evil spirits or human malevolence. To heal a patient required knowing where the patient's social relationships were dysfunctional. The cures that followed required both physical and psychological treatment as well as magical intervention. Patients were not left in the dark about the causes of their illness. If the diagnosis was correct and timely, the antidote would work, or at least so the patient and doctor thought.

In the Americas most African-American care givers were not full-time professionals. Nonetheless black men and women commonly served as "doctors," although their skills were deprecated by whites because they lacked European-based medical training and used magical as well as physical procedures. Within the African-American community, black practitioners—who were more often women than men—handled most nursing, midwifery, doctoring, and dentistry. Despite, and sometimes because of, their comparatively greater reliance upon magic, they were probably as good as, if not better than, their European-American counterparts.

STATUS OF WOMEN

Because the surrounding European-American society generally gave women less independence than was common in Africa, the status of black women generally declined in the North American colonies. The royal festivals of the Caribbean and Brazil honored black queens as well as kings, but in New England and New York only males received recognition. In none of the North American colonies did the economic independence of African-American market women reach the level of the West Indies or Africa.

Still African-American women retained strong personalities and reserved the right to criticize the children they raised, black or white. They were far more economically independent of their husbands than white women and less subservient to their mates than their African sisters. Physically they worked as hard as men. Yet since fewer African women than men were carried to North America, their favors were highly valued by a surplus of suitors and potential mates. Aware of their value, African-American women often raised their status within their own community to a level above their male counterparts.

NATIONAL HOLIDAYS
AND FESTIVAL TRADITIONS

By the middle of the eighteenth century, New England and nearby New York had developed regional variations of what was then becoming an almost universal New World institution—annual rites in celebration of Africa's royal heritage. During these festivals black kings and governors were elected and honored by grand, often satiric, parades followed by several days of feasting and dancing.

In New England, Negro Election Day was far more attractive to the citizenry than the sober formality of European-American public rites, and so the region's holiday celebrations and parade styles became more African American. In New York, like New England, the white holiday observances of Pinkster quickly withered under the competition of rowdier and more amusing black festivals.

In the southern colonies, formal displays of black royalty and officialdom apparently seemed too dangerous. These colonies, unlike the rest of the Americas, did not develop royal festivals although otherwise the basic African-American holiday model was maintained.

Much of the basic African festive style was carried across the Atlantic, and it shaped African-American forms of celebration. Music and dancing were absolute requirements. The custom of celebrating far into the night, a practice that made sense in the tropical heat of the homelands, always annoyed white observers, whose cultural values had developed in cooler climes. Additionally the noise level of black celebrations, which were customarily held out-of-doors, seemed excessive to European Americans, who traditionally celebrated inside. On the other hand, the holiday drinking that irritated white officials was not viewed as different in kind from the consumption of alcohol by the white lower classes whom the blacks were copying.

In general form of march, the African-American royal parades of New England looked like Anglo-American parades honoring the region's white governors; the major differences were in the random firing of salutes, the raucous music, the behavior of the surrounding crowd, and the satirical style of the parades. African Americans were blending African traditions of royal parades and secret society processions into a new African-American style that usually included jesters in exotic costuming as well as honored personages.

Despite the daily oppression of slavery, colonial African Americans did not spend the greater part of their holidays grumbling conspiratorially with each other or tearfully rendering the sorrow songs of Christian spirituals. That was not the African way. Instead most black festivals revolved around good times and featured what the Reverend Francis Le Jau of South Carolina called, "feasts, dances, and merry meetings." And yet, holidays were not simply moments of escapism.

The best humor at black gatherings usually came from attacks on white pretensions, assaults that also served to inhibit blacks from becoming too assimilated in their behavior. Thus a white observer of a South Carolina "Country-Dance" in 1772 noted: "The entertainment was opened, by the men copying (or *taking off*) the manners of their masters, and the women those of their mistresses, and relating some highly curious anecdotes to the inexpressible diversion of that company. . . ." Songs, humorous anecdotes, dances, and folktales were all used to reinforce community solidarity by openly attacking antisocial actions in the forum of social discourse. This was a traditional African form of resistance against the abuses of power.

VIOLENCE

Given the connection between repression and violence, especially in heavily male populations, we might expect that early African-American society would have been extremely violent, but it was not. Blacks readily and continually took part in the communal violence of colonial warfare (and probably would have joined more slave revolts if the numbers and geography had been more promising), but in general they rarely used private violence against either one another or against whites. African Americans preferred wit, ostracism, and public ridicule; the best revenge came from outsmarting an enemy, not in landing a blow.

It was not just European-American power and nascent Christian morality that led colonial African Americans to prefer intellectual and social skirmishing to physical combat. African societies did not accept physical violence directed against neighbors who were, after all, usually kinsmen, nor did they accept the right of revolution against those in authority. In the colonial era, African Americans remained relatively nonviolent because they were in this regard more highly socialized, dare one say more civilized, than the surrounding European-American society.

ETHNICITY

In North America, African Americans developed a new sense of nationality far quicker than their white countrymen or their black brothers in the Caribbean. Specific African ethnicities usually disappeared by the second generation because they no longer seemed relevant to either whites or blacks. Most of the area's African-American marriages were mixed in terms of the spouses' original African nationalities, and the result was a new African-American population sharing a kind of pan-African racial consciousness.

GROWING NATIONALISM

When the revolutionary idea of an American nationality began developing in the late eighteenth century, African Americans were already ahead of the movement having left their individual African ethnicities far behind. The names they gave their children, like the freedom names they took for themselves, were for the most part blandly Anglo-American and assimilationist. But during the revolution, the disparity between rhetoric and reality long evident in white preaching was seen to be putting a double face on white politics as well; African Americans were expected to be patriots to the cause of freedom and equality in a society that denied them both.

Blacks responded with their own overt expressions of nationalism, developing ethnically based institutions such as the First African Baptist Church of Savannah, the Free African Society of Philadelphia, and the African Society of Boston. "African" in these cases did not mean in the style of the homeland. To the contrary, such organizations were developed by the most assimilated African Americans—"We the free Africans and their descendants," as the preamble for the Free African Society in Philadelphia put it. What then did the "African" in the titles of these generally assimilationist organizations mean? It reflected a rejection of white segregationist attitudes by pridefully asserting a double cultural identity for blacks.

These new organizations were both assimilationist and separatist; they accepted far more of European-American culture than they rejected. What they renounced was the racism that tarnished the otherwise universal values of revolutionary America. These principally northern organizations were an assertion by members of the black elite that they accepted the American vision of progress and morality but as independent African Americans, not as slaves or white men's lackeys. These blacks saw their people as a nationality within a nationality; for as the colonial period ended, blacks had become African Americans in name as well as fact.

BIBLIOGRAPHY

Szwed, John E. et al. *Afro-American Folk Culture: An Annotated Bibliography of Materials from North, Central, and South America, and the West Indies.* Philadelphia, 1978.

Wood, Peter H. "'I Did the Best I Could for My Day': The Study of Early Black History During the Second Reconstruction, 1960 to 1976." *William and Mary Quarterly,* 3rd ser., 35, no. 2 (1978):185–225.

Wright, Donald R. *African Americans in the Colonial Era: From African Origins Through the American Revolution.* Arlington Heights, Ill., 1990.

African Background

Herskovits, Melville J. *The Myth of the Negro Past.* Boston, 1958.

Holloway, Joseph E., ed. *Africanisms in American Culture*. Bloomington, Ind., 1990.

Thompson, Robert Farris. *Flash of the Spirit: African and Afro-American Art and Philosophy*. New York, 1983.

Regional Studies

Creel, Margaret Washington. *"A Peculiar People": Slave Religion and Community Culture Among the Gullah*. New York, 1987.

Kulikoff, Allan. *Tobacco and Slaves: The Development of Southern Cultures in the Chesapeake, 1680–1800*. Chapel Hill, N.C., 1986.

Piersen, William D. *Black Yankees: The Development of an Afro-American Subculture in Eighteenth-Century New England*. Amherst, Mass., 1988.

Sobel, Mechal. *The World They Made Together: Black and White Values in Eighteenth-Century Virginia*. Princeton, N.J., 1987.

White, Shane. *Somewhat More Independent: The End of Slavery in New York City, 1770–1810*. Athens, Ga., 1991.

Wood, Peter H. *Black Majority: Negroes in Colonial South Carolina from 1670 Through the Stono Rebellion*. New York, 1974.

Cultural Studies

Epstein, Dena J. *Sinful Tunes and Spirituals: Black Folk Music to the Civil War*. Urbana, Ill., 1977.

Levine, Lawrence W. *Black Culture and Black Consciousness: Afro-American Folk Thought from Slavery to Freedom*. Oxford, 1977.

Raboteau, Albert J. *Slave Religion: The "Invisible Institution" in the Antebellum South*. Oxford, 1978.

Sobel, Mechal. *Trabelin' On: The Slave Journey to an Afro-Baptist Faith*. Princeton, N.J., ppr. ed., 1988.

Vlach, John Michael. *The Afro-American Tradition in Decorative Arts*. Cleveland, Ohio, 1978.

William D. Piersen

SEE ALSO **Festival Traditions; Literature; Magic and Witchcraft; Medical Practice; Recreations; Slavery; and Social Tensions.**

2

SLAVE RESISTANCE

ENSLAVEMENT WAS WIDESPREAD in colonial North America. So also was slave resistance, but it did not always appear that way to historians. From the mid nineteenth to the mid twentieth century, white scholars often portrayed racial slavery as so benign, and African Americans as so limited, that militant opposition seemed neither necessary nor possible. Mainstream historians defined resistance narrowly, in terms of armed insurrection, and stressed the greater number of revolts in the Caribbean and South America. They forgot, as many still do, that while well over ten million Africans were brought to New World plantations by European slave traders, scarcely five hundred thousand—less than 5 percent of this huge forced diaspora—were brought to North America. Overlooking substantial evidence of generations of black opposition (compiled by Herbert Aptheker and others), these writers naively presented the white abolitionist movement as the first "serious" resistance to the peculiar institution.

Much has changed in the late twentieth century. The modern civil rights movement reminded all who opposed discrimination that they were joining a much older and deeper river of black resistance. Firsthand experiences and secondhand reflections about totalitarian and racist regimes in the twentieth century also helped to broaden the discussion of colonial race slavery, prompting new generations of scholars to reflect again upon human capacities to endure and re-

sist exploitation. As a harsher vision of American slavery emerged from the records, some authors stressed the cruel necessity for compliance and outward capitulation among most enslaved persons, most of the time. Others, drawn to the opposite horn of the slaves' dilemma, emphasized that brutality and repression only stiffened and broadened the will to resist.

Both views held much truth, and the ensuing debates have sparked greater interest and deeper research on the subject of slave resistance. Comparative studies, first of all, have allowed closer consideration of the types of enslavement that have existed over time throughout the world. This, in turn, has prompted greater sensitivity to the varieties (and limits) of resistance—personal and collective, spontaneous and planned—that can arise to combat dehumanization. In addition, recent challenges to Eurocentric writing of American history, while not yet widely heard or accepted in the colonial field, have begun to open up the prospect of viewing and understanding the dilemmas of resistance from the perspective of the enslaved non-European, rather than the master. From this vantage point, resistance stops being a problem and becomes a dangerous but alluring possibility; and those who engage in resistance, instead of being renegades and outcasts, appear as variations on an archetypal American theme. After all, the national culture honors those who fight for personal dignity and collective liberty despite overwhelming odds. Eventually, it reveres all those who oppose tyranny and enslavement through their commitment to the ideals of freedom and self-betterment.

INDIAN SLAVERY

Varieties of slavery existed among the diverse inhabitants of North America and Africa long before the transatlantic exchanges initiated by Columbus, and these traditional forms persisted among indigenous people throughout the colonial era. Persons could lose their freedom through capture in war or through sale by elders in order to obtain goods, preserve peace, or pay off debts. Enslavement to another group could involve harsh physical punishment or demeaning labor. Still, such enslaved status was not hereditary and often ended in manumission and assimilation into the group. The European slave trade, unprecedented in the Atlantic world for its scope and brutality, changed these traditional patterns, intensifying warfare and providing an insatiable market for captives. Local leaders who tried to resist these forces found themselves excluded from attractive trade and threatened by rivals willing to exchange prisoners for guns (to be used to capture more prisoners). Those who took part in the new European trade, whether reluctantly or enthusiastically, gained in material wealth, though many discovered that this year's collaborators might become part of next year's cargo.

Even before this new pattern became familiar in Africa, Spanish explorers in America moved to exploit the inhabitants as labor in their hunt for gold. Florida was decimated in the sixteenth century, as captives were exported to the Caribbean, where their frequent suicides by eating cassava poison represented some of the earliest and most poignant resistance to European enslavement. During the seventeenth century, Indians captured in the Southwest were shipped south to the silver mines of New Spain. When English colonists arrived, they, too, soon began to trade in Native American prisoners, enslaving some and shipping others to the West Indies, where they brought a higher price because it was harder for them to escape. By the early eighteenth century white Carolinians were promot-

ing raids across the Southeast that ensnared thousands of Indians.

Numerous "Indian Wars" of the colonial era, therefore, must be understood in this context, from the little-known Gualean Revolt of northern Florida in 1597 to the Tuscarora and Yamasee wars in the Carolinas after 1700. In the West, the eighteenth century would see recurrent local resistance to the continuing subjugation of Indian workers through Hispanic *encomiendas* and Catholic missions. In the north, Eskimos and Aleuts were forced to procure sea otter skins for Russian fur traders, who took women and children as hostages to force men to hunt. Pressured in this way, native Alaskans attacked their exploiters repeatedly, starting in the 1760s.

Though the timing and nature of such resistance, as well as its harsh suppression, varied from place to place, native peoples throughout North America faced common threats. Europeans could mobilize troops with ships and horses, while enforcing their rule with guns and steel swords. (The Spanish also used trained attack dogs.) The ravaging effects of new diseases, the ruthlessness of European warfare, and the unremitting growth of colonial settlements all put Native Americans at a sharp disadvantage. Still, retaliation was commonplace, though rarely so successful as in the dramatic Pueblo Revolt of 1680, when Indians in the Spanish province of New Mexico, forced to work for European masters, instigated a carefully planned and violent rebellion that drove hundreds of Spanish colonists out of the Rio Grande Valley and kept them away for more than a decade.

In the Southwest, a trade in Indian captives persisted for nearly two centuries after the Pueblo Revolt, but several circumstances worked to limit violent resistance by those enslaved. The fact that many of the men continued to be shipped out of the region curtailed organized rebellion somewhat; so did the fact that slavery was not deemed hereditary. Baptism into the Catholic church and the frequent assignment of godparents created linkages that helped to limit exploitation, as did the model for humane, if patronizing, treatment established by many slave-owning priests. Perhaps more important, Indian slaves were widely dispersed throughout colonial households, with no major concentrations where large-scale conspiracies for freedom might materialize. As a result, resistance took on domestic and religious forms, difficult to document and hard to analyze. The degree to which the Indians who provided productive labor at Spanish missions were "enslaved" in some manner remains a matter for debate and exploration, as does the extent to which they resisted this cycle of dependency.

THE BEGINNINGS OF AFRICAN SLAVE RESISTANCE

Native Americans, biologically isolated from the rest of the world for many centuries, suffered horribly from the strange diseases introduced from the Old World. Their populations were rapidly decimated by colonial contact and exploitation, and those who remained proved more useful to the invaders as hunters and allies than as slaves. Within a generation of Columbus's arrival, European powers turned to Africa as an alternative source for labor in the Americas, and Africans enmeshed in this expanding trade promptly began to resist. As with Jews shipped to German death camps in the twentieth century, one huge drawback to overwhelming early resistance by Africans at the point of departure was the absence of accurate information. For if the traffic soon became enormous, it still flowed entirely in one direction; almost no one returned to condemn collaborators and describe the horrors of the distant destination.

The Middle Passage
Nevertheless, resistance materialized from the outset, as Africans escaped from the coffles that brought them to the coast and from the barracoons where they were confined. Each successful act prompted a tightening of procedures that made it harder for those who followed, and this was true on board ship as well. Attempts to escape in port and to commit suicide at sea became so frequent that captains rigged nets to prevent their prisoners from jumping overboard. Hunger strikes proved so frequent that crews often either carried instruments for prying open the mouths of resisters or used hot coals to sear the lips of those who refused to eat. Despite the

enormous odds, scores of violent uprisings can be documented, and those that occurred closest to Africa appear to have had the greatest chance of success. Not only were captives closer to their homelands, but they had not yet been weakened and demoralized by the grueling confinement.

As the Old World receded, the odds for escape grew longer. Few revolts during the middle passage across the Atlantic proved successful, for captains whose profits depended upon limiting shipboard mortality took every precaution to avoid any uprising that would cost lives. Still, potential leaders in the hold remained alert when interacting with members of the crew, for crewmen themselves were often on the brink of revolt against harsh controls and miserable conditions. Indeed, slaves aboard the *Hope,* bound from Africa to the West Indies in 1764, took advantage of an actual mutiny. After the chief mate assumed command, the Africans, hoping to profit from the disorder, rebelled, killing two crew members. Eight slaves died in the uprising. Such revolts, few of them well documented, proved precursors to the resistance that enslaved Africans would generate in the New World.

The Sixteenth and Seventeenth Centuries
Enslaved Africans regularly accompanied early European explorers, and these first African Americans began a long and complex tradition of seeking an alternative existence among Native Americans. What may well have been the first black resistance effort in North America occurred on the Carolina coast in 1526, when enslaved Africans with the ill-fated Ayllón expedition struck back against tyrannous treatment, setting fire to the hut of their oppressors. The ensuing struggle prompted the departure of most of the Spaniards, but some whites and blacks apparently stayed behind to live among the Indians. After Hernando de Soto's massive *entrada* visited the queen of Cofitachiqui in Carolina in 1540, he took her along as a hostage to ensure compliance from neighboring Indians. But she escaped, along with the black slave of a Spanish soldier, and the two returned to her village.

African members of the Narvaez expedition to Florida in 1527 may also have taken refuge among Native Americans. One of four known survivors was Estaban, a slave who joined with

Cabeza de Vaca and two other Spaniards to return to Mexico after a decade among the Indians. Later employed as a guide in the Southwest, Estaban was killed by Pueblo Indians under uncertain circumstances; he may well have been seeking to establish himself as a middleman between two cultures from which he felt removed. In the next century African slaves and their free mulatto offspring would continue to play complex intermediary roles in colonial New Mexico, and there is interesting evidence that one of the instigators of the Pueblo Revolt had African ancestors who had been enslaved by the Spanish.

Meanwhile, with varying degrees of success, the French, English, Dutch, and Swedes had established colonies on the Atlantic coast, and all made some use of African workers. At first the status of such persons was ambiguous, since the enslavement of some arriving Africans proved neither permanent nor hereditary. The Dutch West India Company, for example, bestowed "half-freedom" after years of service, granting the right to marry, acquire property, and move around the colony in exchange for a fixed annual tax. Scarcity of hands meant that blacks as well as whites were issued arms in times of war; slave status was not automatically inherited; and religious belief figured more than racial characteristics in determining social standing.

At first, therefore, imported Africans readily found common cause with European and Indian workers. One of the first known conspiracies in English North America involved both white indentured servants and black slaves who planned to rebel and secure their freedom in Virginia in 1663. In 1672 the Virginia Assembly, faced with bands of fugitive slaves who were raiding plantations, noted that "many mischiefes of very dangerous consequences may arise to the country if either other negroes, Indians or servants should happen to fly forth and joyne with them." Four years later these official fears were realized during the complex uprising known as Bacon's Rebellion. In the latter part of the revolt, servants and slaves made up two-thirds of the rebel army, though government officers offered them freedom to switch sides. The last resisting rebels, a group of "Eighty Negroes and Twenty English which would not deliver their arms," were deceived with promises of liberty, only to be sent back to their masters.

Much changed in the expanding English colonies during the generation following Bacon's Rebellion. With increasing competition for indentured workers from Europe, white laborers could bargain for shorter terms and better conditions. Simultaneously, English participation in the African slave trade expanded, providing wider access to black workers at lower cost. With profits to be made in tobacco and, later, rice and indigo, southern planters moved in the 1660s and 1670s to link slave status firmly to race, making lifelong servitude hereditary for Africans. When Bacon's Rebellion produced an open alliance between white and black workers, it only reinforced the desire of elite leaders to drive a lasting wedge between these two groups. Similarly, frustrated by the close connections between black and red on the frontier, white authorities moved to prevent African Americans from taking part in the deerskin trade, which allowed them to explore opportunities for escape. A South Carolina act of 1731 imposed a heavy fine on anyone employing a "negro or other slave" in the Indian country or in moving goods to and from frontier garrisons and trading posts.

CULTURAL RESISTANCE

By 1700 labor relations in the English colonies had begun to change dramatically, and so had patterns of resistance. Just as Africans found themselves increasingly separated from Europeans by law and custom, their own numbers began to increase dramatically through the burgeoning African trade. Especially in the South, black workers found that their daily contacts were less with Europeans and Indians, and more with a diverse array of African newcomers. For the eighteenth century marked the unchallenged dominance of the British slave trade, and most black citizens trace arrival in North America to this dark period. By 1708 a black majority existed in coastal South Carolina and in parts of tidewater Virginia; two decades later blacks outnumbered whites in French Louisiana.

During the first half of the eighteenth century a larger part of the North American population had been born in Africa than at any time before or since, and this influenced patterns of resistance. Many ideas and practices were brought from the Old World and passed among members of this expanding slave society and beyond. In 1712, when John Barnwell confronted a well-fortified Indian village in eastern North Carolina during the Tuscarora War, for instance, he was informed that "it was a Negro taught them," for an African slave had escaped from a Virginia plantation and was assisting their insurgency. As the regional African-American communities grew in size and self-consciousness, their access to diverse forms of cultural resistance increased.

Indeed, this struggle became all-encompassing. For as Europeans refined their racial arguments and pushed to isolate and demean African workers, every aspect of life became an area of conflict. While whites used every means at their disposal to strip away African cultural independence, blacks sought to preserve a strong identity in the face of devastating odds. In this context, even wearing one's clothes or hair in an African style could become an act of resistance. Such actions could elicit respect and admiration from fellow slaves, anger and retribution from powerful whites. The same was true of cooking African foods such as rice and okra or of playing African instruments such as the drum and banjo. It applied to methods of dancing, speaking, naming, building, moving, marrying, worshiping, and burying the dead.

Slave owners, therefore, could outlaw drumming or curtail African dancing; they could offer—or impose—a select version of the Christian faith. But they could do little to prevent the growth of a separate world in the slave quarters, hidden away from white eyes, where African Americans could—within the harsh material constraints of slavery—speak and eat, dance and dress, worship and mourn more as they chose. Such cultural assertiveness, even though clandestine and intermittent, kept alive prospects for further resistance. While planters felt obliged to tolerate a measure of this resistance to European ways, they realized that such interactions could spawn serious threats to their control.

Poisoning

Poisoning constitutes a case in point. Many Africans arriving in the South brought a wide familiarity with the flora of warm climates, and this kind of knowledge could be shared within the emerging slave community. Not only was poisoning effective, but slaves could obtain the necessary plants from the surrounding countryside, and acts of poisoning were often impossible to prove with the forensic procedures of the time. Women in particular were thought to practice this art, since it required little physical strength and was well suited to the kitchen, where female house servants had regular access to the preparation and serving of the master's food. In Virginia, from 1740 to 1785, more slaves were charged with poisoning than with any other crime except stealing. Enslaved women convicted of using poison could be burned alive, a punishment normally reserved for traitors and witches.

To whites, aware of the animosity created by perpetual bondage, poisoning was a particularly frightening and insidious crime. They knew that those they had enslaved could poison them under the pretense of offering helpful medicines and tasty foods, or could simply pollute a well and infect the public drinking supply. This possibility sometimes led whites to paranoia. In 1740, for example, amid rumors that New York slaves had been plotting to poison the water supply, whites began purchasing bottled water. Colonial assemblies passed laws against poisoning, harshly punishing those who instructed others about poisons, restricting the occasions when slaves could administer medicines, and offering rewards to informants. Enslaved blacks continued to poison, however, and white colonists continued to convict, though they surely imagined some cases and failed to detect others.

ECONOMIC RESISTANCE

Arson

Like poisoning, arson required no special strength and offered an anonymity impossible for most acts of resistance. Enslaved workers sometimes used arson to cover up thefts, but more often they risked burning down houses and farm structures in order to hurt their masters economically, to torment them emotionally, or to destroy them physically. The Negro Act of 1740 in South Carolina, for instance, ordered execution for "any slave, free negro, mulatoe, Indian or mustizoe, [who] shall wilfully and maliciously burn or destroy any stack of rice, corn or other grain." But fires continued to occur suspiciously between October and January, when black Carolinians were forced to work long hours in dusty barns cleaning and packing rice.

In an era of wooden houses and primitive fire protection, urban arson was especially tempting, for a city blaze in windy weather could quickly spread to nearby buildings and create a raging conflagration. Between 1721 and 1723 numerous fires of suspicious origin broke out in Boston and New Haven. In April 1734 in Montreal, a slave named Marie-Joseph-Angélique, convinced that her mistress was planning to sell her, ignited the woman's home and set out for New England with her white lover. The fire spread quickly and consumed forty-six houses as well as a convent and church. Marie-Joseph-Angélique was captured and subjected to an elaborate ceremony in which she was paraded around the city to witness the parts she had destroyed. Afterward, she was publicly hanged and burned, but her lover remained at large and was never found.

In general, the fact that arson was so difficult to prove seems to have heightened the willingness of authorities to try innocent slaves for fires they had not set and to attribute other unexplained blazes to culprits already convicted of arson. On 18 November 1740, barely a year after South Carolina's Stono Rebellion, flames erupted in the center of Charleston, destroying three hundred houses and burning down newly constructed fortifications. The fire handed white residents a huge financial loss and prompted immediate suspicion of slave arson, but no charges could be confirmed.

In New York the following summer slaves were convicted of setting several blazes, including one that destroyed the fort where the governor resided. Shortly after word of the New York fires reached Charleston, a mulatto slave named Kate and her companion, Boatswain, tried to burn a dwelling by igniting a bundle of straw under the roof shingles at night. A neighbor spotted the flames and the fire was put out before it could spread, but both conspirators were condemned to death. According to Charleston prosecutors, Boatswain "looked upon every white Man he should meet as his declared Enemy," and he and Kate were accused of arson, with the "evil intent of burning down the remaining

Part of the Town." Several months later two other slaves were convicted of attempting to set the city's powder magazine on fire.

Sabotage

Arson was not the only means of threatening the economic and psychological well-being of those who considered themselves masters. Wherever labor is expropriated for profit, varied and frequent acts of sabotage occur. Well before European peasants made a practice of using their wooden shoes (sabots) to jam the early machines of the Industrial Revolution, plantation workers in America, enslaved to the market production processes of the "factory in a field," had developed their own ways to limit production. Newcomers feigned ignorance at learning to use wheelbarrows and plows; experienced hands regularly broke hoes and axes, pretending carelessness. Again and again, unpaid workers ruined crops by intentionally picking tobacco leaves too early or by flooding rice fields too much.

Like other workers before and since, colonial slaves came to realize the strength of numbers, undertaking collective actions even when such combinations were strictly forbidden. Black chimney sweeps in Charleston stopped work to protest their conditions, and field hands sometimes risked punishment by refusing an increased workload. In July 1776, at his plantation near Baton Rouge, Louisiana, William Dunbar recorded in his journal how he had made a wager with fellow planters to see whose workers could produce the most barrel staves in a week. Faced with this speed-up, a conspiracy developed across several plantations. Informants named one of Dunbar's slaves as a leader, and the man was bound and put aboard a canoe, "sitting in the bottom of the Boat with his arms pinioned." But in the middle of the river the accused managed "to throw himself overboard & was immediately drowned." To Dunbar, "this was sufficient evidence of his guilt."

While owners constantly sought to accelerate production, enslaved laborers steadily devised ways to hold it back. Since their labor profited only their masters, slaves had little incentive to work hard. Instead, they toiled as slowly as they could without being punished, knowing that this type of resistance was impossible to combat.

If challenged, they could engage in verbal argument, gaining satisfaction from studied insolence while slowing the work process further. In addition to working slowly, slaves also feigned illness to avoid labor. Such malingering might sometimes be caught, but because the slave represented a substantial investment, the slave owner had to use discretion. Working a slave who really was sick could lead to a more serious illness and even death, a heavy financial loss for the master.

"Thieves," Runaways, and Maroons

By slowing the pace of work, slaves were robbing the master of their expropriated labor, but the whole concept of theft itself becomes ambiguous in the context of enslavement. Stolen from Africa and denied the right to accumulate money or possessions, these captives felt little obligation to create wealth for their supposed owners. Not surprisingly, a major form of resistance was the appropriation of some of the fruits of their own labor in terms of food they had raised, products they had made, or goods they would have been able to purchase if compensated for their actual labor. While acts of appropriation occurred individually on a daily basis, from time to time they also took place on a larger scale through organized rings. Such gangs seem to have operated in Charleston and New York in the 1730s and in Richmond and Petersburg in the 1780s. In defining all these acts of appropriation as "stealing," white society overlooked or obscured the basic contradictions underlying its system of racial exploitation.

Nothing illustrated these contradictions more clearly than when enslaved colonists literally "stole themselves" by running away. Many slaves left their plantations to maintain contacts with friends and relatives; others chose to run away when faced with new work assignments, harsh treatment, or the threat of sale. Each person had to decide whether to leave briefly or for good, alone or with others; whether to head for Indian territory or seek the anonymity found in a large seaport or aboard an oceangoing vessel. Enslaved South Carolinians had all of these dangerous options, plus the prospect of Saint Augustine, where Spanish officials encouraged unrest in the English colony by offering the prospect of freedom to fugitive slaves. By the 1740s a small community of black refugees resided just north of Saint Augustine at Fort Mose.

In the South, some runaways joined remote communities of fugitive slaves known as maroons (derived from the Spanish word *cimarrón*, which had been applied in Hispaniola to cattle living in the hills). The Dismal Swamp on the Virginia–North Carolina border sheltered one of the largest maroon communities in North America, while other groups hid in the mountains farther west. When a large number of slaves established themselves in Virginia's Blue Ridge Mountains in 1729, most were captured after a pitched battle. The Englishman John Brickell recalled that there were "above three Hundred joined together" who "had taken Sanctuary in the Woods for some time before they were discovered," and who "did a great deal of Mischief in that Province before they were suppressed." He had seen two dozen of the leaders hanged "for conspiring against their Masters" after being "hunted out by the Indians, who are very serviceable to the Christians in those Parts."

Though Indians and runaway slaves occasionally resided together, especially in Louisiana, the presence of Native Americans along the frontier prevented the establishment of maroon communities as large as those in Central and South America. White colonists practiced "divide and rule" and passed laws early on that pitted Indians against blacks. In 1721, for example, the first royal governor of South Carolina established a treaty with the Upper and Lower Creek, who promised "to apprehend and secure any Negro or other Slave which shall run away from any English Settlements to our Nation" in exchange for blankets and firearms. The Indians received acknowledgment that if a runaway was killed while being apprehended they were "to be paid one Blanket for his Head by any Trader we shall carry such Slave's Head unto."

OVERT REBELLION

Prevented from absconding to the interior and unable to return to Africa, the victims of chattel slavery in colonial North America occasionally resorted to overt rebellion. Their uprisings were smaller and less frequent than those in the Caribbean and South America, where the plantation system was older and larger, the annual influx of Africans was greater, the ratio of black workers to white planters was higher, and the conditions of intensive sugar production in a tropical climate were inhuman in the extreme. Nevertheless, rebellions occurred in all areas of North America, from Alaska to Florida, wherever large numbers of Native Americans or Africans were enslaved. In short, wherever non-European slaves resided, there were attempted rebellions, regardless of the type of work imposed or the nationality of the colonizers.

Studying such uprisings is by no means easy, however. As with other forms of slave resistance, almost all of the documentation comes from white sources. At times it contains gross exaggerations and false accusations; at other times it reflects naive innocence or willful suppression of evidence; therefore the true extent of a rebellion as planned by slaves usually remains unknown. Confessions used in court were often obtained by torture; and accused persons, desperate for clemency, sometimes simply said what authorities wanted to hear. A rebellion occupying several columns in a colonial newspaper may have been simply a small scuffle, exaggerated by the imaginations of fearful whites; whereas an incident that occupies only a line or two may in reality have been a carefully planned blow for liberation.

But certain patterns of armed upheaval can be discerned. For example, participation in colonial slave revolts usually involved both Africans and African Americans. While a plan could originate with courageous newcomers or embittered "country-born" slaves, broad (and risky) coalitions were generally necessary among both leaders and participants, crossing boundaries of religion, language, and ethnic group. For slaves to organize and risk their lives in a revolt, they had to find common ground, both practical and spiritual. In those all-too-few revolts about which we know more than the date, slaves often depended heavily on African religions, Christianity, or a mixture of the two for support in their undertaking.

Moreover, such planned resistance was most often attempted during military crises, economic depressions, and political upheavals. For instance, by the time of the Natchez War in 1729–1730, Africans had recently become a majority in the small Louisiana colony. Taking advantage of the chaotic situation, "the Negroes formed a design to rid themselves of all the French at once, and to settle in their room, by making themselves masters of the Capital, and of all the property of the French." Le Page du Pratz, who helped uncover the plan, found the trusted overseer on the plantation of the Louisiana Company, an African named Samba Bambasa, to be among the leaders, eight of whom were eventually broken on the wheel. The Frenchman learned that Samba had previously "in his own country, been at the head of the revolt, by which the French lost Fort Arguin." Condemned to slavery in America, it was said that "Samba, on his passage, had laid a scheme to murder the crew, in order to become master of the ship; but that being discovered, he was put in irons, in which he continued, till he landed in Louisiana."

Stono, South Carolina, 1739

A decade later it was new arrivals from Angola (perhaps bringing considerable military experience with them) who sparked the largest uprising in British North America, twenty miles (32 kilometers) southwest of Charleston, South Carolina. By the end of the 1730s enslaved persons outnumbered free people in the rice-growing colony by nearly two to one, and the proportion of African-born "saltwater" slaves in the colony had reached its highest point ever. Still able to recall their childhood freedom and unreceptive to life at the bottom of an alien English culture, these persons often proved unwilling to submit to bondage. Jemmy, leader of the Stono Revolt, must have been such an individual. In the fall of 1739 he found himself in a work camp near the western branch of the Stono River, forced to repair the public roads with other enslaved Africans.

Before daylight on Sunday, 9 September 1739, he and nearly twenty others broke into a store at Stono Bridge. They took firearms, executed the proprietors, and then headed south toward Saint Augustine, hoping to be joined by others as they marched. Along the way, they killed the whites whom they encountered and set fire to the plantation houses they passed, sparing one innkeeper because he was "kind to his slaves." Though whites liked to think of their slaves as childlike and incapable of plotting, the

Stono Rebellion proved otherwise. It was carefully timed to take advantage of the confusion in Charleston caused by an epidemic of yellow fever. In addition, the attack was launched the day word reached Carolina that hostilities had erupted between Spain and England, in what would become known as the War of Jenkins' Ear. Moreover, the slaves rebelled a few weeks before a law was to go into effect requiring all men to carry arms to church on Sunday.

Late Sunday morning, Lieutenant Governor William Bull, on his way back to Charleston, spotted the rebels, now numbering between sixty and one hundred. Had he not chanced upon them, their numbers would have continued to grow rapidly. The revolt might have struck such a blow that the development of race slavery in South Carolina would have been arrested by fearful whites. As it was, Bull managed to report the rebellion, and by late afternoon scores of armed and mounted planters had responded to his alert. They caught the escaping band of slaves off guard, wounding or killing at least fourteen and capturing others. A third of the rebels escaped, but the organized march south was broken up. More than thirty blacks and twenty whites lost their lives, and the vulnerability of the repressive slave system was demonstrated to Africans and Europeans alike. One leader remained at large for more than three years before he was captured and hanged.

While the Stono Rebellion forced South Carolina planters to reflect on the slave society they were creating, they emerged from the crisis resolved to keep, and refine, their lucrative system. The assembly enacted a law penalizing owners who mistreated their slaves; and it passed the long-debated Negro Act, which curtailed the movement and assembly of blacks and restricted them from raising their own food, earning money, and learning to read and write. Ironically, it also created a black "school" to spread planter Christianity and train a select group of compliant black leaders. Threatened with the prospect of a growing and increasingly rebellious slave population, the assembly also took steps to discourage the presence of free blacks in the colony, and it passed a law reiterating that one white should be present for every ten blacks on plantations. In addition, a prohibitive duty was placed on new slaves from the West

Indies and Africa, but this law lapsed within a decade.

New York City, 1712 and 1741

New York, with the highest proportion of slaves among the northeastern colonies, witnessed some of the largest slave insurrections in the colonial era. Resistance ranged in New York City from assaulting "the mayor on the face" when he ordered a group of slaves to disband in 1696, to the major insurrections of 1712 and 1741. There were cases of uprisings outside of New York City, as in Newton, Long Island, when a family was murdered by its slaves in 1708; but the larger rebellions occurred in New York City, where enslaved persons were shipped in from Africa and auctioned off on Wall Street.

Such "saltwater" slaves enhanced the prospects for insurrection, because large numbers were regularly added to the local population of the small port. Well before 1712, therefore, New York already had a series of laws to prevent insurrections. A 1684 act prohibited slaves from carrying firearms and from assembling in groups larger than four (in 1702 the number was reduced to three). In 1708 New York got its first "act for preventing the conspiracy of slaves," and in 1710 an ordinance passed in New York City prohibited blacks from being on the streets after dark without a lighted lantern.

It was recently enslaved Africans, including Coromanti (Akan peoples from the Gold Coast in the vicinity of the European fort at Cormantine), who planned and executed a rebellion in 1712. Early in the year two dozen of these slaves, along with several Indians, met to plot a revolt "to obtain their freedom" and "to destroy all the whites in the town." According to one newspaper, they swore "themselves to secrecy by Sucking ye blood of each Others hand," and a free Negro supposedly provided a powder to rub on their clothes that would make them invulnerable. On the night of 6 April, they set fire to a building, planning to slaughter any whites who rushed to combat the fire. They succeeded in killing nine men and wounding seven others, but within twenty-four hours most of them had been captured by soldiers. In a last act of resistance, six rebels chose to commit suicide rather than submit, including a husband who first killed his wife. Twenty-one captives were later executed—some

217

hanged, some burned alive, one broken on the wheel. In the words of the governor, "there has been the most exemplary punishment inflicted that could possibly be thought of."

After the revolt arson by a slave became punishable by death, but despite preventative measures New York slaves continued to resist. In 1741 a larger and more extensive rebellion erupted, involving organized crime and alliances between whites and black slaves. At the time, the city had a population of twelve thousand, of which two thousand were black. A group of slaves—known as the Geneva Club because they broke into a tavern and took several barrels of Geneva gin in 1736—operated a racket in which they stole goods and passed them on to two white men, John Romme and John Hughson, who then sold them back to whites. The government was more than dismayed to learn later that it had in fact purchased stolen butter from this ring for the use of its soldiers.

On 28 February 1741 a small robbery occurred for which Caesar and Prince, two leaders of the Geneva Club, were blamed. The robbery would have been insignificant had a series of fires not broken out in the city in March. Fort George, which housed the governor and contained administrative offices and an armory and barracks, was the site of the first suspicious fire, and others followed. While the robbery was being investigated, Mary Burton, a sixteen-year-old Irish servant indentured to John Hughson, stated that she would talk about the robbery but would not say a word about the fires. From there, conspiracy burst into the minds of the authorities, and the race was on to uncover its extent. In a period of over three months, one hundred fifty slaves were arrested along with twenty-five whites, seventeen of them soldiers.

As the conspiracy grew in the minds of the prosecutors, they found that numerous slaves had been meeting at John Hughson's tavern to plot a rebellion. Cuffee, one of the implicated slaves, was reported to have said at one of these meetings that "a great many people have too much and others too little." The conspiracy grew to include all the traditional enemies of British colonists; not only were slaves rebelling, but they were being aided by Spanish and Catholics with the support of the Spanish king and the pope. In the end, thirteen slaves were burned alive,

eighteen hanged, and seventy banished; four whites were executed as well.

Prosecutors exaggerated the extent of the conspiracy, but their fears did have a foundation. There was an organized crime ring involving both blacks and whites, built upon a common resentment of New York City's wealthy elite. These members of the underclass, black and white, were fraternizing too closely for the comfort of civic authorities. New York slaves had developed another life of which their masters were not aware; and this other half of the city, populated by both enslaved blacks and poor whites, was as great a threat to New York's elite as any violent insurrection. When authorities uncovered the crime ring and linked it to the fires, they promptly executed thirty-five people, though no one had been killed in either the fires or the robberies.

Pointe Coupée, Louisiana, 1795

French and Spanish slave codes provided some protection for enslaved workers brought from Africa, but they could not prevent the plotting of rebellions in colonial Louisiana, the largest of which was conceived in 1795 at Pointe Coupée, 150 miles (240 kilometers) north of New Orleans on the west bank of the Mississippi. Enslaved blacks, who outnumbered whites throughout the Spanish colony, exceeded Europeans seven thousand to two thousand in this particular community. In early April authorities learned of a slave meeting at one of the Pointe Coupée plantations to plot a rebellion, and they swiftly rounded up scores of black inhabitants. As the prisoners were tried, it was discovered that blacks in Natchez had planned to rise up simultaneously with those in Pointe Coupée. Several dozen persons were eventually executed, and the severed heads of resistance leaders were placed atop posts in New Orleans and elsewhere.

The slaves of Pointe Coupée, most of whom were French-speaking, were doubtless influenced by events in Saint Domingue, where a bloody and ultimately successful slave revolution was being waged that would lead to the creation of Haiti as an independent state. Many white refugees had fled to Louisiana with their slaves for safety, and these immigrants may have contributed to local awareness of events on the Caribbean island. Along with the ideological upheavals of the French and American revolutions, the revolution in Saint Domingue served as a model for slave rebellions in the Americas and influenced those in North America well into the nineteenth century, including two of the largest, Gabriel's Conspiracy of 1800 in Virginia and Denmark Vesey's Rebellion of 1822 in South Carolina.

After the conspiracy of 1795, Spanish authorities took steps to prevent a recurrence. First they stopped importation of slaves from the French islands, and later they banned altogether the entry of blacks into Louisiana. Despite the gruesome warnings of severed heads on display, African Americans in the region took part in subsequent plots over the next twelve months and again in 1804. In 1811 several hundred black workers around Pointe Coupée would rebel again in the largest slave revolt in American history.

RESISTANCE AND THE AMERICAN REVOLUTION

If slave resistance occurred most readily and openly when political struggles divided the ranks of the slaveholders, then it is not surprising to find upheaval associated with the era of the American Revolution. When white colonists rallied against the Stamp Act in the streets of Charleston during 1765, their cries of "Liberty!" were soon taken up by black slaves. "The city was thrown under arms for a week," Henry Laurens recalled, "and for 10 to 14 days messengers were sent posting through the province." In April 1775, at the time of Concord and Lexington, a free black pilot in Charleston named Jeremiah was said to have rallied enslaved African Americans on the docks with his prediction that "there is a great war coming" that would "help the poor Negroes." A few months later, Jeremiah was arrested and publicly executed by white patriots who feared that he was plotting a slave revolt with the aid of British authorities.

But even such drastic retaliation could not hide from slaves the fact that colonial society was in turmoil and that those in bondage stood to gain from the upheaval. In 1775 in Saint Bartholomew's Parish, South Carolina, a revolt was uncovered in which one of the leaders had told his fellow slaves that "the old King had rec^{ed} a Book from our Lord by which he was to Alter the World [meaning to set the Negroes free] but for his not doing so, was now gone to Hell, and punishment—that the Young King, meaning our Present One, came up with the Book, & was about to alter the World, & set the Negroes Free." Similarly, a black preacher in Georgia instructed an audience of whites and blacks that "God would send Deliverance to the Negroes, from the power of their Masters, as He freed the Children of Israel from Egyptian Bondage." He fled the colony after angry slave owners determined that he should be hanged for inciting rebellion.

Indeed, similar plots were discovered up and down the Atlantic coast in 1775; and the proclamation of Virginia's Governor Dunmore in November, offering freedom to black men who took up arms against the rebels, further heightened expectations. The British knew that slaves were fighting for different reasons than they were; they tried to refrain from arming them but on some occasions could not avoid it. When French and American forces besieged Savannah in 1779, the British were forced to arm blacks in the town. After successfully fighting off the siege, however, the British found it difficult to disarm the African Americans and "reduce them to their proper obedience and position." Several of these slaves eventually fled to the Belle Isle Swamp and established a colony. They waged guerrilla war for years along the Savannah River, calling themselves soldiers of the king of England, but were eventually defeated in 1786 by militia from Georgia and South Carolina and some Indian warriors. Several thousand black Loyalists obtained passage to Nova Scotia at the end of the war, and in 1792 more than eleven hundred of them chose to migrate to Sierra Leone in West Africa.

But many slaves who had fled to the British ended up as laborers in the army or were sold in the West Indies. A few were eventually given their freedom, but overall, British promises of emancipation were made as military expedients, not moral imperatives. Slaves caught actively aiding the British were hanged as traitors by white Americans. Such was the fate of Sancho, court-martialed in 1781 for offering intelligence and piloting the Virginia waterways for the British army. Even for those who helped neither side or actively supported Washington's army, the end of the war did not bring freedom and independence. The cries of "Liberty!" in the American Revolution, as many embarrassed patriots recognized, applied only to whites. Most African Americans would have to continue their freedom struggle for almost another century.

BIBLIOGRAPHY

Aptheker, Herbert. *American Negro Slave Revolts.* New York, 1943.

Davis, Thomas J. *A Rumor of Revolt: The "Great Negro Plot" in Colonial New York.* New York, 1985.

Frey, Sylvia R. *Water from the Rock: Black Resistance in a Revolutionary Age.* Princeton, N.J., 1991.

Genovese, Eugene. *From Rebellion to Revolution: Afro-American Slave Revolts in the Making of the Modern World.* Baton Rouge, La., 1979.

Greene, Lorenzo J. "Mutiny on the Slave Ships." *Phylon* 5, no. 4 (1944):346–354.

Hall, Gwendolyn Midlo. *Africans in Colonial Louisiana: The Development of Afro-Creole Culture in the Eighteenth Century.* Baton Rouge, La., 1992.

Harding, Vincent. *There Is a River: The Black Struggle for Freedom in America.* New York, 1981.

Holmes, Jack D. L. "The Abortive Slave Revolt at Pointe Coupée, Louisiana, 1795." *Louisiana History* 11 (1970):341–362.

Johnson, Michael P. "Runaway Slaves and the Slave Communities in South Carolina, 1799 to 1830." *William and Mary Quarterly* 3rd ser., 38, no. 3 (1981):418–441.

Kaplan, Sidney. "The 'Domestic Insurrections' of the Declaration of Independence." *Journal of Negro History* 61 (1976):243–255.

Lara, Oruno D. "Resistance to Slavery: From Africa to Black America." *Annals of the New York Academy of Sciences* 292 (1977):464–480.

Mullin, Gerald W. *Flight and Rebellion: Slave Resistance in Eighteenth-Century Virginia.* New York, 1972.

Price, Richard. *Maroon Societies: Rebel Slave Communities in the Americas.* Garden City, N.Y., 1973.

Quarles, Benjamin. *The Negro in the American Revolution.* Chapel Hill, N.C., 1961.

Schwarz, Philip J. *Twice Condemned: Slaves and the Criminal Laws of Virginia, 1705–1865.* Baton Rouge, La., 1988.

Scott, Kenneth. "The Slave Insurrection in New York in 1712." *New-York Historical Society Quarterly* 45, no. 1 (1961):43–74.

Thornton, John K. "African Dimensions of the Stono Rebellion." *American Historical Review* 96 (1991):1101–1113.

Trudel, Marcel. *L'Esclavage au Canada français: Histoire et conditions de l'esclavage.* Quebec, 1960.

Watson, Alan D. "Impulse Toward Independence: Resistance and Rebellion Among North Carolina Slaves, 1750–1775." *Journal of Negro History* 63 (1978):317–328.

Wax, Darold D. "Negro Resistance to the Early American Slave Trade." *Journal of Negro History* 51 (1966):1–15.

Winks, Robin W. *The Blacks in Canada: A History.* New Haven, Conn., 1971.

Wood, Peter H. *Black Majority: Negroes in Colonial South Carolina from 1670 Through the Stono Rebellion.* New York, 1974.

————. "'The Dream Deferred': Black Freedom Struggles on the Eve of White Independence." In *In Resistance: Studies in African, Caribbean, and Afro-American History,* edited by Gary Y. Okihiro. Amherst, Mass., 1986.

Wright, J. Leitch, Jr. *The Only Land They Knew: The Tragic Story of the American Indians in the Old South.* New York, 1981.

Peter H. Wood

SEE ALSO **Crime and Law Enforcement; Farming, Planting, and Ranching; Slavery;** and **The Slave Trade.**

VIII

WAR AND DIPLOMACY

INDIAN-COLONIST CONFLICTS AND ALLIANCES
THE EUROPEAN CONTEST FOR NORTH AMERICA
THE CONQUEST OF ACADIA

INDIAN-COLONIST CONFLICTS AND ALLIANCES

THE BRITISH COLONIES

As with virtually every other aspect of interaction between Europeans and Native Americans, war and diplomacy must be understood within the cultural frameworks that divided peoples from the two sides of the Atlantic. War and diplomacy sprang from closely related cultural imperatives for both Europeans and Indians, but those imperatives set the two societies radically apart. The point is particularly worth stressing because, while diplomacy is readily appreciated as a delicate matter of negotiating cultural differences, something so apparently simple as organized violence often seems universal, even precultural; there are only so many ways, after all, of systematic killing. Yet societies vary widely in their ways of war. Moreover, if the old European maxim that diplomacy is warfare by other means holds any validity, mechanisms of diplomacy must also diverge.

CONTRASTING CULTURES OF WAR AND DIPLOMACY

The gap between European and Native ways of war and diplomacy did not lie in the realm of comparisons between "civilized" and "savage" or "peaceful" and "warlike." The societies of both the colonizers and the colonized were, by any objective measure, prone to extreme acts of organized violence. At the same time, however, both also had powerful counterideologies of peace and elaborate cultural practices designed to suppress intersocietal conflict. And both groups were quite diverse. Generalizations about "the British" must account for ethnic distinctions between the English core and the Celtic fringe, between the localistic world of the countryside and the cosmopolitan outlook of the court, and between the aims of the state and the interests of the private groups who controlled most early colonizing efforts. British colonies, meanwhile, ran the gamut from the religious utopias of New England to ethnically pluralistic New York, New Jersey, and Pennsylvania to the plantation societies of the Chesapeake and the Carolinas. Similarly, discussions of "the Indians"—even those limited to North America east of the Mississippi—inevitably lump together a vast array of linguistic groups and economic and political structures.

English Warfare and Diplomacy
Perhaps the best way to conceive of the difference between English and Native American war and diplomacy is to concentrate upon the respective

roles of individuals and families on the one hand, and larger politico-economic units on the other. In England, as everywhere in the European world, warfare and diplomacy originated with the institutions of the nation-state: the Crown, the Parliament, and the powerful national economic interests that sought to control them. In a way that would have been obvious to any European but utterly foreign to most North American Indians, decisions made at the center worked their way downward, often coercively, to the localized world of village communities, family groups, and individuals. By regulations of economic activity designed to strengthen the position of English merchants compared with those of other nations, by impositions of taxation necessary to finance their international activities, and by drafts of military personnel destined to fight against counterparts from abroad, governments sought to bend the population at large to their will.

English central authorities went to war and conducted diplomacy for any number of reasons, not the least of them religious. Nonetheless, economic motives predominated in European traditions of warfare, even when the parties involved sincerely professed higher ends. States battled over control of international trade routes, over access to important material resources, over colonial riches derived from both commodities and the human labor that produced them, and over revenues that crowns could derive from each of those activities. Meanwhile, although Christianity mandated the pursuit of peace for its own sake, monarchs who claimed such titles as "His Most Christian Majesty" and "Defender of the Faith" seldom conducted diplomacy to halt bloodshed and promote international understanding. Instead, their diplomats pursued the same economic ends as did their warriors, as reflected in the prevalence of such phrases as "amity and commerce" in the titles of their treaties.

In the English colonies, the diplomats and the warriors were usually one and the same. Late-sixteenth- and early-seventeenth-century trading companies tended to place military men in positions of authority and to entrust all dealings with Indians to their purview. Subsequently, the British governors-general who controlled intercultural relations in most of the North American provinces hailed almost exclusively from military backgrounds. More was involved with this choice than a tendency to shoot first and ask questions later. As soldiers, such figures approached intercultural diplomacy primarily as an aspect of military strategy, often with a primary purpose of enlisting native warriors as allies against other Indians or rival Europeans. As veterans of brutal duty in Ireland, on the Continent, or among cutthroat privateers, they approached nearly all human beings with assumptions of distrust and expectations of random violence. As officers their habit of command combined with their class biases and religious prejudices to give them every expectation of imposing their will on peoples they considered undisciplined, savage heathens. In short, little in their background prepared them for serious, mutually respectful negotiations with Indian leaders.

Indian Warfare and Diplomacy

Among Native peoples of eastern North America, starkly contrasting (but not necessarily more noble) mechanisms, motives, and personnel characterized warfare and diplomacy. None of the coastal societies encountered by English colonizers possessed a nation-state form of political organization. Even the most highly centralized—the Powhatan Confederacy of the Chesapeake Bay region—depended more for its unity on reciprocal economic exchanges and ceremonial obligations than on the considerable military might of its paramount leader. Elsewhere in the areas that the English entered in the seventeenth century, autonomous village communities that were loosely connected by ties of trade, marriage, and language prevailed. Within them headmen presided on the basis of kinship, reciprocal obligations, and moral example rather than on the coercive exercise of authority.

In such a cultural milieu, warfare and diplomacy tended to flow from the bottom upward rather than from the political apogee downward. For the most part individuals and families, rather than nations, made war and conducted diplomacy, and they did so for reasons utterly foreign to Europeans. To one degree or another, all of the Indian societies with which the English interacted practiced the "mourning-war." In that cultural pattern—which was most highly developed among the Iroquoian-speaking peoples of the eastern Great Lakes region—wars were waged primarily to seize captives, who would replace decreased members of the community, either literally through adoption or symbolically through ceremonial execution. Thus, although the economic importance of a prisoner's labor or of battlefield plunder should not be underestimated, the grieving families who initiated mourning wars sought emotional more than material satisfaction. The involvement of Native peoples in trade with Europeans gave economic motives an apparently unprecedented significance in their conflicts with both Indian and European neighbors, but mourning remained a central element of warfare.

With familial emotions so paramount and with the potential for initiating warfare dispersed through so many hands, leaders who sought peace had to concentrate as much upon other elements of their own communities, nation, and allies as upon their enemies and rivals. Native diplomacy, therefore, attempted to create conditions by which all concerned would voluntarily forgo war rather than crafting specific agreements based on competitive advantage. To a degree Europeans never ceased to find baffling, therefore, the *process* of treaty making was always far more important to Indians than the results enshrined in a treaty document.

That process proceeded along two parallel tracks. First, in cultures where mourning and warfare were deeply connected, diplomacy had to address the emotions of those who participated in a treaty council. Rites of symbolic cleansing erased anger, grief, and the desire for revenge. Affirmations of reciprocity through exchanges of gifts induced a positive state of mind; so too did such rituals as the leisurely and contemplative sharing of tobacco and food. Ceremonial recitations of the history of ties between peoples, of the agreements made by fathers and grandfathers, stressed the long-term benefits of peace and made contemporary disputes seem insignificant. Proceedings followed an elaborately structured protocol that stressed predictability, fictive kin relationships between peoples, persuasive oral dexterity, and amity; speakers almost never openly disagreed with one another and therefore avoided the kind of divisive issues European diplomats insisted on thrashing out.

The second track of Native diplomacy involved the exchange and redistribution of material goods. During a treaty council, each important statement or proposition was accompanied by a gift of wampum (sacred shell beads) or some other highly valued commodity. Such exchanges served several important functions. On one level they extended the basic principle of economic reciprocity that maintained most extrafamilial social and political relationships in Native villages, thus bringing outsiders and potential enemies into networks of obligation that made them members of a single community. Moreover, gifts testified to the veracity and authority of the diplomat who offered them, for they were material evidence of a broad basis of support among people at home who had banded together to provide them. A leader who gave no presents, by contrast, seemed to speak for himself alone and to have little chance of persuading his kin and fellow villagers to abide by any agreements he made. Finally, the redistribution of gifts brought populations at large directly into agreements made in their names. Not only did material rewards obligate community members to follow the policies of the headmen who obtained them; the presents that they received were material reminders of the peaceful ties that united otherwise potentially hostile communities. Again, the status and emotional climate of the relationship, rather than the specific details of the agreement negotiated, took precedence.

Cultural Confrontations and Accommodations

Thus, while Indian and English cultures shared much—not the least a basic pattern of unity between the functions of war and diplomacy—the specifics of that pattern were deeply incompatible, and the potentials for miscommunication and misunderstanding were great. Where Indian leaders shunned details in favor of establishing a climate of good thoughts, colonial officials sought specific advantages through ironclad agreements enshrined in treaty documents. Where Native diplomats arrived as contemplative men of peace, European officers attempted to enlist warriors and business partners. Where headmen expected gifts as marks of sincerity and reciprocity, governors found beggars seeking handouts and bribes. Where village leaders knew they could not depend on everyone at home to follow their wishes, the English saw treacherous figures who would never keep their word.

It becomes, then, far less surprising that distrust so often prevailed than that representatives of the two cultures ever found the means to transcend their hostilities. Eventually, as English officials learned that they must adapt to the ceremonial expectations of Indian diplomacy, elaborate intercultural treaty procedures evolved that drew far more heavily upon Native than European traditions. Speaking through interpreters, royal governors delivered long speeches of peace and condolence, transferred massive quantities of wampum, cloth, tools, weapons, and other gifts, and endured days of inconclusive ceremonies before extracting a few specific commitments from Native leaders. In the colonial capitals and trading centers of Boston, Albany, Philadelphia, Williamsburg, and Charleston, gatherings of the hundreds of Native leaders necessary to ratify and re-ratify treaty arrangements became common sights, while from the Abenaki villages of present-day Maine to the Iroquois towns of New York and the Catawba centers of the Carolinas, leaders shrewdly adapted to the ways of European statecraft. But that cultural common ground took nearly a century to emerge; in the interim a brittle atmosphere of intersocietal distrust and violence prevailed.

VIOLENT CONFRONTATIONS AND RECURRENT TENSIONS, 1585–1676

European-Native relations in the two major centers of early seventeenth-century English colonization—the Chesapeake and New England—began in very similar ways. In each region tense and violence-prone interactions resulted from the gap between the respective parties' cultures of war and diplomacy, from English officials' assumptions of superiority and habits of command, and from the inability of "civilized" colonists to thrive in alien environments. Differences in cultural orientations among the Chesapeake and New England colonizers and in political organization among the local natives, however, sent the two regions along temporarily divergent paths.

The Chesapeake

A model for Indian relations of the Jamestown colony that was established in 1607 had emerged a generation earlier, during two ill-fated attempts to colonize Roanoke Island, on the Outer Banks of present-day North Carolina. In 1585 initially friendly relations between the first colony and the Native headman Granganimeo rapidly decayed after a silver cup disappeared from the baggage of the expedition's commander, Richard Grenville. The item may simply have been lost, or it may have been taken by an Indian who saw it as a gift owed him as part of the reciprocity characteristic of Native diplomacy. Whatever the case, after only a token effort to seek a peaceful solution, Grenville ordered the village of the supposed culprit burned to the ground. The overreaction was probably born of fear that the Indians might discover how weak the poorly supplied colony really was. During the winter of 1585–1586, the situation deteriorated further, as an epidemic took the lives of many Indians (including Granganimeo), and others on both sides died in skirmishes. In June 1586 Governor Ralph Lane turned a council of peace into a massacre of Granganimeo's successor Pemisapan and his followers; a week later the colonists fled hastily for England.

Part of the first colony's bellicosity is explained by its primary purpose as a base for privateering against Spanish shipping. Yet despite a very different, more agriculturally and family-oriented focus in the second Roanoke venture begun under John White in 1587, the legacy of earlier experiences poisoned relations with the natives and perhaps led to the "lost" colonists' mysterious disappearance. The cryptic message CROATOAN that a subsequent search party found carved on a tree and post at the remains of the settlement, however, has long fueled speculation. Some scholars wonder if the survivors found shelter among the people of that name whose homeland lay just to the southward of Roanoke and with whom both the 1585 and 1587 colonies had maintained reasonably friendly relations. Some scraps of evidence also indicate that this or another group of colonists eventually moved northward to the mouth of Chesapeake Bay to settle with a Native group that would be conquered by Powhatan's forces just shortly before the arrival of a new group of English colonists in that region in 1607.

Whatever the fate of the lost colonists of Roanoke, Powhatan, the paramount chief of the Chesapeake Algonquian confederacy that bears his name, evidently knew well what had happened on the Outer Banks. Moreover, the Powhatans' relations with a Spanish expedition that attempted to establish a Jesuit mission on the York River in 1570–1571 had been unrelievedly hostile. The natives killed the priests, and the Spanish slew some forty Indians in reprisal; the paramount chief's own clan seems to have been deeply involved with both events.

With English memories of Roanoke still fresh, and with military personnel and attitudes predominant among the initial colonists, prospects for peaceful relationships were not high. Nonetheless, Powhatan and such tributary headmen as his Pamunkey kinsman, Opechancanough, had many reasons to welcome the European presence. The paramount chief exercised an uneasy authority over recently incorporated villages within his own confederacy and waged wars with Siouan-speaking peoples to his west and with the Chickahominy closer to home. The trade goods and weapons that the newcomers brought promised both to increase Powhatan's capacity to secure his internal position through the redistribution of rare commodities and to give him a military advantage over his domestic and foreign foes. In return the colonists needed the food yielded by the natives' cornfields.

For a few years, therefore, mutual need balanced mutual distrust to preserve an uneasy peace between the English and the Powhatan. Yet specific English diplomatic and military strategies, like the rest of the policies of the Virginia Company of London, changed rapidly with shifts in power at home. Christopher Newport, the first governor, hoped to integrate the Indians into a bicultural—though clearly English-dominated—society. His approach was epitomized by a 1608 "coronation" of Powhatan, which in English eyes made the Native leader a vassal of James I but from an Indian point of view may have reversed the relationship; Newport came to Powhatan, rather than vice versa, and in exchange for a crown and cloak, the chief gave the Englishman a mantle and a pair of moccasins.

Shortly after this ceremony, the Powhatan tribe began withholding food from the English, who had long since ceased any pretensions to reciprocity in trade, and a state of low-grade warfare followed. For the next year, Council President John Smith kept relations at a less than chaotic level through a policy of carefully controlled military intimidation. Intercultural tensions reached a new plane, however, between 1610 and 1614, when governors Thomas Dale and Thomas Gates proposed to win Indian allegiance to the English by killing all the Native religious and political leaders and kidnapping their children. The plan was never implemented, but skirmishes—some scholars have labeled them "the First Anglo-Powhatan War" —continued.

That phase of conflict ended in 1614, when after the English took hostage Powhatan's daughter Pocahontas, the paramount chief agreed to peace. For the next eight years the colonizers, having discovered the riches to be gained from tobacco cultivation, expanded their land base at the natives' expense and deluded themselves that intercultural relations rested on the friendly footing symbolized by the marriage of Pocahontas to Englishman John Rolfe in 1614. Nonetheless, the Indian side of the equation was much more complex. When Opechancanough became paramount chief in 1618, he resumed the initial strategy of using ties with the English for Native purposes, particularly the acquisition of firearms. At the same time, he fostered a religious and military revitalization movement led among his people by the prophet Nemattanew, whom the English called "Jack of the Feather."

In March 1622 Nemattanew was killed by some English in a suspicious accident. Later that month the prophet's followers struck back, and at least 347 colonists died. A two-year English rampage of revenge followed, wreaking a severe defeat upon Opechancanough's forces and sealing the end of the Virginia Company's disastrous regime on the Chesapeake. The royal officials who took over the colony in 1624, however, embraced no fantasies of intercultural cooperation. Their view of the future of North America was exclusively English.

Between 1644 and 1646 an unsuccessful final military campaign by the aged Opechancanough's people confirmed for the English the lesson the 1622–1624 war had taught: they assumed the inevitable hostility of Indians and found no place for them—even as slave laborers—in their emerging society. As the second major war came to an end, however, the Virginians recognized the folly of perpetual military struggle. In 1646 a peace treaty guaranteed the natives lands north of the York River in exchange for an Indian pledge to pay an annual tribute of beaver skins to the colony. In effect this agreement inaugurated the reservation system that would be so persistent a feature of American history in the future. The concept of an intercultural boundary line, too, would be a recurrent theme in subsequent years.

Yet how little had really changed became apparent three decades later, when Virginians and Indians again found themselves at war. A growing English population—some forty thousand by 1670—resented the economic dominance of the colony by a tiny elite of planters and focused its hopes for the future on the lands north of the York River that had been reserved to the natives in 1646. In July 1675 frontier tensions exploded when a group of Doeg Indians retaliated for the failure of an English planter to pay for goods he had purchased from them. The Virginia government's efforts to keep the peace and enforce the York River boundary were one of many grievances that produced the political uprising known as Bacon's Rebellion.

In September 1675 an unauthorized foray by some one thousand Virginia and Maryland troops surrounded the Potomac fort of the Susquehannock allies of the Doeg (and of the two colonies' governments) and assassinated several Susquehannock headmen. In the full-scale frontier war that ensued, the Virginia Baconites indiscriminately killed Indians, especially those of such previously uninvolved communities as the Pamunkey and Appomatox, whose reserved lands were closest to the plantations.

Ironically, in Bacon's Rebellion European Americans practiced the kind of bottom-up, freelance warfare characteristic of Native societies while government officials stood helpless to prevent them. Despite the suppression of the last Baconites in early 1677, future Virginia rulers, recognizing their lack of power over the colony's frontier residents, followed a relentlessly expansionist policy. In many cases treaties, boundary lines, and reservations proved merely temporary expedients to forestall more self-destructive military tactics.

New England

The early 1620s and the mid 1670s marked important turning points not only for English-Indian relations in the Chesapeake but for the colonies farther north as well. The Virginia war of 1622–1624 coincided with large-scale colonization at Plymouth, and Bacon's Rebellion occurred simultaneously with a cataclysmic intercultural war throughout New England. More than accidents of the calendar were at work, for the Virginia experience in many ways provided a model for events at Plymouth, which in turn set the pattern for much of what occurred in the later New England colonies of Massachusetts Bay, New Haven, Connecticut, and Rhode Island.

Plymouth's hired military specialist, Miles Standish, was familiar with the violent histories of Roanoke and Jamestown which, like nearly all English people, he blamed on Indian treachery. Thus he arrived expecting the worst from the natives and, like Smith, assumed that military intimidation was the only way to deal with them. Such attitudes received an additional twist from Puritan colonists' rhetoric concerning their role as God's chosen people and New England as the New Israel. Indians easily fell into the category of new Canaanites, who had to be crushed if they hindered the divine plan.

At Plymouth, and particularly in its much larger successor, Massachusetts Bay, such basic tendencies toward hostility were, however, countered by at least three forces. First, the same Puritan religious beliefs that made Indians seem potential stumbling blocks to the erection of a New Israel also made New England leaders take seriously their obligation to convert the "heathen" to Christianity. Second, the perceived Native threat was blunted by the demoralization and disruption of Indian life caused by epidemics that struck between 1616 and 1619 and that (providentially, it seemed to the colonists) depopulated much of the coastal area and left the survivors ill-equipped to counter the European onslaught. Third, the absence in southern New England of anything resembling the unitary political order of Powhatan's regime invited an English strategy of divide and rule that tempered hostility to particular native groups with alliances to others.

Four clusters of Algonquian-speaking villages surrounded the Pilgrim enclave: the Massachuset of the bay area named after them, the Pokanoket (Wampanoag) of the Cape Cod region, the Narraganset of present-day Rhode Island, and the Pequot-Mohegan of the lower Connecticut River valley. Disease had most forcefully devastated the Massachuset and Pokanoket, allowing the Narraganset and Pequot-Mohegan to emerge as the major regional powers and placing the surviving Pokanoket, in particular, on the defensive. The Plymouth colonists established their settlement on the site of the village of Patuxet, the population of which had evidently been completely destroyed by disease. The only known survivor was Squanto, who had been captured in 1615 by English explorers who taught him English. Sources variously identify his band with the Massachuset to the north or the Pokanokets to the south and west. Whatever the case, in 1621 he helped the colonists seal an alliance with the latter's headman, Massasoit.

The Pokanoket leader hoped that the newcomers would aid him in his struggles against the Narraganset and Massachuset. For Standish and the English, such an arrangement would not only strengthen their hold on the territory they claimed but aid in opening the lucrative fur trade that lay beyond those two enemies of Massasoit's people. The maturation of the Plymouth-Pokanoket alliance was marked in 1623 when Standish, with the encouragement of Massasoit, led a preemptive strike against a Massachuset village alleged to be plotting an attack against the colony. A major English purpose, however, seems to have been to intimidate any Native leader who might plan to follow the course set by Opechancanough the previous year.

Although the Plymouth-Pokanoket alliance set the basic pattern of divide and rule, the context in which such arrangements operated changed dramatically in the 1630s. In that decade the Dutch established posts on the Connecticut River, from which they traded with the Pequot-Mohegan and the Narraganset. Meanwhile, the Massachusetts Bay colony and its offshoots of Connecticut, New Haven, and Rhode Island grew, cutting Plymouth off from much of its trade with the natives. A multisided rivalry ensued among English colonies, the Dutch, and the major Native groups for control of the region's furs, lands, and wampum supplies, a conflict that reached its climax in the Pequot War of 1637.

The Pequot—trading partners of the Dutch—were apparently seeking to corner the market on wampum, and in the process they alienated nearly all of their Native neighbors, including the formerly closely allied villages of the Mohegan. In the war of 1637, the Puritan colonies allied with the Narraganset virtually to annihilate the Pequot; the penultimate episode was at Mystic Fort, when Massachusetts and Connecticut forces massacred at least three hundred and perhaps as many as seven hundred men, women, and children of that nation. The final event occurred when the Pequot leader Sassacus and some forty followers fled west of the Hudson River and were executed by the Mohawk. When the fighting was over, Connecticut and Massachusetts emerged as the major victors, gaining access to the lands and economic resources of the lower Connecticut River valley that had been Pequot territory and that formerly lay within the Dutch trading orbit. At least briefly the Narraganset profited too, as they became intermediaries in a web of economic transactions involving the exchange of wampum to the Mohawk for furs, which the Narraganset in turn sold to the English of Rhode Island for tools, clothing, household items, and weapons.

As the English colonies' divide-and-rule strategy pursued its logic, however, the Narraganset's turn was next. In 1643 the Puritan colonies of Massachusetts, Plymouth, New Haven, and Connecticut established the New England Confederation. The organization was ostensibly a defensive military alliance, but seems to have been just as much an offensive coalition directed at heterodox Rhode Island and its Narraganset trading partners. By 1645 the Confederation, relying on an alliance with the Mohegan led by the headman Uncas, found various pretexts to declare war against the Narraganset. A combination of military bluffs and intimidation made bloodshed unnecessary, however, and produced a treaty in which the Narraganset yielded much of their land and most of their political autonomy to the English. For the next thirty years an uneasy peace settled across the region, maintained in large degree by English military intimidation. During that period Puritan missionaries enjoyed notable success, particularly among refugee and remnant groups that had survived decades of disease and warfare. The converts coalesced in "praying towns," where they submitted to English political and ideological domination and in many cases sincerely embraced Christianity while preserving their distinct ethnic identity.

Other southern New England natives, however, responded in a quite different manner, particularly after the death of Massasoit in 1661. A new generation of leaders, epitomized by Massasoit's sons Wamsutta and, especially, Metacom (Metacomet), chafed under English domination. The colonizers' apparent contempt for Native aspirations, meanwhile, seems to be reflected in the nicknames they gave the two Pokanoket brothers: Wamsutta was "Alexander the Great" until his death in 1662, when Metacom assumed the role of the ancient Greek leader's reputedly half-wit sibling, "King Philip." If for no other reason than to halt the perpetuation of an insult, the tradition of labeling the massive Anglo-Indian conflict that followed in 1675–1676 as "King Philip's War" ought to be abandoned. Names such as "The Second War of the Puritan Conquest" (the First having been the Pequot campaign), however, stray from scholarly neutrality too far in the opposite direction. The most widely agreed upon alternative—"Metacom's War"—perhaps overstates the Pokanoket leader's role, but at least it bears minimal ideological freight.

In June 1675—apparently before Metacom himself had completed his military preparations and efforts to secure allies among other Indian groups—Pokanoket warriors began attacking Plymouth towns. As the Native victories mounted, nearly all of the southern New England Algonquian peoples joined the war and went far toward a dream of pushing the invaders of all the region's colonies back into the sea. Of some ninety English towns, over fifty were attacked and at least twelve destroyed. A separate and, to the English, equally devastating war erupted on the Maine frontier as Eastern Abenakis acted upon their own long-standing grievances.

In southern New England, the military tide began to turn against Metacom and his allies during the winter of 1675–1676. English forces,

unable to engage their enemies in set battles, waged war against Native corn supplies instead, inducing severe food shortages and keeping the Indians on the run in the most difficult part of the year. Together, the two forms of hardship opened the way to a third, epidemic disease. Metacom and a substantial portion of his forces retreated to a winter encampment north of Albany, where they hoped to replenish their stocks of weapons and enlist additional allies. Instead, they were attacked by the Mohawk who had long been at war with many elements of the southern New England Algonquian coalition and had been encouraged in their efforts by New York Governor Edmund Andros. In the summer of 1676 victorious English forces—with the significant help of their praying town allies—hunted down their enemies, including Metacom himself, who was shot by a Christian Indian. The English paraded the leader's severed head in triumph.

By autumn the war in southern New England was over, and the region's remaining natives—even those who had sided with the victors—quickly lost any vestige of political independence. Before the close of the decade, all had either sought refuge in French Canada or English New York, resettled in one of four remaining praying towns, or found uneasy places as despised individuals in English society. By late 1676, therefore, as Metacom's War in New England and the nearly simultaneous Bacon's Rebellion in Virginia came to an end, European-Indian relations had traveled different paths to much the same destination in each region: natives had been confined to reservations and pushed to the margins of the dominant society.

FROM CONFRONTATION TO ACCOMMODATION, 1676–1754

By the period of Metacom's War and Bacon's Rebellion, the violence-prone character of English-Indian interactions seemed clear. But within that brittle context, perdurable diplomatic strategies were also emerging, based on economic relations and on concepts of intercultural and intracultural balances of power. For most English colonies in the late seventeenth and early eighteenth centuries, the economic benefits of peaceful ties to Indians shrank steadily as the fur trade slipped in relative, if not absolute, importance. At the same time, however, imperial rivalries among the English and the Spanish and, particularly, French crowns made alliances with militarily powerful Native peoples more vital than ever before.

In the midst of this imperial contest, Native leaders throughout the heartland of eastern North America, from the Eastern Abenaki of Maine to the Creek of the Southeast, independently discovered balance-of-power diplomacy as the most effective means of survival. Avoidance of exclusive ties to any single colony preserved vital maneuvering room, while the playing off of one side against another—French or Spanish against English, New Yorkers against Pennsylvanians, Virginians against Carolinians—helped preserve autonomy on a continent otherwise dominated by powerful Europeans.

The Carolinas: Seventeenth-Century Patterns Continue

As the seventeenth century turned to the eighteenth, traders from South Carolina, where English colonization had begun in earnest during the 1660s, reaped great profits from a deerskin trade with Native groups of the interior but also from a traffic in Indian slaves. The latter commerce rested upon the familiar English strategy of divide and rule, for Carolinians seldom themselves raided Native peoples for captives. Instead Indian allies did their dirty work. In such a brutally exploitative situation, it is no surprise that, when Native trading partners outlived their usefulness, violence erupted.

The Westo War of 1680–1683, the Tuscarora War of 1711–1713, and the Yamasee War of 1715–1717 replayed the patterns of 1622, 1637, and 1675: after each conflict vanquished peoples scattered and English colonists expropriated their homelands. The nations that survived in the region either consisted of clusters of refugees who found means of accommodating their powerful neighbors—the new people called Catawba are the prime example—or were, like the Cherokee and Creek, able to maintain alternative trading ties to Virginia or Spanish Florida that gave them bargaining room in dealing with Carolina traders and governors.

Pennsylvania: The Rise and Fall of Peaceful Expansion

As the Carolinas were playing out a new variant on familiar patterns of English-Indian interaction, an apparently quite different approach prevailed in Pennsylvania, where in 1682 William Penn's proprietary colony assumed control of the Dutch and Swedish trading outposts that had been operating on the Delaware River for more than two generations. In stark contrast to the vast majority of his English predecessors Penn, in keeping with his Quaker beliefs, insisted upon peaceful interactions with the natives and a scrupulous policy of purchases of all lands to be occupied by the English. Although Penn's legendary 1682 agreement with the Lenape (Delaware) under the "Treaty Elm" at Shackamaxon (near present-day Philadelphia) is firmly entrenched in European-American tradition, no documentation of such an event survives. That some meeting between Penn and Delaware Valley Indians took place late in that year is likely, however, and the amicable tone of relations that the legend symbolizes is accurate.

But it lasted only for Penn's lifetime. However elevated the intentions of the founder, a basic imperative for Pennsylvania, as for the New England and Chesapeake colonies, was the acquisition of ever more land for a growing European population. Almost inevitably, by the second quarter of the eighteenth century Indian resentments grew. They were vastly exacerbated by the unscrupulous policies of the Penn family's agent, James Logan, who in a series of fraudulent treaties culminating in the "Walking Purchase" of 1737, forced nearly all Native peoples out of the lower Delaware and lower Susquehanna River valleys and placed tremendous pressure on those who clung to lands in the upper portions of those river systems. By the 1740s, then, Pennsylvania's Indian relations had become quite similar to those of New England, Virginia, or the Carolinas.

New York, The Iroquois, and the Covenant Chain

The search for a more lasting new departure in intercultural relations leads not to Pennsylvania but New York, the former Dutch enclave that came under secure English control only in 1674. Several factors set that province apart: the fur trade remained a vital element of its economy well into the eighteenth century; its European-American population, and thus its appetite for Native lands, continued relatively small through the same period; and its intercultural diplomacy fell under the purview of officials directly appointed by the Crown and who thus viewed Indian affairs in a continentwide perspective. The goals of New York's royal governors were no more noble than those of the rulers of other English colonies and, indeed, in many respects they simply rang changes upon the hoary theme of divide and rule. Nonetheless, a framework emerged for stable and peaceful Anglo-Indian relations.

On the Native side of the equation, the shapers of the new intercultural politics were the Five Nations of the Iroquois League, long-time trading partners of the Hudson River colony. Their homelands straddled trade routes leading to New England, New France, and the Chesapeake; moreover, they had long fought against the southern New England Algonquian led by Metacom, the Susquehannock foes of the Baconites in Virginia, and (despite peace treaties of 1665–1667) the French on the Saint Lawrence. To New York governors Edmund Andros (1674–1683 and 1687–1689) and Thomas Dongan (1683–1687), an alliance with the Five Nations against the many Native and French enemies of the Iroquois promised not only to pacify English frontiers but to extend New York's influence in at least three important geographical directions. Similarly, from the standpoint of many Iroquois leaders, the English colony represented a potential ally against Indian and French military rivals and an alternative to the growing French domination of the region's intercultural trade.

The New York–Five Nations relationship evolved in a series of treaties that Andros and Dongan negotiated between 1676 and 1684 with an anti-French faction of Iroquois headmen. In 1676 Andros encouraged the Mohawk Iroquois attack that helped to defeat Metacom. Subsequently, he and his agents at Albany sponsored negotiations that ended both the Iroquois–southern New England Algonquian and Iroquois-Susquehannock wars on terms highly favorable to the Five Nations. In 1677 Andros invited both the dispossessed southern New England Algon-

quian and the Susquehannock defeated by Bacon's forces to resettle north of Albany and in the Susquehanna Valley, respectively, under the joint protection of New York and the Five Nations. These intercultural arrangements created the "Covenant Chain" system of alliances, in which New York on the one hand and the Five Nations on the other claimed to be the principal spokesmen and mediators for English and natives throughout a wide swath of the continent.

Once peace was thus established along much of the intercolonial English-Indian frontier, the Covenant Chain assumed an explicitly anti-French cast, particularly under the leadership of Governor Dongan. In a treaty at Albany in 1684, an anglophile faction of Iroquois headmen placed their lands and peoples under the protection of the English Crown in exchange for vague promises of military support and concrete efforts to establish the Five Nations as intermediaries in trade between Great Lakes Native peoples and Albany. Invigorated by their new military and economic connections, the anti-French Iroquois led their peoples into a renewed war against the Saint Lawrence colony and its Great Lakes Native allies during the mid 1680s. Beginning in 1689, that conflict merged with the broader struggle known in Europe as the War of the League of Augsburg and in the English colonies as King William's War.

The Covenant Chain was a marriage of convenience that grew from the very factors that had produced enmity between English and natives in Virginia and New England; divide-and-rule and mutual advantage linked Andros and Dongan with the Five Nations in much the same way it had thrown together Newport and Powhatan and Standish and Massasoit. In contrast to those earlier cases, however, for at least two generations New York's small population and its economic reliance on the fur trade forestalled the relentless agricultural expansion that had helped to poison earlier English-Indian relationships, and thus the marriage survived. Indian interests, however, ensured that the Covenant Chain relationship would never be exactly the sort of alliance of which English officials dreamed. The transaction that placed Iroquois under the protection of the Crown—and that long buttressed British claims to much of North America—was always controversial; perhaps a majority of Iroquois headmen and their followers rejected it utterly. Meanwhile, the many Native peoples within the Covenant Chain for whom the Iroquois claimed to speak continued to act independently. By the early eighteenth century that category included the Mahican, the Delaware, the Shawnee, and a host of southern refugees from Virginia and Carolina expansionism who had resettled within the present-day boundaries of Pennsylvania.

Neutrality and the Play-Off System

During the War of the League of Augsburg, New York repeatedly failed to live up to what the Iroquois considered to be its military obligations. As a result, by the end of the 1690s a majority of Iroquois had abandoned the always troubling concept of an exclusive alliance with the Hudson River colony. In 1700 and 1701, in two nearly simultaneous sets of treaties with the English at Albany and the French at Montreal that are sometimes labeled "the Grand Settlement," headmen established a framework of neutrality between the French and British empires that, with a few exceptions, would survive for nearly fifty years. The Covenant Chain remained an important mechanism for mediating English-Indian diplomacy, but—despite the contrary assertions of British officials—it ceased to be primarily a military alliance against the French.

Fundamental to the play-off system of diplomatic neutrality pursued by most Iroquois leaders, as well as the headmen of several southeastern peoples, was the stasis that characterized imperial power relationships among the British, French, and Spanish crowns in North America during the first half of the eighteenth century. A sort of cold war prevailed, punctuated by hotter outbreaks in the War of the Spanish Succession (Queen Anne's War, 1702–1713), Dummer's War (1721–1725), the War of Jenkins's Ear (1739–1742), and the War of the Austrian Succession (King George's War, 1744–1748) that nevertheless failed to ignite widespread violence in North America outside the New England-Eastern Abenaki frontier in Maine.

Because the English colonial governments could never count upon Native support should more expansive conflict erupt between the empires, colonial governors had to pay at least some attention to Indian concerns and to expend sub-

stantial sums of money to keep their frontiers quiet and their allies and trading partners in their camp. Thus elaborate intercultural rituals of annual diplomacy and large-scale gift giving became familiar parts of colonial life. The English were forced to adapt to Native traditions of frequent, broadly based personal confirmations of peaceful relationships sealed by exchanges of material goods. Particularly notable intercolonial and multi-Indian treaties occurred at Lancaster, Pennsylvania, in 1722 and 1744 and at Albany in 1754. In each of those agreements, the Iroquois found themselves forced to preserve their own increasingly fragile position between the French and British empires by yielding to the British lands in Pennsylvania belonging to their Native allies in the Covenant Chain, the Shawnee and Delaware.

RENEWED HOSTILITIES, 1754–1775

Indeed, by the period of the Albany Treaty, the balance that had supported Indian neutrality strategies and undergirded intercultural diplomacy was rapidly collapsing. The focus of imperial rivalry had moved from the Great Lakes region and a contest over its fur trade to a struggle over the lands and commerce of the Ohio country. There, the rapidly expanding populations of Virginia and Pennsylvania were repeating the kinds of pressures that had earlier helped to produce Metacom's War and Bacon's Rebellion. Meanwhile, the southwestward shift had moved affairs out of the region in which the government of New York and the councils of the Iroquois could effectively manage events through the now tattered mechanisms of the Covenant Chain. Virginians and Pennsylvanians and Shawnee and Delaware increasingly shaped the course of continent-wide warfare and diplomacy, as the defeats of George Washington and Edward Braddock in 1754 and 1755 revealed.

The Seven Years' War

Those defeats ignited the international conflict known in Europe as the Seven Years' War and in British America as the French and Indian War. Early in the struggle, the Shawnee and Delaware employed their new alliance with the French to strike back at the Virginians and, especially, the Pennsylvanians, who had forced them out of homes farther east and now threatened their lands in the Ohio country. In a different arena and from a different perspective, Virginians and Carolinians used the Seven Years' War as an opportunity to fight for the lands of their Cherokee neighbors, who early in the conflict had sought to pursue the play-off system of diplomacy. As warfare spread and Indian and French victories mounted, Native peoples who still tried to preserve their neutrality found their position increasingly untenable.

In August 1758 the Anglo-American conquest of Fort Frontenac on Lake Ontario tipped the military scales, for it disrupted the French supply lines that supported Fort Duquesne (Pittsburgh) and through it the war-making capabilities of the Ohio country Indians, which were further weakened by smallpox epidemics during the period. In October of the same year, at the Treaty of Easton, Pennsylvania, the Ohio country Delaware pledged to the English their neutrality in exchange for Pennsylvania's renunciation of its previous claims to lands west of the Appalachian Mountains. At the same treaty, diplomatic gifts to the Iroquois leaders who were present secured their guarantee of the arrangement with the Delaware and, within a year, the active enlistment of many of their warriors in the British cause.

These developments were crucial to the British victory over the French that culminated in the fall of Quebec in 1759 and the capitulation of all French forces at Montreal in 1760. Those defeats, confirmed in the 1763 Peace of Paris, destroyed the framework within which Native peoples had been able to play European powers off against each other, for it removed the French and Spanish military presence from North America, east of the Mississippi. At least briefly, unquestioned British dominance among European Americans halted any incentive for imperial officials to preserve the intercultural system of diplomacy that had grown up in previous generations. In official terms the Proclamation of 1763 set the framework for postwar English-Indian relations.

To the extent that it established a boundary between Europeans and natives that roughly followed the Appalachian Mountains, the new policies conformed both to the principles of the Treaty of Easton and to long-standing aims of Iroquois, Delaware, Cherokee, and countless other Native leaders. In almost no other way, however, did the proclamation satisfy Indian demands. On the one hand, the royal government proved powerless to prevent squatters from traversing the boundary and seizing lands supposedly reserved to Native peoples. On the other hand, whatever guarantees that the proclamation offered were couched in language that clearly assumed British, rather than Indian, ownership of the territory between the mountains and the Mississippi. And long before the proclamation was issued, relations had deteriorated significantly as British authorities sought to confine the region's fur trade to army posts and to call a halt to the expensive custom of diplomatic gift giving.

Indian Wars for Independence

Resentment at such stringent exertions of British dominance produced a brief but bloody war between the Cherokee and Virginia in 1760–1761. In the Ohio country, meanwhile, the Delaware religious figure Neolin found receptive audiences for a message of cultural self-reliance based upon the renunciation of European goods. One of his disciples was the Ottawa military leader Pontiac, who preached the expulsion of the British from the Great Lakes region. In May 1763 Pontiac led an assault upon the major British garrison at Detroit that turned into an unsuccessful six-month siege. Almost simultaneously, but apparently without central direction from the Ottawa leader, other Indian forces attacked and destroyed British posts throughout the region; only Detroit, Niagara, and Pittsburgh survived the campaigns. Although fighting continued in "Pontiac's War" for two more years, the British regained military superiority by late 1763. Ironically, the very lack of European trade goods and weapons that Neolin had envisioned was a key to the Indians' defeat.

For financial and practical reasons, British officials subsequently adopted a more conciliatory approach to Indian relations that included a withdrawal from many western posts, a reform of fur trade regulations, and a return to long-standing practices of intercultural diplomacy and gift giving. The Treaty of Fort Stanwix (Rome, New York) in 1768 confirmed the shift through a negotiated modification of the boundary between Indians and Europeans that had been issued by royal fiat in 1763. For the Indians of the Ohio country and the southern interior, however, little had changed.

As a result, the half century after 1763 can be viewed as a period of Indian wars for independence against the domination of first the British and then the United States. "Pontiac's War" was but the first in a series of battles that Native peoples of the interior would wage to preserve their homelands. Later episodes included Dunmore's War in the Ohio country in 1774, the Indian alliances with the British during the war of the American Revolution, the struggle for the Old Northwest that would culminate in the Battle of Fallen Timbers in 1794, and the movement led by the Shawnee Tecumseh and Tenskwatawa ("The Prophet") in the early nineteenth century. With the end of the early eighteenth-century conditions that had created a balance of European and Native forces in North America, relations between Anglo-Americans and Indians returned to the hostility first displayed at Roanoke, Jamestown, and Plymouth.

BIBLIOGRAPHY

General Works

Jennings, Francis. *The Invasion of America: Indians, Colonialism, and the Cant of Conquest.* Chapel Hill, N.C., 1975.
Jones, Dorothy V. *License for Empire: Colonialism by Treaty in Early America.* Chicago, 1982.
Nash, Gary B. *Red, White, and Black: The Peoples of Early America.* Englewood Cliffs, N.J., 1974; 3rd ed. 1992.
Smith, Marian W. "American Indian Warfare." New York Academy of Sciences, *Transactions*, 2nd ser., 13 (1951):348–365.
Sturtevant, William C., gen. ed. *Handbook of North American Indians.* Vol. 4, *History of Indian-White Relations*, edited by Wilcomb E. Washburn. Washington, D.C., 1988. Vol. 15, *Northeast*, edited by Bruce G. Trigger. Washington, D.C., 1978.

Roanoke and the Chesapeake

Fausz, J. Frederick. "Merging and Emerging Worlds: Anglo-Indian Interest Groups and the Development of the Seventeenth-Century Chesapeake." In *Colonial Chesapeake Society*, edited by Lois Green Carr, Philip D. Morgan, and Jean B. Russo. Chapel Hill, N.C., 1988.
Kupperman, Karen Ordahl. *Roanoke: The Abandoned Colony.* Totowa, N.J., 1984.
Lurie, Nancy Oestreich. "Indian Cultural Adjustment to European Civilization." In *Seventeenth-Century America: Essays in Colonial History*, edited by James Morton Smith. Chapel Hill, N.C., 1959.
Vaughan, Alden T. " 'Expulsion of the Salvages': English Policy and the Virginia Massacre of 1622." *William and Mary Quarterly*, 3rd ser., 35, no. 1 (1978):57–84.

New England

Leach, Douglas Edward. *Flintlock and Tomahawk: New England in King Philip's War.* New York, 1958.
Morrison, Kenneth M. *The Embattled Northeast: The Elusive Ideal of Alliance in Abenaki-Euramerican Relations.* Berkeley, Calif., 1984.
Salisbury, Neal. *Manitou and Providence: Indians, Europeans, and the Making of New England, 1500–1643.* New York, 1982.
Vaughan, Alden T. *New England Frontier: Puritans and Indians, 1620–1675.* Boston, 1965; rev. ed. New York, 1979.

The Carolinas

Crane, Verner W. *The Southern Frontier, 1670–1732.* Durham, N.C., 1928.
Merrell, James H. *The Indians' New World: Catawbas and Their Neighbors from European Contact Through the Era of Removal.* Chapel Hill, N.C., 1989.
Ried, John Philip. *A Better Kind of Hatchet: Law, Trade, and Diplomacy in the Cherokee Nation During the Early Years of European Contact.* University Park, Pa., 1976.
Silver, Timothy. *A New Face on the Countryside: Indians, Colonists, and Slaves in South Atlantic Forests, 1500–1800.* Cambridge, England, 1990.

Pennsylvania and New York

Jennings, Francis. *The Ambiguous Iroquois Empire: The Covenant Chain Confederation of Indian Tribes with English Colonies from Its Beginnings to the Lancaster Treaty of 1744.* New York, 1984.
———. *Empire of Fortune: Crowns, Colonies, and Tribes in the Seven Years' War in America.* New York, 1988.
Richter, Daniel K. *The Ordeal of the Longhouse: The Peoples of the Iroquois League in the Era of European Colonization.* Chapel Hill, N.C., 1992.
Trelease, Allen W. *Indian Affairs in Colonial New York: The Seventeenth Century.* Ithaca, N.Y., 1960.
Wallace, Anthony F. C. "Origins of Iroquois Neutral-

ity: The Grand Settlement of 1701." *Pennsylvania History* 24, no. 3 (1957):223–235.

The Ohio Country

Downes, Randolph C. *Council Fires on the Upper Ohio: A Narrative of Indian Affairs in the Upper Ohio Valley Until 1795.* Pittsburgh, Pa., 1940.

Jacobs, Wilbur R. *Diplomacy and Indian Gifts: Anglo-French Rivalry Along the Ohio and Northwest Frontiers, 1748–1763.* Stanford, Calif., 1950.

McConnell, Michael N. *A Country Between: The Upper Ohio Valley and Its Peoples, 1724–1774.* Lincoln, Nebr., 1992.

White, Richard. *The Middle Ground: Indians, Empires, and Republics in the Great Lakes Region, 1650–1815.* Cambridge, England, 1991.

Daniel K. Richter

SEE ALSO **The European Contest for North America; The Fur Trade;** and **Indian-Colonist Contact.**

THE DUTCH AND SWEDISH COLONIES

After ye White people came ye Dutch about New York shot an Indn for pulling Peaches off his trees, which caus'd Wars, & after Peace, ye Indians being settled thick in a Town Near ye Dutch, in a very deep Snow, ye Dutch taking ye advantage kill'd ye Indians only one made his escape, who allarm'd others so that two other Wars & Peaces ensued, ye last Peace lasting untill this late War . . . after ye White people brot Rum & suply'd ye Indians with it, they forgot God & lost their former Devotion. (John W. Jordan, ed. "Journal of James Kenny, 1761–1763," *Pennsylvania Magazine of History and Biography* 37, no. 2 [1913], p. 2)

THUS DID JOHN DOUBTY, a New Jersey–born Delaware Indian living in Ohio in 1762, summarize in his conversation with Kenny the history of relations with Dutch colonists who began moving to his people's homeland in both the Hudson and Delaware river valleys more than 150 years

earlier. Although Doubty's particular order of events differs from that chronicled by Europeans (colonial archives show that the Peach War of 1655 through 1658, for example, followed the 1643 and 1644 winter massacres of Governor Kieft's War), Dutch records corroborate his general assessment. Unlike the Swedes, who maintained generally amicable relations with their Delaware and Susquehannock Indian neighbors during New Sweden's brief existence on the Delaware River from 1638 to 1655, Dutch colonists and Indian people failed to live peaceably with one another along the Hudson River. Devastated by a succession of wars, the Dutch colony of New Netherland first established in 1614 fell easy prey to English seizure in 1664.

The earliest records documenting contact between Indian people and Europeans along the Hudson River, two journals recording Henry Hudson's 1609 voyage to the river that later bore his name, show that the twin themes of trade and war set out in Doubty's narrative dominated intercultural relations in the region from the first. Both reveal the Indians' and Europeans' interest in trade with one another. Records of fights that left at least one seaman and several Indians dead also demonstrate the willingness of both people to use violence to resolve differences.

Seeking profit and power, other Europeans soon followed Hudson to the region. Traders employed by the New Netherland Company built small posts and during the mid 1610s began trading with Delaware Indians along the Delaware River and with Mahican Indian people around Fort Nassau on the Hudson (modern Albany, New York). Floods destroyed Fort Nassau in 1618. The successor corporation to the New Netherland Company, chartered in 1621 as the West India Company (WIC), withdrew altogether from the Delaware and built a new post at Albany, Fort Orange, in 1624. The company purchased Manhattan Island from the Indians for sixty guilders' worth of goods (equivalent to about sixty days' wages for a laborer at the time), and established its main settlement at New Amsterdam, at the southern end of the island, in 1626. European settlers financed by Swedish stockholders established the short-lived colony of New Sweden on the lower Delaware River in 1638.

INDIAN COLONIST CONFLICT: DUTCH AND SWEDISH

Both European settlers and Indians establishing relations with them tried to profit from commerce with one another as they struggled to gain or maintain power over their own lands and lives. Differing more in style (Europeans generally were impelled by personal gain while Indians tended to emphasize communal redistribution) than in substance, both peoples were motivated by spiritual as well as secular considerations. Europeans acted on the assumption that wealth could purchase salvation as well as security. Believing all objects to be spiritually animated, Indian people sought new powers and abilities in European imports.

Finding neither gold nor a northwest passage, Europeans sailing to Indian lands between the Hudson and Delaware rivers settled for what the country offered. Foremost among these were skins, furs, and hollow cylindrical white or purple shell beads known as wampum. No less important were the services of Indian men and women. For the newcomers, Indian men provided information about land, people, and products; guarded colonial frontiers; and hunted and fished. Indian women furnished corn, beans, squash, companionship, and sex to men often forced to live without the company of women from their own countries.

Fascinated by both practical and spiritual characteristics of goods they could not produce themselves, Indian people accepted European iron knives, axes, and awls; glass beads, bottles, and mirrors; copper and brass pots; firearms and munitions; woven textiles; alcoholic beverages; and other imports for their goods and services. Trading posts and traders providing such goods were regarded as sources of wealth and power to be exploited and protected. In the north, Mahicans fought Mohawks seeking direct access to Fort Orange in a series of wars that dragged on for decades. Farther south, Delaware Indians were unable to stop Susquehannocks from driving them farther east into New Jersey away from Dutch and Swedish posts along the Delaware River.

Aware that war depressed trade, WIC officials directed employees to avoid taking sides in conflicts between Indians. The one employee ignoring this directive, Fort Orange commander Daniel van Krieckenbeeck, was killed along with two of his men while accompanying a Mahican war party defeated by Mohawks in 1626. Quickly patching things up with the Mohawks, the Dutch never again openly took sides in Indian wars.

Land was not initially a major bone of contention in the region. Focusing almost entirely upon commerce, neither Dutch nor Swedish trading companies exhibited much interest in obtaining more than small plots surrounding their trading posts. This state of affairs changed during the 1630s as Dutch and Swedish authorities interested in making their colonies self-sufficient encouraged farmers to settle along the Hudson and Delaware rivers. Provincial officials, private citizens, and wealthy feudal landlords known as patroons soon began purchasing land from Indians.

Devastated by epidemic diseases and ravaged by wars with other tribes, few Indians living on lands desired by European settlers were in a position to deny purchase requests. Some, like Mahicans driven eastward after suffering serious setbacks in their war with the Mohawks, sold much of their land along the Hudson River around Albany to the patroon Kiliaen van Rensselaer in 1630 and 1631. Most others employed tactics used by groups like Hackensacks and Canarsees living near New Amsterdam, who responded to excessive territorial demands by selling smaller plots. Accepting low prices offered by insistent Dutch purchasers, Indian people did their best to obligate colonial governments to acknowledge their title to remaining lands. Often retaining rights to hunt, fish, and camp on alienated lands, Indian sellers also frequently demanded that land sales be formally renewed or renegotiated. Prominent sachems like the Massapequa leader Tackapousha and the Hackensack diplomat Oratam achieved or increased influence among their own people as they established and maintained social, political, and economic relationships with colonists by brokering such land sales. In these and other ways, Indian people struggled to use land deeds as informal treaties establishing and maintaining relationships.

ESCALATING CONFLICT

Intercultural relations worsened as European settlers increasingly pressed Indian people for their land, furs, and services during the late

1630s. Laws regulating trade were habitually flouted. Indians living around New Amsterdam particularly resented a tax payable in corn imposed upon them by New Netherland governor Willem Kieft in 1638. To make matters worse, Mohawks and Susquehannocks securing firearms from traders were now demanding tribute payments of wampum or European trade goods from coastal Indian communities. Forbidden under Dutch law to trade for firearms of their own, coastal groups were unable to defend themselves against such demands.

Misunderstanding, fear, and frustration finally turned to anger after a series of unresolved murders and other provocations committed by Indians and European settlers led to open hostilities in the 1640s. Known today as Governor Kieft's War, the conflict devastated New Netherland. Settlements were burned throughout the region, and scores of colonists and hundreds of Munsee people were killed in the fighting. In February 1643 Dutch forces brutally attacked Wiechquaesgeck Indians from Westchester County, New York, who were taking refuge from Mahican attack near New Amsterdam. In 1644 the burning of a large winter village near Pound Ridge, New York, left some three hundred to six hundred Indians dead. Such massacres compelled most Munsees to conclude a treaty of peace with the Dutch on 30 August 1645.

Not all Munsees accepted the treaty. Embittered Wiechquaesgeck refugees living in New Jersey, for example, continued to waylay unwary travelers. Peter Stuyvesant, who succeeded Kieft as governor in 1647, moved quickly to conciliate aggrieved Indian communities. Adjudicating Wiechquaesgeck complaints about lands taken from them in Westchester, Stuyvesant negotiated a new deed to the disputed territory and concluded a separate peace with the Indians in 1649.

By the 1650s Indians and Europeans living in New Netherland had to deal with an increasingly difficult political environment. Mohawks still fighting the Mahicans were involved in a bitter war against the French in Canada that threatened the peace of the region. To the east, New Englanders flooding into Long Island and Westchester County openly called on their countrymen to seize New Netherland for the English Crown. Farther south, Swedish and Virginian traders tried to monopolize the Delaware River trade. Caught in a kaleidoscopic web of often rapidly shifting alliances and antagonisms, Indians and Europeans struggling to survive did their best to play friends and enemies off against one another.

THE PEACH WAR

Preoccupied by political troubles and desperate to increase lagging trade returns after New Englanders seized control of Long Island wampum-manufacturing areas crucial to the Indian trade, Stuyvesant was forced to tolerate excesses of traders and land speculators violating laws protecting Indian lands, lives, and property. Infuriated by Stuyvesant's failure to protect them, Indians living along the lower Hudson River finally took matters into their own hands. While Stuyvesant and the city's garrison were away reducing New Sweden during the autumn of 1655, Indians attacked New Amsterdam.

Named the Peach War, after Indian allegations that a Dutch settler's murder of an Indian woman picking peaches in his orchard had sparked the conflict, the war devastated the colony. Once again European settlers were killed, out-settlements destroyed, and captives taken for ransom. Suspecting a Swedish plot to draw him away (too late, since New Sweden had fallen before word of the Indian attack reached the Dutch expedition), Stuyvesant hurried back to New Amsterdam. Although English settlers demanded Dutch protection, they refused to send troops against the Indians as they did ten years earlier during Governor Kieft's War. Realizing that he had neither troops nor supplies sufficient to retaliate, Stuyvesant was forced to bargain with the Indians for release of the captives. Unable to do more against the Dutch and happy to consolidate their gains without further bloodshed, the Indians stopped their attacks and gradually released ransomed hostages over the next few years.

WAR WITH THE ESOPUS

Reselling Staten Island to the Dutch in 1657, Hackensack Indians and their neighbors gradually let Dutch settlers return to farmsteads established before the war. Farther north, other European settlers returning to lands on the west bank of the mid Hudson Valley at Wiltwyck (today's Kingston, New York) in 1658 received a less-cordial reception from local Esopus Indians. A series of murders and other provocations threatened to develop into open warfare. Subsequent Dutch and Indian efforts to keep the peace failed. Indians who sold some of their lands to compensate Dutch losses were angered when the financially strapped Stuyvesant failed to deliver promised presents. The Dutch, meanwhile, were alarmed and angered by persistent rumors of imminent Indian attacks.

Matters reached a flashpoint on 20 September 1658, when Dutch settlers disobeying orders to keep the peace fired into a group of carousing Indians; they killed one and captured another. The next day, Esopus warriors killed or captured everyone in a party of thirteen men carrying dispatches notifying Stuyvesant of the incident and requesting help. Several hundred other Esopus warriors burned outlying settlements and laid siege to Wiltwyck. Leading a force of 150 men upriver that included 25 Englishmen and as many Long Island Indians, Stuyvesant quickly raised the siege and compelled the Esopus to withdraw into the interior. Unable to follow, Stuyvesant left a portion of his army to reinforce the Wiltwyck garrison and returned to New Amsterdam to await developments.

Stuyvesant quickly moved to stem the spread of the war and isolate the Esopus by renewing friendships with Hackensacks and other Indians living near New Amsterdam in the first formal treaties with these Indians since the outbreak of the Peach War. Cut off from their lower Hudson Valley kinsfolk, chastened by several Dutch raids, and pressured by Mohawk and Susquehannock representatives ordering them to make peace, Esopus leaders surrendered their remaining lands near Wiltwyck and allowed the Dutch to keep eleven of their men sent as captives to Curaçao as hostages for their good behavior at a treaty signed on 14 July 1660. All of these men were gradually returned to their families during the next two years.

War broke out again on 7 June 1663, when Esopus warriors attacked and destroyed an unwanted new Dutch town constructed near their village at the present site of Hurley, New York. Once again, Esopus warriors besieged Wiltwyck, and once again, Stuyvesant dispatched soldiers to drive the Indians away. Led this time by Ensign Martin Cregier, the force of 210 Europeans, African slaves, and Long Island Indians destroyed Esopus settlements, burned their provisions, liberated Dutch prisoners, and killed a number of Esopus people and several Minisink and Wappinger visitors. Negotiating an armistice in the autumn of 1663, the Esopus concluded a peace treaty with the Dutch in New Amsterdam on 16 May 1664.

Acknowledging defeat, the Esopus gave up most of their best remaining lands and accepted Dutch control over their lands and lives. By most measures, Stuyvesant had won a great victory. But nearly twenty-five years of almost constant warfare had exhausted the Dutch. Obsessed by an overwhelming desire for profit, the Dutch almost wholly focused their limited resources on ultimately unsuccessful efforts to make their colony pay. Their failure to make crucial social and cultural adjustments doomed the colony to economic stagnation and collapse. Exhausted and almost bankrupt, Stuyvesant surrendered New Netherland without a shot to the duke of York's fleet on 8 September 1664.

The new rulers of the colony of New York quickly concluded treaties of their own with the Indians of the Hudson and Delaware valleys. Learning from Dutch mistakes, English diplomats managed to establish and maintain an enduring peace with the region's Indian people that lasted for most of the following century.

BIBLIOGRAPHY

Trelease, Allen W. *Indian Affairs in Colonial New York: The Seventeenth Century.* Ithaca, N.Y., 1960.

Weslager, C. A. *The Swedes and Dutch at New Castle: With Highlights in the History of the Delaware Valley, 1638–1664.* Wilmington, Del., 1987.

Robert S. Grumet

SEE ALSO **The European Contest for North America; The Fur Trade;** and **Indian-Colonist Contact.**

THE FRENCH COLONIES

OF ALL THE EUROPEAN powers active in North America, the French were the most successful in their relations with Native Americans, though these relations were not without their difficulties. The French generally managed to earn the respect of the Indians, even those who opposed them, and many became their partners in both trade and war. These relations rested on three factors. The first was economic need. The Indians provided essential skill and labor in the fur trade, and fur was the single most important cash crop for Canada. The French provided Indians with labor-saving and otherwise attractive goods. The second factor was military. The French armed forces were not numerous so they had to rely on Indian allies. At the same time, European weapons, and on occasion the additional manpower, were increasingly important to Indians. Each needed the other if they were to mount a successful opposition to large enemies such as the Iroquois or the English. Occupation of much territory was, in any case, impossible without Indian cooperation. The French also found themselves the beneficiaries, in a sense, of their enemies' actions, attracting everyone alienated by the English and their Indian allies, particularly the Iroquois. The third factor affecting relations was a stronger cultural bond that developed between the Indians and French than between Indians and other Europeans. When Samuel de Champlain established colonies in Acadia and Canada, he decided that the French should learn the Indians' language and adapt to their customs and way of life. Champlain had men live among the people of the area and among trading allies farther away. This became a classic feature of French operations, and individuals representing the different elements of the French colonial enterprise (traders, missionaries, military officers) all went to live among the different tribes. But if an Indian nation opposed French imperial designs, the policy could change markedly and treatment was less than sympathetic.

There were two levels of diplomacy. The first was a grand conference held in Montreal during the early spring. (The same practice was adopted in Louisiana when that colony was established at the beginning of the eighteenth century.) The conference was the major diplomatic event of each year. It originated in the 1640s with the practice of bringing furs in convoys to Montreal. Most of the important negotiations with Indian nations were conducted by the governor general and accompanied by the customary exchange of presents and elaborate festivities. The second level of diplomacy was in the homelands of different Indian peoples, around individual posts or missions in the interior. Diplomatic agents, most often officers in charge of fortified posts or missionaries, kept track of events and the complex internal politics of individual tribes, conveyed messages from the governor to the Indians, and distributed presents.

Other forces, less easy to understand or manage, also influenced relations and the strength of individual nations. Diseases to which Native Americans had never previously been exposed ravaged each tribe soon after contact with whites. Within a short time tribal populations were reduced by at least half in almost every case. Alcohol, for which Indians had limited tolerance, and frequent warfare caused more disruption and further reduced numbers. Such troubles created great psychological stress. These experiences profoundly affected Native society, its culture, politics, and religion. Still, Native North Americans were a major force shaping the course of events more often than has been acknowledged by historians.

RELATIONS WITH THE PEOPLES OF THE ATLANTIC COAST

At the beginning of the seventeenth century, the Micmac numbered about three thousand and occupied the whole of present-day Nova Scotia and the eastern coast of New Brunswick. To the southwest were two small tribes, the Malecite, on the Saint John River, and the Passamaquoddy, on the Saint Croix. The Abenaki comprised several tribes numbering ten thousand in all. The eastern Abenaki, chief among whom were the Penobscot, lived in present-day Maine and southeastern Quebec, ranging up to the Saint Lawrence River opposite the city of Quebec. The western Abenaki, chief among whom were the

Sokoki, lived in present-day Vermont and New Hampshire. From the first days of contact, the French formed good relations with each. This posed problems, since the Micmac, Malecite, and Abenaki were often at war with each other, but the French were able to persuade them to forget their differences and live harmoniously. From this time onward the Malecite and Micmac were constant allies of the French.

Relations with the Abenaki were more complex. In 1613 the English destroyed French Jesuit missions, and throughout the 1620s they carried on a successful trade with the Abenaki. Rapid colonization soon threatened the eastern Abenaki and they began to turn to the French. In the 1640s Abenaki relations deteriorated with the Mohawk and other members of the Iroquois confederacy (allies of the English) who lived west of Abenaki lands. From the 1650s onward the Abenaki were frequently at war with the Iroquois. The Abenaki therefore welcomed French traders, missionaries, and soldiers. In the 1670s Jean-Vincent D'Abbadie de Saint Castin, a part-time military officer and full-time trader, was adopted by the Penobscot, married the daughter of a sagamore, and went on to become one of the principal chiefs of the Abenaki. His influence helped bring the confederacy close to the French. After Saint Castin, the key French agent was the Jesuit Sébastien Râle, who was active from 1694 until the English killed him in 1724.

Pressure on Abenaki lands from colonists touched off a succession of wars with the English. Unprovoked attacks on their villages initially drove the western Abenaki to seek refuge closer to Canada. Then in 1676 the Abenaki were drawn into King Philip's War (1675–1678) during which they mounted a formidable opposition to English colonists and regular troops. Victory was confirmed at the peace, and the English abandoned their northeasternmost coastal settlements. The Abenaki remained inveterate enemies of the Iroquois and readily joined French expeditions against them from 1687 until the general peace of 1701. Their wars with the English (1689–1697, 1702–1713) paralleled the contest for empire among European powers. The French provided weapons and supplies and often joined their Abenaki allies in attacks on English settlements. However, prolonged hostilities eroded the Abenaki population and damaged aged the economy, in which English goods were important. Each time peace was made, trade resumed.

During the eighteenth century the French and their allies found themselves slowly driven back. Port Royal fell to the English in 1710, and at the peace of 1713 the French lost the peninsula of Nova Scotia. Cape Breton Island then became the colony of Île Royale with the new fortress-town of Louisbourg as its capital. French officials tried to create a buffer zone of Indian land between New France and New England by engineering a closer association of the east coast tribes. The Penobscot, however, no longer favored such a close relationship with the French. Preserving their independence and the integrity of their territory became the twin pillars of the Penobscot policy toward both European powers.

Considerations of relative strength, the proximity of the English, and their cheaper trade goods led to complex politics within the Abenaki tribes in which one faction favored the French, another sought accommodation with the English, and a third held out for a neutral position. Differences were settled temporarily when English incursions on Abenaki land and attacks on certain villages touched off Dummer's War in 1722. This time the Abenaki fared less well, and by the terms of the 1725 peace they abandoned western Maine. During the next war (1744–1748) the Abenaki again struck at English settlements that had crept into their territory. The Micmac assisted in the preemptive strike against Nova Scotia in 1744, but they could do little when a large Anglo-American force attacked Louisbourg in 1745 and the supposedly impregnable fortress fell (only to be returned by treaty in 1748). In the Seven Years' War the Penobscot remained neutral, while the other Abenaki, now closer to Quebec and under enemy attack, joined the French and Micmac in expeditions against the English. Abenaki also fought with the French in the Ohio Valley, around Lake Ontario (at Oswego), and in the Lake Champlain corridor.

Then in 1758 the English again seized Louisbourg. As the colonies of New France collapsed, so did the Indian position. When the Abenaki finally made peace in 1764, they were forced to give up much of the best land in their territory.

FRENCH-INDIAN RELATIONS IN SEVENTEENTH-CENTURY CANADA

People of the Northeast

The French presence on the Saint Lawrence River began with the establishment of Tadoussac in 1600 as a fishing and trading station. This was in the territory of the Montagnais, who lived in the region north of the Saint Lawrence and east of the Saint Maurice River, and their close relatives, the Naskapi, who lived inland. In 1603 Champlain began trading with them and in the process entered into an alliance that lasted as long as New France. The principal enemies of these people were the Iroquois of the Iroquois confederacy, with whom they had been at war intermittently since the 1570s. To oppose the Iroquois, the Montagnais needed allies, so they allowed their western relatives, the Algonquin, to trade at Tadoussac and Quebec (1608). The Algonquin lived in western Quebec and eastern Ontario, along the Ottawa River and its tributaries. To the west was an Iroquoian tribe, the Huron, also enemies of the Iroquois confederacy, and they often entered into alliance with the Algonquin and Montagnais.

The French recognized the economic and military potential represented by a coalition of northern tribes and fostered the alliance. In doing this, they became entwined in a Native power struggle which would parallel that between the European powers. Champlain came to the aid of his trading partners in 1609, 1610, and 1615. In battle, opposing sides formed lines in the open; the men wore body armor, carried shields, and shot arrows at each other until one side gave way. On the first occasion, Champlain turned his harquebus on the Iroquois, killing two chiefs. The new weapon touched off a panic that helped New France's allies prevail. Although their range and accuracy was not much better than bows and arrows at this time, muskets deeply impressed Indians with their noise and their ability to penetrate traditional Native armor, injecting a metal charm into the body. Still, it was not until 1622 that the Iroquois confederacy made peace with the French and their allies, a peace that broke down in 1627 following an altercation with the Montagnais. Soon after, the English took Quebec but were obliged to return it in 1632. Two years later, a new peace was made.

The Algonquin hoped they would now be in a position to make the French compete in trade with the Dutch. The Mohawk Iroquois, on whose land Fort Orange (present-day Albany, New York) was built, never favored this and killed Algonquins who went south. This touched off another war that dragged on for years. In 1646 the Mohawk decimated the lower Algonquin. The Algonquin and Montagnais then sought to bolster their position by forming an alliance with the Nippising. The Iroquois prevailed, destroying the Huron (1648–1649), driving the Algonquin to the west (1649–1651), and battering the Nippising (1649–1652) until they moved from Lake Nippising to Lake Nipigon far to the northwest. The concerted efforts of the French and their Indian allies brought about a general peace in 1667. Soon after, the Algonquin returned to the Ottawa Valley, and some Nippising returned to their old homeland. All three nations remained steadfast allies of the French, fighting in expeditions against the Iroquois and the English in each of the wars that followed.

Farther north, around James Bay and Hudson Bay, lived the Cree, close relatives of the Montagnais. The Cree were willing trade partners during the years between 1686 and 1713 when the French managed to hold onto one or some of the posts set up on the coast. Being so distant, however, they did not figure in French military operations, even around Hudson and James bays.

The Huron, Petun, and Neutral

Three Iroquoian people lived north of the lower Great Lakes. The Huron confederacy occupied the lands north of Lake Ontario. It comprised four nations: the Bear, the Cord, the Rock, and the Deer. The Petun were a smaller confederacy at the south end of Georgian Bay. The Neutral lived north of Lake Erie and west of Lake Ontario. The Huron were old enemies of the Iroquois confederacy that lived in what is now upstate New York. In 1615 Champlain finally reached Huron territory where he met their leaders, concluded an alliance, and joined an expedition against the Iroquois.

War dragged on, with only a brief peace from 1622 to 1627. During the 1620s tactics changed as both the Huron and Iroquois resorted to raiding each other in small groups that could remain hidden in the woods. "La petite guerre," as the French called it, had begun. The Spanish would later speak of "guerrilla." Both mean literally "little war."

The 1630s were a period of great stress for the Huron. At the same time that they struggled with the Iroquois, they had to cope with epidemic disease, culminating with a disastrous outbreak of smallpox in 1639. At the same time Jesuit missionaries established several fortified mission centers. Huron society became divided between Christians, always in the minority, and traditionalists who wanted the Jesuits cast out. Some spoke of abandoning their treaty with the French and making peace with the Iroquois confederacy. A combination of Christians and traditionalists who feared and mistrusted the Iroquois defeated the move but the divisions, often rooted in much earlier disputes, persisted.

At the end of the 1640s, the Iroquois confederacy destroyed their three northern neighbors. Almost every year during the decade, the Iroquois attacked the French and their Indian trading partners in the valleys of the Ottawa and the Saint Lawrence. Finally, in 1641, the French traded muskets to the Huron for the first time, in the process accelerating the struggle for a technological edge. By 1648 the Huron had perhaps 120 muskets while the Iroquois had more than 500.

The motivation for the wars between the 1640s and 1660s is debated by historians. One factor was the Iroquois concern for security, particularly the issue of access to muskets for themselves and the use of muskets by their enemies. Aside from the obvious military advantage in possessing such a weapon, Indians at the time perceived a supernatural property in the musket; it was a source of terror to those who did not have them and greatly increased the self-confidence of those who did. Linked to the preoccupation with muskets was a concern about access to the fur stocks that provided the means by which muskets could be obtained. Plundering convoys brought the Iroquois more furs, and consequently more muskets, while it depleted the resources of their rivals. Another factor affecting intertribal warfare was numerical strength. The Iroquois were worried about the

formation of powerful neighbors and also concerned about their own size, especially when war and epidemic disease took so many lives among their people. One solution was adoption. Like many tribes, the Iroquois had a custom of adopting members of Indian populations that they captured during a war. From these considerations emerged a broad plan: the Iroquois confederacy sought to bring all Iroquoian people together in one league—"one people in one land," as they told Father Isaac Jogues in 1643. Iroquoians, like the Huron, the Petun, and the Erie had an option: join or die.

The Iroquois adopted a strategy of reducing the Huron gradually, preventing them from growing crops, and attacking one village at a time, beginning with those on the fringes of Huronia. By 1647 one of the four nations in the Huron confederacy was reduced to seeking refuge among the others. In 1648 the Iroquois attacked two larger settlements and in March 1649 a large Iroquois force destroyed a major center and surrounding villages. The lack of support from the Jesuits (who sheltered in their fortifications with soldiers and a large supply of food) convinced the Huron that their position was untenable. The remaining villages dispersed and ultimately the missionaries also perished at the hands of the Iroquois.

Some took shelter on Christian Island (Georgian Bay, Lake Huron), but starvation ended the attempt to hold out there. A small band of Huron went to Lorette near Quebec City in 1650 where their descendants live to this day. One nation joined the Neutral confederacy. Smaller groups sought refuge with the Petun. To prevent the formation of a new and powerful confederacy, the Iroquois attacked the Petun in the winter of 1649–1650, forcing them to disperse. Many Petun and Huron fled west, together forming what came to be known as the Wyandot.

The Seneca, one of the Iroquois confederacy, then turned their attention to the Neutral who were left alone to face the Iroquois. After major defeats in 1650 and 1651, some Neutral surrendered to the Seneca and were absorbed, while others fled westward and disappeared.

These were grim years for the colony of Canada. Iroquois attacks retarded the growth of settlements and discouraged immigration. Desperate requests from the governor for more soldiers and weapons met with little sympathy in France. Colonists built palisade forts, without cannon, at key locations but the Iroquois soon found routes around them. This development exposed the basic weakness of fortifications in the North American wilderness: they did not assure sovereignty and did not stop the enemy, but merely provided shelter for people and goods. There were never more than one hundred soldiers in the colony at any time during the 1650s, while the Iroquois could field over twenty times that number. When it came, news of the destruction of their Indian friends was profoundly disturbing to the French, although they tried to salvage a spiritually uplifting message from the martyrdom of the missionaries.

The Ojibwa

The Ojibwa lived beyond the Huron territory, north of Lakes Huron and Superior, and also south of Lake Superior, where they are now referred to as Chippewa. Closely related to them were the Ottawa who lived around Georgian Bay and on Manitoulin Island, and the Potawatomi who lived east of Lake Michigan. Together they were more numerous than either the Huron, their longtime trading partners, or the Iroquois. During the 1630s and 1640s Iroquois attacks drove some north and others west. The Potawatomi ventured all the way to the Door Peninsula by Green Bay. Between 1650 and 1665 the Iroquois raided villages and convoys around the Great Lakes. Instead of securing their position, however, the Iroquois alienated everyone around them, assuring the French the everlasting alliance of people in the region. This pattern would be repeated elsewhere in Indian diplomacy and is crucial in the unfolding of Franco-Amerindian relations.

Living in rich fur country, the Ottawa and Ojibwa readily assumed the role of supplying the French, making a long trip eastward and down the Ottawa River to Montreal. With their relatively large population, they became the backbone of the fur trade during the seventeenth and eighteenth centuries and important allies in the French war effort. The French made an effort to secure the relationship by building fortified trading posts throughout Ojibwa territory, most notably Chequamegon (1660–1675, 1692–1760) on the south shore of Lake Superior, Mi-chilimackinac (1665–1760) at the straits (near Mackinaw City, Michigan), and Kaministiquia (1679–c. 1700, 1717–1760) at the western end of Lake Superior (Thunder Bay, Ontario).

In the 1690s the Ojibwa and Ottawa began moving south again, reoccupying parts of what is now Michigan. In a series of bitter battles they forced the Iroquois back out of the territory north of Lakes Ontario and Erie. In 1700 the Iroquois confederacy calmly informed the English that they let the Mississauga, an Ojibwa people, settle around the northwest end of Lake Ontario. This announcement put a brave face on a major defeat—in previous years the Iroquois would never have allowed such a move. Peace, when it came, was the accomplishment of the Ojibwa-Ottawa and allied Indians.

The Iroquois Confederacy

One of the most powerful of all Indian nations in North America was the confederacy of five large Iroquoian nations, living south of Lake Ontario, from east to west: the Mohawk, Oneida, Onondaga, Cayuga, and Seneca. Despite large reductions from disease and war, they could still field 2,250 fighting men in the 1650s. The Mohawk were anxious to maintain their position of influence between the Albany traders and the western nations. They would be the most pro-Dutch and, after 1664, pro-English. The Seneca, the largest nation, at the western end of the lake, were closest to fur territory. The Onondaga in the middle were referred to as "keepers of the fire," maintaining the capital of the confederacy. They were unwilling to be beholden to either and used their access to eastern Lake Ontario, and hence the French, to maintain a position of power. Onondaga were the center of intrigue during the seventeenth and eighteenth centuries during which the Iroquois played the French against the English. Understanding the complexities of internal relations was crucial to the success of agents for any European nation, and the French worked at this assiduously.

During the 1640s the Iroquois changed the way they fought and greatly increased their military might. Between 1639 and 1644 they quickly accumulated muskets from the English and the Dutch. They dispensed with armor (useless against muskets) and equipped ambushing teams with their new weapon. The tactics are familiar to many: the Iroquois often fought in small parties, avoided formal battle patterns, stayed under cover, and attacked the enemy at exposed, ill-defended points. These tactics kept opponents in a constant state of alarm and increased their outlay on military operations. Masters of surprise, the Iroquois blocked exposed trade routes by attacking convoys at many different places. Their new style of war was a great success militarily, economically, and psychologically.

After finishing with the Neutral, the Iroquois turned their attention to other neighbors. In 1651 the Seneca began attacks on the Erie, who lived at the southeast end of Lake Erie. At the same time the Mohawk became embroiled in war with the Susquehannock, former allies of the Huron. This stretched Iroquois resources too thin, so in 1653 they made peace with the French. After struggling for three years, the Erie collapsed and survivors were absorbed by the nations among whom they sought refuge. But the other Indians managed to hold out. For the next three decades the Iroquois were engaged in intermittent war with the Susquehannock, who lived to the south of the Iroquois confederacy, and the Abenaki (particularly the Sokoki) and Mahican to the east.

During the 1653 peace negotiations, Iroquois emissaries invited the French to build a mission similar to the one in Huronia. The Jesuit missionaries soon attracted a group of followers, and in reaction to this, a band of opponents. This time, however, traditionalists prevailed and mounting hostility prompted the priests to abandon the mission in 1658.

In 1660 Adam Dollard des Ormeaux headed up the Ottawa River with seventeen French and forty-four Huron and Algonquin. What they had in mind was to ambush Iroquois hunters; what they met was a force of several hundred warriors. This Iroquois force was to join five hundred warriors on the Saint Lawrence and descend on Montreal. After holding out for a week in an old stockade, the French defendants and their Indian allies were killed or taken away to be tortured to death. Legend maintains that their heroic stand saved New France. But the Iroquois actually turned back for several reasons, and the next year they returned, terrorizing the colony.

Canada was still besieged by hostile Indians when Louis XIV revoked the Company of New France's charter and put Canada under royal rule in 1663. Two years later, Alexandre Prouville de Tracy was given the task of humbling the Iroquois confederacy. He brought with him twenty-four companies of fifty men, including the entire Carignan Salières regiment—a fighting force equivalent to half the colony's population. Tracy began by building a series of forts, then in the autumn of 1666 he headed west with seven hundred soldiers, four hundred settlers, and one hundred Indian allies. He singled out the Mohawk for special attention, even though the Seneca, the largest and most powerful nation, were chief agents in the demise of the Huron and their neighbors. As the army approached, the Mohawk retreated, so Tracy's men set about destroying villages and crops. In 1667 the Iroquois sent an embassy to discuss peace. Canadians credit Tracy, but the peace was at least as much the work of the Indians. The Iroquois were exhausted by four wars on different fronts, none of which was going well. They had been mauled in recent expeditions against the Ojibwa and Algonquin, and they found themselves up against ferocious opposition from the Susquehannock and Mahican.

In 1673 Governor Louis de Buade de Frontenac built a fort named after himself at the eastern end of Lake Ontario. Like all earlier forts in New France, it would be a feeble guard against war parties but useful in gathering intelligence—and as a trade base. In 1679 the Seneca allowed the explorer René Robert Cavelier de La Salle to build a fortified trading post at Niagara, though supply problems made its existence tenuous.

Iroquois politics during the long peace with the French (1667–1682) were complicated by the development of factions bitterly divided on policy. The peace terms with the French had included another invitation to send missionaries, this time to each nation of the Iroquois confederacy. Again, those who favored the Christians confronted those who opposed them. Two sides formed over the issue of the relative merits of their European neighbors.

The French embarked on a policy of relocating converts in 1676. Catholic Iroquois, mostly Mohawk, were settled at Caughnawaga near Montreal. Though reluctant to campaign against their relatives, they could be induced to attack

245

other Indians or the English. But they were much more interested in trading with Albany and, together with the *coureurs de bois* (woodsmen), in carrying on a thriving contraband trade that would frustrate the intentions of both France and England.

Around 1680 the Seneca began raids on their neighbors to the south and west, notably the Illinois, allies of the French. In 1682 a special assembly of the colony's leading inhabitants strongly advised Antoine Le Febvre de La Barre, who had just replaced Frontenac as governor, to attack the Iroquois before the western alliances were destroyed and the fur trade lost. Although he received meager assistance from France, La Barre headed west in 1684 with 850 Frenchmen and 380 Indians. When he reached the edge of Oneida lands, he did very little, merely holding a conference with Iroquois leaders and then withdrawing. Among the Iroquois confederacy, the renewed tensions with the French and the departure of the converts tipped the balance in favor of the traditionalist faction and the remaining Jesuits were forced to leave. In France, Louis XIV was appalled by what looked like a disgraceful campaign and recalled the governor, replacing him with a seasoned soldier, the marquis de Denonville.

The new governor arrived in 1685 with 800 soldiers. He decided more were needed and in 1687 the total was doubled to 1,600. Denonville then embarked on a campaign similar to Tracy's but aimed at Seneca lands. It was one of the largest military operations in French North America until the final years of the colony: 832 troops, 1,030 militiamen, and 300 Indians. The Seneca retreated and Denonville destroyed their villages and crops. He then reestablished Fort Niagara. The next year both sides sought a respite in peace negotiations.

In the summer of 1689 news arrived at Albany that England and France were at war. The Iroquois thought they were now assured of active assistance from the English. Sensing that victory was close at hand, they redoubled their efforts. Fifteen hundred warriors descended on Lachine, a sizable town near Montreal, killing settlers and destroying buildings, crops, and animals. Forts Niagara and Frontenac were now untenable and Denonville recalled the garrisons. He then handed the colony over to Frontenac who had

just been appointed governor for a second term.

French attention concentrated first of all on the English. Early in 1690 they employed Iroquois tactics against the English villages of Salmon Falls, Fort Loyal, and Schenectady, striking terror there just as the Iroquois confederacy had done at Lachine. In October the French turned back an attack on Quebec by a naval force from the English colonies led by Sir William Phips. This victory greatly enhanced their standing with Indian allies. The Iroquois, however, continued to raid the Saint Lawrence Valley, disturbing settlements and reducing the shipments of furs from the interior.

The French then pressed the Five Nations. In 1693 Frontenac sent 100 troops, 325 militiamen, and 200 Indians into Mohawk lands. Again the Mohawk simply retreated, and again their villages and crops were laid waste. In 1695 Fort Frontenac was reestablished, a major operation requiring 336 troops, 160 militia, and between 200 and 500 Indians. In 1696 Frontenac set out with 2,150 French and Indians, this time against the Onondaga and Oneida lands. Once again, the Iroquois retreated and the French contented themselves with destroying everything in sight. The next year the English signed the Peace of Ryswick leaving their Indian allies on their own. War smoldered for three more years but the Iroquois were exhausted. Whereas the confederacy had between 2,000 and 2,500 fighting men in 1680, it had no more than 1,250 in 1700. It was beaten in the north by the Ojibwa, driven back from the Ohio by western tribes, and harrassed from the east by the French and the Abenaki.

The Peace of 1701. In July 1700 the Iroquois confederacy began making overtures for peace. The next summer a large delegation went to Montreal. There the French organized the largest and most elaborate set of Indian-European negotiations ever undertaken. In all thirteen hundred Indians attended, representing thirty different tribes from the Atlantic coast to the upper Mississippi. Everyone eventually agreed to live at peace. They would not strike back if attacked; instead they were to take their grievances to the governor of New France who would obtain redress. In addition, the Iroquois agreed to remain neutral in any future war between France and England. With occasional small lapses, this peace with the Iroquois held for almost sixty years, much to the irritation of the English. It is most often depicted as a triumph of French arms, but this omits important facts. While the diplomatic accomplishment owes much to Louis-Hector de Callières, the new governor general, and his agents among the tribes, much of the fighting that brought the Iroquois to terms was done by Indian allies.

The Illinois and Miami

French explorers first made contact with the Illinois confederacy in 1673. Member nations occupied strategic lands along the Mississippi and ranged over to the Ohio and the Wabash, a territory slightly beyond the present boundaries of the state of Illinois. Although numerous and therefore quite powerful, the Illinois had several enemies. They were closely related to the Miami, who lived south of Lake Michigan. Relations between the two were strained during the seventeenth century, and the French worked hard to sustain peaceful coexistence. In 1680 the Kaskaskia, a member of the confederacy, were attacked by the Iroquois confederacy and their village destroyed. They regrouped near Starved Rock, where La Salle built a fortified trading post in 1682. From this time onward they were firm allies of the French. Traders and missionaries soon followed, building up the relationship. A fortified mission post was built at Cahokia among the people of that name, and Kaskaskia, fortified in 1703, became the economic center of the territory. Factional strife and wars with their neighbors led Illinois tribes to relocate their villages several times. The French finally managed to bring an end to Iroquois raids but then other tribes began to invade Illinois lands.

ANGLO-FRENCH RIVALRY AND INDIAN ALLIANCES

During the wars between France and England, the alliances carefully cultivated by the French proved their value. New France's Indian allies are best remembered for the terror raids that kept the English colonists scrambling during the 1690s and 1700s. Most war parties comprised roughly equal numbers of Indians and French, ranging from thirty to two hundred fifty, a far cry from the "armies" described in some history texts. Indians also appeared among the forces massed near French towns in response to threatened attacks by the English and their allies. French raiding parties achieved results out of proportion to their numbers. Their psychological impact is evident in the enduring images of Indian war in American legend, and in the particular view Americans retained of Indians in the centuries following. Indian allies intimidated the enemy. Together with French soldiers and Canadian militia, they created a perception of Canadian military power—attacks came from many directions and the English found them hard to oppose. They also made it appear that invasion would meet a serious challenge.

There is a striking general pattern in the conflicts between 1689 and 1748. The French usually began with a series of guerrilla attacks meant to throw the enemy off balance. Having thus established the tenacity of their opposition, the French would attempt a larger operation when money, men, and materiel allowed. In the 1690s, most of the effort was directed against the Iroquois confederacy. In the 1700s French efforts focused squarely on the English. But each time they were hampered by supply problems and the size of forces they could assemble and move through the forest. Because cannon were extremely difficult to transport they were not taken—nor did the English use them in the interior. This meant that it was difficult or impossible to attack larger settlements and fortifications. There were desperate years, such as 1706 and 1745, when very few supplies and no troops arrived in New France. The governor was hard pressed to keep his allies actively committed simply because he had little to offer in the way of supplies or support. The other classic feature of the wars was the formation of a determined English counterattack. These attacks avoided Indian opposition by striking from the sea at strategic points of the colony. Phips attacked Quebec in 1690, and Commander Sir Hovenden Walker tried in 1711. Neither offensive was successful, but the French could not always count on good fortune. In 1745 Louisbourg fell and plans were made for another expedition against Quebec.

The policy of relying on Native allies was not without its problems. They had to be supplied with gifts, weapons, goods, and even food, and these became a substantial part of colonial expenditures in the eighteenth century. The Indian military contribution was inconsistent at times—natives would sometimes disappear in the field, so that many parties were equipped at considerable expense only to achieve virtually nothing. The effects of disease, the military threat to Indian homes, and a waning will to fight affected their performance. Finally, Indians were of limited use in conventional battles. Masters of forest warfare, they were not accustomed to massed engagements in regular formations, facing not just men but also artillery. Indeed, French officials repeatedly noted that cannon stunned Indians or set them to flight.

FRENCH POLICY DURING THE EIGHTEENTH CENTURY

Historians have spoken of a shift in French policy toward Canada around 1700. The principal trigger was the collapse of the fur market in 1696–1697. Although one must avoid the terms of modern military thinking (grand strategy did not really develop until the Napoleonic era), a shift in policy clearly did occur between 1701 and 1725. It was a gradual, stumbling process of change, influenced by several considerations, not always clearly spelled out. The first was the demise of fur as a major source of revenue, and a failure to find a replacement. A second, related factor was the sorry state of French finances from the turn of the century onward, making expensive military plans impossible. Only a few specific places, such as Louisbourg, which protected the Grand Banks fishery, were selected for attention. Canada and Louisiana had to make do with small amounts of money, materiel, and manpower. Third, running at cross purposes to French policy were the ambitions of colonials, both for land and for wealth. The fourth consideration was a genuine desire in Versailles and Quebec to stake some claim to territory throughout the continent.

This process was begun by the Canadians, then furthered by the French. In the summer of 1701 Antoine de la Mothe Cadillac established Détroit. Though he hoped to raise his status and his fortune, he also argued that the post would help bring together the western tribes.

The new policy was most obvious after the peace of 1713 when Governor Vaudreuil, over the objections of the minister, built a string of new forts in the interior—bases for trade, diplomacy, and war—among each of the nations allied to Canada. Officers at these posts came to replace missionaries as key diplomatic agents. The objective was to align tribes with the French and thereby hold back the English advance. In the minds of government officials in France, however, considerations were slightly different: if Canada could limit English expansion and power in North America and also draw off resources from the British Isles, France would be better able to pursue its objectives in Europe. The French thus set out to occupy the interior of the continent, encircling the English colonies along the eastern coast.

FRENCH-INDIAN RELATIONS IN CANADA

The Iroquois

Central to French designs was the continued neutrality of the Iroquois. Although worn down, they could revive, and that possibility was increased when the Tuscarora moved north and joined the confederacy in 1722. Peace with the Iroquois required plenty of attentive diplomacy and to this the French committed some of their best agents. The nature of the confederacy made it possible for one tribe (generally the Seneca) to favor the French while another (invariably the Mohawk) favored the English, and others, especially the Onondaga, formed a shifting center. Factions developed, broke down, and reformed, squaring off on many different policy issues. Among the Iroquois, Francophiles struggled with Anglophiles and neutrals. Political tensions were exacerbated and cultural life was disturbed by the activities of Protestant and Catholic missionaries and increased amounts of alcohol.

The Iroquois did not at first accept the 1701 accord as final. They began overtures to the western tribes soon after peace was signed in the hope of bringing them into the English trade network. In 1710 they managed to conclude a treaty with the Ottawa, permitting them to go to Albany and establish a mutual assistance pact for protection against other nations. As attacks on New England continued during the 1700s, the English intensified their efforts to bring the Iroquois into the war but did not succeed until 1711. Some Iroquois ventured to support the attack on Quebec but when it failed, the confederacy resumed a strict neutrality. After the peace of 1713 the Iroquois lost leverage in the west. This was partly the result of developments in the region, and partly the effect of the new entente between Britain and France in Europe.

The threat of Iroquois diplomatic victory in the west, as well as increased competition from English traders, led to an increase in the number of men and forts the French maintained out west. A crucial point in this program was establishing a firmer presence at the western end of the confederacy's territory. After several years of careful diplomacy, the French persuaded the Seneca to allow them to build a fortified trading station. This extraordinary accomplishment was the work of Louis Thomas Chabert de Joncaire, an officer in the colonial troops who had often been among the Iroquois since he was captured and adopted in the 1680s. He mastered their language and understood their mentality, building a formidable reputation both for his counsel and his courage. The new Fort Niagara was begun in 1720 by the Niagara River (present-day Youngstown, New York). A much more powerful stone structure, still standing today, was built in 1725. As a counterbalance, the Onondaga allowed the English to build Fort Oswego. This development marked the shift to a new policy of trying to play the French off the British to preserve Iroquois sovereignty. Neutrality became a way for the Iroquois to protect themselves from the rising strength of the two European powers and their Indian neighbors. Competing posts also led to a price war that was very much to the advantage of the confederacy. In the next war (1744–1748) a desperate shortage of supplies in Canada weakened French relations with several western tribes between 1745 and 1747; nevertheless the Iroquois insisted on neutrality, and only some Mohawk joined English expeditions. The Iroquois also stood by as the French moved in to secure the Ohio Valley in the 1740s and 1750s.

Northern Allies

During the wars with the English in the eighteenth century, the Montagnais, Algonquin, Nip-

ising, and Ojibwa-Ottawa remained steadfast allies of the French, frequently participating in war parties raiding American borders. That did not prevent them from venturing down to Albany, taking advantage of the trading possibilities that resulted from the 1701 and 1710 treaties. The Ojibwa and their relatives benefited from their association with the French. They followed the fur trade westward and took over a huge territory from Lake Superior to Lake Winnipeg, pushing back the Cree in the northwest and the Fox and Sioux in the southwest. They aided the explorations of Pierre Gaultier de La Vérendrye and his associates, but since the Ojibwa were long-standing enemies of the Sioux, they took a dark view of any French move toward the Dakotas. The Ojibwa and Ottawa were drawn into present-day Michigan after 1701 when Cadillac established Détroit. At the same time they consolidated their hold over the territory north of Lakes Ontario and Erie from which they had expelled the Iroquois.

The Fox and Their Neighbors

In the mid seventeenth century, the Iroquois drove the Fox from their homeland between Lake Saint Clair and Lake Michigan to lands just west of Lake Michigan. This probably led to the troubles that arose between the Fox and their new neighbors, the Sioux to the west and the Ojibwa-Chippewa and Potawatomi to the north. The French tried to contain intertribal warfare in the interest of trade but this only further alienated the Fox, who remained at a disadvantage against the more numerous and better-armed Ojibwa. Cadillac's plan of concentrating tribes at Detroit proved to be a major mistake when some Fox moved there in 1712. The new commander thought the Fox aimed at destroying the post and incited other Indians to attack them. After a nineteen-day siege, the Fox abandoned their palisade and fled west under cover of a storm. Pursued and forced to fight, some eight hundred died. The Fox understandably became implacable enemies of the French, attacking traders and their Indian partners. At the same time, French relations deteriorated with the Kickapoo and Mascouten. They had been driven to the lands west of lower Lake Michigan by the Iroquois and had favored the French, but the aggressive behavior of the

Ojibwa, Ottawa, and Potawatomi now turned them into allies of the Fox.

In 1716 an expedition of 425 French and 500 Indians advanced against the Fox. They began a conventional siege of the Fox stronghold, with trenches advancing on the enemy's fortifications. After three days the small cannon that the French brought with them—the first used in the west—blew a hole in the fort, and the Fox accepted a harsh peace.

The Fox soon became embroiled in wars with the Sioux, Ojibwa, and other tribes of the region. The French reopened the war in 1728. The Fox fell out with the Kickapoo and Mascouten, whom the French drew back to their side in 1729. Four hundred fifty troops and militia and 1,200 Indians headed west from Michilimackinac but did not destroy the Fox. A large group of Fox then headed east to seek refuge among the Seneca but were met south of Lake Michigan by a second force of 150 Canadians and 850 Indians. The Fox held out for days, something only possible because the French had no large cannon with them and could not reduce stout stockades. With both sides desperately short of food, the Fox tried to flee in a storm but were discovered and forced to fight a bitter battle. The ragged remains of the Fox tribe took refuge with the Sauk, beginning a close association that has persisted up to the present. When the Fox sought terms, officials were outraged, having believed that the tribe had been exterminated. The French resolved to eliminate the remnants. In 1733 the commander at La Baye (present-day Green Bay, Wisconsin) demanded that the Sauk hand over the Fox. When they refused, he tried to force his way into the village and was killed. The two tribes fled west, pursued by a small French force that failed to make contact.

The tremendous cost of military operations in the far west and the tenaciousness of the Fox forced the French to offer peace in 1737. Meanwhile, the Kickapoo and Mascouten remained allies of the French, waging war against the English and the Chickasaw in the 1740s and 1750s when they were not fighting the Illinois.

The Miami and Shawnee

The Miami occupied the land between the Wabash and Ohio rivers going north as far as the Saint Joseph. They were occasionally associated with the Mascouten and the Shawnee, who lived along the Ohio River but ranged over southern Ohio and Kentucky. Since the 1660s the Miami and the Shawnee had been frequently attacked by the Iroquois, and so the French were able to draw them loosely into their collection of allies. In the early eighteenth century, the Miami were attracted by the goods and prices of English packhorse traders. They relocated several times, moving south and east. Unable to persuade them to move back, the French built two fortified posts: Miami in 1704 at present-day Fort Wayne, Indiana, and in 1717 a second, also called Miami or Ouyatanon after the tribe (now called Weas) on the Saint Joseph River near present-day Lafayette, Indiana. During the desperate years of the War of Austrian Succession (1744–1748), some Miami were drawn to the British cause.

In 1749 Pierre Joseph Céloron de Blainville led a force of 213 Frenchmen on a circular tour through the Ohio region planting lead plates bearing France's claim to the area and holding conferences with the Indians of the region. The show of strength was not completely successful; English traders proved to be well-established. The Shawnee were wooed by the English in the early 1750s but fell victim to raids by the French and their allies.

In 1752 an expedition of 250 Canadians, Ottawa, and Ojibwa seized the British post of Pickawillany (Piqua, Ohio) and killed Memeskia, leader of the Anglophile faction among the Miami. After this, French fort building in the Ohio Valley was tolerated by the Miami and Shawnee whose alliance with France lasted until the fall of the forts in 1758.

FRENCH-INDIAN RELATIONS IN LOUISIANA

In 1699 Pierre Le Moyne d'Iberville founded Biloxi as the first step in carrying out Louis XIV's plan for the settlement of Louisiana. His brother Jean Baptiste Le Moyne de Bienville succeeded him as governor, built a fort along a river above present-day Mobile, Alabama, in 1702, and founded Mobile itself in 1711. It served as the capital until shortly after, in 1718, New Orleans was established. Bienville was recalled in 1723, serving again from 1732 to 1743.

With the Indians of the region, Bienville adopted the approach that worked so well in his native Canada, meeting the leaders of many tribes in person each spring at the capital, and sending agents among the Indians, learning their language and their way of life. But he found it harder to secure close relations with some. Aside from tensions between settlers and Indians, the French had to contend with strong competition from English traders who offered the Indians lower prices, sometimes better goods, and invariably plenty of alcohol.

The Choctaw

The Choctaw lived in what is now southern Louisiana and Mississippi. Many early French establishments were in or near Choctaw lands, including New Orleans, and the French soon won these people to their side. However, English traders reached them around 1714 and a vigorous competition ensued. The French assisted the Choctaw in wars against their old enemies, the Chickasaw, who were assisted by the English. By the later 1730s, the strains of war and the effects of competition between traders led to the emergence of Anglophile and Francophile factions. As a result, the Choctaw could not be induced to fight when war resumed in 1744. Eventually the tribe was torn apart by factional fighting, which was settled after Matahachitoux (Soulier Rouge), leader of the pro-British faction, was killed in 1747 at the instigation of the French. Soon after, the Choctaw attacked a large Carolina trading party. Finally in 1750 the treaty of Grandpré made the Choctaw in effect a French protectorate, banned the English from their territory, and committed the tribe to assist the French against the Chickasaw. Exhausted by previous struggles, the Choctaw did little after the campaign of 1752.

The Destruction of the Natchez

North and west of the Choctaw lived the Natchez in the lower Mississippi Valley. In 1700 d'Iberville and his entourage were treated to a great ceremony by the chief and six hundred warriors, and accounts speak of a remarkable culture. Relations soon soured, especially under Cadillac, who was briefly governor of the colony. Four

Frenchmen were killed by the Natchez in 1716. Cadillac ordered Bienville, now military commander of the Mississippi Valley, to deal with the offenders. The Natchez had eight hundred men, Bienville had thirty-four. Nonetheless, he managed to get hold of those responsible and, so he claimed, had the chiefs condemn them to death. He then persuaded the Natchez to help the French build Fort Rosalie (present-day Natchez, Mississippi).

The presence of the military encouraged settlers to move upriver from the gulf settlements. The Natchez resented the loss of rich farmland and in 1722 tried to expel the settlers. Troops were sent in and the Natchez accepted a harsh peace. In 1729 further expansion impinged on a Natchez village and sacred site. The outraged Natchez massacred the garrison and attacked settlements, killing some 250 French and taking others hostage. The French, with the help of seven hundred Choctaw warriors, then attacked Natchez strongholds and in a six-month campaign inflicted heavy casualties. Of the Natchez who survived, 427 were captured and shipped to Haiti as slaves, while others found refuge among the Creek and Chickasaw.

The ferocity of this revenge shocked the Indians of the region, altering diplomatic conditions for years to come. Moreover, the cost was great and the loss of the Natchez post extinguished the possibility of short-term profit. The directors of the financially troubled Compagnie des Indes, which ran the colony, therefore requested that Louisiana revert to the Crown.

The Illinois Territory

The Illinois territory was annexed to Louisiana in 1717. By this time, however, the Illinois people were less able to assist the French than they had been in the past. They were reduced by disease, alcohol, and nearly constant warfare with the Kickapoo and Mascouten. Soon after, these two tribes were won over by the French but this did nothing to end war with the Illinois. An irony of French diplomacy was that in their bid to extend the network of alliances and trading partners the French made friends with opposing sides in old wars, and in this case it was to the detriment of an important ally.

The French maintained several fortified posts, some relocated as members of the Illinois confederacy retreated southward. The military center of the territory was Fort de Chartres, built in 1718 about eighteen miles (30 kilometers) north of Kaskaskia, which remained the economic center. In a bid to secure sovereignty, the French spent a fortune rebuilding the fort in stone between 1753 and 1756.

The Chickasaw Wars

The Chickasaw, a small warlike tribe, lived east of the Mississippi River in what is now northern Mississippi and Alabama, a strategic location between the main colony of Louisiana and the Illinois territory. They remained firm allies of the English from the time traders first reached them in the 1690s. This, of course, was unacceptable to the French. Open war broke out in 1719 when the French insisted that the English leave and the Chickasaw refused. French and Choctaw parties raided the territory, and the Chickasaw responded by attacking traffic on the Mississippi River. The two sides reached a standoff and accepted peace in 1725.

War broke out again in 1732 when some Natchez took refuge with the Chickasaw. The French demanded that they be handed over and pressed for the removal of the English, both of which the Chickasaw refused. In 1733 Bienville sent the Choctaw and Indians from the Illinois territory against them. The Chickasaw again interrupted traffic on the river. After months of preparations, Bienville embarked on a two-pronged attack in 1736. One column under Pierre d'Artaguiette consisted of 400 French and Indians, the other, under Bienville himself, comprised 600 French and perhaps a thousand Choctaw. They failed to arrive simultaneously. D'Artaguiette and many in his party were killed, and after brief engagements, Bienville himself decided to withdraw.

In 1739 an army of 1,500 headed north from Louisiana, while two detachments from Canada headed south with 325 French and 600 Indians. Impeded by heavy rains and unable to transport the artillery that alone could reduce palisaded villages, the French probably would not have prevailed. In the face of such a large force, however, the Chickasaw sued for peace, handing over some of the Natchez.

The marquis de Vaudreuil, Bienville's successor, was never confident of the armistice, and in 1752 he embarked on a third war that was no more conclusive than the others. Exhausted by the struggle, the Chickasaw chose to remain neutral during the Seven Years' War.

The Creek (Muskogee)

The Creek confederacy occupied lands in present-day Alabama and Georgia. In 1703 English agents incited the Alabama, members of the confederacy, to kill members of a French expedition. The French then began paying the Choctaw a bounty for Alabama scalps, but Bienville soon managed to make peace. In 1714 he visited the Alabama villages and emerged with permission to build Fort Toulouse (1717) on the lower Coosa River near present-day Montgomery, Alabama. It was supposed to block the English from using that route into Louisiana, but English traders carried on regardless. Members of the local garrison, particularly the Frontenot family, married into the local Alabama tribe prompting their overall attachment to the French.

Though courted by the English, French, and Spanish, the Creek maintained a determined independence. They generally preferred English goods but refused to expel other whites. They balanced their dependence on European goods with Europeans' interest in their military might. In 1747 a small party joined the Chickasaw at the English behest and raided French settlements. When the French insisted that they be punished, the Creek replied they would not be drawn into internal war like the Choctaw; if the French persisted, Fort Toulouse would be destroyed. During the Seven Years' War, many agents tried to win over the Creek but the confederacy, confident of its power, remained neutral.

Western Tribes

In 1718 the French ventured up the Red River into the lands of the Caddo and built a fort at Natchitoches (present-day Natchitoches, Louisiana). Traders soon ranged over the territory drained by the Arkansas and Red rivers and established themselves among the Caddo and Wichita who came to dominate trade. This activity led to persistent squabbles, but no full military engagements, with the Spanish. Explorers and traders also ventured southwest from the Illinois territory into the lands of the Osage and Pawnee.

They encouraged the Osage to raid Plains Indians, their traditional enemies, and bring pelts and slaves to sell. Yet again the French found themselves allies of two old enemies. In the 1740s the Osage went on devastating raids through the Arkansas Valley, forcing the Wichita to resettle on the upper Red River.

ANGLO-FRENCH RIVALRY IN THE MID EIGHTEENTH CENTURY

In the Seven Years' War, the direction of French operations was torn between competing policies. Indians figured significantly in the plans of the marquis de Vaudreuil, governor general of New France. He sought to keep the English at a distance by relying on terror raids and drawing off large parts of the enemy with far-flung forts in contested territory. Louis Joseph de Montcalm, commander of the regular forces, did not think highly of Indians and preferred to concentrate forces to assure victory in major engagements, reasoning that it would not be possible to keep the enemy at a distance using guerrilla tactics if he was determined to attack. Eventually English policy changed from one of trimming French territory or regaining their own losses to the complete defeat of the enemy. That was only possible through massed engagements at strategic points.

Indians remained a significant presence in smaller military operations. They made up the majority of fighting men in the small raiding parties along the frontiers from northern Massachusetts (Maine) to the Carolinas. In the Battle of the Monongahela in 1755, 108 French soldiers, 146 Canadian militiamen, and 637 Indians defeated General Edward Braddock's 2,200-man force. But there was quite a difference in the larger engagements. At the siege of Oswego in 1756 there were 1,000 French regulars, 137 marines, 1,500 Canadian militiamen, and 260 Indians whose presence, reviving memories of raids in the past, was meant to intimidate the garrison.

Indians could be a liability in the new way of war, as Montcalm found out the next year. In 1757, three thousand French troops, twenty-five hundred Canadians, and twelve hundred Indians surrounded Fort William Henry in northern New York and it capitulated. Short of supplies, Montcalm decided not to take the garri-son prisoner and let them march off, unarmed, on condition that they not serve for eighteen months. Such action made no sense to the Indians who plundered the prisoners, killing over thirty who resisted and holding several hundred prisoner. This attack, as well as raids elsewhere, served to reinforce Americans' assessment of Indian manners.

Later, though their allegiance helped hold the west for France, there were only small numbers of Indians at major battles such as Carillon in 1758 or Niagara in 1759. At the siege of Quebec there were four thousand troops, eleven thousand militia, and twelve hundred Indians. At the 1760 siege there were few Indians.

Pontiac's War

In the spring of 1763, after more than a year of secret councils, Indians from around the upper Great Lakes determined to remove the English from the west and particularly to fend off encroachment on their lands. Eventually Pontiac, war chief of the Ottawa at Détroit, emerged as the leader. This was more than a military exercise; it involved a religious revival led by the Delaware prophet Neolin (or Neyon) that contained a strong antiwhite element. Unrest turned into a siege of Detroit and soon all forts in the west were attacked and most fell. Pontiac drew support from former allies of the French and from other tribes, notably the Delaware and some Seneca, as well as French or Canadians still living in the west. Neither Detroit nor Fort Pitt (formerly Duquesne) was captured, however, and these garrisons provided some ground for the British to regain control. Though the uprising came apart by the autumn of 1763, it was not until April 1765 that peace was achieved.

Earlier historians accepted contemporary English and American reports that blamed the French in the west for inciting the Indians by suggesting that France would retake Canada. Scholarships however, suggests that the Indians themselves were behind events; if anything, they sought to influence France. More immediately, they sought to protect themselves from the harsh or exploitative treatment they received from English soldiers and traders. Their action was influenced in part by the positive relations that had generally existed with the French. But that time was past, and a new kind of relationship between Indians and whites was beginning.

BIBLIOGRAPHY

Dictionary of Canadian Biography. Toronto, Buffalo, and London, 1966–1979. Volumes 1–5 are an excellent reference on natives and whites active from the seventeenth to early eighteenth centuries and also contain an abundance of information about various activities and wars.

Dowd, Gregory E. "The French King Wakes Up in Detroit: 'Pontiac's War' in Rumour and History." *Ethnohistory* 37 (Summer 1990):254–278.

Eccles, W. J. *Essays on New France.* Toronto, Ontario, 1987.

———. *France in America.* New York, 1972; rev. ed. Toronto, Ontario, 1990.

———. *Frontenac, the Courtier Governor.* Toronto, Ontario, 1959.

Eid, L. V. "The Ojibwa-Iroquois War: The War the Five Nations Did Not Win." *Ethnohistory* 26, no. 4 (Fall 1979):297–324. A remarkable revisionist piece relying on both Indian and white sources.

Ellis, Christopher J., and Neil Ferris, eds. *The Archaeology of Southern Ontario to A.D. 1650.* London, Ontario, 1990. Contains noteworthy essays, especially a very important revisionist history of the Iroquois wars by Conrad Heidenreich.

Frégault, Guy. *Canada: The War of the Conquest.* Translated by Margaret M. Cameron. Toronto, Ontario, 1969. A detailed account of the Seven Years' War from a Canadian perspective. A bit dated, occasionally inaccurate, and in places obviously biased.

Giraud, Marcel. *A History of French Louisiana.* 5 vols. Baton Rouge, 1969–1991. A detailed history to the 1730s.

Haan, Richard. "The Problem of Iroquois Neutrality: Suggestions for Revision." *Ethnohistory* 27, no. 4 (Fall 1980):317–330.

Harris, R. Cole, ed. *Historical Atlas of Canada.* 3 vols. Toronto, 1987–1990. Vol. 1, *From the Beginning to 1800,* has excellent maps detailing many developments.

Heidenreich, Conrad. *Huronia: A History and Geography of the Huron Indians, 1600–1650.* Toronto, Ontario, 1971.

Hunt, George T. *The Wars of the Iroquois: A Study in Intertribal Relations.* Madison, Wis., 1940. This famous account is now distinctly dated. Hunt's thesis that the Iroquois fought for the position of "middleman" in trade is Eurocentric and inaccurate. See Trigger and Heidenreich.

Jaenen, Cornelius. *Friend and Foe: Aspects of French-Amerindian Cultural Contact in the Sixteeth and Seventeenth Centuries.* Toronto and New York, 1976.

Miquelon, Dale Bernard. *New France 1701–1744: "A Supplement to Europe."* Toronto, Ontario, 1987.

Parkman, Francis. *France and England in North America.* 8 vols. Boston, 1851–1884. Still considered an authority by some, although the history is dated and the research limited; there are many factual errors in regard to Indians, and the analysis is flagrantly biased.

Stanley, George F. G. *New France: The Last Phase, 1744–1760.* Toronto, Ontario, 1968. A passable but dated account.

Sturtevant, W. J., gen ed. *Handbook of North American Indians.* 15 vols. Washington, D.C., 1978– . Vol. 4, *Indian-White Relations* (1988); vol. 6, *Subarctic* (1981); vol. 15, *Northeast* (1978). This series is the best general guide to Native North Americans and the bibliographies are exhaustive.

Trigger, Bruce. *The Children of Aataentsic: A History of the Huron People to 1660.* 2 vols. Montreal, 1976. A detailed account.

———. *The Huron, Farmers of the North.* New York, 1969. A useful, brief history.

———. *Natives and Newcomers: Canada's "Heroic Age" Reconsidered.* Montreal and Kingston, Ontario, 1985.

Verney, Jack. *The Good Regiment: The Carignan-Salières Regiment in Canada, 1665–1668.* Montreal, 1991.

Zoltvany, Yves F. *Philippe de Rigaud de Vaudreuil: Governor of New France, 1703–1725.* Toronto, Ontario, 1974.

Jay Cassel

SEE ALSO The European Contest for North America; The First Americans; The Fur Trade; and Indian-Colonist Contact.

THE SPANISH BORDERLANDS

THE SPANIARDS, MORE than any other colonial power that set forth from Europe in the Age of Reconnaissance, were a nation and a society formed by war. If the dissenting Pilgrims who landed at Plymouth Rock in Massachusetts in 1620 were well-suited to build an agrarian colony, then no people were more suited to land in Mexico in 1519 than the Spaniards. Seven hundred years of crusading warfare against the Moors in Spain, the period known as the *Reconquista* or the Reconquest, had more than prepared them for the task of military conquest and occupation.

The Reconquest, an extended period of intercultural contact and conflict, left the Spaniards equipped with a range of institutions and traditions that would be needed in the Americas. The *requerimiento* (a declaration made to infidel peoples), the Real Patronato (the power the Pope had granted the Spanish monarchs), the *presidio* (a frontier garrison), the *encomienda* (a grant of labor and tribute)—all these Iberian traditions would serve the conquistadores superbly in their encounters with the Arawak, Incas, Aztecs, Chichimec, Araucanian, and other Native peoples. That these encounters would result in destruction and enslavement for millions concerned most Spaniards very little. By the time missionaries like the Franciscans and Dominicans appealed to the conscience of the Spanish monarchy, it was too late, at least for the peaceful inhabitants of the Caribbean islands. This essay treats the Spanish military interaction with the Indians of the northern fringe of Spain's American empire. In particular it focuses upon the western and central regions of the Spanish Borderlands.

EMPIRE-TOPPLING

The first warfare in North America between European and aborigine was the campaign against the Aztec Empire, a campaign that ended with the conquest and overthrow of the Triple Alliance of the Mexica, or Mexicans. Although it was for the continent of North America a campaign of unprecedented logistical and military scale, and was also of uncompromising ferocity, it was, in most ways, an example of "conventional" warfare. The destruction of the ruling Aztec elite and army, accompanied by the leveling of their capital city, represented a relatively straightforward goal, and the army of Hernando

Cortés and his Tlaxcalan allies had a clear plan with which to achieve it. Furthermore, the concentration of leadership in a hierarchical system like that of the Aztec Empire meant that its decapitation ended the war and ensured the triumph of the Spaniards and their allies. The Indians whom the Spanish encountered after the establishment of the colony—the nomadic tribes of the borderlands—were another matter entirely.

North of the valley of Mexico lay an enormous arid and semiarid region, peopled mostly by nomadic hunters and gatherers. Although these tribes possessed lineage forms of political authority that regulated their social and political relations with each other, they had no form of government that the Spanish could recognize within the European conception of polity. Furthermore, since they lacked anything resembling tribal cohesiveness, these bands had to be dealt with on an individual basis. Thus the Spanish entered a prolonged period of guerrilla warfare that began with the Chichimec wars in 1540 and was still raging when the Spanish Empire in North America came to an end in 1820. In fact, the wars of the *Gran Apachería,* as the borderlands have been termed, did not truly end until the last independent Apache nation surrendered in the last decade of the nineteenth century, after 350 years of unremitting war against dozens of Indian nations from the mouth of the Colorado River to the forests of eastern Texas.

Twenty years after the fall of Tenochtitlan, the Aztec capital, two events marked the beginning of Indian-Spanish struggle in the borderlands. The first was the Mixtón war, the most serious Indian revolt to shake New Spain; the second was the beginning of the long war against the Chichimec Indians.

THE MIXTÓN WAR

After the Aztecs had been conquered, Spanish *entradas* or expeditions were sent north and south in search of treasure and, the Spanish hoped, yet more Tenochtitlan to besiege. In this the Spanish were disappointed in North America (although some veterans who had been with Cortés joined Francisco Pizarro in time to participate in the conquest of the Inca Empire in Peru).

Beltrán Nuño de Guzmán, a particularly blood-thirsty and cruel conquistador, fled Mexico City and his Spanish enemies there to pursue conquest in the unknown lands to the northwest of the valley of Mexico, in the areas of Michoacán, Nayarit, Jalisco, and Sinaloa, which he named Nueva Galicia. His pillaging and slaving activities there so infuriated the Indians that they finally arose in revolt in 1541. They refused to deliver their tribute, killed the *encomenderos* (to whose service they had been assigned), as well as the missionaries who had been assigned to Christianize them, and fled into the mountains near Guadalajara.

Francisco Vásquez de Coronado was at that moment searching for the legendary Seven Cities of Cíbola in New Mexico, and with him was a very large force of fighting men; thus the kingdom was stripped of defenders. As a consequence the lieutenant-governor of Nueva Galicia was rebuffed in the field by the Indians. He desperately sent for help from Viceroy Antonio de Mendoza in Mexico City. The famed conquistador Pedro de Alvarado happened to arrive from Guatemala with a force of men and was quickly dispatched to the west. Alvarado attacked the Indians at the *peñoles* (cliffs) of Nochistlán, Jalisco, but was forced to retreat. This conquistador, who had survived the disastrous Spanish retreat from Tenochtitlan on the *"noche triste"* (sorrowful night) and triumphed with the conquest of the Aztec Empire, died after his horse fell on him. Viceroy Mendoza was faced with a serious threat to the safety of the kingdom of New Spain. He gathered 450 Spaniards and a large force of Indians, including Tlaxcalans (who had helped Cortés overthrow their Aztec enemies), Tarascan, and even Aztec warriors, and crushed the revolt, killing thousands of Indians and enslaving many thousands more, mostly women and children.

WAR IN THE GRAN CHICHIMECA

During the previous year, 1546, the real impetus to move into the north came when silver was discovered near Zacatecas, hundreds of miles north of Mexico City. Slowly at first and then in increasing numbers, Spaniards flocked to the area to prospect for riches. Within ten years an inspector found thirty-four mining concerns or partnerships operating in Zacatecas with smelters, a labor force of free Indians and black slaves, stores, churches, and ranches to supply the mines. In 1554 silver was discovered at Guanajuato as well, and the north became a major focus of government attention.

Unfortunately for the Spaniards, the road between Mexico City and Zacatecas ran straight through the lands of some of the fiercest Indians in the Americas. The nomadic hunters and gatherers of the northern badlands had always been called *chichimecas* in Nahautl, the common tongue of the Indians of the valley of Mexico and its environs. *Chichimec* had a negative connotation, signifying "dirty, uncivilized dogs." That all of the tribes which had migrated south (including the Aztec), had been labeled *chichimecas* at one time or another mattered little; the term was applied indiscriminately to all of the northern bands. *Chichimeca* became a generic term for the great arid northern wilderness of the borderlands; it connotated both the badlands and the warriors who inhabited it.

The Indians with whom the Spaniards came into contact were actually many small scattered bands; the four major nations into which they were grouped were the Pame, Guamare, Zacateco, and Guachichil. Even compared to the many tribes with whom the Spanish warred in the succeeding centuries, including the Apache and Comanche, the Chichimec were singular for their ferocity. Nudity was their habitual state. They lived in rude huts of brush and survived by hunting or gathering cactus and mesquite plants for food. Their social organization was the small band or group of families. To the Spanish they seemed unspeakably savage and primitive, but the Chichimec were tenacious warriors, used to roaming with complete freedom, and totally unsuited for the labor, urban life, and Christianity that the Spaniards were determined to bring them. Adding further potential for conflict, wagon trains loaded with desirable goods were now rolling through their customary hunting grounds, and horses and cattle were wandering through their lands, both of which they ate before learning that horses had more practical uses. To compound the situation, the Spaniards often seized Indians and forced them to labor on their farms or in their mines. The Chichimec struck back, burning settlements and attacking and looting wagon trains. The Chichimec war had begun.

The Indians' usual method of warfare was the ambush; war parties consisted of forty or fifty braves, but they could also range upwards to several hundred and in one case even as many as a thousand warriors. The Spanish learned that tribes were making temporary alliances in order to exterminate the "palefaces" (la blancura). The Indians would strike at short distance with blood-curdling shouts and rapid shooting of arrows; their painted, nude bodies and war cries were unnerving to the Spanish. The Chichimec prepared for battle by prolonged dancing and often used alcoholic beverages or drugs to induce frenzy. After a successful attack, the warriors would split up into small groups in order to make pursuit more difficult. To some extent these tactics were a common pattern among all nomadic warriors of the borderlands.

The Indians were nothing if not adaptable; they soon learned to send spies into Spanish-Indian towns to learn the Europeans' strength and plans. Major attacks were often preceded by a prolonged period of raiding and livestock stealing. This last tactic could turn mounted Spanish cavalry into foot soldiers. If the tables were turned and the Indians were attacked in their hideouts, they used the terrain (especially caves) to their advantage, fighting tenaciously. Women joined in defending their homes with the weapons of their men. The bows and arrows of the Indians more than matched the Spanish crossbows and harquebuses. The degree to which the Chichimec reed arrows with obsidian tips penetrated their chain mail was astonishing to the Spanish and speeded their adoption of buck-skin armor in place of European metal armor. One Spanish soldier, comparing the Indians of America with the enemies he had known in Europe, commented that the Chichimec fought and skirmished as if they were Moors of Granada. On one occasion he saw four mounted and armored soldiers fall upon one lone Chichimec; the Indian took away the lances of three even as the fourth lance was in his body.

The Chichimec war, setting the pattern for repeated conflicts with other enemies over the centuries, was one of unprecedented ferocity.

Inasmuch as torture, scalping, and cannibalism were traditional Native practices in war, these factors, combined with the Indians' killing of priests and burning of churches, enabled the Spaniards to declare guerra a fuego y a sangre— a war of fire and blood, or full-scale conflict— against the Indians. The New Laws of 1542 had outlawed enslavement of Indians in the Americas, but since the Spanish could declare that the war against the Chichimec was a "just war" against savages who had rejected the call to submission to Spanish authority and conversion to Christianity embodied in the requerimiento, they were able to enslave them legally. The Indians struck back by kidnapping women and children; the women reportedly because of a shortage of females in the Gran Chichimeca, the children because they could be more easily than adults turned into "white Indians"—that is, raised as part of the band until they forgot their heritage and participated fully in all aspects of Indian life, including making war on their former countrymen.

In the first years of the Chichimec war, to about 1560, the Indians primarily raided cattle ranches, or estancias, and looted wagon trains on the roads to the mines. In 1554, for example, the Indians attacked a train of sixty wagons in the Ojuelos Pass, making off with more than thirty thousand pesos' worth of clothing, silver, and other booty, including mules to carry their loot. They also captured Indian women from tribes that cooperated with the Spanish. Increasingly the Chichimec also were taking Spanish weapons and horses and using them for war; swords and even muskets were captured in Indian rancherías (villages).

By the 1560s evidence was mounting that the Indians were growing bolder, raiding Spanish settlements farther and farther south, striking across the Río Lerma near Guadalajara into the lands of Indians the Spanish had already conquered, pacified, and missionized. By the end of 1561 an estimate put the casualties among the Spanish at more than two hundred and among their Indian allies and converts at over two thousand. Property damage to estancias and wagon trains was estimated at more than a million gold pesos and to royal wagons and treasure (the Crown took a percentage of all silver mined) at more than four hundred thousand gold pesos.

The Spanish, in for a prolonged guerrilla war, began to build fortified garrisons near the mines and later along the roads to the mines. The mission of the soldiers in these *presidios* was to patrol the highways and provide escorts for wagon trains. During the course of the Chichimec war, roughly between 1540 and 1600, thirty *presidios* were erected from Mexico City to Zacatecas and beyond to Durango. At first only lightly garrisoned (with an average company of only fourteen men or even fewer) these forts, much enlarged in personnel, were eventually to become the backbone of Spanish military strategy throughout the long Indian wars on the frontier.

In the meantime so ineffective were the small presidial companies in stopping Indian raiding that the viceroy in Mexico City decided on a different strategy, that of a full-scale peace offensive. He prohibited the further enslavement of war captives (something that had driven the Indians to retaliatory fury), freed some of the already enslaved, placed the rest under the care of missionaries, banned all unauthorized expeditions into the Gran Chichimeca, and offered food, clothing, land, agricultural tools, religious instruction, and government protection to the Indians. At the same time intensified war was unleashed against Indian bands that spurned Spanish overtures. The authorities brought in Indian auxiliaries to fight the Chichimec—Tlaxcalan, Otomí, Tarascan, Cholutecan, and Aztec soldiers from the south. Chichimec tribes that accepted peace were quickly turned against groups still fighting the Spanish. The total lack of Indian unity in New Spain, New France, the United States, and elsewhere in the Americas was always a potent weapon of the Europeans against Native Americans.

The war rose to a climax in the early 1580s, when the settlers of the Gran Chichimeca appealed directly to the viceroy to defend them against the Indians. Shortly afterward, the peace offensive started, and a crackdown on illegal slaving of Chichimec by greedy soldiers began to yield results. More groups begged for peace, and the Spanish seeded the frontier with colonies of Tlaxcalan Indians (their invaluable allies against the Aztecs), who were to defend the frontier and, more important, to teach the Chichimec by example to till the soil and to provide a model of Christian, sedentary life. The combi-

nation of bribery and warfare, assisted by the ever-present diseases that so severely depopulated the Indians, gradually brought the war to an end. The prohibition against enslaving the Indians had such a marked effect that it quickly became clear that enslavement alone had been responsible in large degree for perpetuating the war. Diplomacy, evangelization by friars who studied the Indian tongues, the transplantation of Native auxiliaries as defenders and settlers, and the provisioning of both colonizers and pacified enemies from royal funds were the four cornerstones of the settlement of the Chichimec war. By 1600 this frontier was more or less at peace.

REBELLION IN NORTHWESTERN NEW SPAIN

By the end of the Chichimec war the Spanish were already moving north into new territories peopled with many different tribes. Besides nomadic hunters and gatherers, the Spanish encountered *ranchería* peoples in the Sierra Maestra Occidental—the Tepehuan and Tarahumara Indians of the mountains of northwestern New Spain and farther to the north, the Mayo, Yaqui, and Seri of Sinaloa and Sonora. These Indians were sedentary and semisedentary agriculturalists, often moving from homes in the mountain canyons to settlements in the river valleys between planting seasons.

Although the majority of these tribes accepted the presence of Spanish Franciscan or Jesuit missionaries, every tribe revolted against the Spanish. One cause of these rebellions was the exploitative miners and ranchers who followed in the wake of the friars, men who seized Indians for labor or expropriated Indian lands or water. Most of the borderlands is either arid or semiarid, and Indians in the mountain valleys occupied the only sources of water available. Thus conflicts with Spanish settlers were inevitable. Another cause for uprisings was the missionaries themselves. They saw their role as saviors of the Indians; in this capacity they viewed the extirpation of all manifestations of Native religion as essential if "idolatry" and "heathenism" were to be suppressed. They dispensed punishment, often in the form of whippings, to recalcitrant converts or to shamans, the medicine men of the tribes, whom they branded as *hechiceros,* or sorcerers. Their heavy-handed and intolerant behavior often bred resentment, followed by rebellion.

The Tepehuan revolted in 1616, and the Tarahumara rebelled in 1648, 1652, and 1690. In each case hundreds of Spaniards and thousands of Indians were killed when the Europeans mounted their inevitable military retaliation. In 1609 Captain Diego de Hurdaide, the Spanish military commander north of the Sinaloa River, was pursuing a band of Ocoroni Indians (a small nation in northern Sinaloa) when he encountered a new nation, the Yaqui on the banks of the river that was to bear their name. The Yaqui refused him passage across the river in pursuit of the Ocoroni. Unprepared for real battle, he returned with two thousand Indian allies and forty Spaniards, only to be promptly defeated by the Yaqui. Hurdaide then put together the largest army northwestern New Spain had ever seen, four thousand Indian fighters and fifty mounted Spaniards for the conquest of the Yaqui. Again the Spanish were defeated by a reported force of seven thousand Yaqui, who put the Spanish-Indian army to flight and wounded the captain himself. A year went by, during which the Spanish were unable to mount further attacks. Suddenly the Yaqui asked for peace and requested that missionaries be sent to them. The exact reasons why are unclear; one explanation is that the Yaqui learned that the Spanish planned to outflank them by sea.

The Yaqui and Spanish hammered out a peace accord by whose terms the Indians had to give up the Ocoroni leaders who had precipitated the Spanish-Yaqui encounter as well as any arms and horses that they had captured from the Spanish. While not specifically forbidden in the treaty, the Spanish made no effort to send any soldiers or permit settlers into Yaqui country for over ten years after the treaty, and when Jesuits traveled into the Yaqui country to begin their work of conversion, they traveled without the traditional escort of soldiers that had meant so much trouble in previous encounters with Indian nations. The first decades were peaceful ones, and the priests established some fifteen mission villages on the Mayo and Yaqui rivers. But in 1684 silver was discovered at Alamos,

on the edge of Mayo territory, and slowly and steadily Spanish settlers and miners moved into Indian lands. In 1740 the Mayo and Yaqui revolted.

The precise causes were obscure but may have been related to friction between the Jesuits and the governor of the territory, Manuel Huidobro, who, from all accounts, was a poor administrator. Huidobro later accused the missionaries of precipitating the rebellion by whipping the relative of a Yaqui town governor, who sought and received moral support from the civil authorities against the friars. Rumors of maltreatment of Indians spread, and the revolt began when another Indian governor was killed in the lands of the Mayo. Shouting a battle cry of "Long live the King! Long live the Blessed Virgin Mary! Down with bad government!" some six thousand Indians seized possession of all Mayo and Yaqui towns and chased the Spaniards south to Alamos. Huidobro proved his incompetence to deal with the situation, but his lieutenant, Augustín de Vidósola, raised a mixed army of Indians and Spaniards and defeated the Yaqui in two pitched battles, reportedly killing five thousand of the enemy. By the time Yaqui chiefs asked for peace, more than a thousand Spaniards and five times that many Indians had died.

Sonora was devastated, its mines and haciendas abandoned and burned. Vidósola tried and executed four ostensible leaders of the rebellion and deported all Indians suspected of infidelity. The Jesuits returned to rebuild their missions, but their wholesale expulsion in 1767 ended their dream of a peaceful Christian kingdom in northwestern New Spain.

THE GREAT PUEBLO REVOLT

By far the most serious Indian revolt in the borderlands occurred in New Mexico, which had been settled by Juan de Oñate in 1598 and was an isolated Spanish outpost far to the north of the Spanish-Indian frontier, with thousands of leagues of hostile territory in between. New Mexico lacked silver mines, and Spaniards who lived there were small farmers and cattle ranchers. Populated by nine nations collectively known as the Pueblo Indians, the Rio Grande Valley was viewed as a fertile ground for missionary activity by the Franciscans. But the Pueblo tribes proved stubbornly resistant to evangelization.

As in Sonora, the civil and religious authorities were at odds, each side accusing the other of economically exploiting the Indians. For example, Bernardo López, *gobernador* from 1659 to 1662, required Indians from several pueblos to deliver to him hides, salt, and piñon nuts for resale. The friars claimed that Indians were being taken away from both their own village agriculture and that which supported the missions. In return successive governors charged that the missionaries abused and exploited their charges. The Franciscans, like the Jesuits, enforced their authority in the mission villages by corporal punishment, usually whippings administered by mestizo or mulatto *mayordomos*.

Meanwhile the Indians continued to dance their masked kachina dances, offer prayer sticks, and strew sacred cornmeal, which some governors condoned as harmless Native customs. The friars characteristically saw such activity as heretical and idolatrous. Civil officials encouraged the Indians in order to undermine the authority of the missionaries with whom they were feuding.

The situation exploded in 1680 in the great Pueblo Revolt. Drought and crop failure after 1667 had to some extent brought greater cooperation between religious and civil authorities in the province. One Spanish governor even went so far as to support the friars in the suppression of Native religious practices. Some forty-seven Indian leaders from villages throughout the valley were accused of witchcraft, idolatry, or their promotion. This campaign for the eradication of what the Spanish regarded as idolatrous superstition backfired badly.

In 1680 there were between twenty-five thousand and thirty thousand Indians living in the eastern pueblos, divided among the nations of the Piro, Kere, southern and northern Tiwa, Tano, Towa, and Tewa. The "European" population (which included many mestizos, blacks, and mulattoes) was about 2,350, with most living in or near Santa Fe. There were also some 33 Spanish missionaries living among the Indians. Two shamans, Popé and Catiti of San Juan and Santo Domingo pueblos respectively, managed to unite the villages in a conspiracy to expel the Spaniards from the valley. The fact that many of the Indians had been living on the tops of mesas at the time of the Spaniards' arrival testified to the continual state of warfare between themselves and the nomads they called Apache. But resentment of the Europeans served briefly to unite them.

A force of Tano besieged Santa Fe, while in most of the other Pueblo villages Indians killed all the missionaries and other Spaniards they could find. Tewa and northern Tiwa from Taos reinforced the Tano, and the Spanish were obliged (and permitted) to withdraw southward under Governor Antonio Otermín. All the missions were burned, 21 of 33 missionaries were murdered, and 401 of the roughly 2,350 colonists were killed. That the Indians allowed the Spaniards to leave when they could have destroyed them all indicates that their expulsion from Pueblo lands, and not their deaths, was the object of the revolt.

The Spanish pulled back to El Paso del Norte. There they remained for some twelve years. Revenge raids on Tiwa and Kere villages netted some captives, but the reconquest of New Mexico was not seriously attempted until 1692. By then Indian unity had collapsed, and the Spanish under Otermín were able to retake each pueblo individually. The Indians' failure to unite in the face of a common cultural threat, except for brief periods, permitted the Spanish to reconquer them. But the Europeans tread lightly forever after in New Mexico. The friars never reestablished their full authority in Indian villages, and never again was a campaign to eradicate Native religious practices undertaken.

With the suppression of the Pueblo Revolt, the Spanish authorities in Mexico City embarked on a drive to strengthen the defenses of the northern frontier. An expansion of the *presidio* system was undertaken at the same time as new dangers appeared to challenge the Spanish hold on the northern borderlands.

THE APACHE THREAT

In 1700 the decayed, enfeebled, and inefficient Hapsburg dynasty came to an end with the death of its last monarch, Charles II. The Bourbons who came to power in 1714, at the conclusion of the War of the Spanish Succession, embarked on a vigorous program of political, economic, and military reform. During this period pressures on the borderlands grew from the southeast. In addition the Spanish faced the greatest indigenous threat they had ever encountered on the frontier.

As early as Coronado's expedition in search of Cíbola in 1540, the Spanish encountered nomadic hunters in the Southwest, people referred to by the Pueblo Indians as Apache, a name thought to be derived from the Zuñi word *ápachu*, or enemy, a term that the Pueblo applied to their foes, the Navajo. Near the end of the eighteenth century, a Spanish officer described the Apache as divided into nine distinct tribes. To the west of the Rio Grande in New Mexico were the Mimbreño, the Navajo, the Gileño, the Chiricahua, and the Tonto, or Coyotero. To the east were the Faraone, the Mescalero, the Llanero (divided into three groups), and the Lipane. Although they spoke a common language, their customs and practices differed. And, of course, an agreement such as a peace accord with one nation did not necessarily bind another tribe, a fact that was to plague the Spanish until the end of the colonial period. The Spanish, accustomed to European patterns of war and diplomacy, always preferred to deal with a single personage who spoke for all Indians of one nation. However, traditional Native ideas about tribal and even band autonomy and independence did not conform to Spanish ideas about leadership.

Like the Chichimec, the Apache were described as being exceptionally robust, insensible to heat, cold, fatigue, hunger, or thirst. They were hunters and gatherers, living in the most rugged and mountainous regions. The only duty of the men was to hunt and fight. When making war the Apache left their women and children in secluded camps with a guard force and set out in small groups on foot to avoid leaving a trail. Rendezvousing near the enemy, they sent out decoys to lure their pursuers into ambush. When chased themselves they fled at top speed, splitting into small groups to throw off pursuit. If impeded by livestock they had stolen, they killed the animals and drank their blood on the run. They were credited with an almost magical ability to conceal themselves in terrain, to cross mountains and waterless deserts at a pace that killed Spanish horses chasing after them, and

to turn on pursuers if the latter were inferior in number and massacre them in ambush.

To counterbalance this fearsome enemy, the Spanish had the line of *presidios* and the companies that manned them. They also had one big advantage. Living as well in the Gran Apachería were many other equally warlike tribes who hated the Apache as much as the Europeans did. On the southeast were the Caddoan tribes— the Taovaya, Wichita, Kichai, Iscani, and Tawakoni—whom the Spaniards called the *norteños,* or nations of the north. Throughout Texas were the Comanche, traditional enemies of the Apache, as were the Pueblo nations in New Mexico and the Ute to their north. To the west were the Hopi and Zuñi, all of whom warred with the Apache (and each other). In short, the Spanish found a huge, complex mosaic of tribal alliances and enmities of which they made considerable use from the early 1700s on.

THE *PRESIDIOS*

In 1724 Pedro de Rivera set out to inspect the frontier for the viceroy, and found a wholly inadequate defense system in place. It consisted of a paltry 23 military garrisons, divided between 18 *presidios*, 3 squad posts, and 2 *compañía volante* (light cavalry) posts, manned in all by 1,006 officers and men. The strength of the 18 *presidios* themselves varied from a pitiful 9 officers and men to a more respectable 105 soldiers. This force was charged with defending a frontier that stretched from Sonora on the west to eastern Texas. The soldiers were poorly armed and clothed, lacked horses and ammunition, and in many cases were routinely cheated by their officers in matters of pay and supply.

Worse, many of the *presidios* were simply in the wrong place, established at locations of Indian hostility in the past that were now the sites of peaceful Spanish towns. Rivera traveled thousands of miles over a period of three years to make his report to the viceroy. His report was codified in the *reglamento* of 1729, in which the pay of the common soldier, the sites of the *presidios*, the authority of officers, and the duties and obligations of soldiers were set out precisely. Unfortunately, the aim of the inspection was not a better defense force, but economy, the reduction of military costs. The "reforms" cut military strength on the frontier from 1,006 officers and men to 734 soldiers, at a savings of 63,000 pesos. But these economy measures did incalculable harm to frontier defense.

Indian depredations reached new levels by the middle of the century. The Apache, often aided and abetted by runaway mission Indians or by renegade Spaniards, mulattoes, and mestizos, raided everywhere on the frontier, burning towns, stealing cattle and horses, and killing and kidnapping the terrorized citizenry. In Nueva Vizcaya between 1749 and 1763, according to Spanish estimates, the Apache killed more than eight hundred people and destroyed approximately four million pesos' worth of property, all within a two-hundred-mile (320 kilometer) radius of Chihuahua. Some raids took place within a few miles of the city. The Bolsón de Mapimí, a barren and arid badlands located just to the south of the bend of the Rio Grande in Chihuahua, gave the Apache sanctuary in terrain so rugged that the Spaniards feared to give chase there. The Bolsón, in the words of one missionary father, "vomited forth enemies."

At the same time that Indian raids were reaching a crescendo, Spanish imperial responsibilities expanded enormously. The Peace of Paris in 1763, that ended the Seven Years' War, gave Spain the French territories in the Mississippi Valley. Thousands of square miles were added to Spanish defense boundaries at the stroke of a pen. The French were removed as a menace to New Spain and its silver mines, only to be replaced by a more dangerous foe, the English. In addition Russian moves down the coast of California added to the security headaches of the Spanish. As a result, a new investigation of frontier defenses was carried out in 1766, and a new *reglamento* was promulgated in 1772.

Over the years a number of new *presidios* had been erected in Texas and Nuevo Santander (in the extreme east, north of Tampico) as Spanish settlers poured northward to establish new towns, ranches, and mines. Now strategic decisions were made that set defense policy on a new course. *Presidios,* while still the cornerstone of borderlands defense, were augmented with more *compañías volantes,* or flying cavalry companies, more companies of dragoons, and an expanded militia. Furthermore, an important recommendation came from the Marqués de Rubí, who had carried out the inspection. Rubí, after consulting with many frontier soldiers, came to recognize that the Comanche and Caddoan nations were not so much enemies of the Spaniards as of the Apache, and that in the main their attacks on places like San Antonio de Béjar and San Sabá had been retaliations for the Spanish sheltering their Apache foe. Furthermore they generally abided by their word given in treaties and were judged overall to be more trustworthy than the Apache. Accordingly he recommended that an alliance be struck with these nations and that their aid be enlisted to exterminate or reduce the Apache. When this proposal was adopted some years later, it was to become the cornerstone of Spanish Indian policy in the borderlands until independence and the establishment of the Mexican republic.

Once again *presidios* were to be relocated so that they would contribute more efficiently to frontier defense. The frontier troops were raised to the same status as those of the regular king's army. Pay scales were standardized, as were weapons, uniforms, and mounts. Each trooper was supposed to be equipped with a string of six horses and a pack mule, but few were able to muster that many mounts. In order to encourage better marksmanship, each man was to be issued three pounds (1.4 kilograms) of gunpowder per year for making cartridges.

The men who manned these companies on the frontier were a tough breed of soldier. Their lack of discipline and near-total absence of spit and polish appalled regular army officers who inspected them, but those who commanded them came to recognize that they possessed great toughness, stamina, and courage. Although a few regular army companies from Spain were sent to the frontier in the last quarter of the eighteenth century, the greater part of defense on the borderlands fell to men who had been born there.

Less than half of the soldiers in the *presidios* were described on the rolls as *españoles, europeos,* or *criolles* (Spaniards, Europeans, or born in the Americas of European parents). Almost 40 percent were described as mestizos, mulattoes, or persons of other mixed blood castes, known as *coyotes* or *lobos.* The remainder were Indians, who mostly served as scouts. The presidial companies in the east and center tended to be more Spanish; those in the west were more Indian and mixed blood. In fact three militia companies created in Sonora in the 1780s were recruited entirely from Indian villages. Literacy was low among the soldiers, although no lower than among the frontier population at large. But then requirements for enlistment were minimal: recruits had to be at least five feet two inches (1.5 meters) in height, have no noticeable facial defect, subscribe to the Roman Catholic faith, and attest to an understanding of the requirements and penalties of the military code. In addition to caste, enlistment rolls recorded recruits' age, place of origin, and hair and eye color.

The *presidiales* were called *soldados de cuera*—soldiers of leather—since they wore *cueras*. These were leather hides molded into a sort of doublet or jacket, a heavy, knee-length sleeveless coat composed of at least seven thicknesses of leather hides. The *cuera* was supposed to stop Indian arrows. Many were lined with quilted cotton for comfort. (The Spaniards had very early adopted quilted cotton armor from the Aztecs in preference to their own heavy European steel armor.) Beneath the *cuera* the *presidio* soldier wore a short jacket trimmed with red collar and cuffs, breeches, a hat made of blue woolen cloth, as well as leggings, a neckerchief, and shoes. Shortages of equipment on the frontier made these dress regulations the ideal rather than the reality.

The presidial soldier also carried an *adarga*, or oval shield about twenty-two inches (55 centimeters) in height made of buckskin, and a regulation *escopeta*, or musket, a smooth-bore muzzle loader with a thirty-eight-inch (95-centimeter) barrel, that fired a one-ounce (28-gram) bullet. By the rules he was also supposed to be armed with a lance eight to nine feet (about 2.5 meters) long and a sword. Burdened with an eighteen-pound (8.1-kilogram) *cuera*, a four-pound (1.8-kilogram) shield, a musket, a cartridge box, a lance, a sword, and perhaps a pistol, the *presidio* soldier was also supposed to carry twenty-two pounds (9.9 kilograms) of biscuit, twelve pounds (5.4 kilograms) of *pinole* (toasted ground corn), and a copper jar for heating water. Not surprisingly some critics considered the soldiers far too heavily loaded for mobile operations. The *comandante-general*, or commander in chief, of the frontier favored the creation of more light

cavalry companies that would be less impeded by heavy armor and weapons and more able to strike back at Indian raiders. Other reforms included cutting the required string of horses the soldier had to maintain from ten to six, since large herds of horses were expensive and constituted a tempting target for Indian horse thieves.

Garrison life was harsh and unrelenting. The rigors of life on the bleak and arid frontier, with its wearisome patrolling and guarding against Apache raids that might lead at any moment to sudden and violent death, could discourage the strongest of men. Desertion was a constant problem. The muster rolls of the *presidio* at Janos in Nueva Vizcaya in the 1780s show that out of a company of around 145 men, at least 1 and sometimes 2 men deserted every month. Spanish documents are full of descriptions of men deserting from the *presidios* and of the dispatch of parties to hunt them down, a tactic that further weakened the fighting readiness of a company. Sometimes desertions were wholesale rather than individual; when the Spaniards abandoned the Texas missions in 1693, four of ten soldiers escorting the Franciscan friars deserted to live among the Indians. In 1776 a frontier commander wrote the viceroy in Mexico City that a captive who had managed to escape from an enemy village (probably Apache) had reported it to be under the command of a Spanish deserter named Andrés. The Cavallero de Croix, the *comandante-general*, issued a proclamation in 1778 that bemoaned the gravity of the desertion problem, which he blamed in part on the willingness of the region's inhabitants to shelter fugitives.

THE *PROVINCIAS INTERNAS*

In 1776, in order to better organize and prosecute the war against the Apache and other enemies on the frontier, the Crown created a new administrative unit in the borderlands. The Provincias Internas, or Interior Provinces, consisted of Sonora, New Mexico, Nueva Vizcaya (Chihuahua), Coahuila, Nuevo León, Nuevo Santander, and Texas—that is, the entire frontier from the west coast to the border with Louisiana. This vast area was to be governed by a *comandante-general*. Beginning an inspection of the frontier,

263

Teodoro de Croix, the first commandant, assembled the first of a series of *juntas de guerra,* or councils of war, at Monclova in December of 1777. Present was Jacobo de Ugarte de Loyola, governor of Coahuila and an experienced soldier. Ugarte was one of a handful of seasoned fighters who understood the difficulties facing the Spanish in the war in the Gran Apachería.

The officers confronted some grim facts. They were not winning the war against the *indios bárbaros* (barbarous Indians), they were losing it. In the borderlands between 1771 and 1776, 1,674 people had been murdered and 154 captured, 116 ranches and haciendas had been abandoned, and 68,256 head of livestock had been stolen. Croix probed his commanders: What was the numerical strength of the Apache and of the Texas tribes, the so-called *indios norteños*? Should the Spaniards ally themselves with the Comanche (as the Marqués de Rubí had recommended ten years before) or the Lipan Apache? The consensus was for the Comanche and against the Apache.

Continuing his inspection of the frontier, Croix held another *junta de guerra* in Chihuahua in June and July of 1778. In attendance were Ugarte of Coahuila, Pedro Fermín de Mendinueta, the outgoing governor of New Mexico, and Juan Bautista de Anza of Sonora, the incoming governor of New Mexico, a soldier of legendary toughness and a veteran of many Indian campaigns. All approved the proposed Comanche alliance. Croix planned to ask Spain to approve another two thousand men for the frontier. But upon learning that Spain had entered the war against England in support of France and the American revolutionaries, Croix realized he would never get his additional soldiers and that plans for a grand offensive would have to be abandoned. The Crown now wished Croix to make peace with Indian nations as far as possible, and persuade them to settle down near missions and *presidios*.

The twin Spanish stratagem of alliance with the Comanche and what amounted to bribery of the Indians to be peaceful brought a measure of peace to the last decades of the Spanish presence in the borderlands. But this approach was little more than a holding action in the face of an increasingly enfeebled Spanish monarchy that could not afford adequately to defend its vast territory. A few more flying companies of light cavalry were organized, and a few *presidios* were shifted, but essentially the Spanish simply attempted to maintain their defenses in the face of an ever-active Indian threat on multiple fronts. Also pressing on their flanks were increasingly aggressive Anglo-Americans, who replaced the French and English as the prime European threat to the Spanish Empire in the Americas.

INDIAN ADAPTATION AND ACCULTURATION

The Indians of the Provincias Internas, after two centuries of cultural contact with Europeans, both French and Spanish, were not the savage nomads of the Chichimec wars. They were sophisticated in matters of war and peace, adopting foreign methods and materials of war, and were adept in playing the European powers against one another. Spanish law had long forbidden the arming of Indians; the French had no such scruples, however, and sold muskets to many tribes in the trans-Mississippi region. These tribes put pressure on Indian nations like the Comanche, who slowly moved south and west into the territories of other Indians, who in turn pressured the Apache tribes. The Apache ultimately vented their aggressions on the Spanish and other Indians. Thus European actions at one end of the borderlands could have repercussions at the other end of an immense frontier.

Perhaps the worst Spanish military setback in the history of borderland warfare occurred in 1720, when Pedro de Villasur led a party of forty-two Spaniards and sixty Indian allies on a reconnaissance foray into the Great Plains in search of French interlopers. On the South Platte River in present-day Nebraska, the force was attacked by a Pawnee war party and wiped out nearly to a man. The Spanish were never able to determine whether Frenchmen had actually been present in the camp at the time, but they had no doubt that French influence instigated the ambush.

Indians very quickly took to riding horses, which became the chief medium of exchange among members of tribes. Aside from their natural multiplication on the grasslands of the Great Plains, the prime source for more horses was raiding Spanish towns. These Indian forays also netted the natives reinforcement for their bands through the kidnapping of women and children. The Indians sometimes traded these abductees back to the Spaniards in exchange for goods, since they quickly learned that the Spanish would always ransom Christians, even Christian Indians. More often these people were absorbed into the tribes and became Indians themselves.

There were cases in New Mexico where European children had become so thoroughly Indianized that they refused to be ransomed by the Spaniards, preferring to remain with their adopted people. Some Indianized Europeans became leaders among their adopted people. In 1782 the *comandante-general* wrote in a dispatch about one José María Gonzales, captured by Indians (probably Apache) in a Sonora mining town in 1771. This man was identified as leading an attack of three hundred enemy Indians on the pueblo of Cucurpe, in Sonora, in 1781. The raid killed fifty-three people, resulted in the capture of forty-four others (including the apostate's two brothers), and the loss of the entire horse and cattle herd of Cucurpe. Gonzales, known among the Indians as Cayetano, lived in the sierra with an Indian wife and children and apparently had a devoted following among his adopted people. *Comandante-general* Croix urged that every effort be made to apprehend him, dead or alive. Another document from Texas spoke of negotiating a peace treaty with a Comanche chieftain known as *el de los ojos azules*—he of the blue eyes—indicating that the Native leader was either a converted European or the offspring of Europeans. And so genetically as well as culturally the Indians were affected by the Europeans.

The Indians also took up European arms and tactics. Governor Diego de Vargas of New Mexico was campaigning in Ute country when the Ute attacked him by mistake. Under a flag of peace, the Indians explained that the Pueblo Indians, the traditional enemy of the Ute, had, after the great revolt of 1680, taken to hunting in Ute country armed with muskets, mounted on horses, wearing leather hats and jackets, even carrying about a bugle looted from the abandoned Spanish towns. The Ute had taken Vargas's party of Spaniards for a band of their Pueblo enemies.

In 1758 two thousand warriors from the *norteño* tribes killed the missionaries at San Sabá and burned the mission to the ground; they then besieged the *presidio* soldiers in their fort, taunting them and displaying their firearms. When a Spanish retaliatory raid was attempted on an enemy camp on the Red River, the Spaniards found the Indians inside a fortified and moated palisade. The *norteños* fired muskets and even raised a French flag over the stockade. The Spanish were obliged to retreat. They were especially perturbed to uncover in an abandoned camp in eastern Texas signs that the Indians were being taught by Frenchman how to manufacture their own gunpowder, as well as an anvil and tools for repairing muskets.

Spanish and French pressures on Indian nations exacerbated relations among tribes that were already perpetual enemies and combined with the weakening influences of alcohol, disease, and trade that distorted traditional economic patterns to put enormous strains upon the fabric of Indian life. The borderlands had never been at peace; Indians had fought one another for centuries before the arrival of the Europeans. But the colonial powers' propensity for extending their European conflicts into the Americas intensified intra-Indian conflict.

After the Spanish made their strategic decision to favor the Comanche over the Apache, a series of peace negotiations was conducted in the late 1770s. Athanase de Mézières, commander of the Spanish garrison at Natchitoches (the easternmost fort in Texas), found the Comanche a noble people, commending to the authorities their bravery, their skill in war and horsemanship, and, above all, their honesty. Their abhorrence of the cannibalism of the *norteños* and their strict moral code of behavior impressed the Spanish, who, in conformity with the ethnocentrism of the era, believed most Indians, especially the Apache, to be ignorant savages. De Mézières hoped to induce the Comanche to settle on homesteads, and he traded agricultural implements with them in exchange for buffalo hides. The hope of settling the Indians was a vain one, for the amused natives had no inclination to abandon their nomadic buffalo-hunting existence. De Mézières fashioned peace in Texas with the eastern Comanche; with great delicacy Anza made a treaty with the western

Comanche and the Ute of northern New Mexico in 1786.

The Spanish tactic of bribing the Indians to maintain the peace resulted in both annual trade fairs at places like Taos, New Mexico, and the ceremonial presentation of gifts to Indian chieftains in locations like Nacogdoches. In July 1785, for example, 400 Comanches visited Taos to inquire into treaties of friendship with the Spanish. Within the month, 120 more warriors from 25 different *rancherías* followed, trading buffalo meat and hides, tanned skins, and horses to the Spanish and returning several muskets. (The Spanish still disliked the idea of the Indians possessing firearms, although there was little they could do to prevent them from acquiring European weapons.) The Indians showed their sincerity by going so far as to return two captives from New Mexico without the usual ransom. They departed promising to maintain peace with the Spanish and to make war on the common enemy, the Apache.

When a general treaty of peace and friendship was made in the fall of that year, lavish celebrations were necessary. The Spanish governor of San Antonio de Béxar, embarrassed at his empty coffers, asked the chieftains to postpone the celebrations for six months until suitable presents could arrive from Mexico City. The Comanche obligingly agreed. Fortunately, a trader arrived in time with appropriate gifts. The ensuing celebrations lasted three weeks, and the Comanche departed loaded down with ribbons, mirrors, needles, knives, and other items. In Santa Fe in January 1786, Governor Anza welcomed a Comanche leader named Ecueracapa, two hundred other chiefs, and representatives from some six hundred Comanche *rancherías* and negotiated a peace with the western Comanche. The Ute from the north sent representatives to join in the peace. The Apache, enemies of both Indian nations, were boxed in.

Another tactic the Spanish used, with double-edged results, was the deportation of Apache captured in war. Long *colleras,* or chain gangs, of Indian men, women, and children were dispatched south to Mexico City. From there the Indians were often sent to Cuba or other islands in the Spanish Main. But they often escaped from their chains; Seri from Sonora and Apache from other areas were reported to have

made their way back over incredible distances to rejoin their fellow tribesmen in fighting the Spanish.

Spain's powers grew ever more feeble as the eighteenth century ended. It unwisely went to war with revolutionary France in 1793, with the result that men, money, resources, and attention that might have gone to safeguard the frontier were diverted to other corners of the empire. A large group of Indian nations approached the Spaniards with requests for a grand alliance against a new threat, that of American settlers moving south and west in search of new lands to settle and farm. An unimaginative and complacent administration failed to grasp the opportunity being offered. The Louisiana Purchase of 1803 completely altered the strategic situation in the borderlands; the Indians who were allied with the Spanish, especially the Comanche, had to deal with a new culture, one that did not have the benefit of experience from three centuries of war and peace with borderland tribes, and one, furthermore, whose aims and objectives were very dissimilar from those of the Spanish. To the Spanish, the Indians presented an opportunity to bring to the Christian faith people they considered living in darkness. To the Anglo-Americans, the Indians were merely an obstacle to their settlement and peopling of the continent. The extermination of Indian society, a goal that the Spaniards had never contemplated, lay ahead.

WAR IN RETROSPECT

The expansion eastward and westward of a technologically superior West meant cataclysmic change for indigenous peoples from the Americas to the Philippines. But even within the context of imperialism and conquest, there were among the European powers vital differences. Spanish aims in the New World were quite different from those of the French, Dutch, English, and Anglo-Americans. The Spaniards clearly sought the absolute assimilation of Native peoples into their culture, which meant that Indians in the Americas were to be transformed into agrarian Catholic peons, obedient to church and Crown. This was not an unrealistic goal for peasant laborers living in organized, highly stratified

266

societies, like those of the Aztecs and Incas, once these empires had been militarily conquered.

But in the borderlands, the likelihood of fulfilling this goal was less promising. The Spaniards actually did achieve a measure of success with the semisedentary and sedentary tribes of the northwestern *rancherías* and Rio Grande Valley in New Mexico. These people already lived as farmers in semipermanent or permanent villages. The transfer of authority from their traditional leaders to missionary friars or their appointed agents of control was not a cataclysmic change. But the experiment usually failed when the friars tried to institute religious or cultural change with too heavy a hand or too rapidly. It also came undone when Spanish settlers encroached on Indian land or water sources or tried to press-gang Indians for labor in mines or on ranches. The result was revolt, followed by military repression.

Elsewhere on the borderlands, in the vast stretches of the Gran Apachería, where nomads had wandered for millennia hunting game and gathering roots, the goal of assimilation was completely unrealistic. Once the Indians had taken to riding horses, their newfound mobility made settlement and pacification a virtually impossible goal. Until disease, pressure from other Indian nations armed by other European powers, and decades of war forced them to reconsider, most nomadic tribes rejected the plans that Spain had for them. They were eager to accept European things of material value—iron implements, knives, blankets, guns, and above all, cattle and horses—but were resistant to European ideas, which included an exclusive god that would replace their own spirits and deities.

War had existed as a natural state in the borderlands even before the coming of the Europeans. This was because the region was a largely arid zone where resources to sustain life were limited and so were fought over. Of course, war that began as a struggle to survive had become a ritualized way of life and a source of pride in the male-dominated society of the hunting bands. The intrusion of Europeans on the scene, with their superior technology, their mobility, their desirable material wealth, and their exclusive religious ideology wrenched familiar patterns of war and peace into new paths. European pressures and European guns and horses stimu-lated old animosities among nations and gave new opportunities to tribes to expand their territorial hunting areas and their power. The horse gave birth to a new hybrid Indian society, which flourished for only a brief few hundred years before being extinguished at the end of the nineteenth century.

The Spaniards just barely managed to balance war and peace in the borderlands. Strategically overextended and perpetually short of funds adequately to support frontier defense, by the end of the eighteenth century they had managed to concoct a patchwork of alliances which combined bribery and threat in order to maintain peace on an enormous frontier peopled with mutually antagonistic tribes. With the termination of Spanish subsidies at the end of the colonial period in New Spain, the system collapsed. Spanish officers left their *presidios* when Mexico became independent. The succession of warring factions that passed for a government in Mexico City was too preoccupied with internal fighting to pay attention to a distant frontier. With the collapse and abandonment of the *presidio* system, the frontier was wide open, and Comanche and Apache raids resumed deep into Mexico. Not until the last decades of the nineteenth century was a well-organized and permanent regime, the "benevolent dictatorship" of Porfirio Díaz, able to tackle the Indian problem. A series of campaigns by the Mexican and United States armies pressured the last independent Apache bands into asking for peace in 1890.

Indians in North and South America like the Apache, the Araucanian of Chile, and the Tehuelche of Argentina were reduced to accepting government handouts and to living in poverty and misery on reservations, on a fraction of the land that was once theirs on which to roam about freely. But while the military war between Spain and the borderland Indians ended with victory for Europe, a religious, cultural, political, and economic struggle began, a struggle that continues today. Five hundred years after the encounter between America and Europe, Native Americans in both North and South America press for greater autonomy, for political and economic rights, for the restoration of control over their natural resources, and for the reconstruction of their culture and the restoration of their human dignity.

BIBLIOGRAPHY

Archer, Christon I. *The Army in Bourbon Mexico, 1760–1810.* Albuquerque, N.Mex., 1977. The leading study on the only professional army Spain ever maintained in its Mexican colony.

———. "The Deportation of Barbarian Indians from the Internal Provinces of New Spain, 1789–1810." *The Americas* 29, no. 3 (1973):1376–1385. Discusses the policy and consequences of deporting Apache from the borderlands to other areas of the Spanish Empire and includes some excellent stories of individual Indian escapes.

———. "Pardos, Indians, and the Army of New Spain: Inter-Relationships and Conflicts, 1780–1810." *Journal of Latin American Studies* 6, no. 2 (1974):231–255. Spain enlisted Indians and persons of mixed African ancestry in its militia, with sometimes unhappy results, given the prevailing ethnocentrism and racism within Spanish society.

Armijo, Isidro, trans. "Noticias que da Juan Candelaria de esta Villa de San Francisco de Albuquerque de edad de 84 años nació el año de 1692." *New Mexico Historical Review* 4, no. 3 (1929):274–297. An English translation is provided with the original.

Basso, Keith H., and Grenville Goodwin, eds. *Western Apache Raiding and Warfare, from the Notes of Grenville Goodwin.* Tucson, Ariz., 1971.

Bloom, Lansing L., ed. "A Campaign Against the Moqui Pueblos Under the Leadership of Governor and Captain-General Don Phelix Martínez, Beginning August 16th, 1716." *New Mexico Historical Review* 6, no. 2 (1931):158–226. Primary-source narration of an Indian campaign in New Mexico.

Brinckerhoff, Sidney B., and Odie B. Faulk. *Lancers for the King: A Study of the Frontier Military System of Northern New Spain, with a Translation of the Royal Regulations of 1772.* Phoenix, Ariz., 1965. Excellent study of the *presidio* system of the late eighteenth century, with color illustrations.

Daniel, James M., ed. and trans. "Diary of Pedro José de la Fuente, Captain of the Presidio of El Paso del Norte, August-December, 1765." *Southwestern Historical Quarterly* 83, no. 3 (1980):259–278. Good account of a presidial commander.

Depalo, William A., Jr. "The Establishment of the Nueva Vizcaya Militia During the Administration of Teodoro de Croix, 1776–1783." *New Mexico Historical Review* 48, no. 3 (1973):223–249. Describes the expansion of the militia system, which was the key to frontier defense in a time of Spanish economic contraction.

Gálvez, Bernardo de. *Instructions for Governing the Interior Provinces of New Spain, 1786.* Edited and translated by Donald E. Worcester. Berkeley, Calif., 1951. Excellent translation of the revised regulations for the *presidios* in the last decades of the eighteenth century.

Gerard, Rex E. *Spanish Presidios of the Late Eighteenth Century in Northern New Spain.* Museum of New Mexico Research Records, no. 7. Santa Fe, N.Mex., 1968.

Griffen, William B. *Apaches at War and Peace: The Janos Presidio, 1750–1858.* Albuquerque, N.Mex., 1988. Based extensively on primary archival sources of Apache relations with the Spanish, this study centers on the Nueva Vizcaya *presidio* at Janos. Griffen is the author of several other important ethnohistorical studies of central borderland Indians.

Hackett, Charles W. *Historical Documents Relating to New Mexico, Nueva Vizcaya, and Approaches Thereto, to 1773.* Publications of the Carnegie Institution of Washington, no. 330. 3 vols. Washington, D.C., 1923–1937. A vital three-volume compilation of Spanish documents on war and peace in New Mexico and Nueva Vizcaya. A treasure trove of material, especially on the aftermath of the Pueblo Revolt of 1680.

John, Elizabeth A. H. *Storms Brewed in Other Men's Worlds: The Confrontation of Indians, Spanish, and French in the Southwest, 1540–1795.* College Station, Tex., 1975. The finest single monograph on two hundred fifty years of war and peace in New Mexico and Texas. Massive, superbly documented, and quite sympathetic to the plight of Native Americans trapped between warring European powers.

Jones, Oakah L. "Pueblo Indian Auxiliaries and the Reconquest of New Mexico, 1692–1704." *Journal of the West* 2, no. 3 (1963):257–280.

Loomis, Noel M., and Abraham P. Nasatir. *Pedro Vial and the Roads to Santa Fe.* Norman, Okla., 1967. A pioneering book that traces the development of a true border society, part Indian and part European, in the trans-Louisiana-Texas borderlands. Notable for exploring the "French connection" in frontier acculturation.

Matson, Daniel S., and Albert Schroeder, eds. "Cordero's Description of the Apache—1796." *New Mexico Historical Review* 32, no. 4 (1957):335–356.

Moore, John Preston. "Anglo-Spanish Rivalry on the Louisiana Frontier, 1763–68." In *The Spanish in the Mississippi Valley, 1762–1804,* edited by John Francis McDermott. Urbana, Ill., 1974. Analyzes a much-neglected arena of borderland rivalry.

Moorhead, Max L. *The Apache Frontier: Jacobo Ugarte and Spanish-Indian Relations in Northern New Spain, 1769–1791.* Norman, Okla., 1968.

———. *The Presidio: Bastion of the Spanish Borderlands.* Norman, Okla., 1975.

———. "Spanish Deportation of Hostile Apaches: The

Policy and the Practice." *Arizona and the West* 17, no. 3 (1975):205–220. Moorhead's monograph on the *presidio* is the standard work on frontier forts and those who manned them. His work on Ugarte traces the course of Spanish-Indian policy over its most critical period of war and alliance. Moorhead's early death deprived borderland historiography of one of its most energetic and insightful scholars.

Powell, Philip Wayne. *Mexico's Miguel Caldera: The Taming of America's First Frontier.* Tucson, Ariz., 1977. Miguel Caldera, a Spanish soldier who was himself the son of a Spaniard and a Chichimec woman, is an early example of borderland mestization and acculturation.

————. *Soldiers, Indians, and Silver: The Northward Advance of New Spain, 1550–1600.* Berkeley, Calif., 1952. The standard work on the Chichimec war.

Secoy, Frank. *Changing Military Patterns on the Great Plains.* Monographs of the American Ethnological Society, 21. Locust Valley, N.Y., 1953. Examines in a broad context the effect of Spanish guns and horses on Indian war and Indian life among the nomadic hunters of the Great Plains.

Shelby, Charmion, trans. *Revolt of the Pueblo Indians of New Mexico and Otermín's Attempted Reconquest, 1680–1682.* Annotated by Charles W. Hackett. 2 vols. Albuquerque, N.Mex., 1942. Excellent primary source on the Pueblo Revolt.

Simmons, Marc. "Tlascalans in the Spanish Borderlands." *New Mexico Historical Review* 39, no. 2 (1964):101–110. Discusses the crucial role of Mexican auxiliaries in borderland colonization.

Spicer, Edward H. *Cycles of Conquest: The Impact of Spain, Mexico, and the United States on the Indians of the Southwest, 1533–1960.* Tucson, Ariz., 1971. Spicer is one of the deans of borderland ethnohistory. This work remains one of the foremost examinations of long-term effects of acculturation on southwestern Indian groups.

————. *The Yaquis: A Cultural History.* Tucson, Ariz., 1980.

Thomas, Alfred Barnaby. *Forgotten Frontiers: A Study of the Spanish Indian Policy of Don Juan Bautista de Anza, Governor of New Mexico, 1777–1787.* Norman, Okla., 1932.

————. *Teodoro de Croix and the Northern Frontier of New Spain, 1716–1783.* Norman, Okla., 1941. Alfred Barnaby Thomas was among the first of Herbert Eugene Bolton's students to continue his work in borderland history. He translated and reproduced a large body of primary documentation in four volumes on Spanish Indian policy on the frontier.

Peter A. Stern

SEE ALSO **The First Americans** and **Native American Religions;** and various essays in RACIAL INTERACTION.

THE EUROPEAN CONTEST
FOR NORTH AMERICA

For the courts of western Europe, two major objectives of oceanic trade and colonization were revenue and power at home. Rivalry among western European powers motivated much of their involvement in North America throughout the colonial period. Ambitious petitioners to these governments played upon fears and resentments of rival European states in seeking approval or support for voyages of discovery or piracy, for trading monopolies or their violation, for wars against American Indians or rival colonies, and for new settlements or improved fortifications. North America reflected, even more than it affected, the European military dominance that passed from Spain to the Netherlands and then to France and Britain.

BEYOND THE LINE, 1475–1559

Initially belligerence "behind God's back" in the Americas did not disrupt the peace of Europe; displays of power in America could, with minimal consequence, illustrate possession of power to European rivals. This separation began to dissolve as soon as Spain used new American wealth to help fund its European wars. For Spain's rivals the hunt for comparable discoveries failed. North America proved to be a land mass that yielded no fabulous mines and blocked westward

maritime access to the rich trade of the Orient. The contest shifted to attacks on treasures coming from Spanish America, and North America became a potential base for such raids.

Portugal, Spain, and Discovery

Spain and Portugal competed ferociously in the exploration of Europe's eastern Atlantic islands, establishing numerous precedents for later rivalry overseas. The Portuguese traded in slaves, gold, and spices along the West African coast from the 1440s and founded colonies of fishermen, wine producers, and sugar planters in the Azores, Madeira, and Cape Verde islands. Portugal and the Spanish kingdom of Castile both claimed the Canary Islands and each gained written papal endorsement as early as 1344. Although the native Guanches on some of the Canary Islands resisted conquest for nearly two centuries, by the fifteenth century Spanish missionaries had made some converts and Spanish colonists controlled enough Guanches land and labor to produce sugar, wine, and wheat for export to Spain.

The Portuguese-Spanish contest for the Canaries revealed methods of future overseas competition. Each condoned piratical raids on the other's colonial settlements and shipping, and this chronic fighting became part of full-scale war between the kingdoms in 1475. During this

War of Castilian Succession, the Portuguese not only invaded Castile, they also supported the Guanches in the Canary Islands against Castilian colonists. War ended with the 1479 compromise Treaty of Alcaçovas, the first European treaty concerning overseas colonies. It acknowledged Portuguese control of the West African trade and of all the newly discovered Atlantic islands except the Canaries, which were recognized as Spanish. Captured interlopers in either maritime domain were to be treated as pirates, condemned to die promptly and without appeal.

Exploration to the westward of these island bases was not a priority in the next decade. Christopher Columbus, the Genoese sailor experienced in Portuguese oceanic voyages, was not able to find sponsorship for his "enterprise of the Indies" in eight years of petitioning the courts of Portugal, Castile, England, and France. Genoese-born and Venetian-trained explorer John Cabot was equally unsuccessful at the Portuguese and Spanish courts. After Columbus's successful Caribbean voyage of 1492, accomplished with support from Queen Isabella of Castile (1451–1504), European competition emerged quickly.

Ensuing controversies with the Portuguese did not retard Columbus's voyages to consolidate and extend his discoveries, but Portugal threatened to send a powerful expedition in the same direction. Spain gained diplomatic support from Pope Alexander VI, whose *Inter Caetera* of 1493 gave Spain exclusive rights to land, trade, and religious authority in places discovered west of a longitudinal demarcation line drawn one hundred leagues (about three hundred miles, 480 kilometers) west of the Azores and Cape Verde islands. Since the disgruntled Portuguese authorities received no comparable assurances for their African ventures, the planned Portuguese expedition to the west was forestalled only by direct diplomacy between the kingdoms. The resulting Treaty of Tordesillas, signed 7 June 1494, moved the demarcation line to 370 leagues west of the Cape Verde Islands, halfway between that Portuguese territory and Columbus's Caribbean discoveries, and recognized the exclusive rights of each power to exploration, trade, and conquest in their generous respective spheres. The Iberian courts had appropriated and divided all the worlds they might find, without traditional papal confirmation or broader agreement with other rivals.

Although it was unmeasurable, since accurate longitudinal readings were not possible for another 250 years, the Tordesillas line was immensely significant for the subsequent history of the Americas. England's King Henry VII (1457–1509), who had earlier declined the Columbus enterprise, now challenged that line. Following up oceanic voyages of Bristol fishermen and merchants, John Cabot sailed to discover the Gulf of Saint Lawrence region in 1497 and 1498. The Portuguese court sent the Corte Real brothers out from the Azores to test the location of the line in the northwest Atlantic in 1500 and again in 1501, and a Portuguese fishing colony was established on Cape Breton Island from 1520 to 1525. Rapid Portuguese acquisitions in the South Atlantic, Indian Ocean, and China Sea, however, made the Portuguese more supportive of the treaty of 1494, and their interest in North American territory faded. They continued to fish the Grand Banks, but North America's main value to the Portuguese was that it blocked their rivals from direct access to the trading world of the Far East.

French Challenges, 1521–1559

Spain was unchallenged in America for a generation during which its colonists established modest settlements on Española (Hispaniola) and Cuba, but this changed with the Spanish conquest of Mexico in 1521. Rivalry between Hapsburg emperor Charles V (1500–1558), who was also king of Spain, and French king Francis I (1494–1547) would launch nearly forty years of the Hapsburg-Valois wars in Europe (1521–1559). French privateers captured Spanish ships laden with Mexican treasure as early as 1523. France's first official expedition to North America sailed the next year, led by the Florentine navigator Giovanni da Verrazzano, who scouted the coasts between the Carolinas and Nova Scotia searching in vain for rich trade or a passage to Asia. England's Henry VIII (1491–1547) also showed interest in North America in the wake of the success of Hernán Cortés and the claims staked by Verrazzano. Henry VIII sponsored John Rut's exploration of the coast between Labrador and Florida, followed by armed reconnaissance that made his the first non-Hispanic European vessel to enter Santo Domingo harbor (1527–1528). Jacques Cartier's first two voyages in 1534 and 1535–1536 claimed the Saint Lawrence River for France, but subsequent French attempts to found a colony at Cap Rouge, Quebec, lasted for only a few months in 1542–1543. French and English rivals had failed to find gold, silver, or civilizations comparable to the Aztec, Mayan, or Incan cultures and had failed to find a passage to Asia's wealth. The wealth of America appeared to be the wealth that could be taken from the Spanish.

As Spain's fleets became better protected, French harassment of Spanish American settlements intensified, climaxing in the complete destruction of Havana in 1555. The Peace of Cateau-Cambrésis of 1559, which brought the Hapsburg-Valois wars to a close, included an unwritten agreement that any depredations made west of the Canary Islands were not to disturb the peace of Europe. This line was very different from the Spanish-Portuguese line, not only in location, but in diplomatic authenticity and in intent. The Americas were informally acknowledged to be a permanent war zone; there was to be "no peace beyond the line."

SPANISH HEGEMONY, 1559–1621

Philip II (1527–1598), king of Spain from 1556, had excellent reasons for excluding the New World from the formal Cateau-Cambrésis treaty. Spanish claims to exclusive rights in the Americas were thereby maintained at a time when the Americas were becoming a major royal resource. The gold and silver production of Mexico and Peru had grown remarkably, constituting an average of 20 percent of Philip's annual revenues. This bullion was seen by all as the foundation of Spanish power in Europe, paying major armies, funding dissidents in neighboring countries, and backing Spanish government borrowing on a scale that transformed military contests.

Spanish American bullion had a greater impact on European rivalries than did any other colonial commodity, and from 1523 it became the target of pirates, privateers, and expeditions sponsored by Spain's royal competitors. Philip's advisers, however, had inherited and perfected

a convoy system that proved a formidable defense for the treasure fleets. Two well-defended fleets, averaging approximately sixty ships, left Seville's port of Saint Lucar each year for the Canaries and the Caribbean. The spring fleet, the *flota,* sailed for Mexico City's port of Vera Cruz, and the late summer *galeones* stopped at the Panama isthmus port of Nombre de Dios before wintering at better-protected Cartagena. The *galeones* began their return in the spring, timed to meet the Peruvian silver that was being carried by ship and then mule caravan across Panama to Nombre de Dios. The *galeones* and *flota* met at Havana and sailed back to Spain together. For the rest of the sixteenth century, North America was valued most as a base from which to attack these riches, and Spanish assertions of monopoly there and in the Caribbean were predicated on defending the treasure fleets.

French Huguenots
Philip II's emergence as enforcer of the Catholic Reformation made Spanish America a special target of Protestant invaders. As France dissolved into religiously oriented civil wars during the thirty years from 1559 to 1589, the French Calvinist Huguenots attempted a European settlement in North America to serve as a privateering base, a refuge, or both. Admiral Gaspard de Chatillon, count of Coligny (1519–1572), sent out a preliminary expedition in 1562 under the experienced navigator Jean Ribault. A small fort and settlement was established at Port Royal (South Carolina). Unsupported from home for a year, the garrison returned to France, and Ribault to England, just before a Spanish expedition razed the fort. A larger Huguenot fleet, carrying three hundred sailors and colonists under René Goulaine de Laudonnière, laid out a settlement at Fort Caroline (at what is now Jacksonville, Florida) in 1564. Internal dissent, poorly handled relations with neighboring Indians, and famine threatened the settlement, but the following year English adventurer John Hawkins arrived, as scheduled, with provisions and Ribault brought reinforcements.

The Spanish response was swift and decisive. Pedro Menéndez de Avilés commanded a powerful fleet that established what would be the first permanent European settlement in North America at Saint Augustine, Florida, before going on

INTERCOLONIAL BATTLE SITES, 1689–1748

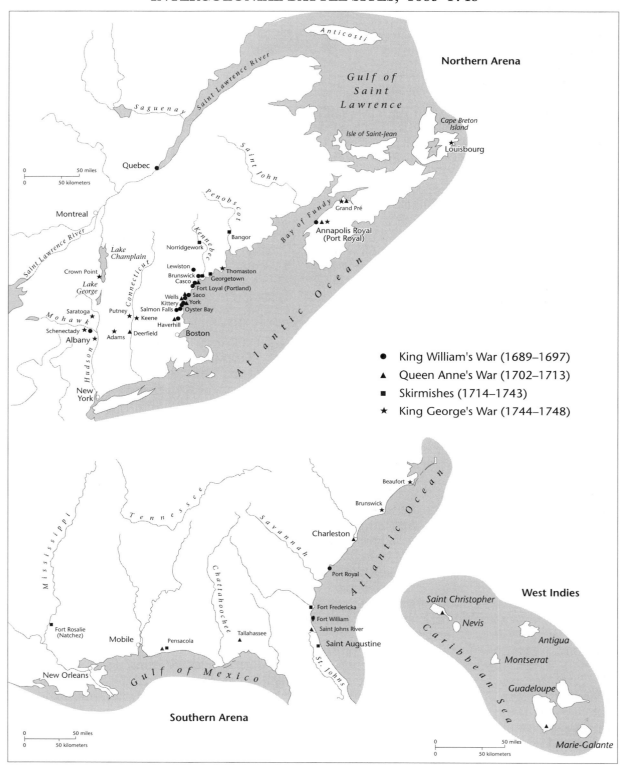

Northern Arena

Anticosti

Gulf of Saint Lawrence

Saint Lawrence River

Saguenay

Saint John

Cape Breton Island

Louisbourg ★

Isle of Saint-Jean

Quebec ●

Penobscot

Montreal ●

Kennebec

Bay of Fundy

★ ▲ Grand Pré
● ▲ ★
Annapolis Royal (Port Royal)

■ Bangor

Norridgework ■

Lake Champlain

Crown Point ★

Lewiston ●
Brunswick ■ ■ Thomaston
Casco ● Georgetown
● Fort Loyal (Portland)
Wells ● ● Saco
Kittery ▲ ● York
Salmon Falls ● Oyster Bay

Lake George

Connecticut

Mohawk

Saratoga ★
Schenectady ★ ●
Albany ★
Putney ★
Keene ★
Adams ★ ▲ Deerfield
Haverhill ●

Boston ●

Atlantic Ocean

Hudson

New York ○

● King William's War (1689–1697)
▲ Queen Anne's War (1702–1713)
■ Skirmishes (1714–1743)
★ King George's War (1744–1748)

0 ⊢——⊣ 50 miles
0 ⊢——⊣ 50 kilometers

0 ⊢——⊣ 50 miles
0 ⊢——⊣ 50 kilometers

Mississippi

Tennessee

Savannah

Chattahoochee

Beaufort ★

Brunswick ★

Charleston ▲

Atlantic Ocean

● Port Royal

Fort Rosalie (Natchez) ■

Mobile ○

Pensacola ▲ ▲

Tallahassee ▲

■ Fort Fredericka
● Fort William
▲ Saint Johns River

Saint Augustine

West Indies

Saint Christopher

Nevis

Antigua

Montserrat

Caribbean Sea

Guadeloupe

Marie-Galante ▲

New Orleans ▲

Gulf of Mexico

St. Johns

Southern Arena

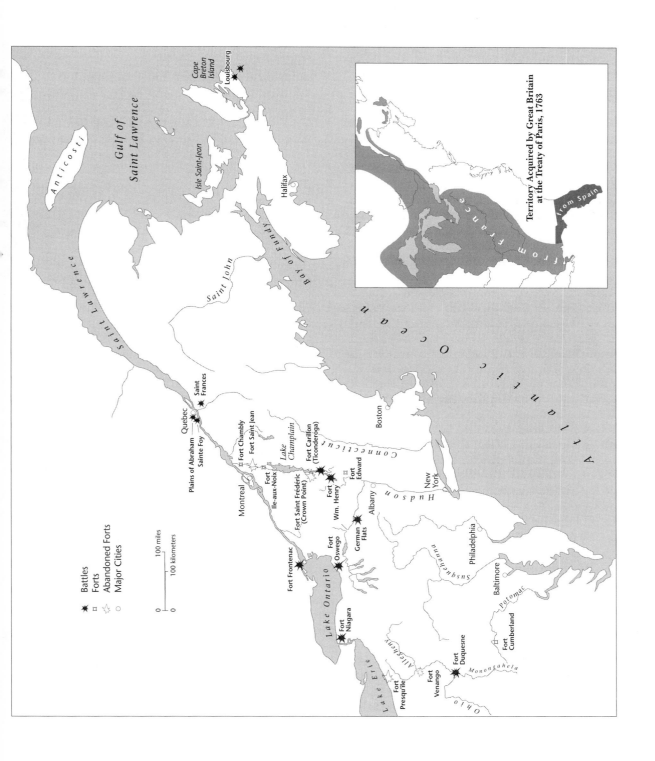

Battles ✹

Forts ⊡

Abandoned Forts ☆

Major Cities ○

0   100 miles

0   100 kilometers

Saint Lawrence

Gulf of
Saint Lawrence

Anticosti

Cape
Breton
Island

Louisbourg

Isle Saint-Jean

Halifax

Saint John

Bay of Fundy

Saint
Frances

Quebec

Plains of Abraham

Sainte Foy

Montreal

Fort Chambly

Fort Saint Jean

Fort
Île-aux-Noix

Lake
Champlain

Fort Carillon
(Ticonderoga)

Fort Saint Frédéric
(Crown Point)

Fort
Edward

Fort
Wm. Henry

Connecticut

Boston

Albany

New
York

Hudson

German
Flats

Fort
Oswego

Fort Frontenac

Lake Ontario

Fort Niagara

Lake Erie

Fort
Presqu'île

Fort
Venango

Fort Duquesne

Monongahela

Ohio

Allegheny

Susquehanna

Philadelphia

Fort
Cumberland

Baltimore

Potomac

Atlantic Ocean

Territory Acquired by Great Britain
at the Treaty of Paris, 1763

from France

from Spain

to storm Fort Caroline. About one hundred defenders escaped to France, but the rest, including Ribault, were killed. A three-vessel French privateering expedition of revenge surprised the Spanish garrison at Fort Caroline in 1567 and returned the brutality of taking no prisoners. Nevertheless the French Florida venture was over. Spanish Saint Augustine remained permanently to warn intruders away from the North American flank of the treasure route. French fishing and fur-trading voyages to the northern coasts were frequent thereafter, especially in the 1580s, but the next French attempt at colonization in North America was not undertaken until the ill-fated Sable Island, Nova Scotia, colony (1598–1603).

English Elizabethans

During his long reign, Philip II's relations with the English court were completely transformed. His marriage to Catholic Mary Tudor (1516–1558), which made him king-consort of England from 1555 until her death in 1558, strengthened traditional trade and diplomatic ties and allowed a few Englishmen access to Spanish navigational training. As Elizabeth I—who reigned from 1558 to 1603—gradually emerged as a leader of Protestantism, English interest in Spain's America became more belligerent. After John Hawkins's third illegal slave trading voyage to the Caribbean ended with his fleet being attacked near Vera Cruz by Spanish men-of-war in 1569, the English returned as pirates, led by Francis Drake. Spain had just become preoccupied with fighting what would be an unsuccessful Eighty Year War (1569–1648) to prevent Dutch independence, a struggle that became truly global after the Spanish conquest of Portugal in 1580 made both empires prey of the Dutch. The Elizabethans helped the Dutch spasmodically in Europe and helped themselves in America. Drake's Caribbean voyages of illegal trade and reconnaissance in the period 1570–1571 were followed by an immensely profitable raid in 1572, conducted in alliance with local Indians and runaway black slaves, which captured three Panama mule caravans carrying silver. Both of the Elizabethan colonizing undertakings in North America—Humphrey Gilbert's in Newfoundland (1583) and Walter Raleigh's at Roanoke Island (1584–1587)—were intended to create bases for raiding Spanish American shipping.

The Anglo-Spanish War (1585–1603) achieved neither party's offensive objectives. Spain's massive armadas failed in attempted invasions of England in 1588 and 1596. Drake's West Indian expedition of 1585 devastated the towns of Santo Domingo and Cartagena but failed to capture the treasure fleet or hold a permanent base. Drake and Hawkins both died on a major Caribbean raid in 1595–1596 that met effective Spanish resistance. Nevertheless, dozens of other English privateers became familiar with American waters, and captured prizes added greatly to England's merchant-marine and commercial resources.

The first Spanish concessions on her American monopoly, couched in ambiguous diplomatic language, soon followed. In the 1604 Anglo-Spanish Treaty of London, which fulfilled the ambition of King James I (1566–1625) for peace, the English insisted that they would respect the Spanish monopoly in America only where it was visible through effective occupation. The Dutch, whose global commerce already mocked the Spanish monopoly, particularly in Spain's newly acquired Portuguese empire, won similar equivocal concessions in the 1609 Antwerp negotiations for a twelve-year Spanish-Dutch truce.

Rival Colonies, 1603–1621

The French and English used the interlude of peace to establish what proved to be their first permanent settlements in North America. Samuel de Champlain accompanied a trading voyage to the Saint Lawrence in 1603. The following year he served as geographer on a venture that explored and carefully mapped Acadia (Nova Scotia) and the New England coast south beyond Cape Cod. The expedition also wintered on the Saint Croix River in 1604–1605 and at Port Royal (Annapolis Royal, Nova Scotia) in 1605–1606 before founding Quebec in 1608. The next summer Champlain accompanied a war party of Hurons and their allies fighting the Mohawk along Lake Champlain. At the same time Henry Hudson, sailing on behalf of the Dutch East India Company, was exploring, trading, and fighting Indians on the river that bears his name. By

1615 the Dutch had a trading post at Fort Nassau (Albany, New York) and a charter to all the land between New France and Virginia.

The English Virginia Company of London established Jamestown in 1607 and Bermuda in 1610, and the first English colony in Newfoundland started that year. Conflict between English and French colonies came quickly. In 1613 a Virginia Company vessel captured a French party attempting to establish a missionary base on Mount Desert Island off the coast of Maine and returned that autumn to burn both the Saint Croix site and Port Royal. The Plymouth branch of the same Virginia Company encouraged the group of Puritan separatists that founded the New England colony of Plymouth in 1620.

DUTCH LEADERSHIP, 1621–1678

The most effective infringement of the Spanish monopoly, and the one that would alter the terms of American settlement everywhere, was the Dutch conduct of their resumed war for independence from Spain. The Dutch West India Company, founded as the truce expired in 1621, focused its attention on the Spanish-controlled Portuguese empire of West African slaves, Brazilian sugar, and oriental spices. A powerful Dutch squadron captured the rich Brazilian capital of San Salvador (Bahia) in 1624, and the diversion of massive Iberian resources to recapture the city in 1625 allowed other intruders to establish themselves in the eastern Caribbean. French and English colonies began on uninhabited Saint Christopher's (Saint Kitt's) in 1624, and English venturers settled Barbados (1625), Anglo-Dutch Saint Croix (1625), Nevis (1628), Providence Island (1630), Antigua (1632), and Montserrat (1632). French conquest of Martinique and Guadeloupe from the tenacious native Caribs began in 1635.

Weakening of the Spanish hold on the eastern Caribbean coincided with a major growth of rival colonies in North America. With the Dutch at war with Spain, and France intriguing in the murderous Thirty Years' War (1618–1648) in Germany, the English strengthened their relative position in North America. Anglo-French commercial and court disputes and En-

glish support for a Huguenot revolt led to war in 1627. The French Company of One Hundred Associates (Compagnie des Cents-Associés) and a new Scottish and English Company were granted conflicting monopolies of the same Saint Lawrence area trade by the royal rivals. In 1628 the English company, headed by merchant Gervaise Kirke of London and Dieppe, sent a small fleet of privateers, including five of Kirke's sons, that captured nineteen French fishing boats, the French post at Tadoussac, and the entire first fleet of the Associates. The unsupplied Quebec settlement survived to face the Kirkes again in July 1629 but was forced to surrender. The Kirkes cooperated with the Scottish promoter of colonies, Sir William Alexander, who established a short-lived colony at Port Royal, Nova Scotia. The Anglo-French war had ended with the restoration of colonies by the Peace of Susa in April 1629, but the English and Scottish claimants did not relinquish their Canadian conquests until 1632. In the meantime the Massachusetts Bay Company, founded in 1629, launched a major migration to its new colony.

The most spectacular and unique success of the Dutch was the capture of the entire Spanish treasure fleet, including all *flota* and *galeones* and two hundred thousand pounds (90,000 kilograms) of silver, off Cuba in 1628. In addition to affording the Dutch West India Company investors a special 50 percent dividend, this capture crippled the Spanish treasury irreparably and weakened its war effort in Flanders. In the Caribbean, Spanish settlements and trade were scourged by subsequent fleets of the Dutch West India Company and by Dutch privateers. The Dutch went on to capture and keep several islands, including Curaçao and Saint Eustatius, bases from which illicit trade with Spanish America flourished once raiding had become less profitable. In the midst of these exploits, the Dutch West India Company made peripheral ventures to establish trading centers at New Amsterdam (New York City), Fort Orange (Albany, New York), and Fort Nassau on the Delaware. In 1639 and 1640 Spain's position was further weakened by disruption of the sailing of the treasure fleets, naval defeats in the English Channel and off Brazil, revolt in its own province of Catalonia, and Portuguese independence.

The Treaty of Münster and Beyond

When the long Dutch war with Spain concluded with the Treaty of Münster of 1648, the Spanish monopoly in America was formally ended. Spain not only conceded Dutch independence but also acknowledged Dutch possessions in America. America ceased to be a continuous war zone "beyond the line" of European diplomacy. The recognition that Spain conceded to Dutch colonies in 1648 would be extended to colonies of England after 1667 and to those of France after 1684. These privateering powers in America had come to possess West Indian plantation colonies both valuable and vulnerable enough to prompt extension to the New World of Europe's diplomatic curbs on war.

The rise of the Dutch from prosperous Spanish colony to independent republic and leading European maritime trading power was accomplished by 1648. The Dutch Republic had become a decentralized country of two million people. The Netherlands, as well as affluent portions of neighboring Germany and France where Dutch traders were influential, experienced prosperity and the birth of retail shopping and advertising associated with a consumer society. The Dutch fostered the growth of mass markets, including those for the previously exotic luxuries of sugar, tobacco, and spices.

The Dutch seaborne empire, built on Europe's most efficient shipping, replaced Spain's as the model of imperial success and provoked economic and military rivalries that affected trade and colonization everywhere. Dutch traders provided capital, expertise, shipping, and markets in introducing sugar production to the English and French Caribbean islands in the 1640s. This "sugar revolution" meant rapid expansion of the West African slave trade and West Indian slavery as well as expanding markets in the West Indies for North American provisions, horses, and lumber. Dutch merchantmen also paid higher prices and offered better products in exchange for the tobacco, furs, fish, and whale products of North America. The Dutch established few and relatively modest settlements in North America, primarily as trading stations. Like the Portuguese, whose oriental empire they had captured, the Dutch controlled a global trading network, not an empire of settlers. New Amsterdam grew slowly from 1624 and was less important than the fur-trading center up the Hudson River at Fort Orange.

The English and French were unable to compete with the Dutch traders and therefore answered with policies of economic exclusion and war. During the English Civil War (1642–1648), England had lost economic and political control of its American colonies. Its reassertion of economic power came with the Navigation Acts, developed in the half century after the first Navigation Ordinance of 1651 and designed deliberately to exclude Dutch shipping from the carrying trade of England and her colonies. The political supremacy of the new English republic was asserted by a naval squadron under George Ayscue, which forced the submission of the defiant royalist colonies of Barbados, Antigua, Bermuda, and Virginia in 1651–1652. Dutch merchantmen, violating an English trade ban against these colonies, were confiscated. As a result colonial staple products were increasingly marketed through London.

Dutch Wars, 1652–1678

War became an extension of trade rivalry favored by the uncompetitive English and French. This forced the Dutch to increase spending on convoys, forts, and marine insurance, thereby lessening their comparative price advantages.

The first of the Anglo-Dutch wars (1652–1654) was a naval war fought in the English Channel and the North Sea. English attacks on homeward-bound Dutch merchant fleets were aided by geography, the prevailing westerly winds, and larger and better armed (though less numerous) naval vessels. The English captured between one thousand and seventeen hundred Dutch merchant vessels with which to expand and improve their merchant marine. Now the English could carry the traffic of the exclusive English trading empire that had already been asserted and defended. North American possessions were largely neutral in this war, though Connecticut forces seized the Dutch fort at Hartford in February 1654. An English naval expedition under Admiral Robert Sedgewick was sent against New Netherland in 1654 but arrived in Boston after the Anglo-Dutch peace. Despite peace with France, Sedgewick used this opportunity to capture all the major settlements in neighboring French Acadia.

THE EUROPEAN CONTEST FOR NORTH AMERICA

The Peace of Westminster in 1654 brought mutual recognition of English and Dutch overseas possessions, but it left the boundaries undetermined and accepted English insistence upon exclusive trade within its empire. Oliver Cromwell, lord protector of England, anxious to end this war between Europe's most powerful Protestant republics, had made two proposals: a union of the two and an agreement to divide the world between them, as the Spanish and Portuguese had done in the Treaty of Tordesillas—the latter proposal indicating English ambitions to take all of the Americas except Brazil. The Dutch had declined both suggestions.

In the wake of this war, Cromwell launched another surprise attack in America without a formal declaration of war, this time against the Spanish West Indies. In 1655 this "Western design" failed in its attack on Santo Domingo but captured the thinly populated island of Jamaica. This raid in America affected England's diplomatic options in Europe. England joined France in a war against Spain (1655–1660) in which English merchant shipping fell to Spanish privateers while the Dutch remained profitably neutral.

The English monarchy, restored in 1660 under Charles II (1630–1685), was slow to follow popular anti-Dutch sentiments, despite incidents in the Baltic, West Africa, and the East Indies and anger over the king's marriage to the Portuguese Catholic princess Catherine of Braganza in 1662. In 1664 the English initiated hostilities in peacetime with predatory raids on Dutch colonies. A naval squadron under Captain Robert Holmes took Dutch forts and ships along the West African coast. Another squadron, under Major Richard Nicholls, captured New Amsterdam in August 1664 without firing a shot. The second Anglo-Dutch war (1665–1667) was not officially declared until the following March, and English disruption of Dutch commerce in the English Channel and the North Sea was pursued successfully for the first year. Fiscal difficulties weakened the English thereafter. In 1667 they were unable to fit out a main battle fleet, and the best of it was lost when the Dutch raided the Medway River dockyards in June 1667. The Peace of Breda was concluded a month later.

This second Anglo-Dutch war had reached America more clearly than any previous European contest. The English capture of New Netherland in 1664 had been one of the provocations for war. Dutch admiral Michel Adriaanszoon de Ruyter (1607–1676) circled the North Atlantic in 1665, retaliating in West Africa, attacking Barbados, and raiding commerce in the Leeward Islands and at Newfoundland. A small Dutch privateering squadron captured an eighteen-vessel English tobacco convoy in the James River, Virginia. The French had joined the Dutch in 1666, offering little effective assistance in the European war but using the opportunity to raid in America. The English colonies on Saint Christopher's, Antigua, and Montserrat were captured and looted by the French. French authority was imposed upon Saint Eustatius and Tobago. Dutch Caribbean trade was severely disrupted, and it never entirely recovered. The Peace of Breda confirmed English possession of New York in exchange for Surinam, and the French exchanged the English portions of Saint Christopher's for Acadia. The allocation of West Indian colonies was stabilized by Breda and would change little over the next century.

France drew the English into an alliance against the Netherlands in 1672, in a war without colonial preliminaries or provocations. France quickly captured four of the seven Dutch provinces by land, but the larger Anglo-French naval forces were unable to gain a clear victory in three major fleet actions the following summer. Parliamentary resistance and popular anti-French feelings forced the English out of the war in 1674. A Dutch squadron recovered the Caribbean islands of Saint Eustatius and Saba from the English before recapturing New York as easily as it had been taken by the English a decade earlier. The colony reverted to the English in exchange for Surinam in the 1674 Treaty of Westminster, which ended English participation in a Franco-Dutch war that continued until 1678.

In this Franco-Dutch contest between Europe's leading army and its leading navy, the Dutch quite logically took the initiative in America. De Ruyter's attack on Martinique in July 1674 failed, however, and French fleets in the Caribbean were able to check Dutch naval and privateering squadrons in 1676. The next year a French squadron under Jean d'Estrées captured the Dutch West African trading station at Goree and the West Indian island of Tobago before being wrecked as it approached the Dutch stronghold at Curaçao. French privateers in European waters and buccaneers in the Caribbean effectively disrupted Dutch trade and that of their Spanish allies, while French armies defeated the Dutch in the Low Countries.

The Peace of Nymwegen in 1678 included French treaties with both the Dutch and the Spanish. France and the Netherlands recognized each other's overseas possessions. France accepted free trade within Europe, reversing prohibitions and discriminatory tariffs that had been in place for a decade but excluding the Dutch from trade in the French colonial empire. The treaty also crippled the new colonial ambitions of the Danish and Brandenburg allies of the Dutch. The French treaty with Spain called for a restitution of all possessions taken during the war but included no mutual recognition of colonies, so French buccaneers still had free rein in the Caribbean.

By 1679 the French had emerged triumphant, and their only challenger in the New World was their erstwhile ally, England. By this time the Spanish had abandoned all pretense to exclusive rights by prior discovery and accepted effective occupancy as the basis for claims. The convention that war and peace in Europe extended to America became fully operational after the Franco-Spanish Truce of Ratisbon in 1684.

ANGLO-FRENCH COLONIAL WARS, 1689–1748

By the 1680s the France of Louis XIV (1638–1715) was the undisputedly dominant power in western Europe. With some twenty million people, France had ten times the population of the Dutch United Provinces, four times that of England and Wales, and nearly three times the population of Spain. Moreover France displayed growing efficiency in royal control of the state, in tax collection, economic policy, and naval power under Jean-Baptiste Colbert (1619–1683), and in the management and training of the largest peacetime army Europe had ever known, under the Marquis de Louvois (1641–1691).

French power was also overwhelmingly internal and therefore less vulnerable than had been either Spanish hegemony, based upon prosperous colonies in northern Europe and America, or Dutch dominance, based upon European and world trade. France, unlike Spain or the Dutch, could not be severely weakened by attacks in America. The Canadian fur industry and the Martinique and Guadeloupe sugar colonies contributed to French wealth and would be defended vigorously, but neither was crucial to France's capacity to make war in Europe.

Serious European interest in America was evident only at the beginning and end of wars fought in Europe. At the beginning there was a race to take news of war to America in the hope that easy conquests of diplomatic value could be made at the expense of unprepared enemies. Once war in Europe approached its end, there were again advantages in using military resources overseas, where they would not inhibit European peace negotiations and might gain fortresses or colonies for diplomatic bargaining. The long duration of the struggle for North America owed much to this pattern of limited and spasmodic European involvement.

War of the League of Augsburg (King William's War), 1688–1697

French aggression along its eastern borders during ostensible peacetime gradually drew its enemies together. From 1686 the Holy Roman Emperor, Spain, Sweden, Saxony, and the Palatinate belonged to the anti-French League of Augsburg. England had been a secret ally of France from 1670 to 1685 but became less reliable during the three-year reign of Charles II's Catholic brother and immediate successor, James II (1633–1701), who faced mounting internal opposition. The Anglo-French Treaty of Whitehall, negotiated in 1686, sought to prevent war in America, which was threatening due to clashing interests in Hudson Bay, Acadia, Iroquois country, and the Caribbean. Peacetime trade between the empires was forbidden by this agreement but never confirmed in trade laws. William of Orange (1650–1702), princely stadtholder of the Netherlands, led an invasion of England in support of rebellion against James II and became joint monarch, as William III, with his wife, James's daughter Mary. He then drew England into the Franco-Dutch war that Louis XIV had already declared. In May 1689 England and the Netherlands joined the League of Augsburg in war against Louis XIV.

Although it remained a sideshow in the massive struggle of armies and fleets in Europe, Anglo-French rivalry intensified in North America during the late seventeenth century. Canadian explorers and traders entering the Ohio Valley and Illinois country in the 1670s and 1680s roused the powerful Iroquois confederacy to war against New France again in defense of traditional hunting grounds and fur-trading networks that supplied the English at Albany. The well-armed and numerically superior Iroquois forced humiliating terms on a French force in 1683. A new governor of Canada, veteran soldier Jacques-Réné de Briasay, marquis de Denonville, was appointed to seek revenge. English competitors in the fur trade were attacked first by an overland expedition that captured three trading posts and the peltry of the Hudson's Bay Company in 1686. The next year a major expedition destroyed Seneca villages and captured English traders among the Iroquois. A peace negotiated in 1688 was not ratified by the Indians. Instead the Iroquois, hearing of the outbreak of the Anglo-French war in Europe in 1689, renewed their own war by attacking and destroying the Canadian settlement at Lachine in the summer of 1689. Simultaneously the Abenaki Indians, who had been at war with New England since 1688, captured the English fort at Pemaquid, Maine. Indian wars against European colonists were reinforced and extended by this Anglo-French conflict but had not been caused by it.

France won the military initiative in America in 1689. In the Caribbean the French were first to deliver news of war and again captured the English portions of the sugar island of Saint Christopher's. The first colonial blows in North America were not struck until early in 1690, when Canadians and Indians raided Schenectady in New York, Salmon Falls in New Hampshire, and Falmouth in Maine. Intended to paralyze numerically superior but politically divided opponents, this initiative also provoked what would become a predictable English colonial response: a major conventional expedition against Canada. Sir William Phips led both the preliminary expedition that captured Port Royal, Acadia, in May 1690 and the ill-fated, two-pronged attack on

Quebec that summer and autumn. Thereafter, with little direct involvement of either mother country, colonial war reverted to occasional raids and supporting initiatives by allied Indians on both sides.

Although the French navy defeated the Anglo-Dutch combined fleet decisively off Beachy Head in July 1690, an Anglo-Dutch victory at La Hogue in 1692 encouraged the French administration to avoid fleet confrontation and to shift even more resources to the army. For the remainder of the war, the French maritime offensive became a very successful privateering war against English and Dutch commerce. English sugar and tobacco fleets were captured in European waters, with the most prizes being taken in 1694 and 1695.

The war in Europe had produced no clear victor, only exhausted belligerents. The Peace of Ryswick ended the war in September 1697, returning all prisoners and possessions taken in North America during the conflict. The North American war, however, may not have been a stalemate. The war had proved particularly hard on the Iroquois, who rightly complained that their English colonial allies had left them unsupported against the Canadians. Besides loss of lives, the Iroquois had suffered from severe dislocation of their fur trade. The Iroquois neutrality treaty of 1701 represented Canada's major accomplishment of this war, in addition to surviving a numerically overwhelming colonial enemy.

War of the Spanish Succession (Queen Anne's War), 1702–1714

The death of the last Spanish Hapsburg king, the sickly Charles II of Spain (1661–1700), had been anticipated for the entire thirty-five years of his reign but still provoked war among the related dynasties of western Europe when it finally occurred. Louis XIV, whose kingdom was bordered by Spanish territory on all land frontiers, had sought the Spanish inheritance by marrying Maria Theresa, the eldest daughter of Philip IV (1605–1665). Louis had pursued the same prize by negotiations with Philip IV and later with William III of England in treaties to partition the Spanish Empire. Louis also fought to acquire the Spanish Netherlands (1665–1668), Spanish possessions in Italy, and finally the global War of the Spanish Succession. His enemies, led by William III, tried to curb France's hegemonic power in western Europe and to gain parts of the Spanish monarchy's vast possessions for themselves.

This European war was more extensive than the last, with major battles along the Spanish coast, the Po Valley, and the Danube. These battles involved larger forces suffering higher casualties, reaching 30 percent in the Battle of Blenheim in 1704 and as many as 190,000 were in the Battle of Malplaquet in 1709. Louis the XIV, having outlived his enemies, his best ministers, and most of his heirs and resources, sued for peace beginning in 1709. Five years later, after a separate peace with England, a cluster of eleven treaties, known collectively as the Treaty of Utrecht, brought this massive war to a close.

The war in America was, in general terms, a strategic rerun of the previous struggle. The Peace of Ryswick had been particularly short and uneasy in the Caribbean, for privateers had become pirates and continued their raiding, and English and French naval squadrons protected trade while awaiting a declaration of war permitting them to strike. This time the English won the race to bring news of war, and they conquered the French portion of Saint Christopher's. In North America the new war did not reinforce existing wars between colonists and Indians, and therefore it began a little more slowly. Again the first blows were struck by Canadian and Indian raiding parties, which attacked New England frontier settlements in the summer of 1703 and destroyed Deerfield, Massachusetts, in February 1704.

The Massachusetts response again centered upon a large expeditionary force to conquer Port Royal and Quebec. After two years of waiting for English help, the New Englanders raided Port Royal twice in 1707 but failed to conquer this privateering base on their own. Ambitious plans for a two-pronged attack on Canada in 1709 aborted when the promised British assistance was diverted to Portugal. (England and Scotland, having shared the same kings for a century, joined to form Great Britain in 1707.) In 1710, with peace negotiations under way in Europe, Britain sent a five-vessel squadron and four hundred marines to assist the New England expedition that took Port Royal and renamed it Annapolis Royal, Nova Scotia. A new govern-

ment in Britain, seeking to position itself well during peace negotiations, sent the luckless Walker expedition to capture Quebec in 1711. In this larger replay of the Phips venture of 1690, some sixty-five hundred men, predominantly seasoned regular troops, sailed in a forty-five-vessel armada to Quebec while twenty-three hundred men traveled overland by the Lake Champlain route. Nine ships of the fleet and nine hundred men were lost in fog and gales in the Saint Lawrence, prompting a decision to abort the attack. The English counterstrike had failed again, and the war in North America was all but over.

Although New France again survived the war against odds so great that surviving meant winning, it lost at the peace table. In a separate peace with the British, France ceded claims to Newfoundland, except for fishing rights on the north shore, and acknowledged British control of Acadia, though the boundaries would still be disputed. Hudson Bay was recognized as British territory as well, and a clause implied British sovereignty over the Iroquois. Saint Christopher's was also confirmed as an exclusively British possession. The British, who sought compensation overseas for a generation of support for France's European enemies, gained more than did British colonies. Hudson Bay and Newfoundland were British commercial enterprises rather than colonies. Nova Scotia became a new royal province, not a political addition to the colony of Massachusetts, which had invested so much in its conquest.

The Peace of Utrecht, 1714–1739

Western Europe was free from a general war for twenty-five years after the peace at Utrecht. Not only did Britain and France refrain from war, they actively cooperated to keep peace in Europe. This Anglo-French *entente*, championed by leading ministers Robert Walpole and Cardinal André-Hercule Fleury, protected the internal stability of both countries during the first years of the Hanoverian dynasty in England and the regency for young Louis XV (1710–1774) in France.

This diplomatic cooperation did not preclude aggressive economic policies that brought rapid and unequal economic growth, particularly in colonial commerce. French West Indian sugar colonies outpaced the British, becoming the major suppliers of cane sugar to Europe. Meanwhile, an independent Spain had become a junior partner in the Bourbon Family Compact of 1733 that closely allied the French and Spanish Crowns, which Europe had fought to keep separate.

In North America the peace was an uneasy truce marked by intense competition for trade and land. British colonial population growth and land hunger brought friction with rival European colonists as well as with Indian neighbors. On the poorly defined southern frontier, the Yamassee War (1715–1718) pitted South Carolina expansionists against the outraged Yamassee and a broad group of their Native American allies, encouraged by the Spanish in Florida.

French development of Louisiana was also rapid during the early years of the peace. The Acadian frontier was uneasy: boundaries were disputed, Acadians refused oaths requiring them to fight their former monarch, British authorities vacillated, and Canadian governors schemed. The Abenaki were driven even closer to the French by the outrages of Massachusetts expansionists before and during Dummer's War (1722–1725). More ominous was the massive French investment in fortifications in North America during the peace. France founded Fort Toulouse (1717) on the Alabama River plus New Orleans (1718) and Louisbourg on Cape Breton Island (begun 1720) to challenge ship access to the two great rivers of the interior, the Mississippi and the Saint Lawrence. The French also rebuilt Fort Niagara (1720) and built Fort Saint Frédéric (1731) on Lake Champlain. These two were not boundary defenses against expanding British settlements but strong forward bases for trade or war. The British responded lamely with poorly designed Fort Oswego (1726) on Lake Ontario. They also built Fort King George (1721) in South Carolina and established the colony of Georgia (1733) on the southern frontier with Spanish Florida. The European governments tried to limit the level of aggression between their colonies, but the rivalries were fierce and the new levels of fortification would eventually mean new levels of warfare in America.

Anglo-Spanish War of Jenkins Ear, 1739–1744

Britain and Spain were at war briefly in 1718–1719 and 1727–1728, but these conflicts did not become prolonged or general. Wholesale British and British colonial violations of trading restrictions in Spanish America during the 1730s were met with bullying by Spanish privateers and *guarda costas*, including one incident in which a Captain Jenkins had an ear severed. Robert Walpole's government negotiated compensation for Spanish confiscations in the Convention of Pardo (1739), but Spain refused to pay in the face of mounting British belligerence. British clamor for a predatory war against Spain overwhelmed Walpole's political resistance, and British naval squadrons in the Mediterranean and Caribbean were ordered to take Spanish prizes as reprisal for nonpayment. In 1739 a small squadron under Admiral Edward Vernon captured Porto Bello on the Isthmus of Panama, inflaming British and colonial enthusiasm for a war that was not declared until later that year.

The major British initiative was a massive amphibious attack upon Cartagena in 1741. Some three thousand Americans, called such by the British authorities for the first time, joined what they thought would be a buccaneering raid but which became a military disaster resulting in the death from disease of more than half of them. Another grand design of British imperial cooperation, like the Walker expedition of 1711, had ended in disillusionment. The war continued for three more years—essentially as a privateering war with minor raiding on the Georgia-Florida frontiers after an exchange of failed invasions in 1740 and 1742—before coalescing with the broader European War of the Austrian Succession.

War of the Austrian Succession (King George's War), 1744–1748

Despite the prelude of Anglo-Spanish conflict in the Caribbean, the War of the Austrian Succession developed from European dynastic upheaval. The sonless Hapsburg emperor Charles VI (1685–1740) had negotiated with the powers of Europe to ensure that his daughter, Maria Theresa (1717–1780), would be accepted as his successor. When Charles died in 1740, the new king of Prussia promptly provoked war by invading Austrian-controlled Silesia. The following year France joined the Prussians in what rapidly became a broader European war. Although Britain and France did not go to war with each other until 1744, Britain's King George II (1683–

1760), in his capacity as elector of Hanover, had led an army successfully against the French at Dettingen the previous year. In 1745, after a major French victory at Fontenoy, France supported "the '45," a Scottish uprising under Charles Edward Stuart against George II that took nearly a year to suppress. The European fighting thereafter proved Prussian and French military superiority. The Peace of Aix-la-Chapelle (1748) ended the war with recognition of Maria Theresa as Hapsburg empress and the Prussian possession of Silesia.

The war in North America was essentially fought with local resources, as had been the case in the two previous Anglo-French wars. The French governor of Louisbourg initiated hostilities by capturing the New England fishing station at Canso, Nova Scotia, in May 1744. As previously, a French raid provoked a New England invasion. New Englanders taken to Louisbourg as prisoners of war learned of the fort's weaknesses and the garrison's dissensions. Upon exchange these prisoners helped Governor William Shirley of Massachusetts to plan the successful attack on Louisbourg in 1745 by a four-thousand-man New England force supported by a Royal Navy squadron of twelve men-of-war. In 1746 the British planned to extend this victory with an attack on Quebec, while the French planned to retake Louisbourg with a massive armada of seventy-six ships commanded by Jean-Baptiste-Louis-Frédéric de La Rochefoucauld de Roye, duc d'Anville (1709–1746). The promised British fleet did not sail, and d'Anville's expedition was destroyed by storms, epidemics, and calms in which food and water shortages occurred and epidemics were aggravated. The three thousand deaths in this fleet exceeded all other losses in the North American war.

Canadian raids increased after the fall of Louisbourg. Abenaki and Micmac warriors forced the conquered Acadians into more active opposition to the British and raided frontier settlements in Maine, New Hampshire, and Massachusetts. In August 1745 Fort Massachusetts was captured and its garrison taken captive to Canada. Saratoga, New York, was captured and destroyed that November by a Canadian and Indian force led by Paul Marin. In the winter of 1746–1747, a daring winter raid on Grand Pré, Nova Scotia, overwhelmed a surprised New England garrison. When Europe made peace in 1748, North America obeyed the requirement to return captures and exchange prisoners.

THE SEVEN YEARS' WAR 1754–1763

Never before had Europeans lavished resources on a fight expressly for North America as Britain and France did between 1755 and 1760. The ancient Anglo-French rivalries for influence in Europe, for trade, and for territory had become global, and North American commerce was increasingly seen by both parties as a significant source of both their own and their rival's power. Appropriately the initial sparks of a global war were struck in the remote forests of the Ohio Valley two years before the war began in Europe resulting in a nine-year war on American soil.

By 1748 British colonial traders and settlers were breaking through the Appalachian mountain barrier into the upper Ohio Valley. In 1749 the Ohio Company of Virginia was granted a charter by the British government to land already claimed by the British, the French, the Iroquois confederacy, and the numerous Indian peoples of various tribes who had settled this hunting area during the previous generation. This British initiative prompted the Canadian government to send an expedition to the area with more than two hundred men and a number of lead plates proclaiming French sovereignty. Canadian conferences with Seneca, Delaware, Mingo, Shawnee, and Miami councils reinforced the suspicion that the lead plates would not substitute for occupation in the coming confrontation. Governor Ange Duquesne de Menneville, marquis Duquesne, took the military initiative in 1752, sending a Canadian and Ottawa Indian raiding party to capture and destroy a Miami settlement at Pickawillany that was friendly to British American traders. By the end of that year he also had a fort built at Sandusky Bay and in 1753 had two more forts erected between Lake Erie and the Allegheny River. The rather quixotic Virginia reply was to send young George Washington to newly built Fort Le Boeuf, bearing an order that the French leave, which was ignored.

By the end of 1753 Virginia's governor was authorized by Britain to use force to expel the French from British-claimed territory in the Ohio Valley. On their way to the forks of the Ohio River in 1754, Washington and a force of Virginia militia ambushed a small Canadian party, killing ten, including their leader, Ensign Joseph Coulon de Villiers de Jumonville, and taking the other twenty-one as prisoners. The "assassination of Jumonville" in peacetime caused both a diplomatic furor when the news reached Europe and the immediate pursuit of Washington's militia by a larger force of French, Canadian, and Indian warriors. Washington, unable to escape, built the aptly named Fort Necessity, which he was soon forced to surrender. French victory was symbolized that summer in the capture and completion (as Fort Duquesne) of an unfinished Virginia fort at the headwaters of the Ohio River. Peace had evaporated in the forests of the Ohio Valley, and the Virginians had initiated more than they could complete. Virginia's active rivalry with Canada was new and had a major impact on colonial warfare. For one thing a population four times that of Canada joined the already unequal colonial contest. For another this leading tobacco colony was important enough to draw unprecedented British support for its ambitions.

British military investment in America began when two understrength Irish regiments, commanded by General Edward Braddock, were sent to Virginia in 1755. The British government of Thomas Pelham-Holles, duke of Newcastle, was apprehensive about costs and the possibility of war with France at a time when Britain had no reliable major European ally. Newcastle was backed into this American commitment by more aggressive voices led by the king's son, William Augustus, duke of Cumberland, captain-general of the British army. The plan was to eliminate ostensible French encroachments on British-claimed territory at Fort Duquesne and Fort Saint Frédéric as well as at Forts Beauséjour and Gaspéreau on the Acadian frontier. This military initiative in America was to be protected by a naval blockade in American waters that was under orders to take or sink French troop ships.

Cumberland's strategy of 1755, with Fort Niagara added as a target when the extent of British colonial recruitment became known, proved a disaster. Despite the advantage of surprise, Vice Admiral Edward Boscawen's squad-

ron captured only two French troop ships in the fogs off Newfoundland. France delivered four times as many regular troops to North America as did the British in the first year of hostilities. Braddock and his army were surprised and destroyed before reaching Fort Duquesne. British colonial forces failed to reach Fort Niagara, and those headed for Fort Saint Frédéric were stopped by a bloody battle at Lake George, after which each side built a fort, British Fort William Henry and French Fort Carillon (Ticonderoga). The only British success was the capture of Acadian Forts Beauséjour and Gaspéreau by a New England force led by British colonel Robert Monckton. The expulsion of the Acadians was among its consequences.

Vaudreuil's Offensive, 1756–1757

War was formally declared in Europe in May 1756, after Britain and France completed a "diplomatic revolution" in their alliances. Britain joined Prussia against France and Austria, resulting in an initial French victory over the British at Minorca matched by Prussian victories over Austria and its German allies. In North America the strategic initiative passed to the French and was exploited effectively by the new, native-born Canadian governor, Pierre-François de Rigaud, marquis de Vaudreuil-Cavagnal. The defeat of Braddock had reinforced Canada's Indian alliances even more effectively than had the raids with which Canada had opened the previous wars, and the Battle of Lake George had displayed the courage of a small group of French regulars. Despite blockades of the French coast, the British Royal Navy failed to catch a convoy bringing one thousand regulars to Canada in 1756. While the British struggled to reorganize their American war, the French captured Fort Oswego in a well-coordinated use of Indian, Canadian, and French troops and methods. Newly arrived general Louis-Joseph de Montcalm-Gozon de Saint-Véran commanded the victors.

The climax of Vaudreuil's offensive came in August 1757. The same combination of Canadian and Indian guerrilla raids followed by formal siege brought French victory at Fort William Henry (Lake George, New York). Montcalm's generous terms for the defeated violated his commitments to Indian allies, and the Indians angrily left, effectively terminating a campaign that was to proceed south to the Hudson River. Meanwhile a British attempt to besiege Louisbourg became a costly diversion. Defeats of the British also continued in Europe, with French victory at Hastenback and the duke of Cumberland's capitulation at Kloster Zeven on 2 September 1757.

Pitt's Offensive, 1758–1760

With British and British American fortunes so low, King George II put the government and the war in the hands of the eloquent and erratic William Pitt (1708–1778). A determined patriot who forced the British to pay whatever was necessary to win in Europe and America, Pitt negotiated a new treaty for subsidizing Prussia and funded a new, enlarged Anglo-Hanoverian army. He also launched a generous requisition system that vastly improved the cooperation of the British American colonies, whatever effects the costs eventually had on imperial relations.

Having decided to pay in Europe and fight in America, Pitt and newly appointed Captain-General John Ligonier developed a new strategy for North America. The target areas remained the same as those of 1755: the Ohio Valley (Fort Duquesne), Lake Ontario (Fort Frontenac), Lake Champlain (Fort Carillon), and Nova Scotia (Louisbourg). British regulars, who had constituted only one-seventh of the British and Americans fighting force in 1755, were now fully one-half of the much-enlarged British forces in North America. The British navy, which delivered the troops and stayed to fight at Louisbourg and Quebec, also blockaded French ports more effectively, curtailing French assistance to Canada.

Despite impressive investment and recovery under Jean Frédéric Phélypeaux, comte de Maurepas, the French navy remained on the defensive. The results, like the means, were different than the earlier British offensive. The careful, unimaginative General Jeffery Amherst, new commander-in-chief of the British forces in North America, conducted the successful siege of Louisbourg at a pace that precluded an attack on Quebec in 1758 and indicated the plodding pace of his army for the rest of the war. Louisbourg and Fort Frontenac fell to the British that year, and Fort Duquesne was destroyed as a British army approached in November 1758. Even

Montcalm's successful defense of Fort Carillon marked the shift of a badly outnumbered Canada to a defensive war that would make poor use of the martial skills of Canadians and Native Americans.

The 1759 campaign was a predictable continuation of the pressure on shrinking Canada. The western Indians grew cautious after the fall of Fort Duquesne. The Iroquois, whose formal neutrality of 1701 had continued despite major breaches in 1755, decided to join on the side of the likely victor. When a battle between Indians on the French and British sides became likely at the siege of Fort Niagara, France's Native American allies withdrew their support after discussion with the Iroquois. Fort Carillon and Fort Saint Frédéric were abandoned on the Lake Champlain frontier at the approach of overwhelming numbers of British troops. The fall of Quebec City in September 1759 was an important symbol, but it was not decisive. The strangulation of Canada was also advanced by two British naval victories that year off Lagos, Portugal, in August and at Quiberon Bay in November.

New France was already defeated in 1759, yet in another sense it was not defeated at all. The battle of Sainte Foy in the spring of 1760 was a rerun of the earlier encounter, with the French under General François-Gaston, chevalier de Lévis, defeating the British on the same Plains of Abraham and then besieging them in Quebec City. The arrival of the British fleet at Quebec in mid May 1760 forced the French to withdraw. When the siege of Montreal ended in the surrender of New France in September, fewer than three thousand defenders faced three British armies totaling some seventeen thousand.

The final solution would be diplomatic. The skilled French foreign minister Étienne-François, duc de Choiseul, began tentative negotiations with Britain as early as February 1760. His task was made easier by the new British king, George III (1738–1820), who was anxious for peace. William Pitt was forced from office, British subsidies to Prussia ended, and Britain entered negotiations for a separate peace with France. Choiseul further strengthened his hand by negotiating an alliance with Spain, bringing the latter into what would be a short and humiliating war in which the British captured both

Havana and Manila in 1762. While the British court was anxious to make peace, British forces in America were still making war. The French West Indian islands of Guadeloupe (1759), Dominica (1761), Martinique, Saint Lucia, Grenada, and Saint Vincent (1762) were all captured.

The Peace of Paris, 1763

The North American war had been won decisively by the British, and the peace confirmed their subsequent cultural dominance there. French power was gone from North America, save for fishing rights at Newfoundland and the small nearby islands of Saint Pierre and Miquelon. Canada, Cape Breton Island, and the portion of Louisiana east of the Mississippi came under British control. Spain ceded Florida to the British, resigned fishing rights at Newfoundland, and recognized the British presence in Honduras. Spain received from France the part of Louisiana west of the Mississippi and regained Havana from the British. France regained her dominant West Indian sugar islands of Guadeloupe and Martinique, as well as Saint Lucia, but ceded the lesser islands of Saint Vincent, Dominica, and Tobago to Britain.

Britain's success was also evident in other territorial settlements: Minorca was restored, Senegal was ceded by France, and the French presence in India was curtailed. France's American empire had paid for France's defeat without loss of the empire's commercial core of sugar islands and fisheries. Britain had gained maritime hegemony without weakening France in Europe. The peace was not harsh, but it alienated Britain's allies without significantly weakening her enemies. French revenge would come with the American War for Independence.

Native American Reaction, 1763–1766

The war that began in the Ohio Valley would also end there. France's withdrawal from North America fundamentally altered the situation of its former Indian allies, customers, and friends. The rivalry between Britain and France in North America had been understood, exploited, and extended by Indians. While intertribal hatreds had been exploited by the Europeans, few Indians were killed by Indians during the Anglo-French wars. France, the less-threatening pres-

ence in North America after 1701, had gained Native American allies while the British had gained only neutrality and trade. Indians withdrew support for New France after 1758 to improve their position during the ensuing disruption, but the Peace of Paris confirmed suspicions that they had been betrayed. European diplomats traded claims of sovereignty over unceded Native American lands.

Between 1760 and 1763, British colonial traders and settlers became numerous in the Ohio Valley, and customary gift giving at conferences with the Indians was suspended by General Amherst as an economy measure. Native Americans spoke of a return of the French both as a hope and a threat, and they valued the remaining French priests and traders. An influential Delaware shaman known as the "Prophet" found wide intertribal support for a rejection of all cultural links with whites. Pontiac, eloquent war chief of the Ottawa, laid siege to the now-British post at Detroit beginning in May 1763. British forts at Sandusky (Ohio), Saint Joseph (Michigan), Fort Miami (Indiana), Fort Ouiatenon (Indiana), and Michilimackinac (Michigan) all fell to the Indians within a month, followed promptly by Venango (Pennsylvania), Fort Le Boeuf (Waterford, Pennsylvania), and Fort Presqu'île (Erie, Pennsylvania).

The British response centered upon a 460-man force sent to Fort Duquesne, renamed Fort Pitt, under Colonel Henry Bouquet. This regular force successfully defended itself against attack by Delaware and Shawnee at the Battle of Bushy Run in August 1763 and went on to relieve besieged Fort Pitt. In October 1763 Pontiac ended the siege of Detroit. British expeditions under Bouquet and Colonel John Bradstreet collected Indian promises of peace and released captives held by many of the tribes that had been involved in the resistance. By royal proclamation of 7 October 1763, the British government addressed Indian concerns by excluding white settlers from the entire trans-Appalachian region and by providing for the licensing of traders there. Hostilities subsided, but final negotiations were not completed until July 1766.

North America, which had mirrored western Europe's shifting rivalries for two centuries, had eventually come to reflect a British dominance that was demographic long before, and after, it became military and diplomatic.

BIBLIOGRAPHY

Andrews, Kenneth R. *Elizabethan Privateering: English Privateering During the Spanish War, 1585–1603.* Cambridge, England, 1964.

——. *Trade, Plunder and Settlement: Maritime Enterprise and the Genesis of the British Empire, 1480–1630.* Cambridge, England, 1984.

Boxer, C. R. *The Dutch Seaborne Empire, 1600–1800.* London, 1965.

Brewer, John. *The Sinews of Power: War, Money, and the English State, 1688–1783.* London, 1989.

Davenport, Frances G., ed. *European Treaties Bearing on the History of the United States and Its Dependencies to 1648.* 4 vols. Washington, D.C., 1917–1937.

Davies, K. G. *The North Atlantic World in the Seventeenth Century.* Minneapolis, Minn., 1974.

Davis, Ralph. *The Rise of the Atlantic Economies.* London, 1973.

Eccles, W. J. *Canada Under Louis XIV: 1663–1701.* Toronto, Ontario, 1964.

——. *France in America.* 2nd ed. Markham, Ontario, 1990.

Elliott, J. H. *Imperial Spain, 1469–1716.* Toronto, Ontario, 1963.

——. *The Old World and the New, 1492–1650.* Cambridge, England, 1970.

Frégault, Guy. *La guerre de la conquête.* Montreal, 1955.

Halpenny, Frances, et al. *Dictionary of Canadian Biography.* 12 vols. Toronto, Ontario, 1966–1990.

Leach, Douglas Edward. *Arms for Empire: A Military History of the British Colonies in North America, 1607–1763.* New York, 1973.

McNeill, John Robert. *Atlantic Empires of France and Spain: Louisbourg and Havana, 1700–1763.* Chapel Hill, N.C., 1985.

Miquelon, Dale Bernard. *New France, 1701–1744.* Toronto, Ontario, 1987.

The New Cambridge Modern History. 13 vols. Cambridge, England, 1957–1990.

Newton, Arthur Percival. *The European Nations in the West Indies, 1493–1688.* London, 1933.

Parry, J. H. *The Age of Reconnaissance.* 2nd ed. Berkeley, Calif., 1981.

——. *The Spanish Seaborne Empire.* London, 1966.

Penrose, Boies. *Travel and Discovery in the Renaissance, 1420–1620.* Cambridge, Mass., 1952.

Quinn, David Beers. *England and the Discovery of America, 1481–1620.* New York, 1974.

Roberts, Penfield. *The Quest for Security, 1715–1740.* New York, 1947.

Savelle, Max. *The Origins of American Diplomacy: The International History of Angloamerica, 1492–1763.* New York, 1967.

Scammell, G. V. *The English Atlantic, 1675–1740: An Exploration of Communication and Community.* New York, 1986.

——. *The First Imperial Age: European Overseas Expansion c. 1400–1715.* London, 1989.

Steele, Ian K. *Guerillas and Grenadiers: The Struggle for Canada.* Toronto, Ontario, 1969.

Trudel, Marcel. *The Beginnings of New France, 1524–1663.* Translated by Patricia Claxton. Toronto, Ontario, 1973.

Wallerstein, Immanuel. *The Modern World-System.* 2 vols. New York, 1980.

Wolf, John B. *Louis XIV.* New York, 1968.

Ian Kenneth Steele

SEE ALSO **The Fur Trade; Indian-Colonist Conflicts and Alliances; Indian-Colonist Contact; Mission Communities;** and **Trade and Commerce;** and various essays in OLD WORLD EXPANSION.

THE CONQUEST OF ACADIA

ACADIA WAS ALWAYS a vulnerable border colony. For the French it was New France's eastern flank, and for the British it was an extension of New England. Its boundaries were never clearly defined. France had understood Acadia to include at the very least what are now the provinces of Nova Scotia, New Brunswick, and Prince Edward Island, while Britain claimed all the territory that extended as far north and east as approximately the Gaspé Peninsula of Quebec. This explains why so much of the history of Acadia was punctuated by struggle between the two crowns for nearly a century and a half from its settlement in the first decade of the seventeenth century to the fall of New France.

THE CAPTURE OF PORT ROYAL, 1710

From the start Acadians, at the time illiterate farmers and fishermen who wanted only to be left alone, regularly found themselves caught in the middle of colonial power struggles in which they themselves took little interest. Title to the colony changed several times and it suffered numerous destructive raids before the final British capture of Port Royal (renamed Annapolis Royal), the principal settlement site, in 1710. When the colony was ceded to Great Britain by the Treaty of Utrecht in 1713, the disputes with respect to its boundaries and the debate as to what constituted Acadie, or Nova Scotia as the British called it, continued. The French, wishing now to minimize their loss, claimed that Acadie's "ancient," or former, boundaries did not extend beyond the Isthmus of Chignecto. Britain insisted that under the French the province had extended as far as Canada in the north and New England in the west. British control over the territory and its French-speaking population thus remained essentially ineffectual for another half century, until the conquest of the rest of New France by British arms nullified the boundary question.

THE "NEUTRAL FRENCH," 1713–1744

The major preoccupation of Nova Scotia's new masters was to secure from the Acadians an oath of allegiance to the British Crown. The latter had the option of either immigrating to French territory—the French retained Île Royale (Cape Breton Island) and Île-St-Jean (Prince Edward Island)—or remaining on their ancestral lands as British subjects. In substance the Acadians were an unpolitical people. They were prepared to submit to British authority, but only up to a point. They resolutely resisted an oath of allegiance not qualified by the recognition of various rights: freedom of religion, the right to remain neutral when France and Britain were at war, continued enjoyment of their property, and the right to immigrate, if they so chose, to French territory.

289

Throughout the 1720s there was a good deal of jousting between master and subject on the matter of allegiance. The Acadians resisted as best they could, encouraged by their priests to regard neutrality as a guarantee of their security. They continued to live peaceably in the province, diking and farming the Bay of Fundy's tidal marshlands and engaging in trade with the Indians and their New England neighbors, without their British masters insisting on the resolution of this vexing problem. Additionally they enjoyed the advantage of a thriving export trade, mostly in grain and livestock, with the new French colony of Île Royale.

For their part the British lacked the power to enforce the regular submission of their new subjects. In 1730 Governor Richard Philipps acquiesced in the idea of neutrality by giving the Acadians a verbal promise recognizing the principle in the event of war between the two crowns. The expression "the neutral French" was used thereafter both by officials and by the Acadians themselves. In the years that followed, the Acadians by and large did remain neutral in the conflict that constantly threatened to erupt around them. The majority believed firmly that neutrality would spare them the unpleasant consequences of war.

Although they were considered an alien and at times troublesome people, the Acadians were valuable to the British in Nova Scotia. For a generation after the conquest there were no permanent English-speaking Protestant settlers in the province. The authorities therefore were forced to depend on the Acadians for foodstuffs, firewood, and other necessities. The Acadians also served as a sort of buffer between the British and France's perennial Native American allies, the Micmac, "ye worst of enemies" as the British described them. They were also valuable to the British in a negative way: by not immigrating to Île Royale, they deprived the French of additional population and considerable livestock.

Conversely, there was harmony between the Native Americans and the Acadians, aided to some extent by blood ties and more importantly by successful missionary activity that attached both the Micmac and the Malecite to the same Roman Catholic faith as the Acadians. The Malecite never felt threatened; they lived in the interior and fished in the estuaries, while the Acadians diked and farmed the marshlands or fished offshore. To them, the Acadians were seen merely as permanent neighbors, middlemen in the fur and feather trades, suppliers of manufactured goods, but never a hostile force.

The British left the Acadians largely to govern themselves through their elected deputies and their priests, who continued to be appointed by the bishop at Quebec. In 1720 Captain Paul Mascarene complained that "all the orders sent to them if not suiting their humors, are scoffed and laughed at, and they put themselves upon the footing of obeying no Government." Nor did the situation improve in time; in 1732 Lieutenant Governor Lawrence Armstrong lamented that they were as disobedient as ever and that they obstructed everything proposed by the authorities. Even the French, before 1710, had found the Acadians troublesome and tainted with "republican principles," partly as a result of decades of neglect by France and partly because of the close ties they developed with New England merchants and traders.

Yet the Acadians were not unruly subjects, nor radical in their aspirations. They saw themselves as caught between the imperial ambitions of Britain and France, each seeking their active loyalty. To survive these pressures, the majority tried to ignore the quarrels they felt did not concern them. Their goals seemed simple: to retain their lands, their Catholic religion, and their friendship with the Micmac; to be tolerated by the British; and to enjoy the trust of the French at Louisbourg and in Canada. And they wished to continue trading with everyone in the region, as before. For the rest they desired simply to be left alone and, hopefully, one day to become subjects of the king of France once again.

THE FRUITS OF WAR

Peace in the region ended early in 1744 with the beginning of the War of the Austrian Succession. The year was a watershed, the eve of the most critical decade in the history of the Acadians. War and its consequences came quickly to dominate the region and its population for nearly two decades. The golden age of Acadia came abruptly to its end as both France and Great Britain realized just how strategically important the region was in their struggle for supremacy in North America. The French had lost Acadia by treaty but, they hoped, not permanently. In the meantime officials at Quebec and Louisbourg encouraged the Acadians to remain loyal to France. They remained valuable as suppliers of grain and livestock to feed Louisbourg.

When war resumed between the two crowns in 1744, the French launched a series of expeditions of regular troops and Indian allies into Nova Scotia, which in retrospect can only be described as halfhearted efforts to regain the province. Each time they passed through it to invest the British fort at Annapolis, they relied on the Acadians for military intelligence, food, transport, and other supplies.

In a general way the Acadians honored their commitment to neutrality, but a score of Acadians nevertheless did take up arms on behalf of the French. Others were compelled by the invaders, or by the prospect of profitable trade, to provide supplies and services. Ample evidence suggests that for some Acadians scruples about neutrality were not insurmountable. The genial Mascarene, now lieutenant governor, was generally satisfied with their conduct, convinced, as he reported in 1744, that those who assisted the French did so only "as force obliged them to it."

Mascarene's assessment notwithstanding, with the return of peace in 1748 the British authorities seriously began to question the Acadians' reliability as neutral subjects. The founding of Halifax the following year heralded a vigorous new effort to secure the province definitively for British interests. At the same time, the Micmac and the Malecite—encouraged and supported by the French at Louisbourg and inspired by the fiery missionary Jean-Louis Le Loutre— were becoming more belligerent in their resistance to British and New England encroachments in the region. Acadians to some degree seem to have supported this Indian activity after 1749. At the very least the Acadians were aware of Micmac comings and goings, especially in the more remote settlements of the province. Because of their fear of Indian reprisals the Acadians rarely reported such movements. Also, they considered the Micmac and Malecite, and themselves, as more permanently established in Nova Scotia, and with better title to the land, than the British.

From the early 1750s, as they groped for a solution to the thorny problem of allegiance, British attitudes toward the French and their Indian allies in the region grew more bitter. With war looming, what particularly alarmed the authorities both in Nova Scotia and Massachusetts was the steady military encroachment of the French after the founding of Halifax. In response to the British establishment of Fort Lawrence on the Isthmus of Chignecto and attempts to blockade the Saint John River, the French built Forts Beauséjour and Gaspereau across the Missaguash River from Fort Lawrence and revived another stronghold at the mouth of the Saint John; thus they enforced their claim to the territory beyond peninsular Nova Scotia. Concurrent with this, the missionary Le Loutre was busily creating a "nouvelle Acadie" north of the Missaguash, to which the inhabitants of the peninsula were being cajoled—and more often coerced, apparently by the threat of Indian reprisals—into moving, certainly against their best interests.

In 1754 London in a general way authorized Governor William Shirley of Massachusetts and Lieutenant Governor Charles Lawrence of Nova Scotia to act in concert to drive the French from the region entirely. This set the stage for the conflagration from which even the unpolitical Acadians could not escape. Events that unfolded in Nova Scotia beginning in the summer of 1754 were clearly part of the continent-wide struggle for domination in North America. Given the circumstances, it is doubtful whether any degree of political sophistication could have extricated the Acadians from the crossfire between the warring imperialists.

THE MATTER OF THE OATH, SUMMER 1755

Although their homeland was being transformed into a place of warlike confrontation, the Acadians continued to insist on their status as neutral subjects by refusing an unqualified oath of allegiance to the British king. From a population of twenty-three hundred in 1714, the community had grown to an estimated thirteen thousand throughout the region in 1755. By then only about half lived under British jurisdiction. Since the founding of Halifax, large numbers had immigrated to the French colonies of Isle Saint-Jean and Île Royale, into "nouvelle Acadie," and to the Saint John River. Belatedly the Acadians were beginning to recognize their masters' determination to create a viable, normative British colony in Nova Scotia. It was dawning on them that the authorities were insisting that the time had come for their "neutral subjects" to take an unqualified, unconditional oath.

It is no simple matter to explain the ultimate decision of the Nova Scotia Council in Halifax to uproot the Acadians, deport them from the province, and disperse them among English-speaking colonists along the Atlantic seaboard. Deportation had been discussed since the capture of Port Royal in 1710, but there were sound reasons not to depopulate the province at the expense of the British and to the advantage of the neighboring French. What occurred in Nova Scotia beginning in the summer of 1755 resulted from a number of converging factors. The principal one was the military buildup by the French in the strategic Chignecto Isthmus at a time when British fortunes in America were going badly. To this may be added Le Loutre's belligerent leadership locally and the persistent refusal of the Acadians remaining in the province to swear an unconditional oath. Finally, there was the rigid and uncompromising temperament of the professional soldier Charles Lawrence, which exacerbated the atmosphere of crisis building in Nova Scotia in 1755.

The removal of the Acadians was essentially a military decision arrived at locally by Lawrence and his council, without the concurrence of higher authority in London. Lawrence was much influenced by Governor Shirley, who shared the conviction that under the prevailing circumstances the region could remain securely in British hands only if the Acadians could be induced to take an unqualified oath or be forced to leave the province.

The impact of this new policy of firmness was first felt in the Minas district in the spring of 1755, when the Acadians were ordered to surrender first their boats, then their firearms to Captain Alexander Murray, the commander of Fort Edward, at Pisiquid. Murray suspected the inhabitants of using their boats to violate the ban on exporting foodstuffs to the French at Louisbourg. While complying with both orders, the Acadians sent a strongly worded petition to Halifax arguing against this imposition.

Meanwhile, Lawrence proceeded with his and Shirley's plan to reduce the French forts at Chignecto. A mixed force of two thousand New England provincials and two hundred and fifty British regulars under Lieutenant Colonel Robert Monckton departed Boston on 19 May 1755. Fort Beauséjour, the key to the French threat to the province, was invested on 13 June. Three days later it capitulated, and a large number of Acadians from the French side of the Missaguash were found in arms within the fort. Although they claimed that they were forced to bear arms, Lawrence ordered them imprisoned pending removal from the province. Fort Gaspereau surrendered on 17 June without a shot being fired. Monckton then ordered the inhabitants of the district to bring in their firearms to Fort Beauséjour (renamed Fort Cumberland), which they did on 25 June.

Back in Halifax, Lawrence and his council were sufficiently encouraged by Monckton's success to press finally for an unequivocal oath of allegiance. On 3 July, with fifteen Acadian delegates present from Minas and Pisiquid, the council discussed the petition objecting to the confiscation of their boats and firearms. Lawrence insisted that they take the prescribed oath. This they refused to do, requesting first a general consultation with the inhabitants they represented. The following day the exasperated council ordered the delegates imprisoned and replaced by new ones. This was the decisive confrontation between the Acadians and the provincial authority, for Lawrence and his council agreed that henceforth any who refused the oath would be removed from the province.

The arrival in Halifax of Vice Admiral Edward Boscawen in command of a large squadron gave the council an even firmer resolve. On 18 July Lawrence wrote his superiors in London of his determination to press for the oath to be taken unconditionally. At the meeting of the council on 28 July, with new Acadian delegates from the Annapolis and Minas districts persisting in the general refusal, the council undertook to settle the matter once and for all. These delegates were summarily imprisoned with the original ones; the government then ordered that measures be taken to remove the entire population from their lands and from the province, and to distribute them among the English seaboard colonies.

THE REMOVAL OF THE ACADIANS, 1755–1758

The removal of the Acadians was organized over the weeks that followed. Lawrence entrusted responsibility to Monckton for the district of Chignecto, including the Chepoudy Bay (Shepody) settlements and Tatamagouche. Lieutenant Colonel John Winslow was assigned the districts of Minas, Pisiquid, and Cobequid (Truro), and Major John Handfield was responsible for Annapolis.

At Chignecto, Monckton ordered all adult males to report to Fort Cumberland, and on 11 August four hundred came and were taken prisoner. By now many families, fearing the worst, were fleeing into the forests in an effort to escape the British dragnet. Raiding parties went out from Fort Cumberland, destroying Acadian homes and barns and rounding up what strays they could. The embarkation began in early September. In six weeks some eleven hundred Acadians from the district had been placed aboard transports. The Chignecto Acadians in Lawrence's estimation were the most rebellious, and he therefore ordered them removed to the farthest colonies, South Carolina and Georgia.

John Winslow, the New England provincial officer who was Monckton's second-in-command at the reduction of Chignecto in June, arrived at Grand Pré (in the Minas district) on 19 August. He convened more than four hundred males to the parish church on 5 September and declared them prisoners. Uneasy because his prisoners outnumbered his troops, Winslow forced 230 of them onto transports anchored offshore. The general embarkation, much-delayed for want of sufficient transport, only got under way finally on 8 October. More than twenty-one hundred Acadians were deported from the Minas

district. At Pisiquid, Captain Murray gathered up another eleven hundred in late October.

At Annapolis the operation was hampered by Major Handfield's insufficient force. Reinforcements eventually arrived from Grand Pré in late autumn, and the removal finally got under way in December. For Handfield, as for Winslow, the task of rounding up and deporting the Acadians—sixteen hundred from the Annapolis district—was "most disagreeable and troublesome," the more so as Handfield was related by marriage to many of his victims.

In all, more than six thousand Acadians were deported from the province in the autumn of 1755. In the confusion that was wrought in each district, many Acadians became separated from their families. Many who escaped actual deportation (including the entire village of Cobequid) joined other, earlier refugees on Île-St-Jean and Île Royale. Others fled north and west of the peninsula, and for the next several years attempted to survive the effects of exposure and starvation in the forests as far as the Miramichi, the Restigouche, and the Saint John rivers. A number of able-bodied Acadians joined the Canadian officer Charles Deschamps de Boishébert's force in his resistance to the steady British advance north of Chignecto.

Later, when the British captured Louisbourg in July 1758, they resumed their deportations. The British rounded up and deported nearly all of the inhabitants of Île Royale and Île-St-Jean to France. Others were captured around Cape Sable, while detachments scoured the north shore of the Bay of Fundy and its estuaries for more Acadians who had eluded the earlier operations. Several hundred from the Saint John and the Petitcodiac rivers escaped and joined earlier refugees on the Miramichi and the Restigouche. Fifteen hundred managed to reach the colony of Quebec.

The removal of the Acadians from Nova Scotia achieved Charles Lawrence's primary goal, to render the province secure for British interests. This he undertook before war had formally been declared between France and Great Britain. When Canada fell half a decade later, the last obstacles to British settlement in Nova Scotia were removed. During the 1760s some eight thousand New Englanders arrived to occupy the former Acadian lands. The least that can be said of Charles Lawrence's role is that he acted callously, indeed brutally. He lacked the imagination to perceive that the removal of the Acadians was unnecessary on military grounds. He secured the decision of his council without reference to or authorization from his superiors in London.

THE DIASPORA

What the Acadians themselves christened the "Great Upheaval" lasted officially from 1755 to 1763, but for many their wanderings continued for a generation or more. Of the majority who were deported in 1755, most were dispersed among the British North American colonies. Others were removed to England and France. The colonies, whose officials Lawrence had not forewarned of this large penurious influx, did not welcome the Acadians. Apart from strong anti-Catholic feeling among the Anglo-Americans, there was an understandable reluctance to assume the financial costs of supporting them, which generally took the form of bigotry, discrimination, and government harassment.

Many Acadians did not live to reach their destinations in exile because of the conditions imposed upon them by their captors. If they survived the passage, makeshift accommodations and inadequate nourishment very often increased their vulnerability to disease, especially smallpox. Those who survived were dispersed within each colony, where they came under the purview of local overseers of the poor, but ultimately only a few Acadian exiles were assimilated into the English-speaking colonies.

As early as 1756 large numbers of deportees undertook to return to their ancestral homes, or at least to create new homes among people of their own language and faith. Some who had been deported to Georgia and South Carolina attempted a settlement on the lower Saint John River, only to be forced by British operations in 1758 to flee farther upstream, and again after 1783, with the arrival of the Loyalists after the American revolutionary war, north to the Madawaska River, and east to Chaleur Bay and the Memramcook-Petitcoudiac district. Other Acadians, exiled in Massachusetts, went north to Canada where they joined those who had escaped deportation in 1755, and founded new Acadias before assimilating in time with the general population of Quebec.

More Massachusetts deportees sailed to Saint Pierre and Miquelon in 1763, and large numbers left New York for Martinique in 1764, and Saint Domingue in 1765. Around the same time exiles in the middle and southern seaboard colonies learned of a growing exodus to Louisiana, which was French until 1763 and whose Spanish rulers after that date were sympathetic to the plight of the Acadians and favored Catholic settlement. In the final years of the decade 90 percent of the Acadians surviving in Maryland and Pennsylvania sailed from the Chesapeake ports to New Orleans.

Several thousand Acadians escaped deportation by fleeing to the wilderness in 1755. Many of these refugees suffered even worse deprivation than those who were deported. Starving, indigent, and decimated, most had no choice ultimately but to emerge from the wilderness and give themselves up to the British detachments.

When Canada fell in 1760, Acadian resistance to British authority in the region collapsed. In the end between two thousand and three thousand refugees, a mere remnant of those who had originally fled, were captured or had surrendered. They spent several years imprisoned in various strongholds around the province. In due course the able-bodied were permitted to hire out as cheap labor on various public works or on behalf of the province's new English-speaking settlers. A small number of refugees had avoided capture altogether and began to gravitate back toward the very settlements they had previously fled.

It was these refugees who in one way or another had remained in the region, more than the returning deportees, who beginning in the 1760s laid the foundations for the reestablishment of the Acadians in Canada's maritime provinces. With strangers inhabiting their former lands, these Acadians—on condition of taking the oath in the prescribed form—were directed in small groups to widely scattered and less favored districts, in peninsular Nova Scotia, Cape Breton Island, Saint John's Island (Île-St-Jean), and along the eastern shore of continental Nova Scotia, soon to become New Brunswick.

Conversely, many liberated Acadians decided they no longer wished to live under British rule in a province where their lives, and the demography of their homeland, had been so fundamentally disrupted. Article 4 of the 1763 treaty allowed the refugees in Britain's North American territories eighteen months to find their way to any French dependency. Thus one group left Nova Scotia for the islands of Saint Pierre and Miquelon, where they joined earlier arrivals from Massachusetts and France. The tiny islands, unfortunately, could not support so large a population of dispossessed exiles, and in 1767 about seven hundred and fifty Acadians were removed by the French government. One hundred and sixty-three went to Nova Scotia, and the rest were taken to France. The next year, the decision was reversed, and several hundred Acadians braved yet another transatlantic removal. These trends continued, with Great Britain deporting the entire population of the archipelago in 1778 after France joined the United States in the Revolutionary War. At the ensuing peace in 1783 about six hundred returned, only to be deported by Britain once again in 1794 during the Napoleonic wars. Finally, more than six hundred brave souls returned to Saint Pierre and Miquelon for the final time in 1815 and 1816, some, conceivably, having suffered as many as eight forcible removals in the sixty years since 1755.

In 1764 a large expedition of Acadians left Halifax for the French West Indies, but soon transferred to Louisiana, which offered a more salubrious climate. More refugees departed Nova Scotia for Louisiana the following year. In all more than one thousand refugees from Saint Domingue, Nova Scotia, New York, Maryland, and Pennsylvania had settled in Louisiana by 1769. Cajuns, as they came to be called, contributed significantly to the development of the nascent, underdeveloped colony. As in old Acadia, they preferred to settle in isolated districts, far from the government in New Orleans, and the Creole-dominated rural districts adjacent to the colonial capital.

However, the Spanish authorities at first settled many in scattered, vulnerable locations along the east bank of the Mississippi to secure the border with British West Florida. Other Cajuns went to the west bank and to the district of Bayou Lafourche where with great difficulty they cleared virgin forests and gradually developed a mixed agriculture. Still others settled in Attakapas and Opelousas, the frontier districts west of the Atchafalaya River. Here on the lush savannahs of the Bayou Teche and Vermillion River valleys they raised cattle and prospered. Four fifths of these latter Cajuns were natives of the Chignecto district of Acadia, where they or their families had raised cattle for generations on the fertile tidal marshlands of the Bay of Fundy.

In 1763 there were nearly thirty-five hundred Acadian refugees in France, mostly deportees from Île Royale and Île-St-Jean and the remote coasts around Nova Scotia, and some eight hundred recently freed from English prisons. Despite a number of schemes to establish them in Brittany, Poitou, Corsica, French Guiana, Saint Domingue, and the Falkland Islands, none succeeded. By the third quarter of the eighteenth century, the independent-minded Acadians were far removed from the institutions of French feudalism, and their future in France looked bleak indeed. Most eventually returned to North America. Some had settled in Saint Pierre and Miquelon as early as 1763, others along the shores of Chaleur Bay a decade later, but most, nearly 70 percent of those still in France in 1784, went to Louisiana.

An expedition of six large merchantmen chartered by Spain transported sixteen hundred Acadians to Louisiana in 1785, a full generation after the upheavals began in 1755. Most chose to settle on the periphery of the original Cajun settlements, especially in the districts of the lower Bayou Lafourche and Mississippi valleys. Others went west to the Opelousas and the Attakapas, nearer long lost relatives. They adjusted rapidly to their new surroundings, thanks to the assistance of the Spanish Crown and the support of their compatriots already long established in the colony. Yet a generation later, at the restoration of the French monarchy in 1815, sixty years after the events of 1755, there were still displaced Acadians in France receiving government pensions.

THE SURVIVAL OF THE ACADIANS

For close to a century before 1755 Acadia's inhabitants, even under the British after 1710, enjoyed an easy prosperity. They developed skills in exploiting the tidal marshes along the shores of the Bay of Fundy and an astuteness in pursuing the trade of their region. They lived far from worldly currents, and because of this, despite a penchant for quarreling, they were essentially a contented people. They suffered no epidemics, food shortages, or famines, as even the more sophisticated and commercially developed Quebec and Louisbourg suffered occasionally. In retrospect one can see that during the late 1740s and early 1750s the Acadians had perhaps lost sight of just how vulnerable they were in British Nova Scotia. They were ill-prepared at any rate for the events that progressively dragged them into the imperial disputes of France and Britain from 1744 onward. By the time the struggle for hegemony in North America was finally resolved by international treaty in 1763, the Acadians had become, with their friends the Indians, the continent's most visible and tragic victims.

A mere half century after the Great Upheaval, the Acadians had greatly surpassed the population figures of their golden age. By 1800 an estimated eight thousand Acadians lived in New Brunswick, Nova Scotia, Cape Breton, and Prince Edward Island, and an equal number in Quebec Province. Around six thousand lived in Louisiana, one thousand elsewhere in the United States, and one thousand in France. Another thousand had migrated to miscellaneous domiciles, for an estimated total of twenty-five thousand, or about twelve thousand more than had lived in the Acadian region in 1755. This represents a rather phenomenal natural increase, especially surprising when we recall this as a period of exceptional hardship and high mortality resulting from exposure, disease, and exhaustion.

Although in the late twentieth century the Acadians are widely scattered geographically, their sense of identity remains intact. Despite the more recent inroads of assimilation and Americanization, many Acadias survive in long-isolated pockets throughout Canada's Atlantic region, on Saint Pierre and Miquelon, in Quebec, Louisiana, and New England, and in several *départements* of western France. The Acadians themselves call this phenomenon *la survivance*, an achievement largely attributable to the remarkable cohesion of the population through the generations. By 1755 nearly every man, woman, and child was linked by bonds of parentage, and every Acadian could claim an ancestor who figured among the pioneers in the first census of 1671. No less during the lengthy migrations of the Acadians and their aftermath than before the Great Upheaval, one can make reference to a single, enormous close-knit family, *la grande famille acadienne*.

BIBLIOGRAPHY

Primary Sources

Akins, Thomas Beakins, ed. *Selections from the Public Documents of the Province of Nova Scotia.* Halifax, Nova Scotia, 1869.

Fergusson, C. Bruce, ed. *Minutes of His Majesty's Council at Annapolis Royal, 1736–1749.* Halifax, Nova Scotia, 1967.

Macmechan, Archibald M., ed. *A Calendar of Two Letter-Books and One Commission-Book in the Possession of the Government of Nova Scotia.* Halifax, Nova Scotia, 1900.

Public Archives of Canada. *The Northcliffe Collection.* National Archives of Canada, MG 18 M, Series 1. Ottawa, 1926. Papers of Lieutenant Colonel Robert Monckton.

———. *Report Concerning Canadian Archives for the Year 1905.* Vol. 2, appendix A, part 3. Ontario, 1906.

Willard, Abijah. *Journal of Abijah Willard, 1755,* edited by John Clarence Webster. Saint John, New Brunswick, 1930.

Winslow, John. "The Journal of Colonel John Winslow of the Provincial Troops, While Engaged in the Siege of Fort Beausejour, in the Summer and Autumn of 1755." In *Collections of the Nova Scotia Historical Society for the Year 1884.* Vol. 4. Halifax, Nova Scotia, 1885.

Secondary Sources

Brasseaux, Carl. *The Founding of New Acadia: Beginnings of Acadian Life in Louisiana, 1765–1803.* Baton Rouge, La., 1987.

———. *Scattered to the Wind: Dispersal and Wanderings of the Acadians, 1755–1809.* Lafayette, La., 1991.

Brebner, John Bartlet. *New England's Outpost: Acadia Before the Conquest of Canada.* New York, 1927.

Clark, Andrew Hill. *Acadia: The Geography of Early Nova Scotia to 1760.* Madison, Wis., 1968.

Daigle, Jean, ed. *The Acadians of the Maritimes: Thematic Studies.* Moncton, New Brunswick, 1982.

Frégault, Guy. *Canada: The War of the Conquest.* Translated by Margaret M. Cameron. Toronto, Ontario, 1969.

Griffiths, Naomi E. S. "The Acadians." In *Dictionary of Canadian Biography.* Vol. 4. Toronto, Ontario, 1979. Introductory essay.

————. *The Acadians: Creation of a People.* Toronto, Ontario, 1973.

Harris, R. Cole, ed. *Historical Atlas of Canada.* Vol. 1, plates 29, 30. Toronto, Buffalo, London, 1987.

LeBlanc, Robert G. "The Acadian Migrations." *Canadian Geographical Journal* 81, no. 1 (July 1970):10–19.

Rawlyk, George A. *Nova Scotia's Massachusetts: A Study of Massachusetts–Nova Scotia Relations, 1630–1784.* Montreal and London, 1973.

Bernard Alexander Pothier

SEE ALSO **French Settlements** and **Interracial Societies, The French Colonies, Louisiana.**

IX

THE SOCIAL FABRIC

REPEOPLING THE LAND

THE BRITISH AND DUTCH COLONIES

INTRODUCTION

EUROPEAN TRADERS AND COLONISTS, as one authority remarks, "did not settle a virgin land. They invaded and displaced a resident population." Exactly how large that population was at the time of contact is unknown. As many as from ten to twelve million Indians may have inhabited North America before the arrival of Europeans, although most authorities accept a lower figure of between four and five million. What mattered to settlers, however, was less overall numbers than the density of indigenous populations in areas of contact. Colonists who immigrated to the Chesapeake in the early seventeenth century encountered a powerful group of tribes, organized under the chiefdom of the Powhatan Indians, which embraced upwards of thirteen thousand people dispersed across some six hundred square miles (1,600 square kilometers) of the tidewater from the Potomac River to the present-day border between North Carolina and Virginia. The total Algonquian population of the region may have been at least double that number. Estimates for New England also suggest large numbers, ranging from 72,000 to 144,000.

Altogether approximately a million Indians lived east of the Mississippi on the eve of British settlement.

The catastrophic decline of Indian populations began well before the British and Dutch arrived, primarily as a consequence of the Indians' lack of immunity to imported diseases. More devastating than the epidemics that periodically ravaged European cities, Old World diseases introduced initially by explorers and colonists in the late fifteenth and early sixteenth centuries relentlessly reduced indigenous populations all across the Americas during the next two hundred years. War and the spread of European settlement comprised other "horsemen of the Indian apocalypse." In mainland and island colonies alike, brutal fighting between settlers and Indians retarded but did not prevent the steady expansion of European settlement. By the end of the colonial period only about 150,000 Indians of the original one million inhabiting eastern North America were left, while in the Caribbean the indigenous peoples had virtually disappeared.

As Indian populations rapidly declined, so European populations grew by leaps and bounds. Table 1 shows the growth of regional populations of British colonies in the seventeenth and eighteenth centuries. Precise figures are unavailable, but estimates reveal impressive annual growth rates among the mainland colo-

Table 1 Regional Populations of British America, 1610–1780 (in thousands)

	New England			Middle Colonies			Chesapeake		
	White	Black	Total	White	Black	Total	White	Black	Total
1610	—	—	—	—	—	—	0.3	—	0.3
1620	0.1	—	0.1	—	—	—	0.9	—	0.9
1640	13.5	0.2	13.7	1.7	0.2	1.9	8.0	0.1	8.1
1660	32.6	0.6	33.2	4.8	0.6	5.5	24.0	0.9	24.9
1680	68.0	0.5	68.5	13.4	1.5	14.9	55.6	4.3	59.9
1700	90.7	1.7	92.4	49.9	3.7	53.5	85.2	12.9	98.1
1720	166.9	4.0	170.9	92.3	10.8	103.1	128.0	30.6	158.6
1740	281.2	8.5	289.7	204.1	16.5	220.5	212.5	84.0	296.5
1760	436.9	12.7	449.6	398.9	29.0	427.9	312.4	189.6	502.0
1780	698.4	14.4	712.8	680.5	42.4	722.9	482.4	303.6	786.0

	The Lower South			The West Indies		
	White	Black	Total	White	Black	Total
1640	—	—	—	14.0	—	14.0
1660	1.0	—	1.0	47.0	34.0	81.0
1680	6.2	0.4	6.6	42.0	76.0	118.0
1700	13.6	2.9	16.4	33.0	115.0	148.0
1720	24.8	14.8	39.6	35.0	176.0	212.0
1740	57.8	50.2	108.0	34.0	250.0	285.0
1760	119.6	94.5	214.1	41.0	365.0	406.0
1780	297.4	208.8	506.2	48.0	489.0	537.0

Source: Adapted from John J. McCusker and Russell R. Menard, *The Economy of British America, 1607–1780,* tables 5.1, 6.4, 7.1, 7.2, 8.1, 9.4; pp. 103, 136, 153, 154, 172, 203.

nies, ranging from 2.4 percent in New England to 4.3 percent in the lower South (North Carolina, South Carolina, and Georgia). Population more than doubled every twenty-five years during the colonial period. In the island colonies the rate of increase was lower at about 1.5 percent per year. By 1700 the total mainland population was in the vicinity of 260,000 and that of the British islands 148,000. Eighty years later they had risen to 2,728,000 and 537,000 respectively. Total populations, however, obscure important differences in racial composition. Only about 2 percent of New England's population was of Afro-Caribbean origin in 1780 compared to 6 percent in the middle colonies, 40 percent in the upper and lower South, and over 90 percent in the British West Indies. The presence of enormous numbers of black slaves in the islands and the South provided the major contrast between the different regions of British America at the end of the colonial period and presaged the political and economic sectionalism of the nineteenth century.

SEVENTEENTH-CENTURY IMMIGRATION

Black and white populations grew from two sources, natural reproduction and immigration. Down to 1780 approaching 900,000 Europeans immigrated to North America and the Caribbean compared to more than 2.3 million blacks. It is worth emphasizing that in terms of the overall number of immigrants, British America was more black than white, and that the majority of settlers arrived in some form of servitude. The two main labor systems—indentured servitude and slavery—were intimately connected. Cheap white labor was vital to the early development of colonial economies and predated the widespread adoption of slavery by several decades.

Magnitude, Pace, and the Social Character of Immigration

British (mainly English) settlers dominated European colonization of North America and the Brit-

Table 2   Sex Ratios of British Servants Who Emigrated to the West Indies, 1635–1739*

Port of Embarkation	West Indies		American Mainland	
	N	Ratio	N	Ratio
London, 1635	836	1717.4	2011	642.1
Bristol, 1654–1680	4260	366.1	5081	309.1
London, 1682–1686	703	368.7	838	246.3
London, 1718–1739	1418	3732.4	1334	1101.8

* N refers to the number of men and women in the sample. Ratio refers to gender ratio. (If Ratio equals 100, then the number of men to women is exactly equal; if 200, then there are two times as many men.)

Sources: London 1635: Hilary McD. Beckles, *White Servitude and Black Slavery in Barbados, 1627–1715,* table 1.6, p. 34; and James Horn, "Servant Emigration to the Chesapeake in the Seventeenth Century," in Thad W. Tate and David L. Ammerman, eds., *The Chesapeake in the Seventeenth Century: Essays on Anglo-American Society,* table 3, p. 63. Figures for Bristol 1654–1689, London 1682–1686, and 1718–1739 computed from data in Farley Grubb, "The Long-Run Trend in the Value of Indentured Servants: 1654–1831," Working Paper No. 90–25, Department of Economics, University of Delaware (June 1990), Appendix, pp. 44–61.

ish West Indies in the seventeenth century. Approximately 400,000 people left Britain for those areas in this period, a ratio of emigrants to domestic population greater than from any other part of Europe. The great majority went to the plantation colonies that produced the major staples of colonial trade, tobacco and sugar. Some 225,000 went to the Caribbean (58 percent) and 125,000 to the southern Colonies, principally Virginia and Maryland (32 percent), compared with about 40,000 to New England and the Middle Colonies (10 percent).

The timing of immigration varied from one part of British America to another. In New England the great majority of settlers arrived between 1630 and 1640; in the West Indies, most came between 1630 and 1660. In the Chesapeake most arrived between 1630 and the onset of the long depression in tobacco prices in 1680, but there was substantial immigration afterwards. Whereas the white population of the Caribbean began to decline after 1660 and a significant flow of people left New England after 1640, the Chesapeake attracted large numbers of British settlers throughout the century. Generally, however, the peak period of immigration occurred within a single generation, between 1630 and 1660, when more than half of all seventeenth-century British settlers arrived.

Different patterns of immigration to the plantation colonies and New England are reflected in the social characteristics of settlers and their motives for leaving Britain. The phenomenal growth of the tobacco industry in Virginia and Maryland and the rapid development of sugar production in the West Indies created a voracious demand for cheap labor. Not less than 70 percent of white immigrants to the West Indies and the Chesapeake were indentured servants, typically serving from four to five years. Most were young, single, and male. The great majority, men and women, immigrated between the ages of fifteen and twenty-five, an age range in which they might well have been in service of one kind or another as domestics, farm laborers, apprentices, or unskilled casual workers. Family emigration among servants was rare, and most were below marriageable age when they left England. Indentured servants were expected to be unencumbered by family responsibilities and therefore able to devote all their energies to working for their masters. In the early years of settlement, men outnumbered women by a factor of between six and seventeen to one, but as the century progressed the sex ratio became more balanced (table 2). Nonetheless both the Chesapeake and the West Indies experienced a serious shortage of women during the period.

Contemporaries were critical of the social character of indentured servants, describing them variously as beggars, petty criminals, prostitutes, and all sorts of riffraff swept from the streets. Recent studies of their origins, however, reveal that they came from a broad spectrum of working people, ranging from the destitute and desperate to the middle classes. The occupational background of servants who emigrated from Bristol and London between 1654 and 1686 is summarized in table 3. David Galenson has identified four main groups: farmers, laborers, men from skilled trades and services, and youths apparently without trades. The largest group of male servants with registered occupations who emigrated from Bristol in the 1650s came from farming backgrounds, followed by men from the textile industry and clothing trade. By the 1680s, however, the proportion of servants specifically identified from farming occupations had dropped significantly, while the proportion of men from the textile and clothing trades, together with laborers, had increased. It is probable that the large numbers of servants whose occupations were not registered when they embarked for America (40–60 percent of the total) came from the lower echelons of society and were either unemployed youths, poor migrants, or casual laborers picking up jobs where they could find them.

Conventionally, colonial historians have stressed the contrasts with New England immigration. Most settlers departing for the northern colonies paid their own passage, left in family groups, were on average considerably older than Chesapeake immigrants, and usually came from skilled or established trades, particularly artisanal backgrounds. In addition, the sex ratio was more balanced. Migration to New England, Virginia Anderson has argued, "was primarily a transplantation of families." This aspect of immigration has been used, in turn, to explain the orderly settlement and relative social stability of New England compared with the chaotic and conflictual societies to the South, where family formation was retarded by the prevalence of servitude and the skewed sex ratio.

These generalizations have been criticized from a number of viewpoints. Richard Archer has suggested that the importance of the family unit in migration to New England has been exaggerated. A third of adult males who immigrated between 1620 and 1649 were single and without any family connection in the colonies. Most were young. Well over 40 percent were less than twenty, and 72 percent were less than thirty. Moreover, during the thirty-year period male settlers outnumbered females by two to one, a ratio similar to that in parts of the Chesapeake in the second half of the century. David Cressy has found that over a fifth of 242 male emigrants who left England between 1635 and 1638 were recorded as servants, and as such belonged to what was, along with textile trades, the largest single occupational category. In short the social characteristics of an important, if neglected, element of New England immigration bore a resemblance to servant immigration to the plantation colonies.

Motives for Emigration

A variety of reasons—national, regional, local, and individual—lay behind emigration in the seventeenth century. At the national level, the most important factor was demographic growth. England's population rose from just over three million in 1550 to four million in 1600 and over five million by the 1650s. In the context of preindustrial societies, this was a massive increase. Growth was most obvious in the slums of the major towns and cities, but in the countryside, especially in marginal areas, rapid increase led to land shortages and deepening poverty. Rising food prices and a decline in real wages after 1550 led to a steady fall in the living standards of the poorer sections of society, while recurrent harvest failures and dearth in the 1590s and from the 1620s to the 1650s led to widespread misery and social unrest throughout southern and central England.

Far-reaching social changes were accompanied by equally important economic changes. The steady advance of commercial agriculture in pastoral and arable areas was encouraged by the growing population and expansive metropolitan and overseas markets. Much interest, too, was shown in initiatives to develop industries in the countryside, particularly in marginal areas. The growth of domestic manufactures from the mid sixteenth century eroded England's traditional reliance on foreign imports and provided new avenues of investment. Experiments with

304

"industrial" crops—rape, flax, hemp, woad, and tobacco—promoted enthusiastically by agricultural improvers of the age, were subsequently transferred to the American colonies where efforts were made to establish industries and crops that had already proven promising in England.

The conjunction of these social and economic developments, together with a switch in direction of English expansionist policies, account for the colonization schemes from the 1560s onwards. With the end of the attempt to retain a beachhead on the Continent after the loss of Calais in 1558, merchants and statesmen began looking westward rather than to Europe for expansion, first to Ireland, then the Caribbean and North American mainland. The two major advantages of American colonization were commercial and social. All kinds of goods and products imported from Europe and Asia could instead, it was argued, be imported cheaply from English colonies in the New World. England's surplus poor, the able-bodied poor and unemployed, could be put to work in the colonies to the nation's advantage. The large-scale transfer of poor to America would create an enormous and growing demand for English goods, thereby stimulating industry at home. Overpopulation would be avoided and the mounting social problems associated with poverty, vagrancy, and underemployment alleviated.

There is little direct evidence regarding why indentured servants, the great majority of the immigrants to the Chesapeake and the West Indies, chose to leave England. Most did not (or could not) record their thoughts in letters, diaries, and memoirs, which might have provided glimpses of the immediate factors that led to their decision to take ship for America. Consequently, much of the evidence is circumstantial.

Poverty appears to have been the principal influence on servant emigration in the seventeenth century. Possibly because it was one of the most obvious characteristics of servants—few who were able to pay the cost of their own passage would have willingly emigrated under indentures—or because it was at the center of much government legislation, poverty appears again and again as a key determinant in the experiences of individuals. Robert Redman, for example, was sent to London to be put on board the *Hopewell* in 1684. "If 9 years or tenn yeares ser-

vice be required," his uncle wrote, "I am contented provided he have his bellefull of food, with cloathes to keep him warm and warm lodgin at night. I could keep him no longer." A group of "pilfering boys that lie day and night in the marketts and streets of this city [London], and having noe friends or relations to take care or provide for them," were indentured to serve in Virginia in July 1684. Jonathan Cole, "a poor boy" who was abandoned in the parish of Coleshurst, London, left for America the following year. Throughout the century parishes and borough corporations routinely rid themselves of the expense and trouble of caring for orphans and unwanted children by indenturing them for service in the colonies.

Emigration from Bristol. The origins of servants who took ship from Bristol in the mid seventeenth century provide further clues about the mechanisms of emigration. Most servants came from populous lowland areas within forty miles (64 kilometers) of the city, which may be divided into three regions: the Severn Valley, north Somerset, and the South Wales coastal plain. These regions were mainly woodland and pastoral areas, devoted to dairy farming, stock rearing, and mixed agriculture. Compared with neighboring uplands they supported relatively dense populations, the result of natural increase and also of the large numbers of migrants who moved to these areas, attracted by the prospect of casual work in farming and a variety of rural manufactures, such as the cloth industry and coal mining. Parishes with extensive common lands and wastes, together with forests and woodlands, were traditional havens of the poor and were noted for their free and open society and the mobility of their local populations. In contrast to the more static populations of the surrounding wolds and uplands, where stronger manorial control and a less diverse economy prevailed, there was constant movement in and out of the marginal lowland areas, and many poor people from the forests of Dean, Wentwood, Frome-Selwood, and Neroche eventually found their way to Bristol and from there to Ireland and America.

Towns also supplied large numbers of servants. Over half of the Bristol servants came from (or had last resided in) urban communities.

Cloth-working towns such as Wells, Frome, Bradford-upon-Avon, Bath, and Malmesbury provided large numbers from the textile and clothing trades, while provincial capitals and county towns such as Gloucester, Salisbury, Monmouth, and Cardiff provided large numbers from crafts and service backgrounds. Towns played a key role in long-distance migration, providing temporary accommodation and work. Many prospective servants moved from their native village to the local market town and then in stages to Bristol before taking the decision to go overseas.

Emigrants from London. The influences that acted upon servants who emigrated from London in the seventeenth century are more difficult to interpret. Without question the city provided the majority of English immigrants to America in this period, but little evidence about their reasons for leaving survives. Migrants were drawn from all over the British Isles, although 40 percent came from the city itself and a further 11 percent from neighboring counties. As in the case of the Bristol servants, most emigrants appear to have moved to the capital in a series of stages. The magnitude of the total migrant flow to London, of which emigrants were a small subset, underlines the capital's enormous attraction throughout the century. During the period London's population rose from about two hundred thousand to approaching half a million, by which time it was one of the largest cities in the world. The whole of this increase can be attributed to immigration, which in the latter half of the century amounted to at least eight thousand persons a year, or roughly half the natural increase of provincial England. London, like the plantation colonies, relied on a sustained and massive influx of immigrants to maintain population growth.

The attraction of the capital lay in its unique role in the political and economic life of the nation. The city was at one and the same time a major industrial center, the country's leading port, the cockpit of national politics and government, a forum for taste, fashion, and display, and an enormous consumer of all sorts of goods and services. London dominated England in a way that few foreign capitals dominated their nations. Throughout the century people from all ranks of society flooded into the capital seeking out relatives, friends, and business connections to better their opportunities. The poor and those without connections looked for work where they could find it. Swelling the already burgeoning suburbs that circled the old inner core of the city, poor migrants replenished the huge mass of underused labor that already existed and that even London's diverse economy could not absorb. Some of those who could not find work moved on or went home, others scraped a living as best they could, while still others were recruited by merchants and their agents for the colonies.

Terms of Employment. This view implies that London, and to a lesser extent other colonial ports such as Bristol and Liverpool, served as reservoirs of cheap labor for the plantations. The supply of potential servants was not constant, and much depended on competing economic opportunities at home (nationally and regionally), but nevertheless merchants could be confident of siphoning off a proportion of the unemployed from the poorer quarters of ports and cities if demand from the colonies was sufficiently high. There is disagreement, however, about how much influence individual servants exercised in negotiating their terms of employment with merchants and how much they knew about conditions in America. David Souden, James Horn, and John Wareing argue that servants had little influence on where they were sent or on the conditions under which they served. Where they ended up and the terms of their indentures were largely predetermined by the demand from colonial planters, the dominant pattern of transatlantic trade at the time they left, and the customs that governed length of service both in England and the colonies.

David Galenson, on the other hand, maintains that a clear correlation exists between age, skill, destination, and length of indenture. Older and skilled servants served shorter terms than the young and unskilled. Similarly, those servants who went to the West Indies received shorter terms on average than those who went to the mainland colonies because conditions of service and economic opportunities for former servants were believed to be worse in the Caribbean. These differentials, according to Galenson, suggest that servants had a degree of leverage in bargaining the terms of their service with recruiting agents, which reflected the market value of their labor.

Insufficient evidence exists to prove either theory conclusively. While older and skilled servants generally did serve shorter terms than unskilled youths, this was wholly consistent with English labor custom and suggests that merchants adopted English practice in constructing an informal "going rate" for the different sorts of servants they recruited that had little to do with individual servants' ability to bargain for better terms. The role of merchants in the organization of the servant trade during the seventeenth century was extremely important. In the absence of state-sponsored schemes, it was largely left to private enterprise to provide the means of peopling the British colonies. Merchants, responding to the demand of colonial planters, governed the direction of the transatlantic servant trade. They and their agents provided the crucial link between England and America. They found and persuaded people to emigrate and provided the capital for transportation.

The root cause of servant emigration at least down to the 1660s was demographic and economic pressure in England, combined with the massive demand for cheap labor in the expanding colonies. The great majority of servants from the towns, cities, and populous lowland regions of southern and central England left their home parishes without the preconceived idea of emigrating and followed the general pattern of migration in this period, moving to neighboring market towns where they expected to find work. Others shifted to industrial areas for the same reason. After a period of tramping the highways, they eventually ended up in one of the major colonial ports—London, Bristol, Liverpool, or Plymouth—where some chose or were persuaded to try their luck laboring in the plantations. Poor emigrants were therefore part of a much larger volume of migration in this period, generated by the development of a national, and subsequently international, labor market. They cannot necessarily be distinguished as having greater vision or enterprise for desiring to leave England than the mass of migrants who, for one reason or another, opted to remain behind.

Not all servants, however, were the passive victims of demographic pressures, economic recessions, and the demand for contract labor in the plantations. Some farm laborers may have decided to swap casual laboring in England for working in the Chesapeake, where at least there was a possibility of one day setting up their own smallholding. Others, impressed by stories of the profits to be made from tobacco, may have been attracted by the prospect of striking it rich. But the degree to which people were able to weigh up opportunities in the colonies should not be exaggerated. Most poor did not have the luxury of considering their future in a detached manner, and it is improbable that they had sufficient information to judge their options in a calculated and rational way. If they had, it is unlikely that so many would have emigrated, because the risk of an early death was too great. Emphasis should be given instead to the constricted world of poor migrants. Poverty and the search for subsistence were the compelling and confining determinants of everyday life. The poorest emigrants indentured themselves to escape from their *immediate* situation—destitution, homelessness, unemployment—rather than because they had a clear concept of what life would be like in America. For many servants short-term, not long-term, imperatives were the driving force behind immigration to the New World.

English men and women provided the great bulk of the human cargoes of the seventeenth century, but there was also a lively trade in Irish servants, voluntary and involuntary. During the 1650s thousands of political and military prisoners were transported to the colonies and sold into servitude following the repression of the Cromwellian campaigns. In 1655 permission was granted to ship a thousand young women to Jamaica, "where they would breed up" the population of the newly acquired island. By the 1660s at least twelve thousand Irish Catholics were scattered throughout the British West Indies. Twenty years later Irish inhabitants comprised a third of the white population of the Leeward Islands. Generally plantation owners held Irish servants in contempt, judging them idle, disobedient, and "good for nothing but mischief." As their numbers increased, so did planter fears of servant insurrection, possibly in alliance with slaves or with French Catholics.

The Chesapeake. In plantation societies the crucial distinction between free and unfree settlers marked the borderline between independence and subservience, wealth and poverty, and opportunity and exploitation. Racial and ethnic differences—black slaves, Irish and Scottish servants—only added emphasis to this vital division.

Colonists who paid their own way went primarily to make money, either as sugar or tobacco planters, factors, merchants, or government officials. "To Parts Beyond the Seas" suggests that the great majority of Chesapeake free immigrants were single, young to middle-aged males from southern and central England. They came from a broad range of occupations but there was a clear preponderance of men from gentry and mercantile backgrounds. Gentlemen tradesmen, merchants, mariners, shopkeepers, and provisioners made up about four-fifths of the sample. In the early years of colonization, some gentry were attracted to Virginia by the prospect of easy wealth and military adventure. Exploration and conquest of foreign lands were thought worthy pursuits for gentlemen, especially when allied to the propagation of the Protestant faith. Hopes that Virginia would furnish fabulous riches to the degree associated with the Spanish *conquista* rapidly faded in the face of the hardships encountered within a few years after the initial settlement in 1607. As it became apparent that the colony was no Mexico or Peru, so the upper gentry and aristocracy lost interest. The typical free emigrant, insofar as one existed, was not so much the representative of England's landed classes as of the mercantile communities of provincial towns and the major ports. Thousands of small and middling merchants and retailers from London and Bristol moved permanently or temporarily to the Chesapeake during the century.

Perceptions of opportunity for free settlers in the New World took a number of different forms. Some early immigrants to Virginia may be best described as provincial *hobereaux,* impoverished gentry and younger sons who gambled on recouping declining fortunes at home. Sir John Berkeley from Gloucestershire, who immigrated in 1620 to set up an ironworks, was described as "estranged from his friends and reduced to poverty." A neighbor, George Thorpe, Esq., "did secretlie flie out of England" in 1620, while another Gloucestershire gentleman, Arnold Oldisworth, was alleged to have owed the Crown £6,000 when he departed for Virginia.

The colonies also provided a distant sanctuary for people who feared that their religious beliefs were becoming marginalized in England, as well as for proponents of new radical sects such as the Quakers. The scale of Puritan migration to the Chesapeake and the West Indies was far smaller than that to New England but was nonetheless significant. Separatist immigrants to Virginia and the West Indies were guided by the same impulses that led their counterparts to Plymouth. They had shared similar experiences in England and on the Continent, espoused a similar theology, and had the same objective of creating a godly community in the New World. Their impact on plantation society was not nearly as significant as that of Puritans in the northern colonies; historians more concerned with the economics of tobacco and sugar or with the development of chattel slavery thus have tended to neglect their influence.

New England. Discussions of the settlement of New England have revolved around the relative importance of religious and other motives in generating emigration. The standard view, reflected in the stress given to the Puritan character of migration, is that religious factors were predominant. It has recently been given renewed emphasis by Virginia Anderson, who argues against an overly economic interpretation. If settlers sought economic opportunities, why did they not go to the Netherlands or to the Chesapeake or Caribbean? And since it was well known by the mid 1630s that New England was no paradise, why did colonists continue to go there? Anderson suggests that the major reason was spiritual gain. The "majority of emigrants," she argues, "responded to a common spiritual impulse in moving to New England." They were well aware of the Puritan temperament of the region and chose to move to that part of the New World where they could live according to their religious principles. Nor did the quest for spiritual wealth necessarily imply material ruin. Puritans believed that as they followed their mission, God would look after His own and grant them, through their own efforts, a modest sufficiency. Some might even improve their economic fortunes, but material gain was perceived as incidental to the religious imperatives that shaped their society.

The emphasis given to religion has been questioned from a number of perspectives. Timothy Breen, Stephen Foster, and David Grayson Allen have argued that religious and economic motives were inextricably interwoven and that it is impossible to arrange the complex admixture of economic distress, religious persecution, and local and individual factors into a neat list of discrete influences ranked in order of importance. Allen's study of emigration from Yorkshire, East Anglia, Wiltshire, and Hampshire concludes that neither religious issues nor economic distress can account satisfactorily for the movement to New England. The intensity of religious persecution, for example, varied considerably from one diocese to another and at different times. Persecution does not appear as a major influence on emigration from Wiltshire and Hampshire, and even in the case of Hingham, Norfolk, where a dispute between the local minister and the Anglican church authorities sparked off the migration of a number of families in the late 1630s, other purely local factors—periodic visitations of plague and the evolution of social and kinship ties in early Massachusetts—were also instrumental in attracting people to America.

Emigrants were not all convinced Puritans. The presence of a sizable group of servants, the majority of whom were young, male, and poor, suggests that similar socioeconomic factors to those that influenced immigration to the plantation colonies may have operated on a proportion of New England migrants. They may have been more concerned about finding work and having the opportunity to set up for themselves after completing their terms than about the well-being of their soul or building a godly commonwealth. Similarly, many free immigrants believed the northern colonies offered bright prospects for commercial agriculture, trade, fishing, and various other profitable enterprises. One cannot rule out that they were influenced by religious factors, but equally one cannot assume that these were primary. An approach recognizing a variety of

motives that blends the "secular and circumstantial" with religious factors offers a more promising line of inquiry than insistence upon the label "Puritan migration," with all that it implies for the subsequent development of New England society.

THE DUTCH COLONIES AND IMMIGRATION

Three main considerations influenced the development of the Dutch colonies in the seventeenth century. First, the United Provinces did not experience mass immigration in the period and in fact tended to attract migrants fleeing religious persecution in other parts of Europe or seeking opportunity in the wealthy cities and ports of the United Provinces during the Dutch golden century. Second, those who were tempted overseas had almost literally the whole world to choose from, such was the expansion of the United Provinces' mercantile empire in the first half of the century. Adventurous young men might seek their fortune in the service of the East India Company in Indonesia, Japan, China, India, and Persia. If they chose to sail west, they might have ended up working on the sugar plantations of New Holland (Brazil), the epicenter of the Dutch West India Company's operations in the Caribbean for thirty years from the mid 1620s, or on the islands of Curaçao and Saint Eustatius. Third, Dutch merchants and mariners focused their energies on trade rather than colonization, and their spectacular success in the former has tended to overshadow their modest achievements in the latter. Dutch traders were ubiquitous in the British-American world of the mid seventeenth century, and they were especially prominent in the West Indies and the tobacco colonies, where some eventually settled.

New Netherland (New York), the most important Dutch colony on the northern mainland, was first settled in the mid 1620s by French-speaking Walloon peoples mainly from the province of Hainault on the border with France (in present-day Belgium). Little is known about their origins or reasons for emigrating. More information is available for the colonists who settled at Rensselaerswyck, a company enterprise organized by the van Rensselaer family on the Hudson River, between 1630 and 1644. The majority of 174 immigrants identified (about 60 percent) were single men in their late teens and early twenties; only about a third of the settlers arrived in family groups. Nearly 40 percent of the men were from farming backgrounds, and another quarter were described as either servants or laborers. The rest came from a wide range of craft and trade backgrounds, particularly woodworking and food-processing occupations, many of whom had been recruited in return for handsome salaries. A large proportion of the colonists came from the inland province of Utrecht, one of the most depressed regions of the United Provinces, which provided more settlers than the far more populous and prosperous provinces of North Holland and South Holland combined. Smallholders and laborers who drifted into Amsterdam were picked up by van Rensselaer's agents, who persuaded them of the opportunities awaiting them in New Netherland.

The character of immigration had changed significantly by the late 1650s and early 1660s. Family migration, rather than the movement of single men, dominated this period, suggesting that the colony had at last become attractive to couples looking for a new start in America. Moreover, the loss of Brazil in 1654 made New Netherland more attractive to Dutch financiers and merchants as a possible entrepôt for the sale of goods and slaves to the expanding British colonies. A thriving Dutch colony on the Hudson could occupy a pivotal role in the development of transatlantic and intercolonial trade; thus the attempt by the West India Company and the Dutch Government to supply New Netherland with colonists after 1657. Ironically, just as the colony appeared to be entering a period of stability and prosperity, it was conquered by the English.

The population of New York was probably in the range of from five to eight thousand at the time of conquest in 1664. From its earliest days, it had attracted ethnically diverse peoples, and by 1673 the majority of New York's inhabitants were non-Dutch. Colonists originating from North Germany made up nearly 40 percent of the population and were joined by British, French, Italian, and Jewish settlers, as well as Danes and Norwegians and a growing number of black slaves. New York quickly emerged as one of the most polyglot of the British colonies.

EIGHTEENTH-CENTURY IMMIGRATION

Two major developments distinguish eighteenth-century American immigration from the earlier period. First, the relative importance of various British regions as producers of immigrants to the colonies altered and, second, the direction of movement changed. During the seventeenth century, several thousand Scottish and Welsh settlers, and possibly as many as from fifty thousand to one hundred thousand Irish, immigrated to the colonies, but the great majority of colonists were of English extraction. During the following century, however, Ulster became the main region of British emigration. About 250,000 emigrants left Northern Ireland compared to 50,000 from Scotland and from 80,000 to 100,000 from England and Wales. In addition approximately 100,000 German-speaking immigrants arrived in British North America between 1683 and 1783, together with several thousand French Protestant immigrants who settled mainly in the South. Four-fifths of British immigrants went to the mainland, principally to the Chesapeake, the Carolinas, Pennsylvania, and New York. The major receptor of the seventeenth century, the West Indies, received only a fifth of the total migrant flow.

Scotch-Irish Emigration from Ulster

Five main waves of Scotch-Irish emigration have been identified down to the American Revolution: 1717–1720, 1725–1729, 1740–1741, 1754–1755, and 1770–1775. The first migration, involving from about two to three thousand people, was caused principally by the expiration of generous leases granted by landowners in the 1690s to attract immigrants from famine-stricken Scotland. Drought, crop failure, cattle disease, and high food prices also contributed to the exodus. Five years later a similar combination of high rents and disastrous harvests persuaded thousands more to leave. Hugh Boulter, Archbishop of Armagh, wrote in 1728 of an infatuation with emigration: "We have had three bad harvests together. . . . The humour has spread like a contagious distemper, and the people will hardly hear anybody that tries to cure them of their madness." Severe food shortages and "dearness of provision" reduced many small farmers and laborers to destitution, encouraging thousands to take up indentures for service in America. The doubling of rents and reduction in the length of leases also induced the better off to emigrate. The "richer sort," it was reported in 1729, believed "that if they stay in Ireland their children will be slaves and that it is better for them to make money of their leases while they are still worth something to inable them to transport themselves and familys to America," than be subjected to the same poverty as their undertenants.

Continuing efforts by commercially minded landlords to improve their land and rents, together with periodic crop failures and the ensuing spiraling cost of food, created the basic preconditions underlying mass migration throughout the rest of the century. But several new factors surfaced. Letters from settlers who had already emigrated encouraged families, relatives, and friends to follow in their wake. To a degree emigration became self-sustaining. Some colonies, such as South Carolina and Georgia, offered cheap land and other inducements to immigrants willing to settle in the backcountry. Finally, in addition to the economic problems caused to tenant farmers by high rents and price rises, slumps in the linen industry had a disastrous effect on thousands of poor cottage-weavers who had multiplied rapidly in the province after 1720. During the climax of emigration between 1770 and 1775, when about thirty thousand migrants left Ulster, a severe recession put roughly a third of weavers out of work. Cottage-weavers and smallholders composed the majority of the members of the Hearts of Steel, a loosely coordinated movement that sought to resist excessive rents and wholesale evictions as well as government troops sent to quell the disorders. Subsequent repression led thousands more to emigrate. Across the eighteenth century, the rapid commercialization of Ulster caused the impoverishment of large numbers of the most vulnerable sections of the working classes in town and country alike and explains why the bulk of emigrants, the displaced poor condemned by contemporaries as idle and worthless, could not raise their passage money and went to America as indentured servants or "redemptioners" (servants given the opportunity to buy their freedom by paying the cost of their passage shortly after arrival).

Eighteenth-Century English Emigration

While little is known about free emigration from England and Wales, it is evident that indentured servants made up the majority of settlers who embarked for America in the eighteenth century, despite their decline in numbers compared to the previous century. Several general similarities in the social character of servants compared with the earlier period are worth noting. As in the seventeenth century, the vast majority of servants were male, young, unmarried, and came from central and southern England. Similar factors—the attraction of the major cities and ports, unemployment, and the search for work—motivated the poor and mobile to leave their native communities for new horizons elsewhere. In the eighteenth century, like the seventeenth, emigration was typically a two-stage process, beginning with a period of moving around in England and ending in arrival at one of the major ports followed by the move to America. Emigration was closely attuned to the volume and direction of internal migration flows.

Nevertheless, there were a number of important changes in the social character of servants. Whereas during the seventeenth century nearly a quarter of indentured servants were women, in the eighteenth century women comprised only 10 percent of registrations. The reasons for the growing preponderance of men are not altogether clear. One suggestion is that as sex ratios became more balanced in eighteenth-century America, the demand for women immigrants fell. Planters could look to native-born women for wives rather than having to rely on female servants shipped from England. The increase in the supply of female labor reduced the need for women servants who had been traditionally employed to do household work and various light tasks around the plantation. An-

Table 3   Occupations of Male Servants Who Emigrated from Bristol and London, 1654–1775 (in percentages)

Category	Bristol 1654–1660	Bristol 1684–1686	London 1683–1684	London 1718–1759	London 1773–1775
Gentleman	1	0	0	0	0
Farmer	30	4	9	11	16
Laborer	9	12	5	6	15
Food and Drink	1	2	2	4	7
Metal, Wood, and Construction	6	7	6	18	29
Textiles and Clothing	10	15	8	14	19
Services	2	2	10	10	14
Not Given	41	58	60	37	0
Total	100	100	100	100	100

Source: Adapted from David Galenson, *White Servitude in Colonial America: An Economic Analysis,* tables 3.1, 3.3, 4.1, 4.5; pp. 35, 40, 52, 57.

other possibility is that there were changes in the supply side of the servant trade. During the seventeenth century, women servants were recruited not only because they were in demand in America but because merchants could not always find enough men. With the drop in the overall numbers of English servants in the eighteenth century, it is possible that merchants were able to recruit a greater proportion of men and, since males consistently brought higher returns than females, increase their profits.

Changes in the occupational backgrounds of male servants who emigrated from London in the eighteenth century are illustrated in table 3. Between the late seventeenth and mid eighteenth centuries, the number of servants registered without a designated occupation fell substantially from 60 percent to 37 percent, while the proportion of men from artisanal backgrounds increased. On the eve of the American Revolution, nearly half the men came from metal, wood, and construction crafts together with the textile and clothing trades. Only about 15 percent came from unskilled backgrounds. It would appear, therefore, that during the period there was a significant increase in the proportion of servants from skilled and semi-skilled backgrounds. Commenting on emigration from England and Scotland in the mid 1770s, Bernard Bailyn has remarked that from neither region was emigration a mass exodus of "destitute unskilled urban slum dwellers and uprooted peas-

ants" but rather was characterized by "certain segments of the lower middle and working classes, artisans and craftsmen with employable skills, for whom emigration would seem to have represented not so much a desperate escape as an opportunity to be reached for."

There can be little doubt that by the end of the colonial period, the social origins of servants had shifted from the lower to lower-middle classes, but it is unlikely that this transition occurred much before the 1750s. While the occupational structure of servants who left London between 1718 and 1759 might suggest a fall in the number from unskilled and lower-class backgrounds, the age of male servants nevertheless indicates a relatively humble status. The average age of those departing in the 1680s was from twenty-one to twenty-two years, compared with between nineteen and twenty for the period 1718–1759 and from twenty-one to twenty-three for 1773–1775.

Although there was a slight decrease in the extent of the city's migration field across the century, London continued to attract migrants from all over the British Isles, but the majority came from southern England. Between 1718 and 1739, from a third to 41 percent of servants came from the capital itself and another 12 percent came from surrounding counties, almost exactly the same proportions as in 1773–1776. As in the seventeenth century, the attraction of London can be attributed to the opportunities it offered to thousands of hopefuls who streamed into the city every year looking for work, swelling the size of London to around three-quarters of a million by 1775. Many thousands of unemployed men, women, and children, a constant feature of the city's population, provided an enormous pool of cheap, surplus labor and potential colonists. The gathering pace of population increase after 1750 and increasing social unrest following the end of the Seven Years' War in 1763 suggest other general causes of emigration in this period.

Scottish Emigration

"The westward reach of the Scots to America," Eric Richards has written, "was a variant of their penetration of England. . . . Lowland Scotland had overcome its provinciality and had become an autonomous source of technological, intellectual, and political ideas, all of which were broadcast across the Atlantic world and within Scotland itself." Spurred on by the economic advantages that accrued in the years following the Union of Parliaments in 1707, merchants and manufacturers quickly took advantage of the benefits of being a partner in one the most extensive trading zones in the world. Clydeside tobacco merchants rivaled their English competitors in Bristol and Whitehaven by the 1730s, and by 1770 Glasgow had overtaken London as Britain's premier tobacco port. In the same period, the volume of Scottish linen exports to America rose by two to three times. The growing contribution of Scotland to the metropolitan economy affected all parts of the country but was particularly noticeable in the Lowlands, where the concentration of towns, population, mineral resources, prime farming land, and capital accentuated age-old cultural differences with the Highlands. During the half century after 1750, Lowland society, like parts of England, experienced rapid population growth, urbanization, and industrialization, encouraging the flow of commerce and technology between the two countries and overseas.

The bifurcation of Scottish society in the eighteenth century had a profound influence on emigration. Lowland migration typically included large numbers of artisans, especially from the industrial West Lowlands that included Glasgow, Greenock, Paisley, and other important textile centers. The area suffered a severe depres-

sion in the early 1770s, reducing thousands of textile workers "to the utmost distress for want of employ," many of whom were forced to emigrate "to prevent them from starving." Three-quarters of 369 emigrants of known occupations from the area who embarked for America just before the revolution came from craft backgrounds.

By contrast the great majority of migrants from the Highlands and Western Isles were recorded as farmers and laborers; relatively few artisans emigrated. Population growth and pressure on the land gave impetus to a movement that had begun as far back as the 1740s. As in eighteenth-century Ireland, the determination of landlords to improve their lands, consolidate holdings, and raise rents had a profound impact on the well-being of the peasantry. Much of the movement from both countries can be explained by the commercialization of agriculture and the resultant dislocation of traditional agrarian society. The large number of poor laborers corresponds more closely than anywhere else in Britain, according to Bailyn, to a displaced rural proletariat.

German Emigration

German-speaking emigrants represented a diverse group of settlers from the territories of the Holy Roman Empire and the Helvetic Confederation. Small numbers arrived in British and Dutch colonies in the early seventeenth century, mainly attracted by the prospect of religious toleration, but it was not until a century later that large-scale emigration began with the movement of some 13,000 people from the Palatinate to Britain in 1709, of which 2,344 eventually settled in New York and another 650 in North Carolina. The pattern of immigration during the rest of the century was far from uniform. Numbers gradually increased from the mid 1720s to the end of the 1730s, fell during the wars of the Austrian Succession, surged dramatically between 1748 and 1754, and thereafter dwindled down to the revolution. Over three-quarters of immigrants arrived in family groups, and most of them entered America through Philadelphia and either settled in Pennsylvania or moved south and west into the backcountry of Maryland, Virginia, and the Carolinas. Across the century after the initial settlement of Germantown in 1683, just under 102,000 German-speaking immigrants arrived in British America.

Southwestern Germany, particularly the Protestant areas of the Palatinate, Hesse, Wurtemberg, and Alsace Lorraine, together with the Swiss cantons of Basel, Bern, and Zurich, supplied the majority of settlers throughout the eighteenth century. The region, "a checkerboard of territories distinct in terms of religion, the composition of their populations, and their customs and laws," represented a major arena for rival dynastic interests during the seventeenth and eighteenth centuries and as a consequence was periodically devastated by war. Against this cycle of destruction and rebuilding, some half a million migrants left the region between the 1680s and the 1780s, mostly for the eastern lands of the Hapsburg Empire, Russia, and Prussia. The flow of Protestant immigrants to North America was but a small part (about 13 percent) of the much broader movement of people out of southwestern Germany.

The destructive effect of war is usually cited as a principal factor behind German emigration. Apart from the obvious point that war hindered long-range migration, however, there is no precise correlation between emigration and periods of war and peace. As in other examples of European emigration, it is difficult to be precise about the significance of individual factors that might have influenced mass movement, such as political or economic crises, demographic fluctuations, war, harvest failure, or religious persecution. A number of religious sects and churches—Amish, Mennonite, Brethren, Quaker, Lutheran, and Reformed—as well as mystics and spiritualists, found America a congenial refuge, but religious persecution was not the main reason for German emigration. Marianne Wokeck has suggested that it is misguided to look for one or two principal causes and argues instead that the political and economic instability endemic to the region provided the general context for emigration, together with the attraction of the colonies and the development of a means of cheap transatlantic transportation.

Wokeck's argument raises important issues. For a variety of reasons, at different times particular regions of Europe emerged as net donors or receptors of migrants. North America was a net receptor throughout the colonial period and its ability to attract settlers was contingent upon the relative attraction of parts of Europe, as well as the development of the means by which people could be transported across the ocean cheaply. British, Dutch, German, and French emigration all depended on merchants and their agents to transform the European migrant into the American settler. In the case of German emigration, British and Dutch merchants in Rotterdam emerged as essential middlemen in organizing the immigrant trade via the development of different strategies by which individuals could be profitably transported. A second aspect of the ebb and flow of emigration was the role played by emigrants themselves. Successful colonists who returned to Europe and spread encouraging reports about life in America stimulated further emigration. By providing information, expertise and, in some cases, material resources Newlanders (returnees from America) facilitated the movement of their fellow countrymen and countrywomen to the colonies.

The importance of family, kinship, and ethnic ties differentiated German emigration from the more impersonal system of servant transportation typified by English and Irish Catholic examples and helped shape the character of German migration. A growing and increasingly prosperous German-speaking community provided the means by which new arrivals could "redeem" the cost of their passage, find work, and adjust to the novel conditions in America. The pattern of German emigration represented a middle way between indentured servitude and free migration and was subsequently adapted and developed on a larger scale during the mass European migrations of the nineteenth century.

CONCLUSION

All the major European powers—Spain, Britain, France, and the United Provinces—established commercial empires in the New World during the early modern period, although their success as colonizers varied considerably. Emigrants from lesser states, such as the Scandinavian countries or the territories of the Holy Roman Empire, either established small-scale settlements or went to the colonies of their more powerful rivals. Small numbers of Finns, Swedes, Danes,

Table 4 National or Linguistic Stocks as Proportion of White United States Population in 1790 (percentages)

State	English	Welsh	Scotch-Irish	Scotch	Irish	German	Dutch	French	Swedish
Maine	77.6	2.2	8.4	4.2	4.8	1.2	—	1.6	—
New Hampshire	81.4	2.3	8.0	4.0	3.7	0.1	—	0.5	—
Vermont	81.4	3.5	7.3	3.6	3.6	0.2	0.2	0.2	—
Massachusetts	84.4	5.3	5.3	2.7	2.5	0.3	0.1	1.2	—
Rhode Island	79.9	2.3	7.0	3.5	2.6	0.1	—	4.6	—
Connecticut	87.1	3.1	4.5	2.2	2.1	0.4	0.1	0.5	—
New York	50.3	3.4	8.7	4.3	4.1	9.1	15.9	4.2	—
New Jersey	50.6	3.6	6.8	3.4	4.1	6.5	20.1	3.8	1.1
Pennsylvania	25.8	3.6	15.1	7.6	7.1	38.0	1.3	0.9	0.6
Delaware	63.3	5.5	9.2	4.6	8.0	2.6	1.3	1.7	3.8
Maryland	52.5	4.6	10.4	5.2	10.9	12.7	0.4	3.0	0.3
Virginia	61.3	6.5	11.7	5.9	6.8	4.5	0.7	2.4	0.2
North Carolina	53.2	6.2	15.8	7.9	8.6	5.1	0.4	2.5	0.3
South Carolina	47.6	6.2	18.9	9.4	8.2	5.5	0.2	3.7	0.3
Georgia	58.6	7.9	12.2	6.1	8.6	3.5	0.1	2.6	0.4
Kentucky	54.8	3.6	16.5	8.3	9.0	4.9	1.2	1.5	0.2
Tennessee	50.6	4.8	17.8	8.9	8.7	6.6	1.3	0.9	0.4
United States	59.7	4.3	10.5	5.3	5.8	8.9	3.1	2.1	0.3

Source: Thomas L. Purvis, "The European Ancestry of the United States Population, 1790," table II, p. 98.

Jews, Italians, Spanish, and Portuguese settlers found their way to the British and Dutch colonies of North America as merchants, farmers, field hands, and religious refugees, together with larger numbers of French Protestants and German-speaking immigrants. Although British America remained overwhelmingly British in terms of the national origins of the majority of white settlers (by the time of the first federal census of 1790, about 60 percent of the white population was of English stock and over 85 percent was of British origin), a significant proportion of German, Dutch, and other Europeans lived in the United States by 1790 (table 4). From these modest beginnings, the foundations of ethnic pluralism, a distinctive feature of modern American society, were laid.

BIBLIOGRAPHY

General

Altman, Ida, and James Horn, eds. *"To Make America": European Emigration in the Early Modern Period.* Los Angeles, 1991.

Jones, Maldwyn Allen. *American Immigration.* Chicago, 1960. Dated but still provides a useful overview.

Meinig, D. W. *The Shaping of America: A Geographical Perspective on 500 Years of History.* Volume 1, *Atlantic America, 1492–1800.* New Haven, Conn., 1986. Ambitious and valuable survey.

Thernstrom, Stephan, ed. *Harvard Encyclopedia of American Ethnic Groups.* Cambridge, Mass., 1980.

European-Indian Relations

Denevan, William M., ed. *The Native Population of the Americas in 1492.* Madison, Wis., 1976.

Fitzhugh, William W., ed. *Cultures in Contact: The Impact of European Contacts on Native American Cultural Institutions, A.D. 1000–1800.* Washington, D.C., 1985.

Jennings, Francis. *The Invasion of America: Indians, Colonialism, and the Cant of Conquest.* Chapel Hill, N.C., 1975. Influential reappraisal of the impact of British colonization on Indian cultures.

Merrell, James H. "'The Customes of Our Countrey': Indians and Colonists in Early America." In *Strangers Within the Realm: Cultural Margins of the First British Empire,* edited by Bernard Bailyn and Philip D. Morgan. Chapel Hill, N.C., 1991. Excellent account.

Salisbury, Neal. *Manitou and Providence: Indians, Euro-*

peans, and the Making of New England, 1500–1643. Oxford, 1982.

Colonial Society

Beckles, Hilary McD. *White Servitude and Black Slavery in Barbados, 1627–1715.* Knoxville, Tenn., 1989.

Cohen, David Steven. "How Dutch Were the Dutch of New Netherland?" *New York History* 62, no. 1 (1981):43–60.

Dunn, Richard S. *Sugar and Slaves: The Rise of the Planter Class in the English West Indies, 1624–1713.* Chapel Hill, N.C., 1972. The best general account of English society in the Caribbean.

Greene, Jack P. *Pursuits of Happiness: The Social Development of Early Modern British Colonies and the Formation of American Culture.* Chapel Hill, N.C., 1988. Valuable synthesis and a provocative argument.

McCusker, John J., and Russell R. Menard. *The Economy of British America, 1607–1789.* Chapel Hill, N.C., 1985.

Nash, Gary B. *Red, White, and Black: The Peoples of Early America.* Englewood Cliffs, N.J., 1974; 2nd ed. 1982.

Rink, Oliver A. *Holland on the Hudson: An Economic and Social History of Dutch New York.* Ithaca, N.Y., 1986.

————. "The People of New Netherland: Notes on Non-English Immigration to New York in the Seventeenth Century." *New York History* 62, no. 1 (1981):5–42.

Roeber, A. G. "'The Origin of Whatever Is Not English Among Us': The Dutch-speaking and the German-speaking Peoples of Colonial British America." In *Strangers Within the Realm: Cultural Margins of the First British Empire,* edited by Bernard Bailyn and Philip D. Morgan. Chapel Hill, N.C., 1991.

European Immigration

Allen, David Grayson. *In English Ways: The Movement of Societies and the Transferal of English Local Law and Custom to Massachusetts Bay in the Seventeenth Century.* Chapel Hill, N.C., 1981.

Anderson, Virginia DeJohn. "Migrants and Motives: Religion and the Settlement of New England, 1630–1640." *New England Quarterly* 58, no. 3 (1985):339–383. Emphasizes the significance of religious motives.

Archer, Richard. "New England Mosaic: A Demographic Analysis for the Seventeenth Century." *William and Mary Quarterly,* 3rd ser., 47, no. 4 (1990):477–502. Questions conventional views of New England immigration.

Bailyn, Bernard. *Voyagers to the West: A Passage in the Peopling of America on the Eve of the Revolution.* New York, 1986. Provides an exhaustive analysis of emigration from Britain in 1773–1776.

Breen, Timothy H., and Stephen Foster. "Moving to the New World: The Character of Early Massachusetts Immigration." *William and Mary Quarterly,* 3rd ser., 30, no. 2 (1973):189–222.

Campbell, Mildred. "Social Origins of Some Early Americans." In *Seventeenth-Century America: Essays in Colonial History,* edited by James Morton Smith. Chapel Hill, N.C., 1959. A seminal study.

Cressy, David. *Coming Over: Migration and Communication Between England and New England in the Seventeenth Century.* Cambridge, England, 1987. Useful discussion of transatlantic connections.

Dickson, R. J. *Ulster Emigration to Colonial America, 1718–1775.* London, 1966. The best study of Ulster emigration in the eighteenth century.

Fischer, David Hackett. *Albion's Seed: Four British Folkways in America.* New York, 1989.

Galenson, David W. "Labor Market Behavior in Colonial America: Servitude, Slavery, and Free Labor." In *Markets in History: Economic Studies of the Past,* edited by David W. Galenson. Cambridge, England, 1989.

————. *White Servitude in Colonial America: An Economic Analysis.* Cambridge, England, 1981. Valuable survey of indentured servitude and the labor market.

Gemery, Henry A. "Emigration from the British Isles to the New World, 1630–1700: Inferences from Colonial Populations." *Research in Economic History* 5 (1980):179–231.

————. "Markets for Migrants: English Indentured Servitude and Emigration in the Seventeenth and Eighteenth Centuries." In *Colonialism and Migration: Indentured Labour before and after Slavery,* edited by P. C. Emmer. Dordrecht, The Netherlands, 1986. Good summary of late-twentieth-century literature.

Horn, James. "Servant Emigration to the Chesapeake in the Seventeenth Century." In *The Chesapeake in the Seventeenth Century: Essays on Anglo-American Society,* edited by Thad W. Tate and David L. Ammerman. Chapel Hill, N.C., 1979.

————. "'To Parts Beyond the Seas': Free Emigration to the Chesapeake in the Seventeenth Century." In *"To Make America": European Emigration in the Early Modern Period,* edited by Ida Altman and James Horn. Los Angeles, 1991.

Miller, Kerby A. *Emigrants and Exiles: Ireland and the Irish Exodus to North America.* Oxford, 1985.

Purvis, Thomas L. "The European Ancestry of the United States Population, 1790." *William and Mary Quarterly,* 3rd ser., 41, no. 1 (1984):85–101.

Richards, Eric. "Scotland and the Uses of the Atlantic Empire." In *Strangers Within the Realm: Cultural*

Margins of the First British Empire, edited by Bernard Bailyn and Philip D. Morgan. Chapel Hill, N.C., 1991.

Salerno, Anthony. "The Social Background of Seventeenth-Century Emigration to America." *Journal of British Studies* 19, no. 1 (1979):31–52.

Smith, Abbot Emerson. *Colonists in Bondage: White Servitude and Convict Labor in America, 1607–1776.* Chapel Hill, N.C., 1947. A classic early study of indentured servitude and convict labor.

Souden, David. "Rogues, Whores, and Vagabonds? Indentured Servant Emigrants to North America, and the Case of Mid-Seventeenth-Century Bristol." *Social History* 3, no. 1 (1978):23–41.

Wareing, John. "Migration to London and Transatlantic Emigration of Indentured Servants, 1683–1775." *Journal of Historical Geography* 7, no. 4 (1981):356–378.

Wokeck, Marianne. "Harnessing the Lure of the 'Best Poor Man's Country': The Dynamics of German-Speaking Immigration to British North America, 1683–1783." In *"To Make America": European Emigration in the Early Modern Period,* edited by Ida Altman and James Horn. Los Angeles, 1991.

James Horn

SEE ALSO **The First Americans; Indian-Colonist Conflicts and Alliances; Indian-Colonist Contact; Medical Practice, Health and Disease;** various essays in LABOR SYSTEMS; and the maps in **Internal Migration.**

THE FRENCH COLONIES

CANADA AND ACADIA

The Context of Peopling

WHAT ADVANTAGES AMERICA might offer to France could be secured only by settlement. Without settlement, there could be no national claim de jure, and no stronghold from which a claim could be defended de facto. The first attempt to people the new land with Frenchmen was that of Jacques Cartier and Jean-François de La Rocque de Roberval, who in the period from 1541 to 1543 established a substantial but ephemeral colony near the site of Quebec, drawing their colonists directly from the jails. Over fifty years later, in 1598, Mesgouez de La Roche left a group of beggars, vagabonds, and convicts on Sable Island off the Nova Scotian coast, from which the few survivors were rescued some five years later.

From the 1580s, European demand for beaver became significant. Thereafter, the search for beaver trade provided the economic motive for penetrating Canadian territory, to which, from the 1620s, was added the motive of proselytizing the native peoples.

Peopling Canada and Acadia with Frenchmen came to be a burden imposed upon merchants interested in beaver pelts and upon the faithful who supported Catholic missions. Although fur-trade monopolists honored their promise to settle immigrants mainly in the breach, there were proponents of colonization among them. Samuel de Champlain and Charles de Biencourt, who had both earned their bread in the beaver trade, presented colonization schemes in 1618 for Canada and Acadia, respectively. In 1626 Isaac de Razilly, a soldier, prepared a memorandum on colonization for Cardinal Richelieu, who in 1627 established the Compagnie des Cent-Associés (One Hundred Associates) as an instrument of state, for which profits were secondary, to colonize and evangelize Canada and Acadia and, in a larger sense, to lay the foundations of a French overseas empire. The captures of Port Royal, Nova Scotia (1627), and Quebec (1629) by the piratical Kirke brothers and the untimely death in 1635 of Razilly, to whom the Cent-Associés had entrusted the colonization of Acadia, dealt major blows to the French colonizing effort. Nevertheless, over the next generation, the Cent-Associés directed a steady trickle of colonists to the Saint Lawrence Valley, either directly or through enterprising seigneurs to whom it conceded lands. The Jesuits (1625), the Montreal Society (1642), the Ursulines (1639), and others brought workmen to Canada to support their establishments.

The scheme of empire, glimpsed in Richelieu's plans, was reformulated in distinctly mercantilistic terms by Jean-Baptiste Colbert, Louis XIV's secretary of state for naval affairs. Colbert invested troops and treasure in Canada to fend off the colony's enemies, to diversify the economic base, and to develop a larger market in Canada for French goods. Although the wars of Louis XIV beginning in 1672 cut short royal largess, the broad Colbertist vision remained intact. But as Canada and Acadia were, economically speaking, marginal to the colonial world, so were colonies in general fated to be marginal to the French world.

Implications for Native Peoples

The heart of New France was the Saint Lawrence Valley from Montreal to the sea. Peopled in Cartier's time by indigenous tribes known as the Laurentian Iroquois, this area was a vacant no-man's-land by the late sixteenth century. The French settlers of the 1630s and later thus repeopled a land long empty. Cartier had ascended the Saint Lawrence seeking a route to Asia. He took land without asking, interfered in Native politics, and kidnapped natives. This gives us some small insight into the relationships that might have developed between the French and Indians had the Saint Lawrence Valley still been settled by Indians in the seventeenth century and had the fur trade not developed as a main reason for France's gaining an American foothold.

Tadoussac, Port Royal, Quebec, Trois-Rivières, and Lachine were all established as fur trading posts. The native Montagnais and Algonquian who lived north of the Saint Lawrence, wanted the goods the French had to trade and wanted the traders' alliance. The French, with their harquebuses, clumsy weapons but sensational in terms of flash, smoke, and noise, were good protection against the Mohawk and kindred Iroquoian who attacked these Algonquian to pillage their beaver-laden canoes. Throughout the history of New France, the fur trade, which involved ever more distant peoples, gave rise to a Franco-Indian interdependence that was both economic and military. This coincidence of interest protected New France and made its settlement possible. Thus in a very real way, the repeopling of the Saint Lawrence Valley by the French rested upon Indian consent and assistance, not only at the time of settlement but also generation after generation, for the entire history of New France.

The Canadian fur trade in the West and Anglo-Indian warfare in the East engendered numerous movements of peoples, including the resettlement of native peoples in the Saint Lawrence Valley. The earliest of all to settle along the Saint Lawrence were Montagnais families, encouraged to take up farming at the reserve of Sillery in 1637. As the Montagnais were not horticultural Indians, it was an unhappy experiment. In 1651 dispersed Huron settled on the Île d'Orléans, later moving to Ancienne Lorette near Quebec City. Mohawk, Oneida, and assimilated Huron settled south and north of Montreal in the later seventeenth century. In the eighteenth century, Abenaki, fleeing the wars with New Englanders, settled at Saint François on the south shore of the Saint Lawrence. When the French settled at Detroit in 1701 they encouraged Huron, Ottawa, Fox, and others to come and establish their fields and villages near their own Fort Pontchartrain, producing a Native concentration where none had been, although disregarding the claims of the Seneca to this strategic passage.

With the exception of Sillery, the purpose of which was assimilation, these Indian settlements were characterized by Native horticulture, Native housing, Native customs, and Native government. Thus the repeopling of the land in the Saint Lawrence Valley was partly undertaken by Indians, in an Indian way.

Modalities of Repeopling

The first impulse of the French was to people New France with the sweepings of the jails and roadsides. Such forced emigration of vagabonds and criminals was again utilized by the French government in the early eighteenth century as a means of populating Louisiana, which was technically within the jurisdiction of the governor of New France. The attempt was not repeated in Canada on any scale after the failures of the sixteenth century. Rather, traders, shippers, missionaries, and colonizers took to hiring men on three-year contracts to clear land, to build, or to work in the fishery. A recruiter, seeking in French ports the rootless men who had drifted from farming the land, signed them up at a tavern, gave them a cash advance, and got them on board ship before they could run away. These *trente-six mois* (thirty-six months), as these contract workers were known, were free at the end of their terms to return to France. Before about 1650 a return passage was usually a part of the bargain. Salary and perquisites distinguished these *engagés* (hired men) from the similar indentured servants in the English colonies.

From earliest times, property rights in New France were expressed in terms of the seigneurial system. Land was granted by the ultimate landholder under the king to others as seigneuries. The holders of seigneuries then attempted to settle them with farmers. One of the earliest examples of this is the concession of Port Royal, Acadia, to Jean de Biencourt de Poutrincourt by Pierre du Gua de Monts, in 1606. Poutrincourt brought to his colony not only *engagés* but also a few complete families. Colonizers whom the Cent-Associés had made seigneurs in Canada—for example, Robert Giffard and Noël Juchereau des Chatelets—returned to their native communities to recruit relatives and other families as well as single *engagés*. Isaac de Razilly, acting for a kind of subsidiary company composed of members of the Cent-Associés, brought *engagés,* soldiers, relatives, and other families who would constitute the nucleus of Acadian settlement to La Hève in 1632. In 1659, the Montreal Society made a similar mixed recruitment in the La Flèche district, from which it had sprung. The Cent-Associés continued to send out *engagés* in its own right annually. While the settlement of New France was by and large an affair of individuals and not of communities, affinities of blood, marriage, and community played a role, particularly in the early recruitments by seigneurs and religious societies. A flurry of speculative *engagements* occurred in the 1650s and 1660s. Shippers in the French Atlantic ports gathered *engagés* and sold their contracts at Quebec.

From 1662 to 1671 the king sent *engagés* to Canada, largely depending upon the expertise of experienced shippers. To offset the preponderance of men that resulted, from 1663 to 1673 the French government also sent to Canada 774 women without other prospects, the so-called *filles du roi.* In 1665 the king sent troops to fend off the Iroquois. Some four hundred soldiers were persuaded to take up land in the Richelieu Valley. Thereafter, soldiers were a major pool of settlers.

Except for ironworkers recruited for the forges at Saint-Maurice (1730s) or craftsmen required for the building of the fortress of Louisbourg on Cape Breton Island (especially 1723–

1745), few *engagés* were brought to Canada in the eighteenth century. The law required a number proportional to a ship's tonnage to be carried on every vessel sailing to every colony except Louisiana, but it was much evaded. Another scheme was to send to Canada salt smugglers and poachers, but few were actually sent and still fewer stayed. All in all, of some twenty-seven thousand potential settlers thought to have debarked at Quebec, less than one third became established. Only a few hundred colonists sailed to Acadia. In the Seven Years' War, their numerous progeny, possibly as many as thirteen thousand people, were deported by the British army or fled into the woods or to nearby French colonies.

LOUISIANA: A DIFFERENT LAND, A DIFFERENT ERA

The eighteenth-century colony of Louisiana was founded by the state for immediate strategic needs, although for the long term, mercantilistic hopes abounded. When in 1712 the new territory was turned over to a state creditor, Antoine Crozat, a monopoly of mines, lands, and trade was conceded in return for peopling at the modest rate of ten young men or women a year. Clearly, putting off a creditor rather than building a colony was the point of this exercise. Undoubtedly, there was genuine hope for development and peopling in the founding of the Compagnie de l'Occident in 1717 (renamed the Compagnie des Indes, 1719), one aspect of John Law's "system" that was supposed to bring France an unprecedented prosperity. The monopolies conferred were considerable, but the peopling requirement ambitious: six thousand settlers and three thousand black slaves in twenty-five years. A propaganda campaign that had no analogue in the settlement of New France accompanied the foundation of the new company.

Business partnerships, some great, some small, received from the company concessions of land *en franc alleu* (freehold), usually four leagues square. (A league ranged from about 2.4 to 4.6 miles [some 4 to 7 kilometers].) Many of the concessionaires were absentee landowners for whom Louisiana was a distant and highly speculative business investment. The continuously inflating currency of Law's bank was the shaky underpinning of their attempts at colonization. Both this attitude of mind and the no-strings-attached land tenure set off the Louisiana experience from the earlier colonization of Canada, with its religious overtones and characteristic seigneurial tenure, and even from Acadia, where seigneurialism never achieved more than a shadowy existence.

Investors sent *engagés* to settle their concessions. The Compagnie des Indes sent Swiss soldiers, who were to build, in case of need to fight, and at the end of their contracts (it was hoped) to settle. Law's attempt to people his own concessions with nearly four thousand Rhineland settlers (few made it beyond the French port of L'Orient) was without parallel in earlier French colonization. The exile of petty criminals, vagabonds, and prostitutes produced results as fleeting as those of Cartier's colonization. More significant were the black slaves from the Guinea coast, some six thousand of whom were brought in the 1720s alone.

Approximately seven thousand immigrants sailed from France to Louisiana from 1717 to 1721, less than a fifth of them forced emigrants. The death rates were as appalling among these Europeans as among Africans. The survivors constituted the nucleus of the population of Louisiana, to which were added some Alsatian immigrants from 1753 to 1759, Acadians from 1765 to 1769, and, of course, the annual shipments of slaves.

A growing plantation colony was not one that could easily find links of interest with the Native population. Predictably, a war over land broke out at Fort Rosalie (Natchez) in 1729 and was not ended until the Natchez Indians were completely dispersed. Conflict was minimized by experienced Canadian leadership, the lagging pace of settlement, and the preoccupation of Native peoples with fighting the English and each other.

BIBLIOGRAPHY

Campeau, Lucien. *Les Cent-associés et al peuplement de la Nouvelle-France, 1633–1663.* Montreal, 1974.

Delâge, Denys. *Le Pays renversé: Amérindiens et européens en Amérique du nord-est, 1600–1664. Montreal, 1985.*

Giraud, Marcel. *A History of French Louisiana.* Vol. 1, *The Reign of Louis XIV, 1698–1715.* Translated by Joseph C. Lambert, Baton Rouge, La. 1974. Vol. 3, *L'Epoque de John Law (1717–1720).* Paris, 1966.

Lanctôt, Léopold. *L'Acadie dès origines, 1603–1771.* Montreal, 1988.

Le Gac, Charles. *Immigration and War: Louisiana, 1718–1721.* Translated and edited by Glenn R. Conrad. Lafayette, La., 1970.

Moogk, Peter N. "Reluctant Exiles: Emigrants from France in Canada Before 1760." *William and Mary Quarterly,* 3rd ser., 46 (July 1989):463–505.

Trigger, Bruce G. *Natives and Newcomers: Canada's "Heroic Age" Reconsidered.* Kingston, Ontario, 1985.

Trudel, Marcel. *The Beginnings of New France, 1526–1663.* Translated by Patricia Claxton. Toronto, Ontario, 1973.

Dale Miquelon

SEE ALSO **The First Americans; Indian-Colonist Conflicts and Alliances; Indian-Colonist Contact; Medical Practice, Health and Disease;** various essays in LABOR SYSTEMS; and the maps in **Internal Migration.**

THE SPANISH BORDERLANDS

As OCCURRED THROUGHOUT NORTH America, sustained contact with Europeans caused a rapid decline in the size of the Native populations. Beginning in the middle and late sixteenth century, Spanish soldiers and colonists started the process of repopulating the northern frontier regions of New Spain and Florida. This essay examines the degree of Indian demographic collapse in Florida, New Mexico, Arizona, Texas, and California; the types of European settlements on the frontier; the size of the settler-military population; and motives for migration to Florida and New Spain's northern frontier.

THE DEGREE OF INDIAN DEPOPULATION

Several generations of scholars have debated contact Indian population size and the scale of demographic collapse from the sixteenth to the early nineteenth centuries. The estimates for Florida have generated the greatest controversy. Anthropologist Henry Dobyns, using what he calls the "disease mortality model," which reconstructs contact population levels by analyzing the mortality caused by epidemics, estimated that the population of one tribe, the Timucua, totaled about 722,000 in 1517, and that, by implication, around a million natives lived in all of Florida. According to Dobyns the Timucua population dropped to almost 37,000 in 1618. Scholars have challenged both the size of Dobyns's estimate and the method and sources used to arrive at the figure. Douglas Ubelaker had estimated the population of the Gulf states, including Florida, at around 114,000, and a substantially smaller figure for Florida. The Indian population living in the territory under Spanish control declined rapidly as a result of disease, warfare, and enslavement. In the mid 1650s, 26,000 Apalachee, Timucua, and Guale converts lived in the Florida missions. In the early eighteenth century, following a series of English attacks on Florida between 1702 and 1704, several hundred Indians lived in missions near Saint Augustine and Pensacola.

The Indian population of the frontier regions west of Florida experienced similar levels of depopulation. Some 80,000 Indians lived in New Mexico in 1598; the numbers dropped to 17,000 in 1679, 10,568 in 1750, 9,732 in 1800, 9,923 in 1820, and 16,510 in 1842. Clearly, the Indian population of New Mexico experienced a drastic decline in numbers in the century and a half following the arrival of the Spaniards in 1598, then recovered and began to grow at a moderate rate at the end of the eighteenth century after having reached a nadir around 1776. What is now Arizona was the northern district of Sonora. An estimated 85,000 Indians lived in Sonora in 1530 and 9,300 in 1790. As many as 5,000 to 10,000 lived in the part of southern Arizona that eventually came under Spanish control; around 400 natives survived in two missions in 1820.

Texas and Alta California (the modern state of California) pose the greatest problem in estimating the degree of population loss, since only a part of the Native population in both provinces lived in mission communities under direct Spanish control. Missionaries in both regions drew converts from increasing distances from the mission communities. The number of Indians living in the Texas missions fluctuated. There were 900 in 1740, 1,480 in 1760, 800 in 1780, and 700 in 1800.

The evidence for Alta California is more complete than for the rest of the borderland region, particularly in respect to the census and, especially, parish registers. Complete runs of baptisms, marriages, and burials survive from the foundation of most establishments until secularization (the transfer of the administration of the missions to state-appointed administrators after 1834). Thus, although distinct in many ways from the population dynamics of missions established elsewhere, a detailed examination of patterns of change in the Alta California missions is illustrative for the other western borderland missions. Some 310,000 Indians lived in the area of the modern state of California in 1769, and an estimated 200,000 to 250,000 dwelled there in 1848, two years following the occupation of the province by the forces of the United States. The Spanish occupied a narrow strip of territory running along the coast from San Diego in the south to San Francisco Bay in the north. Franciscan missionaries established twenty-one missions and systematically congregated the Indians living along the coast. As the coastal population declined, the Franciscans attracted converts from further inland, beyond the area of effective Spanish control. In 1769 some 59,700 Indians lived along the coast, 21,063 in 1820, and 15,225 in the missions in 1834.

The populations of the missions fluctuated as chronically high mortality reduced the number of converts and the missionaries relocated new converts to repopulate the missions. A total of 7,711 Indians lived in eleven missions in 1790, 13,628 in eighteen missions in 1800, 18,680 in nineteen missions in 1810, 21,063 in twenty missions in 1820, and 15,225 in twenty-one missions in 1834. An examination of one mission—San Juan Bautista, established in 1797 in central California, south of modern San Francisco and east of Monterey Bay (see table 1)—documents the process of the repopulation of the mission communities. The population of San Juan Bautista grew during periods of active recruitment and resettlement of Indians, first from the San Benito and surrounding coastal valleys from 1797 to

Table 1. Patterns of Baptisms and Population Growth at San Juan Bautista Mission, 1797–1834

Years	Baptisms of Converts	Births	Burials	Net Gain +/−
1797–1799	315	31	296	50
1800–1809	1,178	325	917	586
1810–1819	180	310	579	−89
1820–1829	902	457	1,039	−320
1830–1834	56	174	355	−125

around 1810, and from the mission in the Central Valley (located east of San Francisco between the Sierra Nevada and the Coast Range) after 1810. The mission population could not grow through natural reproduction because of very high infant and child mortality rates, and thus declined when the number of converts dropped, as occurred in the decade 1810–1819 and again in the 1830s. The pattern documented for San Juan Bautista was duplicated at all twenty-one missions. For example, in the 1820s the number of recruits entering the missions dropped, in part as a result of growing resistance by interior tribes.

PATTERNS OF EUROPEAN SETTLEMENTS

Spanish colonists and soldiers established different types of settlements in Florida, Texas, New Mexico, Arizona, and California. The type that evolved in each region reflected the original motives for colonization. For example, geopolitical considerations were important in the colonization of Florida, Texas, and California, and military garrisons were important settlements in all three areas. French settlement in Florida and Louisiana prompted the Spanish settlement of Florida in 1565 and of Texas in 1690 and again in 1716. English exploration of the Pacific Basin and the beginnings of Russian colonization of Alaska spurred the occupation of Alta California in 1769. New Mexico, on the other hand, began as a mission frontier between 1598 and 1680, and developed as a settlement colony in the eighteenth century. Ranching and farming communities developed alongside missions. The settlement of Sinaloa and Sonora, first colonized in the mid sixteenth century, advanced as the Jesu-

its established missions throughout the region, the government placed military garrisons to defend the missions, silver and gold were discovered, and ranching and farming communities developed to supply a growing market economy. The southern part of what today is the state of Arizona was the northernmost part of Sonora, and the permanent occupation of the area began after 1687.

The Spanish established permanent settlements in Florida after 1565, with most of the soldiers and colonists coming from Cuba. Throughout the period of Spanish occupation the military garrisons at Saint Augustine, Pensacola, San Luís in Apalachee, and other sites were important settlements in the province. Towns grew up around Saint Augustine and Pensacola in East and West Florida, respectively, and during the sixteenth and seventeenth centuries Santa Catalina de Guale, located on Saint Catherine's Island in Georgia, was a third significant community. The Franciscans included some eighty village sites occupied by eleven distinct peoples in an extensive mission system that existed between 1567 and 1704. The most important missions were among the Guale along the Georgia coast and the Sea Islands, and the Timucua and Apalachee establishments west of Saint Augustine.

New Mexico first evolved as a mission frontier during the seventeenth century and, following the Pueblo Revolt of 1680–1692, developed as a settlement colony. A large population of colonists lived in towns and farming hamlets throughout the region. The most important communities were these: Santa Cruz de la Cañada in the Rio Arriba district upriver from Santa Fe; the provincial capital Santa Fe; Albuquerque in the Rio Abajo district downriver from Santa

Fe; and El Paso, established in 1680 by refugees fleeing from the Pueblo Revolt in that year. Local officials also established communities for *genízaros* (detribalized Indians and mixed breeds) at Abiquiu, San Miguel del Vado, Belén, Jarales, Ojo Caliente, and the Analco section of Santa Fe. In the seventeenth century the Franciscans included thirty-six pueblos in their mission system. Following the Pueblo Revolt, the Franciscans did not reassert control over the Hopi west of Albuquerque, in the northeastern part of the modern state of Arizona.

The colonization of Texas in 1690 and again in 1716 came in response to concerns over French encroachments on lands claimed by Spain which could potentially serve as a base for an invasion of New Spain. Los Adaes, a military garrison and community located in eastern Texas, was the administrative center of the province and the principal outpost against French incursions until it was abandoned in 1773. Nacogdoches was a second important settlement in eastern Texas. San Antonio and La Bahía, located on the San Antonio River, were sites of missions and military garrisons around which small communities evolved: in 1731 the Crown sent colonists from the Canary Islands to San Antonio in an effort to increase the size of Texas's non-Indian population, and established a formal municipal government. Following the abandonment of Los Adaes the colonists living in eastern Texas moved to the Trinity River. However, many returned to eastern Texas and reoccupied Nacogdoches in 1779.

The Franciscans established many ephemeral missions in Texas, and other missions occupied several different sites. Between 1718 and 1731, the missionaries established two missions in the San Antonio area and relocated another three from eastern Texas. Three missions existed in the neighborhood of La Bahía in the second half of the eighteenth century, including Refugio, established in 1793. All told, sixteen separate missions existed in Texas at different times and in different locations.

Spanish colonization of what is now Arizona was limited to the Santa Cruz and San Pedro river valleys in the southern part of the modern state. The Pimería Alta, the northernmost district in Sonora, which included southern Arizona, was a mission frontier with some settlement by non-Indians. The government established presidios at Tubac and Tucson, which became population centers as settlers sought refuge from Apache raids. Prior to the 1760s, there were several cattle ranches in the Santa Cruz River valley along the modern Arizona-Mexico border. Finally, there were ephemeral mining camps established throughout the region in the eighteenth and nineteenth centuries. During most of the eighteenth century and the early part of the nineteenth century, the Jesuits and later the Franciscans operated two missions in the Santa Cruz Valley.

The colonial government carefully planned the colonization of Alta California. Between 1769 and 1800 the viceregal government in Mexico City authorized the establishment of four military garrisons at strategic points along the coast (San Diego, 1769; Monterey, 1770; San Francisco, 1776; Santa Barbara, 1782) and three pueblos, settled by colonists from central New Spain and the northern frontier (San Jose, 1777; Los Angeles, 1781; Branciforte, 1797). An implied English and/or Russian threat to California was the catalyst for the occupation of the region, and royal officials were constantly preoccupied by the underpopulation of the province and its vulnerability to foreign invasion. The underpopulation of California remained a concern as late as the 1830s, when the Mexican government sent one last group of colonists to the frontier. As the population of Alta California grew in the first three decades of the nineteenth century, towns developed around the four military garrisons. Between 1769 and 1823 the Franciscans established missions and developed farms, sheep stations, and horse and cattle ranches throughout the territory.

THE SIZE OF THE SETTLER POPULATION

Population data for Spanish Florida are incomplete and focus primarily on Saint Augustine, a garrison town. The military garrison grew slowly. There were some 150 soldiers stationed there in the 1570s and 100 in the 1640s. The number increased to an authorized strength of 400 by the mid 1700s, supplied from the professional Spanish troops stationed in Cuba. In

1598 the population of Saint Augustine was some 700, 1,444 in 1689, some 2,800 in 1759, and 3,561 in 1793. During 1763 and 1764, after Spain ceded Florida to England, the government evacuated some 3,100 settlers and Indians to Cuba and New Spain.

During the period of English occupation of Florida, the government issued land grants, and the recipients of the grants imported agricultural workers. The most important segment of the population, however, was the estimated nineteen thousand Loyalists who fled to Florida during the American Revolution. At the end of the American Revolution, England returned Florida to Spain. During the second Spanish period (1783–1821) Saint Augustine and Pensacola were the most important communities. Several thousand Hispanic settlers lived in the province. The major demographic movement of this period was the migration of hundreds of Anglo-American settlers into northern Florida, many of them entering illegally. A second significant segment of the population was formed by the Minorcans, Italians, and Greeks brought to New Smyrna in 1767 to work on a plantation being created by Andrew Turnbull, a British entrepreneur. Some fifteen hundred contract workers arrived in Florida, and most eventually settled in Saint Augustine.

The history of Spanish New Mexico is divided into two periods broken by the Pueblo Revolt (1680–1692). The pre-revolt settler population of New Mexico was some 200 in 1600; 1,200 in 1630; and 2,347 in 1680. The revolt forced an estimated 2,500 colonists to retreat to the El Paso area, where the decision was made to establish a new community. Around a thousand settlers returned to New Mexico in the 1690s after the reconquest of the province, and the population grew through natural reproduction during the eighteenth century. The settler population totaled 3,809 in 1750, 9,742 in 1776, 28,436 in 1820, and 46,988 in 1842.

Several formal civilian communities existed in Spanish Texas, including San Fernando (modern San Antonio), Nacogdoches, and the short-lived Bucareli, established on the upper Trinity River in 1774 after the abandonment of eastern Texas. Moreover, the *presidios* such as La Bahía became population centers as settlers looked for safety from raids launched by hostile Indians,

and retired soldiers elected to remain in the vicinity of the *presidios* where they had served the king. The non-Indian population of the province was never large, but it did experience gradual growth in the late eighteenth century and first two decades of the nineteenth. There were some 900 in 1740, 1,190 in 1760, 2,150 in 1780, 3,550 in 1800, and 8,000 in 1821.

The non-Indian settler population of what is today southern Arizona grew rapidly during the seventeenth and eighteenth centuries. In 1600 there were six hundred settlers in the region. The number increased to fifteen thousand in 1700, seventy thousand in 1800, and ninety thousand in 1821. Two settlements existed in the Santa Cruz Valley during the late eighteenth century, both *presidios*, and a third *presidio* was located in the neighboring San Pedro Valley for something more than a decade before pressure from hostile Indians forced its abandonment. The two military garrisons, Tubac and Tucson, attracted settlers who sought protection from hostile Indians and markets for agricultural surpluses. In 1764 the combined military-settler population of Tubac totaled 421, and, in 1796, 395 settlers lived at Tucson. Some one thousand to two thousand soldiers and settlers lived in the valley in the early nineteenth century.

The non-Indian population of Alta California was concentrated in the four military garrisons, including the families of the soldiers and of retired soldiers who continued to live at the *presidios,* and the three civilian pueblos. Moreover, small numbers of soldiers with their families were routinely stationed at each mission to protect the Franciscan missionaries and to provide a degree of coercive force to promote the smooth functioning of the missions' social and economic activities. The population of the presidios and pueblos in Alta California totaled 906 in 1790, 2,062 in 1810, 2,959 in 1820, and 4,506 in 1834.

As in other sections of New Spain's northern frontier, Anglo-American and other Europeans settled in Alta California in the first three decades of the nineteenth century. There were two distinct groups. Merchants and sailors who jumped ship and settled in the emerging towns in many cases became Spanish/Mexican citizens, converted to Catholicism, and received land grants from the Mexican government and local officials

in the 1830s and 1840s, following the secularization of the missions. Englishman William Hart-
nell typifies the merchants. He married a local
woman, received a land grant in the Salinas Valley (a coastal valley in central California some
ninety miles [144 kilometers] south of modern
San Francisco) in the 1830s, and between 1839
and 1840 worked for the local government as
an inspector of the missions in the process of
being secularized. The sailors maintained their
separate identity and constituted a hostile group
of illegal aliens. Some married local women. In
1845 fifty-six foreigners lived illegally in the vicinity of Branciforte on the northern shore of
Monterey Bay, cutting lumber and periodically
participating in civil wars between rival government factions.

In 1800 some twenty-eight thousand Hispanic settlers and soldiers lived in Florida, New
Mexico, Texas, Arizona's Santa Cruz River valley, and Alta California. Few native-born Spaniards lived in the five frontier provinces, and
the bulk of the population was of mixed European, Indian, and African ancestry. However,
many colonists, particularly light-skinned individuals brought to the frontier from central New
Spain by the government, frequently claimed
to be Spaniards once they arrived in communities
where their racial heritage was not known, in
an effort to improve their social status and to
differentiate themselves from local Indian populations. Moreover, racial identities assigned to
frontier residents by government officials or
priests were by no means precise. In the 1780s,
for example, the only individuals in Spanish
Texas who had been born in Spain or who could
claim direct Spanish descent were high government officials or members of the families descended from the handful of Canary Islanders
brought to the province in 1731. However, according to a census prepared in 1783, some fifty
years after the arrival of the Canary Islanders,
the non-Indian population of Texas consisted
of 1,577 Spaniards, a mere 125 mestizos (of
mixed European and Indian ancestry), 404 *color
quebrado* (of mixed European, African, and Indian ancestry), and 36 slaves presumably of African ancestry. Similarly, in 1797 the bulk of the
mestizo colonists brought from central New
Spain to settle Branciforte in Alta California
claimed to be Spaniards.

MOTIVES FOR MIGRATION TO THE NORTHERN FRONTIER

Migration to Florida and northernmost New
Spain on an individual basis was limited; the
Crown or its representatives in New Spain and
private individuals were responsible for most settlers and soldiers reaching the five regions studied here. Private individuals organized and financed the colonization of Florida and New
Mexico in 1565 and 1598, respectively, but
throughout the colonial history of both provinces, the Spanish government contributed to
the repopulating of the two regions by sending
soldiers, many of whom remained, to garrison
the military posts established to protect the settlements. In the 1760s an English entrepreneur
organizing a large commercial agriculture operation south of Saint Augustine in Florida imported some six hundred Minorcan and Greek
contract workers, most of whom remained in
Florida when Spain reclaimed the province in
1783.

In Texas and Alta California the Crown organized and financed the initial expeditions that
occupied the provinces in 1716 and 1769, respectively, and established military garrisons which
protected settlers and contributed to the growth
of the population because most soldiers and their
families remained. Moreover, the government
recruited colonists in the Canary Islands, in
Spain, in central New Spain, and in the more
populous regions of northern New Spain to increase the number of loyal citizens living in the
geopolitically sensitive but sparsely populated
provinces, offering land for farming and ranching and a chance to improve one's life. The three
civilian pueblos established by the government
in Alta California were initially populated by contingents of settlers recruited in central New Spain
and Sinaloa-Sonora. The Spanish and later the
Mexican government continued to send soldiers
and small groups of settlers to Alta California
as late as the 1830s.

The Santa Cruz River valley in northern
Sonora was the only area examined here not
settled through government or private colonization schemes, although the soldiers and their
families stationed in the military garrisons established in the valley constituted a large percentage
of the total population. Beginning in the seven-

teenth century, a dynamic market economy developed as a consequence of mining operations. A floating population of miners went from strike to strike to try their luck, and a small number of settlers established farming hamlets and ranches to provide food and leather products to the mining centers. The cattle ranches that operated in the upper Santa Cruz River valley prior to 1764 supplied the mines and, to a lesser degree, the military garrisons. The settlers living at Tubac and Tucson sold food and livestock to the mining camps in central and northern Sonora, and also to the military garrisons.

The historical geographer Michael Swann examines migration patterns in late-eighteenth-century Durango and Chihuahua (now states in northern Mexico), and documents instances of long-distance migration to the frontier from central New Spain. The limited evidence available for the five provinces studied here indicates that, with the exception of the planned colonization schemes promoted by the government, there was relatively little interprovincial mobility. The service records of soldiers stationed in northern Sonora and New Mexico indicate that most of them were recruited in the province where they served or were transferred from garrisons in neighboring provinces. In eighteenth-century Florida soldiers were recruited from the local population for the unit permanently assigned to Saint Augustine and other positions, but Spanish military units were also stationed in the province and rotated periodically between Cuba and Florida.

Detailed censuses of Branciforte and Monterey, located on Monterey Bay in Alta California, in 1845 and 1836, respectively, recorded the places of origin of their residents. In both instances the majority of the inhabitants came from the Monterey Bay area or other parts of Alta California. For instance, 72 percent of the Mexican residents of Branciforte were natives of the Monterey Bay area. The Mexican residents born outside of Alta California were elderly survivors of the early colonization expeditions, government officials sent to the province, or soldiers. However, as the local settler population grew, a large percentage of the soldiers stationed in the province were recruited locally.

Throughout the colonial period royal officials sent convicts to the northern frontier as soldiers and settlers, since it was difficult to entice large numbers of people from central New Spain to migrate, for example, to New Mexico and Alta California. Criminals in New Spain generally ended up in prison or on work gangs leased to private entrepreneurs, such as the operators of *obrajes* (which produced woolens in textile mills located in central New Spain as early as the 1530s). However, it is important to document accurately what crimes the convicts sent to the frontier had actually committed. As was the case with English convicts transported to Australia after 1788, many of the convicts sent to northern New Spain were guilty of minor crimes, not violent crimes such as murder, assault, and robbery. Many of the initial group of colonists recruited in the Guadalajara area (west central Mexico) and sent to Branciforte had committed such crimes as concubinage and carousing in bars, activities frowned upon by royal officials concerned with maintaining strict social control.

CONCLUSION

With the exception of New Mexico and northern Sonora, the northern frontier of New Spain and Florida was populated primarily through the efforts of the Spanish government or of private individuals given extensive political and economic rights over a jurisdiction in exchange for undertaking the organization and financing of colonization. However, all five regions remained sparsely populated, receiving a few migrants besides colonists recruited for various settlement schemes and the soldiers posted to the military garrisons.

The population density was increased in Florida, Texas, and Alta California primarily by Anglo-American settlers, thus hastening the absorption of the provinces by the United States between 1810 and 1846, beginning with West Florida. Anglo-American settlers in West Florida and Texas led revolts against the Spanish and Mexican governments which created short-lived independent republics later annexed by the United States. The Hispanic population of East Florida was outnumbered by Anglo-American settlers by 1821, and the Anglo-Americans in Alta California materially contributed to the occupation of the province by the United States in 1846. Only New Mexico, where Anglo-Americans were a minority, was conquered by outside force. The 1853 purchase by the United States of the Santa Cruz River valley and other districts in the modern states of Arizona and New Mexico (the Mesilla Strip) completed the acquisition of a potential route for a projected transcontinental railroad.

BIBLIOGRAPHY

Arana, Luís. "The Defenses of Florida During the Reign of Charles III, 1759–1788." In *Charles III: Florida and the Gulf,* edited by Patricia Wickman. Miami, Fla., 1990.

Arana, Luís, and Albert Manucy. *The Building of Castillo de San Marcos.* N.p. 1977.

Cook, Sherburne. *The Conflict Between the California Indian and White Civilization.* Berkeley and Los Angeles, 1976. Reprint of studies originally published in *Ibero-Americana* between 1940 and 1943.

———. *The Population of the California Indians, 1769–1970.* Berkeley and Los Angeles, 1976.

Dobyns, Henry. *Their Number Become Thinned: Native American Population Dynamics in Eastern North America.* Knoxville, Tenn., 1983.

Gerhard, Peter, *The North Frontier of New Spain.* Princeton, N.J., 1982

Gutiérrez Ramón. *When Jesus Came, the Corn Mothers Went Away: Marriage, Sexuality, and Power in New Mexico, 1500–1846.* Stanford, Calif., 1991.

Hann, John. *Apalachee: The Land Between the Rivers.* Gainesville, Fla., 1988.

Jackson, Robert. "Causes of Indian Population Decline in the Pimería Alta Missions of Northern Sonora." *Journal of Arizona History* 24, no. 4 (1983):405–429.

———. "Demographic Change in Northwestern New Spain." *The Americas* 41, no. 4 (1985):35–52.

———. "The 1845 Villa de Branciforte Census." *Antepasados* 4 (1980–1981):45–57.

Johnson, Paul, ed. *The California Missions: A Complete Pictorial History and Visitors Guide.* Menlo Park, Calif., 1964.

Kuethe, Allan. "Charles III, the Cuban Military and the Destiny of Florida." In *Charles III: Florida and the Gulf,* edited by Patricia Wickman, Miami, Fla., 1990.

———. *Cuba, 1753–1815: Crown, Military, and Society.* Knoxville, Tenn., 1986.

Lyon, Eugene. "Demographic Trends: Florida and the Gulf." In *Charles III: Florida and the Gulf,* edited by Patricia Wickman. Miami, Fla., 1990.

Thornton, Russell. *American Indian Holocaust and Survival: A Population History Since 1492.* Norman, Okla., 1987.

Ubelaker, Douglas H. "Prehistoric New World Population Size: Historical Review and Current Appraisal of North American Estimates." *American Journal of Physical Anthropology* 45(1976):661–666.

Robert H. Jackson

SEE ALSO **The First Americans; Indian-Colonist Conflicts and Alliances; Indian-Colonist Contact; Medical Practice, Health and Disease;** various essays in LABOR SYSTEMS; and the maps in **Internal Migration.**

INTERNAL MIGRATION

THE BRITISH AND DUTCH COLONIES

THE AMERICAN PROPENSITY to migrate far from family and community is part of American folklore. Discussion of migration in the colonial era evokes the hardy pioneer, his hard-working and self-effacing wife, the struggle with Indians to tame the wilderness, and the creation of settled communities of Englishmen. We have understood, as Richard Hofstadter wrote in 1968, that "the American people shaped their lives with the vast empty interior of the country before them." But that story, however compelling, omits many migrants. The Indian inhabitants migrated during the seventeenth and eighteenth centuries, often over far greater distances than the European settlers who conquered them and confiscated their lands. African and African-American slaves were forced to migrate, first from Africa and then across the colonial South to enrich their masters and sustain international commerce. And Europeans from many places besides England—including Scotland, Ireland, Germany, Holland, and Sweden—reached British North America and often migrated over long distances to form communities of their own. In the case of the Dutch and Swedish, the only non-English peoples to have established their own colonies among the English, inland migration was very limited in scope and significance. Most of it took place after the respective conquests of these colonies (New Sweden by the Dutch, 1655; New Netherland by the English, 1664).

Any discussion of migration immediately raises issues of definition. Nearly everyone resident in early America—Indians, European immigrants, native-born whites, African and African-American slaves—left their paternal home, moving about the countryside. Yet not all of these movements could be called migration; marriage migration, seasonal movement, and short-distance moves to an adjacent village or county, perhaps to land already owned or used by the family, community, or tribe, were part of the normal rhythm of daily life. Often involving setting up a new household just five or ten miles (8 to 16 kilometers) from the old homestead, these movements—even if repeated throughout one's life—hardly disrupted the daily lives of either those who moved or those who stayed behind. Internal migration, as defined here, excludes these kinds of movement but includes movement by individuals, families, or communities over sufficient distances to sever normal social ties with kindred and friends left behind. Such migration raises questions about social and cultural continuity between old and new homes. In the North American colonial context, this usually involved frontier migration, by Indians to an area controlled by another tribe, by Europeans or their descendants seeking to farm lands confiscated from Indians, or by slaves forced by masters or slave traders to move to uncultivated acres.

Far from being an invention of colonists, such forms of internal migration were intimately linked to previous forms of internal movement, both in Europe and North America. American Indians had peopled the continent long before whites arrived, moving in search of fresh game or fertile acres or forced to leave ancestral lands when defeated in war. They did not, however, move to increase production or create surpluses, but just to maintain a subsistence. As English population grew in the sixteenth and early seventeenth centuries—sometimes as much as one percent a year—English families left densely populated rural areas, moving long distances to the fens and wastelands, where they could eke out a subsistence on uninhabited lands, or toward provincial towns or the bustling city of London, where they could find work. Others left home as adolescents to labor in nearby villages as servants-in-husbandry on annual contracts, while still others, dispossessed of their land, tramped the countryside in search of work.

Even though internal migration had been ubiquitous in both America and England before the English arrived in North America, the *form* of migration common in the colonies—coerced population exchanges, and resettlement of forcibly abandoned frontier lands—was new. Internal frontiers were rapidly disappearing in England, but in the colonies white settlers dispossessed the original Indian inhabitants, creating new frontiers. As small farmers came to expect to own land, they spread across the landscape, moving to frontiers. As Marx understood, "the essence of a free colony . . . consists in this, that the bulk of the soil is still public property, and every settler on it can therefore turn part of it into his private property and his individual means of production, without preventing later settlers from performing the same operation." Once on the land, farmers sought to make a competency, a comfortable living, one that mandated some trade of surpluses to procure manufactured goods.

This essay will not only assess the demography and geography of frontier migration—Euro-

pean conquest and colonization, the movements of Indians and Europeans, the development of typical northeast and southwest directions of migration by European settlers and their descendants, age- and-place specific movements, and the levels of persistence in communities—but also will address the cultural and economic impact of migration. Migration played a key role in the transition of seventeenth-century enclaves into eighteenth-century colonies by spreading the white population across the landscape and connecting communities into regions where only isolated settlements had appeared before. Demands of the North Atlantic world economy, in turn, structured the timing and direction of migration. In response Indians were not only forced to move beyond the areas whites and slaves inhabited but also to reorganize themselves into more cohesive confederations to control the lands that remained to them.

The relation between migration and cultural diffusion is very complex. Some scholars, following the lead of Frederick Jackson Turner, insist that the frontier environment transformed European or eastern migrants, creating new men and women more democratic and individualistic than permitted in their older societies. Others insist upon cultural continuity, arguing that migrants brought their culture with them and successfully shaped the environment to meet their expectations. A group of environmental historians has challenged both of these opposed visions. They contend that the environment shaped the migrants at the same time as migrants transformed the environment. New cultures and economies thereby emerged, ones that resembled those left behind but which developed along a far different trajectory.

Migration must not be seen solely in such neutral, apolitical terms. The North American continent was hardly empty when Europeans arrived and began to compete to gain sovereignty over the land. Migration was part of this struggle over control of the continent among such European powers as England, France, Spain, Sweden, and the Netherlands and between Europeans and the Indian tribes. The speed of population growth and dispersion of Indians and various groups of Europeans partially determined the outcome of this centuries-long conflict. Migration by winners and losers in this struggle for

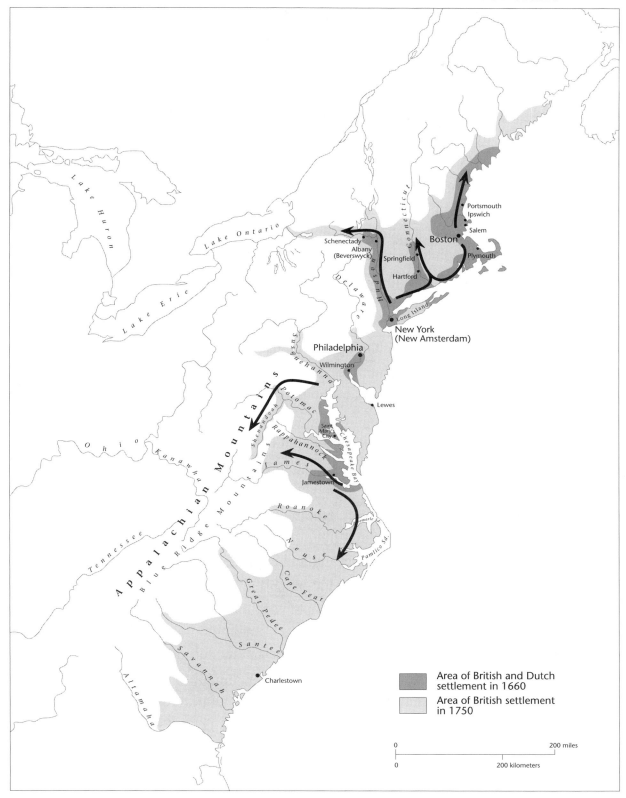

Area of British and Dutch settlement in 1660

Area of British settlement in 1750

0   200 miles

0   200 kilometers

SHAWNEE LOCATIONS AND MOVEMENTS DURING THE COLONIAL PERIOD

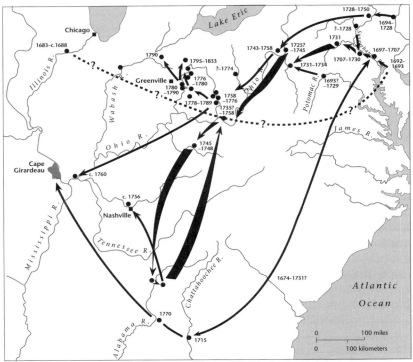

Based on a map in the chapter "Shawnee" by Charles Callender in *Handbook of North American Indians* vol. 15, 1978, Judith Crawley Wojcik, cartographer.

FRENCH EXPANSION INTO NORTH AMERICA, 1600S TO 1750S

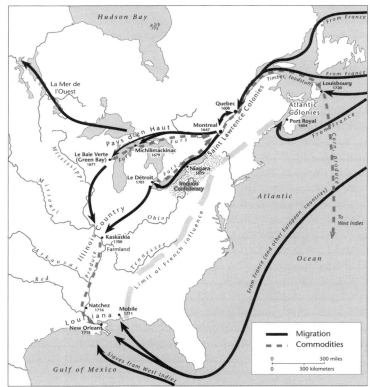

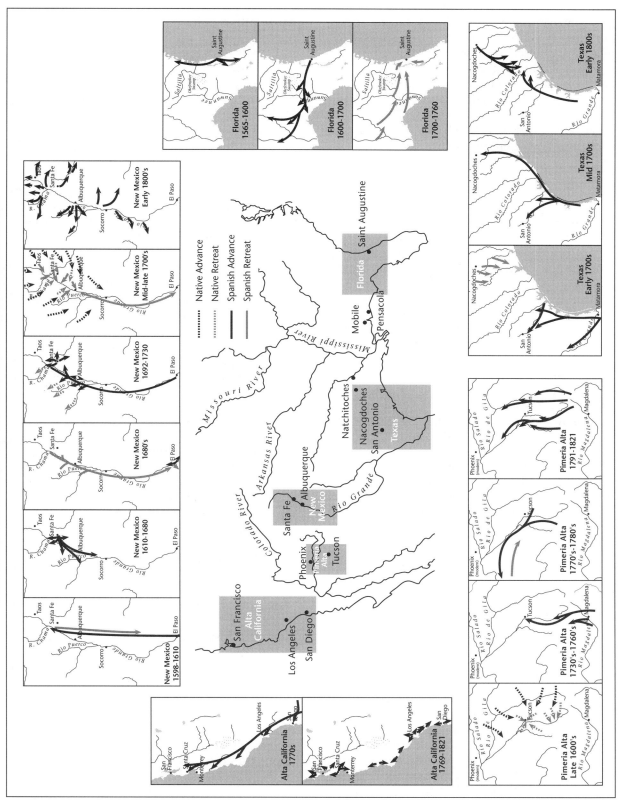

INTERNAL MIGRATION IN THE SPANISH BORDERLANDS

Florida 1565-1600

Florida 1600-1700

Florida 1700-1760

Texas Early 1800s

Texas Mid 1700s

Texas Early 1700s

New Mexico Early 1800's

New Mexico Mid-late 1700's

New Mexico 1692-1730

New Mexico 1680's

New Mexico 1610-1680

New Mexico 1598-1610

Native Advance
Native Retreat
Spanish Advance
Spanish Retreat

Saint Augustine

Mississippi River

Missouri River

Arkansas River

Colorado River

Rio Grande

Florida

Mobile
Pensacola

Natchitoches
Nacogdoches
San Antonio
Texas

Albuquerque
Santa Fe
New Mexico

Phoenix
Pimería Alta
Tucson

San Francisco
Alta California
Los Angeles
San Diego

Pimería Alta 1791-1821

Pimería Alta 1770's-1780's

Pimería Alta 1730's-1760's

Pimería Alta Late 1600's

Alta California 1770s

Alta California 1769-1821

333

the control of land, had far different consequences. If Indian migrants, their tribes decimated by disease and warfare, struggled toward intertribal unity or at least peace, Europeans created new cultures and communities out of familiar folkways and economic and environmental necessity while slave migrants managed, with great difficulty, to create African-American cultures in a hostile environment.

EARLY MIGRATION

The timing of transatlantic migration was no accident. It was part of the commercial expansion of Western Europe and England during the early modern era. England, France, the Netherlands, and Spain sent colonists to North America to trade with Indians (buying furs and skins that were in demand in the mother countries) and to produce agricultural staples such as wheat, tobacco, rice, and sugar. In return they expected to send manufactured goods to their infant colonies, thereby providing work in the mother countries for poor peasants forced off the land. Agricultural products were the only exports from the colonies that would meet European needs; growing colonial agricultural output, in turn, required ever increasing numbers of immigrants and internal migrants willing to "improve" the supposed North American wilderness. Internal migration to frontiers by European immigrants and their descendants, then, was a necessary part of European mercantile policies. However little inhabitants actively participated in such commerce, they were deeply affected by it. Those European-American families who wished to evade full market participation left settled communities where market agriculture existed and moved to lands confiscated from Indians. There they could subsist on goods produced by the community.

Inhabited Lands
Agricultural and hunting tribes of Indians, numbering several million on the eve of initial contact with Europeans, held sovereignty over the land, even if Europeans refused to recognize it. But long before many white colonists had arrived, a majority (sometimes as many as three-quarters to nine-tenths) of Indians had died from diseases like smallpox and influenza brought by trappers, hunters, and traders—diseases to which they had no genetic resistance. Thus weakened, they could put up little opposition to well-armed European conquerors, at least in those coastal areas where they were most decimated by disease. A plague, for instance, struck New England Indians beginning in 1616, leaving the coastline nearly uninhabited. Similar deadly epidemics appeared whenever whites settled in North America; for example, after white traders arrived in the Piedmont Carolinas late in the seventeenth century, a series of epidemics killed nine-tenths of the Catawba population. European colonists eagerly settled on village lands abandoned by Indians after such epidemics.

Yet Indians lived near every initial settlement, thereby preventing rapid internal migration and agricultural expansion. As many as 500,000 Indians inhabited the Eastern coastal plain in 1600, and some 120,000 still survived a century later. By the mid seventeenth century, when Europeans and their African slaves probably numerically dominated the populations of southern New England and Virginia, only 50,000 settlers lived in New Netherland and the English mainland North American colonies. The white and black population of the English colonies reached 250,000 by 1700, but Indians still constituted nearly half the population of the Carolinas. As late as the mid eighteenth century, Indians retained practical sovereignty over much of northern New England, western New York and Pennsylvania, and the Piedmont and mountain South—all areas claimed by England.

Land remained very scarce for white settlers as long as Indians controlled substantial portions of it. Even after Indian population had declined, Indians posed a substantial danger to settlers hungry for Indian hunting lands and corn patches. Constrained by Indian occupation, farm families rarely ventured onto tribal lands until Indians had been driven from them. Few hardy families ventured beyond small, densely populated, coastal settlements. This caution was eminently reasonable; Indians seeking to prevent colonial expansion warred against isolated outlying settlements before striking more densely populated areas. Driven by settler confiscation of their lands, southern New England Indians led by Metacom burned outlying settlements in central and western Massachusetts in 1675–1676, chasing white families to the relative safety of coastal or Connecticut River towns. Notwithstanding Indian defeat and the rapid white repopulation of towns like Deerfield, it took half a century for colonists to move back to all the lands that Indians had contested.

Hostile relations between whites and Indians and the relatively small population of European immigrants and their children, then, constrained opportunities for internal migration by whites in North America during the seventeenth century. After landing on the Saint Lawrence River or at Plymouth, Boston, New Amsterdam, Jamestown, Saint Mary's City, or Charlestown, seventeenth-century migrants from Europe usually stayed a few months or years before traveling inland to found new settlements. When they did begin to migrate, the colonists followed the courses of rivers and the natural contours of the land, rarely traveling more than a two days' trip from the ocean. Their children and grandchildren continued the process, slowly settling the western reaches of rivers that flowed into the Atlantic, barely reaching the flowing hills of the Piedmont by the late seventeenth century.

The English Colonies

Immigration to English mainland North America was far more sustained and intense than it was to either New Spain or New France. Migrants arrived in the continental British North American colonies in every decade from the 1610s to the 1770s. These flows of immigrants, however, were not random; the colonists who went to each colonial region came from particular and different English regions. The great migration to New England in the 1630s, for instance, came mostly from Puritan areas, especially East Anglia; immigrants to the Chesapeake colonies, in contrast, arrived over the entire seventeenth century and came from the south of England, especially London and the surrounding counties. Emigration to the Carolinas, first colonized toward the end of the seventeenth century, originated in the West Indies and (to a lesser extent) from Virginia. Internal migration in the seventeenth century, once immigrants arrived, tended to be isolated within regions, a pattern that suggests little mixing of English cultures within the colonies.

The first immigrants to reach New England in the 1620s and 1630s settled along the coast from Salem to Boston and around Portsmouth or on the upper reaches of the Connecticut River from Hartford to Springfield. Mostly free families and their servants, they achieved very high levels of natural increase, necessitating migration and colonization of Indian lands. Frontier settlers in the Massachusetts Bay, Connecticut, and New Haven colonies spread out from the ten towns they organized immediately after their arrival, founding eighty-two new villages between 1633 and 1675 that were mostly situated adjacent to previously organized settlements. By 1660 migrants had colonized the entire Atlantic coast from southern Maine to southern Connecticut as well as nearly all of the Connecticut River valley. They continued to push westward until forced back to coastal and river villages by Indian warfare in 1675–1676. Given the difficulty of forming new towns in an Indian-dominated wilderness, most seventeenth-century colonists moved to villages near their birthplace, migrating as little as thirty miles during their entire lives.

The first settlers in the Chesapeake region landed on the north bank of the James River, and most early immigrants and migrants moved westward on both banks of the James River or north to the York River. Immigration drove internal migration by Europeans in the seventeenth-century Chesapeake; high mortality and low fertility guaranteed a negative rate of natural increase. But high demand for tobacco in England sustained a substantial immigration of servants, who constituted a majority of the region's adult population until late in the century. Once freed, surviving servants migrated to Chesapeake frontiers to find cheap land. By the mid seventeenth century, these migrants had moved north to the shores of the Rappahannock, Potomac, and Patuxent rivers and east across the Chesapeake Bay to the eastern shore. Others moved directly west, reaching the hills of the Piedmont along the James River by the end of the century. Only late in the century did slave migrants begin to replace white servants as laborers.

Seventeenth-century immigrants to the Carolinas arrived in two separate streams. Beginnings in the 1650s, Virginians moved southeast from the James River area to lands surrounding Albemarle Sound in the far northern part of the region. Although a few families moved from Albemarle south to lands along Pamlico Sound and the Nuese River, these migrants mostly stayed in that region for the remainder of the century. Beginning in the 1670s the other group of migrants moved from Barbados and other islands in the West Indies to the far southern coast of South Carolina, establishing ranches, farms, and plantations on the coast and sea islands surrounding Charlestown. As late as 1720, immigrants and their few descendants had migrated only a few miles inland. Accustomed to living in a slave society, these South Carolina planters quickly imported slaves from the West Indies and later from Africa; by the early eighteenth century, slaves constituted a substantial majority of the population.

New Netherland

Although the Dutch established New Netherland in the 1620s, its European population remained very small until the 1640s and 1650s, when several thousand Dutch immigrants—mostly young unmarried men at first, but including a number of families—landed at New Amsterdam. Many of these men, who became involved in the fur trade with Indians or bought small farms, moved from New Amsterdam and established several villages on nearby Long Island and outposts along the Hudson River as far north as Albany and Schenectady and as far south as Delaware Bay (the Horenkill settlement at Lewes, Delaware). Less than two-thirds of the European residents, however, were Dutch. Several thousand New Englanders migrated to western Long Island, establishing agricultural villages adjacent to Dutch settlements. Small numbers of other ethnic groups—including French, Walloons, Scandinavians, and Germans—lived in New Amsterdam and in the Dutch or English villages.

ACCELERATING MIGRATION: THE EIGHTEENTH CENTURY

At the end of the seventeenth century, after nearly a hundred years of European immigration and internal migration within North America, Europeans had gained but a precarious foothold on the continent. Small settlements were scattered across the Atlantic Coastal Plain, isolated from one another and more strongly linked to London or Paris than to families in nearby settlements. Indians still inhabited coastal areas between European settlements and predominated from just beyond coastal settlements to the Mississippi River. Small, concentrated settlements of hamlets or plantations could be found along the Saint Lawrence River, the Connecticut River, the central and southern New England coast, Manhattan Island and the Hudson River valley as far north as Albany, adjacent to Delaware Bay and to the great rivers of the Chesapeake colonies (in some cases as far west at the fall line), near Albemarle Sound, in southern Carolina on the Stono and Cooper rivers, and in New Mexico along the Rio Grande River.

During the eighteenth century, the level of internal migration increased greatly. As population rose, the children and grandchildren of the original colonists filled in lands distant from rivers and creeks, creating less isolated and more extended agricultural settlements along the Saint Lawrence River, the Atlantic and California coasts, and the Mississippi and Rio Grande rivers. By far the greatest internal movements took place in the British colonies. Massachusetts farmers, for instance, poured over the New York border during the mid eighteenth century, where they eventually constituted a substantial part of the population of several manors. The founding of new colonies in Pennsylvania and Georgia opened hundreds of thousands of new acres for settlement by white migrants. At the same time, whites chased Indians from the backcountry of colonies from Pennsylvania to Georgia, permitting the repeopling of the Piedmont and of the rich agricultural valleys between the Blue Ridge and Appalachian mountains. Immigration from Germany, Scotland, and Ireland played a major role in this process of migration and settlement, but families from coastal areas moved as well to these newly opened regions.

Long-distance migrants followed a north-south axis, splitting into two regional patterns. People born in New York and New England tended to move north and northeast up the Connecticut and Hudson river valleys, settling in northeastern New York, western Massachusetts, and northern New England, or due south into northeastern Pennsylvania. Moves of over a hundred miles (60 kilometers) were far more common in colonies from Pennsylvania south. Migrants in this region—often immigrant families from Germany, Scotland, or Ireland—moved in a southwest direction, from eastern Pennsylvania and the Susquehanna Valley into the Piedmont and mountain districts of Maryland, Virginia, and the Carolinas. A large proportion of immigrant migrant families traveled from Philadelphia to the Susquehanna River, then turned southwest on the Great Wagon Road that went through the mountain valleys of Maryland, Virginia, and the Carolinas. People from the same region often migrated to the same parts of the backcountry, as did a number of Evangelical or Pietistic religious communities. The native-born migrants usually moved from coastal Virginia or Carolina inland to the Piedmont up-country or (less often) to the mountain valleys.

Internal migration in North America by Europeans during the eighteenth century was propelled by the rapid growth of population in the colonies, both from natural increase and from immigration, by changing local opportunities, by perceived population pressure on land (and increased land prices) in older areas, and by inexpensive land on frontiers. But families moved long before population pressure reduced the quantity of available land below subsistence levels. The defeat and exile of Indians at the end of the seventeenth century and beginning of the eighteenth century had opened up so much land for exploitation by Europeans that inhabitants came to expect to be landowners. Settlers strove to own sufficient land not only to provide a competency, but to produce marketable surpluses and provide land for their sons. Migration to a frontier area was often the only way families could accomplish such goals.

Such internal migration took place throughout the colonies. Increasing demand for tobacco and growing population raised land prices in southern tidewater counties, impelling poorer planters to move to Piedmont areas of Virginia. New England yeoman farmers moved westward to New York or northeastward to Maine and New Hampshire to remake small farms; immigrants, not wishing to rent land, moved to thinly populated mountain areas in New York or the South to attain a sufficiency. In the 1760s and

1770s, families moved to parts of Pennsylvania west of the Susquehanna River or to such areas as the Shenandoah Valley of Virginia or Piedmont North Carolina to take advantage of improving markets for wheat in the West Indies and especially in England and Western Europe.

By 1775, after a century and a half of internal migration, Europeans and their descendants inhabited nearly the entire Atlantic Coastal Plain, except for parts of Georgia. Moreover, they had moved to much of the interior, repeopling all of southern and central New England, Pennsylvania east of the Susquehanna River, all of Long Island and the Hudson River valley, all areas of the Chesapeake colonies, and the Piedmont Carolinas. The French and Spanish established new colonies in the Illinois country and Louisiana and expanded settlement in California and New Mexico. Whites (and their slaves) could also be found in enclaves west of the mountains in Pennsylvania, Virginia, and Kentucky. Notwithstanding this internal migration and settlement, however, Indians still inhabited much territory, including northern New England, western New York and Pennsylvania, most of Georgia, and the entire territory west of the Appalachian Mountains to the Pacific Ocean, except for the aforesaid Spanish and French settlements.

Decimated by disease and often defeated in warfare by European settlers, Indians who had inhabited the coastal plain were forced to migrate west, beyond white settlements. These movements began in the seventeenth century but increased greatly during the eighteenth century. The Delaware, for instance, migrated from the Delaware Valley to the Ohio Valley; the Seneca and Erie moved west along the Great Lakes; the Huron (renamed Wyandot) moved from Quebec to southern Michigan; the Tuscarora migrated from North Carolina to join other Iroquoian tribes in western New York. Tribes might be in a constant state of flux; for example the Shawnee, who had lived in Illinois, Alabama, and eastern Tennessee in the late seventeenth century, moved to the Potomac River and eastern Pennsylvania in the early eighteenth century before removing to the Scoito River in Ohio after 1730. Migration to and around the Great Lakes region was especially intense; at least one-quarter of the Indians living there in 1768 were recent arrivals. When they reached their new villages and hunting grounds, these refugees often ran into other indigenous peoples, creating polyglot societies; mid-eighteenth-century northeastern Ohio, near present-day Cleveland, was home to the Mingo (mixed groups from various Iroquois tribes), Mahican, Ottawa, and Ojibwa. Such complex series of migrations created conditions amenable to both intertribal warfare and the development of pan-Indian movements organized to fight Europeans.

THE DEMOGRAPHICS OF MIGRATION

A familial decision by European immigrants or their descendants to move or stay was very complex. Since internal migration to a frontier was expensive, requiring money for travel and land and the foregoing of income while establishing a new farm, only families with some assets could afford to move over long distances. However, frontier landlords or entrepreneurs in such places as New York and Maryland sometimes recruited migrants, thereby mitigating some uncertainty or expense. Migration by landed farm families depended upon the age of the head of household, the number of children in the home, the threat of Indians, perceived opportunities at home or at the frontier, and previous moves by family, friends, or neighbors.

Like almost all migration, movement toward colonial frontiers was selective. Adolescents left home in search of work, often engaging in agricultural labor or perhaps overseeing slaves on a large plantation, but they infrequently migrated over long distances. Men tended to move long distances in their mid twenties, after receiving their marriage portions and after their fathers died. They took with them their wives, probably in their early twenties, but since they had recently married, few children migrated long distances. Long-distance migration declined once men reached their forties, except for the few who moved with grown children.

The general level of opportunity in settled places, critical to migration decisions, can be seen in studies of personal persistence (defined as appearance on two or more consecutive nominal lists—censuses, tax assessments of a village or county). Such studies suggest that few immigrants persisted but that from the mid seven-

teenth to the mid eighteenth centuries, their children increasingly stayed where they had been born. Men with property at all times persisted at higher rates than poor families without land. Such measures, however crudely accurate, fail to capture either migration over the life cycle just discussed or subtle changes over time. After the mid seventeenth century in New England, for instance, families often persisted in one village for decades, but as many as two-thirds of the immigrants' children moved sometime in their lives, often at marriage. One can see similar patterns in the Chesapeake colonies. Four-fifths of former servants in Charles County, Maryland, that were able to gain land stayed in the community as did many unable to rise out of the ranks of laborers or tenants. In total, a quarter of surviving immigrants left Charles County, and about two-fifths departed from Lancaster County, Virginia. Out-migration from the region increased as tobacco prices and the opportunities for ex-servants to find land both declined after 1680.

During the eighteenth century, internal migration changed in contradictory ways. Levels of ten-year persistence in settled areas rose among the grandchildren of original settlers. While most people moved, either upon marriage or as members of families headed by young adults, they tended to move short distances. In New England from 1750 to 1770, from two-fifths to three-quarters of marriages were between people from the same town, and nearly all the others were between residents of neighboring towns. Migrants born in New England between 1701 and 1740 moved just under forty miles (24 kilometers) over their lifetimes; soldiers who enlisted for revolutionary service in Virginia had generally moved to adjacent counties or stayed in their county of birth. The reasons for this pattern of increasing persistence and short-distance migration are clear. Men waiting for their inheritances stayed close to home until their fathers died. Fathers—if they possessed enough land—settled married sons or sons-in-law on unimproved land near their own or on land they had purchased years earlier for speculation or security. Moreover, settlement of the interior proceeded slowly enough during the colonial era so that few areas were completely filled in with European-Americans. Even after their fathers died, men could therefore still find inexpensive land within several days' journey of their current residence.

Nonetheless, long-distance migration did increase absolutely during the eighteenth century, if not in proportion to population. Moves of over one hundred miles (60 kilometers) were more common in colonies from Pennsylvania south, while shorter moves to nearby frontiers were more common in New England and New York. This frontier migration was embedded within the household economy. Most migrants sought to establish the kind of yeoman economic independence possible within an interdependent market environment. Although they usually moved as parts of households (but not as members of a kin group or community), unmarried men (and more rarely women) sometimes moved alone. Since kin groups rarely moved together, except for occasional adult siblings or a father and adult son, frontier families could rely upon few kindred for support during the first years in their new homes.

A form of communal chain migration might have been more common. After early migrants had achieved some economic success, others from their home communities sometimes joined them. Quakers—who frequently migrated over long distances from Pennsylvania to Virginia and North Carolina—may have gained communal support for migration from their meetings that other groups of frontier migrants lacked; on occasion, though, other settlers moved in groups, founding colonies of their old communities. Residents of Andover, Massachusetts, for instance, founded communities in Windham County, Connecticut, in the early eighteenth century and moved to a cluster of towns in New Hampshire and western Massachusetts later in the century. Similar patterns of movement can be discerned in planter migration from the tidewater Chesapeake to Piedmont Virginia.

Poorer men and women rarely accumulated the capital necessary to move to the frontier. They could expect neither land nor other capital from their impoverished parents. With few prospects at home or on the frontier, they moved within settled eastern areas, tramping the roads near their homes searching for work. Transiency became common in settled areas of the northern colonies by the mid eighteenth century, presaging the development of a system of seasonal agri-

cultural and urban employment. Massachusetts warnings out (a legal registration system for poor newcomers) document a growing transient population, mostly young men and women. The young transients of coastal Essex County, often ex-servants, sought agricultural labor at the time of planting and harvest or urban employment in towns near their birthplace. Many rural transients ended up in Boston, working on the docks, in ships, or in workshops. Even after marriage some men and women could not find permanent employment, and over a third of the transients were young families with an average of two children. Those poor young couples from old towns with sufficient resources to migrate to the frontier rarely achieved success; the percentage of families among transients warned out in frontier Hampshire County rose from under half to over two-thirds between 1739–1743 and 1770–1774.

Forms of social organization within colonies, then, greatly influenced patterns of migration. Economic and social constraints against migration, especially among landed families, were very strong. Neither men expecting inheritances nor women fearing loss of neighborhood sociability willingly moved to what they perceived as a howling wilderness. Long-distance migration, when it occurred, was a familial and communal process, involving collective (or chain) migration and financing of movement. Far from the atomistic individuals of our folklore, these familial and communal migrants carried with them cultural norms and expectations for proper social organization in new communities. The making of communities by migrants, therefore, raises the question of cultural or social continuity between older, settled areas and frontiers.

MIGRATION AND THE MAKING OF AMERICAN CULTURES

The culture migrants brought with them clashed with the social relations and environment in their new homes, forcing the creation of new cultural norms. Yet how are we to understand the abundant cultural continuities, even the survival of entire systems of folkways, from England, Scotland, or Africa to North America? One might argue for direct cultural transmission from one region to another. David Hackett Fischer, for one, traces the persistence of British folkways, ranging from speech and naming patterns to systems of wealth, rank, and power. All, he argues, originated in contrasting regional cultures of Britain. Given the relatively homogeneous regional origins of settlers in each North American community, migrants readily adapted old cultural practices. But comparing cultural practices falters because of differences in commerce, markets, and labor systems in the home country, the Atlantic plain, and the Piedmont and mountain frontier.

The social selectivity of migration and the failure of all groups to migrate equally suggest a fragmentary recreation of older cultures in the colonies. Such cultural fragments, Louis Hartz argues, were severed from the home country and then developed independently in the colony, unfolding without competition or conflict; the "liberal" fragment of English society became hegemonic in America, he states, developing without relation to its feudal past. The growth of cultural fragments no more captures how partial cultural transmission inevitably is. Colonies and even regions within colonies were discrete societies, settled by diverse peoples, whose ideologies and social relations could hardly be reduced to unthinking acceptance of liberal ideology.

Alternatively one might argue that colonists invented new traditions, consciously adapting older cultural forms in new situations, applying customs in a new environment and building upon the culture they left behind. Such new traditions commonly appear when old societies profoundly change, sometimes serving to sustain memories of what migrants believed social relations should be. Migration, whether over the Atlantic or from settled region to frontier, obviously severed old social ties, necessitating conscious acts of creation. The making of new traditions in the colonies was both public (distribution of land) and private (naming children).

Only a dynamic model that sets changing productive relations in sending and receiving areas side by side can fully explain cultural invention in new communities. The process begins in the home country or region prior to migration, continues with immigration, and concludes with adjustment or transformation in the new area. Community development, with its invention of new traditions within the productive relations common in the colony, takes place following initial occupation; once set, such traditions change slowly as immigrants come into contact with Indians or other settlers.

The regional patterns of internal migration we have described suggest that North American families of European descent often lived in relatively homogeneous populations. Indians and the offspring of mixed Indian-European marriages (like the Métis) were either forced from European communities or segregated from them; peoples of African descent lived subservient lives and struggled to make their own societies. The French dominated most of Quebec and the Illinois country. English populations—often from the same parts of the realm—predominated in New England and the tidewater South. Small ethnic enclaves of Germans, Scots, Scotch-Irish, and Irish could be found in the middle Atlantic colonies and the backcountry. According to Thomas L. Purvis, by 1790, when the first census was taken, significant concentrations of Dutch lived in New York, and between a quarter and a third of the people in the Carolinas, Georgia, and Kentucky were Scots, Scotch-Irish, or Irish. Pennsylvania was polyglot: two-fifths were German; one-quarter English; and one-third Scots, Scotch-Irish, or Irish. Such aggregate data do not tell the whole story regarding ethnic group concentrations within the states in 1790. Pennsylvania Germans, for instance, lived mostly in the east central part of the state, where they constituted nearly two-thirds of the populace; Scotch-Irish, Irish, and Scots tended to migrate to the western portions of the state; English and Welsh lived near Philadelphia and in the far west. While all Europeans had to interact with one another, the English, Germans, and Scots usually moved from one ethnic enclave to another, thereby making and sustaining peculiar regional and ethnic identities.

The homogeneity of communities of migrants in North America provided a basis for recreating cultures. But the environment that migrants found, the relations of production that structured daily activities, and the nearby presence of other ethnic groups guaranteed that new societies would bear only superficial similarity to the places they left behind. The experience of New England migrants, Scots who went to

New Jersey, and African and African-American slaves, suggests a wide range of possible cultural transfer and documents the ways varying groups invented new traditions.

From England to New England

The family nature of immigration permitted some English settlers to reinvent with remarkable fidelity the cultures they left behind. They often came from a single village or contiguous villages. The land system, the mix of grazing and farming, and local government in the English places of origin and the villages they founded in Massachusetts resembled one another. The Yorkshire settlers of Rawley, for instance, had lived in open-field communities where an individual's lands were scattered in small strips among several fields and totaled only a few acres. When they arrived in Rawley, they set up common fields. For several generations this open-field system persisted because farmers rarely consolidated their holdings. East Anglia settlers of Ipswich recreated the borough government and closed polity found in the towns they had inhabited. The officeholders, like those of English boroughs from which they came, made economic policy. The peculiarities of Ipswich, however, may owe as much to its commercial and urban development as to the origin of its citizens.

Early Springfield shows how commercial activities of a single patron could shape a society. William Pynchon, a Puritan entrepreneur from East Anglia, founded Springfield in 1636 and owned most of the town's land. By 1641 most of the original settlers had left; Pynchon and his son John replaced them with indentured servants he brought from London or Boston. Without the vision of a communal society that motivated some immigrants to eastern Massachusetts, migrants to Springfield came to town searching for economic opportunity. The two Pynchons built a system of patronage and clientage that incorporated most of Springfield's families in its web. By far the wealthiest men in town, they loaned money to most town families. Freed servants and even free immigrants who wished to stay in town usually worked as day laborers or leased land from the Pynchons. In return for credit and an outlet for their produce, tenants developed Pynchon land (without retaining any rights in the improvements) and paid rent. A large majority of immigrants and their children stayed, apparently satisfied by local opportunities to become tenants or enjoy a secure wage.

From Scotland to New Jersey

The Scottish immigration to New Jersey contrasts greatly from that to New England. Since New Jersey, like the other middle colonies, was settled by people from a variety of cultures, Scottish migrants could not set up new societies isolated from alien groups. The Quaker great lairds of northeast Scotland sponsored the initial Scottish occupation of New Jersey in the 1680s. They brought over Scottish indentured servants (families as well as young men) and tenants and set them to work developing their estates. Although the proprietors sought to recreate the wage-labor estates of the Scottish northeast, they had to compromise to attract settlers and placate the New Englanders in their midst. Tenants gained longer terms in New Jersey than in Scotland. Although proprietors refused to sell land to settlers, they gave thirty acres (12 hectares) to every freed servant at the end of his term. About seven hundred Scots, mostly servants, migrated to New Jersey in the 1680s to take advantage of these terms. Ingrained habits died hard, however, and most former servants who stayed in New Jersey either worked as agricultural laborers for their colonial lairds or rented land from them. Emigration from Scotland to New Jersey slowed in the 1690s but picked up around 1720. These emigrants were sponsored by merchant proprietors from the southwest lowlands. Once in New Jersey, they created extensive trading networks among themselves and established liberal leasing policies for their tenants.

During the mid eighteenth century, Scottish immigrants in New Jersey created a cohesive ethnic group whose social relations differed from Scotland's while also varying dramatically from those of the New Englanders in their midst. Scottish immigrants moved from place to place, much as their kinfolk in Scotland. Fathers divided their land among all their sons but expected older sons to find homes elsewhere. Scots in New Jersey moved from one cluster of their countrymen to another, forming intricate social networks with men of similar status wherever they moved. Moreover, a uniform Scottish religion, critical to the formation of the Scottish ethnic group, was born in New Jersey. Scottish Quakers and Anglicans migrated to New Jersey, but their descendants, tiring of conflicts with New England brethren in church and meeting, joined Presbyterian congregations. Once revivalists had successfully converted most of the Scots, they formed a unified Scottish-dominated Presbyterian Church.

Slave Communities

Unlike Europeans, African and African-American slaves moved involuntarily, carried by masters or slave traders from Africa or from the Atlantic coast to frontier staple plantations. While slaves had toiled in the Chesapeake and Carolina colonies from the outset of European settlement, most arrived in the eighteenth century. Between 1700 and 1775, southern planters imported close to two hundred thousand slaves from Africa and (to a much lesser extent) the West Indies. At first most of the Africans went to the Chesapeake, but after mid century the African slave trade to South Carolina and Georgia increased markedly.

Alienated and unhappy, African migrants often ran away or refused to work. Since few women were imported, many of the men could not begin families. Coming from disparate communities, they spoke mutually incomprehensible tongues. Because plantations sizes in the Chesapeake were small, African-born slaves could create communities only by gathering in the woods after dark. Africans slowly accommodated to slavery, and with their American-born children began building African-American slave communities, a process aided by the high rates of persistence within local communities by Africans and their children.

During the mid eighteenth century, few African-American slaves were forced to move more than twenty miles from their birthplaces. But movement by slaves over short distances was pervasive. Slaveowners gave slaves to each of their children. Men tended to bequeath male slaves to sons (to work on their plantations) and female slaves to daughters (to be personal servants). Such inheritance strategies guaranteed the separation of brothers from sisters and children from parents. Inheritance split families apart while concentrating slave families within tidewater Chesapeake and low-country Carolina neighborhoods. Since family members usually lived within traveling distance, "broad" husbands and other kindred could visit with regularity. The pain of family separations, then, were partially mitigated by the cross-plantation slave networks that African-Americans created.

The internal slave trade, which remained small, revolved around local communities as planters sold surplus slaves or executors or creditors organized estate or insolvency sales. Once African Americans predominated in the slave population, planters with sufficient capital to choose preferred them to unseasoned Africans. Like the inheritance system, such sales spread slaves across settled neighborhoods. Small groups of slaves, often recently arrived Africans, were sold from areas with many slaves (such as tidewater Virginia or coastal South Carolina) to areas with few slaves, usually to colonies in the North or to the southern frontier.

As white migrants spread gradually across the South, establishing new tobacco and rice plantations, the wealthier planters among them moved to the area with their slaves and non-slaveholding frontier residents bought Africans from slave traders. Slavery expanded rapidly into Piedmont Virginia, disrupting the lives of some twenty thousand slaves from 1755 to 1782, mostly youths taken from the tidewater by migrating planters or purchased by men already in the Piedmont. But Piedmont planters bought an equal number of Africans during the same period, thereby reducing the demand for native-born slaves by Piedmont tobacco producers. In South Carolina a substantial majority of slaves working in frontier areas were Africans, thereby making the lives of the growing native-born coastal population somewhat more secure.

By the mid eighteenth century, as the slave population grew by natural increase, many Creole blacks had secured a stable, if precarious, family life. Adapting African norms of extended kin relations, they invented systems of fictive kin, entrusting relatives to raise their children when they were sold or otherwise forced to move. They established flourishing communities in the Chesapeake region, where the increasingly large quarters could each accommodate up to twenty occupants, and on the vast plantations of coastal South Carolina and Georgia. The growth in the 1750s, 1760s, and 1770s of evangelical religion, whose churches were created by whites and slaves together, gave slaves a claim to spiritual equality with whites and created a new slave institution, one with liturgical forms (like the call and shout) similar to those found in Africa.

CONCLUSION

Looking back to 1600 from the perspective of 1770, a historian of North America can see the profound changes that English, African, Scottish, Irish, and Dutch immigrants and internal migrants wrought. They displaced thousands of Indians from the Atlantic plain, forcing them to move into the interior, and then established farm settlements out of the wilderness they had created. Most of the colonies they developed quickly became multiethnic and multiracial, which spurred the development of new ethnic communities. This diversity to the contrary notwithstanding, English speakers established hegemony over much territory, and their very high levels of natural population increase presaged their mass migration to the Mississippi River and beyond during the decades after the American Revolution.

BIBLIOGRAPHY

Adams, John W., and Alice Bee Kasakoff. "Migration and the Family in Colonial New England: The View from Genealogies." *Journal of Family History* 9, no. 1 (1984):24–43. Based upon detailed family histories, Adams and Kasakoff map migration patterns from eastern New England to frontiers within and outside that region.

Allen, David Grayson. *In English Ways: The Movement of Societies and the Transferral of English Local Law and Customs to Massachusetts Bay in the Seventeenth Century.* Chapel Hill, N.C., 1981. This study of the origin of immigrants to four Massachusetts towns argues that they replicated the entire social order they had left behind.

Anderson, Virginia DeJohn. *New England's Generation: The Great Migration and the Formation of Society and Culture in the Seventeenth Century.* Cambridge, England, 1991. This detailed study of the migration from England to New England in the 1630s and of internal migration thereafter argues that reli-

gious motivations predominated among immigrants.

Bailyn, Bernard. *The Peopling of British North America: An Introduction.* New York, 1986. Bailyn summarizes the major patterns of immigration to the British colonies and internal migration within them and connects internal migration in England with its counterpart in North America.

———. *Voyagers to the West: A Passage in the Peopling of America on the Eve of the Revolution.* New York, 1986. A massive study of emigration from England and Scotland to the North American colonies in the 1770s, Bailyn's book illuminates the initial settlement by immigrants of backcountry areas from Newfoundland to Florida.

Cole, Thomas R. "Family, Settlement, and Migration in Southeastern Massachusetts, 1650–1805: The Case for Regional Analysis." *New England Historical and Genealogical Register* 132, no. 3 (1978):171–185. Cole analyzes the slow diffusion of selected families between towns in the old Plymouth colony.

Cressy, David. *Coming Over: Migration and Communication Between England and New England in the Seventeenth Century.* Cambridge, England, 1987. Cressy argues that New Englanders emigrated from England for a variety of economic and religious reasons.

Fischer, David Hackett. *Albion's Seed: Four British Folkways in America.* New York, 1989. Fischer exhaustively documents the movements of peoples and cultures from Britain to her continental colonies, arguing for almost a direct transfer of cultural norms.

Galenson, David. "'Middling People' or 'Common Sort'?: The Social Origins of Some Early Americans Reexamined." *William and Mary Quarterly*, 3rd. ser., 35, no. 3 (1978):499–524. This is the best examination of the social origin of indentured servants in the colonies, arguing that they were mostly poor.

Gragg, Larry Dale. *Migration in Early America: The Virginia Quaker Experience.* Ann Arbor, Mich., 1980. Gragg traces Quakers from Virginia to North Carolina and other places.

Hofstadter, Richard. *The Progressive Historians: Turner, Beard, Parrington.* New York, 1968. The section on Turner is the definitive critique of Turner's frontier hypothesis.

Horn, James. "Moving On in the New World: Migration and Out-Migration in the Seventeenth Century Chesapeake." In *Migration and Society in Early Modern England,* edited by Peter Clark and David Souden. Totowa, N.J., 1987. Horn traces migration to the Chesapeake and estimates migration within the region.

Jones, Douglas Lamar. "The Strolling Poor: Transiency in Eighteenth-Century Massachusetts." *Jour-*

nal of Social History 8, no. 3 (1975):28–54. Jones discovers a growing poor, transient population in late eighteenth-century Massachusetts.

———. *Village and Seaport: Migration and Society in Eighteenth-Century Massachusetts.* Hanover, N.H., 1981. A detailed study of two towns, this book documents patterns of persistence and migration.

Kulikoff, Allan. *The Agrarian Origins of American Capitalism.* Charlottesville, Va., 1992. This work includes chapters on white internal migration and on the migration of slaves in the colonial period and new nation.

Landsman, Ned C. *Scotland and Its First American Colony, 1683–1765.* Princeton, N.J., 1985. An evocative examination of the formation of an ethnic group, this volume details the social lives of Scots in Scotland and in New Jersey.

Lemon, James T. *The Best Poor Man's Country: A Geographical Study of Early Southeastern Pennsylvania.* Baltimore, Md., 1972. Lemon maps ethnicity, population growth, agricultural patterns, and persistence in early Pennsylvania.

McDonald, Forrest, and Ellen Shapiro McDonald. "The Ethnic Origins of the American People, 1790." *William and Mary Quarterly,* 3rd ser., 37, no. 2 (1980):179–199. The McDonalds use surnames from the 1790 population census to determine the ethnic composition of the new American states, thereby permitting one to determine patterns of immigration.

Marx, Karl. *Capital: A Critique of Political Economy.* Introduction by Ernest Mandel. Translated by Ben Fowkes. 3 vols. Hamburg, Germany, 1867–1894; paperback ed. 1977–1981. In chapter 33 of volume 1, Marx brilliantly expounds upon the social development of colonies where surplus land exists.

Meinig, D. W. *The Shaping of America: A Geographical Perspective on 500 Years of History.* Vol. 1, *Atlantic America, 1492–1800.* New Haven, Conn., 1986. Meinig places immigration from Europe and Africa and internal migration throughout North America into a broad economic framework.

Menard, Russell R. "British Migration to the Chesapeake Colonies in the Seventeenth Century." In *Colonial Chesapeake Society,* edited by Lois Green Carr, Philip D. Morgan, and Jean B. Russo. Chapel Hill, N.C., 1988. Menard traces the level, rate, and timing of migration from England to the Chesapeake.

Mitchell, Robert D., and Paul A. Groves, eds. *North America: The Historical Geography of a Changing Continent.* Totowa, N.J., 1987. This collection of essays includes valuable articles on immigration, settlement patterns, and migration in all North American regions.

Morgan, Philip D., and Michael L. Nicholls. "Slaves in Piedmont Virginia, 1720–1790." *William and Mary Quarterly,* 3rd ser., 46, no. 2 (1989):211–251. The authors document the movement of slaves—both African and African American—to the Piedmont frontier.

Purvis, Thomas L. "The European Ancestry of the United States Population, 1790." *William and Mary Quarterly,* 3rd ser., 41, no. 1 (1984):85–101. Purvis critiques the methods of the article by the McDonalds cited above.

Rosenberry, Lois Kimball Mathews. *The Expansion of New England: The Spread of New England Settlement and Institutions to the Mississippi River, 1620–1865.* Boston, 1909; repr. 1962. The classic study of internal migration by New Englanders, this work traces New Englanders from the coast to the interior of New England and from New England to New York and the Midwest.

Rutman, Darrett B. "People in Process: The New Hampshire Towns of the Eighteenth Century." In *Family and Kin in Urban Communities, 1700–1930,* edited by Tamara K. Hareven. New York, 1977. By examining migration to New Hampshire and population growth there, Rutman challenges the presumption that population pressure on land intensified internal migration.

Tanner, Helen Hornbeck, ed. *Atlas of Great Lakes Indian History.* Norman, Okla., 1987. Tanner provides maps and text to document the migration of Indians to and within the Great Lakes region from the sixteenth through the nineteenth centuries.

Turner, Frederick Jackson. *The Frontier in American History.* New York, 1920. These reprinted essays capture the essence of Turner's ideas about the frontier.

Villaflor, Georgia C., and Kenneth L. Sokoloff. "Migration in Colonial America: Evidence from the Militia Rolls." *Social Science History* 6, no. 4 (1982):539–570. This article, based upon place of birth and place of enlistment data from muster rolls, is the best statistical study of migration throughout the late eighteenth-century colonies.

Walsh, Lorena S. "Staying Put or Getting Out: Findings for Charles County, Maryland, 1650–1720." *William and Mary Quarterly,* 3rd ser., 44, no. 1 (1987):89–103. Walsh traces opportunity and the propensity to migrate in one Maryland county.

Wood, Peter H. *Black Majority: Negroes in Colonial South Carolina from 1670 Through the Stono Rebellion.* New York, 1974. Wood's book remains the definitive work on the early South Carolina economy and the development of slavery there.

Allan Kulikoff

SEE ALSO **Repeopling the Land** and **Transportation and Communication**.

THE FRENCH COLONIES

UNLIKE THE ENGLISH and Dutch, and the settlers on the northern borderlands of New Spain, the French who settled in the Saint Lawrence Valley had easy access to the interior of the continent. The other European colonizers were confined by geography and the proximity of powerful Indian nations such as the Iroquois confederacy, the Apache, and the Comanche. The French faced no such obstacles and were free to follow the Saint Lawrence and the Ottawa rivers to the Great Lakes, and from there to the Mississippi south to the Gulf of Mexico, or to the Saskatchewan River west to the Rocky Mountains. Other river systems, like the Saguenay, led north to James Bay and Hudson Bay.

Moreover, the French had the means to make use of these great waterways, the birchbark canoe. Of the ten species of birch trees found in the northern part of North America, the most common is the white birch, also called the paper birch, which provided the bark for the canoes. These trees grew profusely in the lands occupied or dominated by the French, but not to the south where the English and the Dutch had established themselves. With some spare bark, wattap (a long, thin, flexible pine root), and spruce gum, the French could take their canoes anywhere on the continent and effect all necessary repairs. Depending on the voyage, the French either used the *canot de maître* (Montreal canoe)—a huge thirty-six-foot (nearly 11-meter) canoe capable of carrying three tons of cargo—or the *canot du nord* (north canoe), a smaller canoe with half the carrying capacity, but which was easier to carry on portage routes and easier to paddle on smaller, shallower streams.

As important were the cordial relations that the French enjoyed with the Algonquin, the Huron, and the Ottawa, relations which other European colonizers were unable or unwilling to culti-

vate. French success in their dealings with Indian peoples was largely due to their ability to adapt to Indian ways. The French learned Indian languages—Algonquian, Iroquoian, and Siouan—in a multiplicity of dialects. In order to keep pace with their Indian guides, the French mastered the skills of paddling canoes, snowshoeing in rough terrain, and dragging fully laden toboggans. They wore Indian style dress: a loose-fitting blouse, *mitasses* (leggings), *braguets* (breechcloths), and deerskin moccasins. French clothes would have been too bulky and too uncomfortable when wet. In their diplomacy, the French observed Indian protocol. Like their hosts, they offered presents as a form of tribute, and they learned to deliver speeches in the customary formal and richly metaphorical style. With the Huron and Ottawa, the French shared an enemy, the Iroquois confederacy. This fact provided an important military dimension to the alliance and ensured the French of continued access to the Great Lakes region.

EXPLORATION AND EARLY ESTABLISHMENTS

The explorers, traders, and missionaries who first traveled to the Great Lakes and beyond were attracted by a variety of factors: minerals, new territories, and a possible route across the continent to the elusive western sea, furs, and souls. For the most part, the Indians tolerated the French presence and welcomed the alliance. Territories were claimed for France, but the Indians remained in complete control of their lands. In fact, territorial claims were made to offset British expansion rather than to open new areas of settlement for the French. Many of those who went west settled at the interior ports and married Indian women. These marriages further strengthened the bonds between the French and their Indian allies and helped ensure continued migration to the *pays d'en haut* (literally, upper country), as the area of the Great Lakes and beyond came to be known.

Michilimackinac
The Great Lakes region provided water access to every point on the continent, and the hub of the three upper lakes soon became a base

from which French travelers commonly embarked. The Michilimackinac post, and the nearby Jesuit mission at Saint-Ignace, were of particular importance. Through this gateway, explorers and fur traders could head north, pass the Sault Sainte Marie rapids, and enter Lake Superior, or they could head west through the Straits of Mackinac into Lake Michigan. Following the shoreline to the Chicago portage, they would cross into the headwaters of the Mississippi River. Michilimackinac was under the control of France's leading western ally, the Ottawa, and they helped to ensure a French presence in the region. By holding this post, the French were able to prevent other European powers from making incursions into the *pays d'en haut*. Its strategic importance was underlined in 1686 when French renegades led a party of English traders to the port. Measures were taken to ensure that a repeat performance would mean a death sentence for the perpetrators.

The Indians who came to Michilimackinac aroused the French interest in exploration of the west by their descriptions of a great river, called "Ohio" by the Huron and "Mississippi" by the Ottawa. Médard Chouart Des Groseilliers and Pierre-Esprit Radisson spent time at Michilimackinac in 1659 before heading north of Lake Superior in search of furs. Louis Jolliet and Father Jacques Marquette spent the winter of 1672–1673 at the Saint-Ignace mission, listening to the accounts of this river told by Indians who were spending the winter season there. When they set out to find this river, they had a reasonably good idea of what to expect. René-Robert Cavelier de La Salle used Michilimackinac as a base for his voyage into the Illinois country in the winter of 1679–1680. Daniel Greysolon Dulhut wintered just to the north, at Sault Sainte Marie, before voyaging to the Sioux country to the west of the Great Lakes in July 1679. As *coureurs de bois* (woods runners) followed these men, Michilimackinac became an important fur-trade center and the first French community in the *pays d'en haut*. With the abolition of the *congé* system of trade licenses by a royal decree on 21 May 1696, many of these traders were effectively cut off from the Saint Lawrence colony. They established themselves permanently at Michilimackinac and married Huron and Ottawa women.

The West and the Southwest

The seventeenth-century French explorers opened the way for exploration in the southwestern and western areas of North America. Louis Juchereau de Saint-Denis, the Canadian who commanded the Fort du Mississippi, traveled extensively in that part of New Spain which is now the state of Texas. In the early part of the eighteenth century, he established French trade with Spanish settlements and traveled as far as Mexico City. Like other French explorers, his success was based on successful relations with Indian nations.

Étienne de Véniard de Bourgmond, yet another of the early-eighteenth-century explorers, treated with the Comanche and enlisted their aid in furthering French interests in the Southwest. As in the Great Lakes and Mississippi, others followed and took advantage of the cordial relations to establish trade.

From the Great Lakes, the French also pushed their explorations westward in search of a route to the western sea, the Mer de l'Ouest. The acting commandant of the Poste du Nord (Post of the North)—a depot for the furs collected from the area north of Superior— Pierre Gaultier de Varennes et de La Vérendrye, learned much about the region from the Assiniboine and Cree who came to trade furs. With support from Governor Charles de Beauharnois de la Boische and Intendant Gilles Hocquart, La Vérendrye embarked on a voyage to find the route to the Mer de l'Ouest.

In the late spring of 1731 La Vérendrye made his way through the many small lakes and rivers west of Lake Superior. From Kaministiquia (Thunder Bay) at Superior's western end, the route was extremely difficult. Weather, rough terrain, and poor portage trails leading in uncertain directions conspired to make progress excessively slow. To make this difficult situation worse, the Sioux who lived to the west of the Great Lakes were bitter enemies of France's Cree allies. Indian goodwill was replaced by open hostility, brutal attacks, and warfare. In spite of these obstacles, and the wavering support of officials who could scarcely imagine the difficulties, La Vérendrye's sons reached a point on the Saskatchewan River known as Fort Paskoya. Like the other explorers who expanded the trading region, La

346

Vérendrye opened an area to trade that extended to the foothills of the Rockies.

IMPERIAL POLICY
AND CHAIN MIGRATION

The explorers had encouraged fur traders to venture into the *pays d'en haut,* but by the end of the seventeenth century the fur trade was near collapse. French interest in western ports, however, revived almost immediately as their strategic value was realized. After 1700 new ports were built to prevent British expansion. The trade in furs was continued in order to preserve strong alliances with the Indian nations. A relatively minor military force in North America—which maintained ports among the various Indian nations—could successfully oppose a much larger British force. French posts from the Gulf of Mexico, the Mississippi, the Great Lakes, and the Saint Lawrence and all the way to the Atlantic coast prevented any British expansion and confined the Anglo-Americans to the areas east of the Appalachian Mountains.

Now a part of imperial policy, the fur trade also acted as a strong pull factor in internal migration. Fur traders were tolerated by the government administration because their presence and "marriage according to custom of the country" strengthened Indian alliances. The trader's way of life was particularly attractive to those habitant farmers of the Saint Lawrence colony who yearned to be free of the pressures of feudal society and many followed their countrymen to the *pays d'en haut.* In three of the more important French settlements in the west—Detroit, the Illinois country, and Michilimackinac—the parish registers and other documents provide good evidence of chain migration that link habitants to fur-trading family members in the west.

The Illinois Country
The Illinois country is a good example of chain migration. This area of the Mississippi Valley was originally settled by French *coureurs de bois,* who found themselves stranded by the decree against the *congé* system and fur glut of 1696. Around 1700 these settlers founded six small villages on the eastern bank of the Mississippi.

Gradually, farming replaced the fur trade as the chief economic activity, and with the establishment of the Province of Louisiana in 1718, the settlements began to flourish. The fertile soil of the rich Mississippi bottomlands was able to nourish enough crops to keep Louisiana supplied. This steady market for Illinois produce proved an important pull factor for migration to the region; almost two-thirds of the migrants came from Canada, and the rest from France.

Of the migrants coming to the Illinois from the Saint Lawrence, fully 40 percent followed their relatives. The others were attracted by the availability of good farmland, open prairie ready for the plow with no need for the arduous clearance of forest and where neither Church nor Crown could inhibit activities unduly. Those who had run afoul of these institutions may have taken the opportunity to begin a new life. This explanation should not be taken too far, however, as the population of the Illinois country did not exceed three thousand at mid century, and a third of the inhabitants were slaves. More oppressive conditions in the Saint Lawrence might have occasioned a greater migration westward.

Detroit
At Detroit the pattern of migration was much more organized. On 4 June 1701 Antoine Laumet (better known by the name he invented for himself, Lamothe Cadillac) and his lieutenant Henri de Tonty embarked with one hundred settlers and soldiers to establish Fort Pontchartrain du Détroit. Although this establishment was given official sanction, many of the migrants who accompanied Cadillac did not really intend to farm. Most were quite familiar with the *pays d'en haut;* many were fur traders who had been at Michilimackinac or the Illinois country. Most went with the intention of trading for the *menues pelleteries,* or furs of animals other than beavers. There was still a large market for such furs in France, and these migrants saw the same possibilities as Cadillac at the Detroit settlement.

Migration Within the
Saint Lawrence Colony
The Canadians were not only a highly peripatetic people on the North American continent, they were also very mobile within the Saint Lawrence

colony itself. Demographic studies of the colony show a remarkable rate of exogamous marriage. Between 1700 and 1760, the period of greater demographic stability, at least 40 percent of marriages involved partners of different parishes. Of that 40 percent, almost 60 percent involved partners coming from distances of twelve miles (20 kilometers) or more.

To a certain degree, the high rate of exogamous marriages may be explained by demographic features such as the elevated rate of all marriages, epidemics, and demographic imbalances caused by military actions. Features of the seigneurial system—such as the division of land—and the attraction of the colony's three towns also contributed to the high rate of exogamous marriage. The salient feature in this explanation remains the river itself. Canadians traveled up and down the Saint Lawrence by canoe, bateau, and schooner in summer and by sleigh in winter. In many cases, Canadians married someone two or three parishes away simply because a young man could travel by river far beyond the confines of his parish, pay court, and return home on the same day. By the 1730s a road was completed along the river from Quebec all the way up river to Montreal, and so horseback travel was also popular. The marriage patterns of this highly mobile society are at marked variance with those in France or in the English colonies to the south. An English colonist, lacking such means of transportation, had few contacts with the world beyond walking distance of his homestead.

FORCED MIGRATIONS

For Canadians, the ease of mobility was one of the most attractive features of the North American environment. The lure of the *pays d'en haut,* the waterways, and the affordable means of transportation all contributed to a high degree of internal migration both from parish to parish within the Saint Lawrence and in the footsteps of the seventeenth-century explorers. But not all migrations can be understood in terms of the opportunities presented by geography and Indian modes of transportation. The unfortu-

nate Acadians remain the most prominent example of a people forced to migrate against their will, but they were not alone.

The Huron who settled at Lorette had been dispersed after the dramatic destruction of Huronia by the Iroquois confederacy in 1649. Some of the Huron had taken refuge with their Ottawa allies; others were adopted by the Iroquois. Still others found refuge among the French. The Jesuit missionaries supervised the mass migration from Huronia to Quebec in the summer of 1650. From Quebec the Huron were sent to the Île d'Orléans, where they suffered numerous harassments. They returned to Quebec in 1668 and were removed to Beauport, to Notre-Dame-de-Foye, to Ancienne Lorette in 1673, and finally to the Saint Charles River in 1697, a series of disruptions that rivals the Acadians' saga.

Some Abenaki were also forced to migrate well beyond their usual homeland, although they were chased out by English colonists rather than Iroquois warriors. The Pigwacket, Arosaguntacook, and some of the Kennebec moved north to land appropriated from seigneurs at Bécancour and the Saint-François River in the year 1724. This was likely the only time in the history of North America that land was taken away from European settlers and given back to an Indian people.

BIBLIOGRAPHY

Briggs, Winstanley. "Le Pays des Illinois." *William and Mary Quarterly*, 3rd ser., 47, no. 1 (1990):30–56.
Eccles, W. J. *The Canadian Frontier, 1534–1760.* New York, 1969; rev. ed. Albuquerque, N.Mex., 1982.
Harris, R. Cole, ed. *Historical Atlas of Canada.* Vol. 1, *From the Beginning to 1800.* Toronto, Ontario, 1987.
Mathieu, Jacques, Céline Cyr, Guy Dinel, Jeannine Pozzo, and Jacques St-Pierre. "Les Alliances matrimoniales exogames dans le gouvernement de Québec." *Revue d'histoire de l'Amerique française* 35, no. 1 (1981):3–32.
Moogk, Peter N. "Manon Lescaut's Countrymen: Emigration from France to North America before 1763." In *Proceedings of the Sixteenth Meeting of the French Colonial Historical Society,* edited by Patricia Galloway. Lanham, Md., 1992.
———. "Reluctant Exiles: Emigrants from France in

Canada Before 1760." *William and Mary Quarterly,* 3rd ser., 46, no. 3 (1989):463–505.

William J. Newbigging

SEE ALSO **The Conquest of Acadia; Repeopling the Land;** and **Transportation and Communication;** the maps accompanying this article.

THE SPANISH BORDERLANDS

FOR THREE CENTURIES Spaniards, Indians, *mestizos,* and mulattos tried desperately to settle and subdue the North American periphery of the Spanish Empire. Unlike the somewhat even push of settlement in the British colonies across the tidewater and into the Piedmont, there was no single advance of a settlement frontier across the borderlands' coastal plains and interior deserts. Nor was there any continuous and sequential extension of settlement up the river valleys that drained the southern half of North America. Instead, Spanish occupation of the vast and challenging borderlands was spatially and temporally uneven. From the very beginning, distinct provincial networks of *presidios,* missions, villages, and towns evolved hundreds of miles from one another. This isolation gave rise to unique regional economies, cultures, and populations within the borderlands. It also meant that the bulk of migration and movement was carried out within each of the separate provinces rather than between them.

The patterns of migration that developed in each province were influenced by several important restrictions unique to the Spanish Borderlands. The great distances that separated settlements from one another and the difficult terrain that characterized much of the borderlands served as a geographical barrier to migration. The lack of significant transportation and trading links between the frontier provinces meant that there was no well-developed economic system that could pull laborers and merchants from one province to the next. Moreover, the virtual absence of mining in Spain's North American colonies removed what was the most important economic force behind migration in other marginal areas of the empire. And if these conditions were not enough to keep internal migration at low levels, the constant threat of Indian incursions and strict viceregal restrictions on individual travel certainly reduced mobility in the borderlands.

Many of these same conditions promoted migration under certain circumstances. Attempts to subdue Native populations through the *presidios* and missions created new frontiers and settlement opportunities for soldiers, merchants, and artisans. The need to cultivate crops and raise livestock for the *presidios* and civil settlements opened up additional opportunities for farming near the northern outposts. As the Spanish settlements expanded their holdings and encroached on Indian lands, uprisings by sedentary peoples as well as depredations by displaced nomadic tribes could force an entire community of missionaries, merchants, and farmers to return to the provincial core.

The interplay of these ecological, economic, and demographic forces created a rich variety of migration patterns in the borderlands. Human movements varied tremendously in distance, direction, and purpose. The migrants themselves moved individually, with their families, or as members of large, recruited communities. And the pull of migration in the borderlands cut across the bounds of race, age, gender, and occupation.

Throughout the Spanish Borderlands, however, three types of internal migration were generally most common. First, there were large-scale, mass colonization efforts that took place in all of the provinces. These movements frequently drew on source populations from the settled core of New Spain or the Hispanic possessions in the Caribbean. In some provinces, such as New Mexico, they took place within decades of exploration and initial reconnaissance. In other places, such as Alta California and Pimería Alta (Arizona), mass colonization did not occur until the end of the colonial period. A second type of migration typical of the borderlands involved the displacement or relocation of Native peoples. Whether forced or free, this type of migration resulted in a labor supply for the missions, the opening of Indian lands for Hispanic colonization, and the gradual assimilation and reduction of the indigenous population. Many other internal migrations appeared in a third form—as rapid bursts of human movement involving a wide range of people. Indian conflicts, ecological disturbances, infrequent mining strikes, and similarly abrupt events affecting the habitability of an area often resulted in the quick advance or retreat of a sizable population. In addition to these more common forms of internal migration, the seasonal movement of free laborers and an ongoing flow of vagabonds characterized several provinces.

Depending upon the local circumstances of economy, demography, and settlement, these patterns of migration might result in the dispersal of population in one province and nucleation in another. They might constitute the initial implantation of settlement in one place, and they might result in resettlement elsewhere. A brief examination of the differences in internal migration patterns among the borderland provinces will illustrate the variety of movement that existed and the range of results that occurred.

THE WESTERN BORDERLANDS

The four provincial settlement clusters of the western borderlands—New Mexico, California, Arizona, and Texas—made up the northern periphery of Spain's most vibrant viceroyalty, New Spain. As a result these isolated western outposts shared the benefits of periodic population and trade flows from the core of Mexico. There was little exchange of goods and people, however, among these clusters. Each province was established and sustained by a different source and flow of immigrants, each was organized and administered for different reasons, and each followed a different path of economic and demographic growth that, in turn, affected its patterns of internal migration. As outposts of the Spanish economy, the western provinces were more closely linked with New Spain than with each

other. It was not until Anglo trade links were forged at the end of the colonial period that the foundation was laid for interregional migration in the borderlands.

New Mexico

The province of New Mexico was the largest and most important outlying core of settlement in the borderlands. This island of European influence was surrounded by desert and hostile Indians, and it remained a closed system of settlement throughout the colonial period. The occupied area of New Mexico included three Spanish exclaves: the upper Rio Grande Valley in the north, a string of missions and other settlements that extended to the west, and the El Paso district in the south. Internal migration in New Mexico resulted in alternating phases of expansion and contraction of the province as Indian depredations influenced the advance or retreat of settlers and the nucleation or dispersal of the province's population.

Many different parties explored New Mexico in the mid 1500s, and mass colonization was initiated at the close of the sixteenth century. Following the illegal and unsuccessful settlement attempt by Gaspar Castaño de Sosa, Juan de Oñate succeeded in recruiting 130 colonists to plant the first European settlement in the center of Pueblo lands in the upper Rio Grande Valley. About one-half of the colonists were from Spain, one-third from New Spain, and the rest from Europe and other areas. The settlement was short-lived, and after three years most of Oñate's colonists had retreated southward. During the next eighty years, however, the flow of settlers from New Spain increased, and Spaniards and *mestizos* slowly spread out from the newly created capital of Santa Fe into the nearby *encomienda* pueblos. Until the late seventeenth century, New Mexico witnessed continuous growth and infilling from Taos to Socorro and throughout the El Paso district.

This expansion ceased in 1680 when the Pueblo Indians rebelled, forcing Spaniards and *mestizos* to retreat from the upper Rio Grande Valley to the El Paso district. Many of the twenty-four hundred migrants continued farther south into present-day Mexico. Others remained near El Paso and slowly dispersed throughout that area. This set off a rebellion of the Manso Indians in the El Paso district. Clearly, the Spanish desire to avoid nucleated settlements and live instead in dispersed *poblaciones* created considerable problems throughout New Mexico.

In 1692 the settlers retook the upper Rio Grande and created several new communities. In response several thousand Indians fled to Moqui fortresses and isolated sites. Others went to live on Spanish haciendas as paid laborers. As the Indian populations thinned out and migrated away from their communities, the Spaniards expanded their holdings in the center of the province. In 1692 the Villa of Santa Cruz was established by forty-four families from Santa Fe. These families were then replaced in Santa Fe by other migrants recruited from Nueva Vizcaya to the south. By the end of the seventeenth century, the Spanish population was once again migrating out from the provincial core and settling new areas.

This expansion slowed again in the eighteenth century as constant raids by nomadic Apache made the margins of the province uninhabitable. These raids, combined with Comanche incursions to the east and Ute depredations to the North, forced Spaniards and Indians alike to withdraw from the edge of the eastern plains and retreat into the Rio Grande Valley and southward, once again, to El Paso.

While this eighteenth-century provincial pattern of expansion and contraction was playing out, many of the existing New Mexican settlements were attracting migrants from the province. Within the individual missions themselves, non-Pueblo Indians were being absorbed into the population. Tlaxcaltecan migrants resettled near Santa Fe and some Apache, Moqui, and Navajo were resettled in the system. At the same time, highly localized migrations fueled the growth of the civil settlements. A 1788 census of El Paso revealed that over 90 percent of the household heads were natives of the district. Most others were from nearby communities.

By the late eighteenth century, as the Apache incursions slowed, population dispersal once again became the rule. Spanish stockmen migrated to the west, away from the Rio Grande, northward into the Chama Valley and eastward to the margin of the Plains. By the time of Independence, as Anglo trade connections were be-

ing solidified, the Spanish population was on a course of expansion that would lead by mid century into Colorado, Arizona, and the Llano Estacado.

In 1821 over three-quarters of the fifty thousand borderland Spaniards lived in New Mexico. Their frontier society was established earlier than any other Spanish exclave in the western borderlands, and it survived despite the 220 miles (352 kilometers) that separated El Paso from the settlements of the upper Rio Grande. Although the Spaniards and *mestizos* had a strong tendency to migrate outward and to settle in dispersed, isolated *poblaciones*, their willingness to migrate back to nucleated settlements during periodic crises kept the province viable. Thus, after two centuries of colonization, retreat, advance, dispersal, and retreat, the settlers of New Mexico had migrated well beyond the original Oñate holdings westward to Abiquiu and Laguna and eastward to the mountain communities of the Sangre de Cristo range. This expansion took place almost entirely through the internal migration of native-born Spaniards and *mestizos*.

California

The province of Alta California had a pattern of internal migration and settlement that contrasted sharply with developments in New Mexico. Although the California coast was reconnoitered by Spain in the sixteenth century, it took British and Russian intrusions along the Pacific Coast to stimulate Spanish settlement at the end of the colonial period. The consequently brief and late history of colonial migration and settlement could hardly compare with the century-long swings of contraction and expansion in New Mexico. Instead, internal migration in colonial California was stimulated by the rapid recruitment of colonists from New Spain and organized into some highly selective and highly directed patterns of movement.

In the mid 1770s colonists from Jalisco, Sonora, and Sinaloa migrated into California to operate farms near the newly founded *presidios* and missions. This first colonizing group included many large families that traveled through Baja California and Arizona to arrive in the province. The provincial government encouraged these and other migrants from northwestern New Spain by offering grants of 120 pesos for two years of occupancy and rations, equipment, and livestock for an additional three years in California. The flow of immigrants continued until 1781, when the Yuma uprising in western Sonora cut off the most significant overland migration route. After that the flow of colonists slowed considerably. To balance this decline in free migration, the government of New Spain resettled a limited number of convicts and orphans in California in the 1790s. The motive was to build a population large enough to block British and Russian settlement attempts.

Within California certain types of settlement attracted specific components of the population. The mission system was the basic element in the settlement framework. Between 1769 and 1790 a chain of twenty Franciscan missions was established from San Diego to San Francisco. These were largely self-sufficient communities made up principally of Indians who resettled and remained on mission lands. *Presidios* also were established in Alta California, and they attracted a mixed population of soldiers and their families. To accommodate the large military population in the province, ranchos were established and granted to disabled and retired soldiers.

The focus of much of California's internal migration, however, was the civilian town. Settled initially by retired Spanish soldiers from the *presidios,* the three towns of San Jose, Los Angeles, and Branciforte began to grow in the last two decades of the eighteenth century. Incentives were used in 1781 to attract settlers to Los Angeles, and skilled artisans who migrated to the pueblo were given government contracts. In 1797 a number of families were recruited from Guadalajara to resettle in Branciforte and augment the small population of retired soldiers and their families. The government extended considerable benefits and privileges to the *gente decente* or non-Indians who migrated into these civilian settlements. By 1821 more than three thousand colonists were scattered throughout California among the ranchos, *presidios,* and missions and in the three small Spanish towns.

Arizona

The northern extension of settlement from Sonora into the land known as Pimería Alta (southern Arizona) created a self-sufficient and isolated borderland outpost with minimal external trade, few linkages with neighboring provinces, and very little internal migration. In a sense, however, conflict with neighboring Indian tribes caused the population of Spanish Arizona to repeat many of the migration patterns (expansion and contraction) that characterized New Mexico.

There was no in-migration or in-filling in Pimería Alta following the sixteenth-century expeditions of Francisco Vásquez de Coronado, Antonio de Espejo, and others. Instead, it was not until the Jesuit mission frontier advanced into the area in the late 1600s that any kind of significant migration took place. The resettlement and nucleation of the Pima into mission-controlled settlements known as *pueblos de visita* was part of the proselytization of the Native peoples. Fray Eusebio Francisco Kino succeeded at converting the Pima and in 1700, despite constant Apache raids, he had established the Mission of San Xavier del Bac near present-day Tucson.

This rearrangement of the Native population was followed by a period of limited immigration and colonization associated with mining and the founding of *presidios*. A short-lived mining boom at Arizona attracted a small number of migrants from Sonora in the 1730s. Later, in the three decades following 1750, the flow of migrants increased as soldiers, their families, and many civilians moved from Sonora to the new *presidios* at Tubac, Altar, and Terrenate. By 1776 these *presidio* populations had grown and, at the fortress and town of Tucson, several hundred settlers could be found clustered around the *presidio*.

Population growth and in-migration from Sonora led to expansion of the settlement core. In 1774 a number of families migrated from Pimería Alta to California. Small, dispersed settlements were established near the confluence of the Gila and Colorado rivers. These were soon abandoned, however, as the Yuma rose up in rebellion in 1781; settlers on the margins of Arizona retreated to the provincial core.

A decade later the cycle of out-migration, recolonization, and expansion was again underway. A new settlement law attracted more Sonoran families north to Tucson, and stock-raising grants pulled many families into the more habitable river valleys of southern Arizona. Between 1791 and 1821 the population of Arizona grew in numbers and density and, at the time of Independence, migration away from the provincial core at Tucson was already underway.

Texas

Of all the outposts that made up the western borderlands, Texas was probably the most tenuously held and the least affected by internal migration. As in California, early Spanish exploration in the sixteenth century was followed by almost two centuries of inactivity, and it was not until Spain perceived a French threat to its North American claims that migration into the area was promoted.

The failed attempt of Robert Cavelier, sieur de La Salle, to establish a permanent French colony at Matagorda Bay in 1685 provoked an equally futile response from New Spain. Initial attempts to proselytize the Teja Indians in the 1690s failed, and the Spaniards retreated. Once a French fort was founded at Natchitoches in 1714, the Spaniards returned to the area and built several missions to reassert their claim to east Texas. The push to establish the eastern missions was followed in 1718 by the founding of a *presidio* and mission far to the west at San Antonio. Three years later, the third cluster of Spanish settlement was laid out at Espíritu Santo (Goliad), where a mission and *presidio* complex was built along the coastal plain.

Beyond these three clusters of Spanish settlement, Texas was virtually uninhabited in the eighteenth century. The missions generally failed to acculturate the small Native populations that were scattered nearby. The Indians were not subjected to *encomienda* and their labor was rarely used outside the missions. Those who survived the introduction of European diseases remained in their Native settlement areas. As Apache raiders pushed into the occupied areas in the mid eighteenth century, the missions became even weaker and, in the east, there was a general retrenchment between the 1730s and 1770s as people retreated to the Trinity River.

The civil settlements at Nacogdoches, San Antonio, and Goliad failed to establish any local migration fields to support their growth, and they were forced to draw populations from distant areas. Many of the settlers at Nacogdoches were drifters and adventurers who had crossed the empty wilderness of eastern Texas. The Goliad settlers were drawn mainly from Querétaro on the central plateau of Mexico. San Antonio's growth was attributable to an influx of Canary Islanders in the 1730s and a number of families who migrated from Nuevo Santander later in the eighteenth century. The only other Spanish settlement of any significance was the town of Laredo, founded on the lower Rio Grande in the mid 1750s.

In 1806, just after the Louisiana Purchase, New Spain sent one thousand troops into Texas to bolster defenses against an Anglo threat. The viceroyalty had long recognized the need to increase the population in the northeastern province of Texas, but by 1811 there were still only seven thousand people counted in the area defined by the three clusters of settlement. This number began to increase ten years later as control of Texas switched from Spain to Mexico.

The vast stretch of land between Nacogdoches and San Antonio remained unoccupied throughout the eighteenth century. In an attempt to populate Texas ahead of a U.S. intrusion, the new government of Mexico promoted colonization of this huge area by authorized outsiders led by commissioned *empresarios* who would recruit colonists, allocate lands, and impose regulations. Thus, it was not until the end of the colonial period that the area between the *Camino Real* (Royal Highway) and the Gulf Coast was filled in by migrants.

In terms of migration, the outpost province of Texas had a unique history in that the missionaries failed to induce the Indians to resettle, there was no ongoing contraction-expansion pattern of settled areas associated with Indian hostilities, and each of the key Spanish settlements relied on a unique migration field outside the province.

THE EASTERN BORDERLANDS

The four western provinces of the borderlands drew what demographic vitality they had from their linkage to New Spain. To the east, along the Gulf Coastal plain from the Mississippi to the Atlantic Coast, there was a Spanish province that was politically important during the colonial period but demographically insignificant. The

Floridas, comprised of the Florida peninsula and Spanish Louisiana, stood as an eastern extension of Spain's North American colonies. This borderland, however, formed the continental periphery of Spain's empire in the Caribbean. Thus, the population histories and migration patterns of people in these eastern lands depended more closely on the development of the island segment of the Spanish Empire and the expansion of the British and French colonies east of the Mississippi. The massive colonization efforts that emanated from New Spain and kept the western borderlands populated played no part in the demographic history of the eastern borderlands.

The Floridas
The bulk of population movements took place on the eastern margins of the Florida peninsula. The Spanish colony that formed in this southeastern corner of North America never had a sizable population and was primarily the setting for several missionary and military frontiers. The Spanish established missions and *presidios* but failed to develop the network of towns and villages found in the provinces of the western borderlands. A significant population of free settlers capable of sustaining a strong commercial base never materialized.

The spread of military and ecclesiastical power in the Floridas was relatively slow. Early expeditions into the area by Pedro Ponce de Léon, Hernan de Soto, and others brought back a wealth of information in the early sixteenth century, but by the mid 1500s, four separate attempts to colonize the peninsula had ended in failure. Finally, in 1565 a permanent Spanish foothold was established at Saint Augustine, where a *presidio* and small community of soldiers, shopkeepers, and traders flourished.

Religious and military attempts to colonize the Floridas were intertwined, and the migration of population out of Saint Augustine soon followed three separate corridors. One thrust of settlement pushed northward through the "Golden Isles," the low coastal islands situated off southeastern Georgia between the mouths of the Savannah River and Saint Mary's River, and along the South Carolina coast. A half-dozen missions were established among the Guale, a sedentary people who inhabited the coastal islands. This northward press of settlement ended about 1700. A second intrusion followed the Saint John River into the interior of the peninsula and southward. Here several settlements were established among the Timucuan people. These communities remained small and never attracted any large numbers of migrants away from Saint Augustine. A third expansion of the Florida colony took place during the seventeenth century and extended across northern Florida to Apalachee Bay and inland to central Alabama. The Franciscans established a string of missions to the Apalachee Indians, and several *presidios* were constructed along the main road that cut through this northern mission field. A lively trade was initiated with the Creek nation in the area, but increasing attacks on the peripheral settlements forced the Spaniards to retreat to Saint Augustine by the mid eighteenth century.

By 1763 the *presidio* and town of Saint Augustine was virtually all that remained of the Spanish presence in eastern Florida. From 1763 until the time of the Louisiana Purchase, the port of New Orleans in West Florida and all coastal settlements and lands west of the Mississippi River fell under Spanish control, but there were no significant consequences that led to the rearrangement of populations. Similarly, a shift from Spanish to British control (1763–1783) of the surviving settlements on the peninsula failed to set off any substantial migration of people. The colony was returned to Spain in 1783, and the population remained geographically and numerically stable until the United States purchased Florida in 1819.

SUMMARY

Internal migration was an important facet of life in Spain's North American colonies. This ongoing process, which involved men, women, and children of all classes, races, and backgrounds, was driven throughout the borderlands by the initial European attempts to colonize and the subsequent, and often immediate, rearrangement of populations as they came to grips with the reality of an existing indigenous population and the limitations of a harsh and challenging natural environment. In most places the bulk of colonial migration was part of the simple expansion and contraction of provincial cores. In many instances, however, people moved within the framework of established settlements; this involved Indians moving from Native pueblos to missions and *mestizos* moving from one hacienda to another. It was the paucity of internal migration between the provinces, however, that had the most significant long-range effect in the borderlands. This lack of human exchange, interaction, and movement allowed distinct regional populations and rich regional cultures to develop in relative isolation over more than two centuries.

BIBLIOGRAPHY

Bannon, John Francis. *The Spanish Borderlands Frontier, 1513–1821.* Albuquerque, N.Mex., 1974.

Garr, Daniel J., ed. *Hispanic Urban Planning in North America.* New York, 1991.

Gerhard, Peter. *The North Frontier of New Spain.* Princeton, N.J., 1982.

Jones, Oakah L., Jr. *Los Paisanos: Spanish Settlers on the Northern Frontier of New Spain.* Norman, Okla., 1979.

Larsen, Clark Spencer, ed. *Native American Demography in the Spanish Borderlands.* New York, 1991.

Meinig, Donald W. *The Shaping of America: A Geographical Perspective on 500 Years of History.* Vol. 1, *Atlantic America, 1492–1800.* New Haven, Conn., 1986.

Nostrand, Richard L. "The Century of Hispano Expansion." *New Mexico Historical Review* 62, no. 4 (1987):361–386.

Officer, James E. *Hispanic Arizona, 1536–1856.* Tucson, Ariz., 1987.

Michael M. Swann

SEE ALSO **Repeopling the Land** and **Transportation and Communication;** and the maps accompanying this article.

THE STRUCTURE OF SOCIETY

THE BRITISH COLONIES

The British colonies in America were settled at first almost entirely by English men and women, but within a few decades four quite different societies existed, all recognizably English yet all American. Some immigrants found soil and climate suitable for large-scale commercial farming. There, a few men became large landowners with numerous laborers and concentrated on raising a staple or "cash" crop such as tobacco or wheat. In other areas the geography allowed farm families to support themselves but permitted only a small surplus, which could be produced without the use of hired hands. Towns appeared in the harbors along the coast, while inland for a thousand miles (1,600 kilometers) from Maine to Georgia the Europeans built new houses and ploughed new land along the "frontier." Each species of settlement was well-known to English men and women; in each the colonials sought to reproduce what they knew; and in each they adjusted the old ways to fit the New World.

BRITISH SOCIETY IN THE SEVENTEENTH CENTURY

British society, in the opinion of its principal families, consisted of two kinds of people: those on top—the better sort, gentlemen and ladies; and everybody else—the lesser, inferior, or common people. The reality was more complex, but clearly one's position depended upon the opinion of others; most important of all, the prestigious families at the top decided the relative rank of everybody else. Economically the possession of large landed estates with plenty of tenants and laborers was essential for the highest rank, and we find the settlers in America struggling to acquire as much land as they could. Also requisite was a title obtained from the king, preferably hereditary and elevating one to the peerage, which entitled one to sit in the House of Lords and be considered part of the nobility. Baronets and knights were not peers (the knights' titles were not hereditary), but still they formed part of the better sort.

So did another group of large landowners called the gentry, among whom a "greater gentry" belonged to families officially recognized as distinguished (by virtue of being armigerous—bearing heraldic arms) and a "lesser gentry" did not. These last outnumbered all the better sort combined and occupied an ambiguous position with no title and no hereditary status; indeed, they were almost indistinguishable from the respectable yeomen farmers. The latter quite often became gentry, a process that involved claiming the rank by writing "Gent." after one's name and persuading other people of one's higher position by gentlemanly behavior, conspicuous consumption, or a good marriage—preferably all three.

Just as the lesser gentry complicated the definition of the British aristocracy, the wealthy city dwellers challenged the meaning of "commoners." The gentry originated in an era when towns were few and small, but by 1700 one out of six inhabitants of England and Wales lived in urban centers, and a century later it was one out of three. At the top of urban society stood businessmen and professionals with wealth, skill, high standards of living, power, and prestige. Unlike the peerage, they possessed no titles and had not inherited their high status; indeed, as many as half were essentially self-made. Thus urban society possessed its own social structure, more open than the rural and with leaders who did not consider themselves common.

EARLY COLONIAL SOCIETY

Of this diverse population the colonists received a few gentry, mostly the lesser, and some prosperous townspeople, but almost none of the economic, social, or political leaders. The exceptions went primarily to the southern coastal area, which offered the best chance to acquire wealth in land and commercial agriculture. During much of the seventeenth century, a time of depression in England, laborers also migrated to the South, where the large landowners needed them until slaves took their place. Later they supplied the need for workers in the towns and on the fertile farms of New Jersey and Pennsylvania. As to the yeomen farmers and skilled workers, the "middling sort," economic and social opportunities at home were fairly good, and they immigrated primarily for religious reasons, first to New England and later to the middle colonies, where good land at low prices promised a better life even to families already owning farms or shops. Nowhere did the colonies replicate the European nobility; only in the coastal regions from Maryland to Georgia did one find the gap between a self-styled gentry and the rest of the world, and even there the gentry came to be colonial born, minus titles, and more open to newcomers than almost anywhere in the Old World.

In general the northern colonies received the largest proportion of farm families and skilled workers while the southern, at least by 1700, were distinguished for their slaves and great landowners. All of them contained the same types of subregions, the same occupational groups, and similar societies characterized by economic classes and a status order. Everywhere one found coastal towns, large-scale commercial farms and small, largely self-sufficient ones, and newly settled regions. In all of these areas mobility, upward or downward in rank and from place to place, was an important element in social change. In each region social institutions performed crucial functions. These similarities helped to reduce the differences between sections and provided, as the people were to say in a later time, cement to the union.

During the first century, most of the colonials lived on small farms varying in size from twenty to two hundred acres (8 to 80 hectares), the higher figure being common in the South, the lower rare outside of New England. The farms resembled those of the English yeomanry in that they were owned by the families themselves. They were considerably less fertile than those of the average English (or Scots, Welsh, or Irish) husbandman and tenant, but of a size that English husbandmen only dreamed of. As a rule colonial families needed forty acres (10 hectares) for subsistence; most of them owned farms much larger, the median size for a middle-aged New Englander being about one hundred acres (40 hectares) and elsewhere around twice that.

The first settlers, their sons, and their grandsons could obtain an adequate amount of land, although speculators with large tracts sometimes forced farmers to rent. By 1700 the colonies contained about 250,000 white families scattered along a thousand miles (1,600 kilometers) of coast and extending, on the average 150 miles (240 kilometers) inland—about 400 acres (160 hectares) of land per family had it all been usable and equally divided, with potentially much more than that for future use. The best quality was becoming expensive, but a man could buy a starter with a year's wages. That continued to be true until about a quarter century before the American Revolution, when some of the young men in the older towns could not find enough affordable land and had to become craftsmen or leave. It was, of course, this long period of opportunity that attracted people from Western Europe, and even in the early 1770s many were settling along the western and northern borders.

Most fortunate were farmers' sons, since their parents already owned land. With the profits of the boys' labor, the fathers could buy enough acreage to endow the average family's two sons, especially since their wives' inheritance would be added on. This process ensured a fairly equal division of the estate and so helped to prevent a concentration of wealth. In colonies such as Virginia, if a man died without making a will all the land (aside from the widow's dower) went to the eldest son, a system preferred by those seeking to imitate the European aristocracy. Ordinary farmers with more than one boy, however, usually made a will dividing the land.

Some fathers, of course, were too poor to provide for all their children, especially men who died young without accumulating much land. Their boys had to start from scratch, competing with laborers. In Britain and in Europe, their chances of obtaining land free of debt were small because the cost was too high and the competition too great. But, in America the odds were about fifty-fifty, since for most of the colonial period land valued at less than $100 per acre in today's money was available nearby. Besides, no more penalty attached to borrowing money for a capital investment than attaches today to a business loan or home mortgage. Trouble arose only in particular cases, especially in the late colonial period, when vacant lands were distant and competition intensified.

SMALL-FARM SOCIETIES

In communities characterized by small farms, the labor supply came almost entirely from children of the farmers and their neighbors. Laborers comprised a fourth or a third of the adult male population, but of these only a fraction formed a permanent underclass, since most of them were in their twenties and would soon marry and inherit a share of the paternal land. Also, they had an alternative to farming: becoming a skilled craftsman. Although such a community bought necessities and some luxuries from outside in exchange for its own surplus, people provided most of their needs with the help of one or more blacksmiths, coopers, carpenters, millers, shoemakers, tailors, tanners, and weavers, depending upon the local economy and population. These craftsmen were very like the farmers, intermarrying with them, attending the same churches, and sharing their culture. Some, like the millers and tanners, ranked economically at the top and often bought large farms. Other craftsmen, such as the shoemakers and tailors, were more often landless, quite poor, and young; they tended to become small farmers if they could.

At the top of the social order and owning relatively large properties were the traders and professionals. Every town or crossroads village had a store, often combined with an inn, where the people not only bought what they needed but sold their surplus. The storekeeper, of course, made a profit on both operations and in normal times became one of the economic leaders, almost always investing in land, which retained some of its status value as well as providing security in case of a depression. He also gained prestige through his contacts with the outside world. Ministers were highly respected, and they were usually well educated, except among the Baptists and Quakers. They were paid as much as the people could afford.

Lawyers appeared on the scene only gradually, the people preferring to settle their own disputes by arbitration or through the church. By the mid 1700s, however, their ability to represent the local people to the outside world, their knowledge, and their higher incomes placed them at the top of the power and economic structures. People chose them for high office even though, as a group, they were sometimes unpopular. So, too, doctors were respected despite their lack of medical knowledge. Schoolteachers were seldom well paid or admired, except for college graduates who taught briefly while preparing for another profession.

Every small community, then, had a status order based to some extent on occupation as well as on relative wealth and merit. Also, certain public offices brought prestige and, usually, property—for example, grants of land from the royal officials. First, since wars were always expected, most colonies established militia companies in every town or county. The captains of the militia became important men, especially since they often served as purchasing agents of military supplies. They received their commission from the colonial governments but were often elected by the soldiers, and in any event local opinion was usually consulted. Second, judges and the more numerous justices of the peace were admired for their knowledge as well as their power. Third, most churches selected members of the congregation to conduct lay as well as secular affairs, such as enforcing many of the laws, aiding the poor, collecting money, and often choosing the minister. These deacons, elders, vestrymen, or wardens were elected for their character rather than their wealth or family. Finally, in New England, New York, and East Jersey, where townships served as units of government, the voters chose a moderator to preside over the town meeting and other officials to conduct community affairs. The most important of these, together with the ministers and church leaders, the judges, militia captains, delegates to the legislature, and men of wealth or prestige constituted the upper class of rural and small-town society.

In Europe and in English counties, almost all of these men were appointed by the kings or local nobility from among the better sort, and where the lesser folk chose them the result was much the same. Among English justices of the peace and judges, at most 10 percent were commoners during the seventeenth century. Probably not more than 12 percent of the British leaders of all types at the county level lacked prominent family background, except in the case of ministers and lay leaders of dissenting churches.

In rural British America such a concentration of authority could not occur, if for no other reason than that experienced men of high status were few, so the provincial governors and the voters had to take what they could get. When a colony was first settled, at least half of those in authority came from families of ordinary property and status with little education and no record of leadership. As time passed a pool of qualified men appeared, but in America status was, on the whole, achieved or bestowed, not inherited. Indeed in rural Chester County, Pennsylvania, a prosperous farming area, as late as 1750 over half of the leaders came from ordinary

families, and the one-third in Connecticut was far greater than in England.

The distribution of property in such small-farm communities was comparatively equal because the great speculative and commercial farming estates rarely appeared in regions of diversified farming. As a rule the top 10 percent of the men did not own over 40 percent of the wealth, perhaps only 30 percent in the hill country, compared with 80 percent in England. Much of this limited inequality was due to the greater wealth held by married men of middle age and the small properties of the young and single. Opportunity certainly did not exist for all; probably from one-fourth to one-third never rose much above the subsistence level, but at the same time few remained truly poor. That was why they had come to the New World.

STAPLE-PRODUCING SOCIETIES

The commercial-farm societies, epitomized by those specializing in tobacco and rice but including the major grain- and livestock-raising economies, differed in several key respects. First, wealthy British landowners, merchants, and royal officials bought or obtained royal grants for huge estates once they knew the value of the land, and a few immigrated. Second, their children and some gentry obtained sizable tracts. Third, part of this land proved to be of excellent quality and soon supported wealthy colonial-born farmers. Fourth, land prices rose so much as to force out many of the small landowners (in some South Carolina parishes, virtually all). Finally, the well-to-do farmers purchased indentured servants and slaves, thus creating an exceptionally large class of dependent laborers.

Although small farmers remained in considerable numbers, the critical characteristics of this society were the large proportion of rich and poor, the difficulty of improving one's status by comparison with the opportunity in small-farm communities, and the concentration of wealth and power. This description depicts an extreme, but the general features mark much of the region along the lower Hudson, Delaware, Potomac, James, and other river valleys along with the coastal lowlands of South Carolina and Georgia, with outliers even in New England (notably part of southern Rhode Island).

At the top of the "plantation" societies were the great landholders, the merchants, the top lawyers, and high-ranking government officials appointed by the king or, in Pennsylvania and Maryland, the Penns and Calverts with their allies. In Maryland the top 10 percent held over 60 percent of the wealth, far less than in England but much more than in the small-farm communities. The wealthy planters eventually dominated the government, law, and churches, though they did not constitute a closed "establishment" because new men, lacking family advantages but possessing ability, joined their ranks.

The middling sort were less important and less numerous in large-scale commercial farming societies than elsewhere, though the degree varied. In the South Carolina Low Country by 1750, they constituted about three-fifths of the whites but only 15 percent of the total population. In Middlesex County, Virginia, where around 1700 the great planters owned 62 percent of the property, the small farmers comprised about the same proportion of the whites as in South Carolina. Since only 22 percent of the population was black in Middlesex, the middle class there comprised half of the people at mid century. Most of the remainder were white servants. As blacks became more numerous, the balance of the two races tended toward (but did not reach) the South Carolina extreme.

In the northern colonies, the proportion of families of the middling sort did not differ greatly from one agricultural area to another. The small farmers dwelled close by the great landowners, though on less fertile land, with smaller plots, and often as tenants. The economic situation of the tenants was about on a par with that of the free farmers because their land, having been selected by the wealthy investors, was on the average superior, and so the tenants' additional profits compensated for the rent. Moreover, the standard of living of the landowning farmers and tenants was about equal. What distinguished commercial-farm society everywhere from the point of view of ordinary residents was less its financial status than the presence of slaves and servants and of the wealthy, who overshadowed everyone else by their influence and prestige.

Mobility for the sons of ordinary farmers was limited in these commercial regions because of high land prices, so the ambitious ones sold out and moved to less expensive parts, generally westward. The free white workers without family connections had far less of a chance once the nearby land was occupied, because they lacked capital. Some of the successful ones found jobs in the towns during periods of prosperity, but towns of any size were very few, so their best bet was to head west. This was especially the case by 1700 or so, when slaves supplied the need for farm laborers and also had become skilled craftsmen. The indentured servants of the tidewater South could obtain land for the asking during the early decades of colonization, but their prospects gradually diminished over time. In Connecticut during the seventeenth and early eighteenth centuries, some 30 percent of the white servants did rise to become free farmers or artisans. If that proportion applies generally, the indentured had probably gained by coming to America, but this figure may be high. They were almost certainly better off physically. The slaves apparently gained in that way too. During the eighteenth century, the birth and survival rate of those born in the colonies permitted a steady population growth, always a good sign. Nonetheless, their surplus earnings of course went to the owners and no one was volunteering for their positions.

Profits did accrue to the business and professional men who shared the top positions with the great landowners. Retail shopkeepers increasingly turned wholesalers, at least as to exports, and ordered from Europe quantities of luxury goods demanded by wealthy customers. Often they invested some of these profits in land, slaves, mills, and money at interest and married the daughters of the leading families, as British merchants did. The ministers earned salaries that enabled them to live in comfort instead of shabby gentility, and they benefited from a generally higher level of culture. Lawyers had rich clients, doctors flourished, and even teachers turned into tutors living with the best families. Thus the presence of a larger lower class combined with good soil to raise the level of living for everyone else.

THE SOCIAL ORDER IN URBAN CENTERS

Colonial towns, almost all in the north, contained no more than 10 or 12 percent of the people throughout the colonial period, but they were important as the centers of culture, commerce, finance, and government. While the small farming communities were distinguished by their numerous middle class and the large commercial farm societies by their people in servitude and great landowners, towns such as Boston and Charleston, South Carolina, were characterized by their large and influential upper class of merchants and professionals, many poor free laborers, and great variety of shopkeepers and craftsmen in between.

The urban better sort differed from the wealthy landholders in that, with some exceptions, they did not fancy themselves to be an elite and did not acquire extensive landed estates, build great country houses, or surround themselves with servants. Insofar as they imitated anyone, they lived like the English middle class, Dutch burghers, or other European bourgeoisie except that their wealth rarely permitted conspicuous display. By European standards they were really only well-to-do, with properties of from £5,000 to £20,000 rather than fortunes of £100,000. Moreover most of them belonged to the Congregational, Quaker, Presbyterian, Dutch Reformed, or low church variety of the Anglican denominations, all of which frowned on ostentation.

Like the Londoners, however, they dominated the cities' major political, religious, cultural, and social institutions and owned at least 60 percent of the wealth. Most important for the internal economic system were the merchants engaged in overseas trade and in wholesaling and banking. The other members of the urban better sort were satellites, deriving their incomes and status from the association, often as relatives. These included the best lawyers, the educated doctors, ministers of the most prestigious churches, top officials, and high-ranking military officers. The most skilled and capable craftsmen overlapped into the upper class, especially if they were large manufacturers (such as shipbuilders) or branched out into trade; successful printers, too, were often allies. The urban leaders did not form a single class, but consisted of various types of the same status who competed with one another nearly as much as they cooperated and who belonged to different political factions.

The urban "middling sort" included from 30 percent to 40 percent of the people. These were the respectable people, the lesser professionals, retail shopkeepers, owners of hostels who rented rooms to the transients, innkeepers, ships' captains, and a great variety of skilled workers from barbers to carpenters. As just noted, the ablest and wealthiest of these rose and merged with the top ranks of society, so that no sharp distinction divided status levels. The great majority earned adequate incomes about equal to those of their country equivalents, with the same range from marginal to comfortable. They were more endangered by depressions and had less security as to food and, in the north, necessary wood for hard winters; these problems, however, came near the end of the colonial period. By that time the largest towns contained almost no woodlots and little farm land for gardens, milk cows, or pigs; major centers such as New York and Philadelphia were receiving a surplus of immigrants, and unemployment increased. The craftsmen, like farmers, varied from almost rich to decidedly poor, in about the same proportion.

Sailors and fishermen were generally poor, partly because as a group they were young and died before they could accumulate any capital or become ships' captains; moreover, jobs were seasonal and fluctuated with depressions and wars. During the seventeenth century, fishing and even many whaling vessels were locally owned by members of the crew or their neighbors; later the size and cost increased while the crews came to include foreigners or, often, Indians or freedmen. The natives tended to be crowded out, and in any case the profits went to the builders of the big ships and the merchants who provided the capital.

Historians disagree about the number of urban poor. One obtains the maximum figure by studying the largest towns, including not only slaves, servants, apprentices, sailors, wage laborers, and journeymen but also independent artisans leaving small estates at their death or paying only a minimal tax, adding widows, using a tax list from a depression year such as followed the Seven Years' War, and concentrating on the eighteenth century. All this can yield a figure as high as 60 percent, of whom half were genuinely poor and the rest living just above the subsistence level. This may be correct for the period just after the Seven Years' War, although if one subtracts widows and nonresidents such as many of the sailors, the figure falls somewhat. Fifty percent would be closer for the earlier decades and considerably fewer for smaller towns. The circumstances of most city laborers, however, differed from those in Europe because they rarely lacked food or other essentials; they were not impoverished. Had that not been the case, immigrants would have ceased to arrive and local farmers' sons would not have tried their luck in the towns.

Thus the cities had a complex status order ranging from the truly poor—whatever their proportion—to the very rich, with different kinds of people at every level. Slaves, of course, ranked at the bottom; they were nonetheless better off than those in farming areas because about half were household servants, and their concentration encouraged cultural and social events as well as family life for some. They did not increase except by immigration, but that was true for city folk generally. White servants, ordinary laborers, and sailors were more fortunate only in their freedom. Few of these had much realistic chance for advancement, although the possibility existed.

Apprentices and journeymen were in a different position. The former were young, indeed often in their teens, and so would not belong to the category of poor adult men. In any case the system enabled parents to start a son in a career, often paying a fee to someone with skill, such as a merchant, a doctor, or lawyer as well as a master craftsman. The apprentice, therefore, might come from the middling and even the upper rank of society and could normally expect to become successful after a further period of training as journeyman, sometimes marrying the master's daughter if his family background permitted. The chances of a journeyman depended upon economic conditions, the degree of population growth or stagnation, and personal ability. In the British colonies, the chances were pretty good to reach at least a level sufficient to support a family, especially before 1760 or so. As to the independent artisans, some—such as tailors—were proverbially poor all their lives, but most might expect to achieve modest pros-

perity in the colonies on about a level with their fathers, after the usual struggle for reputation and customers.

BACKCOUNTRY SOCIETY

After 1700 colonists began to settle in the backcountry, which stretched from Maine to Georgia, up to the foothills of the Appalachians, well away from the coast and often beyond the reach of navigable rivers. For most of the colonial period it was a frontier, and that word will serve if freed of traditional associations. There were two variants. In one a man or group of men invested in a large tract—thousands of acres—beyond the edge of settlement, which could be obtained by an outright grant from the government or purchased for a small fee, since it had little value in its undeveloped state or with Indians still unappeased. Examples from the earlier years are William Pynchon in western Massachusetts and William Byrd in Virginia, both of whom settled and profited, while several big grants in New Hampshire and Maine failed. In later years Sir William Johnson created and occupied a feudal domain along New York's Mohawk Valley, and Lord Fairfax did the same on his five-million-acre (8,000,000-hectare) empire in northwestern Virginia.

The owners had either to sell or rent the land before it would turn a profit, except for that small part that they could cultivate themselves. They had to keep the price down, for neither renters nor buyers had much money and generally could go elsewhere. The four men above opened up land that had not been previously available and attracted settlers, even creating large-scale commercial farming districts on sections with good water transportation and fertile soil. Each such district included other men of high status associated with the great landowner, together with a large number of both yeomen and tenant farmers as well as agricultural laborers, the latter being primarily sons of the settlers. In these respects the society rather resembled a small farming community with the one great family added on top; the concentration of wealth was far greater, but the median was nearly the same. A manor lord, however, not only dominated the people economically but, like a European aristocrat, took the best seat in the church, served as judge, chose the sheriff, led the militia, and attended the legislature, or, if he found any of these positions undesirable, obtained the position for a supporter. Successful landholders were smart enough to get along with the Indians; all except Fairfax were traders.

The other type of backcountry society was an extension of the small-farm variety in that the settlers generally arrived with little capital and tended to settle close together for mutual aid upon the scattered tracts of good soil and along streams. This arrangement was satisfying because they had sometimes lived in communities of that type or belonged to a dissenting religious group seeking cooperatively to worship God rather than to become rich. The great majority of these "pioneers" were farmers and artisans. They chose their leaders partly from members of such few prominent families who joined them but mostly from the best available, men from ordinary background with superior capabilities and often capital.

COHESION AND CONFLICT

This opportunity to settle on good vacant land helps to explain why, despite the inequality of wealth and the existence of obvious social distinctions, so few rebellions occurred other than those by slaves. Even discontent among slaves almost always took the form of individual actions such as running away, an activity favored also by indentured servants. Some historians, most notably Gary Nash, stress the importance of economic classes in early America and cite instances of conflicts pitting the rich and powerful against the poor and oppressed. A case can be made for such struggles during the economic depression that followed the Seven Years' War and again during the revolutionary years, but before the 1760s disputes rarely involved the opposition of people divided solely along lines of wealth. This reflected in part the absence of true poverty: people had enough to eat, and those falling below subsistence were few enough for their neighbors to care for them. Almost everywhere children could become craftsmen or farmers, and even though some might remain journeymen and tenants (the likely outcome in Europe), that

was rarely worth a revolt. Moreover the ordinary white colonials tended to identify their interests with those of the local leaders, electing them to office (along with men like themselves) and supporting key policies such as maintaining discipline over slaves.

The vertical gulf so general in Europe between gentlemen and commoners, and enforced by strong governments and the requirement of deference, existed fully only with respect to slaves and indentured servants during their term of servitude. The colonial leaders would have preferred such a system but could rarely create it. Finally, with some exceptions among the great landowners of South Carolina, Virginia, and New York, the men of high status usually married women from ordinary families, thus integrating the two most important social strata, as did for example two-thirds of Connecticut's leaders and perhaps two out of five of the ministers.

Another variety of conflict, rather more economic and political than social, involved disputes between inhabitants of the backcountry against people of the long-settled area along the coast. The issues included western expansion, land policy, Indian-white relations, and representation in the legislature. Other common conflicts were between residents of small-farm communities and those living in the larger towns or commercial farming areas over such issues as the administration of justice, relations between debtors and creditors, and tax policy. These occasionally became violent but usually were fought out in the colonial legislatures and properly belong to political rather than to social history.

SECTIONAL DIVERSITY

Colonial society also differed along sectional lines: New England and its extensions; the southern colonies, from Maryland to the Spanish border; and the middle colonies, including most of New York, New Jersey, and Pennsylvania with the adjacent counties in Delaware and Maryland. In each of these sections, social changes occurred over time.

The South
During most of the seventeenth century the South, then restricted to the Chesapeake Bay

region, contained mostly small, nearly self-sufficient farms as previously described, though lacking the village centers so common to the north
and in Europe. Since numerous river valleys
crisscrossed the country, the settlers moved
inland quite rapidly once the Native Americans
had been dispossessed. Population growth was
slowed by disease, but immigrants continued to
arrive from England, both as free men and
women with a little property and as indentured
servants who supplied the need for a labor force,
compensating for the high infant mortality. The
good soil and profits from tobacco culture attracted some English gentry and traders with
capital, and after the first few decades their children and the successful farmers formed a native
aristocracy (as their descendants would call it).
The distribution of property nevertheless remained far more equal than in England and
the opportunity for a poor man, even a former
indentured servant, was relatively high.

Toward the end of the century, a series of
changes created the commercial-farm society already discussed. Fundamental was the slowing
of immigration, including servants, which with
the continued high mortality, especially among
newcomers, deprived the ambitious tobacco
growers of an adequate labor force. Slaves provided that force, but their high initial cost prevented most ordinary farmers from buying any.
Consequently, society became increasingly stratified, wealth more concentrated, and the chance
for an ordinary farmer, artisan, or servant to
rise sharply diminished, at least in the older,
settled areas.

The colonists of South Carolina, who arrived
in the late 1600s, telescoped this process, with
slaves becoming a majority by about 1706. Great
plantations also appeared presently in Georgia
and parts of North Carolina. Although small
farmers remained a majority in all of the South
except coastal South Carolina, and although in
many areas they raised wheat, corn, cattle, and
hogs just as did northerners, the tobacco and
rice planters dominated southern society. Their
high prestige derived, of course, from their
wealth, but it also owed something to the English
reverence for landowning; thus even southern
merchants hastened to buy land and slaves to
an extent rare among the wealthy city folk of
England. Also, all of the colonies were dominated

by a royal or proprietary governor and other
appointed officials. The county system of government granted extensive power to these officials
(especially judges and sheriffs), who by the eighteenth century usually belonged to the important
families. Finally, the ministers and vestry of the
dominant Anglican church supported the social
status quo.

Except in a few cases (notably Bacon's Rebellion [1676] in Virginia and the Regulator movement [1766–1771] in the Carolinas), the southern middling sort accepted this social structure.
It had been familiar in England and remained
normal in America. The middle elements formed
a respectable part of society; they could vote
for delegates to the legislatures, which usually
attended to their petitions, and some of them
achieved positions of leadership. In Maryland
during the late 1600s, over half of the delegates
came from ordinary backgrounds, and as late
as 1750 fully a third did so. This may not have
been so true in Virginia and certainly was not
in South Carolina. The effect of the new environment on society became especially evident during
the late colonial period. During this period the
backcountry of the entire South was settled by
thousands of farmers coming, often by way of
Pennsylvania, from all parts of Great Britain as
well as Germany who were not Anglican and
were disinclined to accept the domination of the
great planters. Moreover, more towns began to
appear in the interior. Nevertheless, the distinctive characteristic of the region's society remained the paramount influence of the tobacco
and rice planters, merchants and lawyers, with
the slaves at the bottom.

New England

New England's society resembled that of the
South in the existence of leading families with
sufficient property and prestige to occupy fully
three-fifths of the important positions, religious
as well as secular, which most of them achieved
by popular vote rather than by appointment.
Almost the entire immigration had occurred during one quarter century, bringing a handful of
knights, a few lesser gentry, and some traders
along with their servants. Most of the colonists,
however, were yeomen or craftsmen or both;
and since New England's geography did not encourage large-scale commercial farming, the

original social structure remained fundamentally unchanged.

From the first the region contained numerous small towns and one large one (Boston), presently joined by many other urban centers, which distinguished New England from the South. Also, no major change over time occurred because some of the original immigrants brought with them considerable capital, so that wealth per person began at a fairly high level and was concentrated. Both figures diminished quite rapidly, recovered rather irregularly, and ended in 1770 about where they had begun, though the standard of living did increase. A favorable climate and plenty of food effected a rapid growth of population; indeed, the farmers and artisans produced their own labor supply and so did not have to import workers. Status distinctions were slight relative to those in England and the South, except in the larger towns and a few rural communities. Newport, Salem, Boston, and Portsmouth, New Hampshire, all were characterized by wealthy merchants and professionals, an unequal distribution of wealth, and a large proportion of poor laborers, while the dominating position of Springfield founder William Pynchon and others in the western portion of the Massachusetts Bay colony has attracted much attention because of its near uniqueness. Still, the distinguishing characteristic of New England was the multitude of small farms rather than large estates or stratified cities.

Scholars disagree concerning changes in New England. One group, including Kenneth Lockridge, James Henretta, and Gary Nash, finds the older farming towns becoming overcrowded by the mid 1700s and the principal cities, especially Boston, stagnating, so that the proportion of poor increased and wealth became more unequally distributed. Others, such as Gloria and Jackson T. Main, consider the difficulties local and cyclical, point to an improvement in the overall standard of living, and stress the availability of land to the north and west. In any case the democratic polity of the area's churches, the universal town governments with their popular election of most leaders, the limited influence of the British government except in New Hampshire, and the near absence of a servile class made New England far less oligarchical than the southern colonies.

The Middle Colonies

In many respects the middle colonies were indeed middle. Like the South they had large quantities of fertile soil to provide an agricultural surplus. Whereas in the South this surplus was exported by representatives of British companies in scattered stores or ships, in the middle colonies colonial merchants in New York, Philadelphia, Baltimore, and other port cities conducted most of the trade, as in New England, so that the region was partly urban. Again as in the South, large landowners owned both servants and slaves, though fewer than the tobacco and rice planters, and the colonies possessed an extensive backcountry that gradually opened to settlement. The people, like New Englanders, established townships but lacked local government except in areas settled from New England (East Jersey, most of Long Island, eastern Westchester County, and toward the end of our period, along the Massachusetts and Vermont border).

What especially distinguished the region, however, was its national and cultural diversity. It contained Swedes, Finns, Dutch, Germans, Scots, Scotch-Irish, and a remarkable collection of religious groups. With the exception of some Scottish lairds and Dutch entrepreneurs, most of these immigrants were farmers or artisans with families, though in the eighteenth century some indentured servants and slaves appeared, and of course the major cities contained sailors and other workers. The population consisted primarily of the middling sort, much like that of New England, but with a variety unknown to that English enclave or to the equally English tidewater South.

CROSS-COLONIAL BONDS

While the members of colonial society differed in so many ways, they were united by several important institutions, in particular churches, courts, and governments. The influence of these and other forces bound them into communities; the famous American individualism was based first upon cooperation. During the early years of settlement churches sometimes competed bitterly for supremacy, but by the mid seventeenth century toleration had become the law in Maryland and a few decades later even the New Englanders permitted dissent, though they continued to quarrel among themselves and with others. New York under the Dutch and Pennsylvania under William Penn and the Quakers welcomed any Christian from the start.

In the South the Anglican church at first was nearly universal in the coastal regions, joined even by some slaves. Other Protestants were unwelcome and scarce in the colony until, during the eighteenth-century, Baptists and Presbyterians moved into the backcountry and soon outnumbered the Anglicans who had preceded them. These, like the Quakers and various German sects, allowed their members substantial control over church government and the lay leaders also influenced community affairs outside of the church. Since these leaders came from the whole body of members, they united people of all sorts, except blacks and Indians. The influence of the Anglican church tended to isolate the coastal South, but everywhere else the colonists established very similar religious groups. The congregations gathered at least once a week, uniting a large part—certainly the most influential part—of the community, since many of the colonists had immigrated primarily for religious reasons and most of the others at least pretended some faith. Moreover the meetings were always social gatherings with both political and economic implications.

So also the court meetings brought colonists together. The justices were chosen by the provincial government, not the people, and as learned men they had traditionally come from the better sort, but in the colonies that was not invariably so, if for no other reason than a scarcity of college graduates and of long-established families with high status. The court cases did not simply involve the rich prosecuting the poor; thus, for example, both creditors and debtors belonged to all ranks, the difference being largely one of size, the wealthy owing the greatest amounts. Moreover the cases, like those of today, included all kinds of disputes, criminal as well as civil, interesting to everyone in the neighborhood. Court days, then, were attended by every sort of person—practically the entire community—and even the justices included some ordinary folk.

In the same way, election day brought the voters, at least, to the polls, to be greeted amicably by the candidates, however elevated their rank. Town meetings offered a further opportunity for the people to socialize. So also did weddings, funerals, holidays (rare then), and such joint activities as house-raisings or combined efforts at harvesttime. During the later colonial period, urban, social, and cultural organizations attracted prosperous craftsmen as well as merchants and professionals, as in the case of the Ancient and Honorable Military Company in Boston. Colleges such as the College of New Jersey (Princeton), Franklin's Academy (University of Pennsylvania), Yale, and Harvard extended the friendship of students beyond colonial boundaries, and newspapers circulated widely.

Finally, they were united by wars and their military organizations. Throughout the colonial period and in almost every colony, British settlers fought the Spanish, the French, or both, and were often in battle against Indians. All of the governments established military organizations, the captains of which were selected with some attention to local preference and often belonged to ordinary families. Support for the wars came not only from the backcountry but, for different reasons and in varying degrees, from people everywhere. The last and greatest conflict, the Seven Years' War, ended with a major triumph, shared by all the colonies, that captured a vast new western territory creating new dreams.

BRITAIN AND THE COLONIES: CONTINUITY AND CHANGE

The king and his councillors, the wealthy merchants, and the landed aristocracy of Great Britain, who held most of the property and nearly all of the most important offices and who financed the invasion of North America, hoped to duplicate the social structure that they knew and that they thought best. They came closest on the western shore of the Chesapeake Bay, in tidewater Maryland and Virginia, along the coast of South Carolina, and on the islands of the Caribbean Sea. There they instituted and dominated the Church of England as the intended universal form of worship, established governments that they controlled through high English officials or colonial lords of the land, and created a society with a small upper crust, a large servile laboring class, and some middling "commoners," the farmers and artisans. By the end of the first century of settlement, the high-ranking families held over two-thirds of the property in those regions. Almost every white male belonged to the Anglican church, and the only revolt of any account had been led by one of the highest-ranking planters, Nathaniel Bacon.

Other similarities between Britain and her colonies were more pleasing to the great mass of immigrants, including those from the continent. The high mobility in European towns, at least for those in trade and the professions, and in some areas for movement up into the lower gentry, was also present in the New World. Geographical and horizontal mobility were also as high in America as in Europe.

There were additional continuities. England and the continent contained many small towns and villages where cooperation was customary yet individualism was familiar and where the ordinary folk treated their leaders with genuine respect. So it was in British North America, too. And everywhere in the colonies as in the Old World, even in the small-farm societies, members of the principal families exerted an influence in the church, the army, the government, the courts, and other institutions out of all proportion to their numbers.

But the differences were more profound. Most striking was the absence in British America of a hereditary aristocracy, which in Europe would not even begin to weaken for a century and a half. With few exceptions the colonials who became leaders were at best lesser gentry and more often new men—commoners. Moreover, except for the slaves, the class of dependent poor was much smaller and the proportion of landowning farmers and independent craftsmen far larger than in Great Britain. Even as late as 1774, when the concentration of wealth was perhaps a little higher than earlier, the richest 10 percent, including the great landowners in the South, owned just a little over half of the property, hardly an equal distribution but far more so than in Britain. Moreover in the extensive areas dominated by small farms, the figure was under 40 percent. The wealth per person in the colonies was well below that of England, but the median was certainly higher.

Finally, in the colonies as a whole the major social institutions reflected, much more than in the Old World, the desires of the majority (other than the servants and slaves). Except for the staple crop area of the South, where the wealthy planters dominated the Church of England, the congregations ran their churches democratically and elected their lay leaders from the whole membership, and the militia represented the community, at least through the rank of captain. Even men controlling the political power structure could not dominate the people as did the House of Commons, the councils of the cities, and the judiciary in Britain. For the majority of white colonists, society was far from perfect, but it was a vast improvement on that of the Old World.

BIBLIOGRAPHY

Beeman, Richard R. *The Evolution of the Southern Backcountry: A Case Study of Lunenburg County, Virginia, 1746–1832.* Philadelphia, 1984.

Galenson, David W. *White Servitude in Colonial America: An Economic Analysis.* New York, 1981.

Henretta, James A., and Gregory H. Nobles. *Evolution and Revolution: American Society, 1600–1820.* Lexington, Mass., 1987. A survey, more political than social, stressing internal conflicts.

Main, Gloria L. *Tobacco Colony: Life in Early Maryland, 1650–1720.* Princeton, N.J., 1982.

Main, Jackson T. *Society and Economy in Colonial Connecticut.* Princeton, N.J., 1985.

Nash, Gary B. *The Urban Crucible: Social Change, Political Consciousness, and the Origins of the American Revolution.* Cambridge, Mass., 1979. Excellent on eighteenth-century cities, especially the workers.

Rutman, Darrett B., and Anita H. Rutman. *A Place in Time: Middlesex County, Virginia, 1650–1750.* New York, 1984.

Wrightson, Keith. *English Society, 1580–1680.* London, 1982. The best book on the English background.

Jackson Turner Main

SEE ALSO **Artisans; Colonial Political Culture;** and **Poverty.**

THE DUTCH COLONY

THE CONTOURS OF New Netherland society reflected the colony's history as a possession of the Dutch West India Company (WIC), a commercial enterprise oriented toward the acquisition of wealth. Begun by men who placed secular above spiritual aims, the colony attracted migrants seeking material gain, whether as employees of the company or independently. The social evolution of New Netherland was directly influenced by the company's decision to allow private traders to participate in the lucrative fur trade after 1640, its willingness to accept settlers of diverse European backgrounds in order to populate the vast territory, and its endorsement of slavery as a means of filling the colony's labor needs.

PROMINENCE OF URBAN CENTERS

The centrality of the fur trade in New Netherland's economy led to the prominence of the urban centers of New Amsterdam (New York City) and Beverswyck (Albany). Beverswyck, located just south of the confluence of the Mohawk and Hudson rivers and close to the Indian sources of the beaver pelts that commanded high prices in European markets, grew near Fort Orange after the company surrendered its monopoly of the fur trade. Former company employees, dissatisfied tenant farmers from the Rensselaerswyck patroonship, and new immigrants vied with each other for advantage in the trade. Trading season (the summer months of June, July, and August) was the high point of the year, with local residents as well as merchants from New Amsterdam scurrying to make profitable deals with the Indians who came to town. Yet contrary to the accepted view, only a handful of Beverswyck's men focused their energies exclusively on the fur trade. Most townspeople pursued traditional occupations and engaged in fur trading only to supplement their incomes. By the mid 1650s, when the population had exceeded one thousand, Beverswyck was a diversified community resembling many villages in the Netherlands.

THE SOCIAL HIERARCHY

New Amsterdam's social structure was more complex, with company officials and well-connected overseas merchants dominating town affairs. A few professionals—clergymen, physicians, and teachers—whose superior education and specialized skills entitled them to an extra measure of respect also lived in New Amsterdam by the last decade of Dutch rule. Artisans such as blacksmiths, carpenters, and glaziers practiced their skills full-time, and the town was well-furnished with bakers, butchers, and tavernkeepers. Laborers performed a variety of tasks associated with the life of the seaport, and soldiers employed by the West India Company supplied the community's defense. Indentured servants imported from the Netherlands learned their crafts while assisting their masters. At the bottom of the social hierarchy were African slaves belonging to the WIC and to private individuals. Farmers cultivated crops on the outskirts of the settlement at the tip of Manhattan Island, but most agricultural production was centered in the village of Harlem, founded in 1658 at the upper end of the island, and in the farming communities of nearby western Long Island.

Great extremes of wealth and poverty were unknown in these urban areas during the period of Dutch rule. Nevertheless certain families, such as the Schuylers in Beverswyck and the Van Cortlandts in New Amsterdam, began amassing substantial amounts of property that would form the foundation of their descendants' fortunes. Opportunities to display wealth were still limited in New Netherland's frontier society, but members of the colony's mercantile elite already lived on a grander scale than their artisan neighbors, and the gap would widen in the years after the English conquest. The small number of residents who, because of infirmity or age, lacked adequate resources could depend on the Dutch Reformed church for assistance.

New Netherland boasted several areas of small farms—the Hudson Valley, Schenectady, Long Island, and the territory on the Delaware River captured from Sweden in 1655. Whether Dutch, English, or Swedish, farmers in these regions raised crops primarily to feed their own families while regularly selling surpluses in the marketplace. Farmers varied in the amount of land and livestock they owned, but differences in economic standing were not vast. New Netherland's moderately stratified farming communities also included several craftsmen as well as a handful of African slaves owned by the more prosperous families.

A FLUID AND HETEROGENEOUS SOCIETY

New Netherland was a fluid society, especially in its early years. Men who migrated as employees of the Dutch West India Company or as servants indentured to private individuals could experience a rapid increase in wealth and status as they acquired land, established themselves in trade, or set up shop as craftsmen. Neither was opportunity constricted on account of ethnic background.

Cognizant of the numerous advantages of life in the Netherlands in the mid seventeenth century, the company's directors at the outset realized that Netherlanders alone would never populate the extensive domain of their North American colony. The resulting open-door policy set the stage for the immigration of Europeans of French, German, Scandinavian, and Jewish origins to New Netherland and the emergence of a social order noted for its heterogeneity. A related decision to permit groups of New England Puritans to form towns on Long Island under Dutch governance further differentiated the colony's society, as did the conquest of New Sweden. Concessions to these foreign settlers allowed them to reproduce their own cultural and religious institutions while displaying nominal allegiance to the Dutch West India Company. The colony's cultural complexity acquired another dimension as the number of African slaves gradually increased.

Heterogeneity was most pronounced in New Amsterdam, Beverswyck, and New Amstel, the settlement on the Delaware River ceded to the city of Amsterdam by the WIC in 1657. More than a quarter of New Amsterdam's residents were not Dutch. Europeans from the German states, Norway, Sweden, Denmark, France, and England, as well as enslaved Africans, crowded the streets of the tiny seaport, rubbing shoulders with natives of both rural and urban areas of the Netherlands.

New Netherland was far from being religiously uniform, despite the fact that the Dutch Reformed church was officially established. Lutherans, Quakers, and Jews struggled for the right to practice their faith, while English Puritans on Long Island received permission to worship openly.

Focusing on the diverse origins and beliefs of New Netherland's population, however, obscures the fact that many European immigrants to New Netherland had previously resided in the Netherlands, whose tolerant religious climate and economic prosperity made it a magnet for refugees in the seventeenth century. In Amsterdam and other cities, they absorbed elements of Dutch culture, thereby facilitating their adjustment to New Netherland society. Once in the Dutch colony, individuals from all over the map of Europe came together to worship in the Dutch Reformed church. Whether they married natives of their own country or people of Dutch birth, as frequently happened, their marriages were solemnized there. Moreover, the offspring of foreign and mixed couples alike were baptized in the Dutch Reformed church and encouraged to enroll in the elementary school operated by the church.

To a great extent, then, ethnic divisions in New Netherland society were muted by the diffusion of a common Dutch culture and religion. Ironically, only after the 1664 conquest of New Netherland did confrontation with the English catalyze ethnic consciousness in the colony.

BIBLIOGRAPHY

Bielinski, Stefan. "The People of Colonial Albany, 1650–1800: The Profile of a Community." In *Authority and Resistance in Early New York,* edited by William Pencak and Conrad Edick Wright. New York, 1988.

Boogart, Ernst van den. "The Servant Migration to New Netherland, 1624–1664." In *Colonialism and Migration: Indentured Labour Before and After Slavery,* edited by P. C. Emmer. Dordrecht, The Netherlands, 1986.

Goodfriend, Joyce D. *Before the Melting Pot: Society and Culture in Colonial New York City, 1664–1730.* Princeton, N.J., 1992.

Merwick, Donna. *Possessing Albany: The Dutch and English Experiences, 1630–1720.* Cambridge, England, 1990.

van Rensselaer, Mariana Griswold. *History of the City of New York in the Seventeenth Century*. 2 vols. New York, 1909.

Joyce D. Goodfriend

THE FRENCH COLONIES

ADMINISTRATION

NEW FRANCE WAS DIVIDED into five zones or regions under a governor general at Quebec: Acadia, Labrador and the King's Posts, Canada, the *pays d'en haut,* and the *Mer de l'Ouest.*

Acadia (modern Nova Scotia and New Brunswick) had its own governor at Port Royal, but after the British takeover in 1713 it was restricted to Île Royale (Cape Breton), with the seat of administration at the fortress of Louisbourg; Île Saint-Jean (Prince Edward Island); and the coastal establishments of New Brunswick and the Gaspé Peninsula. The inhabitants of this rump colony were engaged in fishing and hunting marine animals, some fur trading, and minimal subsistence horticulture.

Labrador and the King's Posts were not organized as a distinct *gouvernement.* The Labrador fishing and whaling activities were regulated by a commandant, while the four trading posts on the north shore of the mouth of the Saint Lawrence and Chicoutimi on the Saguenay were reserved to the Crown, closed to settlement, and their trading and fishing activities farmed out. The revenue of these concessions went to meet colonial expenses.

The region on both shores of the Saint Lawrence was known as Canada. It was divided into seigneuries and contained the three principal towns and local districts, or *gouvernements,* of Quebec, Montreal, and Trois-Rivières. This riverine area of settlement was the heartland of social life and commercial activity for the Laurentian and hinterland regions.

From these regions of initial fishing and fur trading activities, and subsequent agricultural settlement and social organization of Acadia and Canada, the French Empire spread into the interior of the continent. The region beyond Montreal, accessible by canoe up the Ottawa or upper Saint Lawrence rivers, was commonly known as the *pays d'en haut* (literally upper country). It comprised Native ancestral territories over which French sovereignty was extended but where colonization was discouraged in the interests of the fur trade, the maintenance of military alliances with the original inhabitants, and missionary work. Detroit, founded in 1701, was the only post with a significant number of French colonists, while Michilimackinac was the hub of western activities.

As trading activities moved farther west, a distinct region known as the *Mer de l'Ouest* (Western Sea) was created, incorporating all the posts beyond Kaministiquia (Thunder Bay) on Lake Superior to the Rocky Mountains. Missions and trade pushed southward from the Great Lakes into the Mississippi Valley, and soon French Canadians, particularly from the Montreal area, established villages such as Cahokia, Kaskaskia, and Sainte-Geneviève, surrounded by agricultural plots. This Illinois country was later detached from the immediate jurisdiction of Quebec and administered from New Orleans.

Louisiana was the farthest point southward reached from the Saint Lawrence–Great Lakes axis, but its effective settlement came directly from France by way of the Gulf of Mexico. This plantation colony was quickly given its own governor, *commissaire-ordonnateur* as a subintendant, Superior Council independent of that of Quebec, and grand vicar to oversee religious activities.

SIZE OF THE COLONIAL POPULATION

In this vast continental colony there were by 1760 only about eighty-five thousand colonists, mostly rural and concentrated near the principal towns of the Saint Lawrence Valley, Louisbourg, and New Orleans. The demographic basis of this colonial society was not as homogeneous as commonly asserted. The approximately twelve thousand immigrants who remained in the colony as "founders" came from diverse metropolitan ethnic backgrounds, speaking a variety of dialects and languages. The colony also absorbed a number of foreigners such as Catholic Scots and Irish, Iberian fishermen and Basques, German artisans, New England captives, and English deserters. To this must be added the results of *métissage* (mixture of races), especially in the upper country, where soldiers and traders often took Native companions either in long-lasting "country marriages" or temporary liaisons. By the mid eighteenth century at posts on Lake Superior, villages of Métis separate from those of the natives and French personnel appeared, marking the advent of a consciously "new nation" or "people-in-between."

There is some debate whether the colonists also developed some sense of distinct identity, which would later develop into French-Canadian nationalism. From the beginning of permanent settlement in the early seventeenth century, a distinction was made between habitants, or "permanent residents," and *hivernants,* or "sojourners." The colonial farmer, who had access to free land and enjoyed a greater measure of liberty and was subject to fewer seigneurial obligations than his metropolitan counterpart, resented any suggestion he was a peasant and preferred the appellation habitant.

There is no doubt that adaptation to the colonial environment and contact with Amerindian peoples aided the development of a set of colonial values and attitudes different from those of the metropole. Royal administrators sent to the colony complained of the independence, self-reliance, and self-assurance of the colonists. They were accused of having adopted the cruel practices of their Native allies in warfare, of having lost a proper respect for those of superior rank, and of having little concern for the education and discipline of their children or the proper support of their clergy. Nevertheless, governors and intendants convinced the Ministry of the Marine that harsh repression was neither advisable nor possible "against transplanted peoples, far removed from their prince" and his enforcement agents. Royal instructions establishing direct rule in 1663 recognized the special circumstances prevailing in this distant colony and ordered that "the general spirit of government

ought to lean in the direction of gentleness," in what historians have since called paternalism.

SOCIAL HIERARCHY

New France, for all that, did not develop either frontier democracy or an egalitarian society. In the decades of earliest settlement, before royal courts, the militia organization, and parochial structures were in place, there was the possibility for the kind of unfettered freedom associated with a frontier region, but the drive for commercial gain through the fur trade required good relations with the Native peoples and the missionaries. Under the administration of monopoly associations of merchants or the Compagnie des Cent-Associés (Company of New France) before 1663, a council had been established with some elected members, but this practice was discarded with the advice that "none should speak for all" (the representative principle), but that each should speak for himself. When the Conseil Souverain (Sovereign Council) was introduced, its members were all appointed by the Crown and eventually given royal commissions. Louisbourg (Île Royale) and New Orleans were eventually given their own Superior Councils.

Egalitarianism was anathema to the spirit of an ancien régime society; it was the hallmark of Amerindian societies, which were supposedly less developed, unorganized, and primitive. Again, in the early stages of colonization, a certain leveling of social classes and distinctions imposed itself, but always without official sanction or encouragement. There were reports of seigneurs who worked their land alongside their *censitaires* (copyholders), of officers who shared the facilities of common soldiers and Native warriors, and of Jesuit missionaries who fared no better than begging Recollets. These reports were confined almost exclusively to the initial "heroic age" before the institutions and customs of the mother country were implanted. Colonial society developed over time in the direction of duplicating in many respects that of the metropole. It was not a question of European fragments developing into a distinct North American society with its own values, social structures, and institutions. New France remained very much a colony of the metropole, an overseas territory, an economic and military "supplement to Europe."

The social class structure of France was much in evidence in the colony, if not as rigid in its delineations or remarkable in its social distancing as in the mother country. The colonial nobility consisted of the descendants of French nobility and propertied colonials with leadership qualities ennobled by the Crown. Most were seigneurs (but seigneurs were not necessarily noblemen in the colony), all were members of a privileged group in civic and religious ceremonials, and they and their sons came to monopolize the officer corps of the Marine troops, except at Louisbourg.

Rank was something the nobility cherished, and the courts protected its privileges, but nobility did not constitute a social class truly because as a group it did not enjoy exclusive superior wealth, education, cultivated tastes, or standard of living. Some nobles resembled poor bourgeois, and some members of the middle classes enjoyed the same standard of living and amenities, without the social privileges, of the nobility.

The bourgeoisie, or middle class, consisted of merchants, seigneurs, and modest entrepreneurs. They were not a homogeneous class and were characterized largely by their urban residence, their preoccupation with business, and their pretentious way of life, which included the possession of domestic servants and slaves. They did invest in supplying the fur trade and military garrisons, in the inshore fishery, in a limited number of small industries, and in shipbuilding and export trade with Louisbourg and the Antilles. Although a number took up a seigneury, there was no opportunity to speculate in land under the landholding system. A number of them were appointed to bureaucratic posts, which, along with the modest fortunes to be made in the import trade, increased the possibility of acceding to noble status through marriage. Whether they were upwardly mobile or not, many affected an aristocratic way of life.

The opportunities for investment in colonial industries and commerce were limited by the restricted market, the paucity of skilled labor, and the few natural resources available along the Bay of Fundy and the lower Saint Lawrence Valley, where settlement was concentrated. The bourgeois tended to engage in conspicuous consumption rather than in reinvestment in colonial enterprises.

In addition to what most French regarded as the unfavorable climate of the colony, there were political and religious restrictions that discouraged metropolitan development of the colonial economy. Since 1627 Huguenots, who were prominent in the commercial and industrial enterprises of the metropole, were unwelcome in the colony. In 1686 several were expelled, among them Gabriel Bernon, who was the wealthiest merchant in Quebec. Also there were mercantilist limitations imposed by France, which discouraged any colonial manufacturing or export trade that would compete with metropolitan enterprises.

Nevertheless, both nobles and bourgeois engaged in illicit trade (in which royal officials collaborated in many instances). This trade flourished for several decades in the eighteenth century between Montreal and Albany, and between Louisbourg and the New England ports. Merchants in Montreal who petitioned for the right to establish a hatmaking industry were refused permission by the Crown. This was probably a wise economic decision, which saved them from almost certain bankruptcy, given the marketing possibilities at the time.

Where private enterprise showed little interest or failed, state enterprise moved in to serve colonial needs. There were two major industrial enterprises: the ironworks of the Forges Saint-Maurice, which went bankrupt and were taken over by the state, and the Saint-Charles shipyards near Quebec, which were operated under royal naval jurisdiction. Supply contracts for the military forces were the greatest source of wealth. Twenty-two individuals emerged as millionaires, at least in paper money if not in gold and silver, during the last decade of French rule in Canada through their activities organized by the Intendant François Bigot and his Grande Société, which had important ties to Protestant and Jewish capitalists in Bordeaux. Bigot, as intendant in charge of colonial finances, and as a member of the Grande Société, which exercised the monopoly for provisioning French and Canadian troops, used state funds to buy supplies at grossly inflated prices from his associates. One-fifth of the profits went to the general contractor, one-fifth to the Montreal and Quebec agents, and three-fifths to silent partners, including the intendant and probably the governor. There were only a few Canadian entrepreneurs "decapitated" by the British conquest in 1760.

The "third estate," or commoners, included minor bureaucrats, local retailers, craftsmen, laborers, farmers, and soldiers. In theory they should have been subject to some upper-class control, but in the colony they often acted quite independently. Artisans, for example, had little group consciousness and were not subject to the strict hierarchical guild system that regulated both quality and quantity of production and progress through the ranks from apprentice to journeyman to master craftsman. What organizations existed were religiously oriented and more fraternal than artisanal in nature. One became a recognized craftsman by practicing one's trade for six years, and one could then train apprentices. Price and quality of goods were regulated by market demand. The state opposed all group organization, and the workers themselves preferred an unregulated system in which they could freely change occupations and residence. Since most commoners, especially rural dwellers, made their own rustic shelters and furniture, there grew up a respect for the handyman as opposed to the skilled craftsman.

Common laborers in the preindustrial towns possessed neither group consciousness nor organization. They were expected to know their place and to show proper deference to their superiors. There was little upward social mobility for the lower class, or *menu peuple*. The educational institutions, limited for the most part to the chief towns, catered to the needs of the aristocracy and bourgeoisie. Parish priests might occasionally sponsor a promising youth at a seminary, but generally the poor, the rural dwellers, and girls had access at best to religious instruction and the most rudimentary schooling. The lower class also lacked the kind of personal contacts that were necessary to improve one's social status in a society where the dominant groups maintained themselves through patronage and clientage.

Clergy

The clergy played a significant role in colonial society at the privileged end of the social scale. The church required large revenues to maintain its privileged position. Initially these came from bequests and revenues of the various religious communities of men and women in the metropole who extended their activities to the colony either in missionary work, chaplaincy duties, social work, or education. Contemplative orders were excluded by the state as unprofitable to colonization. In time the colonial church obtained revenues from its local estates and from privileges and monopolies granted by the Crown, royal subsidies, and a variety of dues payable for services. By the end of the French regime, one-quarter of all cultivated lands belonged to the church and about one-third of the Canadian population lived on these estates, which provided considerable seigneurial revenues. Parish clergy were supported from tithes on cereal crops, but at a greatly reduced rate compared to that prevailing in France.

The national Catholic church as an authoritarian and hierarchical institution reflected the social structure of society. The bishops came from the ranks of the French aristocracy, as did many of the Jesuits who dominated Native missionary work and the Sulpicians who were the seigneurs of the island of Montreal, its town, and seigneuries. Neither had much success in recruiting colonial members, possibly because they did not feel most candidates could meet their educational and devotional standards. The Recollets of the Franciscan family and the secular clergy of the Seminary of Foreign Missions in Quebec (Séminaire des Missions Étrangères) had more success in attracting religious vocations.

The Ursulines at Quebec, Trois Rivières, and New Orleans were an elitist order devoted to hospital work and the education of girls that accepted few colonial novices. Two orders of Hospitallers that came to Canada soon began to attract young women of middle class and aristocratic background to their ranks. The sisters of the Congrégation de Notre Dame, secular and of Canadian origin, were the most popular women's community and extended their network of elementary schools to a number of rural parishes as well as Louisbourg.

The secular diocesan clergy trained at the Quebec seminary, which along with the cathedral chapter remained in the hands of metropolitan clergy. Its recruits came mainly from the urban aristocratic and bourgeois milieu, a few from the artisans, and only two from the peasants. By 1760 about four out of five secular priests were of colonial origin, but more than half the clergy overall still came from France. More important was the fact that the recruitment of parish clergy did not keep pace with population growth. Île Royale and Louisiana together with the Illinois country remained dependent on the missionaries for religious services.

The church fell far short of controlling all aspects of life. Long absences on the part of the bishops invited secular intrusions into spiritual matters. Poor standards of piety and religious knowledge among the clergy, the growing illiteracy of the population, popular resistance to church discipline especially in Louisiana and at Louisbourg, and widespread attachment to superstitious beliefs and practices as well as to the liturgy and ceremonial characterized religious life. Law and community pressure exacted conformity, but as time passed the religious zeal evident at the beginning of the seventeenth century waned. The parish had not yet become the center of social life or the curate its community leader.

Slaves

At the lowest level of the social ladder were the slaves: largely domestic slaves in Canada and Île Royale, agricultural workers in the Illinois country, and plantation laborers in Louisiana. Amerindian slaves in the northern regions, often obtained from the Iroquois who had previously enslaved them, were not preconditioned to servile labor and so were not as highly valued as African slaves purchased in the Antilles.

In Louisiana, plantation workers were imported from the West Indian colonies from 1712 onwards. In 1721 at least forty Negro slaves were sent up to the Illinois country as agricultural laborers and workers in the lead mine. Although the Code Noir of 1685 was promulgated for the Antilles, and registered in Louisiana in 1724, it was applied generally throughout New France in regulating slave-master relations. In Canada the regulations of 1709 adopted its main precepts: slaves were to be encouraged to marry, women were not to be sexually exploited by their masters, children could not be sold away from their parents, and all were to be instructed in the Catholic religion and baptized. The state pro-

tected its interests by ordering that owners could not free slaves without government consent, by forbidding interracial marriages, and by permitting slaves to take masters to court if state regulations were violated to the point of inciting slave rebellion. Even in agricultural work, whether on a seigneury in Canada or an Illinois farm, the slaves worked without overseers in proximity with free men. On the southern plantations conditions were different because many slaves lived in crowded quarters and worked on isolated estates, sometimes under brutal overseers who required certain work quotas. Human bondage was an accepted institution, but in New France it was not based on a concept of racial inferiority.

FAMILY

The family was an important cornerstone in this preindustrial society. It was the family more than the individual that was at the center of social relations, and the Coutume de Paris (Custom of Paris) as applied throughout the colony protected family rights and property, including those of women.

Children generally remained at home until the establishment of an independent household or trade. The rural farm required the labor of the children and functioned as a family unit of production. Little outward affection was shown young children, probably because many did not survive to adolescence. There was some consolation in the popular belief that after death those who had been baptized became angels or "holy innocents."

European concepts of child rearing and training were transplanted, including corporal punishment as a means of inculcating respect for authority, obedience, and moral values. Just as severity of criminal justice was calculated to deter criminality, so strict parental discipline was presumed to educate children in the fear of God, respect for law and order, and civilized manners. The religious orientation of the parental discipline reinforced its authoritarian and punitive qualities. Terrifying images of eternal punishment and diabolical tortures in purgatory and hell menaced the recalcitrant. But many colonial families seem to have neglected their responsibilities, causing more than one intendant to remark on the lack of discipline and respect for authority of the youth as well as their independence and freedom. These observations reinforced the theory that the colonial environment produced a degeneration of cultural and moral standards.

Although the Coutume de Paris protected the inheritance and property rights of women, their roles were exalted chiefly as spouses and mothers. The family was patriarchal, assigning to the husband and father overriding authority and privilege. Marriage contracts setting out the property of each spouse were the rule, and widows were eagerly sought in remarriage because of the property they held. Most adults were married, but they did not enter into marriage at the early age the state wished, nor did they produce the large families civil authorities wished in order to populate the colony.

SOCIETY AT WORK

For the most part the colonists were comparatively well fed and housed. Unlike their counterparts in France, they were subject to no direct taxation, although all males between sixteen and sixty owed militia service without remuneration. In the towns there were strict regulations governing town planning, fire prevention, waste disposal, biweekly markets, and the inspection of weights and measures. In times of shortages, price controls and rationing were imposed. The church supported state regulations through its teachings on just price and community service. Inns and taverns were licensed and operated under strict regulations to avoid what was feared to be the inciting of scandalous and seditious behavior. Medical and hospitalization services were freely available in the major towns.

In this basically law-and-order society, the colonists expected the state to protect their rights. People of all rank resorted to litigation. There were popular demonstrations, even minor riots, when it was felt that the merchants charged excessively high prices in times of shortages, or when the church altered parish boundaries. These were not risings against constituted authority but demands that the system function equitably.

Raised in a rationally conceived, authoritarian, and hierarchical society, the colonists felt secure in the station in which they were born but aspired nevertheless to better their lot. Opportunities for doing so were only slightly better in the colony than in France, but within most ranks conditions were better.

BIBLIOGRAPHY

Dechêne, Louise. *Habitants et marchands de Montréal au XVIIᵉ siècle.* Paris and Montreal, 1974.

Frégault, Guy. *La Civilisation de la Nouvelle-France (1713–1744).* Montreal, 1944.

Hamelin, Jean. *Économie et société en Nouvelle-France.* Quebec, 1960.

Jaenen, Cornelius J. *The Role of the Church in New France.* Toronto, Ontario, 1976.

Lemieux, Denise. *Les Petits innocents: L'Enfance en Nouvelle-France.* Quebec, 1985.

Nish, Cameron. *Les Bourgeois-gentilshommes de la Nouvelle-France, 1729–1748.* Montreal, 1968.

Ouellet, Fernand. *Economy, Class, and Nation in Quebec: Interpretive Essays.* Edited and translated by Jacques A. Barbier. Toronto, Ontario, 1991.

Trudel, Marcel. *Dictionnaire des esclaves et de leurs propiétaires au Canada Français.* Quebec, 1990.

Cornelius John Jaenen

SEE ALSO **Patterns of Community; Rural Life; Social Tensions;** and **Urban Life.**

THE SPANISH BORDERLANDS

GEOGRAPHICALLY ISOLATED AND assigned a predominantly military role of defending the northern boundaries of Spain's American Empire, frontier society nonetheless reflected, in simplified form, the hierarchical structure of the Spanish colonial society. Chronic underpopulation, limited economic development, and the presence of unassimilated Native American peoples all contributed to the development of substantially different patterns. Spanish Borderland society

376

may be described as less ethnically and socially stratified than that of central Mexico or the Greater Antilles, at the same time that it was more economically marginal and egalitarian.

FEATURES OF COLONIAL SOCIETY

Sociedad de castas, a racial hierarchy based on biological mixing among Spaniards, Indians, and Africans, served as the organizing principle of Spanish-American society throughout the colonial period. As Spanish peninsular cultural, political, and economic norms set the standards for behavior within colonial society, proximity to those norms in speech, diet, economic activity, and customs served more than race to define an individual's place within the social structure. The large number of theoretical categories that existed for classifying all manner of racial mixture began to appear more frequently in late-eighteenth century records as the Crown attempted to maintain social control while implementing economic and political reforms. Despite these official efforts, the major social categories, especially in the borderlands, consisted of Spaniard, mestizo, mulatto, black, Indian living within Spanish society, and community Indian.

Because economic success as well as visible physiological and cultural signs of "Spanishness" could contribute to gains in social standing, society underwent a gradual shift toward the Spanish end of the scale in the course of the colonial period. Successful passing could turn the children of a mulatto-mestizo couple into mestizos, and the offspring of a mestizo-Spanish couple into Spaniards. Sufficiently Hispanicized Indians could leave their communities to become "mestizos" in neighboring Spanish towns. Blacks could not only buy their freedom, but if successful enough economically could purchase certificates from the Crown granting them Spaniard status.

Spanish colonial political and economic hierarchies might be said each to contain a distinct, though interrelated, structure from the socioracial hierarchy. European Spaniards generally occupied the highest administrative posts in the Americas—viceroys, captains-general, high court justices, bishops, and the top posts of the numerous religious orders. Middle-level administrators, governors and *alcaldes mayores* and *corregidores* (two names for district magistrates), could

be either Europeans or Creoles. Creoles, that is American-born Spaniards, held considerable power at the local level controlling *cabildos* (town councils), militias, and the parishes. Generally *castas,* members of the racially mixed sectors of the population, found it difficult to obtain administrative posts, although separate mulatto militia units, some with mulatto officers, were not uncommon. Outside their communities, where they elected their own officers, Indians were excluded from the administrative system altogether.

In the economic sphere, European Spaniards controlled wholesale trade between Spain and the principal American metropoles, and had considerable investments in mining and land. Nonetheless, it was the Creoles who controlled the bulk of colonial manufacturing and agricultural production. The artisan guilds as well as the professions and retail trade were also in the hands of Creoles. The *castas* were most often found in jobs requiring manual skills in mining and manufacturing. In agriculture, the *castas* made up the sector of small independent farmers and skilled workers on large estates. Indians, aside from working their communal and individual plots, often served as temporary labor on large estates. Both Native Americans and freedmen of African descent bore a number of economic burdens, including the payment of tribute and forced work quotas.

But race classification alone did not determine an individual's place in Spanish colonial society. Most Spaniards, although members of the group at the top of the social hierarchy, belonged to the laboring sector of the population. Aside from a small minority of families that established *mayorazgos* (entailed estates) or succeeded in obtaining titles of nobility, there was a great deal of movement up and down the social ladder. As an old proverb put it: *padre cajero, hijo caballero, nieto pordiosero* (father a salesman, son a gentleman, grandson an almsman). Although the achievement of "Spanish" status was socially desirable, it did not represent or ensure economic success.

GENERAL CHARACTERISTICS OF BORDERLAND SOCIETY

The immediacy of government and austereness of the economy in the borderlands paralleled a corresponding simplicity in the region's social structure. European Spaniards were few and far between. The Creole contingent, which according to census records made up the majority of the population, was nonetheless the product of generations of race mixing. Because the majority of Indians remained outside Spanish control, the *castas* outnumbered Native Americans within borderland society.

Differentiation in the borderland social structure was conditioned by its distinctly military orientation and only marginally urban character. From Florida to California soldiers, former soldiers, militiamen, and their families made up the bulk of the Hispanic population. Even in New Mexico, where following Juan de Oñate's successful occupation of the region in 1598 the population had lost its military character, the Pueblo Revolt of 1680–1696 led to a remilitarization of Spanish settlement. These soldiers and militiamen were mostly American by birth and often of mixed-blood descent.

Officially only Spaniards, European or American, were to make up the body of military units, yet the scarcity of pure-blooded recruits meant that enlistees often came from the various *castas*. For official reporting purposes some commanders went so far as to list their entire commands as Spanish. Occasionally circumstances forced Spanish authorities deliberately to enlist units made up entirely of mulattoes or blacks. The shortage of school-trained cadets for service on the frontier meant that promotion from the enlisted ranks was not uncommon. Soldiers who could read and write, had exemplary records or had well-connected friends, despite a racially mixed heritage or illegitimacy, could hope to reach noncommissioned officer or higher rank and assume the title of *don*. The extension of the special privileges (*fueros*) granted to both officers and enlisted men contributed an additional measure of social status even to *casta* members of the military. Military service, then, served as a vehicle for social mobility throughout the borderlands.

Overall, agricultural pursuits—farming and ranching—were the most common occupations as well as the sources of most wealth on the borderlands. Most farmers (*labradores*) were small, independent agriculturalists who tended fields of just a few acres themselves or with the help of family members. Theoretically, farmland ownership was open to all racial groups, although most farmers, particularly those with larger landholdings, appear listed as Spanish in census reports. When missions were secularized Indians who had been fully Hispanicized joined the ranks of landowners by acquiring portions of the fields they had worked. Although present throughout the borderlands, agricultural day laborers constituted a considerable proportion of Texan and New Mexican populations. They came from all racial groups and were often former Indian slaves, strays, orphans, and poor relations of more prosperous farmers. Only in late-eighteenth-century Florida were there a handful of planters, most of them holdovers from the British period, who owned plantations and used black slaves as field hands.

Ranching was a common occupation in the borderlands, though less so than farming. As in the case of farming, most ranchers were small operators who participated directly in everyday operations with family members and a few hired hands. Many livestock raisers were former soldiers whose skills for such operations had evolved in the course of long military careers. Like farmers, ranchers were typically listed as Spanish in censuses, whereas ranch hands came from all racial groups. Despite the legal prohibition on horseback riding by Indians, the missions relied on Indian ranch hands to manage the herds under the direction of Spanish or *casta* foremen. Nowhere in the borderlands did ranchers achieve the same social status as the hacienda owners of more central areas in the empire.

Economic conditions limited the urban occupations to the basic trades. Blacksmiths, carpenters, shoemakers, tailors, and masons were the most common artisans on the frontier, along with an occasional silversmith. In most instances, these tradesmen had to conduct a second line of business in order to make ends meet, as the low population levels rarely supplied enough business to support full-time artisanship. Because of limited opportunities for work and training, artisans were often newcomers from the central parts of the empire. Yet, as was true for rural occupations, artisans came from all racial groups, including Hispanicized Indians who had learned their skills in the missions.

Few professional people made their way to the frontier. Parish priests and missionaries were the sole representatives of the vast and complex

Spanish ecclesiastical hierarchy. As in the case of artisans, most clergy came from more central provinces or, as with most of the Franciscans, Europe. Professionally trained doctors and surgeons were extremely rare, except at Saint Augustine. The borderland populations often had to rely on people with practical training or on practitioners of folk medicine. Also, few colonial-period teachers were university educated, aside from an occasional parish priest who offered limited instruction to selected boys.

With the exception of Florida, where the army maintained an elaborate infrastructure and a sizable support population, the limited economic importance and sparse populations along the borderlands generally made for an absence of bureaucrats. An occasional notary did the paperwork required by the colonial government official. Most of the time, however, the borderlands went without notaries because the volume of business did not make the cost of a license worthwhile. The work therefore devolved on elected local magistrates (*alcaldes*) in the few towns where civil government existed; otherwise it fell on garrison commanders, lieutenant governors, or governors.

The lack of civil government in most places meant that garrison commanders, like the governors, provided both military and civilian leadership. More often than not these men were Creoles, many of them born in the frontier provinces. The level of education among the garrison commanders varied widely; some were barely literate, while others came to the borderlands with considerable formal military training and experience. Although many commanders represented families of some social standing either regionally or locally, others were self-made men of humble background.

Frontier governors were predominantly military men; thus they were at the top of both the civilian and military hierarchies. Their royal salaries, routinely augmented by various business dealings while in office, automatically placed them among the wealthiest of their provinces' residents. Often only they and the resident clergy could boast of a formal education. Usually European by birth, some governors were Creoles, and on a rare occasion frontiersmen who had risen through the ranks.

The vast distances, difficult climatic conditions, and sparse populations throughout the borderlands tended to create local societies where the cultural differences between rich and poor were much smaller than in central areas of the empire. Among the few signs of prosperity were control of ranch land; ownership of farmland beyond a subsistence allotment; replacement of the *jacal* (wattle and daub huts) or simple adobe huts with more elaborate multi-room stone or adobe brick structures; acquisition of substantial home furnishings such as chairs, beds, and cupboards; and ownership of domestic slaves.

Aside from government or ecclesiastical position, status within local society was based on and exhibited by length of family residence within the community; location of one's house on or near the main plaza; service in municipal government; and, most commonly, having the appellation *don* attached to one's name. Some families managed to send their sons to New Spain or Cuba for a formal education; educational opportunities on the frontier were sporadic and rudimentary at best.

REGIONAL VARIATIONS

Economic, geographic, and political conditions differed from region to region, giving each province its own distinct characteristics. Florida, the oldest of the borderland provinces (permanently occupied in 1565), nonetheless remained one of the least developed throughout the colonial period. Its society followed the general pattern outlined above, but its Caribbean links and proximity to the Anglo-American colonies gave it distinctive features. A large number of black slaves was always present. During the seventeenth and early eighteenth centuries most slaves were laborers on the various fortification projects; after British withdrawal in the 1780s, many were field hands on the few surviving plantations. During the first half of the eighteenth century Saint Augustine society was also marked by the presence of satellite Hispanicized Indian villages and one community of escaped slaves from the English colonies.

Ethnic diversity marked Florida society during the second Spanish period. High government and civil service posts were in the hands of Spaniards and Cubans, who shared the top of the social hierarchy with a number of British, Spanish, Italian, Corsican, and Floridian merchants and planters. Below them, an equally polyglot population of artisans, tradesmen, and petty merchants, including many of African descent, formed a large share of the population. At the bottom of society were subsistence farmers, fishermen, sailors, and day laborers, followed by the substantial number of black slaves, many of whom worked on plantations.

In New Mexico frontier colonial society reached its most complex form. During the first Spanish period (1598–1680), society resembled early post-conquest Mexican society. The more important of Juan de Oñate's followers received *encomiendas* (grants of tribute from predetermined groups of Indians), giving these families elite status. However, the small Hispanic population consisted primarily of subsistence farmers and ranchers who lived clustered in small groups near their farmlands and ranches. Through the *encomiendas* and other demands placed upon them, the Pueblo Indians were incorporated into Hispanic society in a servile capacity. Pre-revolt New Mexico also had the least military of the frontier societies, containing no formal *presidios* (garrisons) and only a handful of soldiers at Santa Fe.

After the reconquest of New Mexico in the 1690s, society more closely reflected Hispanic society in other parts of the borderlands. Although garrisons at Santa Fe and El Paso and military detachments at the missions contained only a fraction of the Hispanic population, they, along with a more formal militia system, gave society a stronger military character. While the Pueblo Indians remained on the margins of Hispanic society, *genízaros* (detribalized slave or former slave Indians) made up a significant portion of the population residing in Spanish towns. As the number of *genízaros* grew, they sometimes formed their own separate communities on the fringes of Spanish New Mexico. Nonrenewal of the *encomiendas* eliminated the single most important status symbol among the Hispanic population. Social status in the postconquest period was based primarily on the same criteria as in other borderland provinces—service to the Crown, length of family residence in the province, and extent of agricultural and ranching property.

The large Hispanic population living in New Mexico by the end of the colonial period also allowed an urban economy to develop that was a little more diverse than in the other borderland provinces. Sheep ranching in the province provided the raw material for an increasing number of weavers who, at least in Santa Fe, were concentrated in numbers large enough to have a guild by the latter eighteenth century. The population by this time was also large enough to support a number of *santeros*, woodworkers who specialized in carving religious images or painting them on prepared pine canvases.

Hispanic society in Texas centered around the three permanent garrisons established during the province's initial occupation in 1716–1722. The largest and most socially diverse of the settlements was San Antonio, primarily a military center throughout the colonial period. Soldiering became both an occupation and a means of social mobility for many descendants of the *presidio*'s 1718 founders. Another cornerstone of San Antonio society was a small group of royally sponsored immigrants from the Canary Islands who founded the only chartered town in the province in 1731, at the site of the already established San Antonio *presidio*.

Even at the end of the colonial period descent from the Canary Islanders or one of the founding military families was an important status symbol in the community, although certainly not the only one. Chronic Indian hostilities throughout the colonial period limited the expansion of agriculture and ranching, making the ownership of either type of property a clear symbol of wealth and social status. The wealthiest members of San Antonio society combined farming or ranching with retail commercial activities. The majority of the population consisted of agricultural workers, ranch hands, and soldiers.

In what is now south Texas, the settlement that took place under the direction of José de Escandón in the 1740s and 1750s led to the creation of a society that specialized more in ranching than other parts of the borderlands did. Topographic conditions led to the distribution of land in grazing allotments rather than agricultural fields. The result was a large number of Spanish ranching families, some of which came to control vast expanses of coastal prairie. Substantial as this group was, the majority of the population consisted of propertyless Spanish, *casta,* and Indian ranch hands, day laborers, muleteers, and their families.

As was the case in Texas, settlement in Arizona depended on military settlement, which moved into what in the 1740s was far-northern Sonora in the wake of Franciscan missionaries. Military service, along with tending livestock and subsistence farming, were the principal occupations. A handful of officers came from prominent Creole families, but the majority of the settlers were of mixed blood, although some considered themselves Spanish. In the region as a whole there was an almost complete lack of tradesmen; the only ones reported present in the late eighteenth century were a handful of soapmakers at Tucson and weavers at Tubac.

California, the last of the borderland provinces to be settled, relied almost exclusively on military settlers for its base population in the 1760s. Aside from the missionaries, a few officers, and some of the civilian settlers, the presidial and civilian populations were racially mixed. Mission Indians made their way into the Hispanic population but in fewer numbers than in New Mexico or Texas. The nonmilitary Hispanic population consisted of subsistence farmers and a small number of marginal ranchers. Native Americans supplied the bulk of day laborers. Tradesmen were few, and the *presidios* and settlers often had to rely on the services of mission Indian artisans.

INTEGRATING INSTITUTIONS AND FACTORS

The one Spanish colonial institution deliberately designed to serve the cause of social integration was the mission. Where the missionaries were successful the result was a Hispanicized Indian population capable of serving the needs of Spanish Borderland society. As farmers, ranchers, and artisans, mission Indians not only provided for their own and the missionaries' needs, but also for those of neighboring presidial and civilian populations. In some instances the successfully acculturated Indians incorporated themselves into the general Hispanic society through marriage or occupation. After secularization, the missions left behind communities of subsistence

agriculturalists and ranchers as well as substantial labor resources for the Hispanic population.

But the military, too, had its integrative aspects. Throughout the borderlands the *presidios* and garrisons served as magnets for population. As employer of men of all racial categories, the frontier military served to improve their status to some degree. Soldiers upon retirement could often expect a grant of farmland, and if promoted beyond the enlisted ranks, a pension and a degree of social deference. In the absence of civilian government, military order and justice served the needs of entire communities.

The most important integrating economic institution was the ranch. Except for Florida, the north Mexican cattle culture arrived in the borderlands with the mission and the *presidio* in amazingly similar form. Replacing the elaborate and often self-contained hacienda was the more modest ranch. Most ranchers were former soldiers, petty merchants, or artisans who had more in common with their herders and cowboys than they did with *hacendados* and planters. Horsemanship and livestock handling were universally known skills that established one's identity as a frontiersman.

Indian hostility and foreign menace from French traders, English merchants, and Anglo-American farmers were contributing factors to the integration of borderland society. Most frontiersmen understood themselves to be the Crown's first line of defense against aggressors. They often pleaded their cases for favors from the Crown or for justice on the basis of their military service, even when they were civilians. Defense against outside aggressors required unity of purpose among the population, and expeditions and defenses were often mounted by mission Indians and civilian militiamen as much as by soldiers.

In a social context, intermarriage served the cause of integrating society everywhere on the frontier. From an early date the unavailability of Spanish women led the conquistadors to take Indian brides and concubines. This process continued in the far north, where mission Indians constituted a ready supply of wives and female companions for single soldiers and settlers. These fluid sexual boundaries soon included the significant African population present in Florida and northern New Spain. The result was a society in which everyone strove to assert Spanish status through generational "improvements" in their racial mix.

Finally, Roman Catholicism served to integrate the frontier population. The missions produced not only Spanish subjects but syncretic Catholics who joined the Hispanic population in the almost constant pageant of rituals while retaining some aspects of their previous religious practices. Although separated by rank or wealth during services, frontier parishes were too small to admit separate churches or services for the various groups that made up local society.

BIBLIOGRAPHY

Campbell, Leon G. "The First Californios: Presidial Society in Spanish California." *Journal of the West* 11 (1972):582–595.

Gerhard, Peter. *The Northern Frontier of New Spain.* Princeton, N.J., 1982.

Greenwood, Roberta S. "The California Ranchero: Fact and Fancy." In *Columbian Consequences, Volume 1: Archaeological and Historical Perspectives on the Spanish Borderlands West,* edited by David H. Thomas. Washington, D.C., 1989.

Hall, Thomas D. *Social Change in the Southwest, 1350–1880.* Lawrence, Kans., 1989.

Hinojosa, Gilberto M. *A Borderlands Town in Transition: Laredo, 1755–1870.* College Station, Tex., 1983.

Johnson, Sherry. "The Spanish St. Augustine Community, 1784–1795: A Reevaluation." *The Florida Historical Quarterly* 68 (1989):27–54.

Jones, Oakah L. *Los Paisanos: Spanish Settlers on the Northern Frontier of New Spain.* Norman, Okla., 1979.

Landers, Jane. "Gracia Real de Santa Teresa de Mose: A Free Black Town in Spanish Colonial Florida." *The American Historical Review* 95 (1990):9–30.

Officer, James E. *Hispanic Arizona, 1536–1856.* Tucson, Ariz., 1987.

Poyo, Gerald E., and Gilberto Hinojosa, eds. *Tejano Origins in Eighteenth Century San Antonio.* Austin, Tex., 1991.

Scholes, France V. "Civil Government and Society in New Mexico in the Seventeenth Century." *New Mexico Historical Review* 10 (1935):71–111.

Tebeau, Charlton W. *A History of Florida.* Coral Gables, Fla., 1971.

Tjarks, Alicia V. "Demographic, Ethnic, and Occupational Structure of New Mexico, 1790." *The Americas* 35 (1978):45–88.

Jesus F. de la Teja

SEE ALSO various essays in RACIAL INTERACTION.

GENDER RELATIONS

THE BRITISH COLONIES

ENGLISH LAW, CUSTOM, and religion established distinct yet flexible boundaries between the roles and expected experiences of men and women. Men were dominant in politics and society as well as within families; they were responsible for the financial support and protection of their wives and children. Women, in contrast, had a constricted public role, and within the household they contributed unpaid labor and promised obedience to their husbands. Thus men alone held governmental offices and voted for candidates, filled military ranks, and were the ministers and lay leaders of all churches except the Society of Friends and some Baptist and Methodist congregations. Only men could obtain access to professional training, in college or apprenticeships, for the ministry and law.

In other areas, however, gender distinctions were less rigid. In commerce, while men controlled large mercantile houses, women participated as urban shopkeepers and small traders. And though denied entrance to university courses in medicine and the newly emerging field of obstetrics, women were the chief practitioners of midwifery and traditional medicine. Within the home wives were responsible primarily for domestic tasks, but many had sufficient understanding of their husbands'

work to fill in for them when they were absent or ill.

The gender ideology of early modern England contained the contradictory constructs of women's inferiority on the one hand and capability on the other. The English, like other Europeans, believed that men and women had different natures, with males assuming central, dominant, and positive characteristics and females portrayed with marginal, subordinate, and negative traits. Martin Luther reflected this polarity in early modern thinking—casting woman as "other"—when he wrote:

Lest woman should seem to be excluded from all glory of future life, Moses mentions both sexes [in Genesis 1:26–27]; it is evident therefore that woman is a different animal to man, not only having different members, but also being far weaker in intellect[ingenium]. But although Eve was a most noble creation, like Adam, as regards to the image of God, that is, in justice, wisdom, and salvation, she was nonetheless a woman. For as the sun is more splendid than the moon (although the moon is also a most splendid body) so also woman, although the most beautiful handiwork of God, does not equal the dignity and glory of the male. (Elisabeth Potts Brown and Susan Mosher Stuard, eds. *Witnesses for Change*, p. 9. Brackets in original.)

Europeans believed that women were intellectually and morally inferior to men, less able to control their passions, more likely (as in the case of Eve) to make compacts with Satan. Thus while females were weaker physically and mentally, their openness to the devil's deception gave them powers that men should fear and seek to control.

Both the means of subordinating women and recognition of their potential strength permeated English culture in the common law, sexual relations, and religion. Under the concept of unity of person, which was part of common law tradition, a woman and a man became a single entity upon marriage. The husband received legal authority to act for both—to buy, sell, transfer, and bequeath property, retain earnings, sue and be sued, make contracts, and act as guardian of the children. The wife, who as a married woman had the legal status called *feme covert,* could take none of these actions independently; the participation or consent of her husband was required. However she retained the right to dower; that is, the use of one-third of the husband's real estate upon his death.

Even so if the husband became incapacitated or took a long voyage, the wife was often expected to manage his affairs—to become, as historian Laurel T. Ulrich has explained, a "deputy husband." Courts recognized the authority of women in such situations to make contracts and carry on business whether or not they had a formal power of attorney. Thus English common law placed married women in an inferior position but recognized their ability to manage family business. It further testified to women's capacity in the *feme sole* status accorded unmarried women. *Femes soles* retained or, in the case of widows, regained the property rights that married women lost and thus could legally establish businesses and support themselves and their families.

The English women and men who settled in North America also carried with them complicated notions of sexuality. Sexual intercourse was not inherently evil but should be restricted to marriage and even then limited in frequency. Its chief purpose was procreation. Contrary to the nineteenth-century conception of women's lack of carnal desire, early modern English people believed women were fully sexual and in fact had more difficulty controlling their passion than men. According to the best evidence yet found, couples sought sexual satisfaction for both partners. Nevertheless men usually took the initiative in sexual encounters and assumed the position on top during coitus.

Protestant theology also contained contradictory messages on the status of women before God and in the church. On the one hand, Protestant reformers emphasized the individual's relationship with God and made no distinction between the sexes in their ability to achieve salvation. Both women and men had souls and were individually responsible for their sins. In Puritan congregations the elect, or saved, who comprised the church membership, included both sexes; in fact over the course of the seventeenth century, a growing proportion of new members in New England churches were women. On the other hand, the Christian tradition was patriarchal, with its fundamental beliefs in God the Father and Jesus Christ the Son. Reformers further rejected the Roman Catholic cult of Mary and the institution of nunneries, which had given women authority and autonomy in one sector of church governance. With the exception of the Society of Friends and perhaps some early Baptist congregations, all seventeenth-century English and Anglo-American denominations restricted the ministry and lay offices to men. They adopted literally Saint Paul's injunction to the Corinthians,

Let your women keep silence in the churches: for it is not permitted unto them to speak; but they are commanded to be under obedience, as also saith the law. And if they will learn any thing, let them ask their husbands at home: for it is a shame for women to speak in the church. (I Cor. 14:34–35)

Female members had no vote or voice in church affairs beyond the influence they could exert individually and informally on male members.

Thus in the early seventeenth century, when the first North American English colonies took root in the Chesapeake region and New England, the settlers, both men and women, held inconsistent notions about women's nature and proper social role. They recognized women's full humanity but enforced or acquiesced in a subordinate role for women in all socially constructed institutions, including the family, church, government, and commerce. Despite improvements in the material conditions in which some women lived and some modification of attitudes toward white women during the colonial period, the status of female colonists had changed little by the American Revolution. Though historians have uncovered circumstances in which women experienced enhanced autonomy and power—when their numbers were few in comparison with men and during periods of emergency and war—gender inequality persisted in the British North American colonies.

WORK

Most basic of distinctions by gender in the roles of women and men in the British colonies were those of work. While some jobs belonged to women and others to men, considerable overlap existed, and the distribution of appropriate roles varied by class, race, ethnic origin, and individual need or opportunity.

Throughout British North America, women were responsible for domestic tasks, whether they supervised servants and slaves or were the ones who did these necessary and productive, but often menial and monotonous, chores. Their workplace generally included the house and yard. They prepared and served meals, baked bread, cared for children, built fires, carried water and waste, cleaned the house and furnishings, washed and ironed laundry, gardened, tended poultry, milked cows, and made clothing and other household articles. Some women decorated with needlework the bedding and bed curtains that dominated house interiors. Often they hoed crops and assisted with the harvest.

Scattered evidence suggests that women specialized in one or more activities and traded surplus production with neighbors and shopkeepers. Predictably the kinds of manufacturing or service in which they specialized depended upon available resources, including time, skill, and raw materials. For example, women in older settled rural communities were more likely to produce textiles and dairy products than either frontier women, who with their husbands were too busy meeting the challenge of establishing farms, or urban women, who lacked space for spinning wheels, looms, or livestock and could readily purchase manufactured goods and foodstuffs at the market. Historian Carole Shammas has demonstrated that women's work varied by region and

changed over time. A much smaller percentage of women produced butter and cheese in the Chesapeake than in Massachusetts throughout the colonial period. However the proportion of households with spinning wheels grew substantially and similarly in both the Chesapeake and rural New England.

Colonial women took responsibility for a large part of medical care and primary education. Some rendered service as midwives, nurses, and lay doctors. In these capacities, though not accorded the title of doctor, they delivered babies, treated wounds and illnesses, and administered drugs. A woman was probably the first teacher a child faced, for literate mothers taught their own children to read. In New England towns, some women opened dame schools in which they taught young girls and boys the fundamentals of reading. Because the Puritans emphasized personal access to the Bible, as early as 1642 the Massachusetts government required parents to provide reading instruction. Writing skills were considered much less important. Further, women throughout the colonies transmitted skills to young women—their own daughters and those of their neighbors and relatives—in the "art, trade, and mystery" of housewifery or a specific craft such as weaving.

While men's workplace and roles sometimes overlapped with those of women, they avoided domestic chores—women's work—whenever possible. In the countryside, where the majority of colonists lived, men took responsibility for raising and processing the staple crop and delivering their product to market. They also maintained buildings, fences, and implements; determined which fields to plant and which to leave fallow; leased or purchased land; and arranged for the hiring or purchase of field hands. Many farmers also pursued the craft of blacksmith, carpenter, or cooper and served as master to apprentices in those trades and in farming.

In cities, where space was limited, men often kept shop or followed a craft in one room of the house. Urban men were shoemakers, cabinetmakers, brewers, candle makers, blacksmiths, and all sorts of other artisans. They sold merchandise and ran taverns and inns. Their wives often assisted in these activities and took control at the husband's death. Other male residents of the cities worked outside the house as laborers, carters, longshoremen, shipbuilders, house carpenters, masons, ropemakers, and sailmakers. Some went to sea, and others hawked wares from town to town. Men dominated professions, for they alone could acquire a college education or appropriate apprenticeship. Only men served as ministers in all churches except the Society of Friends and some Baptist congregations, were lawyers and judges, assumed the title of doctor, and taught in secondary schools and colleges.

Scholars have debated the question of how women's status changed over time and, in particular, whether increasing commercialization defined gender work roles more rigidly. Most have identified a turning point in the early nineteenth century when, they say, industrialization and the growth of towns and cities throughout the North altered the nature of women's work and encouraged the separation of spheres between the sexes. As families left farms behind and textile factories took over the female occupation of spinning thread, women lost their productive capacity and became full-time nurturers and caretakers of the children and the home.

However, evidence from colonial towns and cities suggests that for some women such changes predated industrialization. Well before the American Revolution or the construction of mechanized textile mills, affluent urban residents purchased rather than produced most of their household needs. These women spent their days managing the home, raising children, visiting friends, and helping the sick and poor, not growing food or making cloth. Their daily activities were to a large extent—though not entirely—separated from their husbands' business affairs. Servants and slaves released these matrons from the onerous domestic labor that even an urban household required.

Nevertheless most women lived and worked on farms throughout the colonial period (and well beyond). The work that a woman performed on a plantation or a farm—the extent to which her sphere of activity was separated from a man's—varied widely by class, ethnicity, and stage of settlement. Under normal circumstances a British colonial farm woman expected to avoid heavy fieldwork, except at harvest, just as her husband eschewed domestic chores. However,

many women and girls worked side by side with men in the fields.

Immigrants to seventeenth-century Virginia and Maryland included female indentured servants who paid for the cost of their transportation by tending a master's tobacco for four or more years. Women were not prized as indentured servants but once purchased by scrabbling planters they were put to the tasks that would yield the greatest return—growing tobacco. In New Jersey and Pennsylvania also, after their founding in the latter part of the seventeenth century, servant women from England, Ireland, Scotland, and Germany spent at least part of their labor in the fields. Indeed German farm women, whether free or bound, customarily tended and harvested crops.

African women, who were captured and enslaved alongside their countrymen, though in smaller numbers, worked in many occupations. In areas like the Chesapeake and the Carolinas with labor-intensive staple crops, most spent long hours planting, tending, and harvesting tobacco, corn, and rice. Anglo-American masters apparently felt no compunction about requiring black women to perform hard physical labor in the fields. Masters differentiated between men and women in the assignment of tasks other than ordinary field work. Only men had the opportunity to become drivers and artisans. Slave women, probably those who were not of prime age for working on the crop, received positions as nurses, cooks, and spinners. Both women and men performed domestic service. At the same time, female slaves were responsible for the household needs of their own families, including laundry, food preparation, and sewing.

In the northern colonies, black women and men performed a wide variety of jobs over the course of a lifetime, a year, or even a day. Without a staple crop that required huge amounts of labor, masters employed slaves in many different kinds of tasks. Agricultural production in the middle colonies and New England centered on livestock and grains that demanded less labor than tobacco or rice. In most parts of the northern British colonies, slaves comprised a relatively small proportion of the rural population, and those who worked on farms were involved in a variety of tasks. For example, one Chester County, Pennsylvania, woman could "do town or country work, but [was] most suitable for the country, as she was brought up there, and is very handy and active in tending cattle and horses, and can do many sorts of out-door work," as reported in the *Pennsylvania Gazette* (1 January 1767). In the northern cities, the vast majority of African-American women performed domestic labor for the families of merchants, innkeepers, artisans, professionals, and gentlemen. Slave men were household servants and cooks, but much more often than women worked at a craft. Men labored on the wharves and as cartmen, sail and rope makers, shipbuilders, and sailors.

INHERITANCE PRACTICES

To assess women's status in colonial British America, many scholars have studied the inheritance practices of husbands and fathers. Because written statements of men's attitudes toward their wives and daughters are rare and exist only for a few well-to-do, literate individuals, historians have turned to wills to capture the gender beliefs of a larger percentage of men. Still, not all classes of men were represented in proportion to their numbers in the population, because the affluent were more likely to leave wills than the poor.

According to English common law and statutes passed by most colonial legislatures, a widow had the right of dower to one-third of the couple's real estate for use during her life. The children or other heirs, if adults, received the other two-thirds immediately and the widow's third at her death. If there was no will, she received one-third of the personal estate if there were children and one-half if there were none. If her husband left a will, he was obligated to grant her dower (otherwise she could contest the will), but he was free to distribute his personalty as he saw fit.

In regard to the rights of sons and daughters, English common law specified primogeniture, with the eldest son normally receiving all of the real estate. Most colonial parents divided their estates more evenly, attempting to provide all of their children with a start in life, whether it be a farm, college tuition, an apprenticeship, livestock, or cash. Even so, gender differences

prevailed, with sons more often receiving real estate and daughters receiving personalty such as slaves, household furniture, or money.

Historians have measured the degree to which husbands adhered to the legal guidelines in making bequests to their wives. The first to use probate records to study male attitudes toward their wives were Lois Green Carr and Lorena S. Walsh. Their pathbreaking article, "The Planter's Wife," describes how men in seventeenth-century Maryland often gave their wives responsibility for managing their entire estates, including the children's share, despite the fact that widows quickly remarried and thereby ceded control of the property to their new mates. The society that fostered such innovative and risky decision making by husbands was highly unstable and fragmented. Mortality was high among adults and children, with the result that marriages on average lasted from just seven to ten years and produced just two or three children who reached maturity. Most adults were immigrants who had served from four to seven years as indentured servants. Men drastically outnumbered women, everyone married late, and few had kin in Maryland. While women experienced an enhanced risk of dying during their childbearing years as a result of malaria, they were younger than their husbands at the time of marriage and therefore often outlived them. With the skewed sex ratio, women married soon after their terms of servitude expired and promptly remarried if their husbands died.

Within this context of high mortality and disrupted kinship networks, husbands chose, perhaps because in their minds they had little alternative, to give greater authority to their wives than was customary in England. The average testator, facing death, had a wife in her thirties, two young children, and no resident father or brothers in whom to trust the family's care. In this situation the husband relied on his wife and hoped she could deter her next spouse from wasting or spoiling the children's estate by cutting down all the trees, exhausting the land, or selling personal effects. In the eighteenth century, when the majority of the Maryland white population was native born and consequently married earlier and had longer-lasting marriages than their immigrant parents, men more often died only after their children reached adulthood.

As a result they more frequently followed traditional English practice in granting control of estates to mature sons rather than to their widows.

In Massachusetts and neighboring colonies also, the demographic structure of society influenced the decisions made by testators. The demographic experience of seventeenth-century New Englanders contrasted significantly with that of Chesapeake settlers but was not altogether distinct. Many early immigrants to New England traveled in family groups; in fact some Puritan congregations transported themselves across the Atlantic Ocean, thus transferring existing kinship and social networks to new towns in America. But as historian Richard Archer has shown, one-third of early male settlers were single, without immigrating kin. The sex ratio was therefore skewed, though not as badly as in the Chesapeake, resulting in early marriage for women, delayed marriage for men, and reliance of young decedents on their widows despite a high probability of prompt remarriage. New England proved to be more healthful than Maryland and other southern colonies, with life expectancies (at age twenty) of almost sixty years for men and fifty-five years for women, the difference resulting from the dangers of childbirth. Couples had an average of eight children and fathers often lived to see their sons and daughters reach maturity. Nevertheless when New England husbands died young, without mature sons, they granted control to their widows.

When testators lived long enough to see sons reach maturity, however, they sometimes adopted a practice that was rare in the Chesapeake: they devised all of their real estate to one or more sons and made the heir or heirs responsible for supporting their mother. Instead of receiving her dower right of one-third of the real estate for life, the widow obtained possession of a room; the right to pass through the house to and from her room; and received firewood, food, use of a horse, and a small amount of cash (or its equivalent in crops) paid annually. Such bequests were also fairly common in rural Pennsylvania, which experienced a large migration of families in the late seventeenth century and had a mortality rate and average family size roughly equivalent to those of New England. Widows in the northern colonies apparently accepted this condition of dependency and rarely contested their husbands' wills. Maryland wid-

ows, in contrast, regularly renounced wills they considered unsatisfactory, thereby enforcing their property rights more successfully than their counterparts in Pennsylvania and New England.

Studies of testamentary practices in New York have demonstrated that ethnicity as well as demographic conditions influenced men's decisions. During the first generations after the English conquest, Dutch colonists retained the tradition of community property within marriage; that is, the wife and husband held property jointly. Dying husbands left most or all of their possessions to their wives, who kept control during their widowhood. Sons and daughters, even if mature at the death of their father, had to wait until their mother died or remarried before receiving their inheritance. When children finally took control, they obtained equal portions, with daughters as well as sons receiving real estate. By the 1730s, however, many Dutch descendants of the early New York settlers had abandoned the custom of community property and adopted English practice. Testators less often bequeathed their entire estates to the widow and were more likely to distribute land to the sons but not the daughters, who received cash payments instead.

RELIGION

While class, race, region, and ethnicity affected a colonial woman's status and well-being in economic matters, the degree to which she could take part in church affairs depended on the religion to which she belonged. In all Christian denominations, women stood equal with men in the eyes of God and were welcomed as members of the community of believers, but the extent to which they could participate in decision making and the ministry varied widely. Among the major denominations of British America, the Puritans and Anglicans narrowly restricted women's role while the Quakers established near equality. Toward the end of the colonial period, female teachers and preachers helped to establish congregations of Methodists and Baptists, but among the Methodists, with the institutionalization of their sect, women lost the opportunity to lead.

Among New England Puritans, women sat separately from the men, could not speak except to sing hymns, and were allowed no leadership role. Their status improved little over the colonial period and in fact probably deteriorated as they became an increasing proportion of members. By 1650 women in Massachusetts and Connecticut comprised 60 percent of church admissions and in some congregations made up as much as three-fourths of new admissions. Despite their increased percentage in church membership, women obtained no greater formal authority.

However, Puritan women challenged these restrictions in a variety of ways. Most often they used their influence, or informal authority, to sway the church fathers. Though men alone had the right to cast votes and sign petitions for new churches, women spurred the establishment of new congregations by convincing their husbands of the need. As settlements grew, families in new areas found themselves miles from the closest meetinghouse. Mothers with small children and elderly worshippers experienced difficulty in traveling three or four miles to meeting. In 1677 women of Chebacco, Massachusetts, went so far as to ignore a legal mandate to obtain permission from the Ipswich town meeting before building a new church and were fined by the county court for their contempt of authority. Women also used their influence and the power of gossip to subvert the position of ministers they considered troublesome. Women of Rowley, Massachusetts, in 1674 successfully opposed the ordination of their young minister, Jeremiah Shepard, at least in part because he was disrespectful to female members.

Other women challenged the seventeenth-century Puritan order more dramatically; their crime in that intolerant society was to express publicly their less-than-orthodox beliefs. The most famous was Anne Hutchinson, who arrived in Boston with her husband and children in September 1634. She was forty-three years old, the mother of eleven surviving children, and a nurse and midwife. A follower of the Reverend John Cotton, she was concerned that people believed they could achieve salvation by living a moral life instead of adhering to the covenant of grace, which taught that salvation could not be earned but rather was bestowed upon the elect by the Holy Spirit. She emphasized the individual's direct communication with God rather than the authority of ministers.

To convince her neighbors of their error, Hutchinson began holding meetings, which were attended by both women and men. She publicly criticized the ministers and magistrates headed by John Winthrop and in 1637 was arrested and brought to trial for defaming ministers. She defended herself well and nearly escaped conviction but then shocked her judges by announcing that God had told her that they would be destroyed. They banished Hutchinson from the commonwealth; with family and supporters, she settled in Rhode Island.

Two other women who confronted the Puritan magistracy were Anne Eaton and Mary Dyer. Eaton was the wife of the governor of New Haven and independently wealthy from a former marriage. As such her opposition to infant baptism and to the town's minister, John Davenport, was especially provocative. She was tried and excommunicated in 1645 but continued to move about the town freely and, supported by other women, persisted in dissent. Mary Dyer had been a follower of Hutchinson and fellow exile to Rhode Island; in the 1650s she became a missionary of the Society of Friends. Dyer decided to challenge the Puritans' stern opposition to Quakerism and went to Boston, where she was immediately imprisoned and exiled. She returned to Massachusetts three more times, despite passage of a law in 1658 prescribing the death penalty for Quakers who defied their banishment. With other Friends, Dyer challenged the law, returning to "look [the] bloody laws in the face." In 1660 she was hanged, having deliberately sacrificed her life to "desire the repeal of that wicked law against God's people." After her execution, in response to pressure from the English government, Massachusetts stopped putting Quakers to death on account of their faith.

Less is known about the status of women in the Anglican church, but clearly women were expected to accept a subordinate role in these congregations as well. Only men could preach, administer the sacraments, and serve on the vestry boards that were in charge of all parish business, including aid to the poor, sick, and elderly. Like Puritans, however, Anglican women wielded informal authority that emanated from their responsibility for religious practice in their families. Eighteenth-century Virginia women supervised preparations for burials and marriages, most of which took place at home. They even managed to convince clergy to conduct some baptisms in their homes, despite the preference of priests to hold them at church.

In contrast to their Puritan and Anglican sisters, Quaker women had a formal role in the authority structure of their church. From the mid seventeenth century, when George Fox gathered followers from the radical sects that flourished during the English Civil War, Quaker leaders included both women and men. Fox's first convert, Elizabeth Hooten, was an early missionary, as were Katharine Evans, Elizabeth Harris, and others who traveled as far as North America, the eastern Mediterranean, and Venice. Twenty-six of fifty-nine missionaries who journeyed from England to America between 1656 and 1663 were women.

Quakers, like other Protestants, believed that both sexes were equal in God's eyes, but the Friends took equality much further. They held that revelation did not end with the Bible, that the Light could bring new understanding. Saint Paul, in his letter to the Corinthians, attempted to end a dispute, not suppress women's voices for all time. The Light now revealed that women should serve as ministers, missionaries, and leaders of the church. Quakers also denied any continuing significance of the fall of Adam and Eve, arguing that equality of women and men returned with spiritual rebirth. George Fox explained that

man and woman were helps-meet in the image of God, and in righteousness and holiness, in the dominion, before they fell; but after the fall in the transgression, the man was to rule over his wife; but in the restoration by Christ, into the image of God, and his righteousness and holiness again, in that they are helps-meet, man and woman, as they were before the fall. (Quoted in Jean R. Soderlund, "Women's Authority," p. 726)

In addition to preaching as missionaries and in their home meetings, Quaker women participated in governing the church. In their own separate monthly meetings for business, they made disciplinary decisions concerning women and girls, supervised marriages, and provided relief to the poor. Many meetinghouses had partitions that could be opened and closed. During meetings for worship, the men and boys sat on one side of the meetinghouse and the women and girls sat on the other, with partitions open. For their monthly business meetings, women and men convened separately, with partitions closed. The separate meetings underscored the authority of esteemed, usually middle-aged and elderly women over the welfare and behavior of younger women and girls. However, women Friends did not have complete equality with the men, because most women's meetings were required to seek the permission of the men's monthly meeting before disowning anyone, while the men did not reciprocate. Even so the men apparently always approved the women's decisions. In addition the men, but not the women, discussed and approved many policies, including such important new disciplinary rules as those concerning oaths, slaveholding, and aiding the military. Despite these instances of gender inequity, the Quakers preserved an expanded role for women as the religion moved from its early years of prophecy toward greater institutionalization.

A century after the founding of the Society of Friends, in the decades leading to the American Revolution, Methodists and Virginia Baptists experienced their initial period of evangelistic fervor. African-American Baptist women participated prominently in revivals and were "expected to have as full an experience as each man; to recount it; to shout and have joy; to be baptized and to continue to witness." They served as deaconesses, disciplined disorderly women, and took part in church societies.

Methodist women were attracted by a similar message, that God speaks directly to each individual, whether man or woman, black or white. They accepted Methodism in greater numbers than men and helped to set up new societies. Elizabeth Piper Strawbridge, for example, with her husband, Robert, sought converts in western Maryland. Other women served as class leaders, including two Philadelphia women: Mary Thorn, who conducted two classes, and Mary Wilmer, who led a class in her home. However, by 1800, when the church hierarchy was in place and churches had been built, Methodist women assumed a much more restricted role.

THE COMMUNITY OF WOMEN

When women exercised authority in colonial British society, as among Quakers and African-

American Baptists, they did so primarily among the community of women and girls. Middle-aged and elderly women took responsibility for supervising the behavior of the female half of the population. They watched over the actions of the community's young women—not just their own daughters and granddaughters—to guard against sexual offenses and disorderly marriages. If a young girl showed signs of departing from the straight and narrow, they warned her of the consequences of sin.

In the Society of Friends, women's meetings dealt most frequently with cases of unsupervised weddings, marriages to non-Friends, fornication before marriage, and bastardy; these constituted the misdeeds of most female offenders. Men, in contrast, were guilty of a much broader range of offenses—from failure to repay a loan to murderous assault—but they too were prosecuted most often for improper marriage and sexual infractions of various kinds. If the Quaker meeting found that the woman or man had committed the offense, and the person acknowledged the wrongdoing, the meeting generally allowed her or him to remain a member. When wrongdoers refused to confess and ask forgiveness, they were disowned. Meeting minutes indicate that men and women were treated with equivalent stringency by their respective meetings.

In New England, though elder women lacked this institutionalized power, they took responsibility for the behavior and well-being of younger women. Historian Laurel Ulrich has shown this most clearly in her discussion of court cases in which young women were sexually assaulted or accused of improper conduct. While the community's senior women were barred from serving as justices or members of juries, they counseled, reprimanded, and aided girls and young women who were the victims or accused perpetrators of crimes.

By law the woman held most accountable for reporting sexual misconduct on the part of women and men was the midwife, a respected and mature member of the female community. She had such official and semiofficial functions as testifying in court as to whether an unmarried mother had named the infant's father during labor, reporting whether an infant was born prematurely or at full term, verifying birth dates, and examining female prisoners to determine whether they were truly pregnant or just claiming that condition to avoid punishment.

More important to nurturing a community of women, however, was the midwife's role in orchestrating the activity that brought women together and excluded men—childbirth. During the colonial period, midwives presided over most births, which were attended as well by a group of female neighbors and relatives. The midwife was the most knowledgeable and experienced person in attendance and was responsible for seeing the mother and child through their ordeal. She was a professional and received payment for her service. Her training probably came from informal apprenticeship with an elder midwife and from witnessing the childbirths of relatives and friends.

Childbirth, or "travail" as the English colonists called it, was imbued with female ritual and tradition. Fortunate women had special bed linen and apparel that they inherited from their mothers. When their time drew near, pregnant women prepared special refreshments with names like groaning beer and groaning cakes to serve to their attendants during the initial stage of labor. During this first stage, the mother walked around and drank herbal teas or alcoholic drinks to relieve the pain. At the time of birth, she squatted on a "midwife's stool," remained standing while supported by two women, or was cradled in another woman's lap. The midwife caught the baby or if necessary assisted its passage through the birth canal. She cut the umbilical cord, not "too short for a boy, lest he prove 'insufficient in encounters with Venus,' nor too long for a girl, lest she become immodest." When complications occurred midwives could often help by manual manipulation of the infant, but they lacked the ability or resources to perform cesarean sections. Sometimes they had to kill and break apart the child; sometimes the mother died. Without modern antibiotics infection was a constant threat. After safe delivery one of the attendants usually nursed the child, for the mother's milk was considered unsafe for several days.

WITCHCRAFT AND CRIME

Elder women—those who were past their own childbearing years—thus carried weight as the guardians and overseers of younger women and girls. They lacked political power, however, and thus were subject, like all women, to the judgments and domination of men. In fact elder women were especially vulnerable as they faced the challenge of fulfilling authoritative and nurturing roles in the community without defying patriarchal prerogatives. During the seventeenth century, middle-aged and elderly women who overstepped gender boundaries were most at risk of being charged with witchcraft, defined legally as making a compact or conversing with Satan. The colonists, like their contemporaries in the Old World, believed that God and the devil both influenced everyday events. Weak individuals, especially women, could be recruited by Satan to perform evil deeds against God's people.

In the British colonies, the Puritan governments of New England prosecuted the great majority of witchcraft cases; this was partly the result of the centrality of religion in their society. Also important in explaining the skewed distribution of witchcraft accusations, however, was the fact that elder women, the people most at risk, were much more numerous in the Puritan colonies than elsewhere during the seventeenth century, when witchcraft hysteria peaked. According to historian Carol Karlsen, in the years 1620 to 1725 about 350 New Englanders were accused of witchcraft. The most famous episode occurred in Salem, Massachusetts, in 1692, when almost two hundred people were accused and twenty persons executed for conspiring with the devil.

In witchcraft cases, including the initial stages of the Salem tragedy, the accused witches were preponderantly women past menopause. They were rarely the well-respected women who counseled young women and delivered babies. Rather they were individuals who in various ways deviated from expected gender roles. They had fewer children than the average woman their age; without sons, a significant number were heirs or potential heirs of estates and thus held greater economic power than most New England women. Some claimed the power of a "cunning woman" to heal and foretell the future; many had been accused of assaultive speech, at a greater rate than women not accused of witchcraft; and they tended to experience conflict within their families and with their neighbors. Revealingly, men of the same age group and

troublesome character were much less likely to be identified as witches. These assertive, outspoken old women challenged accepted gender ideology by claiming their voice and by failing to uphold communal ideals. The sense of empowerment that accompanied aging made them seem especially dangerous to their neighbors.

Historians have also found gender differences in the prosecution of other kinds of crime. In these studies they have distinguished between married and unmarried women and men but for the most part have not included age as a factor in their analysis. Most fundamentally, men made the laws and controlled the courts. Only men could serve as judges and jurors, and they were the great majority of accused, plaintiffs, and witnesses as well. Women committed and were convicted of murder, theft, fraud, and assault, but at rates much lower than men. The prosecution of women most often stemmed from sexual crimes, especially fornication. Their male partners were also accused of these offenses, but men were prosecuted for such a wide range of crimes that for them sex offenses were proportionally less significant. According to David Hackett Fischer, the New England and Chesapeake colonies treated sexual offenses differently. The seventeenth-century Puritans enforced laws against extramarital sex strictly and in a relatively evenhanded manner. Chesapeake authorities were lax in enforcement, but in the cases brought to court women received more severe punishments than men.

Both English common law and colonial criminal statutes distinguished between men and women with regard to their rights and responsibilities. The common law, for example, protected a married woman (*feme covert*) from prosecution if she committed certain crimes in the presence of her husband. The law assumed that she acted under her spouse's instructions. At the same time, the common law hindered (though did not prevent entirely) access of married women to the courts, for they could not bring suit without their husbands' participation. Most basic, a double standard existed in English law, granting property rights in the chastity of women to husbands and fathers. A woman's sexual purity was valued as property, that of her father before marriage and that of her husband after. But wives and mothers had no similar rights in the chastity of men. Thus adultery committed by a woman was considered more serious than if committed by a man. In the words of historian Keith Thomas, extramarital sexual intercourse was "for a man, if an offense, none the less a mild and pardonable one, but for a woman a matter of the utmost gravity." In England, where absolute divorce could be obtained only by act of Parliament, husbands but no wives obtained decrees on grounds of adultery alone.

In colonial Massachusetts, where the governor and council granted divorces, the experience of women was equivalent. Massachusetts, in its legal code of 1648, underscored the notion of a man's property rights in his wife by defining adultery, which was punishable by death, as illicit sexual relations involving a married woman. If a married man and a single woman had intercourse, they committed fornication, which was not a capital crime. In practice magistrates reduced the charges of most people accused of adultery and just a few were put to death for the crime. The same was true in the case of rape, which was also a capital offense in the Bay colony. Then, as now, women had difficulty proving that they had not consented to the act. Men of higher status were likely to escape punishment, while white servants and blacks received harsh punishment for attacks on white women. Consistent with the double standard, rapes were considered trespasses on the property rights of the assaulted woman's husband or father.

The law and system of justice were male-defined and male-dominated. Court cases reflected the gendered value system of society. As historian Mary Beth Norton found in a study of slander cases in mid-seventeenth-century Maryland, different kinds of defamation impelled men and women to take slanderers to court. Men were most concerned when they were labeled cheats or thieves; women more often went to court to protect their sexual reputations. For men, economic well-being required a reputation for trustworthiness in making contracts with other men. Women, whose financial support depended upon the good will of their husbands, needed to maintain a reputation for proper sexual behavior. Relationships with men were most crucial for both men and women. Thus male values and interests defined what constituted proper social behavior.

Actions that affected the operation of the male sphere came under the purview of the courts much more systematically than did activities reserved to women's domain. Men were the plaintiffs and defendants in cases of theft and fraud much more often than women, because men legally possessed most of the property and engaged in public affairs and business. Men turned to the male-controlled judicial system for redress of grievances. If women committed such crimes within their own trading network, they did so much less frequently or, perhaps more likely, resolved the disputes informally among themselves. Women came into contact with the legal system most often when they were accused of a sexual offense or had been sexually assaulted—that is, in cases of fornication, bastardy, adultery, and rape. These cases threatened men's property rights and the communal order, as defined by men. Nevertheless women offenders were not necessarily treated more harshly than men by the courts.

Over the eighteenth century, communities became less concerned with the immorality of fornication and more intent on learning the identity of the father of a child born out of wedlock so that he, and not the local government, would be responsible for the child's support. Whereas a couple could be whipped or fined for having illicit sex during the seventeenth and early eighteenth century, by the time of the American Revolution most prosecutions were against men who refused to marry the mother, the purpose being to obtain financial support for the child's upbringing.

CHILD REARING AND EDUCATION

Historians have written little about gender differences in child rearing in colonial America. The best evidence suggests that children of each sex were perceived to have natures similar to adults and were expected to assume appropriate gender roles. Consistent with Protestant beliefs that females and males had equal access to salvation and a direct relationship with God, parents apparently did not distinguish between girls and boys in the importance of religious training. Infanticide of babies of both sexes was considered a heinous crime. And children all wore similar dresses to about age six, when boys put on coats and breeches.

Nevertheless even young girls and boys received socialization to their future roles. As soon as they were capable, most colonial children began assisting their parents at work. African-American slave children first assumed less physically demanding jobs in their masters' houses and fields, then joined the field crews when they reached their teens. More generally, girls learned to stitch and help with the myriad domestic tasks of their mothers. At teenage they supplied labor at many of the spinning wheels that had become common in rural households from New England to the Chesapeake by the time of the revolution. Boys assisted their fathers in the fields and at other chores. Many children performed these tasks in the homes of other families. New England parents often "sent out" their children to apprentice for a trade, obtain schooling, learn the varied responsibilities of housewifery and husbandry, or assist an elderly or sick relative. Puritans may have conceived this as a way to discipline their offspring more effectively. For whatever reason—discipline, occupational training, or financial exigency—parents throughout the colonies commonly apprenticed and placed their children in other homes.

The amount of formal education that children received varied widely by region and class. The Puritan colonies early mandated instruction in reading to facilitate individual access to the Bible. Probably most New England girls and boys learned to read, but writing was considered a separate skill and less necessary for girls. According to historian Gloria Main, the percentage of Massachusetts females who could sign their names was significantly lower than males, especially in rural districts. Signature literacy actually declined among women after 1660 but then improved during the decades immediately preceding the revolution, possibly as women became more involved in the commercial economy and needed writing skills to engage in trade.

In colonies south of New England, education was voluntary and much more haphazard. In Pennsylvania schools were operated by religious denominations and private teachers but were probably nowhere numerous enough to provide schooling for everyone. As in Massachusetts females were much less likely to be able to sign their names, especially outside Philadel-

phia. Quaker schools provided some free education to African Americans and poor white non-Friends in addition to Quaker boys and girls. Girls gained greater access to education after the mid eighteenth century, but only some daughters of affluent parents pursued academic subjects beyond basic reading, writing, and arithmetic. In Virginia education was even more restricted. While men and women of the upper class were literate, fewer than 20 percent of females of middling status could sign their names, as opposed to about 80 percent of males. Fewer than one percent of African-American slaves could read and write.

POLITICS, WAR, AND
THE AMERICAN REVOLUTION

While education improved for some middling and upper-class women by the outbreak of the American Revolution, even the most educated and fortunate female colonists continued to experience exclusion from political affairs. According to English gender ideology, men and not women participated in government and war. Only men could vote and hold office; only men donned uniforms and took up weapons to protect their homes and their right to political control. If politics and military participation are defined rigidly—according to who voted, held office, and served as regular members of armed forces—then actual practice in the British North American colonies mirrored this ideology of gender roles. Women did not vote, even if otherwise qualified as property holders, and none, as far as we know, formally served as a governor, justice of the peace, or constable. They did not drill with the militia.

Despite this bleak portrait of disfranchisement and dependency, colonial women participated in the body politic in two ways, neither of which permanently altered their subordinate political status. Both roles were consistent with English concepts of gender relations; in both women helped to build and sustain the community, or polity. Foremost was women's responsibility for teaching their children religious and moral precepts and leading their husbands to God. Most British colonists believed that God had a constant impact on their lives—that their behavior and the relationship they maintained with the deity largely determined their well-being. If they, their families, or neighbors sinned, God's punishment would result. War, political unrest, and human suffering were the consequence of moral decay. If the community obeyed God's laws, it would prosper and achieve peace. As moral guardians of their families, women were responsible for raising pious, well-behaved children. They held the key to maintaining a prosperous body politic, despite their inability to vote or hold offices. Even with the creation of the new republic, this primary female political function, to raise their sons to be responsible, moral leaders and citizens, remained substantially unchanged.

In the other role, individual women temporarily substituted for husbands or other men who for some reason could not fulfill their official duties in government or the military. They participated as deputy husbands, and because they had the approval of powerful men, their temporary assumption of male roles was not seriously questioned. Women like Anne Hutchinson and Mary Dyer, whose challenges to the Massachusetts orthodoxy were political as well as religious, experienced exile and execution for improper behavior because they acted on their own authority (or, as they believed, God's). Margaret Brent, Hannah Penn, Hannah Duston, and Mary Hayes also played crucial, even courageous, roles in political and military affairs, but they did so temporarily and with official male consent.

Margaret Brent and Hannah Penn exercised the power of governor in their respective colonies, Maryland and Pennsylvania. Brent was a member of a noble Roman Catholic family of the county of Gloucester, England. In 1638 she immigrated with a sister and two brothers to Maryland, which had recently been founded by Cecilius Calvert, Lord Baltimore. She established a large plantation and, with her family, was influential in the colony. In 1647 Governor Leonard Calvert, the proprietor's brother, died and designated Margaret Brent as his executor. As such she received responsibility for resolving a political crisis as well as settling his estate. Calvert had recently defeated the forces of Richard Ingle, who contested Lord Baltimore's proprietorship, by bringing soldiers from Virginia. Brent had the difficult task of paying these troops with the insufficient funds in Leonard Calvert's estate. Thus to ward off rebellion among the soldiers

and send them home, she used the power of attorney she received as Leonard Calvert's executor to sell some of the proprietor's cattle. She ended the crisis peacefully, and when Lord Baltimore protested that she had overstepped her authority, the Maryland assembly defended her actions. However, when Brent had earlier requested two votes in the legislature, one for herself as a landowner and the other as Calvert's executor, the assembly refused. Her overt political activities concluded with the settling of Leonard Calvert's estate.

Hannah Callowhill Penn was the second wife of William Penn, the founder and proprietor of Pennsylvania. When William Penn had a stroke in 1712, ending his public life, Hannah Penn became the head of the household and took responsibility for Pennsylvania's affairs. Before and after the proprietor died in 1718, she worked with his trusted friends and agents to achieve resolution of the boundary conflict with Maryland, repay debts, and deal with problems concerning the colony's government. While Hannah Penn acted as her husband's agent and did her best to conceal his illness, she capably assumed his duties as proprietor of Pennsylvania.

Wars with Native Americans, and later the American Revolution, temporarily broke down gender restrictions as women assumed responsibilities normally defined as male. Hannah Duston of Haverhill, Massachusetts, became a heroine in 1697 after she was captured by Native Americans. She and two companions killed the Indians, escaped, and brought back ten scalps, of which six were of children. Other women, in the absence of their husbands, protected their homes and children against attack, often disguising themselves as men. Scattered evidence exists that New England frontier women were familiar with firearms and used them when necessary. However, they also took the closest weapon at hand—Hannah Bradley of Haverhill, for example, threw a kettle of boiling soap at her assailant.

During the American Revolution, women similarly defended themselves and their families against aggressors. In 1775 a group of thirty or forty women of the towns of Groton and Pepperell, Massachusetts, dressed in the clothes of their minutemen husbands and took up arms to guard a bridge near their homes. Many other women went further and accompanied armies to battle. Mary Hayes of Carlisle, Pennsylvania, known as Molly Pitcher, was the most famous of women who ended up fighting the enemy. She accompanied her husband when he joined the American infantry, stayed with him at Valley Forge during the winter of 1777–1778, and fetched water for his gun crew at the Battle of Monmouth. When her husband collapsed, Hayes took his place among the crew.

According to one estimate, twenty thousand women traveled with the American army, serving as nurses, laundresses, cooks, and haulers. George Washington set a ratio of one woman per fifteen men and provided that these women would receive regular army rations. His own wife, Martha Washington, accompanied him at Valley Forge and Morristown. Women also served the army as spies, most often by giving warning of enemy movements. Sixteen-year-old Dicey Langston of South Carolina was one who, in order to alert the Americans about British maneuvers, left "her home alone, by stealth, and at the dead hour of night. Many miles were to be traversed, and the road lay through woods, and crossed marshes and creeks where the conveniences of bridges and foot-logs were wanting." Elizabeth F. Ellet published the stories of these heroines in 1851.

Despite formidable contributions of women on the homefront and in battle, statesmen and historians defined the American Revolution as the accomplishment of men. Making war was men's work. If women fought, they did so as the agents of men; everything else they did towards victory was women's work and did not count. Thus, participation by women in the revolution had no effect on the gender ideology that made men the protectors of family and nation. With the creation of a new government based on the sovereignty of the people rather than the king, the political role of women remained essentially the same. They lacked the public voice and unity to claim an equal share in government; they failed to articulate their substantial part in winning independence. Only one state, New Jersey, permitted female property holders to vote, and that was probably an oversight. In any case the privilege was withdrawn in 1807.

Abigail Adams, in a famous letter, asked her husband, John, to "remember the ladies" in creating a new legal code. She wanted an end to coverture, the principle that prevented married women from acting for themselves and own-

ing property. John Adams and his fellow lawmakers in the Continental Congress rejected her request, for they were fully satisfied with the legal and political doctrine that men represent their wives, children, and other dependents in society. According to Adams and his colleagues, to give a woman the vote gave her husband two votes, because he could sway her choice of candidates. Men held legal ownership of the family property and thus had the stake in society that justified their participation in government. They had also risked their lives to establish the republic. No matter that some women legally owned property and most had contributed to the revolution, some by taking up arms.

CONCLUSION

Throughout the colonial period, then, the conflicting concepts of women's capability and inferiority defined gender relations in British North America. English custom, law, and Protestant theology held women responsible for guaranteeing the smooth operation of households, representing and protecting their families in the absence of husbands, and maintaining God's providence over the community but required their subordination to men. Historians have attempted to determine the extent to which women's status changed over the colonial period, some arguing that expansion of the market economy or the American Revolution allowed greater autonomy and opportunity. Others see a decline in women's status as settlements matured and sex ratios evened out. In truth, any attempt to determine whether the status of all colonial women improved or declined over the course of about 170 years would be as difficult to accomplish as the same sort of study for all men. Much more research that is sensitive to economic, racial, ethnic, religious, and regional differences is required before we can understand the range of women's experience in all aspects of their lives, including their relationships with men.

BIBLIOGRAPHY

Archer, Richard. "New England Mosaic: A Demographic Analysis for the Seventeenth Century." *William and Mary Quarterly*, 3rd ser., 47, no. 4 (1990):477–502.

Brown, Elisabeth Potts, and Susan Mosher Stuard, eds. *Witnesses for Change: Quaker Women over Three Centuries*. New Brunswick, N.J., 1989.

Carr, Lois Green, and Lorena S. Walsh. "Economic Diversification and Labor Organization in the Chesapeake, 1650–1820." In *Work and Labor in Early America,* edited by Stephen Innes. Chapel Hill, N.C., 1988. Demonstrates the effect of economic change on the work of African-American slave women and men.

———. "The Planter's Wife: The Experience of White Women in Seventeenth-Century Maryland." *William and Mary Quarterly,* 3rd ser., 34, no. 4 (1977):542–571. A classic study of the effect of demographic conditions on gender ideology.

Cott, Nancy F. "Divorce and the Changing Status of Women in Eighteenth-Century Massachusetts." *William and Mary Quarterly,* 3rd ser., 33, no. 4 (1976):586–614.

———. "Eighteenth-Century Family and Social Life Revealed in Massachusetts Divorce Records." *Journal of Social History* 10, no. 1 (1976):20–43. Uses testimony in divorce cases to investigate social and sexual mores and practices.

Demos, John Putnam. *Entertaining Satan: Witchcraft and the Culture of Early New England.* New York, 1982. The first section contains a valuable profile of accused witches.

DePauw, Linda Grant. "Women in Combat: The Revolutionary War Experience." *Armed Forces and Society* 7, no. 2 (1981):209–226.

Dunn, Mary Maples. "Saints and Sisters: Congregational and Quaker Women in the Early Colonial Period." In *Women in American Religion,* edited by Janet Wilson James. Philadelphia, 1980. Important comparison of theological views concerning women.

———. "Women of Light." In *Women of America: A History,* edited by Carol Ruth Berkin and Mary Beth Norton. Boston, 1979. A thoughtful discussion of Quaker women.

Ellet, Elizabeth F. *Domestic History of the American Revolution.* New York, 1851.

———. *Women of the American Revolution.* 3 vols. New York, 1849–1850.

Fischer, David Hackett. *Albion's Seed: Four British Folkways in America.* New York, 1989.

Frost, J. William. *The Quaker Family in Colonial America: A Portrait of the Society of Friends.* New York, 1973.

Greven, Philip J., Jr. *Four Generations: Population, Land, and Family in Colonial Andover, Massachusetts.* Ithaca, N.Y., 1970. Focuses on the impact of demography and the availability of land on the ability of fathers to control sons.

Jensen, Joan M. *Loosening the Bonds: Mid-Atlantic Farm Women, 1750–1850.* New Haven, Conn., 1986. In-cludes some material from the colonial era but focuses primarily on the post-revolutionary period.

Karlsen, Carol F. *The Devil in the Shape of a Woman: Witchcraft in Colonial New England.* New York, 1987. Uses the prism of witchcraft accusations to evaluate the status of women in Puritan New England.

Kerber, Linda K. " 'History Can Do It No Justice': Women and the Reinterpretation of the American Revolution." In *Women in the Age of the American Revolution,* edited by Ronald Hoffman and Peter J. Albert. Charlottesville, Va., 1989. This volume also contains important articles on inheritance practices, law, and the status of African American and white women.

Kulikoff, Allan. "The Beginnings of the Afro-American Family in Maryland." In *Law, Society, and Politics in Early Maryland,* edited by Aubrey C. Land, Lois Green Carr, and Edward C. Papenfuse. Baltimore, Md., 1977.

Main, Gloria L. "An Inquiry into When and Why Women Learned to Write in Colonial New England." *Journal of Social History* 24, no. 3 (1991): 579–589.

Menard, Russell R. "The Maryland Slave Population, 1658 to 1730: A Demographic Profile of Blacks in Four Counties." *William and Mary Quarterly,* 3rd ser., 32, no. 1 (1975):29–54.

Norton, Mary Beth. "The Evolution of White Women's Experience in Early America." *American Historical Review* 89, no. 3 (1984):593–619. A useful survey of the literature as of the early 1980s; focuses to a large extent on New England women.

———. "Gender and Defamation in Seventeenth-Century Maryland." *William and Mary Quarterly,* 3rd ser., 44, no. 1 (1987):3–39.

———. "Gender, Crime, and Community in Seventeenth-Century Maryland." In *The Transformation of Early American History: Society, Authority, and Ideology,* edited by James A. Henretta, Michael Kammen, and Stanley N. Katz. New York, 1991.

Salmon, Marylynn. *Women and the Law of Property in Early America.* Chapel Hill, N.C., 1986. An excellent comparison of women's property rights in different colonies.

Shammas, Carole. *The Pre-industrial Consumer in England and America.* Oxford, 1990.

Shammas, Carole, Marylynn Salmon, and Michel Dahlin. *Inheritance in America from Colonial Times to the Present.* New Brunswick, N.J., 1987. Contains a useful discussion of inheritance laws in the British North American colonies.

Shiels, Richard D. "The Feminization of American Congregationalism, 1730–1835." *American Quarterly* 33, no. 1 (1981):46–62.

Sobel, Mechal. *Trabelin' On: The Slave Journey to an Afro-Baptist Faith.* Westport, Conn., 1979.

Soderlund, Jean R. "Black Women in Colonial Pennsylvania." *Pennsylvania Magazine of History and Biography* 107, no. 1 (1983):49–68.

———. "Women in Eighteenth-Century Pennsylvania: Toward a Model of Diversity." *Pennsylvania Magazine of History and Biography* 115, no. 2 (1991):163–183. A survey of the literature on colonial women, with emphasis on Pennsylvania.

———. "Women's Authority in Pennsylvania and New Jersey Quaker Meetings, 1680–1760." *William and Mary Quarterly*, 3rd ser., 44, no. 4 (1987):722–749.

Thomas, Keith. "The Double Standard." *Journal of the History of Ideas* 20, no. 2 (1959):195–216.

Tolles, Frederick B. "Mary Dyer." In *Notable American Women, 1607–1950: A Biographical Dictionary*, edited by Edward T. James, et al. Vol. 1. Cambridge, Mass., 1971.

Ulrich, Laurel Thatcher. *Good Wives: Image and Reality in the Lives of Women in Northern New England, 1650–1750*. New York, 1982. The best single work on women in colonial British America.

———. *A Midwife's Tale: The Life of Martha Ballard, Based on Her Diary, 1785–1812*. New York, 1990. Though the diary is post-revolutionary, the book adds considerably to our knowledge of the colonial period as well.

Wilson, Lisa. *Life After Death: Widows in Pennsylvania, 1750–1850*. Philadelphia, 1992.

Jean R. Soderlund

SEE ALSO Civil Law; Marriage; Rural Life; and Urban Life.

THE DUTCH COLONY

THE ROLE OF WOMEN IN DUTCH SOCIETY

GENDER RELATIONS in the early Dutch republic were distinguished by the fact that women enjoyed civil and property rights not generally granted to their sisters elsewhere in Europe. Under Roman-Dutch law, women were not allowed to hold public office, but they could and did run businesses, sue in court, inherit property equitably with their brothers, and will property in their own right. A woman also retained her patronymic after marriage. She might invoke the law against an abusive or reckless husband who endangered her person or the property she brought into the marriage. A married woman in England, France, or Spain had no such recourse; her legal identity was thoroughly merged with her husband's. Despite the growing hegemony of the Dutch Reformed church, the Calvinistic emphasis upon patriarchy was certainly moderated in the United Provinces by concepts of domestic reciprocity deeply embedded in Dutch jurisprudence and Christian humanism.

In the seventeenth-century Netherlands, the ultimate ideals of Christian manhood and womanhood could be achieved only through marriage and family life. The husband and wife were bound in an intimate partnership; their most important functions were the nurturing of children and the advancement of the family's interests, with each partner having a separate sphere of responsibility.

The differentiation between the male and the female world began in childhood. Indeed, daughters were raised to housewifery, and sons were thoroughly trained in the family craft or in some collateral trade. Sons almost always got more formal schooling than daughters, but girls were commonly taught reading, writing, sometimes arithmetic, and at least the rudiments of the family business. In fact, Dutch females were much more involved in the male sphere than were most European women.

Young women went rather casually in the company of men, and foreign observers frequently criticized the considerable freedom allowed Dutch girls in courting and in choosing mates. The premarital conception rate ranged from 15 percent to 20 percent, but bastardy was rare. Moreover, once married, Dutch women were known for their fidelity as much as for their housekeeping skills, acknowledged by native commentators and foreign critics alike. The husband or father was expected to be the undisputed head of the household, and Dutch moralists regularly condemned the shrew or dominating wife, whose existence could hardly be denied. However, the didactic literature also made it clear that the husband should not be the autocrat but rather the senior partner in a family tied together by reciprocal obligations. His primary duty was to provide for the material welfare of the household, especially by maintaining and expanding the family business.

His wife was mistress of the household, basically in charge of all domestic matters, including housekeeping, cooking, maidservants, and children. Although her domain was primarily the household, the wife might well be involved in the family business and even take charge of it if her husband should become disabled or die. Her fate and that of her children might well depend upon it. In fact, the enhanced status and freedom accorded Dutch women flowed directly from the heavy responsibility they were expected to bear as wives and mothers.

WOMEN'S PLACE IN NEW NETHERLAND

Dutch attitudes toward gender were not simply transferred to America. Relations between men and women in New Netherland were shaped by changing immigration patterns and evolving economic and social conditions. Until the mid 1640s, immigration to the Dutch colony was slight, comprising mainly young, single men. Fragmentary records suggest that not more than 25 percent of these early settlers came as family members.

During its first two decades of settlement, New Netherland was disorderly, due to its rough-and-tumble men and rowdy women. The general shortage of women inhibited the development of stable domestic relations. Scarcity enhanced the status of women, but they had to contend with the hardships of the frontier, and even apparent advantages proved to be mixed blessings. For example, while servant girls had plenty of prospective husbands, they also had to deal with unwanted advances from the numerous unattached males, many of whom were much more interested in sex than in marriage.

Becoming director-general in 1647, Peter Stuyvesant believed that family formation was fundamental to the social stability and the economic success of his chaotic little colony. Demo-

graphics were on his side. Changes in the Dutch West India Company's land and trade regulations attracted increasing numbers of settlers, especially young couples with children. Under Stuyvesant, gender relations in New Netherland became fairly reflective of standards and practices in the Dutch republic itself. Laws regarding marriage, breach of promise, adultery, and fornication were regularly enforced. In breach-of-promise suits, usually provoked because the man was having second thoughts, magistrates insisted that the couple proceed with the marriage, unless sexual intercourse with a third party had compromised the betrothal pledge. Considerable effort was made to determine the paternity of bastard children. If the evidence was solid, the accused father had to either marry the mother or make a monetary gift to her and provide for the child.

In terms of courtship and marriage, Dutch custom generally prevailed, leaving matters largely in the hands of young men and women themselves. In the small Jewish community at New Amsterdam and in the English towns on western Long Island, daughters were considerably more restricted by their parents in choosing a mate. However, endogamy in terms of class and ethnic group seems to have been followed throughout the colony, among both whites and blacks. Because of slavery and racial prejudice, black women, both slave and free, faced restrictions on mate selection beyond those prescribed by parental attitudes, about which we know little.

The women of New Netherland were primarily housewives and mothers. However, some women were drawn rather deeply into the family business, compelled usually by a mixture of necessity and opportunity. Mothers were careful to instruct daughters in housewifery, but the distance between the house and the shop was never very great in New Netherland, and girls learned a good deal about the family business, just as they usually went to school as their brothers did and learned literacy skills and basic math. The best estimates suggest that female literacy in New Netherland (45 percent) was considerably higher than that in either Virginia (25 percent) or Massachusetts Bay (33 percent).

Should her spouse die—and Indian wars, epidemics, and shipwrecks took their toll—or become disabled, a wife might well continue the family businesses, although she would almost certainly marry again. Following the death of her blacksmith husband, Heilke Peterse carried on his successful trade in New Amsterdam. Other women—most, but not all, of them widows—became farmers, tapisters, brewers, launderers, bakers, and traders. Linda Biemer has calculated that between 1653 and 1664 there were 134 women in New Amsterdam and 46 in Beverswyck (Albany) sufficiently engaged in commerce to be called traders. Among them were Margaret Backer, Rachel Vinje, Margaret and Heligonda Van Slechtenhorst, and Margaret Hardenbroek.

The extensive involvement of women in the economy of New Netherland is evident from the court records. According to Biemer, women were involved in 1,049 cases (16.5 percent of the total number) in New Amsterdam between 1653 and 1674. Looking at the years from 1648 to 1700, Sherrin Penny and Roberta Willenkin found women party to 538 cases (15.2 percent of the total number) in Beverswyck. In both Beverswyck and New Amsterdam, the cases involving women almost always arose from civil disputes over contracts, goods, or property; women were seldom involved in criminal cases. In disputes between women, other women were frequently called upon to arbitrate. In those cases where women were charged with violating trade regulations, they were usually punished less severely than men; however, women convicted of fornication or adultery were more likely than were their male partners to receive the harshest penalty, banishment. Under Roman-Dutch law, a married woman, unless her separate property rights had been previously defined by an antenuptial agreement, would ordinarily not appear in court except as an agent of her husband. That procedure was certainly not followed strictly in New Netherland, where women had considerable flexibility in making use of the courts.

Antenuptial agreements and joint wills further defined the status of New Netherland women. If life was precarious for men, it was even more so for women because of the hazards of childbirth. Joint wills, whereby spouses left all their property, its management, and the raising of their children to the survivor, constitute perhaps the best evidence that marriage was viewed in partnership terms; they were much favored by Dutch husbands and wives. When the survivor remarried, he or she got half the estate and the children, the other half, divided equally among sons and daughters upon their majority. Either the orphanmasters or the appointed guardians made sure that the property rights of the children were protected in New Netherland. Widows and widowers, before marrying again, especially if they had children by their previous marriage, would almost certainly prepare an antenuptial agreement, under which, for example, a widow could keep property from her first marriage separate from the community property she and her next husband might accumulate. Antenuptial contracts also further defined and secured the property of children vis-à-vis the parent and stepparent.

ENGLISH WOMEN IN THE DUTCH COLONY

Antenuptial agreements and joint wills were not a part of English common law, whereby a woman upon marriage came under the doctrine of *femme covert.* Her property became her husband's property, and only he could dispose of it. Unlike the Dutch wife, the English wife did not enjoy community property with her husband. In fact, as interpreted under *femme covert,* her legal status was merged into her husband's legal status, and she had no independent standing before the law. Unless her husband specified differently in his will, the English widow was legally entitled only to the personal property she brought into the marriage and the dower's third of the real estate belonging to her deceased husband for as long as she lived and remained unmarried. Rather than practicing partible inheritance, whereby daughters as well as sons shared and shared alike, the English on western Long Island were much influenced by the British practice of primogeniture, by which much, if not all, of the land and the personal estate were left to the oldest son. In fact, daughters seldom got more than a small dowry, their mother's clothing, and furniture now and again. Jewish fathers in New Netherland similarly favored their sons and left comparatively little to their daughters.

CHANGES UNDER ENGLISH RULE

Under the terms of surrender in 1664, the British guaranteed to New Netherlanders who became New Yorkers their rules of inheritances and religious liberty. Joint wills, antenuptial agreements, and partible inheritance persisted among Dutch New Yorkers throughout much of the seventeenth century. However, the gradual triumph of English common law increasingly restricted the legal status of women. Increasingly, the widow became simply the fiduciary entrusted to manage the estate for minor children. Indeed, following English practice and tradition, the widow's legal and economic status became much less significant than that of her children, particularly male children. Likewise, partible inheritance gave way to the English practice of favoring the eldest son in particular and sons generally over daughters. The participation of women in the crafts and trades declined steadily, as did the appearances of women in the courts in civil cases, though their prosecution in criminal cases increased dramatically as they were restricted from legitimate economic endeavors. In fact, the Dutch women of colonial New York lost much of the economic freedom and most of the property and civil rights they had enjoyed in New Netherland.

BIBLIOGRAPHY

Biemer, Linda. "Criminal Law and Women in New Amsterdam and New York." In *A Beautiful and Fruitful Place: Selected Rensselaerswijck Seminar Papers,* edited by Nancy Anne McClure Zeller. Albany, N.Y., 1991.

Earle, Alice Morse. *Colonial Days in Old New York.* New York, 1896; repr. 1990.

Gehring, Charles T., ed. and trans. *Fort Orange Court Minutes, 1652–1660.* Syracuse, N.Y., 1990.

Hershowitz, Leo, ed. *Wills of Early New York Jews.* Waltham, Mass., 1967.

Kilpatrick, William Heard. *The Dutch Schools of New Netherland and Colonial New York.* Washington, D.C., 1912.

Kruger, Vivienne L. "Born to Run: The Slave Family in Early New York, 1626–1827." 2 vols. Ph.D. diss., Columbia University, 1985.

Leonard, Eugenie A. *The Dear-Bought Heritage.* Philadelphia, 1965.

Marshall, Sherrin. *The Dutch Gentry, 1500–1650: Family, Faith and Fortune.* New York and London, 1987.

Morris, Richard B. *Studies in the History of American Law.* New York, 1958.

Narrett, David E. "Preparations for Death and Provision for the Living." *New York History* 57, no. 4 (1976):417–437.

O'Callaghan, Edmund B. *Calendar of Dutch Historical Manuscripts in the Office of the Secretary of State, Albany, New York, 1630–1664.* Albany, N.Y., 1865; repr. Ridgewood, N.J., 1968.

Penny, Sherry, and Roberta Willenkin. "Dutch Women in Colonial Albany: Liberation and Retreat, Part I." *De Halve Maen* 52, no. 1 (Spring 1977):9–10, 14.

———. "Dutch Women in Colonial Albany: Liberation and Retreat, Part II." *De Halve Maen* 52, no. 2 (Summer 1977):7–8, 15.

Schama, Simon. *The Embarrassment of Riches: An Interpretation of Dutch Culture in the Golden Age.* New York, 1987.

Shattuck, Martha Dickinson. " 'For the Peace and Welfare of the Community': Beverwyck, 1652–1664." Ph.D. diss., Boston University, 1993.

Singleton, Esther. *Dutch New York.* New York, 1909; repr. 1968.

Van Rensselaer, Mrs. John King. *The Goede Vrouw of Mana-ha-ta: At Home and in Society, 1609–1760.* New York, 1898.

Ronald W. Howard

SEE ALSO **Civil Law; Marriage; Rural Life;** and **Urban Life.**

THE FRENCH COLONIES

THE BOOK OF GENESIS indicates that the roles of men and women were established in the Garden of Eden. Eve, created as an afterthought to Adam, involved her husband in an attempt to emulate God by eating from the Tree of

Knowledge. As punishment she was condemned to painful childbirth and to her husband's rule, he to lifelong toil by the sweat of his brow. Hardship for both sexes and woman's subordination thus emerged not long after creation in the Judeo-Christian tradition. This tradition was enshrined in Western culture.

In law, if not always in custom, European males tended to enjoy superior rights and powers, whether they were lofty heads of church and state or humble heads of families. For a variety of reasons, however, French people in the vast expanse of territory known as New France, which stretched from Cape Breton to the Saskatchewan River to the Gulf of Mexico, dispensed with a number of these separate but unequal practices. Not least of the reasons for change was the influence of the fur trade and the Native peoples who conducted it.

NATIVE PEOPLES

Standing in contrast to the Book of Genesis are the versions of "woman's place" in creation stories of many aboriginal cultures. The Haida Raven was content to begin humankind with two females until they themselves complained; the Iroquois primordial mother fell from the sky and alighted on a turtle whose back later became Mother Earth. Among the Eastern tribes the French first encountered, practice bore some relation to these primordial accounts, resulting in societies that were less patriarchal than that of the French. Among the Iroquois, place of residence was matrilocal, matrons selected and deposed male elders, and women produced and controlled most of the food supply.

Among various Native allies of the French, women became temporary wives and co-workers of fur traders in symbiotic alliances. They paddled canoes, made moccasins, and served as interpreters and trade intermediaries, sometimes themselves initiating the alliances, which brought heightened status and were a step up from what Europeans saw as a slavish existence among the women of some western and northern tribes. It is significant that when the Jesuits stepped in during the 1630s to condemn such relationships, Huron women expressed a preference for these arrangements to leadership by the puz-

zlingly celibate Blackrobes. Mixed fur-trade marriages long remained a feature of the western trade in which Easterners adopted Native customs and marriage practices.

Along the Saint Lawrence where French colonists soon outnumbered natives, there was less compromise. Upholding European traditions, the Jesuits worked through male leaders such as the Huron canoemen, whose conversion to Christianity they rewarded with guns and trading privileges. Ursuline nuns labored (with indifferent success) to turn Algonquian girls into domesticated wives for settlers. Jesuit missionaries to the democratic Montagnais called for the election of male captains and persuaded them to break with their tradition and to chastise disobedient wives physically. To the extent that Eastern Woodlands tribes were accustomed to a balance of power between the sexes, assimilation probably tipped the balance toward the more patriarchal structures of Europe.

EUROPEANS: TRADITION AND CHANGE

In European society and its colonial outposts, women's subordination, though varying according to time and place, had the sanction of law. Husbands had the right to determine the conjugal dwelling and were accountable, as Montreal's French governor warned them in 1650, for any wifely misdemeanors, since "the law established them as lords of their wives." Men were to chastise disobedient spouses, though not to use weapons or to bruise vital organs in so doing. With several important exceptions, husbands had powers of attorney for initiating court actions and for transfer of wealth and most family property. Most formal levers of power were in the hands of male governors, intendants, councillors, civil and judicial officers, members of the church hierarchy, and military officers.

Pioneering people, however, tend to tap whatever talent is available. Emergency or exigency can loosen or transform traditional restrictions, although there is usually an attendant cost. The "emergency" that affected gender relations in New France had three aspects. First, the initial settlements of 1604–1608 suffered a half century of neglect by trading companies and by the

Crown. The colony's existence was so precarious in the years before the establishment of the structures of royal government in 1663 that religious orders assumed much of the burden of publicizing, peopling, and funding the tiny colony to keep it alive. Along with influential Jesuit scholar-martyrs of the period were several remarkable female administrators who possessed the peculiar blend of mysticism and worldly savoir faire characteristic of Counter-Reformation piety. Marie de l'Incarnation, a former Tours businesswoman who established the Ursuline school in Quebec City where both French and Native American girls were taught, wrote some twelve thousand letters, which, like the hair-raising missionary accounts in the *Jesuit Relations,* raised curiosity and cash in France. Jeanne Mance helped compensate for the rather inept leadership of Governor Paul de Chomedey Maisonneuve by obtaining funds from the legendary De Bullion family for a hospital for the beleaguered Montreal of the 1650s; she also secured essential immigrants and troops.

The second aspect of emergency was that few immigrants settled in New France, only about ten thousand in all. Men predominated among those who did come, and only partial remedy was provided in the transport of some eight hundred *filles du roi* (potential brides, with dowries provided by the Crown) between 1663 and 1673. For most of the colony's history, until natural increase solved the problem around 1710, women were in short supply.

The third aspect of the emergency was the vast size of the colonial empire, which kept men away from the main settlement along the Saint Lawrence River for long periods of time. Competition from the Hudson's Bay Company, over-trapping, and the movements of successive Indian allies required fur traders to expand their territory. At the same time, strategic interests created a chain of posts from Louisbourg in present-day Nova Scotia west to Fort Jonquière on the Saskatchewan River and south to Louisiana.

There were also successive conflicts with the Iroquois, the Fox nation, and the English. This meant that men in the fur trade (an estimated 18 percent to 25 percent of adult males in the legal trade and a substantial number in the illegal trade), in the army (with a number of Canadian officers and recruits), or in the militia (all males

aged sixteen to sixty) were in many cases absent from the central settlement for some part of their lives. Many wives and daughters had to adjust to the absence of their husbands and fathers. The probability of losing them was increased by the fact that Canadian brides of the seventeenth century married younger than their counterparts in France and often wed men who were some eight years their senior, and who had a shorter life expectancy than women. On average, women spent about 20 percent of their adult years as widows, with "widow rights" that largely erased women's legal inferiority. Taken together, these factors created an aberrant situation that we might call the Absent Husband Syndrome, the "opportunity cost" of a rather wide range of female activity.

The premature death of a male family member was a hard blow to the survivors in terms of both affection and necessity. The latter is generally conceded to be more important in peasant societies. In the Laurentian colony, which was about 80 percent rural, a family team was so vital to clearing and maintaining a farm that, when brides were available, marriage rates were exceptionally high. Remarriage, especially for those widows with young families, was so swift that the charivaris condemning hasty remarriages in France fell into disuse in the colony. Loss of a working adult could spell tragedy, particularly if the children were not of an age to fill the empty boots. In the agrarian areas of lower Louisiana the population was much more sedentary than in New France as a whole. As a consequence, the social and economic status of women reflected realities in provincial France more closely than those of the Saint Lawrence Valley. The fact that men were around constantly left women with less autonomy as regards economic matters.

SOCIAL WELFARE

The paternalism of church and state enlisted the efforts of both sexes, softening some of the harsher aspects of life in a rather primitive colony that was often at war. Service of men on the seventeenth-century Bureaux des Pauvres, which gave poor relief, and the establishment in Montreal of a general hospital by the Charron brothers for a similar purpose, show that nurturing (or "policing the poor") was not confined to one gender. Studies of lodging and relief suggest the poorest townspeople were female, so women perhaps profited more than men from welfare services, as did the nursemaids for illegitimate children and the midwives who had salaries from the Crown. The population as a whole (with some bias toward urban males) benefited from the work of hospital nuns in Louisbourg, Quebec, Trois-Rivières, Montreal, and New Orleans. Care was provided free of charge, and mortality at Quebec compared favorably with that at French hospitals.

EDUCATION AND LITERACY

In the realm of education, males had the advantage of variety. The Collège des Jesuits founded in Quebec City in 1635 taught seminarians and laymen, and there were training schools for artisans and river pilots. Girls, on the other hand, perhaps had fuller access to the basics, particularly in the seventeenth century when nuns were plentiful, parish priests scarce, and men preoccupied with the heaviest outdoor work. In 1663 Montreal had a school for girls but none for boys. Several studies of ability to sign one's name showed female literacy in Montreal and elsewhere surpassing that of males, although some studies have found male literacy somewhat higher. Late-seventeenth-century female literacy rates seem roughly comparable to those found in New England and more than double the 14 percent rate in France. Girls in all five centers of population benefited from either the genteel Ursuline education or the Congregational sisters' free primary schools in Louisbourg and in Montreal and its surrounding countryside. In Louisiana, boys' education consisted mainly of various kinds of apprenticeship, with slaves as well as freemen being trained for skilled trades. The ten Ursulines who arrived from Rouen in 1727, in addition to running the hospital and the orphanage, gave instruction to European, Indian, and black girls. One observer described the long-term effect as causing the girls to be "less vicious than the other sex."

The religious life offered influence to talented people of both sexes. Though local curés were often native-born, male religious orders did not have the same recruiting power and were slower to "canadianize." On the other hand, some 20 percent of the female elite joined religious orders, some no doubt welcoming this alternative to family life. Humbler applicants of both sexes changed bedpans or toiled in their order's seigneurial fields, while aristocrats and members of the bourgeoisie served as hospital and welfare administrators, teachers, and superiors and as pharmacists and nurse practitioners.

WOMEN AND MEN
IN COMMERCE

Because of the geographic mobility that characterized the male population, a number of women were recruited into forms of activity more typically performed by males. Absent husbands in New France made it particularly likely that female relatives would cover home base, and it was not unusual for men heading west to delegate powers of attorney to their wives. Some women procured supplies or kept accounts, and others produced trade goods; canoes were built by women and girls at Trois-Rivières under government contract. In the colony's first days, Jeanne Enard was an important though unscrupulous trader at Trois-Rivières, while Mesdames de la Tour and Joybert shipped furs from Acadia. In the eighteenth century Mesdames Couagne and Lamothe were substantial merchants at Montreal, as were the Desaulniers sisters, whose Indian trading post was a front for a Montreal-to-Albany smuggling operation.

Husbands in the military created openings for calculating wives. Sometimes the partnership was close, as in the case of the Lusignons, who put Fort Frederic in a state of rebellion in the 1750s because the husband, as commandant, enforced his wife's trade monopoly. Madame Benoît, who directed a Montreal operation in which women made shirts and petticoats for use in the fur trade, was married to the commanding officer at Lac des Deux Montagnes. Pierre Legardeur de Repentigny was a career officer who left moneymaking to his wife, Agathe de Saint Père. She ransomed nine English weavers who had been captured by the Indians, hiring them to work for her and to instruct local families, thereby beginning Montreal's textile industry. Such enterprise did not necessarily secure respect for women in general; Repentigny apparently raped a servant girl in his wife's absence.

Men's preoccupation with military affairs also seems to explain the operation of a large Richelieu lumbering operation by Louise de Ramezay, the daughter of a governor of Montreal. Ramezay, who remained single, lost her father in 1724. First her mother and then Louise ran the sawmilling operation on the family's Chambly seigneury. Going into partnership with the Seigneuress de Rouville, Louise then opened a Montreal tannery and several mills. By the 1750s she was shipping twenty-thousand-livre loads of lumber and expanding the leather business in Montreal. When Louise was growing up, all but one of her brothers had perished. One, an ensign in the French navy, had died during an attack on Rio de Janeiro in 1711, another during a 1715 campaign against the Fox Indians, another in a shipwreck off Île Royale. The remaining brother, almost inevitably, chose a military career over management of the family business affairs. It may be that similar situations accounted for the presence of other female entrepreneurs in iron forging, tile making, sturgeon fishing, sealing, and contract building.

FAMILY AND POPULATION

Separate spheres of activity—public for men, private for women—were not well-developed in New France. Both sexes took to the streets to riot, the only form of popular protest in a colony without franchise or newspapers. Artisanal and farm work took place at home and involved the whole family. The amount of care taken to protect these working units is seen in the legal restrictions on the sale of family property, in the practice of dividing inheritances among all the children in lieu of primogeniture, and in mandatory provision for widows and retired parents. In New France the family's importance may have been enhanced by the absence of other institutions, such as villages and guilds. Family connections and prudent marriages were so crucial to family fortunes that parental consent was required for marriages of "children" as old as thirty. That family and community needs prevailed over personal predilections is suggested by the never-mind-the-courtship marriages of the *filles du roi*, the low rates of illegitimacy, and

the sharp drop in the number of conceptions during seasons of intense farm work or church-prescribed abstinence.

Despite the rarity of passionate love, New France was a healthy place for both sexes, who surpassed their French counterparts in fecundity and in life expectancy. The selectivity factor in immigration, which led primarily the young and healthy to migrate, the abundance of protein from fish and game, the pure water, and the lack of urban overcrowding have all been credited for these statistics. In every age cohort up to age sixty—including, surprisingly, the child-bearing years—women had a life expectancy from one to three years longer than that for men. The gap began narrowing around age forty, by which time peripatetic males had either begun to stay home or had become next to indestructible. Precisely the reverse of the pattern in New England, it is possible that the relatively high life expectancy of young women also owes something to the efforts of the government-subsidized midwives to reduce infant and maternal mortality.

ROLE OF WOMEN

Women in New France stood somewhere between the humiliated female of Genesis and the goddess-provider of Iroquois mythology, while men made their sacrifices to the god of war. Both ancien régime traditions and frontier conditions valorized the family, but trade and combat not infrequently ruptured family life, increasing the burden on the survivors. The frequent absence of husbands did allow women a considerable role in commerce, just as the nearly empty settlement before 1663 had room alongside Jesuit heroes for redoubtable "foundresses" whose teaching orders and hospitals serve Canada to this day.

BIBLIOGRAPHY

Bosher, John. "The Family in New France." In *Readings in Canadian History: Pre-Confederation,* edited by R. Francis and D. Smith. Toronto, Ontario, 1990.
Charbonneau, Hubert, et al. *La naissance d'une population.* Montreal, 1987.

Clio Collective. *Quebec Women: A History.* Toronto, Ontario, 1987. The most comprehensive source.

Leacock, Eleanor. "Montagnais Women and the Jesuit Plan for Colonization." In *Rethinking Canada,* edited by V. Strong-Boag and A. Fellman. Toronto, Ontario, 1991.

Marshall, Joyce. *Word from New France: The Selected Letters of Marie de L'Incarnation.* Toronto, Ontario, 1967. Gives insight into the lives of nuns and their Native and French pupils.

Noble, Stuart, and A. Nuhrah. "Education in Colonial Louisiana." In *French Louisiana: A Commemoration of the French Revolution Bicentennial,* edited by Robert Holtman and G. Conrad. Lafayette, La., 1989.

Noel, Jan. "New France: Les Femmes Favorisées." In *Rethinking Canada,* edited by V. Strong-Boag and A. Fellman. Toronto, Ontario, 1991. Also in *Readings in Canadian History: Pre-Confederation.*

Van Kirk, Sylvia. *Many Tender Ties: Women in Fur Trade Society, 1670–1870.* Winnipeg, Manitoba, 1980.

Jan Noel

SEE ALSO **Civil Law; Marriage; Rural Life;** and **Urban Life.**

THE SPANISH BORDERLANDS

FOR THE SPANISH BORDERLANDS, studies of sex and gender have fundamentally altered the way historians think about social relations, politics, economics, and culture. The distinctions that have often marked the discussion of sex versus gender—that sex is a topic better left to scientists and best understood in essence as biological, while gender is considered primarily a matter of roles, prescriptive and ascriptive, and is the province of social scientists and cultural workers—have also affected the scholarship of men and women. The number of books and articles in this field has increased dramatically, and since the 1980s a range of newer questions about gender has broadened the scope of scholarly research in the former Mexican North.

Different inquiries about men's and women's interactions, about child rearing, and about people's behavior in general are being conducted. One result is that, unlike the older Spanish Borderlands' school, which included women primarily when they were prominent or notorious, the tendency in the late twentieth century is to layer the discussions with queries about social relations.

The following essay assumes that because this research is new and its practitioners carry on investigations in other areas of history, some of the conclusions drawn necessarily remain tentative. Demographic and statistical analysis has yet to be done on many Spanish Borderland communities; the most basic data concerning population, male and female ratios, and female-headed households are unknown. Several preliminary tasks thus face scholars hoping to undertake work in gender studies providing multiple challenges.

One demanding task confronts the scholar who wishes to be sensitive to the amount of attention devoted to one sex or the other. This essay examines gender relations by writing about women. The interactive relationship between men and women, women and children, has not been lost, but has been set aside in favor of tracing by example a newer trend in gender studies and in women's history. Until women are the focus of our work in this way, scholarship will repeat history's refrain: the people who are noticed are those who control. The institutions governed by men, and not individual men, have been assumed to have circumscribed women's activities and responses. It is the institutions who are now temporarily relegated to the background until a better, more well-rounded, conscientious portrait of women can be drawn.

New and inquisitive, the study of gender relations is sometimes also guided by, or mindful of, tradition. Because relations between men and women, and adults and children, are themselves a "borderland," scholars frequently begin their work by delineating social structures and discerning patterns of living in order to trace the institutional framework within which people have lived; the social and physical realities of life allow us to draw conclusions about the situations of women and men, about their differing ideologies, values, and cultures. Silvia Arrom's work on the women of Mexico City in the eighteenth century opens with details about the institutions of the state—family and church. Spanish governance, understood as simultaneously political and social, demanded intricate and familylike ties. Within those webs spun by the church, by governors, by heads of households (mainly men), women existed in supposed protection. Arrom's research and other scholarship on life in the Spanish Borderlands, including the discussions of wife beating, rape, adultery, and abandonment, suggest that the Spanish Empire's apparatuses and those of the Catholic church did not function to meet the demands or needs of the governed, especially the women. Rather, the numerous cases available from the archives of the Catholic church detail a contrary pattern: for the majority of women, and for most residents of the borderlands, life was harsh, conditions rigorous. This fundamental characterization thus serves as the basis for Spanish Borderlands gender studies.

THE SEXUAL HIERARCHY

The sexual hierarchy is important to understand. Its symbolic meanings asserted themselves initially in the "protection" offered women and could be found in the edicts of politicians, bishops, and others. As Elizabeth Perry demonstrated in her work on Spanish medical literature in the era preceding the conquest, women's prescribed roles fell under four categories. Women—doctors and others believed—were virgins, martyrs, witches, or whores. Their ailments, needs, values, and worth derived from these positions; thus situated, it became difficult for women to escape their roles.

Even in arenas and spaces set aside for women—and never really controlled by them, for example, convents—the restrictions imposed by church officials encouraged particular actions as well as forms of resistance. Actively, unmarried women sought segregation from men in the convents; some widows were accepted into the religious orders as well. Regarding patterns or methods of resistance in this period, we know less because they frequently went undocumented by who needed to resist, particularly within institutions like the church. We often configure the

protests of women in the convents by deciphering subtleties in the church documents. The colonial Mexicanist Asunción Lavrin has uncovered many instances of overt defiance and of rearrangement in the cloistered female communities of the New World. In the Spanish Borderlands, the mission systems established by the Spanish conquerors never provided what the priests and other officials had hoped: a refuge within which women and men labored for the benefit of the state. In the hinterlands, the Spanish officials fretted over the lack of "control" the soldiers exhibited; Father Junípero Serra wrote of rape in this language. Women suffered its consequences—abuse and dehumanization. They complained bitterly and often, as the historian Antonia Castañeda reports, about the injustices and failures of the system.

Other colonial historians, especially Ramón Gutiérrez, have suggested that in matters of sexuality, marriage, and seduction, women faced similar challenges; their roles were institutionalized from birth, and any movement beyond the prescribed boundaries could be dangerous. As wives, mothers, and grandmothers, women had their behavior consistently circumscribed, especially when inheritance and property were at stake. Matriarchs occupied honored spaces, but if widowed, their existence depended on their oldest sons, and if wealthy, on strong ties to the church, its priests, or the aristocracy.

Studied from these angles, women's options and choices left much to be desired. In different sites, however, still another picture emerges. The documents of the local courts in New Mexico, Texas, and California suggest that women accepted marriage contracts and sued when these were dishonored; they also were known to reject marriage proposals and, sometimes, to commit adultery and shun matrimonial conventions entirely. Disobedience bred repercussions, but women of the upper classes occasionally escaped the worst punishments—fines, banishment, and public scorn.

THE CLASS SYSTEM

The class system in colonial Mexican society, operating with Catholicism and a racial hierarchy that placed at its apex the "pure-blooded" Spaniard, gave upper-class *criollas,* women of Spanish descent born in the Americas, security when they transgressed social boundaries. In a rigidly pyramidal society—and Mexico and its northern borderlands have been viewed in that way—the upper classes, if not completely immune from the problems of daily life, at least were protected by money or status from ostracism, the worst form of punishment for women in this era.

Despite the fear of rejection, women of the Spanish Borderlands had inherited a history of disobedience. Malinali Tenepal, or La Malinche, who either was sold to the Spanish conqueror Hernán Cortés, or given to him, established a pattern of moving outside the culture's prescriptions. A linguist, conversationalist, and diplomat, she became Cortés's personal translator and mistress. A similar process, but moving toward glorification, accompanied the apparition of the Virgin of Guadalupe in 1531; because she appeared before an Indian, Juan Diego, she came to symbolize the unification of Spanish and Native American causes. The unification served its purposes on a political level, but it also established an ideological pattern that Mexico would follow later: the Virgin of Guadalupe became the nation's mother, and in the colonial period she was looked upon by the poorest classes as their immediate savior. Meanwhile, Malinche became a symbol of the poor relation, referred to always in negative terms.

These two symbols, each deified in its own way—Malinche in secular style, and the Virgin by the organized church—became part of the same order in the matter of roles for women. While colonial society throughout Mexico placed the Virgin of Guadalupe on a pedestal, La Malinche was systematically snubbed (and in the period of independence was resurrected as a traitor to indigenous people, a whore to the Spanish). Both Malinche and Guadalupe were thus bound symbolically, if contradictorily, in folklore and history. Young girls, educated for the most part at home or in the church, were admonished to avoid embarrassing parents, extended family, or elders. Betrayal brought forward the accusation of *malinchismo,* which encoded ever more strongly the desires of a culture regarding proper female deportment. Work undertaken for the church, and supported in its rituals—including acts of charity, good mothering, devoted wife-

liness, and discreet widowhood—was rewarded by communities throughout the Spanish Empire.

WOMEN AND THE LAW

In their relationships with men, who tended to control public institutions, women of the Spanish Borderlands continally exhibited the desire to reject male prescriptives. Court cases demonstrate this trend and, as a source of information, are remarkably underused. Usually incomplete and disorganized, part of state and church archives, the court documents were safeguarded by ecclesiastical authorities as well as by royal appointees. Church courts presided over some of the affairs of the Crown, interpreting the law codes according to local custom as much as anything else. Juridical authority rested in both church and state; some citizens of the borderlands used both court systems or shifted between the two as needed.

Although court records often omit details about the outcome of cases, combining them with the Catholic church's records of disputes heard by its adjudicators makes patterns of male-female relations discernible. Frequently women could not read or write, but a scribe or judge wrote out their testimonials, which were then deposited at the next, higher tribunal. In the case of the church courts, which entertained many different motions and held trials accordingly, the archdiocese offices in Durango received and reviewed the written materials. Some efforts were made to control and standardize legal decisions across the borderlands.

The problems that plagued other colonial regions, like illiteracy, cannot be said to have halted resolving disputes between men and women. The most frequent complaints involved married partners; women argued before the judges the problems of adultery, abandonment, battery, and other abuses. The judges routinely supported women's arguments; when the outcome was unfavorable toward women, the same parties might appear repeatedly before the same judge.

Some female litigants appeared many times before the judges or priests, often with different complaints and several witnesses in tow. Robbery, physical assaults, and character assassination brought people back into court. On the frontier regions of the Spanish Empire, residents tended to use the legal system to resolve what might today be termed petty disputes, but what then were certainly considered more injurious. As one historian of New Mexico notes, questions of honor, concerns over legitimacy (meaning birthrights but also marriage vows), and governed and ungoverned sexuality could result in court hearings. Understood as communal ritual, the hearing, its participants, and its issues suggest that the concerns of litigating women were considered not only legitimate but worth hearing.

How had these rites of community been established? One answer lies in the Spanish legal codes, which contained key provisions supporting women's rights. Since the fourteenth century, women had been accorded the right to sue in a court of law, the right to own property in their family name and to retain it after marriage, and the right to make wills, secure inheritance, and sign documents throughout adulthood. These were unusual prerogatives, but not when they are considered as intrinsic to the Spanish Empire's need for an orderly transfer of property in the New World and the constant concern about implanting Spanish institutions in the frontier regions. The transmittal of institutions functioned to secure the cultural programs of conquest and at the same time offered women an arena that allowed them to air complaints and settle differences.

WOMEN AND THE CHURCH

Few of the women who could be labeled recalcitrant participants in the task of building an empire in the New World, and especially in the regions farthest from the center of Mexico City, escaped reprimands. These took several forms. In the seventeenth century even the best-known and most intelligent women, such as Sor Juana Inés de la Cruz, who at sixteen was living at the royal court and entertaining officials and academicians alike with her command of Latin, science, and literature, came under scrutiny. Intellectual debates with royalty, and philosophical and political arguments with church officials, did not stop Sor Juana from producing feminist poetry. However, she was limited at the convent she entered (1667) by the popular notion that

women were not supposed to engage in scholarly or literary work.

Into the 1700s the church and Crown promulgated these ideas about women, but by then commoners and *criollos* alike were beginning to detest many unpopular decrees, like the *vida común*—an edict that asked convents and nuns to simplify their lives, disengage from anything that could be construed as intellectual or ostentatious, and return to a life of humility. This edict disturbed many of the wealthier nuns who had entered the convents with their dowries, servants, and musical instruments, and who had chosen a religious life based on their understanding that, in the convents, they could live among other women who enjoyed a genteel life somewhat removed from watchful officials, priests, fathers, or brothers.

Eventually, the disgruntlements of women became part of a long series of disagreements between rulers and subjects, between Catholic officials and Catholics born in the New World. Other unpopular actions, like the expulsion of the Jesuits in 1767 and the limitations imposed by the Crown and church on the convents and missions, led Mexico and the people of the northern frontiers on the path toward independence. In that sense, women's roles, preoccupations, and statuses were part of every significant event in borderland history: from the conquests in the early sixteenth century to the 1820s, when Mexico separated from Spain, the concerns of women were formalized within religious and political institutions. To a certain extent, the periods of pronounced political turmoil popularized and highlighted women's causes.

In the Spanish Borderlands, fewer women entered convents, but many resided close to the missions. There the linkage between women and the church was strong. Their activities in the frontier churches might not have been as genteel or as refined as those of nuns in the urban centers of Mexico, but they carved out a special place in the missions. When not actually working in the mission system, women undertook the tasks that kept the churches functioning, from cleaning the priests' robes and dusting the altars to, in frontier New Mexico, climbing ladders to apply stucco to the church walls. On those occasions, mounted on ladders or scaffolds, and wearing garments that resembled pantaloons, women demonstrated how central they were to maintaining the churches, and to Catholicism generally. The evidence does not imply marginalization; rather, women kept Catholicism alive in the borderlands.

NONCONFORMING WOMEN

On the borderland haciendas women performed many tasks and labored to keep the family estate functioning. Some wives served as their husbands' accountants, and many widows kept their families' haciendas and ranches operating long after the men had died. This was not unusual, for women in the colonial period tended to outlive men, and in the northern regions widows frequently did not remarry. Popular prejudices equating remarriage with pronounced sexual desire prevented many women from marrying anew, but so did concerns about the possibility of distilling a family's assets. It is difficult to determine how often women of this period made decisions that represented concessions to broader family concerns or how often they reached independent judgments. The percentage of widows was as high as 18 percent of all adults in some communities. This statistic would suggest that many women did not wish to, or could not, find partners, or—and this conclusion is rarely drawn—that they might have preferred to live without husbands. Irrespective of the problems surrounding their immediate choices or lack of choices, widowhood represented a practical alternative. Because extended families were the norm, few widows and elderly women actually lived alone; rich and poor alike continued to care for children and ran households. Widowhood rarely signified uselessness, and elderly widows were respected members of their communities.

Many scholars have pointed out the irony that some women were respected only in old age. It is, indeed, true that Mexican culture has frequently dropped its misogynistic inclinations in the face of individual women's accomplishments (the women who fought heroically in the independence movements as soldiers or assistants come to mind), but more often than not, the life histories of women in the Spanish Bor-

derlands also suggest that many gaps lay between what was expected of women and what they actually did. Some women could be assured that respect would come to them only in old age; others received it earlier in life.

In wars and battles, the gap between the mythologies and realities surrounding womanhood seemed most pronounced. Some women, during the conquest period, disguised themselves as men to join the military campaigns pushing northward. In early-seventeenth-century Peru, Catalina de Erauso had adopted male identity to "pass." She disguised herself as a man and lived that way for many years, in order to join the military and was allowed to do so by the church and Crown. In the decade leading up to independence, women married to the leaders of independence movements struggled along with their husbands to break away from Spain. To a certain extent, we can argue that the prescriptives associated with womanhood could be suspended, if not entirely erased, by women's individual acts of bravery. Few women, however, received complete absolution if their activities moved them dangerously close to any suspicion of aberration.

Expressions of sexuality outside marriage (male-female) explicitly allowed church and state to denounce individual women. Single charges of witchcraft were unusual; most often this type of accusation was linked to other stigmatizing behaviors, such as licentiousness. Prostitution and adultery ranked highest on the list of punishable infractions. It was, in fact, the dual indictment of immorality and libidinousness that most often brought women before public officials. Notoriety of the Sor Juana or Malinche varieties was one of the gravest offenses a woman could incur, and many avoided it assiduously. If notoriety was coupled with a lesser defect, however, a woman could—and many did—find herself fined and isolated for such minor offenses as gossip or theft.

The worst sexual offense women could commit in the colonial period was adultery. The Catholic church denounced any sexual relations outside of marriage, but a woman found having sexual intercourse with anyone except her husband suffered the most severe penalty. If childless, she could be expelled from her village. If she was mestiza or Indian, the ecclesiastical documents imply, the worst punishments, including death by hanging, could be applied. Although some scholars have suggested that before the conquest indigenous women were similarly restricted from any expressions of sexuality outside the boundaries of marriage, it would be erroneous to take these sorts of comparisons at face value. As the historian Patricia Seed explains in a review of a book on Aztec women, the documents containing information about women's sexuality were mostly written by men; Native American communities had differing views about women's roles, about gender roles. To say, then, that Native American or mestiza women's sexual behaviors were more well-regarded in the Spanish colonial period is erroneous. Women of both groups, and perhaps in both eras, remained at the bottom of the social, economic, and sexual hierarchy; their activities were scrutinized, their transgressions were condemned. Women of all classes and ethnicities could not roam too far beyond their allotted space: the boundaries remained drawn around the institutions of family and church.

That women ventured outside the arenas condoned by colonial society is indisputable. The court records, the ecclesiastical documents, and government sources contain thousands of references to women's sins. The aim of strict regulation appeared to be the control of women and the preservation of institutions dependent on their participation, from the family to the church. To argue women's resistance in the face of such strict authority is neither contradictory nor impractical. Women's lives were governed, regulated, and restricted by individual men and by the institutions of colonial society, but their responses to the rules and rulers did not follow any general pattern of acquiescence.

If we know primarily that women did not always abide by expectations, we know far less about their motives in moving outside the strictures of their society. Women wrote very little, and what men wrote about them is incomplete. For these reasons, historians have shied away from guessing at the purposes underlying the actions of women. This is one direction gender studies will probably begin taking, because the pattern in the archival material is clear: women were burdened by the assumptions of men, but they bypassed many along the way.

In the Spanish Borderlands, women's powers and autonomy were limited, but even documents once thought to depict only men's positions or roles now suggest other possibilities. Male-female relations were intertwined and tension-ridden; but few residents of the borderlands have left the material necessary to portray harmony or happiness. We can assume it existed as much as we know that sorrow, anger, and jealousy characterized social relations. Gender studies suggest that what cannot be assumed is that one existed without the other.

BIBLIOGRAPHY

Arrom, Silvia M. *La mujer mexicana ante el divorcia eclesiastico, 1800–1857.* Mexico City, 1976.
———. *The Women of Mexico City, 1790–1857.* Stanford, Calif., 1985.
Capdequí, José María Ots. "Bosquejo histórico de los derechos de la mujer casada en la legislación de Indias." *Revista general de legislación y jurisprudencia* 132 (1918): 162–182.
Castañeda, Antonia. "Presidarias y Pobladoras: Spanish-Mexican Women in Monterey, Alta California, 1770–1821." Ph.D. diss., Stanford University, 1991.
Couturier, Edith. "Women and the Family in Eighteenth-Century Mexico: Law and Practice." *Journal of Family History* 10, no. 3 (1985):294–304.
Cypress, Sandra. *La Malinche: From Myth to History.* Austin, Tex., 1991.
Douglass, William A. "Iberian Family History." *Journal of Family History* 13, no. 1 (1988):1–12.
González, Deena J. *Refusing the Favor: The Spanish-Mexican Women of Santa Fe, 1820–1880.* New York, 1993.
Gutiérrez, Ramón A. *When Jesus Came, the Corn Mothers Went Away: Marriage, Sexuality, and Power in New Mexico, 1500–1846.* Stanford, Calif., 1991.
Lavrin, Asunción. "Values and Meaning of Monastic Life for Nuns in Colonial Mexico." *Hispanic American Historical Review* 59 (1979):367–387.
Lavrin, Asunción, and Edith Couturier. "Dowries and Wills: A View of Women's Socioeconomic Role in Colonial Guadalajara and Puebla, 1640–1790." *Hispanic American Historical Review* 59, no. 2 (1979): 280–304.
Perry, Elizabeth. "The Manly Woman: A Historical Case Study." *American Behavioral Scientist* 31, no. 1 (September/October 1987):86–100.
Rodríguez Valdés, Maria J. *La mujer azteca.* Toluca, Mexico, 1988.

Salas, Elizabeth. *Soldaderas in the Mexican Military: Myth and History.* Austin, Tex., 1990.

Seed, Patricia. "The Church and the Patriarchal Family: Marriage Conflicts in Sixteenth- and Seventeenth-Century New Spain." *Journal of Family History* 10, no. 3 (1985):284–293.

————. "Marriage Promises and the Value of a Woman's Testimony in Colonial Mexico." *Signs: Journal of Women in Culture and Society* 13, no. 2 (1988):253–276.

Sor Juana Ines de la Cruz. *A Sor Juana Anthology.* Translated and edited by Alan Trueblood. Cambridge, Mass., 1988.

————. *Sor Juana Ines de la Cruz: Poems.* Translated by Margaret Sayers Peden. Binghamton, N.Y., 1985.

Deena González

SEE ALSO **Civil Law; Marriage; Rural Life;** and **Urban Life.**

PATTERNS OF COMMUNITY

THE BRITISH COLONIES

WHEN WE CALL TO MIND the colonial past we evoke a host of hallowed images: Roanoke's first white child, Virginia Dare of 1587 legend; Captain John Smith and Pocahontas of Jamestown fame; selected cavaliers, such as the Lords Baltimore of Maryland; and of course the Pilgrims of Plymouth and the Puritan patriarchs of Massachusetts Bay. Custom requires us at least to mention the pacific William Penn and his Quaker friends and to cite one-legged Peter Stuyvesant of Dutch New York. Additionally, our modern sensitivities now call upon us to give explicit recognition to the presence and contributions of the various colonial blacks, be they indentured, slave, or free. We are also aware of the odd fellows—the communal Moravians of the Carolinas, the Mennonites and other German folk of the middle colonies, and the cantankerous Celts who settled along the low hills of Appalachia with little care and less concern for charter boundaries, deed titles, taxes, or Indian rights. Finally, we pay surprisingly little attention to the individual settlers who came here on their own to pursue their private interests and had no formal connections with the established chartered groups; yet at least one fifth of the European emigrants fall into this category; and it was their material successes that helped support the social fabric of many of the various colonial communities.

We would like to examine this rich early American past first by viewing several of the fishing community settlements on the Atlantic seaboard, second by looking at 1607 Jamestown as the model for all male military fort settlements, then by seeing Virginia as the English ideal of a transplanted and perfected gentry society to be supported by its "servants." After examining the Carolinas' slave society, our next regional focus will be utopian New England, followed by the "holy experiment" of the middle colony Quakers and the cloistered Moravian communities. Finally, we conclude with the hill communities of the Scotch-Irish and a reflection on the many unknown sojourners whose faint footprints graced this desert wilderness and promised land.

The communities established by the people discussed in this essay and others were the vehicles through which most colonists adapted to the New World. They either replicated the communities that they came from in the Old World or modified them to suit the challenge of this new environment; in any case, they were very powerful socializing forces in shaping the American experience.

FISHING COMMUNITIES

Fishing camps gave us our first communities, their charts our first knowledge of the North

American terra incognita; their salted cod was the down payment necessary for European settlements. We do not know the name of the banks fishermen who taught Squanto how to speak English or to use cod as a crop fertilizer, yet their unnamed presence is part of William Bradford's account of Squanto as "a spetiall instrument sent of God," since Squanto's acquired knowledge guided the Plymouth colony. Even more wrapped in historical fog are the Bristol sailors who voyaged the yet barely chartered Atlantic in the 1480s and whose landfalls might well have informed Christopher Columbus's own voyages in the 1490s. But it is these anonymous visitors and sometime settlers—the wandering fisherman, the freelance trapper, the marginal farmer—who deserve pride of place in any survey of early American settlement patterns; they were first both to make their peace with the Native inhabitants and the first Europeans to learn how to live off this strange new land, and they left behind them a legacy of goats, hogs, and peas, which succoured both native and immigrant.

When the 1609 "Tempest" storm wrecked Sir Thomas Gates's Virginia-bound fleet, it was saved from starvation by the "herds of swine" that they found on those Bermuda Islands. Moreover, some of them, by "going native," ensured the partial genetic survival of the original Americans, although neither our culture nor its historians celebrate the creation of the Métis, as do the Canadians. (Anglo-American–Indian miscegenation remains a relatively unexplored research topic.) Finally, their cash crops of fish, pelts, and lumber constituted the first great American staples, without which no colonial communities could have existed. These early pioneers made continual profits while the famous Virginia Company and the patient Pilgrims perennially lost money, and while William Penn, the Quaker social visionary, spent time in debtors prison.

The great problem with these first settlers is that their very marginality has kept them hidden from our eyes; most of them cannot be found on the standard English tax lists, either because they had nothing worth taxing or because they were past masters in evading the king's greedy hands. Nor are they usually part of the genealogical nexus which has been so fruitfully used by the "new" social historians of the 1960s. (But then again we should remember that our vaunted genealogies at present take in no more than 20 percent of the estimated 160,000 settlers migrating to British North America in the seventeenth century, while we lack entirely a genealogical survey for the estimated 585,000 additional immigrants from 1700 to 1775.)

We now know of more than twenty seventeenth-century fishing sites in the Maine area alone, and archaeologists continue to turn up clues about these camps through their detritus, including clay pipes and hidden hoards of Elizabethan gold. We also are aware of the Puritans' hostility toward these early "Founders" of New England, for we have John Winthrop's description of them as "a multitude of rude and misgoverned persons, the very scumme of the land."

It has been only in the latter half of the twentieth century that historians have attempted to assess the fishing communities of Marblehead, Massachusetts, Richmond Island, Maine, and Nantucket free from a bias that labeled their speech as filthy, profane, and abounding in "Clipt Oaths" and to see their relationship to the larger Massachusetts polity. The historian Christine Leigh Heyrman contends that these Marblehead folk were a "volatile mixture of emigrants from the ports of Wales and Ireland" as well as from the French speaking Channel Islands, but their salty references to each other as "a thievish Welsh rogue," "Jearse cheater," and "French dog" ought not to blind us to their creation of a multicultural as well as multiethnic community; Herman Melville's *Moby Dick,* with its sailors of all races, mirrors this truth. Moreover, the absence of most males during the fishing seasons meant that the Marblehead women performed a wide range of occupations and cultivated a significant amount of personal independence; they well merited their reputation as voracious "Amazons." Given a gender ratio skewed in their favor, they could be highly independent in bestowing their favors and in changing their sexual partners. The Richmond islanders came mostly from England's west country, were Anglican traditionalists who feasted rather than fished during the "2 weekes of Christmas tyme" in the 1630s, and had a ten to one male to female ratio.

These three fishing communities—unusual in that some of their historical documents have survived—were all suspected of superstition, sexual irregularity, and irreligion by the Massachusetts Puritans. These suspicions were connected to the fact that Congregationalism had no initial appeal to the folk of Richmond Island, that in Marblehead a substantial part of the population throughout the seventeenth century considered itself either Anglican or Quaker (and described their "Parsecuting Dogs" as being from the "Puritan establishment"), and that Nantucket was in opposition to Massachusetts orthodoxy. Furthermore, these fishing communities offered a limited (yet real) role to their Indians as well as giving unusual recognition to female leaders in the life of the community. Odd, difficult, different, and lacking scribes to tell their tales, they deserve recognition as a significant minority within Puritan New England.

THE CHESAPEAKE

We have honored the 1607 establishment of a fort at Jamestown, Virginia, based on the claim that it was the first permanent English settlement in what became the United States. In reality it was a bachelor garrison under martial law, a starving outpost surrounded by bountiful waters, and a rural retreat for officer visionaries who were busily creating a paradisal community that still has mythic purchase on the American imagination. Its founders envisaged the settlement as a transplant of the top of England's hierarchical pyramid, along with necessary supporting personnel including perfumers, jewelers, tailors, and, of course, manual workers such as coopers and carpenters, who would package the export produce to be supplied by the indigenous population—the pyramid's bottom—much in the manner of Mexico and Peru after the Spanish conquests. This gentry vision of an ordered Elizabethan social structure is the one great constant, consuming ideal in the formation of community life in the Chesapeake throughout the colonial era. Its features were a gentry at the top, a small number of necessary artisans, and a vast supporting population of servants, be they red, white, or black in color.

The 28 gentlemen in the group of 105 first arrivals stood ready to hunt, to pray, and to govern as befitted the pyramid's top. As "Maister Captaine Chester" put the tale, "The lands full rich, the people easilie wonne," the people's gains being "the knowledge of our faith / And ours such ritches as the country hath." The all-male task force was expected, by working in common, quickly to produce a profit for the stockholders who had invested in the Virginia Company. It was assumed that this venture would attract the surplus "fatherless children . . . , or young married people, that have small wealth to live on" who "heere by their labour may live exceeding well: provided alwaies that first there bee a sufficient power to command them," which of course would be provided by the gentry's second sons.

As Governor Sir William Berkeley saw it, Virginia could solve the family dilemma facing "indigent younger Brothers whom the peculiar policy of this Nation condemned to poverty or War," for it would take but a small sum to "enable a younger Brother to erect a flourishing Family in a New World." Simply put, the "heir" would inherit the manor, while the "spare" would colonize Virginia, selecting a mate, if he wished, from a pool of orphaned gentry women as socially disadvantaged as he. (The company in 1621 had decided by this method to supply quality women to the colony's successful tobacco planters.) Such a formula addressed the need for elite continuity as well as for men with practical experience: a goodly portion of these younger brothers, coming from either the south or west of England, had dealt in either London or Bristol commerce. As for innovation, because these younger brothers had been victims of primogeniture, it would become both their desire and their custom to endow all their sons with plantations in the dispositions of their own American estates.

Four realities challenged this ideal gentry community: first, the natives preferred flight to forced labor (and in any case, disease quickly thinned their numbers); second, malaria decimated the English garrison in its Jamestown "fortresse"; third, once reports circulated about forced labor, working by the bell, eating gruel in mess halls, twice a day prayers such as "O Lord defend us from the delusions of the devil, the malice of the heathen, the invasion of our enemies, and mutinies and dissentions of our own people," the common folk decided to stay in England; and fourth, few desired to work solely for the company store—or, as Captain John Smith put the case, no "other motive then wealth, will ever erect there a Commonweale" or draw the English "from their ease and humours at home."

Albeit wealth was a strong motivator, force still remained the first option utilized by the Tudors and Stuarts to achieve their will; poor boys, orphans, and Bridewell inmates were forced to the colony in the belief that "in Virginia under severe Masters they may be brought to goodness." It did not matter that they did not want to be transported and be bound to service—the king's privy council waived their rights in favor of the company's greater good. This quasi-legal method of obtaining workers helped to create the legend that the Chesapeake was settled by "Rogues, whores and vagabonds."

Of course, this legend is in part true—witness the dominance of servitude—and research in the latter half of the twentieth century suggests that a full 75 percent of that region's immigrants came as either forced or indentured servants. But part of it is false; the social background of the vast majority of the immigrants was not criminal or marginal but rather a representative cross section of England's working men and women. Most had had an urban experience before coming to Virginia. We also now know that the vast majority of these immigrants were males and isolates without family or relatives, and with a sex ratio of between three and four males to every one female, most would die unmarried. In fact, with a contract (the indenture) calling for seven years' service to pay transportation costs and an average yearly mortality rate of at least 7 percent, half of all of them were dead prior to receiving their freedom dues and the opportunity of becoming property holders in the New World. In reality, the figures for the earliest years make even more dismal reading: from 1607 to the census of 1624–1625, we count a little more than six thousand arrivals and just over twelve hundred survivors.

In Charles County, Maryland, the average length of marriage before death intervened was nine years. Given the limited number of females—remembering that maids, as the name implies, did not customarily marry while in service—one can infer that a majority of widows

had an active hand in the choice of their second mates.

What then were the norms of community in the seventeenth-century Chesapeake? First, the region's incredible rate of mortality meant that the English social model, with its ideal of patriarchs and generational order and its controlling nexus of kin, did not exist. We see it replaced by the creation in the South of fictive uncles, aunts, and cousins of popular folklore—which shows that the survivors chose their intimate associates even as they adroitly legitimated this change of practice by using traditional kin terms. Second, the short duration of marriages meant small families of about three children per couple, quick remarriages upon the death of one partner, many stepbrothers and stepsisters, and a good deal of tensions, envy, and conflicts over probate. Third, there were more visibly active and powerful roles for women; they had legal power as widows and executors, they were young, and they were sexually active. Fourth, there was a 5 percent chance from about 1635 to 1655 for an indentured servant to move from the bottom into a gentry position. Fifth, this was and would continue to be an immigrant society dependent upon white (and then black) servitude; it would be about a hundred years from 1607 before a majority of the Chesapeake's English population was American born. The colony also included a smaller number of blacks—we estimate about 5 percent of that region's total population in 1680. In the 1620s they were indentured servants, but most of them at least from mid century endured servitude for life. And these blacks, unlike their enslaved brethren in Barbados, had started to form conjugal units that reproduced; some had also created their own semifunctioning communities; their children born there, like most foreign whites, shed the various languages of their parents and "did talk good English, and effect our language, habits, and customs."

All this happened in a society where most men and women had lived the first part of their lives in bound servitude. Moreover, deference was the culturally accepted habit as we see 'democratic' Virginians backing the religious intolerance of their gentry-controlled Anglican vestries just as 'autocratic' Marylanders followed their proprietor's decree of religious freedom for all members of Jesus Christ's 'Holy Churches.' Here life was overwhelmingly rural and isolated save for the gentry's village-like plantations, and where all had been stalked by death. It is no wonder that this community was governed by a mentalité of impermanence, with a gentry calculus favoring silk and silver buttons over permanent dwellings, the better to spend and enjoy large tobacco profits in short lifetimes. The life of risk, the politics of show, the gamble of a horse race, the presence of many workers in the fields all obviously marked the boundaries of gentry rule in tidewater Virginia, Maryland, the lower Delaware, and the northern part of the Carolinas.

THE BARBADIAN-CAROLINA NEXUS

Almost sixty years have past since Charles McLean Andrews, following a prior call of a quarter-century before by George L. Beer, attempted to remind his insular Americanist brethren that U.S. history must surely include Barbados and the Leewards, since those islands "formed a part of the colonial world within which the merchants, agriculturists, and seafaring men of the continental colonies had their being." When the English looked at their empire in the seventeenth century, they saw Barbados, settled by seventy-four males in 1627, as its crown jewel; by mid century its population of thirty-eight thousand easily made it its most populous colony, while sugar made it the wealthiest. It was ruled by a narrow oligarchic plutocracy, assisted by an unhappy group of poor whites and supported by its black slaves—"an heathenish, brutish and an uncertaine, dangerous kinde of people" is the way they were described in the 1661 law code—who outnumbered the whites four to one. The English held a monopoly of arms, the awe and power of technology, and terror over their slaves: as one black put it, the "devil was in the Englishman, that he makes everything work; he makes the Negro work, the horse work, the ass work, the wood work, the water work, and the wind work." As Andrews realized, by the 1660s this small, overcrowded island was in effect "a single great sugar plantation controlled by the crown, owned by absentee planters, and worked by negro slaves." In 1710 the Barbadian Thomas Walduck reflected on this island inhabited by slaves, knaves, and barbarians in quest of wealth and wrote, "Death is thy look and Death in every part," adding "Oh! Glorious Isle in Vilany Excell / Sin to the Height—thy fate is Hell."

The import of Barbados for the continent is that it helped found South Carolina; about half of the 684 lowland Carolina settlers from 1670 to 1680 were from these islands and a third of its governors from 1669 to 1737 were from the Barbadian elite. The colony's plan featured such feudal titles as landgrave and Creole ones such as cacique, along with a hierarchical system of government that John Locke helped draw up. But this was a guise for the Barbadians' introduction of a thoroughly modern and exploitative social order into America, an order based upon a rural black slave majority (with poor whites as the first overseers) and an urban white ruling class that called Charleston home. In Peter Wood's apt words, South Carolina started as "a colony of a colony." Its great rice planters carried little social responsibility, amassed untold wealth, and had the satisfaction of being the masters of the richest mainland colony in the eighteenth century.

These Barbadian-Carolinian planters created a modern community of self-interest that survived for more than a century and a half. It was open to the talents of Huguenots, but following Aristotle, it believed that human beings were naturally unequal, that the English obviously were the top cards, that the Irish and Russians were unfortunate middlings, and that Negroes were at the bottom; they believed further that the top was entitled to the lion's share. Having said the obvious, let us note with an awareness of our own social blindness that these were not evil men, and in their time and place they found praise and honor.

NEW ENGLAND

Just as John the Baptist prepared the way for the first coming of the Christ, so the Pilgrims prepared the Massachusetts Bay area for the Puritans (who expected there the second coming of the Christ in their own time). The 101 Pilgrims who dropped anchor at Provincetown in 1620 already had a generation-old identity as religious separatists from the Church of England and as a network of related families and kind neighbors who had shared exile and "Ancient" grace in Holland. They believed in a self-governing congregation, and some insisted upon an explicit conversion experience as a test for admission to their religious society; it is possible that their Puritan neighbors borrowed this test from them. If they were good farmers, they were also hopeless businessmen who were deeply in debt to their English supporters.

Their salvation from debt came with the business acumen and the ready cattle market supplied by the Puritans' great migration of the 1630s. And that migration of nearly twenty thousand settlers was led by the visionary lay preacher and governor John Winthrop, who thought "the care of the publique must oversway all private respects." Following the precepts of Matthew's gospel, they were to be as a "Citty upon a Hill." Certainly "divine providence" had determined that the settlers would be "riche and poore"— for while these Puritans were utopians, they were not levelers—but more important they would be knit together into an organic whole graced by gospel ordinances. With Winthrop keeping notes, the charismatic minister John Cotton sought out the lost sheep, for "Yea, the Lord gave witness to the exercise of prophecy, so as thereby some were converted, and others much edified." It was this exciting period of revival-like conversions and prophecy akin to that of apostolic times that also inspired the chiliast Captain Edward Johnson to declare that "this is the place where the Lord will create a new Heaven, and a new Earth in, new Churches, and a new Common-wealth together." These were the chosen people in a new Israel; God had covenanted with "them" and "their children." They believed that their Anglo-Saxon ancestors were the elect of Christ, that as reformers they had restored Gospel rule, and that the fruit of their loins was to rule over all other races.

The nucleus of the Bay colony's leaders was college trained and from the East Anglian gentry and their affinities. The rank and file, young and old, followed in family and neighborhood groupings; at two to one, their ratio of males to females was the highest in the colonies, while their one servant in four migrants was possibly the lowest. This revivalist-dominated settlement of the godly and the sexually chaste (the franchise depended upon church membership) branched out in contiguous, though dispersed, villages formed by families of uniform opinions and religious experiences. They, like all seventeenth-century Christians, believed in signs, and they saw that during this "Great Migration" their God had brought 197 out of 198 of their ships to New England without accident, that he had vacated the heathen Indians from the land for their benefit, that he had made the climate mild so that their crops prospered, and that he blessed them with an unparalleled fertility in their families of seven children. Many children meant many marriages, which by the third generation had produced village communities dominated by kin networks.

We have been able to look at the strategies of these mostly self-subsisting farming communities as "revealed in arranged marriages between cousins, marriages of siblings between families," such as a son-in-law's sister marrying her in-law's son, and their generational transfers of land; they yield persuasive evidence that these New Englanders valued above all literate households of fathers, sons, and related females. This was the most literate, most schooled, most free, most record-keeping, most substantially housed, most kin-connected, and most ministered of all the colonial communities. It was also the poorest. It believed in religious freedom for those walking in true gospel order—namely its own adherents—and asked others, such as the dissenter Roger Williams of Rhode Island fame and the antinomian, and possibly protofeminist, Anne Hutchinson, to depart. And for those of its Quakers who felt compelled to return, it offered them the gallows.

New England's two great colleges, Harvard and Yale, when they grew rich with legacies derived from the new wealth of late-nineteenth- and early-twentieth-century America, pietistically collected the heavily documented experiences of their forefathers, which Perry Miller and his disciples in the twentieth century have so intensely studied. We now realize—as Miller did not—that the New England communities were neither the intellectual nor social models for America. Academic historians still rejoice in the records of these communities, which reflect their creation of a unique regional culture, and are mindful of the initial dominance of New England community studies in the formation of our recent historiography. But they now recognize the region's atypicality.

QUAKER SETTLEMENTS

In many respects William Penn's Quaker communities on the Delaware were similar to those of New England; his was also to be a "holy experiment," and he too stressed religious conformity, sexual purity, and the recruitment of families and neighbors. In the decade following their settlement in 1675 of Salem in West New Jersey, the Friends helped shepherd more than eighty-five hundred colonists to either West Jersey or Pennsylvania. Penn counted the ninety arriving ships and observed that "not one vessel designed to the Province, through God's mercy, hitherto miscarried. And God in His and Her mercy intended to continue to guide us if we would only be silent and listen, and open our eyes and see the 'light.'"

There was no need for priests in orders, or ministers with college degrees, or a gentry with its worldly distractions; no need for pockets in jackets, or hat tipping, or fancy language, for all would be addressed as "thee." There was no need for oaths, for were not the brethren always to tell the truth? And no need for armies, for were not the Friends bound to live in peace? Moreover, they had as their collective mission the return to the paradisal norms of our earliest progenitors. Before the fall, God had intended—so preached the founding Quaker, George Fox—that "man and woman were helps-meet in the image of God, and in righteousness and holiness, in the dominion"; after the fall "man was to rule over his wife," but now in these days of joy "in the restoration by Christ, into the image of God, and his righteousness and holiness again, in that they are help-meet, man and woman, as they were before the fall." In this quote we see the essence of Quaker radicalism and how its peculiar readings of Scripture would, in this particular case, have undermined the accepted gender roles and distinctions of Stuart England. And so they

did in the Delaware Valley, with their women preachers, women's meetings, women committee heads, women witnesses to wills, and women's marriage proposals when the Spirit prompted them to speak before men. In all of these matters, they were following their belief that "in souls there is no sex."

The Quakers arriving in the 1680s were mostly common folk from the English Midlands and the border areas, this explaining the origins of their customarily drab gray garments. In addition, the Friends were the first colonials actively to recruit Irish folk and other such foreigners as German and Swiss pietists, thus adding a multiethnic dimension to their communities. The sharp Quaker calculus is evident in this recruitment of like-minded spiritualists and is also apparent in their effort to provide a religious environment friendly to low church Anglican sympathizers. Penn opined that there is "no reason to persecute any man in this world about anything that belongs to the next," and he was unusual in his time for that tolerant position.

At the same time, Penn also believed that both rural and urban environments should be organized to reinforce the Quaker collective discipline. Philadelphia, with its unusual (for the British) quadrilateral street plan spoke of control, as did Quaker designs for nucleated rural centers of "loving neighborhoods" with surrounding farms, much like the hub and spokes of a wheel. In truth, brotherly surveillance played a major part in everyday Quaker life. In no realm was this so plain as in marriage. It was required that the intended couple be in love prior to their union and not as a result of it, the latter being the standard expectation then; that both sets of parents give their approval; and that both the bride's and groom's meetings also bless the intended union. Also there was endless exhortation on the spiritual as opposed to the carnal aspect of marriage, as befitted a sect influenced by Pauline Christianity. In fact, they believed that celibacy had a place in marriage. Not to marry Quaker, to become a party to what Quakers called a "mongrel marriage," meant being ousted from the meeting and, possibly, family disinheritance; it also cast suspicion (and probable censure) on the parents of these carnal children. A significant number of Friends married late in life. The first settlers averaged families of five children—placing them between the Chesapeake and the New England averages. Unusually for colonial America, as many as a fifth of Quaker women may have remained single; if this was their choice, it is yet another example of the Friends' protomodern behavior.

Having been the first to arrive in Pennsylvania, the Quakers took possession of the best farmland and the choicest lots in Philadelphia, exercised great care in trading wheat, attempted to avoid worldly luxury, and as a result of their thrift, careful calculations, and a general habit of observation had become the single wealthiest group in the colony.

The Quakers welcomed the Scotch-Irish as well as Lutheran and Reformed Germans in the 1720s and the cloistered Moravians in the 1740s, with their belief "that there can be no Christianity without community." Thus, by the middle of the eighteenth century, the Quakers were a numerical minority in Pennsylvania; their Quaker party ruled only with the support of its client German folk with the implicit agreement that German might be the language of church and kitchen but English would be the parlance of court and exchange. In the poorer backcountry, Quakers found themselves flanked by increasing numbers of hostile Scotch-Irish, who undermined their pacific policy toward the Indians.

With the commencement of hostilities in the Seven Years' War in 1754 came times of tribulation. Calls for troops and taxes led to the withdrawal of observant Quakers from the Pennsylvania assembly, with power passing to their opponents. Likewise, their attempted neutrality in the American Revolution branded them in the eyes of the winning Patriots as being of questionable loyalty; this in effect delegitimized their role as American social pioneers. In fact it has only been since the turbulence of the civil rights movement that began in the 1950s, and with it the restudying of the roles played by blacks, Native Americans, and women during the colonial era, that the Quakers have been brought back to the historical center stage.

CELTIC MIGRATION

It is estimated that from 1718 to 1775 the poor, overcrowded Celtic fringe of the British Isles yielded 250,000 immigrants to the Americas, half of the eighteenth-century colonial total. They were called Irish, Saxon-Scotch, Ulster Scots, North Britons, people of the borderlands, and Scotch-Irish for the first time in Maryland about 1695. And in today's contemporary ethnic America the eminent and reflective scholar Maldwyn A. Jones sums up the present interpretation that sees these multinamed "Irish," which was the most common term used in the eighteenth century, as sharing a "common Pan-Celtic, nomadic, pastoral, and warlike culture." Moreover, these Irish were religiously diverse; for while Presbyterians constituted about half of these folk, a quarter were Roman Catholics, and the remainder Irish Episcopalians, Quakers, Baptists, and others. It was their traditional warlike characteristics that brought them invitations to settle both the Massachusetts and Pennsylvania frontiers, the intent being that they would serve as buffers between the Indians and the English. They came with their families, their neighbors, their own ministers—or in a few cases, with priests. Some spoke Gaelic, and all seemed to be land hungry; James Logan, the proprietary agent who recruited them, observed that they had the habit of squatting on "any spot of vacant land they fancied" as well as being "hard neighbors to the Indians." One critic saw them as the "scum of two nations," but they had a reputation of being proud and free, with less than a fifth coming as servants. Highly mobile, by the 1750s they had taken over Appalachia by establishing a chain of backcountry settlements on the Great Wagon Road from Pennsylvania to Georgia.

We think they married early by colonial standards. The English clergy considered them sexually promiscuous, and they were also charged with being clannish, dogmatic, nonreflective, and covetous. Without champions in academia, they are the group least in demand for modern study: this, despite the fact that the three million Appalachian folk of the 1990 census constitute the largest continuing "colonial" community.

When these Scotch-Irish looked at the Indian hunting lands west of the Susquehanna, they asserted, in the words of James Logan, that "it was against the laws of God and nature, that so much land should be idle, while so many Christians wanted it to labor on, and to raise their bread." Fortunately for them enough backed the winning side in this rebellion, so that they claimed frontier land as their due. From their culture emerged prototypical western or "country" dress, music, and populism. Moreover, in the nineteenth century they helped to elect one of their own, Andrew Jackson, as the Union's first democratically elected (and ethnic) president. Observe, though, that they neither founded, formed a majority in, nor controlled any colony, and they gained real political power only by compromise, coalition, and cooperation. In this respect they constituted a model for all future immigrant communities in the new nation.

CONCLUSION

We have looked at both the ideals and the realities of community formation in early America: the proud plans for early Jamestown; John Smith's belief that only the possibility of wealth would attract settlers; marching cavaliers; sweating and dying workers in the hot tobacco fields; pious Pilgrims and procreating Puritans; gentle Quakers; and John Locke's fantastic dreams for a feudal Carolina. We have also seen fisherfolk at work with cod as their purpose, poor whites along with the first struggling blacks of unsure status, much servitude, the paying fields of grain and rice, and the less fertile fields of New England, the latter giving testimony that bread (and wealth) alone did not form all of these communities. Moreover, the European traditions of capital cities and concentrating populations, overruled colonial experiences connecting high mortality with overcrowding; death visited both the urban rich and poor; and in the early Chesapeake it helped to promote some of the lowly into the seats of the vacant gentry. We think we know some of the beliefs of the early Virginians and some of the theology of the Puritans, and we try to read with care the minutes of the Quaker meeting, praying to see a faint ray of light.

We historians have our moments of pride when we review the vast modern historical literature, with its Gini ratios and Pearson correlations and note our corrections of the errors of earlier generations of scholars. We also are painfully aware of our use of incomplete data; as we read names of historical actors who helped form their communities, we realize that we know almost nothing about these men and women. Even worse we know of lists burnt during Sherman's march through Georgia as well as those lost in the London blitz that could have added to our understanding of these now-silent early Americans. By remembering these many dead early Americans—those with and without progeny, both the poor and the propertied, the writing men as well as the many unrecorded women— we honor their presence among us. They are all part of an incredible movement that emptied, remade, and expanded concepts of what makes an American community.

BIBLIOGRAPHY

Anderson, Virginia DeJohn. "Migrants and Motives: Religion and the Settlement of New England." *New England Quarterly* 58, no. 3 (1985):339–383.

Andrews, Charles McClean. *The Colonial Period of American History.* Volume 2, *The Settlements.* New Haven, Conn., 1936.

Axtell, James. *The Invasion Within: The Contest of Cultures in Colonial North America.* New York, 1985.

———. "The Vengeful Women of Marblehead: Robert Roules's Deposition of 1677." *William and Mary Quarterly,* 3rd ser., 31, no. 4 (1974):647–652.

Bailyn, Bernard. *The Peopling of British North America: An Introduction.* New York, 1986.

Battis, Emery. *Saints and Sectaries: Anne Hutchinson and the Antinomian Controversy in Massachusetts Bay Colony.* Chapel Hill, N.C., 1962.

Bolton, Charles K. *The Real Founders of New England: Stories of Their Life Along the Coast, 1601–1628.* Boston, 1929.

Bossy, John. "Reluctant Colonists: The English Catholics Confront the Atlantic." In *Early Maryland in a Wider World,* edited by David B. Quinn. Detroit, Mich., 1982.

Breen, T. H. "Horses and Gentlemen: The Cultural Significance of Gambling Among the Gentry of Virginia." *William and Mary Quarterly,* 3rd ser., 34, no. 2 (1977):239–257.

Byers, Edward. *The Nation of Nantucket: Society and Politics in an Early American Commercial Center, 1660–1820.* Boston, 1986.

Carr, Lois Green, and Russell R. Menard. "Immigration and Opportunity: The Freedman in Early Colonial Maryland." In *The Chesapeake in the Seventeenth Century: Essays on Anglo-American Society,* edited by Thad W. Tate and David L. Ammerman. Chapel Hill, N.C., 1979.

Carson, Cary, et al. "Impermanent Architecture in the Southern American Colonies." *Winterthur Portfolio* 16, 2/3 (1981):135–196.

Churchill, E. A. "A Most Ordinary Lot of Men: The Fishermen at Richmond Island, Maine, in the Early Seventeenth Century." *New England Quarterly* 57, no. 2 (1984):184–204.

Cressy, David. *Coming Over: Migration and Communication Between England and New England in the Seventeenth Century.* Cambridge, England, 1987.

Dunn, Richard S. *Sugar and Slaves: The Rise of the Planter Class in the English West Indies, 1624–1713.* Chapel Hill, N.C., 1972.

Earle, Carville V. "Environment, Disease, and Mortality in Early Virginia." In *The Chesapeake in the Seventeenth Century: Essays on Anglo-American Society*, edited by Thad W. Tate and David L. Ammerman. Chapel Hill, N.C., 1979.s

Faulkner, Alaric. "Archaeology of the Cod Fishery: Damariscove Island." *Historical Archaeology* 19, no. 2 (1985):57–86.

Fischer, David Hackett. *Albion's Seed: Four British Folkways in America.* New York, 1989.

Fogleman, Aaron. "Migrations to the Thirteen British North American Colonies: New Estimates." *Journal of Interdisciplinary History* 22, no. 46 (1992):691–709.

Galenson, David W. *White Servitude in Colonial America: An Economic Analysis.* Cambridge, England, 1981.

Handlin, Oscar, and Mary F. Handlin. "Origins of the Southern Labor System," *William and Mary Quarterly*, 3rd ser., 7, no. 2 (1950):199–222.

Hecht, Irene W. D. "The Virginia Muster of 1624/5 As a Source for Demographic History." *William and Mary Quarterly*, 3rd ser., 30, no. 1 (1973):65–92. New York, 1979.

Heyrman, Christine Leigh. *Commerce and Culture: The Maritime Communities of Colonial Massachusetts, 1690–1750.* New York, 1984.

Horn, James. "Servant Emigration to the Chesapeake in the Seventeenth Century." In *The Chesapeake in the Seventeenth Century: Essays on Anglo-American Society*, edited by Thad W. Tate and David L. Ammerman. Chapel Hill, N.C., 1979.

Jameson, J. Franklin, ed. *Johnson's Wonder-Working Providence, 1628–1651*, by Edward Johnson. New York, 1910.

Jones, Maldwyn A. "The Scotch-Irish in British America." In *Strangers Within the Realm: Cultural Margins of the First British Empire*, edited by Bernard Bailyn and Philip D. Morgan. Chapel Hill, N.C., 1991.

Kulikoff, Allan. "The Origins of Afro-American Society in Tidewater Maryland and Virginia, 1700 to 1790." *William and Mary Quarterly*, 3rd ser., 35, no. 2 (1978):226–259.

Lauter, Paul, ed. *The Heath Anthology of American Literature.* Vol. 1. Lexington, Mass., 1990.

Levy, Barry. "'Tender Plants': Quaker Farmers and Children in the Delaware Valley, 1681–1735," *Journal of Family History* 3, no. 2 (1978):116–135.

MacDougal, Hugh A. *Racial Myth in English History: Trojans, Teutons, and Anglo-Saxons.* Montreal and Hanover, N.H., 1982.

Main, Gloria L. *Tobacco Colony: Life in Early Maryland, 1650–1720.* Princeton, N.J., 1982.

Menard, Russell, Lois Green Carr, and Lorena S. Walsh. "A Small Planter's Profits: The Cole Estate and the Growth of the Early Chesapeake Economy." *William and Mary Quarterly*, 3rd ser., 40, no. 2 (1983):171–196.

Morgan, Edmund. *The Puritan Family: Religion and Domestic Relations in Seventeenth-Century New England.* Rev. ed. New York, 1966.

Quinn, David B. "The First Pilgrims." *William and Mary Quarterly*, 3rd ser., 23, no. 3 (1966):359–390.

Quitt, Martin H. "Immigrant Origins of the Virginia Gentry: A Study of Cultural Transmission and Innovation." *William and Mary Quarterly*, 3rd ser., 45, no. 4 (1988):629–655.

Ransome, David R. "Wives for Virginia, 1621." *William and Mary Quarterly*, 3rd ser., 48, no. 1 (1991):3–18.

Roper, Louis H. "Conceptions of America: South Carolina and the Peopling of a Wilderness." Ph.D. diss., University of Rochester, 1992.

Rutman, Darrett B. *Winthrop's Boston: A Portrait of a Puritan Town, 1630–1649.* Chapel Hill, N.C., 1965.

Rutman, Darrett B., and Anita H. Rutman. "'Now-Wives and Sons-in-Law': Parental Death in a Seventeenth Century Virginia County." In *The Chesapeake in the Seventeenth Century: Essays on Anglo-American Society*, edited by Thad W. Tate and David L. Ammerman. Chapel Hill, N.C., 1979.

Salisbury, Neal. *Manitou and Providence: Indians, Europeans, and the Making of New England, 1500–1643.* New York, 1982.

Smith, Daniel Blake. "Mortality and Family in the Colonial Chesapeake." *Journal of Interdisciplinary History* 8, no. 3 (1978):403–427.

Smith, Daniel Scott. "'All in Some Degree Related to Each Other': A Demographic and Comparative Resolution of the Anomaly of New England Kinship." *American Historical Review* 94, no. 1 (1989):44–79.

Souden, David. "'Rogues, Whores and Vagabonds'? Indentured Servant Emigration to North America and the Case of Mid–Seventeenth-Century Bristol." In *Migration and Society in Early Modern En-*

gland, edited by Peter Clark and David Souden. New York, 1988.

Vickers, Daniel. "Work and Life on the Fishing Periphery of Essex, Massachusetts, 1630–1675." In *Seventeenth-Century New England,* edited by David D. Hall. Boston, 1984.

Walsh, Lorena S. "Charles County, Maryland, 1658–1705: A Study of Chesapeake Social and Political Structure." Ph.D. diss., Michigan State University, 1977.

Waterhouse, Richard. "England, the Caribbean and the Settlement of Carolina." *Journal of American Studies* 9, no. 3 (1975):259–281.

Waters, John J. "Family, Inheritance, and Migration in Colonial New England: The Evidence from Guilford, Connecticut." *William and Mary Quarterly,* 3rd ser., 39, no. 1 (1982):64–86.

———. "Hingham, Massachusetts, 1631–1661: An East Anglian Oligarchy in the New World." *Journal of Social History* 1, no. 4 (1968):351–370.

Wells, Robert V. "Family Size and Fertility Control in Eighteenth-Century America: A Study of Quaker Families." *Population Studies* 25, no. 1 (1971): 73–82.

Wood, Joseph S. "Village and Community in Early Colonial New England." *Journal of Historical Geography* 8, no. 4 (1982):333–346.

Wood, Peter H. *Black Majority: Negroes in Colonial South Carolina from 1670 through the Stono Rebellion.* New York, 1974.

John J. Waters

See also **Interracial Communities.**

THE DUTCH COLONY

Bounded on the north by the Mohawk River and the south by the Delaware River, New Netherland constituted a mosaic of disparate communities situated in three major zones of settlement: the upper Hudson Valley, Manhattan and western Long Island, and the Delaware region. Differentiated by economic orientation and ethnic makeup, these communities illustrate the colony's defining characteristics; its commercial focus and its diverse population.

PREEMINENCE OF COMMERCE

The primacy of trade for the Dutch West India Company's (WIC) leaders ensured that New Netherland would be dominated by its two urban centers: New Amsterdam and Beverswyck (originally Fort Orange and later Albany). Initially these towns were WIC trading posts protected by adjacent forts manned by company soldiers. But as knowledge of opportunities in the fur trade spread, individual entrepreneurs moved to center stage, and the presence of the company receded. Demands for greater autonomy by the local population resulted in alterations in the form of government. New Amsterdam, the commercial center at the tip of Manhattan Island, was granted a municipal government in 1653; Beverswyck, the fur-trading center on the Hudson River, had been given an independent administration the year before. Life in these urban communities revolved around commercial exchanges. Linked to the global network of the Dutch trading empire, residents of New Amsterdam and Beverswyck also took advantage of local and regional markets to sell the products of their industry.

Because of the preference accorded trade, rural communities occupied a secondary role in New Netherland. Most were small villages composed of family-owned farms. Inhabitants raised foodstuffs for themselves and sold whatever surpluses they had in the cities. Their daily lives resonated more to the change of seasons, the vagaries of weather, and the currents of local gossip than to the rhythms of the trading calendar. In the patroonship of Rensellaerswyck (surrounding Beverswyck), tenant farmers held leases from the Van Rensellaer family.

THE POPULATION

Once past the frontier stage, New Netherland's communities had a relatively even sex ratio, and families predominated. Research on Beverswyck has shown that after the 1650s marriage was almost universal and large families were the norm.

The diversity that characterized New Netherland's population was graphically displayed in the urban centers of New Amsterdam and Beverswyck, whose residents originated in places across the map of Europe and Africa. But in the rural areas of the colony, geographical separation of cultural groups was the rule. Homogeneous communities of Dutch, English, and Swedes dotted a landscape still largely inhabited by Indians. For the most part, the residents of these villages shared a common ancestry, culture, and religion. They worshiped in their native language in churches of their own design.

Men and women with roots in the Netherlands formed the bulk of the population in the five so-called Dutch towns on western Long Island (in present-day Kings County or Brooklyn): Breuckelen (Brooklyn), Vlakkebos (Flatbush), Nieu Amersfoot (Flatlands), Nieu Utrecht (New Utrecht), and Boswyck (Bushwick). Dutch colonists also clustered in Esopus (Kingston) in the Hudson Valley, Schenectady, and on the Rensellaerswyck patroonship. Gathered into communities at the urging of the WIC administration, these farmers came together to worship at newly organized Dutch Reformed churches. Initially content to submit to the rule of the central government with only a modicum of local autonomy, Dutch villagers began to clamor for greater privileges of self-government after observing their English neighbors in towns to the east.

Communities comprised of English people were incorporated into New Netherland because the WIC encountered difficulties in finding enough settlers for its colony. At a time when opportunities for material advancement abounded and the government was not inclined to enforce religious orthodoxy, men and women were reluctant to uproot themselves from the Netherlands. The company, eager to populate its territory in order to ward off encroachments from the English colonies to the north and south, permitted groups of disaffected New England Puritans to establish their own towns on Long Island in the 1640s. While the particular origins of each town differed, they were all founded by men and women who had initially cast their lot in Connecticut and Massachusetts. Gravesend, the first English settlement on western Long Island, was established in 1643 under the leadership of Lady Deborah Moody, whose religious differences with Puritan authorities in Essex County, Massachusetts, led her to migrate to New Netherland. Other New Englanders settled in the towns of Flushing, Newtown, Jamaica, and Hempstead.

With shared language, culture, and religion, Long Island's Puritan townspeople also drew on their English experience for a model of community organization premised on a high level of popular participation in governance. Their situation as aliens in New Netherland added urgency to their quest for self-rule. They successfully pressed their claims for a substantial measure of autonomy in local affairs by consenting to submit to the authority of the Dutch West India Company.

Early Dutch colonizing efforts on the Delaware River, followed up by the conquest of New Sweden in 1655, resulted in the incorporation of Swedes and Finns into New Netherland's population. Scandinavians dwelt alongside Dutch and members of other nationalities in Fort Casimir, renamed New Amstel when it became a colony of the city of Amsterdam in 1657 and later called New Castle by the English. However, the main settlements of Swedes and Finns on Tinicum Island and adjacent lands remained separate communities and were given virtual autonomy by Director-General Peter Stuyvesant, along with the privilege of practicing the Lutheran faith.

The communal patterns displayed in New Netherland changed little during the early years of English rule. Rural villagers continued to farm in accustomed ways, while the inhabitants of the renamed towns of New York City and Albany still marched to the beat of the marketplace. English immigration began to alter the cultural makeup of several communities, but appreciable change in ethnic ratios was decades away.

BIBLIOGRAPHY

Bielinski, Stefan. "The People of Colonial Albany, 1650–1800: The Profile of a Community." In *Authority and Resistance in Early New York,* edited by William Pencak and Conrad Edick Wright. New York, 1988.

Merwick, Donna. *Possessing Albany, 1630–1710: The Dutch and English Experiences.* Cambridge, England, 1990.

Weslager, G. A. *The Swedes and Dutch at New Castle.* New York, 1987.

Wright, Langdon G. "In Search of Peace and Harmony: New York Communities in the Seventeenth Century." *New York History* 61, no. 1 (1980):5–21.

———. "Local Government and Central Authority in New Netherland." *New-York Historical Society Quarterly* 57, no. 1 (1973):7–29.

Joyce D. Goodfriend

SEE ALSO **Interracial Communities.**

THE FRENCH COLONY

THE PATTERN OF COMMUNITY in France's North American colonies was shaped by the conjuncture of North American geography, French institutions, and the benevolent intervention of the French Crown. Any consideration of the pattern of community in the French settlements, however, must begin with the role played by the Indians of the eastern part of the continent. Their cooperation was the indispensable condition without which the communities themselves could not have developed.

THE SAINT LAWRENCE VALLEY

When Samuel de Champlain established the trading post at Quebec in 1608, he effectively excluded other European nations from laying claim to the Saint Lawrence Valley. Indian nations would not have recognized this claim, but fortunately for the French, the valley was deserted. What happened to the Iroquoians whom Jacques Cartier encountered at Stadacona (Que-

bec City) and Hochelaga (Montreal) remains one of the great mysteries of Canadian history. Archaeological evidence suggests that the men were killed and the women and children adopted by the Huron nation to the west. Disease, introduced by Cartier's men, may also have contributed to their disappearance. In any case, the Saint Lawrence Valley was unpopulated at the time French settlement began and the Algonquian nations to the north welcomed the French presence as a means of protection against the Iroquois confederacy south of the lower Great Lakes.

French settlement in the Saint Lawrence Valley is notable for the lack of conflict over land that marked settlement in New England. France soon established alliances with several Algonquian nations in the north as well as with the Huron and Ottawa nations in the west. This brought them into conflict with the Iroquois, but this threat was overcome by the arrival of the Carignan-Salières regiment in 1665. When hostilities broke out again in 1683, troops of the Ministry of the Marine—the French government department responsible for colonies—and the colonial militia were called upon to deal with the threat. Together with the cooperation of their Indian allies, the Iroquois threat was alleviated and the Canadian settlers were not forced from their land.

With the Saint Lawrence secured, the Canadians were able to settle in riparian communities known as ranges, along the Saint Lawrence and Richelieu rivers. In 1665 at the Jesuit seigneury at Notre-Dame-des-Anges, just north of the town of Quebec, the Jesuits attempted to create a model compact village. Their hope was that the Canadians would settle in these villages, where they would be safer from the Iroquois threat, and where they could be more easily influenced and prevented from interfering with Jesuit missionary work in the *pays d'en haut* (upper country). This attempt was a spectacular failure. In 1691 the intendant Jean Bochart de Champigny called for the formation of compact villages, with a common, and with the services one would find in a village in France. This appeal fell on deaf ears too.

There is some question over the objectives of the intendants; there was a security concern, but the communities would have been easier to govern in small villages. This same question arises with regard to the restrictions placed on settlement to the west of Montreal. These restrictions were made in the name of security against the Iroquois threat, but there was also concern about the habitants gaining easier access to the Ottawa River route to the fur trading regions of the upper Great Lakes, and forsaking farming for the life of a *coureur de bois* (woods runner).

ACADIA

In Acadia (Nova Scotia) the French settlers arrived at a suitable partnership with the Micmac nation. The Micmac had little interest in the marshland along the banks of the Rivière Dauphin (the Annapolis River). The forty families who settled this area after 1640 were welcomed as trading partners by the Micmac, who were already a part of an extensive hunting and trading network. The Acadians were simply incorporated into this system, although admittedly French trade goods made a large impact on Micmac society. Like the Canadians in the Saint Lawrence Valley, the Acadians favored riverfront properties, but because of the marshy conditions, settlement took a markedly different pattern.

The Acadians built dykes of sod from the marshes and reinforced them with branches and logs. These dykes were wide enough to support roads, so transportation was developed away from the river. The small town of Port Royal (Annapolis Royal, Nova Scotia) had a garrison of 150 men by the early eighteenth century, as well as a few officials, merchants, and artisans, but the vast majority of Acadians lived on farms in the river valley. Their fertile fields were well-suited for legumes, but they also grew wheat and other cereals, and they raised all manner of livestock. They farmed mainly for subsistence—each farm had a kitchen garden—but they did a small but regular trade with New England, and Louisbourg, the French fort on the Île Royale (Cape Breton Island), as well as with the Micmac. One of the outstanding features of the Acadian community was its closeness. Many of the Acadians who immigrated and who constituted the nucleus of Acadian society were drawn from the small geographic area of Poitou.

A substantial number were from the same estate and some were already interrelated—hence the cohesiveness and homogeneity of Acadian society. The sense of community was further strengthened by a patriarchal organization and electoral mechanization for the selection of delegates for decision making. These institutions remained informal.

LOUISIANA

A similar lack of formal institutions was the salient feature of Louisiana's colonial development. Here the problem was compounded by the lack of a demographic balance that was so crucial in Acadia. Louisiana was of strategic value to the French, but unfortunately it was founded at a time when incessant warfare and poor harvests had drained France's imperial coffers. By the early eighteenth century there was also a decided lack of enthusiasm among France's merchant community. They wanted no part in colonial enterprise in general; a risky venture like Louisiana was to be avoided at all cost.

Louisiana's geography made it unattractive to merchants and settlers alike. Access to the Mississippi was difficult because of the shifting sand bars and the lack of a good natural harbor. Access to the Gulf itself was less than evident because of the strong British presence in the West Indies, and the danger of hurricanes. Finally there was a decided paucity of resources worth exploiting. Settlers found the hot, humid climate and the swampy terrain uncomfortable, unhealthy, and difficult to farm. The demographic imbalance—caused by garrisons of male soldiers, and a ban on marrying Indian women—was yet another barrier to the establishment of a rural community.

In spite of the economic and geographic difficulties, Louisiana's location was of vital strategic interest and settlement was attempted. Land was granted by the Crown, on riverfront lots, but not in seigneurial tenure as in Canada. When the entrepreneur Antoine Crozat relinquished his trade monopoly in 1717, the Crown renewed its efforts to populate the colony by granting control to a new proprietary regime—the Company of the West and its successor, the Company of the Indies. It was found that the crops that prospered in Louisiana—tobacco, cotton, sugar, indigo, and rice—could be grown profitably with slave labor. Black slaves were sent to the colony as a labor force. Swiss, German, Alsatian, and Italian settlers were sent as well, but many found the conditions intolerable. Many others encountered death as the climate, difficult passages, and hard work combined to exhaust them.

Relations with the Indian nations, especially with the Chicksaw, were abysmal. Settlers had tried to force them to work on the plantations until they discovered that the Indians could escape too easily. The Church too was in a state of disorder with clergymen debating the morality of sanctioning marriages between French men and Indian women against the specific ban by the authorities. Community did not really develop in Louisiana until the late colonial period when the Acadians, after their expulsion in 1755, made their way in large numbers to the mouth of the Mississippi. There they found the underdeveloped, but recognizable vestiges of familiar institutions, and they were able to help in the development of a distinct and vibrant community.

THE SEIGNEURIAL SYSTEM

The most fundamental of the colonial institutions was the seigneurial system, under which territory was governed by a feudal lord and granted according to a code of specified rights and obligations. In the Saint Lawrence Valley, the most developed and most important of France's North American colonies, the system was introduced in 1623 when Louis Hébert was granted a small fief on the outskirts of the trading post at Quebec by the viceroy of New France, Henri, duc de Montmorency. Four years later Cardinal Richelieu granted eastern North America to the Compagnie des Cent-Associés (Company of One Hundred Associates) and obliged them to "subenfeudate," or to grant seigneuries themselves. The Custom of Paris—the legal code introduced in New France in 1640—said little on the subject of land tenure, so various interpretations were put forward.

There is some disagreement on the importance of the seigneurial system. While the region

remained unpopulated, or underpopulated, seigneurs often neglected both their rights and their obligations. Later, however, toward the middle of the eighteenth century, and certainly after the British Conquest, the system took on a renewed importance as rising populations and declining business opportunities made the exploitation of the system more profitable for the seigneurial class. No land was granted in seigneurial tenure after 1763, but the existing seigneuries remained until 1854 when seigneurial tenure was expunged. For the pattern of community in the Saint Lawrence Valley, the seigneurial system is most significant for the manner in which the land was granted.

The company, or later the Crown, granted each seigneury on the Saint Lawrence, or on one of its tributaries. Similarly, the seigneurs granted *rotures* (lots) to the habitants on the rivers as well. Seigneuries were surveyed by the *rhumb de vent*, a perpendicular line drawn back from the bank of the river. This method proved to be inexpensive and efficient. The long narrow shape of the *rotures* was due to the fact that each habitant demanded river frontage. There were several important reasons for this: each family had access to the main artery of transportation; each family lived on its own farm, but relatively close to its neighbors; the lots were easily surveyed with the *rhumb de vent*; each family had access to water and to fishing; and each strip of land was made up of different soil types that allowed for different types of activities. As riverfront lots became scarce, second and third ranges were granted along the roads that ran roughly parallel to the rivers.

CÔTES

As one traveled along the Saint Lawrence River, the farms on either shore gave the impression of one long straggling village from Quebec to Montreal. In reality, there were many different communities, and the habitants identified themselves as belonging to one or another of these "villages," called *côtes*. The *côte* did not correspond with the seigneurial boundaries, but rather to a group of farms within certain natural boundaries, a tributary, for example, or a barren promontory. Admittedly, there were some compact villages, of the type that the authorities had tried to promote. At the time of the British Conquest there were six fairly large compact villages and four hamlets, but they were of little significance to the overall pattern of community.

There were a variety of reasons why the Canadians preferred the *côte* to the type of village found in France. In the first place the rivers were of vital importance in the thriving economy of expedience that was such a vital part of life in the French colonies. The Saint Lawrence led to the heart of the continent and to the fur trading regions of the Great Lakes. Young men could realize substantial profits by taking their canoes to the *pays d'en haut* and trading for furs. These *coureurs de bois* would have been prevented from carrying out this illegal activity had they been settled in compact, easily policed villages. The rivers also provided important fishing and hunting opportunities. Another facet of this economy was the different areas of artisanal specialization within the *côte*. People developed sidelines to farming, such as blacksmithing, carpentry, masonry, and other trades. The members of a community knew which of their neighbors to turn to for certain needs. For goods not provided within the *côtes,* the habitants made a trip to one of the towns, a welcome diversion from everyday life. Succinctly put, these communities developed independent economies within the larger economy that was based on farming and the seigneurial system. In villages this spirit of independence would have been stifled.

THE PARISH

The parish, not the seigneury, was the center of administration within the rural communities. With so few villages, there were also no village officials of which to speak. Whereas in France each village had a common, in New France there were no common woodlots and no officials appointed to manage the common pastures. Each *roture* provided for a family's needs. Furthermore there were no taxes. A land tax, the *taille,* was proposed in 1704, but the governor and the intendant convinced the metropolitan government not to implement it. With no taxes there was no need to elect village officials to act as collectors or assessors. Communities did not come intact

from France, as was the case with the group migrations to New England. The one institution, therefore, that served as the nodal point in the shared experience of the entire community was the Church. The parish became the logical center of the community's official and social life.

The social role of the Church was as important as its official role. The church building was a community gathering place where people met, conducted small transactions, and made announcements. Church was also the place where social status, so significant in a paternalistic and hierarchical society, was made manifest. The seigneur was always entitled to the most prominent pew, nearest the altar and on the right hand side. He was also the first to be sprinkled with holy water and the first to receive the Sacrament. The rest of the pews were allotted upon purchase according to one's social status and were entailed, although this created, at times, bones of contention. Religious processions also illustrated the order of society. The curé (parish priest) always led, followed by the other clergy, then by the seigneur, the captain of the militia, judges, the church wardens, and the rest of the faithful.

Curés

A parish could only be considered complete with the arrival of the resident curé. Many parishes were established as incitements to settlement. In 1685, forty parishes were created, and in 1721 another eighty-two. Some of these were in settled areas. The parish did not correspond with the seigneury. In some cases the parish embraced several seigneuries; in others one seigneury contained two or more parishes. Some of the parishes were served by itinerant priests, and they did not have the same status as a community as did those with their own curé.

The curé was an important member of the community. He was responsible for the registration of births, marriages, and deaths. He acted as a consultant for all manner of transactions, as a trustee for testaments, and as an advisor for legal problems. In his official capacity he presided over the board of wardens, a committee of parishioners charged with the maintenance of the fabric, and of the school if one existed. The curé was also an important contact with the world beyond the parish. Official edicts and announcements were read and posted at the church. Attendance at mass was obligatory—at least in theory—and it was found that this was the most efficient medium of communication. In the other direction, curés were careful to report the transgressions of their parishioners to their superiors in Quebec.

CAPTAINS OF MILITIA

If any member of the community could claim leadership status, it was the captain of militia. This office was created after Louis XIV ordered the governor general to form Canadian men, from the ages of sixteen to sixty, into militia units. A company was formed in every parish under the command of a captain of militia. Although this action was taken because of the very important military function of France's North American colonies, it soon became evident that the captain of militia also acted as a local agent for the intendant. In addition to their military duties—mustering the men, checking their equipment, and training them as a fighting force—the captains of militia were responsible for the maintenance of law and order within their communities. Like the curés, they reported untoward incidents to their superior, in this case, the intendant. They were also responsible for arresting criminals.

In the style of Louis XIV, captains of militia were selected from the habitant class. Their office entitled them to a high status within the community. They were recognized as the voice of authority and, like the curés, as a contact with the outside world. When distinguished visitors stayed in the parish, they were the guests of the captain of militia. That a military captain commanded such respect shows how important the military was in New France. This military organization of the local communities is one of the features of Canadian society that bears underlining.

TOWNS

While the majority of Canadians lived in rural communities, there were also three towns: Quebec, Trois-Rivières, and Montreal. The other centers in the French colonies—Louisbourg, Biloxi, New Orleans, and Port Royal—were little more than military garrisons or trading posts throughout most of the colonial period. The three towns in the Saint Lawrence Valley provided services that were not available in the *côtes*. There were hospitals, the *Hôtels Dieu*, established in Quebec in 1639, in Montreal in 1642, and in Trois-Rivières in 1702. There were also almshouses, the *Hôpitaux Généraux*, and offices of the poor or *bureaux des pauvres*. In each of the three towns there was a court of first instance, the *Prévôté*. These were important as many seigneurs abdicated the expensive responsibility of dispensing justice.

Quebec
In general, all three towns were prosperous and impressive in their architecture, but none more so than Quebec, the capital and administrative center. Situated on the promontory overlooking the Saint Lawrence, the Upper Town dominated the surroundings. The governor-general's residence—the Château Saint-Louis—and the cathedral were most prominent, but there was also a seminary, a Jesuit college, the *Hôtel Dieu*, an Ursuline convent, the bishop's palace, and a Recollet church. In Lower Town the intendant's palace, which housed the Quebec *Prévôté*, the Superior Council, and the gaol, was also evidence of the governing class that dominated the local society. Quebec was also a seaport with docks, merchant warehouses, and taverns dominating Lower Town. This added to the imperial quality of Quebec society; the community of officials and merchants spent a good deal of time in France.

Montreal
While the people of Quebec looked across the Atlantic, Montreal's society looked to the heart of the continent. Montreal was originally founded as a mission settlement by Paul de Chomedy, sieur de Maisonneuve, but soon became the commercial heart of the fur trade. Montreal was well-situated to exploit the Ottawa River trade that led to the upper Great Lakes. It was also an important strategic outpost. Soldiers were garrisoned at Montreal so they could be quickly dispatched to deal with the English, the Iroquois,

or other enemies of France's allies, the Huron and the Ottawa. The town was walled and built of impressive stone buildings. Montreal, like the two other towns and the rows of habitant farms, impressed the visitor with its wealth and order. An officer in Amherst's army described Montreal and its citizens shortly after the capitulation of the French forces to the British on 8 September 1760. He wrote:

On 14 September I had an opportunity of viewing the interior parts of Montreal; and, for delightfulness of situation, I think I never saw any town to equal it . . . The inhabitants are gay and sprightly, much more attached to dress and finery than those of Quebec, between whom there seems to be an emulation in this respect; and, from the number of silk robes, laced coats and powdered heads of both sexes, and almost all ages, that are perambylating the streets from morning to night, a stranger would be induced to believe Montreal is intirely inhabited by people of independent and plentiful fortunes. (Quoted in John Knox, *The Siege of Quebec*. Mississauga, Ontario, 1980, pp. 300–302)

Trois-Rivières

Trois-Rivières was founded where the Saint Maurice River flows into the Saint Lawrence, roughly halfway between Quebec and Montreal. In the early days the town was a fur trade post for the northern fur trade with the Algonquian. Trois-Rivières then developed into a regional center of administration with a lieutenant governor and a royal court, and a center of religious life with a Récollet church and an Ursuline convent. In 1730 iron forges were established on the Saint Maurice River and, after some difficulties, this industry became profitable with Crown assistance. Canoe-making was the other important economic activity.

In spite of their small numbers, the people of French North America—particularly those living in the Saint Lawrence Valley—had a sophisticated and well-developed sense of community. Their ability to coexist with their Indian neighbors and their adaptation of ancestral institutions enabled them to overcome many of the difficulties posed by the new environment. While some attempts to colonize met with scant success, the above observation is indicative of their accomplishment.

BIBLIOGRAPHY

Adair, E. R. "The French Canadian Seigneury." *Canadian Historical Review* 35, no. 3 (1954):187–207.
Eccles, W. J. *Essays on New France*. Toronto, Ontario, 1987. In particular see the following essays: "The Role of the Church in New France," "Social Welfare Measures and Policies in New France," as well as "The Social, Economic, and Political Significance of the Military Establishment in New France."
———. *France in America*. New York, 1972; rev. ed. Markham, Ontario, and East Lansing, Mich., 1990.
Harris, Richard Colebrook. *The Seigneurial System in Early Canada*. Kingston and Montreal, 1984.
———, and Geoffrey Matthews, editor and cartographer. *Historical Atlas of Canada*. Vol. 1. Toronto, Ontario, 1987.

William J. Newbigging

SEE ALSO **Interracial Communities.**

THE SPANISH BORDERLANDS

THE COMPLEX PATTERN of community in the Spanish Borderlands centered on the defensive nature of settlements. In order to block foreign intrusion and bring the indigenous population into the Spanish sphere, three frontier institutions—mission, *presidio*, and pueblo—were utilized. Of these three the pueblo, or town, with its pattern of community will be studied here, with the *presidio* playing a secondary role.

The defensive and isolated nature of the Spanish Borderland frontier, along with restrictive Spanish immigration policy, kept the colonial population from expanding. The frontier territories included not only Spaniards (and to a lesser degree other Europeans) but also mestizos, Africans and mulattoes, and Native Americans. As a result the pattern of community throughout the borderlands is unique in the colonial story.

FLORIDA AND ALABAMA

The colonial history of Spanish Florida is separated into two periods, which were based on defense: 1565–1763 and 1783–1821. The Florida story can be divided between East Florida (Saint Augustine) and West Florida (Pensacola). East Florida was occupied in 1565 by Pedro Menéndez de Avilés both to dislodge the French from Fort Caroline (Jacksonville) and to end the threat to the treasure fleets sailing for Spain. In order to reach his objectives, he brought with him five hundred soldiers, two hundred sailors, and one hundred civilians. On 8 September 1565 Menéndez founded Saint Augustine, a garrison community. Soon afterward he founded a number of *presidios* and settlements in Florida as well as neighboring Georgia and South Carolina. Although these settlements would become the basis for future missions, they were not successful civilian settlements.

Throughout its history Saint Augustine remained a garrison town that relied on government supplies in order to survive. The garrison at Saint Augustine was never completely composed of Spanish-born men because Spain could not fully compensate for normal attrition of the original force. As a result Creoles and recruits from New Spain and Cuba provided the necessary manpower. Later the viceroy sent men convicted of lesser crimes to Florida. During the period from 1658 to 1756, *peninsulares* accounted for 38.3 percent of the population and Spanish Americans comprised 15.8 percent, the bulk of the latter coming from Mexico and Cuba.

Another population source was fugitive slaves from the Carolinas and later Georgia. The first blacks began to enter Florida in 1688 and at first were maintained as slaves. By 1693 the Crown decreed that fugitive slaves who embraced Catholicism would be freed. Governor Manuel de Montiano created between 1738 and 1739 the community of García Real Santa Teresa de Mose, about two miles (3 kilometers) north of Saint Augustine, for them. By 1764 Africans, both freemen and slaves, amounted to 14 percent of the population, making it the largest concentration of blacks in the Spanish Borderlands.

Displaced Indians made an important addition to the population, especially after the English launched raids from Carolina in 1702–1704. Acting as allies, the Indians provided a military buffer against the English, as well as a pool of laborers and farmers. With few Spanish women in the community it was only natural that through marriage or concubinage of Indian women a mestizo population developed.

By the Treaty of Paris, signed on 10 February 1763, Britain received Florida and the local inhabitants, numbering around 3,100 people. Although many left for Cuba, there was an influx of people during the British occupation (1763–1783). A group of Minorcans, Italians, and Greeks had been induced to settle in New Smyrna, south of Saint Augustine, to develop a plantation for Andrew Turnbull. When this experiment failed in 1777, the settlers fled to Saint Augustine. On the eve of the British departure in 1784, there were some 1,992 people in East Florida, including 445 Minorcans.

The cosmopolitan nature of the community continued during the second Spanish period. In 1786 the resident population was 943 (50 percent Minorcans, 31 percent slaves, 9 percent white foreigners, 5 percent Floridians, 5 percent Spanish) with an additional 300 persons classified as "suburban" and 450 troops stationed in the garrison.

The final census taken for East Florida was dated 1815 and included both Saint Augustine and surrounding areas. Within the four wards of the city there were 1,383 persons, of whom 840 were white (61 percent). The total population had risen to 3,729 persons, making Saint Augustine part of a populated area extending from the Saint Mary's River south. It is obvious that the population outside of Saint Augustine was growing at a faster rate than that inside the walls of the city.

At Pensacola the situation was similar to that of Saint Augustine, except for a smaller population. Since its military origins in 1698 Pensacola had maintained close ties with the French at Biloxi and Mobile, which were founded soon after 1698. The Indian pueblos of Escambe and Punta Rosa were utilized as buffers against other Indians. During the years three haciendas developed, but all of them were destroyed in a 1761 Indian uprising. When the Spanish evacuated the garrison in 1763, some eight hundred men left, along with one hundred Christian Indians and some one hundred women. During the second period of Spanish occupation (1783–1821) the population remained below one thousand and was composed primarily of *isleños* and French Creoles, Africans, British, and as the eighteenth century progressed, Americans. The latter were attracted to the Escambia River area because of the arable land; although this was in violation of official policy, the Spanish had little choice but to allow them to remain. At the time of the last census in 1820, there were 713 inhabitants (63 percent white and 37 percent black) living in Pensacola. Along the Escambia River there were 380 white and 73 black Americans furnishing the community with food.

Spain obtained Spanish Alabama with the capture of Fort Charlotte at Mobile in 1780 and administratively made it part of Spanish West Florida, which included Dauphin Island, Biloxi, Pascagoula, Bay Saint Louis, and the offshore islands. The government modified traditional policy by extending religious freedom and providing land grants to Americans in return for an oath of loyalty. As a result many Loyalists from the Atlantic colonies settled along the Tombigbee and Tensaw rivers in southern Alabama. In order to defend the area against Indian raids, Spain created Fort San Estebán de Tombecbé (1789) and Fort Confederación (1794). By 1796 there were 287 people living around Fort San Estebán; they engaged in cattle ranching, and nearly 90 percent were from the United States.

The polyglot, heterogeneous population was composed of Carolinians, French, Spaniards, British subjects, Latin Americans, and blacks from Guadeloupe. In 1785 the population stood at 1,149, and in 1805 it had risen to 1,535. The church records show an unusually high incidence of intermarriage involving Africans, European Americans, and mulatto settlers at Mobile. Between 1785 and 1805 the average white population was 40 percent, of free blacks 8 percent, and of slaves, 52 percent.

NEW MEXICO

New Mexico was settled in 1598 by a group led by Juan de Oñate as a defensive measure against alleged English encroachments in California and to convert the Pueblos. The first soldier-settlers from Zacatecas numbered 129, some with their families. Between the first settlement and 1680,

the colony consisted of missionary establishments and one formal pueblo at Santa Fe founded in the spring of 1610. Although Spaniards tended to be town dwellers, in seventeenth-century New Mexico a different pattern of community developed due to the limited agricultural lands. Some were given land grants and created haciendas while others located themselves along the Rio Grande and its tributaries. They lived on their land where they could watch over their farms and be close to the Pueblo Indian labor force, especially prior to 1680. As early as 1630 there were about 1,050 Spaniards, mestizos, and converted Indians living in Santa Fe and vicinity and 2,900 living throughout the province. The defenseless nature of these communities was seen in the Pueblo Revolt of 1680 when 21 missionaries and 380 settlers were killed; the remaining 2,200 people fled to El Paso del Norte.

At El Paso they formed the nucleus of European-Indian settlements around the mission of Nuestra Señora de Guadalupe, founded in 1659. A fifty-man *presidio* was established in 1683 for the eventual reconquest of the upper Rio Grande valley. Unfortunately, Indian unrest and shortages drove people away, so that in 1684 there were only 1,030 people living in the district. A permanent community had been established, however, that would grow with the addition of people from Mexico, *genízaros* (Plains Indians ransomed by the Spanish and integrated into society), and other Indians.

The revolt and subsequent reconquest by Diego de Vargas in 1693 saw some changes in the pattern of community. Following urban tradition Spanish officials created a number of *villas*: Santa Fe (1609), El Paso del Norte (1680), Santa Cruz de la Cañada (1695), and Albuquerque (1706). Despite the ordinances, the populations of these *villas* remained under twenty-five hundred and they were poorly organized as the settlers continued to live on their farmsteads along the watercourses.

The declining Indian labor force and the introduction of a growing number of Spanish settlers created the *rancho* (a loose agglomeration of small farmsteads) in place of the hacienda. Beginning in 1700 and lasting through the Spanish era the *rancho* was the typical unit of colonization in New Mexico. They were generally referred to as *poblaciones,* or if the population consolidated for mutual defense, as *plazas*. Even when dispersed over several leagues the settlers constructed a church to serve their needs. In the late eighteenth century when there was a lack of priests, laymen created the brotherhood of the penitentes, who oversaw the spiritual needs of the communities.

Besides the Spanish settlements there were a variety of Indian communities. The oldest were the fortified towns of the Pueblos located in the Rio Grande valley. The *genízaros* or ransomed captives from miscellaneous Plains tribes colonized in special villages (Cerro de Tomé, Abiquiú, San José, and San Miguel del Vado) at strategic locations on the frontier. Finally there were a number of unsuccessful attempts at creating *reducciones* or special communities for nomadic Indians.

New Mexico was reconquered in 1693 by Diego de Vargas; the new colonists numbered one hundred soldiers, some seventy families and eighteen friars. Santa Fe was reestablished as the capital, and in 1695 Santa Cruz de La Cañada was founded with forty-five families of *españoles mexicanos* from Santa Fe. At the same time additional settlers from Zacatecas and Sombrerete arrived in Santa Fe. In 1706 the *villa* of Albuquerque was founded, as were other small communities of Christianized Indians and *genízaros*.

Despite the inaccuracies of census reports, a general overview can be developed for the latter years of Spanish occupation. By 1805 the El Paso district boasted some 6,209 people. On 17 December 1817 there were 36,579 Europeans and Indians living throughout New Mexico. If one subtracts 8,788 Pueblo Indians of the Keres and Zunñi linguistic groups, there were 27,791 Spanish-speaking people.

New Mexico was the oldest and largest province in the Spanish Borderlands. The population had increased with the arrival of Spaniards and the incorporation of castes and Indians, and these mixtures were considered part of the "civilized people" on the frontier.

TEXAS

Texas was settled in response to the fear of French colonization along the Gulf Coast. Between 1690 and 1693 a combined military-clerical venture tried unsuccessfully to settle East Texas. The permanent settlements developed during 1716 to 1721 as the French renewed their efforts in Louisiana. In 1716 the expedition under Domingo Ramón and Louis St. Denis led a party of sixty-five settlers into East Texas, where they established a clutch of four missions and the small *presidio* of Dolores on the Neches River. Two years later Governor Martín de Alarcón founded San Antonio de Valero. In 1721 Joseph de Azlor, Marqués de San Miguel de Aguayo, further strengthened East Texas when he established a *presidio* at Los Adaes in modern Louisiana.

In the 1730s a formal civil settlement was established in Texas. On 9 March 1731, fifty-eight Canary Islanders (*isleños*) formed the nucleus of the *villa* of San Fernando de Béxar. This community, along with the *presidio* and five missions, constituted the community of San Antonio. Other presidial communities existed in Los Adaes and to the south in La Bahía.

The settlers of East Texas consisted of some thirty Spanish families living on scattered ranches around Los Adaes in 1767. The latter community comprised some five hundred people—Spanish, French, Indian, African, and castes. When the government attempted to remove them to San Antonio in 1773, they reluctantly complied and the following year were allowed to return under the leadership of Antonio Gil Ybarbo, a local rancher. Although they tried to establish a community, Nuestra Señora del Pilar de Bucareli on the Trinity River, their efforts were ended by Comanche raids. As a result, in 1779 they founded Nacogdoches, the second civil settlement in Texas.

The population of Texas, never large, was concentrated at San Antonio, La Bahía, and Nacogdoches. In 1720 there were fewer than two hundred people in the province. De Aguayo infused the province with several hundred more, and fifty-eight Canary Islanders were added in 1731. By 1777 the total population of Texas was 3,103 of which 46.81 percent was Spanish, 29.52 percent was Indian, 2.73 percent was mestizo, 20.60 percent was "other colored groups," and 0.72 percent was African. For a variety of reasons the population stagnated. In 1790 there were 3,169 people in the province, whereas in New Orleans in 1788 there were 5,338 residents, approximately 66 percent more than in Texas.

The population of Texas came from various sources. The first Spaniards and mestizos came from nearby Mexican provinces; they were followed by the Canary Islanders. Later, whites and Indians arrived from the United States, and in the early nineteenth century there were a number of Frenchmen and Louisianans living in San Antonio and La Bahía. As in New Mexico, class differences were more theoretical than real. The only class rivalry developed among the Canary Islanders, who had an exaggerated idea of their own importance.

ARIZONA

In the late seventeenth century Arizona was an extension of the Sonoran Jesuit missionary frontier. The Jesuit priest Eusebio Kino visited Indian villages in southern Arizona in the 1690s. In 1700 he established the mission of San Xavier del Bac near modern Tucson, followed by the missions of Guebavi and Tumacácori. Through the first half of the eighteenth century stagnation and decline set in, aggravated by Apache raids and Indian uprisings.

In 1752 the *presidio* of San Ignacio del Tubac was founded in the upper Santa Cruz valley. Late in 1776 this garrison was moved to the new *presidio* of San Agustín del Tucson. This location was selected because of its proximity to food-producing Pima villages. This *presidio* protected the frontier from Pima and Apache raids and, theoretically, from Russian advances. Raids continued, as did Spanish campaigns against the Apache. The presidial troops consisted of mestizos, detribalized Indians, veteran soldiers, and noncommissioned and commissioned officers along with their families. Spaniards were in the minority among the mestizos and mulattoes in the garrison. There were also Opata Indian scouts with Spanish names.

The garrison facilitated cultural contact between the Indian and Hispanic populations. In 1793 a successful policy was established to settle the Apache at Tucson. A law of settlement in 1791 encouraged Hispanic families to people the frontier, and it was hoped that Tucson would develop as a *presidio*-related pueblo. Small civilian communities developed at Tucson and Tubac with many families living outside the walls. Social leadership was shared by the chaplain and the *presidio* commander, and Tucson became a primary cultural exchange arena for the Spanish and the Indians. The isolated and hostile environment of the Santa Cruz valley fostered interfamilial and interethnic cooperation.

By 1804 there were thirty-seven Spanish settlers and more than two hundred Indians living in the vicinity of Tucson. Cattle ranching, cotton cultivation, textile manufacturing, and mining were carried out both at Tucson and at Tubac to the south, where by 1816 there were four hundred people in a racially mixed settlement. This frontier did not fully develop, owing to persistent Apache raids well into the nineteenth century.

LOUISIANA AND THE MISSISSIPPI VALLEY

Spain obtained Louisiana by a treaty of cession on 3 November 1762, to compensate for the loss of Florida and to end friction between Louisiana and Texas. At the time of the cession, the main center of population was Louisiana; scattered communities along the Mississippi River terminated at Saint Louis. The majority of people lived between Pointe Coupée and New Orleans; other settlements in the lower Mississippi valley were at La Balize, Attakapa, Opelousas, Avoyelle, and Natchitoches. Upriver there were small settlements at Natchez and Arkansas Post. To the north in the interior there were small trading posts scattered about and the agricultural community of Saint Genevieve, south of Saint Louis.

When news of the transfer of the territory reached the colonists at New Orleans in September 1764, there was consternation and protest. At this time the population of the province was estimated to be between 8,250 and 11,500 inhabitants, over half of whom were of African origin. The whites were primarily of French or French Canadian origin, though there was a small number of other Europeans mixed among them. The French had introduced German, Swiss, Irish, and northern Italian soldier-settlers who remained in the colony. When the transfer became known, many French living in the Illinois country moved across the river, as did the French garrison at

Fort Chartres in 1765, when the British took possession.

Spain reluctantly took possession of the province in March 1766 when Gov. Antonio de Ulloa arrived. The province had a small agricultural base but was primarily concerned with fur trade and commerce. Spain saw to it that the economy of the province was allowed to remain intact and to follow French commercial policies. The defense of the province was foremost in the minds of officials because the English were now on the east bank of the Mississippi and aggressive traders were crossing into Louisiana to trade with the Indians. Forts were established along the river, as was a galley patrol. Both Frenchmen and Spaniards were utilized as administrators throughout the province.

During the Spanish occupation of Louisiana, which ended in 1800, there were a number of efforts to introduce non-Spanish settlers into the province. In 1765 the first Acadians were brought to Louisiana, and they settled to the west of New Orleans in the vicinity of modern Lafayette. In later years their numbers were increased by additional immigration. During the late 1770s, Governor Bernardo de Gálvez established a series of settlements in the lower Mississippi valley for Canary Islanders, Malagueños, and Loyalist refugees from the revolution. The most notable of the numerous Canary Islanders' settlements was located in Saint Bernard Parish, where their descendants still reside.

At various points along the Mississippi River, fear of an aggressive move by Americans into Louisiana caused Spanish officials to allow first Catholic Americans, and later Protestant Americans, to settle. Many French came from the Vincennes area; the Americans hailed from Kentucky, Tennessee, and North Carolina, and many were of German or German-Swiss extraction. They formed a significant portion of communities such as Cape Girardeau, Missouri. In a number of mixed communities like Natchez, Irish priests from the University of Salamanca were sent to minister to the inhabitants.

The less restrictive immigration policy caused a population increase in Upper Louisiana. In 1763 the population was just under 1,000; it increased to 2,703 (74 percent white, 2 percent free black, 24 percent slave) in 1791. On the eve of the Louisiana Purchase there were

10,350—more than half Americans—who lived in isolated and scattered settlements in the uplands just west of the Mississippi.

In Louisiana the population grew steadily over the years. In 1766 it stood at 12,927, and by 1788 there were 36,235 people in the province. In New Orleans—the political capital, economic center, and cultural and social heart of Spanish Louisiana—the population in 1788 was 5,338 and rose to approximately 12,000 by 1800. Upriver at Natchez there were some 1,619 settlers in 1784.

ALTA CALIFORNIA

Although Alta California was explored in the sixteenth century, it was one of the last borderland areas to be settled. In the mid eighteenth century, with the advance of the Russians into Alaska, there was fear in Spain of a foreign occupation of California. As a result, in 1769 there began a military-clerical venture into Alta California comprising over one hundred persons of Spanish blood and eighty-six Christianized Indians from Baja California. Through 1821 four basic types of settlements were established: the missions, *presidios*, pueblos, and *ranchos*.

The missions were established to assimilate the Indians into Spanish frontier society. The province was protected by four *presidios* located at San Diego (1769), Santa Barbara (1782), Monterey (1770), and San Francisco (1776). Although established as military posts, they soon became civilian population centers as well.

The first civilian colonists arrived in 1776, brought to the province by Capt. Fernando de Rivera y Moncada and Capt. Juan Bautista de Anza. The colonists had been recruited principally from Sinaloa and Sonora to provide a population base in Alta California that would provide food for the missions and *presidios*. Anza brought 250 settlers north from Tubac, Arizona, who formed the nucleus for future expansion.

The formal civilian towns were San Jose (1777), Los Angeles (1781), and Branciforte (Santa Cruz; 1797). The first two were created to support the missions and *presidios* with food and supplies, which were costly to import. On 29 November 1777 José Moraga led nine presidial soldiers from Monterey and San Francisco, along with five of Anza's colonists, and their families (sixty-six settlers) and founded San Jose. Before Los Angeles was founded, Governor Felipe de Neve developed specific guidelines for future settlements. Of the forty-six persons who founded Los Angeles on 4 September 1781, only two claimed Spanish blood; the rest were of African, Indian, or mulatto origin. After the establishment of these two towns, settlement was halted due to a 1781 Indian uprising that closed the land route through Yuma, Arizona.

The third civil community, Branciforte, was founded in 1797 for reasons different from those for San Jose and Los Angeles. Once again fear of foreign encroachment caused officials to recruit seventeen settlers from Alta California and Guadalajara who did not want to be there. Branciforte proved to be an unsuccessful enterprise. Besides these official communities, other less formal settlements arose as settlers congregated in the vicinity of missions and *presidios,* creating *ranchos.*

The population increased notably between 1769 and 1821, but it was never large. By 1779 there were 500 persons of Spanish or mixed blood; by 1810 this number had risen to 2,130, and in 1820 there were 3,270 people in the province, or one-tenth of the population of New Mexico at that time.

The residents of Alta California were survivors or descendants of the original settlers, military retirees, or immigrants recruited from Sonora or Sinaloa. The populations of San Jose and Los Angeles were augmented by numerous offspring. In addition, a number of convicts and orphans were shipped to Alta California at various times. The people were officially classified as Spaniards, Indians, mestizos, and slaves but in reality there was little differentiation among the various groups who were known as *gente decente* (decent people) in the civil communities. At times the upper-class residents of the *presidios* looked down on them.

PACIFIC NORTHWEST

In the late eighteenth century international commerce in the Pacific Northwest caused the Spanish to develop plans for settlements to secure their claims to this area. Schemes were made but never carried out to establish settlements at Bodega Bay, California, and at the mouth of the Columbia River. In the 1790s a military post, Santa Cruz de Nuca, was established at Nootka Sound, Vancouver Island, which was the northernmost extension of the borderlands. The small garrison was composed of Spanish and mestizo recruits, especially Catalonian volunteers. During its short existence (1788–1789, 1790–1795) it attracted some American and British seamen, ransomed Indians, and a few Chinese artisans.

In the spring of 1792 a small garrison occupied Neah Bay, Washington, and constructed the post of Núñez Gaona to protect the entrance to the Strait of Juan de Fuca. Although Viceroy Juan Vicente de Güemes Pacheco de Padilla, Conde de Revillagigedo, contemplated a permanent settlement populated by married soldiers, the project was abandoned by that September.

IMMIGRATION

Throughout its history in the borderlands, Spain was reluctant to admit foreign immigrants, though some did enter with or without official approval. Irish officers and recruits were approved foreigners; forced to leave Ireland, these émigrés settled in Spain and joined the armed services. In this capacity they arrived in the New World. Irish names surface often. Alejendro O'Reilly reestablished Spanish control over Louisiana. Hugo O'Conor was commander of the Los Adaes *presidio,* then interim governor of Texas (1768–1771), lieutenant colonel, and inspector of the northern *presidios.* After an Irish brigade took part in the capture of Pensacola in 1781, a number of officers served as governors of East Florida and West Florida until the transfer of the province to the United States in 1821. There were also Flemish administrators such as Alejandro Wauchope and Thomás de Winthuysen and engineers like Jaime Franck at Pensacola.

Besides the Irish, the Spanish utilized detribalized Indians to settle the frontier. The most notable were the Tlascalan Indians employed as scouts, settlers, troops, and teachers. In 1640 several families lived in the barrio of Analco across the river from Santa Fe. During the Pueblo Revolt of 1680 they fled and resettled in El Paso.

Later a few families returned to Santa Fe. Throughout borderland towns small numbers of Indian slaves became part of the communities. Many of them were freed and remained within the population. In the eighteenth century the Spanish ransomed Plains Indians whom they called *genízaros* and settled them in New Mexico, where their descendants remain.

Beginning in the late seventeenth century and continuing through 1767, foreign-born Jesuits were a common feature in remote and isolated frontier missions. A number of Croatian, German, and Italian Jesuits served in Baja California and in Sonora-Arizona.

BIBLIOGRAPHY

Corbett, Theodore G. "Population Structure in Hispanic St. Augustine, 1629–1763." *Florida Historical Quarterly* 54 (1976):263–284.

Crouch, Dora P., Daniel J. Garr, and Axel I. Mundigo. *Spanish City Planning in North America.* Cambridge, Mass., 1982.

Cruz, Gilberto R. *Let There Be Towns: Spanish Municipal Origins in the American Southwest, 1610–1810.* College Station, Tex., 1988.

Dobyns, Henry F. *Spanish Colonial Tucson: A Demographic History.* Tucson, Ariz., 1976.

Garr, Daniel J., ed. *Hispanic Urban Planning in North America.* New York, 1991.

Gutiérrez, Ramón A. *When Jesus Came, the Corn Mothers Went Away: Marriage, Sexuality, and Power in New Mexico, 1500–1846.* Stanford, Calif., 1991.

Jones, Oakah L., Jr. *Los Paisanos: Spanish Settlers on the Northern Frontier of New Spain.* Norman, Okla., 1979.

Landers, Jane. "Gracia Real de Santa Teresa de Mose: A Free Black Town in Colonial Florida." *American Historical Review* 95 (1990):9–30.

Leonard, Olen. *The Role of the Land Grant in the Social Organization and Social Processes of a Spanish American Village in New Mexico.* Albuquerque, N. Mex., 1970.

Magnaghi, Russell M. "Plains Indians in New Mexico: The Genízaro Experience." *Great Plains Quarterly* 10 (1990):86–95.

———. "The Role of Indian Slavery in Colonial St. Louis." *Missouri Historical Society Bulletin* 31 (1975):264–272.

Moorhead, Max L. *The Presidio: Bastion of the Spanish Borderlands.* Norman, Okla., 1975.

Poitrineau, Abel. "Demography and the Political Destiny of Florida During the Second Spanish Period." *Florida Historical Quarterly* 66 (1987–1988):420–443.

Rock, Rosalind Z. " 'Pido y Suplico': Women and the Law in Spanish New Mexico, 1697–1763." *New Mexico Historical Review* 65 (1990):145–159.

Scholes, France V. "Civil Government and Society in New Mexico in the Seventeenth Century." *New Mexico Historical Review* 10 (1935):71–111.

Tjarks, Alicia V. "Comparative Demographic Analysis of Texas, 1777–1793." *Southwestern Historical Quarterly* 77 (1973–1974):291–338.

Viles, Jonas. "Population and Extent of Settlement in Missouri Before 1804." *Missouri Historical Review* 5 (1911):189–213.

Webre, Stephen. "The Problems of Indian Slavery in Spanish Louisiana, 1769–1803." *Louisiana History* 25 (1984):117–135.

Wood, Minter. "Life in New Orleans in the Spanish Period." *Louisiana Historical Quarterly* 22 (1939):642–709.

Russell Mario Magnaghi

SEE ALSO **Interracial Communities.**

RURAL LIFE

THE BRITISH COLONIES

FROM MAINE TO GEORGIA, the British North American colonies remained overwhelmingly rural (thinly populated places without town centers) and agrarian (predominantly agricultural) throughout the colonial era. As late as 1800, more than nine of every ten white and black inhabitants of the new United States, nearly all of them farmers or farm laborers, lived in the country. Carpenters, coopers, blacksmiths, and millers performed essential tasks in the farm economy, but they often owned land and worked as farmers as well as artisans. Typical colonists, whether masters or slaves, lived on isolated farms scattered through the countryside, not in compact villages.

This isolation constrained the social and cultural life of farm families. Farmers and farm wives relied mostly on their families, their neighbors, and kindred who lived nearby for companionship and help in time of need. Other forms of community life were intermittent at best— weekly or monthly attendance at church services, quarterly journeys to town meetings or the county court, occasional visits to stores or taverns. Toward the end of the colonial era, small villages became more common, but these places often contained only a shop or two, a gristmill, a tavern, and a church or county court. Only a minority of the rural population enjoyed even these op-portunities. White women rarely ventured out to village, tavern, or store; white children attended schools irregularly; slaves occasionally visited family or friends on nearby plantations but otherwise had to stay at their quarters.

Such open-country settlement was not inevitable. Colonists had lived in or around compact villages and Indian settlements, very different landscapes indeed. Many had emigrated from the compact villages and open fields still found in much of England; they had worked as artisans in their village shops or traveled daily from their village house to farm their scattered strips of land. Some New Englanders had initially expected to re-create open-field villages, but they soon abandoned the idea. Others had lived in towns or had worked in London before they emigrated. British travelers unfailingly argued that this absence of villages and towns proved the colonies lacked civilization. Indians provided another potential model. Immigrants and their descendants knew about (and sometimes saw) the temporary villages of Native Americans, who set up encampments every season in different places to take advantage of good crop land or rich hunting grounds.

FORMATION OF RURAL HOUSEHOLDS AND COMMUNITIES

How did this landscape, so different from much of England and preconquest America, develop?

The economic underpinnings of the British colonies provide a partial explanation. Colonization was financed by merchant capitalists who pursued profits by importing exotic New World crops, but the first European immigrants to the English North American colonies came, in part, to make independent households, thereby escaping the debased wage labor spread by the development of capitalism in England. Everywhere in the British colonies, families structured their daily activities and community life around the households, where they cultivated crops, made tools, and manufactured clothing, and the marketplaces where they exchanged goods and labor. Household members pooled the income they received from farm and craft activities, thereby ensuring the perpetuation of the household as an economic and social unit. The relationship of the market to the household encompassed the farm (and the division of farm labor between husbands and wives) and the rural community, the local marketplace and the world economy, and linked the daily work of farm families at home and in the community to broader economic exchanges, local, regional, and international.

The world market played a large role in agrarian development of the British colonies. Every farm family in colonial British America had to sell surpluses to ensure the perpetuation of its household. The poorest farmers traded at local markets, and some of the goods they sold wound up in the West Indies or Europe. Farmers who produced small surpluses required credit to buy and cultivate the land that was the basis of their precarious autonomy. Southern tobacco and rice planters were so tied to commodity markets that their year-to-year survival depended upon decent prices for their staples. When English merchants (in whose hands credit originated) called in loans to colonial merchants in times of world recession—as in the late seventeenth century—local farmers could not find capital to expand and had to make do with small plots or even suffer loss of their land. When times improved, farmers bought more land or slaves, increased their consumption of manufactured goods, or moved to frontiers.

Farmers tried to structure the market to meet the needs of their households, the fundamental productive units in colonial agriculture. Not only did farm families produce nearly all the crops sold at market, but household labor provided most of the work necessary to grow crops. Parents and children worked the farm, aided on occasion by a servant, hired hand, harvest laborer, or slave. Women and men worked in households to support their families, dividing tasks in ways compatible with their perceived roles in life. Men cleared land and cultivated the grain, tobacco, cotton, or rice sold in the market; they were joined by their wives and daughters at harvest time. Women cultivated gardens, milked cows, baked bread, plucked chickens, cooked meat, and made clothes. Southern slaves, who made most of the rice and tobacco that planters exported, were subordinate members of the households of their masters, unable to make independent decisions about work and production. Every decision farmers or planters made about farm labor was aimed at becoming self-sufficient, sustaining farm production, and saving money to set their children up on farms of their own.

The environment that immigrants and later settlers found constrained the social activities of farmers in the British colonies. Woods so thick that neighbor could not see neighbor permeated the seventeenth-century landscape, except in the meadows that Indians had been forced to abandon. Farmers first occupied these meadows but soon had to clear farms from the heavily forested lands they considered to be "wilderness." Early colonists traveled on Indian paths or abandoned the land for canoe or boat travel on rivers or streams. To facilitate both marketing of produce and community life, colonists engaged in an orgy of road building, stream clearing, and ferry making that connected every farm to marketplace, tavern, store, and church within several decades of initial conquest of Indian lands. As population grew throughout the seventeenth century, farmers filled in their coastal settlements, and by the end of the century woodlands had disappeared from the oldest and most populous settlements.

Native Americans impinged upon the farms and communities of white settlers as much as the alien environment they found. Indian population in *settled* parts of New England and the Chesapeake colonies exceeded that of whites until the mid seventeenth century, and enough Indians remained (despite fierce epidemics and warfare) until the 1670s to pose an ever-present military threat to settlers. This Indian threat kept colonists from enjoying the seeming abundance of land that surrounded them, creating intensive land *scarcity*. Colonial governments responded to Indian power by encouraging relatively compact settlement by farmers intent upon living on their own farms. Even though colonists refused to congregate in villages, they ventured inland only a few miles, creating farms within easy travel distance of one another. Seventeenth-century colonies were therefore characterized by scattered, but connected, settlements along coasts and rivers. Such prudence helped guarantee safety. In the 1622 Indian war in Virginia, Indians massacred planter families in outlying settlements on the upper James River, but killed far fewer whites in the more thickly settled places nearer the Chesapeake Bay. And in 1676 Metacom's (King Philip's) warriors chased hundreds of families from isolated and outlying settlements in central New England while leaving coastal settlements untouched.

Trade and social exchange on the "middle ground" between Native American and settler influenced British colonial social life as much as hostilities between the two groups. Indian women, who farmed while their husbands hunted, knew how to increase farm productivity in the face of constrained labor. They (and their husbands) burned foliage and underbrush and girded trees before planting corn and other crops in hills beneath the dead trees and tree stumps. To cultivate their growing crops, they used the simplest of hand tools. They continued to use the field until its soil was exhausted, and then moved onto fresh land. Colonists adopted this agricultural system—but put it to use for far different ends than had Native American women. Indians had a subsistence ethic: they planted and harvested just enough to feed themselves, leaving only very small surpluses for tribute or trade with other Indian communities. Colonists, in contrast, expected to exchange surpluses, sometimes of substantial size, with neighbors and at market and therefore cleared and exhausted much more land per person than did Native Americans. Rapid population growth, caused by continued immigration and substantial natural increase, put ever more pressure on Indian corn patches and hunting grounds and led to warfare and confiscation of Indian lands. Once

settlers gained control over the land, a new rural habitat, characterized by permanent structures, new meadows and open ranges, and depleted forests, gradually emerged.

These environmental and cultural imperatives structured forms of community life in rural areas. But in turn, communities—organized around neighborhoods, churches, courts, and other institutions—mediated between households and markets. Farm families depended on neighbors for economic survival. On frontiers, neighbor helped neighbor build houses, raise barns, and harvest crops. Such cooperation continued long after the frontier stage had passed. Neighboring farm men and women exchanged labor and surpluses, raised barns and made quilts together, and borrowed money from one another to finance their operations. To participate in such extensive exchanges, farmers had to accept communal norms concerning planting and harvest times, the division of labor between men and women, and farm management. Informal community life—Sunday church services, market days, court days—cut into rural isolation and sustained communal norms about farming. Farm families gathered at church to pray, to take communion, and to listen to sermons (the most common entertainment of the colonial era), but they also met neighbors, settled (or started) disputes, arranged visiting and dinners, and courted. Creditors and buyers from distant places attended colonial market and court days, creating community networks of great importance in a time when the state played a weak role in the relation between markets and household. The state only regulated prices of labor and some commodities and built crude roads but otherwise did little to encourage economic growth.

The differences between farm communities in the British colonies were as great as the similarities. Regional differences in community organization in New England, Pennsylvania, the Chesapeake colonies, the Carolinas, and the backcountry—the Piedmont and mountain frontier that stretched from Pennsylvania to Georgia—can be explained by variations in the social and geographical origins of immigrants, settlement patterns, the time of settlement, crop regime, and religion. For example, immigrants from different parts of Britain attempted to adapt varying forms of agriculture (communal open fields versus the capitalist model of enclosed farms) and religion (Calvinist versus Anglican) in the new colonies. Neighborliness was far more important in frontier areas, where few other social or communal institutions had developed, than in places long settled. And southern colonists successfully cultivated tobacco or rice, but colonists farther north could only export small surpluses of grain. Such differences were particularly great in the seventeenth century. The contrast between Calvinist semisubsistence farmers in early New England and unreligious (or barely Anglican) Virginian tobacco growers could not have been greater.

Variations remained through the eighteenth century, but as New England farmers participated more fully in the market and families in both regions participated in religious revivals, some convergence of rural communal institutions did occur. To plumb these differences, we need to look in some detail at specific agrarian communities over time. A comparison of agrarian society in the seventeenth-century Chesapeake and New England colonies, where three-quarters of the white and black inhabitants of the British mainland colonies lived in 1700, is a good place to begin.

RURAL LIFE IN THE SEVENTEENTH CENTURY

The first English immigrants to the Chesapeake hoped to find silver and gold, but they soon turned to the more prosaic, if almost as profitable, task of growing tobacco. Planters financed the purchase of numerous indentured servants, nearly all young men, with the proceeds of their tobacco crops and set them to work making that crop. Servants (and planters for that matter) were apparently an unruly lot, unmarried men on the make, whose behavior forced Virginia Company authorities to attempt to impose harsh penal laws. Indians, angered over confiscation of land, rose up twice (in 1622 and 1644), killing many settlers and disrupting whatever social institutions had developed. Intestinal and waterborne diseases killed even more people and reduced life expectancy for the survivors. As Englishmen completed their terms as servants and married the few available white women, fam-

ily agriculture and new communal institutions—centered at the parish church and the county court—gradually emerged.

Seventeenth-century Chesapeake planters placed their entire emphasis on growing tobacco for the market and corn to feed their families and servants. While tobacco prices declined after the 1620s boom, productivity meanwhile grew with sufficient speed to allow planters to make substantial profits for much of the century. With demand for tobacco so high in England and Europe, planters neglected many subsistence activities and imported from abroad nearly everything except the food they ate. As tobacco prices continued their descent after 1675, planter profits plummeted and then disappeared. Some planters who lived in marginal areas turned away from tobacco toward grain-and-livestock agriculture; others continued to depend upon tobacco, but increased the self-sufficiency of their households, buying spinning wheels to make thread or looms to weave cloth, increasing the diversity of their crop mix, or procuring more sheep or cattle. Even those who stopped growing tobacco, however, continued to rely upon foreign markets, for they sent surplus grain, pork, or beef to the West Indies.

Early- and mid-seventeenth-century Chesapeake households were extraordinarily complex. The Chesapeake was a labor-poor but relatively land-rich region, and every former servant wanted to rent or buy a plantation for himself, make tobacco, and achieve upward mobility. Since each planter wanted to produce as much tobacco as possible, he regularly bought English indentured servants to help in the tobacco fields and turned his entire family—often including his wife and adolescent children—to making that crop. If family and servants did not provide sufficient labor to make the crop, a planter might hire as wage laborers former servants not yet able to get land. This labor system persisted until the 1660s or 1670s, when the supply of indentured servants began to decline.

Unwilling at first to import slaves, planters bid up the price of servants and, as a result, most planters had to rely more heavily on family labor. But as the number of servants continued to diminish, wealthier planters turned to slave labor. Between the late 1670s and 1700, slaves replaced servants on most Chesapeake tobacco plantations. The spread of slavery profoundly changed the behavior of whites in Chesapeake households. Planters' wives no longer worked in the tobacco fields, for that labor was reserved for slaves and the white men who supervised them. At the same time, inequality among white households increased because a small minority of white men could afford to purchase slaves, which cost far more than servants had earlier in the century. Poorer planters, then, continued to rely primarily on family labor—probably including that of wives and daughters—to grow tobacco.

By the middle of the seventeenth century, a cohesive group of communal institutions mitigated the heavy immigration, high mortality, and emphasis on staple agriculture characteristic of the Chesapeake region. County courts regulated the economy, setting tax rates, building roads, authorizing ferries, registering land transactions, and—most important—settling disputes over debt and credit. Justices meeting together heard petitions about land and roads, slander accusations, and servant complaints of poor treatment by masters. Quarterly court sessions attracted a substantial proportion of the free men of the community, who had business before the court, wanted to transact business with others in attendance, or wished to observe the proceedings. Individual justices of the peace resolved minor economic disputes and criminal infractions in their neighborhoods, thereby facilitating social peace.

The orphans' court, whose responsibilities were carried out by justices at special sessions of the county court, was especially important in the perpetuation of households. Since immigrants married late and died young, most children could expect to lose one or both parents and live in complex families with stepparents, siblings, and half-siblings. Orphans' courts protected these children by overseeing the estates they inherited and adjudicating disputes between orphans and stepparents. Neither Indian wars nor periodic civil unrest disrupted the operation of local courts for very long.

Many of the first New England colonists immigrated to make a holy commonwealth, unconstrained by the established Church of England, but they could only do so after they had learned to survive on the sometimes inhospitable soil of

that region. Although most New Englanders made their living as farmers, many had left English textile villages and had cultivated only small plots of land. Town proprietors, granted town sites by the colony, maintained strong communal control over land distributions, allocating land to families based upon need, status in the community, or amount invested in purchasing land from the Indians, often excluding tenants or the poor from distributions. Villagers, who had moved together from England, set up new villages collectively with former townspeople and attempted to replicate familiar field systems. Those who migrated from enclosed villages distributed land in compact plots; those who moved from open-field areas attempted to set up open-field systems and distributed plots of arable and pasture land to each family. Conflicts over enclosure broke out in New England's open-field villages whose inhabitants had emigrated from different parts of England, but within a decade of immigration compact farms and isolated farmsteads predominated in every village.

New England was far less favorably situated to take advantage of English demand for agricultural goods than the Chesapeake colonies. Although Plymouth and Massachusetts farmers kept busy in the 1620s and 1630s provisioning recent immigrants, that market disappeared when immigration plummeted after 1640. Barely able to feed themselves on the rocky and infertile soil, seventeenth-century New England farmers reached for self-sufficiency in food, made cloth or candles in their homes, exchanged goods with neighbors, and sold small surpluses at local markets. Byemployments—carpentry or cooperage, spinning or weaving at home—took on added importance in this credit-poor society. Those who lived near water or roads took advantage of the coastal carrying trade, sending grain, pork, beef, or forest products to other colonies; farmers residing in seaside communities often went on commercial fishing ventures part of the year; a few frontier farmers traded in furs.

Household organization varied substantially from place to place in early New England. Farmers who lived in the semisubsistence villages of eastern New England had to rely almost exclusively on family labor, with men working in the fields and women tending their gardens. But family labor sometimes proved insufficient, especially at planting and harvesting times. Only a few indentured servants arrived in these villages, and adults were long-lived, throwing few adolescents prematurely onto the labor market. To alleviate the labor shortage these families—unlike others in early America—hoarded their labor, apparently exchanging labor services with other farmers infrequently. One could find many exceptions to this pattern. Farmers in coastal towns close to markets could buy an occasional indentured servant or hire wage workers to help with planting or harvest. A complex household and plantation labor system developed in the Connecticut River town of Springfield. Most farmers owned some land there, but many of them leased land and worked occasionally for the Pynchons, the wealthiest family in town and the family that owned nearly all the best land. With their income from fur trading, the Pynchons also bought many indentured servants, men they later hired as laborers or tenants.

Blessed with long lives and fortified with an evangelizing mission, rural New Englanders founded strong communities, bound together by socializing with neighbors, church communion, and town meeting. The gradual distribution of town lands encouraged compact settlement patterns, and neighbors lived close enough to visit regularly, exchange goods, and fall into petty disputes. Church and town meeting became more important than the quarterly court session in the Chesapeake colonies. The parish church, founded almost as soon as a town was seated, was central to community life in early New England; most farm families attended church twice weekly, for the Sunday sermon and the Wednesday lecture. Early in the seventeenth century, a majority of inhabitants could relate a conversion experience and therefore become full church members, eligible to take communion and have their children baptized. Towns often linked full voting rights in town affairs to full church membership. Farmers who were neither church members nor shareholders in the town had neither political nor religious rights. The town meetings elected town officials, set tax rates, and allocated land.

Such close communalism bred conflicts between neighbors and social fissures that often rent entire congregations and towns. Selectmen or justices attempted to resolve petty disputes

between neighbors by appointing unbiased mediators to resolve the problem, but community struggles were less easily settled. Any challenge to religious authority as defined by provincial leaders and clergy severed the covenant that bound villagers to one another and rent the province in conflict. Roger Williams's grudging call for religious toleration led to his exile; Anne Hutchinson's report of personal revelation from God and attacks on the clergy as unregenerate tore the colony apart, setting many Bostonians (who supported Hutchinson) against farm villages. Local disputes were ubiquitous. Townsmen fought over the ministers they hired, church policy (what rights the unregenerate children of saints would have), and the location of parish church and town meeting. Outlying farmers, angry over the distant location of church and meetinghouse, often resolved conflicts with other villages by forming a new town and building a new church and meetinghouse. The witchcraft epidemic at Salem built upon tensions between Salem village (Danvers) and Salem town over the rate of commercialization in the town and establishment of a new parish nearer to distant farmers.

The rural inhabitants of Pennsylvania, first peopled by Europeans in the 1680s and 1690s, generally replicated the household structures and market relations of New England. But there were critical differences. William Penn granted large tracts of land to favored associates, who sold smaller parcels to immigrants. Communal control over land was therefore less strong than in New England, and the religious toleration and multiethnic settlement of that colony (by English Quakers, German Pietists, and Scots Presbyterians, for instance) further reduced communalism. Individual farm families joined voluntary communities based upon religion and ethnicity and sustained their own sense of place, separate from that of their neighbors. Quakers, the most important (though minority) group in the province, devised household strategies far different from other colonists. They encouraged female autonomy within farm households (symbolized by the separate and powerful women's meetings), placed great importance on child nurture by parents (and especially by the mother), tried to accumulate sufficient land to give each son a fully operational farm, and insisted that the entire meeting approve every marriage to ensure maintenance of a holy community. These practices presaged the adaptation of capitalist agricultural practices and ideology.

South Carolina, settled by West Indian migrants, resembled early island society more than anyplace to the north. Migrants brought slaves with them and purchased so many more that slaves made up a majority of the population as early as 1715. While white pioneers, nearly all of whom owned slaves, began and managed their plantations and searched for a staple in demand in England, slaves enjoyed some autonomy, clearing land, growing their own food, herding cattle, carrying goods to market, cutting wood, making turpentine, working as craftsmen. But by the early eighteenth century planters, perhaps aided by their slaves, discovered how to grow rice efficiently. Since rice was in great demand in England, planters set their slaves to producing the crop, bought thousands more unseasoned African slaves, and in the process reduced the autonomy resident slaves had previously enjoyed.

RURAL COMMUNITIES IN THE EIGHTEENTH CENTURY

For nearly the entire seventeenth century, the threat of Indians—real or imagined—kept settlers from venturing more than a few miles from coast or riverbanks. But by the beginning of the eighteenth century this danger receded. The white population of each colony overwhelmed that of Indians living within its bounds. Surrounded by whites envious of their lands, they faced defeat and exile everywhere. The timing of this change varied from place to place. In 1676 Nathaniel Bacon's irregulars massacred Virginia Indians, chasing them to the foothills and mountains, opening up millions of new acres to white settlement. That same year, Metacom rose up against New England's settlers and forced their temporary retreat, but in the end his men were defeated and forced from lands they hunted and farmed. Indians held on in the Carolinas for several more decades, but by 1720 whites dominated coastal areas and the sovereignty of the British in all the lands they claimed as colonies was no longer in doubt. The defeat

of the Indians profoundly transformed white rural communities. Whites, who had always lived among (or at least near) Indian villages, isolated themselves from the aboriginal population, and any Indians still within their midst became dependent upon whites for their survival.

Without an Indian threat, settlers no longer needed to conserve precious land. The resulting land abundance changed the rural life of English colonists. Whatever their regional differences, eighteenth-century colonists shared new material conditions, expectations, and rural culture. Immigrants had moved from England to find land, something inconceivable in England. Seventeenth-century colonists owned land far more often than the English, but hemmed in by hostile Indians, their hold over their land was precarious; eighteenth-century farmers came to expect to own land as their birthright. Secure land ownership provided the material base that allowed the formation of new classes of yeomen in all the colonies. During the last half of the eighteenth century, between two-thirds and three-quarters of married men owned land; yeomen, who headed more than half of all rural households, usually owned several hundred acres. Southern yeomen often possessed a slave or two as well. Secure in their homes and on their land, unwilling to borrow recklessly against their landed equity, yeomen sought a sufficiency—an adequate diet for their families, decent clothes on their backs, a well-constructed house. To accomplish these ends, yeomen cultivated food crops, exchanged goods with neighbors, and marketed small surpluses of grain or staples like tobacco. They traded surpluses for British manufactured goods like cloth, pottery, and forks, items that became both cheaper and more available over the eighteenth century. Taking few risks, they rarely became wealthy, but they often accumulated enough land and other property to bequeath sufficient goods to their children, allowing them to form their own households.

Yeomen refused to tolerate any challenge to the security of their land. They knew that without land they could not provide their families with a sufficiency and would fall into poverty. Moreover, they maintained adamantly that they *deserved* to own their land, for only their labor gave land value. Uncultivated land should therefore be inexpensive and free from burdensome taxes. Yeomen formulated this "homestead ethic" most fully when confronted by gentlemen and merchants seeking to call in debts, raise high taxes, hoard and refuse to sell land, or deny farmers protection from robber bands or marauding Indians. These small farmers went far beyond deferential protests and petitions; during the mid eighteenth century, when the security of their land was in danger, yeomen in New York, New Jersey, North Carolina, and South Carolina took up arms against landlords, tax collectors, and merchants.

Yeomen valued the independence from servility, the market, and ruling classes they believed that they had achieved. This independence, predicated upon land ownership, earned yeomen the right, they insisted, to vote and participate in the polity. That independence was sustained by suppressing any independence by farm women. Farm wives everywhere milked cows, cultivated gardens, made clothes (and sometimes cloth), fed their families, cared for children, and trained their daughters in the ways of housewifery. The children they bore guaranteed the perpetuation of their lineage, and their work was essential to the success of the farming operation. But a farm wife had neither legal nor moral authority in her own household. She was legally subservient to her husband, who owned all the family's property, including the land and chattels she had brought into the marriage, and who had the right to punish her for infractions, real or imagined, to his orders. Divorce or even separate bed and board (legal separation) was rarely possible, even if the husband acted brutally. At best a "deputy husband," she had no independent domestic sphere she could call her own; her husband made all decisions about the education of her children and placed no great value on the tasks he expected her to accomplish.

As the population grew, and farmers filled in the often less fertile lands not yet cultivated, unimproved land in older settlements became scarce. Since farmers continued to cultivate fields until the soil was exhausted, and refused to take up the methods of English "improving" farmers, pressure on the remaining fertile land became ever more intense. Yeoman fathers could no longer accumulate sufficient land to give or bequeath farms to their sons, nor could the sons

afford to purchase increasingly expensive improved land. Younger men in all the colonies therefore migrated to new frontiers, located on land Indians had been forced to abandon, and took up unimproved acres rather than fall into tenancy or wage labor. Frontier migration by men seeking land led to a dramatic expansion of settled territory, from a few enclaves around the coasts and on the rivers in 1700 to nearly a continuous band of settlements from southern and central New England to the coastal areas of the Carolinas and Georgia. In New England and the Chesapeake region, settlement reached and even went beyond the Appalachian Mountains. Frontier settlers relied on settled areas and England for manufactured goods and lived close enough to Indians to become embroiled in constant conflict.

The more intensive settlement patterns and higher population densities of the mid-eighteenth-century British colonies threw farmers in rural communities closer to one another and created greater demand for urban services. Tiny hamlets, rural villages, and even towns grew in the older parts of every colony. Larger towns more commonly appeared in coastal New England, southeastern Pennsylvania, and Virginia's Shenandoah Valley, areas where grain production, rural industries such as textiles or shoes, or fishing had developed. These market towns and villages had a substantial resident population, numbering in the hundreds, that served the nearby farm population, processing wheat, lending money, or sewing clothes. Many fewer towns could be found in staple-producing areas like the tidewater and Piedmont regions of the Chesapeake colonies, but even there hamlets containing a tavern, general store, church, several artisan's shops, and perhaps a courthouse dotted the landscape. The village or town center became a center of sociability for men, who regularly shopped at the store, drank with friends at the tavern, had a horse shoed, or attended court sessions. Women, who came to town irregularly, did not share in these new opportunities for sociability but were still usually confined to the farm and their immediate neighborhood.

As a result of increased population density and the growth of towns, eighteenth-century farm men (and farm women to a much lesser degree) enjoyed a fuller community life than had their immigrant ancestors. Visiting and other neighborhood activities became easier, as county courts ordered the maintenance of innumerable country roads, linking nearly every farm with its neighbors and the nearest town. Established churches lost their monopoly, and Anglicans, Presbyterians, Baptists, and Congregationalists could form churches in most colonies, albeit often facing discrimination. Women joined churches in greater numbers than men, perhaps because they were socialized to be more spiritual and because church membership was one of the few outlets off the farm open to them. Court days and town meetings (in New England) became more intensive entertainments for male citizens, for the greater population yielded more controversies, more debt cases, and more problems to resolve. Towns became centers of male sociability: men could attend muster meetings (often more like drinking brawls), horse racing, and election rallies in or near town. On most days, however, farmers remained isolated on their farms, and farmer organizations did not appear until after the revolution.

Religious revivals were so ubiquitous in the mid-eighteenth-century British colonies that nearly every rural American of that period had an opportunity to participate in one or more of them. The revivals covered the entire country over a long period, from the 1730s in New England, through the 1740s and 1750s in the Middle Atlantic colonies, to the 1760s and 1770s in the South. At all these widely separated events, charismatic preachers, eager to convert the multitudes to God's true faith, brought together a cross section of rural population, male and female, free and slave, and urged them to listen, to repent their sins, to be converted. Revivalists persuaded their listeners of the spiritual equality of all women and men, thus sustaining the incipient republicanism of most small farmers. Equally important, revivals revitalized Protestant churches, increasing the proportion of men among members, as well as leading to the formation of many Presbyterian, Baptist, or crypto-Methodist evangelical churches. These new churches not only created new opportunities for farm families to pray together and socialize but provided an institutional base for a new kind of Christian republicanism of great importance during the revolution.

However much the eighteenth-century North and South resembled each other, they remained different. As land ownership spread, labor shortages on the farm inevitably grew. Men who knew they could farm their own land married at youthful ages, in their early to mid twenties, rather than work on their parents' farms. Northern farmers relied upon exchange of labor with neighbors, an occasional hired hand, and particularly upon their own families, especially the large numbers of children their wives bore. In contrast, southern farmers, even yeomen, solved the problem of farm labor with slaves. The high demand for tobacco and rice in England gave wealthy southerners access to slave markets, and yeomen often owned a slave or two, critical additions to scarce family labor. (The many slaves owned by large planters produced most of the rice and tobacco exported to England.) These fundamental regional variations in household labor led to important divergences in rural society and in the relation between market and household that sustained rural life.

New England, with its dense population and rocky soil, suffered from population pressure on land more than any other region. Many communities, unable to feed themselves, had to import food. Farmers searched for more commercial crops or craft pursuits that would permit them to make up for these food deficits. For instance, farmers around Boston and coastal towns probably sent milk and butter, fruit and vegetables, firewood and shingles to urban markets. Household production of thread and cloth, nails, and shoes proliferated and began to be organized in a putting-out system, in which a manufacturer provided the materials, and farmers and farm wives performed labor necessary to turn thread into cloth or leather into footwear. By the end of the colonial era, a few farm towns like Lynn, Massachusetts, began to turn from farming to specializing in shoe manufacturing or other industrial pursuits. Men who wished to continue farming full-time, whose inheritance proved insufficient to buy land in settled towns, moved to new frontier areas in New Hampshire, central and western New England, and the Hudson River valley. Families without an inheritance fell into poverty. Poverty increased throughout the region, forcing many single men and families to tramp the roads searching for work. Some of these people wound up in Boston, where the work they found kept them in dire poverty. Nonetheless, a majority (if an ever-diminishing one) of most New Englanders still lived in rural villages and pursued agriculture on the eve of the revolution.

Farmers in the Middle Atlantic colonies owned far better land, in greater quantities, than did farmers in New England. They were therefore poised to take advantage of the rapidly growing demand for wheat after 1750 in Philadelphia and especially in Western Europe and England. Farmers increasingly turned to commercial agriculture, growing large surpluses of wheat for domestic and foreign markets. As population grew and farmers allocated more and more land to commercial wheat production, land became expensive and scarce. Farmers who wished to take advantage of the new wheat markets, and avoid the heavy transportation costs associated with frontier agriculture, willingly leased land near Philadelphia. Commercial agriculture transformed many farm households. The farm operation became more specialized around wheat production. Rather than grind grain themselves, farmers took their output to a local miller, who accepted a percentage of the grain for his service. The milling industry therefore grew rapidly. Wage labor became far more important for farmers. Since wheat required intensive labor only at planting and harvest, they hired seasonal day laborers rather than employ workers or servants on an annual contract. An insufficient number of laborers, however, accepted harvest employment. To solve their labor problems, southeastern Pennsylvania farmers hired cottagers. In return for help at planting, harvest, and other times, the cottager had use of a small house and a vegetable patch, where some food could be grown. When not needed on the farm, the cottager worked as a craftsman or wage laborer.

Slavery as a labor system intensified in the eighteenth-century South. Farmers in every colony held slaves, but only the staple-producing areas of the Chesapeake colonies, the Carolinas, and Georgia became slave *societies,* in which slaves produced nearly all the exports and whites measured their wealth and status by the number of slaves they owned. Yeomen planters often owned a few slaves but still had to labor in the fields, directing the work of their sons and slaves. Gen-

tlemen planters, in contrast, owned so many slaves of working age that they could hire an overseer and avoid agricultural labor entirely. White women, unless very poor, no longer labored in the fields, for that was considered servile work, fit only for slaves. The wives of slaveholders, moreover, had help with onerous household tasks, such as hauling water, not available to their slaveless neighbors. The system of slave labor created two separate, and highly unequal, communities. Like whites elsewhere, southern planters and their wives could take advantage of church services, court days, and the enticing life of the village. Slaves, especially the African-American slaves who dominated the black population by the eve of the revolution, also enjoyed some family and community life from sundown to sunup but it was far more limited than that of their masters. They often suffered forced separations from their loved ones, when masters sold or bequeathed slaves. Slaves visited nearby plantations to see friends or family (many fathers lived on different plantations than their children); they attended church services, sitting in the balcony, but could rarely listen to their own preachers; and the master or mistress might occasionally send a trusted slave to town on an errand.

Like farmers everywhere, those who lived in the backcountry wanted to send surpluses to market and maintain a comfortable sufficiency for their families. But they had fewer options than farmers elsewhere. Lacking adequate roads, they sent surpluses to market with some difficulty and had to find crops that would survive jarring transport. A majority of frontier families were probably immigrants from Scotland, Ireland, or Germany who traveled down the great wagon road from Philadelphia through the backcountry. They had enough capital to make that journey but not enough to buy land in settled areas or spend much money making frontier farms. Indians, who dominated frontier regions numerically, remained a constant threat. Since frontier families often lived beyond the surveyor's reach, they squatted on the acres they farmed. Therefore, they also constantly feared that someone of greater wealth might receive a grant for their land, have it surveyed, and either chase them from the land or force them to pay for it.

These economic differences notwithstanding, rural communities in the British colonies resembled each other enough on the eve of the American Revolution to make similar responses to English taxation, trade policy, and military occupation in the 1760s and 1770s. Farmers everywhere feared heavy taxation and any policy that might permit confiscation of their landed property. Not only their family's welfare but their own control over their household was potentially at stake. Whig leaders of the revolution mobilized farmers by appealing both to their fears and to their role as sturdy yeomen defending colonial liberties. Many yeomen responded by supporting the revolution, but they did so on their own terms, insisting that they have a major role in the formulation of public policy and in the preservation of their independence, authority in their own households, and liberties they enjoyed as inhabitants of discrete communities. The republic of the United States then can trace its origins, in part, to ideology yeomen used to legitimate their land ownership and their place in society.

BIBLIOGRAPHY

Allen, David Grayson. *In English Ways: The Movement of Societies and the Transferral of English Local Law and Custom to Massachusetts Bay in the Seventeenth Century.* Chapel Hill, N.C., 1981. This study of the origin of immigrants to four Massachusetts towns, three of them agricultural, argues that they replicated the entire social order they had left behind.

Boyer, Paul, and Stephen Nissenbaum. *Salem Possessed: The Social Origins of Witchcraft.* Cambridge, Mass., 1974. Shows that social tensions between subsistence farmers and commercially oriented inhabitants underlay the Salem witchcraft craze.

Carman, Harry J., ed. *American Husbandry.* New York, 1939. This volume, written in the 1770s, is the best contemporary description of agriculture in the North American colonies.

Carr, Lois Green, Russell R. Menard, and Lorena S. Walsh. *Robert Cole's World: Agriculture and Society in Early Maryland.* Chapel Hill, N.C., 1991. Brilliantly evokes the economy of a middling seventeenth-century Maryland planter, by making use of a detailed farm-account book.

Clemens, Paul G. E. *The Atlantic Economy and Colonial Maryland's Eastern Shore: From Tobacco to Grain.* Ithaca, N.Y., 1980. Details the transition from tobacco to grain on Maryland's Eastern Shore in the mid eighteenth century.

Cook, Edward M., Jr. *The Fathers of the Towns: Leadership and Community Structure in Eighteenth-Century New England.* Baltimore, Md., 1976. First devises a typology of eighteenth-century towns and then analyzes community institutions in each type.

Cronon, William. *Changes in the Land: Indians, Colonists, and the Ecology of New England.* New York, 1983. Analyzes differences in land use among Indians and New England settlers, arguing that agriculture profoundly changed the New England landscape.

Fischer, David Hackett. *Albion's Seed: Four British Folkways in America.* New York, 1989. Documents the movements of cultures from Britain to her continental colonies, arguing for almost a direct transfer of cultural norms.

Gray, Lewis Cecil. *History of Agriculture in the Southern United States to 1860.* 2 vols. Washington, D.C., 1933. Standard reference work on southern agriculture; volume 1 covers the colonial era.

Greene, Jack P. *Pursuits of Happiness: The Social Development of Early Modern British Colonies and the Formation of American Culture.* Chapel Hill, N.C., 1988. Most recent synthesis of colonial social history.

Greven, Philip J. *Four Generations: Population, Land, and Family in Colonial Andover, Massachusetts.* Ithaca, N.Y., 1970. The classic account of family, kinship, and inheritance in early New England.

Innes, Stephen. *Labor in a New Land: Economy and Society in Seventeenth-Century Springfield.* Princeton, N.J., 1983. Argues that tenancy and a wage labor system were far more common in early New England than previously supposed.

———, ed. *Work and Labor in Early America.* Chapel Hill, N.C., 1988. Includes valuable essays on farm and family labor in New England, Pennsylvania, and the Chesapeake colonies.

Isaac, Rhys. *The Transformation of Virginia, 1740–1790.* Chapel Hill, N.C., 1982. In this now-classic work, Isaac shows that a plebeian (and yeoman) Baptist culture, centered in Virginia's Southside, challenged the hegemony of tidewater gentlemen in the 1760s and 1770s.

Kulikoff, Allan. *The Agrarian Origins of American Capitalism.* Charlottesville, Va., 1992. Looks at development of the yeoman classes in the colonial period.

———. "Households and Markets: Toward a New Synthesis of American Agrarian History." *William and Mary Quarterly,* 3rd ser., 50 (1993):342–355. Reasons that the metaphor of "markets and households" best synthesizes rural history.

———. *Tobacco and Slaves: The Development of Southern Cultures in the Chesapeake, 1680–1800.* Chapel Hill, N.C., 1986. Analyzes eighteenth-century agriculture, white society, and black society in the Chesapeake region.

Lemon, James T. *The Best Poor Man's Country: A Geographical Study of Early Southeastern Pennsylvania.* Baltimore, Md., 1972. Details agricultural patterns and town formation among various ethnic groups in early Pennsylvania.

Levy, Barry. *Quakers and the American Family: British Settlement in the Delaware Valley.* New York, 1988. Contends that Quakers devised modern families, predicated upon the individualism of each person in the family.

Lockridge, Kenneth A. *A New England Town: The First Hundred Years, Dedham, Massachusetts, 1636–1736.* New York, 1970. The classic account of the organization of consensual communities in early New England and in their demise.

McCusker, John J., and Russell R. Menard. *The Economy of British America, 1607–1789.* Chapel Hill, N.C., 1985. This volume, the standard economic history of colonial North America, includes chapters on regions, on commerce, and on agriculture.

Martin, John Frederick. *Profits in the Wilderness: Entrepreneurship and the Founding of New England Towns in the Seventeenth Century.* Chapel Hill, N.C., 1991. Argues that founders of New England towns were entrepreneurs, out to make a profit, and that they excluded many inhabitants from land distributions.

Meinig, D. W. *The Shaping of America: A Geographical Perspective on Five Hundred Years of History.* Vol. 1, *Atlantic America, 1492–1800.* New Haven, Conn., 1986. Places agricultural development, commerce, and urban development in colonial North America into a broad economic framework.

Mitchell, Robert D. *Commercialism and Frontier: Perspectives on the Early Shenandoah Valley.* Charlottesville, Va., 1977. Argues that commercial agriculture predominated in the early Shenandoah Valley, despite the region's isolation from coastal markets.

Perry, James R. *The Formation of a Society on Virginia's Eastern Shore, 1615–1655.* Chapel Hill, N.C., 1990. Demonstrates that planters in the early Chesapeake quickly created social and kinship networks that mitigated the difficult demographic environment they found.

Rothenberg, Winifred B. "The Market and Massachusetts Farmers, 1750–1855." *Journal of Economic History* 41 (1981):283–314. Argues that farmers in late colonial Massachusetts eagerly participated in markets, searching for the most profitable crops and markets.

Rutman, Darrett B. "Assessing the Little Communities of Early America." *William and Mary Quarterly,* 3rd ser., 43 (1986):163–179. Defines community in terms of social networks and makes a searing critique of studies that define rural community in terms of values and beliefs.

Rutman, Darrett B., and Anita H. Rutman. *A Place in Time: Middlesex County, Virginia, 1650–1750.* New York, 1984. This evocative history of a Virginia county details the early development of a strong community life.

Soderlund, Jean R. *Quakers and Slavery: A Divided Spirit.* Princeton, N.J., 1985. Shows that Quakers owned more slaves than their neighbors until the 1770s, when Friends began to see slavery as an evil.

Tate, Thad W., and David L. Ammerman, eds. *The Chesapeake in the Seventeenth Century: Essays on Anglo-American Society.* Chapel Hill, N.C., 1979. Contains important essays on servant opportunity, communities, and family life in the region.

Vickers, Daniel. "Competency and Competition: Economic Culture in Early America." *William and Mary Quarterly,* 3rd ser., 47 (1990):3–29. An important examination of the ideology of farmers, this essay contends that rural folk sought a competency rather than maximizing profits.

Wood, Peter. *Black Majority: Negroes in Colonial South Carolina from 1670 Through the Stono Rebellion.* New York, 1974. Remains the standard account of the early social and economic history of South Carolina, one that makes slaves and slavery central to its story.

Zuckerman, Michael. *Peaceable Kingdoms: New England Towns in the Eighteenth Century.* New York, 1970. Shows that New England towns remained consensual communities through the eighteenth century.

Allan Kulikoff

See also **Architecture**; **Crafts**; and **Urban Life**; and various essays in economic life and folkways.

THE DUTCH COLONY

Virtually all life in sprawling New Netherland, with its estimated peak population of nine thousand, was rural. Only two "cities" existed: Fort Orange, also called Beverswyck (Albany), and New Amsterdam (New York City). In 1664, the year of the British conquest of New Netherland, the rest of the population was scattered in nine chartered towns, in the patroonship of Rensselaerswyck, and in small villages on Long Island and Staten Island and in the Hackensack and Hudson valleys.

Life in New Netherland, in both rural and urban districts, had a certain international flavor, for only about half of the "Dutch" settlers were actually ethnically Dutch. The rest of them came from other parts of western and northern Europe. Many had previously sought refuge, for political, economic, or religious reasons, in the relatively tolerant and prospering Netherlands. Though most of these persons, in their stay in the Netherlands, had acquired the ability to speak Dutch, had often affiliated with the Dutch Reformed church, and had been assimilated into Dutch culture, they also brought with them to New Netherland remembered elements of their first culture.

An Indian presence, often hostile, and an unwilling African one added other ingredients to rural life in New Netherland. Since the slave trade to New Netherland had been under way since the 1620s, wherever the Dutch settled there were also enslaved Africans—many of whom had been "seasoned" to slavery in the West Indies. The slaves toiled in field and house, thereby contributing their own culture's distinctive features to the melting pot.

As the population grew in the 1640s, 1650s, and 1660s, the quality of rural life in this pluralistic society was determined less by what they held in common than by differences in settlers' backgrounds: the arduous task of clearing and planting the wilderness, close-knit family life, affiliation with the Dutch Reformed church, as well as an ever-present (and realistic) fear of Indian attack. Moreover, there were ongoing conflicts with New Englanders, who claimed a right to the colony's territory and who were as determined as the Dutch to establish their own social, political, and cultural institutions in New Netherland.

THE RURAL ECONOMY

Clearing the land and planting it were the paramount realities of rural life in New Netherland.

The farmer, his family, and his slaves were all involved in these tasks.

To succeed the farmer had to make a yearly profit by selling his surplus crops. It was only by turning a profit that he could afford to develop and improve his holdings, purchase seed, tools, livestock, and slaves, hire day labor as needed, and acquire the niceties to make his life comfortable. Not everyone succeeded, of course, and rural communities were stratified along economic lines. The largest landowners and slaveholders were at the top; a strata of smaller, struggling farmers and tenant farmers were in the middle; under them stood men and women too poor to own more than a cow and a pig; and at the bottom were indentured laborers and slaves.

Artisans contributed their vital skills to the developing rural scene, but agriculture to lay one's own table could hardly be avoided by anyone. And so on the side, carpenters, masons, wheelwrights, shoemakers, blacksmiths, coopers, clerks, weavers, tailors, brewers, surgeons, and shipbuilders cultivated some ground of their own and kept some livestock. Most New Netherlanders also supplemented their incomes by trading with the Indians, peltry for resale being the most desirable item. After 1657 the beaver trade began to decline. This hardship, combined with those unpredictable misfortunes brought on by bad harvests, flooding, drought, and disease, were ever-present crises in the life of rural New Netherlanders of all economic groups.

Incessant work characterized the life of both men and women in rural New Netherland. Men who were often also relatives—for families were large and intimate—helped each other in field clearing, provided mutual assistance in house, barn, and fence building, and shared oxen and slaves. Men also hunted, fished, and fowled together. More isolated from each other than men, women relied mostly on Sunday church services to meet and exchange information and ideas, news and gossip. Women's work ranged from tending the kitchen garden, dairy, and poultry yard to cooking and preserving for a large household, turning fleece and flax into yarn and linen and these into clothing and bedding, and caring for children. Children met at church and also at school, which even in rural New Netherland was open to girls as well as boys, although the quality of the education was poor. Despite their own routine of grueling work and grim deprivations, slaves were permitted to marry and attend church services, almost their only occasion for social interaction with each other. Some New Netherland slaves were freed after a period and allowed to own property and learn and practice a trade.

RELIGION AND SOCIAL LIFE

As the hinterland became populated, the importance of the Dutch Reformed church to rural life in New Netherland cannot be overemphasized. Though few ordained ministers, or *predikanten,* served New Netherland, an order of lay preachers called *voorlesers* (public readers) and *krankenbesoeckers* (comforters of the sick) were authorized by the mother church in the Netherlands and sent over to the colony to minister to the settlers. They were authorized to console the dying, read prescribed prayers and sermons, lead psalm singing, catechize children, and keep the church records. The *voorleser* also functioned as schoolmaster. An ordained minister was required for the sacraments of baptism, marriage, and Communion. For these occasions rural people either traveled to the nearest minister or waited for him to come to them on a quarterly basis. On his visits he boarded with one of the community's more prosperous citizens. It was also the church, through its deacons' fund, that supported the poor, for life was as much as four times as expensive in New Netherland as in the Dutch Republic, and many settlers were unable to provide for their basic needs without assistance.

Throughout New Netherland most rural communities constructed, as soon as they were able, a mill and a tavern, followed soon by church and store. These were the significant meeting places for people isolated on far-flung farms. Miller and tavern keeper, *voorleser* and storeowner were important figures in the life of the rural community, as were *schout* (sheriff) and *schepens* (judges), who saw to order. A jail was also a familiar landmark in rural communities. The most frequent offenses were defamation of character, slander, libel, trespass, debt, and vagrancy.

Social life in rural New Netherland centered around family and church. Families were large, all members of the community knew each other, and many were related by ties of blood and marriage. Holidays—particularly Saint Nicholas's Day (5 December), New Year's Day, Easter, May Day, and Pentecost (around 1 June)—were celebrated in rural New Netherland after the fashion in the Netherlands, with visiting, feasting, drinking, and general merriment. Other festive occasions during the year included market days and fairs, when families and friends could gather and exchange news. Favorite pastimes in New Netherland were sleighing, skating, sledding, bowling, tick-tack (or backgammon), trock (similar to billiards and croquet), picnicking, nutting, berrying, and, always, visiting. In all areas rural life in New Netherland was strongly colored by the customs of the fatherland.

BIBLIOGRAPHY

Donck, Adriaen van der. *A Description of the New Netherlands.* Edited by Thomas F. O'Donnell. Syracuse, N.Y., 1968.

Earle, Alice Morse. *Colonial Days in Old New York.* New York, 1896.

Jameson, J. Franklin, ed. *Narratives of New Netherland, 1609–1664.* New York, 1909.

Raesly, Ellis Lawrence. *Portrait of New Netherland.* Port Washington, N.Y. 1945.

Firth Haring Fabend

SEE ALSO **Architecture; Crafts;** and **Urban Life;** and various essays in ECONOMIC LIFE and FOLKWAYS.

THE FRENCH COLONIES

NEW FRANCE WAS essentially a rural society that developed from trading outposts at Port Royal, Tadoussac, and Quebec. Settlement based on agriculture developed only slowly because of the dominance of commercial exploitation, notably the fishery and fur trade, which required little in the way of overseas support bases.

The missionaries who came to evangelize the Native peoples soon expressed a desire for good Catholic colonists who would provide examples of the type of pious agriculturalists that they wished their nomadic converts to emulate. An agricultural community would also provide the foundation for parish organization and the support of resident priests through tithing. A Recollet missionary urged both the French nobility to send its sons to take up seigneuries and the king to consider emptying the prisons of petty criminals to populate a vast, sparsely inhabited territory. As English settlers moved into North America in significant numbers, it became imperative for France to strengthen her sovereign claims through active settlement of the northeastern approaches first made known by Giovanni da Verrazano, Jacques Cartier, and the Breton and Norman fishermen.

Nevertheless, the search for mines in this new land, the exploitation of its marine resources, and the pursuit of trade with the original inhabitants in exchange for furs did not stimulate either the Crown or merchants to underwrite the costs of establishing settlements. Even Samuel de Champlain's vision of a permanent colony on the lower Saint Lawrence River contemplated a showpiece city called Ludovica, which would be a free port and entrepôt for the France–China trade.

In 1627 Cardinal Richelieu, Louis XIII's first minister, organized 107 noblemen into the Compagnie des Cent-Associés (Company of One Hundred Associates) for the colonization of Acadia and Canada in exchange for a fur-trade monopoly. This company was never able to fulfill its obligations to bring out four thousand settlers. This was due in part to the misfortunes of war and piracy and to the more fundamental reasons that Canada seemed unattractive and that there were few "push factors" in France encouraging emigration to a distant land. It had already been decided that Protestants would not be permitted to found a colony, even if they had been inclined to do so, and peasants and artisans were not free to leave.

A handful of noblemen undertook to bring out settlers at their own expense, as did the Jesuit missionaries, Ursuline nuns, and Sisters Hospi-

tallers who were granted estates by the Crown. Prospects for permanent settlement improved with the introduction of royal government in 1663. Soon soldiers were sent out to deal with French embroilment in an intertribal war that threatened the very security of the three beachheads at Quebec, Trois-Rivières, and Ville Marie (Montreal). "King's daughters," drawn from religious houses of charity, were sent out as brides at royal expense. Captains of vessels sailing for the colony were required to bring out indentured servants. Little by little, seigneuries were surveyed around the principal towns, land was cleared, and agriculture was established on a subsistence basis.

THE SEIGNEURIES

It was natural that the traditional system of landholding of the mother country, seigneurialism, should be introduced along with the Coutume de Paris (Custom of Paris) for regulating inheritance and property rights. The seigneurial system has been seen as a means of colonization, as well as a means of perpetuating the class system of the metropole. Few individuals who accepted a seigneury from the Crown in Canada did much to develop their estates beyond having some land cleared by hired laborers in order to attract settlers who would put their plots into production. The estates were very large in area, and until they became fully exploited the population was scattered and isolated. This necessitated a high degree of self-sufficiency and initiative and encouraged a spirit of independence.

At first, some seigneurs enjoyed a life-style little better than that of their *censitaires*, the peasant farmers who held plots in the seigneury. So there appeared to be a social leveling and reduction of social distinctions on the frontier of settlement. Many of the early seigneurs were unable to provide the stone gristmill and the services of a miller that their state-imposed contracts required. The farmers demanded this essential service, of course, and it was not uncommon for seigneurs to band together or for *censitaires* to pool resources and labor to build a mill.

There seemed to be no shortage of arable land and no reason to doubt its fertility and productivity despite the harsh winters and short growing season. The superiority of seigneurialism over freehold tenure was that there was no initial payment for land; it was free and remained the property of the farmer or *censitaire* and his heirs so long as the annual dues, the *cens et rentes,* were paid.

The seigneury and its farms were laid out in the shape of trapezoidal parallelograms running back from the Saint Lawrence River rather than in the European circular village form. This pattern had the advantages of being easy to survey, of facilitating road construction and maintenance at the rear of the seigneury when a second range of lands was to be conceded, and of giving each of the farmers access to the river for transportation, water, fish, and other marine life. It also provided each farm with a cross section of soil types and vegetation ranging from marshy lowlands, heavier soils for growing cereals, upland meadows, and—at the rear of the property on the highest ground—a woodlot possibly with stone suitable for building.

Settlement took the form of a line of farms along the riverbank, and because of the narrowness of the lots (about 165 yards, or 150 meters) neighbors were much closer than if farms had been randomly dispersed as in the English colonies. This pattern of settlement had some disadvantages because it left the homes accessible to enemy attack from the river, and it also worked against the formation of villages. Only toward the end of the French regime did service centers grow up, sometimes near the church or the manor house.

Seigneuries outnumbered parishes, and since *censitaires* tended to choose lands distant from the seigneur's manor the parish might consist of seigneuries adjoining the church and sometimes a presbytery and school located on their common border. Strong kinship ties developed as relatives tended to settle in proximity to each other, as plots were subdivided among the heirs (both male and female children had protected rights of inheritance), and as neighbors intermarried. When all the land in the riverfront seigneuries was taken up, a second line, or *rang,* of farms was opened up along a parallel interior road. These interior farms were usually acquired by people who were related or already knew each other as neighbors. In this way they maintained

some sense of community. The settlers who moved out into the interior of New France, as far as Detroit or the Illinois country, seem to have formed communities in similar fashion. The colonists in the Illinois country, for example, were almost all from the same parishes near Montreal. Many were related or at least knew each other before moving west.

In Louisiana, the population concentrated itself in the inhabitable territory nearest the coast, largely in a core section along the Mississippi River. The river formed the colony's main artery, extending from just below New Orleans to about one hundred miles (160 kilometers) above it. A second concentration of population developed in the Mobile area, off the Alabama River or the Gulf of Mexico. An economic relationship formed between Louisiana and the Illinois country as the latter produced some of the foodstuffs to feed the soldiers at the different posts in the south, the slaves on the plantations, and the inhabitants of New Orleans.

SUBSISTENCE FARMING

In the lower Saint Lawrence Valley, the region of New France properly known as Canada, subsistence agriculture and peasant households were characteristic of the colonial period. It was a typical preindustrial society in which the farm family produced many of its necessities in the way of food, clothing, shelter, furniture, tools, and implements. In the initial two generations of settlement there was little surplus production and little specialization. Short-lived attempts in the 1670s to encourage the growing of flax and hemp to supply the navy were not repeated.

The Canadian habitant grew cereal crops to provide bread for his family and fodder for his livestock—pigs, sheep, and chickens, as well as the horses of which he was reputedly too fond. The women looked after the vegetable gardens and the poultry and swine, in addition to child rearing. Although they reportedly gave slovenly attention to their household chores, the women carded, spun, knit, sewed, quilted, and wove to the extent that royal intendants praised their resourcefulness and industry.

The men seemed less industrious—in the eyes of royal officials who had no experience of the arduous nature of pioneer agricultural labor such as clearing land and cultivating virgin soils. The habitant made many of his tools and implements, which though often crude were practical in design and efficiency. Similarly, the tables, benches, and beds of the normal household were of domestic manufacture. Just as the few artisans in the three principal towns prided themselves on their diversity of skills, so in the rural areas the settler valued self-sufficiency, independence, and innovation. In adaptation to local conditions, the colonial ideal focused not on the specialized skilled worker but rather on the *bricoleur*—the handyman, or "Jacques of all trades but master of none."

In some measure, the rural adaptation to the rigors of the Canadian climate owed much to the Native peoples, from whom colonists learned about the qualities of various native trees for building, for making furniture and implements, or for constructing canoes and sledges. The new settlers employed food-preservation methods long practiced by the original inhabitants, just as they adopted native plants such as corn and medicinal herbs. The climate was not as favorable to agriculture as it had been in the regions of France from which the newcomers had emigrated. Quebec had only 115 frost-free days on average each year; the winters were extremely cold, while the summers varied between cool and damp and hot and excessively dry. Animals had to be sheltered and provided with fodder during the long winters, which often required the slaughter each autumn of all animals except those absolutely essential for breeding and traction. Caterpillars and grasshoppers often attacked orchards, gardens, and grainfields, and the habitants' defenses often were simply to participate in a novena and ask the priest's blessing on their properties.

The agricultural potential of the region was realized only very slowly. Not only was "making land" by clearing the forests, draining the swamps, and turning over the virgin soils time-consuming labor, but it was made harder by the dearth of efficient tools and implements and the lack of domestic animals available whose power could be harnessed. Fortunate was the man who owned a pair of oxen in the seventeenth century. It took a family about five years to clear three hectares of land (about 7.5 acres), the minimum

for self-sufficiency. Farming methods inherited from France were backward compared to practices in the Low Countries and England at the time. Crop rotation, manuring, and weed control appear to have been foreign to the habitant, therefore royal intendants found it necessary to stimulate better practices through ordinances regulating such matters as the breeding of sheep at the proper season, the upkeep of enclosures, the use of manure as fertilizer, and the control of noxious weeds. Plenty of land had been available during the seventeenth century, but by the 1750s the best soils were all under cultivation. By that time, wheat and peas were being produced in sufficient quantities for sale in the towns, and even for possible export, but the majority of the rural farms were still relatively isolated and distant from markets and service centers.

SURPLUS PRODUCTION

Agriculture was becoming more diversified and there were indications it would soon be commercialized, although the Seven Years' War postponed that realization. Merchants bought up some seigneuries and set up shops outside the three principal towns, but no urban network yet existed. Small villages such as Beauport, Boucherville, Charlesbourg, Pointe-aux-Trembles, Terrebonne, and Verchères acted as service centers for the immediately surrounding rural communities. The vacuum was filled to some extent by traveling vendors, who sometimes bartered goods rather than demanding hard currency in exchange for their wares.

Those who lived closer to Montreal and Quebec could sell some of their small surpluses of milk, butter, cheese, eggs, and poultry at the weekly farmers' market in town. From time to time an ox or cow might also be brought to the abbatoir (slaughterhouse). When it was suggested by the authorities during the privations of the Seven Years' War that horse meat be sold in equal quantities to beef, the farm and town women were scandalized. Not even the governor's suggestion that they tour the abbatoir to see the cleanliness employed in the preparation of horse meat could quell their protests. In the eighteenth century no fewer than seventeen years of poor harvests were recorded in the colony. In 1749, for example, an angry crowd of hungry peasants made its way to Quebec to demand relief; they protested not against the authoritarian administration but rather against the seeming inability of that government to meet the basic needs of the populace. The intendant undoubtedly was reminded of the bread riots that were commonplace in rural France, but at first he could only enact regulations prohibiting begging and vagrancy. As on occasions when the price of bread or salt rose sharply, or parish boundaries were altered without much local consultation, the populace could turn ugly and demonstrate none of the docility and subservience some historians have attributed to it.

The fact that the Coutume de Paris guaranteed that all the children, females as well as males, should share equally in the inheritance of nonnoble land has led some historians to conclude that excessive subdivision of farms quickly ensued. The *censitaire* had always arranged that his children left home upon marriage and settled on their own holding. After the arable land had all been taken up by the early part of the eighteenth century, however, new strategies of survival had to be devised.

Some young couples or families set out, usually in small groups, to pioneer new regions such as the Ottawa River valley or the Illinois country. In some cases the children entered into an agreement drawn up before a notary according to which one or two of the children inherited the entire holding, while the others relinquished their rights for payments in cash or kind over a period of time. Another strategy that grew in popularity was the "donation among living heirs," whereby aging parents entered into a notarial contract with one of their offspring, usually the youngest son still under the parental roof, securing their care in return for title to the property. This arrangement avoided the inheritance-law stipulations, but it still required some indemnification for the other members of the family.

A popular strategy, much deplored by both church and state authorities, was to try to supplement farm income by engaging in the seasonal fur trade. Young men in particular left their parents' farms to be hired as *engagés* in the fur brigades or to illicitly "run the woods" of the upper country, or Native ancestral territories. Most of the manpower capable of handling a loaded canoe and strong enough to manage the numerous portages was recruited in the rural parishes near Montreal. As both the normal load and size of the canoes increased in the eighteenth century, wages remained high and men continued to show an interest in supplementing their farm income as boatmen and *coureurs de bois* (woods runners). Wages also remained high because farming was becoming more attractive and remunerative.

The *coureurs de bois* have generally been depicted as undisciplined, rowdy, and immoral adventurers. When they eventually returned to the rural parishes from whence they originated, however, they were also perceived as bringing valuable supplementary earnings essential to their establishment of a new family on its own plot of land. From the Amerindians they had learned many useful skills—including much about wilderness survival and guerrilla warfare—all of which would be invaluable as they sought to reintegrate into rural life and take their place as farmers and militiamen.

The pattern of seasonal labor being undertaken off the farm by numerous men, while the women and children were left to tend to the necessary chores, became well established. Some men sought to supplement their income by working during the winter months on urban projects, at lumber camps, and at sawmills. Sons of more prosperous farmers turned to wage labor, and a few even set up shops in the villages that were beginning to appear toward the end of the French regime.

THE PROSPERING SEIGNEURY

The seigneurs in the seventeenth century had sometimes found their privileges curtailed and the income from their estates rather limited. A few were even reduced to working their lands themselves and having to relinquish their banal rights to operate a gristmill that their *censitaires* would be obliged both to use and to pay for its services. But in the eighteenth century many seigneurs lived in a fashion befitting their social status. They employed domestic servants and sometimes slaves, followed fashion trends, and exacted a widening range of traditional dues from their subordinates. They insisted now on the *corvée,* or statute labor owed at seeding and harvesting seasons, and even on their monopolies on fishing, quarrying, pasturing, and ferrying. Instead of the frontier egalitarianism and social leveling that appeared in the early decades of colonization, there was now a sense that the colony, like the mother country, was a society of orders, of social distinctions, and hierarchical privilege. It has been characterized as the product of two different rationales: dependency on the fur trade, which was supported by a military elite; and dependency on agriculture, supported by the seigneurial and clerical establishment. It was, first and foremost, a predominantly rural society.

From the small urban beachheads established at the beginning of the seventeenth century, the colony grew outside the towns until by 1706 its population was 75.6 percent rural. At the conquest in 1760, the rural proportion had reached 78 percent and would continue to increase. It was a peasant society as classically defined.

THE ROLE OF THE PARISH

This rural society was also described by visitors, including the scholar Peter Kalm—a Finn and a Lutheran—as deeply religious yet quite independent-minded. The national Roman Catholic church of France, or Gallican church, alone was permitted to engage in missionary work among Native peoples and to hold public worship and offer religious instruction. Although the various religious communities of men and women, including seminaries in both Quebec and Montreal, were established early in the settlement period, the rural regions were only slowly organized into parishes with resident curates. The first bishops, François de Laval and Jean-Baptiste La Croix de Chevrières de Saint-Vallier, hesitated to erect parishes canonically until a region seemed capable of supporting a priest through

tithing and maintaining a minimum of edifices for worship and instruction. In 1681, for example, of twenty-five priests in regular parish charges, only nine held letters of provision from the bishop. Most areas were still being served as missions by itinerant clergy.

Not only did the clergy not exercise much power over the general population in such a case, but the colonists complained of infrequent services rendered by the church and refused to give financial support until such time as they would be adequately shepherded. Scarcely any seigneurs were able to assume the financial burdens of becoming patron founders of a parish church. They did enjoy a few privileges, nevertheless, such as being seated close to the communion rail, being given priority in processions, and sometimes being mentioned in the prayers. The church also upheld the social order.

The temporal affairs of the parish, constituted in law as a self-governing *fabrique,* or parochial corporation, were administered by elected churchwardens, under the guidance of the curate, and this afforded some opportunity for parishioners to assume some prominence among their peers. The parish priest catechized the children to the best of his ability, and he was overjoyed if sisters of the Congregation of Notre-Dame came from Montreal during the summer months to teach both girls and boys rudimentary letters and catechism. Apart from some sixty itinerant lay schoolmasters, who provided some basic education for brief periods in rural communities, there was little provision to escape from the prevalent illiteracy. The literacy level was lowest in the rural areas, where most of the colonists were found. Boys in rural areas seem to have had a slightly better chance than girls of receiving some basic training in reading, writing, arithmetic, and religious studies. The intendant Jacques Raudot opined in 1717 that the colonists felt no pressing need for schooling, valuing practical skills over formal training. His comments ignored the dispersed nature of the population, the absence of compact villages, and the paucity of teachers in the colony, including those with religious vocations.

The parish system became better established by the eighteenth century, but there were still only 114 parishes for about 240 seigneuries at the end of the French regime. There was a shortage of priests to serve the parishes that had been created; the thesis that the colonists were priest-ridden and closely supervised is wide of the mark for this period. Little by little colonial-born clergy were ordained, especially as seculars, but few of these were recruited in the rural parishes. The seminarians came mostly from the aristocratic and bourgeois families, with a marked increase from the artisan class; only 2 of the 195 ordained between 1611 and 1760 were sons of habitant farmers.

The colonists were religious in the sense of accepting the teachings of the church, of observing popular devotional practices, and of remaining firmly attached to the rites and liturgy. But at the same time, they held to firmly rooted popular beliefs in witches, devil possession, and observances officially decried as superstition. They loved the pomp and ceremonial associated with various fraternal organizations, processions, and festive occasions. Yet, the civil power was called upon from time to time to legislate on matters such as Sunday rest and attendance at mass, paying of tithes, maintenance of church properties, and especially respectful behavior in church.

This was not yet the period when the curate was the social as well as spiritual leader of the parish, with social functions organized around the church. Instead, the family was the basic unit in rural communities around which social life revolved. In the countryside, the evening gatherings of ostentatiously dressed women, pipe-smoking men, and courting couples giving themselves to dancing, feasting, drinking, and tale-telling—much of which was condemned by the church—was the common expression of a joyful sense of community. This reflected the gradual replacement of the religion of fear, inherited from the Middle Ages, by a more festive and familial religion and the growing cult of the Virgin Mary.

The parishes became the administrative units of a very different organization and ethos. A 1669 decree required that all able-bodied men between sixteen and sixty years of age, not members of the privileged orders, were to serve in the militia for home defense and military expeditions. A militia captain was named in each parish

to train and lead the unit. The population accepted this unremunerated duty willingly—and effectively, in time of war or threatened civil disorder—because it appeared to serve their self-interest (especially when Iroquois raids threatened the settlements) as well as providing them with issues of clothing, weapons, and ammunition. In the initial period of colonization, the clergy had read the official orders and reported on current affairs, but the militia captains replaced them as official spokesmen for the government, and they organized community activities such as statute labor, police work, local defense, and public-works projects. By attaching the militia to the parish, rather than to the seigneury, the central administration had effectively weakened the leadership roles of both seigneurs and clergy. This was a unique characteristic of Canadian rural communities during the French regime.

Rural life in the colony reflected many of the characteristics of a preindustrial agricultural society. Nevertheless, the local environment, the contact with Native peoples, and the desire of the administration to limit the power of the privileged orders in order to enhance royal power worked together to provide the colony with some unique qualities.

BIBLIOGRAPHY

Charbonneau, Hubert. *Vie et mort de nos ancêtres.* Montreal, 1975.

Dechêne, Louise. *Habitants et marchands de Montréal au XVIIe siècle.* Paris, 1974.

Douville, Raymond, and Jacques Donat Casanova. *Daily Life in Early Canada.* New York, 1968.

Frégault, Guy. *Canadian Society in the French Regime.* Ottawa, 1971.

Greer, Allan. *Peasant, Lord, and Merchant: Rural Society in Three Quebec Parishes, 1740–1840.* Toronto, Ontario, 1985.

Rioux, Marcel, and Yves Martin. *French-Canadian Society.* Toronto, Ontario, 1964.

Séguin, Robert-Lionel. *La civilisation traditionelle de l' "habitant" aux XVIIe et XVIIIe siècles.* Montreal, 1967.

Cornelius John Jaenen

THE SPANISH BORDERLANDS

SPAIN SELF-CONSCIOUSLY set out to foster and support colonization of its vast territories in the Americas, in contrast to other colonial nations. Historically speaking, C. H. Haring argues, the Spanish-American colonies may be divided into two general classes: exploitation colonies and farm colonies. Exploitation colonies were established in environments where a commodity or commodities could be produced on a large scale for export. The large agricultural estates of the tropical zone and the gold and silver mining colonies of Peru and Mexico belonged to the exploitation type. These export enterprises were managed by a small, wealthy colonial aristocracy, and the labor was performed by a large underclass of indigenous peoples or imported slaves.

In contrast farming colonies were founded in regions that lacked such economic advantages. Where limited resources made it impossible to produce for large-scale export, the rationale for Spanish colonization was of necessity different. Such regions were colonized to acquire converts to the Catholic faith, to protect the Crown's empire from encroachment, and for general territorial aggrandizement. The Indian mission and the *presidio* were generally the first colonial institutions established in these ventures; civilian settlers followed on the heels of the priests and soldiers. Settlement in the Spanish Borderlands was generally characterized by this type of colony.

Following the conquest of the Aztec Empire in central Mexico, that rich exploitation colony became the hub of the Spanish Empire in America. Thus, the principal thrust of colonizing efforts in North America came from Mexico. The Spanish colonial enterprise in North America was initiated when Philip II authorized Luis de Velasco, viceroy of New Spain, to undertake settlement of Florida in 1558. The following year the viceroy dispatched fifteen hundred soldiers and settlers to found a colony at Pensacola Bay. However Saint Augustine, founded in 1565 on the Atlantic Coast, became the first continuous settlement within the present limits of the United States. Generally, though, the Spaniards found southeastern North America unsuitable for colonization, and thus settlement in this region was limited and tenuous throughout the colonial period.

Settlement in the borderlands of the U.S. Southwest proved to be the most important colonization effort; it began with a general movement northward from central Mexico initiated in 1540, following the discovery of rich silver deposits in Zacatecas. The cutting edge of this expansion was the established mining colony, with its potential for providing rapid and substantial monetary rewards. Through this type of exploitation, the costs of colonization could be underwritten and handsome profits realized.

Beyond the mineral-rich district of Mexico's central plateau was a vast northwest territory that was claimed by Spain. Despite the hopes and dreams of sixteenth-century explorers and the designs of early colonizers, this borderlands territory ultimately was found to lack such economic advantages. Thus, settlement followed the developmental pattern of farm colonies.

The missions and *presidios* established at the outset in North America have captured our imagination and thus have generally received the greatest historical attention; however, farming and ranching settlements were also an important part of the Spanish program for colonizing the borderland frontier. In fact civilian settlers, who were variously called *pobladores, colonos,* or *vecinos,* far outnumbered friars and soldiers on the borderland frontier.

These *pobladores* were mostly common people of mixed racial background and were drawn largely from the populations living in the frontier settlements of Mexico's central plateau. On this new borderland frontier, further racial amalgamation occurred as members of the various North American Indian groups were assimilated. Through the efforts of these *pobladores*, small farming and ranching communities were founded over a vast North American territory.

Everywhere the Spanish went in North America, considerable effort was directed to founding civil communities. In general these efforts bore more fruit in the United States Southwest than elsewhere on the Spanish Borderlands. These settlements were conceived and developed as self-contained rural-urban units. The *pobla-*

dores maintained their residence in the small towns and outlying satellites; they worked the surrounding land to gain a livelihood and became largely self-sufficient. They were truly people of the country. Thus, the conventional Anglo-American rural versus urban distinction cannot easily be drawn in the Spanish Borderlands.

Over more than three centuries, these *pobladores* and their descendants created an Hispanic society and culture based upon the institutions, beliefs, and practices derived from Spain, which were simplified and adapted to the necessities of different frontier environments. In particular, this distinctive Hispanic tradition is reflected in the contemporary culture of the U.S. Southwest.

EUROPEAN ANTECEDENTS

The Old World roots of the Spanish-American community form must be sketched so that its distinctive qualities can be fully appreciated. From medieval times until the nineteenth century, the small village community was the primary unit of rural social organization, landholding, and agro-pastoral production in Western Europe, as shown by Jerome Blum. In these communities town lots and farm plots were private property; grazing land and woodlands were held in common for the benefit of all villagers. This dual form of landholding accompanied the development of an agro-pastoral economy in which plow agriculture and animal husbandry were closely interrelated and mutually supportive. These communities provided for the bulk of political, religious, and social needs in a highly integrated fashion, making them largely self-sufficient entities.

The Iberian Peninsula experienced a long history of such small agro-pastoral villages. The small pueblo became both the natural territorial unit and unit of society and was so defined in Spanish political jurisprudence. To Spaniards the word "pueblo" traditionally denotes a conception of human community based on place, for it means both a physical place on the surface of the earth and also the people who reside there. Conceptually people, society, and geographical place are integrated. Spanish villagers found it hard to imagine life without close interaction with their fellow community members in all phases of daily activities. Thus, they were predisposed historically to live in compact settlements and to work together to gain a livelihood from farming and raising stock on the surrounding community land.

The boundaries of the village land not only delimited territories for economic exploitation but also separated populations with distinct political and religious identities. Each had its own patron saint and calendar of religious feast days, which were integrated with the annual cycle of village activities. Thus, the Spanish village was a complete, virtually self-sufficient unit of rural society.

THE SPANISH CONQUEST CULTURE IN THE AMERICAS

In Spanish-American history, one immediately encounters parallels to the type of rural social organization found in Spain. Similarly, in the farm colonies, the pueblo became a fundamental unit of rural society and culture. Of course these parallels are not accidental but a result of Spain's formal colonization scheme in the Americas.

To meet the needs of the diverse indigenous populations and geography in the Americas, social and cultural innovation was necessary. Thus, the social forms and culture carried to the Spanish colonies may be thought of as a distinctive "conquest culture," as George M. Foster has characterized it, and was of necessity simplified and standardized. In many respects this culture consisted of idealized forms inspired by the utopian philosophical currents in sixteenth-century Europe. In the Americas the Spanish found seemingly virgin continents where they could impose their ideal conceptions of society, with the hope of creating a New World in the strict sense of the term. Centuries of political factionalism, economic fragmentation, and religious heterodoxy could be left behind in Spain.

To carry out such a large and ambitious colonization, the Crown created elaborate governmental, legal, and religious machinery. Endless sets of instructions and laws dealing with every phase of colonial activity emanated from the administration. Spanish colonists could not undertake settlement on their own initiative;

rather, a license had to be secured from the Crown. Colonization entailed cooperative ventures between government and private citizens. Thus, the character of the Spanish colonial society contrasted strikingly with that of colonies established by the northern European powers, where private enterprise was dominant and operated with much greater autonomy.

Laws for New Settlements

Spanish colonial regulations contained provisions for several types of civil communities, distinguished according to their size and function: *ciudades* (major self-governing cities); *villas* (charted settlements with more limited self-government); and pueblos or *poblaciones* (small unchartered communities that were attached to larger settlements for administrative purposes). There were also *reales de minas* (mining jurisdictions) and haciendas (large private ranches); however, these exploitation communities were uncommon in North America's farm colonies. Other than New Orleans and perhaps Saint Augustine, no North American community ever achieved the status of a *ciudad.*

The basic model for settlements in farm colonies in North America was an idealized version of the Castilian landholding village. During more than three centuries of colonial rule, a massive body of laws and directives was set down pertaining to every aspect of this type of settlement. These regulations and administrative practices applied to the Native American populations as well as to Hispanic settlers and proved to be especially effective in helping Spain pacify and hold new frontiers. Throughout the colonial era, the friars and civil officials alike labored tirelessly to Christianize and incorporate frontier Indians into Hispanic society. Grants of the royal domain to establish farming communities was a principal vehicle employed to accomplish these objectives.

Several types of royal land grants (called *mercedes*) were made to establish these farming and ranching villages, which had similar characteristics. A site for settlement was to be selected in an unoccupied area that could be used without injury to any other community. The sites were to be chosen with attention to the fertility of the land and the abundance of water, as well as the availability of ample common land for pastures, firewood, timber, and other natural re-

sources. In all, a town's land grant was to consist of four square leagues (a league equals 2.6 miles, or 4.2 kilometers) and to encompass both urban and rural segments.

The town was to be laid out in a grid fashion with a central plaza (public square). Standard house lots were to be distributed with sufficient land set aside to provide for future population growth. Beyond the limits of the urban settlement, land was divided into several classes according to its character and potential use. The two most important categories were *suertes* (private farm plots) and *deheseas y tierras de pasto* (communal pastures and grazing lands). Only use rights to the *ejidos* (commonlands) were granted to community members; ownership was held by the community. Water rights for domestic purposes, agriculture, and livestock accompanied the land grant.

It was the intention of the Spanish colonial government to provide each rural community with all of the natural resources needed for self-sufficiency. Settlers were required to occupy the land within three months; to perfect the title, they had to live on the grant and work the land for four years.

RURAL LIFE IN NEW MEXICO

The first permanent North American settlements were established in Florida in 1565, as has been noted, and in New Mexico in 1598; colonization occurred much later elsewhere. For example, settlement in Texas was initiated in 1716 (short-lived settlements had been abandoned some twenty-odd years earlier), in California in 1769, and in Arizona in 1752. As New Mexico was one of the oldest of the colonies and the most successful of them, its civilian population far exceeded that of the other North American provinces throughout the colonial period. For example, near the end of the Spanish colonial regime (1815–1821), the province of New Mexico had 36,579 residents, while the populations of Texas and Alta California numbered only 4,051 and 3,270 respectively.

Therefore, the colonial rural life and civil institutions in New Mexico are presented in this essay as an ideal type. There were variations elsewhere in the Spanish Borderlands, of course,

461

but the shared institutions and common culture are of far greater significance. Oakah L. Jones documented this fact in *Los Paisanos* (1979), his historical survey of New Spain's northern frontier. An exception was the Spanish colonies in the southeastern region of North America, which remained impoverished missionary and military outposts, incapable of supporting themselves by agriculture or raising livestock and thus always dependent upon annual royal subsidies. These conditions were not conducive to the development of strong civil settlements.

Colonization in New Mexico entailed a nucleus of settlement along the Rio Grande from El Paso to Taos, where arable land was found and numerous Native American farming communities had existed for centuries. Indeed, the Pueblo farming communities were one of the principal attractions of the region, since it appeared that they could be readily incorporated into Spanish colonial society.

The roots of Hispanic culture planted here were deep and strong; it is the region of North America where a rural farm community tradition persisted with only modest changes well into the present century. First colonized in 1598 under a contract awarded to Juan de Oñate, the initial settlement was established in northern New Mexico at the confluence of the Rio Grande and the Rio Chama. In 1610 the settlers moved some twenty miles (32 kilometers) south to found the Villa of Santa Fe, where they secured better land and water.

However, because the upper Rio Grande region lay approximately eight hundred miles (1,280 kilometers) beyond the edge of the mining and ranching frontier of northwest Mexico and because few settlers could be supported in this venture made difficult by distance, finance, supply problems, and the environment, seventeenth-century New Mexico was basically a Franciscan missionary enterprise among the Pueblo Indians. The missions were supported by a garrison of soldiers and a small number of civilian settlers in Santa Fe. Santa Fe was the only formally organized municipality prior to the Pueblo Indian Revolt. Santa Fe settlers established *estancias* (small farms) in the outlying region, locating them more often than not near the Indian Pueblos and supporting themselves through raising livestock and collecting Indian tribute. Settlers

attended mass at the missions and relied on Santa Fe to meet other social, political, and economic needs.

The Pueblo Revolt in 1680 was brought on by abusive economic exploitation and repressive Christian proselytizing. In throwing off the colonial yoke, the Pueblo Indians killed many of the Spanish priests and settlers and burned the missions and farms; the Spanish survivors quickly fled south to the El Paso region.

In the 1690s northern New Mexico was reconquered under the leadership of Diego de Vargas. Concessions granted to the Pueblos at this time—forced labor and tribute were not reinstituted—brought about a fundamentally different social order. Pueblo Indian land claims were recognized and protected by law from Spanish encroachment, and limited communal autonomy was granted.

During this period landholding villages became permanently established in New Mexico. However, it should be noted that because of the rugged topography, severe climate, and limited natural resources, this region failed to realize the ideal scheme for Spanish colonial settlement; the compact settlement pattern required to create grid-pattern towns was impractical. For this reason some historians have concluded that there was no genuine urbanism and that colonial officials often submitted greatly exaggerated, even fraudulent reports of their accomplishments in founding new towns. It is the belief of this author that, on the contrary, the civil officials and friars alike displayed a strong and enduring passion for founding towns. These efforts were directed toward Hispanos as well as Indians. In the view of these colonial authorities, urban living as constituted in the landholding town was a hallmark of Spanish civilization and thus a principal objective of colonization on this remote frontier. Indeed, the historical records show that in founding new communities, officials frequently fell far short of what they sought to accomplish, but given the circumstances it seems less than fair to condemn them without reservation for these shortcomings.

A FULLY REALIZED SETTLEMENT

The following description of civilian settlement in New Mexico will focus on Santa Cruz de La

462

Cañada, which became the largest and one of the most fully developed rural communities in the Spanish Borderlands.

Following the reconquest Santa Fe was overflowing with new settlers, and the arrival of additional colonists was imminent. Thus in April 1695 Governor de Vargas issued a proclamation directing that a new settlement be founded in the Santa Cruz River valley, where it meets the Rio Grande. The sixty-odd families who had arrived from Mexico the previous June were ordered to settle in the new villa.

The settlers were charged with the responsibility of defending the town and the territory within its jurisdiction. Since the settlement was likely to face frequent incursions from nomadic Indian bands, Santa Cruz was established with both a civil and military government. The principal officer was named both *alcalde mayor* (chief magistrate, a civil office) and *Capítan de la Guerra* (war captain).

The boundaries of the new villa were recited when the governor put the settlers in possession. Each family was given a house lot; *suertes* were apportioned so that each head of household received sufficient land with which to plant one-half *fanega* of corn (approximately 4.4 acres). The community's *ejidos* (grazing lands and woods) were to be held and used in common.

Founding a new town on the Spanish Borderlands was one thing; ensuring its survival was another. Initially, subsistence proved to be the greatest problem for the Santa Cruz settlers. Plagues of worms and drought and an inadequate supply of agricultural tools brought great suffering and hardship. Settlers also experienced difficulties due to a lack of familiarity with the characteristics of the soils and seasons. Further, in 1695 an epidemic took a heavy toll in sickness and death, contributing to the depressed state of affairs. In these early years, several appeals were directed to the governor requesting permission to abandon the settlement for the above reasons as well as the fear of Indian hostilities.

It appears that the settlement was abandoned on at least one occasion in the ensuing years; a sequence of founding, abandonment, and refounding of settlements was more the rule than the exception on the Spanish Borderlands frontier. In 1704 Governor de Vargas traveled to Santa Cruz and revalidated the grant, as well as fifteen other land grants in the *Alcaldía* (the administrative district of the Villa de Santa Cruz). In addition, several settlers requested new grants. From this point Hispanic settlement in the district was stabilized, and the population began a steady growth that continued throughout the colonial period.

The pattern of settlement in the villa consisted of dispersed *ranchos* (small farms) strung out along the watercourses. This was necessitated by the region's geography; small amounts of arable land and pasturage at any one site limited the population that could be supported. This limitation affected the growth of the town of Santa Cruz itself. The district's *ranchos* were inhabited by expanded family groups, which often included widows, widowers, mothers-in-law, nieces, nephews, and captive Indian servants.

Periodically as the population grew, a loose clustering of kin-linked *ranchos* formed small hamlets or villages known as *poblaciones*, or plazas. (The term "pueblo" was used only for sedentary Indian communities in New Mexico.) These local residential units made it possible to accomplish tasks that required more hands than could be provided by a single household, tasks such as harvesting crops, herding livestock, and undertaking military operations. All able-bodied *pobladores* were expected to provide a prescribed number of days of militia service annually. Plazas were also formed, in part as the result of the cooperative efforts necessary to build, maintain, and operate *acequias* (irrigation systems). A dependable supply of water for domestic and agricultural purposes was critical to the survival of settlers in this semiarid climate. The *acequias* also provided the water power to operate small *molinos* (gristmills).

Hispanic settlers brought with them to the Spanish Borderlands a constellation of arid-land techniques, including both the technical knowledge and the institutional framework to build and operate irrigation systems. Thus irrigation systems have always been an integral part of farming in this region. They have served to integrate man, land, and water over time and space, creating a distinctive rhythm of life in the Hispanic plazas. *Acequia* associations remain, perhaps, the most important community institutions, a visible part of the Spanish colonial legacy.

Subsistence was achieved through a mixed agro-pastoral economy. The irrigated farmland in the valleys produced corn, wheat, beans, and a few vegetables. In addition, small orchards were established. Wild plants and nuts augmented the diet, as did deer and other game. Hunting parties traveled far afield annually to hunt buffalo on the eastern plains.

Keeping herds of sheep, goats, and a few cattle, however, was the most important subsistence activity. In keeping with the Hispanic pattern, animal husbandry was integrated with farming. It involved a genuine wedding of the two types of production so that one supported the other. Grazing was coordinated with the agricultural cycle; the stock was moved to mountain pastures during the growing season and returned after the harvest to graze on the stubble. Their manure helped to fertilize the valley fields so that successful farming could be sustained.

Other important adjuncts to the economy were trading with the nomadic Indians and periodically raiding their *rancherías* (temporary settlements). Horses, weapons, corn, and *punche* (a semidomesticated tobacco) were bartered for dressed hides, meat, and captive women and children. Government-sanctioned punitive raids allowed the participants to take booty—personal belongings, livestock, and women and children.

The division of labor was largely along the lines of age and sex. Domestic chores, infant care, and tending the crops after planting became the responsibility of women, older children, and the elderly. If the household contained servants, they assisted the women with these domestic chores. Men and maturing boys repaired and cleaned the *acequias* each spring, prepared the fields, planted the crops, managed the livestock, and devoted themselves to hunting, trading, and military service.

Labor for all was characterized by considerable mobility. This was a consequence of the irregular, intermittent distribution of arable land, the seasonal movement required by animal husbandry, and the gradual outward expansion of settlement as the population increased. Extended families often acquired rights to farming and grazing land in several localities, and they frequently owned dwellings in several places. Thus, they shifted their residence seasonally as farming and ranching activities required. Also,

they were drawn periodically to Santa Cruz to satisfy governmental, religious, and some social needs.

Government and Religion

Formal governmental and social institutions were quite limited in the Villa de Santa Cruz throughout the colonial period. Despite the gradual dispersal of the population, administration was centered in the town of Santa Cruz, where the *alcalde mayor* resided. He was responsible for enforcing the law, settling disputes, collecting taxes, distributing land, and compiling censuses for the entire *Alcaldía*. In a similar fashion, military affairs were also directed from Santa Cruz.

As the number of plazas somewhat removed from Santa Cruz grew, *teniente alcaldes* were named for the *partidos* (jurisdictional units) of the *Alcaldía*. Judicially, the *teniente* was responsible for settling minor civil cases and, more generally, assisting the *alcalde mayor* in fulfilling his responsibilities. A *teniente alcalde* also had military responsibilities and was aided by several local militia officers. It should be understood, then, that the Villa de Santa Cruz incorporated the small *plazas* as dependent subunits; the community consisted of the urban center and its rural environs, as was the Hispanic pattern.

Leaders emerged out of the local kinship matrix to fill the limited number of formal civil and military positions in the *Alcaldía*. As a rule these appointed leaders were respected senior male heads of the larger and most prominent kin groups, so the structures of authority and decision making along kinship and governmental lines were merged.

The administration of religion in Santa Cruz was at first in the hands of the Franciscans residing at the nearby missions of San Juan and Santa Clara pueblos. At most *pobladores* were given permission to build small chapels, which were visited periodically by the priests. Franciscans invariably were outsiders, and relations with settlers generally were uneasy. Franciscan reports to their superiors abound with derogatory assessments of the level of Catholic orthodoxy and the general moral climate among the *pobladores*.

Sometime during the final quarter of the eighteenth century, in the absence of sufficient clergy to serve the Hispanic settlers, voluntary penitential *cofradías* (confraternities) or *hermandades* (brotherhoods) took over most of the duties normally performed by the priest in the Catholic church. In particular, the *hermandad* guided the community through the important rituals associated with Lent and Holy Week. It also served as an agency to aid the needy.

Trade and Crafts

In general life on this remote Spanish Borderland frontier during the eighteenth and nineteenth centuries was difficult. The settlers lived with the constant threat of loss of life and property as the result of nomadic Indian raids. They also faced periodic epidemics and frequent crop failures in this inhospitable environment. The opportunities to amass wealth were limited. The development of external trade was hampered by the limited ability to produce surpluses for export, the great distances between Spanish colonial provinces, and the crude forms of transportation—horses, mules, and *carretas* (wooden-wheeled carts). The majority of settlers labored principally to achieve a subsistence livelihood; trade occurred largely between nomadic Indian bands and villages within the province. Only a limited number of items were exported from New Mexico, among them mules, sheep, wool, animal hides, and Indian captives.

Relatively few products and manufactured goods were imported, and *pobladores* generally provided for themselves. The region developed its own craftsmen, who made everything from farm implements to furniture and religious images. Adopting indigenous materials and techniques, adobe architecture was developed. A distinctive style of Catholic religious imagery was created by carving and painting on wood and painting on animal hides. Lacking direct access to Spanish-American theater and music, *pobladores* created local traditions.

Education

There were no public schools or colleges in New Mexico until the very end of the colonial period. Most formal instruction was conducted by the Franciscans and directed to young Indians, with the objective of drawing them into the Catholic faith. During the eighteenth century, a few private teachers were available to serve the children of *pobladores* in Santa Fe and Albuquerque, but none resided in Santa Cruz. A handful of elite families were able to send their sons to be educated outside of the province. However, the vast majority of the *pobladores* were without formal education.

In the waning years of the colonial regime, at the beginning of the nineteenth century, primary schooling grew in the province, and public schools were reported to be operating in several communities, including Santa Cruz. Those who attended learned to read and write and to recite the catechism. As a result of these formal efforts and informal learning that occurred at home, it is estimated that approximately one-third of the adult male *vecinos* were literate.

Daily Life

The rhythm of life in the Santa Cruz district was governed by the daily and seasonal cycle of agriculture and animal husbandry, punctuated periodically by the festivities surrounding saints' days, fiestas, and Indian trading fairs. The most important saints' days were San Ysidro Day (in honor of the patron saint of the farmer) and the days honoring the various saints adopted by the different plazas. These celebrations usually entailed a procession where the image of the saint was carried from the church or chapel around the community, followed by a Mass; entertainment for one and all—food, drink, music, and a *baile* (dance)—concluded the celebration.

The ordinary rounds of social life were always simple but satisfying. Visiting the homes of kinsmen, attending church services, weddings, and so forth enriched everyday life. Storytelling, singing, and playing games brought pleasure and occupied many leisure hours.

CONCLUSION

In general the pattern of rural community life described for the Villa de Santa Cruz may be found in all of the Spanish Borderland provinces, except perhaps in the Southeast, where civilian (nonmilitary, nonmissionary) rural life appears not to have developed to the extent it did in California and the Southwest. Colonial towns consisted of self-sufficient, rural-urban jurisdictions; the distinctive Spanish agro-pastoral community tradition incorporated urban living and rural work.

As difficult and, at times, precarious as life was during the Spanish colonial era, Santa Cruz grew from a population of approximately 200 in 1695 to 12,903 in 1817. Thus, at the end of the colonial reign, Santa Cruz was by far the largest and one of the most successful villas in the Spanish Borderlands. This remarkable three hundred-year-old rural community legacy is quite palpable in New Mexico today; it continues to shape and give meaning to the lives of the numerous descendants of these *pobladores* in the Spanish Borderlands.

BIBLIOGRAPHY

Blum, Jerome. "The European Village as Community: Origins and Functions." *Agricultural History* 45, no. 3 (1971):157–178.

Foster, George M. *Culture and Conquest: America's Spanish Heritage.* Viking Fund Publications in Anthropology, no. 27. New York, 1960.

Freeman, Susan Tax. *Neighbors: The Social Contract in a Castilian Hamlet.* Chicago, 1970. See this study regarding the Spanish agro-pastoral village.

Gibson, Charles. *Spain in America.* New York, 1966.

Haring, Clarence H. *The Spanish Empire in America.* New York, 1963.

Jones, Oakah L. *Los Paisanos: Spanish Settlers on the Northern Frontier of New Spain.* Norman, Okla., 1979.

Pitt-Rivers, Julian A. *People of the Sierra.* Chicago, 1961. The classic study of a small Spanish pueblo.

Quintana, Frances Leon. *Pobladores: Hispanic Americans of the Ute Frontier.* Aztec, N.Mex., 1991. Offers a full description of the typical development pattern along the Rio Chama drainage in the Santa Cruz District.

Simmons, Marc. *Albuquerque: A Narrative History.* Albuquerque, N.Mex., 1982.

———. "Settlement Patterns and Village Plans in Colonial New Mexico." *Journal of the West* 8, no. 1 (1969):7–21.

Van Ness, John R. *Hispanos in Northern New Mexico: The Development of Corporate Community and Multicommunity.* New York, 1991.

Weber, David J. *The Spanish Frontier in North America.* New Haven, Conn., 1992.

Wolf, Eric R. *The Sons of Shaking Earth.* Chicago, 1959. See pages 152–175 for a treatment of the influence of European utopian philosophical currents on Spain's design for settling and developing its American colonies.

John R. Van Ness

SEE ALSO **Architecture; Crafts;** and **Urban Life;** and various essays in ECONOMIC LIFE and FOLKWAYS.

URBAN LIFE

THE BRITISH COLONIES

THE CITIES OF THE BRITISH COLONIES in North America were never large in comparison to the urban centers of Europe, Asia, and the Middle East or even compared to the urban centers of New Spain. In 1700 Boston, then the largest North American city, had only seven thousand inhabitants, while New York, Philadelphia, and Charleston were merely large villages of about five thousand, two thousand, and two thousand, respectively. But because they were administrative centers of the colonies as well as seaports through which people and goods passed, they partook of the rapid growth of the colonies themselves in the eighteenth century. By the eve of the American Revolution, Philadelphia had blossomed into the largest North American city, with about thirty thousand inhabitants, while New York and Boston stood at about twenty-five thousand and sixteen thousand, respectively.

In an overwhelmingly agricultural society, only about 5 percent of the eighteenth-century American colonists lived in towns as large as twenty-five hundred. Yet the urban societies were at the leading edge of social change. Almost all the alterations associated with the advent of modern life occurred first in the seaport towns and then radiated outward to the villages, farms, and plantations of the hinterland. It was in the urban centers that the transition first occurred from a barter to a commercial economy, from a social order based on assigned status to one based on achievement, from rank-conscious and deferential politics to contentious and participatory politics, and from small-scale workshop craftsmanship to factory-centered, machine-based production. In addition, the cities were the centers of intellectual life and the conduits through which European ideas flowed into the colonies.

In their earliest years, the urban centers were ethnically and religiously uniform to a considerable degree. East Anglian Puritans settled Boston, Dutch Calvinists founded New Amsterdam (the predecessor of New York City), English Quakers established Philadelphia, and West Indian Anglicans built Charleston. But religious and ethnic homogeneity broke down rapidly in Manhattan in the late seventeenth century and in Philadelphia, Boston, and Charleston in the eighteenth century. After the Peace of Utrecht in 1713, thousands of white immigrants poured into Philadelphia from Ulster, the Rhineland, the West Indies, and other points of the compass. Boston most successfully resisted newcomers of different tongues and religions, but there too, by the eve of the revolution, people of diverse religious persuasions worshiped, though most were English in background. New York City by the end of the seventeenth century was a mélange of Dutch, French, and English settlers with a scattering of Germans, Portuguese, Spanish, and others.

Amid this growing cosmopolitanism, religious persecution, if not religious prejudice, faded in Boston and smaller New England towns. In the process, the early Puritan meaning of community—a collection of like-minded believers who had little use for "strangers"—gave way to the Philadelphia meaning of community—a collection of believers, disbelievers, mystics, agnostics, and nihilists who learned to see themselves linked by material rewards and social necessities rather than by heavenly quests. In this growing acceptance of the idea that diversity could be the cement rather than the dissolver of unity lay the origins of the pluralism that was to become a mainstay of urban American society.

One immigrant group that was largely absent from European towns but figured importantly in the social landscape of North American cities was the African. At the beginning of the eighteenth century, only Charleston had more than a few hundred of these involuntary immigrants. But their proportion of the population grew substantially between 1720 and 1770, spurred by the demand for labor in the growing towns and, during the Seven Years' War (1756–1763), by the nearly complete stoppage of the indentured servant trade. By the mid 1700s more than fifteen hundred Africans lived in Boston, and at least half the white families of New York City owned slaves. In Philadelphia, where those investing in bound labor had chosen Irish and German indentured servants more often than African slaves in the first half of the century, merchants and artisans alike purchased record numbers of Africans during the 1750s. In Charleston, capital of the colony with the highest proportion of slaves in British North America, 54 percent of the city's eleven thousand residents were slaves by 1770.

In the closing decade of the colonial period, this rapid growth of black laborers underwent several important changes. First, slave imports to the growing cities came to an abrupt halt, except in Charleston. The depression following the Seven Years' War convinced many urban merchants and artisans of the advantages of free laborers, whom they could hire and discharge as economic cycles dictated. The growth of abolitionism in the cities in the 1770s aroused increasing pressure against slave imports. All along the northeastern seaboard, the black urban slave populations began plummeting as the imperial crisis arose, since dying slaves were not replaced by new recruits from Africa.

The second change was the rise of free black populations of a few dozen to a few hundred in places like Philadelphia and New York in the 1770s. These were the nuclei of the much larger free black populations that would form after the revolution.

COMMERCIAL GROWTH

In the half century after 1690, Boston, New York, Philadelphia, and Charleston blossomed from urban villages into thriving commercial centers. This urban growth accompanied the development of the agricultural interior to which the seaports were closely linked. As the colonial population rose and spread geographically, satellite seaports such as Salem, Newport, Providence, Annapolis, and Norfolk gathered four to five thousand or more inhabitants.

Trade was indispensable to colonial economic life, and cities were trade centers. Through them flowed colonial export staples such as tobacco, rice, wheat, timber products, furs, meat, and fish as well as the imported goods that colonists needed. The imports included manufactured and luxury goods from England such as glass, paper, iron implements, and cloth; wine, spices, coffee, tea, and sugar from other parts of the world; and human cargo to fill the labor gap. As centers of waterborne and wagon-borne trade, the cities were always filled with mariners, wagoners, carters, and dockhands as well as tavernkeepers to serve the needs of those passing through.

By the eighteenth century, the American economy was integrated into an Atlantic-basin trading system that connected Great Britain, western Europe, Africa, the West Indies, and Newfoundland. In the commercial seaports, the pivotal figure was the merchant. He linked producers and consumers, coordinating a commercial network that reached from the coastal city to the interior villages, plantations, and trading posts and stretched outward across the Atlantic. Frequently engaged in both retail and wholesale trade, the merchant was also moneylender (for no banks yet existed), shipbuilder, insurance agent, land developer, and often coordinator of artisan production. He was also the most frequent source of contributions to build a church, a school, a charity institution, or a civic improvement.

URBAN ARTISANS

Although merchants stood first in wealth and prestige in the colonial towns, craftsmen— known also as artisans, mechanics, and trades- men—were far more numerous. They made up from one-half to two-thirds of the taxpaying heads of household in most urban centers. As they fit themselves into local economies, they ranged up and down the social ranks because they were members of two overlapping hierar- chies: first, the traditional, three-level craft hier- archy of apprentice, journeyman, and master craftsman; and second, the hierarchy of trades in which shoemakers, stockingmakers, coopers, and tailors could usually be found at the bottom; construction craftsmen such as carpenters, glazi- ers, shipwrights, mastmakers, bricklayers, and painters in the middle; and metalworkers such as goldsmiths, silversmiths, and instrument mak- ers at the top.

Work patterns for artisans were irregular, dictated by weather, hours of daylight, erratic delivery of raw materials, and shifting consumer demand. When ice blocked northern harbors, mariners and dockworkers endured slack time. If prolonged rain delayed the slaughter of cows in the country or made impassable the rutted roads into the city, the tanner and the shoemaker laid their tools aside. The hatter depended upon the supply of beaver skins, which could stop abruptly if disease struck an Indian tribe or war disrupted the fur trade. Every urban artisan knew "broken days," slack spells, and dull sea- sons. Ordinary laborers dreaded winter, for it was a season when the demand for labor was at a low ebb and firewood to heat even a small house could cost several months' wages.

Over the many decades of the colonial era, two seemingly contrary developments occurred among the craftsmen of the various urban com- munities. On the one hand, greater occupational specialization came to mark all the growing colo- nial port towns and inland agricultural market centers. A much greater variety of artisans ap- peared, so that joiners—to take one example— would specialize in cabinetmaking, chair making, or clock making. Along with this greater speciali- zation came the arrangement of artisans along a broader spectrum of wealth and status. On the other hand, the passing generations brought greater political involvement by craftsmen. Dur- ing a series of eighteenth-century wars, they wit- nessed wealth becoming concentrated in the hands of merchants and large property owners and economic cycles becoming more pro- nounced. This helped to create a greater feeling of common interest among artisans and to re- shape their understanding of their political rights, responsibilities, and goals.

Among urban craftsmen the belief in the utility and dignity of labor was widespread. The dignity belonging to the creation of a crafted product was based not only on the Protestant concept of calling, where the mason was as wor- thy as the merchant in God's eyes, but also in the notion that no community could exist without the products of its dextrous craftsmen. Craft skill represented indispensable knowledge, and upon that expertise rested a claim to respect and a certain social authority in the community. More- over, craft skill was a form of capital, nonmaterial to be sure, but at least as important as cash or real estate. As a type of capital, artisanal skill became invested in products, and thus chairs, houses, ships, pewter platters, china, and car- riages always bore the personal stamp of their maker or makers and were therefore, in an indi- rect way, his transferred possessions.

In the course of crossing the Atlantic, arti- sans developed a corollary attitude that intensi- fied their belief in the dignity of labor. On the western side of the Atlantic, the incentives for industriousness went beyond a search for "a de- cent competency" because the availability of land and the persistent shortage of labor produced a more fluid social structure. That encouraged greater industriousness. Hector St. John Crève- coeur wrote memorably of an "altering of scale," an embarking on "designs the immigrant never would have thought of in his own country." It was true that the rise to status of master crafts-man was comparatively swift by comparison with the German Palatinate, Ulster, or East Anglia. The prospect of a relatively rapid elevation promoted a more careful use of time and the desire to stay at the workbench longer. Benjamin Franklin's best-selling almanacs were accordingly filled with nostrums about not wasting time and keeping one's nose to the grindstone: "The sleeping fox gathers no poultry"; "Lost time is never found again"; "Sloth makes all things difficult but industry all easy"; "At the working man's house, hunger looks in but dares not enter"; "He that is prodigal of his Hours, is, in effect, a Squanderer of Money."

Such advice made economic sense only for the self-employed, since apprentices and journeymen could not increase their income by working harder or longer. Hence, acceptance of a more intense work ethic spread downward from the master craftsmen only slowly, as lesser artisans protected customary rights to grog breaks and long midday meal hours. But it is notable that while English construction artisans reduced their working hours to ten per day in the early eighteenth century, and most other artisans achieved the same reduction from the traditional dawn-to-dusk regimen, apprentices and journeymen in eighteenth-century American cities kept toiling from first to last light.

Along with the craftsman's belief in the dignity of labor came the expectation of respect in the community. This respect, as given by those above him in the social order, usually came in full measure only when the artisan achieved independent status by controlling his own property and tools, the capital invested in his enterprise, and those he employed to assist him. Reaching this stage required patience, for it took time to learn the "mysteries of the craft" and to accumulate sufficient capital. Few were the young craftsmen who did not covet the greater freedom and control of workplace and work pace that came with achieving the status of master.

Some of the artisan's pride comes through to us in the rare portraits of eighteenth-century craftsmen. When Paul Revere of Boston sat for John Singleton Copley in about 1769, he wanted to be depicted in the workingman's simple linen body shirt and vest, his leather, with his sand-filled pad and engraving tools before him on the work table, and with an unfinished silver teapot cradle in one hand. Joseph G. Cole's portrait of the ninety-three-year-old Boston shoe-maker, George Robert Twelves Hewes, depicts the last surviving member of the Boston Tea Party in 1835 with a countenance displaying "the pride of a citizen, of one who 'would not take his hat off to any man.' " Charles Willson Peale's portrait of John Strangeways Hutton, the Philadelphia mariner who spent thirty years at sea and then became a notable silversmith (and who could still turn out a silver tumbler at age ninety-four) similarly shows the face of a man with a strong sense of self-esteem.

The craftsman's goal of independence was usually set within a broader outlook. Belonging to a trade carried with it an understanding of cooperative workshop labor where master craftsman, journeyman, and apprentice toiled together in service to themselves, each other, and the community. A man was not simply a chair maker in Newport or a pewterer in Savannah, striving independently to make "a competence." He was also a member of a collective body, organized in tiers; and those collective bodies, representing the various trades, made up the laboring part of the community. Men certainly aspired individually—Franklin could not brook the role of apprentice or journeyman and competed fiercely with his fellow printers once he established his own shop in Philadelphia—but this striving was reined in by a collective trade identity that carried with it obligations to the community.

The importance of independence for artisans can be better understood by viewing its opposite—dependence. The extreme form of dependence was the recourse to charity of public poor relief, which signified that a man could not provide for his family. In some cities, such as New York, municipal authorities made sure that the shame of poor relief sunk marrow deep by making all recipients wear a colored badge on their shoulder. Thus, the ability to maintain one's household without falling upon charity was a crucial element in the craftman's respectability.

In their quest for self-respect and the respect of the community, the colonial craftsmen of the American cities had certain structural problems to surmount, such as the wrenching dislocations of a series of wars from the 1670s through the 1760s. In their early stages, such wars created a hefty demand for goods and services that benefited most craftsmen. But war itself led to many craftsmen's deaths, and at war's end, slack times with unemployment and material want often occurred.

Craftsmen also had to overcome another impediment—the attitude of upper-class urbanites who regarded men who worked with their hands as inferior beings. The urban social structure, while fluid in comparison with that of European cities, was presided over by wealthy nabobs who often decried the crossing of status lines. This put craftsmen in an awkward and sometimes anomalous position. They did not always command the respect that they craved because upper-class merchants and professionals often saw them as "mere mechanicks." Therefore the upward mobility of craftsmen and their desire for involvement in community affairs often brought charges of inappropriate striving and misplaced self-importance from those at the top who wished for an orderly society in which the elite led and the masses followed submissively. Since most craftsmen derived their living from "bespoke work"—the fashioning of articles by agreement with a customer who was a shopkeeper, merchant, doctor, lawyer, or official—artisans sometimes found themselves uneasily situated in a clientage system in which their social and political aspirations rubbed against elite notions of how they should behave.

URBAN POLITICS

This was especially true regarding the political involvement of craftsmen. From the very beginning of settlement, artisans saw themselves as public persons with civic interests and responsibilities. This moved them from their shop benches into the streets whenever their interests, or those of the community as they perceived it, were threatened. Many artisans milled among the crowd that attacked the grain-loaded ships and warehouses of Andrew Belcher of Boston in 1710 and 1713 who had threatened bread shortages in the Bay colony's capital by attempting to ship much of the year's wheat harvest out of the province. In Philadelphia a decade later, artisans responded to a severe recession in the early 1720s and to the elite's insensitivity to the plight of craftsmen by flocking to the Leather Apron Club organized for artisans by the populist governor William Keith. From this organization, probably the first artisans' group of its sort in colonial America, they pressured the legislative assembly and swung their votes on election day behind those responsive to their needs.

Such artisan involvement in politics brought howls of indignation from those in the upper stratum of urban society, and artisans had to devise ways of buffering themselves from the withdrawal of patronage that resulted. To the wealthy Philadelphia merchant Isaac Norris, the activities of the Leather Apron Club in the 1720s proved that "the people head and foot run mad," that government was being taken out of the hands of "the Wise, the Rich, the learned" and placed in the hands of "rabble butchers, porters & ragtags." In Boston in the 1730s, the royal governor called the craftsmen's political leader, Elisha Cooke, Jr., "head of the scum" and "idol of the mob."

In the early eighteenth century, craftsmen often entered the political arena gingerly, struggling to overcome a built-in tendency to defer to their betters. But this reticence, if inbred, also had its limits, for artisans prided themselves as the inheritors of the rights of freeborn Englishmen with habits of mind that abhorred subservient behavior.

Episodic in the seventeenth and early eighteenth centuries, the intrusion of artisans into urban politics became more systematic when war in the 1740s and 1750s brought hard times to all the cities. The most politically involved craftsmen, at least those who took to the streets, were probably mostly from the lower artisanry, where shoemakers, tailors, ship caulkers, coopers, and other of the less materially fortunate tradesmen were perched on the knife edge of economic insecurity. In Boston, where economic downturns since the early eighteenth century had caused more suffering than in any other port town, craftsmen joined mariners and laborers by the hundreds in 1747 to stymie Commodore Charles Knowles of the Royal Navy when he tried to fill the depleted ranks of his fleet by sending press gangs to comb the waterfront and dragoon workingmen. Few chairs were fashioned or pewter bowls hammered during several tumultuous days in November when laboring men took control of the town in a facedown with the English commodore.

In Philadelphia during the same year, patrician reaction to newly politicized craftsmen was countered in an urgent public debate. When a French attack on Philadelphia seemed imminent and the assembly procrastinated in mobilizing the militia, Benjamin Franklin appealed to the old sense of dignity and worth in the producing classes. They had always been civic-minded, he reminded them, and now they must step forward to solve a problem that their social betters were cravenly evading. The result was the formation of the Philadelphia Associators, a voluntary militia that became symbolic of artisan strength, respectability, and community mindedness. Franklin played to the idea that craftsmen were the most civic-minded people in the city in his clever *XYZ Dialogue*, a fictionalized debate among three Philadelphians about the volunteer militia act. "X", an artisan, had all the best arguments in his verbal joust with patrician neighbors, as Franklin spread the message that the craftsmen of Philadelphia were the city's bone and sinew.

CHANGING VALUES

In every city during the eighteenth century, new values took hold. In the older, medieval, "corporate" view of society, economic life ideally operated according to what was equitable, not what was profitable. Citizens usually agreed that government should provide for the general welfare by regulating prices and wages, setting and enforcing quality controls, licensing providers of services such as tavernkeepers and ferrymen, and supervising public markets where all food was sold. Such regulations seemed natural because a community was defined not as a collection of individuals, each entitled to pursue separate interests, but as a single body of interrelated parts where individual rights and responsibilities formed a seamless web from which all would benefit.

But as in Europe, American city dwellers began to imbibe new ideas about economic life. The subordination of private interest to the commonweal became viewed by some as a lofty but unrealistic ideal. Prosperity, it was argued, required the encouragement of acquisitive appetites rather than self-denial, for ambition would spur economic activity as more people sought more goods. According to this view, if people were allowed to pursue their own material desires competitively, they would collectively form a natural market of producers and consumers that, while impersonal, would operate to everyone's advantage.

As the North American towns grew and became more tightly imbedded in the Atlantic world of commerce, merchants became accustomed to making decisions according to the emerging commercial ethic that rejected traditional restraints on entrepreneurial activity. If wheat fetched eight shillings a bushel in the West Indies but only five shillings in Boston, then a grain merchant felt justified in sending all the grain he could purchase from local farmers to the more distant buyer, quite apart from the effect this would have on bread prices in his own community. Indifferent to the immediate social effects of economic activity, the heralds of the new order argued that in the long run all would benefit from a more vigorous, unrestrained economic system.

The tension between the new economic freedom that made the individual the social unit of concern and the older concern for the public good that put the community at the center of all rulemaking erupted mostly in times of stress. Many craftsmen, in good times, could unconsciously fuse the new capitalistic mentality and the traditional communalistic ethos into a kind of collective individualism where the values of community-oriented workshop production commingled with new notions of economic rationality and pursuit of profit. The new bourgeois stance was particularly attractive in the more profitable trades, where opportunity for advancement was greatest.

Wartime dislocations such as food shortages and runaway inflation brought the older ethic of considering the community above the individual back to the minds of many urban dwellers. For the most part, the clergy continued to invoke the traditional concept of the corporate community: "Let no man seek his own, but every man another's wealth." But by the mid eighteenth century, the pursuit of a profitable livelihood, not the social compact of the community, animated many city dwellers.

SOCIAL RESTRUCTURING: WEALTH AND POVERTY

Cities have always been places that attract fortune seekers and risk takers, and the North American cities in the colonial period were no different. The growing seventeenth- and early eighteenth-century cities were full of men who had risen to modest wealth from artisan backgrounds. Still young and fluid, the cities were arenas of opportunity for the industrious and bold. Benjamin Franklin was everyone's model of the plucky, shrewd, and frugal leather apronman who might advance rapidly from apprentice to journeyman to master craftsman. Many, like Franklin, watched their wives replace the wooden spoon and earthen porringer at the table with a pewter spoon and china bowl, symbolizing the ascent beyond the "mere competency" that was the artisan's modest goal in the preindustrial era. In Philadelphia about half the artisans who died in the first half of the eighteenth century left personal property worth between £50 and £200 sterling, signifying a comfortable standard of living. Another quarter left more than £200, often including slaves and indentured servants. New England's urban craftsmen did not fare so well, for their economy was weaker in the eighteenth century. But in all the cities, many upward-moving craftsmen could be found.

Population growth, economic development, and a series of wars that punctuated the period from 1675 to 1765 altered the urban social structure. Stately Georgian townhouses rose as testimony to the fortunes acquired in trade, shipbuilding, war contracting, and urban land development. This last may have been the most profitable of all. "It is almost a proverb," a Philadelphian observed in the 1760s, "that every great fortune made here within these [last] 50 years has been by land." Some merchants amassed fortunes, and this trend could almost be measured by the greatly enlarged number of horse-drawn carriages that rolled through the streets—twisted in Boston, curved in New York, and straight in Philadelphia and Charleston. A merchant's estate of £2,000 sterling was counted impressive in the early eighteenth century. Two generations later, some commercial titans had become North America's first millionaires by accumulating estates of from £10,000 to £20,000 sterling.

The rise of Thomas Hancock, upon whose fortune his less commercially astute nephew, John Hancock, would later construct a shining political career, provides a glimpse of how war could catapult an enterprising trader to affluence. As a young man, Hancock, a minister's son, became a bookseller in Boston. An opportune marriage to the daughter of a prosperous merchant provided a toehold in commerce and enough capital to invest in several ships. By 1735 Hancock had made enough money, much of it from smuggling tea, to build a mansion on Beacon Hill. After war broke out with Spain in 1739 and with France five years later, Hancock used his connections with the governor to obtain lucrative supply contracts for military expeditions to the Caribbean and Nova Scotia. He also invested heavily in privateers, who engaged in private warfare against enemy shipping and auctioned the enemy vessels they overpowered. When peace returned in 1748, all Boston witnessed what war could do for a well-connected merchant. The man who had sold books from a tiny shop on Drawbridge Street fifteen years earlier now imported a four-horse chariot from London with the interior lined in scarlet and the doors emblazoned with a heraldic shield.

Another by-product of new urban wealth, which produced a broader middle class than had existed earlier, was the rise of a consumer ethos. The sheer range of articles available for purchase in the cities grew enormously in the eighteenth century, as can be seen in newspaper advertisements, in occupational specialization, and in the inventories of wealth recorded in the probate records when urban dwellers died.

Yet alongside urban wealth grew urban poverty. Both increased impressively in the middle decades of the eighteenth century. A primary cause again was war. While enriching many merchants and suppliers of military goods, war widowed many wives and orphaned many children, who then had to rely on public relief. Boston suffered earlier and more intensively than other towns, its economy wracked after the 1720s by war-induced inflation and heavy taxes and its coffers strained from supporting hundreds of war widows and their fatherless children. By the mid eighteenth century, Boston was the widow capital of the western world, with a widow heading every third household.

In all the cities, poverty spread during the deep recession following the Seven Years' War. Churches provided what they could for their indigent members, but most of the burden had to be carried through heavier poor taxes to provide for public relief. Nobody in the cities of Cotton Mather and William Penn could have imagined a report such as came from the Philadelphia almshouse managers as the Continental Congress was convening to debate independence a few blocks away: "Of the 147 Men, 178 Women, and 85 Children [admitted during the previous year] most of them [are] naked, helpless and emaciated with Poverty and Disease to such a Degree, that some have died in a few Days after their Admission." To control poor relief expenditures, paid for by the special poor taxes, town leaders tightened residency requirements, expelled newcomers from the countryside and other towns, and built large new workhouses and almshouses with harsh daily regimens to control those who qualified for public relief. The growth of princely fortunes amid increasing poverty made some urban dwellers reflect that the conditions of the Old World seemed to be reappearing in the New.

Not only was the incidence of poverty growing in the late colonial period, but so was the proportion of propertyless urban dwellers. As a century of urban growth increased the gap between gentry and common folk, it also began to transform the spatial patterns of working and living and, perforce, social relations. As land values rose, far outstripping wage increases for laboring city dwellers, two historic changes in the social geography of the cities began to occur. First, property ownership became more concentrated in the hands of merchants, professionals, shopkeepers, and speculative builders. As the price of urban land spiraled upward, craftsmen, mariners, and laborers found that a building lot cost four or five years' wages rather than the four or five months' pay it had cost their grandfathers earlier in the century. Hence tenancy rates

climbed from about 30 percent of all households at the beginning of the eighteenth century to about 80 percent one hundred years later.

Second, facing the urban real estate market with wages that increased only slowly in the second half of the eighteenth century, working people were obliged to seek cheaper land and rental housing on the periphery of the city. This, in turn, led to another change—the separation of the place of residence from the place of production. Thus emerged the pattern of concentric residential zones that became common to all growing urban centers of the Atlantic basin. Towns whose neighborhoods had previously been integrated by occupation and wealth now began to develop a core dominated by the wealthy, a surrounding belt containing primarily the middle class, and a periphery populated by the laboring poor.

THE EFFECTS OF ECONOMIC CHANGE

As well as reflecting rising land values, the social geography of the cities changed with the reorganization of work. Early in the eighteenth century, apprentices and journeymen, operating within a household mode of production, had usually lived with the master artisan in a familial setting where residence and work location were merged. By the end of the century, a larger-scale production had led many masters to relocate their shops away from their place of residence. Journeymen usually lived independently of the master, typically in rented rooms or in boardinghouses. Moreover, journeymen began to find themselves in an antagonistic relationship with masters as the traditional pathway from apprentice to journeyman to master craftsman began to clog. The term "walking cities" still applied at the end of the colonial period, because the cities were still small and people of many stations lived within hailing distance of each other. But the social and geographical distance between employers and employees, and between rich and poor, was beginning to grow.

For urban women somewhat different changes were taking place. Throughout the first half of the eighteenth century, business and craft knowledge was a family affair, with urban women very frequently assisting their husbands in retail shops and craft shops alike. This accounts for the many cases in which a widow would carry on her husband's business after his death—as a printer, tavernkeeper, shopkeeper, or even in craft production when she could continue to hire apprentices and journeymen. But female proprietorship began to decline at the end of the colonial period as male productive labor began to shift from the household to a commercial place of business.

As middle-class female proprietorships were beginning to diminish, lower-class female household production in one important area—textiles—began to grow after the middle of the eighteenth century. The first attempts to utilize the labor of poor urban women—and increasingly their children—came in Boston, the American capital of impoverished widowhood. But Boston women balked at the separation of domestic responsibilities and income-producing work, and this resistance played a large part in the failure of the linen manufactory that merchants had opened in 1750. However, women adapted readily to the putting-out system under which they spun thread or wove cloth in their homes while simultaneously discharging family responsibilities. This began a long history of urban women and children of the lower classes in textile work.

ON THE EVE OF REVOLUTION

Political life could hardly help but change as the fast-growing urban centers of North American life emerged from the Seven Years' War in 1763 and almost immediately entered a period of inflamed debate with Great Britain over new imperial policies. The economic downturn that gripped the major towns after 1760 foreshadowed the increasingly volatile market economy that would frame the lives of both merchants and artisans and brought home the lesson that he who took risks in good times sometimes suffered greatly in bad times.

The severe post-1760 depression greatly increased the number of unemployed and poor, challenged the dominant belief that those who were industrious and frugal would succeed, and made merchants question the advantages of a mercantile system designed for the advantage of the metropolitan center of the British Empire. It also shook artisans' confidence in the internal economic system, and intensified class antagonism. In such a milieu craftsmen, mariners, and laborers entered politics with a passion. From their benches, anvils, sawhorses, and counters, from Portsmouth, New Hampshire, to Savannah, Georgia, they became a fount of political energy without which the revolutionary movement could never have been organized.

In every town they joined the Sons of Liberty by the scores, and in some places they began to dominate those beehives of revolutionary ferment. Most conspicuously, laboring people began to exert themselves as a separate political entity in the protests of the 1760s and early 1770s. They spurred foot-dragging merchants to adopt a non-importation policy and organized secondary boycotts of those who did not. They called public meetings to discuss strategies of protest, published newspaper appeals for community-side action, and began to organize their own agendas for changing American society internally. By the early 1770s Philadelphia's artisans were jettisoning their reliance on upper-class leadership, instead nominating men from their own ranks for local and provincial offices. Conservatives within the merchant-dominated elite sputtered that "The Mechanics . . . have no right to *speak* or *think* for themselves." But the craftsmen could not be deterred. By the eve of the American Revolution, many craftsmen in the cities were sitting on the committees that were assuming de facto powers of government, most conspicuously in enforcing community covenants for the boycotting of British goods.

The cities would become the crucibles of revolution not only because of a large and increasingly politicized artisanry, but because the cities had become centers of communication and education in the eighteenth century. Most of the colonial colleges were in or near major cities that functioned as colonial capitals—Harvard, Rhode Island College (later Brown), Yale, King's College (later Columbia), the College of Philadelphia (later University of Pennsylvania), and the College of William and Mary. They produced annually small crops of men adept in verbal and written persuasion and keenly interested in political theory and practice. At the same time, Boston, New York, and Philadelphia became centers of printing and publishing. Newspapers proliferated and the writing and distributing of political broadsides and pamphlets escalated. A new kind of urban figure—the political propagandist—emerged on the scene, and joined in the growing practice of mobilizing the electorate during hotly contested election contests. By the early 1770s the cities were poised not only on the edge of revolutionary leadership but on the cusp of a new world of international commerce, factory production, and modern politics.

BIBLIOGRAPHY

Archdeacon, Thomas J. *New York City, 1664–1710: Conquest and Change.* Ithaca, N.Y., 1976.

Bailyn, Bernard. *The New England Merchants in the Seventeenth Century.* Cambridge, Mass., 1955.

Baxter, W. T. *The House of Hancock: Business in Boston, 1724–1775.* Cambridge, Mass., 1945.

Bridenbaugh, Carl. *Cities in Revolt: Urban Life in America, 1743–1776.* New York, 1955. Bridenbaugh's two works represent the best overall survey of the colonial cities.

———. *Cities in the Wilderness: The First Century of Urban Life in America, 1625–1742.* New York, 1938.

Bridenbaugh, Carl, and Jessica Bridenbaugh. *Rebels and Gentlemen: Philadelphia in the Age of Franklin.* New York, 1965.

Cray, Robert E., Jr. *Paupers and Poor Relief in New York City and Its Rural Environs, 1700–1830.* Philadelphia, 1988.

Goodfriend, Joyce D. *Before the Melting Pot: Society and Culture in Colonial New York City, 1664–1730.* Princeton, N.J., 1992.

Nash, Gary B. *Forging Freedom: The Formation of Philadelphia's Black Community, 1720–1840.* Cambridge, Mass., 1988.

———. *The Urban Crucible: Social Change, Political Consciousness, and the Origins of the American Revolution.* Cambridge, Mass., 1979. Reflects the social history of the last generation and the interconnections between economic development, social change, and politics.

Price, Jacob M. "Economic Function and the Growth of American Port Towns in the Eighteenth Century." *Perspectives in American History* 8 (1974):123–186. Examines urban growth.

Rutman, Darrett B. *Winthrop's Boston: Portrait of a Puritan Town, 1630–1649.* Chapel Hill, N.C., 1965.

Salinger, Sharon V. *"To Serve Well and Faithfully": Labor and Indentured Servants in Pennsylvania, 1682–1800.* Cambridge, England, 1987.

Smith, Billy G. *The "Lower Sort": Philadelphia's Laboring People, 1750–1800.* Ithaca, N.Y., 1990.

Tolles, Frederick B. *Meetinghouse and Counting House: The Quaker Merchants of Colonial Philadelphia, 1682–1763.* Chapel Hill, N.C., 1948.

Warden, G. B. *Boston, 1689–1776.* Boston, 1970.

Wilkenfeld, Bruce M. *The Social and Economic Structure of the City of New York, 1695–1796.* New York, 1978.

Gary B. Nash

SEE ALSO **Architecture; Artisans; Drama; Free Blacks; Poverty; Rural Life;** and **The Structure of Society;** and various essays in FOLKWAYS.

THE DUTCH COLONY

DESPITE THE FACT THAT no more than two thousand people ever lived in the Dutch trading center at the tip of Manhattan Island, New Amsterdam faced a wide range of urban problems. Beverswyck (Albany), with a population of over a thousand by the mid 1650s, encountered similar difficulties on a smaller scale. The director-general and council of the Dutch West India Company's (WIC's) colony began developing strategies for dealing with issues such as sanitation, excessive drinking, and poor relief in the settlement's embryonic years during the 1630s and 1640s. Only after the chartering of a municipal government in New Amsterdam in 1653 did systematic approaches to urban problems become evident. Influenced by precedents set in the towns of the Netherlands but cognizant of the special needs of a frontier outpost, New Amsterdam's burgomasters initiated policies that served the town's population well and laid the groundwork for future elaboration during the English colonial period.

REGULATING NEW AMSTERDAM

The people of New Amsterdam originally lived in wooden houses clustered adjacent to the WIC's fort, but streets were laid out at an early date and brick dwellings began to replace the wooden ones after 1650. Though the scale of the town was minuscule in comparison with that of Amsterdam, the Dutch preoccupation with cleanliness gave sanitation measures a high priority. Municipal ordinances were passed that prohibited throwing refuse into the streets and designated specific sites as garbage dumps. An attempt was made to guard against the dangers of street traffic by ordering carts not to speed.

The WIC's influence on life in New Amsterdam was incalculable. The company's officials, soldiers, and slave labor force constituted tangible reminders of the weight of imperial rule. Policies developed to further the company's quest for profits at times ran counter to the wishes of the townspeople. But as the decades unfolded and increasing numbers of immigrants arrived, local residents attained more power over their own affairs. The inauguration of a municipal government in 1653 in which leading citizens filled the position of burgomaster demonstrates this. Strict government control of the local economy also reflected the wishes of city dwellers.

In keeping with traditional European practice, New Amsterdam's economic life was regulated by the local government. Intending to foster the prosperity of the town's working people as well as to protect consumers from inferior products and price gouging, municipal authorities enacted ordinances to deal with a variety of issues. Market days were set up for inhabitants to purchase needed commodities. Appointed officials monitored the price of goods and inspected their quality. Taverns were licensed and weights and measures regulated. Fearing the competition of strangers and wishing to protect the livelihoods of the city's residents, the burgomasters established the "burgher right" in 1657, which conferred a status akin to that of freeman on the city's workers and allowed them to practice their trades.

FORGING AN URBAN COMMUNITY

In comparison with cities in the Netherlands, the distance between rich and poor in New Amsterdam was not great. Major company office-holders and members of the incipient merchant class were located at the top of the social hierarchy. Artisans and laborers ranged beneath them, with indentured servants and slaves filling the lowest rungs of the social ladder. Town residents unable to support themselves were eligible for aid from the deacons of the Dutch Reformed church. Although opportunities for upward mobility existed, social distinctions were carefully preserved.

New Amsterdam was a vibrant urban community that experienced its share of social disorder. Serious crimes were rare, but altercations and minor infractions of the law were endemic. The major source of heated words and violence was excessive drinking. The denizens of New Amsterdam and the sailors who passed through the port were well supplied with taverns at which to imbibe liquor. Centers of social life, the taverns at best fostered conviviality and at worst provided a context for the venting of emotions that could lead to physical attacks. In an effort to curb the antisocial behavior associated with tavern life, authorities instituted a system of licensing for tavernkeepers at least as early as 1648. Nevertheless, illegal tippling houses proliferated and offenses multiplied. Violators of the law ordinarily were punished with fines or whipping. The occasional felon was banished from the city.

Though New Amsterdam authorities lacked the zeal of Puritan leaders in promoting religion, they did seek to preserve a portion of the Sabbath as sacred time. Accordingly, they prohibited tavernkeepers from serving liquor during preaching but allowed them to tap after the conclusion of afternoon services in the Dutch Reformed church. How seriously church attendees took clergymens' admonitions to cultivate spiritual values can never be known, but urban dwellers were not deterred from enjoying such traditional Dutch recreations as ice skating, sleighing, fishing, bowling, and a version of golf. Folk holidays such as Saint Nicholas Day and Shrove Tuesday were celebrated despite attempts by the Calvinist clergy and the WIC administration to prohibit them.

New Amsterdam residents were far from a literary people, but they cherished their Bibles and saw to it that their children were educated at the school run by the Dutch Reformed church in conjunction with the company. A handful of men assembled private libraries, wrote poetry, and painted, but their output was negligible when contrasted with the works of their countrymen in the Netherlands.

BIBLIOGRAPHY

Goodfriend, Joyce D. *Before the Melting Pot: Society and Culture in Colonial New York City, 1664–1730.* Princeton, N.J., 1992.

Raesly, Ellis Lawrence. *Portrait of New Netherland.* New York, 1945.

van Rensselaer, Mariana Griswold. *History of the City of New York in the Seventeenth Century.* 2 vols. New York, 1909.

Joyce D. Goodfriend

SEE ALSO **Architecture; Artisans; Drama; Free Blacks; Poverty; Rural Life;** and **The Structure of Society;** and various essays in FOLKWAYS.

THE FRENCH COLONIES

PHYSICAL ASPECTS

FRENCH NORTH AMERICA's cities were communities without communal spirit. That is surprising, given their small size. In the 1750s Quebec (founded in 1608), Montreal (founded in 1642), Louisbourg (founded in 1713), and New Orleans (founded in 1718) had no more than eight thousand inhabitants each. With stables, paddocks, stray livestock, and kitchen gardens inside the town walls or palisades, these communities had a rustic aspect; some residents were farmers. Town and country also mixed at the twice-a-week markets.

Despite the towns' modest character, authorities tried to provide these colonial centers of political, religious, and commercial power with the amenities of French urban life. Streets were marked out at an early date. The effect of town planning was not always visible; only Louisbourg

and New Orleans followed the rectilinear grids laid down by military engineers. Urban expansion was also contained, in part, by defensive walls; those who built outside risked having their houses leveled when an attack was expected. Masonry and brick construction was more likely to be found in the towns than the countryside, and urban houses were often two stories high to take full advantage of the small lots. Private dwellings were overshadowed by centrally located churches and government buildings.

PUBLIC ORDER

Regulation of town life came under the general rubric of *la police* which, despite its affinity to "police" in English, was more wide-ranging. *La police* embraced maintenance of thoroughfares and public rights of way; regulation of food markets, craftsmanship, commerce, and weights and measures; fire prevention; repression of crime and begging; and upholding of public morality. People were compelled to show respect for religious ceremonies, taverns were closed during mass, blasphemy was punished, and heresy was to be suppressed. Care of the poor, the orphaned, and the aged was entrusted to the Roman Catholic church rather than to civic authorities.

Policing responsibilities were not pursued with equal zeal, but food sellers and fire hazards received the administrators' continuing attention. Bakers and butchers were licensed to sell wholesome food at regulated prices, the object being to provide townsfolk with an ample supply of bread and beef at the lowest possible price. Fire prevention entailed the regular sweeping of chimneys in winter and enforcement of the increasingly detailed building laws, which required structural features to reduce combustible materials and to hinder the spread of conflagrations from one house to another. Fire-fighting tools and water buckets were distributed throughout Quebec and Montreal, although the fighters usually could do no more than tear down adjacent buildings to arrest the spread of a blaze. Quebec, Trois-Rivières, Montreal, and New Orleans all suffered devastating fires in the eighteenth century. The principles for regulating town life, along with legislative models, were contained in Nicolas de La Mare's *Traité de la police*

478

(1705–1738) and in other French manuals for magistrates.

In France's North American colonies, there was no provision for street lighting, piping water into towns, or for the regular removal of garbage, but each Quebec house was required to have an indoor latrine. Magistrates contented themselves with laws against depositing refuse or waste in the roadways and by requiring butchers to dispose of offal and other unwanted by-products of their trade in the river, which supplied townsfolk with their drinking and washing water. Few townspeople had private wells. Tanneries were banished to the town's periphery because common wisdom held that anything giving off foul odors "corrupted the air" and caused diseases. In Montreal and New Orleans the number of taverns was limited, and, to reduce conflict, each drinking establishment was sometimes assigned to a particular social group or Amerindian tribe. Such lubricious haunts were close to the town's waterfront, where canoes and ships arrived first.

Townsfolk had a minor role in civic administration, because urban regulation was entrusted to royal appointees, namely the *lieutenants-généraux civil et criminel*. In 1673 Governor General Louis de Buade de Frontenac established an elected civic administration for Quebec, consisting of two aldermen and a mayor. Because the French Crown disapproved of autonomous corporations, the governor was told to prevent any further elections. That was the end of representative municipal government in New France. At Montreal the Society of Saint Sulpice appointed officers to its *bailliage* court from 1666 until 1693. That seigneurial court maintained public order in Montreal.

Originally, responsibility for *la police* in New France was shared by various royal officials. Governor General Frontenac, after his arrival in 1672, issued public-order regulations alone or in concert with Quebec's Conseil Souverain (Sovereign Council). The highest civil official was the intendant, whose full title was *intendant de justice, police, et finances*. Frontenac was reprimanded in 1674 for taking advantage of the intendant's absence to issue police regulations and to appoint town magistrates at Quebec. Thereafter, public-order regulations emanated from the intendant, sitting as chairman of the Conseil Souverain.

The continuing role of the councillors in such matters led them to believe that they were the essential agency, and, when they issued a public-order regulation by themselves in 1684, a decree of the king's Council of State voided the law and forbade them to act without the intendant or governor general's presence. The Quebec council made one last attempt in 1714 to assert its jurisdiction over public order, and the claim was firmly rejected by both governor general and intendant. Thereafter, it was customary for local magistrates to rule on *la police* under the intendant's supervision. At Louisbourg and New Orleans a subdelegate or *commissaire-ordonnateur* assumed the intendant's role. In Quebec and Montreal occasional *assemblées de police* were summoned at which leading townsfolk advised magistrates on the pricing of bread and meat; the practice lapsed in the 1720s. As a rule, townsfolk had no right to participate in their communities' affairs. The Spanish introduced municipal government by colonials to New Orleans, and civic administrations appeared in former New France during the early 1800s, under British auspices.

Routine policing of public places fell to law court ushers and *sergents*, who made arrests. In Quebec *archers* (guards) were the forceful arm of the *prévôté* court, while the *archers de la maréchausée* policed the countryside. Whenever there was a major disturbance or resistance to these legal officers, the town major could dispatch garrison troops of that day's watch to assist them. In 1737 a colonial official said that the five hundred soldiers in the Saint Lawrence Valley were "not enough to keep the populace of the towns and countryside in good order." The authorities, however, blamed the soldiery for most crimes at Louisbourg, in Canada, or at New Orleans.

TOWNSFOLK AND COMMUNAL LIFE

Urban society was fragmented. Ecclesiastics, administrators, merchants, craftsmen, and other menials coexisted in the towns without intermixture. Social contact usually was confined to one's own kind and kin. Town residents sometimes gathered to receive newly arrived high officials, to celebrate a royal marriage or birth, or to sing Te Deum in church for a victory or the return of peace. Gunners provided fireworks displays at celebrations. Even in religious processions or in church the devout were carefully segregated by social rank. Worshipers were offended if they were not accorded the precedence and visible marks of respect owed to persons of their standing. Official concern with upholding the social hierarchy and the general preoccupation with asserting one's position kept the townsfolk divided.

In documents a few residents described themselves as "bourgeois de cette ditte ville" and Montrealers ridiculed Quebeckers as "sheep," while the latter reciprocated by referring to the fur-trading center's residents as "wolves." Otherwise, personal identification with cities was rare. Louisbourg's brief forty-five-year existence was twice disrupted by conquest and evacuation of the city, and so it was difficult for this town to develop a community identity.

The lives of townsfolk followed very different paths. Single people, childless couples, and poor artisans rented a few rooms in private homes for a year or more. These tenants sometimes promised to make structural improvements to reduce their rent, in addition to their customary obligation to maintain the house in its original state. One Montreal tenant was instructed not to split firewood inside the dwelling. Their "betters" lived in large houses with a retinue of servants, slaves, and family dependents.

Louisbourg had a large transient population of fishermen, comparable with the *voyageurs* (hired canoemen) who passed through Montreal and New Orleans. Navigation season also brought sailors to the seaports. Amerindian visitors were expected to live in temporary dwellings outside the towns. At New Orleans, Native Americans sold fish and wild game at the public market. A few inns offered shelter for short periods, but travelers were more likely to find lodgings in private homes for want of hotels. In 1744 Quebec had three inns and thirty-seven taverns; Louisbourg had one drinking establishment for every forty-six inhabitants.

Apart from the odd billiard game, drinking, talk, singing, card playing, and gambling were indoor amusements for humble folk. The church had effectively suppressed public theater, but it failed to end mixed dancing, which was also condemned as morally dangerous. The urban

notables and wealthy amused themselves with book reading, evening suppers, private amateur theatricals, and society balls. Less than half of the second-generation colonials could read and write, and so there was insufficient readership to support newspapers or local publications. Outside the church, French colonials had a narrow intellectual life; the arrival of news from Europe in springtime was eagerly awaited, and, in the interval, people speculated freely on the outcome of events in the homeland. For colonial townsfolk, France was the source of all that was admired and worthy of imitation.

Towns had a clear occupational hierarchy even if few callings had any solidarity. Royal officials frowned on secular associations among the lower orders. Churchmen and officials came together to carry out their duties, and merchants were permitted to deliberate among themselves. Because of the comprehensive commercial monopoly of companies exploiting Louisiana from 1712 until 1731, wholesale merchants only appeared in New Orleans near the end of the French regime. Small retailers, itinerant and fixed, existed in New Orleans as in the other French colonies. Manual trades, apart from food preparation and surgery, were open to all comers. Thus, there were no craft guilds in French North America, because there were no occupational privileges to be maintained, and unofficial economic monopolies were illegal. Religious confraternities, whose activities and property came under clerical supervision, admitted people from all groups. Even these inoffensive associations were rare; only five existed in New France. Three had begun as craft confraternities. It was rare for an occupational group to possess any corporate identity. Despite this lack of collegiality, people were keenly aware of occupational ranks.

Taking Quebec's population in 1744 as an example, the 5,200 residents divided into five ranks. At the top were 52 senior administrators, court officials, and military officers. Many were seigneurs who, like Louisiana's plantation owners, maintained a town residence. In the second rank were 66 merchants and traders; 24 law clerks, court ushers, scriveners, and notaries; followed by 10 of the highest craftsmen, such as master builders and silversmiths. Unfortunately, the enumerator did not enter the nunneries, cathedral, hospital, hospice, or other religious houses that distinguished the colonial capital.

Socially, the religious belonged to the second rank.

The third order contained 260 craftsmen of whom 80 were in the building trades, 34 were leatherworkers, 32 were bakers or butchers, about 30 were metalworkers, and 26 made clothes. Quebec's role as a port was reflected in the presence of 70 sailors or navigators, 25 coopers, and a dozen shipbuilders and auxiliary tradesmen. Personnel of the King's Shipyard were omitted, since they were indentured workers from France who seldom intended to remain in the colonies. Maritime tradesmen tended to live in the Lower Town with many merchants. Specialized trades, such as clockmaking, cutlery, and chairmaking, had a scattering of representatives. Four transient peddlers from France, who provoked many complaints from colonial retailers, were also present that year.

The fourth rank of Quebec's European population consisted of 44 carters, a score of day laborers, 8 gardeners and chimney sweeps, a half-dozen apprentices, and 5 *voyageurs* whose handsome earnings gave them access to more secure and estimable positions. They, tanners, and masonry builders had the best chances of social advancement; promotion in the civil administration and garrison troops required patronage by the king's officials. Outside Quebec's polite society were 47 Amerindian or black slaves, 5 Protestants, 2 Englishmen, and 14 bastards.

Cultural diversity made French North America cosmopolitan and the concentration of administrative, military, religious, and commercial functions in Quebec and New Orleans made them cities in spite of their small populations.

BIBLIOGRAPHY

Clark, John G. *New Orleans 1718–1812: An Economic History.* Baton Rouge, La., 1970.

Crowley, Terry. *Louisbourg: Atlantic Fortress and Seaport.* Ottawa, 1990.

Lachance, André. *La vie urbaine en Nouvelle-France.* Montreal, 1987.

Reid, Allana G. "The Nature of Quebec Society During the French Regime." *Canadian Historical Association Report of the Annual Meeting* (1951):26–35.

Peter N. Moogk

SEE ALSO **Architecture; Artisans; Drama; Free Blacks; Poverty; Rural Life;** and **The Structure of Society;** and various essays in FOLKWAYS.

THE SPANISH BORDERLANDS

SPANIARDS BROUGHT across the Atlantic a concept of the town as part of Spanish life and as a device of local government. Their commitment stimulated the rise of towns from the Strait of Magellan in the south to the so-called Spanish Borderlands in the north, that tier of present-day states of the United States bordering the Gulf of Mexico and the international boundary with the Republic of Mexico. The development was reinforced by the Crown's policy of placing emerging municipalities directly under royal officials, in order to curb the power of adventurers with contracts from the kings for the conquest of large domains.

ORDINANCES GOVERNING THE PLANNING OF A TOWN

The settlement of colonists in towns was also fostered by the need to protect small groups of aliens determined to live amid, and dominate, large Native American societies. The rule that Christians must not be scattered across the country was expressed in the original instructions of 16 September 1501 to Frey Nicolás de Ovando, governor of Española, and was more or less observed in the course of Spanish colonization in America. During the reign of Philip II (1556–1598) the policy was spelled out in the *ordenanzes de pobladores* of 1573, which were ultimately incorporated in the Laws of the Indies.

Although the regulations dealt with establishing a town, they affected a larger area. The emerging municipality, according to its size variously called *ciudad* (city), *villa* (city of second rank), or pueblo (town), covered the community and the lands for the colonists, together with a body of water and a stand of trees. Then there were building lots, reserved for future settlers, and the king's land, which all could use. The government house, chapel, and other official structures faced the plaza. Each settler received a building lot (*solar*) in the town and gardens and fields (*suertes*) of the surveyed pueblo lands. Adjacent to the town were the lots (*ejidos*) for newcomers. Beyond these pueblo lands were the pastures (*dehesas*), which could be bought and sold, while *solares* and *suertes* could be neither divided nor sold but only inherited. The pueblo used the royal lands (*tierras realengas*) as commons (*propios*), or leased them for income.

The towns of the borderlands bore the marks of the ordinances, despite many variations. In Florida and California colonization followed conquest and was intended to keep out European rivals. In the cases of New Mexico, Texas, and to some extent California, the spark for colonization came also from the millennial visions of Franciscans searching for mission fields. The northern rim of New Spain attracted few settlers after the Coronado and the De Soto expeditions had undermined the illusions of easy riches.

The Indian pueblos of New Mexico and Arizona, which conquistadors encountered on their roads to Cíbola, testified to town life long before the arrival of the Spaniards. With the prehistoric appearance of agriculture and the diffusion of crops and pottery from Central America into the far Southwest, complex cultures emerged. One of them, now called Anasazi (Navajo for "ancient ones"), used cliff and open-site dwellings, which between the eleventh and thirteenth centuries produced large population centers. At the time of the Spanish conquest, each Indian pueblo, surrounded by its farmland, constituted an independent political unit. The Spaniards did not incorporate the political or physical structures of the Indian pueblos into their urban world. Despite the distance from the sources of their culture, the Spaniards followed traditional practices modified by the colonial experience.

ADAPTATION OF THE ORDINANCES TO THE BORDERLANDS

In the isolated settings of the borderlands, with its limited resources, officials were more con-

cerned to secure the outskirts of the Spanish world than to extend into a hostile environment the details of the town planning ordinances. If implemented completely, they would have affected most aspects of the settlements, since they included orders to leave Indian towns undisturbed, to lay out streets in accordance with the prevailing winds, and to share water from irrigation ditches. Each feature taxed officials' abilities to hold the settlers to the plan and to adapt it to sometimes hastily selected sites. At times, soldiers thwarted all plans by making themselves at home in conquered Indian towns, while making no attempt to colonize their conquest. Furthermore, during most of the sixteenth century, towns combined the several functions that were later served by *presidio*, mission, and pueblo as separate frontier stations for soldiers, missionaries, and settlers. Often, the urban dynamics and the complex institutions continued to blur the distinctions.

The missions contained pueblo features anticipating the time when the Native Americans would join the empire not only as laborers but also as Christian townspeople. The families of married soldiers and ordinary settlers modified the military character of the *presidios*. At times, a pueblo close to a mission and a *presidio* produced frictions between settlers, missionaries, and soldiers, which stifled the growth of the civil settlement. These and other circumstances limited the effectiveness of the town planning ordinances. The emergence of Saint Augustine, Santa Fe, San Antonio, and Los Angeles, the major examples of Spanish town building in the borderlands, reflected the adjustments to local needs.

MAJOR BORDERLAND TOWNS

Saint Augustine, the oldest European city in the United States, was founded in September 1565 by Pedro Menéndez de Avilés, as a base to destroy the Florida beachhead of French Huguenots near the mouth of the Saint Johns River and to protect the passage of Spanish treasure ships through the perilous Florida Straits. A three-year contract with the Crown charged him to conquer at his expense the coast between the Florida Keys and Newfoundland, making him the proprietor of any conquest. Located roughly thirty-three miles (about 53 kilometers) south of the river's mouth, Saint Augustine began as a ditch hastily dug around the council house of the Seloy village of the Saturiba Indians, but appropriate ceremonies immediately made it a true Spanish municipality.

Despite setbacks, Saint Augustine survived. Provisions were scarce, supplies uncertain, and starvation frequent. The Native Americans set the first fort on fire; French and English privateers harassed the Florida coast. The king sent reinforcements but he also sent Menéndez on new assignments, and the Council of the Indies began to convert his family's proprietorship to a Crown colony. Slowly, Saint Augustine showed traces of the long-standing Spanish pattern of planned communities. After the haphazard beginning at a bay barely suited for shipping, the town was laid out on higher ground. Initially, the houses were half-timbered structures of wattle and daub with cypress support and thatch roofs. An early view of the town, dating from Francis Drake's attack in 1586, shows a dozen blocks located some distance from the fort that guarded the entrance of the harbor.

In the 1580s Saint Augustine had about three hundred inhabitants. Possibly one third of the households included a woman; and perhaps half of the women were Native Americans, skilled in finding food and preparing meals. Their wares and practices predominated in the outwardly Spanish town. By the turn of the sixteenth century, a good proportion of the native-born residents were mestizos or mixed-bloods. Black slaves of the king worked on the fortifications. Amy Bushnell has found that the rich had their own black slaves as well as Indian slaves from other parts of the empire.

Saint Augustine's decline began roughly in the 1580s, when silver mining directed the Crown's concern for settlements to northern New Spain. The Villa de Santa Fe became the first Spanish town west of the Mississippi. In 1610 Governor Pedro de Peralta founded it as capital of New Mexico, on the banks of a small tributary of the Rio Grande, at the foot of the Sangre de Cristo Mountains. Two years earlier Juan de Oñate, who since his 1598 conquest of the northernmost province had been concerned more with searching for Coronado's elusive Quivira than with the government of New Mexico, had resigned its governorship. Oñate had used as headquarters successively two Indian pueblos,

which he named San Juan de los Caballeros and San Gabriél. Ramón Gutiérrez writes in *When Jesus Came, the Corn Mothers Went Away* that Peralta was instructed to build a Spanish town where the colonists could "live with some order and decency." In 1620, when disease unwittingly introduced by the conquerors had reduced the number of Pueblo Indians in New Mexico to seventeen thousand from eighty thousand in 1598, one hundred Spaniards lived in Santa Fe.

The emergence of Santa Fe, despite its small population of forty-eight heads of families, immediately provided a center for Spanish affairs in New Mexico and an outpost in the southern Rocky Mountains. The town added an additional focus to the interaction between colonists, Franciscan missionaries, and government officials. Administrative buildings, now called the palace of governors, graced the north side of the plaza. Other government structures and a church rose in its vicinity. These features, reinforced by the rectangular street pattern, reflected planning. By the next century, however, one of the few maps showing the town during the 1760s indicates that after the Pueblo Revolt (1680–1692) and the reconquest of New Mexico the settlers had somewhat dispersed from the compact town.

The appearance of the borderland pueblos reflected only partially the royal instructions. Civil, military, and missionary functions characterized the pueblo of San Fernando de Béxar (often called San Antonio de Béxar). San Antonio was the first and most successful colonial civil settlement in Texas, which in 1811 was officially elevated to the status of a *ciudad*, the only one within the limits of the present continental United States. Established in 1731 to augment the colonization of the northern frontier, it was located on the San Antonio River. There the pueblo shared the site of a former Indian village with the *Presidio* of San Antonio de Béxar and the Mission of San Antonio de Valero (later known as the Alamo), both founded in 1718.

A group of ten families from the Canary Islands, having been increased to fifteen by marriages along the way, formed the nucleus of the pueblo. Next to it, however, separated only by the church placed at one end of the plaza, the older *presidio* had earlier attracted colonists from Coahuila, Saltillo, and Nuevo Léon, following a pattern of soldier-settler movements. To promote the civil settlement, it received its own name, Villa de Béxar; and by 1731, when the *isleños* (islanders) arrived, the civilians at the *presidio* had increased to about twenty-five male heads of households. *Presidio, villa,* and pueblo faced the mission on the east shore of the river. In 1762, with French Louisiana and its capital, New Orleans, passing into Spanish possession, the transfer of the provincial capital to Béxar added distinction that the population growth did not merit.

More than two centuries after Philip II had promulgated the *ordenanzes de pobladores,* tradition still shaped the plan of Los Angeles. Appropriately it became the only town in Spanish California at times referred to as *ciudad.* When Los Angeles was established in 1781, officials adjusted the layout of its plaza, building lots, streets, and fields to the local conditions, but the 1779 instructions of Governor Felipe De Neve sought to approximate the ideal. He located the pueblo in the vicinity of the Río Porciúncula de Nuestra Señora la Reina de los Angeles, as the Portolá expedition had called the river in 1769. The governor considered it and the Río de Guadelupe in the north, where in 1777 he had founded San José as the first civil settlement in Alta California, as the best locations in his province to produce grain for the newly established missions and *presidios.* El Pueblo de Nuestra Señora la Reina de los Angeles de Río de Porciúncula rose where a dam and an irrigation canal could be built conveniently.

The site was not far from a former Indian village whose residents now lived for the most part nine miles (14 kilometers) to the northeast at the Mission San Gabriel Arcángel, established in 1771. The site was also close to where the road from the mission crossed the river, but out of the reach of floods, which had impaired the development of San José. At the plaza the San Gabriel road coming from the east turned southwest into the direction of Cahuenga Pass. From the plaza the Pacific Ocean could be reached at the San Pedro landing without crossing the river.

The ethnic composition of the early inhabitants reflected the cosmopolitan character of an empire curtailed by religious orthodoxy, as well as the extent to which intermarriages between Spaniards, Native Americans, and African Americans produced new groups of people for the colonization of the borderlands. The original twelve settlers of Los Angeles and their families were recruited from the poor of Sinaloa, in northwestern Mexico, and these forty-six colonists represented mixtures of Native Americans and African Americans, with faint traces of Spanish blood. More than half of them were African American or part African American. Only among the Native American settlers were there families whose members belonged to the same race. The first alcalde, the highest municipal officer, was an Indian, José Vanegas.

URBAN LIFE IN
THE BORDERLANDS

In the borderlands, as in the northern parts of New Spain in general, the small number of settlers erased racial boundaries. Hardships stimulated interdependence and toleration. Pure-blooded people were the exception, but many mixed-bloods passed as Spaniards, and friars registering settlers often did not give an ethnicity unless it was Spanish. The loneliness of the isolated settlements bonded people, and sodalities reinforced the ties. The changes of the seasons, the threat of Indian attacks, and the actions of officials enlivened daily life in the small farming communities. Family gatherings provided spontaneous festivities in a social calendar shaped by religious holidays. Celebrations and dances added diversion to the necessity for cattle round-ups. When not zealously defending their prerogatives on the local scene, secular and ecclesiastical authorities shared the official features of civic affairs.

The local government was in the hands of the *cabildo* or *ayuntamiento.* A pueblo had an *alcalde* (a judge with certain legislative powers), four *regidores* (town councilmen), one *alguacil* (constable), and some minor officials. The selection of officials varied. In a newly conquered area, the founder of the town usually nominated the first officials. Afterward, annual elections frequently rotated members of a few allied families in office.

CONCLUSION

Together with mission and *presidio*, the municipality was a significant tool of colonization that proved to be the most durable of the three frontier institutions. Unlike their counterparts in Spain, the borderland towns enjoyed less self-government because they were subject to a hierarchy of officials in the Viceroyalty of New Spain. *Pobladores* (colonists) or *vecinos* (town residents), however, enjoyed local self-government, enhanced by the distance from Mexico City. Trade and commerce broadened the agricultural base, but without mines the towns did not stimulate development. Spanish town planning added to urbanization a measure of stability that was frequently absent in the part of North America settled by English-speaking people. The slow growth and the small number of residents shielded human and natural resources from the apparent progress, as well as the destructive effects, of urbanization.

BIBLIOGRAPHY

Bancroft, Hubert Howe. *History of California.* Vol. 3. San Francisco, 1884. A good starting point for new insights into the beginnings of Los Angeles.

Blackmar, Frank W. *Spanish Institutions of the Southwest.* Baltimore, Md., 1891. Remains a useful guide to key documents.

Borah, Woodrow. "European Cultural Influence in the Formation of the First Plan for Urban Centers That Have Lasted to Our Times." In *Actas y memorias del XXXIX Congreso Internacional de Americanistas.* Vol. 2. Lima, Peru, 1972. Succinctly presents the large context of the subject.

Bushnell, Amy. "The Noble and Loyal City, 1565–1688." In *The Oldest City: St. Augustine, Saga of Survival,* edited by Jean Parker Waterbury. Saint Augustine, Fla., 1983. Provides comments on the emergence of Saint Augustine, Santa Fe, and San Antonio, with good references to the literature.

Crouch, Dora B., Daniel J. Gar, and Axel Mundingo. *Spanish City Planning in North America.* Cambridge, Mass., 1982. With Cruz, below, one of the rare general studies.

Cruz, Gilbert R. *Let There Be Towns: Spanish Municipal Origins in the American Southwest, 1610–1810.* College Station, Tex., 1988.

Gutiérrez, Ramón A. *When Jesus Came, the Corn Mothers Went Away: Marriage, Sexuality, and Power in New Mexico, 1500–1846.* Stanford, Calif., 1991.

Poyo, Gerald E., and Gilberto M. Hinojosa, eds. *Tejano Origins in Eighteenth-Century San Antonio.* Austin, Tex., 1991. Jesús F. de la Tejás essay entitled "Forgotten Founders" provides valuable information on the settlement of San Antonio.

Reps, John W. *Town Planning in Frontier America.* Princeton, N.J., 1969.

Gunther Barth

See also **Architecture; Artisans; Drama; Free Blacks; Poverty; Rural Life;** and **The Structure of Society;** and various essays in FOLKWAYS.

MEN IN ARMS

THE BRITISH COLONIES

EUROPEANS PENETRATED THE Western Hemisphere about 1500, just as a revolution in European warfare was beginning. Inevitably, this military revolution profoundly influenced the English colonization of North America.

EUROPEAN REVOLUTION IN WARFARE

Firearms, light enough to be carried by a man, reliable enough to shoot under field conditions, and effective enough to kill at a hundred paces, were the most visible aspect of the new European warfare. But changes in organization came earlier and may have had more profound consequences. By 1500 European aristocracies that had justified and defended their high social status by controlling the military function had clearly lost their monopoly. Plebeian foot soldiers—infantry—had defeated and displaced aristocratic armored horsemen throughout Europe even before infantry firearms became a significant factor on the battlefield. The reasons for this shift to infantry were various and complex and are still disputed. Crucial, however, was the experience that a large body of trained, disci-

plined infantry, even when armed with no more than swords and pikes, could defeat a large body of cavalry encumbered by heavy armor and crippled by an aristocratic disdain for obedience to orders. European monarchies increasingly depended on hired infantry—mercenaries—to enlarge their territories, suppress their ever-rebellious aristocrats, and expand and exploit their tax bases.

The revolution in warfare put a premium on skill, training, discipline, and experienced leadership to the disadvantage of those who had only numbers, weapons, and enthusiasm; professional soldiers—regulars—would dominate European warfare throughout the era of colonial American history. The centralizing consequences of the military revolution accelerated the process of change. By 1600 the English, a century behind Spain and Portugal and years behind the French, had fully absorbed the new firearms technology and tactics and undertaken their own colonization of America.

DEFENDING THE FIRST COLONIES

John Smith, the legendary hero of the first successful English colony, founded at Jamestown in 1607 on the Chesapeake Bay, was a striking exemplar of the European military revolution. Of obscure social origins, Smith made his way in life as a professional soldier. The violent split in the western Christian church had carried him as a young man into the service of Dutch Protestant rebels fighting to free themselves from Spanish Catholic rule. As a Protestant English volunteer in the Dutch wars, Smith learned the latest lessons in military technology, tactics, and discipline; he gained additional military experience fighting in Hungary for Christian forces against the Muslims. After a series of fabulous adventures that carried him as far as Russia, Smith returned home just in time to be hired for his military skills by the Virginia Company when it assembled a new team of colonists and leaders. The mission of this new team was to repair the failure of an earlier company venture on Roanoke Island in the 1580s when a colony had been mysteriously wiped out, either by Native resistance or by the Spanish, who had destroyed a coastal colony of French Protestants farther south in the 1560s. In any case the new English colony, precariously planted on a swampy island named for King James I, depended heavily for its survival on a capacity for self-defense, and it was this dependence that enabled Smith briefly to play his heroic role in American history.

In the New England colonies, founded soon after Virginia, experienced soldiers, veterans of religious warfare and the military revolution in Europe, played roles comparable to that of Smith in early Virginia by training and leading armed English colonists in war. Myles Standish and John Underhill in Massachusetts and John Mason in Connecticut were among the most prominent of these early military leaders. All brought to their conduct of war against Native Americans the same brutal attitudes and methods that were evident in contemporary wars against Catholics and infidels in Europe, as well as in the English pacification of Ireland.

The Virginia colony, like every subsequent English settlement in North America, at least until the conquest of the Dutch colony of New Netherland (New York) in 1664, was initially a private venture. New York, established in a second wave of English colonization after 1660, was an exception in that the duke of York, its proprietor, was also the brother of King Charles II, and brought to his venture a small English fleet and force of regular soldiers. Against unfriendly natives or hostile Europeans, the English colonists, who had claimed as their own the coastal strip between Spanish Florida and the Saint Lawrence Valley, could not look to England for military protection but only to themselves. All colonial ventures were expected to profit the mother country and their investors; since none of these early English mainland colonies turned much of a profit, large military outlays by the English government for their defense were out of the question.

Comparison with the French and Spanish colonies and with the European West Indies helps to clarify what happened in the English mainland colonies—the future United States. The Spanish found gold and silver in abundance and during the sixteenth century saw a large Native population almost destroyed by its lack of resistance to European diseases. Enormous wealth from America funded the Spanish armies sent to reconquer Europe for Catholicism as well as the warships that protected the treasure fleets; a few Spanish forts and professional garrisons at key points in America were easily affordable. A Native population devastated by epidemic disease posed only a minor problem of military control. The French after 1600 began much as the English did, relying on private enterprise. However, the economic value of the Newfoundland fisheries and the Laurentian fur trade, plus the growing strategic importance of the Saint Lawrence colony in coping with a hostile England, enabled Louis XIV to justify sending substantial numbers of professional soldiers to Canada after 1660.

During the seventeenth century both France and England quickly developed rich sugar-exporting economies worked by African slave labor on the smaller West Indian islands. These nations also established island bases for a lucrative but illegal trade with the Spanish colonies, thus again providing good reason to pay for garrisons of professional soldiery, whose mission was as much to put down slave rebellions as to defend the valuable little islands from external attack.

THE MILITIA SYSTEM

The sheer economic value of sugar colonies like English Barbados and French Guadeloupe, plus their large African slave populations, induced English and French governments to pay most of the costs of military garrisons in the West

Indies. But in the mainland English colonies the military situation was radically different from that in all the other European colonies in America. The key feature of this radical difference was population, both Indian and Anglo-American. The Native population near the English colonies, while decimated by the same diseases that had previously destroyed so much of the Indian population of Spanish-held America, recovered more quickly and never lost its capacity for serious military resistance. Quickly armed by Dutch and other European merchants with the latest military technology, the "English" Indians endured a relationship with the American colonists that became a complex medley of dependence and hostility involving the regular exchange of foodstuffs, furs, firewater, and firearms and punctuated by bouts of the most brutal violence, in which European weapons, not arrows and tomahawks, predominated on both sides.

Meanwhile, if the efforts of Spanish and French Catholic missionaries to win the hearts and control the minds of Native Americans seem to have been far more effective than those of Anglo-American Protestant missionaries, some of the explanation is demographic: the numbers of American colonists grew at a spectacular rate from the seventeenth century to the American Revolution in 1776. Already reaching a quarter million by 1700, that population had grown tenfold when its leaders declared independence from Britain. In no other European empire was there anything comparable to the heavy immigration and high rate of natural growth characteristic of the American colonies, and the difference was fundamental to the endless military pressure felt by Indians along the common frontier.

At the same time, a rapidly growing colonial population made self-defense a feasible military option for the Anglo-Americans. Among the early laws enacted in almost every American colony were acts requiring adult males to perform military service. A few occupations—including clergymen, college students, millers, and public officials—were usually exempted, and in time nonwhites came to be excluded. With the exception of Pennsylvania, founded by William Penn of the pacifist Society of Friends and requiring no compulsory military service until the American Revolution, each colony established a militia,

enrolling virtually the entire adult white male population. Captains in their localities and colonels in their counties were required to muster and train the men on their rolls several times each year and in an emergency to assemble and lead their companies and regiments against the enemy.

The militia system evolved naturally from the conditions of life in the earliest colonies. Every man was expected to be armed, but no man could easily be spared from useful labor to be a full-time soldier. Nor was there any evident need for full-time soldiers; relations with the Native population were always tense and complex, but open hostilities were at worst sporadic. The dreaded European threat was very slow to develop. So the early English colonies got by on what they could afford: the part-time soldiers of a compulsory militia. That the colonial militia also had roots in medieval English military organization, before the peasantry was effectively disarmed in the seventeenth century, is often mentioned but is hardly relevant. A growing European population in the colonies and a fluctuating but rarely severe degree of danger meant that a widely diffused military obligation was an adequate response. Unsatisfactory by contemporary European military standards, an armed population suited American conditions.

Militia Weaknesses

The diffused nature of military obligation under the militia system, however, had glaring inadequacies. Officers' commissions in the colonial militia were honorific, tendered by the colonial governor and reflective of social and political status rather than military knowledge or competence. Meeting and training every two or three months for a day under such leadership could hardly produce the disciplined and skillful troops needed to fight effectively with firearms, even against an enemy who employed what colonists called a "skulking way of war," marked by Native warriors striking by surprise and fleeing quickly, often ambushing any party of militia that tried to pursue them. Militia units when called to active service were notoriously unable to keep themselves clean, healthy, or even in some acceptable degree of order. Twice, in 1622 and 1644, citizen soldiers failed to prevent devastating surprise attacks on the Virginia colony, and similar stories of militia failure, often abject, appear elsewhere throughout colonial history.

Sheer numbers on the colonial side, along with the inability of the Native economic base to sustain prolonged warfare, regularly meant ultimate victory for the colonists in their conflicts with Native peoples, but only after wars that were more like massacres, with noncombatants on both sides the principal victims. Almost from the outset, a search began for a more effective military alternative to reliance on a widely shared military obligation. After a disastrous Indian war in New England in 1675–1676, a bloody conflict in 1676 in the Chesapeake that led to the overthrow of the colonial government of Virginia, and a perceptible rise in the threat posed by France and its empire to the English colonies, the search for military alternatives became more urgent.

From Militia to Volunteers

One obvious military option got much attention but little or no action until very late in the colonial period. Regular troops from England and warships on American station had many advocates, especially among hard-pressed Americans themselves and those in London most concerned with colonial policy. But it was simply too costly to be accepted by the House of Commons, and in a political culture suspicious of standing armies, too dangerous as well. Besides (so the argument ran), the feckless Americans, far more numerous than their potential enemies, ought to be able to defend themselves, if given a modicum of munitions and better leadership. As the early private colonies fell more and more under control of the Crown, men with substantial military experience in Europe increasingly came to be appointed to royal governorships in America.

Some of these former soldiers, like Alexander Spotswood, governor of Virginia from 1710 to 1722, studied the weaknesses of the militia system and tried to find feasible remedies. Spotswood's critique, the work of an intelligent, energetic soldier who had served under the duke of Marlborough and would later make Virginia his permanent home, deals only with the military situation of his own colony but is applicable to the other English mainland colonies. The key

problem, Spotswood argued, was that the more affluent Virginians, as well as their servants, were evading military service simply by paying the legal fine levied against absentees from scheduled militia musters. Poor men, who could not afford to pay fines, were doing all the military duty but were naturally bitter about it. Officers, he noted, being also gentlemen, were not even subject to fines for absence; furthermore, if they had political ambitions, they would court popularity by canceling militia musters. Spotswood was sure that Virginians were capable of becoming excellent soldiers, but he was also sure that the Virginia militia, as it stood, was the worst in the British Empire.

Spotswood's remedy was to excuse most men from military service, commuting their obligation to a modest annual tax (a few pounds of tobacco) and using the revenue to recruit a smaller, better force. His reformed militia would rely less on compulsion than on monetary incentives and would be both more economical and fairer to all parties. A selective militia could muster more often, train more seriously, and learn discipline more readily from picked officers who knew more (and cared more) about the business of war. Spotswood's plan was never adopted, in part at least because some Virginians claimed to fear that their governor might use a newmodeled militia to rule by martial law; but rough, improvised versions of Spotswood's ideas were what the mainland colonies, including Pennsylvania, actually did in trying to wage war when, from the 1690s onward, their military problems began to grow.

In an emergency whole companies and regiments of militia were not called into active service; that in effect would have removed most of the manpower of an area from the labor force. Instead the militia was mustered only for recruiting purposes. Provincial authorities set a quota of men needed from each locality and county. Often a bonus for enlistment and the promise of daily pay and rations would attract enough volunteers to fill the quota, but if voluntarism failed then other methods might be tried—an additional bonus raised from local donors or a lottery in which any loser might try to find a substitute to serve in his place. Compulsion was a last, undesired resort, and even then colonial draft laws often targeted those who were indi-

490

gent, unemployed, and without settled residence—"loose and strolling persons" was typical language. The key point is that no law or ethic absolutely required a particular person to serve; anyone obligated to serve might, if he or his family had the means, hire someone else. It was unfair: but less so, as Spotswood noted, than a universal compulsory system that was even more easily evaded by the well-off.

What Spotswood did not have in mind was that military units raised in this quasi-voluntary fashion, by monetary inducement, would be so hastily formed and quickly dispersed. Typically, a colonial regiment in wartime was formed from militia volunteers in the spring, completed by drafts if needed during the summer, and disbanded before winter. Officers for these wartime units were recruited from among the more vigorous, ambitious, and warlike militia officers, sometimes by offering them a promotion in rank, but there was none of the year-to-year continuity of training and shared service that Spotswood had seen as a key advantage of his proposed reform. Most units broke up after each campaigning season, and the process began anew each spring.

An occasional exception occurred when a particular outpost needed to be garrisoned through the winter months and a colony government induced a fraction of the annual contingent to stay on for that purpose. Similarly, many colonies paid small groups of rangers, sometimes mounted, to patrol a sensitive portion of the colonial frontier through all or most of the year. These semiprofessional specialists were usually recruited from frontier settlements and provided some of the legendary characters of colonial military history, like Robert Rogers of New Hampshire. But the basic pattern was the recruitment of volunteers each wartime year from the pool of semiskilled manpower represented by the militia.

A maritime counterpart for the voluntary mobilization of colonial soldiers may be seen in the chief American contribution to British seapower. While some colonial governments attempted to maintain a small warship or two, a far more important role was played by privateering. Privateers were armed ships built in America and manned by sailors recruited from the docks of Boston, Marblehead, Newport, New York, Philadelphia, and Charleston by the hope of a small fortune in prize money. Legally authorized to attack French and, usually, Spanish merchant shipping, privateers were hardly more than legalized pirates. French privateers working from Louisbourg, Martinique, and other bases were both aggressive and effective against British and American trade, thus encouraging Anglo-American officials to make a reciprocal effort to sever the more vulnerable French transatlantic lifeline to its colonies. The general importance of privateering in colonial warfare is suggested by its impact on pacifist Pennsylvania, where enemy privateers raiding in Delaware Bay led the Quaker-dominated assembly to accede to Benjamin Franklin's plan for a volunteer land force to defend the colony in 1747. Whatever its strategic value, and that was debated, privateering notoriously drew American manpower away from the less appealing service on land and always made the recruitment of volunteer soldiers in wartime more difficult.

The high point of the voluntary system came in 1745, when William Shirley, the royal governor of Massachusetts, mobilized over three thousand volunteers from all the northern colonies and sent them on more than fifty hired ships against the great French fortress at Louisbourg on Cape Breton Island. Joined opportunely by a small squadron of the Royal Navy, which had been cruising in the Caribbean, this great New England crusade defied the odds by forcing the Louisbourg garrison to capitulate. The low point of the volunteer system had come five years earlier, when the British government adapted it for an expedition against the Spanish Empire. British officers had recruited about thirty-five hundred provincial volunteers from eleven colonies for service in an American regiment, which joined the British ships and troops assembling at Jamaica. But unlike the 1745 attack on Louisbourg, the expedition's attack on the Spanish seaport of Cartagena was a major fiasco. The American troops sickened and died "like rotten Sheep," and hundreds of survivors were forced to serve as sailors in the British Navy.

Not all American volunteers in 1740 and 1745 came from the enrolled militia. Many were fugitive servants, fleeing the labor contracts with which they had paid their passage across the Atlantic. Some were African Americans, either freemen or runaway slaves, welcomed by recruiting officers although militia laws barred them from carrying arms. A few were Native Americans, who were actively recruited to serve with the small paid ranger companies stationed along the American frontier. All three categories of men could be found in numbers on board colonial privateers as well.

In other words, real military service tended to migrate downward to the lower levels of society, attracting those most vulnerable to economic appeals, while the militia structure incorporated the existing social structure of elites, taxpayers, families, and settled residents. The growing divergence between volunteer forces and the militia system varied in degree from colony to colony and depended on the wartime demand for military manpower. New England, with its fairly compact and cohesive towns, probably drew a larger proportion of its volunteers from the organized militia than was the case in other regions, where contract servitude, chattel slavery, and pervasive migration created alternative pools of military manpower.

Despite differences from one English colony to another, and an overall trend toward the use of volunteer forces recruited each wartime year instead of mobilizing the organized militia for war, the life of the American colonial soldier on active service varied little from one decade to the next, and from one place to another. Racial minorities were always present. The entire units of African Americans that played an important part in defeating the Yamasee Indians in 1715 disappeared as the white population grew. Nevertheless, the difficulties of recruitment necessitated that individual African Americans serve, however much racial prejudice, like that expressed by George Washington early in the American Revolution, may have argued otherwise. Native American soldiers, in tribal bands cooperating with British and American forces, but also as individuals recruited for their skills in scouting and tracking, were rarely absent from colonial military life. The military companies of settled natives from Stockbridge, Massachusetts, gained a certain fame as part of the ranger forces led by Robert Rogers. But just as these minority soldiers were often mistreated and disparaged by their white comrades, colonial laws haltingly

tried to exclude them from the dubious honor of bearing arms in the militia.

Similarly, the law excluded servants, indentured to their masters for a period of years, from military service, sometimes specifying that immigrant servants from Ireland were not to bear arms. Motives behind these legal exclusions were mixed: partly the desire to protect property, partly the fear of insurrection by an aggrieved underclass, and partly simple racism, even when directed at the despised Irish of whom several hundred thousand had migrated to the Anglo-American colonies.

The officers and sergeants who commanded these colonial soldiers might, to professional eyes, appear very like the men themselves: civilian-soldiers, raw amateurs dragged from their farms and shops to march, fight, and die. But a closer look shows that the leaders were often leaders in the civilian world from which the soldiers came. Whether appointed by the royal governor or elected by the men they commanded, the typical colonial military officer carried his authority less by right of military rank than by being a mature, more prosperous farmer, or the son of a county justice, or a seaport merchant. The key to his position lay in his ability to recruit volunteers for war; men joined because they knew, respected, and perhaps even liked the men who commanded them.

In this pattern of voluntary recruitment lay the apparent weakness of colonial American forces; when soldiers refused to obey, whether to stand and fight, or to dig and use latrines, there was very little most colonial captains and sergeants could, or would, do about it. Rarely was a colonial American soldier whipped, as men often were in the British Army and Navy, for failing to carry out orders, and almost never was an American shot or hanged.

British officers serving with Americans were shocked by the lack of discipline in the colonial units, and aghast at the filthiness and disorder of their encampments. A limited number of women, usually soldiers' wives, served with British regiments in the field, and these women earned their rations by washing, cooking, and nursing, helping to maintain an important degree of order and cleanliness. Nothing comparable existed in colonial Anglo-American units, certainly not in those from New England, nor even in the more permissive colonies to the south. European observers sometimes ascribed poor discipline to the military ignorance of American officers, but in fact standard European military manuals sold well in the colonies, and American officers, aware of their deficiencies, did what they could to remedy them.

The American colonial soldier, only conditionally obedient to his commanders, usually wearing not a uniform but only the clothes in which he left home and perhaps carrying a musket and blanket issued to him, but just as often providing even these for himself, was not the kind of hard-bitten, desperate infantryman on which the European military revolution had been made. Whatever his motives for enlisting—economic need, youthful impulse, or religious belief (most wars were against heathen or Catholics)—the colonial soldier knew that, if military service became too unpleasant or dangerous, he could simply walk away. Desertion was a chronic and serious problem in all armies during the seventeenth and eighteenth centuries, so in this respect American soldiers were hardly unique. The articles of war provided for severe punishment of colonial deserters, and other laws made the harboring of deserters a crime. But colonial American soldiers, walking away from active service, also knew they could count on sympathy and shelter in the civilian world, not only from families and neighbors if they could reach home, but from strangers as well. Even when deserters were detected, few local magistrates did much to bring them before the law.

European military officers found it difficult to understand, much less accept, the conditional nature of colonial military service, and to realize that beyond the enlistment bounty (often supplemented by local subscription to avoid the need to draft anyone) or the promised grant of land that had enticed the American colonial to become—temporarily—a soldier, there was very little except persuasion to keep him steady in the arduous task of war. Such soldiers were, by European standards, promising material, bigger and healthier if less docile than the typical British, French, or German recruit. But they often proved, especially in a crisis or under severe hardship, ungovernable and unreliable, and it

was this growing perception that led to the final transformation of the colonial military system.

BRITISH REGULARS

A major change in the military system of the American colonies was taking shape by the middle of the eighteenth century. The generally unsatisfactory wartime performance of both colonial militias and provincial volunteers precipitated the change, and the rapidly growing importance of the colonies in the British imperial economy facilitated it as Anglo-French conflict in America reached a climax in the 1740s and 1750s. As noted, the British government had long been averse to the costs and risks of stationing its own troops and ships in North America.

Exceptions were made for the West Indian islands, where African slaves vastly outnumbered white sugar planters, hostile French colonies were near by, and the economic value of these colonies justified the military expense. Lesser exceptions were made in Newfoundland, where a few companies of regular troops tried to police the fisheries; in New York, where four companies of regulars stayed on from the British force that had seized the colony from the Dutch in 1664; and in South Carolina, where a small group of regulars was stationed in the 1720s for defense and police. Police, in fact, more than defense, may have been the military mission that could persuade the British government to deviate from its general policy that Americans should provide their own military forces. Preventing slave insurrection, keeping order among fishermen, and stopping occasional riots and rebellions were tasks better suited to regular troops, especially when colonial militiamen were among the rebels and rioters, as they sometimes were.

The beginning of change can be discerned in the 1730s, with the establishment of the last mainland colony, Georgia, as a military buffer against Spanish Florida, and in the 1740s, with the decision to build up a naval base at Halifax, Nova Scotia, to counteract Louisbourg, which was returned to France in peace negotiations in 1748. Regular forces in South Carolina and Georgia were increased, and several regiments were posted in Nova Scotia. Even so, as late as

1754 there were less than a thousand British regulars in those mainland colonies that in 1776 would join to become the United States. The great change came in 1755, when war with France flared once again.

This time London did not simply tell the Americans to do their own fighting but sent two British regiments to Virginia. In the years of war that followed, thousands of British regulars crossed the Atlantic to confront the French, who for almost a century had relied heavily on regular troops to defend their outnumbered colonists in Acadia and the Saint Lawrence Valley. British regiments replaced some of their battle losses by recruiting from the colonial American population, but far more Americans served in better-paid and more lightly disciplined provincial units. A promise of reimbursement from London encouraged colonial assemblies to vote the funds needed to recruit thousands of volunteers. The military quality of the provincial units so mobilized did not impress most British officers, and there was constant friction between British and American forces. Although this climactic Anglo-French war was finally won when French Canada surrendered, credit belonged largely to the British navy and army, aided by small bands of Native Americans and colonial rangers; the American role was confined mostly to the drudgery of warfare—building roads and hauling and guarding supplies.

A famous contemporary painting, Benjamin West's *The Death of Wolfe*, historically inaccurate in many respects but tremendously popular in both Europe and America, captured perfectly the ambiguous military result of this final war to defend and expand the British-American Empire. The British general James Wolfe is seen dying after his army has won the key battle for Canada. He is surrounded by his officers, most resplendent in British uniforms. A British grenadier grieves, a pensive Indian scout sits at the feet of the dying commander, and a green-clad American ranger brings news from the battlefield. But nowhere does the ordinary American soldier or officer appear, because almost none of them were at the battle of Quebec in 1759, having by that time been relegated to a secondary and inglorious part in the war.

The political ramifications of this major change in British military policy for America are well known. At the end of the war in 1763, Parliament accepted a decision to keep a large, expensive force of regular troops in the American colonies. Whether these troops were to defend the colonies against hostile Indians and Europeans or to control unruly Americans by armed force was a question raised at the time and not easily answered. Americans protesting the taxation required by this new force argued that never had a regular garrison for colonial defense been less needed, with the French driven out of Canada and the Spanish out of Florida and all the territory between the Appalachians and the Mississippi under British control. British officials simply inverted the argument, insisting that the new territories and their Native population demanded an unprecedented degree of effective imperial control if Anglo-American security was to be maintained. As the dispute escalated to military confrontation, the British resorted to their American garrison as a police force, while the Americans themselves had arms and years of recent military experience with which to mobilize resistance.

CONCLUSION

How much the more than 150 years of colonial military experience, so different from that of contemporary Europeans, shaped American society before 1776 is a difficult question. Little evidence supports the idea that widespread ownership of firearms created an exceptionally violent culture. Evidence is better that the colonial militia reinforced the social (and racial) order while also fostering a proto-democratic local resistance to "central authority." Yet the "right to bear arms" later written into the Federal Bill of Rights as an explicit statement of a colonial tradition, a right formally though not actually denied to Native Americans, African Americans, and other unfree persons, but a "right" as routinely ignored in practice by free white Americans, never carried much sense of being an ethical obligation, at least not after the earliest years of colonization when every male had to be armed and pressed into service when danger threatened. At the same time, the sheer number of colonial Americans who had seen some active military service played a vital role in demystifying the military professionalism of an armed British presence that had grown so quickly after 1755, and in enabling the colonies to free themselves, by force of arms, from British hegemony.

BIBLIOGRAPHY

Anderson, Fred. *A People's Army: Massachusetts Soldiers and Society in the Seven Years' War.* Chapel Hill, N.C., 1984.

Cress, Lawrence Delbert. *Citizens in Arms: The Army and the Militia in American Society to the War of 1812.* Chapel Hill, N.C., 1982.

Ferling, John. *A Wilderness of Miseries: War and Warriors in Early America.* Westport, Conn., 1980.

Gipson, Lawrence H. *The British Empire Before the American Revolution.* Vols. 6–8, *The Great War for the Empire.* New York, 1959–1964.

Johnson, James Michael. *The Military in Georgia, 1754–1776: Militiamen, Rangers, and Redcoats.* Macon, Ga., 1992.

Leach, Douglas Edward. *Arms for Empire: A Military History of the British Colonies in North America, 1607–1763.* New York, 1973.

Malone, Patrick M. *The Skulking Way of War: Technology and Tactics Among the New England Indians.* Lanham, Md., 1991.

Melvoin, Richard I. *New England Outpost: War and Society in Colonial Deerfield.* New York, 1989.

Pargellis, Stanley M. *Lord Loudoun in North America.* New Haven, Conn., 1933.

Parker, Geoffrey. *The Military Revolution: Military Innovation and the Rise of the West, 1500–1800.* New York, 1988.

Peckham, Howard H. *The Colonial Wars, 1689–1762.* Chicago, 1964.

Shea, William L. *The Virginia Militia in the Seventeenth Century.* Baton Rouge, La., 1983.

Shy, John. *Toward Lexington: The Role of the British Army in the Coming of the American Revolution.* Princeton, N.J., 1965.

Steele, Ian K. *Betrayals: Fort William Henry and the "Massacre."* New York, 1990.

John Shy

SEE ALSO **The European Contest for North America; Independence; and Indian-Colonist Conflicts and Alliances.**

THE DUTCH COLONY

SOLDIERS WERE a constant presence in New Netherland throughout its history. They accompanied the first colonists in the 1620s, and they stood on the ramparts of Fort New Amsterdam in 1664 when an English war fleet forced the colony's surrender. In some years soldiers made up a majority of Europeans voyaging to the colony. The number of professional West India Company soldiers serving in New Netherland ranged from about 150 in the 1620s to a battalion strength force of about 550 soldiers in 1664. They were scattered in a series of forts from Fort Orange in the north to Fort Casimir on the Delaware River. In fact military forts dominated the architecture of the colony's largest settlements.

The West India Company built and rebuilt forts in New Netherland: two large ones, at New Amsterdam on Manhattan Island and Fort Orange near the confluence of the Mohawk and Hudson rivers, and two smaller ones on the Delaware River. Fort New Amsterdam was the largest. First constructed in 1626 and rebuilt completely in the 1630s, it towered over the rough clapboard and reed houses set aside for the settlers. Forts were the largest construction projects undertaken by the company in New Netherland, and their maintenance was a constant expense.

PROFESSIONAL SOLDIERS

New Netherland was a far different experience for West India Company soldiers than it was for free burghers or even company employees. Even by seventeenth-century standards, life was harsh for the professional soldiers of the company. Within the company's domain, soldiers comprised the core of the male-dominated societies that first developed in the "factories" established to conduct company business. New Netherland was not much different in this regard from other company outposts. Until the 1640s single men, many of them soldiers, constituted the majority of Europeans in the colony. They were often a bad-tempered and disagreeable lot, given to hard drinking and brawling. Knife fights were commonplace, as were disputes over gambling.

A soldier's pay depended on rank and assignment, but few junior officers and virtually no enlisted men were likely to save much after their terms had expired. By calculating that 1 florin equaled .09 sterling in the seventeenth century and that 1 pound sterling came to approximately $110 in 1991, one finds that 1 florin equaled about $9.90 in 1992. On this basis, an ensign, for example, earned between $356.40 and $396.00 per month, whereas the senior company merchant received from $594.00 to $891.00 per month. Sergeants earned $178.20, corporals $118.80, and common soldiers $79.20. In addition each soldier received a ration allowance from the company store, although some complained that prices were as much as 140 percent higher than in the fatherland.

Enlistments averaged from three to four years, a relatively short period by the standards of the day. One reason for this may have been that the company had to compete with rising employment in the Netherlands. The company sometimes resorted to *zielverkoopers,* or soul-sellers, to round up likely looking young lads off the streets of Amsterdam and Rotterdam. It was an international group, to say the least.

Germans comprised the largest contingent of non-Dutch professional soldiers. They came from all over the Germanies, many of them veterans of the Thirty Years' War. Many others were former soldiers in the various Dutch national armies organized for the war with the Spanish Hapsburgs. The second largest number of foreigners came from Scandinavia, especially Denmark and Sweden. English, Scots, Irish, and Swiss generally made up the rest. Dutch nationals accounted for about 50 percent of the enlisted men. Among officers, Dutch nationals were better represented, owing to the importance of fluency in the Dutch language.

Most soldiers were housed in barracks built within the walls of the forts. A typical barrack housed from ten to twenty soldiers in dormitory-like accommodations. In the barracks built at Fort New Amsterdam and Fort Orange, there was little privacy. Sanitation facilities were shared privies. Cooking facilities were usually provided by a large hearth at one end of the rough-hewn log structures.

Corporal punishment was an accepted means of discipline in the seventeenth century, and the soldiers who served with the great trading companies endured much from the lash. Part of the difficulty facing garrison commanders in the chartered territory derived from the monotonous, backbreaking work to which company soldiers were subjected. In Curaçao, admittedly one of the worst postings in the company's domain, soldiers were frequently drafted to work the salt pans—a backbreaking ordeal that involved cutting salt cakes from a shallow pan filled with seawater at high tide, or tidal pan, after the sea water had evaporated, hauling them on wheel barrows to the wharf, and stacking the cakes aboard ships bound for New England and the fatherland. In the equatorial heat of Curaçao, cutting salt was a job usually reserved for slaves, but when the number of slaves was short, company commanders did not hesitate to use soldiers. Soldiers were also used to repair the fort and fish the shallow lagoons of the island to supplement their rations.

In New Netherland, largely owing to the more temperate climate, a soldier's life was somewhat less taxing than life in Curaçao or along the West African coast. Nonetheless most WIC soldiers longed to complete their enlistments and escape the harsh, regimented life.

Many of the soldiers had had combat experience before being posted to New Netherland. For example, the contingents of soldiers accompanying directors-general Willem Kieft in 1638 and Peter Stuyvesant in 1647 appear to have included a high percentage of veterans from the Dutch national armies, men who had had years of experience in combat against the Spanish armies throughout the Low Countries.

Soldiers who had served in the Dutch army under Maurice of Nassau, prince of Orange, or his successor, Frederik Hendrik, were arguably the best-trained and most battle-hardened troops in Europe. Drilled in the new tactics pioneered by Prince Maurice, Dutch army veterans were expert in the use of the matchlock musket, so named because the firing mechanism required the holding of a lighted match to a primed gunlock. In fact the complex series of steps required to fire and reload the matchlock musket dictated a new approach to battle and, some scholars argue, a revolution in European military tactics.

Prince Maurice, university-trained in the classics and mathematics, analyzed the firing and reloading of matchlock muskets and broke the process down into forty-two positions, that he named and to which he then assigned a specific word of command. He had his officers drill his soldiers in executing each step in unison. After a row of musketeers and arquebusiers (those using heavy matchlock muskets) fired their weapons, they marched to the rear between the lines of the next advancing row. There they cleaned and charged their weapons, prepared the match, and marched forward for the next volley. The result was a marked increase in the frequency of fire. Volleys were more effective in stopping enemy advances, and the shock effect was spectacular. Consequently, Maurice's innovations tended to increase the number of guns in European armies while reducing the number of pikes. The Dutch armies were known for their musketeers, as the Swiss had once been known for their pikemen.

Most WIC soldiers in New Netherland were equipped with matchlock muskets. The arquebus, or heavy musket, was also used by company soldiers, but its weight generally confined its use to garrison defensive positions. In addition the half-pike was a favorite weapon for close-in fighting. During a war with the Algonquian coastal tribes in 1641, Director-General Willem Kieft asked permission of the heads of families to arm the company slaves with hatches and half-pikes to serve beside European musketeers. Most military expeditions in New Netherland contained some pikemen.

Officers wore swords, and most soldiers carried some bladed weapon, ranging from a saber to a short sword. Since most colonial battles were tooth-and-claw affairs against Native Americans, the proficient use of hand weapons in desperate hand-to-hand combat usually meant the difference between victory and defeat.

Company soldiers in New Netherland were theoretically there to protect the colony against foreign conquest and to protect company employees and settlers from the Indians. In fact their most frequent operations were raids against

villages of Native Americans. Often these raids degenerated into genocidal assaults on undefended women and children. Soldiers of the company were infamous for their brutality against Native Americans, as the following eyewitness account of a raid on a coastal Algonquian tribe in 1644 attests:

The moon was then at the full, and threw a strong light against the hills so that many winter days were not brighter than it then was. On arriving there the Indians were wide awake, and on their guard, so that ours [our soldiers] determined to charge and surround the houses, sword in hand. . . . They [the Indians] were also so hard pressed that it was impossible for one to escape. In a brief space of time there were counted one hundred and eighty dead outside the houses. Presently none durst come forth, keeping within the houses, discharging arrows through the holes. The general perceived that nothing else was to be done, and resolved . . . to set the huts on fire, whereupon the Indians tried every means to escape, not succeeding in which they returned back to the flames preferring to perish by the fire than to die by our hands. What was most wonderful is, that among this vast collection of men, women and children not one was heard to cry or to scream. According to the report of the Indians themselves the number then destroyed exceeded five hundred. Some say, full seven hundred . . . our God having collected together there the greater number of our enemies, . . . from which escaped no more than eight men in all, and three of them were severely wounded. (J. Franklin Jameson. *Narratives of New Netherland*, pp. 283–284)

The Dutch attack on the colony of New Sweden in 1655 was the only operation in the history of New Netherland to employ European tactics effectively. The conquest of New Sweden was accomplished by sheer force of numbers in a combined naval and army operation that was the largest ever mounted in North America to the time. The expedition consisted of 7 ships, 317 soldiers (both militia and company soldiers), and a company of combat marines. After forcing the surrender of Fort Casimir (near present Newcastle, Delaware) on the lower Delaware River, the force pushed on up river to Fort Christina, the Swedish stronghold. Surrounding the Swedish fort, Director-General Stuyvesant set up nine artillery pieces in a perimeter outside the wall. Dutch soldiers then began systematically killing off the settlement's goats, cattle, sheep, and poultry. Stuyvesant was prepared for a long seige when, to his surprise, the Swedish governor Johan Rising surrendered.

THE MILITIA

Civilians were involved in every military operation in the colony's history. They fought beside professional company soldiers against the Indians and the Swedes and assisted (somewhat reluctantly) in the building and rebuilding of the colony's forts. Colonists were expected to defend the colony. In the Provisional Orders, which governed the colony from 1624 to 1630, the colonists were bound to observe all "alliances and treaties with foreign princes and potentates," although "by so doing they should be involved in war with others, their neighbors, and even be obliged to take the field." Yet it was not until the establishment of town charters in the 1640s and 1650s that a true citizens' militia developed.

Burgher rights implied service in the *schutters,* or militia, and the formation of the *schutters* followed quickly on the heels of the granting of town charters. The largest was organized in New Amsterdam by the Court of Burgomasters and Schepens in 1653. Believing that an English attack might be imminent, the magistrates resolved that "the burghers of this City shall stand guard in full squads over night at places, to be decided upon by the Director General." Elsewhere in the colony, the *schutters* drilled and stockpiled munitions in the expectation of war with New England.

In New Netherland, as in the fatherland, the militia reflected the status hierarchy of male society. The officers of the burgher guard represented a cross section of the town's leading citizens, and the elaborate panoply of military drill and ceremony served as reinforcement of the rank-ordered society. In the Indian wars of the 1650s and in the conquest of the Swedes on the Delaware, the militia served alongside company soldiers as auxillary troops but took their orders only from their own officers and the director-general.

The chain of command in New Netherland was relatively short. The resident director-general was the commander-in-chief of all armed forces in the colony, including naval vessels while in port. Below him were the garrison commanders at Fort Orange and the two forts on the Delaware River, Fort Nassau and Fort Casimir. Garrison commanders were usually commissioned captains or majors. Most company-sized units also had an ensign or lieutenant. The non-commissioned ranks included sergeant, corporal, lance corporal (*Landspassaat*), and private. Uniforms were not common, although officers usually had military costumes made at their own expense.

By the 1650s the reliance on professional company soldiers that had characterized the military strategy of the colony since the 1620s was changing. It is not possible to estimate accurately the costs of maintaining a military presence in New Netherland, but it clearly was a significant drain on the West India Company. In 1644, for example, the bureau of accounts reported that since the year 1626 a total of 515,000 florins ($5.1 million in 1991 dollars) had been spent on New Netherland, most of which had gone toward the military. The last years of the colony's existence witnessed an even larger expenditure on military affairs. Thus, it seems probable that at least one cause of the West India Company's financial failure in New Netherland was the cost of maintaining so many men in arms.

BIBLIOGRAPHY

Boxer, Charles R. *The Dutch in Brazil, 1624–1654.* Oxford, 1957.
———. *The Dutch Seaborne Empire: 1600–1800.* New York, 1965.
Fernow, Berthold, ed. *The Records of New Amsterdam from 1653 to 1674.* 7 vols. New York, 1897.
Gehring, Charles T., ed. and trans. *Fort Orange Court Minutes, 1652–1660.* Syracuse, N.Y., 1990.
Gehring, Charles T., and J. A. Schiltkamp, eds. and trans. *Curaçao Papers, 1640–1665.* New Netherland Documents, vol. 17. Interlaken, N.Y., 1987.
Jameson, J. Franklin, ed. *Narratives of New Netherland, 1609–1664.* New York, 1909.
McNeill, William H. *The Pursuit of Power: Technology, Armed Force, and Society Since A.D. 1000.* Chicago, Ill., 1982.

Oliver A. Rink

SEE ALSO **The European Contest for North America** and **Indian-Colonist Conflicts and Alliances.**

THE FRENCH COLONIES

ALL THE COLONIES of New France were involved in war for more than half the period of the French regime. Some of the enemies they faced—notably the Iroquois, the Natchez, and the English—had populations larger than their own at the time war broke out. Some—most notably the Iroquois and Chickasaw—were ferocious opponents and skillful warriors. Others, such as the Creek, were numerous and powerful but maintained a careful neutrality. The English, though disunited and disorganized, had access to the latest technology and thus might be able to mount a serious challenge to French claims. In such circumstances the military was bound to be an important presence in colonial society.

THE MILITARY SERVICES

The structure of command was quite simple when trading companies ran the colonies. Each had a small administration headed by a governor. Organization gradually became more complex under royal rule. The governor-general of New France was commander in chief of all French forces in North America. His residence was at Quebec, but he spent much time at Montreal, the center of the fur trade, in the spring and summer. Below him in each colonial capital was the local governor. In practice he had considerable freedom to direct affairs as he saw fit. Acadia (present-day Nova Scotia, New Brunswick, Prince Edward Island, and Maine), Île Royale (Cape Breton Island), and Louisiana (the northern Gulf Coast and the Mississippi River valley)

were in effect separate entities, though they cooperated as necessary with Canada. In the principal towns—Quebec, Trois-Rivières, and Montreal in the case of Canada—there was a *lieutenant du roy* and a major who assumed intermediate command and certain administrative tasks. From 1687 to 1714 there was a commandant of the troops in Canada, but that office was abandoned as superfluous and a cause of friction. In the Seven Years' War, when units of the regular army were sent, a general staff was appointed, headed by a *maréchal de camp* (major general), which was the position held by Louis Joseph, marquis de Montcalm, from 1756 to 1759. All were supposed to be subordinate to the governor-general and, when in the area, to the town governors. In addition each colony also had at least one military engineer to supervise construction of fortifications.

Early Regulars
The trading companies were not willing or able to fund major military enterprises. In the early decades, there were few men referred to as soldiers anywhere. In Canada there were barely enough soldiers, aided by colonists, to repulse Iroquois attacks in the 1630s and 1640s. In 1645 two companies totaling perhaps one hundred arrived, but the numbers soon declined. In 1661 Governor Pierre Dubois Davaugour brought one hundred soldiers, not nearly enough to oppose the Iroquois confederacy, who could field up to twenty-five hundred.

In 1663 Louis XIV decided that the Crown should assume direct control of New France. Continued trouble with the Iroquois led Versailles to take strong action. Alexandre Prouville de Tracy was appointed lieutenant general of all French colonies in the Americas in 1663 (the only such appointment ever made). The king sent the Carignan Salières regiment and four other companies; in all, some twelve hundred men. After helping to bring the Iroquois to terms in 1667, they were withdrawn, though four hundred officers and soldiers remained in the colony as settlers. By the end of 1669, five companies of fifty men had been raised in France for Canada and one for Acadia. Thereafter only a handful of soldiers were sent from time to time to stiffen the garrisons.

The *Troupes de la Marine*

In 1683 renewed hostilities with the Iroquois led Versailles to send soldiers to Canada again. This time they were drawn not from the regular army but from the *troupes de la marine,* the French marines. These troops were raised by the navy, which was responsible for the colonies, for duty at naval bases, on ships, and in the colonies. Some writers refer to them as colonial regulars, but this implies that they were regular troops raised in the colonies and maintained by them, which was not the case.

The marines formed the nucleus of defense forces in New France for three-quarters of a century. Each company had a captain, lieutenant, and ensign, though at various times there were additional officers. Canada received three companies of 50 men in 1683. The total rose each year until there were 35 companies in 1688, for a maximum strength of 1,750. It was cut to 28 companies in 1689, then to 30 men per company in 1699. For the first half of the eighteenth century, the standing army in Canada consisted of marines numbering in all 900 men—less than a regiment. In the face of a mounting challenge from the British and British colonists, the number was increased in 1750 to 30 companies of 50 men. Companies were expanded to 65 men in 1756, for a total of 1,950. The following year the corps reached maximum strength, with 2,600 men in 40 companies.

These numbers are a bit optimistic, however, since companies were seldom up to strength. Also, scattered over a territory exceeding one thousand kilometers (620 miles) from east to west and taking days and weeks to move any great distance, the troops could seldom be said to be a substantial presence on the ground, except perhaps in concentrations around cities. Whatever their quality they would not suffice to defend Canada or go on a major military expedition.

Smaller numbers of marines were deployed in the other colonies comprising New France. Twenty-five soldiers were sent to Terreneuve (Newfoundland) in 1687 and stationed at Plaisance (Placentia). In response to repeated raids in the early 1690s, the garrison was increased to 40 then 60. When war resumed in 1701, the king brought the garrison up to three companies of 50 men. For any major operation, more men had to be sent in, and any time the English at-

tacked, the marines were not strong enough to hold the position. They were sent to Île Royale after Newfoundland was transferred to the English in 1713.

In Acadia the ragtag collection of soldiers who had fought in the early years was joined by a company of marines posted to the capital, Port Royal (Annapolis Royal, Nova Scotia) in 1686, and a second company was sent there in 1687. From 1689 the garrison there stood at three companies of fifty men. They were hardly enough to oppose the large expeditions sent by the English, and in 1710 the colony was lost permanently.

To avoid a repeat of this disaster, the French spent a tremendous sum of money fortifying Louisbourg, capital of Île Royale, now a colony on its own. Seven companies of marines were sent at the outset. By the 1720s there were ten, alongside which there were companies of the Karrer regiment, Swiss troops in the pay of France. The fortress fell in 1745; after it was returned in the peace of 1748, twenty-four companies of marines were stationed there.

Louisiana had few troops initially. Jean-Baptiste Le Moyne, sieur de Bienville, had no more than 35 soldiers at his disposal in 1714, when trouble first flared with the Natchez. After the Crown assumed control of the colony in 1731, a small number of marines were sent. Persistent trouble with the Spanish, the English, and neighboring Indians led to increases until there were 20 companies. During the warfare of 1745–1748, they were joined by 149 Swiss mercenaries for a total of 835 soldiers and officers. There were 21 companies of marines during the 1750s.

The Militia

Under royal rule the people of New France were subject to two kinds of military service, both a form of labor tax. First, they might be called to serve as soldiers in the militia either in the field, on war parties, or at home to repel invaders. Second, they might be required to provide labor (the *corvée militaire*), working on the construction of fortifications, other installations, and military roads, transporting supplies, and so on.

The militia was actually set up by the habitants themselves in 1647. With little help coming from France, they were obliged to assume responsibility for their own defense against the

Iroquois. The service was regularized by Louis XIV in 1669. Each parish formed its own militia company comprising all able-bodied men between fifteen and sixty. They were led, ideally, by a captain of the militia, aided by a lieutenant, ensign, and sergeants. The key figure was the captain, who also had important civil functions. He was chosen from among the most distinguished and capable people in the parish; the post was an honor, without pay.

The small number of troops led to a heavy reliance on the colonial militia. But the population of Canada was not large either. The militia numbered in all 2,250 in 1683, 4,500 in 1700, around 8,000 during the war of 1744–1748, and between 10,000 and 12,000 in the 1750s. The number that could actually be deployed, however, was limited by the fact that calling out a large force might well cripple the economy and jeopardize the military supply system. In the east coast colonies, the militia was much smaller and far less impressive. In Louisiana the sparse, slow-growing population could hardly contribute many men. Between 1744 and 1760 the figure hovered about the 400 mark. For that reason far more soldiers had to be sent to deal with military threats.

Regular Troops, 1754–1760

In 1754 the British government began to reinforce its military position in North America by sending battalions of regular troops. The following year France responded by reinforcing its colonies. The marines could not be expanded rapidly enough to meet the challenge; moreover, they were generally thought to be no match for soldiers from the regular armies of England, France, and other European countries who had been thoroughly trained in conventional warfare and had ample combat experience in large-scale formal engagements. So instead the government sent units of the *troupes de terre* (so called because many took their names from the provinces of France where they were raised).

Each battalion numbered 557 men and was under a lieutenant colonel. There was one company of grenadiers under a captain, lieutenant, and subaltern, and 12 companies of fusiliers each under a captain, lieutenant, and ensign. Four battalions went to Louisbourg and another four to Canada. By the autumn of 1755, there were

2,250 regulars in Canada. The figure rose to 3,600 in 1756 and 4,800 in 1757. The figures might have been higher had not epidemics and naval warfare reduced the number of reinforcements that reached North America.

MILITARY SERVICE

Commissions and Promotion

In the seventeenth century, the French army became the finest in Europe. It contained many excellent officers, well trained and experienced. Commissions and promotions, however, were not conferred solely on the basis of ability or distinguished service. Political or family connections helped, as did money. In the eighteenth century, such practices, along with financial and political troubles, led to a degeneration of the army. A good many men were advanced without having shown the requisite competence or diligence.

In the marines, commissions and promotions were based on several considerations: seniority, talent, zeal, connections, favor, and birth. None of this was unusual for that era. The most significant difference from other services was that commissions could not be purchased. There was a real competition among aristocrats in Canada to get into the marines, and this generally assured authorities of a good choice. It also led to the gradual Canadianization of the corps.

For many Frenchmen Canada was not an attractive place to serve, and more than one officer managed to contract a convenient illness before having to set sail. The easiest way to find good men for the officer corps was to draw on the local population. Many local men, lacking opportunity to advance in the small force in Canada, eagerly took positions in Île Royale, Louisiana, and, on occasion, in the West Indies.

Promotion appears to have been based primarily on seniority. For much of the time, there were few major engagements in which officers could distinguish themselves, and in wars where many saw some action, the fairest arrangement was to promote all those who served in a comparable manner according to who had served the longest. Still, promotions based on ability or outstanding service certainly did occur. In addition officials could reward those who served with distinction by giving them the much-coveted Cross

501

of Saint Louis. The mass of officers, then, were of solid ability. A small number were extraordinary.

Training

During the second half of the seventeenth century, training in the French army was thorough and exacting. Maneuvers and the training required to execute them well were intended to get the most out of both the men and their weapons and to compensate for their limitations. The action of loading, aiming, and firing was reduced to twelve movements executed to the command of a drum beat. The limited range of weapons gave men very little time to reload before the enemy might be upon them.

Experience led forces everywhere to favor two kinds of formations. The line, usually three ranks deep, depended on the firepower of the musket followed by a bayonet charge. The column, only a few ranks wide but many ranks deep, depended on the effect of an attack by a narrow, long formation on a small portion of an enemy line. To learn how to maneuver in formation, officers and soldiers required at least eighteen months of training and then several years of experience. To perform well in the heat of battle required severe discipline.

It was veterans of this system who came out to Canada with Lieutenant General Tracy. In the eighteenth century, the army deteriorated. The quality of officers was much more variable; some lacked spirit and many were given to intrigue against each other. Indifference crept into the training and discipline of soldiers. These were the sort of men who came out with the marquis de Montcalm.

The training of the marines varied from outstanding to pathetic. Officers who came from France had some experience serving in regular units. Officers who began their careers in Canada received a little instruction, very little drill, and plenty of experience, which began when they were admitted (from ages fifteen to twenty) as cadets in the ranks of the soldiers. They were expected to serve on war parties and in garrisons. In this way they became familiar with the land and the manner of warfare in North America.

Of all groups in the colony, these men were the most adept at guerrilla warfare and the most intimately familiar with the territory through which they moved. They were the mainspring of Canadian military operations. But few Canadian officers could master larger formations and the more ambitious elements of regular warfare. It was often alleged that officers rarely took the time to train their men properly. Soldiers, many of whom arrived from France as raw recruits, had to learn by experience, like everyone else in the colony. Relatively small, and fragmented into still smaller units, the *troupes de la marine* were not a cohesive disciplined force, nor were they a professional corps.

Troops in Acadia and Newfoundland were frequently said to be a sad sight. Those stationed at Louisbourg formed something more like a conventional garrison, though training and discipline often left much to be desired. The small detachments in Louisiana during the early years were not distinguished. With time and transfusions of Canadian officers, the colony developed an army much like the one in Canada.

Because of the limited military value of the soldiers sent from France, colonial authorities continued to rely on the militia. Officials in Canada often alluded to the quality of these men. Officials in Versailles came to do the same, usually to justify doing little to strengthen the marines. Like the soldiers, the militia got its best training in the field. Born in Canada, the men were familiar with the terrain and accustomed to the climate. By the 1690s, after years of relentless war, the militia was quite formidable. The militia was very much a North American force; it could not be expected to cope with regular warfare. Moreover, in practice there were not enough officers to direct it, and like any militia, it had a tendency to melt away if kept in the field too late in the season. The Louisiana militia was much smaller and did not grow out of the same traditions. Its performance in the field varied from adequate to unimpressive.

Service

Many troops served only in town garrisons, except in time of war. Only the best soldiers and the most experienced officers served on the frontiers, in Canada's western territories, or in the Illinois territory of northern Louisiana, though promising new men would be added so that they could develop their skills. In Louisiana, noncommissioned officers and soldiers, often of mediocre ability, were rotated between New Orleans and the frontier posts. Generally, Canadian wartime expeditions consisted of 25 percent marines, from 40 percent to 50 percent militia, and from 25 percent to 35 percent Indians, except for the smaller raiding parties, where half or more were Indians. By contrast, in Louisiana the militia played little or no role in expeditions. Marine officers provided most of the leadership for combined forces. Despite recurring hardships, mutiny was rare. There were brief risings at Fort Niagara in 1687 and 1730, both easily put down without bloodshed. At Louisbourg there were more serious mutinies in 1744 and 1750. More often soldiers resolved their distress by deserting.

Officers in the marines performed a remarkable range of other functions. As commanders at the posts set up among most of the allied Indian nations, they were agents for the Crown in its dealings with tribes on whom the French relied heavily in the fur trade and in military operations. Although major negotiations were conducted by the governor general at Montreal, vital work had to be conducted by the officer on the spot. Men who showed a talent for languages or a capacity for understanding the Indian way of life were gradually given greater responsibility. Commanders gave out presents, conveyed messages to and from the king and governor, and kept an eye on the fur trade, upon which good relations were founded. Much of the later exploration of the interior was undertaken by military officers such as Pierre Gaultier de La Verendrye and his sons; they provided information on which a fuller understanding of North American geography was based.

With the arrival of the *troupes de terre* in 1755, the system of command began to break down. Intrigue was rife throughout the French world. Senior officers in the field could not forget that many around them and at the court might be scheming to have them removed or to shift the blame for failure onto them. Everyone was writing letters about everyone else. There was friction between army and marine officers, both of whom looked down on the other. They quarreled over tactics. Some French army officers were repelled by the Indian and Canadian way of fighting, which seemed to them both unprofessional and barbarous. The Canadians did not disguise their disgust at the regulars' inability and unwillingness to endure the hardships of the wilderness. They also objected to the much greater pay that the army received. The esprit de corps that had formerly been so impressive in the Canadian armed forces was eroded by mistrust and a mounting sense of almost inevitable failure.

SOCIAL RELATIONS

Class

The command structure of the armed forces in New France reveals part of the way in which a system of classes was transferred from the Old World to the New World. As in the French army, officers were aristocrats and soldiers were commoners. The aristocratic origins of some are open to question—dubious aristocrats who firmed up their credentials over a couple of generations were common enough in France. The king ennobled few Canadians, and relatively few commoners held commissions. The armed forces therefore were not a mechanism for upward social mobility. By contrast the militia was drawn from the common people of Canada. The bond between the two was that marine officers who usually led combined forces were increasingly born in Canada or settled in the colony, giving them a broad sense of common interest.

Mentality

Two important features of life in Canada owed much to the armed forces: the military ethos that suffused society and a sense of identity with Canada. The *mentalité militaire* was an age-old feature of the nobility, and those serving as officers in the marines generally displayed the customary martial ardor. Officials often remarked on the general determination to be involved in military enterprises and the ferocious courage of veterans. They were also astonished at the hardships that the marines were willing to endure in the field. The soldiers, generally reluctant recruits from France and sometimes deserters from European units, were not as ardent, though at any time a core of about one-quarter of the men were good enough to be assigned to arduous duty.

The most tenacious fighters, as everyone observed, were the Canadian militia, and as a result commanders relied on them more than on their troops. Raised in harsh circumstances, frequently facing war, and influenced by the legacy of desperate struggles in the early years of Canada, these men were formidable fighters. Canada was a society with a strong military tradition. Many people showed a readiness to fight and a confidence born of a history of success in the face of adversity. From this arose the commitment to *la survivance,* or survival, which has remained a central feature of the French Canadian mentality.

In the French world of Louis XIV and Louis XV, there may not have been the elaborate cultural concept of nationality that developed in the nineteenth century, but the records do indicate that the men who settled or were born in Canada were marked out as different. On lists, officers were frequently distinguished as "canadiens," an early indication that a sense of distinct identity was forming. One might suggest a division into colonials and metropolitans similar to that usually discerned in the English colonies, where loyalties would eventually be clearly divided. Those who tied their fortunes to the colony and were comfortable with its distinctive way of life might be called colonials, while those who were passing through might be called metropolitans.

The Canadianization of the officer corps had the effect of alienating some of the influence of the court, especially since there were not that many French noblemen anxious to serve in Canada. Given the limitations of the colony and the potential attractions of France, it is remarkable that very few Canadians went elsewhere to further careers begun in Canada and that when they did, it was usually to do a rotation in Île Royale or Louisiana. The militia was deeply committed to Canada, which in part accounts for its dogged determination against the odds over the years. France to these men was almost a separate entity.

THE TROOPS AND THE ECONOMY

The troops who came to New France provided a limited number of settlers, but as all these were men, it was a lopsided contribution. Several officers and some four hundred soldiers from the Carignan Salières regiment came to Canada in 1668. Small numbers of soldiers from the marines settled in each decade between 1683 and 1760. Elsewhere, the troops represented an even smaller factor in the settlement of the land. All but the severely wounded were shipped back to France after the colony fell, but a good many had deserted and dissolved into the countryside. Very few settled in Newfoundland, Acadia, or Île Royale, and most who did were forced to leave when the colonies fell to the English. In Louisiana the contribution of marines was limited by their small numbers (until relatively late), high level of transience, and appalling mortality rate. Large numbers of enlisted men did, however, remain in the colony following the general discharge of 15 September 1763.

As befits an aristocracy, the officers who settled in Canada were granted large estates, or seigneuries. They received between one-quarter and one-half of all land grants in each decade from the 1660s to the 1750s, making them second only to the Catholic church in the ranks of major landowners. Very few, however, had much influence over agricultural development, which was largely determined by the habitants to whom seigneurs granted lands for farms. Like most aristocrats the officers were not particularly interested in agriculture. Even among those who were interested, few had sufficient capital to do much. Officers looked on their lands as a source of revenue, but since farms were developed slowly, the estates provided only a modest income.

In 1685 the king allowed noblemen in New France to engage in commercial activities without losing their aristocratic status. The nobility, however, did not have substantial resources. This made aristocrats keen to make money but reluctant to invest. In typical aristocratic fashion, a fair amount of officers' income was spent on conspicuous consumption. A very few set out to further the development of industries, notably timber, tileworks, and iron and copper mining. None was a conspicuous success, and much of what was accomplished was the work of civilian associates or successors. Officers insinuated themselves in the fur trade, but their slender means meant that they could contribute little. Instead, most aimed to skim off a portion of the profits being generated. At times the government tried to prohibit officers' involvement in trade, but for the most part, officers posted west managed to turn a good little profit out of their military assignments.

As consumers and laborers, the soldiers' impact on economic development was also limited. They had very little money to spend and therefore represented an insubstantial consumer force, except when it came to alcohol. The troops provided a modest and declining amount of unskilled labor and smaller amounts of skilled and semiskilled labor. Many arrived with a trade but were often apprentices still training to become masters. Louisiana soldiers had to hire themselves out as laborers, fishermen, and so forth to survive economically during the Seven Years' War. A less positive contribution came in the form of crime. Soldiers figured prominently in the ranks of accused, and many of their crimes were economic (theft, counterfeiting, arson).

Far more important to the economy of New France than the troops' economic activities was the business that military operations brought to colonists. The armed forces paid handsomely for supplies and services, particularly food, building materials, and transportation.

SUPPLYING THE ARMED FORCES

A basic pattern runs through the entire period of French royal rule: in peacetime, the Minister of the Marine (in charge of the navy and the colonies) wanted consumption kept to a minimum; when war was imminent or had broken out, he authorized large increases. This system depended on the capacity of suppliers to provide the quantities needed in the time available. The French generally did well enough on the limited scale of peacetime operations, but they were sorely pressed when orders greatly exceeded these levels.

What held things up was the lack of money. The minister tried to keep costs as low as possible by purchasing as little as possible. Restricted commercial operations stemming from long years of limited peacetime spending by the government led to production lags during war. Moreover, on occasion during both war and peace, sufficient funds simply could not be found to purchase supplies or pay for goods already received. Finance was at the bottom of much of the logistical strain afflicting operations in French North America, as it was for most government activities in ancien régime France.

Weapons

The principal weapon of the marines, regulars, and militia was the smooth-bore, flintlock, muzzle-loading musket to which a bayonet could be affixed, making it both a fire and a shock weapon. In North America the preferred design was 3.5 French feet (3.7 English feet or 1.13 meters) long, weighing 5 kilograms (11 pounds). It was shorter and lighter than the standard military issue, which made it easier to use in the woods. At this time the French excelled at manufacturing muskets. With a few memorable exceptions, the weapons sent to New France were reported to be good, and those used in trade were highly prized by the Indians. The principal problem with French muskets, as with those of the English, was that they were largely handmade, and the parts were not interchangeable. Repairs had to be done by gunsmiths, and after several repairs muskets became unserviceable.

Even with plenty of skill or training, a man could fire no more than three times a minute. The maximum range was between 150 to 200 meters (about 490 to 660 feet), but if the aim was to hit a man, the best one could hope for was 100 meters, and for a sure shot, the distance dropped to around 50 meters. These were hardly rapid-fire, deadly accurate devices of destruction. This fact is often overlooked when discussing tactics in colonial North American wars.

In practice few cannon were used outside the major cities or bases (that is, Louisbourg, Quebec, Montreal, Mobile, or New Orleans). Because cannon were very difficult to transport, only small guns were installed at forts. Then in the 1750s, large cannon were shipped great distances to many forts in the interior, a move that caused severe logistical strains. No cannon were used in the field anywhere in North America before the 1750s, with a couple of exceptions when small two pounders were used against palisaded Indian villages. Cannon were hauled to Fort Assumption (Memphis, Tennessee) during the Chickasaw wars, but large guns were not used against the Chickasaw in a major engagement in the field or in a formal siege.

505

Beyond logistical problems was the difficulty of producing enough cannon. Almost all guns used in North America (except a few in Canada) were cast in France. Production of cannon was one area in which the French navy always had difficulty, and only on occasion did the army, with its better facilities, assist. By contrast, gunpowder was usually reported to be satisfactory, and colonial officials noted that it was consistently better than English powder.

Clothing

The distinctive white and blue uniforms of the marines looked splendid when a well-appointed company was on parade. But shipments were of variable quality and more than a few times were insufficient even for the relatively small number of men in each colony. Much of the uniform was made of heavy woolen material, fine in winter but unbearable in the hot, humid summer. A lighter model was used in Louisiana, but the weather still reduced men to abject misery. The boots shipped from France were frequently the despair of soldiers, since they were often ill-fitting and poorly made. Nonetheless all colonies relied on France; uniforms were not made by colonial producers. However, soldiers in Canada and Louisiana adopted parts of the Indian or Canadian garment, not just to make good the shortfalls in shipments but also to cope with the weather and facilitate movement in the wilderness. Militiamen generally had to fend for themselves, though at times they were given some items. The men of the *troupes de terre,* beneficiaries of a superior supply system, fared better until the British Royal Navy seized consignments intended for the colonies.

Food

Assuring adequate quantities of food was a substantial problem for the military in North America as it was for armies everywhere at the time. In Europe, however, much was obtained by foraging, and the meat and grain supplies of the home country were seldom very far away. In North America, armed forces soon left the agricultural base far behind them and precious little could be obtained from the forest, especially if Indian snipers were nearby. Canadian expeditions were seldom large enough to occupy developed land in enemy territory for long, so they could not live off the enemy. The military was thus very dependent on its own agricultural base.

In the seventeenth century, most food had to come from France because colonial farmers did not produce a sufficient surplus. During the eighteenth century, Canada could provide much of the wheat and peas required but never more than half of the meat. Other colonies could not do nearly as well. If there was a harvest failure, or if shipments failed to reach their destination because of the weather or enemy action, the troops were in serious trouble.

In Canada during the 1750s, the number of troops increased ninefold, and there were sharp increases at Louisbourg and in Louisiana. Orders for bread to feed the armed forces in Canada increased from 462,640 livres (French pounds) in 1749 to 8,883,000 livres in 1757. Not surprisingly, such a huge rise in demand over a few years, during a period of mediocre harvests, caused a major crisis and contributed to galloping inflation. More surprising, however, was the success the French had in finding food and getting it to the colonies despite the British Royal Navy. Many people went hungry at times during the last years of New France, but nowhere did they starve.

THE CANADIAN WAY OF FIGHTING

The principal stroke of genius in Canadian military history came in devising tactics that enabled the French to make the most of rather limited resources. For this they were substantially indebted to Indians—both allies, such as the Algonquian, Abenaki, and Ojibway, and, of course, their most powerful enemy, the Iroquois. Historians have referred to it as guerrilla warfare, a term that entered the language in the Napoleonic era. Canadian officials spoke of *la petite guerre* ("little war" which in Spanish is *guerrilla*). Irregular forces fought small-scale, limited actions against orthodox military forces or lightly defended colonists. War parties made skillful use of surprise and combined great mobility, good marksmanship, and extremely aggressive combat. They could cover long distances in any season, strike swiftly, then disappear before the enemy could muster a substantial force to counterattack.

506

The French exploited the value of terror (demoralization) and disruption (demolishing materiel and facilities). The psychological effect of raids could be potent, with an impact out of all proportion to their scale. Guerrilla operations left an indelible impression on the American psyche, just as the Iroquois fury against Canada passed into legend in Quebec. Characteristically, Americans speak of "the French and Indian wars," the two being, in a sense, indistinguishable. But guerrilla tactics were not without their own shortcomings. Such warfare was essentially defensive in strategic terms, striking at the enemy's edges and trying to keep him back. When they could, the French organized large-scale forces that were closer in nature to conventional operations, aimed at the defeat of an enemy and, on occasion, the seizure of a position.

La petite guerre was vicious and terrifying, and so just as the French made a great effort to end the menace of the Iroquois confederacy, the English colonists tried to bring an end to the menace of New France. For the Americans, organizing was no small challenge; however, when the English got their affairs in order, the French faced a serious challenge. Incompetence and dissension, disease, and misfortune frustrated attacks on Canada in 1690, 1709, and 1711, but the English eventually managed to take peninsular Acadia (1710) and Louisbourg (1745, though it was returned). Finally, during the Seven Years' War, the English tipped the scales by increasing the number of troops involved and switching to conventional European-style warfare, with massed forces attacking vital military bases and nerve centers of New France.

BIBLIOGRAPHY

Brown, George W., David M. Hayne, and Francess G. Halpenny, eds. *Dictionary of Canadian Biography.* Vols. 1–4. Toronto, Ontario, 1966–1979. An excellent source not only on individuals but also on events and activities.

Charbonneau, André, Yvon Desloges, and Marc Lafrance. *Quebec, the Fortified City: From the Seventeenth to the Nineteenth Century.* Ottawa, 1982. A magnificent work with plenty of detailed information.

Eccles, W. J. *Essays on New France.* Toronto, Ontario, 1987.

———. *France in America.* New York, 1972; rev. ed. 1990.

———. *Frontenac, the Courtier Governor.* Toronto, Ontario, 1959.

Frègault, Guy. *Canada: The War of the Conquest.* Translated by Margaret M. Cameron. Toronto, Ontario, 1969. A detailed account of the Seven Years' War from the Canadian perspective that is now a bit dated (the original edition was published in French, 1955), occasionally inaccurate, and in places obviously biased.

Fry, Bruce W. *"An Appearance of Strength": The Fortifications of Louisbourg.* Ottawa, 1984.

Miquelon, Dale. *New France, 1701–1744: "A Supplement to Europe."* Toronto, Ontario, 1987.

Parkman, Francis. *France and England in North America.* 8 vols. Boston, 1874–1896. The author died a century ago; anyone still referring to him as an authority on any subject should not be trusted. The series is still reprinted, and some imagine that it has value. While it is eminently readable, the history is dated, the research is limited, the analysis is flagrantly biased, and there are important factual errors.

Stacey, Charles P. *Quebec 1759: The Siege and the Battle.* New York, 1959. A detailed account with a pro-English slant.

Stanley, George F. G. *New France: The Last Phase, 1744–1760.* Toronto, Ontario, 1968.

Steele, Ian K. *Betrayals: Fort William Henry and the Massacre.* New York, 1990.

———. *Guerillas and Grenadiers: The Struggle for Canada, 1689–1760.* Toronto, Ontario, 1969.

Verney, Jack. *The Good Regiment: The Carignan Salières Regiment in Canada, 1665–1668.* Montreal, 1991.

Zoltvany, Yves. *Philippe de Rigaud de Vaudreuil, Governor of New France, 1703–1725.* Toronto, Ontario, 1974.

Jay Cassel

SEE ALSO **The European Contest for North America; Independence;** and **Indian-Colonist Conflicts and Alliances.**

THE SPANISH BORDERLANDS

ALMOST IMMEDIATELY FOLLOWING the conquest of the Aztec Empire by the Spanish conquistador Hernán Cortés and his soldiers in 1521, the

Crown dispatched its armies north from Mexico City into a vast area stretching from Texas through New Mexico and Arizona on into California. (The southeastern borderlands—stretching from present-day Florida to Louisiana—are not treated in particular here, since their military traditions were more in conformance with those in metropolitan Latin America.) Over a period of three centuries in this harsh and unforgiving environment, Spain developed distinctive institutions including the mission, designed to introduce Native peoples to Christianity and control the supply of Indian labor, and the *presidio,* or fortress, which served both to protect the civil population and deter the advance of other colonial powers. Although the mission is the better known of these two frontier institutions, the *presidio* and its soldiery may be the more significant in terms of ability to protect and extend Spanish civilization throughout the borderlands and suitability to the frontier.

The history of men in arms in the borderlands is an anomaly in the history of Spanish expansion in the New World: virtually the entire continent of South America was conquered before the borderlands were subjugated. For three centuries (1550–1850) the borderlands remained a terra incognita of lonely frontier outposts at which soldiers and friars alike toiled in obscurity.

As Spain urbanized after the sixteenth century, it devised its American empire on a metropolitan model derived from Roman law in which power emanated to the far reaches of the New World from capital cities such as Lima, Bogotá, and Mexico City, with both wealth and influence diminishing as one moved away from the viceregal seats of government. Moreover, the northern reaches of the borderlands presented formidable obstacles to explorers and invaders alike. The natural challenges included vast arid plains, forbidding mountains, parching drought, and hostile Indian tribes, who received the generic designation of the Chichimeca or "mad dogs." Having determined early on that no northern passage to the Orient existed through the borderlands, a passage that might have permitted Spain's European rivals to access the silver mining areas of northern Mexico, and because no advanced wealthy Native tribes inhabited the area, Spain occupied the northern borderlands

primarily as a buffer zone to protect the settled metropolitan areas of Mexico rather than as an integral part of the viceroyalty. Therefore the mission and *presidio* developed as distinctly frontier institutions.

MILITARY DEPLOYMENT IN THE BORDERLANDS

Despite the popular notion that the twenty-nine *presidios* that the Crown established throughout northern Mexico by the mid eighteenth century formed a strategic line of defense, the creation of these forts was primarily a reactive measure. Forts were constructed in areas where large concentrations of hostile Indians threatened small groups of Spanish settlers. Because these Native settlements were not evenly distributed throughout the area, neither were the companies of Spanish soldiers stationed in the region. Whenever a Native rebellion occurred, such as the Pueblo Indians' revolt in New Mexico against the Spanish presence in 1680, attention was paid to the adequacy of the borderland *presidios* in protecting mines and settlements. Otherwise these lonely outposts were rarely considered in military planning efforts.

Spain originally developed the *presidio,* taken from the Latin *praesidium,* meaning a frontier military base utilized for defensive purposes, during the seven centuries of armed conflict against the Muslim invaders known as the *Reconquista.* From these bases the Christian kings took the offensive against the Muslim Kingdom of Granada, which fell in 1492, the same year that Christopher Columbus claimed America for Spain. As a result the institution was transferred to the New World intact, along with the concept of knighthood and the career at arms. This development occurred precisely as this ethos was being replaced in Spain by a return to civil precepts with the conclusion of seven centuries of nearly continuous warfare. In this sense the career at arms was reborn in America in the persons of Hernán Cortés and Francisco Pizarro and their intrepid *conquistadores.* The *presidio,* especially in the borderland region of the Viceroyalty of New Spain (Mexico), gained new stature as an instrument of imperial policy.

The difficulty of stationing large contingents of troops in the borderlands, due to problems associated with the supply and rotation of forces, meant that Spain early on established a tradition of dispatching small garrisons of soldiers, and occasionally their families, to defend the region. Occasionally this force was supplemented by friendly Indian forces that could gain privileges by serving as allies to protect the fort against hostile tribes. This device was initially utilized by Cortés, who in 1519 employed Tlaxcalans against the Aztec warriors during the conquest of Mexico and even sent these peaceful, Christian peoples to defend entire Spanish towns such as Saltillo to the north of the capital. With the discovery of the rich silver mines at San Luís Potosí and Zacatecas, the use of friendly Indian allies, an inexpensive means of furthering imperial ambitions employed by all the colonial powers, was further enhanced. In addition, under the reign of Phillip II in 1562, regional militias were conscripted as a means of defending urban areas. This constituted a significant shift away from the feudal model of warfare developed during the reconquest of Spain, when soldiers were privately sponsored and paid by individual nobles or particular families. Thereafter, in Mexico, these local militias were raised, trained, and deployed by officers whose salaries were paid by the royal government. This was an important step in the professionalization of the armed forces.

An outstanding example of military settlement under the old order is Juan de Oñate's military occupation of New Mexico. The viceroy of New Spain, the second Don Luís de Velasco, in 1595 contracted with Oñate, the scion of a wealthy and prominent Spanish family of Mexico, which had prospered in the silver mining economy of Zacatecas. Following two decades of service to the Crown against the troublesome Chichimecas, Oñate contracted with Velasco to recruit and pay for two hundred men, fully equipped and provisioned. In addition Oñate agreed to provide one thousand cattle, one thousand sheep, one hundred goats, three hundred horses, and substantial quantities of supplies for the settlement. The viceroy agreed to send five priests and a lay brother at royal expense, along with artillery pieces and a six-year loan of 6,000 pesos. For his service as *adelantado*, literally "the one who goes forth," Oñate received the titles of governor and captain-general with full authority from the Crown, as well as the use of sizeable numbers of Indians, which carried with it the right to collect annual tribute owed to the Crown. Over time, however, the contract was modified by subsequent viceroys to reduce the *adelantados'* powers and maximize those of the Crown. Following two years of traversing the arid plains of Kansas and numerous defections, the Oñate expedition crossed the Colorado River in 1604. As late as 1607, Oñate was moved to resign his commission and proclaim the venture a massive mistake that, he contended, had cost his family 400,000 pesos. By 1609, however, the promise of conversion of thousands of Pueblo Indians by the Franciscan missionaries attached to the expedition led to the decision to designate New Mexico as a province of New Spain and to establish the capital in Santa Fe, only two years following the English establishment of Jamestown. This model of conquest and pacification was utilized throughout the western borderlands during the sixteenth century.

During the sixteenth century in northern Mexico, the Hapsburg rulers of Spain, particularly Philip II, used a combination of military force and missionary zeal to bring newly conquered tribes into the sphere of the imperial government. Far more than the Bourbon Crown, which governed Spain in the eighteenth century, the Hapsburgs were obsessed with not only conquering the nomadic Indian peoples but also Christianizing and acculturating them into the Spanish state, albeit in a subordinate position. As the royal *presidio* and its garrisons, supported by resident militia, emerged as the major instrument of military policy at the conclusion of the sixteenth century, the quasi-feudal era of the Conquest and its *conquistadores* were replaced by a period characterized by a larger colonial administration reflecting a more coherent military policy.

By the seventeenth century, the career at arms began to evolve within the framework of a developing, more peaceable society. To a large degree, the *presidios* mirrored the tensions and conflicts within frontier society. Far from the centers of civil power, corruption and often inept administration emerged in the military as they did in civil institutions. Frontier officers engaged in ranching and mining enterprises to supplement their meager incomes and to provide for their families while acting as patrons and overlords to their men, whom they treated as virtual vassals. In the realm of warfare, the abilities of mobile, hostile Indian tribes such as the Apaches, who were excellent horsemen and who were capable of striking quickly and disappearing with equal rapidity, forced the Spanish to adopt new strategies and tactics, which included counterinsurgency in the form of *compañias vulantes,* or "flying companies," cavalry forces that could pursue the marauding natives on horseback and attack them in their villages. This tactic in turn required larger contingents of infantrymen to protect herds and civilians while the cavalry was engaged in these pursuits.

By the seventeenth century, the concept of conquering the Native peoples was dismissed throughout the western borderlands, not only because of the sheer disparity in numbers but also because their labor was the Spaniards' most valuable commodity. The earliest *presidios* amounted to little more than camps of four or five men, although these regular soldiers' armament and rudimentary knowledge of military tactics, such as flanking maneuvers, did much to equalize their fighting capacity with that of larger groups of natives. By the latter part of the sixteenth century, as the natives adapted Spanish strategies and tactics to their own situation, the Crown increased the size of presidial garrisons to approximately twenty-five men led by a captain, assisted by *alfereces* (ensigns), *sargentos* (sergeants), and *cabos* (corporals) who commanded smaller units within the garrison. Oftentimes soldiers were granted titles to small plots of land for their use in raising food rather than paid a salary. Only in the eighteenth century did the Crown commission and salary soldiers in these units. Because of the irregularity of the terrain and the variety of marauding forces, the actual size of units in the field varied and was not specified. Patrols and *escollas,* or escorts, were normally from four to six men, with flying companies numbering up to two hundred men when the situation so merited.

Over time the size of presidial garrisons was established at fifty men, although rarely was this number of *plazas* (places) ever filled, requiring the presidial commander to recruit auxiliaries, often from the militia ranks. It was not unusual

for a garrison to have only one-fifth of its specified roster of men, with certain of these individuals permanently assigned to guard another area apart from the garrison where they were local residents. Because units and individuals were frequently detached, one cannot speak of a standard table of organization from regimental size down to the company or platoon. The same can be said of *presidios* themselves: certain of them were legally established and acknowledged, while others were de facto *presidios,* resulting from the detachment of troops to a particular area. In both cases, need dictated organization in a frontier environment. With the adoption of an extensive package of military reforms by the Bourbon monarchs after 1763, the lack of preparation and organization that characterized the early borderland military became apparent.

On paper at least, *presidios* were governed by a captain, who was sometimes outranked by a sergeant major, a military commission frequently granted to the provincial lieutenant governor or mayor (*alcalde*). Although the Spanish military command was hierarchical, based on rank and status, higher civil offices also sometimes carried military rank and privilege in a conscious effort to keep all officials dependent on the Crown as the final arbiter of power and position in a society that worshiped titles. When factors of social class and the ability to purchase offices is considered, it is clear that rank and power were oftentimes subject to interpretation and the relative strengths of the officeholders. Beneath the captain served the *alférez,* or lieutenant, who was sometimes referred to as a *teniente,* or someone who held the captain's powers in the field. Indeed, references to Spanish military titles often had less to do with rank than the duties each individual performed during warfare. Enlisted men were normally *soldados,* meaning foot soldiers or mounted dragoons. Companies of soldiers were led by *sargentos,* who were charged with the duties of supply, discipline, accounting, and instruction.

Civilian settlers—ranchers, merchants, and miners—often received commissions in the militias that served as adjuncts to the professional soldiery. Militia companies were under the nominal direction of a *maestre de campo,* or "field marshal," who frequently raised and outfitted the company at his own expense, often in response to a particular need to engage unruly natives. *Maestres* were assisted by *tenientes*, who could exercise the authority of the senior officer when the officeholder was absent, or a lower-ranking *ayudante*, who could not. As will be made clearer below, these *presidios* and their complements of soldiers—regulars and militiamen—were both part of and separate from the civilian populations that they protected. Within the *presidio*, which was expected to be as self-supporting as possible, a social hierarchy existed based on rank and birth. Hence, a whole series of social and economic relationships are appended to the term *presidio* as it evolved in the borderlands.

The character of presidial life, as has been sketched above, was tedious and difficult and thus shunned by those who could pursue a better livelihood. Garrisons were small but often increased in size as numbers of settlers, merchants, miners, and missionaries entered the borderland provinces. Isolated from the royal government in Mexico City, abuse of Native peoples by all of these groups and corruption within the military ranks were commonplace. Not infrequently in the seventeenth century, the smaller *presidios* in the remote, mountainous areas of the Spanish Borderlands in northern Mexico were overrun and their civil communities destroyed, although sometimes the Spanish presence was revived after a time. While the causes of Native revolts are a matter of debate, mistreatment by the Spaniards along with a fierce desire to maintain their traditional practices and folkways loom large in any collection of grievances. And because the Spaniards often returned in force and dealt out swift and remorseless punishment to rebel communities, the cycle of Native protests and Spanish counterattacks continued unabated during the period.

THE PUEBLO REVOLT

Perhaps no event in borderland military history evinced the fragile nature of presidial life and the enormous power of the hostile Native population of the *Gran Chichimeca,* or region of northern Mexico, as did the Pueblo Revolt of 1680. While the Spanish advance along the middle corridor from Mexico City northwards to New Mexico in the sixteenth century had been orderly,

the westward push into California and the eastern invasion of the Gulf region had been more difficult. The nomadic tribes of New Mexico were unaccustomed to the concept of overlordship, in contrast to the higher civilizations to the south such as the Aztecs, who had subjugated the neighboring tribes of the valley of Mexico. During the mid sixteenth century, for example, the Chihuahua region was engulfed by revolt as Indian bands burned haciendas and ranches as well as Jesuit missions. The fierce Tarahumara tribe of this mountainous region successfully kept Spanish forces sent against them at bay, although over a period of time the influx of Spanish settlers, drawn to the mines, reestablished order.

By the year 1670, the upper Rio Grande valley of New Mexico, pacified earlier by the Oñate expedition, numbered about 2,800 Spaniards, a majority of these in the capital of Santa Fe or nearby pueblos. Despite earlier hopes the Spanish settlement had not produced great wealth, as had the mines of Zacatecas and Guanajuato in the southern sierras. Stockraising and farming existed largely to supply the mines to the south with needed goods. This situation was exacerbated by a power struggle between royal governors and missionaries for control of the Native population. The former asserted the hegemony of the civil administration and the preeminence of using Indian labor for civil projects while the latter demanded that all else should be subordinated to the goal of Christianizing the indigenous peoples.

The revolt that broke out in 1680 can be viewed as the natural result of a clash of cultures that began with Cortés's footfall into Mexico a century earlier. Yet it was actually the most striking instance of a larger, less-noticed phenomenon: incessant Native opposition to Spanish domination of their material, personal, and religious lives. Unlike other, smaller revolts, however, the Pueblo Revolt both prevented further Spanish colonization to the north and threatened the stability of the entire concept of territorial acquisition by ejecting the Spanish from the territory. Coming as it did after nearly a century of Spanish occupation, few military authorities foresaw the massive outburst of violence that was a response to incessant and growing demands on the Indians to produce wealth for the

Spaniards. The loss of an entire province not only shocked Spanish authorities but presaged the need for massive military reform in the Spanish Borderlands during the eighteenth century.

In contrast to other, more limited revolts that both preceded and followed the Pueblo uprising of 1680, the Pueblo leadership sought the complete expulsion of the Spaniards and the eradication of their culture in New Mexico. Striking simultaneously over the span of the entire province from many pueblos, the Indians prevented isolated Spanish settlements from taking refuge in Santa Fe, which was placed under siege on 15 August after more than four hundred Spaniards had been killed. Although the Spaniards of Santa Fe broke the siege and retreated downriver, the *juntas de guerra*, or war councils, determined that the trained military and civilian allies were no match for the vengeful Indians. Reflecting the Spaniards' outrage and wounded pride, the viceroy in Mexico City ordered Governor Antonio de Otermín to recover the province but characteristically provided little wherewithal to do so. Otermín was forced to march northwards to Santa Fe with 146 soldiers and 112 Indian allies. Fortunately for the Spanish, some of the Pueblos felt compelled to seek a pardon due to their fear of attack by their Apache rivals to the east, although far larger numbers of Pueblos to the north refused to submit, foiling Otermín's efforts to reoccupy New Mexico. For a decade the province remained under Native control; it was the first time that the Spanish had lost control of any New World province since the days of the Conquest.

Not until 1692 was a sufficiently powerful force assembled in El Paso to recapture Santa Fe, although the absolute numbers—forty soldiers, ten residents of El Paso, three Franciscans, and fifty Indian auxilliaries—seem laughably small by modern standards of warfare. By October fifteen pueblos in addition to Santa Fe had surrendered, although the triumph proved to be short-lived. Spanish authorities in Mexico City, however, were impressed that the reconquest was effected without bloodshed and, most important, without expense to the Crown, which was in the throes of an economic crisis brought about by Spain's inability to compete with its European rivals. The viceroy immediately ordered that the *presidio* of Santa Fe be reestab-

lished with one hundred regular troops and recruits from the northern mining towns, along with 12,000 pesos to undertake the rebuilding. The expedition obtained one hundred soldiers from the Zacatecas region in early October 1693 and, along with seventy families and nearly four thousand head of livestock, left for Santa Fe. The repacification of New Mexico seemed close at hand.

Yet the recapture of Santa Fe in December 1693 was only the first step of a longer, grueling effort to win the hearts and minds of the over twenty Indian towns that remained hostile to the Spanish presence. Fully three more years of Indian raids and Spanish counteroffensives marked the reconquest of the province. While the Pueblos were pacified, the Apache and Zuni tribes challenged Spanish authority well into the next century. Thereafter, New Mexico formed an outpost against the westward advances of the French in the lower Mississippi valley and a valuable cog in New Spain's northern line of defense.

While the Pueblo Revolt dominates the military history of the late-seventeenth-century borderlands, the successful efforts of the Pueblo tribes encouraged other Indian groups to attack Spanish settlements. In the wake of the Pueblo Revolt, Spanish military commanders became fully aware of the limitations of their garrison forces and the foolishness of deploying small *escoltas,* or escorts of civilian or religious travelers in Indian territory. If anything, the failed Pueblo Revolt hardened the hatreds existing between Native peoples and Spanish occupants due to the mass execution of the Indian ringleaders that followed. By the end of the century, militia rolls were expanded as Spanish commanders went on the lookout both for signs of Native unrest and the newer threat of French intervention into Texas. However, the report of a military inspection of the province in 1693 by Field Marshal Don Joseph Francisco Marín spoke to the reasons for the collapse of New Mexico earlier.

BOURBON MILITARY REFORMS

The Marín report constituted both an assessment of the status of the borderland military in one important province at the end of the seventeenth century and a harbinger of the reforms to come by the mid eighteenth century. A Knight of the Order of Santiago, Marín produced a report that is the most professional assessment of the borderland military situation existing for the later seventeenth century. Among other things it frankly recognized that manpower in the area was limited, a fact hardly acknowledged by inflated tables of organization developed in Madrid. Moreover, the Pueblo massacre had resulted in a net loss of civilian population as settlers fled to El Paso and other areas of relative safety. Marín and others had begun to realize that Spain's future ability to protect New Spain by holding onto the western borderland frontier was predicated on an increase in civil settlements or pueblos. By the eighteenth century under the Bourbon monarchy, Spain would implement Marín's observations into effect as part of an imperial administrative and military reorganization designed to preserve Spanish America in a modernizing world. After a century of inaction, the emphasis on form and legality would be replaced by substance and practicality under the secular Bourbon monarchs.

Unlike the Anglo-American borderlands of the eighteenth century, the Spanish Borderlands were primarily a defensive frontier. The Bourbon military reforms were an example of "defensive modernization"; that is, measures taken to strengthen military forces for the purpose of preventing the French from entering Texas from the Mississippi valley and the Russians from invading Alta, or Upper California, from their outposts in Alaska. Bourbon advances in metallurgy and mining had revived the silver mining economy of northern Mexico, providing the economic wherewithal to energize the economy of New Spain that in turn allowed for changes to be carried out in the borderlands.

The most notable of the reformist Bourbon monarchs, King Charles III (1756–1763), recognized clearly that his most dangerous European enemy was England and accordingly entered into a Family Compact with his French cousin Louis XV in 1756. This decision was quickly followed by Spain's entrance into the Seven Years' War (1756–1763) against England that, although fought against a European backdrop, extended to the New World, where Spaniards and Frenchmen fought the English for control of Canada (the French and Indian War) and also fought

England in the Caribbean. Spain's devastating loss to the English, which resulted in the cession of western Florida (although the more valuable Cuba was retained), meant that England now had American bases from which to confront directly a weakened Spain in America. Knowing full well of the aggressive nature of the Anglo-American colonists, Charles III and his principal ministers set forth in the wake of the Peace of Paris in 1763 a plan of administrative efficiency for the Spanish American colonies that accentuated imperial defense. New Spain was placed under the military command of Lieutenant General Juan de Villalba y Angulo, captain general of Andalucia, who was appointed as General Commandant and Inspector General of the Army of New Spain. To train and discipline the weak and inexperienced militias of the viceroyalty, Villalba was placed in command of the American Regiment, composed of both Spaniards and foreign mercenaries, both of whom were thought to possess better military discipline and temperament than the Creoles, or American-born whites, mestizos, or mixed bloods, and blacks, who made up the bulk of the American armies. Upon his arrival in New Spain in 1764, Villalba soon turned his attention to the military situation in the borderlands of the viceroyalty.

Apart from the enhancement of coastal fortifications, especially those in and around Vera Cruz in the Gulf of Mexico, the primary bulwark against Spain's European rivals, no problem was more central to the defense of New Spain than the borderland frontier. Villalba's task of reorganizing the dispirited defenses of an area that had never been truly pacified was based on the expanded use of professional soldiers. In addition Villalba's field marshal, the marquis de Rubí, had by 1766 completed an inspection of the northern frontier that recommended repositioning the *presidios* in order that they form a more strategic line of defense as well as training the soldiery and enforcing discipline. Many of these suggestions were embodied in a set of military regulations that were published in 1772 and set the pattern for the defense of the borderlands for nearly a century afterwards.

Over the course of the eighteenth century, Bourbon viceroys and military commanders of New Spain, the most notable examples being the marquis of Croix and his powerful visitor general, José de Gálvez, began to fashion a military structure that was both efficient and modern by the standards of the time. Fully aware of the daunting factors of distance, shortages of funds, and corruption, these shrewd administrators promulgated a series of military regulations that to the unitiated may seem naive attempts to carry out the ideals of imperial policy in an area unsuited to European regulations. However, by forcing colonial administrators to obey a bewildering assortment of rules, the Crown on the one hand allowed local governors a limited amount of flexibility. On the other hand it forced these same individuals to carry out a far larger number of royal decrees. This duality maintained the Crown's authority in the face of particularism and self-interest. The Bourbon administrative structure, far from being a rigid monolith, was in fact a flexible and responsive hierarchy that used the power of appointment and removal from office to maintain order and obedience. Bureaucratic self-interest became integral to the system, with officials forced to recognize the Crown's hegemony in order to retain their positions.

A theme that runs through the military history of the eighteenth-century borderlands is the transition of the *presidio* from a seventeenth-century quasi-military institution with a sizable civilian component into a military enclave operated by professional soldiers functioning independent of and apart from the civil towns and missions of the area. As strategic defense became of paramount concern to the Crown, military garrisons took on the primary role of defending against and subjugating Native peoples such as the Apaches, a task that the mission fathers had carried out a century earlier. As might be expected, the shift guaranteed increasing conflict between presidial commandants and order priests, a schism made more serious as professional soldiers replaced local officers with ties to the community. In addition, *presidios* began to assume offensive responsibilities along with their traditional defensive roles.

Prior to the 1772 *Regulation and Instruction for the Presidios of New Spain*, the borderlands were fortified by twenty-nine *presidios*. Located far from the seat of power in Mexico City, they were characterized by disrepair and apathy, staffed by a few officers and men from the northern provinces of New Spain, who were recruited

locally, paid badly, and lacked discipline, skills, or military bearing. Indeed, under the Hapsburgs presidial commandants normally subcontracted for the services of townsmen to fill the ranks while presidial troops worked as laborers or tradesmen and viewed themselves as civilians rather than soldiers. Poverty linked together the missionaries, townspeople, and soldiers, with few economic or social distinctions separating them except at the margins of the social ladder.

What altered this situation after 1772 was that under the Bourbon monarchs military inspectors refused to conduct routine military inspections of these costly, inefficient, undermanned, and corrupt garrisons but rather prepared detailed reviews that could be utilized before the courts to prosecute offending officers and men. No longer was the testimony of commandants accepted without verification, and the account books of any given *presidio* were closely scrutinized by royal accountants to determine where officers were overcharging soldiers for supplies and if they were conspiring with Mexico City merchants regarding the prices charged for uniforms. Muster rolls (*libros de asiento*) and the payroll and expense ledgers (*libros de cuentas*) were surrendered to the inspectors, and the officers were sent approximately five miles away from the garrison during the inspection so that they could not influence the review. Payrolls were no longer to be padded by adding the names of fictitious or even deceased men onto the rolls. Since inspectors general could close *presidios*, reduce ranks, and cut forces if the work of the king was not, in their opinion, being conducted, their reviews began to have the desired result of promoting efficiency and honesty. Following the official investigation, a secret review of the concerned officers' conduct was carried out. Testimony from disinterested witnesses was collected and compiled. If charges were filed, the inspector could judge the matter or pass it on to a military trial judge. Although the Bourbon military received extensive military privileges (*fueros*), frequent reviews and inspections also significantly improved military standards of conduct and professionalism.

THE MILITARY IN CALIFORNIA

The establishment of a military presence in Alta, California, after 1768 reflects the seriousness with which the Bourbon Crown took the matter of defense during the latter part of the eighteenth century. In addition, a review of the California military during the eighteenth century illustrates both the evolution of the frontier *presidio* and the efficacy of that institution in a frontier setting. Finally, the California military demonstrates the adaptive nature of Spanish frontier institutions over time and the impact that these adaptations had on post-colonial society.

The Four Presidios

With the expulsion of the Society of Jesus (Jesuits) from America in 1767, the Crown moved quickly to replace clerical authority with civil and military force. These military changes underscored Spain's fear that the English might eventually discover a Northwest Passage thereby opening all of the Pacific to aggression. In response, Inspector General Gálvez dispatched Lieutenant Pedro Fages and twenty-five Catalonia volunteers to California by sea to receive Governor Gaspar de Portolá, who had left Loreto, a *presidio* located approximately two hundred and fifty miles (400 kilometers) northwest of Cabo San Lucas in Baja California, the capital of the Californias, to reconnoiter the California coastline. Beginning in 1769 four *presidios* were established: San Diego (1769), Monterey (1770), San Francisco (1776), and Santa Barbara (1782). Earlier, the Bourbons had developed standardized plans for new *presidios* that were not to be simply fortresses but fortified settlements, each intended to shelter a garrison of soldiers and their families. Located some two thousand to four thousand feet (5,400–10,800 meters) from shore in order that hostile cannon from enemy ships could not reach them, the *presidios'* batteries overlooked California's primary harbors to protect commercial shipping. Although the *presidios* could not deter invasions all along the coast, they were fully sufficient to deter attacks by the large but disunited groups of California's Indian tribes. Moreover, the sheer difficulty of fortifying an area as remote as California illustrates the rational and orderly efforts of the Bourbon bureaucrats and their state-financed public works, which at long last began to create the ideal form of imperial military force that had for so long been only a promise in Spanish America. Although the California military remained more a symbol of Spanish power than an actual military presence, it demonstrated the lessons learned in the borderlands since the sixteenth century and furthered the objectives of the Spanish state.

All four of the California *presidios* consisted of buildings grouped in a quadrangle enclosing a parade ground, with the buildings themselves enclosed within a defensive perimeter wall made of dirt or adobe. The main gate faced the ocean to signify Spain's recurrent concern with trade and seaborne invasion while the church was located directly in view across the parade ground, symbolic of the role played by the church in Spanish society and law. The California *presidios* contained military housing, garden plots, and horse corrals inside the walls—the latter reflecting a lesson learned from garrisons in Arizona and Texas where Indian raids killed guards and stole horses, thus hindering efforts to pacify Native bands. In contrast to earlier borderland experience, California Indians were forbidden to own or ride horses, this being a deterrent to attack on these garrisons. Outside of the *presidios*, a dry moat separated the ten-foot-high (3 meter) defensive wall from the surrounding environs. Invaders had to surmount an embankment surrounding the moat and scale the wall, during which time they were exposed to fire from rooftops and parapets. Military architecture thus aided *presidio* defenses. Although foreign visitors often disparaged the rudimentary nature of these forts, to the 130,000 California Indians they were effective deterrents to rebellion, a major objective of the Spanish Crown.

The California *presidios* demonstrated the maxim that strategic concerns in so distant an area as California were often subordinated to the needs of Spaniards to survive in a hostile environment. The San Francisco *presidio*, located on a bay that the Spaniards called "a marvel of nature," had a budget of only 14,000 pesos, the annual salary of forty privates. Supply lines to furnish additional men or materiel were unreliable. All four "fortresses" of California, in fact, lacked men and arms to constitute an effective deterrent to foreign attack. San Diego's *presidio*, for example, was established on a footing of two officers, with a lieutenant in command and fifty-two enlisted personnel. Yet over one-half of these troops were detached at the missions within the presidial district as guards while others were perennially away acting as cowboys on the king's *rancho* or performing duties for the commandant. Married soldiers often lived with their families inside the *presidio's* walls while single troops resided on nearby ranches where they worked as cowboys or in the civil trades. Moreover, since the San Diego *presidio* was located five miles (8 kilometers) inland closer to Native towns, it was situated to repel a seaborne invasion. Since the San Diego area was thinly settled, recruits had to be obtained from the civil town of Los Angeles, one hundred miles (160 kilometers) to the north. In 1793 the British admiral George Vancouver called San Diego the weakest of the California *presidios,* although it managed to protect the area missions and maintained a Spanish presence in the south. Learning from the San Diego experience, the Spanish built future *presidios* on high ground overlooking the ocean.

Over time military inspectors in California came to recommend greatly enlarged cavalry forces with the mobility to repulse seaborne attacks along the coast as well as to track down Indian renegades who retreated into the area's huge Central valley after raiding coastal settlements. The Monterey *presidio,* located "a gunshot from the beach," had a company of eighty men, although approximately half of this complement lacked swords, lances, muskets, and pistols. More than half were never issued saddles or heavy leather *cueras,* long sleeveless garments, made of seven plies of deerskin, which gave the cavalry lancers the name *soldados de cuera* (leather jacket soldiers). These jackets protected their wearers from Indian arrows except at short range, and symbolized the defensive nature of Spanish military occupation throughout the borderlands, especially in the Californias. Although effective against the arrows and stones of Indian tribes, the leather jackets were anachronisms in an era of more advanced military technology such as possessed by the Russians and English. The jackets represented warfare of an earlier era and of a civil nature, not the type of warfare needed to protect the Pacific Coast against modern European navies. Similarly, the Spanish lance—virtually unchanged since the days of the Reconquest, consisting as it did of a shaft with a thirteen-inch (325 millimeter) iron blade—reflected the fact that ammunition was in short supply on the borderland frontier and that the lance required little maintenance. Advancement in military technology during the Age of Enlightenment was primarily a European, urban phenomenon. In the borderlands, warfare was modern in concept but fought with the same armament as had existed in the sixteenth century.

The borderland militia reflected the ethnic character of northern New Spain, with mixed bloods making up a majority of the enlisted force and even the officer corps. What came to distinguish the California soldiery, however, was the fact that regulars, the professional forces sent to the province, were small in number, and upon their departure their places were taken by local recruits. Thus, unlike the other borderland regions, by the time of Mexican independence California's military, closely intermarried, had some of the characteristics of a military caste, including extensive landholdings.

The *presidio* of San Francisco, founded on 17 September 1776, was established on a footing of thirty-two men and was thereafter hardly ever at full strength. Lack of timber and proper adobe meant that for much of the era the fortress was constructed largely of mud. As late as 1787, the population of San Francisco numbered no more than 130 persons, including dependents and other civilians. In 1782 the *presidio* of Santa Barbara, the fourth and last *presidio* established in California, had a company of fifty-two men, drawn from the *presidios* of San Diego and Monterey and commanded by a lieutenant, demonstrating the relative lack of experience of the California officer corps. Although the overall size of the California presidial establishment varied between 146 and 218 men, small in relation to the land mass and Indian population, the army was uniformly successful in carrying out its three objectives: protecting the California provinces from attack; protecting the missions; and assuring the establishment of civil towns. Both foreign visitors and European priests, whose comments are taken literally by historians, disparaged this force in comparison with Spanish American or European armies, which were far better trained and disciplined. Yet the fact remains that New Spain held California for over a century without incident, thanks to the presence of its presidial forces.

The strength of the cattle-growing economies of the Monterey and Santa Barbara *presidios* stands in contrast to the presidial economies of San Diego and San Francisco, where ranching was less successful. Santa Barbara showed the greatest growth due to its benign climate and fertile land. By 1790 the pueblo held 68 families numbering 237 persons. By 1810 this number had grown to 850 residents, 500 of whom lived in town with the balance residing on the surrounding *ranchos*. As we have established, the presidial population was made up of a very few Spaniards from the veteran Catalonian Volunteers and some Peninsular priests. The balance of presidial society was composed of settlers who came from the humblest strata of northern Mexican society. Most were unskilled laborers, largely mestizos (Indian and white admixtures), mulattos (black and white), or *zambos* (black and Indian). That they were largely illiterate can be demonstrated by the fact that not one resident of Los Angeles could sign his or her name when lands were granted in 1786. Both the low pay and the hardships associated with the overland journey from Sonora assured that the population of the California garrisons included men who had been freed from jail on condition that they make the journey. Although the initial expeditions carried no women, most officers eventually brought their families with them or married locally, while enlisted men often cohabited, legally or illegally, with Indian women. Records indicate that by 1790, two-thirds of the presidial forces were married, indicating a respectable group that had begun to function primarily as settlers rather than soldiers given the lack of need for a strong military posture. Military service records and reports demonstrate that in addition to herding cattle, soldiers worked as laborers, mail carriers, farriers, butchers, and shoemakers. Although this was not consistent with Spanish military policy, it demonstrates the adaptation of Spanish frontier institutions when flexibility was required for survival.

The Presidial Officers

Despite the fact that California presidial society was drawn from subordinate social groups in comparison with the armies in Spain and Mexico City and regardless of the isolation imposed by the frontier, the society was not democratic in any sense. The hierarchy based on rank and status within presidial society, particularly the officer corps, looked down upon the unlettered, unskilled civil settlers. Although none of the presidial officers were Spaniards, much less nobles, as members of the *gente decente,* or whitish middle groups, they considered themselves superior to the largely mestizo and black settlers as well as to the artisans, mechanics, and enlisted men in the garrison companies. Their status was difficult to maintain, however, due to the fact that the military budget authorized for California was always hopelessly in arrears and salaries were hardly ever paid on time or in full.

Moreover the frontier forced cooperation on its inhabitants, which tended to blur social distinctions that prevailed in more settled regions. When Admiral George Vancouver, the English commander of the *HMS Discovery,* visited the San Francisco *presidio* in 1792, he dismissed the fort as rudimentary, unsuited to defend against either Indian attack or seaborne invasion. Indeed, Vancouver wondered in print why Spain had even bothered to settle an area so cut off by sheer distance from the rest of the civilized world.

In some areas presidial poverty was so extreme as to draw attention. In the Mission San Luis Obispo, for example, visitors remarked that the Indians were better dressed than the presidial escort. So forlorn were these troops that lack of clothing sometimes prevented them from attending Mass. In comparison to the two-room hut with a dirt floor that was the residence of Hermengildo Sal, the commandant of the San Francisco *presidio,* the Russian fort at Bodega Bay to the north boasted luxurious carpets, glass windowpanes, a piano, and a well-stocked library.

Yet the critical comments of foreign visitors and members of the clergy are only valid insofar as they compare the California presidial army with European armies. With respect to the Spanish objectives in holding the borderland frontier, the army of New Spain in California was adequate, successful, and credible as an institution of colonization and pacification.

During its half century of Spanish domination, California was ruled by a military governor resident in Monterey. Under the presidial regulations enacted for California in 1781, the four fortresses were placed under the command of lieutenants. Of this senior command, only one, Captain Don José Joaquín de Arrillaga, was of Spanish birth, having formerly commanded in Loreto, the capital of Baja California. The other nineteen commanders were of decent birth, nine being natives of the *presidio* of Loreto, presumably the sons of presidials there. None had been commissioned due to birth, but rather had become officers only after enlisting in the ranks and serving for several years in this capacity. Indeed, the California presidial ranks were devoid of *soldados distinguidos* (distinguished soldiers), men of high birth who were able to outfit themselves and provide their own horses in exchange for a cadetship. Yet over time the formalities of birth and rank seem to have softened in the California military as opposed to the metropolitan military establishment in Mexico City. In 1827 French naval officer Bernard Duhart-Cilly remarked that the rank and file California presidials were considered the social equals of their officers and accorded the honorific title of Don, and that they even aspired to marriage with the commanders' daughters. More interesting is the fact that presidial commanders awarded the sons of soldiers with noble status, which allowed them to enter the ranks as cadets. This indicates not only that second-generation presidials were regarded as a de facto provincial nobility, but also that they apparently had the economic wherewithal to furnish horses and outfit themselves in a fashion undreamed of by their fathers. The military as a vehicle of social mobility in California distinguished it from the military in many other parts of the Spanish Borderlands.

It is difficult to provide a detailed social profile of a military for which there is little primary-source information. Certainly the soldiers' lives were far from glamorous. Military duties were sporadic, consisting of expeditions into the interior, defending against Indian revolts, escorting mission fathers throughout the province, and caring for the king's livestock. Far more time was spent ranching or in the trades or in leisure pursuits such as bear hunting, which formed an important aspect of the *rancho* life, so prized for its gentility and indolence. Not surprisingly soldiers sent on the initial Anza and Portola expeditions of discovery sought to return to northern Mexico when their tours of duty were up, but their requests were routinely denied. After settlements were established in California, however, desertion in the ranks seems to have been far less of a problem there than in metropolitan Mexico. While this is no doubt due to the fact that finding refuge in the close-knit *rancho* society was difficult, the preponderance of local marriages and land grants indicates that a majority of the soldiers eventually came to accept life in California and the future it afforded. When soldiers were rotated or deserted, their places were taken by boys from the presidial communities who had reached their sixteenth birthday. By preference these young men aspired to live on *ranchos* where they could ride and aspire to the life of a *hidalgo* (literally *hijo de algo*, son of someone). If this was not possible, they preferred to enlist in the militia, since this form of service left their civilian status intact as opposed to the regular army, which was more rigorous and lacked social status. Military tribunals spoke frequently about the difficulty of requiring second-generation presidials in California to perform manual labor as had their lowborn forebears. Thus the deterioration of the military career in California is apparent by the last quarter of the eighteenth century with unpaid soldiers living on sprawling cattle ranches. This decline coincided with and was influenced by the rise of the *Californios*, a local nobility who were to govern California under Mexican rule until the arrival of the Anglo-Americans after 1846.

Social Mobility

Life in the California *presidios* provided the opportunity for social advancement for numerous prominent families of the nineteenth century, including the Alvarados, Arguellos, Carrillos, Moragas, Ortegas, Picos, and Vallejos, to name but a few. Ensign Don Hermengildo Sal, for example, came to California with the Anza expedition in 1776, having been conscripted into the army as a penalty for some undisclosed crime. Showing a facility for administration, Sal was placed in charge of the military warehouse in San Francisco from 1778 to 1782 before being promoted to sergeant at Monterey. Three months later he was promoted to the rank of ensign and dispatched to San Francisco. In 1795 Sal was commissioned as a lieutenant and served as acting commandant in San Francisco from

1791 to 1794, serving out the balance of his career as commandant in Monterey until 1800. Similarly the commandants in San Francisco and Santa Barbara, Ensigns José Dario Arguello and Felipe de Goycoechea, were granted commands for the skill they demonstrated in distributing public lands to civil settlers in Los Angeles and in transferring presidial treasuries, this last no easy task in a dangerous and corruption-prone environment. Presidial schools, staffed by *inválidos,* or retired soldiers, provided the rudimentary skills in writing and arithmetic that served to permit career advancement for many of these individuals. These career patterns indicate clearly that, in California, administrative talent rather than military prowess was the key to promotion. Here, distance from the top of the command chain meant that common sense and organizational skills were prized commodities.

Another factor in the social mobility afforded to frontier settlers and presidials were the *mercedes,* or licenses from the governors, to grazing lands. Presidial commandants were allowed to grant soldiers land as a means of enhancing their self-sufficiency and producing additional foodstuffs, all at no increase in cost to the royal treasury. While presidial commandants were forbidden to own *ranchos,* records indicate that these regulations were not strictly enforced. Ensign José María Verdugo possessed 433 square miles (692 square kilometers) and five thousand head of cattle, while Sergeant Luís Peralta was granted the use of the lands encompassing the present cities of Berkeley, Oakland, and Alameda. Indeed, a listing of the largest *ranchos* in California in 1831 indicates that many of the *rancheros* were former presidial soldiers. *Rancho* grants were particularly prevalent in the Santa Barbara–Monterey areas, where grazing conditions were optimal.

Several consequences derived from these grants. First, soldiers whose status was corporately derived now achieved a new status as freeholders in an economy increasingly given over to ranching. Second, the growth of the *rancho* and the freedom of ranch life made it more difficult to recruit men to the career at arms. Indeed the growth and prosperity of the Monterey–Santa Barbara areas in California during the nineteenth century, at the expense of San Diego and San Francisco, probably resulted from these land grants. Only with the new wave of immigration following the 1849 gold rush was the balance redressed as the seaports of the Pacific Coast, oriented toward the world outside, assumed their present importance in the California economy. Probably the most remarkable feature of the land grants, however, was the fact that the presidial grantees and their families formed extended clans which acquired additional land after the California missions were secularized by the Mexican government in 1834. These *Californios* consolidated their power as a virtual indigenous nobility, a situation far different than that of the soldiery of settled New Spain, whose status, based on their role as conquistadores, was usurped in the sixteenth century by a wave of bureaucrats and civil settlers.

In general, surveys of military service records (*hojas de servicio*) indicate that throughout the eighteenth century the frontier *presidio* developed from a simple organizational structure to one that was more complex, particularly after the Jesuits were expelled from Latin America in 1767 and the military began to assume certain of their duties. Usually military standards of justice were more stringent than those of civil society and punishment, by flogging or incarceration, was severe. Presidial records are replete with lawsuits concerning disputes over women, money, or commercial transactions as well as ones stemming from theft and drunkenness; but what these chronicles of wrongdoing do not reveal is the fact that the *presidios* were also vehicles for advancement and social mobility and that many presidial soldiers or their descendants became the most influential men in late Spanish or early Mexican California. Ensign José Dario Arguello, for example, an officer of non-noble birth from Queretaro, Mexico, was regarded by the time of independence in 1821 as the most influential and respected man in California. His son, Don Luís, capitalized on his father's name and succeeded him as commandant in San Francisco in 1806, using this post as a point of leverage from which to defeat a Spaniard for the governorship in 1822. Yet another Arguello son, Don Santiago, was appointed by the Mexican government to serve as commandant of the four southern California missions and was the owner of a fifty-thousand-acre (20,000-hectare) *rancho* in the Mission Valley area east of San Diego. There are such stories for each of the four *presidios* at century's end. By 1846 American Consul General Thomas Oliver Larkin contended that Mexican California was effectively dominated by forty-six arrivistes who had risen to power from the social and economic bases of their *ranchos* rather than from any inherited wealth. This aspect of military life in California appears distinctive from other parts of the Spanish Borderlands where soldiers do not seem to have consolidated wealth or power to any similar degree, probably due to the relative strength of civil institutions and the presence of royal limits on individual autonomy.

CONCLUSION

In sum, the profession of arms in the Spanish Borderlands achieved significant exploration and conquest thus expanding the viceroyalty of New Spain to a large degree. Thereafter, the Spanish military presence during the seventeenth and eighteenth centuries was defensive in nature, designed to avert the loss of the valuable silver mining provinces to the south rather than to expand Spanish power northwards, where Spain's European rivals held sway. Beset by financial difficulties and the distractions of the Napoleonic Wars, Spain was never able to do more than make a perfunctory attempt to fortify the borderlands; however, its military presence was sufficient to deter domestic violence in most areas, the exception being the Pueblo Revolt in New Mexico in which the Spanish were driven from that province. Despite numerous regulations and ordinances that constituted serious efforts at military reform after 1763, the borderland military remained severely under strength, inadequately equipped, and poorly trained; yet it was able to retain control of the borderlands and allow the eventual expansion of civil settlements.

In California, lack of reinforcements and supplies reached an extreme. Therefore, in that region the Crown had to reward military self-sufficiency by giving the soldiers virtual freedom to trade with the same foreigners whom the Crown sought to exclude; namely, the English, the French, and the Russians. The practice of making land grants to the same individuals accorded these freedoms meant that presidial society on the frontier was markedly less rigid than in the more settled parts of the viceroyalty, where birth, skin color, and occupation dictated social status. Areas such as California were never closely tied to the viceregal government as were more established presidial towns such as Santa Fe. Society developed sui generis, with illegal trade and commerce being conducted from the seaports and *ranchos* along the coast. If the English neglect of its colonies can be called benign because it allowed them to develop on their own, no less can be said of Spanish lack of interest in California. Blessed with a good climate, abundant livestock, and freedom from imperial restrictions, life in the far western borderlands, some felt, was preferable to that in Europe at the end of the eighteenth century. With no previous status to build upon, many presidials and settlers focused upon the present and future of their new homeland and resolved to influence its government, consisting of an independent group of leaders little affected by the vicissitudes of imperial politics during the turbulent period from 1810 to the establishment of Spanish American independence in 1821. The decline of royal power during this period accompanied the deterioration of the career at arms, and the secularization of the missions marked the Mexican government's final break with Spain's legacy of "Cross and Sword."

BIBLIOGRAPHY

Archer, Christon I. *The Army in Bourbon Mexico, 1760–1810.* Albuquerque, N.Mex., 1977.

Bannon, John Francis. *The Spanish Borderlands Frontier, 1513–1821.* New York, 1970.

Brinckerhoff, Sidney B., and Odie B. Faulk, eds. *Lancers for the King: A Study of the Frontier Military System of Northern New Spain, with a Translation of the Royal Regulations of 1772.* Phoenix, Ariz., 1965.

Campbell, Leon G. "The First *Californios*: Presidial Society in Spanish California, 1769–1822." *Journal of the West* 9, no. 4 (1972):582–595.

Faulk, Odie B. *The Leather Jacket Soldier: Spanish Military Equipment and Institutions of the Late 18th Century.* Pasadena, Calif., 1971.

Moorhead, Max L. *The Presidio: Bastion of the Spanish Borderlands.* Norman, Okla., 1975.

Naylor, Thomas H., and Charles W. Polzer, eds. *Pedro de Rivera and the Military Regulations for Northern New Spain, 1724–1729.* Tucson, Ariz., 1988.

————. *The Presidio and Militia on the Northern Frontier of New Spain: A Documentary History.* Vol. 1, *1570–1700.* Tucson, Ariz., 1986.

Powell, Phillip Wayne, *Soldiers, Indians and Silver: The Northward Advance of New Spain, 1550–1600.* Berkeley, Calif., 1962.

Priestley, Herbert I. *José de Gálvez, Visitor-General of New Spain, 1765–1771.* Berkeley, Calif., 1916.

Sánchez, Joseph P. *Spanish Bluecoats: The Catalonian Volunteers in Northwestern New Spain, 1767–1810.* Albuquerque, N.Mex., 1990.

Leon G. Campbell

SEE ALSO **The European Contest for North America; Independence; and Indian-Colonist Conflicts and Alliances.**

SOCIAL TENSIONS

THE BRITISH COLONIES

THE PHRASE "SOCIAL TENSIONS" implies conflict between groups or between individuals who represent groups. From the Jamestown toehold in 1607 to the triumph over France in 1763, the British colonies were riven with such tensions, the origin, quality, and manifestation of which varied, both with time and with place. Some of the tensions played out in the colonies could also be found in Europe, indicative of the strong ties to the Continent. Others could not, signifying the beginnings of a distinctly American society. In whatever form, tension was fundamental to colonial life.

How are we to understand this strife? In 1676 a great rebellion shook Virginia. The royal governor, Sir William Berkeley, was toppled. Battles were fought and people died. An extraordinary meeting of the House of Burgesses passed unprecedented laws. British armed forces were called in to put the rebellion down. At first glance it seems like a dress rehearsal for what happened in the same place a hundred years later.

Indeed, historian Thomas Jefferson Wertenbaker, in *Torchbearer of the Revolution*, described the uprising led by Nathaniel Bacon in just those terms. But it was nothing of the kind. Despite the violent fall of Sir William and somewhat later of his northern counterpart Sir Ed-

mund Andros, white colonials had no desire for independence in the early days of colonial America. We will misunderstand them utterly if we see them only from the perspective of the revolution.

Nor should we think of them as generic, timeless "colonists" in tricorn hat and knee breeches, or bonnet and long gown. Colonial America was triracial. Native Americans and African Americans were participants, not bystanders, and none of them fitted the tricorn-hat and long-dress stereotype. The stereotypes fail even for whites. Colonial history covers some one hundred and fifty years and there were vast differences between the initial British invaders and the people of the mid-eighteenth-century provinces.

Colonial strife stemmed from three distinct sets of problems, each roughly congruous with a different epoch. In the early seventeenth century the issue was the transfer of British power, people, and ways to a distant land. The second epoch spanned the late seventeenth century and the early years of the eighteenth. Its problems grew from continuing attempts by Native Americans to deal with the white invasion, from British conquest of other European settlements, from the beginnings of African America, and from the changes that half a century of white colonial life had wrought. The third set of problems emerged in the middle of the eighteenth century, as Britain's American provinces matured and became both more and less like the mother country.

MIGRATION AND INVASION

More than a century elapsed between Columbus's Spanish beachhead and the first successful British colonization. During that interval the Tudor monarchs Henry VII, Henry VIII, and Elizabeth I transformed England from a late-medieval society into an early modern kingdom. One effect of this was the release of enormous social and cultural energy. When Shakespeare wrote in *King Richard II* (1595) of "this royal throne of kings, this scepter'd isle . . . this earth, this realm, this England," he was expressing the new pride of the English in themselves.

But the era also generated problems with which many English could not cope. Writing far below Shakespeare's level, a doggerel poet took thirteen verses to describe a degenerate England where "New Captaines are come that never did Fight / But with Potts in the daie and Puncks in the night." Each verse asked rhetorically, "And is not ould England growne new?" The visions, energies, failures, and frustrations of an England that had been transformed—all these crossed the Atlantic.

The complexities of the late Tudor and early Stuart years were in evidence in the founding of both Virginia and Massachusetts. The ventures emerged from urban England's new commercial culture, for each colony began as a joint-stock company the purpose of which was to mobilize capital and make money. But their royal charters also gave them the mission to rule conquered territory; to that extent they demonstrated the medieval world's direct union of political and economic power. Each company persuaded a cross section of English society to move to America. Both proved commercial failures, and neither directly returned a penny to their investors.

But they produced very different results. The Virginia Company remained a commercial venture until its collapse in 1624, seventeen years after it founded Jamestown. The Massachusetts Bay Company abandoned the profit motive in 1631, within a year of founding Boston.

Virginia

Early Virginia's English cross section was defined in terms of class and occupation, spreading from gentlemen, knights, and the sons of archbishops and earls to servants and foot soldiers. Virtually all were young and male. The Puritans who went to Massachusetts were mostly of the "middling sort." They formed a cross section in terms of demography, not class, with women and men and the old and young all represented from the start.

The earliest tensions among white Virginians sprang from the intense pressure for gain that lay upon them. Most were used to danger, but not to hard work in primitive conditions. They expected to conquer and loot, not to labor. But little loot came to them. Instead they faced a shortage of foodstuffs so severe that some turned to cannibalism to survive.

Prosperity came a decade after the founding, with the discovery that sweet West Indies tobacco would grow in Virginia soil. Until 1630 returns were very high and Virginia boomed. But tobacco required labor. During the boom time, and for decades after it, most of that labor came from English "servants," lured by promises of a better life once they had worked off the cost of their passage.

Virginia's servants were people for whom England had no place. They came from the streets of London, sometimes from the jails, and from the counties of the West Country, where massive social change was forcing farm people off the land. What they found was cheap land that men greater than themselves controlled, and political power in the hands of those same men. They themselves provided cheap labor, and watched as high profits were returned to the landowners. The scenario was deadly. Some three thousand English migrated to Virginia between 1618 and 1621 only to disappear completely from the historical record. Disease and Indian warfare account for some of these premature deaths, but not for all. Runaways, if captured, faced the prospect of being hanged, burned to death, "broken upon wheles . . . staked . . . [and] shott to death." All of these punishments were meted out in the single year of 1612. A servant's life was difficult in England too. But there the church, the courts of law, the hiring fairs that offered an annual chance to change one's master or mistress, and the presense nearby of family members gave some protection. If it came to it, a person could run away to London. Virginia offered none of these protections.

Massachusetts

Gain posed a problem in Massachusetts as well, but on different terms. Preaching on shipboard in 1630, Governor John Winthrop articulated a vision of social harmony in which he called on his fellows to "be knitt together in this work as one man . . . entertaine each other in brotherly Affeccion." He knew what had happened in the Chesapeake and did not want anything like it. Material conditions favored his hope. The region never developed a high-return, labor-intensive staple crop. Its people were not averse to improving their lives. But most of them went to settle, not to get rich.

Despite their shared Puritan faith, the New England founders were a diverse lot. Some came from parts of England where communal village ways were still strong. These people took Winthrop's words seriously, trying to establish a consensual way of life in the American forests. The very name Concord, Massachusetts, speaks to the point.

The founders of such places worked out careful, detailed town covenants. They distributed land according to standing and social need, not according to what a person could pay or seize. They planted their crops in medieval-style open fields, not on separate farms. They created political structures (the towns themselves), religious structures (Congregational churches), and structures of personal life (strong patriarchal families) that bound individuals tightly. Open-field farming rarely survived the lifetimes of the founders. But most of the rest proved enduring.

Kenneth Lockridge has called one such place in Massachusetts, Dedham, a "Christian utopian closed corporate community." But other New Englanders lived differently. From Boston's founding, it was a capital and a major port, not a farming town. Fishing camps like Marblehead were wild, rough places. Springfield, in the Connecticut Valley, began as a fur-trading post and became the domain of two men, the father and son William and John Pynchon. Their widespread connections, ownership of the best land,

and ability to extend or deny their patronage gave them unquestioned control.

Within a general framework that valued order and cohesion, each of these situations produced its own tensions. The problem for the would-be utopias like Dedham was that any change meant decline, and change was bound to come. The first serious problems erupted in the form of the mid-seventeenth-century church dispute over the Half-Way Covenant. At issue were the founding generation's children, who had been baptized in infancy but were not experiencing the adult conversions required for full church membership. Now they were marrying and seeking full membership regardless, so their own children could be baptized. It marked America's first gap of generations: the American-born children were simply not following the pattern prescribed by their English-born parents.

Elsewhere, New Englanders felt recurrent tension between individuals' desires to improve themselves and the general Puritan belief that community came first. Like the generational issue, this expressed itself first as a theological dispute. In 1636 informal religious gatherings hosted by the Boston midwife Anne Hutchinson provoked bitter factionalism. Among the issues were abstract theology (Hutchinson's claim that God could reveal His will directly, bypassing the formal church), discipline (her encouragement to her followers to scorn ministers whom she considered unconverted), and gender (Hutchinson's being a woman was a challenge to an exclusively male structure of authority).

But the problem of commerce lurked beneath. Hutchinson's own husband was a merchant. Her challenge to formal authority implied greater freedom for people like him to do as they saw fit with their property. Only four years later another Boston merchant, Robert Keayne, had to endure a public trial for doing just that. The charge that cost him his good name was that he had taken "six-pence in the shilling profit; in some above eight-pence; and in some small things above two for one." The memory stung Keayne until his death.

Relations with Native Americans

Whatever their other differences, Virginia and Massachusetts proved much the same in their relations with Native Americans. Virginia projected an Indian college. Massachusetts put the image of an Indian and the words "come over and help us" on its seal, and actually brought a few Indian boys to Harvard. But the major theme was conflict and open war.

The Powhatan Indians of the lower Chesapeake were suspicious of the English from the start, and the Virginians established a record of astonishing violence and incompetence with them. One instance makes the point. In 1610, when infant Jamestown was totally dependent on Indian corn for survival, it sent out an expedition that annihilated the nearest town, burned its growing crops, captured its queen and drowned her children before her eyes, and then put the queen herself to the sword.

The only real surprise about the major attack that the lower-Chesapeake Indians finally launched in 1622 is that they took so long to make it. It failed, and the English concluded that the Indians could justly be made slaves. Whom they could not enslave, they set out to kill. Poisoned wine distributed at one negotiation led to the deaths of perhaps two hundred Indians who had come in good faith to parley.

Warfare broke out in 1636 between Puritans and the Pequots of what is now eastern Connecticut. The Reverend Thomas Shepard attributed the war to the "Pekoat furies" launching an unprovoked attack. A Native American might have told it differently. The New Englanders proved as determined as the Virginians to have Indian blood. Shepard's eyewitness account describes graphically what they did:

At last . . . there wigwams were set on fire which being dry & contiguous on to another was most dreadfull to the Indians, some burning some bleeding to death by the swoord . . . vntill the Lord had vtterly consumed the whole company except 4 or 5. girles they tooke prisoners & dealt with them at Seabrooke as they dealt with ours at Wethersfeeld. (Perry Miller and Thomas H. Johnson. "The Autobiography of Thomas Shepard," pp. 472–473)

Shepard left to the imagination what dealing with those "girles" actually meant.

Here was "social tension" indeed. But more was involved than violence. Native Americans had a tradition of hospitality and they manifested it toward the newcomers. Indian corn kept both Virginians and the Mayflower Pilgrims of Plymouth alive during the "starving times" of their first years. Over the course of the colonial period far more Indian ways were adopted by whites than were white ways adopted by Native Americans.

Not only were the Indians different in their costume, diet, and language, but in their sense of personal relations, property, authority, the sacred, and the profane. An Indian selling land did not think the act meant giving up all rights to it; an English person who was buying could conceive of the bargain in no other terms. Moreover, Native Americans confronted whites against the background of their own divisions. Shepard called the Narragansetts the "ancient enemies of the Pekoats." They aided the Puritans, not their fellow Indians, in 1636.

The whites brought trade goods and alcohol, and each affected the Indians. The Europeans wanted furs: beaver from the northern tribes and deerskins from the southern ones. Entering the trade bound the Indians into transatlantic networks of production and exchange. For some tribes, like the Micmac of Nova Scotia, the trade meant destruction. For others, like the small groups that coalesced into the Catawba of South Carolina, it meant a fundamental rearrangement of life. For still others, most notably the five Iroquois nations of New York, it meant successful warfare and the winning of unprecedented power.

The whites brought their beliefs as well as their goods, and they tried to win the Indians over to them. Sometimes they succeeded, but they had no idea of the fearful psychological price that Indians who accepted those beliefs and abandoned their own culture had to pay. They brought animals, plants, and microbes, and these made an impact as well. The catastrophic epidemics that reduced the Native American population by as much as 90 percent during the sixteenth century are now well understood. That demographic disaster conditioned every other aspect of Indian-white relations. But even a settler's stray pig wandering into an unprotected Native American cornfield or shellfish bed could generate violence.

Pigs, disease, firearms, alcohol, Christianity, and strange people: these made America a "new world" as much for its natives as it was for the invaders. Tribal names that are now familiar to us—Catawba, Cherokee, Creek—signify Native American groups that came together in an attempt to withstand the pressures imposed by the strangers who had come unbidden upon them.

THE SETTLEMENTS BECOME PROVINCES

In 1675 war broke out again. It happened simultaneously in both Virginia and Massachusetts, but the events were distinct. What began as Indian warfare on the Virginia frontier spread east in the form of Bacon's Rebellion and laid bare the problems of a whole society. In New England, King Philip's War was a concerted, cross-tribal attempt to keep the whites from taking any more land and perhaps to push them back.

Other essays in this encyclopedia explore native-settler warfare. The important point here is that these conflicts began an era of trouble that changed colonial life in fundamental ways. By 1700 neither Virginia nor Massachusetts was what it had been in 1660. By then, conquered New York, newly settled Pennsylvania, and emergent Carolina had joined Virginia and Massachusetts as major British provinces and were beginning to display problems of their own.

Virginia was now seven decades into its seventeenth-century ordeal. In many ways it had settled down. Women had joined the colonists. "Seasoning" was enabling the settlers to survive the Chesapeake's climate and diseases. The tobacco boom was over, and the atmosphere was no longer one of get-rich-and-get-out. People were beginning to build the networks, families, and institutions that made for productive societies.

Servants and Slaves in the South

A growing number of late-seventeenth-century Virginians were black. The story of the arrival of the very first Africans aboard a Dutch ship in 1619 is familiar to us. But their experience over the following half century is less so. Its outlines are these. They came to a brutal land where whites were miserable both to one another and to the natives. The Africans came without whatever rudimentary social protection being English

carried. But they did not come initially into slavery. Legally, the institution had not yet taken shape, and the Africans became servants. They and their English fellows worked together, lived together, slept together, and ran away together. Some won their freedom. By mid century there was a free black community whose members called the Eastern Shore (the peninsula between the Chesapeake and the Atlantic) "myne owne ground." In 1676 black people joined whites in insurrection.

In the aftermath of Bacon's Rebellion the society that we associate with Virginia's colonial image began to replace the ramshackle world that the first Virginians knew. The great plantation houses, courthouses, Anglican churches, and taverns that became Virginia's characteristic architecture were more than buildings. They were places where white Virginians acted out the patterns that allowed them to live together on better terms than had been possible amid the brutality of the seventeenth century.

The price was paid by black people, for in the aftermath of the rebellion Virginia became a slave society. By 1700 black and white Virginians were in fundamentally different legal situations and the number of Africans being imported was rising rapidly. If a white servant came to Virginia, it was to work for someone whose own fortune was meager and who had scratched together enough to afford the low price such a servant commanded. The Africans were coming to work for richer people who could afford to buy them in sizable numbers despite the higher price they commanded. Rich whites and poor ones remained very different sorts of people. But by the early eighteenth century the difference that really counted was race.

The Dominion of New England

In New England the Puritans won King Philip's War and sold most of the Indians whom they captured into slavery far away. But they paid a heavy psychological price. In their self-centered view of the world, the war itself could only be seen as a token of God's displeasure with them. Worse was to come.

Most New Englanders had supported the Puritan Revolution in England in the 1640s. Some had even returned to England to take part. After the Stuart restoration in 1660, New Englanders harbored regicides who fled the anger of Charles II. They were free of serious English control, whether they lived in Massachusetts, the Pilgrim colony of Plymouth, Rhode Island, or Connecticut.

For all these reasons the Crown decided in 1686 to amalgamate all the New England provinces, New York, and New Jersey into a single Dominion of New England. A placeman and fortune hunter named Sir Edmund Andros became its governor, to rule without an elected assembly. Politically the Dominion was a disaster, and it collapsed in 1689 when news arrived that James II had been overthrown and William and Mary had taken his place. The Dominion fell most swiftly in Massachusetts. How it fell reveals some of the tensions that New England was feeling by then.

Two issues were at stake, each turning in a different way on the problem of local communities. Part of the problem was legal: the towns owed their corporate existence to provincial governments that technically had no right to create them. This meant that the towns lacked the power either to make separate land grants or to hold land in common. They had done both, of course.

Andros saw his opportunity. He was not so foolish as to try to seize all of Massachusetts or Connecticut. But he knew that he could force individuals to seek confirmation of their titles, with a fee to himself each time. Since common lands belonged to the Crown, not to the towns, he could grant them anew to whomever he chose, including himself. His choice of the college town of Cambridge as one of the first places to despoil of its common demonstrates how little mind he paid to local sensitivities. When news of the Glorious Revolution arrived, farmers from throughout eastern Massachusetts converged on Boston to overthrow Andros and clap him in jail.

Andros had won support from some New Englanders, mostly men like Springfield's John Pynchon. Pynchon accepted one responsibility after another, including a post on the nonelected council, several judgeships, a militia colonelcy, and the important informal tasks of recommending other militia officers and securing the submission of Connecticut. Not every local leader identified so completely with the regime. But the simple fact of having held office under the Dominion became reason for a man to lose his power. Pynchon, who had ruled over Springfield, now faced defiance from a man who had been a mere sergeant in his militia regiment. Dedham rejected all selectmen who had held any office in the Andros years. Only one ever held that highest town office again.

Salem and Witchcraft

New England's late-seventeenth-century crisis abounds in drama. But the witchcraft trials that took place in Salem Village, Massachusetts, in 1692 provide the greatest drama of all. The events were profoundly abnormal. But in their very abnormality they provided a grotesque image of the pressures that historical change was imposing on daily life.

The belief in witchcraft was not peculiar to Salem. It provided a widely accepted way of explaining what some people thought and how they behaved. Understanding requires a sensitivity not only to witchcraft's normality as part of life but to its complex gender dimensions. The conventional image of the witch as female has a historical basis. But many of the people who brought accusations were also women. Witchcraft scares pitted women against each other as well as men against women.

What is most important about the Salem events is not that witchcraft was alleged, or that women were central to it. It is how accusations that might have brought personal tragedy in other places brought a whole community to grief.

Part of the problem was the heated atmosphere of 1692. By then New England had endured King Philip's War, the loss of the original Massachusetts charter, and the tribulations of the Andros era. To this self-styled new Israel, an outbreak of witchcraft seemed the final proof that its God had abandoned it. Another factor was Salem Village itself, which had never built the dense structures that held other places in New England together. Neighboring Andover experienced more accusations during the crisis than Salem Village. But there the accusations did not lead to panic and death. The reason lies in the differences between the two places.

Politically, the village was only a part of the larger town of Salem. It enjoyed neither a town meeting to resolve its conflicts nor public officials to take credit for achievements and bear responsibility for wrongs. Hierarchical Springfield and closed, corporate Dedham both had leaders who could be purged when the Andros regime ended, thus purging evil memories of the regime. Salem Village did not.

Little good came from the village's Congregational church. Founded in contention, the church had never been able to hold a minister of any quality. In 1692 its pastor was Samuel Parris, who lacked the prized Harvard degree and who came to the ministry after a failed business career. The village did enjoy the strong, patriarchal families that were characteristic of rural New England. But one historian has described the inner life of such families as "fierce communion" even where paternal authority and village structure held them together. In Salem Village authority failed and the two chief clans, the Porters and the Putnams, were at odds.

The affair began when a few adolescent girls were caught toying with the occult and brought charges of witchcraft against some older women. The first accused were socially defenseless, like the slave Tituba, who had been teaching them what she knew of conjuring, or the outcast Sarah Good. Throughout New England these were exactly the sort of women who were likely to find themselves at the wrong end of a witchcraft charge. But the accusations spread, to more respectable women like Rebecca Nurse and her sister Sarah Cloyce, to men, including the village's former minister, George Burroughs, and outside the village itself to very prominent people. Even Lady Phips, the spouse of the newly appointed royal governor, found herself accused.

The reason was that the village lay astride the central fault line of New England society. Most of its people were farmers like the ones in Dedham or Andover, who sought primarily to keep to themselves. It would be misleading to describe these people as peasants. Commerce touched their lives constantly, and compared with European villagers their roots in the land were shallow. But their suspicions of the outside world were strong. In 1675 Andover actually voted to deny to any man the "liberty . . . to sell, or transport any cedar out of the town,

either in shingles or otherwise" on penalty of a heavy fine.

If part of Salem Village looked west and sought insularity, another part looked east toward the bustling port with which the village shared its name. When the fury of accusations, trials, and executions burst, accusers like the Putnams may not have linked what they were doing to their own nostalgic and impossible vision of social order. The more respectable accused may not have linked their lethal predicament to their own greater openness to the outside world. But the correlation is strong in each case.

The Colonies in Transition

By the late seventeenth century British North America included more than the Chesapeake and the New England provinces. Dutch New Netherland, founded not long after the English established Jamestown, began as a colony of fur traders centered on Fort Orange (Albany) and New Amsterdam (New York City). The British conquered it in 1664 and renamed it New York. Dutch or British, New Yorkers faced neither the problems generated by the Chesapeake's staple-crop economy, nor those that stemmed from New England's combination of belief in its own divine mission and tension between mercantile and small-village ways. But New York felt tensions of its own.

New York had embraced slavery almost from the start and it eventually acquired the largest African-American population outside the zone of plantations and staple crops. At one time, New York City's slaves accounted for 20 percent of its people. Twice during the eighteenth century, in 1712 and 1741, those slaves attempted insurrections.

A second source of tension was the social patterns that both the Dutch authorities and the conquering English imposed upon the rich lands of the Hudson valley. To encourage settlement the Dutch created neo-feudal patroonships, and one, Rensselaerswyck, took permanent form. It sprawled across almost eight hundred square miles (960 square kilometers) of the upper Hudson valley. The conquering English granted many manors on the same model. Not all of them lasted. But Livingston, Cortlandt, and Philipsburgh became major entities, the first two and Rensselaerswyck enjoying the privilege of electing their own members to the provincial assembly. If the manor lord was not the member himself, he decided who would be.

The third source of tension was boundary uncertainty. No borders were clearly drawn in early America, but New York and New England represented places that were different in ethnicity, language, and social system. New York and Connecticut resolved the issue fairly easily, but New York and Massachusetts did not. A detailed map drawn as late as 1774 showed the New York manors of Rensselaerswyck and Livingston overlapping the Massachusetts towns of Pittsfield, Lenox, Stockbridge, and Great Barrington. While the land lay empty, there was little problem. By the time that map was drawn it was another matter.

Pennsylvania and the Carolinas only really began to face internal tension in the eighteenth century. Their early records simply foreshadowed what would come. Pennsylvania's Quakers thought of themselves as an unconventional people living out their faith, not a chosen people called by God to live apart. Their attempted utopia was liberal, not communal. They never created closed communities. They felt no ambiguities about holding private property, whether it was town lots in Philadelphia or separate farms in the surrounding "best poor man's country."

With Indians, with non-Quakers, and among themselves, they sought reciprocity and openness, not dominion and exclusivity. One consequence was good relations with Native Americans until well into the eighteenth century. A second was a multicultural society. Pennsylvania became bilingual, but its German speakers were voluntary migrants, not conquered subjects like New York's Dutch.

It did face problems, however. The province's openness led to settlement by people who rejected Quaker teaching, including pacifism. A second problem turned on William Penn, whose intent it was to be a patriarch. Despite its liberal qualities, Pennsylvania was a feudal holding. Its governorship descended from father to son in the Penn family. All public land belonged to them as well. Even Penn's fellow Quakers disputed the extent of his power. While he resisted their encroachments, Penn realized that a great deal was at stake.

Carolina's beginnings were also feudal, with a grant by Charles II to eight loyal men he wanted to reward. Like other royal grantees, including Penn, Calvert of Maryland, and the gentlemen who controlled large parts of New Jersey, these people called themselves "proprietors." They envisaged a vertical society that they would dominate and they hired the philosopher John Locke to work out a hierarchical pattern of hereditary titles and landholdings.

Neither the first proprietors nor Locke ever saw Carolina. Socially it became not a stable hierarchy but rather the "colony of a colony." Its first settlers were Barbadians. They brought no visions with them, just their hard West Indian experience, and black people.

Africans quickly accounted for more than a quarter of the young colony's people. Carolina had not yet found its staple crops: rice, indigo, and later tobacco and cotton. It survived by trading deerskins and by herding semi-wild cattle on the first American open range. Indians hunted the deer; Africans herded the cattle, drawing on their ancestors' long experience on the West African savannahs. In historian Peter Wood's words, "it is even possible that the very word 'cowboy' originated through this set of circumstances."

MATURITY AND ITS DISCONTENTS

South Carolina owed its long-term prosperity to rice, not deerskins and cattle. Black slaves built the elaborate works of hydraulic engineering that turned the province's coastal swamps into productive fields. They, not whites, knew how to grow the crop, which was as familiar to West Africans as it was exotic to the English. But as with Virginia tobacco, the ensuing boom was lethal.

The boom occurred in the 1720s and 1730s. Africans were already the majority, and now their number rose dramatically. Only sixty-seven Africans came to the province in 1716; more than seventeen hundred came in 1726. But boom-time Carolina killed them faster than they could arrive. There were perhaps twenty-six thousand by 1734 and some fifteen thousand more came by 1740. In that year, however, the total black population stood at barely more than thirty-nine thousand. Despite its very high rate of importation, the province was experiencing a net population loss.

Black Carolinians had no reason to accept their condition, and they did not do so. Forms of protest included arson, escape, poisoning their captors, attempting to aid the Spanish in Florida, and simple "uppityness." Their most dramatic resistance was the Stono Rebellion of 1739, in which sixty people died. Even before the rebellion, lowland whites lived in fear of what they had created.

By this time Virginia, too, was importing Africans in large numbers. Both provinces brought in roughly twice as many men as women. Like Carolinians, black Virginians suffered badly. Roughly one in four was dead within a year of arrival, primarily from respiratory diseases caught during the first winter. But three-quarters did survive, and Virginia's black population began to grow. The province's boom time was long in the past and servants, not slaves, had felt its effects. But however oppressive the slavery that Virginia Africans entered, their Carolina fellows had it worse.

As Africans begat African Americans, a gap began to open up between the two groups. The Africans spoke their own tongues; they had little resistance to American diseases; at first each was alone, and many remained so. If an African ran away, it was to the wilderness. But African Americans spoke English; they survived American conditions better; simple numbers let far more of them form families and from families came communities. If one of them ran away it was to join a spouse, a parent, or a child in a different place.

Order and Tension in Virginia

Whites were always the Virginia majority, and the planters' great achievement was to convince lesser whites that planter rule was good for all. After 1700 everything worked for them. Slavery and racism were basic to the new Virginia. So was its economic structure. The tidewater gentry lived along the shoreline and lesser people lived inland. But both grew tobacco. A great planter might handle the marketing of a smaller neighbor's crops, creating ties of clientage and obligation between the two. The same gentleman might command his yeoman neighbor in the militia,

sit in judgment when the yeoman brought a dispute to the county court, entertain him at the annual barbecue, and be a vestryman of the Anglican church where the whole district worshiped.

Politics counted, too. By modern standards Virginia, like the rest of the colonies, was deeply undemocratic. Women, Native Americans, and blacks were barred from voting. But most adult white Virginia males eventually did acquire enough land to vote. Elections were public. Lesser men did not seek high office, and it took courage to vote in the open air against one's patrons' wishes. But the freeholders could still deny a wayward gentleman the seat in the Burgesses that signified full membership in the elite. Southern populism began here.

On these foundations white Virginians built a distinctive, intensely masculine public culture, which taught them to prize what they had. That culture laid great stress on self-display and self-assertion. But it also set the rules that allowed one Virginian to assert himself and another to submit. Competitive drinking, dancing, horse racing, and sometimes dueling or wrestling; an Anglican church whose real God was the planter class; the customs of the courthouse, election day, and militia muster; even the balanced architecture of a mansion facing the James or the Rappahannock rivers: all these expressed that culture. It made white Virginian males the most cohesive people in the colonies. But tension did develop.

It expressed itself in religious form, with the mid-century emergence of the Baptist church. Converts stopped dancing, drinking, and horse racing. Rejecting the stratified world of Anglican prayer and ritual, Baptist services celebrated a community of brothers and sisters. The Baptists even welcomed slaves. Any situation that brought black and white together threatened everything the planters had built.

The persecution in 1771 of Elder John Waller asserted the power of the planters but also expressed their fears. While Waller was leading a hymn, the Anglican parson, the sheriff, and some others disrupted the meeting. The parson kept

running the End of his Horsewhip in [Waller's] mouth, Laying his Whip across the Hym Book &c. When done Singing [Waller] . . . was Violently Jerked off of the Stage, [they] Caught him by the Back part of his Neck [,] Beat his head against the ground . . . Carried him . . . some Considerable Distance, where a Gentleman [the sheriff] Give him . . . Twenty Lashes." (Rhys Isaac. *The Transformation of Virginia*, pp. 162–163)

But Waller "Went Back Singing praise to God, Mounted the Stage & preached with a Great Deal of Liberty."

Success and Change in New England

If white Virginians created a synthesis, New Englanders were dealing with a synthesis in decay. They even invented their own word for it: "declension." The problem began almost immediately, and it only worsened when succeeding generations had to deal with the heroic image of the Puritan founders. Virginians chose to forget what had gone before. New Englanders remembered incessantly and found themselves wanting.

Part of their problem was their own demographic success, for they became the world's healthiest people. In England a person was old at fifty; white Virginia life expectancy was even less; everywhere the Indians were dying. But first-generation English men and women in the Massachusetts town of Andover found themselves living to more than seventy.

The reasons included diet, ample fuel during cold winters, low population density, a stable society, and the absence of the South's diseases and fierce exploitation. Even childbirth posed relatively little problem, at least by the standards of the time. Women became pregnant as often as their European counterparts. They carried more pregnancies to completion and the infants were more likely to reach adulthood. In the first generation their death rate during the childbearing years was actually lower than that of men.

These demographic blessings produced their own problems. One was the experience of old age on an unprecedented scale. The perhaps unconscious response was New Englanders' patriarchal families, with fathers controlling children well into adulthood and thus guaranteeing their own support. A second problem was a real population crisis in some places, as New England's numbers inexorably doubled by natural increase every quarter century.

Rural New Englanders were feeling real pressure. By mid century between 30 percent and 50 percent of all brides were giving birth less than eight months from marriage. After as much as three generations of stability, townspeople were beginning to move: north to New Hampshire or the District of Maine or westward to the hilly country between the Connecticut River and the Hudson. Both premarital sex and migration expressed a weakening of the control that parents had long wielded over their children.

But as Yankees approached the uncertain New York–Massachusetts boundary, they encountered New Yorkers who had very different ways. In the Hudson valley there already were great estates. More were projected north of Massachusetts, where both New York and New Hampshire claimed all the land between the Hudson and the Connecticut. In one heiress's words, landlords expected "simple felicity . . . among the amiable and innocent tenants we were to have."

But to New England migrants, tenancy meant the same nightmare that Sir Edmund Andros had tried to impose on their ancestors. They resisted: with sporadic mid-century rioting in the uncertain Taconic-Berkshire borderland, as major participants in a tenant rebellion that swept the Hudson valley in 1766, and with outright insurrection in the Green Mountains between 1765 and 1777, whose eventual result was the creation of the separate state of Vermont. Vermont's Green Mountain Boys fought two separate American Revolutions, one against the distant British and their threatening taxes, the other against New York and its hated "land jobbers."

In central New Jersey, too, migrant New Englanders and uncertain land titles combined to cause strife. The East Jersey proprietors claimed the region by royal grant; New England migrants who had settled Newark and Elizabethtown claimed their land by direct Indian purchase. Rioting ensued in mid century and it made the region ungovernable for several years. The settlers even established their own "goal" (jail) in the woods.

Whether they migrated or stayed put, New Englanders were used to finding religious means for dealing with social problems. In the late 1730s and the early 1740s they found the Great Awakening. It was not confined to them; people from Pennsylvania to newly founded Georgia experienced it as well, making it the first genuinely American social movement. In New England it had complex effects. One was to shake towns and established churches, as long-serving ministers lost their pulpits for being unconverted. Orthodox Congregationalists tried to crush the revival by invoking the authority of provincial governments. But "New Light" Congregationalists, "New Side" Presbyterians, and Baptists resisted, turning religion itself into a political issue.

Perhaps the greatest effect of the Awakening was to provide a cultural means for dealing with social changes that by now were profound. The New England ideal of community was not dead. But the Puritan social order that had expressed it was under ever greater pressure from individualism, whatever form that took.

The tension had always been there: the cases of Anne Hutchinson, Robert Keayne, the Half-Way Covenant, and the Salem witches had all been bound up with it. Now sexual behavior that earlier New Englanders would not have tolerated, migration out of towns that were used to stability, and the disruption of century-old churches by militant Evangelicals proved too much.

The Awakening offered a powerful message: a sinner who sought mercy could find it. It offered as well to replace tight, binding structures that could no longer be endured with the ecstatic union of people who were saved despite themselves. But to accept the message and enter the new communion was to acknowledge that sin, meaning social tension, individualism, and change, could not be avoided.

Landlord-Tenant Conflicts

New York's landlord-tenant system had problems with migrant Yankees; it also created problems for itself. A manorial grant with neo-feudal rights was meaningless if there were no tenants. But in the mid eighteenth century the estates were filling up.

By then such neo-feudal privileges of manorial status as holding a "court leete" and a "court baron" had fallen into disuse. When the redoubtable Sir William Johnson sought the title of manor for his Mohawk valley estate in 1769 the royal governor refused it. But neither the waning of strictly feudal ways nor Johnson's inability to acquire another title made any real difference. Like the lords of Livingston Manor, Rensselaerswyck, and Philipsburgh, Johnson ruled his community. On all of these estates a long lease did give the right to vote. But the elections were held at open polls, and few tenants would publicly challenge the landholder's will. Moreover, these tenants knew they would never own their farms. The value of whatever "improvements" they made would in the end accrue to the lord.

Some landlords, including Johnson, established good tenant relations in a paternalistic way. But others incessantly raised rents, extorted other obligations, and evicted unproductive tenants. Direct tenant resistance was as much a cause of unrest on the estates as the clash between New York and New England ways. On the troubled manor of Livingston the problem was worsened by common knowledge that the estate rested on outright fraud.

Unrest became rebellion in 1766. Evictions by the landlord Beverly Robinson from his estate on "Philipse's Highland Patent" in northern Westchester County sparked armed resistance that spread all the way to Albany. Tenants formed their own militia companies, broke jails, and carried out evictions of their own. They even marched on New York City, though they stopped short of the city line. It took red-coated British troops to put the rising down.

The tenants may have expected help from poor people in New York City; one of their spokesmen said so. But they got none. Nor had help been forthcoming for Pennsylvania's Paxton Boys when they descended on Philadelphia three years earlier. On the contrary, even Quakers there decided that it was time to learn to shoot.

The two risings were not the same: the March of the Paxton Boys began with the murder of friendly Indians by frontiersmen who were under attack and who could not find their real enemies. But the way that New Yorkers and Philadelphians alike responded to the marches suggests that the problems of the countryside and those of the town were quite distinct. It took the revolutionary crisis to bring city and countryside into a single movement, and even then the coalition proved fragile.

The British Ports

Boston's Puritan heritage, New York's black people and its Dutch, Philadelphia's smaller slave population and its Germans, the absence anywhere of the sort of urban network that surrounded a place like Birmingham in the English midlands: all these qualities indicated that these towns and English ones were different. Events like the 1712 and 1741 New York slave conspiracies would not have happened in Britain at all.

But the colonial ports were still British outposts. As a young artisan Benjamin Franklin moved readily from his native Boston to Philadelphia, but just as readily from Philadelphia to London and back. A major merchant like New York's Oliver DeLancey might have direct connections of family, interest, and friendship to English people in high places. In DeLancey's case this meant being the brother-in-law of a knighted member of Parliament and the uncle of titled aristocrats. His brother James could even call on the good offices of his old Cambridge tutor, who had become archbishop of Canterbury.

Like such connections, the social tensions that white urban Americans displayed are the measure of how British their towns were. In both Britain and the colonies, a town's central institution was its controlled market. Paternalistic officials regularly intervened to balance commerce and welfare. Commerce meant people's right to trade their property. Welfare meant an adequate supply of necessities like bread, salt, and firewood at prices consumers could afford. New York's "assize of bread," regulating the size, weight, and quality of the ordinary brown loaf, had many counterparts elsewhere.

If control failed, upheaval became legitimate. An eighteenth-century commodities riot was not mindless violence; it meant acting out well-understood rituals of popular price-setting. These rituals were what Lieutenant Governor Thomas Hutchinson of Massachusetts meant when he called "mobs, a sort of them at least . . . constitutional" in 1768.

The memory of the great English upheavals of the early and middle seventeenth century also crossed the sea. This expressed itself most powerfully in Boston, where crowds marked Pope's Day each 5 November with parades, effigies, bonfires, and sometimes fights. As Guy Fawkes Day, it remains an English celebration, commemorating the discovery in 1605 of the "Popish Plot" to bomb Parliament. In eighteenth-century Boston, and to some extent in New York, it became an annual festival of misrule, a carnival time when social relations were inverted and crowds ruled the street. Like most carnivals it was usually harmless, boisterous fun. But this moment of inversion did point unwittingly toward the possibility of whole worlds turning upside down, and not on a temporary basis.

CONCLUSION

Thoroughgoing, rapid, violent, popular, permanent change: this was precisely what the American Revolution brought. But to repeat the point with which this article began, no colonial either expected such change or wanted it until the very eve of independence, not much before 1774 or even 1775. Why did tensions that seem so profound not lead to greater upheaval during the colonial period itself?

No society can endure without trying to resolve its own problems, and colonials did try to resolve theirs. The village culture of New England, the peaceable Quaker kingdom of the Delaware valley, and the planter synthesis of eighteenth-century Virginia all offered American answers to the question of how people can live together.

Moreover, colonial America sprawled over a vast distance. It included many different political units, economic structures, and ways of life. Working people in New York City who depended on the marketplace for bread, Hudson valley tenants who wanted to own the land they farmed, and New Englanders trying to maintain village ways as they moved into the Berkshire hills: all of these faced "social tensions." But it took the oppressive British policies of the 1760s to force colonials to think of themselves as facing a common plight. Until then there was no particular reason for any group to take on the problems of any other.

Underpinning all other tensions, perhaps, was the most intractable and most profoundly American problem of all—race. Only a seafaring

New Yorker could have reason to know what black people endured in the Carolina lowlands. Only with long memory could eighteenth-century tidewater Virginians or New England Yankees draw the connection between their own ancestors' bloody treatment of the Indians and what the Paxton Boys did on the Pennsylvania frontier in 1763. But New York and South Carolina both used mass executions to crush slave rebellions. Whether frontier warfare took place along the York and the Rappahannock in the 1620s, along the Connecticut and the Housatonic in the 1670s, or along the Allegheny and the Monongahela in the 1760s, the way the whites waged it was much the same.

All of the colonial era's tensions, even those of race, were expressed during the revolution that brought the era to an end. They contributed powerfully to what made the events surrounding the War of Independence genuinely revolutionary. In important ways the people of the early republic had to face very different social tensions from those of the late colonies. But colonial social tensions did not begin or even foreshadow the American Revolution. It had no torchbearers. On the contrary, it was a political revolution, begun for reasons that lay outside British colonial society, that made possible the resolution of some of that society's social tensions.

BIBLIOGRAPHY

Allen, David Grayson. *In English Ways: The Movement of Societies and the Transferal of English Local Law and Custom to Massachusetts Bay in the Seventeenth Century.* Chapel Hill, N.C., 1981.

Axtell, James. *The Invasion Within: The Contest of Cultures in Colonial North America.* New York, 1985.

Bailyn, Bernard, ed. *The Apologia of Robert Keayne: The Self-Portrait of a Puritan Merchant.* New York, 1964.

Bailyn, Bernard. *The New England Merchants in the Seventeenth Century.* Cambridge, Mass., 1955.

Bonomi, Patricia U. *A Factious People: Politics and Society in Colonial New York.* New York, 1971.

Boyer, Paul, and Stephen Nissenbaum. *Salem Possessed: The Social Origins of Witchcraft.* Cambridge, Mass., 1974.

Breen, T. H. *Tobacco Culture: The Mentality of the Great Tidewater Planters on the Eve of Revolution.* Princeton, N.J., 1985.

Breen, T. H., and Stephen Innes. *"Myne Owne Ground": Race and Freedom on Virginia's Eastern Shore, 1640–1676.* New York, 1980.

Bushman, Richard L. *From Puritan to Yankee: Character and the Social Order in Connecticut, 1690–1765.* Cambridge, Mass., 1967.

———. *King and People in Provincial Massachusetts.* Chapel Hill, N.C., 1985.

Countryman, Edward. *A People in Revolution: The American Revolution and Political Society in New York, 1760–1790.* Baltimore, Md., 1981.

Cronon, William. *Changes in the Land: Indians, Colonists, and the Ecology of New England.* New York, 1983.

Demos, John P. *Entertaining Satan: Witchcraft and the Culture of Early New England.* New York, 1982.

Greven, Philip J., Jr. *Four Generations: Population, Land, and Family in Colonial Andover, Massachusetts.* Ithaca, N.Y., 1970.

Heyrman, Christine Leigh. *Commerce and Culture: The Maritime Communities of Colonial Massachusetts, 1690–1750.* New York, 1984.

Innes, Stephen. *Labor in a New Land: Economy and Society in Seventeenth-Century Springfield.* Princeton, N.J., 1983.

Isaac, Rhys. *The Transformation of Virginia, 1740–1790.* Chapel Hill, N.C., 1982.

Jennings, Francis. *The Invasion of America: Indians, Colonialism, and the Cant of Conquest.* Chapel Hill, N.C., 1975.

Karlsen, Carol F. *The Devil in the Shape of a Woman: Witchcraft in Colonial New England.* New York, 1987.

Koehler, Lyle. *A Search for Power: The "Weaker Sex" in Seventeenth-Century New England.* Urbana, Ill., 1980.

Kulikoff, Allan. *Tobacco and Slaves: The Development of Southern Cultures in the Chesapeake, 1680–1800.* Chapel Hill, N.C., 1986.

Lemon, James T. *The Best Poor Man's Country: A Geographical Study of Early Southeastern Pennsylvania.* Baltimore, Md., 1972.

Lockridge, Kenneth A. *A New England Town: The First Hundred Years.* New York, 1970; rev. ed. 1985.

Maier, Pauline. *From Resistance to Revolution: Colonial Radicals and the Development of American Opposition to Britain, 1765–1776.* New York, 1972.

Merrell, James H. *The Indians' New World: Catawbas and their Neighbors from European Contact through the Era of Removal.* Chapel Hill, N.C., 1989.

Miller, Perry, and Thomas H. Johnson, eds. *The Puritans.* New York, 1938. Includes "The Autobiography of Thomas Shepard."

Morgan, Edmund S. *American Slavery, American Freedom: The Ordeal of Colonial Virginia.* New York, 1975.

———, ed. *The Founding of Massachusetts: Historian and the Sources.* Indianapolis, Ind., 1964.

Morison, Samuel E. *Builders of the Bay Colony.* Boston and New York, 1930.

Nash, Gary B. *The Urban Crucible: Social Change, Political Consciousness, and the Origins of the American Revolution.* Cambridge, Mass., 1979.

Rutman, Darrett B., and Anita H. Rutman. *A Place in Time: Middlesex County, Virginia, 1650–1750.* 2 vols. New York, 1984.

Wall, Helena M. *Fierce Communion: Family and Community in Early America.* Cambridge, Mass., 1990.

Wertenbaker, Thomas Jefferson. *Torchbearer of the Revolution: The Story of Bacon's Rebellion and Its Leader.* Princeton, N.J., 1940.

White, Shane. *Somewhat More Independent: The End of Slavery in New York City, 1770–1810.* Athens, Ga., 1991.

Wood, Peter H. *Black Majority: Negroes in Colonial South Carolina from 1670 Through the Stono Rebellion.* New York, 1974.

Edward Countryman

SEE ALSO **Crime and Law Enforcement; Crises of Empire; Indian-Colonist Conflicts and Alliances; Indian-Colonist Contact; Magic and Witchcraft; Repeopling the Land; Revivalism and the Great Awakening; Slave Resistance;** and various essays in THE SOCIAL FABRIC.

THE DUTCH COLONY

ANGLO-DUTCH ANIMOSITY

PEOPLE OF DIVERSE backgrounds and beliefs coexisted, at times uneasily, in New Netherland. Discord in the colony arose from three distinct sources: the clashing interests of Long Island Puritans and Dutch authorities, the heterogeneity of the population of Dutch towns, especially New Amsterdam, and the determined efforts of minority religious groups—Quakers, Lutherans, and Jews—to gain the right to worship in public from a government opposed to toleration.

English Puritans had been permitted to found towns on Long Island beginning in the 1640s. In light of ongoing Anglo-Dutch rivalry and the proximity of the Puritan settlements in New England, the English who lived in these towns posed a threat not only to the colony's security but to its equanimity. When war erupted between the Netherlands and England in 1652 after Parliament's passage of the Navigation Act of 1651, immediate repercussions were felt in the Dutch colony. Infuriated residents of Connecticut and the New Haven colony, driven by suspicions that the Dutch were supplying arms to their Indian neighbors, prepared to attack New Netherland. Their example galvanized Long Island's Puritans to mount their own challenges to Dutch authority and in the process stir up ethnic animosity. Leaders like John Underhill and George Baxter fomented anti-Dutch feeling among Long Island's English in towns such as Hempstead, Flushing, and Gravesend. Although the end of the first Anglo-Dutch war in 1654 quashed overt resistance on Long Island, the ties between English subjects and their Dutch rulers in New Netherland remained tenuous during the final decade of the colony's history.

ELEMENTS OF SOCIAL STRAIN

The towns settled by the Dutch were by no means free of social strain. Because of its heterogeneous makeup, New Amsterdam on occasion experienced strife between members of different European groups, but such episodes tended to be personal in nature. Since no European was prohibited from participating in the economic life of the community on the basis of nationality, and since social and personal contacts between non-Dutch and Dutch were commonplace, interethnic tension was limited. Intermarriage between non-Dutch and Dutch people was not unusual, and colonists of all backgrounds were encouraged to worship at the Dutch Reformed church.

Africans forced into the status of slaves by people of European ancestry had reason to dislike their masters, but overt protests against the slaveowners were sporadic and individualized. The fact that slavery was not incorporated into the laws of the Dutch colony, the existence of realistic prospects of manumission for slaves belonging to the Dutch West India Company (WIC), and the slaves' gradual acculturation to European ways may have deterred uprisings.

DISPUTES AMONG RELIGIOUS GROUPS

The most visible conflicts in New Netherland were not interethnic quarrels but disputes among members of religious minority groups and the WIC administration. These highly charged contests over religious freedom involved three separate groups that sought the right to worship openly in the colony in which they had settled: Quakers, Lutherans, and Jews.

Quaker missionaries spread their message on Long Island in the late 1650s, winning converts in the English towns of Flushing, Jamaica, Gravesend, and Hempstead. Director-General Peter Stuyvesant had allowed English Puritans to found churches on Long Island, seeing no conflict between their form of reformed worship and that of the Dutch Reformed church. But in Stuyvesant's eyes, the radical teachings of the Quakers posed a threat to religious and social peace in the colony, and he attempted to silence adherents of the Quaker faith. Stuyvesant's repressive measures were protested in the Flushing Remonstrance for freedom of worship, but to no avail.

Substantial numbers of Lutherans from the Netherlands, Germany, and the Scandinavian countries transplanted themselves to the Dutch communities of New Netherland. Seeking to call their own minister and to worship openly, the Lutherans were rebuffed by Stuyvesant, whose actions were condoned by the directors of the WIC despite the intervention of the Lutheran Classis of Amsterdam. Stuyvesant, supported by the Reformed clergy, would only sanction gatherings of Lutherans in private homes and went so far as to deport a Lutheran minister who had been sent from the Netherlands to preach to his co-religionists. Ironically, Stuyvesant pursued a contrary policy on the Delaware after the capture of New Sweden. There, Swedish Lutherans were allowed to practice their faith freely.

Jewish refugees from the former Dutch colony in Brazil, which had fallen to the Portuguese, arrived in New Amsterdam in 1654 and soon experienced the hostility of town residents. Actively persecuted by Stuyvesant and the Dutch Reformed clergy, who sought to ban them from New Netherland, they turned to Amsterdam's powerful Jewish community for help. The directors of the WIC, reminded of the investments Jews had made in the company, decided to override Stuyvesant and ordered that the Jews be allowed to remain in New Amsterdam without molestation. Though denied the privilege of building a synagogue, New Amsterdam's Jews were given permission to worship together in private.

Although cultural differences continued to spark conflict between individuals after the English conquest of New Netherland, the policy of religious toleration instituted by the duke of York in his new colony ensured that those groups which had been harassed by the Dutch administration would no longer be denied the freedom to worship openly. Lutherans, Quakers, and Jews were allowed to practice their faiths in New York.

BIBLIOGRAPHY

Pratt, John W. *Religion, Politics, and Diversity: The Church-State Theme in New York History.* Ithaca, N.Y., 1967.
Rink, Oliver A. *Holland on the Hudson: An Economic and Social History of Dutch New York.* Ithaca, N.Y., 1986.
Smith, George L. *Religion and Trade in New Netherland: Dutch Origins and American Development.* Ithaca, N.Y., 1973.

Joyce D. Goodfriend

SEE ALSO **Crime and Law Enforcement; Indian-Colonist Conflicts and Alliances; Indian-Colonist Contact; Repeopling the Land; Rural Life; Slave Resistance;** and **Urban Life.**

THE FRENCH COLONIES

NEW FRANCE DID NOT ESCAPE social tensions any more than any overseas outpost of a European imperialistic power; from the inception of royal government in 1663 there was a consciousness of the need to maintain internal peace, order, and good government. An anonymous memorandum on colonization issued at the time stated,

"It seems that the general spirit of government must incline more to the side of leniency, it being very dangerous to use severe measures against transplanted peoples." This was especially so in Canada, where colonists were "far removed from the majesty of their prince" and his armies, and where using absolute power might prove ineffective and so encourage colonists to "readily forget respect and submission."

The extent of the "corrosive" influences of the Canadian frontier upon the region's transplanted French population is a hotly contested issue in Canadian historiography. Clerico-nationalist historians have portrayed New France as a pious, conformist, "purified society," whereas partisans of a Turnerian frontier thesis of colonial history have seen it as egalitarian and robust. The true nature of the colony would seem to lie somewhere between these two interpretations.

Canada and Acadia witnessed no slave revolts as in the Antilles, no serious bread riots as in the metropole, no mass desertion of troops, no urban crime waves, no political or religious rebellion against constituted authority. Despite the apparent social order and harmony, remarked upon by visitors such as the eighteenth-century Finnish botanist Peter Kalm, who thought Canada was heaven compared with the Anglo-American colonies, religious, social, and economic tensions did exist. Cases where the militia was called upon to furnish aid to the civil power—when government officials issued ordinances threatening severe punishments and bishops issued *mandements* (writs) threatening sanctions and even excommunication, and when military discipline was evoked—belied underlying, long-suppressed pressures. The list of capital crimes was long and the inquisitorial system of justice most daunting.

RELIGIOUS TENSIONS

Religious tensions existed from the moment the first fishing vessels trading furs as a sideline touched North American shores. Many of the early venturers were Protestants who saw their liberties increasingly circumscribed as colonization progressed. In 1627 the Company of One Hundred Associates excluded both Huguenots and the foreign-born from permanent residence, although both categories of unwanted immigrants slipped in occasionally. Once in the colony, these "undesirables" faced unrelenting pressure to conform to the religious norms. Pressures to abjure the Reformed religion were greatest when young people wished to marry, when land grants and trading licenses were issued, and when one landed in the hospital. A miller accused of casting a spell over a young woman was executed for "relapsed heresy." Although there was never any formal toleration of Protestant worship in the colony, the colonial authorities made no concerted effort to deport Huguenots such as Gabriel Bernon, Quebec's leading merchant, until 1685. These actions are understandable in the context of a state that was religious and a church that was national. Uniformity was imposed for both religious and constitutional reasons.

Royal and religious authorities deemed diversity inherently dangerous for both colonists and Native peoples. The latter had noted both dissent and deviation from orthodox teaching and practice among the French, which tended to confirm the Amerindians in their traditionally tolerant beliefs and resistance to conversion. The missionaries were particularly upset that their labors resulted in factionalism among the Hurons and Iroquois, as traditionalists and Catholic converts vied for power. Iroquoian women were particularly opposed to the missionaries, who decried matriarchy, and so were Algonquian women, whose increased work loads as a result of the fur trade seemed to justify polygamy.

These tensions in the missions were also reflected in the colonial parishes, as the immigrant clergy sought to impose post-Tridentine discipline. There was some local feeling that although the parish clergy were increasingly Canadian-born, drawn from the middle and artisan class, the metropolitan French retained control of the episcopacy, the seminaries, and prestigious communities such as the Jesuits, Sulpicians, and Ursuline sisters. Bishops François de Laval and Jean-Baptiste Saint-Vallier felt it necessary to issue *mandements* ordering the faithful to pay their tithes; women to dress modestly, especially when receiving Communion; workmen to observe Sunday rest; innkeepers to close their establishments during divine service; and men and boys of the congregation to refrain from retiring to the back of the church during the sermon to smoke and "swear the Holy Name of God and the Blessed Virgin" or to race their horses around the church. Church officials occasionally called upon the chief civil authority, the intendant, to enforce congregational maintenance of parish property and payment of the tithe, which had been reduced from one-thirteenth of the cereal crop to one-twenty-sixth with a twenty-year initial exemption because of the colonists' opposition. Some parishioners threatened their curates when parish boundaries were altered against their wishes. The clergy succeeded in imposing censorship of literature and theater, to the disgust of military officers in particular. But it never succeeded in banning the brandy traffic with the Indians or in suppressing smoking, dancing, and popular festivities. To the clergy's credit, witch-hunting was discouraged although the populace believed in witchcraft, folk healers, and a variety of charlatans.

SOCIAL CONTROL

Social tensions existed in a milieu where class and rank were of paramount importance. The common people were officially regarded as potentially dangerous and rebellious and, therefore, as requiring constant control. Group organizations—even craft guilds—were discouraged on the principle that "each should speak for himself, and none for all." Although the seigneurial ranks were not drawn exclusively from the nobility, the officer corps of the Marine troops was reserved in time to the sons of the colonial military nobility. Most persons convicted of major crimes were soldiers and lower-class males; the victims of violence were often women and native people. Louisbourg, Acadia, and Louisiana had disproportionately high rates of judicial proceedings. Amerindian slaves were more numerous than African slaves in Canadian households, while on Louisiana plantations the reverse was true. Only in Louisiana do we read of runaway slaves and popular objections to *métissage*, especially liaisons between blacks and Amerindians. State and church officials in Canada deplored the prevalence of "running the woods," on the grounds that it retarded marriage and agricul-

ture; encouraged immorality; and defied the authority of the father, the priest, and the seigneur. On the other hand, popular feeling appears to have been more favorable; the *coureurs de bois* (young men engaged in illicit trading in the hinterland) were seen as acquiring valuable practical experience that would be put to use as militiamen and *habitants,* and as supplementing farm income.

ECONOMIC TENSIONS

Economic tensions were also important in colonial life. There were shortages of food and supplies when crops failed, metropolitan imports were interrupted, and war intervened. Rationing and price controls, strongly supported by the church's teaching on just price, were imposed. But sometimes popular unrest preceded state intervention. When Montreal merchants increased the price of salt during a shortage in 1704 and again in 1705, a mob began to gather, demanding governmental intervention. Similarly, during a 1749 bread shortage in the towns, a popular demonstration elicited government action. Economic necessity was the root cause, and the protests were aimed not against established authority but at convincing a paternalistic administration to fulfill its role. Ten years later, the women of Quebec threatened the governor when war requisitioning resulted in the order that beef was to be sold only with equal amounts of horsemeat. Metropolitan soldiers were accustomed to eating horsemeat, but the Quebec housewives were scandalized and declared horsemeat consumption un-Christian, as the horse was "the friend of man." Offers to have them visit the *abbatoirs* to ascertain the quality of the meat only led to further threats, and the governor rescinded the order.

There were also economic tensions among the soldiers. Karrer's regiment of Swiss mercenaries mutinied at Louisbourg in 1744 because of poor pay, inadequate housing, inferior food, and brutal officers. A strike in the royal shipyards near Quebec in 1741 revealed yet another grievance. Skilled workers hired in France on contract were under naval discipline, while Canadian unskilled workers were hired seasonally, by the day. The metropolitan workers complained of poor housing and unfair working conditions when local workers were better paid and given leave during inclement weather. Intendant Gilles Hocquart found it necessary "to repress at the outset, and once only, by imprisonment and irons, their mutiny, which went to the point of resisting the orders of their commandant." The strikers soon recognized their error and became docile.

Constituted authority was always prepared to deal harshly with insubordination and lower-class protest. There was no working-class consciousness that would have induced Canadians and metropolitans to cooperate in the protection of their economic interests. Instead, a certain aloofness persisted between the colonials and the metropolitans. It would be premature to speak of a Canadian nationalism existing at this time, but the tensions were there to nurture such sentiments after the British conquest.

BIBLIOGRAPHY

Crowley, Terence, " 'Thunder Gusts': Popular Disturbances in Early French Canada." Canadian Historical Association, *Historical Papers/Communications historiques,* 1979.

Jaenen, Cornelius J. "French Views of New France and Canadians." In *Proceedings of the Sixth and Seventh General Meetings of the French Colonial Historical Society,* edited by James J. Cooke. Washington, D.C., 1982.

Lachance, André. "Women and Crime in Canada in the Early Eighteenth Century, 1712–1759." In *Crime and Criminal Justice in Europe and Canada,* edited by Louis A. Knafla. Waterloo, Ontario, 1981.

Moogk, Peter N. " 'Thieving Bugger's and 'Stupid Sluts': Insults and Popular Culture in New France." *William and Mary Quarterly,* 3rd ser., 36, no. 4 (1978):524–547.

Ouellet, Fernand. "The Formation of a New Society in the St. Lawrence Valley." In *Economy, Class, and Nation in Quebec,* edited by Fernand Ouellet and Jacques Barbier. Toronto, Ontario, 1991.

Séguin, Robert-Lionel. *La Vie libertine en Nouvelle-France au XVIIe siècle.* Montreal, 1972.

Cornelius John Jaenen

SEE ALSO **Crime and Law Enforcement; Indian-Colonist Conflicts and Alliances; Indian-Colonist Contact; Repeopling the Land; Rural Life; and Urban Life.**

THE SPANISH BORDERLANDS

THE STRUCTURE OF COLONIAL Spanish-American society mirrored in some ways the hierarchical system found in Spain during the *antiguo régimen.* In the New World, however, race became a much more pronounced determinant of social status, and, although far from the rigid "pigmentocracy" that some have described, the colonial order rested squarely upon racial identity. In general, those who filled the ranks of the lower economic strata tended to be Indian, black, or *casta* (racially mixed). Conversely, high-level civil and ecclesiastical officials, as well as the "great families" who controlled much of the agricultural and mineral wealth, if not the top positions of government, tended to be *españoles* (Spaniards). They reinforced their elite positions by modifying the Iberian ideal *limpieza de sangre* (purity of blood) and fitting it to the multiracial circumstances of the New World. It should be noted, however, that in all parts of Spanish America "racial" designations were somewhat fluid, and they generally reflected cultural affinity more than biological attributes.

Perhaps to a greater extent than elsewhere, the borderlands afforded an environment conducive to social mobility. These provinces lay at a great distance from the rest of the empire, leaving them vulnerable to attack, and the settlers' survival depended upon intergroup cooperation. Still, these people shared with their counterparts elsewhere in the Hispanic world common views regarding the construction and proper expression of social standing. Inevitably, conflicts arose. When they did, the complex and delicate interplay of racial, economic, and political issues at times pushed to the limit the colonial ideal of an orderly social hierarchy.

SOCIAL DIVISIONS

Compared with the multidimensional urban centers of the viceroyalty—Mexico City, Guadalajara, or even Durango and Zacatecas—social arrangements in the borderlands were relatively simple. A limited *rico* (wealthy) class developed in some areas at a rather late date, but no "great families" achieved the status or wealth evident elsewhere in the empire. While the generalized poverty of the borderlands had a leveling effect on society, distinct groups nevertheless existed that sought to consolidate or enhance their positions within the local social hierarchy. The diverse aims of these social groups at times conflicted, accounting for much of the tension in society.

As occupants of the upper strata, colonial administrators possessed the insignia of their hierarchical station—they were pure-blood Spaniards, *peninsulares* (born in Spain), and embodied the authority of the king. As representatives of the Crown, and as career bureaucrats or military officers, provincial governors from Florida to California placed great importance on fulfilling the directives of their superiors. Above all else, the guiding principle for these Crown appointees was the maintenance of harmonious and peaceful relations among all inhabitants of their jurisdictions. This prime directive often stood at odds with the aims of those who sought to promote their particular positions. Hapsburg-era governors (to 1700) differed somewhat from this profile. Typically having purchased their offices and seeking a return on their investment, governors in seventeenth-century New Mexico, for example, squeezed all they could from the province. The Bourbon policy of merit-based appointment in the early eighteenth century brought significant relief, however, and a new class of bureaucrat was able to gain more from an exemplary review of office than from bald economic exploitation. Generally speaking, provincial governors represented a source of moderation and control over the activities of local social groups, and their actions normally reflected the Crown's aim of limiting the power of any particular bloc.

Like civil officials, the clergy enjoyed the status and the privilege that went with their positions of authority and their racial purity. Concerns of the religious elite, however, were considerably narrower than those of the governors. In the borderlands, missionization was the principal reason for clerical presence. Indeed, at different times all of the borderland provinces save Louisiana experienced periods of vigorous evangelization among the Indians. Mission fathers also ministered to the Hispanic settlers and, as agents of the Holy Office of the Inquisition, sought to maintain religious orthodoxy and purity of thought. In promoting and defending their multiple endeavors, missionaries frequently clashed with civil administrators and settlers over a variety of issues.

Below the administrators of the colonial regime stood the Hispanic settlers—*los paisanos*—a group that displayed considerable racial and economic diversity. As elsewhere in Spanish America, social status depended upon a variety of factors, including wealth, prestige of occupation, and race. If frontier conditions weakened the racial hierarchy found in other parts of Spanish America, most Hispanics in the borderlands still claimed to be *español* (Spanish). And they did so precisely because they recognized the preeminence of that designation. Not all *españoles* were of the provincial elite, but the elite were invariably *españoles*. In some areas, several families distinguished themselves economically—mainly by raising livestock—and a *rico* class emerged by the end of the colonial period. Pursuit of their economic goals at times brought members of this group into conflict with missionaries, civil officials, or Indians. These elite families played an important role in the second tier of colonial government, and during the constitutional phase of the early nineteenth century they eagerly took part in local representative assemblies. The Crown's policy of preferment of *peninsulares* for high-level government posts does not seem to have been a major cause for local discontent in the borderlands, unlike other regions.

Though subordinate in the social hierarchy, other Hispanics of various racial mixtures often shared many of the cultural values of their social betters. These farmers, artisans, and soldiers displayed considerable respect for the authority of the Crown, the church, and the family, which undergirded the social ideal of community harmony and cooperation. Thus, in a precapitalist, patriarchal environment where mutual social obligations were important, the lower strata of *paisanos* normally identified with the aspirations and aims of the larger community. Little evidence suggests that a "class" struggle characterized social relations among Hispanics.

Distinct from all others, because of their juridical and cultural identifiers, were Indians. As with Hispanic *castas,* we know little of their aspirations beyond mere survival. While Indians occupied the lower rungs of the social hierarchy, the Crown viewed them as minors to be protected by the law and instructed in the Christian faith. Their defense was considered an important obligation of both civil and ecclesiastical officials. Mission activity in much of the borderlands altered drastically the lifeways of many local Native inhabitants. Some Indian groups disappeared altogether or found their cultural identities altered beyond recognition. Secularization of the missions in Texas and California brought results for Native Americans that ranged from integration into the larger society as laborers and ranch hands to flight beyond the limits of Hispanic control. The experience of the Pueblo Indians of New Mexico differs significantly, however. Their political arrangements and modes of economic exploitation were compatible in large measure with Spanish notions of orderliness. Various Pueblo groups not only survived the period of Spanish sovereignty, they also became vital components of colonial New Mexico society as artisans, producers of foodstuffs, and members of the provincial militia.

A more specific irritant among social groups in the Spanish Borderlands was the competition for sparse resources. Land and water were the most readily exploitable and were the cause of frequent disputes. Access to and control of these vital resources meant nothing less than survival in the borderlands. Often bitter and acrimonious conflict over land and water—especially in the Southwest—pitted both individuals and groups against one another. Yet nothing like the later range wars of the American West developed in these regions while they were under Spanish control, which perhaps reveals the generally cooperative, communally oriented character of Hispanic frontier life, as well as the degree to which the Crown maintained effective control of its subjects.

For example, in San Antonio, where five missions lay in the midst of the Hispanic population, a three-way struggle over these precious commodities emerged between Franciscans, Canary Islanders, and other civil settlers. Typically, the Crown played a mediating role in resolving these conflicts, and no group gained a clear-cut advantage. By the end of the eighteenth century, as *isleños* merged with other settlers and acquired

a *tejano* identity, and as missions became secularized, individualistic litigation replaced group action.

Like their Hispanic neighbors, Pueblo Indians in New Mexico also litigated over land and water rights. Their consistent and often successful use of the Spanish legal system to defend their territorial base was crucial in their cultural survival. Indians in other parts of the borderlands did not engage in group litigation because they were under the much closer scrutiny and care of the mission fathers, who litigated on their behalf.

Like land and water, Indian labor figured as another exploitable commodity, and social tensions in the borderlands at times centered on this issue. In California, missionaries kept a watchful eye on their neophytes to ensure that they remained in the mission, isolated from the temptations of nearby pueblos and *ranchos.* Indians were not only souls to save for God, but also valuable workers who were necessary for the successful operation of the mission economy. For the emerging nonmission ranchos, Indians represented potential labor as tenders of livestock, artisans, and farmers. Evidence from Texas, too, indicates that neophytes there left the missions and merged into the local civilian population of San Antonio as laborers. Missionaries often expressed concern that they were losing their workers. Similarly, a great struggle between clergy and civilians over the allocation of Pueblo labor caused a calamitous political rift in New Mexico during the seventeenth century.

MANIFESTATIONS OF SOCIAL TENSIONS

Inhabitants of the borderlands shared notions of a proper social order that they expressed in innumerable ways in their individual and group behavior. Most social tensions emerged in behaviors that challenged the social ideal. Authorities often treated these departures from the norm as the aberrant behavior of individuals and imposed varying degrees of correction and guidance to reaffirm the values of the culture. Instances of group violence were rare, but notable exceptions existed.

The Pueblo Revolt of 1680 looms as perhaps the most violent manifestation of social tensions in borderland history, and it serves well to illustrate how the conflicting aims of various groups contributed to social conflict. Prior to the rebellion, Indians in New Mexico had been subjected to two formidable institutions that had strong economic dimensions—the *encomienda* and the mission. The *encomienda*—a system of private labor and tribute jurisdiction—became especially abusive under a corrupt seventeenth-century civil administration. Harsh tribute and labor quotas made life miserable for the Native inhabitants. While Franciscan missionaries repeatedly sought to ameliorate this suffering at the hands of civilians, they, too, subjected the Pueblo to strict mission discipline and persecuted with rigor traditional Native religious practices. In the struggle for control of the province, the Franciscans used their most powerful weapon—the Inquisition—to cow the rival bloc. Both groups pursued their particular aims with selfish abandon.

Drained of labor and resources by both systems, faced with demographic decline, and, by the mid seventeenth century, under attack by mounted Apache raiders, the Pueblo rebelled in August 1680. Uncharacteristic political unity made possible their initial triumph. The Pueblo destroyed mission churches, government documents, and most other vestiges of Spanish rule, and surviving Hispanic settlers fled for their lives southward to El Paso del Norte (present-day Ciudad Juárez).

Spaniards returned, led by don Diego de Vargas, and recolonized the upper Rio Grande Valley in the 1690s, but relations between the Pueblo and the Hispanics entered a new phase of pragmatic accommodation. The oppressive *encomienda* became a thing of the past; the new Hispanic settlers were mostly freeholders of small farms who relied on their own labor. The mission system reappeared, but in a weakened version that allowed considerable expression of Pueblo ceremonialism. New Mexico had taken on new strategic importance internationally. To hold the province, the Crown seemed determined to play a more vigorous role in balancing the aims of different groups. For their part, the Pueblo recognized Spanish political authority, became crucial constituents in provincial military defense, and used the courts to resolve conflicts with Hispanic neighbors. The Pueblo Revolt of 1680 represents a watershed in Spanish-Pueblo relations, for after that episode the Pueblo negotiated in colonial society from a much stronger position.

Another culturally distinct group also rebelled against Spanish rule. French-speaking Louisianans rose against the first governor of Spanish Louisiana in October 1768, shortly after the effective change of sovereignty. Perhaps suspicious of a "foreign" presence, and angered by the antismuggling and antiprofiteering measures of Governor Antonio de Ulloa, New Orleans merchants fomented a rebellion that played on the economic fears of the local population. Recognizing his untenable position, Ulloa fled the province to avoid bloodshed. Spanish rule returned authoritatively in the figure of General Alejandro O'Reilly, who disembarked at New Orleans with some twenty-one hundred troops in August 1769. O'Reilly quickly restored political hegemony, brought the rebel leaders to justice— he executed five—and granted amnesty to all other participants. He also restructured the political and judicial systems of the province, instituting a policy of significant local participation in key institutions such as the *cabildo*. From that point, French- and Spanish-speaking Louisianans enjoyed relatively harmonious relations.

Collective social tensions also emerged in Texas in the proto-independence uprising of 1811. Linked to the larger movement of Fathers Miguel Hidalgo y Costilla and José María Morelos y Pavón in central Mexico, the San Antonio rebellion espoused the same egalitarian and pro-American principles. A retired militia captain, Juan Bautista de las Casas, pronounced in favor of the revolutionaries and successfully ousted royalist Governor Manuel María de Salcedo. Bolstered initially by the enlisted personnel at the San Antonio garrison, Las Casas maintained control of the province for nearly two months. However, Las Casas's arbitrary actions, his alienation of the local upper crust, his failure to rally the masses, and the misfortunes of the Hidalgo movement all conspired to weaken his position of leadership. With little difficulty, royalist sympathizers turned him over to Spanish forces, who tried him and found him guilty of treason. While the Texas rebellion of 1811 failed, as did the Hidalgo and Morelos movements, it signaled an early challenge to the social ideals of the *antiguo régimen*. Important and dramatic as they might be, these scattered instances of violent social tensions are exceptional in colonial borderlands history. Less explosive manifestations of social conflict were far more common.

Because racial identity was so important, tension in society often surfaced in the form of racial slurs. Predominantly of mixed blood, Hispanic settlers in the borderlands nevertheless referred to themselves as *españoles* (Spaniards), a term that they surely believed placed them in the upper echelons of the colonial hierarchy. Attacks upon one's "Spanishness" were not taken lightly, and racially tinged "fighting words" might easily bring latent hostility to a head.

Consider the confrontation between two New Mexicans of note, Fernando Durán y Chaves and Juan González Bas. Having been appointed in 1712 as the new *alcalde mayor* of the Albuquerque district, González Bas appeared before Durán y Chaves to take possession of the office. Don Fernando refused to receive him, saying that the governor had sent "an Indian for an *alcalde*." González protested that he was a "good man and not an Indian," but this only enraged don Fernando, who labeled his antagonist a "dishonorable lying Indian dog" and proceeded to assault him physically. With the aid of bystanders, Juan González Bas managed to escape the wrath of don Fernando, as well as of others of the Durán y Chaves clan who pursued him with swords and knives as he made his mounted getaway. Fernando Durán y Chaves's eminent position in New Mexican society undoubtedly saved him from any severe punishment, but the provincial governor did insist that he apologize to *alcalde* González Bas, who then dropped his civil and criminal suit against the patriarch.

If spectacular, the racially charged episode just described was not extraordinary. Because of the construction of colonial society, racial designators might degrade an adversary and reaffirm one's superior position. Significantly, both parties in this incident shared a dim view of what it meant to be Indian. Epithets such as "Indian dog," "mulatto," and *"morisco"* (a Mexicanism for mulatto-Spanish mix) appear frequently in the trial records throughout the borderlands, often in connection with some altercation.

Not surprisingly, social tensions between *peninsulares* and *criollos* also revealed themselves in the context of race. Royal and ecclesiastical officials from outside the province, who were almost invariably from Spain, often employed derogatory racial terminology in their descriptions of the local citizenry. Fray Juan Agustín Morfi, for example, described the members of the *cabildo* of San Antonio, most of them descendants of Canary Islanders, as "a ragged bunch of every color"; of the *alcaldes mayores* of New Mexico, he wrote that they were "unfortunates without education or breeding, mostly half-breeds with an occasional Spaniard." Those on the margins of colonial society, too, were quick to note and to manipulate its racial distinctions. A Spanish missionary reported in 1743, for example, that the Calusa Indians of south Florida demanded that the Spanish feed and clothe them, but "not with burlap, which they detest as identified with blacks."

The manifestation of social tensions in racial terminology reveals the far-reaching importance of race in the construction of identity in Spanish colonial society. Racial categories may have been fluid in the borderlands, but it is evident that nearly all components of colonial society recognized the importance of racial distinctions. In employing them, they replicated and perpetuated the hierarchical social order found throughout the Spanish colonial world.

BIBLIOGRAPHY

Castañeda, Carlos E. *Our Catholic Heritage in Texas, 1519–1936.* 7 vols. Austin, Tex., 1936–1958.

Gutiérrez, Ramón A. *When Jesus Came, the Corn Mothers Went Away: Marriage, Sexuality, and Power in New Mexico, 1500–1846.* Stanford, Calif., 1991.

Jones, Oakah L. *Los Paisanos: Spanish Settlers on the Northern Frontier of New Spain.* Norman, Okla., 1979.

Kessell, John L. *Kiva, Cross, and Crown: The Pecos Indians and New Mexico, 1540–1840.* Washington, D.C., 1979.

Poyo, Gerald E., and Gilberto M. Hinojosa, eds. *Tejano Origins in Eighteenth-Century San Antonio.* Austin, Tex., 1991.

Scholes, France V. *Troublous Times in New Mexico, 1659–1670.* Albuquerque, N.Mex., 1942.

Charles R. Cutter

SEE ALSO **Crime and Law Enforcement; Indian-Colonist Conflicts and Alliances; Indian-Colonist Contact; Mission Communities; Native American Religions; Repeopling the Land;** and various essays in THE SOCIAL FABRIC.

X

FOLKWAYS

RECREATIONS
HOME AND HEARTH
FESTIVAL TRADITIONS
DRESS
MANNERS
TRAVEL AND LODGING

RECREATIONS

SPORT AND RECREATION are the most underrated and underrepresented aspects of colonial North American history. Because leisure activity involves deliberate decisions as to the discretionary use of time, the fundamental values and conditions of society are revealed more clearly in how people play, sport, and recreate than in how they work, war, or worship. Yet Native Americans, thanks to anthropologists, are the only people whose "sporting culture" has received serious study. Amateur historians have long recognized the importance of recreation, but only since the 1970s have academics begun to study the social, cultural, and economic importance of sport.

Conventional wisdom held that British colonists—and by implication all colonial North Americans—had "little time or inclination for fun and games." The pioneering historian of sport in the United States, John Betts, declared, "Fighting Indians, clearing new lands, and building towns allowed little time for most colonists to devote to merrymaking. Only after two centuries of settlement in the New World would sport become an important institution in American life." As recently as 1978 the then leading text in the field, *Saga of American Sport,* stated, "The most significant point that can be made about sport in colonial America is how insignificant it was to the lives of most colonists."

The research of historians and ethnographers demonstrates that scholars have severely underestimated both the pervasiveness of sporting cultures and the popularity of recreational pastimes. People found—or made—considerable time for recreations and embraced leisure activities as a precious commodity not to be taken for granted. Realizing that sometimes a game was just a game, they also recognized that play was purposeful as an important instrument of social control and cultural conditioning. Recreation was an almost universally popular activity, and most people spent more time participating in leisure pastimes than in any other endeavor except labor. Nonetheless, much research remains to be done, especially on New France and the northern borderlands of New Spain, before one can truly appreciate the importance of sport and recreation in the daily lives of colonial North Americans.

DEFINITIONS AND THEORIES

Western Europeans and North Americans did not systematically categorize leisure activities prior to the nineteenth century. "Amusements," "diversions," "pastimes," and "recreations" were all-inclusive terms embracing activities as diverse as ball games and horse races, boxing and fishing, dances and quilting bees, musical performances and theater productions. "Play," "games," "recreations," and "sports" were used interchangeably or not, depending on participants and circumstances.

This essay emphasizes those leisure-time physical activities—recreations (informal, individual endeavors), play (spontaneous, nonserious activity), games (rule-bound play), contests (formal tests of individual skills), and sport (organized, physical competitions)—that not only mirrored cultural values and behavioral norms but also dramatically effected changes in belief systems and behavioral patterns. (Treated only in passing are children's toys and games, adult games of chance, sporting equipment, and those activities later included among the "fine arts." Nor is consideration given to such leisure pursuits as singing, playing musical instruments, sewing, reading, writing, and drinking.) Sport and recreation were both pleasurable and purposeful pursuits which were deeply integrated into the social life of a given community, reflected and reinforced cultural traditions, and enhanced the creative impulses and ego gratification of individuals and groups. No less important, they served as an outlet for repressed antisocial feelings and as a mechanism for fostering group solidarity and social cohesion. Recreational activities and attitudes were not static but evolved in concert with changes in material conditions and cultural circumstances. These pastimes thereby affected social structures, networks, and relationships.

NATIVE AMERICAN RECREATIONS

Sports and recreations played a more prominent role in the lives of Native American peoples than any other inhabitants of colonial North America. Universality amid diversity best characterizes the recreations of Indians. The approximately five million Indians living north of modern Mexico (one million east of the Mississippi River), speaking over three hundred languages and many more dialects at the onset of European colonization, exhibited remarkable similarity in sporting activities in terms of both form and function. Physical, competitive recreations were integral parts of virtually every phase of their existence. Although Indians frequently engaged in recreations purely for pleasure, the activities termed "sports" were intimately related to tribal ceremonials and rites: to cure illness, prepare for war, ensure the fertility of plants and animals, or pro-

duce rain. In some cases—for example, the Iroquois Thunder Ceremony, the Arkansas divination contest between the Earth People and Sky People, and the Jicarilla Apache adolescent male "relay race"—it is impossible to distinguish between the sacred and the secular natures of the activity.

Indian recreations blurred the distinction between work and play. Children's games turned on preparation for adult roles. Women transformed utilitarian crafts into artistic creations. Dances brought all age groups and both sexes together in an activity that was frequently both ceremonial and recreational. In addition to deriving pleasure and provisions from hunting and fishing, adolescent and adult males participated in contests of strength and dexterity—archery, wrestling, footracing—that honed survival skills. While individual sports were important in conferring personal status and tribal leadership roles, group games played the most important role in Native American cultures.

Games between or among tribes, villages, or clans were often violent and preceded by careful preparation, including adherence to dietary restrictions and sexual abstinence. Group sports were approached and executed with a seriousness that reflected their important political, social, and economic functions. Intergroup contests were used for a variety of ends, including resolving disputes short of war, (re)allocating economic resources, and exchanging goods and services. Intragroup sport was a principal mechanism of cultural maintenance—discharging religious functions, promoting group identity and gender roles, and developing leadership and decision-making models.

Characterized by tribal cohesion and ceremonial play, Indian recreations more closely resembled the popular village pastimes of Europe than the recreations of the British, French, or Spanish colonies. The major exception was the absence of animal blood sports, perhaps an expression of the Native American respect for and reliance upon wildlife. It was, then, the sacralization and communalization of play that most distinguished Indian from European sport.

Native American recreations also illustrate the transcultural universality of certain basic games and contests. Despite regional and tribal variations, ball games were conspicuous in virtually every Native American community. Tribes from Canada to the Gulf of Mexico and on the Great Plains—but not the Southwest—played variations of the game known as *baggataway* or lacrosse in the Great Lakes region and stickball in the Southeast, the oldest North American sport in terms of origin and continued existence. Games involving kicking and throwing balls were universals. Like stickball, kickball games generally involved competition between tribes, villages, or clans and were played over great distances, sometimes from one village to another. Other ball games—handball, volleyball (sans net), dodgeball, and juggling—were intravillage activities. Southeastern Indians played a game involving tossing a ball into a receptacle atop a pole.

Indian women participated in sports as well as recreations. Except for male exclusivity in those sports directly associated with religious functions, such as stickball and the hoop-and-javelin throw of the Pueblo peoples, women played most of the games that men did. The nature of their participation varied. Sometimes women joined in the games with men and at other times played by themselves; sometimes they used men's rules and equipment, and sometimes played with modified rules and equipment. When not participating in games, girls and women were conspicuous spectators. Given the matrilineal organization of some Native American societies, Indian women were accorded a greater political and recreational role than in European cultures.

Although Native American games were little affected by Europeans, Indian hunting and fishing techniques and some sports were adopted by Europeans. Indians competed with whites only in certain activities, usually recreations or physical contests. This was because Native American games generally involved a religious or political dimension absent in European sport. The major exception was gambling. As inveterate gamblers, Indians found French and British frontiersmen eager to bet on contests. The frontiersmen even proved anxious to play games of chance. Whites were not involved, at least with Indians, in the heavy gambling that accompanied intertribal competitions. Although there was little sporting assimilation between Native Americans and Europeans, recreational activities greatly facilitated cultural accommodation between Indians and the white colonists.

THE SPANISH BORDERLANDS

As with the British and French empires, recreations in New Spain reflected the purpose of Spanish colonization but were to a much greater degree influenced by environment and the indigenous population. From the 1520s and 1530s Spain was intent upon the political, economic, and religious conquest of Native society. Conquest led to acculturation in most of the Viceroyalty of New Spain, the region north of the Isthmus of Panama, as well as to the south in the Viceroyalty of Peru. However, accommodation was the rule in the northern Mexican provinces. Because Spanish authorities were unable to gain effective control over the scattered pueblos of New Mexico, the Native peoples remained physically isolated and culturally autonomous. Similarly, the Spanish towns, missions, *presidios,* and haciendas widely dispersed across the high desert frontier had little contact with each other and even less with the Indians.

As a result, the Spanish Borderlands featured two distinct social and recreational worlds—the one Indian and the other Spanish. And each was remarkably traditional: the Pueblo culture did not change fundamentally during three hundred years of Spanish rule, while the early Hispanics developed a distinctive borderland culture as their numbers were not increased appreciably by emigrants from Mexico or Iberia.

Spanish recreations mirrored a remarkably traditional and class-oriented society. There was a broad demarcation between the *ricos* (wealthy) and poor on the one hand, and the descendants of the hidalgos (original landed nobility) and those lacking honor and privilege—Indians and slaves—on the other. Occupation and pigmentation created numerous other, often fine, class lines. More class-conscious than British or French colonials, the Hispanos were the most faithful in continuing the traditional Old World games and recreations of children and adults. Recreational ethnocentricity undoubtedly reflected their status as a conspicuous minority in a forbidding land surrounded by the personification of "savagery."

549

Ironically, drama, an entertainment usually reserved for the elite, was a favorite leisure pastime of the entire Spanish community. In fact, the first known North American plays were performed in 1598—the first in April, in a meadow near the present city of El Paso, and the second in July, entirely on horseback at the San Juan pueblo. There being no meaningful distinction between folk plays and professional theater, every Spanish village had a troop of entertainers who staged plays and musicals. Also popular were the *matachinas,* or ballad dances. (Indians traditionally performed dance-dramas but with rare exceptions did not incorporate the Spanish variety or perform with Spaniards.) Plays invariably evoked historical or traditional religious themes, thereby dramatically reinforcing cultural values. Children's games were heavily imitative of adult life and oriented toward cultural conditioning, whether of class, religion, or gender.

Class distinctions were visible in the most popular pastime in New Mexico, the fiesta. Wealth and status determined the magnitude and opulence of the parties celebrating personal, civil, or ecclesiastical events. The fiesta was the major social activity with a decidedly New World flavor; the colonial music and dances were not linked to the folk music or folk dances (such as the flamenco) of Iberia. In fact, fiesta folk dances displayed marked regional variation and pronounced Indian characteristics.

Fiestas were accompanied by a variety of games and contests, usually involving gambling. In the same manner and for the same psychological and social imperatives as planters in the southern colonies, the caballeros (gentlemen) of the northern borderlands of New Spain wagered frequently and recklessly on the roll of the dice, the turn of a card, the spin of a roulette wheel, or the speed of a horse. On occasion entire ranchos changed hands. Those of lesser rank were no less fond of gambling, but tested their luck and skill mostly in private or in taverns. Significantly, the favorite rendezvous in Santa Fe was a gambling saloon.

Aside from the transculturally popular field and combat sports, Spanish men displayed their masculinity and effected male bonding through the *corridas de caballo y de gallo.* Horse races were sprints, not run on organized oval courses. Most popular was the *corrida de gallo*—the bloody "rooster race" derived from the Moors. The contest began with two teams of riders facing each other, seventy-five to one hundred yards (68 to 90 meters) from a hen or rooster buried up to its neck. On signal one rider from each team attempted, at full gallop, to grab the bird. If successful, the horseman and his comrades rode off, chased by the "losers," who tried to snatch away the chicken. The prize frequently changed hands, and the "race" continued until little or nothing remained of the bird. Another version, *correr el gallo,* was a group event in which riders raced en masse toward a rooster, head and neck greased, that was tied by its legs to a stake driven into the ground. The horseman who successfully snatched away the bird was pursued by the others, who pulled the fowl to pieces. This southwestern group version of "gander pulling" was primarily a male activity, although in some villages women (*las galleras*) participated. The "rooster race" was the lone Spanish sport adopted by the Pueblo peoples.

Ultimately, the greatest impact on Spanish recreations came not from Indians or Mexican migrants but from Anglos. Opened in 1821–1822 and extending almost eight hundred miles (1,280 kilometers) from Westport (now Kansas City), Missouri, to the New Mexico capital, the Santa Fe Trail brought hordes of Americans into the Spanish Borderlands. In addition to turning squalid Santa Fe into a raucous, wide-open outpost, the growing number of Americans, many of whom settled in the region, brought cultural baggage as well as trade goods. In time "hispanized English games" and American sports first supplemented and then surpassed traditional Spanish recreations, especially in the larger towns of Albuquerque, Santa Cruz, Santa Fe, and El Paso. The coming of the Americans completed the enduring, distinctive tripartite cultural life, including recreations, of the southwest: Anglo, Hispanic, and Indian.

NEW FRANCE

Notwithstanding explorations as early as 1535, New France did not develop as a viable colony until the first permanent settlement at Quebec in 1608. For a century and a half the French colony territorially dominated the continent, embracing the entire region north of the Saint Lawrence River and extending southward through the Mississippi Valley to the Gulf of Mexico. But because of the nature of French colonization, New France exerted little influence in North America other than in Anglo-French military and diplomatic affairs. That France undertook colonization in North America not to create a homeland for migrants but instead to block British continental expansion while exploiting the natural resources of the area through commercial intercourse with Indians, meant that the colony never developed a significant European population. Thus the French settlers retained their language and religion but otherwise created a new culture, including recreations, because of demographics, environment, and the proximity to large numbers of Indians.

It was demographically impossible to sustain traditional French popular recreations in the New World. Organized around civic holidays, harvest festivals, and ecclesiastical celebrations, the *fête populaire* of the ancien régime was a communal affair wherein the village, neighborhood, or guild determined the nature of the activities. (In contrast with England, traditional French society had no concept of personal leisure time.) Such popular recreations were impossible in New France, where seventy thousand residents of French ancestry in 1760 (the vast majority being colonial-born) lived in an area twenty times larger than France. Rugged mountains, dense forests, and an abundance of lakes and rivers influenced recreational opportunities, as did extreme winter conditions for upward of six months in what is now known as Canada and the Great Lakes region. Recreations in New France thus were of three distinct varieties: (1) those of the indigenous Native American populations performed apart from the French; (2) those resulting from cultural interchange between Indians and Europeans; and (3) those reflecting the traditions of France and practiced mainly in and around Montreal, Quebec, and Trois-Rivières.

Unlike the British colonies, New France had no frontier in the sense of an expanding line of European settlement. The primary French contacts with the numerous Algonquian or Iroquoian villages were made by Jesuit priests, *coureurs de bois* (trappers or traders), voyageurs (salaried transporters of trade goods and people), and soldiers. Although limited by widely scattered forts and trading posts, such contact proved critical in shaping recreational activities. In the *pays d'en haut* (a general term for the Great Lakes region meaning "middle ground"), Frenchmen quickly learned techniques of hunting and fishing from Indians and transformed modes of transportation into competitive sports—canoeing and footraces in summer and skiing, ice skating, and snowshoe races in winter. Missionaries and frontiersmen frequently participated in physical contests, against each other or Indians, in order to impress the Native Americans with their courage and strength, and thus gain respect. Footraces were the most popular form of competition between Indians and Frenchmen, and, following the Native American tradition, were distance events, typically five kilometers (just over three miles) long. (Indians also adopted European ways, and by the 1680s commonly affixed sails to canoes for travel and sporting purposes.) Most sporting events were informal, although Kaskaskia was famous for annual canoe races. With livestock in short supply, the few horses in the colony were used for work and travel, not racing. Gambling was a way of life in the backcountry, and the French found the Native Americans, especially the Illinois, eager to participate in gaming activities. Military and combat contests, such as target shooting and wrestling, were also popular backcountry recreations, as were such work variants as tree felling and rail splitting. In contrast with the British, French frontiersmen seem not to have continued the bloody animal sports of the Old World or adopted the New World pastime of "gouging."

Lacrosse demonstrates the difficulty in ascertaining the extent of recreational acculturation. The stick-and-ball game named lacrosse by the French because the stick resembled a bishop's crozier was played by virtually every tribe in New France. It also bore striking similarity to the popular French game *la soule* (and the medieval *shouler a la crosse*), played by teams from neighboring parishes or villages. The basis for lacrosse was likely the Indian game, adopted readily by the French because of its similarity to *la soule*.

RECREATIONS

Recreations in New France reflected a paternalistic, hierarchical society where church and state exercised greater control over life than elsewhere in North America. Rigid class distinctions separated the pastimes of nobles, military and government officers, the middle class, and an extensive "lower order" composed of farmers, garrison troops, urban laborers, traders, and trappers. Class conventions often broke down in the backcountry, except on military posts, but were strictly followed in the population centers, especially Quebec, the seat of the intendant. In 1727 the intendant, Claude-Thomas DuPuy, authorized the opening of a Quebec billiards parlor on condition that laborers not be allowed to play on workdays. Montreal and Trois-Rivières offered a more varied and relaxed recreational environment with fives (handball), bowls, battledore (badminton without a net), shuttlecock, and various ball games enjoying popularity. Taverns, offering spiritous beverages as well as gambling activities ranging from Pharaoh to roulette, were the recreational centers for the urban lower classes, while the French elite favored dinner and dancing parties, hunting excursions, and riding or racing carriages (calèches) in the summer and sleighs (carrioles) in winter. Numerous court cases arising from the disorderly conduct and verbal assaults so offensive to a society preoccupied with rank resulted from recreational rivalries, especially those involving gambling. Neither yeomen farmers (habitants) nor peasants who worked seignorial estates had as much time as their British counterparts for recreations other than field sports and the collective work-socials associated with rural life because of the intensity of labor during the short growing season.

The cession of New France by conquest to Great Britain in 1763 fundamentally altered recreational life. As in the mother country, New France developed no systematic distinction between work and play or the concept of recreation for recreation's sake. However, sport follows the flag and, aided by extensive Scottish immigration to Canada, British sporting traditions quickly spread into the former French Empire. Curling was introduced by British soldiers during the Seven Years' War, and the codification of ice hockey and lacrosse, the first organized team sports, commenced shortly after British occupation. Quebec had a formal horse racing course in 1764 and a turf club by 1789. Sports and recreations, relatively underdeveloped and culturally unimportant in New France, expanded dramatically in variety, sophistication, and social significance in British Canada.

BRITISH AMERICA

Founded considerably later than New Spain and contemporaneously with New France, the British Empire in North America (1607) rapidly moved to a position of political, economic, and military dominance in North America despite occupying only the eastern seaboard of the continent. The same is true for British recreational activities, which exhibited much greater variety, complexity, and popularity than those of other colonial or Native peoples. The explanation extends beyond the facts that Protestantism encouraged sport more than did Catholicism and that Britain established self-sufficient, permanent settlements in North America whereas France and Spain focused on the economic exploitation of the environment and indigenous populations. Reinforced by governmental and intellectual sanctions, the folk games and recreations that swept western Europe from 1500 to 1800 flourished most widely in the British Isles, producing a deeply rooted sporting culture and consciousness that influenced the recreational activities and attitudes of British America.

The hard realities of establishing viable communities in the wilderness initially retarded the development of recreational activities, but an extensive and distinctive American sporting culture soon appeared. Some Old World pastimes were replicated, but many were modified, some were abandoned, and a few uniquely American sports were created owing to the demographic and settlement patterns, ethnic and racial heterogeneity, and abundance of land that constituted a markedly different recreational environment. (The twelve contiguous Atlantic Coast colonies and Delaware were three times the size of Great Britain with only one-third of the population; as late as 1790 approximately 4 percent of colonials lived in cities of more than eight thousand residents, and outside New England the vast majority of people were scattered across the countryside or dispersed along the coastline or navigable rivers.) Moreover, it was impossible to perpetuate the sporting life of Great Britain without the social, cultural, and legal influences that had both defined and regulated English recreations. The absence in America of an aristocracy privileged by law undermined the customary distinctions between elite or gentry and popular or vernacular recreations. The indigenous colonial elite that emerged by the eighteenth century did not, except for landed gentry in the South, become principal patrons of sport, as had the upper class in England.

Colonial recreations also escaped the close scrutiny and regulation of an established ecclesiastical hierarchy and centralized civil authority. Neither the church calendar, with its numerous feast days, nor the traditional agricultural festivals, which occasioned village folk games in England, were implemented in America. Sabbatarianism was the lone Old World influence to affect recreations in British America significantly. Efforts to ensure that the Lord's Day was observed religiously was part of the evolution of late medieval to early modern Christianity in western Europe, but only in England did the conservative religious impulses combine with political struggles and economic forces to produce Sabbatarianism. To Puritans popular recreations and profanation of the Sabbath were linked not only because the former were considered to be inherently licentious but also because they were thought to interfere with worship, promote idleness and dissipation, disrupt community order, undermine the new Protestant gospel of work, and distract males from social and familial responsibilities. Restrictive Puritan sporting policies gained ascendancy during the Commonwealth of the 1640s and 1650s, then were replaced by a far more liberal attitude toward recreations following the Stuart restoration in 1660.

Every British American colony enacted laws prohibiting Sunday sport, whether "honest recreations" such as hunting and bowling or "unlawful pastimes" such as gambling and bear baiting, but the nature and implementation of Sabbatarian statutes varied according to time, place, and circumstance. Enforcement was especially strict in New England, where all secular and sectarian holy day celebrations, including Christmas, as well as all labor, recreations, travels, and "idle" activity were banned. While less restrictive than in Congregational New England, Sabbatarianism was pervasive throughout Middle Atlantic colonies, particularly in Pennsylvania where the Quaker dominated legislature expanded a 1682 ban of "rude and riotous sports" into a comprehensive set of 'blue laws.' Preachments and practices did not always coincide in the southern colonies, but Sabbatarianism remained the rule until the mid eighteenth century.

Sabbatarianism eroded during the early eighteenth century. With the growing secularization of society, the rise of cosmopolitan urban centers, and the liberalizing effects of the Enlightenment, legislative and ecclesiastical proscriptions against sport and recreation increasingly clashed with the preferences of the citizenry. It was simply impossible to enforce laws and admonitions which did not meet with the approval of residents: Regulating tavern amusements was one thing; suppressing outdoor recreations, quite another. Besides, the religious pronouncements regarding sport were ambiguous, even contradictory: Few persons could easily reconcile the encouragement of "healthful" recreations with the never-on-Sunday limitation. In addition, proponents of sport ranging from Boston clergyman Joseph Seccombe to Philadelphia humanist Benjamin Franklin openly advocated recreations from educational, religious, and secular perspectives. Not even the fundamentalist religious revival known as the Great Awakening, which swept over the colonies in the 1730s and 1740s, could counter the burgeoning sporting culture. By the mid eighteenth century, recreational pastimes enjoyed unprecedented popularity throughout the colonies.

Adapting British Pastimes to New World Conditions

At first glance, British American recreations resembled English pastimes. Colonials imported and reprinted sport literature, most notably John Newbery's *A Little Pretty Pocket-Book* (1744), containing the first American reference to "Base-Ball." Many familiar games received only slight local modification—tennis, battledore and shuttlecock (badminton), tipcat (batting a wooden spindle), oystering, pall mall (croquet), hoop rolling, marbles, hopscotch, leapfrog, kite flying, quoits (horseshoes using rings), ninepins, bowling, and numerous variants of hide-and-seek. Especially popular were games in which balls made of material ranging from leather to inflated animal bladders were kicked, thrown, or batted—

fives (handball), cricket, rounders, stoolball, town ball, baseball, football, soccer, and several species of old cat (a variation of tipcat that involved tossing a ball instead of tipping a piece of wood). But these games were almost exclusively the province of children and adolescents; references to adult colonials participating in Old World communal folk games are rare.

Adults, responding to the environmental and cultural conditions of the New World, favored "natural" sports instead of "contrived" ball games. Thus their recreations were largely pleasurable variants of utilitarian activities. Field sports—hunting, fishing, shooting, and archery—were ubiquitous. Modes of transportation—swimming, horseback riding, sailing and rowing boats, hiking, and running—were easily transformed into recreational activities, although winter sports—skating, hockey, tobogganing, and sleigh riding—were confined to northern climes. Combat sports derived from military preparedness—boxing, wrestling, cudgeling, and fencing matches—were staples of male subcultures. Cockfighting, bullbaiting and bearbaiting, and other blood sports involving animals, vestiges of religious sacrificial rites, were commonplace if illegal. And gambling, whether involving games of chance or contests of physical skill, were exceedingly popular in their own right and provided the impulse for other sporting events. Except for solitary recreations, scarcely a sporting activity occurred without wagers.

If recreations resembled English pastimes in form, they differed significantly in performance and perception. Field sports, naturally popular in an overwhelmingly agricultural society, were far more democratic activities in America because of the absence of class restrictions on participation and the ready availability of open land. But access led to overkill, for without hunting and fishing regulations, sportsmen soon depleted local wildlife and had to travel ever greater distances for game. Because the horse was both the symbol and the reality of work and transportation, pride in stock led inevitably to horse racing for competition and gambling. But whereas horse racing in England was an elaborately staged "sport of kings," in America it was largely an informal pastime of the people. Formal contests held at specialized facilities became increasingly popular in urban areas during the

eighteenth century; run on grass courses in the English manner instead of on dirt tracks, they were match races between two horses, not field races of multiple steeds. Occasionally intercolonial matches occurred, but interregional racing was unknown.

Given the primary concern with establishing new settlements in a veritable wilderness, the historically close relationship between work and play was particularly pronounced. Quilting bees and barn raisings, tree fellings and log splittings, turkey shoots and deer hunts were either recreation or labor, depending upon the purpose and social setting of the activity. In contrast with the growing demand for legislation against cruelty to animals in England, the immigrant mentality of conquering and taming the frontier found expression in blood sports. Fight-to-the-death contests in pits between gamecocks bearing razor-sharp steel gaffles on their spurs were especially popular, as were baitings, wherein six or eight dogs were loosed upon a tethered bear or bull, usually in an enclosure, until the dogs were killed or the beast was incapacitated. "Gander pulling," originated by the Dutch, graphically symbolized the contest between man and beast: A man galloping a horse or standing in a boat attempted with bare hands to jerk the head from a greased goose suspended from a tree or a rope stretched across a street or stream. Similarly, a fascination with combat sports was a logical extension of constant military preparation necessitated by the persistent threat of armed attack or war. And in place of the traditional ecclesiastical holidays that regulated communal folk sport in England, Americans substituted commencements, commercial fairs, and civic rites—elections and court days, training or muster days—which maximized instead of controlled recreations.

The colonial sporting life differed from the English heritage in other respects. Because class lines were both less distinct and more fluid, recreation was more a matter of individual or group initiative than organization by a paternalistic ruling elite, except in certain parts of the South where planters sponsored horse races and masters controlled the sporting life of slaves. Moreover, sports and recreations were not performed on separate space, except for race courses. Recreating in forests and open fields posed no problems, but sporting in cities and towns was another matter; playing games, shooting guns, and racing horses in the streets, marketplaces, town commons, and churchyards endangered persons and property. Sport was also more a participant than a spectator activity. A crowd might happen to observe a boxing match or ball game, but save for selected horse races and cockfights, there were few events staged for an audience. That there was little or no role differentiation between participants and spectators, sometimes even during the course of a game, likely heightened the social and psychological importance of the activity for everyone. However, colonial sports were not democratic. Participation and spectating were often restricted by age, gender, race, religion, ethnicity, or condition of servitude.

Recreational diversity was the norm as peoples from throughout western Europe and black Africa brought distinctive ethnic pastimes to British America. Because colonial society lacked integrating influences, notably the absence of transcolonial institutions along with primitive means of communication and transportation, recreational rules, unwritten and determined by local customs and preferences, varied from village to village, colony to colony. Meaningful only to participants or residents of the immediate locale, sporting events, save for selected horse races, were neither recorded nor reported. Given the marked diversity and parochialism of sports and recreations, the games British colonial peoples played are best viewed from regional, sectional, age-group, ethnic, gender, and class perspectives.

New England

New England constituted both a distinctive geographical region and a particular state of mind. During the seventeenth century, ethnic and religious homogeneity, along with distinctive settlement patterns, produced quasi-theocratic corporate communities at both the town and provincial levels. New Englanders resided in towns similar to the villages of Britain but did not replicate English folk games. The Protestant reformers who fled to America immediately abolished the traditional ecclesiastical calendar of feast days and legislated against the popular communal games associated with them. Also, widely scattered hinterland towns precluded significant in-

tercommunity recreations among a people who possessed a greater sense of community than elsewhere in America save for Indians and African slaves. The lone occasion for communal sport was training day, when local militiamen gathered for a little military drill and considerable drinking and gambling, as well as wrestling, running, jumping, and target shooting competitions. Not a few New Englanders pursued in private recreations they avoided in public, but they avoided all such activities on the Sabbath.

Negative attitudes toward sport were intensified because of the Puritan (Protestant) work ethic that decried idleness while promoting the notion of an "elect" or "chosen" people that demanded physical attributes consonant with the spiritual grace of "visible Saints." Consequently, nowhere else in America was Sabbatarianism enforced so strictly as in New England.

Puritan Congregationalists were not prudes or ascetics for whom pleasure itself was sinful. Nor were their attitudes toward physical activities dogmatic, save for Sunday abstinence. The nature and purpose of the activity, and the age of the participant, were critical considerations. Children participated freely in playtime activities, including ball games on the town commons or village green. For adolescents and adults, Puritan divines encouraged exercise and selected recreations related to one's calling or conducive to health. They condemned activities that might arouse physical and emotional passions, promote immorality, divert attention from one's familial and work responsibilities, and become pleasurable ends in themselves, to the detriment of one's commitment to God. Upon reaching majority, adults abandoned childish pastimes and publicly pursued recreations and exercises designed to promote physical and emotional well-being. Privately they engaged in table games of chance or intellectual skill, and not a few pleasurable or illegal recreations.

Puritan pronouncements regarding sporting activities stemmed less from sectarian than from secular considerations. Keeping the Sabbath holy and preventing licentiousness were genuine religious concerns, but the determined suppression of sport reflected a desire to maintain social conformity and control. Hence the toleration of youths' games played off the streets and with "good order" coupled with persistent opposition to the invariably contentious and debauched vernacular folk games associated with pagan festivals.

The secularization and commercialization that produced the cultural transformation from Puritan to Yankee both compounded the theological ambiguities about recreational pursuits and increased sporting opportunities. Participation in sports was discouraged but not eliminated. By a 1677 proclamation of the Massachusetts Council "that vanity of Horse racing, for mony" was banned from public roads and permitted no closer than four miles to any town; on the eve of the revolution there were still no formal race tracks in New England. Nevertheless, races were held in towns near Boston and throughout Rhode Island, the latter featuring Thoroughbreds and "Narragansett pacers." Field sports, favored by church and state authorities, remained the most popular recreational activities. In the region's two urban areas, Boston and Newport, Rhode Island, cockfights, bowling, and a host of like sports flourished in and around taverns. And student-initiated sports flourished at primary schools as well as at Harvard and Yale colleges. During its first century, New England's mantle of leadership passed from pious preachers to urbane merchants; growing participation and acceptance of sport and recreation formed part of an increasingly diversified and cosmopolitan social order. If New England recreations were increasingly less restrained religiously by the mid eighteenth century, the Puritan legacy, along with strict Sabbatarianism, had an unmistakably inhibiting effect on the development of sport in the region.

Middle Atlantic

Recreations in the Middle Atlantic colonies were far more diversified and popular than in New England. Established shortly after the Restoration amid renewed enthusiasm for sport, New York, New Jersey, Pennsylvania, and Delaware collectively encompassed the range of sporting environments—sparsely settled frontiers and yeoman-dominated hinterlands, seacoasts and mountains, small villages and urban centers. Most important was the ethnic and religious diversity of the four provinces. Originally the site of Dutch, English, Scottish, and Swedish colonies, the region attracted emigrants from numerous northern European counties after the establishment of British hegemony. The English were a majority, but the populace included Dutch, Flemings, Germans, Huguenots (French Protestants), Scots, Scotch-Irish, Swedes, Spanish Jews, Walloons, and Africans free and slave. In addition, New York and Pennsylvania had the largest Indian populations among the British colonies.

The diverse cultures created a colorful recreational tapestry. New Sweden (1638–1663) and the formation of a Scottish enclave in East New Jersey in the 1680s were short-lived experiments, but the Scots and Swedes perpetuated their recreational pastimes. Residing primarily in rural New Jersey and Pennsylvania, both groups were particularly fond of games of chance, horse racing, and communal frolics or "bees" occasioned by barn raisings, butcherings, and harvests. Swedes carefully distinguished between draft horses and racehorses, while Scots imported their Highland (later Caledonian, after the Roman name for Scotland) Games featuring dancing, music, and athletic contests of Celtic origin: footraces, putting the heavy stone, tossing the caber (pole), throwing the hammer, pole vaulting for distance, hurdle races, jumping from running or standing starts, and the hop step and leap.

New Netherland (1624–1664) contributed much to the region's recreational life. Sport played a major role in Dutch society. Although artists in Europe and North America depicted people at play (including Native American sports) in thousands of paintings and woodcuts, the Dutch were the preeminent illustrators of recreations. They also initiated the practice of setting aside separate space for sport activities. New Amsterdam's Bowling Green was reserved for the favorite Dutch game, a variant of curling played on grass instead of ice in which balls ("bowls") were rolled as near as possible to the "jack." Selected ponds or fields, depending on the season, were reserved for *kolven*. Using sticks curved slightly at the bottom, Dutchmen whacked balls across the ground or ice toward posts in a game that was the American forerunner of golf, ice hockey, and field hockey. Bowling and "golf" spread throughout the colonies, as did gander pulling. Dutch winter sports—iceboating, coasting (sledding), sleigh riding, and ice skating for pleasure or distance competition—became popular throughout the Middle

Atlantic colonies and, to a lesser degree, in New England. (The popularity of skating was related to the Dutch use of steel blades instead of the English and Scandinavian practice of attaching bones to boots.) Other *volksvermaken* (folk pleasures) did not catch on elsewhere. One was "truck," a tavern sport wherein players used a cue to drive a ball through a wire wicket on a billiard-like table. Others were animal "sports" associated with Old World folk games. *Papagaaischieten* ("shooting the parrot"), an annual marksmanship event following Pentecost, featured live targets. Another was "cat clubbing," a sport in which contestants took turns hurling a club at a suspended barrel containing a feline; when the barrel finally broke, thereby releasing the cat, participants attempted to capture the crazed creature and then let the cat go after it was caught.

The English conquest of New Netherland in 1664 broadened the Dutch sporting heritage while curtailing traditional folk games. The transformation of horse racing from informal contests to organized sport began in 1665 when Governor Richard Nicolls, the father of racing in America, established the continent's first race track on the plain at Salisbury (Hempstead) on Long Island. Named New Market after the famous English course, it was a two-mile (3.2 kilometer) oval turf course featuring one-lap races. In 1668 Nicolls awarded the winner of the spring and fall match races an engraved silver porringer, America's first sports trophy. The personification of New York's sporting culture, William Burnett, governor from 1720 to 1728, possessed when he died in 1729 "nine gouff clubs, one iron ditto and seven dozen balls" in addition to a fishing rod, three fowling pieces, and four cases of fencing foils. The English also introduced fox hunting, which spread quickly into rural New Jersey and Pennsylvania.

New Jersey and Pennsylvania were havens for field sports. In these colonies other recreations developed slowly amid tensions pitting pietistic Calvinists and Quakers against liberal Anglicans and Presbyterians. This was particularly true in Pennsylvania, where in addition to Sabbatarian statutes the legislature repeatedly enacted laws banning all forms of gambling as well as "needless and vain sports and pastimes." Disallowed by the privy council in England, the

sweeping acts "Against Riots, Rioters, and Riotous Sports, Plays and Games" were attempts to retain traditional Quaker doctrine and social discipline in an increasingly cosmopolitan society. Sports and recreations flourished during the eighteenth century in New Jersey and the Quaker Commonwealth notwithstanding governmental and religious disapproval. For example, when the New Jersey Assembly abolished horse racing in 1761, a Dutch-owned mile-long track along the Hudson River in Paulus Hook (now Jersey City) became part of the New York City racing circuit. While never as popular as in New York, horse racing was symbolic of the rise of organized recreations in New Jersey and Pennsylvania, with the former specializing in breeding stock for neighboring colonies and the latter sponsoring races. Philadelphia's Race Street led to the initial racing grounds, and later Centre Square contained both an oval course and a mile-long straight race path.

European folk games were not perpetuated in the Middle Atlantic colonies less because of Sabbatarianism, the absence of the traditional church calendar, or restrictive legislation than because of population dispersal. With the exception of New York City and Philadelphia, villages tended to be small market centers because farmers lived on the land they worked. The agricultural fairs and harvest festivals held throughout the Middle Atlantic colonies featured more recreational than commercial activity, but nothing akin to English folk games occurred. With numerous bays, estuaries, and navigable rivers indenting the coastlines, boating was popular, but field sports were the recreation of choice for most residents in the agrarian Middle Atlantic colonies. New York City and Philadelphia were the centers of urban sports for the northern and southern halves of the region, respectively.

The South

The climate, geography, racial composition, settlement patterns, social structure, and modes of agricultural production that so markedly differentiated the South from the rest of British America also produced significant recreational variations within the region. Only the institution of African slavery and the concomitant plantation system unified a region whose colonies were established at lengthy intervals, in contrast with the close chronological founding of the pre–(British) Civil War New England and post-Restoration Middle Atlantic provinces. The Chesapeake colonies, Virginia (1607) and Maryland (1632), significantly predated the post-Restoration Carolinas (South 1663, North 1691) and Georgia (1732). Charles Town (Charleston), South Carolina, was the lone urban center. With the most dispersed regional population, the South developed localized and rural recreational patterns. Isolated farms and plantations worked against traditional communal sports, but biannual "publick times" or "court days" provided recreational opportunities as well as an occasion to transact legal and commercial business. Paradoxically, the South simultaneously exhibited the most faithful replication of upper-class English recreations and the most distinctive folk pastimes in British America.

The personal accounts of both visitors and residents as well as public records attest that nowhere else in North America were sports embraced so widely, openly, and enthusiastically as in the South. Notwithstanding early and repeated legislation imposing strict Sabbatarian observances and prohibiting gambling and "unlawful games," sports and recreations flourished due to the migration of Cavaliers after the English Civil War, the tolerance of the established Anglican church, the development of quasi-autonomous plantation societies, and a physical environment conducive to year-round outdoor pastimes. Most important, the planter aristocracy infused society as a whole with a strong sporting ethic by embracing the cult of leisure. Mostly Anglican, and thus free of "puritanical" theological inhibitions, the planter class consciously attempted to imitate the life-style of the English landed gentry, for whom conspicuous participation in sport and recreations was a cultural imperative.

The premier leisure pastimes of the South were boating, dancing, hunting, gambling, cockfights, and horse races. The first three activities mirrored class distinctions, while the latter trio involved a cross section of society. Gambling fever reached epidemic proportions throughout the South, with bets placed on uncertainties ranging from political elections to games of chance. That wagers might involve a year's income, an annual crop, slaves, or an entire personal estate expressed in extreme form the importance of gambling as a cultural symbol of the social conventions of the region's ruling planter class and the high-risk nature of an unstable economy based upon a few cash crops. Cockfights, held clandestinely in New England and disapprovingly in the Middle Atlantic colonies, were conducted openly throughout the South and featured selectively bred and trained gamecocks as well as birds imported from Britain. Plantation owners were the principal sponsors of "mains" or matches, but the bloody sport was popular with all races and classes because of its intimate connection with gambling and cultural imperatives.

The same was true of horse racing, which to an even greater degree expressed the cultural dynamics of Southern society. The passion for horse racing originated in Virginia with impromptu quarter-mile match races between ordinary saddle stock run on country roads or over narrow paths cut through forests and fields. Bred first in Virginia, the quarter horse, known for quick bursts of speed but lacking in endurance, spread throughout the South and eventually gained greatest notoriety as the mount of the cowboy. Maryland and South Carolina mimicked Virginia's passion for horse racing, and by the end of the seventeenth century mile-long oval turf courses offered an alternative to quarter-horse sprints that was more conductive to spectating (and thus to gambling). Horse racing reached new heights with the importation between 1730 and 1770 of some 176 English thoroughbreds bred for endurance. The result was an increase in the number of formal race courses, the development of breeding farms and new training techniques, the founding of jockey clubs, and a new form of competition. Unlike the one-lap races in New England and the Middle Atlantic colonies, Southern horses usually competed in best-of-three four-mile heats.

Southerners were, in a word, obsessive about sport because it was so intimately interwoven with the cultural values and social structure of the region. As elsewhere, by the mid 1700s the Great Awakening and a growing number of Evangelicals produced deep-seated tensions between proponents and opponents of sport. But the debate was especially charged not only because of the South's unique sporting milieu but also because it revealed the special significance of class, gender, and race in the recreations of the region.

Class. Without rigid class lines determined by law or custom, British colonials attached firm social meanings to the fluid concepts of "better," "middling," and "lower" sorts. Initially determined by familial association, class quickly became defined more by wealth than by social status. Well-born aristocrats and lowly common folk alike recreated and created their own sporting traditions. Although less is known about the recreations of the lower than of the upper classes, the field sports and the communal recreations of farmers and townspeople were far more common leisure pastimes than the elite social and sporting activities of the landed gentry and urban merchants.

American upper classes were not patrons of sport as were their British counterparts, but they did significantly influence the recreational attitudes and aspirations of society at large. They were the most conspicuous participants in recreations simply because they had at their disposal the most discretionary time for leisure pursuits and the money to import sporting literature, animals, and equipment or to engage in such expensive activities as owning racing boats or thoroughbreds. While emphasizing recreations that reinforced their privileged social status, such as lavish balls, cotillions, and musical and theatrical performances, the elite also participated in popular physical recreations. Exercising near exclusivity in recreations such as falconry and fencing or participating as a group apart in sports such as horse racing and cockfighting, they simultaneously promoted the commonality of sport as a means of inculcating cultural values across class lines, underscoring their own elite status, and mediating changing societal relationships in a fluid social order.

The South illustrates most clearly the class dynamics of recreations. Unlike the mercantile elite of New England and the Middle Atlantic colonies, who preferred formal socializing and nonphysical games to sporting contests, Southern gentlemen embraced both refined gentility and raw physicality. Recreational class lines were more sharply drawn in the South because social status was less fluid and more tied to lineage than elsewhere in British America. A few sports like fox hunting, which increased in popularity in the Chesapeake region by the 1730s with the importation of English hounds and red foxes, were the exclusive domain of the elite. Most often, however, common activities were distinguished by class differences. Aristocrats attended elegant dancing assemblies, while the lower orders socialized at hoedowns. Wealthy sportsmen hunted on horseback, while those of lesser rank tramped through the woods. The planter elite demonstrated courage and physical prowess through genteel forms of boxing and calculated duels, while common folk bashed each other with cudgels (stout sticks held horizontally) and engaged in unrestrained fighting and wrestling matches. The gentry preferred organized horse races on turf courses, while the middle and lower classes favored impromptu quarter-horse sprints. And while persons of great and meager means alike attended cockfights and horse races and placed bets, it was the gentry who owned the birds and horses and wagered sizable sums. Spectators often represented a cross section of society, but participants were rarely from different classes.

Southern recreation was more than fun and games. Through sporting conventions and behavior the planters not only reinforced the values of their class but also demonstrated to the populace that they indeed possessed superior wealth and culture, and thus rightfully dominated the political and economic life of the community. Just as slavery served to unify and stabilize hierarchical white society, so the Southern elite used sport as an important means of effecting privilege and maintaining hegemony.

Gender. The hegemony of the elite was, of course, a paternalistic one, inasmuch as colonial recreations throughout British America were influenced by gender even more than by class. Originating as an extension of hunting and combat skills, sport was a pervasive form of male bonding and masculine ritual. Individual tests of strength, dexterity, and courage were both rites of passages for adolescents and demonstrations of manhood for adults. And organized hunting parties, whether replete with lavish equipage and ceremonies for the upper classes, or conducted at night by rifle-bearing and dog-braying "lesser sorts," was more a social event than a sporting activity. Even intellectuals like Thomas Jefferson felt the obligation: "From the circumstances of my position, I was often thrown into the society of horse-racers, card-players, [and] fox hunters." Sport was a critical component of Southern masculinity and social unification, simultaneously separating and joining men of different races and stations in life.

Although recreational roles were less rigidly defined than in Europe, American women did not participate as openly or extensively in sporting activities as their English counterparts. Rank, race, region, and religion shaped the recreations of colonial women. Still, they could and did participate in physical recreations, whether sailing and boating on rivers and ocean, bowling with men, running footraces (American versions of the English "smock" races), ice skating and sledding, or competing at archery, cricket, stoolball, and shuttlecock. Horseback riding was a favorite pastime, and women occasionally raced, sometimes against men but mostly against other women. Hunting and fishing were common pastimes, and the numerous women who owned and operated taverns were expert in the games of chance played by their mostly male clientele. The presence of women as spectators (and bettors) at horse races and other competitions suggests a sporting interest beyond mere socializing; indeed, by the mid 1700s women were encouraged by special seating and promotions to attend sporting events.

As with men, the degree of female participation in sporting recreations progressively increased southward from New England. But until well into the eighteenth century, women's recreational activities, whether playing cards or fishing, were usually conducted in private. Public participation in recreations other than dances, musical concerts, tea parties, and sundry bees were exceptions rather than the rule, especially for upper- and middle-class women. For middle- and lower-class women leisure activities were primarily extensions of labor. Needlework, gardening, spinning matches, candle-dippings, and quilting bees, for example, were domestic chores mitigated by self-gratification, socialization, or competition. Functioning as "good wives" as well as "deputy husbands," married women, irrespective of social class, had much less time for leisure

pursuits than their husbands because of household responsibilities. Females participated actively in recreations, albeit not to the same extent or in many of the same sports as males. Inasmuch as women's recreational activities were both ancillary and complementary to those of men, they served to define and control gender roles in colonial society.

Race. Because of pervasive racism in all British colonies, African Americans, free or slave, were discouraged or prevented from openly perpetuating their recreational heritages. However, they shared one fundamental recreational characteristic with Europeans—it was a man's world. Moreover, black women, whether wives or domestic servants, were confined more to hearth and field than white women, who enjoyed far greater opportunities for individual activity or group association.

Free black males, most of whom lived in urban areas north of the Mason-Dixon Line, participated in the same recreations and sports as lower-class whites. However, given racism and social conventions, African Americans usually recreated separately from whites except as spectators at sporting events. Although New York City laws prohibited adult slaves from playing games or congregating within the city limits, urban life necessitated a freedom of movement that undoubtedly facilitated recreational interaction between blacks, slave or free. Public collective recreation of both sexes was limited to rousing communitywide celebrations associated with Shrove Tuesday, Guy Fawkes Day (or Pope's Day) in Boston, and Pinkster Day (derived from the Dutch word for Pentecost), featuring dancing and sundry amusements in New York City. There is little evidence of an African-American sporting community in the North, even among slaves.

The situation was different in the hierarchical and biracial South, where plantation slaves created a close-knit sporting community in response to residential segregation and indefinite servitude. African Americans, slave or free, participated in both white and black recreational worlds. In the former they played openly and equally with white children, but as adults they performed support roles. Blacks rowed racing boats as well as pleasure crafts for whites, raced and trained horses, handled gamecocks, and joined whites as spectators at races and fights. Occasionally slaves were the focus of sporting events, as in the case of bare-knuckle fights and wrestling matches staged by planters or the "footraces for Negro girls" held at Maryland fairs in the 1740s. (Whether the runners were slave or free is unknown, but black women participated publicly in segregated contests regardless of the racial composition of the spectators.)

The most distinctive and revealing African-American recreations occurred in "the quarters," the slave dwellings physically and culturally apart from the world of the plantation owner. Slaves passionately pursued recreations because of a unique conception of work and play. Whereas the workplace was the key to wealth and identity for Europeans, recreation assumed critical personal and social meanings for individuals unable to achieve a sense of self-worth and group recognition through labor because of their legally subservient status. For plantation slaves "play" not only facilitated group solidarity and socialization but also, because it occurred away from white supervision, promoted a sense of freedom and individual achievement essential for psychological survival in a brutally exploitative system of human bondage.

Masters controlled the amount of leisure time available to slaves, but they clearly had more "free" time than is generally recognized. Recreation, not work, was the rule on weekends, during inclement weather, or on holidays, especially Christmas, which brought seven to ten days of rest in addition to presents. Slaves also devoted a considerable portion of their discretionary time at night to amusements. Makeshift equipment and impromptu rules were the norm. Ironically, the favored house servants enjoyed more privileges but had less leisure time than the field hands because of the demands of the "big house."

Like whites and free blacks, slaves enjoyed a variety of recreations that were both purposeful and pleasurable. Hunting and fishing, the preeminent pastimes, supplemented diets, often provided income, served as a rite of passage for young boys, and functioned as a mechanism for male bonding. Slaves were addicted to gambling, eagerly wagering money or prized possessions at craps or cards, marbles or horseshoes, boat or horse races, and cockfights. Gambling was pervasive in African cultures for reasons that transcended economics, but African Americans viewed gambling as one of the few means of increasing their material possessions. Men and boys alike were fond of tests of individual physical skills—running, jumping, swimming, throwing—not only because they were enjoyable competitions but also because they were among the few means of attaining personal respect and social status.

Slave recreations reflected the fears and frustrations of bondage. Just as adults rarely boxed or wrestled publicly for sport, youngsters, who normally did not do field work until adolescence, fostered social cohesion by avoiding games that were combative or based on the elimination of participants. They also mitigated emotional torments through games involving role-playing such as Hiding the Switch (a kind of tag wherein the one "caught" was whipped instead of tagged) and accompanying hopscotch and jump rope with songs and chants voicing anxieties or criticism of whites. Whether through the ring games of children or the "ring shout" of adults, slaves expressed symbolically feelings that could not be openly articulated in the restrictive plantation environment.

Because African Americans were denied participation in the recreations of their homelands, slaves in particular had to devise new leisure pastimes. There is no evidence of the survival in North America of the ball games of the Bantu-speaking peoples, the favorite board game of the Ibos (*okwe*), the pan-African betting game (*wari-solo*), or the spear-tossing and wrestling contests that fostered social rank and leadership roles among men. The absence of indigenous African sports stemmed not only from white opposition but also from acculturation produced by the commingling of numerous African cultures as well as European traditions.

However, African heritages were manifested clearly in song and dance. The "ring shout," the "Buzzard Lope," and "Patting Juba"—group dances accompanied by rhythmic hand-slapping and singing—are traceable directly to West Africa. Considerably more fluid and given to improvisation than the staid uniformity of the reels and minuets of planter society, African American dances were often tests of physical prowess, occasions for individual expression, and opportunities to earn the praise of peers.

While slaves used recreations to bolster self-esteem and group solidarity, masters encouraged such pastimes as a means of maintaining a healthy and "contented" labor force. Despite laws against slaves using firearms, many planters chose to ignore the law and provide guns to their bondmen for hunting. Similarly, planters encouraged Sunday amusements despite Sabbatarian strictures against recreations. And numerous masters did nothing to curtail the illegal movement of slaves from plantation to plantation or to sites of sporting events. Ultimately, recreations benefited both master and slave; a means of instilling personal and group pride among slaves, it also served to dull the impulse of insurrection.

FRONTIER SPORTS

The greatest recreational disparity in British America was sectional, the marked contrast between the burgeoning western frontiers from Pennsylvania southward and the established eastern coastal areas. The environment, physical and cultural, influenced the nature of frontier recreations. Settlers quickly adopted Native American fishing and hunting techniques, but they shunned Indian sports save for lacrosse in New York and Pennsylvania. Field sports were dominant on the fringes of settlement because they provided sustenance. Some backcountry recreations were tests of strength—tugs-of-war, tossing quoits (twenty-to-sixty-pound stones instead of iron rings), and throwing the maul (caber or hammer). Others were contests of agility—footraces, broad jumps, high jumps with or without poles, and leapfrogging over horses or teams of oxen. Combat and blood sports were especially popular because the harshness, primitiveness, and danger of frontier life bred a conquest mentality, a need to dominate the environment and its wildlife. Frontier fascination with gratuitous cruelty found expression in animal-baitings and gander pulls as well as the macho sports of bare-knuckle fighting and "gouging." "Gouging," a brutal, no-holds-barred combination of boxing and wrestling, featured disfigurement or dismemberment as combatants bit, butted, choked, kicked, stomped, tore out tongues and eyeballs, ripped off noses and ears, and even crushed or removed testicles.

Legislation against such barbarism was ineffective because, however cruel or sadistic, "gouging" both reinforced and reflected the social and economic realities of the frontier. Besides a conspicuous correlation among the violence, bloodletting, physicality, and uncertainty of work and play, the absence of institutional and cultural restraints of the more settled portions of the colonies led to a breakdown of social conventions and an elevation of self-reliance and aggressive individuality. There were few means other than demonstrations of physical prowess and courage for males to gain identity and status in the backcountry. Indeed, Westerners relished resisting Eastern efforts to reduce the brutality, disorder, and inequity of frontier sports and deliberately affected a contrary social order. Favoring quarter horses, they were contemptuous of the turf course races dominant in the tidewater, just as they preferred raucous hoedowns to staid balls and communal bees to genteel parties. Like men, backcountry women worked and played hard, and were handy with rod, reel, and rifle. On balance, considerations of class, gender, and race were less significant in the backcountry than elsewhere in the colonies.

URBAN RECREATIONS

Compared with the primitive sports and inchoate traditions of the frontier, urban recreations reflected a dramatically more refined and mature sporting culture. Prior to the eighteenth century there was little difference between town and country leisure pastimes, but the growth of cities created a distinct environment that simultaneously featured the best and basest of recreations. Still small by global standards on the eve of the revolution, the major colonial cities exerted powerful influences as the social, economic, and political centers for their respective hinterlands and regions. The same was true for large towns such as Annapolis and Williamsburg, whose populations increased dramatically during fairs or legislative and general court sessions. Although urban growth reduced the space available for sports, causing a steady move toward outlying areas, the recreational opportunities for both children and adults were far more varied, numerous, and organized than in the rural and frontier areas. Moreover, the recreational life of colonial urban areas closely resembled that of English cities. Indeed, the first international sporting event in North America, a cricket match between "Americans" and Englishmen, occurred in New York City in 1751.

Class consciousness created separate sporting spheres in every city and town of appreciable size. Theaters, music halls, dancing schools, fencing academies, card assemblies, and literary clubs afforded the sophisticated entertainments of high culture to the wealthy. Upper classes combined sporting and socializing in angling and boating societies modeled after Philadelphia's Schuylkill Fishing Company (1722) or jockey clubs, first organized by turf enthusiasts in Charleston in 1734. Intellectuals, tradesmen, and politicians also formed their own clubs and associations that featured recreational activities. Separate sporting facilities symbolized and reinforced the importance of rank in urban recreations. Communities as diverse as Philadelphia and Williamsburg offered both oval turf courses for upper-class horse racing and straight-path tracks for middle- and lower-class racing. Williamsburgers, depending upon class, bowled on greens next to taverns, the "good bowling green" near the marketplace, or the manicured lawn at the Governor's Palace. The only urban sport popular in Britain not to gain favor in America was pugilism (formal, rule-bound, stand-up boxing), probably because of the relatively small size of the laboring class in colonial cities.

Despite repeated efforts to maintain order and decorum, recreations exacerbated urban problems. Numerous laws attempted, with uneven results, to protect persons and property from the dangers inherent in playing ball games, "gunning," and running races on foot or horseback within city limits. Changes in attitudes toward nature and animals, as well as a desire to effect a "civilized" image, produced laws against blood sports, but bearbaitings, rattings, and cockfights continued. Similarly, laws to curb gambling, prostitution, and the "disorderly" behavior of "lesser sorts" such as unskilled laborers, sailors, apprentices, "untrustworthy strangers," and blacks were ineffectual. The inability of social,

political, and religious leaders to control urban recreations stemmed partly from an inability to enforce the laws but primarily from the frequent if clandestine participation of middle- and upper-class males in "low-life" activities. The result was a two-tiered sporting culture. While "proper" Philadelphians conspicuously pursued and publicized their genteel recreations, bullbaitings and cockfights took place in the back streets of the Helltown district or just outside the city limits at Society Hill.

Given the long-standing relationship between sports and spirits, the tavern became the center of colonial leisure activities. Taverns, also called public houses or ordinaries, were scattered throughout the countryside. In cities and towns they emphasized recreation over room and board. There were 177 taverns in Boston in 1737 (about 1 per 25 adult males), 334 in New York City in 1752, and 117 in Quaker-dominated Philadelphia in 1756. The principal off-work meeting and gathering place, the tavern offered food and drink as well as an array of recreational activities, all of which turned on gambling. In addition to card, dice, and board games, taverns possessed recreational equipment not otherwise available to most people—billiard tables, shuffleboards, nine-pin alleys, bowling greens, and skittle grounds—and also hosted illegal animal sports. As opposition to drunkenness, gambling, and illicit sports increased, taverns assumed class distinctions. The upper and middle classes patronized coffeehouses serving only coffee and chocolate in the London tradition or exclusive taverns offering elegant repasts as well as polite recreations. Lower-class males, frequently joined by their betters, patronized "low Tippling houses" or unlicensed dramshops and grogshops. Functionally, the tavern was a man's world wherein alcohol and recreations facilitated masculine posturing and male bonding.

REVOLUTION AND REPUBLICANISM

The reinvigorated opposition to moral laxity and extravagance that coalesced in many colonies by 1750 heightened the pre-revolutionary political and economic disputes between Britain and her American colonies. For many Pietists and Evangelicals, popular recreations and sports symbolized the growing decadence and "Anglicization" of colonial society. Grounded on the principles of virtue and simplicity, the nascent ideology of republicanism found expression in the provision of the Association adopted by the Continental Congress in October 1774, calling upon people to "discountenance and discourage every species of extravagance and dissipation, especially all horse-racing, and all kinds of gaming, cock-fighting, exhibitions of shews, plays and other expensive diversions and entertainments." Provincial congresses and local revolutionary committees followed suit, and after 1776 state governments legislated against extravagant indulgences, including "Idle sport."

Such laws had little impact on field sports and only diminished popular recreations, which simply became less public and more private. Wartime austerity and hardship reduced the time devoted to recreations except in the military, where Continental soldiers engaged in numerous sports—including a ball game called "base" at Valley Forge. After the war, republican ideology and the utilitarian aura given to sport by the military combined to make "virtuous" recreations an important part of the new republic.

CONCLUSIONS

African, European, and Native American sporting heritages were important components of the social and cultural tapestry of colonial North America. There was little recreational exchange between Indian cultures and the various European societies, except for white adoption of Native American hunting and fishing techniques. Because of their religious and ritualistic nature, Indian recreations remained largely immune to European influences. European recreations, on the other hand, exhibited significant adaptation, if not abandonment, of Old World traditional pastimes because of the new environmental, demographic, and institutional realities of North America. Although the sporting heritage of the British colonies would, through Canada and the United States, modify and ultimately dominate the recreational life of the entire continent, the unique traditions of African, French, Spanish, and Indian peoples persist in various places and to various degrees. Nonetheless, sports and rec-

reations have produced the most widespread and effective acculturation and assimilation in North American history, with the "American" sporting ethic emerging predominant.

The United States is markedly different from other nations in terms of the multiplicity, organization, and pervasiveness of its sporting pastimes. The origin of the peculiar American devotion to sport and recreation is to be found in the British colonies, where widespread participation in games, contests, and physical pastimes inherently turned on, and thus reinforced, the credo of individualism, liberty (freedom), and the pursuit of happiness.

BIBLIOGRAPHY

Baker, William J. *Sports in the Western World.* Totowa, N.J., 1982; rev. ed. Urbana, Ill., 1988. The most comprehensive study of "Western" sport to date.
Baker, William J., and James A. Mangan, eds. *Sport in Africa: Essays in Social History.* New York, 1987. The three essays on aspects of precolonial recreations by John Blacking, Sigrid Paul, and Thomas Q. Reefe have excellent bibliographies.
Baldwin, Gordon C. *Games of the American Indian.* New York, 1969.
Betts, John Rickards. *America's Sporting Heritage: 1850–1950.* Reading, Mass., 1974.
Blanchard, Kendall. *The Mississippi Choctaws at Play: The Serious Side of Leisure.* Urbana, Ill., 1981.
Brailsford, Dennis. *Sport, Time, and Society: The British at Play.* London, 1991.
Breen, Timothy H. "Horses and Gentlemen: The Cultural Significance of Gambling Among the Gentry of Virginia." *William and Mary Quarterly,* 3rd ser., 34 (1977):239–257.
Carson, Jane. *Colonial Virginians at Play.* Williamsburg, Va., 1965.
Carter, John Marshall. *Sports and Pastimes of the Middle Ages.* Lanham, Md., 1988.
Cross, Gary. *A Social History of Leisure Since 1600.* State College, Pa., 1990. A comparative study of leisure in Great Britain and the United States.
Culin, Stewart. *Games of the North American Indians.* Washington, D.C., 1907.
Durant, John, and Otto Bettman. *Pictorial History of American Sports: From Colonial Times to the Present.* Cranbury, N.J., 1952; rev. ed. 1965.
Gorn, Elliott J. "'Gouge and Bite, Pull Hair and Scratch': The Social Significance of Fighting in the Southern Backcountry." *American Historical Review* 90 (1985):18–43.

Guttmann, Allen. "English Sports Spectators: The Restoration to the Early Nineteenth Century." *Journal of Sport History* 12 (1985):103–125.

———. *From Ritual to Record: The Nature of Modern Sports.* New York, 1978.

———. *A Whole New Ball Game: An Interpretation of American Sports.* Chapel Hill, N.C., 1988.

———. *Women's Sports: A History.* New York, 1991.

Hervey, John. *Racing in America, 1665–1865.* 2 vols. New York, 1944.

Holt, Richard. *Sport and the British: A Modern History.* Oxford, 1989.

———. *Sport and Society in Modern France.* Oxford, 1981.

Howell, Maxwell L., and Reef A. Howell. *History of Sport in Canada.* Champaign, Ill., 1981; rev. ed. 1985.

Jable, J. Thomas. "Pennsylvania's Early Blue Laws: A Quaker Experiment in the Suppression of Sport and Amusements, 1682–1740." *Journal of Sport History* 1, no. 2 (1974):107–121.

Lucas, John A., and Ronald A. Smith. *Saga of American Sport.* Philadelphia, Pa., 1978.

Lucero-White, Aurora. *Los Hispanos: Five Essays on the Folkways of the Hispanos.* . . . Denver, Colo., 1947.

Macfarlan, Allen A. *Book of American Indian Games.* New York, 1958. A "handbook" that categorizes and describes prominent Native American games.

Malcolmson, Robert W. *Popular Recreations in English Society, 1700–1850.* London, 1973.

Rader, Benjamin G. *American Sports: From the Age of Folk Games to the Age of Televised Sports.* Englewood Cliffs, N.J., 1983; 2nd ed. 1990.

Rice, Kym S. *Early American Taverns: For the Entertainment of Friends and Strangers.* Chicago, Ill., 1983.

Struna, Nancy L. " 'Good Wives' and 'Gardeners,' Spinners and 'Fearless Fearless Riders': Middle- and Upper-rank Women in the Early American Sporting Culture." In *From "Fair Sex" to Feminism: Sport and Socialization of Women in Industrial and Post-Industrial Eras,* edited by J. A. Mangan and Roberta J. Park. London, 1987.

———. "Puritans and Sport: The Irretrievable Tide of Change." *Journal of Sport History* 4, no. 1 (1977):1–21.

Strutt, Joseph. *The Sports and Pastimes of the People of England.* London, 1801.

Wiggins, David K. "Sport and Popular Pastimes: Shadow of the Slavequarter." *Canadian Journal of History of Sport and Physical Education* 11, no. 1 (1980):61–88.

Larry R. Gerlach

See also **Drama; Music and Dance; Rural Life;** and **Urban Life.**

HOME AND HEARTH

THE HISTORY OF HOME and hearth in the British colonies is about the material world and the comportment of those who occupied and used it. It is as diverse as the individuals who lived it and as variable as the experiences they shared. Documentary sources discuss the world of the house from either the vantage of legal issues around the valuation, assessment, and litigation of property or from the incidental perspective of trial narratives, diaries, letters, household accounts, and other comparative written sources. However, the history of home and hearth is largely archaeological in the sense that objects ranging from standing houses to the excavated contents of trash pits and cellar holes provide the most compelling evidence about how people actually structured and furnished the world of domestic experience. The following essay addresses three interrelated aspects of the history of hearth and home: home as artifact, home as personal domain, and home as social symbol.

The history of home and hearth in the British colonies begins with understanding the chronological and regional development of housing. The history of housing in the colonial period is related to, but different from, the history of architecture in the sense that it deals with the ways in which people occupied and defined household space rather than matters of style and construction. Housing in the British colonies went through an extended series of transformations that began with the introduction of traditional British ideas of house form into the colonial landscape and concluded with the functional redefinition of the house. Because each stage overlaps the others and aspects of the earliest stages endure into the nineteenth century, it is necessary to measure each by the introduction of new values and ideas in the organization of domestic space. We invariably discover the reality and textures of domestic life and architecture at the local and individual level, but the broad pattern of hearth and home provides a measure of continuity across regions.

Central to evaluating houses is the notion of house form—the organization of space in and around the house. Not only were there many competing notions of house form in the British colonies, but those forms were subject to variation and change over time and across regions and specific circumstances ranging from personal preference to environmental constraint. Because the spaces people design and inhabit express their sense of self and their orientation to the world and society they inhabit, changes in the type and organization of household spaces signify major shifts in worldview and social orientation at their most basic and intimate level. Folklorist Henry Glassie puts it eloquently:

The skins of houses are shallow things that people are willing to change, but people are most conservative about the spaces they must utilize and in which they must exist. Build the walls of anything, deck them out with anything, but do not change the arrangement of the rooms or their proportions. In those volumes—bounded by surfaces from which a person's senses rebound to him—his psyche develops; disrupt them and you can disrupt him. ("Eighteenth-Century Cultural Process in Delaware Valley Folk Building," p. 43)

The greatest distinctions in housing throughout the colonial period were between regions and between standards of living and domestic life related to social class. Despite important differences in construction, chimney placement, decoration, and landscape, for example, the spatial experience of a one-room house in colonial New England was fundamentally the same as it was in the Chesapeake Bay country. The textures of those spaces, however, could be quite different. Yeomen farmers in both regions would have found some comfort in the familiarity of each others' surroundings even as they remarked on very obvious differences in the quality of domestic life.

REGIONAL DIFFERENCES

We should not undervalue the importance of regional life-styles in the organization of home and hearth. First, the regional British origins of early settlers influenced the types of houses and households created in the colonies. David Hackett Fischer, for example, identifies four regional British cultures and traces their historical course in the American colonies. For example, the British settlements of Philadelphia and its backcountry reflected traditions found in Yorkshire and eastern Wales. Old World ideas and customs found expression in everything from house plans to foodways. Historians tend to oversimplify the complex transmission of Old World culture into New World circumstance. Although we can trace the Pennsylvania settlements to their origins with some precision, we find that colonists were quick to modify ideas and apply them in new, creative ways to their New World circumstances. Thus, the transplantation of folk custom was dynamic. A key factor in that dynamism was the expectation of improved material and

social circumstances. Settlers were also quick to modify certain aspects of home and hearth relative to environmental and economic constraints as well as through the observation and emulation of other settler cultures. For example, Middle Atlantic British colonists adopted the practice of building their houses of log—a technique they learned from the construction traditions of neighboring Continental settlers. On the other hand, they preserved the organization of culturally familiar household spaces and usages. Cooking, for example, made use of New World ingredients such as corn in Old World recipes. Thus, the texture of certain dishes changed, but the customary ideas informing their preparation remained intact.

Second, the extreme variability of material and demographic circumstances produced significant changes in the appearance and operation of households. The difference between the comparatively healthy climate of New England and the miasmatic and disease-prone environments of the tidewater South exercised a direct influence on life span and subsequently on how people built and occupied their houses. In the Chesapeake the archaeological record of the seventeenth and early eighteenth centuries reveals a preference for slightly built houses framed on posts set in the ground. The corresponding interpretation of home and hearth addresses the economic and social instability fostered by fluctuating tobacco prices, high mortality rates, and the uncertain descent of property through inheritance. The trappings of home and hearth mirrored the fluid quality of material life in the early colonial tidewater South, where planters invested in such items as fancy imported ceramics, brass sundials, and other amenities. Even hoe blades, judging by the numbers found in the bottoms of backfilled wells, seem to have been treated as a consumer disposable by tidewater planters. The middling farmers and town folk of New England and the upper reaches of the Middle Atlantic colonies show a marked preference for durable houses and households furnished with fewer fancy goods. Both drew on the same options for the spatial organization of home and hearth, but they articulated the details in very different terms.

The distinction between home defined by one undifferentiated living space and more complex two-, three-, or four-room arrangements, however, was dramatic. The houses of the Virginia plantation owner or the New England merchant intimidated the yeoman from either region. As the colonial period unfolded, architectural distinctions and their attendant social separations became increasingly obvious.

The first century in the history of hearth and home in the British colonies began with the introduction of a number of British house forms into the new American settlements and concluded with the emergence of almost standardized regional housing styles by the early 1700s. Typical houses built during this period tended to be based on so called "open plans" where people entered directly into the main part of the house. The most commonly built houses from northern New England to the lower South were one or two rooms in plan and generally rough in appearance and finish. Other dwelling types were also erected and occupied, such as palisaded houses and large dwellings three-rooms long with a narrow entry passage at one end.

ONE-ROOM HOUSES

The one-room dwelling was by far the most common. The typical single-room house averaged 18 by 20 feet, or 360 square feet (about 32 square meters), and was only a single story tall. As late as the early 1800s, as much as two-thirds of the housing in some southern and Middle Atlantic settlements contained no more than 450 square feet (some 41 square meters) of interior living space. In the older, settled areas of New England, however, the frequency of one-room houses began to decline. By the close of the eighteenth century in central Massachusetts, for example, a scant 10 percent of all houses contained less than 450 square feet (41 square meters) of interior living space. In the coastal settlements of late eighteenth-century southeastern Delaware, on the other hand, more than three-quarters of all houses enclosed less than 450 square feet. While there were regional differences in terms of carpentry techniques, interior finishes, and durability, one-room houses throughout the British colonies represented pretty much the same type of space for the majority of peo-

ple, regardless of place. The major regional and class differences in these spaces were based on how people furnished and lived in these houses.

The best one-room houses in the colonial period were provided with a wattle-and-daub chimney hood or masonry chimney stack, one or two windows, finished interior walls, and a floored loft. The worst were dirt floored, open to the roof where the smoke from cooking fires swirled around the soot-blackened rafters and filtered out through a hole in the roof, windowless, and devoid of interior finishes more sophisticated than planed boards and beveled framing timbers. Such houses were ill-lit, smelly, and noisy, stifling in summer, and bitter cold in winter.

The contents of these tiny houses varied according to the means of the inhabitants. The poorest residents of the Chesapeake, for example, furnished their houses only with chests and coarse bedding. They cooked their meals in a common pot and ate from bowls using spoons or fingers or just drinking the contents. Rhys Isaac characterized these folks as " 'squatters or leaners' " who "rested slumped on the floor, or crouched on the boxes and chests that were the only ubiquitous items of furniture." Their situation was not entirely dissimilar from poor seventeenth-century New England households, where boxes, chests, and bedding also provided the most basic furnishings.

Better one-room houses contained additional furniture such as a bed, chair, squared four-legged stools (called forms) or benches, and a table. The most affluent single-room householders crammed their houses with even more goods in a pattern that would become increasingly common by the end of the colonial period. One Chester County, Pennsylvania, resident packed his single room with a bed, three tables, a half-dozen chairs, a chest, cooking utensils, and other items. It can be imagined just how crowded the one-room house was when we remember that these houses typically lodged six or more inhabitants as well as all the household activities and rituals that attended cooking, spinning, weaving, dining, visiting, birth, illness, and death. A late-eighteenth-century poem from New England captures the quality of life in a single-room dwelling such as continued to be occupied by poor farmers and tenants in the years after the revolution:

It was on a little eminence that this little cottage stood
Compris'd of logs piled up enclosed in a wood
I met the rural Cottager and then as I shall say
We interchanged Compliments and past the time of
 Day

And when our conversation had ended on the spot
He kindly invited me to walk into his cot
But when I was within I solemnly declare
A maide sat in the corner which caused me to Stare

And half a dozen Children all dirt from feet to head
And on the bed the wife who had lately got to bed
Four Chaires a Chest a Table two beds a sive a chest
Was all the parlors furniture I solemnly protest

This house not being divided one room it did contain
It having but one window was very dark within
Now Reachal served supper it being late at night
We had to feel for victuals because there was no light.

(Peter Banes. *Early American Probate Inventories,* pp. 151–152)

TWO-ROOM HOUSES

Within the family of open plans, the difference between the social and domestic organization represented by houses of one room and those containing two or more is startling. Studies of early colonial housing written over the last century have mistakenly cited the two-room or hall-parlor dwellings as the most representative dwellings of colonial settlers. One of the causes for this faulty assumption has been the tendency to see New England housing as representative of dwellings in the larger British colonial landscape. The quality of housing and the organization of household life now identified with the Chesapeake Bay settlements (especially before 1720) expresses a very different reality, which is that one-room houses were much more common. We have only begun to understand just how exceptional two-room houses were in the scheme of domestic space. The two-room house was not just one room larger; it represented an entirely different notion of home. Differences in the quality of interior ornament, the value and quality of furniture, and the numbers and types of possessions within each room enabled

householders to construct interior hierarchies.

The division of architectural space provided for the segregation of domestic functions. From the Carolinas to New England, household inventories for two-room houses routinely recognize a hall and parlor. The hall, also designated by terms such as common room, outer room, the "house below," or kitchen, was the room typically entered from the outside in the South and Middle Atlantic regions and was the setting for all the basic household functions of cooking, dining, and domestic work. In addition to the large cooking hearth (which in the northern and middle colonies often contained a built-in bake oven for breads and pies), the hall held tables, boxes and chests, seating furniture, and cooking utensils. Although some households were equipped with extensive cooking items, the basic complement included a kettle, frying pan, and iron pot along with sundry earthenware storage jars, milk pans, baking dishes, and pipkins.

The best room in the house was the parlor. Usually finished with more costly and pretentious architectural trim, the parlor (also known as the inner room, chamber, and best room) generally served as a downstairs sleeping chamber and private sitting room. Again, household inventories taken throughout the British colonies bespeak a common sensibility despite regional variations in housing design and finish. The parlor typically contained the best furniture, including the most expensive bed and specialized items such as tea tables of better woods like walnut and mahogany, caned and upholstered chairs, curtains, and mirrors. The contents of the parlor typically occupied more floor space than did those of the hall, were more valuable, and tended to be more fragile. The parlor, paradoxically, functioned as the space in the house most closely associated with privacy and the display of socially significant possessions such as silver plate and tea ware.

Two-room houses in colonial cities differed significantly from their rural counterparts in the allocation of household functions. From Charleston to Boston, the most public room at streetside served commercial purposes ranging from workshop to counting house. The back room assumed the uses of the hall, often containing cooking and dining functions except in cases where separate kitchens were located either in cellars or back buildings. The parlor or best room occupied the second floor front of the house, where it overlooked the street below. This room also tended to be the most elaborately finished in terms of architectural paneling and the quality of furniture. Behind the parlor stood the back chamber. Like rural hall-parlor houses, two-room urban dwellings situated the best room away from public access but equipped it with the trappings of status and display.

Regional differences between urban houses of America's colonial seaport cities became more pronounced through the eighteenth century. The best two-room houses of New England, for example, possessed a central chimney stack with back-to-back fireplaces. Typically erected with a heavy timber frame, these houses contained a lobby-like entry with a stair to the second-floor sleeping chambers. Comparable dwellings in the Chesapeake Bay region were only a single story in height and heated by chimney stacks set outside the gable ends. The frame construction of these southern houses was much lighter and more ephemeral than those associated with early New England settlements. The two-room houses of the Delaware Valley presented yet another alternative. The best of these dwellings were two stories in height and built variously of brick, stone, and wood. Log construction, a method of construction not found in British regional building, was the most common. These houses most often were heated with fireplaces located in a chimney stack built inside each gable. The interiors tended to be more elaborately paneled than their southern counterparts and often were equipped with architectural furniture in the form of built-in cupboards and storage closets.

The history and character of house form in the British colonies presents us only with the image of an uninhabited architectural shell, but the distinction between the house as an artifact and as the setting for familial and social interaction is critical to our understanding of hearth and home. The organization of space within the home has fueled debate over questions of gender and household organization. As Laurel Ulrich argues, the house may have been the property of men, but in many ways it stood as the domain of women. "By English tradition," Ulrich writes, "a woman's environment was the family dwelling and the yard or yards surrounding it." The

housewife's "domain" embraced the kitchen, garden, washhouse, milkhouse, cellar, and buttery. Women's ability to create a home depended on their skills in the "art and mystery of housewifery." Thus, the skills women possessed made the difference between what we would consider simple shelter and the comfort of home. To claim and maintain their domain required the abilities to build and tend fires, bake, cook, garden, operate a dairy, process textiles, and, in town settings, conduct business. For women with servants under their control, the requisite skills extended to the management of domestic labor.

The man's domain within the house was caught up in the material display associated with the parlor. Yet the division of male and female domains within the household is not as neat as this division suggests. Eighteenth-century Anglo-American women labored in the fields in rural areas at critical times in the harvest, working along with their husbands, children, and servants. In urban areas women conducted business, particularly in the management of small retail shops and taverns. In the history of home and hearth, they were active participants in the design of their houses and the organization and maintenance of the spaces around their dwellings. Still, women's skills are associated most concretely with the domain of the hearth.

Women were not only the producers in the home, they were the healers. Professionally trained physicians, even in the late eighteenth century, were comparatively rare, especially in rural areas, and most medical advice and cures for everything from burns to toothaches were dispensed within the home. Recipes for poultices, teas, and various efficacious decoctions composed an essential category of knowledge most often associated with women in colonial America. In this sense home medicine was an extension of cookery. Healing also required other skills including midwifery, setting broken bones, and nursing.

Healing practiced in the home followed the principles of natural folk medicine, which relied on a knowledge of the medicinal properties of naturally occurring plants and minerals. The need for early Americans to acquire a knowledge of New World medicine both in terms of cures and ailments was reflected in an advertisement printed in the *Pennsylvania Gazette* in 1734 with the publication of *Every Man His Own Doctor; or the Poor Planter's Physician,* "prescribing plain and easy Means for Persons to cure themselves of all or most of the Distempers incident to this Climate, and with very little Charge, the Medicines being chiefly of the Growth and Production of this Country." The household store of remedies also may have included some imported prepared cures like Turlington's Balsam of Life, Dr. Bateman's Pectoral Drops, or Dr. Godfrey's Cordials, along with "all sorts of Druggs, and Chymical and Galenical Medicines." These early "patent medicines" typically were sold in small bottles or earthenware jars. While the role of women in Anglo-American home healing had its roots in British folk society, many of the ingredients and recipes reflected the traditions of other cultures, especially those of Native Americans and Africans, as well as elements of Old World superstition and magic.

THE DOUBLE-PARLOR HOUSE

Even as certain open-house forms—especially one- and two-room dwellings—emerged in the early colonial period as favored options, others failed to gain sustained currency and dropped from common use by the end of the seventeenth century. Thus, the first stage in the development of hearth and home represents both a sort of winnowing-out process and the emergence of distinctive regional trends in house form developed within the context of broadly conceived notions of Anglo-American housing. Certain open-plan dwelling types, such as the double-parlor house, much favored in rural England and introduced into the British colonies, eventually proved unsuccessful in a New World setting. Finally, although the experience of living in two-room houses was analogous across regions, the appearance and details of those houses were not.

The emergence of regional patterns in housing is significant to considerations of home and hearth in the British colonies because it underscores how quickly settlers veered from British precedent. Available building materials, labor shortages, and other factors contributed to the emergence of regional trends, but the most significant cause appears to have been how quickly the character of British settlements became

American as English-speaking settlers interacted with Native American, Dutch, Scandinavian, German, and African people and cultures. Certainly the influence of African folkways on the British settlements of the Chesapeake and Carolina Low Country are among the most thoroughly documented. The preference in the South for separate outbuildings, particularly those related to food storage, preservation, and preparation, has been associated with African traditions. In a very different context, the German settlers of Pennsylvania introduced their Anglo-American neighbors to continental baking and household heating practices. Thus, by the 1720s the British qualities of home and hearth increasingly reflected elements of cross-cultural exchange and regional preference. By the early eighteenth century, the image of hearth and home in the British colonies assumed less an Anglo-American than a regional American character.

Even as regional preferences became increasingly distinctive in the eighteenth century, certain British house forms were being dropped from the general repertoire of Anglo-American dwelling design options. The contrast between the popularity of the double-parlor houses throughout England and their eventual disappearance in the colonies, for example, suggests a great deal about the ways in which the house, the basic building block of hearth and home, was rethought by the rural and urban elite in the eighteenth century. The English double-parlor house was a dwelling three rooms long and one room deep with an interior arrangement accommodating a kitchen, common room, and parlor. Some double-parlor houses possessed a narrow passage between the hall and parlor, while others provided access directly into the body of the house. The separation of household functions into different spaces represented social status in the seventeenth and early eighteenth centuries. This developing social status provided the context for the further structural transformation of elite households during the later colonial period.

The Philadelphia town house commissioned by settler John Claypoole in the 1680s is representative regarding several key points about the planning and appearance of the double-parlor house in the seventeenth century. Claypoole's expectations for the new dwelling were modest, as he indicated in a 1682 letter: "I would have him to begin to build a house. . . . If it be but a slight house like a barn, with one floor of two chambers and will hold us and our goods and keep us from the sun and weather, it may suffice." Claypoole noted in a second letter,

As I said before, I hope there will be a little house built for us, if it be but like a barn, and if possible, let there be a cellar made, to keep some wine and other liquors cool in, that I intend to take with me, for it's like we shall come there in very hot weather. (James Claypoole. *James Claypoole's Letter Book*, p. 180)

Upon his arrival in Pennsylvania, Claypoole immediately enlarged his house into a three-room arrangement: "To this I built a kitchen of 20 foot square where I am to have a double chimney, which I hope will be up in 8 or 12 days." The completed twenty-by-sixty-foot (6 by 18 meter) shell with its three rooms, cellar, rough appearance, and unfinished fireplaces stood as a mansion of enviable size and quality in the first years of Philadelphia's settlement. The arrangement of Claypoole's house, however, was not unique to Philadelphia or the Middle Atlantic colonies.

Archaeology in Virginia and Maryland has uncovered a number of similar houses. The plantation house at the Clifts in Westmoreland County, Virginia, in the 1670s, for example, displays the same extended definition of household space with cooking functions located at one end of the house, a common room or hall in the middle, and the parlor, or best room, at the other end. The main body of the nearly eighteen-by-forty-two-foot (5.4 by 12.6 meter) plantation house, with its two heated rooms sharing a single hearth at one end of the house and a narrow passage and service bay at the opposite end, also incorporated a back room and a small closet in the form of wings. The "Manner" house at the Clifts stood in sharp counterpoint to the quarter that faced it. Having just one room with an unfinished interior and a smoke hole in the roof instead of a chimney or fireplace hood, the quarter represented the common household environment of the vast majority of farmers, servants, and slaves.

Three-room plans like the Clift plantation house were built throughout the Chesapeake and

were considered "large and commodious" by their builders and occupants. The Clifts house, like Claypoole's, presented an orderly progression from an unheated storage room and passage at one end to the best chamber at the other. The middle of the house was occupied by the hall—the largest and most important space in the dwelling. Like many of its contemporaries in the Chesapeake, the plantation house, quarter, and yard were enclosed in a palisaded or fenced compound.

Three-room houses like the Claypoole townhouse and the Clifts plantation house were also erected in New England. As interpreted by Robert Blair St. George, the Bray Rossiter house and lot developed in Guilford, Connecticut, in the 1650s demonstrates not only the use of an extended house plan with parlor, buttery, hall, and kitchen but also reveals the importance of setting these houses in their larger environment. The Rossiter compound, more than any other, demonstrates the fact that notions of hearth and home included gardens, workrooms, and farm buildings.

Dwellings like the Clifts, Claypoole's townhouse, and Rossiter's domestic compound represented a form of elite expression that drew heavily on familiar British notions of household planning and open-house forms. Archaeology in the Chesapeake has revealed other houses and complexes like the Clifts, and architectural studies in the Delaware Valley have documented houses similar in design to Claypoole's that were built in the early eighteenth century. Given their general acceptance in the British Isles, their recorded use in the British colonies, and their documented association with the colonial elite, why did the image of hearth and home represented by these buildings lose currency?

The answer to this question rests in understanding not only what typical houses were like in the colonial period, but also how the image of home nurtured by the elite was changed to make once subtle distinctions more obvious. As a group, double-parlor houses were larger, better finished, and spatially more elaborate than their neighbors, but they still reflected the importance of direct "open" access into the hall or heart of the dwelling. The statement of social distances signified by separating kitchen and parlor was obvious and familiar, but in the end it was insufficient. Double-parlor houses simply failed to signify enough of a dramatic break with lesser houses.

"CLOSED" OR GEORGIAN DWELLINGS

The symbolic shortcomings of open plans for the Anglo-American social elite's houses heralded a major transformation in the organization of hearth and home. Neoclassically inspired or "Georgian" houses expressing aesthetic and social values of balance, symmetry, restricted access, and hierarchy were the new choice for the rural and urban elite. These "closed" dwellings incorporated unheated stair halls or passages and specialized sitting, dining, entertaining, and business rooms into their overall arrangements. Where access into open plans led directly into heated living spaces, entry into closed plans was filtered through the Georgian stair hall or directed around back to service wings or domestic outbuildings. While the earliest examples of these so-called Georgian houses appeared as early as the 1690s in New England and by the 1720s in the plantation South, they failed to gain general currency until the mid eighteenth century. Even then they remained the property and affectation of the plantation, mercantile, and professional elite.

The hallmark of the Georgian house was a balanced front, which usually included five openings across each floor with a centrally placed doorway. The exterior placement of openings telegraphed the interior arrangement. The centrally placed door, finished in the most pretentious houses with paneled and pedimented surrounds, opened into the unheated stair passage or hall. The windows illuminated the rooms on either side. The exterior and interior geometry of the Georgian hall functioned in sharp counterpoint to the more irregular fenestration and open plans of one- and two-room houses. The visual quality of Georgian houses united these buildings as symbols of social and economic power across regions. Thus, while the Georgian mansions of the Connecticut River valley elite and the South Carolina Low Country gentry were visually distinct in details of ornament and construction, they shared in their closed plans and the quality of their exterior and interior

ornament an unmistakable affinity, wherein local architectural expression was tempered by larger cosmopolitan tastes. In many instances the regional quality of exterior appearances belied elaborate interiors.

Visually powerful, these houses were never the property or the homes of more than a distinctive and powerful minority. The majority of Anglo-Americans continued to build and occupy one- and two-room houses long after the American Revolution. And despite the massive importation of commodities associated with the consumer revolution and rising standards of living, they continued to inhabit their old open-plan houses in much the same way as earlier generations. The difference was that the Georgian house represented elite aspirations in a new way. The organization of the Georgian home was the material expression of new distinctions based not so much on old categories of social rank as on the newly acquired power of property and wealth.

Admittance into the house via an unheated stair passage, which typically contained an open stair leading to the upper floors, represented a dramatic break with the older open plans where people entered directly into the principal working and living room of the home. This segmentation of domestic space is underscored by the relegation of cooking and household work to the back of the house and the location of display in the front. The hall often contained extra dining tables and chairs and could function as a reception or sitting room. In Middle Atlantic and southern houses one room in depth, the rooms on either side of the hall were furnished as a dining room and a parlor. Cooking and other activities associated with foodways and household industries were typically placed in cellars, wings, or separate outbuildings. In houses two rooms deep, the two additional rear rooms served variously as sitting rooms, offices, back parlors, kitchens, or downstairs sleeping chambers.

Dining rooms identified by name in inventories contained the expected primary dining table, sets of chairs, built-in or freestanding cupboards for the storage and display of silver plate, glass, fine ceramics, and, occasionally, bookcases. Parlors, on the other hand, offered considerably more diverse furnishing possibilities. Some were furnished as formal sitting and entertainment rooms, while others were equipped variously as dining rooms, offices, and downstairs sleeping chambers. Although the term parlor implied the best room, it denoted no standard function. In fact, the best room of the house appears to have doubled as both a private family space and public room for special occasions. Thus, the furnishing strategies for both dining rooms and parlors were ambiguous to the point where the furniture associated with one specialized space was not infrequently found in another.

Sleeping arrangements also changed with the advent of Georgian houses. Some householders continued the old pattern of keeping the best bed in the parlor, but more and more often chambers with beds, chests, chairs, and stands occupied the uppermost floors of the house. Not only did the idea of functionally specific sleeping rooms (some still having the aspect of private parlors where people could socialize and dine) gain currency, but so too did the tendency to limit the occupants of a bed by number and gender. Infants and small children slept in the same room as their parents until they were old enough to share quarters with their siblings. Domestic servants in elite households were increasingly likely to have their own quarters—usually located over the kitchen at the point farthest from the best parlor and parlor chamber. Occupants of one- and two-room open-plan houses also created more or less private chambers of the type associated with the specialized spaces of the Georgian house.

Household Goods and Food

The closed quality of the Georgian house was expressed not only through the introduction of the central stair hall as a social buffer and the increased specialization of rooms such as sleeping chambers, but also in the display of furnishings within the house. As the standard of living, measured in terms of a wide selection of consumer goods, skyrocketed through the third quarter of the eighteenth century, the social meanings attached to the acquisition and display of those goods became more and more expressive of class-based social distances. Kevin Sweeney associates this transition with the outward appearance of furniture and the introduction of a new stylistic vocabulary. Tables, for example,

"clearly document a concern with display, comfort, and gentility" among the wealthier members of rural communities and urban society. No single aspect of home life more clearly conveys this transition than the glass and ceramics associated with food preparation and presentation in the eighteenth-century home.

"The emphasis on food as social display," archaeologist Anne Yentsch states, "brought attention to distinctive table settings and increasingly sophisticated and/or ostentatious (that is, magnificent) ways to serve food in wealthy homes." The dinner and tea equippage found in the homes of urban merchants from Boston to Charleston, for example, provided the basis for a mannered discourse centered on the rules of gentility, etiquette, and social comportment. More than one eighteenth-century visitor to the British colonies commented on the disjuncture between what they perceived as the rough exterior aspect of houses and the pleasant and familiar trappings of polite society represented by interior furnishings and entertainments. In this regard they missed the point that these fine houses functioned in at least two contexts. First, despite the perception of exterior plainness, these houses generally represented a standard of living expressed in local architectural terms that was attainable only by the wealthiest. The exterior of the house communicated local hierarchy in the local language of housing. Second, the interior world of taste and manners represented a unifying function where, for example, the material language of the dinner table and the polite discourse of dining connected like-minded individuals through familiar rituals such as conversation, musicales, and gaming. The interior of the house communicated solidarity through the international knowledge and application of etiquette.

The social associations made through a shared appreciation of fine things, as well as the knowledge of how to use them in proper fashion, simultaneously separated the homes of the elite from their immediate, lesser neighbors and allied them with a cosmopolitan community of like-minded individuals scattered throughout the Atlantic basin. A silver tea service carried by an English trader who died in Norfolk, Virginia, at the close of the eighteenth century, for example, represented both economic and social capital. The silver tea set could be pawned or pledged as collateral for cash loans or used as the basis for business entertainments in rented lodgings. In the latter role, a tea service represented the ability to evoke a specific image of home space and a corresponding element of genteel domesticity in an unfamiliar setting.

The heightened complexity of Georgian foodways extended beyond the opulence of table settings to the meal itself. The rites of formal dining exercised by the "rich and opulent," as Yentsch observes, was associated with "more elaborate food preparation; mastery of complex recipes; purchase of rare, expensive, or out-of-season ingredients." Roast meats and fowl, baked tarts and pastries, steamed vegetables, imported wines, and exotic fruits served on English, French, and Chinese ceramics nourished both body and social ambition. Poor and middling farmers and urban laborers and artisans, by contrast, continued to subsist on bland, colorless one-pot meals such as the standard dinner described by Laurel Ulrich for New England farmers: "For ordinary days the most common menu was boiled meat with whatever 'sauce' the season provided—dried peas or beans, parsnips, turnips, onions, cabbage, or garden greens." Diet varied across regions with availability of different types of local produce. The herring, clams, and oysters available to people living on the Atlantic seaboard were not as accessible to inland settlers, but they could be purchased in public markets and stores as readily as rice, tea, coffee, coconuts, and other culinary exotica.

However, the most significant distinctions between foodways, like houses, were not by region but by wealth and social class. The world of formal dining from Boston to Charleston was illuminated by candles and lamps reflected in sconces and mirrors; the less affluent in the same cities consumed their meals from wooden bowls by guttering firelight or the flicker of twisted rush tapers wedged into the exposed carpentry joints of their houses. This hierarchical quality of foodways extended even to basic kitchen equipment. Mid-eighteenth-century Philadelphia merchants advertised "London pewter of several sorts, as dishes, plates, porringers, tankyards, mugs, basons, spoons, dram bottles and sucking bottles" and "all Sorts of Copper work, viz. Tea ketlles, Coffee-Pots, Warming Pans, Copper-Pots, Sauce-pans, Dutch Ovens, and

Stew-Pans." The acquisition of advertised household goods associated with amenity and specialization was an option open to all, and it was exercised to varying degrees by individuals associated with all economic classes; the ability to acquire impressive assemblages, however, remained the option of a wealthy minority. Most kitchen hearths, for example, continued to make do with two or three iron pots and pans and miscellaneous assortments of coarse-bodied earthenwares. Extensive sets of copper cookware were generally associated with the households of the rural and urban elite and were more likely to be handled by servants than the householders.

The Georgian Style as a Symbol of Transformation

The appearance and expression of closed plans coincides with three historic processes: the redefinition of living and service functions in the house, the increased availability and acquisition of goods associated with the consumer revolution, and a pronounced trend toward social segmentation in everyday life. The elaboration of space within Georgian houses describes more than just the insertion of a stair passage between the old hall and parlor. The new plans represented a fundamental realignment in the social geography of the house. Rooms on the ground floor were now divided by the social space of the stair passage instead of the partitions that served to screen the hall from the parlor in two-room houses. The result was the creation of social buffers within the house itself. As a consequence the organization of hearth and home in the Georgian house expressed a social hierarchy of unequal stature and access. The carefully contrived hierarchies expressed within the house through architectural trim, furnishings, and social interaction expressed larger patterns of community interaction and social hierarchy in Anglo-American society at large.

The transformation of home, self, and society symbolized by Georgian houses was articulated throughout the British colonies from the mid eighteenth century into the mid 1800s and is seen as a major phenomenon in colonial American social history. In the Chesapeake, Rhys Isaac observed, "The increasing consciousness of individual separateness, already evident in the spatial divisions in the gentry houses of 1740, was slowly becoming more general." The social usage of

Georgian architecture, Isaac concluded, "would be apparent not only in modified social custom (as in the closing of doors once hospitably opened to strangers) but also in the altered internal arrangement of common planters' houses."

James Deetz voiced the same conclusions for New England in a larger material culture context: "Not only is the Georgian style an imposed order, it is totally mechanical in its integration, and its characteristic balance, symmetry, and order speak to us in the same way as do individualized graves and markers, and matched individual sets of china." In the Middle Atlantic colonies, the spatial conventions of Georgian architecture were both disruptive and desirable: "disruptive because the passage removed entry into the heated, lived-in portions of the house by at least one more distance, desirable because those who opted for the new convention were the same individuals most concerned with expressing their social separation from the community at large."

The advent of the Georgian house did not signal the total abandonment of "open" houses. Folks in the British colonies continued to build and occupy hall and hall-parlor houses, but they did so with an expanded social sensibility of class and home represented by the Georgian house. The images of hearth and home that emerged at the close of the colonial period increasingly reflected rifts in the Anglo-American social landscape. In the years after the revolution, the symbolism and sociology of hearth and home would continue to document the paradoxes of diversity and division, hierarchy and community, self and society with a compelling eloquence and veracity found in few other historical surces.

BIBLIOGRAPHY

Benes, Peter, ed. *Early American Probate Inventories.* The Dublin Seminar for New England Folklife Annual Proceedings, 1987. Vol. 12. Boston, 1989.

Carson, Cary, Norman F. Barka, William M. Kelso, Gaarry Wheeler Stone, and Dell Upton. "Impermanent Architecture in the Southern American Colonies." *Winterthur Portfolio* 16, nos. 2 and 3 (1981):135–196.

Claypoole, James. *James Claypoole's Letter Book: London and Philadelphia, 1681–1684.* Edited by Marion Balderston. San Marino, Calif., 1967.

Cummings, Abbott Lowell. *Rural Household Inventories, Establishing the Names, Uses and Furnishings of Rooms in the Colonial New England Home, 1675–1775.* Boston, 1964.

Deetz, James. *In Small Things Forgotten: The Archaeology of Early American Life.* Garden City, N.Y., 1977.

Demos, John. *A Little Commonwealth: Family Life in Plymouth Colony.* New York, 1970.

Fischer, David Hackett. *Albion's Seed: Four British Folkways in America.* New York, 1989.

Garrison, J. Ritchie. *Landscape and Material Life in Franklin County, Massachusetts, 1770–1860.* Knoxville, Tenn., 1991.

Glassie, Henry. "Eighteenth-Century Cultural Process in Delaware Valley Folk Building." *Winterthur Portfolio* 7, no. 1 (1972):29–57.

———. *Folk Housing in Middle Virginia: A Structural Analysis of Historic Artifacts.* Knoxville, Tenn., 1975.

Herman, Bernard L. *Architecture and Rural Life in Central Delaware, 1700–1900.* Knoxville, Tenn., 1987.

———. *The Stolen House.* Charlottesville, Va., 1992.

Isaac, Rhys. *The Transformation of Virginia, 1740–1790.* Chapel Hill, N.C., 1982.

Michel, Jack. " 'In a Manner and Fashion Suitable to Their Degree': A Preliminary Investigation of the Material Culture of Early Rural Pennsylvania." *Working Papers from the Regional Economic History Research Center* 5, no. 1 (1981):1–83.

Nagy, John C., ed. *Accessible Archives CD-ROM Edition of Pennsylvania Gazette: Folio 1, 1728–1750.* Malvern, Pa., 1991.

Neiman, Frazier D. *The "Manner House" Before Stratford (Discovering the Clifts Plantation).* Stratford, Va., 1980.

St. George, Robert Blair. "Bawns and Beliefs: Architecture, Commerce, and Conversion in Early New England." *Winterthur Portfolio* 25, no. 4(1990):241–287.

———. " 'Set Thine House in Order': The Domestication of the Yeomanry in Seventeenth-Century New England." In vol. 2 of *New England Begins: The Seventeenth Century.* Catalogue of the Exhibition Held at the Museum of Fine Arts, Boston, May 5–August 22, 1982. 3 vols. Boston, 1982.

Sobel, Mechal. *The World They Made Together: Black and White Values in Eighteenth-Century Virginia.* Princeton, N.J., 1987.

Sweeney, Kevin M. "Furniture and the Domestic Environment in Wethersfield, Connecticut, 1639–1800." In *Material Life in America, 1600–1860,* edited by Robert Blair St. George. Boston, 1988.

Ulrich, Laurel Thatcher. *Good Wives: Image and Reality in the Lives of Women in Northern New England, 1650–1750.* New York, 1982.

Upton, Dell. *Holy Things and Profane: Anglican Parish Churches in Colonial Virginia.* New York, 1986.

_____. "Vernacular Domestic Architecture in Eighteenth-Century Virginia." *Winterthur Portfolio* 17, nos. 2/3 (1982):95–119.

Yentsch, Anne. "Minimum Vessel Lists as Evidence of Change in Folk and Courtly Traditions of Food Use." *Historical Archaeology* 24, no. 3 (1990):24–53.

Bernard L. Herman

SEE ALSO **Architecture; Crafts; Gender Relations; Recreations; Rural Life;** and **Urban Life;** and various essays in FAMILIES AND THE LIFE COURSE.

THE DUTCH COLONY

Their [the Dutch at Albany] kitchens are likewise very clean, and there they hang earthen or delft plates and dishes all round the walls. . . . They live here very frugally and plain, for the chief merit among them seems to be riches, which they spare no pains or trouble to acquire, but are a civil and hospitable people in their way, but at best rustic and unpolished.
Dr. Alexander Hamilton, *Itinerarium*, 1744

WITHIN THEIR HOMES the Dutch lived through much of the eighteenth century in a manner little changed from that of their forefathers. Their rooms, "large and handsome," according to Hamilton, retained a traditional medieval aspect recognizable on both sides of the ocean. All were constructed alike, usually with a large Dutch fireplace dominating one wall. Large, smooth ceiling beams were supported on exposed wall posts between which were doors and windows painted red or blue-gray, all of which contrasted with the austerely whitewashed plaster walls. Furnishings gave each room a distinctive purpose and appearance. Both in the towns and on the farms, homes of at least modest pretensions—something to which the Dutch aspired—had a kitchen and a *groot kamer* (big room), while the cellar and second floor remained a space for storage, only rarely used for habitation.

THE ROOMS OF THE HOUSE

The kitchen was more of a general-purpose room than it is today. It was used not only for preparing and serving meals but also for storing possessions, for entertaining everyday visitors, for some family members to sleep, and as a place for keeping everyone warm in winter. The Dutch fireplace was especially suited to a busy kitchen and was well equipped with kettles, pans, saucers, trivets, trammels, andirons, and a cast-iron fireback. Without jambs the hearth was unusually large, making possible the preparation of several dishes at once. Against a wall stood a *pottebank*, a cupboard of shelves for storing and displaying useful pottery, dishes, and pewter. One or more tables and several turned chairs completed the essential furnishings. On the wall might hang a *lepelrekje*, a Dutch spoon rack on which each person hung his spoon between meals. Placed under her feet—and petticoats—a foot stove served the lady of the (drafty) house well as a portable heater.

The *groot kamer* was like our conception of a parlor: a room of good taste and fine possessions used to entertain special people. Warren Johnson, an Irish visitor to Albany in 1760 to 1761, noted that "a Dutch Parlor has Always a bed in it. & the man & woman of the House Sleep in it. their Beds are good, for they Mind noe other Furniture." Since Dutch homes contained few rooms but large families, beds in varying forms were often placed in every room. They included beds enclosed by doors, four-poster bedsteads hung with fine textiles, and pullout beds. In the better homes, a fine *kas* or Dutch cupboard was filled with valuables such as silver, textiles, pottery, and porcelain. However the most expensive silver probably was locked away in an iron chest and shown only on special occasions. Tables, upholstered or caned chairs, the family Bible, portraits and Scripture paintings, a mirror, decorative earthenware upon the *kas* and mantle, and polished brass hearth tools all combined to create the intended effect of well-earned affluence, which for a Calvinist was a demonstration of God's grace.

FOOD AND DRINK

The Swedish naturalist Peter Kalm visited Albany in 1749 and 1750 and remarked on the habits of the Dutch, including their meals, which he found very different from those of the English. Breakfast, at seven, consisted of tea with milk, bread and butter, slices of dried beef, and sometimes grated cheese—over which "the host himself generally says grace aloud." For midday dinner they had milk or buttermilk with bread along with boiled or roasted meat, and a large salad with vinegar. Sometimes they also had Indian *sappaan* (porridge). Supper included bread and butter and pieces of bread in milk, and as Kalm ruefully states, usually "there was the same perpetual evening meal of porridge made of corn meal. . . . It was put into a good sized dish and a large hole made in its center into which the milk was poured, and then one proceeded to help oneself." Others, however, described a rich diversity of foods. Charlotte Lennox, who spent part of her childhood in Albany around 1740, wrote,

Immediately after the tea equipage was removed, a large table was brought out, and covered with a damask cloth, exquisitely white and fine; upon this table were placed several sorts of cakes, and teabread, with pots of the most delicate butter, plates of hung beef and ham, shaved extremely fine, wet and dry sweetmeats, every kind of fruit in season, pistacchio and other nuts, all ready cracked . . . the liquors were cyder, mead and Madeira wine. —All these things were served in the finest china and glass. (*Euphemia*. Vol. 3, p. 34)

WIVES, DAUGHTERS, AND HOUSEWORKERS

Domestic work was the province of the *huisvrouw* (housewife) who, depending on her or her husband's affluence, did the gardening, cooking, and other housework with her daughters or supervised the house slaves in this work, as her husband worked with other slaves on the farm or in his trade. New York households had more slaves than any other northern province. While the Dutch viewed themselves as the most liberal and democratic of Europeans, they found justification for slavery in the Bible and used it to attain the wealth to which they believed they were entitled. As Anne Grant commented, "Amidst all this mild and really tender indulgence to their negroes, these colonists had not the smallest scruple of conscience with re-

gard to the right by which they held them in subjection."

As for daughters, Anne Grant remembered her own childhood in Albany around 1760:

The girls, from the example of their mothers, rather than any compulsion, became very early notable and industrious, being constantly employed in knitting stockings, and making clothes for the family and slaves; they even made all the boys' clothes. This was the more necessary, as all the articles of clothing were extremely dear. (*Memoirs of an American Lady*. Vol. 1, p. 90)

DOMESTIC CULTURE

Despite increasing English influence, many Dutch held to their old values, especially their language and Dutch Reformed faith. The large Dutch Bible, from which the head of the family read daily, was the focus of family devotions. It was a repository of family history, its Old Testament stories recalled meaningful parallels in Dutch history, and its engravings had inspired the Scripture tiles on the fireplace and the paintings on the wall. The *groot kamer* was more a shrine to *Patria* than a room for living; it was the family's equivalent of the community's church. The events that took place there served to intensify the faith and renew the culture. Along with its silver, earthenware, and porcelains, the *groot kamer* was utilized at *Kindermaal* (a women's gathering to which gifts for a newborn are brought), weddings, and funerals to celebrate and grieve together at life-cycle events.

The years of peace and prosperity between 1763 and 1776 proved to be the watershed for these Dutch customs. Especially in inland settlements like Albany, what had been self-consciously preserved until then quickly succumbed to the overbearing influence of a heavy British wartime presence. The old ways faded from practice and then, finally, from memory.

BIBLIOGRAPHY

Blackburn, Roderic, and Ruth Piwonka. *Remembrance of Patria: Dutch Arts and Culture in Colonial America, 1609–1776.* Albany, N.Y., 1988.

Grant, Anne. *Memoirs of an American Lady: With Sketches of Manners and Scenery in America, As They Existed Previous to the Revolution.* London, 1808; repr. 1901. Anne McVicar (1755–1838) (later the wife of the Reverend James Grant) of Scotland lived with her parents mostly at Albany from 1757 to about 1763 (the period of her *Memoirs*) and then in Vermont until about 1770.

Hamilton, Alexander. *Itinerarium, Being a Narrative of a Journey . . . from May to September, 1744.* Edited by Albert Bushnell Hart. St. Louis, Mo., 1907. An Annapolis physician, Hamilton (1712–1756) (no relation to the Alexander Hamilton of later fame) wrote this journal while touring the northern provinces in 1744.

Kalm, Peter. *Peter Kalm's Travels in North America.* Edited by Adolph B. Benson. 2 vols. New York, 1937. Peter [Pehr] Kalm (1716–1779), a Swedish naturalist, collected scientific data in North America for Linnaeus between 1748 and 1751.

Lennox, Charlotte. *Euphemia.* 4 vols. London, 1790. Charlotte Lennox (1727?–1804), like Anne McVicar Grant, was a young daughter of a military officer at Albany (ca. 1738–1742). She recorded her memories of the town in this novel.

Singleton, Esther. *Dutch New York.* New York, 1909.

Wilcoxen, Charlotte. *Seventeenth Century Albany: A Dutch Profile.* Albany, N.Y., 1979.

Roderic Hall Blackburn

SEE ALSO **Architecture; Crafts; Gender Relations; Recreations; Rural Life;** and **Urban Life;** and various essays in FAMILIES AND THE LIFE COURSE.

THE FRENCH COLONIES

THE MID-EIGHTEENTH CENTURY European visitor's first impression of the French colonial home in North America, urban or rural, regardless of social class, was based upon its creature comforts vis-à-vis those of a comparable metropolitan dwelling.

CANADIAN RURAL DWELLINGS

Unlike contemporary French peasant homes and ancillary structures, the rectangular house of the Canadian habitant, built of squared timbers laid horizontally between upright posts, was grouped with other farm buildings to form an inner courtyard. The front door opened into a large common room having a floor of wide spruce or pine planks and partitions, if any, of vertical tongue-and-groove boards. The attic's trap door was reached by means of a small narrow stairway against one wall. Homes usually had either one double roughcast chimney in the center or a single one at each end.

The habitants used the stone fireplace for both heating and cooking; only the colonial elite could afford one of the cast-iron stoves made at the Saint Maurice forges near Trois-Rivières after 1740. Wood, sometimes charcoal, served as fuel. Placed on andirons or spit-racks and set ablaze, burning firewood generated considerable heat, particularly when fanned by bellows. Colonial cooks were adept at regulating the flames to produce copious and varied meals. Food was grilled or toasted on a gridiron, boiled or cooked in an iron boiler or caldron mounted on a trivet or suspended from a hook, or fried in an iron frying pan. Fat was collected in a dripping pan, and skimmers and strainers were used to remove grease from liquids. Bread was baked in a stone or brick oven built into a side wall of the fireplace or in a lean-to known as the *fournil.* Completely separate exterior ovens of earth, stone, or brick were less common. Afterward, bakers used the residual heat to bake in pots or deep dishes cakes, meat, fruit, maple-syrup pies, and beans with salt pork. Food preparation and preservation required specialized utensils and storage containers. The average home had iron or copper scales for weighing food and other materials, measuring vessels to determine capacity, and sometimes glassware for both storage and table use.

The kitchen sink was a hollowed-out slab of stone with a groove in the back, set against a hole in an exterior wall. The hole, which declined away from the house, was plugged by a wooden stopper; to drain the sink, the plug was removed.

At meals family members sat not on one side of a narrow dining table with their backs to the fireplace as in Europe, but on either side of a folding table (set with a coarse cloth). After mealtimes, the table was placed against a wall of the common room and used for other purposes. Pieces of silverware and china were sometimes used to decorate the table. Food prepared in pewter bowls or basins was eaten from pewter, bronze, or brass plates (occasionally French faience or Canadian pottery) with pewter spoons and iron forks; everyone drank from tin cups. As in Europe, diners used their personal knives whenever necessary.

While European peasants had to make do with a few crude sticks of furniture, Canadians furnished their homes with the work of Canadian joiners (*menuisiers*) in the enduring Louis XIII and Régence styles. Chests providing limited storage were far less ornate. Some families also preserved a dome-topped, leather-covered chest brought from France by the original settlers; Canadian ones in a similar style were covered in sealskin. Flat-top chests of Canadian pine served not only to store clothing and bed linen, but also as seats and tables.

Hosts offered overnight guests a four-poster bed (in some habitant homes since before 1700) or the warmer, but less luxurious, *cabane*—or enclosed bed, with one or two doors—common in homes without stoves. Sleepers reposed on feather mattresses (common since 1720) or straw palliasses and bolsters or pillows covered by pillow cases, between sheets and under various types of quilted coverlets. Copper bed warmers containing hot embers heated the sheets beforehand. Coffer benches, which also served as a step, could usually be found next to the beds. Babies slept in pine or birch cradles, usually with four posts: a cord attached to one post allowed the mother to rock the child without having to get out of bed. Mirrors were tin or bronze, framed in wood.

Country homes often had pine armoires (wardrobes), buffets, built-in cupboards, dressers and buffet-dressers for the storage of food and utensils. Some buffets had two single-folding doors, a drawer above each; others consisted of two parts, one above the other, having four doors and two drawers in all. Chairs, which supplemented benches, were commonly in one of two styles: either "open-frame," where the only back support was the frame and the seat was of wood, or "rush-seat" (referred to as *à la capucine*), with the back supported by two or three crossbars as well as by the frame. Armchairs, if not imitations of the seigneur's chairs, had straw or rush seats; stools, if low, doubled as footstools and if high, as stepladders.

Buckets and pots were kept in bucket-benches. Women used a dough box, a primitive-looking trough-shaped chest on legs, hollowed with an adze from a section of pine log, to knead dough and store food. They made butter in a wooden or stoneware churn.

Iron, pewter, or tin oil lamps (dish-like, with handles), torches in pewter holders, and tallow candles made in molds and held in copper, pewter, brass, or wire chandeliers provided light. Portable lanterns, cylindrical with conical covers, allowed light to filter through perforations in the metal shell that prevented the wind from reaching the flame. The fuel was beluga-whale or seal oil.

Rural homes also contained other decorations, furnishings, utensils, and implements, including red leather caskets for papers and valuables, razors, tortoiseshell combs, scissors, pins and needles, spinning wheels, flax choppers, and tinder and stone for lighting fires. Some homes had religious ornaments and images. Muskets and powder horns, animal traps, harpoons, fishing line and nets, snowshoes and toboggans were stored for outside use.

Habitants used the *fournil,* or back kitchen, not only for baking but also for making butter, carding wool, dressing flax, and curing tobacco. Containers such as wooden barrels, basins, vats, and tubs were used for various purposes. A stone, wood-revetted icehouse, in which snow was packed, doused with water and frozen, stood near the house; the resulting ice was covered with sawdust and used during the hot summers to preserve food. Some people cut blocks of ice from rivers and stored them in the same icehouses.

Masons constructed wells, for security reasons, in cellars under isolated seventeenth-century Canadian rural houses, which were really small forts. After 1700 they built wells outside, near farm buildings. Before pumps were introduced, colonists raised the water chiefly by a crank, occasionally by a pole. As to sanitation, the use of latrines tended to be rather haphazard until an ordinance of 1676, repeated in 1706, required all householders to have them—at a convenient distance from the residence. Earthenware chamber pots were in common use.

OTHER FARM BUILDINGS

New France's colonists preferred wooden barns—raised by carpenters and joiners and outfitted by a blacksmith with heavy hinges and other iron accessories—to their masonry counterparts, which provided poor insulation for the severe winter. The excellent roofs were thatched, made of boards, or sometimes made of elm bark in Indian fashion. Farmers generally partitioned barns into two squares, separated by a central area. Wooden cattle sheds, and stables for the ever-present horses, built of horizontal timbers and vertical posts in various combinations, complemented the barns. Exterior baking ovens stood a short walk from the house, to spare the dough from freezing in winter and to spare the baker a long, impractical trip to some distant seigneurial communal oven.

THE SEIGNEURIAL MANOR HOUSE

Though few seigneurs were affluent, their homes reflected the owners' elevated social status. Most seigneurial residences were two-story, rectangular, stone structures built around solidly pegged frames. The typical house's openings were decorated with ornamental ironwork, while the interior woodwork was finely crafted. Partitions and floors were constructed of good quality wood. Heavy stone chimneys, flanking the side walls, serviced the kitchen area and the larger living area, each of which had an individual entrance.

The manor house boasted embellishments rarely found in habitant homes: there would be more china, imported pottery, and silverware, and a wider variety of tasteful Canadian furniture crafted in French-derivative styles: single-door, two-door, and four-door pine armoires, built-in cupboards for the storage of food and dishes; one- or two-tier glazed buffets that doubled as bookcases; food lockers (often built in) with one or two doors and slats for ventilation; and chairs, armchairs, tables, commodes (chests of drawers), and glass mirrors in wooden frames. Affluent colonists also owned upholstered or caned beechwood armchairs imported from France and fine Canadian beds with relatively luxurious bedding.

The seigneurial cook used pepper mills, nutmeg graters, coffee grinders, fish kettles, baking pans for meat pies, dripping pans for collecting fats and juices, basting ladles, and warming pans.

TOWN HOUSES

Although most urban dwellings accommodated extended families, apprentices, and domestics, they were no more crowded than those of contemporary French provincial towns. Most Quebec houses tended to be of stone construction. Crowded close together, narrow structures stood two or three stories high. Most residences in Montreal and Louisbourg were wooden, the former of *pièce-sur-pièce*, the latter of *piquet* construction. Since professionals and tradesmen ranging from the poorest of the artisans to the wealthiest merchant, notary, or physician usually worked in their homes, residences contained both occupational and domestic furnishings, all reflecting individual economic status. Silversmiths, coopers, masons, blacksmiths, joiners, and shoemakers were the most prosperous colonial artisans. These artisans partitioned their buildings into workshops or offices, kitchen-living rooms, and bedrooms: as families grew, bedrooms were subdivided, and partitions or bed hangings improvised to provide occupants a semblance of privacy. In larger, more expensive homes (such as those of merchants), parlors and dining rooms were separate from kitchens.

Stoves, capable of radiating heat more effectively than fireplaces, were in general use. Whether constructed of cast iron or sheet iron, or of brick with a metal door, top plate, and stove pipe, stoves varied in size. At Louisbourg, the standard was brick stoves built in the autumn and dismantled in the spring.

Kitchen utensils and tableware in urban settings resembled those of country homes, but with a greater range of quality and quantity, even among artisans, and demand for these goods was sufficient to sustain a brisk second-hand trade. Only the bourgeois and the more affluent of the artisans enjoyed the use of the roasting spit. In poorer families, simple pots were often adapted to do the work of kettles, while gridirons were used under frying pans. Pewter was initially commonplace but French pottery gradually replaced worn pewter vessels. Silverware, whether of Canadian or French manufacture, was rare, and the use of cups and saucers of different sizes for tea and for coffee was confined to the elite. At Louisbourg, where French West Indian, and New England goods changed hands, colonial households also contained English glass and Chinese export porcelain.

The homes of the affluent also contained console tables, chests for storage of linen and clothing, chests of drawers, clocks, chandeliers, mantelpieces, and desks, as well as damask, calico, or heavy serge bed hangings. Most artisans' homes, on the other hand, were rather bare, though most contained folding tables, numerous, fairly simple chairs, and buffets. Benches were rare, as were wardrobes and chests. A few homespun curtains, a few framed pictures, a mirror or two, perhaps a crucifix and the odd cheap trinket, appeared in sharp contrast to the more numerous and varied decorative objects of the affluent.

In contrast to small, essentially one-room rural homes, the poorest urban dwelling boasted at least one bedstead and other furniture in a separate bedroom. The poorer the family, the fewer the number of bedsteads or cots and the more crowded the sleeping arrangements. The creation of more bedrooms through the use of thin movable partitions (as at Louisbourg) was less effective in preserving the privacy of the master bedroom than the alternative of providing feather mattresses, palliasses, and bolsters for the night in other rooms and storing them out of the way during the day. Bedding varied among homes, with the number of coverlets and comforters, their condition and their quality distinguishing economic classes. Few artisans could afford, even secondhand, the bed hangings seen in merchants' homes.

BIBLIOGRAPHY

Donovan, Kenneth. "Communities and Families: Family Life and Living Conditions in Eighteenth Century Louisbourg." *Material History Bulletin,* no. 15 (summer 1982):33–47. For interiors at Louisbourg, see especially pp. 41–47.

Franquet, Louis. *Voyages et mémoires sur le Canada en 1752–1753.* Montreal, 1974. Astute observations on colonial society in the 1750s by an eminent military engineer.

Genêt, Nicole, Louise Décarie-Audet, and Luce Vermette. *Les Objets familiers de nos ancêtres.* Montreal, 1974. An illustrated glossary of the French names of everyday objects used during the French colonial regime. Those who recognize by sight European objects of the seventeenth and eighteenth centuries, and know a little French, will be able to identify the English names of many of the objects.

Hardy, Jean-Pierre. "Quelques aspects du niveau de richesse et de la vie matérielle des artisans de Québec et de Montréal, 1740–1755." *Revue d'Histoire de l'Amérique française* 40, no. 3 (Winter 1987):339–372. For interiors in the two towns, see especially pp. 355–372.

Kalm, Peter. *The America of 1750: Peter Kalm's Travels in North America: The English Version of 1770.* Edited by Adolph B. Benson. New York, 1966. Observations on North American colonial society in the late 1740s by a Finnish botanist (a Swedish subject), a former student of Linnaeus.

Palardy, Jean. *The Early Furniture of French Canada.* Toronto, Ontario, 1963. A pioneering work by an artist, connoisseur, and eminent consultant on Canadiana. Profusely illustrated.

Séguin, Robert-Lionel. *La Civilisation traditionnelle de l' "habitant" aux 17e et 18e siècles.* Montreal, 1967. A reference work based chiefly on estate inventories and other documents. More descriptive than interpretive.

Frederick J. Thorpe

SEE ALSO **Architecture; Crafts; Gender Relations; Recreations; Rural Life;** and **Urban Life;** and various essays in FAMILIES AND THE LIFE COURSE.

THE SPANISH BORDERLANDS

ON THEIR TREK into North America, the pioneer families of the Spanish Borderlands took with them everything they needed to establish their frontier civilization: the will to succeed and prosper, a knowledge of the fundamental technologies of farming and ranching, and the basic survival kit of seeds, livestock, and tools.

The detailed inventory lists of the colonizing expeditions of Don Juan de Oñate to New Mexico in 1598, and Don Juan Bautista de Anza to

California in 1776, provide a glimpse of the material culture that the settlers had at their disposal. While the colonists of New Mexico went at their own expense and took whatever they could muster, those that settled Alta California were sponsored by the government and received clothing, implements, supplies, and animals. These expeditions themselves were like good-sized towns in motion. As *carreta* wagons and thousands of head of livestock voyaged north, families carried on with their lives. Babies were born and baptized, marriages were performed, and people died and were buried along the way.

Family life in an honor-bound, patriarchal culture provided well-defined gender and age roles as well as behavioral parameters that defined male and female authority and responsibility by conventions of deference and obedience. And, since frontier colonial society offered no formal institutions of learning, such as schools, the family was responsible for socializing and teaching children. In a curious custom that taught patience, compliance, and respect, any adult, even a stranger, could demand and receive a drink of water from a child. The child was obliged to drop everything, get the water, and stand silently and attentively with arms crossed over the chest while the adult finished drinking, no matter how long it took.

Like a king in his court, the father lorded over the family, demanding love, allegiance, and respect in exchange for providing the material goods of life. An equal partner under the law as far as property was concerned, the wife and mother played the dominant role in rearing children and maintaining the household. Her ceremonious deference and subservience to her husband was rewarded by her family's reverence.

Bonds of familial devotion and loyalty were extended to the larger community through ritual kinship systems. Sacraments of baptism, confirmation, and marriage, which the church regulated and blessed, all required godparents and sponsors. Parents invited friends and neighbors to become co-parents with them—*compadres* and *comadres* (co-fathers and co-mothers). Ritual kinship also helped to incorporate slaves and servants into the larger households. These *genízaros* (detribalized enemy Indians) were promised their freedom as they were assimilated into Hispanic culture. Many were freed upon marriage; in any case, their children were by law born free. Communities were united by kin and ritual kin relations to such a degree that everyone was related in some way, which insured social harmony and well-being. To break these familial bonds was to commit sacrilege, a disgrace that could occur only because of tragedy or passion.

Despite the obvious rigors and mortal perils of the frontier, colonists went forth with the knowledge that their lives could improve in their new homes. The peasant immigrant could become a *hidalgo* (son of great worth), a nobleman who controlled land, livestock, and the labor of Indians. However, the *encomienda* system of assigning Indian labor to colonists was unsuccessful and short-lived in the north. Unlike their brethren in the south, the Pueblo Indians of the borderlands were unaccustomed to and resentful of paying annual tributes to the Spanish. Settlers soon learned that the price of their opportunity would be not only the sweat of their own toil but also the blood spent defending their homes and families—first from the rebellious Pueblo and later from surrounding enemy tribes, such as the Apache, Comanche, Navajo, and Ute. The household slaves and personal servants taken as spoils of warfare from the enemy nomads were small recompense for the sacrifices of life on the New Mexico and Arizona frontiers. In California the pacification of the Indians was so complete that colonists there sacrificed less and prospered more than had their countrymen who settled the inland provinces.

What the colonists found most valuable in the business of everyday life can be found in the wills they drew up and the *herencias* (inheritances) that they bequeathed their heirs. First to be listed would be *bienes raices* (rooted goods) or properties, houses, fields, and orchards, followed by the *bienes muebles* (movable goods). Prominent also on the lists were livestock, stores of staples and grains, diverse pieces of clothing, weaving, hides, saddles, ceramics, religious images, iron objects of all descriptions, including *cavadores* (hoes), *navajas* (knives), *hachas* (axes), *martillos* (hammers), *cazos* (kettles), *tinamaistes* (trivets), *frenos* (bits), *clavos* (nails), and even scrap iron. The scarcity of wooden furniture is evident

584

on these lists, even well into the nineteenth century, especially in the inland settlements. In New Mexico a wealthy family might have but a small collection of rustic furniture—a *mesa* (table), perhaps, several *silletas* (straight-backed chairs) or *tarimas* (backed benches), a *petaquilla* or *baúl* (trunks), and a *trastero* (freestanding wooden cupboard) for the kitchen.

A SPARTAN EXISTENCE

It can be said that the major economic activity for the inland provinces of Arizona, New Mexico, and Texas was basic subsistence. Although no settlement was completely self-sufficient, all had to struggle to survive on the isolated frontier. A monetary system based on several kinds of silver *pesos* was in effect, but most trade was based on barter. Eventually a surplus of trade goods was produced, and annual *conductas,* or oxendrawn wagon trains, were driven south with herds of sheep, down the Rio Grande valley in the late fall. The *carretas* (carts) were loaded with woolen Rio Grande weavings, *teguas* (moccasins), tanned hides, dried meat, chile, and *piñones* (pine nuts). They returned with materials unavailable in the north, such as iron, implements, and a few luxury goods. In Arizona and New Mexico, wealth was measured by the number of animals and servants a family owned. Both rich and poor shared a similar inventory of implements, although in different proportions.

The exception to this Spartan frontier standard was, of course, California, whose natural bounty, ready availability of mission Indian labor, and accessibility to commerce by sea created a *rico* (wealthy) class who set the mark for opulence in the northlands. The Californios could easily import luxury goods such as furniture, silk clothing, porcelain, and lacquer ware from the Orient via the Philippines. Early English and American travelers were treated quite generously, and their enthusiastic descriptions of their hosts in diaries and letters contributed to the legend of halcyon California.

HOUSING

The first permanent dwellings inhabited by Spanish Borderland colonists were typical multifamily pueblo apartment blocks, lent to them by the Tewa Indians, of the pueblo of San Juan de los Caballeros, for the fall and winter of 1598. In contrast to the homes they had left behind in Mexico and southern Spain, these apartments had smaller rooms, no chimneys, and fewer doors. Smoke from indoor cooking or heating fires simply escaped through an opening in the roof, which also served by ladder, as an entrance.

Pueblo dwellings were made of rock masonry, mud, and straw, although the latter two materials were puddled and formed by hand. The making of adobes, or earthen bricks, is an Arabic technique that the Spanish settlers introduced to the Americas. The roof was made of whole, peeled timbers crosslaid with a cover of sapling sticks and packed earth. Doorways were low so that they could be easily barricaded against enemies or covered with a blanket or hide to keep out the cold. Daylight entered through doors, the ceiling smoke hole, or through inset panes of natural selenite, a translucent mica. The construction of these Native dwellings was so similar to what the settlers already knew, and was so perfectly adapted to the climate of the northlands, that scarcely any changes were made when Hispanic villages were built.

Besides the adobe brick, the major introduction was the chimney, which was constructed in a corner where two of its four walls were already present. The efficient *fogón,* the rounded adobe fireplace that the chimney ventilated, was eventually adopted by the Indians, as was the exterior beehive-shaped Moorish oven. The firelight of the *fogones* was the major source of nightlighting, since candles were scarce and reserved for use on altars during religious occasions. Outdoor lighting was provided by *luminarias,* or bonfires, built from brands of *ocote,* or pitch wood.

Security was still a concern, so adobe houses were built fortresslike, with a patio and well in the center, solid walls to the outside, a main gateway with heavy gates, and a *torreón,* or defensive tower, in one of the corners. Doors and windows opened inward to the protected patio, the center space of family life. The interior would start with a single room, which was added to as the family grew. Floor plans were shaped as an L, a T, or a U, according to the lay of the land, the southern exposure, or the orientation of the house toward the road. Although descent was patrilineal (traced through the father), settlement patterns during colonial times were matrilocal, meaning in this case that a newly married couple would become a part of the bride's extended family household until they could build their own addition onto the family house.

The major difference between Indian and Hispanic dwellings was not the style or materials of construction but the size of the rooms. The metal tools of the Spanish settlers enabled them to fell larger trees, making possible the impressive open spaces of the churches. The larger multipurpose rooms of one-story Hispanic homes differed from the Indian dwellings, which consisted of rows of smaller cubicles in one or more stories. Many Hispanic homes had a *sala,* or great room, for larger family and community gatherings—receptions, dances, vigils for saints, and wakes for the dead.

INTERIORS

Since both finished lumber and furniture were scarce, settlers relied on built-in features, such as *nichos* (niches), *banquitos* (masonry benches), and *alacenas* (built-in cupboards). After plastering, interior adobe walls were coated with a slip of colored clay applied with a piece of sheepskin. A surprising variety of natural clay colors—from gypsum white to yellows, umbers, and siennas—were available. Some walls, such as those under *portales,* or porches, were often plastered in a two-tone pattern, with a lighter color above a dado strip of darker colored plaster that blended into the floor. Occasionally, geometric floral designs would be painted with colored clay over the lighter plaster. Walls along *banquitos* and later ceilings were sometimes lined in cloth.

The major decorative touches of colonial houses were devotional in nature. Every family kept an altar that served as the focal point for group prayer. Adorning it were crosses, hand-dipped beeswax candles, and images of the saints who were important to the spiritual life of the family. These images might include carefully framed commercial prints brought from Mexico, as well as locally made *retablos* (painted wooden tablets) and *bultos* (wooden carvings). Since so few imported religious objects reached the inland provinces, regional styles evolved that became known for their simplicity and grace.

People often slept in the room where the main fire was tended; in smaller houses, this was also the kitchen. In larger houses, separate sleeping rooms had their own fireplaces and were furnished with nothing more than a long pole suspended by ropes from the ceiling, on which hung the blankets and other bedding that at night would be extended over sheepskins on the floor or on a *banco* (wider masonry bench). *Colchones,* or mattresses, consisted of a homespun cotton *manta* or woolen *sabanilla* cloth, both filled with wool or straw. *Camaltas,* or high beds, became the fashion in the nineteenth century. Indian slaves and servants occupied their own separate quarters.

The production of cloth and weaving was a cottage industry in which the men, women, and children of many families participated, especially in New Mexico where there was a good supply of wool. Wool was washed, carded, spun on the *malacate* (hand spindle), and dyed with natural colors from local plants and minerals or with precious imported dyes like cochineal, brazilwood, and indigo. In New Mexico the distinctive Rio Grande style blankets and *sarapes* with colorful bands, diamonds, and stars were produced by families and in *obrajes* (specialized weaving shops) located in larger settlements like Santa Fe. A regional embroidery style based on the *colcha* stitch also developed, and women in their spare moments embroidered woolen *sabanilla* cloth with colorful floral designs. The root of the *amole,* or yucca plant, was used to wash these fabrics; soap made at home from animal fats, lye from wood ashes, and starch from bran were also used.

COOKING AND PLANTING

In the typical household, the kitchen was the most important room. Meals were prepared directly over the fires of the *fogón,* or corner fireplace. Summertime cooking in more southerly desert areas was done in outdoor kitchens, which featured the *estufa,* a waist-high, built-in counter stove made of adobe with holes for pots to be set on. Not all families were fortunate enough to have iron appliances such as *tinamaistes* (trivets), *parrillas* (grills), or *comales* (griddles) on which to bake corn or wheat *tortillas.* Because the Pueblo Indians made beautiful and practical ceramics, the settlers produced almost no pottery. The European potter's wheel, which dominated ceramic production in the south, was rejected in the north, where traditional Pueblo coil ware was the rule. From snakelike ropes of clay the Indians made *tinajas,* large jars for water and grain storage, and *ollas,* or cooking pots. *Jumates* and *jicaritas* (gourds) were used as dippers and ladles, and forks and spoons were so precious they were listed in wills.

As in all the other parts of New Spain, a unique cuisine developed in the northlands; it was a regional synthesis of Mediterranean and Mesoamerican ingredients. In a barter economy these foodstuffs were traded and for frequent festival occasions, food was further distributed by communal feasting. The staples included well-adapted native varieties of blue and white corn, beans, and squash, plus European staples like wheat and garbanzos, which did well in northerly latitudes. There, temperate climes were very similar to those of the Spanish settlers' homeland, so they were able to cultivate wheat.

Both Indians and Europeans revered their staple grains: in Christianity, the sacramental body of Christ is made of wheat, and in the Pueblo religion sacred cornmeal is sprinkled for both blessings and a ceremonial feeding of the spirits.

Like corn, wheat was most often consumed in the form of the flat, round *tortilla*. The *tortilla* is the basis for all the well-known delicacies of Indo-Hispanic cooking—*tacos, enchiladas, burritos*. Since the preparation of corn tortillas was so complicated and time-consuming, only families with servants could enjoy them on a regular basis. In contrast, wheat flour could very quickly be made into tortillas. Wheat flour was also used for *buñuelos* or *sopaipillas* (fried bread), baked bread, and *biscochitos* (sweet biscuits). Every good-sized farming valley had at least one water-driven stone mill for grinding flour, which would then be measured in *almudes,* a shoe-box-sized scoop.

Other important European domestic plants introduced by the settlers included peas, *habas* (fava beans), tree fruits (apples, peaches, pears, and apricots), grapes, melons, and secondary grains such as barley and oats. In the Mediterranean climate of California, grapes, citrus fruits, figs, and pomegranates thrived.

Surprisingly, the Indian farmers of the north did not cultivate any varieties of chile until it was introduced to New Mexico by the settlers and their Tlaxcalan servants. Other native American foods later introduced in the north by the Hispanic settlers were the Andean potato and the Mexican tomato. Onions, garlic, and oregano were popular condiments, although wild varieties of all three already grew there.

Of incalculable economic importance and considerable ecological impact was the introduction of the Old World domestic animals, including cattle, sheep, goats, pigs, and chickens. Indians who before the coming of the Spaniards had always hunted for their meat were impressed with the control that missionary priests had over the animals they bred, raised, gave as gifts, and offered up for slaughter. Much has been written about the impact of the horse on the history of the Americas. Equines were primarily draft animals, but many a horse and burro were gratefully sacrificed in times of famine or privation. Slaughtering larger animals, such as cattle and pigs, was customarily done during cold winter months, to help avoid spoilage.

Dehydration was the prevalent form of food preservation, achieved by sun drying. Both domestic and game meats, such as buffalo, were dried into *carne seca,* or jerky. Since pork spoils so easily, it was preserved with *adobo,* a marinade made from red chile, salt, and garlic. All varieties of fruit could be sliced and dried into *orejones,* or "little ears." Many vegetables were also dried to be used in winter months: *Rueditas,* or "little wheels," were dried, round slices of squash; *tasajos* were dried strips of melons or pumpkins. *Chiles* were gathered into colorful strings, or *ristras,* and hung from *portales* (porches) to dry. Most grains and legumes dried naturally in the fields, but young corn ears were harvested, roasted, and dried to make *chacales,* or *chicos,* as they are called in New Mexico; they were cooked alone or to sweeten a pot of beans.

Everyday fare included *chaquegüe* (thick blue cornmeal mush), tortillas, beans, chile, goat or cow cheeses, and soup, which could contain combinations of whatever vegetables or meats happened to be available. Known as *caldo* and *cocido* in Arizona and California, New Mexicans called it by its old Spanish name, *puchero*. The most common everyday beverage was *atole*, or cornmeal gruel seasoned with salt. The more exotic and imported chocolate and coffee were expensive but available, and were enjoyed for special occasions. Travelers and soldiers depended on the most portable and easily prepared food, especially *pinole,* a sweet meal made from ground parched corn. Saddle bags also contained jerky and dried fruits and vegetables.

Seasonal fare was most elaborate for the Christmas season, when every conceivable and available delicacy was prepared for the celebration. Pork was the favorite meat of this time of year and the *matanza* (slaughter) was and still is the communal feast celebrated whenever a pig was butchered. All of the by-products were enjoyed, including *chicharrones* (cracklings), sweet and salty style *morcilla* (blood sausage), *chorizo* (pork sausage); the meat found its way into *tamales* and a *nixtamal* (white hominy) stew called *posole.* Pit cooking of sides of beef and other kinds of meat is a technique the Spanish learned in the Caribbean; called *barbacoa* (barbecue), it is practiced in large-scale ranching regions such as Texas. Such feasts and the customary exchanges of food they occasioned insured the sharing of the land's bounty among all.

Lent was the other season observed by the preparation of special foods. Spring was a time of natural scarcity and, appropriately, the major Lenten theme was one of fasting and sacrifice. The feasts of Lent and Holy Week, if not excessive, were certainly sumptuous. Meatless stews of corn and beans, chile made with *torta de huevo* (egg fritters), fish, and side dishes of greens and dried vegetables were the rule. A special sprouted-wheat-flour pudding called *panocha* was the greatest delicacy. The symbolism of rebirth was suggested by the sprouting wheat, but as simple sugars are released from the starch in the process, this dessert was one of the only sweets in the colonial diet. Some farms processed sorghum cane and made syrup; the only other available confection was expensive *piloncillo* (little cones of raw sugar), brought overland from Mexico and saved for making chocolate or other special treats.

Folk medicine, because it depended so completely on the knowledge of local herbs and curative plants, was in many ways an extension of the culinary arts. Several European herbs and spices, such as *manzanilla* (chamomile) and *romero*

(rosemary), were introduced; others, such as *yerba buena* (mint), had wild varieties in both Europe and the Americas. Settlers quickly learned from the experience of their Indian neighbors which local plants were useful in reducing a fever, stopping bleeding, settling a stomach, or calming the nerves. Many local aromatic and bitter plants were adopted into the family medicine chest, but one of the favorites was *oshá* (wild celery), a cure-all for everything from colds to repelling rattle snakes. Folk healers like *curanderas* (curing woman) and *parteras* (midwives) practiced their arts much as they did in Mexico or Spain, based on the precepts of humoral pathology, the major Western medical theory and practice prior to the nineteenth century. A kind of folk psychology was also practiced by these healers to cure the detrimental effects of envy, a contributing cause of folk maladies such as *mal de ojo* (evil eye), *susto* (frights), and *nervios* (nerves).

If food preparation was the special domain of women, the cultivation and husbandry of that food was the domain of men. Irrigation farming required a great degree of organization and cooperation; consequently, men were occupied with maintaining their *acequias* (ditches) and tending their fields for the greater part of the year. Ranching in the northlands soon grew to be a major industry and the technology of large-scale stock raising was pioneered there. In California and Texas, cattle herds grew to unprecedented size. By the mid eighteenth century, millions of sheep roamed the sparse pastures of New Mexico and between a quarter- and a half-million per year were driven south to Mexico for sale. Another undertaking reserved for the men was defense, since all able-bodied males were members of the local militia, participating in defensive actions and retaliatory raids against enemy Indians.

Almost all settlers knew and practiced the most basic survival skills of the frontier. The majority of family heads were listed simply as farmers on census documents, meaning that they probably knew just enough about everything to get by. It is not until the late eighteenth century that more specific trades and occupations appear in any numbers on the census. Broad basic knowledge, self-reliance, and the ability to improvise were the most important qualities in a colonist. And the family was by far the most important frontier institution in the colonization of the northern borderlands. Their history is not so much the story of military campaigns, missionaries, and governors, but rather the story of frontier families living their everyday lives.

BIBLIOGRAPHY

Bunting, Bainbridge. *Early Architecture in New Mexico.* Albuquerque, N.Mex., 1976; repr. 1988.

Campa, Arthur L. *Hispanic Culture in the Southwest.* Norman, Okla., 1979.

Gilbert, Fabiola Cabeza de Baca. *The Good Life: New Mexico Traditions and Food.* Santa Fe, N.Mex., 1949; repr. 1986.

Hall, Elizabeth Boyd White. *Popular Arts of Spanish New Mexico.* Santa Fe, N.Mex., 1974.

Horgan, Paul. *Great River: the Rio Grande in North American History.* New York and Toronto, 1954.

Sánchez, Nellie Van de Grift. *Spanish Arcadia.* Los Angeles, 1929.

Enrique R. Lamadrid

SEE ALSO **Architecture; Crafts; Gender Relations; Recreations; Rural Life;** and **Urban Life;** and various essays in FAMILIES AND THE LIFE COURSE.

FESTIVAL TRADITIONS

THE BRITISH COLONIES

OLD WORLD

FESTIVALS OF THE SEVENTEENTH and eighteenth centuries in Great Britain were a complex legacy of the celebrations of many religious and ethnic groups. Historic events of the Celts, Saxons, Normans, and other Native or invading groups left their marks on the yearly cycle followed by the British. The religious rites of Druidism, Celtic and Roman Catholicism, and Protestantism vied for allegiance; and secular celebrations developed around these formalities in many traditional, reformed, and syncretized variations.

Different practices and attitudes toward festival events in the British colonies were shaped by the opposing political and religious factions in the homeland. Since many early rituals were integrated into the Catholic calendar, the official British festival calendar was controlled by the current ruler's attitude toward Anglican, Protestant, and Roman Catholic celebrations.

NEW WORLD

Festivals in the British colonies were commemorated with greater freedom and diversity than in the mother country. This was due to a new class structure, the settlement patterns of regional English groups, and the integration of other ethnic and racial groups' events into their own festival cycles. The difference in climates and growing seasons also contributed to the divergence. The use of both the Julian and Gregorian calendars and their eleven-day difference further confused the dates of a festival.

The Puritans and the reforms of the short-lived Cromwellian era so dominated early New England that both Christmas and May Day were outlawed as frivolous celebrations in the seventeenth century. It was the pre-Christian parts of these spring and winter rites emphasizing merrymaking that offended these Christian fundamentalists. In the Anglican-dominated South, both Christmas and Whitsuntide continued to be observed in the Old World tradition.

With the acceptance of the Gregorian calendar in 1752, two nativity traditions developed. "New Christmas," on 25 December, emphasized the religious and family aspects; and "Old Christmas" underscored the traditional and community dimensions and was celebrated variously between 4 and 8 January. Old Christmas was marked by visits from two Old World frights. Old Nick was a Devil figure who, as an old man or black man, accompanied the gift giver, Saint Nicholas, distributing switches or coal to bad children. He later merged with Saint Nick and today remains only as the mild threat of "you'd better be good." The Hobby Horse was a flying demon who carried bad children away. The Old World frights left a small present for good children or a warning for those who were bad. Traditional English mummer morality plays were presented in some communities. These dramas were acted out from house to house by masked beggars during festive seasons. Their common theme was the death of evil and resurrection of good with stock characters such as the doctor and dances such as the Morris and sword dances. The play about Saint George slaying the dragon was one of the most popular. A few of these plays were still being performed in the early twentieth century in isolated areas of the Upland South.

In the regions of New York and New Jersey populated by the Dutch, Whitsuntide or "Pinkster" was observed with a week of merriment and revelry. Slaves were allowed to participate in this holiday, and it soon took on the character of an African celebration with its use of drums, dancing, processions, and sales stalls. Pinkster celebrations continued in the New York British colony, especially in Albany, until 1811, when these principal attractions of the celebration were forbidden by law. The festival soon lost its appeal and died out.

In Britain, thanksgiving celebrations were declared annually for many national events for which prayers and feasting were appropriate. Lammas Day, the British wheat-harvest festival, occurred on 1 August and was the basis of the Pilgrim's Thanksgiving. This tradition became important in New England, since the harvest coincided with that in the homeland. First celebrated in 1621, Thanksgiving became an annual event in New England after 1631. In the South and the middle colonies, the harvests came at different times, and celebration of the Old World festivals were less important. Although Thanksgiving was regularly observed in some regions of the new nation, it did not become a national event until the middle of the nineteenth century.

The occasions for public festivities in the colonies included many Old World holidays and New World events. Events such as observances of royal birthdays and anniversaries of rulers' ascension to the throne, as well as college commencement days and the election or appoint-

ment of local provincial government officials, all became occasions for celebration. They were marked with bell ringing, bonfires, parades, firecrackers, banquets, dancing, and drinking. Sports, including English football, horse racing, cockfighting, and bullbaiting, were popular events. Everyday activities of shared work such as hunting, fishing, or agricultural "bees" were usually attended with community festivities when the work was concluded. Even a hanging of a notorious criminal became grounds for a holiday.

The military musters of the New World were not for a militia of the upper class but rather for the local farmers and merchants. The time after the morning drills was considered a holiday and was marked by footraces, sporting events, drinking, gambling, and fighting. After the revolution a satire of these early festivals called the Fusileers was observed around the Fourth of July with parades and the wearing of masks.

The festival of Guy Fawkes, a direct result of a suspected "Catholic" conspiracy to blow up Parliament in 1605, was both a political and religious festival in the colonies; 5 November was an official feast day in the Anglican church's Book of Common Prayer until 1859. It was celebrated in the colonies with the ringing of bells, sermons on patriotism, bonfires, and the parading of the effigies of Guy Fawkes, the Pope, and the Devil. As the revolutionary movement grew in the New World, Guy Fawkes Day became more important as an opportunity to burn effigies of British politicians and rulers in protest against the unfair treatment of the colonies.

FESTIVALS IN THE NEW NATION

After the revolution, elements of the British festivals were incorporated into the new nation's emerging holidays. The first Fourth of July contained the same elements as earlier royal anniversary events. Masking, license, and political satire became common themes in the emerging patriotic celebrations. The New England Thanksgiving became a celebration of Native American foods (turkey, pumpkin) that had saved the early settlers. Many of these festive events became official national, regional, or state holidays. Others were combined with related festivals of different ethnic groups, integrated into local or regional folk tradition, or slowly disappeared.

BIBLIOGRAPHY

Chambers, R., ed., *The Book of Days*. 2 vols. Edinburgh, 1861.

Coffin, Tristram P. *The Book of Christmas Folklore*. New York, 1973.

Cohen, Hennig, and Tristram Potter Coffin, eds. *The Folklore of American Holidays*. Detroit, Mich., 1987.

Douglas, George William. *The American Book of Days*. New York, 1948.

Eights, James. "Pinkster Festivities in Albany Sixty Years Ago." In *Collections of the History of Albany*, edited by Joel Munsell. Vol. 2. Albany, N.Y., 1867.

Forbes, Allyn B. "Social Life in Town and Country, 1689–1763." In *Commonwealth History of Massachusettes*, edited by Albert Bushnell Hart. Vol. 2. New York, 1966.

Bruce R. Buckley

SEE ALSO **African-American Culture; Manners; Music and Dance; Native American Religions;** and **Recreations;** and the various essays in THE SOCIAL FABRIC.

THE DUTCH COLONY

DISTINCTIVE FESTIVAL TRADITIONS marked the yearly calendar in New Netherland. Festivals took place on religious and secular holidays such as New Year's, Shrove Tuesday, and Whitsunday and on seasonal and weekly market days. The civil and church authorities repeatedly tried to ban them all to no avail.

New Year's in New Netherland was an occasion for riotous behavior that included the firing of guns and excessive drinking. In 1652 Brant Van Schlichtenhorst, director of the patroonship of Rensselaerswyck, complained that on New Year's Eve the soldiers "shot burning fuses on the roof of the patroon's house and also on the house of the Director," setting the latter afire. The reveling became so serious that in December 1655 Director-General Peter Stuyvesant and his council declared, "whereas experience has manifested and shewn us, that on New Year's and May days much Drunkeness and other irregularities are committed besides other sorrowful accidents such as woundings frequently arising therefrom, by Firing, Mayplanting and Carousing," they thenceforth prohibited on these days "any Firing of Guns, or Planting of May Poles, or any beating of Drums, or any treating with Brandy, wine or Beer."

Shrove Tuesday, which is the day before Ash Wednesday and the beginning of Lent, traditionally has been a time for festivities such as Mardi Gras among the French. "Riding the goose" constituted the main folk activity associated with Shrove Tuesday among the Dutch. This custom consisted of riding on horseback past a greased goose suspended by a rope and attempting to pull off its head. The Dutch Reformed church disapproved of this custom, and the director general and council banned it repeatedly. But like many folk customs, it continued despite official disapproval. In February 1655 the court in New Amsterdam was informed that "the country people intended Riding the Goose again as they did last year," despite the fact that it had been banned the year before. In 1654 Abraham Stevenson de Croat, a Croatian living in Beverswyck (Albany), was fined for walking along the streets on Shrove Tuesday dressed in women's clothing. The magistrates of New Amsterdam eventually declared that Shrovetide was a "pagan and popish feast," even though it was "looked at through the fingers in some places in Fatherland."

PINKSTER: A CREOLE CELEBRATION

Whitsunday, or Pentecost, was known as *Pinkster* among the Dutch. Its religious significance was to commemorate the appearance of the Holy Ghost to the Apostles after Christ's crucifixion. In its folk manifestation, Pinkster was a springtime carnival festival. There is documentary evidence of its celebration among both the Dutch and their slaves during the eighteenth and nineteenth centuries, and it probably was celebrated earlier as well. In 1786 a Scottish physician named Alexander Coventry, who lived in Hudson, New York, noted in his diary, now in New York State Library's collection:

It is all frolicing to-day with the Dutch and the Negro. This is a holy day, Whitsunday, called among the Dutch 'Pinkster,' and they have eggs boiled in all sorts of colors, and eggs cooked in every way, and everybody must eat all the eggs he can.

Two days later Coventry noted that they were "still frolicing Dutch Pinkster." In 1797 a traveler named William Dunlap described a Pinkster celebration among the Dutch farmers along the Passaic River in New Jersey:

The settlements along the river are Dutch. It is the holiday they called Pinkster and every public house is crowded with merry makers and wagon's full of rustic beaux and belles met us at every mile. The blacks as well as their masters were frolicking and the women children looked peculiarly neat and well dressed. (New-York Historical *Collections* 1 [1929]:65)

In the early nineteenth century, blacks from Albany and the surrounding countryside would assemble on the day following Pinkster on "Pinkster Hill" under the leadership of a slave known as King Charles, who dressed in the costume of a British soldier. He led blacks in dances described as "the original Congo dances as danced in their native Africa," accompanied by fiddle, flute, fife, Jew's harp, pipe, drum, banjo, and tabor, the last three of which were African instruments. The drums were "eel-pots covered with dressed sheepskins," and a song was sung with the African refrain: "Hi-a-bomba-bomba-bomba."

In April 1811 the Albany Common Council banned the Pinkster celebration on the ground that it was not in keeping with the strict tenets of the Dutch Reformed church. It was also implied that there was something subversive about a celebration involving riotous behavior on the part of so many blacks. The Pinkster celebration rapidly faded around Albany after 1811.

In his 1845 romance *Satanstoe*, James Fenimore Cooper described a Pinkster celebration in New York City:

By this time, nine tenths of the blacks of the city, and of the whole country within thirty or forty miles, indeed, were collected in thousands in those fields [the Pinkster ground], beating banjoes, singing African songs, drinking, and worst of all, laughing in a way that seemed to see their very hearts rattling within their ribs. . . . The features that distinguish a Pinkster frolic from the usual scenes at fairs, and other merrymakings, however, were of African origin. . . . Among other things, some were making music, by beating on skins drawn over the ends of hollow logs, while others were dancing to it, in a manner to show that they felt infinite delight. This, in particular, was said to be a usage of their African progenitors.

From these descriptions it seems that Pinkster was a Creole celebration combining European traditions with African survivals and was akin to the carnival celebrations in New Orleans, the Caribbean, and South America. Ironically the celebration of Pinkster on Long Island survived longer among blacks than among the Dutch. In 1874 a local historian wrote: "Poor *Pinkster* has lost its rank among the festivals, and is only kept by the negroes; with them, especially on the west end of this island, it is still much of a holiday."

MERRYMAKING ON MARKET DAYS

Market days were also a time of revelry. In New Netherland the trading season (*handelstijd*) for furs and agricultural products was from 1 May through 1 November. One activity associated with this time was the *papegaai-schieten* (shooting the parrot). The members of the burgherguard would compete with each other by shooting from the edge of a wide circle at a wooden parrot on a pole. There was also much drinking, cavorting, and enactment of role reversals. In 1661 one man in New Amsterdam who was often in debt mockingly attacked a merchant, accusing the creditor of being the debtor in their relationship, but the violence spiraled out of control.

There was also a tradition of revelry on agricultural market days. There were both weekly and annual market days in New Netherland. At first Monday was the weekly market day, and there was an annual Free Market, starting the first Monday after Saint Bartholomew's Day (2 September) and continuing for ten days. In 1641 a Cattle Fair was established on 15 October and a Hog Fair on 1 November. In 1656 the director-general and council changed the market day to Saturday.

The city markets became a venue for dancing competitions among the slaves and free blacks, a tradition that continued into the nineteenth century. In 1862 Thomas F. Devoe described in *The Market Book* the activities at Catharine Market in New York City as follows:

The first introduction in this city of public "negro dancing" no doubt took place at this market. The negroes who visited here were principally slaves from Long Island, who had leave of their masters for certain holidays, among which "Pinkster" was the principal one when, for "pocket-money," they would gather up everything that would bring a few pence or shillings . . . and bring them with them in their skiffs to market. (p. 344)

They would compete with each other at dancing on a wooden board, which was called a "shingle." They supplied the rhythm by beating their hands against their legs and tapping their heels. A hat was passed around for each dancer, with the best dancer getting the most money.

The festival most associated with the Dutch today is Saint Nicholas Day, honoring the patron saint of Amsterdam. It is celebrated in the Netherlands on 6 December. However there is no evidence that this saint's day was celebrated in New Netherland. The association of Saint Nicholas with Christmas was the result of the nineteenth-century writings of Washington Irving and Clement Moore.

BIBLIOGRAPHY

Cohen, David Stevens. *The Dutch-American Farm.* New York, 1992. Discusses various Dutch festivals, including New Years, Shrove Tuesday, and Pinkster.
———."In Search of Carolus Africanus Rex: Afro-Dutch Folklore in New York and New Jersey." *Journal of the Afro-American Historical and Genealogical Society* 5, nos. 3 and 4 (1984):149–162. Describes the blending of Dutch and African traditions in the Dutch culture area.
Devoe, Thomas F. *The Market Book.* . . . 1862; repr. 1970.
Merwick, Donna. *Possessing Albany, 1630–1710: The Dutch and English Experiences.* New York, 1990. Analyzes the *handelstijd* celebrations in Albany and New York City.

White, Shane. "Pinkster: Afro-Dutch Syncretization in New York City and the Hudson Valley." *Journal of American Folklore* 102, no. 403 (1989):68–75. Argues that the Pinkster celebration in nineteenth-century New York was a black rather than a continuous tradition.

David Steven Cohen

SEE ALSO **African-American Culture; Manners; Music and Dance; Native American Religions;** and **Recreations;** and the various essays in THE SOCIAL FABRIC.

THE FRENCH COLONIES

THOUGH THE BUSINESS of settling and colonizing the North American continent was an enormous and difficult task, the colonial community was not without its pleasures. Humans are profoundly social animals, and even on the harsh New World frontier, explorers and settlers managed to find time to celebrate. Many of these early frontier celebrations were simple, homemade versions of Old World cultural expressions and customs brought over in the collective memory of the frontiersmen. Some of these were based on rituals associated with the calendar cycle, especially the annual renewal rituals that occur in French and Western European tradition between the Day of the Dead (1 November) and Easter or May Day. Others were simply celebrations of community and reunion eagerly improvised by *voyageurs* (fur traders) and *coureurs de bois* (woods runners) when they found themselves together for a brief moment.

CREATING AN ESPRIT DE CORPS

During the winter of 1606–1607, just after the founding of the first French settlements in New France and Acadia and even as the first French settlers were struggling to survive the incredibly difficult conditions they encountered in their new homeland, one of the leaders of the Acadian colony, Jean de Biencourt de Poutrincourt, established the Ordre de Bon Temps (Order of Good Times), at the suggestion of Samuel de Champlain, to help lift the spirits of the beleaguered little community. As Marc Lescarbot described the system, "Each man . . . was appointed Chief Steward in his turn, which came round once a fortnight. Now this person had the duty of taking care that we were all well and honourably provided for."

In addition to providing an occasion of good cheer, the Ordre de Bon Temps also cleverly served to motivate the members of the community to participate in the provision and preparation of quality meals by making a ritual out of hunting, fishing, cooking, and eating. Everyone involved felt responsible for the maintenance of this improvised festival. Lescarbot noted that

there was no one who, two days before his turn came, failed to go hunting or fishing and to bring back some delicacy in addition to our ordinary fare. So well was this carried out that never at breakfast did we lack some savoury meat of flesh or fish, and still less at our midday or evening meals; for that was our chief banquet, at which the ruler of the feast or chief butler, whom the savages call Atoctegic, having had everything prepared by the cook, marched in, napkin on shoulder, wand of office in hand, and around his neck the collar of the Order, which was worth more than four crowns; after him all the members of the Order, carrying each a dish. (*The History of New France*, p. 343)

The festivity of these events contributed to the social and physical well-being of this fragile community, creating an esprit de corps while helping to prevent such maladies as scurvy (by then the settlers had discovered how to make spruce beer) and malnutrition.

Analogous, though less-formalized, practices in the rest of New France served similar purposes. Voyageurs and *coureurs de bois* found occasions to celebrate the moments when they found themselves gathered together. These rencontres or rendezvous were typically celebrated with ritual feasting—as stores and providence would allow—and animated with songs and stories. Eventually many of the songs and stories they had carried from their European French tradition were adapted to reflect the realities of

their new surroundings. The wide-open frontier, where almost anything seemed possible, fostered the development of a strong tall-tale tradition based on fantastic hunting, fishing, and farming stories, featuring incredibly abundant game, fish, and crops. Songs also began to reflect such colonial features as new flora and fauna and especially the long winters in traditional lyrics such as "La plainte du coureur de bois":

> Vraiment l'hiver est long
> Le printemps ennuyant.
> Nuit et jour je soupire,
> C'est de voir ce doux printemps
> De voir ce doux printemps
> Celui qui reconsolera
> Ces malheureux amants
> Avec leurs amours fort loins . . .

(The winter is truly long. / Longing for the spring, / Night and day I sigh / To see sweet spring, / To see sweet spring / That will console / These unhappy lovers / Whose loves are so far away . . .)

NATIVE AMERICAN CELEBRATIONS

Contact with Native Americans also provided for festive occasions, as trappers and settlers alike observed and eventually joined the local tribes during their ritual ceremonies. Le Page du Pratz, for example, described the yearly cycle of moon-oriented festivals among the Natchez:

The Natchez begin their year in the month of March, as was the practice a long time in Europe, and divide it into thirteen moons. At every new moon they celebrate a feast, which takes its name from the principal fruits reaped in the preceding moon, or from animals that are then usually hunted. (*The History of Louisiana*, p. 319)

The most elaborately described of these Natchez moon celebrations was that of the Great Corn, with singing, dancing, improvised folk drama, and a ritual feast. Contact with such Native American festivities provided entertainment and socialization for French colonials, especially during the earliest years in New France where French explorers and settlers were drawn to tribal cultures. Missionaries whose goal it was to convert the Indians to Christianity frequently complained that the French instead were being converted to heathenism by the Indians.

MARDI GRAS

European settlers did not arrive in the New World without pagan-influenced rituals of their own. As Pierre Lemoyne, sieur d'Iberville, and his party of explorers were going up the Mississippi River on 3 March 1699, they realized it was the date of an annual festival in their own French tradition—Mardi Gras, the day before Ash Wednesday. Known as Shrove Tuesday on the Roman Catholic liturgical calendar, Mardi Gras means "fat Tuesday" and is celebrated as the last day before the Lenten fast begins. According to legend, Iberville declared a Mardi Gras celebration on the spot, and his men sang and drank wine.

Evidence from several French American communities from Louisiana, up the Mississippi Valley through Missouri to the Illinois country, across the Great Lakes to Quebec, and over to the Canadian maritime provinces of New Brunswick, Nova Scotia, Prince Edward Island, and Newfoundland indicates that there was a pattern of similar traditions involving questing or mumming occurring on different dates from New Year's Day through Mi-Carême (mid Lent) to celebrate the New Year. In many parts of French North America, this renewal ritual was called *la guillannée* and has been described by Rosemary Hyde Thomas as "a cohesive symbol of the old French culture that once flourished everywhere in the French settlements of Mid-America."

Popular in the Saint Genevieve district (in Missouri), in Vincennes, Indiana, in the old Illinois country, and at least as far as Quebec, *la guillannée* was essentially a French mumming tradition and included features associated with the French *fête de la quémande* (a ceremonial begging festival), such as mock begging, improvised drama, and ritual role reversals. Groups of ten to twenty participants, all male, often disguised with reversed coats, red scarves, and blackened faces, with stockings over their heads, and sometimes clad in Indian or *voyageur* garb or colonial finery, visited two or three dozen households during the day, performing a traditional questing song and dancing in exchange for refreshments or money. They could be accompanied by musicians, especially a fiddler, and *la fille aînée*, one of the men dressed as a woman. The song,

as reported by Carl Ekberg (p. 321), describes some of the events of the ritual:

> Bonsoir le maître et la maîtresse
> Et tout le monde du logis!
> Pour le premier jour de l'année
> La Guignolée nous vous devez.
> Si vous n'avez rien à nous donner
> Dites-nous le!
> Nous vous demandons pas grand'chose
> Une échinée
> Une échinée n'est pas grand'chose
> De quatre-vingt dix pieds de long;
> Encore nous demandons pas grand'chose,
> La fille aînée de la maison
> Nous lui ferons faire bonne chère
> Nous lui ferons chauffer les pieds
> Nous saluons la compagine
> Et la prions nous excuser.
> Si l'on a fait quelque folie
> C'était pour nous desennuyer
> Une autre fois nous prendrons garde
> Quand sera temps d'y revenir
> Dansons la Guenille, dansons la Guenille,
> dansons la Guenille!

(Good evening, master and mistress / And to everyone else who lives with you! / For the first day of the year, / You owe us La Guignolée. / If you have nothing at all to give us / Tell us of it right away! / We're not asking for very much, / A chine of meat or so will do. / A chine of meat is not a big thing, / Only ninety feet long. / Again, we're not asking for very much, / Only the oldest daughter of the house / We will give her lots of good cheer, / And we will surely warm her feet. / Now, we greet your company, / And beg you to forgive us please. / If we have acted a little crazy, / We only meant it in good fun. / Another time we'll surely be careful / To know we must come back here again. / Let us dance la Guenille!)

The Missouri *guillannée* closely resembles the questing procession common in rural French Louisiana and associated with the Mardi Gras. There bands of masked participants roam the countryside collecting the ingredients for a communal gumbo, to be prepared and eaten in the evening before a masked ball that traditionally lasts until midnight when Ash Wednesday opens the Lenten period of fasting. An analogous song described similar events:

> Capitaine, Capitaine, voyage ton flag.
> Allons se mettre dessus le chemin.
> Capitaine, Capitaine, voyage ton flag.
> Allons aller chez l'autre voisin.

(Captain, Captain, wave your flag. / Let's get on the road. / Captain, Captain, wave your flag. / Let's go to the next neighbor.)

> Les Mardi Gras se rassemblent une fois par an
> Pour demander la charité.
> Ça va aller de porte en porte
> Tout à l'entour du moyeu.

(The Mardi Gras gather once a year / To ask for charity. / They go from door to door / All around the hub.)

> Les Mardi Gras viennent de tout partout,
> Ouais, mon cher bon camarade.
> Les Mardi Gras viennent de tout partout,
> Mais tout à l'entour du moyeu.

(The Mardi Gras come from all over, / Yes, my dear good friend. / The Mardi Gras come from all over, / Well, all around the hub.)

> Les Mardi Gras viennent de tout partout,
> Mais principalement Grand Mamou.
> Les Mardi Gras viennent de tout partou,
> Tout à l'entour du moyeu.

(The Mardi Gras come from all over, / But primarily from Grand Mamou. / The Mardi Gras come from all over, / All around the hub.)

> Voulez-vous recevoir
> Mais cette bande de Mardi Gras?
> Voulez-vous recevoir
> Mais cette bande de grands saoulards?

(Do you wish to receive / This band of Mardi Gras? / Do you wish to receive / This band of great drunkards?)

> Les Mardi Gras demandent la rentrée
> Au maître et la maîtresse.
> Ça demande la rentrée
> Avec toutes les politesses.

(The Mardi Gras request permission to enter / Of the master and mistress. / They ask for permission to enter / In all politeness.)

> Donnez-nous autres une petite poule grasse
> Pourqu'on se faise un gombo gras.
> Donnez-nous autres une petite poule grasse
> Tout à l'entour du moyeu.

(Give us a fat little hen / So that we might make a rich gumbo. / Give us a fat little hen / All around the hub.)

> Donnez-nous autres un peu de la graisse,
> S'il vous plaît, mon caramie,
> Donnez-nous autres un peu de riz,
> Tout à l'entour, mon ami.

(Also, give us a bit of cooking fat / If you wouldn't mind, my dear, And give us a little rice, / All around [the hub], my friend.)

> Les Mardi Gras vous remercient bien
> Pour votre bonne volonté.
> Les Mardi Gras vous remercient bien
> Pour votre bonne volonté . . .

(The Mardi Gras thank you kindly / For your generous good will. / The Mardi Gras thank you kindly / For your generous good will.)

Other versions of the Louisiana French Mardi Gras song mention *la fille aînée* and the intention to heat her feet, just as in the *guillannée* song. Although these lyrics were collected in the 1970s, we now know that these songs and the events associated with the country Mardi Gras go back to medieval France and even earlier. The elements of this celebration over the centuries, therefore, including the colonial period, are likely similar, though there are few direct references to the ritual and no descriptions.

FESTIVITY IN DAILY LIFE

In addition to liturgical or calendar festivals, daily life in the French colonies eventually included festive occasions of a more secular nature. Ekberg describes what the occasion of a visit from a traveling salesman might have been like in Sainte Genevieve, for instance: "The entire day was probably a festive occasion—with much eating, drinking, and a dance in the evening." Wedding festivities likely went on well into the night. Further, as towns developed on the frontier, they invariably included drinking and gaming establishments that provided festivity on a daily basis, to the consternation of local missionaries. Ekberg mentions an abundance of taverns and billiard halls in Sainte Genevieve, and bars, music halls, and houses of prostitution figure prominently in most descriptions of early New Orleans. Settlers throughout the Mississippi Valley and up into New France also regularly eased the strain of daily work by meeting at night with family and neighbors to play music, sing, and tell stories, sometimes until quite late in the evening.

The consistency of certain folklore features, such as ballads and folktales, as well as the questing festivals, would seem to indicate that there was continuity throughout these far-flung regions of colonial French North America, which on one extreme bordered on the Arctic and on the other, on the tropics. This festivity often caused the French settlers to be described as frivolous—especially by their Anglo-American observers. Nevertheless, it was also an important expression of the cultural continuity that gave the new residents of Louisiana, the Illinois country (where they were influenced by their African, Spanish, and German neighbors), Canada, and Acadia (influenced primarily by their Scottish, Irish, and English neighbors) a sense of community and identity and a way to survive the hardships and tedium of daily life on the frontier.

BIBLIOGRAPHY

Ancelet, Barry Jean. *Capitaine, voyage ton flag: The Traditional Cajun Country Mardi Gras.* Lafayette, La., 1989.

———. "La Truie dans la berouette: Une étude de la tradition orale en Louisiane." Ph.D. diss., Université Aix-Marseille I, 1984.

Ancelet, Barry Jean, Jay Edwards, and Glen Pitre. *Cajun Country.* Jackson, Miss., 1991.

Brasseaux, Carl A. *The Founding of New Acadia: The Beginnings of Acadian Life in Louisiana, 1765–1803.* Baton Rouge, La., 1987.

Carrière, Joseph Médard, ed. *Tales from the French Folk-lore of Missouri.* Evanston, Ill., 1937.

Egan, Thomas J. "Vincennes, Indiana: Echoes of French Popular Culture." Ph.D. diss., Monash University, 1990.

Ekberg, Carl J. *Colonial Ste. Genevieve: An Adventure on the Mississippi Frontier.* Gerald, Mo., 1985.

Fortier, Alcée. *Louisiana Folk-tales, in French Dialect and English Translation.* Boston, 1895.

Le Page du Pratz, Antoine Simon. *The History of Louisiana.* Translated by Stanley Clisby Arthur. London, 1774; repr. New Orleans, La., 1947.

Lescarbot, Marc. *The History of New France.* 3 vols. Translated by W. L. Grant. Toronto, 1907–1914.

Robin, C. C. *Voyage to Louisiana.* Abridged translation, with annotation, by Stuart O. Landry. New Orleans, La., 1966. Originally published as *Voyages dans l'intérieur de la Louisiane, de la Floride occidentale, et dans les isles de la Martinique et de Saint-Domingue, pendant les années 1802, 1803, 1804, 1805, et 1806.* 3 vols. Paris, 1807.

Tassin, Myron, and Gaspar Stahl. *Mardi Gras and Bacchus: Something Old, Something New.* Gretna, La., 1984.

Usner, Daniel H., Jr. *Indians, Settlers, and Slaves in a Frontier Exchange Economy: The Lower Mississippi Valley Before 1783.* Chapel Hill, N.C., 1992.

Barry Jean Ancelet

SEE ALSO **African-American Culture; The Conquest of Acadia; Manners; Music and Dance; Native American Religions;** and **Recreations;** and various essays in THE SOCIAL FABRIC.

THE SPANISH BORDERLANDS

THE CYCLE OF TRADITIONAL festivals in the Spanish Borderlands provides not only a window into the religious, secular, and political life of the community through the seasons but also an index of both the religious assimilation of Indians and their relations with Hispanic settlers.

Before it was imposed on the Americas, Christianity already had a syncretic dimension. Rooted deeply in the pastoralism of Near Eastern tribes, Christianity was successfully grafted onto the solar cults and belief systems of agricultural peoples as it spread through the Mediterranean. In the New World as they had in the Old, missionaries superimposed the Christocentric calendar which emphasized the birth and death of Jesus while projecting those events onto the cosmological calendar of solar, lunar, and stellar events. Christmas and the feasts to commemorate the saints always fall on the same dates each year, as part of the solar calendar, while Lent, Holy Week, Easter, and Corpus Christi are movable feasts whose dates change in accordance with the phases of the moon. A season of excess and celebration begins in December, which in the northern hemisphere follows the harvest; it extends until the beginning of Lent, a season of penance and privation and a time for new planting. In the agricultural cycles of the northern hemisphere, then, the times of abundance and want correspond with the religious calendar.

Spanish missionaries were quick to analyze the values and practices of Native American religions. Paraliturgical pageants (many based on traditional *autos sacramentales* or mystery plays) were staged by priests to dramatize Christian teachings and rival Native ceremonials. Besides religion, ideology and history were also taught in these observances, some of which directly recalled the Spanish conquest. As early as 1633 Fray Estevan de Perea prescribed a three-part ritual of greeting, battle, and submission to be reenacted in popular festivals. These elements were already the central feature of folk plays like "Moros y Cristianos" (Moors and Christians), performed to edify the Indians and entertain the Spanish colonists.

For many Native groups the ceremonial distribution of wealth and gift giving was very important, so the friars also incorporated these features into Christian festivals. Characteristics of revered Native deities were attributed to Christian saints, as in the well-known example of the Aztec goddess Tonantzin and the Virgin of Guadalupe, who, according to religious legend, appeared to the Indian Juan Diego on the hill of Tepeyac, the site of the ruined temple of Tonantzin. Native rites of penance and sacrifice were adapted to Lenten and Holy Week celebrations. Summer solstice rites became part of the feast of Corpus Christi whose ceremonial monstrances resemble sunbursts. The rival midsummer feast of San Juan featured ritual bathing since on that day, all the waters of the earth are holy. Although Christianity is hostile to other religions, in the New World as in the Old, its strategy involved incorporation rather than obliteration of its converts' previous beliefs.

The church streamlined the liturgical calendar for its missionary programs in the Americas. The prodigious pantheon of legendary and historical European saints was modified and considerably reduced. New emphasis was placed on the Holy Family (Jesús, San José, Santa Ana, the multiple aspects of Santa María); an inner circle of saints pertinent to Spain (Santiago, San Lorenzo, San Isidro); Spain's principle religious orders (San Francisco, Santo Domingo, San An-

tonio, San Agustín, San Ignacio); and new saints from the Americas (San Martín de Porres, Santa Rosa de Lima). Because geographical features and new settlements were often named after saints, a close examination of maps of the Americas will reveal this revised list of saints. This cosmographic practice served as a way of sanctifying space, of incorporating barbarous lands into the sacred realms and calendar of Christendom.

The necessity of defining sacred space was ongoing, however, and did not end by claiming territory and founding settlements. Every festival was accompanied by processions demarcating and redefining secular and sacred space in each community, year after year. Sacred personages emerge from their sanctuary centers to tour the peripheries and avenues of the settlement, accompanied by its inhabitants. On the spiritual level, a procession reenacts the continuing journey of life and the progress of Christian humanity towards a New Jerusalem. On a temporal level, it marks the passing of another year in the life of the community.

The settlements of any given area of Spanish America were socially united by their observance of the traditional feasts. Every population center would celebrate the major feasts of Christmas (Noche Buena, Santos Inocentes, Santos Reyes [Christmas Eve, the Holy Innocents, the Holy Kings]) and Easter (Carnaval, Cuaresma, Semana Santa, Corpus Christi [Carnival, Lent, Holy Week, Corpus Christi]), as well as the feast for the dead (Todos Santos, Todas Almas [All Saints, All Souls]), and selected Marian feasts (Guadalupe, Candelaria, Carmen, Soledad, etc.)

FEASTS FOR THE LOCAL PATRON SAINT

The most elaborate celebration was usually reserved, however, for the local patron saint, in whatever season the date happened to fall. This calendar of patronal feasts usually marked the visitation and commerce patterns between Spanish and Native American communities in a particular region. All across the Spanish Borderlands the structure and functions of these feasts were quite similar. Each year a priest or community group selected the mayordomos for the honor and responsibility of organizing and sponsoring the annual fiesta. The mayordomos solicited contributions to cover the expenses; it was their duty to refurbish and decorate the church. Walls, benches, and floors were washed, the saints were dressed in their finest clothes, and the altar was adorned with provisions of the season.

The day before the fiesta, religious services were celebrated in the church, bonfires were lit throughout the town, and a large number of people made confession so that they would receive communion on the following day, during the principal mass. Processions carried the saint around the town between the church, the chapels, and homes of the previous and next year's mayordomos. On the day of the fiesta, enthusiasm and happiness reigned throughout the town capturing all its inhabitants, from the youngest to the oldest. Foods of the season were abundant. Local musical groups provided entertainment, and the local poet sang old romances and corrido ballads, as well as more recent compositions. The largest halls of the town held dances; towns held games for the children, horse races, and rooster pulls. The community was renewing itself for the coming year.

A DUAL ROLE

The church wanted to ensure its place at the very center of community life, providing nourishment for body and soul. Traditional fiestas supported this dual role by creating opportunities for both religious edification and release from the tedium of everyday life. Excessive behavior that would not be appropriate during other times of year was permitted during fiestas. Symbolic inversion of social, political, and gender roles were often enacted, especially during the feasts of the carnaval season.

Nonreligious dimensions and functions of the festival also extended to nationalism and the patriotism associated with the emergence of Spanish America's independent republics. In the eighteenth century, the authorities promoted festivals that celebrated kingship, popular allegiance, and reverence toward the Crown and

its symbols. At first, these celebrations were grafted onto major feast days, such as Corpus Christi and Santiago, the patron saint of Spain. In New Mexico, the succession of Fernando VI after the death of his father was celebrated in 1748 on 25 January, the feast of the Conversion of Saint Paul, one of the patron saints of the Franciscan missionaries.

In the early nineteenth century, with the rise of the Spanish American republics, nationalism gained status as a kind of secular religion, and holidays such as Independence Day came to be celebrated separately. Both tradition and change in religion as well as politics are expressed in the popular festival a "time out of time" in which people still reenact their history, confirm their faith, renew their communities, and express their joys and frustrations.

BIBLIOGRAPHY

Adams, Eleanor. "Viva el Rey." *New Mexico Historical Review* 35, 4 (October 1960):284–292.

Brandes, Stanley. *Power and Persuasion: Fiestas and Social Control in Rural Mexico.* Philadelphia, Pa., 1988.

Brown, Lorin W. "Fiestas in New Mexico." *El Palacio* 48 (1941):239–245.

Brown, Lorin W., Charles L. Briggs, and Marta Weigle. *Hispano Folklife of New Mexico: The Lorin W. Brown Federal Writers' Project Manuscripts.* Albuquerque, N.Mex., 1978.

Campa, Arthur L. *Hispanic Culture in the Southwest.* Norman, Okla., 1979.

Espinosa, Aurelio M. *The Folklore of Spain in the American Southwest: Traditional Spanish Folk Literature in Northern New Mexico and Southern Colorado.* Norman, Okla., 1985.

Gutiérrez, Ramón. *When Jesus Came, the Corn Mothers, Went Away: Marriage, Sexuality, and Power in New Mexico, 1500–1846.* Stanford, Calif., 1991.

Enrique R. Lamadrid

SEE ALSO **Manners; Mission Communities; Music and Dance; Native American Religions;** and **Recreations;** and various essays in THE SOCIAL FABRIC.

DRESS

THE BRITISH COLONIES

DRESS, AS A SYMBOL of social status, was a major concern of both seventeenth- and eighteenth-century societies. However, as a symbol it experienced both a shift and an evolution from one century to the next: in the seventeenth century personal appearance embodied station and economic wealth through the wearing of certain articles of dress, while in the eighteenth century one expressed primarily economic wealth through the donning of fashionable apparel. Therefore, while in both centuries dress stood for status, the determinants of that status were different. More specifically, in the seventeenth century, dress communicated a person's identity; description of an individual's clothing was admissible positive identification of that person in court. Further, even though a person might be able to afford a garment, if it was unfitting his or her "station," it was considered improper. While many of these attributes of status continued to matter at the most elite levels, in the eighteenth century a growing economic middle class—neither landed gentry nor destitute—effected the shift from "station" to economic wealth as the dominant determinant of wardrobe etiquette. This class could afford the newest fashions, and purchased them. In this manner they bought visible status, the ability to dress as a person of elevated social class, and thus equated social class with wealth.

In both centuries dress also had value beyond its communicative powers: it represented tangible economic value as currency in legal and business transactions and settlements. In addition, all recognized a person's right to clothing consonant with his or her status: even prisoners and town poor were provided with apparel, and court records spelled out how the clothing requirements of a decedent's family should be met.

THE SEVENTEENTH CENTURY

Seventeenth-century society expected one's station in life to be easily visible in personal appearance. Legitimate display of one's rank was thought helpful in preventing the blurring of the social classes. But that rank belonged to the man, for a woman's position emanated first from her father's and then from her husband's social position; it was his position her dress depicted. For children, who after age seven were dressed as miniature adults, the status conveyed through dress was that of their father.

That not all agreed with this posture is evident in the sumptuary legislation written to maintain social distance between the elite and the rest of the population. Aside from social

603

markers (such as public service and education), the New England legislation also contained an economic marker—£200—as the dividing line between the assumed elite and the rest, non-elite. Further, in turning enforcement of the legislation over to the elite or those exempt from the law, it allowed the upper class some control over maintaining a visible socioeconomic separation through personal appearance.

The 1651 Massachusetts law exempted from prosecution magistrates or other public officers, any settled military officer or soldier, and "any other whose education and employment have been above considerable degree, or whose estates have been considerable, though now decayed." Only gentlemen were permitted to wear gold or silver lace and buttons, points (ribbons, sometimes with gold or silver tips) at the knee, great boots (with wide, softly falling tops), and new fashions in general. However, it was left to the discretion of the town's selectmen to determine which articles constituted dressing above one's rank and ability "in costliness or fashion of their apparel in any respect." Women of elite rank were permitted silk and tiffany hoods or scarves, and bone (a bobbin lace) lace above 2 shillings per yard, and new fashions in general. While few specific items were mentioned, it is clear that wearing new items of apparel and amassing a wardrobe were not considered appropriate for any but the elite. And it was hoped that the upper class would temper itself.

Furthermore, society had become sufficiently complex that determining an individual's social position was increasingly a local matter, aside from the few guidelines provided in the legislation. In 1651 the Massachusetts Bay General Court stated its position that excess was particularly apparent among "people of mean condition, to the dishonor of God, the scandal of their profession, the consumption of estates, and altogether unsuitable to their poverty." The court did, however, acknowledge that it was difficult to set down rules "suitable to the estate or quality of each person." Transgressors were assessed at the tax rate suitable to their displayed dress.

Much earlier, in 1619 the Virginia Assembly had taken a similar approach when it provided that every person should, if unmarried, be assessed according to his apparel, and if married,

according to the clothing belonging to himself and the members of his family. About mid century the assembly passed a law similar to the New England laws, which prohibited the introduction of garments containing silk, or the introduction of silk in pieces except for hoods and scarves, or of silver, gold, or bone lace, or of ribbons wrought with gold and silver. Connecticut's sumptuary legislation mirrored that of Massachusetts Bay.

The last wave of sumptuary legislation came in New England during King Philip's War (1675–1676) and cited "vain, new fashions . . . poor and rich [persons], with naked breasts and arms [low-cut necklines and uncovered forearms], [and] addition of superfluous ribbons, both on hair and apparel." The 1675 legislation was an expansion of the earlier attempts at regulation; everything mentioned previously as contrary to the "ends of apparel" was still illegal. Flaunting of social class and wearing silk hoods were apparently the most frequent transgressions.

The text of the laws, as well as citing £200 as the minimum qualifier for elite status, was similar to earlier English sumptuary laws. However, the same rules when transplanted to New England had very different results: whereas only 10 percent of the English could be considered elite, approximately one-quarter of Massachusetts Bay colony inhabitants could be. Under Connecticut's more liberal laws, with a £150 qualification for elite status, closer to half of the population around Hartford in 1671 could adorn themselves in elite attire. The reasons likely lie in the large number of middle-class individuals and sons of wealthy English migrating to the colony, and in the economic prosperity that many found in the new land. This large number also helped to fuel consumer demand for new apparel, and eventually to equate "social status" with economic wealth.

For men in the British colonies, particularly in New England, status was communicated first through the quality of wool breeches, jackets, and coats, and secondarily through the fineness of their linen shirts and neck cloths. People continued to upgrade the type and quality of the cloth before becoming overly concerned with adding accessories. Once these were of sufficient quality, accessories such as rings, handkerchiefs, silver-headed canes, and hatbands contributed to an overall classification of elite. For all classes blue, gray, and black were the most acceptable suit colors. Even so, at least one elite gentleman cut a fine figure in his orange three-piece suit. White was the most popular color for shirts.

The most clearly recognizable occupation by dress was seaman, normally considered lower status and near the periphery of society. Notable for its colors and patterns—for example stripes—a seaman's outfit consisted of loose trousers/drawers, a red cap, and a double-breasted coat. Not even New England ministers were recognizable by their dress, which more nearly approximated that of gentlemen as allowed by law.

Although a woman's dress varied by class, it did not vary in the same way a man's did. Women of every rank appear to have worn a shift of the same or similar grade of linen and cut. It was not the shift, however, but first the style and then the cut of the articles worn on top of it that varied by social class. Gowns were more prestigious than coats (skirts) and wescote (bodice). Fine wool was more prestigious than coarse wool but less so than silk. However, the coats and wescotes were not made of silk. As with the men, once a certain level of status was achieved through garments, women's accessories served to further enhance their perceived position. Age does not appear to have been a variable in whether one dressed fashionably.

Within these broad characterizations it is clear that a common dress experience existed between colonies from the start. Captain John Smith preserved the list of articles the Virginia Company thought was necessary to the comfort of the immigrant to Virginia: a Monmouth cap, a type of collar known as a falling band, shirts, waistcoat, suit of canvas, suit of frieze, one suit of broadcloth, Irish stockings, garters, shoes, and points.

Very similar are the items on "A List of Apparel for 100 Men" in the records of the Massachusetts Bay colony, and widely assumed to be the wardrobe for a man: shoes; stockings; garters; shirts; suits of doublet, and hose of leather, lined with oiled skin leather, the hose and doublet with hooks and eyes; one suit of Norden Dussens (a fabric) or Hampshire kersey; bands; plain falling bands; a waistcoat of green cotton, bound with red tape; a leather girdle

(belt); Monmouth caps; a black hat lined at the brim with leather; red knit caps; a pair of gloves. This was amended to include a mandillion (a type of capelike overgarment) lined with white cotton, breeches and waistcoats, a leather suit of doublet and breeches of oiled leather, and leather breeches to wear with the other suits. The records also mention a complete suit of armor, a bandoleer, a fowling piece, and a sword, items also thought necessary in Virginia.

Some of the differences between the lists can be attributed to climate: those to the north would require additional caps, gloves, and outergarments to keep warm in winter. But, in general, these basic wardrobes are remarkably similar. And why not? There is now evidence that not only were there similarities in dress among the British colonies but that these similarities transcended national borders into the mother country, the French colonies, and France.

Although the basics of a seventeenth-century wardrobe were similar, there were also important socioeconomic distinctions as well as regional variations. The variations between regions, including between nations, appear more on the order of fabric preferences, trimmings and color, and modifications due to climatic considerations. The Reverend Francis Higginson, writing from Salem in 1630, gives us a good comparison between clothing necessary in England and what he had become accustomed to wearing in New England. In Virginia the same items and styles, fabrics, and colors appear in men's probate inventories as in the New England colonies; the women, however, are a somewhat different story. In Virginia, the women exhibit a wider range of fine fabrics: brocades, flowered fabrics, velvets, and calicoes; use of metallic in fabric; trims and jewelry. In New England there is less frequent mention of calicoes and cotton in general for garments other than shifts, and few pearls and gold jewelry.

Green aprons also seem to belong more to New England. However, the colors red and blue come up repeatedly in inventories of women's clothes, especially for coats (skirts). At least in New England the red coats and red bays wescote were associated with lower-class dress. Bridget Bishop, who was hanged for witchcraft at Salem in 1692, was identified in court records as wearing a red coat, which signified her social class, rather than the black coat commonly associated with witchcraft.

In New England there were more overgarments, such as mantles and cloaks, and muffs; further north, even more styles of winter wear were improvised in response to the cold and snow. Perhaps the need to acquire seasonal apparel robbed northerners of the money to buy the accessories, such as lighter fabrics, trimmings, and jewelry, that southerners—given the year-round, warm temperatures—could purchase with their capital.

Exchange between the colonies is evident in marriage and mercantile records, letters, and diaries. There is also evidence of trade in second-hand clothing locally, between colonies, and with England; colonial records further show that Connecticut residents and government purchased ready-made clothing from Massachusetts Bay and New York. Inhabitants of New England were always able to purchase their wardrobes ready-made, but it was never a choice that would set them apart as upper class and distinguished. They also always had the choice of patronizing a personal clothier or of making the garments themselves. Equally apparent is that those with sufficient funds did not buy their best clothes ready-made, choosing instead to have them custom-made; some sent for the latest style from London. The social class of the population was expressed in dress, and each knew and tacitly accepted the sartorial conventions that accompanied rank.

THE EIGHTEENTH CENTURY

Even as the essence of the rules and differences set down earlier in the century continued, by the 1690s a blurring of the social ranks was visible. In general, that the elite should dress as such was understood; the issue concerned those whose buying power was outpacing their perceived social prestige. While most appeared content with this new wealth and happy in their quest for fashion, others spoke out against the perceived excesses and undue attention paid to the pursuit of visible status through apparel. In 1692 the Reverend Cotton Mather of Boston addressed the problem of people spending in-

creasing amounts on adornment, stating that clothing should distinguish people's ranks in society and that "the women which go as none but those who are above her do or can, shows herself to be as much out of wits as out of her place. And she that will not cut her coat [skirt] according to her cloth does but put a fools coat upon her." Mather further noted that "she that will have more on her back than can readily come of her purse [finances], deserves to be stripped as the fine Jay was of her borrowed feathers. Nevertheless, Vain Glory may insinuate itself into the rich and great, as well as the poor."

By the end of the seventeenth century the old social order was challenged by the rising merchant class and its money. With mass marketing and expansion of available goods, and the economic means to purchase, what earlier had been possible only by occupying the appropriate social station was now for sale: visible status. Clearly it seems that in the time leading up to the revolution, each region simultaneously paid attention to what the known world thought was appropriate and new and fashionable, and to the mode in its territory. Thus there was a selection, available to the elite, inside a larger trend toward new styling and garment types, and expansion of the wardrobe, resulting in regional variations upon a theme. Consequently, travelers between colonies commented on the strange fashions, all the while recognizing the basic garment type and the status of the wearer.

Men's clothing during this century was a variation on the theme set in the previous century: breeches, waistcoat, coat (to form a suit), linen or fine cotton shirt, neck cloth, stockings, hat, and shoes. The styles, including length and volume, varied over time; the most ornamented garment was the waistcoat. In colder weather a surcoat, or overcoat, was added, perhaps with a muff. Wigs enjoyed seasons of popularity. While wool was the most prevalent fabric for men's suits, other fabrics such as velvets were also worn. Items of undress, or more casual wear, included gowns (also called banyons), caps, and morocco leather slippers.

Women's clothing also continued the trend, initiated in the previous century, of adding a gown (a one-piece garment) to the basic wardrobe of coats, wescotes, or bodys worn over a chemise or shift. (The bodys consisted of two pieces, fastened at the back and the front.) The gown could be made in a wide variety of fabrics from wool to silk brocade and velvet. It was the primary garment, which changed design and fabric in accord with the whims of fashion and signaled upper social status. The gown could be worn over separate boned stays for a fashionably stiff upper torso, with a hoop to support the skirts of the gown and petticoats. The gown could be worn open from the waist down in front, showing off the petticoats, which were often elaborately decorated. Apparently this basic wardrobe was a starting point, and as one could afford it, one would add newer styles, more extravagant fabrics, and accessories, thus communicating that coveted more elevated status.

With this equation of wealth and status, dress could be used to reveal one's social aspirations rather than one's true social position. Where once social class carried an implicit set of social and economic criteria, now one's economic position became more important, as one could acquire the trappings of a person of "better" means. Furthermore, with the increased population, it was becoming more difficult for people to know every person and his or her "true" position.

The equation of visible status with economic wealth helped create exciting new items of fashion. These items included fans, hoops, hair combs, and face patches for women and buckles and hair powder for men. As incomes continued to rise, the number and range of available items did likewise, with a resultant expansion in a person's wardrobe; "newness"—or "fashion"— rather than garment style became the status marker. A commercialization of fashion was part of the larger shift toward a consumer society, as more people could afford those items which had traditionally been out of their reach. This in turn led to a specialization in fashion marketing, both by item and by audience. There is also evidence of an expanded secondhand market in even higher status items, such as Spitalfields silk gowns for ladies, which *could* have included the British colonies as well as England. By the end of the eighteenth century one could truly talk of a culture of consumption. And so, on the eve of independence, Americans wrapped themselves in their dreams, clothed as who they wanted to be, not necessarily who they truly

were, confident of their ability to hold onto that dream as long as their purses continued to expand. This image is still part of our cultural baggage.

BIBLIOGRAPHY

Back, Francis. "S'habiller à la canadienne." *Cap-aux-diamants,* no. 24 (Winter 1991):38–41. Description of what can be considered French Canadian dress in the mid eighteenth century.

Bruce, Philip Alexander. *Economic History of Virginia in the Seventeenth Century.* 2 vols. New York, 1895; repr. 1935. Good description of dress and discussion of sumptuary legislation.

Craven, Wayne. *Colonial American Portraiture.* Cambridge, England, 1986. Excellent discussion of social, economic, religious, and occupational backgrounds of the sitters, their attire, and the current location of the portrait for the period until 1790.

Earle, Alice Morse. *Two Centuries of Costume in America, 1620–1820.* 2 vols. New York, 1903; repr. Rutland, Vt., 1971. Remains unsurpassed as the best general history of American dress.

Fischer, David Hackett. *Albion's Seed. Four British Folkways in America.* New York, 1989. Dress is one of the folkways discussed.

Higginson, Reverend Francis. *New England's Plantation.* Essex, Mass., 1908.

———. "A True Relaton of ye last voyage to New England made ye last Sumer, begun ye 25th of April being Saturday, Anno Doi 1629." In *Chronicles of the First Planters of Massachusetts Bay 1623–1636,* edited by Alexander Young. New York, 1970.

Lemire, Beverly. "Reflections on the Character of Consumerism, Popular Fashion, and the English Market in the Eighteenth Century." *Material History Bulletin* 31 (Spring 1990):65–73.

Montgomery, Florence M. *Textiles in America, 1650–1870.* New York, 1984. An unsurpassed and comprehensive dictionary of textiles based on original documentation.

Rexford, Nancy. "Clothing and Personal Adornment." In *Encyclopedia of American Social History,* edited by Peter Williams, Mary Kupiec Cayton, and Elliot Gorn. New York, 1993. This excellent essay describes the garments of seventeenth- and eighteenth-century whites and Native Americans, as well as the sources available for their study.

Thirsk, Joan. "Popular Consumption and the Mass Market in the Sixteenth to Eighteenth Centuries."

Material History Bulletin 31 (Spring 1990):51–58.

Trautman, Patricia. "Dress in Seventeenth-Century Cambridge, Massachusetts: An Inventory-Based Reconstruction." In *Early American Probate Inventories,* edited by Peter Benes. Boston, 1987. Contains a glossary of apparel terms with modern description, and line drawings of representative men's and women's dress.

———. "When Gentlemen Wore Lace: Sumptuary Legislation and Dress in Seventeenth-Century New England." *Journal of Regional Cultures* 3, no. 2 (1983):9–21.

Wright, Meredith. *Put on Thy Beautiful Garments: Rural New England Clothing, 1783–1800.* East Montpelier, Vt., 1990. Excellent for discussion of individual garments. Includes scaled patterns.

Patricia A. Trautman

SEE ALSO **Manners; Rural Life; The Structure of Society;** and **Urban Life.**

THE DUTCH COLONY

CLOTHING WORN BY New Netherlanders during the period of Dutch administration (1614–1664) denoted social status and the Dutch cultural heritage. While the design and items of apparel were similar for all classes, the quality of textile used—fine or coarse—differentiated the status of merchants, farmers, and other working persons. After the English takeover of New Netherland (ca. 1680–1750), only upwardly mobile, patrician Dutch families sported European fashions and Anglican styles. In the longer term the Dutch in urban areas like New York and Albany adopted, albeit gradually, styles being imported by the English. Nonetheless, a significant segment of the colonial Dutch rejected both English cultural pressure and changing European fashion; this segment of the Dutch population retained the increasingly archaic garment styles of the mid seventeenth century for more than 150 years (through 1800).

WOMEN'S COSTUMES

During the seventeenth century, women wore separate, layered pieces consisting of petticoats (the outer skirt) topped by a shirt and a vest-like garment with detachable sleeves, or *rockje* (plural *rockjen*). This distinctive smock-like jacket extended to the hips and was worn either loose or caught at the waist with a narrow belt; the *rockje* might be either short or long sleeved and made from either silk, wool, or linen. Petticoats were usually black (although red was occasionally favored), and garment pieces for the upper body were often brightly colored—red, blue, yellow, green, or purple. Long sheer white linen aprons hung to the hemline, which was usually ankle length.

In the seventeenth century, such garments seem to have been worn by women of all classes; it was the quantity of garments and the type and quality of textile that distinguished their social status. Wardrobes of prosperous individuals included garments made of gauze, mohair, and damask. Rare and costly cotton was little used for costume until just before the revolutionary era; fur was occasionally used to trim winter garments. Garments worn by other classes were more limited in number, color, and variety of textile, which included less fine and even coarse types of wool, linen, and occasionally silk. The petticoat and *rockje* resulted in a comfortable costume that could easily be adapted to the needs of work, social status, and weather. Dresses are not mentioned in seventeenth-century inventories but do appear in eighteenth-century portraiture.

Several types of white linen caps or coifs, commonly cited in early inventories, were an important part of women's costume. Madame Sarah Knight mentioned one type in 1704 as "French muches wch are like a Capp and a head band in one, leaving their ears bare."

Layered garments created the distinctive style noted by Madame Knight, who observed that Dutch women of the middle class "differ from our women, in their habitt go loose." For older women and women living in rural areas, this type of dressing prevailed up to and even after the era of the revolution. Traveler William Strickland noted in 1794: "The women in their external appearance are the perfect copies of their ancestors, or the modern inhabitants of the retired Provinces of Holland. . . . Exactly such figures may be seen in old Dutch paintings."

MEN'S COSTUMES

Headgear and neckwear characterized the male wardrobe. Ruffs were worn into the 1670s, although cravats—early on a lace or linen scarf tied in a bow with long ends—rapidly supplanted them beginning in the mid seventeenth century. Other ribbon-like bands were also worn as neck ornament. Black hats were most common, although various ornaments, such as gold lace, identified the municipal official, tradesman, or merchant. The best hats were made from felted beaver hair; other kinds of caps were worn for riding, sleeping, and keeping warm; fur hats were used in particularly cold climates. Jackets, worn over shirts, topped breeches, which covered the knees. Coats and cloaks constituted outerwear. Black, tan, and gray were typical colors for men's clothes, while shirts and other linen pieces were white. Breeches were made from all kinds of available textiles—including even leather—depending on the circumstances in which they were to be worn.

CHILDREN'S CLOTHING

Netherlandish paintings of the seventeenth century and New York eighteenth-century portraits confirm that children's costume was a miniaturized version of adult clothing. Knitted items, including *rockjen*, waistcoats, petticoats, shoes, stockings, and other children's garments were stored away, presumably saved for future use by cousins and the next generation. Swathing clothes, typically colored red, were used for infants and very young children.

JEWELRY AND WROUGHT ORNAMENTS

Articles of personal adornment enriched costumes of both men and women. *Oorysers* (ear irons), or earrings, were common. Pewter, brass,

silver, and gold buttons and buckles were important costume accessories. By the 1670s, gemstones—some probably of paste—were common. Madame Knight noted that the uncovered ears of Dutch women were "sett out with Jewells of a large size and many in number. And their fingers hoop't with Rings, some with large stones in them and many Coullers as were their pendants in their ears, which You should see very old women wear as well as Young."

These articles were made by local craftsmen beginning about 1680. Additionally, gold signet rings, silver-mounted daggers, gold rings, silver key rings, silver girdles, and silver chatelaines appeared throughout the colonial period. Two forms traditional in the Netherlands were worn in New York. Wedding crowns, customary in provincial Netherlands, were important personal property in the seventeenth century. New York–crafted gold rosettes, worn at the throat and secured with strings of beads, pearls, or coral were depicted in early New York portraits.

SHOES, STOCKINGS, AND UNDERGARMENTS

Although no wooden shoes are documented among the Dutch colonists until an early-nineteenth-century advertisement for *sabots*, records of leather shoes, boots, and pattens are plentiful, and tanners and shoemakers were relatively numerous. Imported Spanish leather was especially prized. On the other hand, Dr. Benjamin Bullivant of Boston, who visited New York in the summer of 1697, observed that the young women of the city went barefoot, except on Sundays. Stockings were usually made of knitted silk or wool (some of the latter imported from Iceland) but might also be of leather or woven cloth. Undergarments included linen and knitted goods. A type of sash called a health belt was customary in the seventeenth century. Textile accessories included gloves, mittens, pocket handkerchiefs, and night neckerchiefs.

CONCLUSION

Clothes worn by New Netherlanders and their cultural heirs—whether prosperous merchants or common farmers—are best seen in paintings and printed works by seventeenth-century Dutch artists like Adriaen Van Ostade, Emanuel de Witte, and Gabriel Metsu and in New York portraits from the first half of the eighteenth century. The portraits, whose subjects were members of the prosperous middle class, document the Dutch love of color and fine fabrics and bring to life the cultural conflict experienced by the Dutch. Sometimes Dutch heads are depicted atop bodies draped in gowns plainly copied from English mezzotints, and at other times they are atop Dutch bodies garbed in colorful stripes, checks, floral patterns, or rich brocades sewn up in provincial interpretations of eighteenth-century styles. Colonial New York Dutch inventories supplement these images with information about quantities and qualities of the textiles used.

BIBLIOGRAPHY

Andrews, Wayne, ed. "A Glance at New York in 1697: The Travel Diary of Dr. Benjamin Bullivant." *The New-York Historical Society Quarterly* 40, no. 1 (1956):55–73.

Bernt, Walther. *The Netherlandish Painters of the Seventeenth Century.* Translated by P. S. Falla. 3 vols. New York, 1969. Contains numerous examples of the costume of all social classes as illustrated by Dutch artists.

Blackburn, Roderic H., and Ruth Piwonka. *Remembrance of Patria: Dutch Arts and Culture in Colonial America, 1609–1776.* New York, 1988. Includes portrait illustrations of many eighteenth-century men, women, and children, documenting their clothes as well as their faces. It also illustrates several examples of surviving costumes.

Earle, Alice Morse. *Colonial Days in Old New York.* New York, 1895.

Knight, Sarah. *The Journal of Madame Knight.* Reprint. Boston, 1970.

Saunders, Richard H., and Ellen G. Miles. *American Colonial Portraits, 1700–1776.* Washington, D.C., 1987. Colonial New York Dutch subjects are well represented, and there is opportunity for comparison with other colonial costumes.

Singleton, Esther. *Dutch New York.* New York, 1909. Provides a fine social history of the Dutch, but with regard to costume, it must be emphasized that she wrote about diverse peoples in Dutch New York and not only the New York Dutch population.

Strickland, William. *Journal of a Tour in the United States of America, 1794–1795.* Edited by Rev. J. E. Strickland. The New-York Historical Society Collection. 19 vols. New York, 1971.

Ruth Piwonka

SEE ALSO **Manners; Rural Life; The Structure of Society;** and **Urban Life.**

THE FRENCH COLONIES

Canada

DURING THE EARLY YEARS of colonization in Canada and Île Royale, settlers mostly depended on clothing that they had brought with them from France. New attire could also be procured at some expense from Europe, and with time made locally, using dressed skins or imported fabrics.

FASHIONABLE DRESS

Noble families who were present in both Canada and Île Royale (a French colony from 1713 to 1758 covering present-day Nova Scotia and Cape Breton Island) attached importance to aristocratic values, including that of elegant dress. Clothing that was fashionable, richly made, and answered to their need appeared with the development of towns. Yet there was a time lag of more than a year between the birth of a new style in France and its appearance in the colony, since ships from the Continent came only annually.

Depending on their status, women for more formal occasions wore gowns of silk, taffeta, or velvet, but rarely brocades woven with silk thread. Clothing was not quite as elaborate as in France. Nevertheless, much was spent on feminine wardrobes, and an elegant one had a high value, equal to that of a simple dwelling.

Styles followed those of the mother country. During the seventeenth century styles included stiff-bodied gowns, and in the eighteenth century the gown *à la française,* a gown with a loose back consisting of two box pleats—single, double, or treble—stitched down at the top and then flowing free, and *casaquin,* a loose gown cut at hip level and worn with an underskirt. Gowns featured a décolletage, even though from the 1680s until the end of the French regime, female parishioners in New France were strictly admonished by the church not to bare their bosoms and shoulders. Riding habits were also worn, and long cloaks, predominantly of brown, gray, or blue, were worn as outerwear. At times fashionable women even painted their cheeks, made up their eyes, and curled and powdered their hair.

For underclothing, women generally wore a chemise, a garment similar to a short nightgown. On top of this went a corset, and finally an underpetticoat. Drawers also may have been worn. Chemises could in addition have been worn as nightgowns.

Men's underwear was simpler than women's. It consisted only of underdrawers, which actually were not always worn, for the long tails of men's shirts often assumed a protection role similar to that of underwear. Very sporadically, *camisoles* (undershirts) were also worn. Nightshirts were sometimes used.

As did the women, fashionable men on the whole dressed as they did in France. The principal items of clothing in the seventeenth century were various types of breeches, including fashionable so-called petticoat breeches, which were excessively full and trimmed with ribbon, and the doublet, which was a short jacket. Later, the *justaucorps,* a longer coatlike covering for the upper part of the body, became modish and replaced the doublet. Various types of wool were popular fabrics; velvet was sometimes worn. Silver or gold buttons and braid sometimes ornamented clothing. On occasion, the sword or cane was carried and the wig was worn, changing in type as styles evolved. However, on the whole dress of the upper classes was more austere than in France.

One form of highly fashionable male attire in both centuries was the dressing gown. In a 1670 portrait attributed to Frère Claude François Luc, Intendant Jean Talon is depicted in a brocade dressing gown with a lace-trimmed shirt and full-bottomed wig. A garment for private, indoor wear, the dressing gown was always worn over shirt and breeches, although its style evolved and changed with time.

Children's clothing followed European models. Little girls in the colonies from the age of three or four mimicked their elders in fashionable dress, but boys continued to wear skirted garb until about six years old, when they were breeched.

EVERYDAY DRESS

During the early part of the colonial period in New France, female rural wear for everyday folk consisted of corset bodices worn with chemises and petticoats (as skirts were known), the latter being shorter than those in fashionable wear. In Canada only, these petticoats rose eventually to mid calf, revealing the influence of Indian custom. A neckerchief and an apron usually completed the costume. A short cape, called a mantelet, was also popular. Some time in the second quarter of the eighteenth century a jacket or short gown, descending below the waist to the upper thigh or as far down as the knee, began to be worn; it covered the chemise, except at the neck and sometimes at the elbows. In these garments, cut was simple, as was the fabric. Yet an element of color was more prevalent here than in male garb of a similar type. The lower classes in the towns also dressed themselves in such attire.

For country folk, the most characteristic male garment was the *capot,* a hooded overcoat usually fashioned of rough heavy wool but sometimes made of leather, beaver fur, or a blanket, material eminently suited for the rigors of the weather. Its style had evolved from the French seaman's hooded coat and came into existence during the late seventeenth century. However, it was only by the mid eighteenth century that rural dress *à la canadienne,* meaning in the characteristic style worn in Canada, emerged. It was a current term and meant clothing that was rural, worn mostly by ordinary folk. At this time the typical *capot* was dark blue. It was in the same period that the use of domestically produced handwoven cloth became widespread in rural clothing. The *capot* was also present on Île Royale. However, in this maritime colony, it re-

DRESS: FRENCH

ferred to a seaman's hooded coat, usually made of a type of unbleached cloth or canvas. Ordinary rural folk also sported the so-called woolen tuque (a cap or "bonnet" customarily worn by French peasants and sailors). Its use in New France was thought to have been established under the term tuque in the mid eighteenth century. "Bonnets" were made of cotton or linen rather than wool and were also worn on Île Royale.

In general, male rural clothing, as in France, was a looser, more simplified version of fashionable clothing made of rough cloth in somber colors. This type of attire would also be worn by the lower classes in urban centers. Garb such as this changed little, and frequently little if any clothing was available for a change, especially in the country. During the winter it was not unusual, particularly in the early years of New France, for a needy family, especially the women and children, to remain indoors (encabané) because of a lack of protective clothing. Children dressed similarly to adults.

Indian attire played its role in the evolution of rural dress à la canadienne. Both men and women wore Indian-type footwear with moccasin construction. Shoes were known as souliers sauvages (Indian shoes), while boots of similar construction were referred to as bottes sauvages. The rural inhabitants made this footwear, which was essential to the use of snowshoes, from the skin of farm animals. As in rural France, wooden shoes (sabots) were also part of the rural wardrobe. While men and women on Île Royale had wooden shoes, moccasin-type footwear was little used. For inclement weather, they wore galoches, or galoshes.

Male rural dwellers adapted the mitasses, leather leggings used by the Indians for protection from underbrush in the forest, and eventually constructed them from cloth. On Île Royale, a similar accessory was referred to as a gaiter, and they were made not of leather but rather of linen or wool.

The woolen sash that characteristically cinched the wraparound rural capot in New France had an Indian connection, this item having been popular Indian wear. As with the woolen tuque, it was not worn on Île Royale, with its milder maritime climate.

Characteristic not only of rural wear, but also of urban clothing, was the use of fur in

headwear and mittens in New France. In the eighteenth century, men occasionally dressed themselves in whole coats of beaver, with the fur outside.

On Île Royale there was not the preponderance of fur and wool as in New France because of the milder weather. In addition the Amerindian influence on clothing on the island was only lightly felt, as it lacked the connection with the fur trade. Rather the economy of the maritime colony was based on its fishing industry. Its records of inventories and sales after death reveal that ordinary fisherman used various types of rough cloth, including sometimes leather, for their dress. Their attire mainly consisted of loosely cut breeches, a vest and/or jacket, and a shirt, with the addition of the capot (in the previously mentioned maritime sense) or a long overcoat. Fishermen's boots were worn, as well as leather aprons for particular kinds of work.

The coureurs de bois (woods runners) and voyageurs in New France, who spent much time in the forest in connection with the fur trade, opted for practical dress. In the early years of this colony, as an outergarment for protection in the winter, they sported a square-shaped covering of skin, fringed above and below, as did the Indians. These men also selected at times Indian-type garb, made from dressed skins and embellished with fringe. They also dressed in knee-length loosely cut pants or breechcloths called brayets, fashioned of wool or leather, which left the lower part of the legs bare. These could be covered with stockings or mitasses, to be removed if a shallow body of water must be crossed. Moccasin-type footwear and a cotton or linen shirt generally completed the ensemble. Later, depending on the weather, loosely cut jackets or vests with breeches of rough cloth were worn along with the capot. As with the other various types of clothing worn in these colonies, there was considerable variety in the final costume effect.

CONCLUSION

Fashionable clothing in the colonies of both Canada and Île Royale was similar; it was elegant and was influenced by that in France, but more austere and one year or more behind the time. However, there were more variations in the everyday or rural clothing of the two colonies, owing to their different climatic conditions and the occupations of their inhabitants. By the time acknowledged rural dress *à la canadienne* had become a reality in Canada during the mid eighteenth century, Île Royale no longer existed. However, certain aspects of garb *à la canadienne* continued to exist for some time in the region that became the province of Quebec. It was worn there by everyday folk until the early twentieth century, more than a hundred and fifty years after the demise of this French colony.

BIBLIOGRAPHY

Audet, Bernard. *Le costume paysan dans la région du Québec au xviie siècle.* Ottawa, 1980. Describes male, female, and children's clothing, 1670–1710, on the Île d'Orléans, Quebec. Main source is clothing entries from seventy-five notarial inventories after death. The subject, that of pre-Conquest clothing in New France, is difficult, since costume and clear visual evidence of it hardly exist, and newspapers were nonextant.

La Grenade, Monique. "Costume at Louisbourg: 1713–1758. Men's Costume." Louisbourg, Nova Scotia, 1972. Unpublished manuscript. Discusses male costume on Île Royale, based primarily on entries from notarial inventories after death.

———." Le costume civil à Louisbourg: 1713–1758. Le costume féminin." Louisbourg, Nova Scotia, 1971. Unpublished manuscript. Follows same approach for female costume.

Séguin, Robert-Lionel. *Le costume civil en Nouvelle France.* Ottawa, 1968. Discusses both rural and fashionable clothing of the period using primary sources, mostly notarial inventories after death from Montreal, Quebec City, and Montmagny.

Jacqueline Beaudoin-Ross

SEE ALSO **Manners; Rural Life; The Structure of Society; and Urban Life.**

Louisiana

LOUISIANA COLONIAL DRESS reflected a cultural amalgamation of Latin, Anglo, German, African, and Native American influences, as well as adaptations to the environment and available resources. Material evidence for dress in eighteenth-century Louisiana is very sparse, owing in large part to the region's rot-prone climate and numerous fires, hurricanes, and floods. The following discussion therefore relies heavily on documentary research in estate inventories, census and import/export records, travelers' accounts, and other primary sources. What documentary and physical evidence that has survived by its nature illuminates most clearly dress among the upper echelons of society, although an attempt has been made to look at several socioeconomic and racial groups.

LAVISH STYLES AMONG THE UPPER ECHELONS

During the colonial period (1699–1803) Louisiana residents made their own clothes and such accessories as hats, gloves, wigs, and shoes; commissioned both local and metropolitan craftspersons to make them; or purchased them from retailers. Merchants imported cloth and ready-made goods from France, England, Anglo North America, Spain, and the Caribbean islands; Louisiana also attracted skilled tradesmen from those regions. For example, French ship manifests from 1718 and 1719 listed twelve tailors, eleven shoemakers (including one who made wooden shoes), seven wigmakers, a hatter, fifteen weavers, a maker of gold and silver cloth, four silk workers, and a buttons-maker as passengers. By the 1790s New Orleans (total population of some 1,800) alone boasted at least twenty tailors, fifty-nine seamstresses, twenty-two shoemakers, three tanners, three hatters, and six wigmakers, several of them free persons of African descent. Numerous slaves also manufactured clothing, headdress, and accessories for their masters and other clients.

Some affluent Louisianians maintained accounts with their personal tailors in France; frequent trips abroad kept their measurements, as well as their wardrobes, current and fashionable. More humble colonials, and those living in the countryside, harvested raw materials such as cotton or wool, spun thread, wove cloth, and sewed all or a part of their wardrobes (or ordered their African and Amerindian slaves to do so). Even well-to-do settlers had to rely on local resources when warfare or neglect cut off foreign supplies. Toward the end of the colonial period, however, goods from France and the fledgling United States flooded Louisiana markets.

Estate inventories, portraits, and travelers' accounts indicate that most Louisianians—Amerindians and some Africans excepted—attempted to imitate their European counterparts, while partly modifying their clothing choices to endure the hot, humid, hostile environment. They adopted some practices from Native inhabitants and Africans (going barefoot and wearing scanty, light clothing in the summer), but rejected others (tattoos, topless attire, and short skirts, for example). Popular colors were scarlet or crimson, blue, white, black, and gray; the most common types of cloth were cotton, toile (heavy cotton), linen, silk, dimity, chintz, calico, *cotonnade* (coarse homespun cotton), broadcloth, taffeta, camlet, nankeen, and muslin. Ornamentation included needlework and embroidery, gold and silver braid, silver lace, gold edging on buttonholes and vests, lace trim on shirts and cravats, large cuffs, and the abundant use of silver, brass, bone, wood, and even goatskin buttons.

Louisiana males dressed much like Europeans. During the day they wore collarless shirts, collars, cravats, vests or waistcoats, short or long breeches, stockings, shoes, and jackets, overcoats, or capes (depending on the season). They wore nightshirts or dressing gowns at night and casually around the house. Although an occasional set of drawers or underpants graced men's wardrobes, few undergarments appeared in inventories. Early-eighteenth-century men wore long, loose, straight vests or jackets, but later adopted the flared, shorter, tight-fitting waistcoats and the coats with cutaway pointed tails that Europeans were wearing. Suits comprised of waistcoats, breeches, and coats were often of the same ornamented material. Uniforms of all colors and cloth appeared in estate inventories and portraits, pointing to the numbers, importance, and status of the military in Louisiana.

Men adorned their heads with tricorne hats, beaver hats (*castors*), Segovia and Spanish caps, and various cloth caps. Bobbed cuts and natural queues were popular hairstyles among all sectors of society, but there were enough colonists with the money or taste to keep several wigmakers

and powder manufacturers in business. Wigs sported horizontal curls and queues and were powdered with flour no longer fit for internal consumption.

Both men and women wore stockings: silk ones for best, woolen ones in cold weather (rarer than in France or Canada), and thread or cotton ones for everyday wear. Men also wore stirrup stockings, leather leggings, and Segovia socks. Leather and Spanish garters held one's stockings in place. Both genders also wore gloves and mittens.

When dressing, colonial Louisiana women first put on chemises or chemisettes, corsets, and any number of underpetticoats (not quite the underwear we know today) or occasionally a hoop (*panier de femme*), then outerpetticoats or skirts and dresses. Dresses commonly had décolleté necklines, with ruffles bordering the neckline and half- or three-quarter-length sleeves. Popular outerwear included short loose jackets (*casaquillas*), cloaks, mantelets, and shawls. Parasols protected women from the intense sun. They also carried or wore handkerchiefs and fichus. Inventories rarely listed jewelry among women's possessions, but portraits and travelers' accounts attest to the wearing of earrings and necklaces.

From their portraits and inventories it appears that Louisiana women rarely wore wigs, or that these wigs were of natural colors rather than powdered. Women commonly pulled their hair away from their faces into low or high coiffures, frequently with ringlets down the back. In addition to caps and bonnets, women decorated their heads with turbans, feathers, beads, and ribbons, all popular in Europe during the mid to late 1700s.

Indeed, the lavish tastes of Louisiana women frequently caught the attention of visitors. Shortly after landing in New Orleans in 1727, Marie Madeleine Hachard, an Ursuline nun, wrote to her father in France, "Notwithstanding the expense [the women] are dressed in velvets and damasks covered with ribbon." Although he condemned the "tone of extravagance and show in excess of one's mean" as observed in "the dress of the women," Pierre Berquin-Duvallon in general approved of the changes in women's clothing styles he had witnessed during a two-and-a-half-year (1799–1802) stay in New Orleans:

Not three years ago, almost all of them wore short petticoats, and long jackets with lengthened skirts, the upper part of their clothing being of one color, and the lower of another, and all the rest of their dress in proportion; they were brave with many ribbons and few jewels. . . . The richest of embroidered muslins, cut in the latest styles, and set off as transparencies over soft and brilliant taffetas, with magnificent lace trimmings, and with embroidery and gold embroidered spangles are today fitted to and beautify well-dressed women and girls; and this is accompanied by rich earrings, necklaces, bracelets, rings, precious jewels, in fine, with all that can relate to dress. (*Vue de la colonie espagnole du Mississipi,* p. 287)

Scanty evidence on children's dress indicates that girls and boys were outfitted much like their parents, young ladies in dresses with décolleté necklines and ruffles and young men in trousers, shirts, cravats, and jackets.

AFRICAN-AMERICAN DRESS

Free women of African descent imitated and sometimes surpassed the fashions of white women, thereby attracting attention, resentment, and eventually regulation. In Article 6 of his government edict (1786), Governor Esteban Rodríguez Miró admonished free black women not to don fancy headdresses, plumes, or gold jewelry; he reserved these items for white ladies of quality. Free blacks also had to wear their hair flat or, if in a coiffure, covered with a kerchief. Apparently Miró's orders had little effect. Thomas Ashe, an early-nineteenth-century English visitor, noted differences between white and free black feminine attire and free blacks' use of their designated kerchief headgear: "The dress of the White ladies is very plain and simple. The robe white, fastened under the breast with a diamond pin, and the hair in the form of a coronet, connected by small bands of precious stones and pearls." By contrast, free black women's

petticoats are ornamented at the bottom with gold lace or fringe richly tasseled; their slippers are composed of gold-embroidery, and their stockings interwoven with the same material. . . . A kind of jacket made of velvet, fitted tight to the shape, and laced or buttoned in front, with long points hanging down

quite round the petticoat, and trimmed at the end with pearl tassels, is also worn; and on the shoulders of the jacket is fastened a cloak made of gauze, or some such light material, which hangs as a loose train to the ground. . . . Their most general head-dress is either a handkerchief of gold-gauze braided in with diamonds, or else chains of gold and pearls twisted in and out through a profusion of fine black hair. . . . The bosom is covered with solitaires, composed of every different kind of jewels. (*Travels in America Performed in 1806,* vol. 3, pp. 269–271)

Evidence for free African-American men's dress is even scarcer than that for women. It most likely was similar to white men's dress because travelers and officials did not describe it as being unusual or try to regulate it. A Spanish decree for regulation of the New Orleans free black militia issued in 1801 described uniforms of the Battalion of Free Pardos (light-skinned blacks) as a white jacket with inlaid collars and gold buttons, trousers, round hat with a crimson cockade, and black half boots. Members of the free moreno (dark-skinned black) battalion dressed similarly but in a green jacket with white buttons and lapels.

Although urban slaves could acquire fine attire, the majority of African slaves had small, poor wardrobes. Runaway slave advertisements indicate that men usually wore trousers and a shirt, sometimes a jacket or coat and a hat. Women wore gowns and kerchiefs fashioned into turbans; few of either gender possessed shoes. Clothing materials included cotton, linen, wool, flannel, and occasionally silk. According to one traveler, "during the entire summer, the slaves are not clothed. The natural parts are concealed only by a bit of cloth which is fastened at the girdle before and behind, and which has kept in all of North America where the French live the name of *braguet* [breeches or breechclout]." Winter wear included "a shirt and a woolen covering made in the form of a surtout [overcoat]. The children often stay naked until they reach the age of eight, when they begin to render some service."

AMERINDIAN DRESS

The clothing of Louisiana Amerindians was also sparse. Accustomed to the summer heat, both

615

men and women dressed only their lower bodies: men with a breechcloth of deerskin dressed white or dyed black, or those living near French settlements with one of coarse limbourg fastened by girdles; women with pieces of the same materials covering them from waist to knee. Women also fashioned cloaks from mulberry tree bark and swan, turkey, or duck feathers. Boys and girls went unclothed until ages twelve and eight respectively. With colder weather men put on deerskin shirts and long trousers that covered the entire leg. M. Le Page du Pratz noted, "If the weather be very severe, they throw over all a buffalo's skin, which is dressed with the wool on, and this they keep next to their body to increase the warmth." Females wrapped one cloak around them and looped another one under their right arms and fastened it over their left shoulders. Women wore nothing on their heads, but men wore feathers. Native Americans further adorned themselves with tattoos, paints, and necklaces, bracelets, armbands, and rings made of shell, bone, iron, pearls, European trade beads, and silver coins.

ADAPTATION BY THE ACADIANS

Perhaps the most adaptable of European-origin settlers in Louisiana were the Acadians, who arrived in large numbers in the 1760s and 1780s. Warm climes and scarce sheep compelled the Acadians to forsake their red- and black-dyed woolen garments in favor of clothes and stockings made of the coarse homespun cotton called *cotonnade*. They also exchanged their accustomed moose leather moccasins for deerskin ones, and found wooden shoes (*sabots*) impractical and bare feet very comfortable during the summer. For headgear, women replaced woolen shawls draped over their heads with cotton sunbonnets (*garde-soleils*). The research of Carl A. Brasseaux shows that the usual dress of South Louisiana Acadian men included collarless, loose-fitting shirts of undyed or white *cotonnade* and knee-length breeches of indigo blue. The usual female costume consisted of ankle-length skirt of striped *cotonnade*, a cotton corset, and a decorative vest.

CONCLUSION

Thus, like most Europeans who settled in the New World, white Louisianians tried to replicate that with which they were familiar, but found that they had to adapt what they considered elements of "civilization" to new environments and materials. In such a permeable society as Louisiana, where Native Americans and African Americans outnumbered them throughout the colonial period, white settlers also incorporated some components of these groups' dress into their own.

BIBLIOGRAPHY

Ashe, Thomas. *Travels in America Performed in 1806.* 3 vols. London, 1808.
Berquin-Duvallon, Pierre. *Vue de la colonie espagnole du Mississipi, ou des provinces de Louisiane et Floride occidentale, l'année 1802.* Paris, 1803.
Brasseaux, Carl A. *The Founding of New Acadia: The Beginnings of Acadian Life in Louisiana, 1765–1803.* Baton Rouge, La., 1987.
Glasgow, Vaughn. *L'Amour de Maman: La tradition acadienne du tissage en Louisiane.* La Rochelle, France, 1983.
Hachard, Marie Madeleine. *The Letters of Marie Madeleine Hachard, 1727–28.* Translated by Myldred Masson Kosta. New Orleans, La., 1974.
Le Page du Pratz, M. *The History of Louisiana.* London, 1774.
Perrin du Lac, François Maire. *Voyage dans les deux Louisianes, et chez les nations sauvages du Mississippi, par les États-Unis.* Paris, 1805.

Kimberly S. Hanger

SEE ALSO **Manners; Rural Life; The Structure of Society;** and **Urban Life.**

THE SPANISH BORDERLANDS

THE SETTLERS WHO PARTICIPATED in the colonization of the northern borderlands of New Spain all came with the hope of improving their social status, of becoming hidalgos—wealthy land owners or, literally, "sons of great worth." While dress was the most immediate and visible expression of a person's occupation and social standing, its functional and social purpose was so self-evident that it is only summarily described in colonial-era testaments and military documents. The first truly detailed descriptions of the border folk were made by nineteenth-century travelers, but their readings of what they saw were usually clouded by their culture shock and by their mixed feelings toward their hosts.

One of the more complete lists of everyday clothing can be found in the recommendations that Captain Juan Bautista de Anza made to the viceregal authorities who sponsored the 1776 settlement of San Francisco, in what was then Alta California. Each settler family was paid in advance in the form of clothing, tools, and livestock. There was little trouble recruiting colonists, because the list included such useful items as underwear, breeches, hose, shirts, jackets, buckskin boots, buttoned shoes, capes, hats, and even handkerchiefs for the men; and for the women petticoats, stockings, chemises, jackets, shoes, *rebozos* (shawls), and even ribbons. The list for children was similar, since they dressed like miniature adults.

The problem with documentary accounts, such as chronicles and travel diaries, is that the word for a piece of clothing can often refer to several different designs or styles. In places such as New Mexico, seventeenth-century terms are still used, even to apply to twentieth-century styles: pants are still called doublets (*calzones*), for example; socks, hose (*medias*); blouses, bodices (*cuerpos*); dresses, tunics (*túnicos*).

Because vocabulary can be so imprecise, most of what is known about the evolution of dress in New Spain and Mexico comes from examining contemporary visual images, including the Mexican codices (pre-Contact Indian picture books), colonial portraiture, the famous series of paintings depicting the caste system of New Spain, religious paintings and sculptures, rare eighteenth-century historical paintings such as the Felipe von Segesser buffalo hides, and nineteenth-century travel and local color paintings. Colonials always had their eye on European styles—intending to imitate or outdo them—but

were obliged to make do with the demands and materials of a different natural and social environment. Likewise, the dress of the Native Americans modified as a visible index of their cultural and religious assimilation.

MILITARY APPAREL

The earliest image of dress in New Spain is the Spanish conquistador, fully equipped with a complete suit of Hapsburg armor and all the accoutrements. It is also the most stereotypical image. In actuality, since most of the initial exploratory and colonizing expeditions were privately financed, only a few of the wealthier soldiers owned such complete armor. Other than armor and arms, there were no prescribed uniforms for sixteenth-century soldiers. Except for the leather *adarga,* or oval shields and side arms, soldiers dressed like ordinary townsfolk. Most considered themselves fortunate if they possessed a piece or two of armor, a *salade* helmet, a breast plate, or a coat of chain mail. Within weeks of invading Mexico, the conquistadores had already adopted the *escaupil,* native Aztec quilted cotton armor, which was light and quite effective in repelling arrows and lances.

Expeditions in 1519 to the northern borderlands of New Spain assumed a style of Native armor made of stitched layers of hardened leather. It was well adapted to the style of frontier warfare the colonial militias would be obliged to wage. Before long, the pieces of European metal armor taken by the Don Juan de Oñate expedition to New Mexico in 1598 were forged into more useful tools, such as agricultural implements, axes, and knives. The practical leather or *cuera* armor was, by the eighteenth century, a standard piece of military equipment. Captain Gaspar de Portolá, one of the military leaders in the settlement of California, penned this description of a *soldado de cuera* in Monterey in July 1769:

The soldiers wore their sleeveless leather jackets and carried on the left arm shields made of two thicknesses of bull hide with which they protected both themselves and their horses from arrow wounds. A fall of leather called the *armas* hung from each side of the saddle to protect the thigh and leg while riding through brush. Their offensive arms were the lance, which they managed with great dexterity on horseback broadsword, and short musket. (Nettie Van de Grift Sánchez. *Spanish Arcadia*, p. 161)

Dragoons of the remote *presidio* outposts of New Mexico, California, and Texas, as well as their citizen militia compatriots, closely fit this description.

INDIAN INFLUENCES

Besides the vestments of warfare, the major Indian contribution to mestizo dress in New Spain was the *rebozo* shawl. When the Spanish came, they found Indian women wearing loose-fitting cotton tunics and strips of cotton cloth that they wrapped about themselves. Still worn by Indian women today, the *huipil* is a long, open-necked, almost sleeveless blouse that hangs from the shoulders and is worn like a dress. *Huipiles* and similar garments called *quechquemitles* were often decorated with embroidered friezes and feathers. Over these garments they wore shawl-like strips called *mamales, tocas,* or *sabanitas,* which were woven on the strap loom and whose chief purpose was to carry babies or bundles.

With the establishment of the caste system, the Royal Audiencia of New Spain issued an ordinance in 1582 specifying the uses of certain clothing. It specifically forbade mestizo, Negro, and mulatto women to wear Indian dresses. The ordinance was responsible for the preservation of Indian dress, on the one hand, and, on the other, the promotion of the *rebozo.* Although mestizo women were prohibited from dressing like Indians, they could not afford the dresses, high-collared cloaks, and head-covering capes that Spanish women wore. The popular option was the *rebozo,* which was encouraged by the church as a head covering during Mass. Over the years, these traditional shawls came to be finely crafted and ornately decorated. Woven and used throughout the borderlands, they often took on regional characteristics and names, such as the *tápalo* shawl of New Mexico. The quality of weave, colors, and decoration was an index of the wealth and social standing of their owners among the middle and popular sectors of society.

The Indian men the Spaniards encountered were dressed in simple cotton loincloths called the *maxtle,* which were worn alone or with garments such as large cotton cloths. These cloths were worn wrapped about the body and knotted at one shoulder. This mantle-like cloth was the origin of the serape, the male counterpart of the *rebozo,* which underwent a similar development. With the introduction of sheep and wool, heavier *frazadas,* or blankets, were woven by Indians on the new foot loom brought from Spain. In the more temperate and colder climes of New Spain's northern borderlands, these blankets served as clothing.

After the conquest, Indians were attracted to garments denoting social status. Individuals of some standing in the new order wore gloves as a mark of their authority. Footwear was also an outward sign of status. By the end of the sixteenth century, the increasingly Hispanicized Indians of the south were wearing plaited breeches, shirts, hats, and shoes, along with their traditional mantle.

ARISTOCRATIC EXCESS

When the military conquest of Mexico was consolidated, the wealth of mining and livestock interests enriched the new lords of New Spain, especially those in favor with the Crown. Anxious to surpass their contemporaries in France and Spain, the new lords achieved unprecedented levels of ostentation and exaggeration. They spent fortunes on clothing, a state of affairs reflected in the detailed portraits of noblemen and the viceregal court. Luxurious fabrics from the Orient arrived on the great galleons docking at Acapulco. Velvet was used in everything from gowns and suits to shoes and bonnets. Silk was used for stockings and to line garments of all kinds. Doublets were made of satin lined with taffeta. For the more modest or penitential fashion statement, mourning clothes consisting of loose gowns and long hoods were made of baize or course cloth. Everyday clothing for both sexes, capes, coats, and cassocks were made of damask.

Women's wardrobes consisted of skirts, petticoats, French basques and underskirts, and doublets made of Dutch linen, damask, and Rouen linen, with armed or French sleeves. Colored cloth was highly prized, and the most coveted shades of burgundy, purple, and blue were also the most expensive. An abundance of silver and gold braiding as well as pearls adorned the costumes of both men and women, and by the beginning of the seventeenth century, the ruffed collar had reached enormous dimensions. The Europeans of the New World had succeeded in outdressing their kinsmen across the ocean. King Felipe IV (Philip IV) attempted to restrain this vestmental exuberance with his sumptuary decree of 1623 prescribing moderation in public dress, but the lords and ladies of New Spain paid it no heed.

The stylistic vogues and whims of the aristocracy continued their evolution into the eighteenth century, imitating the bewigged fashions of the French court. Notable visitors such as emissaries and ambassadors, as well as celebrated explorers such as Alexander von Humboldt, created sensations wherever they went. Local tailors were soon contriving for their patrons the novel styles they had seen abroad. By the nineteenth century, the bits and pieces of imitated European styles were blended and adapted by middle and popular classes to emerge as an independent cultural synthesis—the national costume.

REGIONAL AND NATIONAL "TYPES"

Popular and regional styles of dress were well documented by Mexican *costumbrista* (mannerist or local color) painters who roamed the countryside documenting types and "typical dress" in portraits that emphasized clothing rather than individual people. The celebrated *china poblana* and *charro* types emerged in these paintings, as well as in music and literature, as the romantic ideals of Mexican mestizo culture. The seductive *rebozo,* a low-cut blouse, and full skirt were the trademarks of the *china,* whose name came not from the Orient but from an old caste term. *Poblana* referred either to her popular origins, *del pueblo,* or to the claim that her origins were in that most typical of Mexican cities, Puebla. The dashing *charro* figure is the silver-studded horseman with broad *sombrero* and *chaparreras* (chaps) who idealizes Mexico's equestrian culture. A revival of interest in this type after the Mexican Revolution of 1910 makes the *charro* a familiar, if not emblematic, figure in the visual imagination.

On the northern frontier, fragments of these popular and aristocratic styles arrived haphazardly whenever travelers or new colonists arrived, bringing news from the south. Clothing styles along the borderlands differed according to the wealth of the settlers and the frequency of their contacts with the south. Because of its access to the sea, the gentle clime, and the easy availability of the labor of mission Indians, California was both more "up to date" and wealthier than the interior provinces, where wealth was measured mostly by larger numbers of sheep or cattle. Anglo-American travelers were impressed by the hospitality and earthy ostentation of the California *rancheros,* and their detailed descriptions of their dress and leisurely ways are legendary. The historian Hubert Howe Bancroft synthesizes various descriptions in his summary of the sumptuous and festive dress of the ruling *Californios*:

A broad-brimmed hat of dark color, gilt or figured band round the crown, lined under the rim with silk; short silk or figured calico jacket; open necked shirt; rich waistcoat, if any; pantaloons open at sides below the knee, usually of velveteen or broadcloth, and trimmed with gold lace, or short breeches and white stockings; deer-skin shoes, dark brown and much ornamented; a red sash round the waist and the whole covered with a poncho or sarape. The last-named garment was always a mark of the rank or wealth of the owner, and was made of black or dark blue broadclothe with velvet trimmings, for the rich, down to the coarse but showy blanket poncho of various colors used by the poorer classes. The women wore gowns of silks, crepe, calico, etc., according to means, made with short sleeves and loose waist worn without a corset; shoes of kid or satin, saches or belts of bright colors; and almost always necklace and earrings. (Nellie Van de Grift Sánchez. *Spanish Arcadia,* pp. 366–370)

A traveler in New Mexico was less likely to encounter individuals of the *Californio's* degree of wealth. Yet the few Nuevo Mexicano merchants who made fortunes on the trade of the Santa Fe Trail are described in similarly obsessive detail, down to estimates of the cost of their "costumes." Unfortunately, these same travelers were much less interested in describing the dress of more modest classes, whom they readily dismissed as "rabble." Descriptions of women's dress are similarly prejudiced with Puritan ideals of feminine modesty and proper behavior. Because of their comfortable, loose-fitting dresses, low-cut blouses, and uncorsetted figures, Anglo-American observers assumed that the morals of these women must be lax as well. For lack of more compelling political reasons, many of the same commentators applauded the Mexican American War as a noble endeavor destined to straighten the loose moral fabric of the republic to the south.

CONCLUSION

As one of the most intimate and overt forms of material culture, dress reveals how the person relates to the natural and social environments. The evolution of clothing styles in the Spanish Borderlands is a visible index of the cultural relations and historical struggles that have evolved there. The Hispanization of the Indian could be seen in the trousers and hat or dress and footwear that he or she used. Likewise, the naturalization of the European settler was obvious in the *rebozos* and serapes they adopted in their new homeland. The excesses of the colonial aristocracy were as evident as the sumptuous and garish styles they indulged in. With independence from Spain and the emergence of republican government came the emergence of national types like the *charro* and the *china poblana*. Social class and social aspirations were still expressed outwardly in dress. The poor as well as the wealthy continued to don whatever finery they could afford, and their culture, occupations, and politics were literally worn right on their sleeves.

BIBLIOGRAPHY

Ballesteros, José Ramón. *Origen y evolución del charro Mexicano.* Mexico City, 1972.

Carrillo y Gariel, Abelardo. *El Traje en la Nueva España.* Mexico City, 1959.

Castelló Yturbide, Teresa. "La Indumentaria de las castas del mestizaje." *Artes de México* (nueva época) no. 8, (verano 1990):73–78.

Castelló Yturbide, Teresa, and Marita Martínez del Río de Redo. "El Rebozo." *Artes de México* 18, no. 142 (1971):1–96.

Cisneros, José. *Riders Across the Centuries: Horsemen of the Spanish Borderlands.* Drawings and text by José Cisneros; biography by John O. West. El Paso, Tex. 1984.

Hotz, Gottfried. *Indian Skin Paintings from the American Southwest: Two Representations of Border Conflicts Between Mexico and the Missouri in the Early Eighteenth Century.* Translated by Johannes Malthaner. Norman, Okla., 1970.

Van de Grift Sánchez, Nellie. *Spanish Arcadia.* Los Angeles, 1929.

Enrique R. Lamadrid

SEE ALSO **Manners; Rural Life; The Structure of Society; and Urban Life.**

MANNERS

THE BRITISH COLONIES

IN THE MODERN AGE, manners appear anachronistic. Emily Post seems irrelevant, etiquettes in general artificial and even hypocritical. Cynics gibe that the old codes of conduct taught a man to act like a gentleman without requiring that he be one. Curmudgeons complain that the purpose of politeness is to make guests feel at home when they wish they were.

In the colonial era, manners seemed a more serious matter. The ceremonious aspects of social relations occupied the attention of persons of ability. Cotton Mather composed manuals of comportment. Benjamin Franklin dispensed maxims of propriety and prudence. George Washington wrote out for himself more than one hundred "rules of civility and decent behavior in company and conversation."

Astute interpreters of society have often sided with such colonists. Ralph Waldo Emerson observed that manners "make the fortune of the ambitious youth." Edmund Burke considered manners "more important than laws," since laws depended so largely upon manners. Alexis de Tocqueville concluded that the causes and effects of democracy in America were "to be found in the circumstances and manners of the country more than in its laws."

In our own time, too, shrewd social scientists have seen that rituals of deportment and demeanor are not as shallow as they seem. Erving Goffman insisted, indeed, that "the gestures which we sometimes call empty are perhaps the fullest things of all." Norbert Elias showed in sumptuous detail how very full such apparently empty gestures could be.

Elias traced the emergence of modern civility to the sixteenth century and the publication of a little treatise on the subject by the Dutch Renaissance humanist Desiderius Erasmus. Elias took the astounding popularity of the tract as a token of the civilizing project that swept Europe in the early modern era and an expression of the ascendant self-interpretation of the Western world. He took the rudeness that repelled the Dutch pedagogue as evidence of the actual state of manners at the time.

By inverting the injunctions that ran through the manual, Elias revealed the crudity of the society that Erasmus set out to reform. It was a society in which courtiers and country people alike ate with their fingers, slurped their soups and sauces right off their plates, drank from common goblets, and shared food as readily as utensils. More than that, it was a society that Erasmus believed beyond real transformation. He advised merely that men and women with pretensions to politeness not lick greasy fingers or wipe them on coats, not quaff from common vessels without first wiping their mouths, not

621

"offer something half-eaten to another." "If you cannot swallow a piece of food," he urged, "turn round discreetly and throw it somewhere." Later courtesy books continued in the same spirit, recommending only that readers blow their noses into their hands rather than onto the table-cloth or that they spit under the table rather than on it.

BECOMING "ENDURABLE TO EACH OTHER"

In the era of American settlement, refinement was a recent, and tenuous, achievement in northern Europe. Emerson caught the precarious purchase of the modern West on cultivation in his dictum that the "service" of manners was to make us "endurable to each other: to get people out of the quadruped state; to get them washed, clothed, and set up on end." Elias added to that collective contribution of manners an individuating element. He held that "a very specific change in the feelings of shame and delicacy" shaped a shift in social standards that contributed to the formation of both the superego and the isolated ego. On those alterations he predicated the appearance of almost a new species, *homo clausus,* in the early modern age. *Homo clausus* evolved a sense of the self as an entity entirely interior, encased within the body. *Homo clausus* acquired an understanding of each person's independence of all that existed beyond the body by learning to control bodily functions and manage emotions as men and women of the Middle Ages never had.

Before the seventeenth century, the peoples of northern Europe were unconcerned about maintaining modesties or containing rages, griefs, and joys. By the time of the Tudors and Stuarts, aspirants to gentility were beginning to inhibit both their anger and their jubilation. By the time of the American Revolution, the earl of Chesterfield could dismiss "frequent and loud laughter" as the manner in which the mob expressed its silly joy at silly things. The unconstrained merriment of the masses had become as vulgar, in the new view, as unconstrained coughing and sneezing.

There were Americans of the eighteenth century who embraced the new manners almost as avidly as the English did and who struggled for self-control almost as ardently. Southern planters sought a stoicism they called "philosophy" on occasions that would once have called forth an expressive intensity of feeling. Northern merchants and men of business held themselves to a strict accounting in the containment of impulse. Members of the Society of Friends gave up in the New World the ecstatic quaking that had gained them the derisive name by which they were generally known in the Old. Tidewater magnates abandoned the anything-goes aggression of their ancestors for the ceremonious codes of pugilism and dueling, which displayed their capacity to hurt and kill with cool restraint and emotional disengagement.

But for every Virginia planter such as William Byrd, who held his sorrows in check, there were a hundred Americans who reveled in the hedonic release that the frontier fostered. For every Philadelphia entrepreneur such as Benjamin Franklin, who contrived methods for monitoring moral progress, there were a hundred who disdained such discipline. For every Quaker who eschewed states of spiritual possession, there were a hundred who sought such transports in the religious revivals. For every elegant gentleman who spurned rough-and-tumbling, there were a hundred backwoodsmen who gloried in stomping, biting, gouging out eyes, and tearing at testicles.

Throughout the eighteenth century, American manuals of manners enjoined the same restraints that Erasmus had exhorted two centuries before. Eleazar Moody's "163 Rules for Children's Behavior" (1715) aimed, above all, to curb animal impulse in the author's New England audiences: "Eat not too fast, or with greedy behavior," "stuff not thy mouth so as to fill thy cheeks," "go not singing, whistling, or hollowing along the street." His "Eight Wholesome Cautions" warned against diverse vices "whereunto young men are too much addicted." His "Ten Short Exhortations" demanded that his readers' "recreations be lawful, brief, and seldom." It was ironically apt that the Boston schoolmaster's academy was located off Prison Lane.

Christopher Dock's "100 Necessary Rules of Conduct for Children" (1764) promulgated the same insistence on instinctual denial among youth of the middle colonies. The Pennsylvania pedagogue recommended to his pupils that they "avoid everything that indicates excessive hunger, such as looking greedily at food." And his animadversions against robust appetite extended beyond food to drink—"It is very bad form . . . to drink such large draughts that one must snort"—and to all other bodily functions—"Do not form a habit of constantly . . . digging the nose, violently panting, and other disgusting and indecent ways."

All the guides to civility promoted the containment of carnality. But as Franklin's Poor Richard wryly recognized, they could only "give advice." They could not "give conduct." Dock would not have had to inveigh against people undressing in public or putting half-eaten food back in the serving dish or licking their plates if they did not routinely do so. He would not have had to beg his readers to let uneaten food "lie on the table" if it were not their habit to stuff it into their pockets.

A NEW SOCIETY BRINGS NEW RULES

The refinement of American manners was a Sisyphean task. A century ago, Frederick Jackson Turner argued that it was bound to be so. The flight from Europe to the frontier exposed colonists to experiences of perennial rebirth in wilderness primitivity. And certainly the first settlements in British America did display the dissolution of tradition and the collapse of communal bonds that Turner postulated.

All the colonies endured rampant disorder in their early days. All of them remained susceptible to riot and tumult to the time of the revolution. None of them had a police force competent to preserve public order, and on the far and near frontiers of provincial society such a force would not have been welcome if it had existed. In the backcountry, men upheld their honor in face-to-face relations rather than legalistic ones. Affronted, they fought "like tigers and bears . . . biting one another's lips and noses off, and gouging one another—that is, thrusting out one another's eyes—and kicking one another on the cods, to the great damage of many a poor woman."

All was transformed on the edge of the dark forests of the New World. As a seventeenth-century visitor to Boston observed disdainfully, "neither days, months, seasons, churches, nor inns [were] known by their English names." As he might have added, neither holidays, houses, laws, land tenures, nor government quite resembled those in the mother country, either. Indeed, no place in America was exactly like England. None had the same weather, religion, or recreations. None grew the same crops, ate the same food, married the same way at the same ages, or died at the same rates. All had to contend or coexist with the natives. All enslaved Africans. And all held out prospects of land ownership and political participation unprecedented in Britain.

The equality that prevailed in the American provinces made manners as imperative as it made them problematic. In Europe, sharp social cleavages kept the rabble at a distance from the refined. In America, people mixed promiscuously. In Europe, social relations were modeled on what John Kasson called "the one-sided deference rituals of the court." On the western shores of the Atlantic, they were governed by "more symmetrical assurances of mutual respect."

The diffusion of property and political entitlements dissolved many of the distinctions between social strata that were the stuff of daily relations in the Old World. And so did a myriad of minor observances. Dress and speech did not infallibly disclose social rank in America. Sports were not segregated by social class. Militia duty was not a perquisite only of the most substantial men of the county—the ones who could afford the equipage—and the remaining nine-tenths of the people were not kept unarmed. Indeed, the colonies obliged all able-bodied men between sixteen and sixty to serve in the militia and accorded all free men the right to bear arms.

As a new vernacular culture expressing new possibilities of parity emerged in the New World, an old ethos gave way. The harvest feasts provided by the manor lord did not survive the ocean crossing; the cornhuskings that began to appear in America at the end of the seventeenth century were egalitarian gatherings. Tocqueville would one day catch the tenor of the transformation: the effect of equality was "not exactly to give men any particular manners, but to prevent them from having manners at all."

The specter of such radical reduction of ritual haunted a few of the colonists from the first, and it preyed upon more of them as affluent elites established themselves. As folklorist Robert St. George wrote, "the most pressing issue" facing the first Puritans was one of "cultural reproduction." The migrants held values of hierarchy, but there were no nobles and few of the lesser gentry among them. They were "dependent on difference" for their sense of social balance, but they were themselves overwhelmingly yeomen. They therefore "had to create among their homogeneous ranks a means of establishing social difference once and for all."

But they could not create what they had to create, and neither could other settlers elsewhere. They could confer the old roles on new actors in order to avert social chaos, but they could not confer legitimacy on their new leaders. "Plain, illiterate husbandmen" could not claim customary deferences just because they were elected to the legislature. Commoners could not carry on ancient gradations just because they were appointed justices of the peace. The people knew too well, as a royal governor said, the origins of the first families, "and the ordinary sort of planters, [who] have land of their own, though not much, look upon themselves to be as good as the best of them."

American farmers simply could not be kept from privileges and pleasures that had been, in England, prerogatives of the elite. All could hunt in the nearby woods as only the king's friends hunted in the royal deer parks. All could eat meat as only the lord's companions ate in the manor halls. All could dress as ambition and inclination prompted.

Virtually every American colony enacted laws restraining upstarts from affecting what the Virginia Burgesses called "excess apparel." But virtually every colony found such sumptuary legislation useless. Distillers and drovers appropriated the garb of the grandees when they rose a little in the world, and their wives were as much "partners in the general disorder" as they were. The wealthier were never by virtue of their wealth worthier in the eyes of the people they tried to overawe.

In much the same way, almost every locality appointed its most impressive figures to lead its militia. But almost every locality discovered that the carnival conditions of muster day dissipated social distinctions rather than deepening them. Observers commented that, amid the general drunkenness, officers and troops alike lacked "the least grain of discipline." Every soldier "supposed himself equal to his commander."

Men of eminence might pattern their behavior on what they remembered or could learn of the landed gentry or the city swells of the mother country, but others understood that, in the very nature of the American character, there could be "no degree of subordination." Rich planters and merchant nabobs might proclaim that their children had "better be never born than ill-bred," but it was not easy to breed them well without a hereditary aristocracy to set standards of deportment and without any extensive experience of the usages of the best society of the Old World.

Sometimes, strangers pierced the pretensions of the well-to-do. The British colonial officer Edward Randolph would dismiss the merchant-princes of Boston as "inconsiderable mechanics." The French journalist Jean Pierre Brissot de Warville would lampoon the planters of the Chesapeake as men who blew their noses indifferently "with their fingers or with a silk handkerchief."

As often, the magnates made themselves ridiculous. To the time of the revolution, for instance, both ladies and gentlemen wore "big wigs." The wigs were so cumbersome that they could not be worn without special training. They fell off, or turned on the wearer's head, or showered the room with their powder at the least abrupt or incautious motion. Men had to shave their heads to make them fit properly. Women had to sleep with their necks on wooden blocks to keep from spoiling the wigs, since they had to last for months. The increasingly elaborate arrangements were held together with clotted dairy cream or flour paste, which caused skin diseases and infestations of vermin, to say nothing of itching and a foul smell. Yet, before the great fêtes in Philadelphia, demand for hairdressers was so great that many patrons had to have their hair done at four in the morning.

Under such circumstances, deference was little more than a delusion. Provincial parvenus spoke of it, but their inferiors did not accord them much of it. As the English economist Walter Bagehot explained, "No difficulty can be greater than that of founding a deferential nation." Certain classes in certain nations could command deference because they had always commanded it and because they inherited a pomp that seemed to make them worthy of it. But in a new colony, such respect could not be secured, for it had never been given to what was "proven to be good" in the first place, only to what was "known to be old."

Even in the idealizations of the American courtesy manuals, rules that bid a suitable submission to superiors were never as numerous as the injunctions that presumed a more democratic demeanor. The counsel that Washington copied in his youthful efforts to acquire civility called for a generalized considerateness of others, regardless of their social station, more often than it demanded deference to those of loftier rank. The "Necessary Rules" that Dock propounded sought far more steadily to inculcate a loving carriage toward all than to instill subordination. The teachings that Moody set before his students emphasized self-control markedly more than they promoted subservience to authority.

Outside such preachments, deference was even less evident. In the great diaries of the putative patriarchs—Samuel Sewall, William Byrd, Landon Carter—that afford us our most intimate view of personal relations in the provinces, the diarists expressed emotions ranging from resignation to raging resentment that they could never compel even obedience, let alone honor, from their families, friends, and neighbors. In the lamentations of ministers and magistrates, it becomes clear that all authority could be contested in early America.

Everywhere, pastors found themselves "hired by the year like the cowherds" in the old country. Everywhere, they learned that if they did not preach to their congregation's liking, they could "expect to be served with a notice" that their services would "no longer be required." And everywhere, they were at once respected and "reviled, insulted, and scoffed at" by a "headstrong, giddy populace." As the European visitor Gottlieb Mittelberger said of Pennsylvania, and might equally have said of other settlements, it was "the heaven of farmers and the hell of preachers."

Public officials met with even more disrespect than clergymen. Constables had to contend with citizens who thought a warrant "good for nothing" and indeed thought nothing of threatening to blow the constables' brains out if they tried to serve one. Justices of the peace were set upon with swords and clubs. Military officers were challenged to fight by men who refused to serve under "any man [they] could lick." One of the last proprietary governors of North Carolina reported that his predecessors had all "lived in fear of the people," and a missionary stationed in the same province maintained that a proprietor himself, "were he here, would be looked on no better than a ballad singer."

THE REJECTION OF RITUAL

The unsettled societies of British America were singularly susceptible to transgressions of civil ceremony. Colonists unpersuaded of the propriety of all power over them resorted again and again to desecration of the rituals of governance. North Carolinians bound a constable neck and heels and smeared feces over his face. A New Jersey man declared his disdain for authority when he addressed its representative as "thou sheriff, thou turd." The regulators in the Carolina backcountry evinced their opinion of the courts of justice "when they took from his chains a Negro that had been executed some time, and placed him at the lawyers' bar, and filled the judge's seat with human excrement." A Dutchman in New York carried his contempt to a more abstract plane when he swore he "valued no English law more than a turd." And an Englishman in Massachusetts assailed the ultimate aegis of order in that colony when he insisted that he "did not care a turd for God in heaven or on earth."

The colonies were simply not societies that stood on ceremony. If, as Erving Goffman suggested, communities can be distinguished by the extent of the ceremonial life they sustain, the minuteness of its specification, and the affect that attends it, then provincial America was extraordinarily impoverished in its ceremonial idiom. Ritual was resented from the first by the Puritans of New England and the Quakers of the middle colonies. It was rejected later by the ascendant Evangelicals of the South. And the iconoclasm of the sects expressed accurately the cultural thinness that obtained everywhere in early America.

In such a society, the cultivation of manners rarely reflected any spontaneous pleasure that settlers took in ceremonial elaboration or performance; until late in the provincial period it rarely represented a mark of authentic ascriptive standing. It was, overwhelmingly, a means of advancing ambition or of seeking status. As a popular almanac of the period advised, "Tell me thy manners and I'll tell thy fortune."

Arrivistes signified their success by striving to "live in the same neat manner, dress after the same modes, and behave exactly as the gentry [did] in London." Others of elevated aspiration did the same, to the extent that their income allowed.

Aspirants could not afford the houses, furniture, or appurtenances that arrivistes could, but they could buy the same books. Imported manuals of refinement always found a ready market. From Henry Peacham, Richard Brathwaite, and Richard Allestree in the seventeenth century to John Gregory and Chesterfield in the eighteenth, they went through far more editions than could ever have been bought by the modest number of nabobs in the New World.

The courtesy books always assured anxious readers that genteel manners were readily accessible. Indeed, the manuals defined such manners in terms of outward behavior that could be appropriated easily rather than in terms of temperaments or tastes that might have demanded a deeper development. Of the 110 rules of civility that Washington copied so sedulously, just one referred to conscience. The other 109 were precepts of unrelenting concern for appearance. A host of them asserted explicitly the priority of external image over inner feeling and urged unabashedly the subordination of personal conviction to public opinion.

Colonists who matured under such a regime of exteriority developed confidence in their conduct but no comparable assurance about their comprehension of the subtleties of style and sensibility. Their insecurity appeared in their abasement before their English correspondents when they ordered goods from the metropolis. On items ranging from clarets to carriages and from waistcoats to watches, self-styled gentlemen and ladies stipulated nothing more than that everything be "of the best sort" or in "the latest fashion."

But gentility did not demand aesthetic sense, or ethical sensitivity either. Samuel Johnson might jeer that Chesterfield taught "the morals of a whore and the manners of a dancing-master." The lord's *Letters* were studied assiduously anyway. John Adams might asperse the "superficial accomplishments of gentlemen, upon which the world has foolishly set so high a value." The world paid him no mind, because he could not "dance, drink, game, flatter, promise, dress, swear with the gentlemen, and talk small talk and flirt with the ladies."

Dress and dancing were crucial. The great botanist John Bartram was warned by a fellow Friend to buy new clothes before traveling to Virginia, "for though I should not esteem thee less, to come to me in what dress thou will, yet these Virginians are a very gentle, well-dressed people, and look perhaps more at a man's outside than his inside." And Virginians did attend more to others' carriage than to their character. When William Byrd went to a dinner and ball for the provincial council, he recorded in his diary only his assessment of the dancers and his chagrin that the president of the council wore "the worst clothes of anybody there." When a new governor arrived in Williamsburg, he declared his gratification to discover that "the gentlemen and ladies are perfectly well-bred, not an ill dancer in my government."

Dress and dancing alike allowed men and women who had not been well bred at all to move in circles beyond their birth. Manners were meant to set the "better sort" at a secure social distance from the motley masses, but manners that could be acquired as readily as dress and dancing enabled those who rose from the ranks to close that social distance. Such manners were democratic despite themselves, an "illuminating phase," as historian Arthur Schlesinger said, of a "leveling-up process" that extended a prospect of gentility to all who made money. A fine fortune could provide the clothes that made the man and the "graceful motions" that elegant dancing demanded as well. For such motions could be mastered "soon," according to the courtesy books, with the tutelage of "a good dancing-master."

A NASCENT CONSUMERISM AND ITS LIMITS

Money also made possible the other amenities by which the eighteenth century increasingly measured civility. Porcelain, portraits, and silver plate, bedsticks, books, and fine brocades, spices, spoons, and tea service—all these and more ceased to seem luxuries and began to define decency as the consumer revolution advanced.

In the seventeenth century, the implements of a gracious domesticity were minimal. Houses themselves, especially in the South, were "mean and little" compared with those in England, and even the ones that were more than a single-celled enclosure had no rooms with specific functions such as dining rooms, living rooms, or bedrooms. In the early years of settlement, families ate from a board nailed to a trestle rather than at a dining table, and for generations they sat for meals on chests rather than chairs, if they sat at all. In the Chesapeake colonies, only one household in three had either chairs or benches. Middling families as well as poor ones often lacked all bedding; only the richest had bedsteads, and even they had not nearly as many bedsteads as they had members of the household. In such settings, where people of means still squatted or stood for meals, still slept on the floor, still fed from common plates and drank from common vessels, still ate with their fingers, and still had no plumbing and put no premium on cleanliness, manners were of little moment. There were no stages on which to perform them, no sites at which to see them, no audiences to applaud them.

By the middle of the eighteenth century, some things were altered. Like Ben Franklin, who began with a china bowl and a silver spoon and eventually accumulated several hundred pounds' worth of plate and porcelain, Americans had commenced their infatuation with the creature comforts of consumerism. As historian Stephanie Wolf noticed, their ancestors had needed but a chest or two to carry all they owned across the Atlantic Ocean. Their grandchildren would require whole Conestoga wagons to carry all they had collected across the Appalachian Mountains.

Nonetheless, the reach of the consumer revolution was limited. Only a minority of Americans of the eighteenth century were acquiring the equipage of conviviality and constructing stages on which to enact it; only the top tiers of colonial society were amassing the means of refinement and absorbing the cultural values to appreciate them. Even as civility advanced, rudeness persisted everywhere in provincial America.

Some colonists in the settled regions mastered the niceties of tea service. Many colonists moved toward the western mountains. By 1776 the population of the backcountry alone was equal to the population of all of British America in the last decade of the seventeenth century. Frontier settlers lived in rude huts when they cleared their first land, and in badly built hovels with wooden chimneys even after they established themselves.

Indeed, most white Southerners lived in tiny one- or two-room houses all through the eighteenth century. When William Byrd built a structure "of a few rooms" for the manager of one of his out-plantations, the man's neighbors admired it "as much as if it had been the grand vizier's tent in the Turkish army." When Byrd traveled in the back parts, he sometimes slept outside sooner than crowd in a cabin where "all pigged lovingly together."

The impermanent architecture of the poor and middling multitudes precluded refinement as surely as the great Georgian houses of the gentry provided a dazzling setting for its display. Large numbers of Americans remained almost utterly outside the sphere of civility, and large numbers of those within could do little more than learn its precepts and yearn to put them into practice. To the time of the revolution, there were never more than forty grand Georgian plantation houses in all of Virginia. Even among the elite that dominated the vestries, the county courts, and the House of Burgesses, the splendor of a Westover, Byrd's James River plantation, was never the norm.

Northerners generally lived in larger houses than Southerners, but their houses were more meagerly outfitted with the amenities of the emergent etiquette. Even among the richest part of the population of New England, hardly more than half the households had so much as a single fork, and only a quarter had any fine earthenware. Among the rest, still fewer had anything more than a pathetic handful of the array of items that modern scholars take to be indicative of the nascent consumer consciousness. As late as 1776, according to the leading students of the subject, "living conditions were still primitive" for most Americans.

The conviviality that obtained across most of America during most of the provincial period was not the mannered sociability of the magnates at their dinners and dances but the rough camaraderie of plain people at their taverns and tippling houses. The genteel complained constantly of the impertinence that they encountered when they ventured outside the sanctuary of their own homes and clubs, but their complaints were unavailing. Ferrymen and farmers did not defer to—or even comprehend the code of—the nouveau-riche nabobs who aspersed them. The "lower orders" never thought their "licentiousness" required the regulation that the "better sort" were always so eager to attempt.

Tension between democratic assumption and genteel arrogation was inevitable in a society such as early America, where masses of modest yeomen and mechanics rubbed shoulders routinely with men of sudden fortune. And the defeat of gentility was inevitable as well in a society where the gentry could not consolidate themselves to dictate terms of deference to the rest.

The new norms of civility arose, as Elias argued, in the new context of the courts and centralized states of Europe. In the absence of those institutions and of the courtiers and civil servants who attended them, the carriers of those new codes in the New World had no way to constitute themselves coherently. They were bound to be at odds not only with presumptuous inferiors but also with one another. The settlers could not come to any real solidarity as a class of gentlefolk because they shared so little beyond the standards of gentility they imbibed from books. They could not establish themselves as a consolidated American elite in a setting where every colony and every locality was in large measure a law unto itself. They could not maintain much mutual regard across their diverse communities when they could command so little homage within them.

So none of the new lords and ladies of the land ever quite convinced their peers of their own gentility, any more than the entire ensemble of them ever quite managed to impress their manners on the rest of the population. Few of the gentry elsewhere thought well of the New Englanders. George Washington found them "an exceeding dirty and nasty people." William Beekman of New York decided that they were "damned, ungrateful, cheating fellows" and refused to extend credit to them after a succession of disappointments. New Englanders in turn perceived New Yorkers as immoral and Southerners as hypocrites. A Maryland man of distinction decried the "gross, smutty expressions" he heard at a very exclusive Philadelphia club. And so it went. It was not easy to be part of a mannered gentry in a land of democrats, and it would not be much easier for generations to come.

BIBLIOGRAPHY

Bushman, Richard. "American High-Style and Vernacular Cultures." In *Colonial British America: Essays in the New History of the Early Modern Era,* edited by Jack Greene and J. R. Pole. Baltimore, Md., 1984.

Cable, Mary, and the editors of *American Heritage. American Manners and Morals: A Picture History of How We Behaved and Misbehaved.* New York, 1969.

Carr, Lois Green, and Lorena Walsh. "The Standard of Living in the Colonial Chesapeake." *William and Mary Quarterly,* 3rd ser., 45 (1988):135–162.

Carson, Cary, Ronald Hoffman, and Peter Albert, eds. *Of Consuming Interest: The Style of Life in the Eighteenth Century.* Charlottesville, Va., 1993.

Elias, Norbert. *The Civilizing Process.* Vol. 1. *The History of Manners.* Vol. 2. *Power and Civility.* New York, 1982.

Fischer, David Hackett. *Albion's Seed: Four British Folkways in America.* New York, 1989.

Goffman, Erving. *Interaction Ritual.* Garden City, N.Y., 1967.

Gorn, Elliott. " 'Gouge and Bite, Pull Hair and Scratch': The Social Significance of Fighting in the Southern Backcountry." *American Historical Review* 90 (1985):18–43.

Hawke, David. *Everyday Life in Early America.* New York, 1988.

Kasson, John. *Rudeness and Civility: Manners in Nineteenth-Century Urban America.* New York, 1990.

McKendrick, Neil, John Brewer, and J. H. Plumb. *The Birth of a Consumer Society: The Commercialization of Eighteenth-Century England.* Bloomington, Ind., 1982.

St. George, Robert. "'Set Thine House in Order': The Domestication of the Yeomanry in Seventeenth-Century New England." In *New England Begins: The Seventeenth Century,* edited by Jonathan Fairbanks and Robert Trent. Boston, 1982.

Schlesinger, Arthur. *Learning How to Behave: A Historical Study of American Etiquette Books.* New York, 1946.

Shammas, Carol. "The Domestic Environment in Early Modern England and America." *Journal of Social History* 14 (1980):3–24.

Thompson, Peter. "'The Friendly Glass': Drink and Gentility in Colonial Philadelphia." *Pennsylvania Magazine of History and Biography* 113 (1989):549–573.

Wolf, Stephanie. *As Various as Their Land: The Everyday Lives of Eighteenth-Century Americans.* New York, 1993.

Wyatt-Brown, Bertram. *Southern Honor: Ethics and Behavior in the Old South.* New York, 1982.

Michael Zuckerman

SEE ALSO **Dress; Rural Life; The Structure of Society;** and **Urban Life.**

THE DUTCH COLONY

DUTCH FOLKWAYS WERE GRADUALLY and selectively transferred to New Netherland. They were propagated by the settlers themselves, the government of the Dutch West India Company (WIC), and the Dutch Reformed church.

By the time of the British conquest in 1664, the population of New Netherland numbered perhaps ten thousand persons, about half of whom were probably ethnic Dutch. Of the others, however, many—if not most—had lived in the Netherlands, adopted Dutch manners and morals, and learned the language before coming to America. In any case ethnic and religious pluralism was the dominant cultural characteristic of the Dutch republic itself, where thousands of refugees fleeing religious and political persecution, war, and economic hardships had found a new home. Moreover although New Netherland was even more culturally diverse than the fatherland, Dutch law and custom prevailed throughout the colony, excepting the five towns on western Long Island founded by New Englanders. There English law and custom held sway, protected by charters from the New Netherland government. Even among the New Englanders, however, the influence of Dutch law and custom was felt by 1664.

TRANSPLANTING SOCIAL CUSTOMS

For almost two decades after settlement began in 1624, New Netherland was primarily a series of trading posts and scattered farms. Immigration was just a trickle, consisting mostly of young unmarried men plus a few occasional families. Riotous beer drinking and knife fighting, both quite common in the Dutch republic, occurred with disturbing regularity. The first Reformed preachers on the scene were appalled not only by that but by the extent of sexual immorality, in particular the "commingling" of male colonists and Indian maids. Indeed New Netherland became known in both Virginia and New England as quite a rowdy place. By the late 1640s, however, thanks largely to reforms in land tenure and trade instituted by the WIC, immigration increased sharply, with young couples in particular settling in the colony. This shift in demographics favored domesticity and social stability, and it was encouraged by both the Reformed church and by Director-General Peter Stuyvesant, who from 1647 to 1664 presided over the transformation of New Netherland from a trading outpost into a commercial and agricultural colony.

New Netherland increasingly reflected the culture and society of the Dutch republic, the most urbanized, commercial-oriented, and literate nation in Europe. Dutch society was largely bourgeois and middle-class, with its leaders drawn primarily from successful merchants. Under both Roman-Dutch law and Dutch tradition, women had more rights and freedom than elsewhere in Europe. From the beginning in New Netherland, women participated in trade, took disputes to court, and inherited property equally with their brothers. As in the Dutch republic, life in New Netherland centered on the family, where relationships between parents and children and among siblings were reciprocal; they were bound together by mutual responsibility and affection.

The Dutch family was almost always nuclear, with particular emphasis placed upon rearing children; in New Netherland the family would reflect those same characteristics in structure and sentiment. Husbands and wives usually made joint wills, which specified that the survivor inherited all the property and had the responsibility of educating the children. By contrast in New England and among the English on western Long Island, women surrendered both their legal identity and property to their husbands upon marriage. Under English common law, wives ordinarily could not will property, and the eldest son usually inherited the bulk of the family estate.

As was the Dutch practice, New Netherland parents usually allowed their sons and daughters considerable latitude in selecting a mate. However, leading families like the Philipses, the Schuylers, the Van Cortlandts, and the Van Rensselaers tended to intermarry. Indeed the family's business interests and political influence were advanced through marriage alliances, both in the Netherlands and in America. A patrician class of sorts certainly emerged in New Netherland, but it consisted mostly of families who had risen from decidedly middle-class circumstances.

Dutch family rituals were also widely followed in New Netherland. Both Director-General Stuyvesant and the Dutch Reformed clergy encouraged family formation, which began with marriage, usually marked by community celebration. The birth of a child, in particular his or her christening, was also generally accompanied by communal festivities. The Dutch were constantly accused by foreigners of being much too affectionate and permissive toward their children. Similar complaints were raised by Peter Stuyvesant in New Netherland. In fact nothing was more important to New Netherland parents than the education, material success, and marital happiness of their offspring. Relations between children and parents were generally very close. (Interestingly if wills are any indication, New England parents often felt considerable distrust and antagonism toward their children; however, it is extremely rare to detect such feelings in the probate records of non-English New Netherlanders.) Even at funerals, the Dutch custom of eating well and drinking to excess was practiced in New Netherland. The evidence is solid that New Netherlanders, whether Dutch or not, focused largely upon the family itself, placing the congregation and the community in decidedly second and third place in terms of their commitment.

Director-General Stuyvesant and the Dutch Reformed *domines,* or clergy, failed in their efforts to make New Netherlanders conform to Calvinistic orthodoxy. Religious convictions remained a family matter, as it was in the Dutch republic. However, Stuyvesant and the Reformed *domines,* through colonial ordinances and sermonizing, respectively, improved manners and morals among the settlers. Laws prohibiting cohabitation without marriage were more rigorously enforced, though neither informal marriages, fornication, nor prostitution were wiped out. To little avail local magistrates also tried to restrict the playing of such dangerous games as pulling the goose, well-known in the fatherland. The incidence of knife fighting certainly declined, though defamation and slander suits, staples of local courts in the United Provinces, if anything increased with time in the Dutch colony. Lampoon writers were numerous, testifying to the strength of literacy among the settlers.

Schooling was very important in a mercantile society like the Netherlands, and so it was in the Dutch colony. Instruction in reading and writing frequently began in the home and was continued at church and school. Catechetical training was especially important to fifteen Dutch Reformed *domines* recruited to New Netherland. The Reformed catechism was also taught by the twenty official schoolmasters who served before 1664. They propagated not only religious beliefs but also literacy, as did the twelve or more private schoolmasters, some of whom were probably Lutheran or Quaker.

Eighty years ago William Heard Kilpatrick concluded that New Netherland was more literate than most of the English colonies. His data indicated that male literacy was 80 percent in Beverswyck and Midwout (later Albany and Flatbush), compared with 60 percent in Virginia in the seventeenth century and 74 percent among the eighteenth-century German immigrants to Pennsylvania. Later analysis by Kenneth Lockridge suggests that New Netherland males were even more literate than the men of early Massachusetts. Of course Dutch women in New Netherland were more likely to be literate than women in the English colonies, even in Massachusetts Bay. Stuyvesant and the *domines* could not turn New Netherland into a Calvinistic commonwealth, but, along with the schoolmasters, they contributed mightily to making it as literate as the Dutch republic.

BIBLIOGRAPHY

Biemer, Linda Briggs. *Women and Property in Colonial New York: The Transition from Dutch to English Law, 1643–1727.* Ann Arbor, Mich., 1983.

Christoph, Peter R. "The Colonial Family: Kinship and Power." In *A Beautiful and Fruitful Place: Selected Rensselaerswijck Seminar Papers,* edited by Nancy Anne McClure Zeller. Albany, N.Y., 1991.

Earle, Alice Morse. *Colonial Days in Old New York.* New York, 1898; repr. 1965.

Kilpatrick, William Heard. *The Dutch Schools of New Netherland and Colonial New York.* New York, 1912; repr. 1969.

Lockridge, Kenneth. *Literacy in Colonial New England: An Inquiry into the Social Context of Literacy in the Early Modern West.* New York, 1974.

Raesly, Ellis L. *Portrait of New Netherland.* New York, 1945; repr. 1965.

Schama, Simon. *The Embarrassment of Riches: An Interpretation of Dutch Culture in the Golden Age.* New York, 1987.

Singleton, Esther. *Dutch New York.* New York, 1909; repr. 1968.

Van Deursen, A. T. *Plain Lives in a Golden Age: Popular Culture, Religion, and Society in Seventeenth-Century Holland.* Translated by Maarten Ultee. Cambridge, England, 1991.

Zumthor, Paul. *Daily Life in Rembrandt's Holland.* New York, 1962.

Ronald William Howard

SEE ALSO **Dress; Rural Life; The Structure of Society;** and **Urban Life.**

THE FRENCH COLONIES

THE SEPARATE COLONIES THAT comprised New France—Canada, Acadia, Île Royale, and Louisiana—had one thing in common, society in all of them was status ordered, hierarchical, with the three estates of France clearly delineated: clergy, nobility, commoners. Jean-Baptiste Colbert, Louis XIV's minister in charge of the colonies, made it clear in 1667 in a dispatch to the intendant at Quebec, Jean Talon, that this was how colonial society was to be established, to mirror that of the mother country.

Yet in the colonies in the seventeenth century, as in France, there was a considerable degree of social mobility both up and down—men married down, women up—but in the eighteenth century upward social mobility declined; society became more stratified, the second estate becoming virtually a caste. Thus attempts were made to stop presumptuous members of the third estate from aping their betters. In 1721, for example, they were forbidden to carry swords.

It was this second estate, the nobility, that dominated and set the tone of society throughout New France, but good manners—defined as consideration for others—were demanded of all the components of society. People in all walks of life were expected to be polite and courteous, even to the enemy when at war, before and after striving to slaughter them.

CANADA

The Swedish botanist Peter Kalm, a member of the Swedish Academy of Sciences, wrote after visiting Canada in 1749,

The common man in Canada is more civilized and clever than in any other place of the world that I have visited. On entering one of the peasant's houses, no matter where, and on beginning to talk with the men or women, one is quite amazed at the good breeding and courteous answers which are received, no matter what the question is. One can scarcely find in a city in other parts, people who treat one with such politeness both in word and deed as is true everywhere in the homes of the peasants in Canada. (*The America of 1750.* Vol. 2, p. 558)

He was even more impressed by the courtly manners of the Canadian nobility and the Jesuits; he compares colonial French refinement very favorably with what he had encountered in the English colonies, writing: "The difference between the favour and politeness which is my lot here and that of the English provinces is like that between heaven and earth, between black and white."

Others were equally impressed with Canadian politesse and the *douceur de vie,* or the comforts and gentleness of life, found in the colony. Comte Louis-Antoine de Bougainville, General Louis-Joseph de Montcalm's aide-de-camp, remarked that the Canadian farmers were not peasants but considered themselves far above that; they were habitants and did not resemble the surly, ignorant peasants of France in any way whatsoever. A main reason for this was indubitably that the untaxed Canadians were far better off economically than the taxed-to-death French peasantry.

More commentary is provided by Major John Livingston of New England, who voyaged to Quebec in 1710–1711, purportedly to effect an exchange of prisoners of war. He was lavishly entertained with banquets, dinner parties, music, and dancing such as he apparently had never experienced before: "The Govr Genll had a supper this night, where at least 50 persons of distinction and ye whole entertainment in great splendor."

All that was just one side of the coin, the noblesse aping the manners and fashions of Versailles and Paris. They were, as a French Jesuit, Father Pierre-François-Xavier de Charlevoix, remarked, extremely profligate, spending their income before they had it in hand, leaving their heirs little but debts. They were as proud as peacocks and as poor as church mice, believing sincerely that *bonne renommée vaut mieux que ceinture dorée* (a good name is better than riches). What they sought was *la gloire,* renown—not wealth. They were also quick to respond to a slight, real or imagined, and duels were commonplace events. The habitants behaved in similar fashion. An insult to a person, or a member of his or her family, demanded an instant response. (Revealingly, the worst insult that could be made toward a woman was to label her *putain,* or whore.) In such circumstances, men and women went at each other with whatever came to hand— fists, club, sword, stones. A man's honor and that of his family had to be upheld, no matter what. Court records are replete with such incidents, and for every case that went to court there were likely a dozen that did not. The Canadians were not litigious; they preferred to settle accounts directly in time-honored fashion.

Early in the eighteenth century the habitants in some Canadian parishes began to display a marked lack of respect for the clergy. They arrived at mass intoxicated, argued and quarrelled in the church lobby, walked out as soon as the curé began his sermon, scuffled and sang raucous songs during religious processions. The civil authority, the intendant, had to intervene to restore order, with ordinances imposing severe penalties on those committing such offenses.

LOUISIANA

The situation was much the same at Île Royale, a garrisoned naval fortress and fishing outport. In Louisiana, the picture was somewhat different, owing to its initial years of desperate struggle in a very hostile environment for Europeans. There the settlers for many years also had to cope with the pathetically inadequate support provided by France. Only the introduction of a large black slave labor force eventually made the colony politically and, almost, economically viable. The institution of black slavery, with slaves outnumbering the white population, inevitably had a profound effect on the mores and manners of the dominant white element in Creole society. Whether this was for good or ill is a moot point. Indubitably the slave labor force provided the masters with the income and leisure time to enjoy the finer things in life; to entertain and be entertained in a manner aping the lesser nobility of France. By the mid eighteenth century the nonindigenous population was less than nine thousand, four thousand of them being originally from Europe. Yet at a banquet given in honor of Governor Louis Billouart de Kerlerec upon his arrival at New Orleans, three hundred persons are reputed to have attended, half of them richly dressed women. It was claimed that the occasion would have done honor to such an entertainment in the wealthier cities of Europe. The colony had surpassed the mere survival stage and had established a firm toehold of French civilization even in darkest America.

SPANISH LOUISIANA

In 1763 France ceded Louisiana to Spain. Once the Spanish authorities became securely established they and the French Creoles got along quite well. They had much in common—their Roman religion, concepts of personal honor, craving for renown, contempt for parsimony, and a marked detestation of the crass Anglo-American traders who were establishing themselves in New Orleans.

In Canada after the British conquest of 1760 and the cession of the colony and its dependencies by France to Great Britain in 1763, the British military officers and royal officials, all imbued with the manners and ethos of the aristocracy, quickly shed their initial animosity to the ancient foe, the French. They soon found the manners and mores of the remaining Canadian nobility, clergy, and common folk much more to their liking than those displayed by the crude, money grubbing, unscrupulous Scots, English, and American traders who swarmed into the colony with or in the wake of the army at the conquest. Thus, in French Canada the old regime manners of New France, marked by courtesy, politesse, gentility—*la douceur de vie*—have in many ways survived as a legacy down to the present day.

BIBLIOGRAPHY

Bégon, Marie Isabelle Elisabeth Rocbert de la Morandiere. *Lettres au cher fils: Correspondance d'Elisabeth Bégon avec son gendre, 1748–1753*. Montreal, 1972.

B[oonefois?], J-C. *Voyage au Canada fait depuis l'an 1751 à 1761 par J.-C. B*. Quebec, 1887; repr. Paris, 1978.

Bougainville, Comte Louis-Antoine. *Relations et mémoires inédits pour servir à l'histoire de la France dans les pays d'outremer*. Edited by Pierre Margry. Paris, 1867.

Brunet, Michel. *Les Canadiens après la conquête, 1759–1775: De la revolution canadaienne à la revolution americaine*. Montreal, 1969.

Charlevoix, Pierre-François-Xavier de. *Histoire et description générale de la Nouvelle-France*. 3 vols. Paris, 1744.

Eccles, W. J. *France in America*. Rev. ed. Markham, Ontario, 1990.

Franquet, Louis. *Voyages et mémoires sur le Canada*. Quebec, 1889.

Gadowry, Lorraine. *La noblesse de Nouvelle-France: Families et alliances*. Montreal, 1992.

Kalm, Peter. *The America of 1750: Peter Kalm's Travels in North America*. Edited by Adolph B. Benson. 2 vols. New York, 1966. The English version of 1770, revised from the original Swedish, with a translation of new material from Kalm's diary notes.

Kerkkonen, Martti. *Peter Kalm's North American Journey*. Studia Historica, I. Finnish Historical Society. Helsinki, 1959.

Landry, Yves. *Orphelines en France pionnières au Canada: Les filles du roi au XVIIe siècle*. Montreal, 1992.

Moogk, Peter N. "'Thieving Buggers' and 'Stupid Sluts': Insults and Popular Culture in New France." *William and Mary Quarterly*, 3rd ser., 36, no. 4 (1979):524–527.

Moore, Christopher. *Louisbourg Portraits: Life in an Eighteenth-Century Garrison Town*. Toronto, Ontario, 1982.

Neatby, Hilda. *Quebec: The Revolutionary Age, 1760–1791*. Toronto, Ontario, 1966.

Séguin, Robert-Lionel. *La vie libertine en Nouvelle-France au dixseptième siècle*. 2 vols. Montreal, 1972.

Terrage, Marc de Villiers du. *Histoire de la fondation de la Nouvelle-Orléans*. Paris, 1817.

————. *The Last Years of French Louisiana*. Edited by Carl A. Brasseaux and Glenn R. Conrad. Translated by Hosea Phillips. Lafayette, La., 1982.

W. J. Eccles

SEE ALSO **Dress; Rural Life; The Structure of Society;** and **Urban Life.**

THE SPANISH BORDERLANDS

HOW TO ESTABLISH hegemony and how to control the daily behavior of the colonial population in such a way as to ensure the expansionist interests of the colonial project and the allocation of limited resources were the two concerns that led to the introduction of a Mediterranean code of honor in the Spanish Borderlands. The code prescribed how individuals should behave in public and private and how deference should be paid to others, in short, the manners that governed individual behavior. This code was not a formalized set of universal laws. It varied over time and by place and was adapted to specific regional needs.

HONOR AND VIRTUE

In Spain honor was ascribed to those who fought the infidel; in the Americas it belonged to those who subjugated the "pagan" indigenous populations. This code justified the superordinate status of the Spanish colonists, the subordination of the indigenous peoples, and the enslavement of large number of detribalized Indians. The code of honor also structured and defined the limits of social interactions and discouraged patterns of behavior that extended beyond the acceptable communal norms.

Distinguishing the honored from the dishonored was a relatively simple task when the colonial project began. One possessed honor if one were white and Christian, and if one had been granted a title of nobility for involvement in the conquest. However, as the social fabric became more intricate through miscegenation, population expansion, and the resulting competition for limited resources, the process of evaluating honor status became more complex. Race, religion, ethnicity, occupation, ancestry, ownership of land, and individual behavior all came into play. Honor was not the exclusive domain of the nobility or the landed gentry since class distinctions were not as marked on the borderlands as they were in other areas of New Spain and Europe. Opportunities for vertical movement or social advancement existed as well. Landowning peasants could also possess honor. The code of honor, nonetheless, did serve to maintain social distance particularly as it pertained to marital contracts.

That the entire community abided by the code of honor, and that all social interactions were governed by the need to maintain individual and, by extension, familial honor is borne out in ecclesiastical and civil documents. In these we find clues regarding how one could lose honor. A sure way was by not keeping one's word. An *hombre de palabra* (man of his word) who did not keep his word lost honor. Therefore the phrase *mientes* (you're lying) could elicit a violent response, one worthy of restoring the accused man's honor.

A man who could not control the behavior of his sons lost honor, as did the son who disobeyed his father. In order to restore his honor, the father of a dishonorable adult son could, in extreme cases, resort to *maldición* or cursing ("May the earth part and swallow you"), or he, as the sole possessor of *patria potestad*, paternal authority, could administer physical discipline. It was not uncommon to do so even to sons who had reached the age of maturity. That this prerogative could be claimed by the mother is recorded in an account of Juan N. Cortina, a Texan folk hero who in a meeting of reconciliation with his estranged mother, handed her his riding crop and knelt to receive her blows in the presence of fellow military officers. A man who could not control his slaves or servants likewise lost honor.

Public flogging of thralls or servants gone astray was a sure way to demonstrate that one was a man of honor. Shaming adult Indian males in this manner was commonly used to undermine indigenous social structures, which were based on respect and submission of youth to the community elders. Since adult male slaves were more likely to be rebellious, the majority of household servants were females and their children. The latter were often also the master's or his son's children. While there were laws that prohibited such unions, the code of honor paradoxically sanctioned them. Sexual conquest, particularly of the spoils of victory, added to male honor.

Female virtue was an important component of the honor code. A single woman who surrendered her virginity before marriage dishonored herself and her family. In order to maintain family honor, fathers and brothers were obliged to protect the virtue of their women from other males who gained honor through sexual conquest. Thus vigilance, chaperoning, and seclusion (though the latter did not go so far as to include the Mediterranean custom of concealing the woman's face with a veil), were methods used to keep women's virtue intact. That such vigilance may have had another motive—to control the family wealth through control of the matrimonial "match"—is not out of the question. Unlike Roman law, Spanish law allowed women to inherit, to bequeath, and to possess the dowry after marriage, and to own property though the latter might be administered by the husband. Furthermore, a dishonored daughter was severely devalued on the marriage market. Her condition could also place economic strain on the family in that the dowry would have to be increased in order to attract a suitor.

The numerous recordings of litigations involving cases of seduction attest to the fact that the code of honor was not always successful in controlling sexual behavior in Spanish colonial society. What is of interest in these cases is that legal, and sometimes ecclesiastical, intervention could contribute to the restoration of honor. The authority in charge of the case could rule, for example, that the offending male restore the woman's honor either by marrying her or by paying her a sum of money.

Married women were not exempt from concerns over virtue and honor. An unfaithful woman brought extreme dishonor to her spouse. One method a husband used to restore his honor was by publicly shaming his wife. This could involve cutting her hair or flogging her, though the latter was not a legally sanctioned practice. It was also customary to place the unfaithful wife in *depósito* (literally, in deposit) with some respectable member of the community while the husband pursued a suitable solution.

It is true that the code of honor limited the role of Hispanic women in colonial society, but never were they as severely affected by it as were the most oppressed of the lot, Indian women. In their Native cultures, women held a high status level because of their involvement with food, the primary ingredient of cosmic harmony. Women's sexuality was also a source of power and authority, for through it women not only gave birth to new generations, but they also tamed malevolent spirits. Outsiders were frequently associated with evil. It was thus the role of women to neutralize potential evil by engaging outsiders in sex, regardless of their own marital status. Extramarital sex for indigenous women was not tinged with shame as it was for Europeans; it was in fact a source of empowerment.

When Native American women engaged in sex with Spanish soldiers, two conflicting codes collided. The women acted to protect the community from evil, while the men gained honor through appropriation of the spoils. However, the alterns did not recognize the significance of the actions of the subaltern, but rather they relegated, through the valuative nature of the code of honor, Indian women to the bottom rung reserved for the dishonored of the dishonored. Once they entered captivity the degree of abuse some of these women received at the hands of their masters and their master's sons increased drastically.

RESPECT IN THE BORDERLANDS

With regard to actual patterns of etiquette in Hispanic communities, we do not have much documentation, for Spanish language chroniclers were much more interested in documenting the way of life of the indigenous populations. We can infer, however, from the copious documentation of the customs and traditions of the Mexican period recorded by early arrivals from the United States that those customs had their origins in the colonial period.

The concept of *respeto* (respect) appears frequently in the literature of early Anglo visitors. Its roots lie in the respect automatically ascribed to the father under patriarchal ideology, but in the Spanish Borderlands it was extended to include all community elders. To what extent the behavior of the indigenous groups may have influenced Hispanic custom in this regard has not been examined, but there is indeed a striking resemblance in attitude toward elders in both groups. *Respeto* was embedded in everyday language. All adults were addressed with the emblematic form of respect, *usted*, while children, servants, and Indians were addressed in the familiar *tú*. The infantile status of the latter and hegemonic control were thus linguistically reinforced.

A son or daughter, even in adulthood, did not dare smoke in front of a parent. To do so was a sign of *falta de respeto* (lack of respect). Women engaged freely in smoking but were not allowed to flaunt a lit cigarette. Unlike men who could hold the cigarette between the fingers, women held the cigarette between the thumb and the forefinger shielding it with the rest of the hand.

Young people removed their hats and stood in the presence of adults, never leaving a room without permission. A young boy did not dare take a drink of water until after having offered the gourd to adults present. If the latter accepted, the young person stood with arms crossed while the adults drank. *Respeto* was extended to neighbors by taking to their homes a sample of a specially prepared dish.

Outsiders were also extended *respeto* through generous hospitality. In northern New Mexico, California, and Texas the phrase *ésta es su casa* (this is your home) was repeatedly heard by strangers, and the cordial treatment that followed was proof of the sincerity with which it was uttered. Again, it is not clear to what extent Indian customs may have influenced Spanish settlers, but it is clear from the early chronicles that the latter were repeatedly impressed by the hospitality of various Indian groups.

CONCLUSION

The high value placed on respect and honor no doubt contributed to conviviality in the Spanish Borderlands. We must not, however, fall into the trap of romanticizing a way of life that demanded a high price from those who were not born into a privileged class reserved for those committed to a colonial patriarchal ideology.

BIBLIOGRAPHY

Arrom, Silvia Marina. *The Women of Mexico City, 1790–1857.* Stanford, Calif., 1985.

Campa, Arthur Leon. *Hispanic Culture in the Southwest.* Norman, Okla., 1979.

Gutiérrez, Ramón A. *When Jesus Came, the Corn Mothers Went Away: Marriage, Sexuality, and Power in New Mexico, 1500–1846.* Stanford, Calif., 1991.

Gutierrez de Pineda, Virginia, and Patricia Vila de Pineda. *Honor, Familia, y Sociedad en la Estructura Patriarcal.* Bogotá, 1988.

Erlinda Gonzales-Berry

See also **Dress; Rural Life; The Structure of Society;** and **Urban Life.**

TRAVEL AND LODGING

Travel and lodging in early America took a variety of forms, and the ease of getting from place to place and the hope of finding a comfortable place to rest were constrained by a variety of factors. To give just one example, the early-eighteenth-century traveler to the Carolinas would have been hard-pressed to find an inn, yet taverns were spaced at fairly regular intervals throughout southeastern Pennsylvania. Similarly, while taverns were plentiful in New England towns and abundant in the northeastern port cities, they were virtually absent along the route that connected Mexico City to Santa Fe.

Travel, before the introduction of regularized coach or stage routes, was uncommon. The vast majority of colonists rarely ventured farther than the distance from home to church. Most travel occurred as part of work—peddlers or traders to exchange goods, judges to preside at the circuit court, colonial representatives to attend the legislative assembly. The mode of transportation employed depended to a great degree on the traveler's social and economic status. Water travel was a favored form, but it was not always an option since it depended upon both geography and an individual's economy. On land, poorer folks used foot power; the wealthier members of colonial society moved about on horses or traveled and transported their goods in carriages and wagons.

This essay focuses on the tavern as a multifaceted institution whose specific character depended upon whether it was large or small, urban or rural, and whether it catered primarily to a local clientele or to strangers. The essay also explores the range of methods of travel available in early America.

TRAVEL THROUGHOUT THE COLONIES

Travelers throughout the colonies relied both on land and water transport. Early New England roads, called "trodden paths," were often trails blazed and walked by Indians. These paths were frequently little more than slight indentations in the ground. The shoes of the colonists and the hooves of cattle deepened the trails. As the use of horses became more common, the trails widened and gradually became large enough to accommodate carts, wagons, and carriages.

The earliest path, noted by the General Court in 1639, was the Plymouth or Coast Path, which linked Boston and Plymouth. Two paths started in Cambridge, Massachusetts, and ended in Albany, New York. The Old Connecticut Path ran through Marlborough, Grafton, Oxford, and Springfield, Massachusetts, on its way to Albany. The New Connecticut Path went through Grafton and on to Worcester and Brookfield, finally reaching Albany. Other paths were linked with these: the Bay Path, for example, left the Old Connecticut at Wayland and wound its way through Marlborough to Worcester, Oxford, Charlton, and Brookfield, where it joined the Hadley Path and went on to Hadley to rejoin the Old Connecticut Path.

Walking was the primary means of getting around in early New England. However, it did not take long for horses to replace feet for all except the poorest members of society. The young Benjamin Franklin followed a typical route from Boston to Philadelphia. Almost totally without money as he made his way in 1723, Franklin traveled partly by sea and then walked from Amboy to Burlington, New Jersey. Carriages were financially out of reach for all but the wealthiest. The American carriage, unlike the English, was lightweight and was a continental variety.

Various techniques were used to improve the poor quality of the roads. One technique was the corduroy. Logs were laid side by side across the road in order to make roads passable by carts and later by larger wagons. Marshy places and chuck holes were filled with saplings and logs. Once a network of roads was created, ferries and bridges linking those roads were built. A "cart bridge" was built in 1633 to connect Boston to Roxbury; by 1639 ferries ran to Chelsea and Charlestown.

Water transportation was the method of choice, both for personal travel and for moving goods. Even in Pennsylvania, where the roads were among the best in the colonies, the agricultural production of the colony was moved to market on small boats over a system of inland waterways. Water travel was used almost exclusively between the settlements of Boston, Salem, and Plymouth. Most roads were rough, sometimes no more than the original Indian paths, and river and stream crossings were perilous; water transportation was far more reliable and damaged produce far less. Water systems not only connected the hinterlands to the capitals but also linked the colonies with the larger world. According to one source, "it was easier and less traumatic in good weather to sail from London to Boston than to reach Charleston from Massachusetts by horse."

The situation in the Chesapeake region was similar to that in New England. Planters were concerned primarily with moving tobacco from their farms to market. Because tobacco was ex-

tremely bulky and fragile and tended to disintegrate if bounced around on bumpy roads, tidewater planters relied on a system of inland waterways. In sparsely settled areas or in regions without streams and rivers, farmers used Indian paths; as the population density increased, they dug additional roadbeds to connect the existing paths. The "three-notche'd road" that linked the Shenandoah Valley to the falls of the James River provides a good example. Most roads were built upon the orders of the courts; in 1733, for example, the colonial court in Goochland County, Virginia, ordered that "a road be cleared from Mountains . . . in the most convenient way." After such a roadway was completed, local planters often petitioned the county courts for bridges to be built over the smaller streams and ferry service to be instituted at the larger ones.

Public roads remained inadequate until well into the eighteenth century. In Prince Georges County, Maryland, in the early 1700s, for example, only fifty miles (80 kilometers) of public paths existed, and roads linked scattered neighborhoods along the Potomac River and eastern branch of the river with other settlements on the Patuxent River. Transportation problems in the region were ameliorated when planters united to petition for bridges and roads. By 1739 295 miles (472 kilometers) of public roads existed in the British colonies, more than five times the number by 1700. Not only could crops be moved more efficiently, but the improved road system enhanced visiting among neighbors. For men, this included stopping at the local tavern after the day's business had been transacted.

In the three French colonies on mainland North America—Acadia, Canada and its western dependencies, and Louisiana—travel was primarily by water. Only in Canada were there roads; one, constructed in the seventeenth century, was a military road running from la Prairie de la Magdeleine, then across the Saint Lawrence River from Montreal to Fort Chambly on the Richelieu River. In the eighteenth century, a road (le Chemin du Roy) was built from Quebec to Montreal, but most goods between the two towns were freighted by boat; people normally traveled by canoe, bateau, or schooner. In winter, the frozen Saint Lawrence River provided an easier route for sleighs than the overland route, but below Trois-Rivières the ebb and flow of the tide—up to twenty feet (6 meters) at Quebec—made the ice treacherous. The farmers along the river were required by law to mark a safe route with spruce trees and tramp down the snow with their oxen after a heavy fall. From Montreal to western Canada, travel was by *canots de maître,* crewed by eight to ten voyageurs, following the Ottawa River to Michilimackinac, then on to Kaministigoya at the western end of Lake Superior, and from there by five-man *canots du nord* to the Saskatchewan River and across the prairies. The other route used ran from Montreal up the Saint Lawrence by canoe to Fort Frontenac at the eastern end of Lake Ontario, then by barque to Niagara, by portage around the falls, then by barque to Detroit and beyond. In Louisiana, the rivers were also the main travel routes, especially because the settlements were ranged along the Mississippi and its tributaries and at the mouth of the Mobile River. In Acadia, during its brief existence as part of the French Empire, settlements were located along the south shore of the Bay of Fundy, and travel here too was primarily by water.

Canada, with its larger and less dispersed population numbering approximately eighty thousand by 1760, was the heart of the French Empire in America. The governor-general resided at Quebec. Unlike their peasant ancestors in France, most of whom never ventured farther than the next village, Canadians voyaged far and wide. Despite the vast distances, there was considerable traffic between Quebec, the Illinois settlements, and New Orleans, while the Saint Lawrence drew settlers to the far west or downstream and on to the West Indies.

Within Montreal and Quebec the upper Class Creoles used sedan chairs in bad weather. Urban residents were required by law to keep the wooden sidewalks in front of their houses in good repair so that, as a Montreal judge sternly ordered, elderly gentlemen and pregnant ladies could walk in safety; small boys caught making ice slides on the streets were severely punished, and pigs found roaming loose were shot by the town archers and their carcasses delivered to the local hospital. After the spring thaw urban dwellers had to have the winter's collected debris cleared away and the potholes filled in.

The senior officials in their frequent trips from Quebec to Montreal, during the ice free months, made use of the intendant's bateau. Colonel Louis Franquet, an engineering officer making a tour of Canada's fortifications in 1752, described the boat as being flat bottomed with a main and top sail, crewed by eleven oarsmen and two steermen. It had a cockpit for passengers some six to seven feet square (almost 1 square meter), benches all the way around covered with blue cushions; along the sides were canvas screens to protect against the spray, a blue canopy overhead served as a sunscreen and a red, oiled canvas tarpaulin could be rigged in wet weather. The boat was well stocked with food, wine, and liqueurs for the trip.

Like colonists elsewhere in North America, inhabitants of the Spanish Borderlands did not travel far from home. However, by 1580, not long after the Spanish conquest of Mexico, a "royal road" (*Camino Real*), dotted with camps, towns, ranches, and garrisons and linked by wagon trains, ran north and west about 850 miles (1,360 kilometers) from Mexico City. This route remained the primary road north until the end of the sixteenth century, when Don Juan de Oñate discovered that he could bypass the vast expanse of desert that extended to Big Bend on the Rio Grande and was able to chart a course for Santa Fe. In 1609, the year Santa Fe was established, the town became the terminus for wagon trains traveling from Mexico City. These wagon trains were subsidized out of the royal treasury, and, after a series of official reorganizations of the route in 1630 and 1664, were required to make the round trip from Mexico City to Santa Fe every three years. Travel to Santa Fe took about six months; six months was required to distribute the cargo; and the return took an additional half year.

Wagon trains that traveled between Mexico City and Santa Fe normally consisted of thirty-two wagons organized into two sections that were further divided into two divisions of eight wagons each. Each section of sixteen wagons was supervised by a wagon master, and the caravan was escorted by a company of twelve to fourteen soldiers commanded by a captain. In addition, the trains were accompanied by a herd of beef cattle, spare draft animals, and service wagons that carried additional wheels, fabric for the wagon covers, axles, spokes, iron tires, tallow, and tools. The wagons were capable of carrying four thousand pounds each (1,800 kilograms) when fully loaded, and each required a team of eight mules.

Wagon trains were established, in theory, to supply and maintain the missions near the road. They did, however, have an important secular purpose as well, since they represented the only form of transportation along the route. As they headed north from Mexico City, the trains carried not only friars and missionary supplies, but settlers, government officials, baggage, mail, and merchandise. On the return trip, the trains transported returning officials and friars and the produce of the settlers.

Camino Real was a long and dangerous route, and the caravans were meant to provide reliable service as well as protection for travelers. However, colonial travel everywhere was dangerous. A French officer, Colonel Louis Franquet of the corps of engineers, noted that Canadian sleigh drivers always traveled at top speed with no regard to life or limb and would not allow themselves to be overtaken. As a result, the *carioles* frequently overturned, tossing driver and passengers into the snow. Colonists everywhere reported accidents on horseback or difficulties crossing swollen rivers and creeks. Sudden storms, drops in temperature, and the steamy heat of the South all inhibited travelers' movements.

Women traveled infrequently, and when they did, they were usually accompanied by male escorts. Women travelers were not guaranteed any better accommodations than those available to men. In her 1704 journey from Boston to New York, Boston resident Sarah Knight was shown to a room with many beds and in the middle of the night was awakened by men arriving to sleep in the same room.

In January 1673 regular mail service was instituted linking New York and Boston. Before regular stage routes were established, mail carriers were required to assist anyone who wished to travel in their company. The carriers covered their routes on horseback and delivered the mail to a local tavern, where it was spread out on a table for the locals to claim after paying the postage. As late as 1763, the Postmaster General of the colonies, Benjamin Franklin, listed only forty-eight post offices in operation. In areas without post offices, mail continued to arrive

and depart from taverns. The colonies below Maryland were without regular postal service as late as 1774 and had to rely on a system whereby ship captains deposited the mail in port cities and private riders would be paid fees to deliver it. The situation in North Carolina was typical. The mail for the entire colony was delivered to Wilmington.

Travel in the colonies improved markedly as regular stagecoach routes were inaugurated. The first, in 1752, covered the fifty miles (80 kilometers) from Burlington and Amboy in New Jersey; from these terminals passengers could connect with ferries traveling to Philadelphia or New York. In 1766 Philadelphia and New York were linked by stagecoach; in good weather, the trip took two days. A year later, a route was established between Boston and Providence, operating in the summer. By 1770 stagecoaches connected Salem with Boston, and the following year Boston and Portsmouth, New Hampshire. Stagecoach service was slow to develop in the South. Regular packet boat service, however, operated from New York, Boston, and Philadelphia to Charleston.

The stagecoach created the first reliable transportation system available to the colonists, and by the late eighteenth century, travel had increased markedly. Coaches made travel easier and cheaper. Many stage drivers linked up with tavernkeepers, either informally or via contracts, and stopped at selected taverns with their passengers on a regular basis. Some of the stops were merely to refresh horses and riders; at others, food and lodging were provided to passengers. In the cities, stagecoaches departed and arrived at specific taverns, and tavernkeepers often acted as ticket agents.

While the stagecoach provided a reliable form of transportation, it was far from comfortable. President Josiah Quincy of Harvard described his trip from Boston to New York: "We generally reached our resting-place for the night if no accident intervened at ten o'clock, and after a frugal supper went to bed, with a notice that we would be called at three next morning, which generally proved to be half-past two." Regardless of rain or snow, Quincy wrote "the traveler must rise and make ready by the help of a horn-lantern and a farthing candle . . . sometimes getting out to help the coachman lift the coach out of a quagmire or rut." Travel increased markedly after the revolution as turnpikes—toll roads with gates every few miles—appeared. The first two turnpikes were constructed in Virginia and Pennsylvania in 1785 and 1792, respectively.

TAVERNS—THE CENTER OF THE COMMUNITY

Taverns were the hotels and motels of early America in an age when distances seemed vast and transportation was slow. Officially, taverns were intended for the "Conveniency and Accommodations of Travelers," and colonial statutes stipulated that they were to provide nourishment and lodging for humans and their horses. A 1692 Massachusetts law was typical: "The ancient, true and principal use of Inns . . . is for the Receipt, Relief and Lodging of Travellers and Strangers, and the Refreshment of persons upon lawful Business." Maryland lawmakers in 1694 required that, in addition to stables for horses, tavernkeepers have "12 good beds of feather or flock with covering . . . if running a public house at the [colonial] capital." Taverns in other locations needed only six beds.

In order to accommodate strangers, taverns located outside cities were most often on public roads, spaced every three to four miles (about 5 to 6 kilometers). Since people traveled both by land and water, taverns appeared as quickly as roads and bridges were constructed or ferries were operational.

Early American taverns, however, filled needs beyond those of the traveler. They were also the focal point of community life for local residents. Day-to-day personal contact, whether among members of an extended family, business acquaintances, or friends seeking a service, a commodity, or just the latest news, was typical of early American society. Many of these contacts took place in local taverns. Locals met to smoke a pipe, to try their luck at games, to share news and gossip, to receive mail, to conduct business, or simply to talk while sipping a friendly glass of spirituous liquors. The relationship of tavern to town was so important that the General Court of Massachusetts passed an ordinance in 1656 making towns that did not have a tavern liable to a fine. At times, taverns substituted for courts,

schools, stores, or hospitals. Thus, they were a source of comfort and shelter for those away from home and for those who simply wanted to get away from home for a while.

The Tavernkeeper

All colonies passed laws to control the tavern trade. The term "ordinary," for example, which was interchangeable with "tavern," indicates that prices for food and drink were set by an ordinance. In addition to meeting legal requirements concerning the provision of food and lodging, landlords were required to be licensed if they wished to serve spirituous liquors. To obtain these licenses, renewed annually, prospective tavernkeepers had to petition the county court for permission to "keep a house of entertainment," explaining why they wanted to become tavernkeepers and why they were suitable for the position. The requirements for winning a license appear to have varied somewhat from colony to colony and from town to town; however, because of the important role taverns played in accommodating travelers and in community life, magistrates everywhere took a number of factors into consideration. Most important was density. It made sense for taverns to be spaced at regular intervals along major roads for the convenience of travelers. On the other hand, magistrates feared that licensing an excessive number would encourage excessive drinking among the local inhabitants. In addition, they refused licenses to proprietors who were of questionable character.

Location often made the most persuasive argument. No matter where the petitioner resided, whether Chester County, Pennsylvania, or Suffolk County, Massachusetts, the vast majority of license requests noted that the house was "conveniently located." Thomas Spring of Weston, Connecticut, petitioned the court for a license in January 1750, pointing out that "a publick highway has been lately laid out, . . . from Watertown thro Newton, Weston part of Natick and Sudbury to Framingham"; since there was no public house within fifteen miles (24 kilometers) he requested a tavern license. In October 1727 Judah Richards was granted a tavern license because she resided on the public road; her application included the observation that "her habitation is conveniently scituated for retailing strong liquor" in the town of Dedham, Massachusetts.

Individuals who operated ferries or who lived near ferries and bridges were also good candidates for tavern licenses. John Chade of Birmingham, Pennsylvania, kept the ferry over Brandywine Creek, and his house and ferry were on the road leading from Nottingham to Philadelphia. In September 1736, he was granted a tavern license to keep a public inn "for the convenience of travellers." Licenses were also granted when the house met the needs of a particular clientele. Henry Russell's license was renewed in 1682 because those who worked at sea depended on having a convenient tavern; Russell entertained "ffisher men and Seamen with diet and lodging at [his] house."

Some petitioners took a different approach, arguing that they were being oppressed by the great numbers of travelers who stopped at their private residences seeking food and lodging. Without a proper license, the petitioners stated, they had to turn away the visitors since it would be illegal for them to dispense the proper hospitality. Garrett Brumbbough of Coventry in Chester County, Pennsylvania, was "frequently oppressed with travellers whom he is obliged to entertain . . . on the great road which leads from Philadelphia to the iron works and from thence to Conestoga." His request for a taverkeeper's license was granted. William Boyd in August 1738 claimed the same problem. He lived in Sadbury, Pennsylvania, on the "great road leading to Lancaster . . . and travelers [were] passing and repassing frequently calling for refreshment and lodging to the damage of your petitioner and great fatigue of his family."

Colonies also granted licenses as a form of poor relief. John Reed, who petitioned for a license to keep a tavern in Chester County, Pennsylvania, in 1757, had been employed laying boards on a kiln but was injured when the beams broke. "His leggs brocken and the doctor not taking care to do his duty in curing him, he has lost the use of his leg," stated his petition. Reed hoped to be granted a tavern license because he was "utterly unable to support himself by any labour whatsoever." Similarly, Thomas Jones of Charlestown, Massachusetts, was granted a license to retail wine and liquors because he had been "for a long time held under

bodily weakness and distemper together with a total deprivation of his sight whereby his estate is greatly impaired." He claimed to be unable to provide for his family by any other means and without hope of recovering. David Morgan of Haverford Township in Chester County, Pennsylvania, combined two criteria, location and need, and successfully petitioned for a license. His wife, he wrote, was "an ancient and lame woman and his dwelling house [was] convenient for the entertainment of such as travel the great road leading from philadelphia to the forks of brandy wine."

Women, often widowed and responsible for maintaining their families, commonly petitioned for tavern licenses. While women held approximately 30 percent of the tavern licenses in Boston and Philadelphia, they were less frequently tavernkeepers in the rural areas of the colonies where they were fewer in number. Elizabeth Bond's petition was typical. In 1738 she asked that the Massachusetts magistrates grant her permission to sell liquor in small measure from her home. Bond claimed that she was "left a widow with a considerable charge of small children and having no way to maintain them but by my hard labour." Bond's request was allowed.

Regulating the Trade

In addition to controlling the granting of licenses, the colonies regulated the tavern trade in other ways. Tavernkeepers were told what they could sell, at what prices, to whom, in what quantity, on which days of the week, and at what hours. The cities of Boston and Philadelphia prohibited tavernkeepers from extending credit to mariners. Gaming and gambling were discouraged. A Massachusetts law attempted to control drinking by limiting the amount of time patrons could spend in the tavern; the tavern door was to remain closed until one hour before sunset and customers were to drink no more than one-half pint (roughly one-quarter of a liter) of wine at one sitting. Most travelers, however, were exempt from the regulations. Furthermore, blacks, apprentices, servants, and seamen were not permitted inside a tavern without permission from their masters or captains.

In contrast to the social concerns that led to the institution of laws governing the establishment and operation of taverns in New England

and in the Chesapeake region, the motivations for the regulation of taverns in seventeenth-century New Netherland was economic. The earliest laws governing the sale of alcoholic beverages in that colony included provisions requiring tavernkeepers to pay an excise tax on beverages they purchased and forbidding them from brewing their own beer.

During Peter Stuyvesant's administration (1646–1664), lawmakers took note of the quantity of alcoholic beverages that were being consumed, Stuyvesant complaining that one-quarter of the city of New Amsterdam contained "brandy shops, Tobacco or Beer houses." While the Dutch required that tavernkeepers be licensed, they did not limit the number of licenses issued. Drinking among the colonists does seem to have been a problem; in 1662, a law was passed to prevent citizens from pawning family possessions in order to buy alcoholic beverages. Although the English passed new laws when they took control of New Netherland in 1665, the new regulations had little impact.

Taverns abounded in the French mainland colonies of Canada, Louisiana, and Acadia, as well. At New Orleans the authorities sought to limit the number of taverns to six, plus two canteens to serve the soldiers of the garrison. The two canteens might have sufficed for the two hundred troops stationed there in 1744, but they were certainly inadequate by 1751, by which time the garrison population had increased to one thousand, bringing the total population of New Orleans to about five thousand.

The tavern trade was also well regulated in French Canada. In 1726 all Canadian taverns were required to display a branch of evergreen over the door to identify themselves, and all were forbidden to sell spirits after 9 P.M. Liquor was to be served only in rooms furnished with tables and benches—in other words, not in bedrooms. Gambling and rowdy behavior were strictly forbidden. Soldiers could not be served before noon, and servants ordering liquor had to have a chit signed by their masters granting them permission to imbibe. In addition, servants were limited to no more than two quarts (roughly 2 liters) of beer, a quart of wine, or a pint of eau-de-vie (a fruit brandy). Tavernkeepers were forbidden to accept in payment household goods such as linen, silverware, or crockery from youths, soldiers, or servants.

In 1710 the stern intendant Raudot reduced the number of taverns in Montreal to nineteen, nine of them set aside for the Indians and allocated to the different nations to prevent tribal massacres. The highest incidence of crimes brought before the Montreal Court was, by far, that of selling liquor to the Indians. Some unscrupulous tavernkeepers kept what was known as "the Indian barrel" into which the dregs from all the tankards and glasses, beer, wine, or brandy, were dumped, then served surreptitiously to the Indian customers. The practice came to view when a soldier was charged with assaulting a tavernkeeper. His defense was that having ordered a glass of wine he was served from the Indian barrel. He was acquitted.

The amount of wine and spirits imbibed by the Canadians was indeed startling; by the end of the seventeenth-century, with an estimated population of fifteen thousand, they consumed about 1 percent of Bordeaux's annual wine production. Beer was brewed locally, also a form of beer from spruce needles that was an excellent safeguard against scurvy. In the eighteenth century the upper class became partial to Spanish wine—most likely sherry—and Madeira. A favorite way to start the day was a piece of bread dunked in cognac.

While the courts in every colony prosecuted violators of tavern laws—from those who drank too much, too often, and too late to those who operated houses without licenses or who ran "disorderly houses"—the laws appear to have been difficult to enforce. Similarly, while Canadian laws forbade rowdiness in taverns, the number of cases that began with fighting among officers over cards and dice and that ended in duels suggests that the attempts at regulation were not overly successful.

Characteristics of Early American Taverns

The type and quality of taverns varied enormously. A case in point involves George Plimn's tavern and the Indian Queen, both in late-eighteenth-century Philadelphia. While Plimn's tavern was a typical small inn, the Indian Queen was known for its elegance. The one public room in Plimn's tavern, furnished with a walnut desk, a table with six chairs, and four framed pictures, also contained the tools of the drink trade: pewter measures, a keg, bottles, three glasses, and scales and measures. A room in the back, simply furnished with a bed and table, was available for overnight guests. Accommodations at the Indian Queen contrasted dramatically with those at Plimn's. The Indian Queen consisted of many buildings with large halls and with many small apartments used for lodging. Each chamber was elegantly furnished with a "bed, bureau, table with drawers, a large looking-glass, neat chairs and other furniture."

Although the quality of accommodations offered by taverns within cities ranged markedly, rural establishments were more uniform and typically were simple and functional. The Wellfleet Tavern in Cape Cod, which operated from 1690 to 1740, can serve as a model. On the first floor were two public rooms, one on either side of the chimney. It is not clear where guests slept. However, archaeological excavation reveals that another room may have extended the length of the building and provided sleeping accommodations.

Taverns did not vary only in size. They also differed in the services they offered. In addition to selling a wide range of beverages, including punch, toddy, cider, bitters, grog, beer, rum, wine, slingers with various flavorings, brandy, and batesman's drops, taverns provided food, and some even specialized. One river-town tavern was known for its salmon, another for its oysters. An old Dutch tavern was noted for head cheese, while near Philadelphia, catfish suppers were popular. In addition, some taverns, especially those located in rural areas, operated as small shops, selling beef, butter, eggs, veal, lamb, and beverages in quantity. The Moulder's tavern in Philadelphia had a chair for hire and could arrange day labor if a peddler needed assistance unloading his wares. Many colonial taverns functioned as lending institutions and provided short-term loans of small amounts of cash.

Taverns were the social centers of towns and hamlets in the French colonies as they were elsewhere. Cards, dice, and billiards were favorite amusements, and meals were served. In many taverns, a slatted wooden drum about four feet (about 1 meter) in diameter, with its two sides about half that length, was mounted beside the fireplace; an ingenious system of cords and pulleys connected it to the spit inside the fireplace.

When a haunch of venison or half a dozen carrier pigeons, capons, or other fowl had to be roasted, a dog was placed inside the drum and induced to walk, thereby rotating the drum and the spit. Some tavernkeepers kept a room in the cellar, its walls lined with blocks of ice, to keep wines cool in summer.

While taverns existed in the southern and Chesapeake colonies, there were fewer than in other regions, and those there were tended to cluster at county seats or colonial capitals. Taverns in Williamsburg, Virginia's eighteenth-century capital, were typical. When the House of Burgesses was in session, these spacious, well-appointed taverns were filled to capacity and provided food and lodging and a large range of entertainment, from billiards to dancing, to the colony's legislators. Because the distances between farms were so great and the number of towns so few, travelers depended more often upon private homes for lodging. Indeed, plantations were expected to house travelers; the entertainments associated with tavern life elsewhere in colonial America were offered in the plantation house, from lodging to drinking, smoking, gambling, gaming, and dancing. Joseph Oxley's ministerial tour through the colonies in the 1770s highlights the regional variations faced by travelers. At times in the southern and Chesapeake colonies, this English Quaker's only option was to knock on doors and beg accommodations. Occasionally he and his party were forced to camp outdoors.

Taverns attracted a regular clientele. When Benjamin Henry Latrobe visited the small village of Newcastle in Hanover County, Delaware, in 1797, he described a tavern scene that was intimate and congenial, claiming that virtually all the adult males of the town were present in the billiard room. As magistrates made their regular court rounds, they tended to stay at the same taverns each time they made their circuit. Dockside ordinaries catered to mariners and unskilled laborers, while those in the middle of the cities drew a wealthier clientele whose members made business deals with glasses in their hand.

When members of society's elite gathered in taverns, they participated in the ritual of toasting and reassured each other in various ways that they imbibed properly. When the marquis de Chastellux visited Philadelphia, he found it "absurd and truly barbarous practice, the first time you drink and at the beginning of dinner, to call out successively to each individual to let him know that you drink to his health." Josiah Quincy, in his travels from Boston to South Carolina, reported in a diary entry dated 7 March 1773 that "I toast all the friends, Sir. Each gent gave his toast round in succession." The social luminaries of colonial America gathered in taverns to toast each other, to be the wittiest, to participate in social rituals, and to separate themselves from the lower orders.

The number of taverns grew everywhere in the eighteenth century, but especially in the cities, where they reflected the increasing economic and social divisions among the urban population. Taverns continued to be places for travelers to stay and for locals to find familiar companionship with drink. But the types of taverns varied. In the port cities, like Philadelphia, New York, and Boston, waterfront grog shops catered to the laboring classes, while more genteel establishments sold rum and punch to the city's elite. By the eighteenth century, few city taverns were simply private homes opened to travelers. Urban taverns were clearly designed with the commercial trade in mind and often contained public rooms downstairs and sleeping quarters on the second floor.

Eighteenth-Century Accommodations
Through the eighteenth century, other forms of public houses emerged, especially in cities: coffeehouses, boardinghouses, and hotels. The first coffeehouse in the colonies opened in Boston in 1678, a few decades after a similar establishment first appeared in London, and was advertised as "a publique house for retailing of Coffee and Chocolato." Similar establishments appeared in Philadelphia and New York, but not until the late eighteenth century. Coffeehouses functioned much like taverns; indeed, colonial laws did not distinguish between them. Both served food, alcoholic beverages, and coffee, and both provided overnight accommodations to travelers. Coffeehouses differed from urban taverns primarily because they drew their clientele from a more narrow segment of the population, catering primarily to the merchant community.

Boardinghouses fulfilled different needs than taverns. Taverns were notoriously loud; and visitors had to be prepared for all kinds of possibilities, from sharing beds with strangers to enduring midnight disturbances. Boardinghouses solved some of these problems. They tended to be more private and quieter, in part because their primary function was to provide overnight lodging and they therefore did not offer entertainment or allow drinking. Many did not even serve food; typically, guests would eat at a tavern and perhaps participate in the evening's entertainment before returning to sleep. Boardinghouses also were less expensive to stay at, since most offered a weekly rate, whereas taverns charged by the night.

As the eighteenth century progressed, the number of boardinghouses increased dramatically. In Boston, for example, there were forty-five boardinghouses in 1789; that number rose to sixty-eight by 1796. Hotels, which developed in the late eighteenth and early nineteenth centuries combined the best of both worlds—public rooms for drinking, dining, and entertainment and private chambers separated from the public areas for sleeping.

CONCLUSION

Taverns and travel were mutually dependent. The tavern served a vital role in providing travelers with food and drink; since travel was slow and dangerous, the warm glow of the tavern fire welcomed strangers. However, taverns were important as centers of community life as well. Except in the Spanish Borderlands, where sparse settlement and accommodations in homes served travelers, the tavern filled a vital role in providing travelers with food and drink; that same fire beckoned to the New Englander after the cold church meeting, to the Canadian and New Netherlander after work, and to the Philadelphia resident when weather slowed labor. No matter where, New England or New York, Canada or Virginia, the local male citizens gathered to drink a "friendly glass" or try their luck at games of chance. By the late eighteenth century, although other institutions arose that provided some of the same functions, taverns did not disappear, but continued to serve strangers and the locals.

BIBLIOGRAPHY

British Colonies and New France

Clark, John G. *New Orleans 1718–1812. An Economic History.* Baton Rouge, La., 1970.
Conroy, David. "The Culture and Politics of Drink in Colonial and Revolutionary Massachusetts, 1681–1790." Ph.D. diss., University of Connecticut, 1987.
Earle, Alice Morse. *Home Life in Colonial Days.* New York, 1898; repr. 1975.
———. *Stage Coach and Tavern Days.* New York, 1915.
Garvin, Donna-Belle, and James Garvin. *On the Road North of Boston: New Hampshire Taverns and Turnpikes, 1700–1900.* Concord, N.H., 1988.
Kalm, Peter. *Travels in North America by Peter Kalm.* Edited by Adolph B. Benson. 2 vols., New York, 1966.
Kulikoff, Allan. *Tobacco and Slaves: The Development of Southern Cultures in the Chesapeake, 1680–1800.* Chapel Hill, N.C., 1986.
Lathrop, Elsie. *Early American Inns and Taverns.* New York, 1926.
Rice, Kym S. *Early American Taverns: For the Entertainment of Friends and Strangers.* Chicago, 1983.

Thompson, Peter. " 'The Friendly Glass': Drink and Gentility in Colonial Philadelphia." *Pennsylvania Magazine of History and Biography* 113, no. 4 (October 1989):549–573.

The Spanish Borderlands

Moorhead, Max. *New Mexico's Royal Road: Trade and Travel on the Chihuahua Trail.* Norman, Okla., 1958.
Scholes, France V. "The Supply Service of the Mexican Missions in the Seventeenth Century." *New Mexico Historical Review* 5 (1930):93–115, 186–210.

New Netherland

Scott, Kenneth. "New Amsterdam's Taverns and Tavernkeepers." *De Halve Maen* 39, no. 1 (April 1964):9–10, 15.

Sharon V. Salinger

SEE ALSO **Local Government; Rural Life; Transportation and Communication;** and **Urban Life;** and various essays in FOLKWAYS.

XI

FAMILIES AND THE LIFE COURSE

FAMILY STRUCTURES
SEXUAL MORES AND BEHAVIOR
MARRIAGE
CHILDHOOD AND ADOLESCENCE
OLD AGE AND DEATH
NATIVE AMERICAN FAMILIES AND LIFE CYCLES

FAMILY STRUCTURES

THE BRITISH COLONIES

THE "ENGLISH" FAMILY

EVERY HUMAN SOCIETY defines the family in its own way but usually the definition includes a co-resident group of people related to each other by blood or marriage. In much of seventeenth-century England, the customary co-resident kin group consisted of a married couple and their children. This nuclear family might also temporarily expand to encompass unmarried persons who performed labor services or an elderly widowed parent who would otherwise live alone. When such persons entered the household, they became subject to the authority of the husband/father who was "master" of the family and responsible to his neighbors and the community for the good behavior of all those under his roof.

Nuclear families formed the fundamental units of English social organization. Family membership dictated one's personal identity and social status, and families rather than companies carried out most of the productive work of early modern England. Family enterprises utilized their members' labor to provide subsistence, acquire amenities, and preserve or expand their capital resources. Female members took primary responsibility for housekeeping, laundry, cooking, and child care, whereas the males' tasks often took them further afield. In farming, members of both sexes carried out some chores in common, such as harvesting, but performed others according to age and gender.

The conjugal pair married for life in England and normally could not separate but were expected to live together peacefully. Ideally based on love and mutual respect, their marriage endured as a sacred union (although when one partner died, the survivor was free to marry again). Marriage did not take place until both partners brought together enough resources to live separately from their parents, and from other kin. The spousal relationship took preeminent importance in most people's lives, superseding all other ties.

Wives were their husbands' subordinates with no separate legal identities. Upon marriage, a woman became dependent on her husband just as, until then, she had been dependent on her father. A married woman could not make contracts, operate a business, or draw a will without her husband's consent. Although the relationship between husband and wife was unequal, his power over her did not extend to life or limb. English mores permitted "correction" by a husband but did not condone brutality. Nor could a husband keep his wife secluded at home. Foreign visitors to England remarked on the freedom of married women there to go abroad as they pleased.

Within the home, married couples shared the duties and obligations of parents toward their children, although the father took precedence in matters relating to the outside world. Children born to a couple belonged to both and not to grandparents or other kin. If one parent died while the children were still young, the other assumed full control of the children and the estate. But, if a widow remarried, she and her new husband had to legally promise—together, before a judge—to give the children their inheritance when they came of age. A widower, however, was under no such obligation even if his deceased wife had possessed property in her own right prior to marriage with him.

Children were expected to love and obey their parents, who loved and cared for them in return. Ideally, children publicly and privately addressed their parents with formal respect, did as they were told, and spent their time in constructive activities contributing to the family's income and well-being. Religious catechizing buttressed these prescriptions and warned of satanic dangers awaiting the disobedient or indolent child. Parents had both the right and the obligation to "correct" their wayward offspring with force, if necessary, but it was to be "lovingly" and temperately applied. Some historians argue that the preferred mode of child rearing stressed absolute subjugation of the child's will to the parent's, but it is unlikely that this or any other style of child rearing prevailed over all classes of society. People who kept diaries or wrote letters expressed great love and deep concern for their children at all stages of their growing up.

It was the duty of parents to protect their children from accidents and to provide them with food, clothing, and shelter suitable to the family's circumstances or to make arrangements with an employer or master who would undertake to do so. Society expected parents and masters to train children as useful members of society who would be financially self-supporting as adults. Parish officials took charge of paupers' progeny and bound them out to someone in return for their labor service until they reached adult age: twenty-one for men and eighteen for women.

Most families in England drew their subsistence from farm work, although fewer than half could claim property rights in land. Entitlement to the use of land came in two principal forms: manorial leases or freehold tenure. In both cases individuals inherited or purchased the right to use specific pieces of ground, which under freehold tenure could be freely bought and sold. Although individually owned private property was gradually emerging as the typical claim on social resources, most such property was vested in heads of families whose discretionary powers over family real estate never quite fought free of long-standing legal and customary restraints during the early modern period.

Title to property owned by a married couple normally resided in the husband, unless the wife owned land prior to marriage or inherited it, in which case he might use it but not sell it. Marriage gave her a lifetime claim to a share in their real estate, usually one-third. Called "dower," this right prevented him from mortgaging or selling their land without her legal permission, obtainable only in a private interview by a judge. Without it, would-be buyers and mortgageers ran the risk of losing it if she went to court to recover her dower after her husband died. She could take her dower rights with her if she remarried, but they lasted only while she lived, and she could not sell or bequeath them.

Except for their wives' dower, English fathers were legally free to dispose of the family's assets as they saw fit. Most surviving wills of the period, however, reveal a pervasive loving concern for their children's future. If the father left no will, English laws or local customs of intestacy directed the distribution of the net estate. Under common law, all the freehold land went to the oldest surviving son, or, lacking a son, to all the daughters in common. The inheriting son yielded to his father's widow her dower for life, after which her land reverted to him. Of the personal estate, one-third of what remained after the bills were paid went to the widow outright, and the remaining two-thirds was divided among sons and daughters equally.

The practice of giving all the freehold land, saving dower, to the eldest son, is known as primogeniture, and was unusual in Europe at the time. Even in many parts of England local custom directed other modes of inheritance, such as giving the land to the youngest son, who continued to live at home, or to all the sons equally. Many fathers making wills followed the latter practice,

650

and it is easy to understand why, for it seems intrinsically more equitable. Yet the argument for giving all of the land to one son was based on sound economic reasoning. In order to support a family, farms needed to be some minimum size and to contain a desirable mix of arable land, pasture, meadow, and woods suitable to the kinds and quantities of crops and livestock raised locally. To break up a working unit in order to satisfy children's claims destroyed this capability. Giving the farm to one couple to operate maximized its revenues, out of which the heir could pay his siblings their shares of the estate, although it might take years to do so.

Since most people in early modern England did not own land, laws and customs dealing with intestacy did not concern them much nor did they normally write wills. Landless husbands and wives supported their families by means of wage labor, and as soon as a child was able to do so, he or she left home to work as apprentice to an artisan or as a servant in husbandry. As many as three-fifths of the English population aged fifteen to twenty-four worked as farm servants. "Putting out" a child to a skilled craftsman often required paying a fee in advance plus supplying the apprentice with new clothes. "Service," on the other hand, normally cost the parents nothing, but placing the child with a good family required "connections." In southeastern England, it was common for even relatively affluent families to do this. If the child earned no more than room, board, and clothing, the savings to the parent were still substantial, and the child might learn a useful skill in the process. People also believed that children should not be allowed to "waste" their time, which would damage their character and endanger their souls. Perhaps, too, parents found it difficult to enforce work discipline with their own offspring. In any case, custom in the most populous part of England encouraged parents to send children away as a form of education that would provide them with an experience considered good for them.

Adult servants usually retained their own earnings, which for those whose parents were poor became the sole foundation of whatever career they might build for themselves. If they wished to start a family of their own, they had no choice but to save their wages, because custom demanded that they be prepared to pay for separate lodgings and be able to support children. Until then, individuals generally lived in the households of their parents or with their employers. As many as one-quarter of all adults in seventeenth-century England never married at all, and those who did wed at an advanced age by world standards: men generally between the ages of twenty-seven and thirty-two and women at twenty-two to twenty-six. The older ages reflected for many the long waiting time for a designated heir to succeed to his father's farm or the delay necessary for wage laborers to accumulate the wherewithal for setting up housekeeping.

Rates of illegitimacy and prenuptial pregnancy were very low in this period. Given the apparent ignorance of contraceptive methods before the eighteenth century in England, one must conclude that the overwhelming majority of sexually mature individuals abstained from extramarital intercourse despite the late age at marriage and the large proportion never marrying. Although property considerations necessarily played a major role in the timing of the decision to marry and in the choice of a spouse, personal attraction was also important. The church forbade parents and guardians from forcing young people to marry against their will and counseled vigorously against alliances based solely on money. Parents and kin generally accepted the need for mutual compatibility between prospective couples.

In courtship, the initiative normally lay with the young man, at least in classes below those of the upper gentry, but his father or principal friends often acted as go-betweens to help him win the consent of her parents or friends. Among well-to-do and wealthy people, such negotiations included explicit agreements by the two fathers on the "settlements" of land or other kinds of property that they would grant their children at the time of the marriage. These negotiations could be lengthy and precarious when stakes were high. The more property at risk, the greater the role played by parents and kin in the courtship process.

A major purpose of Christian marriage was for the spouses to satisfy each other emotionally and physically, and the natural product of fulfilling this purpose was conception. Many people thought that conception itself could only take place when partners enjoyed simultaneous orgasm. The English couple expected children of their union and did not attempt to avoid them by interfering with "Nature's way" or "God's will." On the other hand, mothers did not simply bear children at the maximum possible biological rate. One study calculated that intervals between births in families having at least six children averaged only twenty-three months in wealthy parishes but extended to twenty-seven months in poor parishes. Such evidence strongly suggests that parents exercised some discretion over conception, perhaps by extending the period of breast-feeding or by temporary abstinence.

Not all babies survived. Infant and child mortality varied widely among the different regions of England, but approximately one-third of all children died before reaching adulthood. This is a high death rate by modern standards but was not immoderate for the times. Parents did not accept the inevitability of loss, and those who could afford to paid for doctors and medicine in their efforts to keep their sick children from dying.

Once they became adults and gained independence, children had no compelling obligation to remain in touch with their parents, although self-interest might dictate otherwise. English law did not require them to succor parents in need, unless the parents were unable to work. Thus parents facing the infirmities of old age were expected to make their own arrangements. Those with a house and land attempted to hang on to their home as long as they could, but one finds occasional contracts in which a son agreed to provide room and board to his parents in return for title to their property. Some men wrote wills that sought to ensure sons' "dutiful" behavior toward their mother by making bequests to them conditional on providing her with a room in the house, farm produce, firewood, and services. It is not clear how she could win enforcement of these terms should her sons default, but in any case, most elderly people lived alone or with an unmarried child or grandchild. If an old person needed assistance, a neighbor provided it for pay or the parish might make such arrangements.

Children of the propertyless class did not abandon their parents so much as move to where the jobs were. England in the seventeenth century was a land of restless mobility as a growing proportion of the population came to depend on wages. Heads of families bought their food in shops, paid rent for their shelter, and when times grew tough, they moved on. Many of the most mobile were simply unemployable, but the fortunes of the others depended on the times, and the times were mostly bad in seventeenth-century England. These were the years when the principal lure of the English plantations in the New World lay in their economic promise. Historians Wrigley and Schofield have calculated that more than two-thirds of the net growth of the English population between 1640 and 1690 went to colonies in the New World.

There were other reasons for venturing across the Atlantic, one of the most powerful being the guarantee by some colonies of the freedom to practice religious beliefs that did not conform to those of the national church. Religious motives brought entire families to the New World, in contrast to the lure of good wages that attracted mostly young single people, particularly males. The dominant motive among an immigrant flow influences its demographic and social makeup, which in a colony's early years means its initial population as well. Immigration to Maryland prior to 1675, for instance, consisted almost entirely of young men who had indentured themselves for a term of four or five years. By contrast, families dominated the immigration to Massachusetts in the 1630s. Too few marriageable women meant frustrated bachelorhood in Maryland, whereas a more proportionate mix of ages and sexes in Massachusetts helped smooth its early transition to a well-functioning society.

The local environment into which immigrants settled, on the other hand, affected the evolution of family structures by imposing a specific set of physical constraints on human activities. Each new society in the New World emerged as the unique product of a particular group of people responding to the promises and limitations of the specific place in which they located. Hence, the story of families in British North America is best told regionally. Nevertheless some generalizations are important.

Common to most families throughout the British colonies were basic "English" attitudes about marriage and the family that the immigrants had brought from home. Foremost among these was the centrality of the family to the community and the state. As in England, heads of families governed their affairs and freely allocated family resources, including members' labor. Parents could apply physical chastisement to all their dependents. Children and servants owed obedience and respect to both their master and mistress and were to practice honesty, celibacy, and sobriety. Once children reached adulthood and servants completed their terms they were free to depart, but only in order to place themselves under another's rule until they could afford to marry. Sexual activity was for married people only, and marriage was a lifetime contract with a single partner with whom one expected to live apart from other kin and to have children together. Brides surrendered their separate legal identity and their property to their spouses, so that women normally achieved independence only when they were widowed and if they possessed sufficient property to support themselves and their dependents. These rules formed the foundation of all institutions relating to the free family everywhere in the British colonies in North America.

The principal differences in family structures between the regions arose from the social origins and demographic makeup of their immigrants, the nature of the environment into which they settled, and in some cases the presence of nonconformist religious beliefs.

THE ENGLISH FAMILY
IN THE CHESAPEAKE

The English began moving into low-lying lands around the Chesapeake basin early in the seventeenth century, the principal part of the immigration concentrating in the period 1630 to 1675. During this time only a relative handful of men with capital ventured their lives and fortunes to create tobacco plantations, perhaps 15 percent of all the white immigrants to the region that included Virginia, Maryland, and northeastern North Carolina. Their labor-intensive crop required a continuous supply of new workers from home as their servants died or completed their terms. Workers consisted mostly of single young men who had indentured themselves for four or five years. When their time was up, servants

who had survived the arduous labor and the epidemics, dysentery, and malaria set about making an English life for themselves.

Freed men enjoyed a modest prosperity in the early years but freedom from sickness proved a rare luxury. Malaria became endemic, doing the most harm to pregnant women for whom the African strain, probably introduced in the 1680s, proved especially lethal. Shallow water tables contaminated easily, and passengers aboard each new ship arriving in the Bay might carry ashore a fresh cargo of deadly microbes.

Epidemics from Europe struck down the Native population as well, undermining their military defenses so substantially that the English achieved control of all the area west to the Piedmont by 1675, enabling plantations to spread up the creeks and rivers deep into the country. The scarcity of women and the continuing toll from disease, however, sorely constrained population growth. Six times as many English went to the Chesapeake in the entire seventeenth century as founded New England in the 1630s, yet the sizes of the population in the two regions were almost identical in 1700. Only a third of indentured servants survived their service, and only half of the freed men ever married. Because of early death, the average marriage did not last a decade.

Such a population in so hostile an environment could not reproduce itself by natural means. More than half of the Anglo-American babies born in the Chesapeake succumbed before reaching adulthood. The odds against adult survival were such that children could expect to lose one parent by age fifteen and the other before age twenty-five. Surviving spouses remarried quickly, and their children found themselves living with a stepparent who had brought along children from a previous marriage. Then came half-brothers and -sisters to add to the burgeoning household, which might also include servants and boarders.

The language of letters and court records provides little insight into how people managed the emotional demands of living amidst such circumstances. The importance of the wife and mother was probably greatly enhanced by the scarcity of kin among a population of former servants. Court decisions and men drawing wills put widows in charge of the children and their estates, despite the near certainty that they would remarry, which placed their children's inheritance under the control of a stepfather. Maryland's government charged a special Orphan's Court with supervision of their estates to ensure that stepfathers and guardians did not subvert the children's economic interests, but the court never removed a child from a household in which the mother was living.

In a society where parents died early, children had to grow up in a hurry. It was easy, by European standards, for young people to acquire the economic independence required to marry and set up a separate household. Land was abundant and cheap once the Native Americans were gone, and livestock proliferated freely as they roamed the unfenced woods. Moreover, the kit of tools necessary to farm the light soils of the tidewater did not require a sizeable outlay. Thus the age at marriage before 1740 was young by English norms: native-born men married at age twenty-three or twenty-four, although in the Rutmans' study of Middlesex County, Virginia, the grooms (who may not have been native-born but were not former servants) were two or three years older. Women born in either colony married at eighteen or nineteen, reflecting their scarcity. Later generations did not marry quite so young.

Although the English in the Chesapeake continued to regard extramarital sex as wrong, 10 percent to 20 percent of Anglo-American brides were already pregnant by the time they wed, many more than back home. Since native-born women in one Maryland county who had lost their fathers were three times as likely to be pregnant at their weddings than those whose fathers were still living, fathers who could do so apparently continued to play their traditional roles even in the wild western fringes of the British empire.

The man who successfully found a wife acquired all the power over her and her property that he would have enjoyed were they still in England, while she obtained full common-law rights of dower. These were better protected in the southern colonies than in the north, perhaps because there the sex ratio was more even and mortality more moderate. While the laws of intestacy in the Chesapeake replicated those in England before 1690, more than half of married men wrote wills in order to override them.

Indeed, two-thirds gave their widows more than they would have received without a will, and half gave land to their daughters as well as their sons. Widows whose husbands had shortchanged them readily contested unsatisfactory wills in court, where they obtained the equivalent of the portions allowed under intestacy, as they could have in England prior to 1690.

Mortality levels remained high in the tidewater areas over the entire colonial period, even for people born there. Parents continued to lose more than half their children before they reached adulthood. Native-born parents, who married at an earlier age, had more children than immigrants. Among long-lived couples in Middlesex County, Virginia, wives bore seven babies on average, about the same number as produced by women surviving their childbearing years in England, but only three or four of those children lived long enough to start families of their own.

The second and later generations were able to construct and extend networks of kin in order to help each other in times of family crisis. They named their firstborn after their own parents. Later ones were named after themselves, their siblings, and other kin, cherishing the broadest possible connections while staunchly continuing the English pattern of strict separation of households with property transmittal confined to their own children.

Men fortunate enough to survive into their sixties generally lived in their own homes attended by a second wife or a grandchild. Widows who had not remarried were more likely than widowers to live with a married son who had taken over the home plantation, although they often possessed a life interest in the house itself as part of their dower.

The growth of population in the eighteenth century made it increasingly difficult for fathers to establish their children on plantations near their own. Poorer and middling planter families began selling out to prosperous slave owners and moving up into the Piedmont regions, where they found themselves farther away from the ships fetching tobacco but where the water was cleaner and the mosquitoes fewer. Mortality probably fell substantially, with the result that families grew in size: increasing numbers of children survived into adulthood and fewer parents died before their late fifties.

At the same time, women's status deteriorated. Changes in the laws and in testamentary practices nibbled away at the autonomy of widows. Dying fathers sought to exert greater control over their children's futures by creating entails, setting up trusts, and even appointing guardians. In parts of Maryland a majority of fathers writing wills placed some sort of limitation on bequests of land, and one-third did so for slaves. In several Virginia counties the use of entails alone ran as high as 20 percent of testamentary arrangements. Brothers of testators or grown sons replaced the widow as executor of the estate, while increasing numbers of wills limited dower to widowhood, in effect forbidding widows to remarry. Dower became defined by courts and by husbands as a right to a share in the income from the land, rather than the right to use and manage the land itself. Meanwhile fathers generally granted daughters portions equal in value to their younger sons', but fewer gave them land, often substituting slaves if they could afford them.

The age at marriage climbed for both sexes. In Middlesex County, Virginia, the mean age of men at first marriage after 1740 rose to 27.5. For women the mean age had reached twenty before 1730, rose to twenty-one in the 1730s, and to twenty-two in the 1740s. A study of top wealth-holding Virginia families, however, shows the men marrying at age twenty-eight from 1735 through 1744 and at thirty in the next decade, but their women continued to marry before age twenty.

In general, family structures in the tidewater regions remained more heterogeneous than in England or in the northern colonies due to the frequent breakup of families caused by early death. The nuclear family endured, however, as the basic residential and property-holding unit of white society and as the fundamental source of personal identity and social status, despite the widespread fondness for reciting comprehensive genealogies on both sides of the marital bond.

THE ENGLISH FAMILY
IN NEW ENGLAND

Whereas the immigration of 125,000 English men and women to the Chesapeake occurred over many decades and consisted overwhelmingly of poor young individuals who had indentured themselves, the settlement of New England took place almost entirely within a single decade and consisted predominantly of families with children. Heads of these families were motivated as much by religious concerns as by economic ones. As a group, the emigrating Puritans came principally from the middling, propertied strata of society in southern England, but they were not entirely homogeneous. Almost half were artisans and craftsmen of various sorts, and there were hundreds of college-educated men who had trained as ministers, lawyers, or doctors.

As a result, early New England possessed far fewer full-time farmers and a much larger class of leaders than did European colonies elsewhere in North America. At the other end of the social scale were the servants who accompanied many of the families, plus a sizeable number of venturesome young men hoping to make their fortune. Together these constituted about one-fifth of the fifteen to twenty thousand immigrants, making the ratio between the sexes more uneven than in England but not as one-sided as in the Chesapeake.

New England's natural environment also contrasted with the tidewater's. Hilly terrain, rocky soils, and a much shorter growing season made farming difficult. Away from the coast, cattle could not forage successfully in winter, requiring shelter and hay for as much as a third of the year. On the other hand, winter's cold temperatures killed off many disease organisms, and good drainage ensured safer drinking water and a shorter mosquito season. The early termination of immigration and rural isolation also cut short the career of epidemic diseases crossing the Atlantic. Consequently most of New England provided a far more wholesome environment than did settlements in the tidewater and Low Country of the south.

Another major advantage enjoyed by the English immigrants to Massachusetts Bay was their ease of access to the clearings of the original owners. European diseases had drastically reduced Native American populations in the northeast along the Atlantic coast. Whole villages lay vacant as straggling survivors regrouped to protect themselves from hereditary foes and aggressive new intruders. Leaders of the English colonists took advantage of the vulnerability of indigenous inhabitants to negotiate advantageous land transfers as well as peace treaties.

Although large-scale immigration to New England lasted little more than a decade, the population thereafter grew naturally because men and women married young, and people lived longer. Studies based on family genealogies show life expectancy for adults to have been among the greatest anywhere, most men living into their sixties and women into their late fifties. About two-thirds of first marriages lasted more than twenty years, and probably fewer than one out of fifteen women died in childbirth. Women who lived through the end of their childbearing years bore their last baby at an average age of thirty-nine and had eight to nine offspring, of whom six or seven survived into adulthood.

Given these healthy conditions, remarriage between young adults—and households containing stepchildren and half-siblings—was relatively uncommon. Congruently, parents had lively expectations of seeing their grandchildren and perhaps even a great-grandchild or two.

Women born in New England did not marry quite as young as their counterparts in the Chesapeake, averaging twenty or twenty-one in the initial decades, when there were fifteen men for every ten women. By the 1650s the average age of women at marriage rose to twenty-two or twenty-three, and this figure remained stable for the next hundred years.

New England families took longer to accumulate the wherewithal to endow their children, of whom there were far more born and surviving than in the south and for whom the capital investment necessary to set up farming was significantly greater. Hence, parents did not encourage early marriage. Nonetheless, New England grooms—like those in the Chesapeake—were young by English standards (at an average age of twenty-five or twenty-six), and the proportion never marrying in either region was far lower than at home.

The family system inherited from England prevailed in New England with certain modifications. Puritan leaders enforced the sexual code more rigorously, made marriage a civil contract subject to law, permitted divorce in certain situations, made women even more dependent on their husbands, and took a more active interest in the education of children. The central importance of the church-town relationship in early

New England tended to magnify the authority of male heads of households, who consulted together regularly about a myriad of important decisions, among which those about the disposition and use of town commons probably loomed largest in the minds of their children.

Parents in New England usually expected to provide the housing and capital needed by their children to marry, and thus they retained the right to exercise some influence in their children's choices. In New England, more parents were alive to exert control, and in at least one town in Massachusetts, fathers retained authority even over their married sons by withholding title to their land.

Given the tight curbs over access to land wielded by the towns and by long-lived parents, the prospective groom probably more often than in the Chesapeake chose a partner who would please his parents and whose own parents would encourage the match by offering a generous marriage portion. The willingness of children in New England to wait for their parents' consent is well demonstrated by evidence of their sexual restraint prior to marriage: the first child born to couples in the seventeenth century came soon, but not too soon. This self-discipline waned in the eighteenth century, when prenuptial pregnancy and illegitimacy became common throughout the British Empire.

Early diaries and correspondence of New England colonists reveal loving, concerned parents who agonized over their children's illnesses and fretted over the state of their souls and of their development as future citizens. They spanked when necessary but preferred to pray for guidance. Wills and court records provide extensive insight into the nature of ordinary family relationships. Testators with wives and children in New England generally concentrated their bequests entirely within the nuclear family, despite the extensive kin networks existing among the region's founding generation. Only the well-to-do made additional gifts to siblings and cousins or to the church and minister. Husbands with no surviving children generally left their entire estates to their widows rather than to brothers or nephews.

The average age of men drawing wills was some fifteen years older than in the Chesapeake, and there were far more heirs making demands on their estates. Fathers steered a perilous course in trying to provide for so many children while accommodating their widows, trimming their sails according to the particular situation in which they found themselves. As a general rule, the ages and gender of the children dictated the terms: very young children were left entirely to the care and discretion of the mother, who was seldom hindered from remarrying. With older children, the father might direct their apprenticeship or education, and with children in their mid to late teens, he commonly specified the value and content of the bequests they were to receive from their mother when they came of age or married. In all these cases, testators usually appointed their wives as sole executors. With a son near twenty-one or older, the father made him co-executor with his mother and dictated all shares, sometimes in great detail; thus, the eldest son customarily enjoyed little discretion in distributing the family estate, even when entrusted with its management.

Sons normally received specific parcels of land with no values attached, whereas daughters got personalty expressed in cash sums. Where bequests in land can be evaluated, such as in an inventory, daughters seemed to have made out as well as younger sons. The oldest son often received more than the rest, either in conformity with the legal rule of a double portion or in exchange for paying off creditors, shouldering the dower demands, and distributing the remaining shares.

More than half of the married men in New England failed to leave wills, despite biblical injunctions to leave their houses in order, and in cases of intestacy, the eldest son received a double portion of both the land and personalty—instead of all the land, as he would have under English common law. The rest of the children each received single shares without regard for sex. (Connecticut courts, however, usually divided the land among the boys and the personalty among the girls.) When the farm could not be divided without harming its income-making potential, as happened frequently in the eighteenth century, the court awarded it to the oldest son who would agree to take it. He had to post bond guaranteeing that he would pay his mother an annual amount equal to one-third of the rent the farm would command in the local real-estate market. He also agreed to pay his siblings their shares in cash, which might require him to mort-

gage the farm. When the estate debts or the obligations to siblings and mother proved too burdensome, the designated heir simply sold the farm to pay off everyone.

Once past their childbearing years, women lived longer than men. While the majority of men who lost their spouses remarried within a few years, widows past childbearing age seldom did so, a social trait that also continues today. When such widows became numerous, as they did in the older settlements of New England in the eighteenth century, society may have found them burdensome. Children of a widow who lived a long time found themselves still sending her remittances as part of her dower even as their own children were beginning to ask for their portions. One way to fulfill their obligation was to send a capable child to live with her as a helper. Estate settlements and wills of the eighteenth century show this to have been a relatively common arrangement even for men.

Widows and widowers in New England seldom chose to live with married children and give up their independence. Since a widower usually married again, he continued to head his own household. A widow often continued to live in the home she had shared with her husband, either alone or with an unmarried child or grandchild. She might rent a room or apartment nearby or move to a large town such as Boston. When she needed help, she called on a neighbor or nearby kinswoman. If she became disabled, she might move in with a favorite daughter.

Many eighteenth-century testators, however, gave their widows no choices. Numerous wills from New England's rural interior contain detailed instructions from fathers to the son inheriting the farmhouse directing which rooms and furniture were to be hers and that she was to have the right to use the oven, the well, and specific parts of the yard and barn. He might also direct annual provisions such as grain, wool and flax, apples from the orchard, firewood, and meat, plus cows, sheep, and perhaps the use of a horse to go to meeting and even a little money on a yearly basis. It is hard to imagine how wills such as these could be fairly enforced, yet they are common, and one wonders what actual recourse a widow might have had if, say, her daughter-in-law turned hostile.

In New England, as in the Chesapeake, the eighteenth century saw changes in testator behavior favoring sons over widows and daughters. Young husbands on the point of death became less likely to trust their widows with the sole executorship of their estates and began to attach conditions to their bequests that encroached on wives' autonomy and dower rights. Older testators showed a greater tendency to exclude their widows entirely from management of the estate and to restrict their bequests to the period of widowhood only, despite the fact that remarriage rates for widows were falling.

THE ENGLISH AND WELSH QUAKER FAMILY IN THE MIDDLE COLONIES

When the Dutch surrendered their territory between New England and the Chesapeake in the 1660s, they opened the region to colonization by their neighbors. Despite an influx that soon eclipsed their majority, Dutch family practices persisted in ethnic enclaves well into the eighteenth century, but English inheritance practices and treatment of women gradually superseded their own.

These middle reaches between New England and the Chesapeake came to be occupied by English, Welsh, Scots, and Irish of several denominational faiths, plus Germans possessing a wide variety of religious beliefs. Eastern Long Island and East Jersey were colonized by New Englanders; West Jersey and Delaware hosted British-born immigrants of Quaker and Anglican persuasion; while descendants of the Dutch occupied northern New Jersey, the Hudson Valley, and the west end of Long Island. Germans and Scotch-Irish entered the colonies through several Atlantic ports, but Philadelphia in particular funneled this vast movement of families through the river systems of southeastern Pennsylvania and eventually southward into the "backcountry" of Virginia, the Carolinas, and Georgia by way of the Shenandoah Valley.

The shores of the lower Delaware Bay, lying in the present states of New Jersey, Pennsylvania, and Delaware, were initially colonized by a small number of Dutch, Swedish, and Finnish families. The principal immigration into the area, however, began after Quaker leaders achieved proprietary control of the region and their adherents started emigrating from the north of England,

Wales, Ireland, and the lower Rhine Valley between 1675 and 1715. This movement resembled New England's in the numerous groups of families of modest means arriving in hopes of practicing their religious beliefs without government harassment. As in the Chesapeake earlier, however, there was also a continuing influx of poor young persons binding themselves for terms of service in order to pay their passage.

On some ships' passenger lists from the 1680s, servants made up as much as three-quarters of the total. Altogether, about twenty-three thousand settled the Delaware Bay region before 1715, of whom maybe half came as members of families. Males probably outnumbered females, perhaps by as much as two to one. Quakers and their sympathizers composed about two-thirds of all immigrants during these years, and most came from poor and sparsely populated rural districts in the north midlands of England, the home of 85 percent of Quaker meetings in the country. Another fifth came from Wales and Ireland. Probably less than 5 percent came from southeastern England, where most of the emigrants to New England had originated.

Early settlers in the middle colonies gained access to land by simple purchase of large lots, already surveyed, through proprietary land offices, and people spread out at once on their own separate farms. Despite the dispersed pattern of settlement, Quaker meetings offered the faithful stronger community bonds than characterized even the most insular towns of New England, since membership was voluntary and ignored the uncommitted.

The social and economic structure of the middle colonies emerged as a hybrid of the regions to the north and south: mixed farming by families predominated, but tenancy was common and there was a large class of servants and wage laborers continually refreshed by new arrivals. The steady influx of immigrants created a brisk demand for farmers' livestock and products, the income from which enabled them to amass hundreds of additional acres. The richness of the soils, the longer growing season, and the superb transportation network of streams and rivers emptying into Delaware Bay equipped early settlers to compete successfully with the longer-established colonies for coastal and overseas markets. Prosperous Quakers even acquired slaves, although many were troubled by the buying and selling of fellow human beings.

Local Native Americans cooperated in making early Pennsylvania a haven for free men. Proprietor William Penn had persuaded surviving Lenni Lenape and others in the region that his province would guarantee them sanctuary from advancing Europeans and raiding Iroquois. He set aside large areas over which they could settle and hunt, while arranging for an orderly advance of whites. His policies worked to the advantage of both groups for many decades until they were undercut by corrupt officials and outflanked by the imperial rivalries of France and Britain.

Agrarian communities and families experienced peaceful prosperity in early Pennsylvania. The climate was less rigorous than New England's and, except for the lower Delaware Bay, healthier than the Chesapeake's. Scanty public records do not permit an adequate reconstruction of birth, marriage, and death rates but studies using county probate records and the minutes of Quaker meetings suggest something about family structures in the area.

Despite the fact that Quaker women could earn great prestige within their religious community, they enjoyed fewer property rights and less autonomy in economic matters than their counterparts in other colonies. Neither testators nor courts in Pennsylvania trusted widows to care for their children's estates without close supervision. In Bucks County, the proportion of wills excluding widows entirely from executorship rose from one-fifth before 1730 to close to half afterwards.

Men used wills to benefit their children at the expense of their wives. Only a quarter of testators gave their widows as much as the laws of intestacy allowed. Another quarter tied down their widows by arranging for room in the family house and provisions in lieu of dower. If she challenged the will in court, she received one-third of the *net* value of the real estate after the payment of all outstanding debts, and no more. No other colony gave creditors precedence over widows' dower.

As in New England, Pennsylvania laws of intestacy substituted the double portion for primogeniture and granted equal shares to other children regardless of sex. Fathers writing wills usually gave younger sons as much as older ones, as in New England and the Chesapeake, but tended to give larger shares to sons than daughters. Quaker testators were more likely than others to make significant bequests to kin outside the nuclear family, a practice common in north Wales and adjacent parts of England.

The greater importance given relatives in this culture may have predisposed parents to seek and accept outside help in rearing and disciplining their children. While the nuclear family remained the norm as a residential and work unit, the Quaker monthly meetings shared with the parents the responsibility for their children's upbringing. Quakers were encouraged to raise their children strictly but without the use of force and with no intention of breaking the child's will, a pattern appearing in some English and New England families. The men's and women's meetings regularly sent older members out into their communities to review and counsel families in the inevitable crises afflicting them.

Nowhere is the power of these meetings more in evidence than in their obtrusive inquiries into courtship behavior. The age at marriage for both sexes was about the same as in New England or a little older. But Quakers not only required an aspiring suitor to win the assent of both sets of parents prior to commencing courtship but made sure that the young people could withstand a thorough scrutiny into their character by Quaker elders before marrying. To remain in good standing, Quakers must marry Quakers and they both must be well supplied with the necessaries for independent living. It was particularly important that the young couple marry for spiritual, rather than sexual, feelings toward each other. Winning approval could take many months, during which time prospective spouses took great care to avoid scandal. Given these hurdles, it is not surprising that prenuptial pregnancy rates among Quakers were near zero and that some 15 percent never married at all.

The stresses imposed by rigorous Quaker discipline, the high value placed on keeping children within the fold, and an ascetic view of sexual relations may account for a gradual reduction in their family size. The average number of births among Quaker women completing their childbearing years fell from seven or eight for women born before 1730 to six for women born between 1731 and 1755 and then to only about five to those born between 1756 and 1785. Since Quakers in 1750 formed the third largest religious denomination in the British colonies of North America, their unusual family practices hold special interest for the history of the American family.

DIVERSE POPULATIONS IN THE MIDDLE COLONIES AND SOUTHERN BACKCOUNTRY

English Anglicans

The middle colonies attracted a more-or-less continuous but relatively small-scale stream of non-Quaker English immigrants throughout the eighteenth century. These were generally adherents of the Church of England who may have experienced difficulty adapting to the multiplicity of faiths in the area. As a group, they have not won much attention from social historians so their family practices remain obscure. It seems safe to assume that those who arrived too poor to pay their fare would normally have been young, unmarried, and highly mobile. Those arriving with families and resources probably practiced customs similar to those of the yeoman, artisan, and mercantile classes of the south of England.

Scotch-Irish Presbyterians

Groups of families from southern Scotland and Ulster in Ireland began immigrating in large numbers to British North America about 1720. The overwhelming majority entered through the port of Philadelphia and found their way to the frontier of settlement. They shared Presbyterian loyalties and harbored strong anti-Anglican and anti-Quaker sentiments. Their family practices are difficult to document, because they kept few records themselves and were greatly disliked by Quaker, German, and English neighbors for their aggressiveness and disrespect for authority. The only safe generalizations that one may make include a comparatively young age at marriage for women, numerous children, and probably long life expectancy. Husbands and fathers may have wielded even more authority over their dependents than in New England.

German Families of Various Ethnic and Religious Backgrounds

Refugees from religious persecution in the Rhine Valley began appearing in the middle colonies as early as the 1680s, but the major migration from Germany took place in the middle decades of the eighteenth century. Most Germans found their way to Philadelphia by way of the Netherlands and, like the Scottish and Ulster families, quickly moved to the nearest frontier, leapfrogging already settled areas, so that each fresh group of immigrants worked its way farther westward and southward, the later arrivals reaching the "backcountry" of South Carolina and Georgia before the American Revolution.

They were far from being a homogeneous immigration, coming from vastly different parts of the Rhine Valley and founding a variety of churches and sects. Social historians are only just beginning to investigate German family practices in systematic fashion, using marriage and baptismal records kept by churches and probate records where these appear useful. In Germantown, Pennsylvania, marriages of the 1750s, the grooms averaged thirty years of age and the brides twenty-five, but these high ages declined to twenty-five for the men and twenty-two for the women by the 1770s, similar to levels among contemporary Anglo-Americans. Among Schwenkfelders marrying between 1735 and 1764, brides in this German sect were five years older than the Anglo-American average, offering striking evidence that when the bonds of corporate religious unity were sufficiently strong, as with Quakers, they could resist powerful secular forces. Late age at marriage contributed to a significant reduction in fertility among the Schwenkfelders, with only five to six children born to completed families. Other published German-American fertility rates also look low, but these appear to be the consequence of inadequate records.

Germantown wills show fathers giving gifts of cash to adult children and then sending them out on their own. Rather than parceling out land among the heirs, testators more often ordered that the land be sold and the proceeds divided. Fathers generally attempted to equalize lifetime gifts to children of both sexes, but in the earliest wills daughters received a marriage portion only, whereas sons also collected a share in the estate settlement.

When there were no children, a married testator in Germantown usually gave his whole estate to his widow and made her sole executor without penalty for remarrying. This pattern also characterized married but childless testators in New England and the Chesapeake, though not among Quakers. Of the testators with children, however, more than half excluded their widows entirely from executorship, a high proportion by any standard in the colonial period. When children were young, Germantown testators usually made the widow joint executor with power to sell, whereas New England and Chesapeake testators would have entrusted the estate entirely to their widows, at least before the late colonial period. Most Germantown wills stated that the widow would forfeit her share if she remarried or that she would lose all but her legal dower right in the land.

ENGLISH AND OTHER EUROPEAN FAMILIES IN THE LOWLANDS

Families of English immigrants with slaves arrived in the Charleston, South Carolina, area from Barbados in the 1680s, where they were gradually joined by a small and ethnically mixed stream of newcomers from other colonies. The outbreak of wars with the indigenous peoples in the early part of the eighteenth century devastated both populations. Despite these inauspicious beginnings, overseas demand for plantation-grown rice eventually made South Carolina and Georgia the richest colonies on the continent and home to many thousands of African slaves.

The marshy coasts and swampy interior of eastern South Carolina and Georgia proved a charnel house for whites and blacks alike, more deadly than the Chesapeake tidewater. High mortality and low fertility meant small families, few children surviving to adulthood, early parental loss, and frequent remarriage, which created heterogeneous families with stepchildren, half-siblings, and orphans. Age at marriage for native-born spouses seems to have paralleled Virginia's.

Intestacy provisions and dower rights closely followed English practice. Older and wealthier testators favored devices for perpetuating property within the patrilineage, even more than did those in Virginia. Nearly half of all fathers writing wills used trusts, entails, or other arrangements to control heirs' use of land and slaves. They were particularly prone to use life estates for their bequests to daughters in order to protect the property from avaricious sons-in-law and ensure its descent to the testators' grandchildren. As in New England and the Chesapeake, men with wives and children did not make significant bequests outside of the nuclear family.

Because of their short life expectancy, most fathers in the coastal lowlands left quite young children. In such cases, testators gave their widows far-reaching powers over the estate and the children, just as they did in like circumstances elsewhere in the British colonies. With the presence of older children, however, a testator cut back the powers awarded a widow and trimmed her share of the estate. The long-term trends toward favoring children over widows and encroaching on widows' autonomy prevailed as elsewhere. Although the proportion of Charleston wills excluding the widow entirely from the executorship had reached 36 percent in the 1760s, southerners did not tie their widows to an abject dependence on sons' provision of room and board, as did so many northerners in Pennsylvania and New England.

CONCLUSION

Whereas high mortality and a plantation economy probably made family structures in South Carolina and Georgia similar to those of the Chesapeake tidewater, too little is known to speculate about trends in the sex ratio and the treatment of women. Nor have historians studied English families of Anglican or Presbyterian affiliation in the middle colonies. What is available on the English so far strongly suggests that non-Quaker immigrants transplanted a common system of rules about marriage and the family.

Demographic manifestations of this system in the colonies deviated from the home country principally because of the greater accessibility of land everywhere but also because of local circumstances such as land usage and mortality rates. These demographic indices include age at marriage, proportion ever marrying, number of children born to completed families, proportion of children surviving to adulthood, remarriage rates, proportion of people living beyond age sixty, and so forth. The demographic makeup of the colonial population, in terms of the sex ratio and age structure, may have directly influenced the relative autonomy granted to widows and the patterns of bequests contained in wills, but certain types of religious affiliation and inherited custom may actually have been more important. These latter clearly shaped attitudes toward spousal relations and child rearing among Welsh Quakers and perhaps among German Schwenkfelders as well.

The widespread ownership of land in the colonies meant that more colonial parents, proportionate to the home country, were in a position to exercise economic control over older children. Yet the greater ease of accumulating assets for setting up separate housekeeping, on the other hand, undermined parental constraints among the lesser-propertied classes. Economic opportunity lowered the age at marriage for men relative to England's by several years wherever the population of women was great enough that any man who wanted to marry was likely to find a partner. A comparatively young age at marriage for women increased the number of children under the care of parents, although high rates of death and morbidity in the southern tidewater and lowlands prevented even half from surviving into adulthood there. Early parental death promoted high rates of remarriage, extending the kin network and making stepchildren and half-siblings common. Respect for kin pervaded southern customs of speech and hospitality and influenced the choice of children's names, yet fathers strictly confined the disposition of property to their own legally begotten children.

Hence the regional variations in the demographic makeup of testators and in the numbers and ages of their children strongly affected observed inheritance practices and testator treatment of widows. A lopsidedly male sex ratio in the early South, a product of the continuing arrival of young males attracted by economic opportunity, gave women greater control over the marriage market. This, in turn, enabled them to win more evenhanded bequests from their fathers and perhaps better treatment as wives and widows. Meanwhile, a more balanced sex ratio and longer life expectancy in early New England tended to empower men at the expense of their wives and children.

Quaker discipline nullified any advantages women and children might have derived from local circumstances in the middle colonies, making both groups even more economically dependent on the patriarch than they were in New England. New England and the middle colonies actively forwarded the legal changes under way in England with respect to land transfers and inheritance practices, which had the effect of narrowing the property rights of married women. Pennsylvania laws and Quaker practices went furthest in this direction despite the great religious and moral authority wielded by Quaker women.

Local environmental circumstances modified only the demographics of Anglo-American family behavior in each region, without disturbing the underlying system of values inherited from England. But the system itself began to change in the eighteenth century, as witness the empirewide rise in the rates of illegitimacy and prenuptial pregnancy. A gradual modification of demographic profiles in longer-settled parts of the colonies may account for certain other trends in common across regions. In wills from both the Chesapeake and New England, far fewer daughters received land as part of their portions, and fathers in both places showed a greater inclination to give more to the eldest sons at the expense of the other children. In both regions and in Pennsylvania, as well, an increasing number of husbands excluded their widows from executorship while making bequests to them conditional on not remarrying.

Not all trends traveled across regional boundaries, however. Chesapeake fathers began to encroach on mothers' guardianship of minor children, whereas New England fathers and courts did not. New England fathers began to reduce daughters' size shares in the estate but Chesapeake fathers did not do so, perhaps because more of the latter used conditional bequests to daughters in order to secure the property to their grandchildren. The average age at marriage in the Chesapeake rose after 1740 for both men and women but particularly for the men, whereas it declined in eighteenth-century New England before beginning an upward climb late in the colonial period. In general, the position of women and of younger children tended to decline in both north and south. Any argument about the possibility of cultural convergence prior to independence, however, must exclude the Quakers of Pennsylvania: the exceptional Quakers were increasingly able to utilize their meetings to strengthen personal and family discipline and to isolate themselves more successfully from Anglo-American material forces.

This survey of family structures has been stronger on describing quantitative factors than on the quality of the relations between husbands and wives and between parents and children, the living context of the statistics. There are passages of great beauty in the occasional correspondence between husbands and wives that has survived from England and the colonies, and diaries provide glimpses into the love and care with which many cherished their wives and children.

Such bits of evidence are testimony to what was *possible* for the people and the time, though not necessarily what was common. The wise and temperate John Winthrop of seventeenth-century Boston esteemed his devoted wife but fumed at the impertinence of women who spoke in public. The easygoing William Byrd of early eighteenth-century Virginia enjoyed the company (and sexual favors) of women and doted on his children, but he and his hot-tempered wife were capable of the coarsest brutality toward the enslaved members of their "family." The quality and intensity of family relations probably varied between households as much then as it does now. The principal differences in family life in the past were the greater frequency of family crises of death and illness, the legally encoded dependent status of women, and the rarity of divorce.

BIBLIOGRAPHY

The following are all published studies. Much of the material on New England in the preceding

essay, however, rests on unpublished work by the author.

Archer, Richard. "New England Mosaic: A Demographic Analysis for the Seventeenth Century." *William and Mary Quarterly*, 3rd ser., 47 (1990):477–502. The most up-to-date and comprehensive demographic study of New England to 1675.

Ariès, Phillipe. *Centuries of Childhood*. London, 1962. A pioneering work, which argues that until the late seventeenth or early eighteenth century, European children past infancy were treated as little adults. The researches of Macfarlane and Pollock have largely demolished this interpretation.

Calvert, Karin. "Children in American Family Portraiture, 1670–1810." *William and Mary Quarterly*, 3rd ser., 39 (1982):87–113.

Carr, Lois Green. "Inheritance in the Colonial Chesapeake." In *Women in the Age of the American Revolution*, edited by Ronald Hoffman and Peter Albert. Charlottesville, Va., 1989. The best single article on this subject.

Demos, John. *A Little Commonwealth: Family Life in Plymouth Colony*. New York, 1970. A pioneering study of this New England colony, utilizing modern theories of psychology to analyze laws, wills, and church and court records through 1690.

Fischer, David Hackett. *Albion's Seed: Four British Folkways in America*. Oxford and New York, 1989. A major synthesis of demographic patterns related to the family.

Greven, Philip J., Jr. *Four Generations: Population, Land, and Family in Colonial Andover, Massachusetts*. Ithaca, N.Y., 1970. A social and genealogical history of an eastern Massachusetts community organized in terms of generations, with a sustained study of the inheritance of land. Concentrates on relationships between fathers and sons.

———. *The Protestant Temperament: Patterns of Child-Rearing, Religious Experience, and the Self in Early America*. New York, 1977. Relates child-rearing patterns to religious *style* rather than doctrine: evangelical, moderate, and liberal-genteel.

Houlbrooke, Ralph A. *The English Family, 1450–1700*. London and New York, 1984.

Lee, Jean Butenhoff. "Land and Labor: Parental Bequest Practices in Charles County, Maryland, 1732–1783." In *Colonial Chesapeake Society*, edited by Lois Green Carr, Philip D. Morgan, and Jean Russo. Chapel Hill, N.C., 1988.

Levy, Barry. *Quakers and the American Family: British Settlement in the Delaware Valley*. New York and Oxford, 1988. The current authority on the topic, based on careful research on both sides of the Atlantic. The author may overstate contrasts with New England. Very valuable, nonetheless.

Macfarlane, Alan. *The Family Life of Ralph Josselin, a Seventeenth-Century Clergyman: An Essay in Historical Anthropology.* Cambridge, England, 1970. Very thoughtful exploration of a Puritan diary, which establishes the warm emotional basis of one man's family.

———. *Origins of English Individualism.* New York, 1978. Argues that as early as the thirteenth century in large areas of England land sold readily as an ordinary commodity, opening the doors to capitalism. Associated with this is a modern family structure: a nuclear, independent household in which relations between spouses were paramount to all others. This argument is carried forward in Mcfarlane's *Marriage and Love in England: Modes of Reproduction, 1300–1840,* published in Oxford and New York in 1986. It is a brilliant and controversial survey of the English family that argues for its "modern" character in as early as the thirteenth century.

Main, Gloria L. "Widows in Rural Massachusetts on the Eve of the Revolution." In *Women in the Age of the American Revolution,* edited by Ronald Hoffman and Peter Albert. Charlottesville, Va., 1990. Based on wills and other records of the probate court.

Menard, Russell R. "British Migration to the Chesapeake Colonies in the Seventeenth Century." In *Colonial Chesapeake Society,* edited by Lois Green Carr, Philip D. Morgan, and Jean Russo. Chapel Hill, N.C., 1988. The most up-to-date estimates.

Morgan, Edmund S. *The Puritan Family: Religion and Domestic Relations in Seventeenth-Century New England.* Boston, 1944; repr. New York, 1966. Based on sermons, prescriptive literature, diaries, and court records. Argues for a distinctively Puritan approach to courtship and marriage, relations between husband and wife, parent and child, master and servant.

Narrett, David. "Men's Wills and Women's Property Rights." In *Women in the Age of the American Revolution,* edited by Ronald Hoffman and Peter Albert. Charlottesville, Va., 1990. Compares Dutch and English inheritance practices in colonial New York.

Pollock, Linda A. *Forgotten Children: Parent-Child Relations from 1500 to 1900.* Cambridge, England, 1983. Uses diaries on both sides of the Atlantic to argue that early modern English and Anglo-American parents were not callously indifferent toward their children nor did they shield themselves from the pain of grief when a child died.

———. *A Lasting Relationship: Parents and Children over Three Centuries.* Hanover and London, 1987. An anthology from English and American diaries and correspondence, organized chronologically within topics such as childbearing, child rearing, daily life, education, illness, and death.

Rutman, Darrett B., and Anita H. Rutman. *A Place in Time: Middlesex County, Virginia, 1650–1750* and *A Place in Time: Explicatus.* New York, 1984. A systematic study that provides the best available picture of family and community life in a tidewater county from settlement to 1750.

Shammas, Carole, Marylynn Salmon, and Michel Dahlin. *Inheritance in America: From Colonial Times to the Present.* New Brunswick and London, 1987. An important study providing systematic overview of the laws of inheritance in the colonial period, accompanied by comparative cross-sectional studies of Pennsylvania wills, which unfortunately does not distinguish between Quakers and other decedents.

Slater, Peter Gregg. *Children in the New England Mind: In Death and in Life.* Hamden, Conn., 1977. Uses diaries plus pamphlet and sermon literature to explore the idea of infant damnation in Puritan thought and its effect on parental bereavement.

Stone, Lawrence. *The Family, Sex and Marriage: In England, 1500–1800.* New York, 1977. A brilliant but misguided work based on a broad range of materials, which makes it still useful.

Walsh, Lorena S. " 'Till Death Us Do Part': Marriage and Family in Seventeenth-Century Maryland." In *The Chesapeake in the Seventeenth Century,* edited by Thad W. Tate and David L. Ammerman. Chapel Hill, N.C., 1979. An excellent demographic study.

Wells, Robert V. *The Population of the British Colonies in America Before 1776.* Princeton, N.J., 1975. A convenient overview.

Wrigley, E. A., and R. S. Schofield. *The Population History of England, 1541–1871: A Reconstruction.* Cambridge, Mass., 1981. A major source for English demographic statistical estimates of the seventeenth century.

Gloria Lund Main

SEE ALSO **African-American Culture; Gender Relations;** and **Home and Hearth.**

THE DUTCH COLONY

THE FAMILY IN NEW NETHERLAND, in both form and function, reflected the influence of Dutch law and tradition on the one hand and of colonial American conditions and experiences on the other. In the seventeenth century, the Dutch were well in advance of other Europeans in undergoing what social scientists have labeled modernization. The Netherlands possessed the most urbanized, the most commercially oriented, and the most literate society in Europe. Moreover, since the early Middle Ages, women in the Netherlands had exercised civil and property rights generally denied those of their gender in Britain, France, and Spain. Dutch women retained these legal rights after marriage, thereby making domestic relations significantly reciprocal, if not equitable, not only between spouses but also among siblings. Dutch law and custom favored the rule of partible inheritance, by which children, both male and female, received more or less equal shares of the family estate. In fact, judging from what we know about family structure and domestic relations in Europe generally, the Dutch led in the demographic transition from the patriarchal, extended family toward the companionate, nuclear family.

Erasmus and other Dutch humanists had long celebrated the conjugal family and looked askance at overweening parents-in-law. In the Netherlands and elsewhere, Protestant reformers generally rejected marriage as sacrament and embraced marriage as civil contract based on mutual familial interest and consent. Dutch Calvinists preached mutuality in spousal relations, in terms of both affection and duty, even though the Reformed church always emphasized the headship of the husband and father. In fact, familial reciprocity was the fundamental organizing principle in Dutch domestic life, moderating the stern patriarchal character of Calvinism.

Dutch households were typically smaller, more tightly organized, and freer from extended family domination than those elsewhere in Europe. Men and women usually married in their mid to late twenties; half the women who married in seventeenth-century Amsterdam were between the ages of twenty-four and twenty-eight. Family structure, particularly in Holland and Friesland, was typically nuclear, with a mean family size of four—a father, mother, and two children. In England, where the rule of primogeniture provided that the eldest son should

inherit the bulk of the family estate, the mean household size was five.

The primacy of the conjugal family in Dutch life was pervasive, supported by law as well as tradition, reinforced by the decentralized governmental system resting on town and provincial authority, and particularly suited to the pluralistic culture of the young republic. By patronizing the school and congregation of its choice, the family perpetuated ethnic and religious diversity in the Netherlands, much to the chagrin of the Reformed clergy who strove for Calvinistic conformity.

Yet the very dominance of the conjugal family fostered an ethos of domesticity that contributed significantly to unifying the heterogeneous peoples of the Dutch republic. The primary motifs in Dutch literature and art were familial. As historian Simon Schama explains it, the Dutch defined themselves as a people not so much through some transcendent nationalism as through their structuring of domestic relations. Simply put, the fate of the nation was portrayed as the fate of the family writ large. Indeed, the political and economic organization of the United Provinces was based largely on family alliances and extended kinship associations.

ADAPTING FAMILY PATTERNS TO NEW NETHERLAND

The Dutch family would have to adjust to the early American wilderness. Thirty Walloon families were among the first settlers to arrive in New Netherland in 1624. Over the next two decades, most of the immigrants who trickled into the colony were young, unattached males, much more interested in the main chance than in marriage. Women were in short supply. Domestic relations were strained in this turbulent and rather primitive society, whose court records bear witness to the presence of numerous lawless men and lewd women, some married to each other.

By the mid 1640s, immigration picked up significantly, thanks largely to several years of peace with the Indians and to the Dutch West India Company's (WIC) relaxing its restrictions on trade and land tenure. Thereafter, most of the settlers came as families, usually young couples, with small children. Demographics were shifting sharply in favor of domesticity. As one provincial official wrote in 1653, "Children and pigs multiply here rapidly and more than anything else." According to the best estimates, the population increased from five hundred in 1629 to twenty-five hundred in 1645 and jumped to about nine thousand in 1664.

Becoming director-general in 1647, Peter Stuyvesant presided over the transformation of New Netherland from a fur-trading outpost into a commercial and agricultural colony. Increasingly, Dutch law and custom regarding domestic relations were reflected in joint wills, prenuptial agreements, apprenticeship indentures, and other court records. Data on mortality rates are fragmented and impressionistic, but spousal death, both wives and husbands, was commonplace, as was the remarriage of survivors, especially before the 1650s. The overall infant death rate in New Netherland was very likely much higher than the 18 percent estimated by Sherrin Marshall for the Dutch gentry, who averaged 4.3 children born per family. Looking at the Albany Dutch between 1680 and 1700, Alice Kenney has reckoned the number of children per marriage at six. Kenney also suggested that the Albany Dutch married several years earlier than their cousins in Europe. However, the leading families intermarried and consolidated their political and economic influence very much like the patriciate in the Netherlands.

Given the relative weakness of other social and economic institutions in New Netherland, the family played an even more dominating role there than it did in the Netherlands. The household was not only the basic economic unit but also the primary educator, the place where the young received much of their occupational, literacy, and religious training. The incomplete and developing nature of New Netherland society accentuated the reciprocal nature of Dutch family life, with the status of women and children improving because their labors were so desperately needed. Wives and daughters not only managed and maintained the household but were often much involved in the family business and sometimes continued farming, trading, or practicing the family craft after the husband or father had died. In their joint wills, spouses usually left their share of the estate to the survivor, knowing full well that the property interests of the children would be legally protected should the surviving spouse remarry.

Stuyvesant and the Reformed dominies wanted to impose Calvinistic conformity upon heterodox New Netherlanders. However, the directors of the WIC insisted that religious toleration granted the family in the Netherlands likewise prevail in their North American colony. A sizable minority of the settlers were not ethnic Dutch (some estimates say almost 50 percent), but most of them had lived in the United Provinces before migrating to America and came originally from regions of Germany or France that shared many traditions with the Netherlands, including those concerning marriage, the status of women, and the rights of children.

FAMILIAL TRADITIONS AMONG BLACKS, INDIANS, AND NEW ENGLANDERS

Among the peoples of New Netherland least affected by Dutch familial traditions and practices were Africans, both slave and free, New Englanders who settled on western Long Island, and Indians. By 1664 as many as eight hundred Africans were scattered throughout the colony. They were slaves except for perhaps one hundred or so free blacks, most of whom lived in New Amsterdam, where the largest number of slaves (more than three hundred) could also be found.

Under Roman-Dutch law, mulattos and free blacks were free to marry, raise children, and will property, just as whites could do. Until the 1650s, however, black family formation was limited by a shortage of females. Some free blacks were married to slaves with the approval of the slaves' owners, several of whom, like Peter Stuyvesant, encouraged stable domestic relations for their chattel. Slave families were always precarious, with spouses usually living in different households and parents separated early from their children. Extended kin and friendship networks sometimes provided nurture that slaves' children were unable to get from their natural parents because of forced separation.

Numbering perhaps one thousand by 1664, erstwhile New Englanders settled five towns on western Long Island under Dutch jurisdiction. They had privileges of self-government and were allowed to follow English customs and traditions with regard to domestic relations. Unlike their Dutch neighbors, they embraced a strongly patriarchal family structure, did not accord women property rights, and favored primogeniture in inheritance.

Although certainly not under the jurisdiction of the WIC, the Indians were the most numerous peoples on the lands the Dutch claimed as New Netherland. The Mahican, Iroquois, and Delaware were all matrilineal in organization, with several nuclear families, usually closely related, living in the same longhouse. The women possessed considerable influence in tribal councils; although the chiefs were always men, they almost always inherited their claim to leadership through the mother. The men were hunters, warriors, and diplomats, and the women raised the crops and the children, prepared the meals, and skinned the animals. The Indians treated premarital sex rather casually, and divorce among the Mahican and Iroquois was simply a matter of choosing another mate. When separation or divorce occurred, the husband left the longhouse, and the wife kept custody of the children. Although well suited to their way of life, domestic relations among the Indians were not much appreciated by most New Netherlanders, especially the Reformed dominies, who roundly condemned the "savages" for their permissive attitudes toward sexual relations.

AFTER THE CONQUEST

After the British conquest in 1664, English law and customs governing the family gained official status in New York; however, the Articles of Capitulation guaranteed the property rights and patterns of inheritance of New Netherlanders, most of whom remained in New York and clung tenaciously to joint wills and prenuptial agreements until near the end of the seventeenth century. Even as they began to accept English legal forms, Dutch New Yorkers generally maintained the substance of their traditional familial practices, including companionate marriage and child-centered domestic life.

BIBLIOGRAPHY

Christoph, Peter. "The Colonial Family: Kinship and Power." In *A Beautiful and Fruitful Place: Selected Rensselaerswijck Seminar Papers,* edited by Nancy Anne McClure Zeller. Albany, N.Y., 1991.

Goodfriend, Joyce. "Black Families in New Netherland." In *A Beautiful and Fruitful Place: Selected Rensselaerswijck Seminar Papers,* edited by Nancy Anne McClure Zeller. Albany, 1991.

———. "Patricians and Plebeians in Colonial Albany, Part III: Family Reconstitution." *De Halve Maen* 45, no. 3 (October 1970):9–11.

———. "Patricians and Plebeians in Colonial Albany, Part IV: Community Analysis." *De Halve Maen* 45, no. 4 (January 1971):13–14.

———. "Patricians and Plebeians in Colonial Albany, Part V: The Silent Tradition." *De Halve Maen* 46, no. 1 (April 1971):13–15.

Kenney, Alice P. "Private Worlds in the Middle Colonies: An Introduction to Human Tradition in American History." *New York History* 51, no. 1 (1970):4–31.

Kruger, Vivienne L. "Born to Run: The Slave Family in Early New York, 1626–1827." 2 vols. Ph.D. diss., Columbia University, 1985.

Marshall, Sherrin. *The Dutch Gentry, 1500–1650: Family, Faith and Fortune.* New York and London, 1987.

Penny, Sherry, and Roberta Willenkin. "Dutch Women in Colonial Albany: Liberation and Retreat, Part II." *De Halve Maen* 52, no. 2 (1977):7–8, 15.

Raesly, Ellis Laurence. *Portrait of New Netherland.* New York, 1945; repr. Port Washington, N.Y., 1965.

Rink, Oliver A. *Holland on the Hudson: An Economic and Social History of Dutch New York.* Ithaca, N.Y., 1986.

Schama, Simon. *The Embarrassment of Riches: An Interpretation of Dutch Culture in the Golden Age.* New York, 1987.

Sturtevant, William C., gen. ed. *Handbook of North American Indians.* 20 vols. Washington, D.C., 1978. Vol. 15: *Northeast,* by Bruce G. Trigger.

Van der Woude, A. M. "Variations in the Size and Structure of the Households in the United Provinces in the Seventeenth and Eighteenth Centuries." In *Household and Family in Past Times,* edited by Peter Laslette and Richard Wall. Cambridge, Mass., 1972.

Van Deursen, Arie Theodorus. *Plain Lives in a Golden Age: Popular Culture, Religion and Society in Seventeenth-Century Holland.* Cambridge, Mass., 1991.

Ronald William Howard

SEE ALSO **African-American Culture; Gender Relations;** and **Home and Hearth.**

THE FRENCH COLONIES

AS IN THE OTHER preindustrial societies, the family in the French colonies was an institution of fundamental importance, arguably the most important of all social institutions. The Catholic church in Quebec taught generations of children and preached to their parents that the French Canadian family was the last bastion against the dangers of modern, urban, and secular values. Clerical historians encoded the mythology. Identifying the historical family in the midst of the intellectual edifices constructed around it poses a challenge. The following assessment, based largely on more extensive research on Canada, applies to Acadia and Louisiana in its reflections on general values.

DEMOGRAPHY OF FAMILY

Before 1700 the European population in Canada reflected a disequilibrium between the sexes due to the early predominant immigration of single males. The census of 1666 for the island of Montreal (including the total rural and town population) indicates that 38 percent of all ages were female. At the census of 1681 this had increased to 43 percent (44 percent for the whole colony), and by the end of the century the proportion of women in Montreal was approaching equality with the proportion of men. Patterns of celibacy were also skewed by the early gender imbalance. Twenty-one percent of all Montreal-area house-

holds in 1681 were singles, almost all bachelors. Excluding nuns, there were few unmarried women over the age of twenty: bachelors outnumbered them ten to one. All but a few of the remaining households were simple conjugal families, following the common European pattern in which family households consisted usually of married couples with or without children or of a surviving parent with children. The mean number of children per family was a little more than four in the seventeenth century, declining somewhat in the eighteenth century as demographic patterns adjusted to the end of high immigration and its attendant flood of marriages and births.

In the first half of the eighteenth century, the birthrate in the Saint Lawrence colony fluctuated around fifty-five per thousand, and the marriage rate around ten per thousand. These rates were relatively high and translate into an average of seven children born per marriage. Mortality rates at roughly thirty to thirty-five per thousand were similar to those in Europe, as was infant mortality (deaths before one year) at 25 percent. The average age of women at first marriage was 22.0, about two years younger than in France; that of men at 27.7 was less exceptional. With little immigration, offset by some emigration, these reproductive factors translated into a population that doubled every twenty-five years or so. A key factor is the high rate of marriage, and of early remarriage among widows. The experience of giving birth on average every two years was shared by more women, and was less interrupted, in Canada than in France. In its relentless war of attrition against disease and infection the Canadian population had the upper hand only in numbers.

SUPERINTENDING THE FAMILY: CHURCH AND STATE

The prescriptions of religion and law tell us more about elite social ideology than about popular familial behavior. Both church and state in Canada encouraged farming, family life, and large numbers of children, but we cannot conclude that the profile of Canadian family life was owing to these encouragements. The *Rituel du diocese de Québec* of 1703, written by the ascetic bishop

Jean-Baptiste de la Croix de Saint-Vallier, offered severe warnings against fun or pleasure in any aspect of a couple's relationship from courtship to death. Lengthy formal betrothals were discouraged, lest couples took them to permit sexual license before the wedding. The stated purpose of marriage was for the procreation of Christians, with the act of lovemaking to be performed "with modesty and shame." For the encouragement of large families, this was a mixed message at best.

It was only within the sacrament of marriage that sexual relations were allowed. Patterns of premarital conceptions and illegitimate births were comparable with those in France—similar overall rates, with a disproportionate number in urban areas. In Canada, 23 percent of unwed mothers remained single. The mother married before the child was born in 37 percent of cases. About one-tenth of pregnancies out of wedlock ended in court, indicating that the common experience was a private settlement between families. While the father was held to his responsibilities to support the child, through marriage to the mother or otherwise, he subsequently suffered little social censure. The unwed mother, however, lost honor and reputation. Her disgrace could be mitigated only by subsequent marriage. The creation of a new family brought moral absolution. The same double standard applied in cases of adultery, which were always brought against women. Loyalty was essentially a wife's duty.

The royal government took measures to encourage population growth and the settlement of families on farms. The sponsored emigration of orphaned daughters (called the "king's girls") in the late 1660s and early 1670s to provide wives for the large number of single men in the colony was certainly effective: they married quickly on arrival. However, measures at the same time to place fines on bachelorhood and to provide bounties for families with ten or more living children were fruitless. At most, only 8 percent of families by the eighteenth century could have qualified for the bounties. More to the point, it is not credible from what we know of peasant family strategies that the least thought would have been given to producing ten children over a twenty-year period in order to receive at the end what could be earned in two seasons as a

canoeman to a fur-trade post on the Great Lakes.

Age at marriage and frequency of pregnancies obeyed the command of culture, custom, and necessity, not legislation. Peasant women married relatively early because their useful contribution to the family economy, with few opportunities off the farm, ended sooner. Peasant men married later because it took time to convert a concession of virgin land into a farm that could support a family. The seasonality of births indicates a notable drop in conceptions during Lent, a time of religiously prescribed sexual abstinence. The proscriptions of canon law against birth control through abstinence or onanism at other times may also have been followed, though pressures on the household economy would have argued for limiting rather than increasing family size.

THE COUTUME DE PARIS

For elites and lower social orders alike the family was the prime institution of social and economic security. The Coutume de Paris (Custom of Paris), the civil law applied throughout New France, embodied the obligations and rights of family members with regard to property and personal relationships. The foundation of family law was to provide for the widow and to protect the inheritance of the children against alienation of the patrimony. A few salient principles and provisions of the Coutume underscore these objectives.

A young couple wishing to marry, and thereby to create a new family, was not permitted to do so casually. The age of majority was twenty-five, before which children required authorization of parents or guardians in the management of property. The same age applied for parental permission for a daughter to marry. A son required such permission from his father until age thirty, and even then had to observe prescribed formalities (three successive written pleas) to overcome formal opposition. These requirements reflect a deep distrust of youthful judgment and a serious regard for the family and its means of security. Nonetheless, we know from demographic data that most men married before age thirty and most women before age twenty-five. Parental permission was evidently granted routinely. The marriage act bestowed authority upon the new family regardless of the age of husband or wife.

Marriage launched an enterprise for mutual economic survival of family members. To this end the law provided for community of property (*communauté de biens*) between husband and wife, almost always stipulated in a marriage contract signed and witnessed by relatives before a notary prior to the marriage ceremony. The law clearly recognized the husband as master of the family—of both persons and *communauté de biens*. The notion of a single authority was deeply embedded in the hierarchical assumptions of the ancien régime, with women almost always subordinate to men. The husband's authority is reflected in the heading of article 225 under title 10 of the Coutume de Paris, "Husband master of the *communauté*," and "The husband is lord." However, the authority granted to the husband was neither absolute nor arbitrary. He was required to manage prudently, consult his wife and other relatives on important family decisions, and exercise his authority with respect, compassion, and gentleness. If he failed in his duties, his wife was empowered to seek protection in the law. This could be difficult and costly, but she could also expect her own family's support in her suit.

Discord within the family leading to marriage breakdown was rare. It is most clearly documented for the upper classes, who had easier recourse to the courts. Overwhelmingly the wife initiated the demand for separation. A disproportionately high number of separation cases involved remarriages: 41 percent of demands for physical separation (a matter for church tribunals) and 36 percent of those for separation of property, the most common demand. Alcoholism and physical and verbal violence are cited, but the most frequent grounds were "familial irresponsibility"—an inability to support the family or failure to participate in family life.

In case of a husband's financial misadventure, the wife—or widow, as the case may be—was protected by various privileged claims against the *communauté*. Her dower rights, or pension stipulated in the marriage contract, were immune from the claims of other creditors, including her own children, during her life. She was also empowered to renounce the *communauté* and to withdraw her portion if the family enterprise was threatened with bankruptcy, either through common misfortune or reckless dissipation by her husband.

FAMILY LAW AND THE ELITE

Among the elites—merchants, public officials, military officers—the more arcane complexities and ambiguities of family and property law were likely to be tested. For these educated, propertied, and privileged classes the family enterprise required for its security the manipulation of power, influence, and wealth. Appropriate marriage alliances were the prime consideration in protecting the family's position and securing its inheritance. Networks of well-maintained family relationships were essential to ensure support and favor in the promotion of business and careers in a world wholly dependent upon patronage, loyalty, and trust.

Commercial wealth increasingly challenged both the restrictions on the alienation of family property and the privileged claims of widows and inheritors to indebted estates. Elite families with social position to maintain were more likely to insist upon the letter of the law in protecting their family patrimony from alienation. Thus they guarded the distinction between bequeathed property, or *propres*, the alienation of which was strictly forbidden, and *conquêts*, which were earned or purchased and could be disposed of more freely. A family's fortunes could be either advanced or depressed by marriage, so children of the elite class were not at liberty to marry whomever they wished. The decision was a family one, exercised in the first instance by the parents. The fact that most marriages were between individuals occupying the same social position indicates that security against misfortune was the dominant concern.

FAMILY STRATEGY IN COMMON LIFE

For the 80 percent of families who lived by farming, family practices were simpler and more flexible. It is noteworthy that, notwithstanding the demographic disequilibrium of the seventeenth century and the oft-claimed influence of the fur trade in distracting Canadian males from traditional farm and family life, the behavior of colonists steadfastly followed family structures and customs brought from France. Notarial documentation reveals family strategies that placed a premium upon reciprocal obligations, equality of treatment, and mutual agreement.

If anything, the Canadian environment reinforced these values and the family solidarity they reflect. An abundance of land without an abundance of alternative livelihoods kept children on the farm during their growing years and encouraged the reproduction of conjugal farm families each generation. The modest value of land and possessions encouraged pragmatic distribution of inheritances and contributions of members to the family income. The authority of the husband so pronounced in the Coutume de Paris is practically invisible in the evidence of family consultations and negotiations that regulated obligations and entitlements in common practice. Even though legal authority belonged to the husband, there is great evidence that wives shared in decisions of property and household management. Parental authority in the choice of spouses was also less evident. Some clauses of the Coutume that preoccupied the elites, notably the conversion of inherited land into *propres* and unequal gifting of property among heirs, were often ignored.

The object of these apparent deviations, however, was to ensure equity. The unequal distribution of property among children was seldom to favor some and disadvantage others. Rather, it reflected ways of recognizing the unequal expenditures among siblings of time and care in fulfilling several family obligations, usually toward the upkeep of aging or widowed parents. Thus, the ample notarized records of marriage contracts, sales, gifts, debts, testamentary donations, and other acts among family members represent an ongoing account within the family of the state of each member's inheritance. Overwhelmingly, the outcomes reflected a concern to distribute inheritances equally among all children.

The most notable variation to the above family structures and practices was to be found in Louisiana where the early dearth of European women resulted in widespread concubinage of French male colonists and Amerindian and African slave women. Notwithstanding the ban against mixed marriages by the French government, the local clergy continued to sanction them in order to reduce the sin of fornication and the scandal of concubinage. A sizable mulatto population developed with extensive manumission. Before 1730 probably half of all marriages in the Illinois country were mixed. Everywhere inheritance practice was governed by the Coutume de Paris, though there were exceptions, sometimes disputed, when Amerindian widows chose to act on their own customs.

The family in New France was unquestionably the fundamental social institution ensuring employment, security, and affection. The purposes it served and the values it embodied were customary and inherited, brought by immigrants who never saw themselves other than as members of families. Family structures were in large measure independent of the public, religious, and legal institutions established, though these held many values in common. In the nineteenth and twentieth centuries, the traditional French-Canadian family was ascribed mystical properties by a generation of conservative elites who grasped for eternal certainties in a rapidly changing world. Nevertheless, the family continued as always to be remarkably adaptable.

BIBLIOGRAPHY

Bosher, J. F. "The Family in New France." In *In Search of the Visible Past: History Lectures at Wilfrid Laurier University, 1973–1974,* edited by Barry M. Gough. Waterloo, Ontario, 1975.

Charbonneau, Hubert. *Vie et mort de nos ancêtres: Étude démographique.* Montreal, 1975.

———, et al. *Naissance d'une population: Les Français établis au Canada au XVIIe siècle.* Montreal and Paris, 1987.

Cliche, Marie-Aimée. "Unwed Mothers, Families, and Society During the French Regime." In *Canadian Family History,* edited by Bettina Bradbury. Toronto, Ontario, 1992.

Dechêne, Louise. *Habitants et marchands de Montréal au XVIIe siècle.* Paris and Montreal, 1974.

Du Molin, Charles. *La Coutume de Paris conferée avec les autres coutumes de France, . . .* Paris, 1666.

Ekberg, Carl J. *Colonial Ste. Genevieve.* Gerald, Miss., 1985.

Harris, R. Cole, and Geoffrey J. Matthews, eds. *Historical Atlas of Canada.* Vol. 1. Toronto, Ontario, 1987.

Henripin, Jacques. *La population canadienne au début du XVIIIe siècle.* Paris, 1954.

Henripin, Jacques, and Yves Péron. "The Demographic Transformation of the Province of Quebec." In *Population and Social Change,* edited by D. V. Glass and Roger Revelle. London, 1972.

Jaenen, Cornelius J. *The Role of the Church in New France.* Toronto, Ontario, 1976.

Johnston, A. J. B. *Religion in Life at Louisbourg, 1713–1758.* Kingston and Montreal, 1984.

Landry, Yves. *Orphelines en France pionnières au Canada: Les filles du roi au XVIIe siècle.* Montreal, 1992.

Moogk, Peter N. *"Les petits sauvages:* The Children of Eighteenth-Century New France." In *Childhood and Family in Canadian History,* edited by Joy Parr. Toronto, Ontario, 1982.

———. "Rank in New France: Reconstructing a Society From Notarial Documents." *Histoire Sociale/Social History* 8 (1975):34–53.

O'Neill, Charles Edwards. *Church and State in French Colonial Louisiana: Policy and Politics to 1732.* New Haven and London, 1966.

Savoie, Sylvie. "Les couples en difficulté aux XVIIe et XVIIIe siècles: Les demandes de séparation en Nouvelle-France." Masters thesis, Université de Sherbrooke, Quebec, 1986.

Trudel, Marcel. *Introduction to New France.* Toronto, Ontario, 1968.

Zoltvany, Yves F. "Esquisse de la Coutume de Paris." *Revue d'histoire de l'amérique française* 25, no. 3 (1971):365–384.

S. Dale Standen

SEE ALSO **African-American Culture; Gender Relations;** and **Home and Hearth.**

THE SPANISH BORDERLANDS

THE 1984 EDITION of the Spanish Royal Academy's *Diccionario de la Lengua Española* lists thirteen meanings and historical uses of the word *familia* (family). Family is defined as

1. A group of persons related to each other who live together under the authority of one. 2. The number of servants (*criados*) a person has, even if they do not live in his house. 3. The group of ascendants, descendants, collaterals, and affines in a lineage. . . . 6. The body of an order or religion, or a considerable part of one. 7. One's immediate kin. . . . 9. A group of individuals who share a common condition. 10. A large group of persons. . . . 13. (Biology and Zoology) A taxonomic group that consists of several natural types which possess a large number of common characteristics. (Vol. 1, p. 630)

Explaining usage, the *Diccionario* states that *en familia* (within family) means "without strangers, in intimacy."

The *Diccionario's* definition of family summarizes the rather long and complex history of this institution and idea. Today, we equate family with immediate kin and relatives. That which is within the family is intimate, within the private walls of the home, and devoid of strangers. But if we focus carefully on the historical genealogy of the word *familia,* we find that in its antique meanings it was tied neither to kinship nor to a specific private space or house. Rather, what constituted *familia* was the relationship of authority that one person exercised over another. More specifically, *familia* was imagined as the relationship of a master over his slaves and servants. This essay traces the evolution of the concept of *familia* from a servile authority relationship into a kin group, into a private domestic entity, and then into a religious association.

The etymological root of the Spanish word *familia* is the Latin word *familia.* Roman grammarians believed that the word had entered Latin as a borrowing from the Oscan language of a neighboring tribe. In Oscan *famel* meant slave; the Latin word for slave was *famulus.* The second-century novelist Apuleius wrote that "fifteen slaves make a family, and fifteen prisoners make a jail." The Roman jurist Ulpian gave more precision to the term, explaining in the second century A.D. that "we are accustomed to call staffs of slaves families. . . . We call a family the several persons who by nature of law are placed under the authority of a single person." Family thus initially referred to the hierarchical authority relationship between people. This relationship could be based on marriage and kinship but was not limited to these situations. The family relationship is implicit in the definition of the word *pater* (father): the *paterfamilias* was the legal head of a *familia,* whereas the biological father was called the *genitor.* Only a man could exercise *patria potestas,* legal authority over anyone under his command, even if he himself was an unmarried man.

Many of the antique meanings of the word *familia* persisted with some modification into the seventeenth century, undoubtedly because of the revival of Roman juridical thought in canon law and in the legal institutions of the fifteenth-century Iberian kingdoms. By the early part of the seventeenth century, Sebastián de Covarrubias in his 1611 dictionary, *Tesoro de la Lengua Castellana o Española,* defined *familia* as "the people that a lord sustains within his house." Covarrubias concurred that *familia* was of Latin and Oscan etymology and explained that "while previously it had only meant a person's slaves," the word's contemporary meaning then included "the lord and his wife, and the rest of the individuals under his command, such as children, servants, and slaves." Citing contemporary seventeenth-century usage, Covarrubias quoted the section of the legal code known as the *Siete Partidas* that stipulated, "There is family when there are three persons governed by a lord."

The 1732 *Diccionario de la Lengua Castellana,* prepared by the Spanish Royal Academy for King Philip V, repeated Covarrubias's discussion of *familia* almost verbatim. The only "new" meaning of the word family was one referring to "the body of a religion, or a considerable part of it." The textual example cited to illustrate this usage was: "Many are the Holy Families that occupy themselves seeking the salvation of souls." *Padre de familia* (father of the family) was defined as "the lord of the house, even though he may not have any children. He is so-called because of his obligation to exercise the role of father for everyone that lives under his dominion." *Hijo de familia* (child of the family) was that person "who has not taken the state [of marriage] and remains under the father's authority."

By the seventeenth century, both in Spain and in Spanish America, the *familia* was a jural unit based on authority relationships that were established primarily, though not exclusively,

through marriage and procreation. Family was tied to a particular place, to a *casa* or house in which the lord and his subordinates lived. The *casa* was a domestic kingdom, much as the public realm was the king's domain. Family was thus synonymous with authority, kinship, and household.

The centrality of the *casa* or house as the physical entity that defined the familial space had important ramifications for family structure. The house was the basic unit of social differentiation. Every census, every demographic report, every civil and criminal investigation took the *casa* as its basic unit of analysis and implicitly assumed a set of authority relations dominated by the household head in all matters. In early modern Spain and New Spain *casas* were large and small, rich and poor, nuclear and extended, but nonetheless equal in that everyone belonged to a household through principles of consanguinity, through marriage, or through some misfortune leaving them an orphan, slave, or stray.

James Casey and Bernard Vincent maintain that the majority of Christian households—two-thirds to be exact—in seventeenth- and eighteenth-century Spain were nuclear in form and contained on the average 2.7 persons. As one moved up the social ladder, so too the size of the household increased, through the usual addition of aging and widowed parents, destitute kin, and servants and slaves. The average size of these households was 4.5 persons. Members of the nobility and liberal professions (lawyers, doctors, scribes) usually reported one or two servants or slaves. Laborers, journeymen, and heads of poor and humble households resided with their wife and perhaps one or two children, but rarely anyone else. Only among artisans was it common to find an apprentice living with his teacher.

Spanish legal and philosophical tracts from the seventeenth and early eighteenth centuries equated kinship with consanguinity. The commingling of natural substance through procreation engendered blood relations. And these blood ties, first and foremost, were the cement that bound parents and their children as family in households. Ties of affinity created through marriage were important as well, but they were quite secondary in structuring the solidarities, obligations, and legal rights that family entailed.

Juxtaposed with this secular restrictive theory of family rooted in relationships of blood, authority, and coresidence was a much more expansive religious model of kinship advocated by the Catholic church. In Christian theology every person has both a body and a soul and is thus both a natural and a spiritual being. One's jural standing in the community of Christians is initiated through baptism, the sacrament of spiritual regeneration. According to theologians, baptism rivals the very act of physical procreation. Saint Thomas Aquinas explained in the *Summa Theologica* that through baptism the child is "born again a son of God as Father, and of the church as Mother." Once a person is incorporated into the mystical body of Christ through baptism, that person becomes a member of an extensive global community linked by ties of spiritual kinship.

These diametrically opposed models of kinship, one restrictive and the other expansive, one secular and the other religious, were at the center of much of the conflict that characterized relations between families and the Catholic church in Western Europe from the sixth to the seventeenth centuries. Indeed, similar controversies would be played out anew in the Americas as the juridical status of the Indian was defined. In the long history of these disputes the issue of power most bothered the church; this concern perhaps reflected its own hegemonic aspirations in society. The church was always suspicious of a father's absolute authority over members of his household and constantly tried to set limits to the exercise of that power. Tightly integrated families and households were developing into mighty lineages, kingdoms, and protonations, threatening the universalist community the church sought to create and to control.

To weaken the power that families had developed through exclusivist practices, the church defined and tried to enforce an expansive theory of spiritual kinship in all realms of life. Relationships of the spirit required Christians to act in certain ways; by getting individuals to behave in these prescribed ways, the church ultimately hoped to limit the power of fathers and households.

As noted in the entry on family in the *Diccionario de la Lengua Castellana*, marriage was the life-cycle event that created a family and that ended a child's unmediated submission to the family's head. Matrimony, as the ritual act that sanctified the creation of family, was in the hands of the Catholic church. To weaken the power of families, the church defined a very extensive theory of impediments that prohibited certain classes of persons from being joined.

Of greatest importance to the church was incest, or the prohibition of marriage between close blood relatives. Starting at the Council of Elvira (c. A.D. 300), the church began prohibiting marriage between persons related to the fourth degree of consanguinity (that is, three generations removed from the common ancestor). This prohibition was extended to the seventh degree of consanguinity at the Council of Rome in A.D. 1059. To understand how restrictive this incest restriction was, imagine a couple in each of six generations giving birth to two children. The consanguinity impediment to marriage would eliminate 2,731 "blood" relatives of the same generation from choosing one another as mates. Jean Flandrin has argued in *Families in Former Times* that the intent of such consanguinity impediments was clear. As family solidarity increased, the church extended the consanguinity impediments to marriage in the hope that by forcing exogamous marriages it could weaken the power of families.

The power that fathers exercised within the family over wife, children, and slaves was also a very complex and, at times, contradictory issue for the church. The Fourth Commandment enjoined children to "honor thy father and mother," a stricture further elaborated in Saint Paul's Epistle to the Ephesians (5:22 to 6:9). Saint Paul urged Christians to obey God as wives, children, and slaves obeyed the master of the house: "Wives, submit yourselves unto your own husbands, as unto the Lord. . . . Children, obey your parents in the Lord. . . . Servants, be obedient to them that are your masters . . . with fear and trembling . . . with good will doing service as to the Lord." According to Saint Paul, the kingdom of heaven was governed by rules identical to those that governed terrestrial kingdoms.

Nevertheless, the church also maintained a healthy skepticism about the untrammeled exercise of patriarchal power and through its theory of spiritual kinship consistently tried to limit its exercise. Biological parents were simply the earthly custodians and guardians of the children of God, or so argued clerics and theologians.

As the tempering of kinship solidarities through the enforcement of incest impediments increased the church's power, other methods of regulating matrimony provided the church with the means to subvert parental, marital, and seignorial power. Throughout the Middle Ages and into the late twentieth century, the church has always maintained that for a marriage to be valid and legitimate, the partners must enter the marriage of their own volition, freely consenting, and without fear of pain or coercion. On this point, canon law embraced the Roman legal maxim on marriage, that *consensus facit nuptias,* or consent constitutes the nuptial.

Before the Council of Trent (1545–1563), all that was theoretically necessary for two individuals to be married was consent and conjugation. Canon lawyers maintained that because marriage was a bond in natural law and, since the expression of mutual consent—usually through sexual intercourse and occasionally through gift-giving and contract—constituted the sacramental act, any union meeting this requisite was valid. Just as a person could be incorporated into the mystical body of Christ through a covert baptism of the faith to avoid persecution, a man and a woman might similarly be joined secretly in marriage. For the marriage to be considered legitimate in the eyes of the church, it also had to be blessed and witnessed by a priest.

The desire to subvert parental power, particularly the power to arrange marriages to create or expand kinship ties, led to the prohibition of such secret or clandestine marriages at the Council of Trent. Here the church fathers concluded that for a marriage to be valid and legitimate, a priest had to perform the matrimony and had to ascertain beforehand whether the partners were freely exercising their consent. Since many marriages in early modern Europe were arranged solely for the expansion and consolidation of family fame and fortune, here was the mechanism by which the church could and would undermine the exercise of paternal control, be it with children, servants, or slaves. If children truly wanted to marry despite parental objections, the church would marry the couple, just as it would refuse to marry those individuals who it suspected were being forced into marriage against their personal will.

UNIQUE PROBLEMS IN SPANISH AMERICA

All of the concerns that locked the church and families in struggle in Spain from the fifteenth to the seventeenth centuries—the limits of paternal authority, the intensity of blood relations, and the establishment of family through marriage—were carried over into the American colonial empire and renegotiated there under slightly different terms. The nature of the struggle between patriarchs and priests was radically different in Spanish America because the Catholic church and the Spanish state had been joined through the *Real Patronato* (royal patronage) of the late fifteenth century. The concessions of royal patronage, codified in a series of papal bulls that dated to the final years of the Spanish Reconquest, assured the Spanish Crown that in return for its proclaiming and defending Catholicism as the one and only true religion in the realm and for promising to convert the infidel in newly conquered territories, the pope would reciprocate by granting Spain's kings far-reaching rights over the regulation of the church. What the *Real Patronato* meant for the legal regulation of family in the Spanish colonies of North America was that no separate form of family civil law would exist. Family law was church law, a condition that persisted until the 1770s when the "enlightened" Bourbon monarch Charles III moved aggressively to secularize society and to limit the power of the Catholic church in everyday life.

The conquest of America and the extension of Spanish juridical forms into the Spanish colonies presented the monarchy with new issues that would be resolved through the extension of antique principles. Perhaps the most nettlesome of all the issues Spain's kings, theologians, and canon lawyers had to arbitrate in the New World was the juridical status of the Indian. Did the Indians have souls? Were they born into a natural state of slavery? If so, did the absolute authority of a lord over the members of his household extend to those Indians who were awarded to the first conquistadores in tributary grants of entrustment (*encomiendas*)?

Flowing from the juridical definition of the Indian were other equally complex issues. Should Indians be allowed to establish families through marriage? If so, who were appropriate matrimonial partners? Were Native mating practices comparable to marriage, and would the previous celebration of such rites be recognized by the church? Was the indigenous domestic hearth a moral terrain comparable to the Spanish house?

Spanish jurists and theologians grappled with these questions. The Indians most definitely had souls, they concluded, and therefore had to be baptized and incorporated into the faith. Indians could be bought and sold as slaves and incorporated into their master's household, particularly if captured as prisoners of just war. The nature of the relationship that should exist between an *encomendero* (holder of an *encomienda*) and the Indians "entrusted" to him produced long legal disquisitions. According to Spanish law, Indians were considered free vassals who were under the age of majority. As "children," the Indians required special protection and tutelage. Under the rubric of familial tutelage and protection, entire Indian villages were entrusted to the Spanish conquistadores for Christianization, in return for which the *encomenderos* could extract personal labor and tribute payments in foodstuff, hides, and cloth.

Throughout the early years of America's conquest, *encomiendas* were brutally exploitative relationships. The Crown tried to abolish the *encomienda* in 1542, but a rebellion in Peru slowed the law's enforcement. After 1542 the *encomienda* no longer carried a right to Indian labor and the number of generations an *encomienda* could be inherited was limited. Finally, in 1721 the institution was abolished. Those Indians who survived the *encomienda* had learned that the authority of a father over those under his care could be gentle and loving but also vicious and cruel.

Because the Indians were considered mere children before the law, the issue of Indian marriage also proved to be a complex question for both the church and the state. Since marriage was the bedrock on which families were formed, the church consistently proclaimed the right of

Indians to marry freely and held that the marriage canons of the Council of Trent would regulate all marriages in Spanish America. Marriages between Spaniards and Indians were legal and encouraged. The only marriages that were explicitly prohibited were those between the servants of a local governor or viceroy and Indians held in *encomienda* and those between royal officers and local women. In this latter case the fear was that the marriage would compromise the officer's loyalty to the Crown. The law also asserted that persons of mixed racial ancestry had to consent freely to marriage but seen by the law as minors they were urged to seek the permission of their father or master.

One of the most interesting problems that Spanish law had to resolve was the legal status of those conjugal unions established by Indians prior to their conversion to Catholicism. Polygamy was widely practiced in the Americas and so the immediate issue was which of a person's several wives would be deemed the Christian wife. The sixteenth-century Pope Paul III resolved the issue by proclaiming that the first woman who had intimate sexual contact with a husband had to be recognized as the legal wife. But if a man did not remember which of his several wives had been his first, he was free to choose one with whom he would be sacramentally united. The husband had to separate himself from the other women and to dower them and any children produced through these unions.

An equally complex problem faced by civil and ecclesiastical authorities was defining the residential unit that was morally valorized as the familial home. The indigenous populations of America lived in a variety of domestic and household arrangements before their conquest. Spaniards were accustomed to imagining the familial *casa* or household as the residential unit on which kinship was based and in which feeding, socialization, sleeping, sexual activity, and domestic religious rituals occurred, but the relationship between such functions and the household was not similarly defined in indigenous societies. Native American societies gendered spaces differently and drew sharper lines between male and female space. Feeding, sleeping, sexual activity, and domestic rituals did not always occur in the same space; more often than not, they took place in different spaces. For example, among nomadic bands, where animal skins and natural vegetation provided shelter, it was not uncommon for camps to have men's and women's "huts" and for a campfire or hearth to be used jointly by the senior women responsible for cooking. Men spent large amounts of their time together on hunts. They returned to their matrilineal hut with meat and foodstuff and, depending on circumstances, exercised their sexual rights in whatever locale was available.

Similar arrangements existed among sedentary agriculturalists. Houses were owned by women, and within the house's walls resided grandmother, mother, and daughters. Sons and husbands provided these households with labor and meat but did not reside or sleep within them. Men resided in lodgehouses or in the ceremonial chambers of esoteric religious societies, in which they also ate when the women delivered food. Men who enjoyed sexual rights to a particular woman through marriage would enter her mother's house at night, but by daybreak they had returned to the men's lodge.

One of the goals of Spanish colonization was the transformation of the Indians into model Spanish Christians and the restructuring of their societies to conform to Spanish familial and marital ideals. Nomadic bands with fluid housing arrangements were congregated into villages of nuclear households. Where households had been sexually segregated, husbands were now forced to live with a sacramental wife under a common roof, thus fundamentally transforming Native rules of kinship, residence, and sexual behavior. Property rights routinely were taken away from Native women, altering matrilineal forms of reckoning and descent, and vested in men, initiating the triumph of patrilineal rule over mother right.

THE SPIRITUAL FAMILY

As was noted earlier in this essay, the church was suspicious of the strong blood ties that bound biological families and constantly militated to weaken those links through the regulation of marriage. On the Spanish Borderlands, as elsewhere in Spanish America, the church coupled its ecclesiastical marriage policy with a spiritual model of family in its effort to achieve its ends. Unlike the natural family that was concerned with patrimonies and worldly authority, spiritual family concerned itself only with the salvation of souls. The religious model of spiritual family, known as *compadrazgo,* existed in every part of the Spanish Empire during the colonial period, both in the cities and in the countryside and among the conquerors and the conquered alike. *Compadrazgo,* or what in English is often referred to as godparenthood or spiritual coparenthood, dictated that any Christian receiving the sacraments of baptism, confirmation, or matrimony had to be sponsored in the ritual of incorporation into the Christian community by a set of godparents. The *compadrazgo* ties established through the celebration of one of these sacraments rested on three roles—parent (*padre/madre*), child (*hijo/hija*), and godparent (*padrino/madrina*)—and created three sets of relationships: one a natural kinship tie between a parent and child and the other two, ties of spiritual kinship, one between child and godparents and one between parents and godparents. The godchild was referred to as an *ahijado/ahijada* by his or her *padrino* and *madrina.* The parents and godparents referred to each other as *compadres,* or coparents.

Throughout the Spanish Borderlands there were permutations in this model, deviations in custom that evolved over time from this unitary ecclesiastical core. Such modifications were frequently the result of the secularization of public life, and as this secularization occurred, it was not uncommon for a godparent to be selected to sponsor a child's first haircut. From the late eighteenth century on, it has been standard for communities also to select *padrinos* to serve as patrons for the staging of secular festivals and public pageants associated with a town's foundation and with its patron saint's feast day. Similarly, when a person makes, purchases, or is given an unconsecrated icon, a godparent is chosen to sponsor the icon's consecration.

Compadrazgo was rooted in a cultural conception of the person as both a natural and a spiritual being, as Stephen Gudeman has argued. Such dualistic cultural conceptions were by no means unique to Spanish America. What was unique to Spanish Catholic law and practice, Gudeman has suggested, was the belief that these two aspects of a person were quite distinct and as such had to "be entrusted to different sets of persons: the natural and spiritual parents."

The profane secular world of kinship, that realm of existence created through blood and substance and rooted in material life, belonged to the natural family. But before a person could enter into the Christian religious and moral community, they had to be baptized. Through baptism a person attained juridical standing in the eyes of the church. Indeed, baptism prefigured the very death and resurrection of Christ, for through this sacrament one died to the world of nature and was reborn as a spiritual child of mother church.

In The New Testament, Saint John articulated the scriptural foundation for this meaning of baptism:

Jesus answered, and said to him: Amen, amen I say to thee, unless a man be born again, he cannot see the kingdom of God. Nicodemus saith to him: How can a man be born when he is old? Can he enter a second time into his mother's womb, and be born again? Jesus answered: Amen, amen I say to thee, unless a man be born again of water and the Holy Ghost, he cannot enter into the kingdom of God. That which is born of the flesh, is flesh; and that which is born of the Spirit, is spirit. (John 3:3–6)

The fact that *compadrazgo* ties were considered spiritual ties meant that the obligations and responsibilities they entailed were primarily moral and spiritual. Godparents were supposed to counsel and guide their godchildren, leading them to eternal salvation and God by ensuring that they complied with the laws of the church. Relationships between *compadres* were also of a spiritual nature. Relationships of trust between *compadres* ensured that the spiritual tie preempted the operations of the profane world marked by envy, greed, lust, suspicion, and conflict.

During the colonial period the conflict between the spiritual and the natural person was best demonstrated in the baptism of captured slaves who were pressed into domestic servitude. In colonial New Mexico, 3,294 Indian slaves were baptized between 1693 and 1849. In 280 of these cases the officiating priest recorded the names of the godparents and their relationship to the slave. Fourteen percent of the slaves had their owners listed as the godparents. An owner/

nonowner combination served as *padrinos* in 20 percent of these christenings. But in 65 percent of the cases, no apparent relationship existed between the slave's godparents and the master. A more striking pattern emerges in the godparenthood information on the children born to slaves in captivity. Only in one out of 113 baptisms were the child's godparents also its parents' masters. Seven owner/nonowner combinations acted as godparents. But in 92 percent of the baptisms, the child's *padrinos* were totally unrelated to the slave's master.

Why were masters not preferred as baptismal godparents? Gudeman and Stuart B. Schwartz have proposed that the answer lies in the ideological clash between baptism and slavery. In Christian theology a person is made of body and soul. Baptismal sponsorship creates a spiritual bond between the baptized person and the godparents that entails obligations of protection, instruction, and succor. Unlike slavery, a bond of domination over human volition expressed as control over another person's body and signified through servility, baptism bespeaks an equality born of participation in the mystical body of Christ. Thus, two rather incompatible states, spiritual freedom and physical bondage, were brought together when the church insisted that captives be baptized. The contradiction was resolved by the selection of a sponsor other than the slavemaster to witness the baptized person's liberation from original sin and rebirth into Christ's salvation. Masters themselves may have refused to serve as godparents, fearing that to do so would abrogate some of their temporal powers over the slave. And certainly when slaves chose *padrinos* for their children, they invariably avoided choosing their owner to participate in their children's spiritual salvation.

CONFRATERNITIES

A second religious model of family, known as *cofradías* (confraternities) or brotherhoods, existed in the Spanish Borderlands. Confraternities originated in Europe during the twelfth century as voluntary associations of the Christian faithful committed to the performance of acts of charity to alleviate poverty and vagrancy. In an era before social services were provided by the state, pressing social needs accelerated the formation of brotherhoods. Victims of catastrophe, disease, or unemployment found their basic needs met through the works of mercy performed by the confraternities, while the members of the confraternities, by performing such acts, gained grace and indulgences, considered sure routes to personal sanctity and eternal salvation.

The word confraternity and its Spanish equivalent, *cofradía,* were derived from the Latin *confrater,* or cobrother. The idea behind the confraternity was that persons should live together like brothers with a particular code of conduct. Such associations existed in ancient Rome with purely secular objectives; the brotherhoods that were established in the Spanish Borderlands were defined by Christian tradition and canon law.

According to ecclesiastical dictates, a confraternity was a group of lay persons dedicated to the promotion of a particular devotion to Christ, to the Virgin Mary, or to the saints. *Cofradías* required episcopal sanction and were governed by statutes stipulating the rules of their ritual practices, membership rules, dues, required works of piety and mortification, and festival days of observance. Despite great differences in devotional practices, the common thread that bound most brotherhoods was their obligation to lead model lives of Christian virtue, to care for the physical welfare of the locality's needy, and to bury the dead and to pray for the salvation of their souls.

The ecclesiastical sanction that confraternities enjoyed and the familial language in which their organization was delineated made them fitting outlets for the expression of broad-based social affinities. As equal members of the mystical body of Christ joined in spiritual brotherhood, residents of a community could momentarily put aside the enmities and distrust that typically marked the interactions of families, households, and clans in the borderlands for acts of communal solidarity.

In Florida, New Mexico, Texas, and California, membership in one or more confraternities was a natural and essential part of the religious identity of every explorer, conquistador, colonist, and slave. As soon as a church was constructed and Mass celebrated at any locality, the establishment of confraternities followed.

While the form of Catholic confraternities was remarkably uniform throughout the world, their meaning and significance were apparent only at the parish level, in the relationships confraternities had with each other. Thus, for example, it was not uncommon to find in any particular town both vertical and horizontal confraternities.

The vertical confraternities integrated a town's social groups, joining rich and poor, Spaniards and Indians, slave and free. By emphasizing mutual aid and ritually obliterating local status distinctions, these confraternities often diffused underlying social tensions into less dangerous forms of conflict. In place of overt social antagonisms, parish confraternities squabbled over displays of material wealth, the splendor of celebrations, and the precedence due the group.

In Santa Fe, in Saint Augustine, and in San Antonio, vertical confraternities of this sort were formed in the early eighteenth century. Santa Fe, for example, had three such confraternities in 1729 dedicated to the devotion of the Blessed Sacrament, the Poor Souls in Purgatory, Our Lady of the Rosary, and Saint Michael. Fray Atanasio Domínguez reported in 1776 that the Santa Fe members of the Confraternity of Our Lady of the Rosary (also known as Our Lady of the Conquest) included soldiers, peasants, and aristocrats who communally celebrated the defeat of the forces of evil through the subjugation of the Pueblo Indians. On the feast days that commemorated the Virgin's conception, purification, nativity, and assumption, her devotees carried her jeweled statue through Santa Fe's streets while the royal garrison fired salvos; the celebration ended with dances, dramas, and bullfights.

If vertical brotherhoods integrated disparate classes, the horizontal confraternities mirrored a locale's segmentation, or those status inequalities based on race, honor, and ownership of property. Thus, relationships of domination and subordination were articulated through these confraternities. The social supremacy of the Spanish gentry was expressed through its opulent confraternity rituals and celebrations to various saints. Dominated groups, such as Indians and slaves, also expressed their dignity and collective identity with acts of piety that rivaled those of their oppressors.

A symbolic opposition existed in Santa Fe during the eighteenth century between the Confraternity of Our Lady of the Light and the Confraternity of Our Lord Jesus of Nazareth, popularly known as the Brothers of Darkness. The former was founded in Santa Fe in 1760 by Governor Francisco Marín del Valle. The confraternity owned a private chapel, which by contemporary standards was the most ornate in town, and had sumptuous furnishings, rich vestments for worship, and a large endowment of land and livestock. Its membership numbered 236 in 1776 and consisted of Santa Fe's elite Spanish families. Founded originally as a counterpoint to the overwhelming power of the Franciscan friars in the town, the brotherhood provided the gentry with an institutional mechanism for negotiating conflicts with the Franciscans and with a way of avoiding contact with the town's lower classes during religious services.

The Confraternity of Our Lord Jesus of Nazareth, on the other hand, was composed primarily of *genízaros*, or detribalized Indian slaves. Bound by their veneration of the passion and death of Jesus Christ, the Brothers of Darkness displayed their piety through acts of self-mortification, including flagellation and cross-bearing, culminating each Good Friday with the crucifixion of one of its members. "The body of this Order is composed of members so dry that all its juice consists chiefly of misfortunes," wrote Fray Atanasio Domínguez, describing the poverty of this confraternity in 1776. It had no membership records, accounts, or endowment and indeed had to borrow ceremonial paraphernalia from other confraternities for its services.

Cofradías initially were formed in the Spanish Borderlands as a response to individual and collective needs for physical and spiritual succor. Though indigents at times were given meat from illegally slaughtered livestock, and widows of soldiers killed in Indian warfare were regularly paid royal stipends, very little else was provided by the state to indigent members of the community. The need to care for the poor, for the sick, and for the elderly gave rise to the confraternities in the borderlands. *Cofradía* statutes enjoined brothers to provide mutual aid in the form of charitable acts, religious instruction, and burying of the dead. Given the high rates of mortality on the northern frontiers of New Spain and the

limited access to the official sacramental rituals of the Catholic church, *cofradía* membership guaranteed at least a Christian burial. Indeed one of the greatest communal acts a brotherhood's member could perform was to participate in constructing a casket for a deceased brother, digging his grave, and praying for his soul.

GROWING SECULARIZATION

From 1492 until the mid eighteenth century, the definition of family was strictly regulated by the Catholic church, be it in the tempering of secular exclusivist kinship practices or in the extension of expansive ecclesiastical spiritual notions of kinship. The Council of Trent regularized much of church law on family and marriage and ensured that the council's canons would be enforced uniformly throughout Christendom. Though there were secular monarchical attempts to whittle away at the church's power over family formation and regulation, those attempts proved minor and insignificant.

It was not until the ascendancy of King Charles III to Spain's throne in 1759 that a civil form of family law started to take shape. Charles III initiated a far-reaching set of administrative, social, political, and economic reforms, popularly known as the Bourbon reforms. One of the reforms' central objectives was to limit the power of entrenched interest groups in society, including that of the nobility, the church, and the guilds. King Charles III moved rapidly to end the church's hegemony over private life. To accomplish this, the Crown began secularizing the missions on the Spanish Borderlands, removing the Indians from ecclesiastical tutelage and letting them become private citizens. The number of missionaries funded from the king's coffers to proselytize in the borderlands was sharply reduced, and secular settlements were promoted. The amount of land owned by the church and cultivated with Indian labor was sharply reduced, and the church was ordered to pay the Indians for whatever work they performed. In the area of marriage, in 1776 a royal pragmatic was issued requiring all children, under pain of disinheritance, to obtain explicit parental permission to marry. Increasing the role of the state in setting laws for marriage reduced the prerogatives of the ecclesiastical law, and the state now asserted that the church had authority only over the sacramental aspects of marriage. All other aspects, such as consent and property, were matters of state.

The Bourbon reforms represent an attempt by King Charles III to impose the model of the absolutist monarch, with its clear lines of power, and to structure the family as a domestic monarchy ruled by the father. The state's explicit aim was to deprive the church of its power to intervene in familial matters and ultimately to subordinate the church to the state.

The result of the Bourbon reforms with regard to families in the Spanish Borderlands was quite clear. By removing missionaries and secularizing both the missions and society at large, the reforms reaffirmed the power of patriarchs as domestic lords. The authority exercised by the head of state was reproduced on a small scale in the authority of the head of the household. With the disappearance of the missionaries, too, the regulation of spiritual life increasingly fell to the community through its *cofradías* and *compadrazgo*. Though the church as a bureaucracy was, in the end, subordinated on the borderlands, its power to define the individual as both a spiritual and a natural person remained. In the long run, this was the legacy the church bequeathed to family on the Spanish Borderlands. Family represented an authority relationship, a domestic space, and blood ties, but, just as important, it represented a communal sense of membership in the body of Christ.

BIBLIOGRAPHY

Adams, Eleanor B. "The Chapel and Cofradía of Our Lady of the Light in Santa Fe." *New Mexico Historical Review* 22, no. 3 (1947):327–341.

Adams, Eleanor B., and Fray Angélico Chávez, eds. and trans. *The Missions of New Mexico, 1776: A Description by Fray Atanasio Domínguez.* Albuquerque, N.Mex., 1975.

Arrom, Silvia Marina. "Women and the Family in Mexico City, 1800–1857." Ph.D. diss., Stanford University, 1978.

Baroja, Julio Caro. *Razas, Pueblos y Linajes.* Madrid, 1957.

Casey, James, et al. *La familia en la España mediterránea (siglos XV–XIX).* Barcelona, 1987.

Covarrubias, Sebastián. *Tesoro de la Lengua Castellana o Española.* Madrid, 1611.

Dunkle, John R. "Population Change as an Element in the Historical Geography of Saint Augustine." *Florida Historical Quarterly* 37, no. 1 (1958):3–31.

Flandrin, Jean-Louis. *Families in Former Times: Kinship, Households, and Sexuality.* Cambridge, England, 1979.

Foster, George M. "Cofradía and Compadrazgo in Spain and Spanish America." *Southwestern Journal of Anthropology* 9 (1953):1–28.

———. "Godparents and Social Networks in Tzintzuntzan." *Southwestern Journal of Anthropology* 25 (1969):261–278.

Griswold del Castillo, Richard. *La Familia: Chicano Families in the Urban Southwest, 1848 to the Present.* Notre Dame, Ind., 1984.

Gudeman, Stephen. "The Compadrazgo as a Reflection of the Natural and Spiritual Person." *Proceedings of the Royal Anthropological Institute of Great Britain and Ireland* (1971):45–72.

Gudeman, Stephen, and Stuart B. Schwartz. "Baptismal Godparents in Slavery: Cleansing Original Sin in Eighteenth Century Bahia." In *Kinship Ideology and Practice in Latin America,* edited by Raymond T. Smith. Chapel Hill, N.C., 1984.

Gutiérrez, Ramón A. "From Honor to Love: Transformation of the Meaning of Sexuality in Colonial New Mexico." In *Kinship Ideology and Practice in Latin America,* edited by Raymond T. Smith. Chapel Hill, N.C., 1984.

———. "Honor Ideology, Marriage Negotiation, and Class-Gender Domination in New Mexico, 1690–1846." *Latin American Perspectives* 44 (Winter 1985):81–104.

———. *When Jesus Came, the Corn Mothers Went Away: Marriage, Sexuality, and Power in New Mexico, 1500–1846.* Stanford, Calif., 1991.

Herlihy, David. "Family." *American Historical Review* 96, no. 4 (1991):2–35.

Laslett, Barbara. "Household Structure on an American Frontier: Los Angeles, California in 1850." *American Journal of Sociology* 81, no. 1 (July 1975):109–128.

———. "Social Change and the Family: Los Angeles, California, 1850–1870." *American Sociological Review* 42, no. 2 (April 1977):268–291.

Mintz, Sidney, and Eric R. Wolf. "An Analysis of Ritual Co-parenthood (Compadrazgo)." *Southwestern Journal of Anthropology* 6 (1950):341–368.

Ots Capdequí, J. M. *El Estado Español en las Indias.* Mexico City, 1941.

Real Academia Española. *Diccionario de la Lengua Castellana.* Madrid, 1732.

———. *Diccionario de la Lengua Española.* Madrid, 1984.

Siebert, Wilbur H. "Slavery in East Florida, 1776 to 1785." *Florida Historical Quarterly* 10, no. 3 (1932):139–161.

Smith, Raymond T. *Kinship Ideology and Practice in Latin America.* Chapel Hill, N.C., 1984.

Tjarks, Alicia V. "Comparative Demographic Analysis of Texas, 1777–1793." *Southwestern Historical Quarterly* 77, no. 3 (January 1974):291–338.

———. "The Demographic, Ethnic and Occupational Structure of New Mexico, 1790." *The Americas* 35, no. 1 (July 1978):45–88.

Von Wuthenau, A. "The Spanish Military Chapels in Santa Fe and the Reredos of Our Lady of the Light." *New Mexico Historical Review* 10, no. 3 (1935):175–194.

Weigle, Marta. *Brothers of Light, Brothers of Blood: The Penitentes of the Southwest.* Albuquerque, N.Mex., 1976.

Ramón A. Gutiérrez

SEE ALSO **African-American Culture; Gender Relations;** and **Home and Hearth.**

SEXUAL MORES AND BEHAVIOR

THE BRITISH COLONIES

THE BEDCHAMBER is the least accessible room in the house of history. This is particularly true of the American colonial period. We can get a sense of "official" mores from sermons, advice books, and other elite pronouncements, but it is much harder to uncover what ordinary people thought about sex. As to their sexual behavior, we must rely mainly on the questionable generalizations of outside observers and people in authority, or what came to light in court cases. Judging sexual behavior via the misbehavers is a risky business. Even arriving at rates of misbehavior is obscured by the loss of many records.

There are breaks in this dense cloud covering the sexual landscape of the thirteen colonies, however. Some intimate letters, diaries, and spiritual and secular autobiographies have survived. The testimonies of random witnesses in court cases unconsciously reveal popular sexual mores. Demographers have proved highly inventive in extrapolating from surviving statistics and in projecting back from better-documented periods.

This article first explores the shared sexual mores imported from England that had been conditioned by the values of the European Reformation, before describing early colonial regional variations in morals and behavior, concentrating on New England and the Chesapeake. We then examine changes in the century before Independence caused by fresh waves of immigration, the formation of new colonies, and the maturation of older societies.

THE SHARED ANGLO-EUROPEAN PROTESTANT TRADITION

The sixteenth-century European Reformation caused some major changes in sexual mores and behavior. As a result of breaches with Rome, clergy were allowed to marry, monasteries were dissolved, and sexual sins were reevaluated. Fornication was no longer a mere venial sin; it was now considered mortal, "a sin which shutts [offenders] out of the Kingdome of Heaven." Sodomy became a capital offence in England in 1533. The formal interventionist power of the priesthood, through confession for instance, gave way to the Protestant idea of the priesthood of all believers, with its emphasis on individual responsibility, and to the spiritualization of the household—the undiluted religious and moral authority of the Protestant patriarch within each nuclear family. In general, the Reformation claimed to reinstate the sexual continence and purity that Saint Paul had demanded among early Christians.

Although the Counter-Reformation had succeeded in eliminating the worst decadence from the Roman church, this did not deter Protestant propagandists from waging a prurient hate campaign. Many of their followers were convinced that those popes, cardinals, bishops, priests, and friars who were not insatiable fornicators and adulterers were sodomites and pederasts. Monasteries and convents, they believed, were sinks of sexual promiscuity and perversity. This mudslinging emphasized the newfound respectability of Protestantism and especially of its most stridently anti-Catholic wing, Calvinist puritanism.

English immigrants to North America in the first three-quarters of the seventeenth century shared many similar values about sex. They accepted that sexual activity outside marriage was sinful, that marriage should be delayed—often for a decade or more after puberty—until the couple could be economically self-sufficient, that regular coition within marriage was essential, and that society had a right and obligation to regulate what would today be regarded as private relationships. They were generally agreed that the first line of such control of individual passions and desires was the household. Young people should always be "under family government," never "single livers."

If parents or masters and mistresses proved ineffective, then it was normal for the community to step in, either with semiformal warnings followed by formal presentment and prosecution or with informal deterrents like gossip, slander, or physical shaming. The emigrants from England also concurred that if a pregnancy occurred, culpability was lessened by marriage. If a man denied paternity, the mother's word during the agony of labor was believed, and her nominee must support the child. Most people, though not squeamish, valued modesty. There was also a general revulsion against sexual violence, bestiality, homosexuality, and infanticide, all capital offenses under English law. Both shaming punishments—standing before a congregation in a white sheet with the offense written on a paper hat, or on the gallows in a halter—and corporal punishments were commonly used, along with fines for those who could afford them. These reflected the perceived seriousness of offenses. Ten to fifteen stripes or forty to fifty

shillings were the norms for fornication. Thirty-nine stripes or as much as twenty pounds were the penalties for adultery, sexual violence, and prostitution. Penalties in different colonies tended to become more similar over time.

A hazardous import from England was ignorance or misinformation about sex. Judging from such popular works as *Aristotle's Masterpiece* (1684) or *Aristotle's Problems* (1595), which were well-known in the colonies, it was generally believed that sperm originated in the spinal cord, that men could mate with animals, that copulation during menstruation produced monsters, and that women as well as men produced seed. Common treatments for syphilis included the prescription for a sufferer to sleep as soon and as often as possible with a "sound woman." Some abortifacients and aphrodisiacs were similarly dangerous. Conception was regarded as impossible without mutual orgasm.

Historians are deeply divided over what may have been the prevailing attitudes toward intimate marital relations. Some have argued that couples and particularly their parents were more concerned about the economics of marriage and "the corporate merger of two families" than physical attraction or emotional suitability, that spouses treated each other coolly, and that sex was essentially patriarchal gratification on demand. According to Lawrence Stone, a peasant might well grieve more over the death of a cow than the death of a wife. Other critics regard this view as altogether too bleak. While recognizing the widespread beliefs that "there belongeth more to marriage than two payre of bare leggs in a bedd" and that enslavement to passion and desire was generally distrusted, these historians affirm that romantic love and tenderness coexisted with financial considerations, that erotic accomplishment was valued, and that women were understood to have authentic sexual needs. The "mutual comfort" of the marriage service was, according to this school of thought, physical and emotional as well as material.

EARLY COLONIAL CONTRASTS

Some attitudes, misconceptions, and prejudices were common to most early immigrants. But marked differences in sexual mores and behavior between colonies also arose, from the dissimilar demographic, economic, and interracial conditions and from the dominance of Puritanism in New England.

Virginia had from the first been dedicated to agricultural profit-making and attracted a few adventurers with capital and many with fortunes to make. For much of the seventeenth century its population, and that of its sister Maryland, reflected these factors. The environment took a frightful toll on its settlers. Nearly 90 percent of the immigrants arrived as poor indentured servants pledged to work off their passages in the tobacco fields. A huge gender imbalance existed among these marginal, ill-nourished arrivals: six males to every female in the early days, and still two and a half to one in the last third of the seventeenth century. The death rate from disease among the thousands who poured in reached 80 percent in the first generation. Even by 1700 adult-male life expectancy was only in the mid forties.

Indentured servants had to stay single; most men on the tobacco coast had to wait until their mid or late twenties before they were free to marry. Some, like the one out of every four decedents in Maryland, never had the chance. Women servants married younger, around age twenty-three. Such was the demand that suitors would redeem women servants' unserved time and "still think they had a good bargain." Native-born women married very early—the mean age in Somerset County, Maryland, between 1648 and 1669 was 16.5 years—and married often, if they survived. Such serial marriages helped offset the chronic shortage of women.

The infrastructure of the young tobacco colonies was rudimentary. There were few clergy and no church courts, the traditional English seats of moral and sexual discipline. Family life was ruptured with frequent deaths. In one typical Virginian county, one or both parents had died before half the children reached age thirteen. Community and extended family networks of advice, example, and control were therefore brittle or nonexistent. Premature adulthood and the need to look to one's own survival made privatism a way of life in the ill-supervised Chesapeake counties.

The comparison with Massachusetts is dramatic. There, and in most of New England, emigration was a single-surge peopling of the wilderness with extended kinship networks and a strong chain of command among these "middling sort" of people. Sex ratios were nearly balanced by the 1650s thanks to burgeoning natural increase. Large numbers of clergy arrived during the 1630s to organize churches, and an effective and respected magistracy supervised colonial mores from the start. Many of the founders proved long-lived—one-sixth of East Anglian men lived into their eighties. Social cohesion, family discipline, and community control were far more possible in such an environment.

Puritanism in New England made the contrast with the Chesapeake starker. Shaking the filth of a decadent and godforsaken mother country from their feet, these utopian refugees set about creating a Puritan Zion. They suppressed English folk festivals like Mayday, midsummer day, and the twelve days of Christmas, notorious for their sexual excesses among young people. Marriage ceased to be a sacrament and became a civil contract assented to before a magistrate. Divorce with remarriage became a hard-earned possibility. High standards of sexual morality were demanded. The death penalty was introduced in 1631 for adultery. Couples guilty of extramarital sex could be ordered to marry and baptism was denied premaritally conceived infants unless their parents showed genuine contrition. Young women could not be courted without parental permission, but parents could not unreasonably delay marriages. The "discipline of the senses" led to a general rigor against moral "pollutions." "Holy Watchfulness" was required of friends and neighbors because it was a God-provoking sin to condone or permit sin in others.

Were the Puritans of New England sexually repressive? Some scholars cite the adolescent and adult sexual guilt of Cotton Mather, Michael Wigglesworth, and humbler spiritual autobiographers like John Dane. Such people, indoctrinated since infancy with Puritan dogma, thought of the physical as polluting and vile; they must journey on an introspective "pilgrimage through the deceits of the heart" before achieving spiritual rebirth. As they fought their "anguished battle with desire" they suffered the "horrors of an enflamed conscience": depression, self-hatred, anorexia, even suicide. Wigglesworth sought divine forgiveness for "intemperate use of the marriage bed," and Edward Taylor wrote poetic meditations depicting himself as a feminized bride of Christ.

Other scholars, however, doubt the typicality of such self-flagellation. The identification of sex with dirt was biblical quotation rather than Puritan invention. John Winthrop, Thomas Hooker, Anne Bradstreet, even Cotton Mather in a more confident mood and Michael Wigglesworth after his second marriage, celebrated the pleasures of married sexual relations and sympathized with the pull of romantic attachments. They loved their partners in the full sense. Failure or refusal to satisfy a spouse's sexual needs was recognized grounds for divorce in New England. Many offspring of elite parents (Cressy Mather, John Cotton, Jr., or John Elliott III, for instance) were convicted of sexual misdemeanors, suggesting furthermore that injunctions against permissive parenting were preached rather than practiced. Puritan youth might acknowledge parental forms, but their culture was independent, sexually curious, and erotically experimental. The twenty-six social "companies" of young people in Middlesex County, Massachusetts, during the 1660s enjoyed an autonomy far from repressed.

The differences in the moral climates and social controls of the Chesapeake and New England are mirrored in their records of sexual behavior. Indeed, the fact that there are many more surviving, well-entered records in the northern colonies symbolizes the closer supervision and tighter discipline there. Reasons for prosecuting sexual offenses also differed. In the Puritan colonies, fornication was treated as a moral outrage, even when couples subsequently married. In the Chesapeake, however, loss of a pregnant and nursing woman's services and the avoidance of public support for bastards were higher priorities. New England officials were adept at issuing warnings and preventative orders to couples at risk. Husbands who arrived in northern colonies without their wives were required to reunite with all convenient speed. Temptations like mixed dancing, provocative dressing, and night rendezvouses were condemned by preachers and forbidden by law. In the South, few premarital fornicators were indicted. There was similarly no apparent concern there about masturbation, which, given the sex

ratio, was probably common for men. In New England, however, preachers inveighed against this "trick of youth" as detestable. In the early plantation of New Haven, male mutual masturbation was made a capital offense.

Statistical comparisons are fraught with problems, but certain differences and developments are clear. Extramarital sex was extremely uncommon in early New England, but slowly increased by the end of the seventeenth century. The incidence rate in Essex County, Massachusetts, in 1640 was 2.7 per thousand people per decade. This had risen in the 1670s to 9.8. Nonetheless it remained a great deal lower than either England or the southern colonies.

Pregnant brides as much as unwed mothers had been guilty of extramarital sex, but they had been able to persuade the child's father (or occasionally another man) to marry them. Indeed, he had probably made some sort of promise before cajoling her to "have to do" or "commit folly" or "have fellowship" or "do the act" with him, as contemporary euphemisms described coitus. The subsequent marriages were usually of the shotgun variety, rather than pregnancy resulting from betrothal license. In seventeenth-century England, one out of five brides arrived at the altar expecting her first child. Though marriage ages were often seven or eight years younger in Maryland, the same fraction of native-born brides had already conceived there. One out of three former servant women in Maryland was pregnant before marriage, as were as many as two out of three in some Virginia counties. The one southern exception to this widespread sexual indiscipline was that of unmarried women whose fathers had survived and could supervise their courtship.

Figures for New England derived from court convictions, church confessions, or family reconstitution paint a very different picture. In Middlesex County, Massachusetts, the bridal pregnancy rate derived from court convictions was 1.1 percent of all newly married couples during the 1650s. This rose to 1.7 percent in the 1690s. In more urbanized Suffolk County, Massachusetts, the premarital fornication conviction rate in the 1680s was 5 percent, similar to Essex County in the 1670s. The courts used a seven-month birth after marriage rule. First babies born within nine months of their parent's marriages (derived from family reconstitution statistics) represented 9.4 percent of firstborns in late-seventeenth-century Andover, Massachusetts.

A similar disparity can be seen in records regarding bastardy. In England between 1581 and 1630, illegitimate births represented 3 to 4 percent of all births, responding to economic fluctuations. Somerset County, Maryland, averaged a 6-percent rate of illegitimate births in 1666 and a 12-percent rate by 1694. For Middlesex County, Virginia, the rate was 14 percent in 1700. By contrast, Middlesex County, Massachusetts, averaged only .5 percent in the 1650s, a figure that rose to .9 percent in the 1690s. Suffolk County, which included the port of Boston, averaged a 1.6 percent bastardy rate during the 1680s. The high rate in the Chesapeake of illegitimate births occurred despite laws that required indentured single mothers to serve an extra two-year term and directed that masters who fathered bastards on maidservants lose their services.

Two other ways men satisfied their extramarital sexual demands were with prostitutes or with black slaves. Six New England women from ports like Boston or Charlestown in the seventeenth century were described as "bawds" or "whores," notably Alice Thomas in 1672. In Middlesex County, Massachusetts, half a dozen women who bore more than one bastard were members of what has been called the "subsociety of the bastardy-prone" identified in early-modern England. Prostitution in the rural Chesapeake was virtually unknown. William Byrd's attempts to find a whore in colonial Williamsburg as late as 1721 drew a blank. Despite some early coupling with Indian women in Virginia and John Rolfe's diplomatic marriage to Pocahontas, this "abominable mixture" quickly became too dangerous in the South.

The slave quarters were a more promising avenue of sexual conquest for white males, even though there was an official taboo against non-white sexual contacts. In 1630 Hugh Davis, a freed Virginian servant, was "soundly whipped before an assembly of Negroes and others for abusing himself to the dishonour of God and the shame of Christianity by defiling his body by lying with a Negro." This revulsion produced antimiscegenation laws in all colonies. Nonetheless white men did mate with slave women, particularly on the tobacco coast. Visitors commented on the large number of mulattoes, and Virginia needed a law in 1662 to regulate the caste of such offspring. White women also had affairs with blacks, on average one each year according to records in seventeenth-century Maryland.

There is little evidence of sexual violence in the records, though some masters probably forced their will on servants and slaves. In New England such "lascivious carriages" were rare, averaging one per decade in Hampshire County, Massachusetts, and two per decade in more densely populated Middlesex. The women threatened almost always managed to shame their assailants into retreat—suggesting they hold a finger in the fire to get a foretaste of hell or reminding them that God sees in the dark. Throughout seventeenth-century New England, six men were hanged for rape and forty-two were severely whipped for attempting rape.

Other male sexual preferences like pederasty, homosexuality, or bestiality were capital offenses, but in court were hard to prove, requiring two witnesses to specific acts. Between 1642 and 1673, of ten New Englanders accused, five were hanged for sexual contact with animals, including seventeen-year-old Thomas Granger of Plymouth whose partners allegedly included a mare, a cow, two goats, five sheep, two calves, and a turkey. A New Haven man was hanged for pederasty and two male youths and two women were indicted for same-sex liaisons. Puritan terror of "effeminacy" reinforced popular revulsion in restricting male homosexual activity. In Virginia, Richard Cornish, a sea captain, was hanged for sodomy; subsequently a few suspects were examined by justices, but no other cases came to trial.

Marital sexual relations are far more difficult to investigate given contemporary modesty or silence on the topic. Beyond the husband's duty to provide and the wife's duty to manage household and farmyard, couples were expected to be loving partners and sex was an acknowledged expression of mutuality. Compelling evidence from both regions' court records and private sources gives testimony that many unions were loving and sexually fulfilling. Some of this evidence comes from onlookers' responses to unhappy marriages, brought to the limelight by prosecutions for disorderly living, adultery, or petitions for separation, maintenance, or divorce. Again, the record is far fuller for New England, because matrimony was so much more closely supervised there. In the southern colonies, shortage of ministers meant that most people married themselves. A Virginia minister in the early eighteenth century wrote, "If no marriage was valid unless registered in the parish book, it would bastardize nine out of ten people in the country." Unions were often brief, sundered by early death; families frequently "blended" offspring from previous marriages.

Escape from unhappy relationships could be similarly informal. Adultery in Virginia was treated as leniently by the courts as was fornication. Up to 1681 only one formal separation could be recalled, on the grounds of Giles Brent's appalling cruelty. In New England, 128 divorce petitions produced 98 known divorces. Grounds were commonly desertion, adultery, bigamy, or impotence. Eighty-one petitioners were wives, thirty-five were husbands. Most of the seventeen cases of domestic discord found recorded for Middlesex County, Massachusetts, between 1649 and 1699 involved people at the bottom of the social scale. There were 134 cases of adultery and the noncapital offense of "adulterous carriages" (noncoital sex) totaled 134 throughout New England. Only four of those are known to have hanged since juries proved reluctant to convict and judges to sentence. Where details have survived, husbands or wives sought solace from sexually incompatible unions in relationships with neighbors or servants. The passion they professed for their lovers contrasted starkly with contempt or hatred for their spouses.

By the last quarter of the seventeenth century, changes were occurring in the colonies that both reduced the contrasts between New England and the Chesapeake and added new complexities to the picture of later colonial sexual mores and behavior.

THE CENTURY BEFORE INDEPENDENCE: THE NEW IMMIGRATION

The population of the early English colonies had been reasonably homogeneous. Despite English regional variations, and ideological, economic, and religious differences, the new settlers shared a common English heritage. During the period 1676–1776, waves of new immigrants flooded North America from different backgrounds. They peopled new colonies like New Jersey, Pennsylvania, the Carolinas, and Georgia, and surged into the unsettled backcountry. We briefly explore the sexual mores and behavior of three of these groups: the Quakers, the Germans, and the Scotch-Irish.

The Quakers

Like the Plymouth Pilgrims, the members of the Society of Friends who settled New Jersey and Pennsylvania beginning in the 1670s and 1680s were seeking refuge from a contaminating Old World in their new Holy Commonwealth. Their "gathering out" involved a cleansed moral and sexual discipline, encouraged by tender nurturing of the good seed over the bad, "holy conversation" over carnal talking, love over lust. Quakers regarded the nuclear family as a bastion against worldly temptation. Gender relationships were egalitarian and child-centered. Innocence was fostered within the affectionate home; young people were taught to "despise the shame" of sin, and waywardness was punished by withdrawal of love. Marriage was often delayed until the late twenties or early thirties, especially among poorer Friends, and children were encouraged to stay at home until then. Unions outside the Society were condemned. Above families stood separate monthly meetings of men and women who intrusively supervised marriage plans and disciplined members. Between 1684 and 1725 only 4 percent of disciplinary cases involved extramarital fornication.

Many early settlers in Pennsylvania were non-Quaker indentured servants. Penn's Great Law of 1682 (subsequently revised in 1700) governed the conduct of all colonists. Initially reformative in aim, it rejected capital punishment for sexual offenses but reflected a "heightened squeamishness against lust." Single masters who seduced their serving maids were forced to marry them. Adultery was harshly punished. Shame punishments were employed in early Philadelphia. In 1693 a pregnant bride had to stand for fifteen minutes by the whipping post with a placard reading "Here I stand for an example to deter all others." After 1717 laws and penalties came into line with England's.

Among Friends, though, the moral molding process, disgust at "animal passions," and the threat of disownment often produced prudery and "a mild sexlessness." The ideal married love was "pure and true" rather than erotic. Some radical Quakers encouraged marital celibacy except for procreation. By the eve of the revolution some Friends perhaps were practicing family limitation, since completed family size fell from seven children to five.

Pennsylvania's Quakers grew in number from twenty-two hundred in 1690 to thirteen thousand in 1770, and although the first generation of members had conformed to the Quakers' virtuous ideals, indiscipline among young people began to grow after 1712. By the 1730s there were fifteen cases of premarital fornication reported each year; thirty years later the number of cases annually had doubled. By the 1770s monthly meetings were dealing with eighty sexual offenses each year. Marriage to nonmembers, often by poorer Friends, became a growing concern, especially as it usually involved prior sexual relations. Acting lenient, issuing official pronouncements against a "backsliding generation," warning against flirtations and unsuitable liaisons, and spying on the young at fairs all failed to preserve the Society's reputation for exemplary sexual restraint. After 1755 a puristic group succeeded in reimposing old standards. Disownments soared; the Society turned in on itself as a tribalistic sect.

The Germans

Mennonite Germans, similar in faith to the Quakers, began arriving in Pennsylvania in 1683; they were followed by Dunkers (Seventh-day Baptists) and Schwenkfelders. Mass immigration of Germans began in 1709 and attained high annual volume after 1727. Many of these came from the Rhine Palatinate in southwest Germany and were "church" Germans, either Lutherans or Calvinistic "Reformed." By 1776 a quarter of a million Germans had settled in North America, a third of them in Pennsylvania. Later arrivals established stable communities down the Appalachian Piedmont or in northern areas like the Mohawk Valley in New York.

The sects insisted on endogamy and often their sexual beliefs were ascetic or spiritualized. The primary emotional relationship for the Pietist was with God, and sexual intercourse within marriage was solely intended to heighten God's glory by begetting more little Pietists. The Ephrata Cloisters, founded by Johan Conrad Beissel in 1730, required that men and women reside in separate living quarters. The Moravians, who settled in Bethlehem, Pennsylvania, and Salem, North Carolina, after 1742, lived in emotionally segregated "choirs" of single brothers, sisters, and married people. Carnality was suppressed and "earthly marriage" was controlled by the elders. In 1749 fifty-six individuals were wed on the same day. The major problem was a sex ratio of seven single brethren to every single woman. "Our greatest need is for a shipload of sisters," their leader wrote to Germany. After the 1770s the Moravians' religious exclusivity collapsed, and the choir system gave way to a family organization.

Church Germans were more sexually conventional. Often living on dispersed family farms, parents exercised considerable moral control over their children. In the urban village of Germantown, however, sexual discipline began to fray after the 1740s. One out of four brides among third- and fourth-generation settlers was pregnant at her shotgun wedding, though the bastardy ratio of forty-four out of more than five thousand baptisms, or less than 1 percent, was extremely low. Greater population stability after 1760 was reflected in the lowering of the marriage age for men from thirty to twenty-five and for women from twenty-five to twenty-two. Sectarian divisiveness ultimately weakened the sexual sanctions of organized religion.

The Scotch-Irish

By 1776 there were also a quarter of a million Ulstermen, or Scotch-Irish, in America, pioneering a great arc of backcountry from western Pennsylvania to the upper Savannah. In Northern Ireland, the Presbyterian church organization with its university-trained ministry had imposed a severe moral discipline through kirk sessions, which dealt with cases of sexual immorality. Access to Holy Communion was restricted by a system of issuing tokens to the visibly pure, and lack of contrition for premarital sex led to excommunication.

Where these Ulster Calvinists settled in communities, this social control could be replicated, but all too often, replication proved impossible. Social cohesion was weakened by the pioneers' "astonishing mobility," likened by William Byrd to that of the Goths and Vandals. They also lacked moral example. The first two generations faced a desperate shortage of sufficiently qualified men to serve the ministry. Those in office were too often a disgrace to their cloth, as were the presbyteries that condoned their lapses. Seven out of eighteen Old Side, or antirevivalist, ministers in 1741 had been found guilty of sexual immorality. One had been caught in bed with a prostitute and another had frequently made advances to churchwomen.

Wilderness conditions were said to induce a "coarseness and indecency" among those who lacked deep inner piety. The frontier had been identified with sexual laxity ever since Thomas Morton of Merrymount, New England, or runaways from Jamestown had "gone native" with squaws. The crudity of life "quite out of Christendom" was symbolized by the naming of two Lunenburg County, Virginia, waterways: Ticklecunt Branch and Fucking Creek. The county's historian criticizes the concomitant "negligence and immoral lives" of three short-stayed ministers along with the "relaxed private morality of the Lunenburg elite and their continuing lack of concern for public morality" in failing to present fornicators and adulterers to court. In upcountry North Carolina during the 1760s one indentured servant woman gave birth to five bastards under three different masters and two others had three mulatto offspring each. Repeated illegitimate births were commonplace.

Historians' sources for backcountry mores are usually visitors, missionaries, or officials from the east. William Byrd, surveying the North Carolina–Virginia backcountry in 1733 left disdainful descriptions of the promiscuous "Lubbers." North Carolina was a frequent haven for runaway wives "to pig lovingly together" with other men, according to one missionary. The Anglican missionary Charles Woodmason reported that in Round Camden, South Carolina, between 1766 and 1772, there lived within his cure

5 or 6,000 ignorant, mean, worthless, beggarly Irish Presbyterians, the scum of the earth and refuse of mankind. They were very poor, owing to their extreme indolence. . . . Hence their many vices—their gross licentiousness, wantonness, lasciviousness, rudeness, lewdness and profligacy. They will commit the grossest enormities before my face, and laugh at all admonition. (Richard J. Hooker, ed. *Caroline Back Country on the Eve: Journal of Charles Woodmason,* p. 60)

Such "white Indians," who often relied on hunting for subsistence, were the basis of outlaw gangs that included slaves and mulattoes on the run and "many women and girls . . . very deep in the foulest of crimes and deeds of darkness not to be mentioned." Some women had been kidnapped, "though now bold in sin and too abandoned ever to be reclaimed." By the 1760s, however, there were signs of sexual discipline in the backcountry. The vigilante Regulators of the Carolinas included among frontier undesirables whores, whom they "whipped and drove off." Respectability was on the march.

CHANGES IN EIGHTEENTH-CENTURY SEXUAL MORES AND BEHAVIOR

New arrivals had introduced complex variations to colonial morality and sexual practice. They were most influential in new colonies of the mid Atlantic and southern regions. New England was least affected by the new immigration. Other forces were nonetheless creating important changes in longer-settled areas.

As colonies matured and became more complex and socially differentiated, as imperial influence and interests became more pervasive and insistent, as prosperity raised both material expectations and (in the South) life expectancy, as religious zeal ebbed and flowed when revivals shook complacency, so changes in attitudes toward sex and sexual relationships were bound to occur. Here we examine four interconnected changes: (1) The decriminalization, privatization, and liberalization of sexual behavior in New England; (2) the stabilization and increased control of sexual relationships in the Chesapeake; (3) urbanization; (4) the effects of religious revivalism.

Liberalization in New England

The small group of men accused of sexual offenses in early Middlesex County, Massachusetts, usually confessed their sins and acknowledged their paternal responsibilities. By the 1660s, however, suspects were commonly trying to evade public admission of guilt and some unwed mothers were protecting their lovers by nominating richer candidates to support their bastards. Evidence indicates that, starting in the 1690s, some fathers were providing liberal maintenance on a private basis, but adamantly demurred from having their misdeeds paraded in court. By the 1740s, in many areas of New England, fornication was becoming effectively decriminalized for men, provided they "saved the town harmless" by maintaining their offspring—or even better, by marrying the child's mother, however tardily. In Middlesex, the percentage of fornication prosecutions in the 1740s was less than half that of the 1720s. Between 1760 and 1774, 200 out of 210 sexual prosecutions concerned bastardy and the enforcement of child support. By the end of the century, actions against mothers of illegitimate children had also disappeared from the court records. Unsupported single mothers sued for paternity payments without incurring prosecution. Similar changes were occurring in Pennsylvania after the 1740s and 1750s. The old identification of sin with crime had been broken.

Parallel to this development was the steep rise in the incidence of premarital sex, traceable from vital records and the confessions of church members. In eight Massachusetts churches, six couples confessed in the first decade of the century, thirty-six in the third, and fifty-five in the fourth. A pre-1700 New England incidence of 11.1 percent doubled in the next sixty years and rose to an annual average of 33.1 percent in the period 1760–1799. In 1740 one out of every five Concord, Massachusetts, brides was pregnant; by 1800 it was two out of five. In Hingham, nearly half of the lower orders in the community were pregnant at marriage. In revolutionary Maine the figure was as high as 38 percent. The bastardy rate seems to have remained low, however. In Middlesex it was 77 percent in 1764. Families and communities were failing or refusing to enforce sexual discipline on the unmarried, especially the less affluent. This increased adolescent sexual autonomy, though most marked in New England, was also occurring in other colonies, in England, and in western Europe.

To one scholar, this "will to be free" manifesting in premarital sex is part of a whole process of urbanization, industrialization, and modernization, a new expression of sexual love superseding a largely unemotional, physical satisfaction. The issue is hotly debated: other scholars point to intergenerational discontinuities arising from greater geographical mobility, especially to towns, land hunger, and the dispersal of communities. Some contemporary and modern observers have argued that economic fluctuations hold the key, with prosperity enhancing marriage prospects and loosening premarital inhibitions.

Stabilization of the Chesapeake

The ill-controlled sexual standards of tobacco colonies underwent considerable changes in the eighteenth century. In Middlesex County, Virginia, for instance, forty women were convicted for bearing bastards between 1680 and 1720; in the following thirty years, despite rising population, the number had declined to nine. Although the amount of sexual activity among the unmarried probably increased, unplanned pregnancy was now more often followed by marriage.

Demographic changes played a major part in this greater sense of responsibility. A modest decline in the death rate and a sharp fall in white immigrant indentured servants led to a population able to reproduce itself by the 1690s. As a result, Chesapeake gender ratios came closer to being balanced by 1710. The century before Independence saw a thickening of social networks. After thirty years of settlement nearly half the families of Middlesex County, Virginia, in 1687 had local kin or affinal ties. Two out of three families in revolutionary Middlesex went back to 1706. Tidewater society was becoming more stratified, with elite families imposing their sexual standards on the subordinate social classes.

Survival, gender balance, and residential stability all conspired to enforce greater supervision on unwed whites. The average marriage in one southern Maryland county doubled in duration to twenty-two years, with nonelite couples as the main beneficiaries of greater life expectancy. Parents were surviving to watch over their adolescent offspring, daughters especially, who now stayed home longer and married later. Kin or neighbors could now buttress or replace this supervision. Community control actually increased in the tidewater region in contrast with New England decline.

These changes should not be exaggerated. When the newly appointed Anglican commissary James Blair in 1690 proposed to "revive and put into execution the ecclesiastical laws against . . . whoremongers, fornicators and adulterers" he was stalled by opposition in the House of Burgesses. The established church was insufficiently and ineffectively staffed to enforce a crackdown on sexual liberty. Twelve out of fifty-five benefices were vacant in 1724, parishes were still often twenty-miles (32-kilometers) long, and clerical quality was uninspiring or worse. The year 1718 saw the beginnings of convict transportation, mainly to the Chesapeake. This collection of some twenty thousand "filth and scum," "prostitutes," and "shameless creatures" did nothing to improve moral standards. Masculinity in Virginia was often measured by aggressive virility and social belligerence. Sexual restraint depended on the inhibiting influence of female virtue.

Urbanization

Benjamin Franklin's first business partner, Hugh Meredith, wrote of his moral degeneration in 1720s Philadelphia: "I was bred a farmer and it was folly in me to come to town . . . to learn a new trade." Larger towns, and especially seaports, are notorious for attracting vice and ensnaring the young. Even in seventeenth-century Middlesex County, Massachusetts, the main port, Charlestown, had cornered the lion's share of sexual crimes, thanks to its mixture of grass-widows (wives of seamen absent at sea) and footloose mariners from elsewhere idling in port. Even in New England, urban vice gradually became organized and commercialized. In 1713 Cotton Mather recorded of his native Boston, "I am informed of several houses in this town where there are young women of a very debauched character . . . unto whom there is a great resort of young men." In the century

before Independence, the Royal Navy and the army added periodically their contingents of ever-eager customers. Between 1693 and 1769 more than one-fourth of all sex crimes to reach the Massachusetts assizes were from Boston's Suffolk County. In 1771 an outraged mob "routed the whores" plying for trade in the city's Whitehall. Just down the coast, Newport, Rhode Island, had a famously discreet brothel run by "the Negress Madam Juniper."

New York, a multiethnic settlement and base for privateers, quickly acquired an unsavory reputation. Already in 1655 it had a small group of prostitutes "red, white, and black" and one in every eight of its houses was a tavern; in such drinking dens, according to John Adams, "Diseases, vicious habits, bastards, and legislators are frequently begotten." Between 1696 and 1776 the city was responsible for all but twenty-six of the 193 disorderly house prosecutions in the colony. In the 1740s the platform at the Battery had become a well-known place to pick up whores. Thirty years later, Manhattan was alleged to have five hundred prostitutes with such colorful names as Quaker Fan Bambridge or Man-Of-War Nance Bradshaw. When King's College (Columbia University) was proposed in 1747, the city's bad name spurred a strong but unavailing lobby for a rural site. Antagonism seemed vindicated when it was discovered that the new gates to the college were immediately adjacent to a red-light district. Philadelphia had its "Helltown," where Quaker child-rearing could so quickly be undone. The adjacent "urban village" of Germantown betrayed many of the demoralizing features of urban life: weakened family and community cohesion, cultural, ethnic, and religious heterogeneity, mobility, poverty, and anonymity.

The only urban area in the South was Charleston, South Carolina. As a social center for the pleasure-seeking planters of the steamy low country, it catered to the double standard of the region, which prohibited divorce and expected a chaste formality among elite women while condoning widespread male promiscuity. As early as the 1730s, *The Charleston Gazette* was publishing bawdy poetry and correspondence about the sexual charms and appetites of "Ladies from Ginny." In 1754 a Scotch-Irish madam in Pinckney Street was presented for "keeping a most notorious brothel and a receptacle for lewd women." A visitor in 1773 observed "but one gentleman who professedly keeps a Negro mistress and he is very much pointed at. . . . but by the dress of the [black] girles . . . I have no doubt of their conversations with the whites, but they are carried on with more privacy." Despite all this alleged dissipation, prosecutions for fornication and bastardy before the Charleston Court of General Sessions between 1769 and 1776 were only 1.6 percent of the 597 cases tried. The privatization of sex that these figures represent was pioneered in urban areas as both their lure and their snare.

Religious Change

On the eve of the American Revolution, the great jurist William Blackstone intoned: "Christianity is part of the laws of England." In colonial America religion and sexual morality were intertwined. Personal desires and passions were inhibited not only by pragmatic considerations, but also by religiously informed conscience along with family and community legal norms and values. The responses of ordinary people to immoral invitations—"For shame!" or "God sees!" or "Devil take thee!"—demonstrate that Christian teaching deeply infused popular morality.

The revivals of the 1720s and 1730s culminating in the Great Awakening had considerable impact on sexual behavior. Despite contemporary and later denunciation of "enthusiasm" as an encouragement to sexual license, revivalism in New England and Virginia (and elsewhere) led to a revitalizing of sexual standards and a reemphasis of sexual guilt. Incidence of fornication confessions in New England church records, on the rise before the Awakening, fell sharply in its wake. Men were more liable to conversion than women in the New England revival. Newfound male moral sensitivity moved toward the reimposition of rigorous discipline and greater self-control. The fact that revivals attracted younger, unmarried people suggests that the most sexually vulnerable age-group would be inhibited by a reawakened sense of sin and self-discipline. Cedric B. Cowing concludes that "there is every reason to believe that the sexual morality of the New Lights was as good or better than that of any of their eighteenth-century rivals" and that the Awakening, rather than being

"an orgiastic interlude . . . retarded the drift to worldliness and sexual laxity," which, as we have seen, was already under way.

Of these two countercurrents—one leading toward liberalization and sexual expressiveness, the other toward "delicacy" and self-control— the second was to prove the stronger. In 1776, however, Victorian respectability was still some way off.

CONCLUSION

How much did sexual mores and behavior change in the 169 years of the Anglo-American colonial period? Claims have been made that they altered beyond recognition. Such developments as the increase in privacy and the privatization of sexual behavior, greater physical, material, and psychic security, repression giving way to greater permissiveness, the romanticization of both sexual and marital relations, the eroticization of youth, and the growing emphasis on affection and expressiveness all combined, in colonies as initially dissimilar as Virginia and Massachusetts, to produce a sexual and affective revolution.

Explorations of local records and popular culture challenge this interpretation. "Affect" always seems to have played an important part in courtship and marriage. Emotional closeness and erotic stimulation had been valued since the late Middle Ages. Early colonial repression of children and youth has been exaggerated; both normally enjoyed nurture and self-expression. Change in colonial circumstances is undeniable; a revolution in sexual behavior and morality is not.

Firm conclusions are prevented by insufficient evidence. Despite impressive research in these areas, the colonial bedchamber remains a tantalizing mystery.

BIBLIOGRAPHY

Beeman, Richard R. *The Evolution of the Southern Backcountry: A Case Study of Lunenberg County, Virginia, 1746–1832.* Philadelphia, 1984.

Bridenbaugh, Carl. *Cities in Revolt: Urban Life in America, 1743–1776.* New York, 1955.

693

Carr, Lois G., and Lorena S. Walsh. "The Planter's Wife: The Experience of White Women in Seventeenth-Century Maryland." *William and Mary Quarterly*, 3rd ser., 34, no. 4 (1977):542–571.

Cott, Nancy. "The Eighteenth-Century Family and Social Life Revealed in Massachusetts Divorce Records." *Journal of Social History* 10, no. 1 (1976):20–35.

Cowing, Cedric B. "Sex and Preaching in the Great Awakening." *American Quarterly* 20, no. 4 (1968): 624–644.

Davies, Kathleen M. " 'The Sacred Condition of Equality': How Original Were Puritan Doctrines on Marriage?" *Social History* 5, no. 4 (1977):563–580.

Flaherty, David H. "Crime and Social Control in Provincial Massachusetts." *Historical Journal* 24 (1981):339–360.

———. "Law and Morals in Early America." *Perspectives in American History* 5 (1971):201–253.

———. *Privacy in Colonial New England*. Charlottesville, Va., 1972.

Gladwin, Lee. "Tobacco and Sex: Some Factors Affecting Nonmarital Sexual Behavior in Colonial Virginia." *Journal of Social History* 12, no. 1 (1978):57–75.

Greenberg, Douglas. *Crime and Law Enforcement in the Colony of New York, 1691–1776*. Ithaca, N.Y., 1976.

Greven, Philip. *The Protestant Temperament: Patterns of Child-Rearing, Religious Experience, and the Self in Early America*. New York, 1977.

Hiner, N. Ray. "Adolescence in Eighteenth-Century America." *History of Childhood Quarterly* 3, no. 3 (1975):253–280.

Hooker, Richard J., ed. *Caroline Back Country on the Eve: Journal of Charles Woodmason*. Chapel Hill, N.C., 1953.

Isaac, Rhys. *The Transformation of Virginia, 1740–1790*. Chapel Hill, N.C., 1982.

Jordan, Winthrop D. *White over Black: American Attitudes Toward the Negro, 1550–1812*. Chapel Hill, N.C., 1968.

Koehler, Lyle. *A Search for Power: The "Weaker Sex" in Seventeenth-Century New England*. Urbana, Ill., 1980.

Kulikoff, Allan. *Tobacco and Slaves: The Development of Southern Cultures in the Chesapeake, 1680–1800*. Chapel Hill, N.C., 1986.

Leites, Edmund. *The Duty of Desire: The Puritan Conscience and Modern Sexuality*. New Haven, Conn., 1986.

Levy, Barry J. *Quakers and the American Family: British Settlement in the Delaware Valley*. New York, 1988.

Lewis, Jan. "Domestic Tranquillity and the Management of Emotion Among the Gentry of Prerevolutionary Virginia." *William and Mary Quarterly*, 3rd ser., 39, no. 2 (1982):135–149.

Lockridge, Kenneth A. *The Diary, and Life, of William Byrd II of Virginia, 1674–1744*. Chapel Hill, N.C., 1987.

Marietta, Jack D. *The Reformation of American Quakerism, 1748–1783*. Philadelphia, 1984.

Morgan, Edmund S. "The Puritans and Sex." *New England Quarterly* 15, no. 4 (1942):591–607.

Nobles, Gregory H. "Breaking into the Backcountry: New Approaches to the Early American Frontier, 1750–1800." *William and Mary Quarterly*, 3rd ser., 46, no. 4 (1989):641–670.

Oaks, Robert. " 'Things Fearful to Name': Sodomy and Buggery in Seventeenth-Century New England." *Journal of Social History* 12, no. 3 (1978): 268–281.

Parkes, Henry Bamford. "Morals and Law Enforcement in Colonial New England." *New England Quarterly* 5, no. 3 (1932):431–452.

———. "Sexual Morality and the Great Awakening." *New England Quarterly* 3, no. 3 (1930):397–419.

Rutman, Darrett B., and Anita H. Rutman. *A Place in Time: Middlesex County, Virginia, 1650–1750*. New York, 1984.

Shorter, Edward. *The Making of the Modern Family*. New York, 1975.

Smith, Daniel Blake. *Inside the Great House: Planter Family Life in Eighteenth-Century Chesapeake Society*. Ithaca, N.Y., 1980.

Smith, Daniel Scott, and Michael S. Hindus. "Premarital Pregnancy in America, 1640–1971: An Overview and Interpretation." *Journal of Interdisciplinary History* 5, no. 4 (1975):537–570.

Stone, Lawrence. *The Family, Sex, and Marriage in England, 1500–1800*. New York, 1977.

Thompson, Roger. "Attitudes Towards Homosexuality in the Seventeenth-Century New England Colonies." *Journal of American Studies* 23 (1989): 27–40.

———. *Sex in Middlesex: Popular Mores in a Massachusetts County, 1649–1699*. Amherst, Mass., 1986.

———. *Unfit for Modest Ears*. London, 1979.

Walsh, Lorena S. " 'Till Death Do Us Part': Marriage and Family in Seventeenth-Century Maryland." In *The Chesapeake in the Seventeenth Century: Essays on Anglo-American Society*, edited by Thad W. Tate and David L. Ammerman. Chapel Hill, N.C., 1979.

Wolf, Stephanie Grauman. *Urban Village: Population, Community, and Family Structure in Germantown, Pennsylvania, 1683–1800*. Princeton, N.J., 1976.

Zuckerman, Michael. "William Byrd's Family." *Perspectives in American History* 12 (1979):255–311.

Roger Thompson

SEE ALSO **African-American Culture; Civil Law; Crime and Law Enforcement; and Gender Relations.**

694

THE DUTCH COLONY

Sᴇxᴜᴀʟ ᴍᴏʀᴇs in the seventeenth-century Netherlands were shaped by regional folkways, Catholic and Calvinist teachings, and Dutch familial ethos. Local tradition and Christian doctrine inspired laws punishing sexual relations outside of marriage; the punishment depended not only upon the offense itself but also upon the jurisdiction in which it occurred. Prostitution was everywhere deplored and illegal, but prostitutes were generally tolerated in Amsterdam and in other Dutch cities, despite sporadic arrests and prosecutions. Homosexuality, although classified by the Dutch as "the unnatural vice" and made punishable by death, was only occasionally prosecuted in the seventeenth century. Young lovers caught fornicating were expected to marry; if the girl became pregnant, both law and custom almost always dictated marriage.

The most popular Dutch poet and moralist, Jacob Cats (affectionately called "Father" Cats), a Calvinist, praised the joys of marital sex. The Dutch generally accepted that view, though a few Calvinist commentators cautioned husbands and wives lest their passion for one another degenerate into lust and desecrate the marriage bed itself! Sexual desire led naturally to marriage, Father Cats was pleased to note, and with marriage came children, the nurturing of whom was the primary purpose of the family. Cats endorsed sexual intercourse for pleasure as well as for procreation, emphasizing that the resulting physical and emotional intimacy deepened the bonds between husband and wife, thereby strengthening the family. In fact, marriage manuals discussing sexual relations circulated widely among rich and poor alike. Of course, Dutch cultural norms strongly condemned premarital and especially extramarital sex. Dutch writers and artists reiterated the theme that illicit sexual behavior dangerously jeopardized cherished domestic relationships.

Dutch parents usually accorded their daughters considerable freedom both in dating and in choosing a mate, much to the surprise and censure of most foreign observers. The courting practice known as "bundling" (sharing one bed while fully dressed) in England was especially well established in north Holland. Dutch couples certainly had the opportunity for premarital sex, but the extent to which they took advantage of it is not clear. In parts of Gelderland, the prenuptial conception rate was almost 15 percent in the seventeenth century, and it neared 20 percent in south Holland in the eighteenth century. However, baptismal records indicate that the illegitimacy rate was relatively low among the Dutch, about 1 percent of births, far below the European average for bastardy in the seventeenth century. Therefore, whatever the incidence of sex before marriage, the Dutch took their parental responsibility quite seriously, and they were overwhelmingly monogamous. Foreign observers bore witness to the legendary fidelity of Dutch wives. Although the double standard existed in the Netherlands, Dutch males were constantly reminded in print and in paintings of their duty as husbands and fathers.

REGULATING MORES IN NEW NETHERLAND

The Dutch brought their sexual mores with them to New Netherland, where the shortage of women worked against confining carnal passions to marriage. For at least twenty years after settlement began in 1624, New Netherland was populated primarily by young, unmarried males, whose amorous exploits among complaisant Indian maids, servant girls, and other men's wives scandalized the preachers, Patroon Kiliaen Van Rensselaer, and officials of the Dutch West India Company (WIC). During these early years in particular, the fur trade was accompanied by considerable socializing between New Netherland men and Indian women. Iroquois, Delaware, and Mahican society, organized along matrilineal lines, allowed both young men and young women considerable sexual freedom. Indian cultural norms aside, laws against adultery and fornication simply were not well enforced. A New Netherland official reported in 1628 that the English of Plymouth "speak very angrily when they hear from the savages that we live so barbarously in these respects, and without punishment."

Enforcement did improve, and court records of the 1630s are sprinkled with cases concerning illegitimate children, breach of promise, adultery, and even prostitution. By the late 1640s, increased immigration began to correct the sexual balance and favored domesticity in New Netherland. Director-General Peter Stuyvesant encouraged this trend toward family formation in many ways, including the diligent pursuit of the paternity of children born to unwed mothers. Most of the latter were young servant girls, some of whom were no doubt victimized by older men, though others were likely motivated by love or by the desire to escape servitude by marrying. The magistrates usually ordered unmarried offenders to wed, unless the social distance between the two was too great. In that case, as in the Netherlands, the father might escape marriage by making some monetary provision for both the child and the mother.

Under Stuyvesant, Dutch sexual mores increasingly prevailed in New Netherland and were enforced by law. The frontier practice of couples living together, sometimes even having children, without benefit of clergy profoundly disturbed the Dutch dominies and the director-general. Stuyvesant's efforts at encouraging wedlock culminated in 1658 with the promulgation of an ordinance reiterating the illegality and sinfulness of cohabitation before marriage. The law required couples not to delay the wedding once their banns were proclaimed.

In terms of bastardy and premarital conception, Alice Kenney found that the Albany Dutch in the late seventeenth century replicated Dutch cultural norms. Very few illegitimate children were baptized in the Reformed church of Albany, far fewer than the 1 percent estimated for Holland, though the baptismal records are not conclusive. Infants born to the Albany Dutch within eight months of marriage numbered about 28 percent. This figure suggests a somewhat higher rate of premarital pregnancies than prevailed in the Netherlands, though much the same commitment to family relations obviously prevailed.

Stuyvesant did not eliminate prostitution in New Amsterdam, but repeat offenders were banished, and fornicators were regularly fined, banished, or ordered to marry. Of three men charged with sodomizing young boys between 1646 and 1664, two—one of whom was a repeat offender—were sentenced to particularly gruesome deaths. One was ordered publicly choked and his body burned to ashes, and the other

was tied in a sack and drowned in the river.

Court records kept over the course of New Netherland's forty-year history, particularly from the 1630s on, reveal relatively few charges of rape or sexual assault. However, sexual innuendo was the most common cause of slander suits, and no one was exempt from such malicious gossip, not even the director-general himself or the preacher's wife. Many arguments over debt ended with one party accusing the other's wife of being a whore. The marital fidelity of husbands as well as wives was often questioned. In fact, sexual gossip was rife, with women participating as fully as men. Sometimes there was substance to the charge of lascivious conduct.

Reformed dominies and local magistrates worked closely to expose and prosecute adulterous affairs. The most notorious involved Laurens Duyts, a farmer from Holstein, convicted in 1658 for adultery and for selling his wife into adultery. Duyts was sentenced "to have a rope tied around his neck, and then to be severely flogged, to have his right ear cut off, and to be banished for 50 years." Adultery was the primary grounds for divorce under Roman-Dutch law, and at least two divorces were granted in New Netherland, both to men whose wives were deemed guilty of extramarital sexual relations.

Regardless of their race, status, or nationality, settlers living under the jurisdiction of the WIC were expected to conform to its ordinances. Among black New Netherlanders, heterosexual relations were limited not only by the imperatives of slavery but also by the chronic shortage of women. The high sex ratio of men to women improved among blacks in the 1650s, however, much as it did for the whites of New Netherland. What evidence there is indicates that marriage relationships were sought after and prized by both slaves and free blacks. One of the two men executed for sodomy was black. Despite the general shortage of black females, there is no evidence that homosexuality was more prevalent among blacks than among whites.

As for the English in the chartered villages on western Long Island, sexual conduct was regulated by their own town courts, whose records are especially slight before the late seventeenth century. Like the Dutch, the English settlers prohibited and punished sexual relations outside of marriage. Like their cousins in the towns on eastern Long Island and in New England, they limited the freedom of young women far more than their Dutch neighbors did. However, their opposition to New England orthodoxy had led them to New Netherland, reducing their dependence on the Puritan communalism that shaped New England culture, including its sexual mores.

The greatest challenge to both Dutch and English sexual mores in New Netherland came from the Indians. Among the Mahican, Iroquois, and Delaware, premarital sex was regarded as natural. After marriage, Mahican and Iroquois custom permitted either spouse to dissolve the marriage simply by choosing another mate. The Delaware allowed polygamy but strongly condemned adultery, unless one's spouse approved of the liaison. During the early decades of settlement, sexual relations between male colonists and Indian women were fairly common, despite official efforts to discourage the practice. However, as the sex ratio among the settlers became more balanced, sexual relations between the settlers and Indians was no longer viewed as a problem. Nevertheless, Dutch Reformed dominies and English preachers alike recited the Indians' casual sexual habits to warn against the barbarous influence of the American wilderness.

BIBLIOGRAPHY

Gehring, Charles T., ed. and trans. *Fort Orange Court Minutes, 1652–1660.* Syracuse, N.Y., 1990.

Kenney, Alice. "Patricians and Plebians in Colonial Albany, Part II; Aggregations." *De Halve Maen* 45, no. 2 (1970):9–11, 13.

O'Callaghan, Edmund B. *Calendar of Dutch Historical Manuscripts in the Office of the Secretary of State, Albany, New York, 1630–1664.* Albany, N.Y., 1865; repr. Ridgewood, N.J., 1968.

Schama, Simon. *The Embarrassment of Riches: An Interpretation of Dutch Culture in the Golden Age.* New York, 1987.

Singleton, Esther. *Dutch New York.* New York, 1909; repr. 1968.

Sturtevant, William C., gen. ed. *Handbook of North American Indians.* 20 vols. Washington, D.C., 1978. See Vol. 15, *Northeast,* edited by Bruce G. Trigger.

Van Deursen, Arie Theodorus. *Plain Lives in a Golden Age: Popular Culture, Religion and Society in Seventeenth-Century Holland.* Cambridge, Mass., 1991.

Van Laer, Arnold J. F., trans. *New York Historical Manuscripts: Dutch,* edited by Kenneth Scott and Ken Styker-Rodda. 4 vols. Baltimore, Md., 1972.

Ronald William Howard

SEE ALSO **African-American Culture; Civil Law; Crime and Law Enforcement;** and **Gender Relations.**

THE FRENCH COLONIES

IN THE MID SEVENTEENTH century the French settlers in Canada were people of strict, puritanical, and prudish morals. However the authorities, clerical and secular, soon had cause to be concerned. The immigrants who subsequently arrived proved to be a mixed lot, some of them swept up off the streets of Paris and La Rochelle. To make matters worse, until the second decade of the eighteenth century, there was a serious imbalance of the sexes, far more men than women. Thus the women could pick and choose a husband, while only one man in six or seven could hope to marry.

MORAL OFFENSES IN CANADA

In 1672 Governor General Louis de Buade de Frontenac pleaded with the minister of marine to have more women sent to the colony because the sexual imbalance was producing serious moral disorders: some women had taken more than one husband. Twelve years later Intendant Jacques de Meulles complained that the six girls sent to the colony that year had proven to be La Rochelle streetwalkers, whom he would have liked to ship back to France, but, he added, they would be easy to marry off. This case was the exception, not the rule. The vast majority of women sent to Canada in the great wave of emigration in the decade of the 1670s were very straitlaced. Indeed the records of the court at Montreal for the period 1664–1760 reveal that moral crimes brought before that court represented less than 1 percent of the cases heard.

The first mention of anything akin to prostitution occurred in 1675 when the Conseil Souverain (Sovereign Council) at Quebec received complaints that loose women were flooding into the town from the surrounding parishes to prostitute themselves when the annual ships arrived from France. From the court's records it is clear that most of these women had husbands away in the west with the fur brigade. They appear to have pined for a little male company, and what better than a sailor ashore after a two-month voyage. These women were not prostitutes, merely enthusiastic amateurs, but the Conseil Souverain would have none of it. Two of them were arrested, fined, and banished from the town; all others of the same ilk were ordered to take themselves off or feel the sting of the lash.

In 1686 Governor General Jacques-René Brisay de Denonville noted that there were a few prostitutes in the colony. He and Intendant Jean Bochart de Champigny proposed to ship them to France, but the minister of marine vetoed the proposal. He ordered that they be put to hard labor, hauling water from the river to upper town Quebec and sawing wood in plain view of the townsfolk. The work and public shame would, he hoped, induce them to mend their ways. In the eighteenth century there is hardly a mention of prostitutes in the public records. Most likely the authorities and the people at large chose to ignore the matter; yet the most common insult offered women of the lower class was *putain* (whore).

Seduction was quite another affair, far from uncommon, and for every case that came to public attention there must have been scores that were kept under wraps. It has been reliably estimated that 8 percent of Canadian children were conceived out of wedlock by parents who subsequently married. From time to time irate fathers went to court to demand redress of grievance, upon finding their daughters pregnant. The usual demand was that the seducer be compelled to provide for the support of the mother and her child, and the courts invariably complied. Members of the nobility and higher bourgeoisie very rarely made public the disgrace their families had suffered, for disgrace it most certainly was. Usually such families made their own quiet arrangements when it was discovered that a daughter had been indiscreet.

What is significant is that women of all classes made every effort to conceal their shame,

even going so far as to risk an appointment with the *maître des hautes oeuvres* (hangman). There were four possible solutions to the problem of babies born, or about to be born, on the wrong side of the blanket: have an abortion, commit infanticide, deposit the baby wrapped in swaddling clothes on the church steps or at the door of a wealthy family, or give it to the Indians, who cherished all children no matter whence they came. This last practice must have been all too common, since one intendant issued an *ordonnance* forbidding it. Abortion was regarded as a heinous crime, and all found guilty of it went swiftly to the scaffold. Infanticide was dealt with in like manner. During the French regime seven women were charged with the crime, three of them found guilty and hanged.

Abandoned babies became wards of the Crown (*enfants du Roi*). Upon their discovery they were taken in charge by the Crown prosecutor, who gave them over to a wet nurse, paid by the Crown. At eighteen months they were given into the care of honest families, who virtually adopted them, being held responsible for their well-being until the age of eighteen. The steady increase in the number of foundlings as the eighteenth century wore on is an indication of the decline in moral standards in the colony, mirroring the conditions in France and England.

Adultery was regarded as a very serious offense by both the church and the Crown. When a cuckolded husband dispatched his wife's lover summarily to the next world, he could expect to receive sympathetic treatment by the judges of the Conseil Superieur (Superior Council). They usually rendered the requisite death sentence and then sent the case to the king with a strong recommendation that the condemned man be granted a letter of remission and a pardon, which were always forthcoming.

Given that the age of majority was twenty-five, and that men had to have their parents' consent to marry before they were thirty, some impatient couples sought to get around the impediment by the custom of *marriage à la gaumine* whereby while attending mass, in the presence of the Holy Sacrament, the congregation, and two witnesses, they would stand and declare their vows just as they would have done in a regular marriage ceremony. From that point on they conducted themselves as man and wife. The practice was named after a certain man called

Gaumin who initiated the custom in the late sixteenth century. Both the church and the Crown strove to stamp out the custom, and the last known instance of the practice appears to be dated January 1789.

Illicit liaisons between Canadians and Indian women within the central colony appear to have been rare. In the seventeenth century several Canadian men took Indian women to wife, some of them prominent members of society, but a Canadian woman who took an Indian for husband was scorned. In the far west, the *pays d'en haut* (upper country), the Canadian fur traders there for an extended period took Indian girls as wives, according to the custom of the country, for the duration of their stay. The custom came to be known as "savoring the wine of the country."

Within the Canadian settlements there were some cases of rape that appeared before the courts, and the punishment varied according to circumstances. In many instances the guilty man was ordered to pay compensation to the victim's family, and were she to prove to be pregnant, he had to make provision for her and the child until it was able to support itself. In some cases the sentence was far more severe, again depending on circumstances: the galleys for life or the hangman's rope. The rape of a child always led swiftly to the gallows.

Only three cases of sexual perversion have come to light. In 1648 a soldier drummer was tried and sentenced to death for this sordid crime but the sentence was commuted upon his agreeing to accept the post of hangman, which meant that he would be reviled by all and sundry for ever after. In 1691 Nicholas Daussy de St. Michel, Intendant Champigny, informed the minister that Lieutenant le Sieur de Saint-Michel, accused of having committed several "infames et houteuses" (foul, sordid, filthy acts) with young soldiers in his company, had been tried by the Conseil Souverain and ordered banished in perpetuity from Canada. Ironically, some eight years later that same intendant had to account to the minister on reports that some members of his household were leading scandalous lives. Champigny replied that some years earlier his *maître d'hôtel* had formed a "vicious relationship" with one of the valets. He had promptly discharged the valet and ordered the *maître d'hôtel* to mend his ways or else begone.

There were several cases of bigamy, and likely far more than ever came to the attention of the authorities. Frenchmen whose wives remained in France immigrated to the colonies and there acquired new wives.

LOUISIANA: MISCEGENATION

In Louisiana during the early years there was an acute woman shortage, and hence liaisons with Indian women became the order of the day. The practice was particularly prevalent in the Illinois country, where a few hundred Canadian fur traders had settled. In 1713 Jean-Baptiste du Bois du Clos, the *commissaire-ordonnateur,* reported that twelve young women, selected by Bishop Jean-Baptiste de la Croix de Chevrières de Saint-Vallier on the basis of their good morals, had arrived from France "but [were] so ugly and ill made" that the Canadians coming down from the Illinois country had rejected them out of hand. These men had, he explained, little regard for a woman's virtue so long as she be well built. Therefore rather than marry these hags, they had gone back to the Illinois country, declaring that the comely Illinois girls were far more to their liking. The clergy insisted that the Canadians living in concubinage with Illinois women be married according to the rites of the church, even though the Crown discouraged, then forbade, Canadian-Indian marriages.

In lower Louisiana, black slaves were early declared to be an economic necessity, for without them the colony would amount to nothing. In 1719 the first shipment of 450 slaves was brought in by the Compagnie de l'Occident, and during the ensuing decade over 6,000 were imported. By 1739 there were 4,000 in the colony, but two-thirds of them had been born there; the death toll was high. The availability and defenselessness of the female slaves rendered prostitution unviable, except perhaps at Mobile and New Orleans with their garrisons and the periodic arrival of seamen.

Concubinage of white masters and black slaves led to serious social problems, as masters manumitted their concubines along with their mulatto offspring. Beginning in the mid eighteenth century, as in the West Indies, freed Negroes and mulattoes began to compete with the poor white artisans, creating racial friction. The number of octoroons or individuals descended from black ancestors increased, and the women, who were renowned for their beauty, competed with the Creole women for the favors of the French planters, officers, and merchants.

MORALITY IN ACADIA AND ÎLE ROYALE

In Acadia (present-day Nova Scotia and New Brunswick) the settlers generally had the same morals as the Canadians. Prior to the cession of the colony to Great Britain in 1713, the French settlers were always on good terms with the Micmac and Malecite Indians. French fishermen had long been accustomed to having temporary liaisons with Indian girls. The Acadian colonists continued the custom, but the clergy saw to it that concubinage resulted in marriage according to the rites of the church.

Things were different on Île Royale, all that remained in French hands after 1713. At Louisbourg, a garrisoned fortress seaport, the male-female ratio in 1724 was ten to one and in 1752 six to one. Leaving aside the garrison soldiers and visiting seamen the ratio was never less than three to one. Yet the morals of the populace were no worse than in the other colonies and better than in some. There were remarkably few prostitutes, and only two cases of seduction, where redress was sought, came before the Conseil Supérieur.

For a bride to be pregnant on her wedding day was not looked at askance. By law all unmarried women were required to declare their pregnancy to the local authorities. Between 1722 and 1744, 13.3 percent of brides were with child; between 1749 and 1757 the percentage was down to 9.8. For comparison Bristol in Rhode Island with a population of one to two thousand in 1740 (half that of Louisbourg) had prenuptial conception rates of 10 percent between 1720 and 1740 and 49 percent between 1740 and 1760. In England in the eighteenth century between one-third and one-half of all brides were pregnant when they married. All in all then the morals of the French in America appear to have been no better nor worse than those of the other European colonists.

BIBLIOGRAPHY

Boyer, Raymond. *Les crimes et les châtiments au Canada français du XVIIe au XXe siècle.* Montreal, 1966. Virtually a *cri de coeur* by a professor of chemistry who spent some years in jail as a political prisoner. Contains much well-documented information. See chapter 8.

Brasseaux, Carl. "The Moral Climate of Louisiana." *Louisiana History* 27, no. 1 (1986):27–41.

Cliche, Marie-Aimée. "L'Infanticide dans la région de Québec (1660–1969)." *Revue de l'histoire de l'Amérique française* 44, no. 1 (1990):31–59. Scholarly use of the documents.

Donovan, Kenneth. "Family Life in Eighteenth Century Louisbourg." Ms. Rpt. Parks Canada, Louisbourg, Nova Scotia, 1977. Sound scholarship.

Johnston, A. J. B. *Religion in Life at Louisbourg, 1713–1758.* Kingston and Montreal, 1984. Scholarly and very thorough.

Lachance, André. *Crimes et criminels en Nouvelle-France.* Montreal, 1984. See Chapter 4, "Les crimes contre les moeurs."

———. *La justice criminelle du Roi au Canada au XVIIIe siècle.* Quebec, 1978. A basic work.

———. "Women and Crime in Canada in the Early Eighteenth Century, 1712–1759." In *Crime and Criminal Justice in Europe and Canada,* edited by Louis A. Knafla. Waterloo, Ontario, 1981. A useful brief survey of the literature.

Séguin, Robert-Lionel. *La Vie libertin en Nouvelle-France au XVIIe siècle.* 2 vols. Montreal, 1972. An ill-digested mass of useful information.

W. J. Eccles

SEE ALSO **African-American Culture; Civil Law; Crime and Law Enforcement;** and **Gender Relations.**

THE SPANISH BORDERLANDS

SEXUALITY IN THE Spanish Borderlands is a difficult topic to describe comprehensively. If one wants to survey the broad range of practices and behaviors that were deemed "sexual" both by the European colonizers and by the subjugated and nominally conquered indigenous populations of the area, the exercise very quickly becomes one-sided, ethnocentric and presentist in purview. As moderns living in the secular industrialized countries of the West, we have very definite ideas about what we regard the "sexual" to be. Whether it be in defining the sexual and asexual, what is heterosexual, homosexual, and bisexual, or pathologies that are thought of as "sexual," those categories come to us largely through the medical discourses of nineteenth-century sexual science. Today we take those categories for granted. We regard the reasoned ideas of sexual science as the "true" and "natural" order of things.

For the inhabitants of the Spanish Borderlands, natives and Europeans, the nineteenth-century categories of sexual science would have been unintelligible. Instead, the religious discourses of the Roman Catholic church, expressed by priests and theologians in biblical exegesis and juridical pronouncements, in confessional manuals and manuals for the administration of the sacraments, provided the basic coordinates that oriented the Christian body in relationship to its soul and provided the dominant imaginative architecture through which sexuality was defined. As Spain's official state religion, the Roman Catholic church was charged with the regulation of social life, and thus the record of how the church defined appropriate sexual behavior in the Spanish Borderlands is extensive. Daily, in teachings from the pulpit and in confessional boxes, clerics disseminated the church's vision of a properly ordered body politic and the function of sexuality in it. Transforming its ideology into behavior through the penances imposed by its disciplinary agents—local priests, judges in ecclesiastical courts, inquisitors of the Holy Office—the church inscribed on physical bodies the social order it envisaged.

Yet despite the power of the church to impose its vision of a proper sexual order, other models of personal erotic comportment constantly challenged, subverted, and threatened to undermine that order. Among the Spanish colonists of the borderlands there was what might be called a secular or "folk" model of sexuality. We know of these ideas and practices primarily through the repressive apparatus of the church, through the workings of the Inquisition, and through the ruminations of clerics who often

lambasted as pagan and sinful these alternative notions about procreation, about the body, and about the function of sexuality. As society gradually became secularized in the eighteenth century, these ideas were increasingly embraced by state functionaries to undermine the power of religious models among Catholics.

Likewise, a whole variety of complex practices and ideas about the sexual existed among American Indians. These too were deemed sinful and demonic by the friars, who often admitted baldly, at times almost gleefully, that they had been able to repress these behaviors only by resorting to brute force. In fact, one can interpret the whole history of the persecution of Indian women as witches by the learned men of the church as a struggle over these competing ways of defining the body and of regulating procreation, as the church endeavored to constrain the expression of desire within boundaries that clerics defined as proper and acceptable. The subordination of these indigenous peoples of the Spanish Borderlands, the fact that their voices survived only as encoded by clerical quills in judicial dockets, makes it quite difficult to study the integrity of indigenous thought and practice regarding sexuality.

What follows below, then, is a discussion of the models of sexuality that the three major social groups of the Spanish Borderlands articulated: clerics, civilians, and Amerindians. Given the primacy of the church in daily life until the end of the eighteenth century, the documentary record allows us to describe the clerical model best. Bear in mind that given the antiquity and population density of the New Mexican colony in comparison to the sparse and ever-precarious colonization attempts in Florida, Texas, and Alta California, the evidence presented here comes primarily from New Mexico and only secondarily from these other nodes of colonial settlement. When the historical evidence indicates that the New Mexican patterns sharply diverged from patterns in Florida, Texas, and Alta California, that fact is noted.

THE ECCLESIASTICAL MODEL OF SEXUALITY

Since antique times the fathers of the Catholic church had defined the human being as constituted of body and soul. The body, base and vile, was but a transitory vessel for the eternal soul, whose spiritual journey to God was assured only through a virtuous life sanctified by the sacraments. Clerics maintained that given the sinful quality of the flesh, the persons whom God most favored were those who had forsaken the flesh and the vainglories of the world for a life of virginity and chastity. Mystical marriage to Christ and a union with God was the highest state of spiritual perfection to which one could aspire. The 1563 marriage canons of the Council of Trent made this point clear: "Whoever shall affirm that the conjugal state is to be preferred to a life of virginity or celibacy, and that it is not better and more conducive to happiness to remain in virginity or celibacy than to be married, let them be excommunicated."

Theologians viewed human marriage as a less desirable state that had only been elevated to a sacrament by Christ as a *remedium peccati,* a remedy for humanity's inherently sinful state. The primary function of marriage was the reproduction of the species, and only quite secondarily an institution for the peaceful containment of lust. Thus most of the prescriptive literature produced by theologians and moral philosophers during Spain's colonial period did not focus squarely on sexuality. The topic surfaced only tangentially as part of larger discussions of marriage contained in the Ten Commandments. "Thou shall not commit adultery" and "Thou shall not covet they neighbor's wife," or glosses on these Sixth and the Ninth commandments, were the textual points at which extensive discussions of sexual matters often appeared.

The church maintained that marriage was the normative institution that assured the regeneration of the species, the peaceful continuation of society, and the orderly satisfaction of bodily desires. When couples channeled their sexual desires toward the explicit aim of procreation, they fulfilled God's natural design. The two most important objectives of marriage, explained Father Clemente Ledesma in his 1695 *Confesionario del despertador de noticias de los Santos Sacramentos,* a guide for the administration of the sacraments in Mexico, were procreation and the satisfaction of the *débito conjugal,* the conjugal debt that required reciprocal sexual service.

Historian Asunción Lavrin explains that in colonial New Spain conjugal intercourse was imagined as a contractual sexual exchange. Married couples could, so to speak, request a regular servicing of the debt by their partner and were duty-bound to pay it. Sex could be withheld only if it was requested too frequently, during periods of illness, or during religiously motivated temporary vows of chastity. Lavrin notes that confessional manuals counseled men to avoid excessive requests for sex and enjoined women to be charitable and understanding in giving what was requested of them.

According to confessors and theologians, the line between duty and sin was a very fine one. Couples were constantly counseled not to be overwhelmed by lust, thereby losing control of their rational faculties. In his *Espejo de la perfecta casada* (1636), a manual for the Christian education of married women in Mexico, Father Alonso de Herrera cautioned that an excessive display of lust in marriage was tantamount to the sin of adultery. "Engaging one's wife like an animal, inflamed by the libidinous fires of desire, is a very grave sin," Herrera warned.

Churchmen often frenzied themselves with the minutiae of marriage, prescribing exactly where and in exactly what position the conjugal act should occur. "The natural manner of intercourse as far as position is concerned," advised the seventeenth-century Spanish theologian Tomás Sánchez in his *De sancto matrimonii sacramento,* is for "the man [to] lie on top and the woman on her back beneath. Because this manner is more appropriate for the effusion of the male seed, for its reception into the female vessel." Railing in condemnation about the *mulier supra virum* (woman above man) coital position, Sánchez continued: "This method [of intercourse] is absolutely contrary to the order of nature. . . . It is natural for the man to act and for the woman to be passive; and if the man is beneath, he becomes submissive by the very fact of his position, and the woman being above is active." Sánchez added: "Who cannot see how much nature herself abhors this mutation? Because in scholastic history it is said that the cause of the flood was that women, carried away by madness, used men improperly, the latter being beneath and the former above."

Engaging in sex in places other than the conjugal bed was frowned upon by priests, but apparently without much effect. It was not uncommon for lovers to report that they had consummated their affections "in the woods," "by the river," or in some isolated physical setting. The 1712 admission by Santa Fe resident Juana Carrillo that she had enjoyed the affections of a man while "out in the fields" during the spring planting aptly characterizes the type of spaces that proved expedient for the consummation of desires. Provided that churches, chapels, and shrines were not desecrated by such acts, priests had little formal authority to do much about it.

Catholic theologians continually asserted that the "natural" function of marital sexual intercourse was procreation. All uses of the sexual organs that did not have this as their ultimate aim were deemed "unnatural" and punishable as violations of natural law, whatever one's marital state. The sin of Onan (onanism), or masturbation, was evil because men wasted their seed in ways incapable of reproducing human life. Though women undoubtedly masturbated, the activity attracted the clerical gaze—so to speak—only when women's autoeroticism went beyond tolerable bounds or when, as a result of odd circumstances, ecclesiastical authorities discovered that a woman had masturbated her partner in ways that did not have a reproductive end.

Sodomy, or rectal intercourse with a partner of either sex, was the "unnatural vice" precisely because it was nonprocreative. Its only function was sexual pleasure. The prosecution of this sin was quite gender and class specific: most tolerated among elite men, most punished when discovered among men of lower castes and classes. In 1789, for example, Florida governor Vicente Manuel de Zéspedes deported for trial and punishment six soldiers from Saint Augustine for having sexual relations with young boys. Destitute Gaspar Reyes complained to the Inquisition in 1606 that one of Santa Fe's friars had gotten him drunk and tried to use his posterior part for nefarious end. No action apparently was ever taken against the friar.

Perhaps because clerics considered women the weaker sex in need of male supervision, or perhaps because of their own sense of priestly modesty, cases of heterosexual sodomy aroused less attention than the homosexual analogue.

Women engaged in sodomy—or *amores secos,* as it was then called (literally "dry loves"; that is, "dry" in comparison to "wet" vaginal sex)—as a way of maintaining their premarital virginity while still consenting to the sexual desires of their suitors. Sodomy was also a common form of birth control. Ecclesiastical court dockets involving broken promises of marriage frequently noted, that, as Santa Fe's Juana Rodríguez explained in 1705, she had consented to *amores secos* with Calletano Fajardo because he had promised that she would be his wife. Unfortunately for Juana, Calletano developed amnesia. The onset of such a memory lapse was a common strategy men employed to avoid prosecution for their actions. Since they had not deflowered a maiden, which was an actionable offense before the law, this strategy usually proved successful as a way for men to avoid any punishment for their behavior.

Bestiality, though quite infrequently reported in the Spanish Borderlands, was similarly defined as a deviation from "natural" heterosexual marital intercourse and stringently punished. In 1800 an eighteen-year-old soldier stationed at Santa Barbara, California, was found guilty of mounting his mule for other than transportation. Both he and the mule were executed and publicly incinerated, the flames purifying their wicked flesh. In a 1770s New Mexican case involving a young Indian boy from Isleta Pueblo and a cow, charges against the boy were dismissed because the lad had not yet reached the age of reason. He did not understand the gravity of his sin, the judge opined. Repeatedly the ecclesiastical judge queried whether the cow had been standing up or lying down. The boy, having never apparently understood the question as posed by the interpreters, failed to answer satisfactorily. Whether being in one position or the other would have spared the cow's life will never be known.

As addressed by the Sixth and Ninth commandments, the two sins that most threatened the social order based on marriage were adultery and lust. Adultery violated the sexual exclusivity of the sacramental bond of matrimony, created the possibility of illegitimate children, occasioned the spread of disease, and potentially could disrupt the peaceful order of life. As for the unfettered expression of lust, the Jesuit priest Father

Gabino Carta categorizes the subject thoroughly in his *Práctica de confessores: Práctica de administrar los sacramento, en especial el de la penitencia* (1653), a manual for the administration of the sacrament of confession. He explained that lust was the most evil of emotions because it occasioned such heinous mortal sins as fornication, adultery, incest, rape (*estupro*), abduction (*rapto*), sins against nature (masturbation, sodomy, bestiality), and sacrilege. Carta defined fornication as any sexual act outside the sacrament of marriage. He differentiated rape from abduction, the former as forced sexual intercourse, the latter a violation compounded by the victim's abduction. Having sex with a priest or nun or having sex in sacred places were but two of the sacrileges Father Carta had in mind when he cautioned about the excesses of lust.

In addition to these base-level mortal sins stemming from lust, Father Carta articulated a second layer of mortal sins caused by taking morose delight (*delectación morosa*) in one's sexual fantasies. If a person lusted vicariously watching someone else in the sexual act, if one fantasized about sex with a particular person while masturbating, or if one took pleasure recalling sexual dreams after awakening, yet another mortal sin was committed. In short, any sexual activity that was eroticized outside the bonds of marriage, in either fact or fancy, motivated solely by the pursuit of pleasure, was sinful. Such behavior alienated the soul from God and endangered personal salvation.

THE SECULAR MODEL OF SEXUALITY

Unlike the religious who came to the Americas to save souls, having forsaken the pleasures of the flesh and the materiality of the world for a spiritual life, the Spanish conquistadores were propelled by dreams of fame and fortune. For the largely young and single Spanish men who militarily conquered New Spain's northern frontier and laid the groundwork for its colonization, fame was measured through one's honor and fortune through the spoils of conquest—gold, tribute, land, slaves, and women. Save salt, mineral wealth was nonexistent in the borderland. Vacant land was more abundant. If the products of this land were to become as good as gold, it would only be through the exploitation of forced labor, be it from tributaries or slaves.

Indian women became the alchemists who transformed labor into gold, for through their reproductive capacities the sexual violence of the conquistadores in short order produced illegitimate mixed-blood children begotten to serve. The Spanish conquest of America was thus a sexual conquest of Indian women. Through rape and rapine the Spanish soldiers subjugated the Indians, interpreting the subjugation as supreme acts of virility and prowess. One gleans from a reading of the clerical chronicles of the Spanish conquest in Florida, New Mexico, Texas, and California the horrors that marked the event. Fray Francisco Zamora swore before God that he had witnessed the native men of New Mexico stabbed and knifed because the soldiers wanted their wives. "I know for certain that the soldiers have violated them [the women] often along the roads," Zamora wrote. Father Joseph Manuel de Equía y Leronbe said that he had heard the conquistadores shouting, as they went off to their debaucheries: "Let us go to the pueblos to fornicate with Indian women. . . . Only with lascivious treatment are Indian women conquered."

Whereas the priests who initiated the spiritual conquest of America's Indians relied on the lexicon of sin to describe the process, the Spanish soldiers and colonists understood and explained their behavior through the language of honor. As conquerors of the land, by royal writ, they became men of honor with all the rights and privileges of the Peninsula's aristocrats. As men of honor their status was supreme, forcefully lording it over others and seizing the best fruits of the land as their own. In public and in private, men established their honor by asserting their virility and sexual prowess, simultaneously protecting the *verguenza*, or sexual shame, of their womenfolk from assault by others.

A man's honor could be enhanced or diminished through his acts of conquest, be they through seduction or rape. But a woman's shame, intimately tied to her sexual purity, was a limited asset that could only be lost or tarnished, never restored. Since a woman's honor always reflected on that of her menfolk, women were usually under the vigilant care of fathers, husbands, brothers, and sons. Of course, female seclusion varied by class; social ideals became behavior only when material resources were not otherwise employed. In the households of the lower classes and castes, and in households where men were not often in residence, it was always much more difficult both to seclude women, given their requisite activities in public, and to fend off assaults to their honor.

In the initial years of each region's settlement, before stable families had been established, it was not uncommon for the soldier-settlers to sexually assault Indian and lower-class women. Most cases of rape were not litigated, but when they were, the accused men maintained that what had transpired was a seduction, not rape, and that the woman had been won over by blandishments and charm. If the victim was Indian, she was often blamed for the incident; for as a group of New Mexican soldiers confessed regarding their excesses with Pueblo Indian women in 1601, the women "have no vices other than lust."

Research by historians Carmen Castañeda and François Giraud on rape in eighteenth-century New Spain indicates that the majority of victims were women under the age of nineteen who were not carefully guarded by their families. They were assaulted while home alone or off on errands without male supervision. While women of the upper classes, of Spanish and mestizo origin, were less often victims than African slave and indigenous women, women of all races and status were raped. Single men between the ages of twenty and thirty who were outside tightly integrated webs of kinship—such as itinerant merchants, muleteers, and seasonal day laborers—were the typical rapists.

Although raping a woman was considered a repugnant, antisocial crime, guilty men received rather insignificant punishments for it. Exile, public shaming in the stocks or tied to the gibbet, and monetary compensation for the woman were the ways in which most cases were resolved. In extreme cases, corporal punishment, with up to two hundred lashes, might occur. Nonetheless, since a man enhanced his honor through displays of virility, the greatest and most permanent dishonor belonged to the raped woman and to her kinsmen who had not protected her from assault.

Female rape victims were the persons who socially suffered most from this crime. They were often publicly humiliated as loose and shameless women. Their families frequently blamed them for inciting the passions of strangers and kin. If the rape involved incest, they were removed from their homes and placed in a house for wayward women to thwart a father's, brother's, or uncle's incestuous desires. In *Los Recogimientos de Mujeres* (1974), Josefina Muriel describes the way these women were isolated from their families and all but forgotten in these cloistered institutions.

Rape pitted the male prerogatives of conquest against the church's desire to regulate society by containing the expression of lust within marriage. Thus when church officials were faced with the report of a rape, their response focused primarily on the woman's dishonor, on minimizing the public damage that her reputation might suffer. Priests usually dealt with this sin by keeping the assault as secret as possible. Clerics feared that other young men, by hearing of it, might be moved to similar violence.

The penances that the church imposed on rapists illustrate clearly the fundamental conflicts between ecclesiastical theory and the ideal of sexual conduct embedded in the honor code. In the eyes of the church, the only sinner was the rapist. His penance usually amounted to prayers and corporal works of mercy, signs of contrition for the absolution of his sin. The raped woman was guilty of no sin. But according to the honor ideology, she and her family were the persons who remained defamed and dishonored until the assault was avenged. If the rapist prevailed in the blood feud that might be precipitated by the rape, his honor was enhanced by the sexual conquest.

Indian and African slave boys and men were also the victims of rape. But in the cultural lexicon of the Spanish colonists, such assaults were the prerogatives of conquest and neither a crime nor a sin. Between men such acts of violence were part of the physical rhetoric of humiliation by which conquered men were transformed symbolically into effeminates and dominated as "women." Raping defeated warriors was a supreme act of virility and prowess.

Church and state officials believed that the only way in which social stability would be established in colonial territories was by creating stable families through marriage. Repeatedly the kings of Spain and the bishops of America urged their subjects to take local women in matrimony, thereby assuring the reproduction of the race and an orderly society. In the Spanish Borderlands, particularly in those settlements founded after 1690, about half of the colonists brought their families. A man who came alone but who had a wife in Spain or central Mexico sometimes sent for her later. As historian Dolores Enciso has demonstrated, some contracted bigamous marriages, denying that they had a wife elsewhere. The rest of the single men were forced to turn to the local supply of women for legal brides.

Before the early 1800s marriages were arranged by parents solely for the protection, consolidation, or expansion of wealth. Children could and did express their personal desires, but their opinions rarely were decisive in the selection of a mate. Marriage was a lifelong, indissoluble bond, the church maintained. The logical result of such a law was that arranged marriages were often loveless matches, full of domestic discord, and quite routinely punctuated by adulterous liaisons. Silvia Arrom has shown that though a form of legal separation known as ecclesiastical divorce was possible, it was granted only in extreme cases and primarily to elites.

Adultery was a sin in canon law. Both the male and female were equally culpable of having sinned, but it was usually only the woman who suffered consequences. Men were urged to return home and to make a *vida mariable* (a marriageable life) with their spouse. If they continued in their philandering and were discreet with their mistresses, they could escape the attention of the authorities. Women who desecrated the matrimonial bond, however, were given penances; they might be shunned and exiled to remote towns, with threats to their livelihood should they return. In cases of adultery we again see the different definitions of sexuality that existed in canon law and local honor codes. By the code of honor, adultery was a sign of virility for a man; the urge to dominate was deemed natural to the species. Adulterous women were dishonored for engaging in such behavior. But the greatest stigma fell on the cuckolded husband whose wife had not been restrained and kept from such dishonorable behavior.

The biological by-products of philandering husbands, of priests who failed to keep their vow of chastity, and of young unmarried men who exploitatively sowed their seed outside of marriage were illegitimate births. Whether one looks at sizable towns—Santa Fe, San Antonio, Saint Augustine—or smaller outposts, the result was the same: roughly 50 percent of the population was born outside of wedlock; the percentage was much higher among Indians and slaves. In a study of the northern Mexican mining town of Charcas, Marcelo Carmagnani calculated that for mulattos the incidence of illegitimacy was 65 percent in the period 1635–1639 and 75 percent in 1650–1654. Claude Mazet found roughly similar levels of illegitimacy in her study of San Sebastián parish in Lima, Peru, during the sixteenth and seventeenth centuries.

How those who bore the stigma of illegitimacy were treated has long been a topic of debate in colonial Spanish American historiography. Ann Twinam and Thomas Calvo have each argued that while the stigma of illegitimacy was substantial in law, in the day-to-day behavior of communities it did not seem to matter much. Nevertheless, illegitimate aspirants to educational opportunities and honorific posts were often hampered because they lacked a known and honorable father. Partly in response to such desires for upward mobility, and largely to gather extra cash, at the end of the eighteenth century the Spanish monarchy began selling writs of legitimacy, known as *gracias al sacar*, a topic splendidly illuminated by Twinam in her research.

INDIGENOUS SEXUALITY

When the Spaniards arrived in the borderlands in the early 1500s, they found numerous indigenous groups with equally various lifeways. At the simplest level were the nomadic bands that hunted and gathered for their subsistence. Bands could have anywhere from twenty to five hundred persons in them, foraging and hunting broadly in territories they defined as their own. The Apache, the Comanche, and the Ute are but a few of the band societies the Spaniards encountered. Much more complex were the *ranchería* peoples, so called by the Spanish because they were sedentary horticulturalists who lived in dispersed huts surrounded by their crops (*rancho* in Spanish means farm or ranch). The Indians of Alta California and Florida were often described as living in *rancherías*. At the most complex level of social organization were the sedentary farmers who lived in large towns (or *pueblos*); towns that numbered anywhere from five hundred to ten thousand inhabitants. The Pueblo Indians of New Mexico and Arizona were so named because they were best characterized by town life.

For many of the Indian inhabitants of the borderlands, sexuality was at the very center of their religious and cosmic order. Sexuality promoted fertility, it assured regeneration, and it was fundamentally equated with the holy. The sexual feats of the gods were celebrated. Those gods who bisexually combined all masculine and feminine potentialities into one—such as the Zuni god Awonawilona, the Navajo First Man/First Woman, the Hopi Kawasaitaka kachina—were particularly revered. In the natural world, sexuality was everywhere, from the regenerative activities of the animals to the erotic toponyms that local inhabitants gave the earth, names that translate as Clitoris Spring, Girl's Breast Point, and Buttocks-Vagina, for example. Among humans, few boundaries other than those against incest constrained erotic behavior and its forms (heterosexuality, homosexuality, and bisexuality). In religious ritual the Indians sang of sexuality and copulated openly to awaken the earth's fertility, to assure that the gods blessed them with fecundity and peace. Sexual intercourse itself was deemed a symbol of cosmic harmony because it united in balance all the masculine forces of the sky above with all the feminine forces of the earth below.

Yet beyond these rather general statements, what we specifically know about the sexual ideologies and practices of indigenous groups in the borderlands comes to us largely through the writings of the friars whose responsibility it was to convert the Indians to Christianity. Given that the clerical lexicon for the description of sexuality knew only sins, indigenous practices posed complex cognitive problems for the friars and present rather more complex interpretive problems for modern historians.

The nexus that existed in the indigenous world between sexuality and the sacred was re-

pugnant to men who had vowed themselves to lives of chastity. Franciscan descriptions of native sexual ideology and practice must be read with this bias in mind. There is little doubt, however, that the Indians were really as sexually frisky as they were described. The ribaldry of their "orgiastic" dances, the "lewdness" of incorporation rituals that ended in intercourse, and the naturalness with which they regarded the body and its functions are all too well documented from various points of view to be dismissed as clerical anxiety. But did the Indians live in a state of unbridled lust, as the friars constantly complained? I think not.

The goal of the Franciscans was to lead the Indians to God. To keep them on the path, the Franciscans established a regime of sexual repression. They justified what they did by telling the readers of their letters, reports, and denunciations that the Indians lived in wicked debauchery in a society devoid of sexual rules. Anthropologists attest that every society has rules governing sexual comportment, especially about such things as incest. Thus when we read the 1660 Inquisitorial denunciation of Fray Nicolas de Chavez, who states that when New Mexico's Pueblo Indians staged the kachina dance they frolicked in sexual intercourse "fathers with daughters, brothers with sisters, and mothers with sons," we must ask: What rhetorical end did such statements play in the contestation between Indians and Spaniards over the place and meaning of sexuality in a well-ordered society? The friars clearly felt that sexuality could only transpire within the bonds of marriage. By describing the sexual mores of the Indians as incestuous, the friars thus gained authorization to repress Native sexual activity.

Historical records from Florida, Texas, New Mexico, and California indicate that clerical anxiety over the "wretched" indigenous flesh had four principal focuses. The fact that at contact most Indian groups did not wear clothing was a constant concern. Vast amounts of energy were spent getting the Indians to wear clothes, hoping that by so doing they would eventually develop a European and "civilized" sense of modesty and shame toward their bodies. Equally important was the prohibition of Native religious rituals, particularly those performed by women to vivify the earth, which, according to the friars, were the work of the devil—characterized by lewdness, random promiscuity, and debauchery.

Extensive amounts of clerical ink was spent on the North American Indian *berdache*, whom the friars described as male whores addicted to the wicked sin of sodomy. The *berdache* (from the Arabic word *bradaj*, meaning male prostitute) were individuals of one anatomical sex who took the dress and performed the activities of a different gender. Though there are a few reports of females who took the gender attributes of males, the overwhelming evidence is of men transvested as women, performing women's work and offering sexual service to other men. The Spanish chroniclers who mentioned the *berdache* listed various reasons for this gender crossing: parental assignation of a child to one gender as a substitution for lack of a child of another gender, the choice of a gender better suited to personal inclinations, religious or ritual election, and the imposition of another gender as humiliation. Since the 1970s a fair amount of scholarly attention has been focused on the *berdache*, allowing us to conclude that in those societies in which they were observed, the gender system was much more fluid than our own, that gender was less tied to anatomical sex and more so to status, and that the gender ideology allowed for intermediate and third genders.

Finally, a well-ordered Christian society required chastity before marriage, fidelity within the nuptial state, and lifelong indissoluble monogamy. Indian men and women were forced to conform, abandoning those wives they had taken in polygamy and, if serially married, returning to their first wife.

The clerical campaigns to purify the Indian flesh, tied as they were to much more extensive and intensive programs of Christianization, met with varying amounts of success. Mission life offered nomadic bands little in terms of material benefits, and it was among the nomads of Texas, New Mexico, and Florida that Christianization was least successful. The *ranchería* peoples of California perished under mission rule, largely from disease and work; the repressive sexual regime only made matters worse. Only sedentary farmers with well-integrated societies managed to survive the conversion process; the Pueblo Indians of New Mexico and Arizona are the best-studied example. The Pueblo Indians survived

by resisting their domination, by violently rebelling in 1680 and temporarily putting an end to the Spanish colony, and by clandestinely maintaining their native religious ways after their 1693 reconquest. Here the friars were forced to admit that their labors, except in the most superficial ways, had been quite fruitless. In essence, the Pueblo Indians had clung to their ancient traditions and practices.

While the centuries of contact between Spanish colonists and Indian groups resulted only in superficial Christianization and Hispanization, extensive mixing between and among cultures did occur at the material and biological level. European metalwork, plant species, and livestock became common aspects of Indian life. Large numbers of children were born outside of wedlock to mistresses, domestic slaves, and subject Indian women as a result of seductions and rapes; for the Spanish colonists of the borderlands the biological mixing that transpired everywhere created a mestizo, or mixed blood, society.

How this mestizo population affected the mores of the nominally Spanish population of borderland towns and villages can be gleaned by examining reported cases of witchcraft. Such cases became endemic in the last quarter of the eighteenth century. Indian and mestiza women were repeatedly accused by Spaniards of practicing sinister love magic. These women allegedly knew how to make ligatures to attract the affection of a man, how to keep or intensify a particular love, and how to hex and render impotent the genitals of an unfaithful mate. Since many Indian and mestiza women living in Spanish towns worked as domestics, it was usually through food and waste products that they were alleged to have worked their craft. The accusers were Spanish women whose husbands were philandering with their slaves, "loose" mestiza women, and Indian mistresses. Obviously, witchcraft was the only possible explanation for such behavior. Husbands who wanted to avoid the pain of law were all too happy to confess that they were bewitched, victims of the work of the devil and not of their own desires.

The reports of Indian and mestiza witches practicing in the borderlands allow us to glean the way in which indigenous sexual values and practices were slowly and covertly being diffused into Spanish society. The tempo at which this occurred increased as a result of the Bourbon reforms in the last quarter of the eighteenth century. In these decades the secularization of the missions began. As one parish after another was taken from Franciscan control and given to a secular priest, or a priest not belonging to an order, the power that the friars previously had to dictate social behavior evaporated. Many parishes, in fact, were left without priests, and once such places were devoid of overt repression, Native and secular ideas and behaviors about sexuality became increasingly more important.

One gets an idea of how profound the Bourbon reforms were, specifically the curtailment of church power in daily life, by examining the stated motives for marriage given by candidates between 1693 and 1840. When the friars asked New Mexican men and women why they wished to marry, the most common responses recorded between 1693 and 1790 were religious and obligational. Individuals wanted "to serve God," "to save their souls," and to put themselves "in a state of grace." By the end of the eighteenth century the responses, though likewise formulaic, had changed radically. The change is particularly striking in that the responses were recorded in ecclesiastical documents. José García of Albuquerque declared in 1798 that he wanted to marry María López "because of the growing desire that we mutually have for each other." Juan José Ramón Gallego, a resident of Jémez, wanted to marry Juana María because, he said, "I fell in love." While previously love and desire would not have been acceptable justifications for seeking a marital partner, after the 1770s young men and women increasingly married for reasons of love, physical attraction, sexual passion, and other likes and dislikes.

One can conclude on the basis of this marital evidence that by the 1770s the ecclesiastical model of sexuality had been eroded by the large-scale biological mixing. Given the weakened ability of the church to root out paganism, indigenous ideas about sexuality were diffused more broadly. Finally, the formal assaults on church power by the Spanish state assured the eclipse of the ecclesiastical model of sexuality in society. Private sexual life was radically transformed as part of the revolutionary changes that precipitated colonial independence from Spain.

BIBLIOGRAPHY

Alberro, Solange, ed. *La actividad del Santo Oficio de la Inquisición en la Nueva España, 1571–1700.* Mexico City, 1982. See especially Alberro's article "El discurso inquisitorial sobre los delitos de bigamía, poligamía y solicitación" and Serge Gruzinski's "Matrimonio y sexualidad en México y Texcoco en los albores de la conquista o la pluralidad de los discursos."

———. "Inquisición y proceso de cambio social: Delitos de hechicería en Celaya, 1614." *Revista de dialectología y tradiciones populares* 30 (1974):346–357.

Allen, Paula Gunn. "Lesbians in American Indian Cultures." *Conditions* 7 (1981):67–87.

Arrom, Silvia M. *La mujer mexicana ante el divorcio eclesiástico.* Mexico City, 1976.

———. *The Women of Mexico City, 1790–1857.* Stanford, Calif., 1985.

Behar, Ruth. "Sex and Sin: Witchcraft and the Devil in Late Colonial Mexico." *American Ethnologist* 14 (1987):35–55.

———. "The Visions of a Guachichil Witch in 1599: A Window on the Subjugation of Mexico's Hunter-Gatherers." *Ethnohistory* 34, no. 2 (Spring 1987): 115–138.

Blackwood, Evelyn. "Sexuality and Gender in Certain Native American Tribes: The Case of Cross-gender Females." *Signs: Journal of Women in Culture and Society* 10, no. 1 (1984):27–42.

Callender, Charles, and Lee Kochems. "The North American Berdache." *Current Anthropology* 24, no. 2 (1983):443–470.

Carmagnani, Marcelo. "Demografía y sociedad: La estructura social de los centros mineros del norte de México, 1600–1720." *Historia mexicana* 21 (1972):419–459.

Castañeda, Carmen. "La memoria de las niñas violadas." *Encuentro* 2, no. 1 (1984):41–56.

———. *Violacíon, estupro y sexualidad: Nueva Galicia, 1790–1821.* Guadalajara, Mexico, 1989.

Enciso, Dolores. "Bígamos en el siglo XVIII." In *Familia y sexualidad en la Nueva España,* edited by Seminario de Historia de las Mentalidades. Mexico City, 1982.

Estopañán, Sebastián Cirac. *Los procesos de hechicerías en la Inquisición de Castilla la Nueva (Tribunales de Toledo y Cuenca).* Madrid, 1942.

Flandrin, Jean-Louis. "Sex in Married Life in the Early Middle Ages." In *Western Sexuality: Practice and Precept in Past and Present Times,* edited by Philippe Ariès and André Béjin. Oxford, 1985.

Giraud, François. "Viol et société coloniale: Les cas de la Nouvelle-Espagne au XVIII siècle." *Annales:*

Economies, Sociétés, Civilasations 41, no. 3 (May–June 1986):625–637.

Gruzinski, Serge. "Confesión, alianza y sexualidad entre los indios de Nueva España." In *El placer de pecar y el afán de normar,* edited by Seminario de Historia de las Mentalidades. Mexico City, 1988.

Guerra, Francisco. *The Pre-Columbian Mind: A Study into the Aberrant Nature of Sexual Drives, Drugs Affecting Behavior, and the Attitude Towards Life and Death, with a Survey of Psychotherapy in Pre-Columbian America.* London, 1971.

Guilhem, Claire. "La Inquisición y la devaluación del verbo femenino." In *Inquisición española: Poder político y control social,* edited by Bartolomé Bennassar. Barcelona, Spain, 1981.

Gutiérrez, Ramón A. "From Honor to Love: Transformations of the Meaning of Sexuality in Colonial New Mexico." In *Kinship Ideology and Practice in Latin America,* edited by Raymond T. Smith. Chapel Hill, N.C., 1984.

———. "Honor Ideology, Marriage Negotiation, and Class-Gender Domination in New Mexico, 1690–1846." *Latin American Perspectives* 12 (Winter 1985):81–104.

———. "Must We Deracinate Indians to Find Gay Roots?" *Out/Look* 1, no. 4 (1989):61–67.

———. *When Jesus Came, the Corn Mothers Went Away: Marriage, Sexuality, and Power in New Mexico, 1500–1846.* Stanford, Calif., 1991.

Hidalgo, Mariana. *La vida amorosa en el México antiguo.* Mexico City, 1979.

Hurtado, Albert L. *Indian Survival on the California Frontier.* New Haven, Conn, 1988.

———. "Sexuality in California's Franciscan Missions: Cultural Perceptions and Sad Realities." *California History* 71, no. 3 (1992):370–385.

Kamen, Henry. *Inquisition and Society in Spain in the Sixteenth and Seventeenth Centuries.* Bloomington, Ind., 1985.

———. "Notas sobre brujería y sexualidad y la Inquisición." In *Inquisición española: Mentalidad inquisitorial,* edited by Angel Alcalá. Barcelona, Spain, 1984.

Lavrin, Asunción, ed. *Sexuality and Marriage in Colonial Latin America.* Lincoln, Neb., 1989. See especially contributions by Asunción, Ruth Behar, Richard Boyer, Thomas Calvo, and Serge Gruzinski.

López Austin, Alfredo. *Cuerpo humano e ideologia: Las concepciones de los antiguos nahuas.* 2 vols. Mexico City, 1980.

Monroy, Douglas. *Thrown Among Strangers: The Making of Mexican Culture in Frontier California.* Berkeley, Calif., 1990.

Morgan, María Isabel. *Sexualidad y sociedad en los aztecas.* Toluca, Mexico, 1983.

Mörner, Magnus. *Race Mixture in the History of Latin America.* Boston, 1967.

Muriel, Josefina. *Los Recogimientos de Mujeres: Respuesta a una problematica social novohispana.* Mexico City, 1974.

O'Neil, Mary. "Magical Healing, Love Magic, and the Inquisition in Late-Sixteenth-Century Modena." In *Inquisition and Society in Early Modern Europe,* edited by Stephen Haliczer. London, 1987.

Ortega, Sergio, ed. *De la santidad a la perversión.* Mexico City, 1985. See especially contributions by Dolores Enciso and Jorge René González Marmolejo.

Perry, Mary E. "The 'Nefarious Sin' in Early Modern Seville." *Journal of Homosexuality* 16, no. 1 (1988): 67–89.

Ponce, Dolores. *El Nuevo Arte de Amar: Usos y costumbres sexuales en México.* Mexico City, 1990.

Quezada, Noemí. *Amor y magia amorosa entre los aztecas.* Mexico City, 1975.

Roscoe, Will. "Bibliography of Berdache and Alternative Gender Roles Among North American Indians." *Journal of Homosexuality* 14, no. 3 (1987):81–171.

———, ed. *Living the Spirit: A Gay American Indian Anthology.* New York, 1988.

———. *The Zuni Man-Woman.* Albuquerque, N. Mex., 1991.

Seminario de Historia de las Mentalidades, eds. *El placer de pecar y el afán de normar.* Mexico City, 1988.

———. *Familia y sexualidad en Nueva España.* Mexico City, 1982. See especially contributions by Dolores Enciso and Alfredo López Austin.

Whitehead, Harriet. "The Bow and the Burden Strap: A New Look at Institutionalized Homosexuality in Native North America." In *Sexual Meanings: The Cultural Construction of Gender and Sexuality,* edited by Sherry B. Ortner and Harriet Whitehead. Cambridge, England, 1981.

Williams, Walter. *The Spirit and the Flesh: Sexual Diversity in American Indian Culture.* Boston, 1988.

Ramón A. Gutiérrez

SEE ALSO **African-American Culture; Civil Law; Crime and Law Enforcement;** and **Gender Relations.**

MARRIAGE

THE BRITISH COLONIES

ENGLAND

Sexual Behavior and Marriage Formation

ASSUMPTIONS ABOUT MARRIAGE differed between England and the British colonies on many points, while for others, traditional attitudes prevailed on both sides of the Atlantic. The major themes discussed below—sexual behavior and marriage formation, marital rights and obligations, and separation and divorce—will highlight differences and similarities in attitudes and behavior. Often, forces beyond the control of settlers shaped the institution of marriage. Occasionally, ideological commitments played an active role in changing Old World standards. As in many areas of colonial life, the struggle between continuity and change forced the colonists to face their most basic assumptions.

English custom and law designed the institution of marriage to control sexual relations and to ensure the proper care of children, including the orderly transfer of property from one generation to the next. The primary right and obligation of marriage was sexual. Marital partners could not deny each other sexual access, and to be legal a marriage had to be consummated. If either partner were unable to have sexual in-

tercourse, the marriage could be annulled. Male impotence was always difficult to prove, however, and only a physical blockage that prevented penetration made a woman unmarriageable. A failure to bear children was not evidence of sexual inadequacy, and was therefore no grounds for annulment or divorce.

In seventeenth- and eighteenth-century England, men and women alike tended to view frequent sexual intercourse as a basic human need: healthy, necessary, and enjoyable. For much of the early modern period, women were considered more carnal than men. Writers argued that women's "less-developed intellects" could not temper so well their sexual appetites. Unmarried women were required by social custom to remain virgins, but customs of courtship allowed considerable experimentation, and bridal pregnancy was common, especially in plebeian society. Prenuptial pregnancy rates of 15 percent to 20 percent were the norm until late in the eighteenth century, when they rose to roughly one third of all pregnancies. Although pregnancy before marriage was punishable under church law, communities generally paid little attention to the offense. It did not damage significantly a woman's reputation, although it might be used against her later if she transgressed in other ways.

Among the elite, greater pains were taken to protect the sexual purity of daughters. In the seventeenth century, wealthy parents exerted considerable control over courtship and the choice of their offspring's marriage partners, with children frequently having merely the right to veto their parents' arrangements. Since the publication of Lawrence Stone's *The Family, Sex and Marriage in England, 1500–1800* (1977) historians have debated the degree to which parents surrendered their right to choose marriage partners for their children in the eighteenth century. Most now believe that the later period witnessed a change in patterns of courtship granting children increased control. Greater emphasis was placed on affection and respect between spouses, although matters of property remained important and children were expected to choose marriage partners from their own social class.

Sexual relations that were not followed by marriage, and extramarital liaisons, were not accepted as casually, particularly if they resulted in offspring. Children born out of wedlock were considered shameful evidence of parents' wrongdoing, the sinful product of uncontrolled lust. The law granted them no legitimate inheritance claims, although they did have a legal right to support during childhood. Social condemnation of illegitimacy arose from two sources: Christian belief in the sinfulness of fornication and adultery and neighbors' unwillingness to support children abandoned by their fathers. The parents of illegitimate children received punishments from ecclesiastical courts and parish churches, and they often faced informal ostracism or persecution from neighbors as well. Lapses in behavior nonetheless remained common among laboring people and small farmers. Illegitimacy ratios calculated for England in the seventeenth and eighteenth centuries show that anywhere from 1 percent to 5 percent of births occurred outside of marriage. It was very rare for a daughter of wealthy parents to give birth to a child outside of marriage.

Marital Rights and Obligations

The community demanded certain kinds of behavior from married couples. Many of these were codified in the law, but some were not. Folk customs maintained standards that could not be enforced in courts of law, although judges frequently based their decisions in cases of marital discord on neighbors' testimony. A woman's primary obligation to her husband was sexual fidelity. A double standard of sexual morality made his adultery less serious than hers, on the theory that she could impose a false heir on him unknowingly. Male honor also demanded her absolute obedience, particularly in sexual matters. Alternatively, contemporary writers of both sexes advised women to overlook the sexual lapses of their husbands: they were unimportant as long as a man fulfilled his primary obligation of financial support. Only cruelty or abandonment in conjunction with adultery led to general condemnation of male conduct.

Within the home, society expected women and men to exert themselves for the good of the family unit. The work that both performed was directed at providing for children and needy relatives, as well as for each other. To that end, women's marital obligations included caring for young children, the training of older daughters, household management, medical care, and assisting husbands in their occupations. Men were expected to provide for the material needs of their families, train older sons, and assist wives in certain kinds of household management such as care of livestock. A gender-based division of labor was strict, but exceptions were made in times of stress, particularly for families of lesser means. Men might care for the sick, just as women might reap the grain at harvest time.

Neighborhood praise went to spouses who lived peacefully together with their children, maintaining a standard of living through joint effort that was commensurate with their social position. When couples did not meet their obligations, neighborhood criticism could be severe. A woman might be censured by neighbors who believed she spent too much time away from home and neglected her work. Frequent visiting or even the sharing of work was frowned upon if family needs were not met. Matrons tried to balance the legitimate demands of neighbors—for assistance at childbirth or help with sick children, for example—and the demands of their own families. Husbands considered their anger or even physical violence justified if their wives did not stay by their own firesides.

In recognition of the man's primary role as breadwinner, society demanded that husbands provide their wives and children with a comfortable subsistence. Because newlyweds seldom lived with their parents for more than a brief period of time, if at all, marriage had to be delayed until couples acquired the property necessary to establish their own households. Most Englishmen could not marry until their late twenties, while women were generally a few years younger. Married men who refused to work for the support of their families met general condemnation. Less restricted to the home than their wives, their primary focus still had to be on its maintenance. When husbands did not give their wives and children adequate food, clothing, and essentials such as cooking utensils and bedding, the community stepped in to regulate behavior. Women who suffered from neglect, defined according to the social status of their husbands, could apply to local shopkeepers for credit on their husbands' accounts. Men could not refuse to pay for articles purchased by their wives in this fashion, and if they attempted to do so, the courts required payment, seizing husbands' goods if they remained uncooperative. This practice was referred to as the doctrine of necessities.

All property that a wife and husband accumulated, and all money or barter that they earned, belonged to the family unit. It was a husband's exclusive right, however, to manage family property. He could decide how money should be spent, or what goods exchanged, and his wife could not thwart his will or deny him possession of her earnings. A wife's personal property (defined as movables—clothing, money, books, and so forth) belonged to her husband absolutely. Her control was greater over any real property (lands and buildings) she might have brought to the marriage and to the real estate they possessed as a couple. She had the right to support from their realty, and therefore her husband could not sell or permanently alienate it (in a long lease, for example), without her consent.

A husband's obligation to support his wife extended beyond the grave. Although he could disinherit his children in his will, he could not disinherit his widow. She was entitled to dower, a one-third share in any realty he had owned during the marriage. Dower was designed in English law to provide widows and young children with support. Few men disinherited their children; the cultural importance of a man's lineage was too great. Dower served to protect children and widows primarily in instances of insolvency, when creditors could otherwise claim a man's

entire estate to pay his debts. In such a case, a widow's dower claim gave her a maintenance, which she was obliged to share with her minor children. Only after her death could creditors step in to seize their part of a man's real property.

Personal property did not have the same protections under early modern English inheritance law. All of a man's personalty could be taken to pay his debts. Widows of insolvents had no rights to personal property beyond the bare necessities—a dress or two, a bed, some cooking utensils. Even the personalty they had brought into the marriage could be seized to pay husbands' debts, including such personal items as clothing, jewelry, or family Bibles. At the beginning of the seventeenth century, widows possessed dower rights in personalty as well as realty. That right eroded gradually over the century, until men everywhere in England had the right to bequeath all of their personalty to whomever they pleased. Women could be denied their own personal items, beyond the essentials, if their husbands chose to disinherit them.

The law regarding marital property was so damaging to women's interests that members of the elite sought ways to circumvent it. Under English equity law it was possible for couples to create binding contracts giving married women rights to separate property. Among landed families of wealth, fathers negotiated property settlements before marriage, generally in the form of trusts, which gave daughters and grandchildren greater financial security than was available to them under the common law. These contracts also guaranteed that a daughter's inheritance would remain in her father's family should her husband become insolvent. Although most settlements were initiated by fathers, they could be created by couples either before or during marriage. Postnuptial settlements were created most frequently in cases of rising indebtedness. Wealthy widows also relied on separate estates when they remarried. Separate estates could guarantee them continued control over their deceased husbands' estates, for their own protection and that of their children. Significantly, in most cases a man had to agree to the creation of a separate estate. It was not binding under the law unless he signed it before witnesses. Only in the case of inheritance did a man lose his right to consent. Propery could be willed to a married woman "to her sole and separate use," and her husband had no right to disallow the arrangement. Otherwise, his property rights under the common law remained inviolable, subject to separate use only with his consent.

Separation and Divorce

Informal networks of neighborly concern and criticism helped keep many couples within the boundaries of acceptable marital conduct. Among those whose marriages totally collapsed, desertion was the most common response. For couples of small means, desertion meant little more than an informal separation—one spouse, usually the husband, would move some distance away. Often spouses remarried with the tacit approval of their communities, although this was not legal. One form of plebeian self-divorce was the wife sale, in which a husband led his wife to market by a halter and sold her at auction, almost always by prior arrangement to the woman's paramour or a relative.

Informal divorce arrangements could be dangerous for women. If a husband decided to return, his former wife possessed no legal right to refuse him a place as head of the household. While men rarely tried to reestablish marital relations, they did occasionally return to take property accumulated by women in their absence. Without formal separation decrees, women's ability to prevent such theft was minimal and depended solely on community support. For persons of wealth, then, informal arrangements were unsatisfactory. They turned to the courts for help in the form of divorce or, more frequently, separation decrees.

Absolute divorces with the right to remarry, or divorces *a vinculo matrimonii*, were granted by ecclesiastical courts solely to couples whose marriages were determined to have been void from the outset. Bigamy, sexual incapacity, and blood relationship (consanguinity) were reasons for absolute divorces. The marriage thus was considered never to have existed at all, and all children of such unions became illegitimate. Divorces from bed and board, or divorces *a mensa et thoro*, were formal separations arranged by ecclesiastical courts. They did not allow remarriage, but rather formalized terms under which spouses could establish separate households and renounce their sexual obligations. Divorces *a mensa*

et thoro could be obtained for adultery, desertion, and cruelty. Children of the marriages remained legitimate, and innocent women were guaranteed support from their husbands' estates. In a case of desertion without word for at least seven years, remarriage was possible, on a presumption of death. If the deserter reappeared, the new marriage could be annulled, but it did not have to be, according to the wishes of the abandoned spouse.

For men of great wealth, the inability to remarry in cases of their wives' adultery was intolerable. Therefore, beginning late in the seventeenth century an absolute divorce with the right to remarry was made available. It could be obtained by private bill from the House of Lords, providing the husband had obtained a divorce *a mensa et thoro*, from the ecclesiastical courts and also had won a civil suit for damages against his wife's paramour. This process was so expensive, however, that only the very rich could afford it, and so cumbersome that most unhappily married men failed to seek it. Before 1760 the process was restricted largely to those who needed to produce a male heir in a legitimate marriage. Between 1670 and 1799 only 131 private divorce bills were enacted in the House of Lords. No woman obtained one until 1801 when the double standard of sexual morality for women and men began to erode before the law.

ENGLISH CULTURAL ASSUMPTIONS AND COLONIAL EXPERIENCE

Sexual Behavior and Marriage Formation

Colonial settlements in British North America produced significant variations on patterns of English sexual behavior and the formation of marriage bonds. Puritan and Quaker religious ideals, demographic disruption caused by disease and climatic conditions, and class differences in dominant immigrant groups all acted as determinants of behavior. The colonies that were least successful in transferring English standards to the New World were those in the Chesapeake and the lower South, but all of the colonies witnessed change.

Conditions of immigration and settlement were so harsh in the seventeenth-century Chesapeake region that settlers were unable to reproduce the way of life they had known at home. Much of the best research on demographic disruption focuses on Maryland, but many characteristics of that region appeared in Virginia as well. Particularly important for the institution of marriage was an imbalanced sex ratio. Before 1700 the ratio of male to female immigrants arriving in Maryland was approximately three to one. In addition, marriage formation was hindered by the rules on indentured servitude, which forbade marriage without the consent of master or mistress. As many female immigrants to the Chesapeake came as servants, a large percentage of the potential bride pool was unavailable at any point in time. Only if a man possessed the means to purchase a female servant's time could he marry her. As a result, in the first decades of settlement many men died unmarried, and their age at first marriage rose compared with Englishmen. Age at first marriage dropped for the small number of single, free women who immigrated, while for servant women it remained comparable with the English norm.

Women who immigrated to seventeenth-century Maryland as servants frequently bore children out of wedlock, probably more often than servants in England. According to Lois Green Carr and Lorena Walsh, at least 20 percent of Charles County servants were presented at court for this offense between 1658 and 1705. The premarital pregnancy rate also was high; in seventeenth-century Somerset County about one-third of immigrant women already were pregnant at marriage. This was considerably higher than English rates of about 15 percent to 20 percent during the same period. Clearly, the condition of servitude carried a risk for women in the seventeenth-century Chesapeake. The skewed sex ratio placed them in demand as sexual partners, yet the law forbade them to marry. Settlement on isolated farms limited the role of both neighborhood opinion and formal institutions in controlling sexual behavior. And finally, almost all servants came to the colonies in adolescence or early adulthood, and without their families. As a result, they lost the protection kin could provide against sexual temptation or exploitation.

Bearing a child out of wedlock did not damage a woman's chances to marry once her period of service was over. Only a handful of women remained spinsters, and it may have been a desire to improve their marital prospects that prompted many women to emigrate in the first place. Certainly women in the lower ranks of society were more likely to marry landholders in the colonies than they were in England. In the seventeenth-century Chesapeake, some degree of upward mobility was possible for women and men who labored diligently. A harsh reality for couples who married in the early colonial South was the likelihood that one of them would die within a decade. Although pregnancy made women particularly vulnerable to diseases such as malaria (rampant in the Chesapeake), men's older age at marriage meant that most would die before their wives. Remarriage—and quickly—was the norm for Chesapeake widows.

As the population of the colonial Chesapeake stabilized toward the end of the seventeenth century, certain characteristics of marriage changed. Native-born women in Maryland and Virginia married considerably younger than both immigrants and Englishwomen, almost always before age twenty-one. They also lived longer, because of their better adjustment to the native diseases and climate, and the greater care with which more experienced settlers managed their water supplies. As a result they produced more children than their mothers, and the colonial population began to grow by natural increase. The better health of their husbands meant marriages lasted longer, and remarriage was less common than in the earliest decades of settlement.

Unbalanced sex ratios also affected the marriage prospects of Africans who came to North America as slaves. English colonists preferred to employ men as agricultural workers, and therefore slave traders transported more men than women. In the seventeenth century, high morbidity and mortality rates decimated the African population in North America and hindered marriage formation considerably. Enslaved Africans also had difficulty establishing stable relationships in the early decades of settlement because most slaves lived on small, isolated farms and were forbidden to travel without the permission of their owners. Language and cultural differences further alienated potential partners.

The problems facing African slaves changed somewhat in the eighteenth century. As the population in many areas came to be predominantly native born and more planters employed large numbers of slaves, it became possible for more slaves to marry according to their own customs. The children of slave mothers were defined under the law as slaves, and therefore some owners, exploiting a potentially valuable asset in the reproductive lives of enslaved women, began to encourage partnerships as a way of increasing their wealth in slaves.

To the north, in seventeenth-century New England, the laws and customs regarding marriage and family evolved much differently from those of the Chesapeake. For many, although certainly not all, immigrants, settlement was motivated as much by religious zeal as a desire for economic advancement. Women came to New England at almost the same rate as men, and usually with their families. Although young laborers did come to work as servants, the majority of early New Englanders worked on their own small family farms. The region was less dependent on unfree labor than the tobacco-dominated economy of the South. Conditions of life for servants in New England more nearly resembled those of the mother country than they resembled the tobacco colonies. Therefore, although age at first marriage dropped in New England, it never reached the extremes found in Maryland and Virginia. Women tended to marry in their early twenties and men in the mid twenties.

The presence of stable families, and the importance of the Puritan churches to so many settlers, led to the creation of towns in New England. Close-knit settlements dominated by conservative Puritan religious and secular authorities led to more restrictions on sexual activity and marriage formation than existed in the loosely settled Chesapeake region. Sexual offenses were treated harshly in court, church, and community. Together, these forces produced lower illegitimacy and bridal-pregnancy rates than occurred elsewhere in the English colonies or in England itself. At mid century, for example, the New England premarital pregnancy rate was half that of England. In addition, couples faced greater parental control over marriage. Unlike the situation in the Chesapeake, New England

men and women generally lived to old age. As a result, parents were able to help their children make marriage decisions. They also controlled the timing of marriage by bestowing or withholding the land and goods necessary for creation of a separate household.

The healthy New England climate contributed to a high degree of stability within marriage. Most couples spent their entire lives together and remarriage, particularly for widows, was less common than in the Chesapeake region. Seventeenth-century New England couples produced more children than was the norm in either England or Maryland and Virginia. An important result of the birthrate was the relatively early creation of a predominantly native-born population in New England. Chesapeake settlers did not see natural population increases until near the turn of the century.

As the eighteenth century progressed, the colonies became more similar in their morbidity rates, mortality rates, and amount of illegitimate sexual activity. Colonies that were settled later in the colonial period did not experience some of the extremes that characterized the early seventeenth century. The influence of Puritanism waned, settlers learned more about avoiding and controlling disease, and sex ratios evened out. Families became more stable in the Chesapeake region and lower South, which remained an almost entirely rural, agricultural society. Urbanization in areas of New England and the middle colonies produced new stresses on marriage not unlike some of those experienced in the early colonial South, but most of the region remained rural.

One of the most striking developments of the late colonial period was a relaxation in attitudes toward premarital sexual relations. Although bridal-pregnancy rates climbed steadily throughout the colonial era, they rose significantly after mid century. By the end of the eighteenth century, about one-third of women were pregnant at marriage, whereas the average before 1680 was about 8 percent. Some communities reported rates as high as 50 percent. Explanations for the rise in illegitimate births and premarital conceptions vary, but the same trend occurred in England and Western Europe. It is part of an unsteady cyclical rise continuing through to the present day, punctuated by two periods of decline: the mid seventeenth and late nineteenth to early twentieth centuries. To contemporaries, the seventeenth-century decline undoubtedly made the mid-eighteenth-century rise seem aberrant, whereas with historical hindsight we can see it as part of a general trend.

Most historians believe the eighteenth-century rise in illicit sexual activity occurred in response to two main forces. First, they have noted a conjunction between increased sexual activity before marriage and changing attitudes toward courtship and parental control over marriage. Once people had the power to choose their own marriage partners, sexual compatibility became a primary criterion between spouses. In the eighteenth century sexual relations before marriage served as a trial of that compatibility, as well as proof of love and for many, perhaps, a symbol of commitment. For some the "experiment" failed, and women who became pregnant bore their infants out of wedlock, to their own and their families' shame. Second, the rise in illegitimate births and premarital pregnancies coincided with a drop in age at first marriage and a rise in the fertility rate. These trends perhaps signal people's greater willingness to marry and conceive during periods of economic prosperity, growth, and optimism. For the American colonies, as for much of Western Europe, the last half of the eighteenth century was a time of expansion and confidence in the future.

Among most enslaved African Americans, sexual purity before marriage and sexual fidelity after marriage were impossible. Most colonies did not recognize marriages between slaves as legitimate, and forbade interracial marriages as well. Slave marital unions jeopardized the primary purpose of enslavement: total subjection of the worker's will to the owner's economic need. Some slaveholders encouraged African customs of marriage or instituted informal marriages in the English tradition, as a way of encouraging the formation of stable families. This occurred most often in the North, where people generally owned fewer slaves and worked in close quarters with them. Other whites refused to acknowledge even the informal partnerships recognized within the slave community as binding. They indiscriminately separated spouses, changing work assignments or selling wives and husbands as the need arose. Partly as a result of these

unstable conditions, sexual exploitation of enslaved women was common. For women, sexual abuse was one of the harshest features of the slave system.

Marital Rights and Rules on Divorce

The settlers relied on their English legal heritage when establishing rules on sexual behavior, marital property, and work roles. Many aspects of the law remained the same, but some changes also occurred that reshaped familiar customs significantly. Granted the right to adjust English law to New World conditions, colonial leaders rewrote the rules in such areas as dower, separate estates, and divorce. The result was thirteen different legal systems, for no two colonies arrived at exactly the same solutions to the legal problems of the period.

Lawmakers in New England and Pennsylvania were the most committed to revising aspects of English law they disliked. As radicals and reformers, they felt obliged to establish new rules to reflect more closely their own views on proper marriages and property relations. Settlers in New York, Maryland, Virginia, and South Carolina, however, attempted to duplicate rather than to change English forms, as a way of maintaining continuity with the lives they had enjoyed in England. For the most part, they admired the English legal system and tried to imitate it as nearly as they could.

Reforms often were attempts to simplify English rules on marital property, which in some areas had become complicated and expensive. The right of Englishwomen to disapprove land conveyances initiated by their husbands, for example, resulted in extra procedures and fees that seemed unnecessary to reform-minded colonial men. Thus, wives in seventeenth-century Connecticut were not allowed to join their husbands in selling or mortgaging family lands. A husband's signature was all that was needed to validate a conveyance (family property and the lands the woman brought into the marriage) until well into the eighteenth century. To solve the problem of widows' dower right, Connecticut provided that widows should receive dower only in the lands their husbands owned at death, rather than in all the lands owned at any time during marriage. Even after Connecticut lawmakers recognized the right of women to join in conveyances in 1723, they continued to grant dower in the more restrictive fashion. Similarly, Pennsylvania widows received dower only in lands that were clear of debt. Creditors held claims to all of a man's realty as well as his personalty in Pennsylvania, thus eliminating the complications and protections of the English dower system in cases of insolvency.

Rules such as these were based on a literal reading of the legal concept of marital unity. In English law, unity of person had been developed to define the legal positions of spouses as interdependent, but many exceptions had evolved by the middle of the seventeenth century. Some exceptions were designed to protect wives in their legal dependency, and it was these that the Puritan and Quaker lawmakers attacked. Their efforts at simplification of the land law, then, were also attempts to reshape the legal definition of marital property. They disliked rules recognizing women's independent property rights within marriage, as well as those that assumed men would not always act in the best interests of their families.

Coercion, a fully developed principle in English law, was largely ignored in these colonies, due to reformers' emphasis on unity of person. English courts recognized that husbands might sometimes attempt to force their wives to execute conveyances against their best interests. To protect women from male coercion, English law relied on the private examination, a separate questioning of a wife by a court official at the time of a sale or mortgage. In theory, the private examination was a time when she could express her willingness to execute a conveyance or, alternatively, ask the court's protection in opposing her husband's wishes. While traditionally minded colonists in Virginia, Maryland, and South Carolina adopted English law on private examinations, reformers in New England and the mid-Atlantic region did not. In these jurisdictions, lawmakers assumed that men would always act in the best interests of their wives and children when conveying property.

The reformers' dislike of separate marital interests can explain other deviations in the laws of New England and Pennsylvania. Most striking, perhaps, is the Puritan attitude toward separation and divorce. Whereas the English system was designed to facilitate legal separations, the Puritans preferred absolute divorce with the right to remarry. They believed God saw more room for sin in separations than in remarriages. Although absolute divorce remained rare in New England until the end of the colonial period, and was always a social disgrace, it was available for desertion, continued absence without word, uncontrollable hatred or cruelty, female adultery, and male adultery accompanied by desertion or cruelty. The distinction in female and male adultery standards reflects the double standard of sexual morality that prevailed in early modern Anglo-American society.

With the exception of Pennsylvania, the other colonies did not attempt to follow the Puritan example on divorce. At the end of the colonial period (1773), Pennsylvania lawmakers enacted a private divorce bill similar to those granted by Parliament, but it was voided in England. Outside of New England absolute divorces and legal separations could be obtained only for the same causes as justified them in England. They were meant primarily to protect the property of spouses who chose to live separately. In the colonies, as in England, legal separations became the tool of the wealthy, while the poor and even those of average means relied on informal arrangements. Desertion was common in the colonies, and evidence on wife sales has surfaced, as well as other technically illegal procedures such as arbitrations that granted estranged couples the right to remarry.

The Puritans' antipathy to courts of chancery led to another radical reform of English law. They refused to establish separate courts of equity in America, thereby undermining enforcement of broad areas of the law, including trust estates. Although jurisdiction over certain areas of equity—mortgages, for example—was transferred to the courts of common law, trusts never were given that explicit recognition. As a result, they could not be enforced in the courts of colonial Connecticut and Massachusetts. Here again is evidence of the Puritans' emphasis on the concept of marital unity. They disliked equitable separate estates, which allowed female independence within marriage and facilitated legal separations. Although some New England couples did create separate estates, they were unprotected in doing so. When disputes arose, the parties had no vehicle for adjudicating their differences. The colonies of New York, Pennsylvania, Virginia, Maryland, and South Carolina provided for the enforcement of trust estates, either through separate courts of chancery or in courts of common law. Colonies such as New York and those in the South that did not have an ideological opposition to chancery enforced marriage settlements most strictly, following English precedent in this complicated area of the law.

Colonial reforms of English property law had both harmful and beneficial effects on women's, and family, interests. Although women lost some degree of control over marital property in the Puritan and Quaker strongholds, low mortality and morbidity rates, emigration in family groups, and settlement in towns all led to greater marital stability in early colonial New England than in the South. Protection for widows and young children perhaps became more important in colonies where disease and death were the most prevalent. With marriage, as with many areas of colonial life, varying conditions of settlement led to sharply divergent cultural, social, and legal assumptions. The meaning of marriage shifted not only with emigration from England, but also in response to the unique conditions of life in each of the colonies.

BIBLIOGRAPHY

English Background

Laslett, Peter, Karla Oosterveen, and Richard M. Smith, eds. *Bastardy and Its Comparative History.* Cambridge, Mass., 1980.

MacFarlane, Alan. *Marriage and Love in England: Modes of Reproduction, 1300–1840.* Oxford and New York, 1986.

Stone, Lawrence. *The Family, Sex, and Marriage in England, 1500–1800.* New York, 1977.

Marriage in the Colonies

Kulikoff, Allan. *Tobacco and Slaves: The Development of Southern Cultures in the Chesapeake, 1680–1800.* Chapel Hill, N.C., 1986.

Norton, Mary Beth. "The Evolution of White Women's Experience in Early America." *American Historical Review* 89 (1984):593–619.

Spruill, Julia Cherry. *Women's Life and Work in the Southern Colonies.* New York, 1938; repr. 1972.

Ulrich, Laurel Thatcher. *Good Wives: Image and Reality in the Lives of Women in Northern New England, 1650–1750.* New York, 1982.

Colonial Demographic and Legal Studies

Carr, Lois Green, and Lorena S. Walsh. "The Planter's Wife: The Experience of White Women in Seventeenth-Century Maryland." *William and Mary Quarterly,* 3rd ser., 34 (1977):542–571.

Salmon, Marylynn. *Women and the Law of Property in Early America.* Chapel Hill, N.C., 1986.

Vinovskis, Maris A., ed. *Studies in American Historical Demography.* New York, 1979.

Walsh, Lorena S. " 'Till Death Us Do Part': Marriage and Family in Seventeenth-Century Maryland." In *The Chesapeake in the Seventeenth Century: Essays on Anglo-American Society,* edited by Thad W. Tate and David L. Ammerman. Chapel Hill, N.C., 1979.

Marylynn Salmon

SEE ALSO **African-American Culture; Civil Law; Gender Relations;** and **Interracial Societies.**

THE DUTCH COLONY

MARRIAGE CUSTOMS in the Netherlands were fashioned by both religious teachings and civil traditions. As Catholics and Calvinists readily agreed, marriage alone sanctified sexual relations between men and women. Marriage legally and morally began the conjugal family, the central and dominating institution in Dutch life and thought in the seventeenth century. In fact, the Dutch explained their nationality in domestic terms, describing the family as a microcosm of the republic itself.

If the family was well ordered, if husbands and wives and parents and children were playing their respective roles responsibly, the republic would surely prosper and be secure against enemies from without and within. However, if the family was disorderly, if husbands and wives shirked their familial duties, the republic would surely be imperiled. Dutch moralists, like the very popular poet and politician Jacob Cats, claimed marital harmony was crucial not only for the success of the family but also for the very survival of the nation. "In our Netherlands," he exulted, "God be praised, there are no yokes for the wife, nor slaves' shackles or fetters on her legs."

True enough, marriage was basically reciprocal among the Dutch, a partnership, though the husband was definitely the senior partner. Under Roman-Dutch law, women retained property and civil rights after marriage. Because of the rule of partible inheritance, daughters commonly inherited equally with their brothers, and brides frequently brought as much property into marriage as their grooms, occasionally even more. Women could and did run businesses and engage in trade, sometimes with their husbands, sometimes without them. Already well established by the time of the Reformation, the Dutch concept of marital reciprocity was further strengthened by the Protestant view of marriage as a civil contract.

Dutch parents generally left mate selection in the hands of their offspring. Mutual affection and sexual attraction were essential ingredients for marriage, acknowledged the Calvinistic Cats and other moralists; however, as Cats especially pointed out, young people should marry within their own class and with the advice and consent of their parents. Marriage alliances, after all, were fundamental to the extended kinship network upon which politics and business were organized in the Netherlands. In the marriage itself, the husband and wife had separate but complementary spheres, both of which were carefully described in the highly popular marriage manuals of the day. As head of the household, the husband ran the family business, through which the material well-being of family members was sustained. The wife managed the household and nurtured the children. Cats described her as a paragon of virtue, the consummate housekeeper, fully capable of assisting her husband if necessary in the family business.

MARRIAGE CUSTOMS IN NEW NETHERLAND

In New Netherland, the Dutch West India Company (WIC) enforced the laws and encouraged the traditions of the Dutch republic regarding marriage. Among the first colonists sent to New Netherland in 1624 was Bastiaen Jansen Krol, Comforter of the Sick, who had special dispensation from the Amsterdam Consistory of the Reformed church to baptize infants and solemnize marriages, even though he was not yet approved for ordination. However, for the next twenty years or so, marriage and domestic life generally suffered because the relatively few immigrants who came were mainly young, unmarried men, and women were scarce. Reliable statistics on mortality are not available, but spousal death due to childbirth, Indian wars, wreckage at sea, and disease made remarriage common, particularly among widows, several of whom are known to have remarried two or three times.

Especially during these early years, servant girls attracted many suitors, some of whom promised marriage and later had second thoughts. Numerous women and at least one man brought suit for breach of promise, and because Dutch law recognized betrothal as the beginning of the marriage process, magistrates almost always urged that the wedding still take place, particularly if the couple had engaged in sexual intercourse. Under official pressure, the reluctant lover usually went ahead with the marriage.

Coming to New Netherland in 1647, Director-general Peter Stuyvesant sought to regularize domestic relations, including marriage practices. His efforts were increasingly successful, thanks to the arrival of larger numbers of emigrants from the Netherlands, consisting overwhelmingly of young married couples. Urged on by the Dutch Reformed dominies, Stuyvesant condemned and prosecuted illicit cohabitation. He also promulgated ordinances requiring that marriage banns be published at least twice in the town or village where the couple was well known and that, once the banns were published, marriage should follow in due course. In two instances, Stuyvesant declared weddings illegal because they were held without the full approval of the couple's parents. On other occasions, the director-general and his council investigated to make sure that servant girls were not being coerced into marriage by their parents. Such intervention was exceptional, however; the young people themselves played the major role in choosing their mates. Endogamy in terms of race, ethnic group, and class generally prevailed in New Netherland.

Under Stuyvesant, the expanding use of joint wills and antenuptial agreements implies that the reciprocal marital relations of the Dutch republic were being replicated in New Netherland. In most joint wills, the husband and wife agreed to leave their community property to the survivor, usually with no strings attached. Joint wills indicated that both spouses had confidence in the other's ability not only to manage their property competently but also to protect the inheritance of their children. Antenuptial agreements, however, were written by widows or widowers before remarrying to protect the property rights of their children by the previous marriage or to keep their own property separate from the community property they and their future spouses might accumulate together. Either way, the antenuptial contract in Roman-Dutch law is important because it provided wives with a legal identity separate from their husbands. To a considerable degree, the reciprocity characteristic of Dutch marriages was intensified in New Netherland, where frontier conditions demanded exceptional cooperation between husbands and wives to maintain the household, raise the children, and succeed economically.

As in the old country, a wedding in New Netherland was an occasion for celebration, not only for the two families directly involved but for the community in general. Tradition dictated a series of suppers for the intended bride and groom, and even families of modest means felt compelled to maintain the custom. Their friends and neighbors joined in and contributed to the festivities. Food and drink were always plentiful, though of varying quality, depending upon the economic status of the couple.

By 1664 marriage and family life in New Netherland were probably approaching the demographic portrait painted by Alice Kenney of the Dutch settlers of Albany from 1680 to 1800. According to Kenney, the median age for marriage for women was twenty-three and for men, twenty-six. That 28 percent of first-born children arrived within eight months of marriage is suggestive of the extent of premarital coitus, but hardly conclusive. At any rate, recorded instances of bastardy were few in both Beverswyck

(now Albany) and New Amsterdam. Once married, couples usually could expect to have a child about every two years for the next fifteen years or so. During the last years of the seventeenth century, Kenney estimates, the average number of children being born to Albany families was between five and six. How many children survived is not known. Infant mortality rates were high elsewhere in colonial America, and this was likely the case in New Netherland as well.

The affective relationship between husband and wife in New Netherland is difficult to gauge. Throughout the seventeenth century, something very much akin to the companionate marriage of modern times was emerging in the Netherlands. There are signs that the same was occurring in the Dutch colony. True affection certainly bound Jeremias Van Rensselaer and Maria Van Cortlandt, about whose marriage we know more than that of any other couple in New Netherland. Director of the family patroonship, Jeremias reassured his mother that he and his young wife got "along well in the household." The "best thing I would wish for on earth," he continued, would be to have a long life with Maria. Before his death in 1674, Jeremias and Maria had seven children, one of whom died. They gloried in their children and always referred with tenderness to one another. Indeed, they enjoyed what appears to have been a thoroughly companionate marriage. According to Lawrence Stone, such affection did not come to characterize English marriage for another hundred years. The joint wills, though often formalistic in tone and style, provide further evidence of emotional bonding of spouses.

Of course, some marriages were very stormy, and a few cases of brutal wife beating reached the courts. The magistrates were always reluctant to intervene, insisting that disputes between husbands and wives were private matters. However, in a few extreme cases, the husband and wife were ordered to live apart. At least two divorces were granted in New Netherland, both to men who charged their wives with adultery. Two women got annulments, both because their husbands were guilty of bigamy.

Dutch law and tradition regulated the conjugal relations of most New Netherlanders, including those of many free blacks and slaves. Almost all the free blacks were former slaves of the WIC, and many of them were married to slaves, whose owners usually encouraged marriage. A number of black marriages were recorded by the Dutch Reformed churches in both Beverswyck and New Amsterdam. Other black marriages, especially among the slaves, were sanctioned by rituals brought from Africa and from the West Indies. In their chartered towns on western Long Island, English settlers generally followed the laws and customs of New England regarding domestic relations. Puritan communalism and English common law both subordinated the wife to her husband, whether in New England or on western Long Island. The English on Long Island also exercised more authority over their children's courting and marriage than did the Dutch of New Netherland.

In contrast to Puritan patriarchy, matriarchy prevailed among the Mahican, Iroquois, and Delaware Indians, the three most powerful Indian groups living between the Connecticut and Delaware rivers on lands claimed by the Dutch as New Netherland. The women raised the crops and the children, and the men hunted and made war. Descent was traced through the mother's line. Women gave stability to their culture, not men who were constantly moving about, either hunting or making war. Oral traditions passed across the generations sanctioned their marital arrangements.

The Delaware roundly condemned adultery, unless by mutual consent. However, among the Iroquois and Mahican, marriage was a matter of free choice, and either the husband or the wife might dissolve the relationship simply by taking another mate. Only the prohibition on interclan marriage limited their choice of mates. Although well suited to the Indian way of life, such open marriages were denounced by Dutch dominies and Puritan preachers alike.

TRANSFORMATION OF MARRIAGE PRACTICES

Following the surrender of New Netherland to the British in 1664, Dutch marriage practices gradually gave way to English customs and common law. By 1700 few Dutch Yorkers continued to use joint wills or antenuptial agreements, both documents that protected the separate legal identity of the widow and wife, whose status suffered as a result of the change. Similarly, the Dutch rule of partible inheritance gave way to the English custom of favoring the eldest son in particular and sons generally over daughters in dividing the family estate. Under English common law, the wife had no community property rights, nor was she to sue or be sued except as the agent of her husband. Upon his death, she had dower rights to one-third of her husband's estate for her livelihood. However, upon her death, that share too reverted to her children.

BIBLIOGRAPHY

Biemer, Linda. "Criminal Law and Women in New Amsterdam and New York." In *A Beautiful and Fruitful Place: Selected Rensselaerswijck Seminar Papers,* edited by Nancy Anne McClure Zeller. Albany, N.Y., 1991.

Christoph, Peter. "The Colonial Family: Kinship and Power." In *A Beautiful and Fruitful Place: Selected Rensselaerswijck Seminar Papers,* edited by Nancy Anne McClure Zeller. Albany, N.Y., 1991.

Earle, Alice Morse. *Colonial Days in Old New York.* New York, 1896; repr. 1990.

Fernow, Berthold, ed. and trans. *The Minutes of the Orphanmasters of New Amsterdam, 1653–1663.* New York, 1902.

———. *Records of New Amsterdam, From 1653 to 1674.* 7 vols. New York, 1897.

Gehring, Charles T., ed. and trans. *Fort Orange Court Minutes, 1652–1660.* Syracuse, N.Y., 1990.

Goodfriend, Joyce. "Black Families in New Netherland." In *A Beautiful and Fruitful Place: Selected Rensselaerswijck Seminar Papers,* edited by Nancy Anne McClure Zeller. Albany, N.Y., 1991.

Grant, Anne. *Memoirs of an American Lady.* Edited by James Wilson. 2 vols. London, 1808; rev. ed. New York, 1901.

Hershkowitz, Leo, ed. *Wills of Early New York Jews.* Waltham, Mass., 1967.

Kenney, Alice P. "Private Worlds in the Middle Colonies: An Introduction to Human Tradition in American History." *New York History* 51, no. 1 (1970):4–31.

Kruger, Vivienne L. "Born to Run: The Slave Family in Early New York, 1626–1827." 2 vols. Ph.D. diss., Columbia University, 1985.

Leonard, Eugenie A. *The Dear-Bought Heritage*. Philadelphia, 1965.

Morris, Richard B. *Studies in the History of American Law*. New York, 1958.

O'Callaghan, Edmund B. *Calendar of Dutch Historical Manuscripts in the Office of the Secretary of State, Albany, New York, 1630–1664*. Albany, N.Y., 1865; repr. Ridgewood, N.J., 1968.

Penny, Sherry, and Roberta Willenkin. "Dutch Women in Colonial Albany: Liberation and Retreat, Part I." *De Halve Maen* 52, no. 1 (1977):9–10, 14.

———. "Dutch Women in Colonial Albany: Liberation and Retreat, Part II." *De Halve Maen* 52, no. 2 (1977):7–8, 15.

Schama, Simon. *The Embarrassment of Riches: An Interpretation of Dutch Culture in the Golden Age*. New York, 1987.

Singleton, Esther. *Dutch New York*. New York, 1909; repr. 1968.

Shattuck, Martha Dickinson. " 'For the Peace and Welfare of the Community': Beverwijck, 1652–1664." Ph.D. diss., Boston University, 1993.

Stone, Lawrence. *The Family, Sex, and Marriage in England, 1500–1800*. New York, 1977.

Sturtevant, William C., gen. ed. *Handbook of North American Indians*. 20 vols. Washington, D.C., 1978. Vol. 15: *Northeast*, edited by Bruce G. Trigger.

Van der Woude, A. M. "Variations in the Size and Structure of the Households in the United Provinces in the Seventeenth and Eighteenth Centuries." In *Household and Family in Past Times*, edited by Peter Laslette and Richard Wall. Cambridge, Mass., 1972.

Van Deursen, Arie Theodorus. *Plain Lives in a Golden Age: Popular Culture, Religion and Society in Seventeenth-Century Holland*. Cambridge, Mass., 1991.

Van Laer, Arnold J. F., ed. *Correspondence of Jeremias Van Rensselaer, 1651–1674*. Albany, N.Y., 1932.

———, trans. *New York Historical Manuscripts*, edited by Kenneth Scott and Ken Styker-Rodda. 4 vols. Baltimore, Md., 1974.

Van Rensselaer, Mrs. John King. *The Goede vrouw of Mana-ha-ta: At Home and in Society, 1609–1760*. New York, 1898.

Wallace, Anthony F. C. *The Death and Rebirth of the Seneca*. New York, 1969.

Ronald William Howard

SEE ALSO **African-American Culture; Civil Law; Gender Relations; Interracial Societies; and Native American Families and Life Cycles.**

THE FRENCH COLONIES

ONE OF THE GREAT QUESTIONS in French North American historiography concerns New France's exceptional rate of natural population growth. New France boasted some three thousand settlers in 1663; one hundred years later the population of New France had reached more than seventy thousand, of which only ten thousand were immigrants. Conventional orthodoxy held that Canadian women married early and remained in a perpetual state of pregnancy, with a few celebrated examples of child brides cited as evidence.

THE RATE OF MARRIAGE

Demographic research in the latter half of the twentieth century, however, provides a better and more complete explanation for New France's remarkable population growth. Demographer Jacques Henripin maintains that between 1700 and 1730, the mean age of marriage was 22.4 for women and 26.9 for men. Allan Greer's study of the lower Richelieu region argues, with reassuring consistency, that in the second half of the eighteenth century the mean age at marriage was 22.4 for women and 26.6 for men. These figures are consistent with others in colonial North American historiography, and are only slightly lower than corresponding figures for Europe.

Similarly, the birthrate appears to have been only slightly lower than had been imagined. On average, women gave birth every two years. Wives who survived to the age of fifty would have, according to Henripin, an average of 5.65 living children. Henripin estimates that one quarter of all children died in the first year of life, while half perished before reaching the age of twenty. In underpopulated New France the authorities justifiably regarded such figures with consternation. In 1719, Jean de la Croix de Saint-Vallier, the second bishop of New France, related that there were too few midwives in the colony, and too few arriving from France. In 1730 the intendant Gilles Hocquart repeated the demand, emphasizing that more than ever midwives were needed in the colony.

The explanation for the population's dramatic increase must also take into account the high rate of marriage. In New France the marriage rate was between 18 and 24 per thousand; in France at the time the rate was 16.5 per thousand. The rate of remarriage in New France was 163 per thousand. Widows remarried, on average, 38.4 months after their husband's death; widowers waited an average of 25.5 months before remarrying. These figures help to explain the persistence of the custom of *charivari*, in which young people created disturbances in the homes of newly wedded couples whose May-December relationships had offended the community's sensibilities.

New France's exceptionally high rates of marriage and remarriage resulted from local economic, cultural, and political pressures. The need to obtain sufficient resources to establish an economically viable, independent household constituted the principal barrier to marriage. Land, a critical resource in any rural, agrarian society, was relatively abundant in New France, thereby eliminating a major economic barrier to marriage. But New France was plagued by a chronic labor shortage, meaning that children were extremely important.

Economic incentives toward marriage were reinforced by cultural pressures. In the French colonies many metropolitan social institutions were underdeveloped. In the absence of guilds and villages, marriages were the main social events of everyday life. In the long winter months, when there was less work to do and while the fruits of the harvest were plentiful, Canadians celebrated marriages in parties lasting several days.

Marriages were also important politically. Family economic and political strategies were more important than individual ones in New France. Marriages were seen as a means of family advancement. The business side of marriages is best seen in the marriage-contract negotiations, routinely signed by several family members, and marriages were successfully blocked on occasion by disapproving family members. Young people sometimes responded to their parents' objections with *sommations respectueuses* (respectful submissions), duly notarized, formally pleading for reconsideration. While the right partner could improve a family's status at all levels of society, marriages were especially important politically among the governing class. Nepotism was a completely acceptable form of patronage throughout the French Empire, and it was practiced openly with important results.

THE ROLE OF CHURCH AND STATE

The Catholic church and the colonial government also encouraged marriage. The church's attitude toward marriage was plain enough: marriage was meant for procreation. The state took this one step further, making the augmentation of New France's population a top priority. In a letter to Intendant Claude de Bouteroue on 5 April 1668, Minister Jean-Baptiste Colbert established augmentation of the colony's population as the intendant's sole objective. Colbert also outlined a program in which families with ten or more children were to be provided with a pension of one hundred livres. Families with twelve or more living children were to receive double this amount. Men who married before the age of twenty were to be offered twenty livres, as were women who married before the age of sixteen. Conversely, the parents of such individuals who had not yet married were subject to fines, barring justification.

Nor did Colbert stop at bribery and threats. In these same instructions to Intendant de Bouteroue, he suggested that for the good of state and religion, the Jesuits were to be ordered to stop interfering with French-Indian relations. Marriages between these groups were to be encouraged, and Indian children were to be raised as French citizens. In addition, young French women were to be supplied with a dowry by the state and sent to New France as *filles du roi*, or daughters of the king, in an attempt to alleviate the colony's demographic imbalance. Colbert's aggressive policies initially produced results, but successive French administrations did not pursue them as vigorously.

The church exercised a more lasting influence on colonial marriage patterns. Church ritual left no doubt in the colonial mind regarding the purpose of marriage. Immediately following the ceremony the nuptial bed was sprinkled with holy water while the priest chanted prayers and exorcisms. Marriage was the only relationship in which sex was permitted, and the small number of illegitimate children in the early years of the colony shows that premarital chastity and the insolubility of marriage were popularly accepted.

The church was a dominant force in the French settlements, but the Canadians exhibited a rather independent attitude toward it, as demonstrated by the letters of the *curés* (parish priests) complaining of various transgressions and by the persistence of popular customs such as the curse known as *nouage de l'aiguillette* (thought to render couples barren), the *charivari*, and the *mariage à la gaumine*.

The last practice, named for the first person to marry in this fashion, became popular in the early eighteenth century. Couples who encountered family opposition to their proposed marriage simply appeared at a regular service and declared themselves married at the end of the mass. The church took a dim view of such impiety, and Bishop Jean-Baptiste de la Croix de Chevrières de Saint-Vallier put a virtual end to these marriages by issuing a *mandement* (pastoral letter) on 24 May 1717 that threatened excommunication for the contracting parties.

The church's uncompromising position regarding *mariage à la gaumine* is clearly elucidated in Saint-Vallier's *Rituel*, published in 1703. Marriage is compared metaphorically with the alliance between Christ and the church. As one of the seven sacraments, marriage could not be profaned by the mere satisfaction of earthly passions. The *Rituel* also exhorted married couples to pardon one another's faults and to love each other in a chaste manner. Passion was to be disregarded at all costs and one's energy was to be channeled into the Christian education of one's children.

Marriages between French traders or soldiers and Indian women were a matter of grave concern to the church. Colonial policy regarding such unions changed following the failure of Colbert's scheme to assimilate Indians through marriage and education. Governor Philippe de Rigaud, marquis de Vaudreuil, feared that as French men married women of different nations, the risk of colonial disintegration increased. He

was afraid that these men would take opposing sides in intertribal wars. Minister of Marine Jérôme Phélypeaux, comte de Pontchartrain, was persuaded by Vaudreuil's dire warnings of dangerous divisions.

This issue was most important in early Louisiana, where there were very few French women. Henri Roulleaux de La Vente, named pastor of Mobile by Saint-Vallier, issued a scathing report on Louisiana on his return to France in 1710. He railed against the settlers' Indian concubines and lack of religion, and he maintained that either young women of good character be sent to the colony, or that legal marriages to Indian women be permitted. The *commissaire ordonnateur* Jean-Baptiste Dubois Duclos, who performed the same role as the intendant in Canada, opposed the latter suggestion, arguing that Indian women were more successful at assimilating French men than vice versa. Furthermore, the missionaries had not yet learned Indian languages and, therefore, had not successfully converted Indian women to Christianity. The Conseil de Marine (Council of Marine) saw logic in these arguments and voted on 1 September 1716 to uphold a ban on such marriages. The Louisiana Superior Council voted on 8 December 1728 to uphold the ban yet again. Meanwhile, many missionaries defied the ban and sanctioned these marriages, which they viewed as preferable to allowing these couples to live in sin. Many of these marriages were sanctioned in the Great Lakes region, in the Illinois country, and in Louisiana. Indeed by the 1720s, Franco-Indian couples were demanding their rights under the colonial legal code, the Coutume de Paris (Custom of Paris).

CUSTOM OF PARIS

The legality of marriages in the French settlements is important because of the protection afforded wives by the law. The Coutume de Paris, introduced in New France in 1640 and made the colony's only legal code in 1664, gave women a relatively strong position in their marriages. While New France was by no means an egalitarian society, the principle of male authority that operated in New England, was less evident in New France.

Under the Coutume de Paris, all possessions were owned jointly in a community of property for the duration of the marriage. In some cases, this community of property could be continued by a surviving spouse, up until the point where he or she remarried or when his or her children reached majority. There were certain exceptions. Property was classified as *meubles* (movable goods) and *immeubles* (mainly land), and the *immeubles* that belonged to either partner before the marriage did not form part of the community of property. Similarly, property acquired by inheritance after the marriage, known as *propres,* did not belong to the community of property. The husband, it is true, had the right to use the fruits of the property—rent or interest—as he saw fit, but he needed his wife's written consent before making any transactions concerning the property held under the community.

The wife also had the right to refuse her share in the community of property, if on dissolution the debts were found to outweigh the assets. Men did not have a similar right. If the assets outweighed the debts, the wife took her share, one half of the value of the inventory of the *meubles* and her own personal belongings. The other half went to the other heirs, usually the children. More protection still was afforded by the dowries written into these contracts to assure women of some financial protection. *Douaires,* a fixed amount of money that would be paid to the wife on the husband's death, took precedent over all other claims against the estate. The *préciput* guaranteed the survivor a certain specified amount of money, or the right to claim certain specified goods, at the time of dissolution. It should be noted that *conquêts,* goods acquired through labor rather than through inheritance, became part of the community of property, and thus a part of the survivor's estate.

WIDOWS

The wife's control over the estate gave women the opportunity to administer the husband's business after his death. The word *veuve* (widow) appears in the title of many firms in ancien régime France, and some widows of New France were prominent in business as well. Eléonore de Grandmaison carried on after her second hus-

band's death, renting lands on the Ile d'Orléans to the dispossessed Huron and organizing trading ventures with the Ottawa. Following her husband's death in 1733, Thérèse de Couagne took over her husband's interest in the Saint Maurice ironworks and loaned money to merchants. Marie-Anne Barbel was perhaps the most successful of all. When her husband died in 1745, she obtained a monopoly on the commerce of the Baie des Esquimaux (Hamilton Inlet, Newfoundland), and the lease for the Tadoussac fur trade. She also expanded his real estate holdings, acquiring new properties in Quebec City. She relinquished the community only upon her retirement.

Within marriage, too, women could be legally entitled to conduct business. Barbel herself was responsible for the business while her husband was exploring the Labrador coast. Similarly Charlotte Françoise de Juchereau de Saint-Denis, the wife of François Dauphin de La Forest, remained very active in business while her husband commanded Fort Pontchartrain (Detroit). Agathe de Saint-Père, one of New France's most active and energetic innovators, was deeply involved in the business life of the colony. Her husband, Pierre Legardeur de Repentigny, whether through indolence or good sense, gave her full control of all of his dealings while he campaigned in the west. Agathe de Saint-Père experimented with new fabrics and with dyes; she built looms and saw New France through a cloth shortage. Such successes were another reason for the popularity of marriage in the French settlements.

BIBLIOGRAPHY

Greer, Allan. *Peasant, Lord, and Merchant: Rural Society in Three Quebec Parishes 1740–1840.* Toronto, Ontario, 1985.

Henripin, Jacques. *La Population canadienne au début du XIIIᵉ siècle.* Paris, 1954.

Noel, Jan. "New France: Les Femmes Favorisées." In *The Neglected Majority: Essays in Canadian Women's History,* edited by Alison Prentice and Susan Mann Trofimenkoff, Vol. 2. Toronto, Ontario, 1985.

O'Neill, Charles Edwards. *Church and State in French Colonial Louisiana: Policy and Politics to 1732.* New Haven and London, 1966.

Zoltvany, Yves F. "Esquisse de la Coutume de Paris." *Revue d'histoire de l'Amérique Française* 25 (1971):365–384.

William J. Newbigging

SEE ALSO **African-American Culture; Civil Law; Gender Relations**: and **Interracial Societies;** and **Sexual Mores and Behavior.**

THE SPANISH BORDERLANDS

DURING THE MORE than two hundred years between the establishment of Spain's first colonial settlement in Florida (1565) and its last in Alta California (1769), marriage on the Spanish Borderlands was the principal basis of Hispano-Christian society. It was also an important instrument for achieving the sociopolitical conquest and assimilation of indigenous peoples. Defined and regulated by Roman Catholic canon and Spanish civil law, marriage on the borderlands was rooted in Spanish social mores and practices. Those mores were transferred to the increasingly multiracial and multicultural societies in the frontier we now know as the states of Arizona, California, New Mexico, and Texas. The period of Spanish colonial rule spanned the Reformation, the Counter-Reformation, and the Enlightenment in Europe. During that time, Hispano-Christian attitudes toward sex, sexuality, and the institution of marriage varied and changed, as did the ecclesiastical and civil laws governing them.

These changes mirrored the broad ideological, sociopolitical, and economic issues contemporaneously debated and contested in Europe and in the colonies. They also reflected marriage patterns and practices of the indigenous populations, who adjusted to but did not necessarily accept the repressive sexual norms that regulated Spanish Catholic sexual relations within and without the institution of marriage.

MARRIAGE IN POST-REFORMATION EUROPE

The Reformation successfully challenged the medieval theological concept of marriage codified in the canon law of the Roman Catholic church. Church laws regulated the institution of marriage and informed contemporary social attitudes. The theological concept of marriage was modeled on the ascetic ideals of the religious life, which held up celibacy as a state preferable to marriage. This ideology relegated marriage to a secondary, imperfect class or estate. Moreover, canon law defined numerous impediments to marriage between individuals who had either physical or spiritual ties of kinship and thus could place legal obstacles before couples wishing to marry.

Medieval theologians denounced sexual emotion as proof positive of the loss of self-control and disobedience deemed to have characterized Adam and Eve's fall from grace. Sexual intercourse, they argued, could never occur without sin because pleasure was always accompanied by sin. Thus, sexual intercourse was a sin even in marriage because it "was a beastly activity that turned the mind away from spiritual contemplation." Accordingly, marriage had only two valid purposes in the medieval Roman Catholic ideology: the avoidance of fornication and the procreation of legitimate children. Despite the bias against sex and marriage, canon law upheld the ecclesiastical principle—rooted in the notion that all Christians are free to choose a vocation—that each person is free to marry according to his or her own will. Marriage could take place only between two individuals who had freely consented to share this Sacrament. Thus, the canon recognized a clandestine, or "secret," marriage that occurred without parental permission and without public knowledge or witnesses.

Reformation theology and practice shifted the emphasis of the norms and values of virtuous Christian behavior from the religious ideal to the secular, material plane. Rejecting the medieval view of marriage as a distinctly inferior and burdensome institution, the Reformers exalted marriage as the foundation and nucleus of society—the divine instrument for achieving social stability and reform. They replaced the medieval Catholic ideal of chastity with the ideal of conjugal affection. Moreover, they exalted the patriarchal nuclear family as the solution to the contemporary crisis in domestic relations, and the home as the cradle of citizenship, the place where God-fearing, obedient, virtuous, self-sacrificing, and altruistic citizens were formed under the authority and tutelage of the father.

Protestant Reformers defined and added a new reason to marry: "mutual society, help, and comfort that spouses could give one another both in prosperity and in adversity." Thus, spiritual intimacy became an additional purpose of marriage. Now sanctified and elevated to the status of "holy matrimony," marriage, or the married state, became the ethical norm to which virtuous Christians, including Protestant clergy, should aspire. Protestant Reformers also determined that under certain circumstances, marriage was dissoluble. Initially, a wife's adultery was the only ground for divorce. In time, however, adultery by the husband, as well as desertion and severe cruelty by either spouse, became justifications for divorce.

To institutionalize the norms conceptualized and defined by theologians, secular governments had either to authorize existing political, religious, and social structures to incorporate them or to create new structures for doing so. To effect these changes, secular governments wrested legal control of marriage from the Catholic church. They established lay-dominated marriage courts, which supplanted or severely restricted canon law and episcopal courts, and vested control over the new, secular marriage ordinances in these courts. Two pivotal elements in the new laws—parental consent and public ceremony—were now required for a proper Christian marriage. The new legislation made it illegal to marry in secret or without parental consent.

Responding to the need for reform posited by the rise of Protestantism, the Council of Trent (1545–1563) enacted new marriage legislation for the Roman Catholic world. It decreed that betrothal, or the "promise of marriage," was binding and irrevocable if the couple had sexual intercourse. It abolished clandestine marriage by establishing a definitive ritual of marriage, which required the posting of banns for three consecutive weeks, a ceremony performed by a priest, and witnesses to this ceremony.

Finally, the Tridentine Council reaffirmed both the indissolubility of marriage and the orthodox Catholic idea that marriage required the consent of both parties. Although the Roman Catholic church firmly believed that the interests of the patriarchal family and society—especially the preservation of the social order—were best served when parents exerted control over their children and marriage occurred between equals, no ecclesiastical legislation required parental consent to marry or endorsed forced marriages. Rooted in the doctrine that salvation could be attained only through personal actions and intentions, the canon protected individuals from being coerced into marriage.

SPANISH ATTITUDES TOWARD SEX, SEXUALITY, AND MARRIAGE

Spain remained unalterably tied to the Roman Catholic church, and its civil law reiterated the concepts and laws of marriage contained in canon law. Civil legislation retained considerable leverage by reinforcing inheritance and property rights and strengthening the patriarchal family as a social unit. The Catholic church and ecclesiastical courts, however, retained jurisdiction over the institution of marriage and prenuptial conflicts. Of special import to the principle of consent in marriage was the post-Tridentine rejection of the Spanish medieval law that had allowed parents to disinherit children for marrying without their consent or against their wishes.

At the same time, the egalitarian principles of Catholic doctrine were juxtaposed to, and often conflicted directly with, the Spanish cultural idiom of honor, an ideology of personal subordination to familial concerns. Honor, which was used to maintain differential access to and control over the means of production, divided society along both a vertical (honor-status) and a horizontal (honor-virtue) axis. Established during the Spanish Reconquest, the vertical dimension provided a single continuum, a hierarchy of status, to reward persons active in expanding the realm. On this axis, honor was an awarded and ascribed status. Its maintenance and perpetuation depended, however, on the honor-virtue continuum. Honor-virtue divided society horizontally according to class and reputation, which was based on ideal social conduct. This division established a social order of precedence.

Ideal social conduct differed by gender. For women, it centered on sexuality, requiring them to be virginal if single, faithful if married. For men, it centered on conquest, domination, and protection, which included protecting the honor (sexual reputation) of females in the family. These qualities maintained the patrimony and perpetuated an honored image of the self across time. Moreover, locating the honor of women in sexuality and that of men in other, nonsexual qualities resulted in extreme sexual oppression of women and a double standard of sexual behavior.

An individual possessed individual honor and, because honor was inherited through the blood, a family possessed collective honor. Each person's conduct affected both his or her individual honor and family honor. Precisely because precedence at the upper social levels guaranteed control over resources, the greatest conflicts over virtue occurred within the aristocracy and the elites and between these social classes and the church.

Although the post-Reformation concepts of marriage—as a desirable state and as a means of achieving spiritual and physical intimacy—also took root in Spain, Spanish attitudes toward sex and sexual relations both within and without marriage did not change markedly. Human sexuality, as an unending challenge to the spiritual side of humankind, remained a source of constant preoccupation for the church. The concept of sexual behavior as a dialectic of flesh and spirit—two antagonistic forces engaged in unceasing battle—remained.

Thus, the church continued to repress sexuality and sexual union, and to stress restraint and control, while downplaying release or fulfillment. Single persons were to exercise self-restraint and to abstain from all sexual activities and thoughts that could lead to sexual arousal. They were exhorted to resist the sin of lust, which consisted of engaging in any of the sexual practices forbidden by the church. In particular, the Sixth Commandment defined the seven manifestations of lust, all of which were conducive to mortal sin. These included fornication, adultery, incest, rape, abduction, sins against nature (masturbation, sodomy, and bestiality), and sacrilege. Sex during specified periods (menstruation, the final stages of pregnancy, and certain holy days) and any type of contraception except abstinence were also prohibited. Moreover, the church retained consanguinity to the fourth degree and spiritual kinship as impediments to marriage.

Although physical love was a legitimate expression of conjugal love, meaning that sexual intercourse could legitimately take place in marriage, sexuality in marriage was defined and regulated in a contractual manner. The sexual act was a "duty," a debt to be paid upon request. Both spouses were not only entitled to it but obligated to perform it at the behest of the other. Since denying the marital obligation to one's mate was a mortal sin, presumably each person would be a willing, consenting participant in fulfilling the marital duty.

CANON LAW IN CONFLICT WITH CIVIL LAW

Defining marriage as a sacrament intended for the procreation and education of children and for companionship, aid, and deterring lust, the model for marriage embodied in the canon law was more egalitarian than that expressed in civil law. Although the church discriminated against women and recognized the husband as head of the household and family, it gave rights to wives and curbed the freedom of husbands to a much greater degree than did the state.

Canon law granted husbands and wives equal rights and obligations to meet the intended purpose of marriage. They were to aid one another and share responsibility for their children; their mutual consent was necessary for sexual intercourse to "propagate the species"; and both were required to be faithful. Failure to fulfill these duties was grounds for separation. Although only death or annulment could dissolve the marriage bond, the church could authorize an "ecclesiastical divorce," meaning a separation of bed and board permitting the couple to remain married but to live in separate residences and not to sleep together.

Adultery was cause for such a separation, and the penalty applied equally to either spouse: the guilty person lost his or her share of the community property and paid the court costs; the innocent party gained custody of the children. The basis for these egalitarian principles was that canon law considered justice principally in terms of the relationship with God and not with society.

These egalitarian principles were teachings rather than legal prescriptions because the church was powerless to enforce them. With excommunication its only viable penalty—one seldom imposed in domestic matters—the church could not punish husbands who committed adultery, disregarded their wife's wishes in rearing children, or forced their wife to have sexual intercourse. Ecclesiastical courts became involved only when one of the spouses sought a separation. While they remained together, husband and wife were under the exclusive jurisdiction of civil law and the civil courts, which regulated temporal matters.

Under civil law, a married woman was bound by the same discriminatory laws as all women, and by other restrictions as well. To compensate the husband for the support, protection, and guidance he was legally required to provide, the wife owed him nearly total obedience. She was compelled to reside with him and to accept his authority over every aspect of her life. Once married, a woman relinquished sovereignty over most of her legal transactions, property, and earnings. A husband represented his wife and controlled most of her legal transactions and belongings. He could act in her name without her permission, but she needed his permission to perform most legal acts. Although a married woman could own property, and the law curtailed the husband's legal rights over it, he nevertheless controlled most of it. A married woman retained ownership of her dowry, and the husband could not alienate the principal from her; nevertheless, he could, and usually did, control it. Property arrangements and questions concerning the guardianship or tutelage of women remained the province of civil law.

Precisely because they had the capacity to reproduce and were pivotal elements in the structure of property and the provision of parti-

ble and bilateral inheritance—by which daughters inherited equally with sons—women were held to the strictest, most repressive standards of sexual behavior. Moreover, *limpieza de sangre,* or genetic purity free from intermarriage with non-Christians, determined who could hold office or enjoy privilege. It depended directly on female chastity. Thus, the control of women's sexuality was enforced by the legal, moral, and religious codes of Spanish Catholic society. Early misogynist ideas reflecting a negative view of women remained embedded in medieval theorists' depiction of women as sexually insatiable and incapable of controlling their sexual urges. Since a woman's sexuality, specifically her virginity, was a pivotal issue in matrimonial negotiations, honor required that a woman's reputation be free from scandal. Therefore, males strictly supervised female sexuality. Since an inappropriate marriage or sexual relationship could introduce a person of unacceptable ancestry into the family, honor also required that parents exercise strict authority over negotiations leading to their children's marriage.

Very real tensions and conflicts existed between the egalitarian principles of the canon law regulating marriage and the discriminatory principles of civil law favoring men. Civil laws were enacted by the state, which, on the one hand, supported the ecclesiastical principles of marriage but, on the other hand, had vested economic and sociopolitical interest in the marriages of its subjects. The conflict between the spiritual principles of canon law, which supported an individual's free choice of mate, and the temporal principles of civil law, which supported parental authority because marriage affected a family's economic and sociopolitical status, gave rise to bitter disputes within families over the choice of a marriage partner. In the final third of the eighteenth century, the state wrested legal control over marriage from the church.

Although the church defined a set of rules to guide humanity in the unending struggle between the spirit and the flesh, the final choice of behavior rested with the individual and his or her own free will. Sin, like love, was voluntary. And, in fact, since the 1970s the question of love, conceptualized as an expression of will, has occupied a central place in the historiography of marriage and the family in early modern Europe.

THE NATURE OF THE FAMILY AND RELATIVE FREEDOM OF MARITAL CHOICE

Scholarly debate has focused on the conflict between marriage for love and marriage for interest. To what extent, historians have asked, were marriages based on the free will, or love, of the individuals, and to what extent were they purely contractual arrangements between families and based on family interest—primarily material considerations and social prestige? Until the 1980s, scholars generally concluded that family interest was the principal consideration in marriage, that it was normatively approved as the legitimate motive for marriage, and that marriages in early modern Europe, arranged by parents or other kin, were loveless.

The standard history of the family in western Europe posits that the traditional patriarchal family began to give way to the more egalitarian family during the eighteenth century. Correspondingly, the pervasive, traditional authority in social life was eventually superseded by pervasive individualism, which engendered a different approach to marriage. These changes were but one result of the long dramatic shift brought about by the forces of capitalism. Positing a link between capitalism and individualism, Patricia Seed and other historians concluded that the "self-seeking mentality engendered by capitalism spread into noneconomic areas of life, and the wish to be free emerged as romantic love." This wish to be free ultimately led to marriage for love throughout Europe.

Newer studies by Ramón Gutiérrez, Steven Ozment, and Seed, however, have found that, during the sixteenth and seventeenth centuries, the patterns in Spanish societies were different from those in the rest of Europe. In the Iberian Peninsula and the Americas, personal choice of a conjugal mate was rooted not in an ideological individualism brought about by the rise of capitalism but in classic canon law and cultural ideas about the expression of personal will and the importance of honor.

In the Spanish world, the Hispanic Counter-Reformation during the baroque era rejuvenated the teachings of Thomas Aquinas and reinforced a powerful ecclesiastical tradition. Love became an expression of human rational faculties and of individual will. In daily life, however, family interest and considerations of status and kinship took precedence. Love, which glorified personal autonomy and portrayed sexual passion as an intrinsic desire of the species—natural, free, and egalitarian—was considered subversive. The egalitarianism of love was antithetical to the status concerns of the family and to relations of authority in the home.

Despite the contradictions and conflicts between secular and ecclesiastical law, Spanish Catholicism continued to protect the right of marital choice, and in that sense to defend marriage for love. This differentiated Spain from other European societies (whether Protestant or Catholic), where secular control of marriage prevailed and parental control over marriage was the norm.

The extent to which couples in sixteenth- and seventeenth-century Spain actually married for love, or to express their own will, cannot be determined from extant records. Ecclesiastical court documents reveal that, despite the canonical decree of free will, parents went to great lengths, including violence and every imaginable form of coercion, to pressure their children into marrying the person who could best advance the family's material interests. In order to preclude conflict when children reached marriageable age, some parents betrothed and arranged marriage alliances for their children at birth or in infancy.

Nonetheless, sons and daughters turned to the ecclesiastical courts when parents or other kin tried to pressure them into an unwanted betrothal or marriage. Some petitioned these courts when parents tried to stop them from marrying the person of their choice. The church prevented parents from halting such marriages by removing children from parental custody, marrying couples secretly, or dispensing with the banns and neglecting to inform parents of the marriage.

When parents and children were at odds over the choice of a marriage partner, each side often could count on support from some family members and others in the network of kin and community. Kin might pressure the child to acquiesce to parental choice, or they might serve as a place of refuge or *depósito* for the child while the court investigated the case.

Although the seeds of values stressing individualism and notions of love as personal choice were embedded in Spain's ideology of honor and in its Christian theology, parents intensely contested the individualism affirmed by these values. While church doctrine consistently attempted to protect personal and individual desires, enforcement was generally in the hands of lower clergy, whose discretionary powers to interpret the law gave rise to a variety of practices. Some clergy firmly supported parental privilege on the ground that the natural authority of the father over his children fully accorded with the will of God. In these instances, friars often pressured children to obey their parents. This was often the case in the Americas, where marriage, the institution that regularized inheritance of status and property, was critically important to the imposition and maintenance of Spanish colonial domination.

MARRIAGE ON THE BORDERLANDS

Interracial Marriages

The earliest marriages in Spain's American colonies were interracial. During the early, military phase of Spanish expansion across successive American frontiers, royal officials sometimes promoted interracial marriages between Spaniards and Christianized Indian women in order to establish political, military, and economic alliances with indigenous groups. Often, priests and missionaries promoted interracial marriage as a means of stopping sexual violence against Indian women and of arresting the rapid spread of concubinage and other illegal unions. Intermarriage also functioned to acculturate indigenous people to the sexual values, marriage patterns, and social norms of Spanish Catholic institutions.

These were often in conflict with, and diametrically opposed to, the sexual values, norms, patterns of marriage, and social institutions of the diverse indigenous peoples in the Americas.

For these peoples, concepts of morality were generally not tied to sexuality and sexual mores were not repressive. Some Native cultures, including the Pueblo of New Mexico, accommodated a "third sex," known as half-men/half-women by Native people and called the *berdache* by sixteenth-century Europeans. These individuals were biological males who, as a result of a sacred vision or selection by the community, assumed the dress, occupations, mannerisms, and sexual behavior of females in some sexual and homosexual relationships and marriages.

Among the Acoma Pueblo of New Mexico, who likened human life to plant life, celebration of sexual desire was an activity necessary for the harmonious continuation of life. The Acoma believed that children, like seeds planted deep within Mother Earth and fertilized by the sky's life-giving rain, came forth from their mother's womb, grew into adults because their parents and other seniors bestowed life-sustaining gifts upon them, and repeated the cycle of life by engaging in the activity that engendered the next generation. However, throughout the process of growing, marrying, and becoming part of the community, children, or juniors, obtained unreciprocated gifts from or through their parents and other seniors, and thus incurred debts and created bonds of obligation they had to fulfill. Pueblo life was structured by rules of reciprocity that governed gifting and structured generational obligations. Marriage, the mark of transition from junior to senior status, was enmeshed in gift exchange. Exchange of equal amounts of wealth between the households of the bride and the groom validated the marriage. Once this was accomplished, it was followed by a marriage ceremony.

A universal marriage pattern did not exist among indigenous cultures. Some societies practiced premarital sexual intercourse, others did not. Some practiced serial monogamy, others practiced polygamy. In most societies, divorce was possible at the initiation of either spouse. In some cultures, same-sex marriage was practiced by select individuals. The basis of selection varied across different Native American communities. In some cases the selection was rooted in the individual's personal, sacred vision. In other cases, the family of origin selected the individual. In still others, someone else—an elder or shaman—selected the person or persons.

From the very beginning, Spanish colonialism required that indigenous marriage patterns be extirpated and that Indian people be Christianized and married according to Spanish Catholic law and tradition. The centuries-long efforts of officials to impose Spanish Catholic norms and patterns, often through the use of corporal punishment, were not entirely successful. Although Indian people did marry according to Spanish laws and customs, they continued to practice their own marriage patterns and traditions as well.

From the outset, officials of both church and state perceived the departure of single Spanish males to the expanding American frontiers as a major threat to the empire's social institutions and sociopolitical stability. They feared the new, fluid social conditions that were giving rise to unprecedented multiracial, multiclass societies, and illicit sexual relations. To impose order and gain firm control of social development in the Americas the Hapsburg Crown, beginning in 1505, elaborated an extensive body of legislation to address the problem of connubial separation, promote the marriage of single men, and facilitate the emigration of Spanish women to the American colonies. The policy of "domestic unity" explicitly provided economic incentives for married men to bring their spouses with them and for single men to marry and settle in the colonies, which were subject to the same laws, social mores, and patterns that informed the institution of marriage in the Iberian Peninsula.

These incentives extended to the borderlands that stretched in an uneven but well-defined line from Texas through New Mexico and Arizona to California. Once the first *presidios* (military forts) and missions were established in the region, and Indian populations began to be congregated in mission compounds, presidial companies began recruiting married soldiers and their families to staff the borderland outposts. Similarly, colonizing expeditions explicitly recruited married settlers to plant agrarian communities along the great frontier arc from eastern Texas to San Francisco Bay.

On the military frontier, the unbalanced sex ratio prompted some officials to promote marriage by recruiting single women as marriage partners for single soldiers, settlers, and convicts. In the 1790s California's governor, Diego de Borica, tried to recruit "good wives, strong young single women for convict settlers." He subsequently petitioned viceregal authorities in Mexico City for "young healthy maids" for the agrarian settlers, and later still for "one hundred women." Precisely because marriage stabilized society, established legitimacy for purposes of inheritance, and was the basis of population growth on isolated frontiers entirely dependent on natural increase, borderland officials strongly supported and promoted it.

Marriage on the borderlands was defined and regulated by the Roman Catholic canon and Spanish civil laws, social mores, and practices governing marriage on the Iberian Peninsula and the rest of the Americas. Among indigenous peoples, however, acceptance of and adherence to these norms varied across time and space according to the degree of acculturation. Indigenous people residing in the mission compounds had largely converted to Christianity, and married accordingly. However, Amerindians in California until the early nineteenth century rebelled against the missionaries' efforts to enforce Christian norms of marriage and sexuality by running away, effecting revolts, and, in one case, by killing the mission's priest. In New Mexico, however, Christian marriage was a symbol of social status and a measure of acculturation among the landless, freed *genízaros* (slaves and tribalized Amerindians captured by the Spaniards and pressed into domestic service).

Marriage Patterns and Class

Although the settled Spanish-mestizo population adhered to the values of Spanish Christian society, marriage patterns varied according to social class and status. On the militarized frontiers of California and Arizona, Spanish Borderland society consisted of three major classes: Spanish governors, military officers, and priests; noncommissioned officers and soldiers; and artisans and agrarian settlers. The governors, missionaries, and most of the commissioned military officers were *españoles,* either peninsular or American-born Spaniards. Few of this group remained in California after their term of service expired. The rest of the population was racially mixed and included varying combinations and blends of Indian/Spanish, Spanish/African, and Indian/African. In California, civilian settlements were established and subsidized by the Department of War—rather than, as in New Mexico, by a royal charter of incorporation, which conferred honor and aristocratic or noble standing—and a nobility class did not exist. The paucity of research on all regions of the borderlands except for New Mexico enables one to discuss only New Mexico in detail.

Society in the Kingdom of New Mexico consisted of four population groups and "three classes of people . . . superior, middle, and infamous." The nobility, the superior or dominant class of approximately fifteen to twenty families, were *españoles*. Their sense of aristocracy derived from the legally defined honor granted by King Philip II to New Mexico's colonizers in the 1595 charter of incorporation. Below them, the landed peasants, the far more numerous middle group, were of mestizo origin but identified as *españoles* to differentiate them from the Indians. The *genízaros*, primarily of Apache and Navajo origin, were considered sociocultural outcasts, or infamous, and occupied the bottom rung of New Mexico's social hierarchy. A fourth group, the Pueblo Indians, lived in their own economically independent and politically autonomous towns. Although they were a vanquished class who rendered tribute and labor to the nobility, their legal rights and the integrity of their villages and lands were protected by the Crown.

Among Spanish-mestizo families who had property and titles to transmit and high status to maintain, marriage served to perpetuate the material and symbolic patrimony of the family—its material resources, its honor, and its reputation. Marriage united two properties, joined two households, and created a web of familial alliances. In marriage, the honor of the family took precedence over all other considerations, and conflicts often arose when the desires of the children differed from those of their parents and other kin. Love, which glorified personal autonomy, was considered a subversive sentiment that undermined familial needs and group solidarity. It made individuals forget their social obligations.

Parents sought to manipulate their limited material resources, the patrimony, in order to maximize the gains associated with marital alliance; that is, to enhance and perpetuate the family's status. Moreover, the options available to parents for securing acceptable or advantageous spouses for their children were dictated by the number of children in the family, their birth order, and their sex.

Spanish law entitled every legitimate child to an equal share of the patrimony, but practices varied. Large landholders adhered to male primogeniture to keep their property intact. In these cases, a disproportionate amount of the parents' premortem resources was committed to the eldest son, who became heir to the political rights over the group and the person responsible for the name and reputation of the family. The marriage alliance of the eldest son, then, was of singular import. The entire family's public status, including the possibility of securing honorable partners for his unmarried siblings, was diminished if he entered into an inappropriate alliance.

Daughters, whose dowries were absorbed into the husband's assets, did not enhance the patrimony. Thus, families frequently sought to marry their daughters off as quickly and as inexpensively as possible. Securing an appropriate mate for a daughter who had experienced a prenuptial dishonor, such as the loss of virginity, incurred added expense. Despite parental efforts to control the sexuality of young women, daughters sometimes engaged in premarital sex as a strategy to marry the person of their choice. Unless there were major impediments, which could usually be breached, sexual intercourse with a promise to marry was binding on both parties.

Among the noble and propertied families of the borderlands, parents generally arranged marriages for their children, sometimes at the child's birth or in infancy. This may have been especially true in the early colonial period, when the sex ratio was especially unbalanced and single "Spanish" women were in extremely short supply. In cases of primogeniture, if the eldest son married well and the family's position was secure, parents might permit their other children some flexibility in the selection of a spouse. Nevertheless, conflicts over marriage choice arose between parents and their offspring.

Parents frequently used threats, intimidation, and force to convince a child to marry. Children sometimes filed complaints against their parents, but most complaints in colonial New Mexico were filed by males against the parents of a woman they wanted to marry. The complaints usually charged the parents with forcing their daughter to marry against her will or with preventing her from marrying the person of her own choice.

In 1710 Joseph Armijo of Santa Fe appealed to the provincial ecclesiastical judge, Fray Miguel Muñoz, to intervene on his behalf because María Velasquez was, against her will, being prevented by her parents from marrying him. Armijo, whose first appeal to Fray Lucas Arebalo, the local priest, had been stymied, also charged that priest with wrongdoing. Armijo argued that it had been previously determined that María wanted to marry of her own free will and for Fray Lucas to say that she "had a sudden change of heart" was highly suspect and scandalous. Armijo charged that her alleged "change of heart" was the "product of bad advice which ignored the decrees of the Holy Council of Trent which prohibited this type of influence and excommunicated for such counsels while a person was in isolation." Fray Muñoz determined that Fray Lucas had acted illegally and ordered a new investigation. When María and José affirmed their desire to marry, they were married.

Parental concern over marriage choice centered on the issue of *calidad* (social status). Parents sought to marry their children to someone of similar *calidad*. *Igualdad de calidad* (equality in social status) between marriage partners was a reigning principle in hierarchical colonial societies stratified, among other axes, along racial lines. Parents strenuously objected to matrimonial alliances when a disparity, whether of race, occupation, or legitimacy of birth, was too great. Although historians such as Oakah Jones, Ramón Gutiérrez, and Leon Campbell have observed that racial and class lines were blurred on the borderlands, the Spanish aristocracy was bent on retaining and reproducing its property, status, power, and privilege.

Despite parental preference for arranged marriage, other elements, including a person's status and a family's history of fertility, mediated the extent to which arranged marriages could be enforced. These and other variables often conditioned whether a son or daughter responded to family duty or to personal sentiment,

resisted or acquiesced to parental choice, or sought another solution.

Among the peasant class that enjoyed rights to communal land grants and practiced partible inheritance, parents also chose their children's mates. Upon taking a bride, each son received a share of the family's land and was allocated space based on a given number of beams (*vigas*) in the parental home. If existing space was too limited for such arrangements, rooms were added to the house or a separate building was constructed nearby. Peasant daughters seldom received land rights at marriage because the husband's family was expected to have land. Women's dowries usually consisted of household items and livestock.

Parents in wage-earning and landless peasant families did not supervise their children's selection of a spouse. Moreover, families who had no property to transmit or who did not subscribe to the cultural and marital ideals of either Spanish or Pueblo society found little reason to enter into a sacramental Christian marriage. Consequently, landless peasants, *genízaros,* and wage earners were more apt to enter into consensual unions and relationships based on personal desire or love. Moreover, since establishing a conjugal residence required money, individuals who wished to marry had to wait until they had accumulated the necessary resources. Until then, many lived in common-law marriages or other forms of consensual unions.

The marriages of servants and slaves were arranged by the heads of the households they served. Records for colonial New Mexico reveal that servants sometimes filed complaints against nobles for forcing them into marriage; they seldom won such appeals.

In her complaint to the prelate at Santa Fe in 1621, one of Governor Juan de Eulate's female slaves charged that the governor had forced her to marry against her will and that even though she was now married, he continued to demand sexual favors. Similarly, Juan Bautista Saragosa complained in 1640 that Governor Luís de Rosas forced him and Polonia Varela, the governor's retainer, to marry. Polonia and Juan both stated that they had married under duress: Polonia because she feared the governor who "was such an absolute lord that with or without law he trampled on everyone." Juan did so because the governor kept him in the stocks without food and threatened to whip and gibbet him unless he married Polonia.

Marriage and the Bourbon Reforms

In 1760 a royal *cédula* (decree) was passed, which required members of the military corps and other officials to obtain royal permission to marry. The 1760 decree was passed to reinforce the hierarchies of social class and race that structured the military and the royal bureaucracy. Its passage coincided with the departure of Spanish troops for the colonies during the Seven Years' War (1756–1763); these troops were soon followed in New Spain by an established standing army. In the colonies, because social class was not as rigid as in Spain, racial mixing, consensual unions, miscegenation, and concubinage were common. Consequently, military officers had greater opportunity to establish "undesirable" social and sexual alliances and to marry outside their social class and race.

The *cédula* of 1760 focused specifically on the quality and wealth of the woman whom an officer with the rank of captain or above proposed to marry. In order to receive royal permission, or license, to marry, the officer had to submit documents detailing the woman's class (nobility, landed gentry, and so forth), economic circumstances, and purity of blood. A committee screened the application and verified the woman's background. Applications approved by this committee were sent to the king, who, by signing them, granted the couple royal permission to marry. Any officer who defied the committee lost his commission and was dropped from the military corps. Through the granting of royal permission, the state controlled the social and racial composition of the ruling class and ensured the reproduction of this social and racial elite.

Until the latter part of the eighteenth century, canon and civil law upheld the doctrine of freedom of choice in marriage. On 23 March 1776, however, King Charles III issued the Royal Pragmatic on Marriage, a pivotal piece of social legislation in the series of economic, administrative, political, social, and military reforms designed to assert the power of the imperial state, restore Spain's international prominence, and overcome the crisis of production in the American colonies. Collectively, these were known as the Bourbon reforms.

The Royal Pragmatic on Marriage prohibited the legitimation of unequal unions and required, under penalty of disinheritance, that all persons under the age of twenty-five obtain formal parental consent to marry. The decree declared that wide disparities in the status of marital candidates were detrimental to the economic prosperity of honorable families and weakened their social exclusivity. It aimed to preserve the status of the dominant classes by preventing unequal marriages that would "offend family honour and threaten the good order of the state."

By enforcing the doctrine of freedom of choice and by marrying children against their parents' wishes, the Catholic church eroded parents' authority over their children and contributed to the moral collapse of society. Shifting the emphasis from the sacred to the profane, Charles III gave precedence to the secular aspects of marriage as a civil contract that legitimized progeny, established inheritance and property rights, and formed the basis for the accession of honors. The king, however, cautioned parents not to interpret their authority as the right to force a mate upon a child. Parents could oppose only marriages that "offended the honor of the family or jeopardized the integrity of the state."

Extended to all of Spain's territories on 7 April 1778, the Royal Pragmatic on Marriage became law in New Mexico that same year but did not reach California until 1779. The law specifically aimed to prevent the marriage of whites with blacks, mulattoes, and other *castas* of African origin. It did not require parental consent for the "marriage of Negros, mulattoes, *coyotes,* and other such individuals with each other, except for those who serve in an official capacity or otherwise distinguish themselves by their reputation."

The royal legislation on marriage (the *cédula* of 1760, the Royal Pragmatic of 1776, and related decrees of 1783 and 1796) was a key element in Charles III's drive to strip the church, and other corporate bodies, of special privilege and power and to assert the secular authority of the state. The Bourbon concept and locus of power centered on the patriarchal household, which became the symbol of good government.

The Bourbon legislation on marriage expanded the legal scope of parental control and constrained the power of the clergy to impinge upon it. It deprived the church of exclusive control over marriage and extended the role of the civil judiciary in private life by establishing civil courts to hear marriage cases. Finally, to undermine the power of the church and the lower clergy, King Charles allied himself with male heads of household. In doing so, he reaffirmed the principle and fact of inequality between husbands and wives by giving fathers control over the marriage of their children. A mother could concur with, but not dissent from, the father's decision.

In 1783 the Crown passed a law forbidding wives to give money to a child disinherited for marrying against the express wishes of the father. The law denounced the "lack of subordination of wives to husbands" and exhorted wives to "recognize the authority of their consort as the head of the family" and to accept his judgment. In addition to preventing unequal or interracial marriages, the new marriage laws required the obedience of wives as a guarantee of social cohesion.

Whereas the social policies of the Bourbon reforms were restrictive, as the marriage decrees indicate, the economic policies were expansive. Within these contradictions, new values asserted an individualism and egalitarianism initially rooted in the doctrine of freedom of choice in marriage. The new conditions and corollary values extended to the borderlands, where social change in the latter half of the eighteenth century was accelerated by population growth, expanded areas of settlement, greater racial mixing, economic development, and increased wealth.

Changing values and mores concerning the place of the individual in marriage and in the larger community were accompanied by profound behavioral changes, which were particularly evident in New Mexico, the oldest and most populous of the borderland colonies. Examining the behavioral changes in that colony, Gutiérrez charts that by 1800 individualism and love had appeared in the matrimonial documents as reasons for wishing to marry. Prior to 1800 couples used the term *amor* (love) to refer either to Christian love, a sentiment displayed out of duty, or "natural" love stemming from lust and referring to illicit sexual activities. By the turn of the century, however, the term *amor* no longer referred to illicit acts but to love born of passion. Romantic love, which advocated the free expression of pas-

sion and underscored the notion of personal autonomy and individual desire, was sufficient reason for choosing a spouse.

SHIFTING MARRIAGE PATTERNS ON THE BORDERLANDS

Marriage and marriage patterns on the borderlands changed with global socioeconomic and political changes driven by Spanish colonial policies and with changes in local circumstances and conditions. Although many couples did not register their marriage, matrimonial records for those who did reveal that the following changes took place from the beginning to the end of the colonial period: the mean age at marriage decreased, the age gap between spouses narrowed, racial exogamy increased, and an acute racial consciousness developed.

By the end of the eighteenth century, women in New Mexico outnumbered men by a ratio of ten to eight. In this colony, the mean age at first marriage between 1760 and 1810 declined from 25.5 to 23.3 years for men and from 19.4 to 15.5 years for women. The age gap between New Mexican spouses narrowed dramatically from the late seventeenth to the end of the eighteenth century: between 1670 and 1739 only 22 percent of all persons marrying took a spouse of similar age or just one year older, but 50 percent did so by 1800. The increase in racial exogamy in the Bourbon reform era may have been more pronounced in New Mexico than in California. In the latter colony, racial exogamy appears to have been greatest during the earliest years of military occupation and does not appear to have exceeded 15 percent throughout the colonial era. In both colonies racial exogamy increased during the 1820s.

Until the Bourbon reforms of the 1770s, control of the institution of marriage rested with the Catholic church. During this period, marriage was viewed as a spiritual sacrament and a vocation to be entered into by free choice and volition. The authority of the church protected the individual's right to freedom of choice. With the Bourbon reforms, the state asserted its authority over the church and defined marriage as a secular institution that regulated inheritance of status and property, and was thus essential to the integrity of the state. Identifying the power of the state with the power of the head of household, the state essentially rescinded the right to freedom of choice in marriage by giving parents—specifically fathers—authority to select appropriate marriage partners for their children. However, changing the locus of authority from the spiritual to the temporal, which coincided with the growth and commercialization of New Mexico's economy, provided the climate and conditions that gave rise to the secular values of individualism and romantic love. By the beginning of the nineteenth century, the notion of personal autonomy and the importance of selecting a mate on the basis of individual desire were increasingly evident on the Spanish Borderlands.

BIBLIOGRAPHY

Ariès, Philippe. *Centuries of Childhood: A Social History of Family Life*. New York, 1962.

Arrom, Silvia Marina. *The Women of Mexico City, 1790–1857*. Stanford, Calif., 1985.

Boyer, Richard. "Women, La Mala Vida, and the Politics of Marriage." In *Sexuality and Marriage in Colonial Latin America*, edited by Asunción Lavrin. Lincoln, Neb., 1989.

Campbell, Leon G. "The First Californios: Presidial Society in Spanish California, 1769–1822." In *The Spanish Borderlands: A First Reader*, edited by Oakah L. Jones, Jr. Los Angeles, 1974.

Castañeda, Antonia I. "Presidarias y Pobladoras: Spanish-Mexican Women in Frontier Monterey, Alta California, 1770–1821. Ph.D. diss., Stanford University, 1990.

Gutiérrez, Ramón. "From Honor to Love: Transformation of the Meaning of Sexuality in Colonial New Mexico. In *Kinship, Ideology and Practice in Latin America*, edited by Raymond T. Smith. Chapel Hill, N.C., 1984.

———. *When Jesus Came, the Corn Mothers Went Away: Marriage, Sexuality, and Power in New Mexico, 1500–1846*. Stanford, Calif., 1991.

Jones, Oakah L., Jr. *Los Paisanos: Spanish Settlers on the Northern Frontier of New Spain*. Norman, Okla., 1979.

Miranda, Gloria. "Gente de Razón Marriage Patterns in Spanish and Mexican California: A Case Study of Santa Barbara and Los Angeles." *Southern California Quarterly* 63, no. 1 (Spring 1981):1–21.

Moorhead, Max L. "The Soldado de Cuera: Stalward of the Spanish Borderlands." In *The Spanish Borderlands: A First Reader*, edited by Oakah L. Jones, Jr. Los Angeles, 1979.

Ozment, Steven. *When Fathers Ruled: Family Life in Reformation Europe*. Cambridge, Mass., 1983.

Perry, Mary Elizabeth. *Gender and Disorder in Early Modern Seville*. Princeton, N. J., 1990.

Seed, Patricia. *To Love, Honor, and Obey in Colonial Mexico: Conflict over Marriage Choice, 1574–1821*. Stanford, Calif., 1988.

Shorter, Edward. *Making of the Modern Family*. New York, 1975.

Stone, Lawrence. *The Family, Sex and Marriage in England, 1500–1800*. New York, 1979. Abridged edition.

Antonia I. Castañeda

SEE ALSO **African-American Culture; Civil Law; Gender Relations;** and **Interracial Societies.**

CHILDHOOD AND ADOLESCENCE

THE BRITISH COLONIES

CHILDHOOD AND ADOLESCENCE are universal, yet culturally defined, stages of life. Until the 1970s historians of the family generally accepted the hypothesis that children in the premodern era were submerged within the adult world as miniature or little adults and that adolescence hardly existed as a distinct stage of life. However, there is increasing recognition that the history of childhood and adolescence is far more complex and that, however much seventeenth- and eighteenth-century life may have differed from that of the late twentieth century, adults saw and treated childhood and youth (the term commonly used for adolescence in the colonial period) as distinct phases of life.

This essay starts with an examination of the history of childhood and adolescence in England on the eve of colonization and then summarizes the major demographic characteristics of the colonies as they affected children and adolescents. This is followed by a life-course analysis of the experience of children and adolescents from birth to adulthood, stressing both those dimensions of life that were the common experience of children and those that reflected cultural and class differences.

ENGLISH BACKGROUND

On the eve of the English colonization of North America, the English population was surprisingly young by modern standards. As Peter Laslett has observed: "We must imagine our ancestors . . . in the perpetual presence of their young offspring." Nearly half the population was under the age of twenty, with the median age ranging from the low to mid twenties. Infant and childhood mortality rates were high. For example, in eight parishes during the years 1550–1649, about one child in four died before the age of ten.

Family size, especially among the poorer ranks of English society, was relatively small. The cost of establishing new families encouraged women and men to delay marriage. Women commonly married in their twenties, and marriages were often broken by death, thus limiting the years in which women might conceive children. Within marriage the intervals between births ranged from twenty-four to thirty months, a pattern that was due primarily to the contraceptive effects of nursing. The rich, however, had more children because the fertility of upper-class families was enhanced by younger ages at marriage, better diet and housing, and wet-nursing and because a higher proportion of their children probably survived to adulthood. Nonetheless the most privileged English families averaged only about four children.

Children sometimes grew up in complex households, the size and structure of which were determined in large measure by a family's status. As a rule the higher a household's income, the larger and more complex was its membership, for rank and income enabled families to employ a range of servants and other retainers. While households might be complex, children did not necessarily spend much time with their parents or even in their parents' household. Among prominent families children might be put out to wet nurses as infants and reared principally by governesses and tutors. While the children of less privileged families were likely to spend their early years at home, many entered apprenticeships and service in other households before puberty and sometimes as early as age seven. Fragmentary data suggest that between puberty and marriage, as many as two-thirds of the boys and three-quarters of the girls lived away from home. Although large numbers of both boys and girls lived away, there were more reasons to keep boys at home, as they could eventually take over lands worked by their fathers or learn their fathers' trades at home.

Service and apprenticeships in other households not only removed children from parental authority but also created problems of social control, especially among adolescents. There is ample evidence for the existence of an adolescent subculture, particularly in urban areas, where large numbers of adolescents could congregate away from the supervision of their masters.

Edmund S. Morgan has suggested that the practice of placing children in other households, at least in seventeenth-century New England, may have had a sound psychological foundation.

The child left home just at the time when parental discipline causes increasing friction, just at a time when a child begins to assert his independence. By allowing a strange master to take over the disciplinary function, the parent could meet the child upon a plane of affection and friendliness. At the same time the child would be taught good behavior by someone who would not forgive him any mischief out of affection for his person. (*The Puritan Family*, p. 78)

Morgan's hypothesis stresses affection between parents and children and objective discipline on the part of a master, while overlooking the ways in which adolescents could avoid supervision by parents and masters and seek the companionship of their peers. Nonetheless it is important to recognize the patriarchal order of families both in theory and in practice—namely, the preeminent role of fathers and masters and the strong emphasis placed on hierarchy, status, order, and, hence, discipline.

This pattern appears to have transcended religious affiliation, appearing in families of both Anglican and Puritan persuasion. The emphasis on discipline can be seen in references, especially among Puritans, to "breaking" a child's will, in the widespread use of corporal punishment to discipline students, servants, and apprentices, and in a notable concern with outward manifestations of deference and respect toward one's elders and superiors.

As might be inferred from the obligations of service and apprenticeship, formal schooling for many children was limited in both quality and duration. Educational attainment, as measured by signature literacy (that is, the ability to sign one's name), was closely correlated to social class, occupation, and gender. Not surprisingly the clergy, lawyers, and schoolmasters were the most literate groups, with literacy levels declining down through the social orders from gentlemen, yeomen, tradesmen, and craftsmen to husbandmen, farm laborers, and building workers. Signature literacy levels among women were comparable to levels attained by men in the lowest orders, with little more than 10 percent of women able to sign their names. Thus opportunities to become fully literate were directly correlated to one's status and prospects in life. Children who were placed in service to other families were unlikely candidates for extended education. Most parents could at best hope that their children would learn to read; writing and other skills derived from formal education were the province of a relatively privileged few.

Not only did children and adolescents frequently move from their households of birth into other households, but there were larger patterns of movement within sixteenth- and seventeenth-century English society, with many individuals and families moving from village to village and from village to city, particularly London. As James Horn has emphasized, the movement from England to North America was, in part, an extension and elaboration of patterns of movement within an already mobile society.

COLONIZATION AND DEMOGRAPHY

The English population of seventeenth-century Virginia and Maryland was shaped by the demographic characteristics of the immigrants and by the environment that they encountered upon arrival. Most settlers were young, unmarried male servants. Relatively few persons arrived in family groups, and the obligations of servitude postponed the opportunity to establish families. Thus the immigrant population scarcely resembld a stable, settled society and was, in fact, numerically dominated by late-adolescent males.

The environment that the settlers encountered was hostile by any standard. While some lost their lives at the hands of Indians, far more fell prey to diseases to which they had had little exposure: malaria, dysentery, and typhoid, for example. Many colonists ffound Virginia and Maryland an early graveyard rather than a land of opportunity, with life expectancies short for all persons regardless of age, gender, and social class.

The composition of the immigrant population and the environment in which it lived had important effects on family life and, hence, on children and adolescents. Many servants died before their service was completed, and men in their early twenties were likely to live for only another twenty to twenty-five years. Since those men who survived outnumbered available women, women married quickly, while at least some men necessarily postponed marriage or never married. Marriages were unstable, with women particularly vulnerable to illness and death during childbearing. Widows quickly remarried, while widowers entered a highly competitive market for marriage.

Under these conditions of life and death, Creole children (those born in America of immigrant parents) were likely to become members of new, complex, and impermanent households. As Darrett B. Rutman and Anita H. Rutman have noted:

A father might give way to a stepfather, an uncle, a brother, or simply a friend of the deceased father; a mother might well be replaced by an aunt, an elder sister, or a father's 'now-wife,' to use the wording frequently found in conveyances and wills. The children themselves would run a wide gamut of ages and be related to each other in a variety of ways. (*A Place in Time*, p. 118)

Toward the end of the seventeenth century, the structure of the Chesapeake population began to change. Unencumbered by the obligations of indentured servitude, Creole women married earlier than their mothers and could therefore bear more children. With declining numbers of white immigrants, the native-born white population increased both absolutely and proportionately, and the sex ratio became more balanced.

As immigration from England decreased, there was a growing reliance on African slaves among planters. While the African and African-American population of the Chesapeake colonies remained small for much of the seventeenth century, increasingly large importations of Africans and natural increase swelled the African-American population from roughly 15 percent in the early eighteenth century to 38 percent by the end of the colonial period. During the same years, the proportion of Africans and African Americans in South Carolina rose from nearly 43 percent to some 60 percent.

A preference for young male African slaves resulted in demographic patterns that were similar to those among white servants. The sex ratio was imbalanced and opportunities to establish family relationships were limited. Many men had to postpone marriage, while women married young. When plantations were small and had few slaves, husbands and wives frequently lived on separate plantations, and children almost invariably lived with their mothers.

As the African-American population grew through natural increase and more numerous importations, the context of family and household life changed. With a more balanced sex ratio, men were able to marry earlier and in greater numbers. While large numbers of husbands and wives continued to live on separate farms and plantations, the emergence of complex kinship networks afforded opportunities for mutual support and a greater measure of identity separate from the white world. As Allan Kulikoff has observed,

A slave who lived with many Africans in a place where continual heavy importation of blacks kept the proportion of Africans high was more likely to adopt African customs than the slave who lived where importation was sporadic, the proportion of immigrants among black adults low, and the numbers of whites great. (*Tobacco and Slaves,* p. 318)

Not all Africans and African Americans were slaves, for some arrived as servants and others bought their freedom. Among the most closely documented free African Americans were those who lived on Virginia's Eastern Shore in the seventeenth century. For these men and women, the family was, according to T. H. Breen and Stephen Innes, "the central institution," providing "an opportunity to become fully human, to give and receive affection, to express intimate thoughts, to achieve a measure of security in an otherwise frenetic environment, to consider a future that included children as well as grandchildren."

For both white and African-American children in the Chesapeake colonies, life held many uncertainties. For white children these arose in large measure from the cruel demography of the early Chesapeake. For African-American children, uncertainties stemmed not merely or perhaps even primarily from demography but from the dynamics of an institution from which there were virtually no chances to escape and that used them and their parents for its own ends.

In contrast to the Chesapeake region, conditions in the New England and Middle Atlantic colonies provided a substantially different context for the lives of children and adolescents. While there were more males than females among the settlers of New England, the first generation more closely resembled a mature population, containing all ages, ranks, and conditions. Many arrived in family and household groups, comprising not merely parents and children but sometimes elderly people as well as servants.

The white settlers of New England escaped most of the diseases that afflicted their southern counterparts. The favorable environment, com-

bined with the composition of the immigrant population, resulted in extraordinary growth. Most women married in their early twenties, rates of maternal, infant, and childhood mortality were low in comparison to the Chesapeake experience, life expectancies for those who survived childhood and adolescence were quite high, and completed families (those in which the mother survived to menopause) were common and large. Thus among first-generation families in Andover, Massachusetts, the average completed family was 8.3 children, with 7.2 surviving to age twenty-one. In the absence of significant immigration after the first generation, New England's rapid population growth resulted from relatively early marriages among women and relatively low rates of childhood and maternal mortality.

As the population expanded through the generations, disease and death rates rose. With a more densely settled population, increased commercial contacts with the outside world, higher levels of internal movement of people and goods, and a greater proportion of poor individuals and families, diseases circulated more easily and with more devastating effects. Boston and other port towns were especially vulnerable to influxes of smallpox, while successive waves of diphtheria (commonly called the throat distemper) ravaged the countryside in the mid eighteenth century and proved particularly lethal to children. As a result New England became a less healthy region in which to live. For example third-generation families in a town like Andover were still large in numbers of births, with completed families averaging 7.6 children, but only 5.5 children survived to adulthood. These and other data suggest that the eighteenth century witnessed something of a demographic convergence, with the Chesapeake population possibly experiencing lower rates of morbidity and mortality (the data are by no means conclusive) and New Englanders experiencing higher rates.

The founding and settlement of Pennsylvania in the last decades of the seventeenth century added yet another dimension to the demography of early America. Pennsylvania soon became an ethnically diverse society, attracting settlers, Quakers and non-Quakers alike, from England, the Continent, and, later, Northern Ireland. The rapid growth of Pennsylvania's population reflected continuing waves of immigration throughout the colonial period and a healthy environment that allowed for rapid natural increase.

In the burgeoning population of colonial America, children and adolescents not only made up a majority but also had a substantial impact on the adult world. In material terms the sheer numbers of children may have acted as something of a brake on the economy of young households, absorbing resources for food, clothing, and other aspects of their care. As children matured, however, they became increasingly productive and contributing members of families and households. Children also played a role in important familial decisions, particularly in the allocation of resources within families and households and across the generations.

CONCEPTION TO ADULTHOOD

From conception to adulthood, it is possible to delineate the major stages in an individual's life. Although some children were conceived and born outside the bonds of matrimony, rates of illegitimacy were generally low. The prenuptial conception of children was relatively more common, especially among Creole women in the Chesapeake colonies and, increasingly in the eighteenth century, among New Englanders. This upward trend in prenuptial sexual activity occurred in England as well, reflecting what may have been a pervasive and fundamental shift in societal control over and attitudes toward sexuality and courtship.

Childbirth took place in the home and was usually attended by a midwife (or at least by a woman experienced in matters of childbirth) and neighboring women. Male family members typically played no role at childbirth other than to gather midwives and other women. Miscarriages and stillbirths, when the woman herself survived, had little effect on the fertility cycle, as women quickly conceived again after stillbirths and neonatal deaths.

Parents, and particularly fathers, welcomed the birth of male children. One indication of this attitude is the fact that proportionately fewer girls than boys were recorded in the birth records

of New England towns. Thus in eighteenth-century Westborough, Massachusetts, 117.6 births of male children were recorded for every 100 females. (The ratio in the United States is currently about 105 to 100.) The causes of this underregistration are not clear. It is most unlikely that the underregistration of female births reflected infanticide, but one may speculate that fathers were less likely to record their daughters' births promptly and were less scrupulous in recording the birth of a female child in the event of a neonatal death (death within one year of birth). The male line determined a family's surname, and males owned and controlled the intergenerational transmission of most real property. As John J. Waters has observed of seventeenth-century Barnstable, Massachusetts, "the central aspect of traditional peasant life in New England was the concern for a house and lands, a fruitful wife, and oxen and sons to till the soil and thus to place a man's name upon the land," and he suggests that a patriarchal society favored higher survival rates among males.

Entering the World

Three major events for which considerable evidence survives marked the child's entrance into the world: parents' choice of names for their newborns, baptism, and the nursing of infants. According to the Rutmans' study of Middlesex County, Virginia, settlers selected names from a universe determined by their English background; children's names in Middlesex County were generally correlated with children's names in England. Name sharing among the generations was common; more than three-quarters of male children were given the names of their fathers, grandfathers, or uncles, while nearly 70 percent of female children bore the name of their mothers, grandmothers, or aunts. Parents tended to name first sons and daughters after paternal grandfathers and maternal grandmothers and then to name second sons and daughters after themselves. Thus parents' choices of names for their children embedded them into networks of kinship.

The Puritan settlers of New England rejected their English antecedents and stressed the importance of biblical forenames. It was more common in New England than in Middlesex County, Virginia, for both the father's and the mother's first names to descend to a son and to a daughter, and New England parents were more likely to name first sons and daughters than second children after themselves. New England parents (as well as their Middlesex counterparts) also used necronyms; that is, they named a new child after a deceased child. Toward the end of the colonial period, middle names became increasingly common and were often chosen from last names (for example, a maternal grandparent's surname).

The importance of kin is also apparent in African-American naming practices. Parents frequently named children after themselves or other relatives but never for their masters. African names, or names derived from African traditions, appear to have been common among slave families in South Carolina, although the Rutmans find that only about 5 percent of slaves in Middlesex County bore African names, with the rest having names deriving from the dominant pool of common English names and which, they argue, were probably determined by the masters.

The study of naming patterns, particularly outside New England, remains an open field. It is not clear, for example, whether other ethnic or religious groups (for example, the Germans or Quakers) transferred traditions of child naming from the Old to the New World.

The importance of preserving kinship ties through naming practices may have reflected the pervasive instability of the nuclear family in the Chesapeake and the important roles that extended kin played in providing nurturance and identity for children. For African Americans, surviving records suggest that family and kinship ties thrived most readily on large plantations. Thus among the nearly four hundred slaves owned by Charles Carroll of Annapolis, Maryland, in 1773, more than three-quarters lived with other immediate family members. Nearly all children under age five lived either with both parents (77.5 percent) or with their mothers (18.3 percent). While the proportion of older children living with both parents declined (59.3 percent of children aged from five to nine; 53.7 percent of children aged from ten to fourteen), only a few children (7.4 percent) lived in households that contained no kin whatsoever. By contrast children born to mothers on small plantations were more likely to live apart from their fathers.

While all children received names, only some children were baptized as infants. Antiquarians and historians have long noted, sometimes with mild astonishment, that members of the Puritan or Congregational churches of New England brought infants to church for baptism on the day of their birth, if a Sabbath, or on the very next Sabbath, sometimes enduring considerable hardship to obtain this Sacrament in winter months. In this the Puritans were not unique. Since at least the mid sixteenth century, the Church of England had admonished its members to bring their children to church for baptism at the earliest possible opportunity. While there was considerable variation in the interval between birth and baptism, in the seventeenth century most Anglican children were baptized within a fortnight of birth, whereas by the end of the eighteenth century the interval in some English parishes had lengthened for many children to as much as fifteen months. While comparable data are not available for Anglicans in the American colonies, scattered settlement patterns and a shortage of Anglican pastors may have resulted in significant delays in the baptism of at least some children.

The nursing of infants received some commentary and documentation during the colonial period—commentary in the form of admonitions in prescriptive literature, documentation in terms of recorded instances of nursing, difficulties experienced by mother and child, and the timing of weaning. Occasional references to pewter and glass nipples indicate that some infants were bottle-fed, and some infants in relatively prominent families were wet-nursed. Most women, however, breast-fed their infants from necessity and cultural preference. Few families could afford to hire wet nurses, and even when the means were available, cultural values emphasized the importance, for mother and infant alike, of maternal breast-feeding. Some women had difficulties nursing, as references to cracked nipples and infections appear in diaries and correspondence, but most women chose, when they had a choice, to continue to nurse their children. By contrast many wealthy English women ignored the advice of physicians and Puritan writers and employed the services of wet nurses, a pattern that continued well into the eighteenth century.

Mothers occasionally arranged to have their children nursed for short periods by other lactating women. This practice occurred when it was difficult, dangerous, or inconvenient for the infant's mother to nurse. Thus if the precarious health of a new mother made it difficult for her to nurse her infant, another nursing mother could breast-feed the child while its mother regained strength. Women planning short trips might leave their infants to be nursed by other mothers for a day or two. There were natural limitations on the duration of these nursing exchanges, as mothers had to resume breast-feeding before their own milk dried up.

African-American infants, like their white counterparts, were breast-fed by their mothers, but the context of their daily existence differed substantially from that of white children. Their mothers were likely to be employed in fieldwork and therefore tended to the physical needs of their children near the fields. After they were weaned, children spent much of their early years in the company of other children, perhaps under the care of a grandmother or other elderly woman who was no longer used as a fieldworker.

Whatever the conditions of nursing for both free and slave mothers, the frequency of childbirth and sheer numbers of infants meant that in any given community, many women of childbearing age would either be lactating or pregnant or occasionally both.

Mortality

Infants and young children experienced high rates of mortality by modern standards, as they were exposed to diseases and conditions that the modern world has eliminated or can more effectively prevent or treat. Data on childhood mortality is elusive, as the births, to say nothing of the deaths, of many children were not recorded. Nonetheless it is clear that conditions were not uniform throughout the colonies or throughout the colonial period. Infants and children faced an especially harsh environment in the seventeenth-century Chesapeake, where dysentery, typhoid, and malaria were, in the view of some historians, pandemic. In Maryland, for example, as many as one-third of male children died by the age of one, and as many as half or

more died before the age of twenty. In the New England colonies, conditions were more favorable to survival in the seventeenth century, but the growth of population and trade in the eighteenth century resulted in the rapid spread of epidemic disease and higher mortality rates among infants and children. Finally, throughout the colonial period the populations of urban areas experienced high rates of disease and mortality.

While parents experienced frequent bereavement through the deaths of spouses and children, so, too, were children likely to be bereaved by the death of one or both parents. Thus in one Virginia county nearly 75 percent of all children lost at least one parent by age twenty-one or marriage, whichever came first.

With relationships between parents and children likely to be broken by parental death in the Chesapeake colonies, ties with kin and neighbors had great importance. Since fathers could not realistically anticipate living to see their sons and daughters reach maturity, they commonly made early provision for the well-being of their children, especially their sons. These provisions included the transfer of legal title over livestock to their children, provisions in wills that sons attain early control over their inheritances, and the naming of wives, other relatives, or friends to administer their estates. Orphans' courts came to play an important role in the lives of children, protecting inheritances and overseeing the education and training of orphans.

The Crowded Household

The relentless cycle of conception, pregnancy, childbirth, nursing, and weaning, which ended only at menopause or a woman's death, resulted not only in large families but also in crowded households. Rare was the child who had his or her own bed, much less a room that was not shared with other siblings or adults. Privacy was a luxury that few could afford or even imagine.

In large and sometimes complex households, it was common for older children to assume responsibility for the care and supervision of younger sisters and brothers while parents focused their energies and attention on the work required to sustain a household. Older children thus served as figures of authority and as role models for younger children. The resulting ties of affection and respect among children are evidenced in the frequency with which parents named their children after their own sisters and brothers.

Households eventually became less crowded when children married and established separate households. Until then families could relieve the crowdedness by sending children to work in other households or, in the case of teenage boys, arranging for apprenticeships. In the early stages of a family's evolution, when there were only small children, a family might hire older children or adolescents as workers. When there were few or no remaining children, a family might again hire workers to replace children who had married or were serving as apprentices. In the intermediate stages of its development, a family might be self-sufficient in terms of labor and even have a surplus of children who could work in smaller households.

Childhood

Little documentation about the day-to-day experience of early childhood survives; parents and others were more likely to record exceptional rather than routine events. Thus toilet training, a child's first steps, the development of language skills, daily care, and even the extent and manner of discipline for small children elude, for the most part, the historian's eye. There is some evidence that male and female infants and children were dressed similarly, perhaps in a long gown. How long this lasted is largely a matter of conjecture, although there are recorded instances of boys who began to wear breeches at the age of three. Anne Bradstreet recognized that a child's clothing affects his or her mobility and recommended against clothing that would impede a child's movement, "A prudent mother will not cloth her little child with a long and cumbersome garment; she easily forsees what events it is like to produce, at the best, but falls and bruises or perhaps somewhat worse."

Falls and bruises were a natural accompaniment to the development of motor skills and curiosity, and while some children may have attended school as early as age three, most children under the age of six or seven were allowed to play. As Puritan minister John Cotton observed, "their bodies are too weak to labour, and their minds to study are too shallow." As a result,

Cotton was content that the first seven years be "spent in pasttime, and God looks not much at it." While adults might generally supervise a child's activities, or assign that task to an older sibling or servant, records of accidents and deaths indicate that supervision was sometimes lax.

Leisure activities have been most closely documented for the southern colonies, particularly among well-to-do Virginians. While some girls played with imported dolls and tea sets, and boys with formal toys such as a miniature coach and horses, most children inevitably made do with less expensive toys such as homemade dolls, marbles, tops, balls, toy soldiers, or other items that merchants carried among their wares. Outside, children played a wide range of games, including hopscotch, leapfrog, hide-and-seek, rolling a hoop, flying kites, and various games using balls. As children grew older, pure play became increasingly integrated into work tasks and ceremonial occasions—quilting parties, huskings, barn raisings and house-raisings, militia training, and election and court days. Some play required participation by both sexes, particularly parlor and courtship activities, while other leisure pursuits, such as hunting and fishing, were segregated by gender.

Discipline. While children might "run about," as one diarist noted of his children's activities, parents sought to teach them appropriate behavior and disciplined them when they challenged authority or broke the rules. Historians have reached no consensus with respect to the role and type of discipline that parents were likely to employ. English evangelical Protestant males such as John Robinson, George Whitefield, and John Wesley recommended that parents undertake to break a child's will at a very early age. Women, however, and particularly mothers, had primary, if not exclusive, care of infants and small children but left few records of their approach to discipline.

One notable exception is twenty-three-year-old Esther Edwards Burr's description of her treatment of her first child, ten-month-old Sally:

She has been Whip'd once on *Old Adams* account, and she knows the difference between a smile and a frown as well as I do. When she has done any thing that she surspects [*sic*] is wrong, will look with concern to see what Mama says, and if I only knit my brow she will cry till I smile, and altho' she is not quite Ten months old, yet when she knows so much, I think tis time she should be taught. But none but a parent can concieve [*sic*] how hard it is to chastise your *own most tender self.* I confess I never had a right idea of the mothers heart at such a time before. I did it my self two, and it did her a vast deal of good. If you was here I would tell you the effect it had on her. (*The Journal of Esther Edwards Burr, 1754–1757*, p. 96)

In the absence of other first-hand accounts, Burr's example can only be taken as suggestive rather than typical of practice among New Englanders.

Advice on child rearing in New England stressed the need for children to be respectful and obedient—for example, by rising when their parents entered the room, speaking only when spoken to, and obeying cheerfully and without hesitation. Corporal punishment was always a possibility, but those who offered advice to parents preferred that children be verbally admonished, reasoned with, and possibly shamed into obedience rather than physically coerced into submission. Furthermore parents were urged to refrain from disciplining their children in anger.

Regarding Quaker parents, Barry Levy has pointed out that "the memorial literature shows that even the best mothers held in reserve a repertoire of artful skills: restraining, admonishing, praying, advising, reproving, and occasionally lashing. The best mothers were stubborn, if gentle, authoritarians, not indulgent wafflers."

Outside the Puritan and Quaker traditions, some parents approached the matter of discipline in a more lenient fashion. For example the children of prominent eighteenth-century planters in the Chesapeake colonies were given free rein and apparently little coercion. Reason, gentle persuasion, and good example, rather than the rod of discipline, were regarded as the most appropriate approaches to achieving good manners and behavior. Little evidence survives to show how families of lesser economic means, more limited education, and less gentle breeding treated their children.

Work. Most children had to work at relatively early ages. While a Protestant or Puritan work ethic might extol the virtues of labor and lament the snares of idleness, the facts of economic life in a premodern and overwhelmingly rural society dictated a child's early participation in useful work. Beginning with the simple tasks and errands that a child could carry out under the direction of a parent, older sibling, or other adult, a child's work experience evolved in duration and complexity with his or her physical stature, dexterity, and understanding. It is difficult to pinpoint the ages at which children began productive work, but scattered examples suggest that it was certainly as early as age seven. This does not mean that parents or masters demanded work that was beyond the capacities of a child. As Anne Bradstreet observed, "A wise father will not lay a burden on a child of seven years old which he knows is enough for one of twice his strength."

Boys' work throughout childhood and well into adolescence revolved around the barn, fields, woodlot, and herds, while girls' work focused on the household, hearth, textiles, garden, dairy, and poultry. A boy's first tasks might include running simple errands on foot or horseback, cutting firewood, tending cattle, leading oxen or a horse while his father, an older brother, or hired worker handled a plow. A girl's first tasks almost certainly included work related to making, cleaning, and repairing textiles; tending vegetable gardens and poultry; preparing food; and cleaning cooking utensils.

Learning for both boys and girls was by observation and direct experience, with older siblings and adults initiating the child into the world of work. As the child matured, and if there were younger siblings, he or she might gradually assume the role of teacher, passing on to younger children the skills acquired through observation, imitation, and repetition.

On southern plantations, African-American children appear to have begun field or other work by the age of seven. In the timing of productive work, their experience resembled the children of white farmers, although the context was significantly different. Initiation into the world of work sometimes coincided with forced separation from family and friends, with children sent or sold to other farms and plantations.

From a master's perspective, there was little to be gained by separating an infant or small child from its mother and other kin. But once a child began performing productive work, his or her value and usefulness could enter more directly into a master's calculations. The settlement of sons on separate lands, the payment of debts, a decision to move to new lands, and the death of a master and the dissolution of his estate all provided occasions when slave family members might be separated. There is little evidence that masters, executors, or creditors regarded the maintenance of family ties as a major variable in making practical decisions about the disposition of property. A few surviving records of runaways suggest the emotional impact of such forced separations on adolescents who resisted the discipline of strange masters and fled to the comfort and protection, however illusory, of family, kin, and friends.

Education. For most white parents, formal education for children, especially girls, held a lower priority than the children's initiation into the world of work. However great the abstract benefits of learning to read, write, and do simple arithmetic, the immediate economic needs of feeding and clothing a family held greater sway.

There were regional, gender, and class differences in the availability of schooling for children and levels of literacy that they attained. A concern for literacy, at least in terms of an ability to read the Bible, was widespread in New England, leading to legal mandates for towns to support schools and teachers. The acquisition of literacy skills depended upon a variety of circumstances: parents' social status and ability to allocate time or money for education, access to teachers and schools, and the values that a particular culture placed on education.

Reading and writing were learned at different ages and sometimes in different contexts. Increase Mather's recollections provide an important clue: "I learned to read of my mother. I learned to write of Father, who also instructed me in grammar learning, both in the Latin and the greeke Tongues." Instruction in reading and writing was gender based; reading was often learned in the home and frequently under the mother's guidance, while writing was learned under the tutelage of a man, especially in a class-

room. The first steps in learning to read were oral and rote: listening to others read aloud, repetitive exercises in memorization, recognition of letters and words, and a focus on a limited number of printed items, notably the Bible, catechisms, and primers. These and other books were, in David D. Hall's phrase, the "steady sellers" of English and American printers and booksellers; they were materials central to Protestant culture that were frequently reprinted and passed down from generation to generation.

So strong was the cultural value of reading in New England that few persons appear to have been unable to read printed materials. Evidence for other parts of colonial America is less systematic, and historians generally believe that greater numbers of people outside New England could not read. This conclusion is based on a number of circumstances, including a less intense post-Reformation emphasis on literacy, more scattered patterns of settlement, and fewer printers and booksellers.

The acquisition of writing skills was generally begun at an older age and in a more formal context, typically a school or under the guidance of a tutor. Fewer children, especially girls, acquired writing skills. Of those New Englanders who left wills in the mid seventeenth century, only about 60 percent of the men and one-third of the women could sign their names, according to Kenneth A. Lockridge. By the end of the eighteenth century, nearly 90 percent of the men and 45 percent of the women could sign their names.

While studies by Ross W. Beales, Jr., Gloria L. Main, Joel Perlmann, and Dennis Shirley have shown that Lockridge underestimated rates of female signature literacy in late eighteenth-century New England, the culture clearly placed far more value on a boy's ability to write than on a girl's. For example apprenticeship indentures, when they included provisions for education, typically obliged masters to teach boys to read and write and girls to read and sew. These, of course, were minimal expectations, and some children had far greater opportunities and attainments, but the cultural bias was clear: girls—and women—had far less reason and fewer occasions to write.

Education was often episodic rather than systematic. Thus the seasonal demands of an agricultural economy and the immediate contributions that the work of children and adolescents could make to their families prompted parents to defer, limit, or deny educational opportunities to their children. The experience of Abraham Pierson, who was born in Killingworth, Connecticut, in 1756, illustrates the sometimes haphazard nature of schooling, the role of parents, the separate stages in the acquisition of reading and writing skills, and the role of the Bible.

While I was young I had but little opportunity of going to School having Sometimes not more than 5 or 6 weeks Schooling in a year and at most not more than 10 weeks and many years there was no School at all but notwithstanding the little Schooling I had yet being instructed by my Parents I became able when about 7 years old to read tolerable well in a Bible So as that when I was 8 years old I had almost read the Bible through[.] I read once every morning Constantly when there was no School and began to learn to write and within a few years I made Some Progress in Arithmetic learn'd the Ground Rules and Several other useful Rules. ("Abraham Pierson's Journal," *Bulletin of the Connecticut Historical Society* 15, no. 3 [1950]:18)

Some boys, of course, far exceeded Pierson's educational attainments. Parental wealth and aspirations and, in some cases, exceptional talent enabled some youngsters to attend grammar schools or to receive instruction from tutors and then attend one of the colonial colleges.

Occupations. For virtually all girls and for many boys, the choice of a calling—that is, one's eventual occupation if not status in life—was hardly a choice at all. For girls the almost inevitable destiny was marriage and children; the status and image of the spinster were hardly enviable. For boys, too, marriage was the culturally desired norm, but boys did have some range of choice with respect to occupation. Most would eventually engage in farming or in trades closely related to the rural economy. A few, blessed by talent and parental social position, could aspire to a wider range of occupations and stations. The structure of the local economy had a significant if not determining influence on a boy's opportunities.

The example of Benjamin Franklin is instructive. While possessed of enormous talent and ambition, Franklin may nonetheless have been fairly typical of boys growing up in an urban environment like Boston. His father introduced him to a range of possible occupations, but his family's needs strongly influenced the choices that his father made. Franklin would have understood Boston minister Benjamin Colman's description in *Early Piety Again Inculcated* (1720) of youth as a *"chusing time."* Addressing a young urban audience in 1720, Colman reminded them, "Now you commonly chuse your *Trade;* betake your selves to your business for life, show what you incline to, and how you intend to be imploy'd all your days. Now you chuse your *Master* and your Education or Occupation." He continued, "And now you dispose of your self in *Marriage* ordinarily, placed your *Affections,* give away your hearts, look out for some *Companion* of life, whose to be as long as you live."

Most boys experienced a kind of informal apprenticeship in agriculture, learning from their fathers, older brothers, or other adults. Beginning with their earliest chores, their training would be virtually complete by their mid teens. At that point their strength, coordination, and skills would be equal to most farming tasks. The experience of girls, although less well documented, roughly paralleled that of boys, for they also developed skills and experience in the many-faceted dimensions of housewifery.

Adolescence

As children matured into adolescents, their skills as workers became an increasingly valuable asset, with the output of their labor exceeding the cost of their maintenance. In a growing family, the labor of older children helped to provide for younger children. For their part younger children could be sent into service in the homes of older married siblings. Scattered evidence suggests that it was not uncommon for poorer families to place sons and daughters as workers in more affluent households.

Some adolescent males were placed in formal apprenticeships, with their fathers negotiating the terms with prospective masters. For many youth such arrangements were relatively short, lasting perhaps three or four years and ending by the age of twenty-one. The master assumed the role of the father, providing for the youth's bodily needs, training him, and, when appropriate, meting out discipline. Orphans were also bound out, with their terms typically lasting until age twenty-one for boys and eighteen for girls. Not all apprenticeship arrangements proved successful, for some boys were unequal to their masters' expectations. The master and the boy's father would then dissolve the indentures, and father and son would seek another calling more suitable to the boy's talents and temperament.

Adults acknowledged the maturation of young people in many ways. In New England catechetical classes for children before puberty included both boys and girls; after puberty boys and girls were separated. Orphans in their early teens were permitted to choose their guardians, and by their mid teens, boys were eligible for militia service.

For those few boys whose parents had higher aspirations than manual work, attendance at one of the colonial colleges provided opportunities both for education and for immersion in an adolescent subculture. The ages of college students in the colonial period were more diverse than those of today's students, with some freshmen only twelve or thirteen years old and others in their twenties. Nevertheless the disciplinary records of the colonial colleges offer ample evidence of adolescent high spirits and sometimes collective resistance to adult norms and efforts at control. Students were fined, demoted, compelled to make public confessions, suspended, and expelled for infractions ranging from setting off firecrackers and firearms, ringing bells, lighting bonfires, breaking windows, staying out late, drinking, and brawling among themselves or with groups of local servants and apprentices.

College students were not the only adolescents whose behavior, real or imagined, worried parents, ministers, and public officials. Militia training, huskings, elections, court days, house-raisings, and barn raisings provided occasion for the competitive display of strength and dexterity, feats of daring and bravado, and, always, a chance to impress members of the opposite sex. Not surprisingly ministers and other keepers of public morality inveighed against all the unnamed activities that might be encour-

aged by "tavern-haunting" and "vain company-keeping."

Servants and apprentices caused special concern, especially when they lived in towns or at least near taverns. Court records contain actions against servants and apprentices for sneaking out at night; congregating in sheds and barns and on the streets; frequenting those taverns whose keepers were known to welcome their patronage; singing; playing cards, dice, and other games; and engaging in other forbidden activities ranging from petty theft and vandalism to sexual intercourse. For some apprentices and servants, as well as college students, living away from home provided a degree of autonomy and independence from parental if not adult control. But, as Roger Thompson has demonstrated with respect to seventeenth-century Middlesex County, Massachusetts, the disorders about which masters, ministers, and magistrates complained cannot be attributed solely to the less advantaged ranks of society.

A review of all the cases of sexual misdemeanors and group activities, embracing at a minimum some six hundred adolescents, shows quite clearly that bastardy-prone girls or problem families at the bottom of the social scale only contributed a tiny proportion to the total of adolescent offenders. (*Sex in Middlesex*, p. 102)

In the Chesapeake colonies, fathers appear to have condoned and sometimes encouraged a larger degree of autonomy among their sons as the latter approached majority. This may have resulted from parents' sense of their own mortality and from more relaxed attitudes toward the strictures of organized religion. Relations between the generations were not always smooth, for the legal records contain references to sons who disobeyed their parents, guardians, and stepparents, challenged other authority, squandered their inheritances, and broke the law.

Daughters of Chesapeake families sought their autonomy in different ways. Most immigrant women had been forced to postpone marriage, if not sexual activity, until the end of their indentures. Their daughters were reared in a society where men significantly outnumbered women, and, unencumbered by the obligations of servitude, Creole females became sexually active and married much earlier than their mothers. Thus while immigrant women typically married in their mid twenties, some of their daughters married in their early teens, and most married by age twenty-one.

Conditions in early Virginia and Maryland thus created a hothouse environment in which, according to Lorena S. Walsh, "the life cycle of growing up, marrying, procreating, and dying was compressed within a short span of years." Many children never lived to experience adolescence, and adolescence itself, however turbulent, may have been shortened, at least for females, by the necessities of marriage and parenthood. For some males adolescence may have been cut short by the responsibilities of fending for themselves in a world without parents, but the lack of parental guidance may have had other results, especially for those who were landless and without prospects of early marriage. For example the unrest of Virginia society in the 1670s, marked most notably by Bacon's Rebellion, may in part have reflected the existence of large numbers of rootless young men whose passions were no longer constrained by indentured servitude but whose status and resources afforded few opportunities.

Courtship and Marriage

For most young men and women—late adolescents—courtship and marriage marked the crucial transition from adolescence to adulthood. There were marked differences in courtship patterns and freedom from parental supervision and control. In the seventeenth century, the unbalanced sex ratio in the Chesapeake colonies placed a high premium on women, with the result that most women married much earlier than their counterparts in the middle and northern colonies; indeed some became sexually active at early ages, even while still indentured servants. Young men appear to have had greater latitude and to have been more self-directing in their courtships than their northern contemporaries. As the white population became more balanced by gender and longer lived in the eighteenth century, courtship patterns among the sons and daughters of elite planter families became more formalized and, to some degree, stilted. Notions of romantic love, including elaborate statements of affection in prose and poetry, increasingly played an important role. How the less affluent

and less literate conducted their courtships remains obscure.

Parents, if they were still alive, naturally hoped that their children would marry well. This almost inevitably meant marriage to a person from a comparable or higher economic background, although both Puritans and Quakers strongly emphasized the importance of marrying persons of piety. Among seventeenth-century New Englanders, there were strong intrafamilial considerations as well. A study of marriage patterns in Hingham, Massachusetts, found that marriage according to birth order, at least for female children, was common. While this suggests a strong parental role in the timing of marriage, by the middle of the eighteenth century this pattern had been substantially weakened—and, along with it, a significant measure of parental control had been surrendered. Courtships were increasingly initiated and controlled by the participants, not their parents. And while parents might still seek to influence their children's choices, they could no longer as effectively deny those choices as they once had. The loosening of parental control is also apparent in the increasing rates of prenuptial pregnancies among eighteenth-century New Englanders. Indeed at least for New Englanders the conception of children before marriage may have been the ultimate expression of autonomy and resistance to parental wishes.

Among Quakers strong familial and religious concerns helped to direct youth toward marriages with their coreligionists. Quaker youth who married outside their religion risked being disowned by both family and meeting. While Quakers in the early years of settlement were largely successful in directing their children toward approved marriages, successive generations proved more resistant to parental guidance, and larger numbers of Quaker children married non-Quakers.

With marriage those who had been children and adolescents now had the responsibility of rearing their own children. The cycle from conception and birth to infancy and childhood, education and training, and courtship and marriage would be repeated. At the same time, new generations faced different challenges and changing ideas about childhood and adolescence. Eighteenth-century Americans increasingly tended toward ideas about childhood that regarded the child as unique and innocent. Ahead lay the child-centered and sentimental world of the nineteenth-century family.

BIBLIOGRAPHY

Axtell, James. *The School upon a Hill: Education and Society in Colonial New England.* New Haven, Conn., 1974.

Beales, Ross W., Jr. "Studying Literacy at the Community Level: A Research Note." *Journal of Interdisciplinary History* 9 (1978):93–102.

Bradstreet, Anne. *The Works of Anne Bradstreet.* Edited by Jeannine Hensley. Cambridge, Mass., 1967.

Breen, T. H., and Stephen Innes. *"Myne Owne Ground": Race and Freedom on Virginia's Eastern Shore, 1640–1676.* New York, 1980.

Burr, Esther Edwards. *The Journals of Esther Edwards Burr, 1754–1757.* Edited by Carol F. Karlsen and Laurie Crumpacker. New Haven, Conn., 1984.

Carson, Jane. *Colonial Virginians at Play.* Williamsburg, Va., 1989.

Cremin, Lawrence A. *American Education: The Colonial Experience, 1607–1783.* New York, 1970.

Cressy, David. *Literacy and the Social Order: Reading and Writing in Tudor and Stuart England.* Cambridge, England, 1980.

Demos, John. *A Little Commonwealth: Family Life in Plymouth Colony.* New York, 1970.

Frost, J. William. *The Quaker Family in Colonial America: A Portrait of the Society of Friends.* New York, 1973.

Greven, Philip J., Jr. *Four Generations: Population, Land, and Family in Colonial Andover, Massachusetts.* Ithaca, N.Y., 1970.

———. *The Protestant Temperament: Patterns of Child-Rearing, Religious Experience, and the Self in Early America.* New York, 1977.

Hall, David D. *Worlds of Wonder, Days of Judgment: Popular Religious Belief in Early New England.* New York, 1989.

Hawes, Joseph M., and N. Ray Hiner, eds. *American Childhood: A Research Guide and Historical Handbook.* Westport, Conn., 1985.

Horn, James. "Servant Emigration to the Chesapeake in the Seventeenth Century." In *The Chesapeake in the Seventeenth Century: Essays on Anglo-American History,* edited by Thad W. Tate and David L. Ammerman. Chapel Hill, N.C., 1979.

Kulikoff, Allan. *Tobacco and Slaves: The Development of Southern Cultures in the Chesapeake, 1680–1800.* Chapel Hill, N.C., 1986.

Laslett, Peter. *The World We Have Lost.* New York, 1965.

Levy, Barry. *Quakers and the American Family: British Settlement in the Delaware Valley.* New York, 1988.

Lockridge, Kenneth A. *Literacy in Colonial New England: An Enquiry into the Social Context of Literacy in the Early Modern West.* New York, 1974.

Macfarlane, Alan. *The Family Life of Ralph Josselin, a Seventeenth-Century Clergyman: An Essay in Historical Anthropology.* Cambridge, England, 1970.

Main, Gloria L. "An Inquiry into When and Why Women Learned to Write in Colonial New England." *Journal of Social History* 24 (1991):579–589.

Mintz, Steven, and Susan Kellogg. *Domestic Revolutions: A Social History of American Family Life.* New York, 1988.

Morgan, Edmund S. *The Puritan Family: Religion and Domestic Relations in Seventeenth-Century New England.* New York, 1944; rev. ed. 1966.

Perlmann, Joel, and Dennis Shirley. "When Did New England Women Acquire Literacy?" *William and Mary Quarterly,* 3rd ser., 48, no. 1 (1991):50–67.

Pollock, Linda A. *Forgotten Children: Parent-Child Relationships from 1500 to 1900.* Cambridge, England, 1983.

Rutman, Darrett B., and Anita H. Rutman. *A Place in Time: Middlesex County, Virginia, 1650–1750.* New York, 1984.

Slater, Peter Gregg. *Children in the New England Mind: In Death and in Life.* Hamden, Conn., 1977.

Smith, Daniel Blake. *Inside the Great House: Planter Family Life in Eighteenth-Century Chesapeake Society.* Ithaca, N.Y., 1980.

Stone, Lawrence. *The Family, Sex, and Marriage in England, 1500–1800.* New York, 1977.

Thompson, Roger. *Sex in Middlesex: Popular Mores in a Massachusetts County, 1649–1699.* Amherst, Mass., 1986.

Walsh, Lorena S. " 'Till Death Us Do Part': Marriage and Family in Seventeenth-Century Maryland." In *The Chesapeake in the Seventeenth Century: Essays on Anglo-American Society,* edited by Thad W. Tate and David L. Ammerman. Chapel Hill, N.C., 1979.

Waters, John J. "The Traditional World of the New England Peasants: A View from Seventeenth-Century Barnstable." *New England Historical and Genealogical Register* 130, no. 1 (1976):3–21.

Wells, Robert V. *Revolutions in Americans' Lives: A Demographic Perspective on the History of Americans, Their Families, and Their Society.* Westport, Conn., 1982.

Wrightson, Keith. *English Society, 1580–1680.* London, 1982.

Ross W. Beales, Jr.

SEE ALSO **African-American Culture; Dress; Gender Relations; Schools and Schooling; and Slavery.**

752

THE DUTCH COLONY

ANY CONSIDERATION OF childhood and adolescence in New Netherland should begin in the Dutch republic. Demographer Philippe Ariès and other scholars believe that Europeans in the Middle Ages generally lost even the limited understanding that Roman culture had possessed of child development. If that is true, and Ariès's brilliant interpretation has yet to be fully refuted, one should also acknowledge that the Dutch were the first Europeans to rediscover childhood, or at least to celebrate the child in their art and literature.

In the seventeenth century, the Dutch family was increasingly child-centered, devoted not only to nurturing the child but also to preparing the young for life and labor as adults. The Dutch did not use the term adolescence or understand much about the dynamics of that transitional stage from childhood into adulthood. Rather, they spoke of infancy, childhood, and youth, the latter stretching rather vaguely well into adulthood. However, the Dutch were particularly solicitous toward young men and young women, granting them considerable independence and freedom. There were even signs of an emerging "youth culture" in the United Provinces, especially Holland.

In post-Reformation Europe, Dutch parents had the reputation for spoiling their children. Foreigners especially criticized the Dutch for their excessive indulgence and "unmeasured tenderness" toward the young. Even Dutch moralists, like the very popular Calvinist poet Jacob Cats (affectionately called "Father Cats") emphasized that children needed affection quite as much as discipline. In the graphic arts, Dutch painting took a rather comprehensive and realistic look at children. Gone were the miniature adults of the Middle Ages and the Cupid-like putti of Peter Paul Rubens. Children—babes, toddlers, boys, and girls—were portrayed on their own terms, in the street, in the household, at work and at play, being good and being bad, and having fun.

In the Netherlands, the experiences of childhood and adolescence were conditioned largely by the immediate family but also by other influences, such as church, school, and apprenticeship. The family, especially parents but close relatives as well, assumed an important role. Father Cats insisted that infants should be breastfed by their mothers, regardless of class and rank, and the evidence is overwhelming that they were. Moreover, Cats urged fathers to take an active role in nurturing the young, though the mother obviously had the lion's share of early child-rearing responsibility. The kind of parent-child relationship Cats called for surely promoted what we today call bonding. Even the Dutch practice of tightly swaddling the newborn, Simon Schama suggests, likely increased the infant's feeling of security and probably agitated the child less than it has modern critics. The young, both boys and girls, generally got some formal education, if only at the local schools supervised and subsidized by the Dutch Reformed church. Children in the lower and middle classes were taught reading, writing, and some arithmetic and received religious instruction to supplement what they learned at church.

In terms of occupational training, apprenticeship in the crafts or trade awaited most boys, who might be formally indentured or else simply put to work with their fathers or relatives. Girls might be contracted out as servants or, more likely, taught housekeeping by their mothers or other relatives, depending upon the economic status of the family. Girls usually learned something of the family business or craft, but housewifery skills were of primary importance for daughters. Sons of the upper classes often attended one of the many Illustrative Schools (like small colleges today) and one of the three chartered universities, where they could earn a professional degree in law, medicine, or theology.

Marriage also played an important role in the future economic well-being of any young person, and both men and women were urged, by Cats and by other popular advisers, to consider carefully the family status of potential mates. Despite the liberty parents allowed their children in dating, endogamy by class generally prevailed.

CHILDHOOD IN
NEW NETHERLAND

In contrast to the fatherland, New Netherland possessed a thinly populated frontier society, where preachers and teachers were in short supply. For two decades after the first Dutch settlers arrived in 1624, immigration to the Dutch colony remained slight, made up largely of young men, some of them adolescents, and a few young women and girls. The young men and boys generally worked as farmhands or assisted skilled craftsmen, and the young females were mostly house servants. In the 1640s immigration increased sharply, with young couples predominating among the new settlers. The number of children burgeoned, as did public concern for their welfare, particularly after Peter Stuyvesant became director-general in 1647.

Stuyvesant described the children of New Netherland as spoiled and undisciplined, prone to running the streets, and likely to be influenced by the bad example of the morally loose men and women who haunted the numerous taverns of New Amsterdam. His solution was to encourage schooling on a regular basis, formalize apprenticeship arrangements, impose stricter regulations on taverns and tapsters, and increase penalties for disorderly behavior among old and young alike. New Netherland was a rowdy place, and its children were much involved in the adult world, whether living and working with their parents or apprenticed to someone else.

Under Stuyvesant, if a child lost one or both parents, his or her property rights were protected by prenuptial agreements and appointed guardians. Guardians, sometimes named in wills or else appointed by the orphanmasters, strengthened the law and tradition regarding children's property rights. Apprenticeship agreements became more formalized and were increasingly based on notarized indentures. The master stood in loco parentis and could discipline youngsters under his care, but the courts were known to intervene and release apprentices from abusive masters and mistresses. The few cases of sexual abuse of children heard by the courts carried severe punishment, even death in two cases involving homosexuality.

In New Netherland, parent-child relations were generally harmonious, with evidences of genuine affection bonding mother, father, and children. Childbirth was the most important ritual in the family cycle, beginning with the lying-in and ending with the christening of the babe. Among the Dutch settlers especially, merrymaking and feasting always accompanied the christening, as relatives and friends of the couple became more tightly linked through the naming of godmothers and godfathers. Jeremias and Maria Van Rensselaer, the New Netherland couple about whom the most is known, took obvious delight in their six children, keeping grandparents informed of their antics and health, especially the latter, because infant mortality rates were high throughout seventeenth-century America. Prenuptial agreements and joint wills provide further indication of parental affection as well as concern for their offspring, whether in infancy or young adulthood.

The experience of young New Netherlanders increasingly included some schooling, which by the 1650s was available either through town schools or through independent schoolmasters in all the villages of the colony. Schooling was important to the commercial economy of the Netherlands, of which New Netherland was a part. More important, though, was learning a trade, which usually began early within the youngster's own household. Poor children or orphans might be apprenticed at an early age, thereby securing for them a surrogate household, but craft apprenticeship usually did not begin in New Netherland until the young man was near or in his teens.

Although apprenticeship was being used extensively by the 1650s, both for the poor and the orphaned and for young, aspiring craftsmen, Dutch New Netherlanders liked keeping their children at home, or else working and learning in the home or shop of a relative. Even so, New Netherland parents seemed less concerned with restricting and supervising young adults than with helping them advance their own economic ambitions. Groups of young men came together for work and play, especially for such games as Pulling the Goose, which New Netherland officials associated with drinking and fighting. In later years, children of the Albany Dutch were said to divide themselves into several companies for work and play and would usually choose a mate from their particular group. That practice, or something very like it, may well have begun in New Netherland. All of this is suggestive of a preindustrial youth culture, and the freedom allowed the young in Dutch society surely encouraged it.

Most non-Dutch white settlers in New Netherland more or less followed Dutch law and tradition regarding child-rearing, children, and youth. However, the English who migrated from New England and founded towns on western Long Island followed their own customs. Pertinent facts are admittedly few, but despite political and religious differences with their New England brethren, the English of western Long Island apparently accepted Puritan teachings on child-rearing, just as they did on other family matters. These teachings included the ideas that children were tainted by original sin and that their willfulness needed to be broken, for sparing the rod would surely encourage the child's evil nature. Unlike their Dutch counterparts, the Reverend John Robinson and other Puritan moralists viewed nurturing almost exclusively in terms of disciplining the child; parental affection was suspect and likely to lead to indulgence, and from such indulgence came disrespectful children and dissolute youths.

The fear that they might not be stern enough with their own children was probably the primary motive behind the New England practice of apprenticing children during the crucial years of puberty. The English on Long Island very likely utilized apprenticeship in this fashion; their households were rather patriarchal, with wives and children thoroughly subordinated to husbands and fathers by law and custom. Interestingly, wills and court records from the late seventeenth century make it clear that considerable tension and even outright resentment troubled the relationship of the Long Island English and their offspring. Such parent-child antagonism seldom plagued Dutch New Yorkers, whose child-rearing techniques and rules of partible inheritance were less likely to arouse resentment among the young.

Black New Netherlanders, slave or free, raised their children against the backdrop of slavery and racial prejudice. The evidence is meager, but what there is gives poignant testimony to slave parents' hope of liberating their children through baptism into the Christian faith. Slaves could never be certain their children would not be sold away from them, and such separations did occur, despite the general desire of Dutch slave owners to keep black families together.

Much influenced by Dutch culture and law, free blacks had more control over their children's destiny than did slaves. They could and did will them property. Blacks, slave and free, many of whom were artisans and farmers, taught their children skills that would serve them well as adults. The slave children on Stuyvesant's bowery (farm) got a school teacher in the 1650s, compliments of the director-general, and one may assume that the able pedagogue taught the children of free blacks there as well. Free black parents on occasion apprenticed their children to whites to provide them with decent food and clothing and with job experience. The very fact that the free black population of New Amsterdam not only survived but expanded and continued to grow in English New York demonstrated exceptional cross-generational cooperation that almost certainly was instilled during childhood and adolescence.

Free from the domination of either Dutch or English culture, the Indians in the lands called New Netherland raised children according to their own traditions. The culture of the Eastern Woodland Indians varied, but the tribe about which we know the most, the Seneca, was representative of the Iroquois or Five Nations, which became the most powerful Indian confederation in the region. Iroquois society was matriarchal, with the mother raising the children while the father was gone for weeks and sometimes months hunting, making war, or pursuing diplomatic missions. Seneca mothers tightly swaddled their infants and were especially solicitous of their needs, so much so that European observers condemned their "dangerous Indulgence." However, the Seneca went well beyond the Dutch in encouraging independence and assertiveness among the young.

Toddlers and young children pretty much had the run of Indian villages and were seldom chastised. Between the ages of eight or nine and puberty, gender roles began to be delineated, with girls doing chores in the village and boys roaming the woods, hunting, wrestling, and pretending to make war. The boys usually divided into bands that often became the basis for war or hunting parties when the boys grew up. The boys were seldom supervised by adults, but they tended to get along quite harmoniously.

Both boys and girls went through a ritual at puberty that marked their entrance into the adult world. The freedom granted Seneca children was intended to inculcate personal toughness, self-reliance, and independence, and it worked remarkably well.

AFTER 1664

The British conquest of New Netherland in 1664 affected childhood in early New York in several ways. Although Dutch attitudes toward child-rearing were perpetuated among many families, English common law gradually supplanted Roman-Dutch law throughout the province, limiting the legal rights and economic roles of women, which also found expression in the way boys and girls were educated. The English tradition placed less emphasis upon schooling for girls than Dutch custom, and the decentralizing of both schooling and religious training that took place following the English takeover meant that the village or town government or maybe even just a group of interested parents or a religious congregation would be the primary sponsor of the local schoolmaster. Indeed, the lack of the provincial government's funding of or coordination for schooling and worship in early New York meant that the family remained the determinative institution shaping the personality and skills of the young. The ethnic diversity of the settlers was perpetuated because of the dominating role of the family.

BIBLIOGRAPHY

Ariès, Philippe. *Centuries of Childhood.* Translated by Robert Baldick. London, 1962.

Christoph, Peter. "The Colonial Family: Kinship and Power." In *A Beautiful and Fruitful Place: Selected Rensselaerswijck Seminar Papers,* edited by Nancy Anne McClure Zeller. Albany, N.Y., 1991.

Earle, Alice Morse. *Colonial Days in Old New York.* New York, 1896; repr. 1990.

Fernow, Berthold, ed. and trans. *The Minutes of the Orphanmasters of New Amsterdam, 1653–1663.* New York, 1902.

———, ed. and trans. *Records of New Amsterdam, from 1653 to 1674.* 7 vols. New York, 1897.

Gehring, Charles T., ed. and trans. *Fort Orange Court Minutes, 1652–1660.* Syracuse, N.Y., 1990.

Goodfriend, Joyce. "Black Families in New Netherland." In *A Beautiful and Fruitful Place: Selected Rensselaerswijck Seminar Papers,* edited by Nancy Anne McClure Zeller. Albany, N.Y., 1991.

Grant, Anne. *Memoirs of an American Lady.* Edited by James Wilson. 2 vols. London, 1808; rev. ed. New York, 1901.

Howard, Ronald William. "Apprenticeship and Economic Education in New Netherland and Seventeenth-Century New York." In *A Beautiful and Fruitful Land: Selected Rensselaerswijck Seminar Papers,* edited by Nancy Anne McClure Zeller. Albany, N.Y., 1991.

Kenney, Alice P. "Private Worlds in the Middle Colonies: An Introduction to Human Tradition in American History." *New York History* 51, no. 1 (1970):4–31.

Kilpatrick, William Heard. *The Dutch Schools of New Netherland and Colonial New York.* Washington, D.C., 1912.

Kruger, Vivienne L. "Born to Run: The Slave Family in Early New York, 1626–1827." 2 vols. Ph.D. diss., Columbia University, 1985.

McLaughlin, William. "Dutch Rural New York: Community, Economy, and Family in Colonial Flatbush." Ph.D. diss., Columbia University, 1985.

Morris, Richard B. *Studies in the History of American Law.* New York, 1958.

O'Callaghan, Edmund B. *Calendar of Dutch Historical Manuscripts in the Office of the Secretary of State, Albany, New York, 1630–1664.* Albany, N.Y., 1865; repr. Ridgewood, N.J., 1968.

Schama, Simon. *The Embarrassment of Riches: An Interpretation of Dutch Culture in the Golden Age.* New York, 1987.

Singleton, Esther. *Dutch New York.* New York, 1909; repr. 1968.

Sturtevant, William C., gen. ed. *Handbook of North American Indians.* 20 vols. Vol. 15, *Northeast,* edited by Bruce G. Trigger. Washington, D.C., 1978.

Van Laer, Arnold J. F., ed. *Correspondence of Jeremias Van Rensselaer, 1651–1674.* Albany, N.Y., 1932.

———, trans. *New York Historical Manuscripts,* edited by Kenneth Scott and Ken Styker-Rodda. 4 vols. Baltimore, Md., 1974.

Van Rensselaer, Mrs. John King. *The Goede Vrouw of Mana-ha-ta: At Home and in Society, 1609–1760.* New York, 1898.

Wallace, Anthony F. C. *The Death and Rebirth of the Seneca.* New York, 1969.

Zumthor, Paul. *Daily Life in Rembrandt's Holland.* New York, 1963.

Ronald William Howard

SEE ALSO **African-American Culture; Dress; Gender Relations; Schools and Schooling;** and **Slavery.**

THE FRENCH COLONIES

COLONIAL CIVIL LAW, derived from the laws of the Viscounty and Provostship of Paris, upheld a patriarchal model of the family and placed a wife and children under one man's *puissance paternelle* (paternal authority). Dependents could not live apart or manage property without his consent or approval. Legally, a child was a minor until age twenty-five or marriage. The father's authority over his household was to be comparable to a divine-right monarch's power over his kingdom. In practice, the ideal of the omnipotent paterfamilias was compromised: colonial conditions brought a partial emancipation of children and wives from paternal authority.

The colonial population was a young population. In the Saint Lawrence Valley from 1698 to 1734, 44 percent of the total European population was under the age of fifteen. That percentage was higher in outlying settlements and in rural areas. The number of children and the intimate proximity in small dwellings strained the parental capacity to impose discipline. Households of the elite were enlarged by servants and relations beyond the nuclear family. The law provided for an equal division of the parental estate among all legitimate progeny, and so a threat to deny one child its fractional inheritance did not carry great force.

An average family had about six living children; the number would have been higher were it not for deferred marriage and high infant mortality—in the early eighteenth century 45 percent died before reaching their tenth year. It was not wise to become too attached to such fragile beings. French colonials did not practice effective contraception; married women bore children at two-year intervals until about the age of thirty-five.

The scarcity of cheap servants and workers in the colonies compelled a father to heed his dependents' wishes. Their labor was essential to the family's welfare. Children were economic partners as well as legal dependents. Child labor was needed in the workshop and on the farm, and colonials preferred not to rely on strangers. By our standards, a child's productive labor began early in life: at the end of infancy and well before the legal age of majority.

INFANCY

The period of infancy was confined to the first seven years of life. Delivered in bed at home with the help of a midwife or some other woman, the newborn child entered a network of family obligations that was enlarged at baptism. At the baptismal ceremony soon after birth, two godparents promised to have the child instructed in "the Catholic, Apostolic, and Roman" faith. By custom, they were expected to aid the child's establishment in later life. One of the two Christian names given to each child at baptism was that of the godparent of the same gender. The other name would be a traditional family name or that of a favorite patron saint: Marie was preferred for girls, and Joseph was nearly as popular for boys, followed by Jean, Pierre, and François. Patron saints were expected to exercise influence on behalf of their namesake in the celestial realm as much as a godparent would in this world. Birthdates were soon forgotten, yet the feast day of one's patron saint was celebrated annually. In a culture that thought in terms of clients and patrons, the saints' goodwill had to be won. Their intercession with the Almighty could ensure one's good fortune.

The growing infant progressed from a swaddling cloth to loose covers, and when ambulatory to a shift with leading strings attached to the back. The dress was the same for boys and girls. Infants of wealthy families had rattles, made of silver, bone, and wood and adorned with bells and a teething bar or ring at one end. Older children superintended toddlers and walked with them, gripping the leading strings to arrest a fall.

At this stage very little was expected of the infant. On farms the youngest ones might only be asked to scare birds away from ripening crops. Between the ages of seven and twelve, youngsters acquired regular duties: herding livestock, fetching firewood and water, scraping boots, cleaning out the hearth, emptying chamberpots into the outdoor privy, and helping in the kitchen garden. At harvest-time, farm boys aided their fathers in mowing hay and in cutting grain, while the women raked and stooked the crop. Older sons assisted in sowing crops, in threshing and winnowing grain, and in cutting down trees. Canadian men were all reputed to be skilled axemen.

TENDRE JEUNESSE

As if to mark the transition from infancy to "tender youth"—the stage before puberty—children were dressed in a miniature version of adult attire after the age of seven. This does not mean that they had ceased to be children; archaeological finds and estate inventories list toys and tiny furniture for the young. Some playthings, such as crockery, dolls, sailboats, swords, drums, and small cannons, were an introduction to the adult worlds of commerce, domestic life, and war. Poor children fashioned game counters from broken dinnerware, dice from bones, marbles from clay, and whizzers from fragments of slate or builders' lead. Increasingly, their time was occupied with family responsibilities rather than with play.

ADOLESCENCE

Puberty, which usually came between the ages of twelve and fourteen, admitted one to a third stage of life. After puberty children attended catechism classes of the parish or missionary priest. They heard an abridged account of Bible stories, were given an explanation of holy days, and learned rote answers about Roman Catholic doctrine and rituals. A child was to be taught to fear God and to respect his parents. Instruction might be compressed into a three-week pe-

riod before the child's First Communion, but catechism was a form of universal, institutional education in the French colonies.

If the overworked clergy could manage it, or if a feminine religious order were present, the young might receive additional instruction in reading, writing, arithmetic, and, occasionally, in Latin, which was the language of the mass. Bright boys with a religious vocation were favored candidates for further, free education. Daughters of leading families customarily received instruction in skills such as reading, writing, arithmetic, and, occasionally, Latin, and in good manners and needlework. Such elementary education occupied one or two years; farming families would not forgo a child's labor for even that period. As a consequence, illiteracy increased in the countryside from one-third in the immigrant generation to over one-half among native colonials.

Secondary education was reserved for boys from fee-paying, notable families and those destined for the priesthood. Lay teachers were rare, and secondary schooling, like most institutional education, was a function of the church. Philosophy, rhetoric, theology, and Latin dominated the college curriculum taught by priests.

Formal education beyond catechism was often a matter of good luck. An orphan with several relatives in the colony would be provided for by an assembly of kin. Although all sides were represented in the assemblage, adult males of the paternal lineage were preferred as guardians. An uncle or older brother assumed the guardian's role with help from the others. If a child were orphaned before the age of twelve and had no close family in the colony, then the future was bleak. Foundlings and prepubescent paupers were placed by court officers and widows as domestic servants with families that promised to provide the children with food, shelter, and clothing. Impoverished widows were forced to dispose of their children in this fashion. Foster children were bound out until the age of eighteen or even until twenty-one. There was no assurance that they would be taught a manual trade or be given instruction in more than catechism. Only foundlings sponsored by royal officials or poor children accepted by religious houses were protected from brutal exploitation. Child paupers provided a cheap substitute for indentured servants and slaves in eighteenth-century French North America. Their progression to self-determination was delayed.

PREPARATION FOR ADULTHOOD

Entry into the last stage before adulthood came between the ages of fifteen and seventeen. Boys were enrolled in the colonial militia at sixteen, and the French Crown was pressed to accept younger boys from well-born families as officer-cadets in the garrison troops. Others left the paternal home at this stage to work as servants or apprentices in another household. Most craft apprentices serving the standard three-year term were indentured in their sixteenth or seventeenth year. Only those wanting to learn the trade in a shorter period paid something to the craft master. Free training and the absence of guild controls over admission to a trade meant that craft apprenticeship flourished in the colonies. Apprentices took the place of journeymen, who were rare, and artisans welcomed able-bodied assistants. Craft apprenticeship was the most widespread form of secular, formal education in New France. A sense of family solidarity and collective interest made Canadians extremely sensitive to injuries or offenses committed by an outsider against family members, and they readily protested ill-usage by masters and aided the flight of aggrieved apprentices.

Although trained for a career and canonically able to wed by age twenty, French colonials deferred the establishment of a new household for a few more years. Girls could marry at twenty or twenty-one, because a dowry was not required except for an arranged marriage between members of the elite. Rural brides brought no more than a trousseau of clothes and bed linen, and their parents offered, at most, some livestock, a bed, and, perhaps, temporary shelter in the parental home—benefits sometimes deducted from the bride's future inheritance. Colonial men of the humble classes put off marriage until they were twenty-six or twenty-seven in order to accumulate capital to set up their own farm or workshop and to acquire or build a house. In the eighteenth century, work as a laborer, journeyman or, better still, as a *voyageur* (hired canoeman) transporting canoe-loads of trade goods and furs between Montreal or New Orleans and the western posts provided money for a later, independent establishment. As in New England, family autonomy was prized, and few hastened into matrimony before they could set up an independent household. Government encouragements to early marriage had little apparent effect; the marriage of adolescent girls observed in the 1600s ceased once the sexes achieved numerical parity in the European population.

The large number of sexually mature, unmarried men in the colonies—including garrison soldiers—had natural consequences. In the Saint Lawrence Valley during the 1700s *recorded* births out of wedlock increased from 2 per thousand to 12.2. About 6 percent of Canadian brides were pregnant at marriage; widows were twice as likely to be in that condition at their weddings. An unknown number of bastards were given to Amerindians or killed at birth. Many European males also received their sexual initiation among the less-inhibited aboriginal peoples. The genetic contribution of French colonials to the Native population was greater than the reciprocal gain from a few dozen Christian marriages to Amerindian women in white settlements. Church records do not present a complete picture of premarital sexual behavior in the colonies.

FILIAL OBLIGATIONS

Visitors from France criticized Canadians for being too indulgent of their children and accused youngsters of lacking gratitude and affection for their elders. These criticisms reflected the weakening of paternal authority and the assertiveness of dependents. Some children had to be legally coerced into caring for their aged parents. As a safeguard against such neglect, countryfolk increasingly deeded over the family farm and its livestock to one son who accepted full responsibility for them in old age. His obligations were spelled out in a notarized contract, which even specified the quantities of wine, liquor, and tobacco to be provided annually to the retired parents. The other children, having been relieved of that obligation, received a proportionately smaller share of the parental estate and were free to go where they pleased. In this way the patriarchal family upheld by the civil law and sanctioned by religion was reconciled with the independence of the children and their consequent geographic and occupational mobility.

BIBLIOGRAPHY

Lemieux, Denise. *Les petits innocents: L'Enfance en Nouvelle-France.* Quebec, 1985.

Moogk, Peter N. *"Les petits sauvages:* The Children of Eighteenth-Century New France." In *Childhood and Family in Canadian History,* edited by Joy Parr. Toronto, Ontario, 1982.

Peter N. Moogk

SEE ALSO **African-American Culture; Dress; Gender Relations; Schools and Schooling;** and **Slavery.**

OLD AGE AND DEATH

THE BRITISH COLONIES

THE END OF THE LIFE course, no less than its beginning and intermediate stages, tells us much about family and social relations, economic arrangements, and religious practices in times past. Historians of early America explore old age and death in the British North American colonies in terms of popular attitudes, individual experiences, and social changes.

What did people think of old age? How many people lived to be old? How did the elderly expect to be treated? How were they actually treated? How did people view death, and how did they prepare for it? The answers to such questions are complex.

The answers are still very preliminary, limited primarily to New England and secondarily to the Chesapeake colonies, but inspiring some truly remarkable research and analysis. What historians have found so far certainly brings into sharper focus the unity as well as the diversity of British American society and culture. Indeed, colonial Americans looked upon—and even experienced—old age and death differently depending upon their economic and social status, the region in which they were born or settled, and the particular decades during which they lived.

OLD AGE

The population of Anglo-America was relatively young. As late as 1790, the median age was only sixteen; life expectancy at birth was about forty, and less than 2 percent of the population was sixty-five or older. In contrast, the median age in 1990 was slightly less than thirty-three; life expectancy at birth was about seventy-five, and 13 percent of the population was older than sixty-five. While the elderly became increasingly numerous in the twentieth century, their status apparently declined.

Why were aging men and women seemingly accorded more respect and deference in early America than in twentieth-century America? David Hackett Fischer suggests that the relative scarcity of elderly people in British North America made them more appreciated. Even more important was the respect for elders propagated by the Judeo-Christian heritage of the settlers themselves. Most important of all were the standards of a traditional, barely literate society in which land, occupational skills, useful knowledge of all kinds, and social and political leadership were all transmitted in very personal ways from older people to the rising generation.

Old age was ambiguously defined throughout early America. No clearly marked role exits—such as the end of parenting or occupational retirement—separated mature adulthood from old age. Couples in their forties and fifties might feel old, having outlived many of their cohorts and having worked hard for decades. Yet owing to high fertility, extremely high child mortality, and late marriages, those parents who survived might well be in their late fifties or early sixties before their youngest child left home. Extended child-rearing duties and the continual need to provide for themselves meant that older couples could seldom afford to retire. Consequently, despite their advancing years and declining physical strength and energy, housewives, farmers, merchants, and craftsmen usually continued their routine chores until they became enfeebled or died. So did most preachers, doctors, lawyers, and many political leaders. In fact, much of the esteem accorded the elderly was likely due to their continued involvement with and importance to colonial society.

Old age alone did not assure esteem or deference; longevity had to be joined by other characteristics such as wealth, wisdom, piety, knowledge, and family or political leadership for the elderly to be highly regarded in colonial society. Public respect for aging men and women was everywhere conditional, bestowed rather liberally upon upper- and middle-class white males, but conferred less generously upon women and sparingly upon slaves and the poor generally. In addition to social and economic influences, colonial attitudes and experiences regarding aging varied significantly depending upon regional folkways.

New England

Old age became far more common in colonial New England than the youthful bias of the age structure or conventional wisdom suggest. Varying from town to town in the second half of the seventeenth century, the proportion of people older than sixty ranged from about 4 to 7 percent, with those younger than age twenty usually representing well over 50 percent of the total; relatively few old people made the Great Migration to New England during the 1630s. Among the adult population (more than twenty years old), the proportion of those older than sixty ranged from 8 to 14 percent. Life expectancy was 64.7 for adult males and 62.1 for adult females in Andover, Massachusetts, and 69.2 for males and 62.4 for females in Plymouth colony. Comparable figures for Middlesex, Virginia, are sharply lower because of the deadly disease environment of the Chesapeake: 48.8 for married males and 39.8 for married females (see table 1 for comparative data).

New England's reverence for the aged increased steadily during the second half of the seventeenth century as the immigrant population, which had been youthful and disproportionately male, became more gender balanced and began to grow older. Indeed, the founders of New England were imposing patriarchs, fathering large families and living long enough to enjoy their grandchildren. They usually kept control over their property until death, thereby giving their sons good reason to be properly deferential if not obsequious.

In New England during the eighteenth century, patriarchal authority waned somewhat, in part because fathers had less land to pass on to their sons. Nevertheless, respect for the elderly continued to increase. Seeing in the white hair and wrinkled visage of the elderly the very image of the divine, Puritan preachers were fond of quoting Prov. 16:31, "A hoary head is a crown of glory," and 1 Tim. 5:1, "Rebuke not an elder, but entreat him as a father . . . the elder women as mothers. . . ." These biblical injunctions were common among preachers throughout the colonies, but nowhere else in British America were they so zealously propagated in speech and in print or so thoroughly internalized in popular thought and action than in New England.

The Puritan ideal of old age was epitomized by the "elder-saint," the aged and devout Christian, whose cultural significance was rooted in the Calvinist doctrines of predestination, election, and limited atonement. In fact, a long life was generally interpreted as a sign of divine election by a people never certain of their own salvation or their fate after death. The old were venerated for yet another important reason, one based on the communal nature and spiritual quest of New England society. If the Puritan "city upon a hill" was to succeed, if the young were to complete the holy errand begun in the wilderness, they must learn from their elders. As interpreters of a heroic past, the aged were accorded priority seating in the meetinghouse, given preference in communal deliberations, and otherwise treated with deference. The vehemence with which the young were enjoined to honor their

Table 1 Life Expectancy of Colonial White Males

County	\multicolumn{6}{c}{Life Expectancy at Age}
	20	30	40	50	60	70
Charles Parish, Va.	20.8	16.4	11.8	9.5	6.9	4.0
Charles County, Md., immigrants	22.7	17.4	13.2	10.3	10.0	5.5
Charles County, Md., natives, 1652–1699	26.0	20.4	15.6	12.0	9.3	7.0
Middlesex County, Va., 1650–1710	28.8	19.4	13.0	7.7	5.8	3.6
Perquimans County, N.C., 17th century	30.5	24.4	19.4	13.7	11.3	9.9
Perquimans County, N.C., 18th century	30.2	23.1	16.6	12.1	8.7	6.1
Salem, Mass., 17th century	36.1	29.2	24.1	19.1	14.5	10.0
Salem, Mass., 18th century	35.5	30.3	25.3	19.6	14.5	10.0
Andover, Mass., 1670–1699	44.8	38.7	31.4	23.5	15.2	10.2
Andover, Mass., 1730–1759	41.6	36.3	28.4	24.5	17.2	10.4
Plymouth, Mass., 17th century	48.2	40.0	31.2	23.7	16.3	9.9

Source: James M. Gallman. "Mortality Among White Males: Colonial North Carolina," *Social Science History* 4, no. 3 (1980):306.

elders betrayed more than a hint of social as well as spiritual anxiety. Indeed, even as the public vision of a Calvinist commonwealth faded, the elderly, who personified the weakening connection with the Puritan past, became all the more celebrated.

The Delaware Valley

In the Delaware Valley, ideas and customs associated with old age were shaped by Quaker values of family and community. Quakers emphasized domesticity and were very child-centered. According to Quaker beliefs, the elderly deserved respect because they served as "nursing fathers and mothers to the young." Parents particularly were expected to embody this exalted role, but kinship or even age was less important than simply instructing the young in godly conduct. To be a nursing father or mother meant loving, caring for, and teaching youth to maintain "godly conversation." It also meant living the faith and setting the example in conduct and speech for young Quakers.

The Chesapeake and the Low Country

By comparison, not until well into the eighteenth century did the life expectancy of Virginia and Maryland planters improve enough for them to develop a domestic patriarchy in which seniority was the central organizing principle, reflecting the increasingly hierarchical organization of Chesapeake society generally. Respectable old age in Virginia was best represented by the "elder-patriarch," particularly the man of wealth and political influence. Deference might also be shown to aging men and women of humble circumstances, including even slaves. The same was almost surely true of the Carolinas and Georgia, where life expectancy was even shorter than in the Chesapeake.

The Backcountry

Longevity alone meant little to the Quakers and German Pietists of Pennsylvania; there were old reprobates as well as young ones. Much the same attitude toward old age was held by the people along the colonial frontier. Many if not most backcountry settlers were Scotch-Irish in birth, Presbyterian in faith, and patriarchal in family disposition. Perhaps less than 1 percent of western settlers were older than sixty-five; frontier life was hard enough for young adults, much less the elderly. Nevertheless, increasing numbers of men and women grew old in the backcountry, and a few backcountry patriarchs became known for investing their money, labor, and skill in protecting and sustaining the surrounding community. Fischer explains that such men became like the clan chieftains of the British borderlands and were accorded considerable deference. Their wives and other elderly women known for long service to family and friends were likewise highly esteemed. Old age in conjunction with contributions to the general welfare of the community inspired public respect on the frontier of early America.

Common Denominators of Old Age

Even for those treated with the utmost deference, and regardless of ethnicity, religion, economic status, or local custom, the last years of life were often troubling, marred by physical and mental decline, sickness, and a debilitating sense of uselessness. "Old Age is a dry and barren ground . . . a state of weakness and of much infirmity," wrote William Bridge, a fellow of Harvard College, in 1679. Other commentators agreed. Increase Mather, although venerated in Puritan Massachusetts as an elder-saint and community leader, spent the last decade of his life feeling increasingly forgotten and at times bitterly depressed. "God preserve my head," Virginia's William Byrd II wrote fretfully at the age of sixty-six, "and grant I may not lose my memory and sense." Similarly, Massachusetts judge Samuel Sewall worried for years that his advancing age and declining health might compromise his effectiveness; he decided at seventy-five that the time had come finally to leave the bench. Few New England magistrates stayed in public service to such an advanced age; most left office several years before they died.

If respect for the aged was everywhere prescribed in early America, intergenerational conflicts nevertheless arose and manifested themselves in varying expressions of resentment, even in Puritan New England. Part of the reason for such tensions, wrote Cotton Mather in 1727, was the tendency of "old folks" to remain in charge, both in politics and in economic life, until their diminished capacities became embarrassing. Of course, adult children were legally responsible for the well-being of aging fathers and mothers, and there are celebrated court cases from throughout the colonies in which elderly parents complained of abuse or neglect at the hands of their children.

Economic Status and Old Age

Particular folkways notwithstanding, economic status was usually the common denominator in community attitudes toward the aged. Upper- and middle-class males usually retained enough property to be fairly secure in their old age, both economically and psychologically. Those people who had little or no property, however—such as widows, slaves, and the poor generally—ran the risk not only of grievous economic hardship but also of public contempt and ridicule.

Widows. Aging women surrounded by their children, grandchildren, or even great-grandchildren were accorded much the same respect and deference as their patriarchal husbands, in some cases even more. In fact, the matriarchal influences that Laurel Thatcher Ulrich has so ingeniously interpreted for New England existed throughout colonial America, though in widely varying degrees. Years of experience as wives and mothers made older women the acknowledged experts in household manufacturing, caring for the sick, and midwifery. They possessed status and influence because they were important to the general community as well as to their respective families. Upon the death of her husband, however, the lion's share of the family estate might go to a woman's children. The aging widow thus became dependent upon her children, and they were responsible under law for her.

The death of her husband always altered the status and authority of the wife and mother, but the condition of widowhood varied. New England husbands who made wills usually provided well for their wives. Most husbands left their wives much more than their legal "thirds." If a widow was dissatisfied with what her husband had left her, she could always claim "dower rights" of one-third of the real property only.

In Virginia and Maryland, high death rates led husbands to empower wives with much more authority over their estates than English common law traditionally allowed; that too changed after 1700, as both spouses apparently began to live longer and as domestic patriarchy began to assert its influence over Chesapeake society, including probate law. Given the rising standard of living, however, widows were probably materially better off in the eighteenth century than ever before, despite the obvious decline in their legal status.

Wealthy widows could always find husbands, but most widows were not wealthy. Nor were they mostly young in seventeenth- and eighteenth-century New England. Remarriage was not the norm there as it was in the Chesapeake—where widows are believed to have remarried quickly, possessing property enough to attract husbands for themselves and fathers for their children—and probably in the Carolinas before 1700, when mortality rates were exceptionally high and men greatly outnumbered women because of the morbidity associated with childbirth. The numbers of widows in the older towns of early New England were substantial. During the eighteenth century, marriages in the South began to last longer because of improved adult life expectancy. By the 1770s widows on the Chesapeake were usually more than forty years old. Because of an unfavorable sex ratio, they, like widows in New England, faced difficulty finding a husband if they wished to remarry.

Older women bereft of family and income were among the poorest people in the colonies; many had to depend upon public charity for survival. Some twelve hundred widows lived in Boston in 1743, reportedly "1000 of them poor," out of a population of slightly more than sixteen thousand. Most of the references to the poor in Cotton Mather's diary refer to destitute widows; the Puritan divine wrote in 1728 that "a State of Widowhood is a state of Affliction; and very singularly so, if the widow is bereaved of . . . Support." Even if the husband had provided well for her, the widow often found herself assigned a single room in the household she formerly managed but which had passed to her eldest son.

Although prosecutions for witchcraft were largely limited to New England, beliefs in magic, spells, and witchcraft were widespread throughout colonial America, and the popular image of witches that colonists had carried from the Old World undoubtedly aroused some ambivalence toward elderly women. In both England and Europe, the stereotypical witch was an old woman, usually bent and withered, malicious in tongue and vicious in temperament. According to Carol Karlsen, of those women accused of witchcraft in New England, 58 percent (119) were older than forty, and 18 percent (37) were older than sixty. Between 1620 and 1725 widows and married women older than forty were decidedly more likely to be tried and convicted of witchcraft. Of the twenty-eight Salem cases brought to trial, thirteen involved women older than sixty; eleven of those thirteen were convicted, and eight were executed. The fifteen cases involving women between forty and fifty-nine resulted in eight convictions and four executions.

Karlsen maintains that older women, particularly widows, were especially vulnerable to accusations of witchcraft; women of childbearing age were seldom accused. Virtually all of the older women accused of witchcraft also deviated in other ways from the ideal of a venerated saint. Karlsen notes that at least 20 percent—and probably more—of the women accused were also desperately poor, and therefore all the more helpless against such charges. On the other hand, perhaps as many others are known to have been either moderately or very well-off, largely because they had recently inherited property. Such women, if they had sons or brothers to protect their interests, were much less likely to go to trial or be convicted than those who did not. Behind such accusations, Karlsen suggests, lay a deep resentment against women controlling property in a patriarchal society. Being older, or at least beyond childbearing age, apparently made some women all the more likely to fall prey to this particular manifestation of misogyny in New England.

Slaves. If elderly white widows sometimes faced difficult problems, slaves generally found old age increasingly precarious. Older slaves might be highly prized and respected because of what they knew, what they could teach others, and what they could still do in terms of craftsmanship or managing crops. Other slaves, especially their own children and grandchildren, typically treated the elderly with respect and compassion, regarding them not only as teachers and care-givers but also as beings who were suspended between the spiritual and earthly worlds.

Indeed, it was common for younger slaves to go out of their way to take care of their elders. Nonetheless, the quality of life that old bondsmen enjoyed depended mostly upon their masters.

Some masters provided small garden plots for their elderly bondsmen. But others sold off old slaves for whatever they could get or manumitted them and denied any responsibility for their survival thereafter. The Maryland legislature protested in 1752 that "sundry Persons in this Province have set disabled and superannuated Slaves free who have either perished through want or otherwise become a Burthen [sic] to others." Three years later, after it was discovered that 20 percent of all free blacks in Maryland were "past labour or crippled," as compared with 2 percent of white males, Maryland prohibited manumission by will and fined masters who did not feed and clothe their old and sickly slaves properly.

Care of the Aged

Whether white or black, slave or free, early Americans knew that if they lived long enough a time would come when they could no longer care for themselves. Almost always possessing some property, aging white colonists maintained their economic self-sufficiency and avoided living as dependents with family or friends for as long as possible. They did so by marshaling resources, doing what they could for their children, but holding back assets for their old age.

Some aging parents arranged for one of their children, or perhaps another relative or a friend, to live with them in their declining years, arranging by contract or will to compensate them for services rendered. One elderly testator left "all my neat cattle and sheep and horse-carts, chains, plow, and tool" to his cousin "in consideration that he is to move his family and come to live with me and my wife Lynn during our lives and carry on our husbandry affairs."

Some older colonists were so poor they had to ask for public help. Arrested in 1741 for operating a public house without a proper license, Alexander McKensie and his wife pleaded successfully for special permission from the Philadelphia Common Council to remain in business, being "old and infirme and his wife a Cripple."

Municipal officials in New York and Boston as well as in smaller towns occasionally bent the rules so that older people might make their own way and not become dependent upon alms. Local magistrates might warn away a poor old man or woman known to be from another jurisdiction, but they usually tried to care for their own old people, poor and ailing. An impoverished widow, for example, might be paid by the magistrates to room and board an elderly man or to nurse a sickly widow.

By the 1750s perhaps a third of the people living in the poorhouses of colonial cities were elderly men and women. The treatment they received varied, of course, but it was better than nothing. They were given care and sustenance, but little else. Records listed them as Sarah, "an old maid," or "Old Richard," or "Old Hammond." In the context of early America such appellations were pejorative, even degrading, and the poverty-stricken elderly well knew it. Sickly and suffering, without family or friends, most of them had little to look forward to except perhaps death.

DEATH: NUMBERS AND IMPACT

Death shaped the contours of early American life, both in terms of social structure and social psychology. During the entire colonial era, mortality rates remained high by today's standards. Even in seventeenth-century New England, one of the healthier places in British North America at the time, 28 percent of infants and young people died before the age of twenty. After age twenty, life expectancy for both male and female was in the sixties by 1700; however, the living were more impressed by the young dying around them than by their own longevity (see table 1).

In the disease-ridden Chesapeake and Carolinas, on the other hand, life expectancy for adult males was from ten to twenty years less than in New England. Southern women, particularly susceptible to malaria during pregnancy, were more apt to die than males until the age of forty, after which wives were likely to live longer than their husbands. In the eighteenth century, infant and childhood mortality in New England increased somewhat along with the population of towns since diseases could spread among the population, and life expectancy may well have declined slightly. Evidence is less developed for the eighteenth-century South, but life expectancy in the Chesapeake and Carolina tidewater does seem to have improved especially for adult men and women. This development paralleled the growth of a native-born population that possessed greater resistance to endemic diseases than did immigrants.

The middle colonies have yet to receive the demographic scrutiny given New England, or even the South. In New York, New Jersey, Pennsylvania, and Delaware—except for the growing cities of Philadelphia and New York—mortality rates may well have approximated those of New England, given the similarity in climate and geography. Among twenty-five Quaker settlers in Pennsylvania before 1700, Barry Levy calculated an average life expectancy of sixty-seven. Unlike New England, however, the middle colonies after 1700 continued to attract large numbers of European immigrants who brought illnesses with them and who fell victim to endemic diseases during the "seasoning" they invariably experienced. Philadelphia and New York, together with the surrounding hinterlands, were particularly hard hit by epidemics. Overall mortality in the middle colonies must have been lower than in the South but higher than in New England.

During the seventeenth century, life expectancy at birth in New England has been figured at 42.5 for males and 41.8 for females. Life expectancy was longer, however, once people attained the ages of twenty, thirty, or forty years old. At age thirty, for example, a New England male born between 1620 and 1649 could expect to live to age sixty-two.

Life was much shorter and more sickly for both children and adults in the colonial South because of the harsh disease environment there. In the seventeenth century, malaria (known as fevers and agues) and dysentery (called the bloody flux) were endemic—and periodically epidemic—throughout the colonies. These diseases were the primary culprits behind devastating death rates in the South, however, particularly in the Chesapeake tidewater and the Carolina and Georgia Low Country. Infants and children were especially vulnerable. Southerners who sur-

vived bouts of malaria or dysentery might still be weakened and later succumb to such diseases as influenza, pneumonia, and particularly tuberculosis, which was probably the greatest killer overall in the colonies.

Expressing a common lament of southern parents, Colonel Landon Carter of Sabine Hall wrote in 1757, "It is necessary that man should be acquainted with affliction and 'tis certainly nothing short of it to be confined a whole year in tending one's children. Mine are now never well." In the seventeenth century, from 40 to 50 percent of the white children born in the Chesapeake died before age twenty. In the Carolinas, the evidence so far suggests that mortality among infants and children was even more staggering. In Christ Church parish, located in the deadly Low Country, the mortality rate reached 86 percent. Of white males who did live to age twenty, scarcely 15 percent of the immigrants and only 20 percent of the natives would live to age sixty in the Chesapeake. Considerably less than 10 percent lived that long in the Carolina Low Country, compared to 65 percent in parts of seventeenth-century New England (see table 1 for comparative figures).

During the eighteenth century, life expectancy among southern whites rose primarily because of an improving standard of living and a growing native-born population possessed of greater immunity against endemic diseases, including the deadly West African falciparum malaria. Like elsewhere in Anglo-America, smallpox inoculation and quarantine procedures greatly limited that scourge in the colonial South; southern planters also began to associate malaria and yellow fever with swamps and (more gradually) dysentery with unsanitary conditions.

Although childhood mortality in the Chesapeake declined during the early eighteenth century—men generally lived nine years longer and the number of women living to forty increased from 50 percent to 75 percent—the South continued to lead the continental colonies in morbidity and mortality, to which slavery and the slave trade contributed significantly. In the early eighteenth century, more than half of the slaves imported to the Chesapeake died within ten years of their arrival, most within their first year there. Fragmentary evidence suggests that newly arrived Africans faced much the same fate in South Carolina and Georgia. African women bore few children, no doubt because they arrived malnourished and were especially sickly. Their daughters, however, like the daughters of white indentured servants, began to conceive at a much earlier age and gave birth to many more children than their mothers. African Americans also possessed the sickle-cell blood trait that gave added protection against malaria, and African mothers passed on to their infants partial immunity against yellow fever, another disease, like malaria, endemic to West Africa. At the same time, however, slaves (both children and adults) proved much more vulnerable than whites to respiratory diseases like pneumonia, pleurisy, and especially tuberculosis.

Mortality rates had a significant impact on colonial marriages. Data from the Chesapeake indicates that most marriages there did not last seven years because of spousal death, and the average length of marriages was only about ten years. Long-lived New Englanders were not likely to marry more than once. In the early Chesapeake, most surviving spouses did remarry. Because women married younger than men did, it was not unusual for a surviving wife to marry three times. Remarriage was often the only option a young widow had of providing for herself and her children. Immigrant husbands who made wills usually named their wives executors, depending primarily upon them to look after both their property and their children. A few planters simply left their estates to their widows. More often, the widow had use of the entire estate or else the dwelling plantation for her lifetime. As the native-born population grew and life expectancy increased in the early eighteenth century, longer marriages began to prevail. Domestic patriarchy began to restrict the role of wives, who were generally supplanted as executors by elder sons or other relatives.

Parental loss occurred early and on a scale in the Chesapeake and Carolinas unknown in the rest of the colonies or in England. Relatively few New England parents died before their children were married and had children of their own; most lived into their sixties. On the other hand, most children born in the colonial South could expect to lose at least one parent, or even both, before age eighteen. Anita Rutman and Darrett Rutman report that fewer than one-third of children in Middlesex County, Virginia, who survived to eighteen still had both parents. Almost one-third were orphans, and slightly more than a third had lost one parent. The Rutmans' study of Middlesex County indicated that a cooperative network of family and friends would emerge to provide solace and security for a youngster who had experienced the trauma of parental loss.

Remarriage often meant that children from one marriage would be joined with children from another, not always happily. Fathers frequently directed by will the disposition of their children, sometimes instructing that sons should receive their inheritance before their majority (twenty-one years old), thereby freeing them early from their dependence upon a stepfather. The county orphans' court, composed of sitting justices of the peace in the Chesapeake, was a judicial innovation that developed to care for the fatherless and their property. In South Carolina, the Court of Chancery, the royal council in its judicial mode, handled orphans' affairs. The orphans' court not only appointed guardians and found homes for orphans but also heard complaints against stepfathers and other guardians. The evidence is that the orphans' courts worked fairly well, looking conscientiously into charges of abuses against children and their property. Occasionally, the court removed minors from the households of guardians who abused them or despoiled their property.

Although statistics varied from north to south, large numbers of infants and children throughout colonial America did not live to adulthood. Parents and grandparents recognized that infants were fragile, death-prone creatures. "Like as a bubble, or the brittle glass," was the way Anne Bradstreet described a grandchild who had died. Puritan moralists, for example, warned parents against becoming "too fond of your children and too familiar with them" and urged "keeping constantly your due distance." To become too attached to such delicate little beings was to invite shattering disappointment, but there is nonetheless significant evidence of strong parent-child bonds and of deep grieving by fathers and mothers over the death of children, even over stillborn infants. In the seventeenth century especially, however, and whenever families were struggling against economic hardships, parents might not have either the time or the energy for prolonged mourning despite their natural inclinations. They often had to work tirelessly just to sustain the living. During epidemics, omnipresent death forced them to channel their anxiety toward preserving their remaining children.

DEATH AND DYING: ATTITUDES AND PRACTICES

Early Americans were fatalistic about death, in part because they came into such close contact with the dying. People in Anglo-America almost always died at home, usually with their family and friends around them. The way people died and the response of the living in terms of mourning and burying the deceased reflected the particular folk culture of which they were a part. Ideas and customs associated with death shed light upon what colonial Americans thought of themselves, family relationships, and community life.

Puritans

The way one died was crucial to New England Puritans, whose anxiety led them to look for signs of salvation in dying as well as in living. The mystery of divine election was unsolvable, of course; but deathbed scenes of Puritan saints young and old provided guidance. Narratives of these events were avidly written and propagated throughout the Puritan community and across its generations. Almost invariably, the dying saints lamented their own sinfulness and deplored missed opportunities for serving the Lord, thereby reinforcing the Puritan emphasis on striving after godliness. Much of this was aimed at the "rising generation," those young people upon whom the future of Puritanism depended.

Death and dying became major preoccupations of Puritan ideology. Forcing children to view the corpse—to look into the very face of death, as it were—whether of a loved one or neighbor, coupled with teachings on the uncertainty of salvation, meant that the young would likely experience much the same anxiety over death that their parents felt. The only known

relief from such spiritual uneasiness was doing God's work, that is, following the instructions laid out by the elders, the keepers of the Puritan ideal of a biblical commonwealth. Children were thus conditioned to fear death and worry about their chances for eternal life. All this sometimes provoked a morbid introspection that drove more than a few young Puritans to distraction; some actually wasted away and died in the throes of salvation angst. The funeral sermons for such youthful saints—usually detailing the spiritual agony the tormented little souls had suffered—would in turn be used to reinforce the message that life was precarious, death terrible, and salvation uncertain.

Funerary practices in early New England were simple and austere. Once the corpse had been viewed and prayed over, it was of little consequence or interest. Indeed, because Puritans disapproved of embalming, fancy funerals, and lavish tombs, the bodily remains were treated rather perfunctorily. A quick burial, often late in the day, was followed a few days later by a simple funeral sermon. A plain granite rock or rough piece of wood generally served as a marker. Self-restraint was expected of the deceased family at both the burial and funeral and was generally maintained, despite the most heartrending of circumstances. Only at the meal following the burial did emotions generally break loose, often after excessive drinking.

As the seventeenth century progressed funerals became more elaborate, usually including a finely crafted coffin, covered by a pall, with mourners receiving such tokens as scarves, ribbons, cloaks, gloves, or rings. By the late seventeenth century, carvings of skulls, hourglasses, and other symbols of death appeared on gravestones. Funeral sermons at the gravesite became common after 1700. The meal following the burial took on the trappings of a memorial feast, reflecting the shift toward a more spiritually optimistic faith.

By the middle of the eighteenth century, New Englanders were even writing longingly of death. A poem published upon the death of Mary Williams in 1749 read:

> But shall we mourn? Our Loss is great.
> Yet greater is her Bliss.
> She's gone to dwell with Jesus Christ,
> And see him Face to Face!

Sentiment had triumphed over fear and uncertainty regarding death and salvation. The funeral in New England thenceforth primarily served to help reconcile the aggrieved family and the community to the loss of the deceased. The grim face of death on the gravestone was replaced by winged cherubs and weeping willows.

Dutch New Yorkers

Although Calvinistic too, Dutch New Yorkers did not dwell on death; nor did they suffer the salvation angst characteristic of early New Englanders. While fearing their own demise, Dutch New Yorkers dealt with death largely in terms of their own familial-oriented folkways, taking what consolation they could from their religion, ever hopeful of eternal life. They remained devoted to the funerary customs brought from the Netherlands. Such practices followed a fairly set form, intended both to console the family and to celebrate the life of the deceased.

As in the Dutch republic, mourning among Dutch New Yorkers was often intense; but something of a pragmatic fatalism characterized their response to death. Despite the hurt and sense of loss, life had to go on. They, unlike the Puritans, more or less assumed that a heavenly reward awaited the deceased, unless his or her earthly life had been especially evil.

Among Dutch New Yorkers, caring for the sick was both a family and community concern, and so was dying. The Reformed church employed "consolers of the sick" whose duties included visiting, talking to, praying with, and reading the Bible to those who were gravely ill. Ideally, the dying man, woman, or child would expire in the midst of his or her loving family, with close friends and neighbors in attendance. The latter played a major role in laying out the corpse, preparing the house for mourning, and arranging the funeral procession and church services. The *aanspreecker,* or funeral inviter, appropriately dressed in black, would then make his rounds, calling upon all the friends and relatives of the deceased. One did not attend a funeral without a proper invitation.

Tradition called for the corpse to be laid out in the largest room in the house, usually called the *doed-kramer,* or dead room. The casket would be made of sturdy wood and covered by a dark shroud, which in turn was partly covered by the pall of fringed black cloth. Mirrors throughout the house were often covered, and friends and relatives kept watch over the deceased all night. Large amounts of food, drink, and tobacco were usually provided to funeral guests, even when the family of the deceased was not well-off. The funeral service would be preached at home as often as at the church; it was followed by a procession, led by the pall-bearer carrying the casket to the graveyard. Burial would be attended primarily by men, accompanied by only the closest female members of the family. The deceased was frequently buried in the church itself. Afterward, the mourners were typically given scarfs, gloves, handkerchiefs, or monkey spoons, usually made of silver and named on account of their figurine handles. They would continue drinking—good wine or liquor were by custom requirements at funerals—and eating special foods like "dead cakes," sometimes becoming quite boisterous.

The Society of Friends

Like the Puritans, Quakers and other pietistic groups in the middle colonies avidly recounted deathbed scenes, but for very different reasons. Fischer has described Quakers as optimistic fatalists: somewhat apprehensive, but primarily approaching death as the beginning of the apotheosis of the godly, the ultimate reward for Christian living, the doorway to eternal life. Nothing like the morbid introspection of the Puritans disturbed the Quakers' fundamental faith that the godly were due and would achieve glory in heaven.

The ideal death was one in which the dying reassured the living that heaven beckoned and that earth no longer held any appeal. Above all, those in the throes of death were expected to instruct the living, not only in terms of dying but also in living the Christian life. The dying were the ultimate teachers of the faith. A dying ten-year-old boy instructed his mother to live the simple life and gave the assembled company a short speech on salvation, whereupon his grandmother reportedly cried out, "*Oh Lord! That* this young Branch, should be a Teacher unto *us old Ones.*"

Quakerism emphasized simple funerals. Friends grieved deeply over the death of loved ones, but their faith condemned excessive mourning as manifestation of a proud and vain spirit. Funeral processions were discouraged, and interment in a plain wooden box was preferred. John Woolman, a Quaker minister and essayist, instructed that his coffin be made of ash rather than oak, because "Oak . . . is a wood more useful than ash." The body was usually wrapped in a plain cloth, woolen in England and linen in America. In the seventeenth century a meeting for worship was held after the burial. But in the eighteenth century, the meeting was convened before the burial. At the gravesite, Friends had an opportunity to speak before the coffin was lowered into the ground. Whether grave markers should be utilized created considerable controversy; the London Yearly Meeting in 1766 finally recommended the removal of all markers from Quaker graves. Wakes were denounced by founder George Fox as "heathen custom," though they reportedly continued in some quarters, as did the custom of having cakes and sweetmeats for funeral guests. Generally, though, funerals were not elaborate, and gifts were not given to mourners.

The Chesapeake Planters

Chesapeake planters were remarkably nonchalant about dying. Living in the midst of much sickness and death, they reveled in earthly pleasures and scorned religious rigors, taking consolation in the latitudinarianism of eighteenth-century Anglicanism. "They seem all to be free of any terror at the Prescence of death," wrote Philip Fithian in 1774, regarding the children he taught at Nomini Hall, the plantation of Colonel Robert Carter. Carter himself spoke of death in matter-of-fact fashion. "If he could have his Wish," Fithian said of Carter's views, "he would not lie longer than two days; be taken with a Fever, which should have such an unusual effect on his Body as to convince him that it would be fatal, and gradually increase till it affected a Dissolution." Carter explained that his affairs were such that he could dictate a will in five minutes.

Chesapeake planters knew they could never take life for granted; they always had to be prepared for death, which, like so much else associated with the rise of domestic patriarchy, was ritualized. In fact, the planters usually projected an aloofness toward death that was not only calm and calculated but almost cold-blooded. Consider the entry William Byrd II made in his diary

the day the secretary of the House of Burgesses literally slumped into Byrd's arms and died. "This made a great consternation," Byrd wrote, with no further comment except to say he dined at two on some wild duck. Upon the death of his infant son Parke, Byrd congratulated himself for containing his grief and lamented his wife's inability to do likewise.

Byrd nonetheless worried considerably about death at times, as did other Southern planters, especially when he or other family members fell ill. It is even tempting to speculate that the celebrated hedonism of Byrd and other planter grandees was partly their defense against an abiding anxiety about the precariousness of life.

Mourning and grieving at funerals were acceptable in seventeenth-century Virginia and Maryland; but then one had to get on with living. Funerary customs, however, changed in the eighteenth century along with attitudes toward death and dying: by the middle of the eighteenth century, emotions about death and dying were expressed more freely, and attitudes and behavior reflected increasingly affective familial relations. State funerals for wealthy and prominent individuals remained as lavish as ever. The one for Governor William Botetourt in 1770 outdid all others in terms of its large procession, the draping in black of Bruton Parish Church in Williamsburg, and extravagant displays of grief. Instead of being buried in parish-church lands, families increasingly interred their loved ones at home; it was also common to have the funeral sermon preached at home rather than at church.

African Americans in the Chesapeake

African Americans in the South believed they would continue their kinship lines in heaven. Some black Christians absorbed the whites' concept of backsliding from grace, but most had undergone such an ordeal of convictions before their conversion that once saved they felt saved forever: thus, slaves were generally more sure than their white masters that heaven awaited them after death. Since black Christians almost always linked heaven and dying together, death was overwhelmingly seen as at once liberating and healing.

Blacks retained their African customs regarding the importance of the funeral. If the death ritual was not done right, the departed soul might not be satisfied and could haunt the living. The funeral itself was an emotional affair, with much shouting and crying and lots of preaching, much of it praising Jesus and heaven. A secondary funeral sermon preached some weeks after the first was also customary, another vestige of African culture. Black graveyards were often characterized by mounded graves marked by seashells or relics of the deceased.

The religious interaction of blacks and whites in eighteenth-century Virginia meant that whites absorbed much of the black view of death, funerals, and heaven. Attitudes toward the family, in terms of affective relations, contributed mightily to the convergence of black and white responses. Blacks and whites attended church together, went to each other's funerals, and borrowed from each other in worship. Indeed, African Americans talked about heaven and sang about the joyous homecoming there with deceased relatives long before such ideas were beginning to make their way into the sermons and hymns of burgeoning Methodists and Baptists. The influence of black Christians upon the white religious community, especially with regard to death and dying, is too obvious to be ignored.

Settlers in the Backcountry

Western settlers dealt with death in ways that reflected the endemic violence of their society. Death rates were not as high in the backcountry as in the tidewater, though higher than in eastern New England. Even so, Indian wars, outlaw raids, and the everyday hardships of frontier living reminded people that death could come at any moment. There was, in fact, a sense of foreboding, of incipient danger, that arose from the inchoate nature of frontier society. As Charles Woodmason wrote of the Carolina backcountry, "When the Bands of Society and Government hang Loose and Ungirt," the people had to "be constantly on the Watch, and on our Guard" against rogues and criminals of all kinds. Yet backcountry folk spent little time speculating about heaven or hell; they were too oriented to daily living. Westerners were focused primarily on the struggle to survive, facing death with courage and grace, and only secondarily concerned with what awaited them after death. What was important was dying well, making that last battle a worthy one.

Scotch-Irish emigrants from the British borderlands brought their customs regarding death to the American frontier, where they found an environment similar to the one they had left. News of a death led neighbors to stop working until after the burial. In the house of the deceased, dishes were removed from cabinets, mirrors covered or taken down, and clocks stopped. Neighbors "laid out" the body, putting a plate of salt and soil on its stomach, symbolic of the spirit and flesh, respectively. Usually the corpse was kept at home for one or two days, some of the neighbors and family members keeping wake during the night. Neighbors dug the grave, and everyone in the community was expected to come by, pay their respects to the family, and touch the corpse, young and old alike, whether they liked the deceased or not. Plenty of food, drink, and often tobacco were provided for the guests. Should a dog or cat jump over the body, the animal was immediately killed, given the superstition that the next person it jumped over would surely die. If a preacher were handy, a sermon might proceed the interment. Otherwise, a prayer at the grave would suffice. Funerals were a vivid reminder of communal needs in a very individualistic society.

CONCLUSIONS

If colonial Americans did not die young from childbirth or contagious illness, they might sooner or later succumb to degenerative diseases, like heart trouble or cancer, associated with advancing age. Nonetheless aging and dying were always much more than biological facts. Indeed, an evolving pluralistic culture projected assorted expectations for each stage of life, including and in particular the last. Their immediate surroundings, together with the traditions and customs they inherited, made early Americans perceive and experience old age and death from various vantage points; but those perceptions and experiences were remarkably consistent with particular folkways.

Appreciation for the aged in colonial times rested to a great extent on the ties of close and personal relationships. The old and the young and everyone in between shared much the same space and therefore lived in a continuum of shared experience. Colonial families and communities existed in an intimate world of shared love and labor, happiness and sorrow, suffering, and finally death. Because sickness and mortality were so commonplace the distance between life and death did not seem that great, and death was very much an acknowledged part of life. Religion, or rather the belief in a caring God, loomed over the colonial world, contributing significantly to the dignity of old age and bringing the realm of the living more closely into communion with the realm of the dead. Despite the fearsome possibility of hell, the expectation of heaven made death all the more bearable and approachable, for both the young and the old.

BIBLIOGRAPHY

Old Age

Archer, Richard. "New England Mosaic: A Demographic Analysis for the Seventeenth Century." *William and Mary Quarterly*, 3rd ser., 47 (1990):477–502.

Conner, Karen Ann. *Aging America: Issues Facing an Aging Society.* Englewood Cliffs, N.J., 1992.

Cray, Robert E., Jr. *Pauper and Poor Relief in New York City and Its Rural Environs, 1700–1830.* Philadelphia, 1988.

Demos, John. *Entertaining Satan: Witchcraft and the Culture of Early New England.* New York, 1982.

———. *A Little Commonwealth: Family Life in Plymouth Colony.* New York, 1970.

———. "Old Age in Early New England." In *The American Family in Social-Historical Perspective*, 2nd ed., edited by Michael Gordon. New York, 1978.

Elliott, Emory. *Power and the Pulpit in Puritan New England.* Princeton, N.J., 1975.

Fischer, David Hackett. *Albion's Seed: Four British Folkways in America.* New York, 1989.

———. *Growing Old in America.* Expanded ed. New York, 1978.

Greven, Philip J., Jr. *Four Generations: Population, Land, and Family in Colonial Andover, Massachusetts.* Ithaca, N.Y., 1970.

Haber, Carole. *Beyond Sixty-Five: The Dilemma of Old Age in America's Past.* New York, 1983.

Karlsen, Carol F. *The Devil in the Shape of a Woman: Witchcraft in Colonial New England.* New York, 1987.

Keyssar, Alexander. "Widowhood in Eighteenth-Century Massachusetts: A Problem in the History of the Family." *Perspectives in American History* 8 (1974):83–119.

Kulikoff, Allan. *Tobacco and Slaves: The Development of Southern Cultures in the Chesapeake, 1680–1800.* Chapel Hill, N.C., 1986.

Levack, Brian P. *The Witch-Hunt in Early Modern Europe.* London and New York, 1987.

Levy, Barry. *Quakers and the American Family: British Settlement in the Delaware Valley.* New York, 1988.

Lewis, Jan. *The Pursuit of Happiness: Family Values in Jefferson's Virginia.* New York, 1984.

Lockridge, Kenneth A. *The Diary and Life of William Byrd II of Virginia, 1674–1744.* Chapel Hill, N.C., 1987.

———. *A New England Town: The First Hundred Years. Dedham, Massachusetts, 1636–1736.* New York, 1970.

Morris, Richard Brandon. *Studies in the History of America Law: With Special Reference to the Seventeenth and Eighteenth Centuries.* New York, 1958.

Salmon, Marylynn. *Women and the Law of Property in Early America.* Chapel Hill, N.C., 1986.

Smith, Daniel Scott. "Old Age and the 'Great Transformation': A New England Case Study." In *Aging and the Elderly: Humanistic Perspectives in Gerontology*, edited by Stuart F. Spicker, Kathleen M. Woodward, and David Van Tassel. Atlantic Highlands, N.J., 1978.

Sobel, Mechal. *The World They Made Together: Black and White Values in Eighteenth-Century Virginia.* Princeton, N.J., 1987.

Ulrich, Laurel Thatcher. *Good Wives: Image and Reality in the Lives of Women in Northern New England, 1650–1750.* New York, 1987.

Mortality

Carr, Lois Green. "The Development of the Maryland Orphans' Court, 1654–1715." In *Law, Society, and Politics in Early Maryland: Proceedings of the First Conference on Maryland History, June 14–15, 1974*, edited by Aubrey C. Land, Lois Green Carr, and Edward C. Papenfuse. Baltimore, Md., 1977.

Carr, Lois Green, and Lorena S. Walsh. "The Planter's Wife: The Experience of White Women in Seventeenth-Century Maryland." *William and Mary Quarterly*, 3rd ser., 34, no. 4 (1977):542–571.

Carville, V. Earle. "Environment, Disease, and Mortality in Early Virginia." In *The Chesapeake in the Seventeenth Century: Essays on Anglo-American Society*, edited by Thad W. Tate and David L. Ammerman. Chapel Hill, N.C., 1979.

Duffy, John. *Epidemics in Colonial America.* Baton Rouge, La., 1953.

Gallman, James M. "Determinants of Age at Marriage in Colonial Perquimans County, North Carolina." *William and Mary Quarterly*, 3rd. ser., 39, no. 1 (1982):176–191.

————. "Mortality Among White Males: Colonial North Carolina." *Social Science History* 4, no. 3 (1980):295–316.

Kammen, Michael G. *Colonial New York: A History.* New York, 1975.

Laslett, Peter. *The World We Have Lost, Further Explored: England Before the Industrial Age.* New York, 1984.

Logue, Barbara J. "In Pursuit of Prosperity: Disease and Death in a Massachusetts Commercial Port, 1660–1850." *Journal of Social History* 25 (1991):309–343.

Merrens, H. Roy, and George D. Terry. "Dying in Paradise: Malaria, Mortality, and the Perceptual Environment in Colonial South Carolina." *Journal of Southern History* 50 (1984):533–551.

Patterson, K. David. "Disease Environments of the Antebellum South." In *Science and Medicine in the Old South,* edited by Ronald L. Numbers and Todd L. Savitt. Baton Rouge, La., 1986.

Rutman, Darrett B., and Anita H. Rutman. " 'Non-Wives and Sons-in-Law': Parental Death in a Seventeenth-Century Virginia County." In *The Chesapeake in the Seventeenth Century: Essays on Anglo-American Society,* edited by Thad W. Tate and David L. Ammerman. Chapel Hill, N.C., 1979.

————. "Of Agues and Fevers: Malaria in the Early Chesapeake." *William and Mary Quarterly,* 3rd ser., 33, no. 1 (1976):31–60.

————. *A Place in Time: Explicatus.* New York, 1984.

————. *A Place in Time: Middlesex County, Virginia, 1650–1750.* New York, 1984.

Smith, Daniel Blake. "Mortality and Family in the Colonial Chesapeake." *Journal of Interdisciplinary History* 8, no. 3 (1978):403–427.

Vinovskis, Maris A. "Mortality Rates and Trends in Massachusetts Before 1860." *Journal of Economic History* 32, no. 1 (1972):184–213.

Walsh, Lorena S. " 'Till Death Us Do Part': Marriage and Family in Seventeenth-Century Maryland." In *The Chesapeake in the Seventeenth Century: Essays on Anglo-American Society,* edited by Thad W. Tate and David L. Ammerman. Chapel Hill, N.C., 1979.

Wells, Robert V. "Quaker Marriage Patterns in a Colonial Perspective." *William and Mary Quarterly,* 3rd ser., 29, no. 3 (1972):415–442.

————. *Revolutions in Americans' Lives: A Demographic Perspective on the History of Americans, Their Families, and Their Society.* Westport, Conn., 1982.

Wood, Betty. *Slavery in Colonial Georgia, 1730–1775.* Athens, Ga., 1984.

Wood, Peter H. *Black Majority: Negroes in Colonial South Carolina from 1670 Through the Stono Rebellion.* New York, 1974.

Wrigley, Edward Anthony, and Roger Schofield. *The Population History of England, 1541–1871: A Reconstruction.* Cambridge, England, 1989.

Death and Dying

DeSpelder, Lynne Ann, and Albert Lee Strickland. *The Last Dance: Encountering Death and Dying.* 3rd edition. Mountain View, Calif., 1992.

Earle, Alice Morse. *Colonial Days in Old New York.* New York, 1896.

Fithian, Philip Vickers. *Journal and Letters of Philip Vickers Fithian, 1773–1774: A Plantation Tutor of the Old Dominion.* Edited by Hunter Dickinson Farish. Williamsburg, Va., 1943; repr. Charlottesville, Va., 1978.

Frost, J. William. *The Quaker Family in Colonial America: A Portrait of the Society of Friends.* New York, 1973.

Geddes, Gordon E. *Welcome Joy: Death in Puritan New England.* Ann Arbor, Mich., 1981.

Jackson, Charles O., ed. *Passing: The Vision of Death in America.* Westport, Conn., 1977.

Ludwig, Allan. *Graven Images: New England Stonecarving and Its Symbols, 1650–1815.* Middletown, Conn., 1966.

Pinckney, Eliza Lucas. *The Letterbook of Eliza Lucas Pinckney, 1739–1762.* Edited by Elise Pinckney. Chapel Hill, N.C., 1972.

Shackelford, Laurel, and Bill Weinberg, eds. *Our Appalachia: An Oral History.* New York, 1977.

Shammas, Carole, Marylynn Salmon, and Michel Dahlin. *Inheritance in America: From Colonial Times to the Present.* New Brunswick, N.J., 1987.

Singleton, Esther. *Dutch New York.* New York, 1909; repr. 1968.

Smith, Daniel Blake. *Inside the Great House: Planter Family Life in Eighteenth-Century Chesapeake Society.* Ithaca, N.Y., 1980.

Smith, Dorothy H. "Orphans in Anne Arundel County, Maryland, 1704–1709." *Maryland Magazine of Genealogy* 3, no. 1 (1980):34–42.

Stannard, David E. *The Puritan Way of Death: A Study in Religion, Culture, and Social Change.* New York, 1977.

Vinovskis, Maris A. "Angels' Heads and Weeping Willows: Death in Early America." In *The American Family in Social-Historical Perspective,* edited by Michael Gordon. 3rd edition. New York, 1983.

————. "Death and Family Life in the Past." *Human Nature* 1, no. 1 (1990):109–122.

Weir, Robert M. *Colonial South Carolina: A History.* New York, 1983.

Woodmason, Charles. *The Carolina Backcountry on the Eve of the Revolution: The Journal and Other Writings of Charles Woodmason, Anglican Itinerant.* Edited by Richard J. Hooker. Chapel Hill, N.C., 1953.

Ronald William Howard

SEE ALSO **Gender Relations** and **Marriage.**

THE DUTCH COLONY

THE DUTCH IN THE SEVENTEENTH century generally viewed the aged with respect and even reverence, in part because so many people died young. Mortality rates have not been calculated for the United Provinces, but because of epidemics and infection, death was omnipresent and capricious, claiming significant numbers of children as well as adults. Infants were especially vulnerable, with a mortality rate estimated to be above 18 percent. Catholics and Protestants alike believed that the precariousness of life in this world made preparations for life in the next all the more important. Like other Europeans, the Dutch dealt with the social and personal trauma of death through family and community rituals, thereby regularizing their mourning in the face of deepest grief. Even among the poorer classes, funerals were usually accompanied by considerable eating, drinking, and gift giving in remembrance of the deceased.

The relatively few Dutch men and women who lived into their sixties or beyond were regarded as especially blessed or especially lucky; either way, they were usually admired for their longevity. Moreover, in the bourgeois society of the Dutch republic, people's economic and political power tended to increase with age, giving the young another good reason to be appropriately deferential toward their elders. Most important of all, the reciprocity at the heart of Dutch family ethos dictated that the old should be treated kindly because of the nurture and assistance they had supposedly provided the young throughout the years.

The dominant images of the elderly in Dutch culture were positive, epitomized by the pious widow at her prayers or the aging craftsman at his work. Of course, the elderly now and again were presented in sinister terms, manifested occasionally before 1650 in charges of witchcraft against aging men and women but more generally apparent in paintings of an old hag seen as procuress, personifying the ugliness of lust and its constant threat to stable family relationships. However, the Dutch wanted the elderly to be both dignified and honored, even as they knew that aging meant declining physical and mental capacity and, ultimately, death.

There was no retirement as such; men and women were expected to work in their respective spheres as long as they were able. Once superannuated, they were usually cared for by their children, grandchildren, or other relatives. If they were poor and their children were unable to assist them, the elderly became objects of charity, receiving aid from either the Dutch Reformed church or another legally recognized religious congregation, or perhaps from the town poor fund. Given the reciprocal relations within the Dutch family and the custom of partible inheritance, aging Dutch parents were not likely to arouse either the resentment or the jealousy of their offspring. In many cases, the elderly certainly were the objects of veneration and affection, though just how closely reality approximated the cultural ideal is impossible to say.

OLD AGE IN NEW NETHERLAND

The Dutch brought their customs and attitudes regarding old age and dying to New Netherland, whose youthful population contained comparatively few older people. However, surviving to old age was certainly crucial to accumulating wealth and prestige in the Dutch colony. Families like the Van Cortlandts, Schuylers, Beekmans, and Phillipses owed much to the longevity of their founding fathers. As in the fatherland, when the elderly became unable to work, they were usually cared for by their children or, if they had the resources, hired someone to care for them. Otherwise, in order to survive, they had to get support from the church or from the town government. According to the deacons' account book for Beverswyck (Albany), the number of the elderly assisted by the Reformed church increased steadily as the seventeenth century progressed. Similarly, the English towns on western Long Island found it necessary to assist several of their elderly and infirmed citizens. Obviously, many of the aging poor in New Netherland and early New York enjoyed little of the reverence and respect associated with the idealized version of old age embraced by both the Dutch and English settlers.

DEATH

Death was commonplace in New Netherland, due primarily to disease, Indian wars, storms at sea, and the perils of childbirth. Reliable statistics are not available, but numerous references to widows, widowers, and orphans and to the untimely deaths of both children and adults suggest high mortality rates. Spouses and parents took care to protect the property rights of their survivors, as they had done in the fatherland.

By the time of the English conquest in 1664, Dutch funeral customs were also becoming well established, thanks largely to the efforts of Reformed dominies and to shifting immigration patterns in the 1650s that favored domesticity. Dutch New Yorkers would remain extremely loyal to the death rituals of their forebears, all of which have been carefully detailed in works by Alice Morse Earle and Esther Singleton. Death was a communal affair, with relatives, friends, and neighbors playing major roles in laying out the corpse, preparing the house for mourning, and arranging the funeral procession and church service. Gifts were often given to mourners, and large amounts of food and drink turned some funerals into rather rowdy celebrations in honor of the deceased.

As in the Dutch republic, mourning over the death of loved ones was frequently intense, but something of a pragmatic stoicism characterized funerary rituals; despite personal loss and its hurt, life had to go on. In fact, although they too were Calvinists, adherents of the Dutch Reformed church were much more likely to assume that salvation and heavenly reward awaited the deceased than to agonize over life after death as did the more introspective English Puritans.

Unlike adherents of the Dutch Reformed church, who did not dwell on death and dying, New England Calvinists, including those English settlers who came to western Long Island, developed what amounted to almost an obsession with that subject. Death itself among the English of New Netherland was dealt with communally, much as it was among the Dutch Reformed. Blacks, slave and free, seem to have combined African customs with Dutch and English practices and beliefs regarding death and dying, but the records provide regrettably few details.

Somewhat more is known about how the Iroquois dealt with the Great Destroyer, the Being that is Faceless, as they called death. The Seneca deeply mourned deceased loved ones, marked the melancholy occasion with many speeches and much weeping, and regarded their graves as almost sacred. The dead were frequently buried in a sitting position, in a grave lined with wood or bark, and surrounded by goods they would need in the next world. This world was vaguely thought to be a rather pleasant place. Ritual mourning lasted for nine days, followed by the death feast, after which it was hoped the soul of the departed would finally be on its way. Souls reluctant to leave for the next world were known to menace the living.

Among the Iroquois, the aged were respected and venerated as keepers of oral traditions, history, and skills essential to successive generations. Similarly, those settlers who grew old in New Netherland were respected for their experience, whether it was in the fur trade, farming, or a craft. As a reward for their long and faithful service, the Dutch West India Company even freed a number of older slaves, although one may well question the motives of the company in freeing slaves after their usefulness had declined.

BIBLIOGRAPHY

Corwin, Edward T., and Hugh Hastings, eds. *Ecclesiastical Records of the State of New York.* 7 vols. Albany, N.Y., 1901–1916.

Earle, Alice Morse. *Colonial Days in Old New York.* New York, 1896; repr. 1990.

Fernow, Berthold, ed. and trans. *The Minutes of the Orphanmasters of New Amsterdam, 1653–1663.* New York, 1902.

Gehring, Charles T., ed. and trans. *Fort Orange Court Minutes, 1652–1660.* Syracuse, N.Y., 1990.

Goodfriend, Joyce. "Black Families in New Netherland." In *A Beautiful and Fruitful Place: Selected Rensselaerswijck Seminar Papers,* edited by Nancy Anne McClure Zeller. Albany, N.Y., 1991.

Hershowitz, Leo, ed. *Wills of Early New York Jews.* Waltham, Mass., 1967.

Kenney, Alice P. "Private Worlds in the Middle Colonies: An Introduction to Human Tradition in American History." *New York History* 51, no. 1 (1970):4–31.

Kruger, Vivienne L. "Born to Run: The Slave Family in Early New York, 1626–1827." 2 vols. Ph.D. diss., Columbia University, 1985.

McLaughlin, William. "Dutch Rural New York: Community, Economy, and Family in Colonial Flatbush." Ph.D. diss., Columbia University, 1985.

Marshall, Sherrin. *The Dutch Gentry, 1500–1650: Family, Faith, and Fortune.* New York and London, 1987.

Morris, Richard B. *Studies in the History of American Law.* New York, 1958.

Narrett, David E. "Preparations for Death and Provision for the Living." *New York History* 57, no. 4 (1976):417–437.

O'Callaghan, Edmund B. *Calendar of Dutch Historical Manuscripts in the Office of the Secretary of State, Albany, New York, 1630–1664.* Albany, N.Y., 1865; repr. Ridgewood, N.J., 1968.

Raesly, Ellis Laurence. *Portrait of New Netherland.* New York, 1945; repr. Port Washington, N.Y., 1965.

Schama, Simon. *The Embarrassment of Riches: An Interpretation of Dutch Culture in the Golden Age.* New York, 1987.

Singleton, Esther. *Dutch New York.* New York, 1909; repr. 1968.

Stannard, David E. *The Puritan Way of Death: A Study in Religion, Culture, and Social Change.* New York, 1977.

Sturtevant, William C., gen. ed. *Handbook of North American Indians.* 20 vols. Vol. 15, *Northeast*, edited by Bruce G. Trigger. Washington, D.C., 1978.

Van Deursen, Arie Theodorus. *Plain Lives in a Golden Age: Popular Culture, Religion and Society in Seventeenth-Century Holland.* Cambridge, Mass., 1991.

Wallace, Anthony F. C. *The Death and Rebirth of the Seneca.* New York, 1969.

Ronald William Howard

SEE ALSO **Gender Relations** and **Marriage.**

THE FRENCH COLONIES

SEVENTEENTH-AND-EIGHTEENTH-century records present major problems for historians trying to establish the characteristics of any particular population. New France, however, produced some exceptionally fine documents for births, marriages, and deaths, and Canadian demographers have studied them closely. Although old age and death are complex subjects, elements of the basic picture can be presented here.

DEMOGRAPHICS

French colonies had a relatively young population in the seventeenth century. By 1663, 50.6 percent of the Europeans in the main colony of Canada were aged between newborn and nineteen years, 36.3 percent were twenty to thirty-nine, while 11.1 percent were forty to fifty-nine and 2 percent were sixty or over. An impression of conditions by the mid eighteenth century can be gained from data for the city of Quebec (table 1).

Table 1. Age Profile of Population in Quebec City, 1744

Age	Male	Female
0–4	317	324
5–9	359	358
10–14	355	320
15–19	234	313
20–24	173	272
25–29	164	200
30–34	166	148
35–39	150	148
40–44	151	137
45–49	113	107
50–54	96	86
55–59	52	49
60–64	46	34
65+	58	53
total	2434	2549

Source: Danielle Gauvreau. *Quebec: Une ville et sa population au temps de la Nouvelle France*, p. 210.

The impact of death can be gauged from figures for mortality (table 2).

Table 2. Mortality of People Born in Canada, 1640–1729 (rate per 1000)

Age	Male	Female
0	141	129
1	57	57
5	20	24
10	20	15
15	24	34
20	46	43
25	41	57
30	58	76
35	57	82
40	75	108
45	89	86
50	132	88
55	159	146
60	214	168
65	270	254
70	426	325
75	509	390
80	569	691
85	783	833

Source: Hubert Charbonneau. *Vie et mort de nos ancêtres: Études démographiques*, p. 133.

French families in the colonies enjoyed a high fertility; the average final size for families in Canada was 6.7 children. But alongside that was a high level of infant mortality. Depending on period and place, figures could run from 129 to 246 per 1,000. By comparison, figures for infant mortality in rural England at this time hovered around 122–153, but in France they were 172–275. Once a child had passed his or her first birthday, however, the child's chances were much improved.

The mortality figures for mothers are also strikingly high, ranging between 1.1 percent and 2.1 percent of the women who gave birth. Around 11 percent of deaths occurred within twenty-four hours, so relatively few women appear to have died from the actual birth process. Most deaths (60 percent) occurred between the second and fourteenth day following childbirth, suggesting that infection was the principal cause. The number and frequency of births also increased the risk of a fatal pregnancy.

High mortality at the outset of life, and significant levels in middle years, appreciably reduced the life expectancy of Europeans in the French colonies. At birth both sexes had a life expectancy of 35.5 years (combined figure for all generations, 1640–1729).

CAUSES OF MORTALITY

The most significant cause of death in most ages was undoubtedly infectious disease. Agricultural crises brought on by crop failure or economic disruptions (often related to war) could increase mortality, though not to the extent that they did in Europe. Accidents (drowning, fires, falls, injuries from animals and implements, etc.), hitherto underrated by historians of the period, have emerged as a leading cause of death among adults. War was important, but historical demographers have determined that it has been overrated for the period before the outbreak of the Seven Years' War. Recalculation by John A. Dickinson indicates that the effect of the Indian wars between 1609 and 1666 was exaggerated by popular memory. It was more severe in the later Iroquois wars (1683–1701) but still not devastating.

ATTITUDES TOWARD OLD AGE AND DEATH

As demographic historians have admitted, it is difficult to establish particular characteristics of family life in the French colonies. There are only limited narrative sources, so most historians have avoided saying much beyond the basic data. A few general observations, however, are possible.

People considered themselves and others around them to be old once they reached their later forties, however there was no general sense of an age limit among the French in the colonies. Many would work for as long as they were able— usually until shortly before their death. Older people were generally treated with deference, especially as fathers remained at the head of the family's affairs. Among the elite, wealth and influence tended to increase as a man's career progressed. There were, however, those who became quite decrepit. More than a few reports from colonial officials note that particular employees or officers had become *entièrement caduc* (entirely decrepit) and it would be a mercy to them and a help to operations if they were relieved of their functions.

The aged would generally be cared for by their family, as required by law and in keeping with a culture that emphasized familial connections not only in terms of affection but also in economic matters. Parents were also, of course, controllers of the estate, which gave children a certain incentive to look after them if need be. Most of the old would therefore be in the care of children and relatives. It was possible for parents to hand over the business, farm, or other estate to children before death (by means of a *donation entre vifs*, or living will) in return for a guaranteed amount on which to maintain themselves. Not all children fulfilled their commitments. The reasons are often not clear but court records suggest both neglect and, more common, economic difficulties. Nonetheless, such deeds of gift became increasingly common in the eighteenth century.

Communal facilities increased as the colony matured and the old and poor increased both in absolute numbers and relative to the rest of the population. Some government employees and a very few "deserving poor" received direct assistance from the king. The government, however, was reluctant to pension off employees because that would cost money—a pension in addition to the ongoing cost of filling the office. Others were cared for in almshouses called *hôpitaux généraux* supported by the king and church. The one in Montreal was established in 1688 but did not function properly until the later 1690s. It cared only for men, at least until the 1740s. Another at Quebec (1692) cared for both sexes.

Attitudes toward death itself were shaped by French and Catholic traditions. The influence of the church in the French colonies has been a topic of dispute for some time. Early settlers and missionaries created a staunchly Catholic society, comparable to the strongly Protestant settlements in New England, but subsequent generations were less fervent. The church was more prominent in cities than in the countryside. For much of the time, it was difficult to assure adequate numbers of clergy. Most parish clergy do not appear to have been charismatic leaders wielding a strong influence that would produce a fervent religiosity.

In this climate, most French colonists do not seem to have agonized about death, although concern for the life hereafter assured a degree of commitment to the Catholic church. People were matter-of-fact about death. In war, the French copied the stoicism of Indians, gravely accepting the death of fathers, sons, and friends in combat. Widowers and widows frequently remarried. This does not reflect on their feelings for the departed spouse but rather on economic necessities in an age when families had a wide range of economic functions and each member played an important role. The death of a child was certainly tragic but it was quite a common event. This probably limited many people's expectations at the birth of a child and their distress at a death.

Little is known about actual funerals. Records are terse, even for so distinguished a figure as Governor Philippe de Rigand de Vaudreuil, who died in 1725. In keeping with custom, a funeral would be a communal event in which the family, relatives, friends, and neighbors all participated. Ideally, when a person was close to death a priest would be called to provide the last rites. After death, a wake would begin; the corpse would be laid out and the house placed in mourning. The next day, the priest would return to meet the body, sprinkle it with holy water, and then the body would be taken in procession to the church where a requiem mass was celebrated. Most funerals were humble affairs, however, grand ceremonies were arranged for key figures like Bishop François de Montmorency de Laval and Governor Louis Buade de Frontenac—ceremonies providing one final testament to their social status. In the European tradition, a dinner would be offered to the mourners after the burial. In Louisiana, funeral processions evolved into sometimes festive parades bearing the corpse to its final resting place.

Most graves were marked by a simple cross. There were few large funerary monuments and no ostentatious buildings. According to Catholic practice, a certain number of masses were to be said for the dead, and everyone was to be remembered on All Souls' Day (November 2). There are few instances of special projects being undertaken to preserve the memory of the deceased—foundations, buildings, and so on, though a few wealthy colonists left sizable sums for various religious purposes.

BIBLIOGRAPHY

Charbonneau, Hubert. *Vie et mort de nos ancêtres: Études démographiques.* Montreal, 1975.

Charbonneau, Hubert, Real Bates, and Mario Boleda. *Naissance d'une population: Les Français établis au Canada au XVIIe siècle.* Paris and Montreal, 1987.

Dickinson, John A. "La guerre iroquoise et la mortalité en Nouvelle-France, 1608–1666." *Revue d'histoire de l'Amérique française* 36, no. 1 (1982):31–54.

Gauvreau, Danielle. *Québec: Une ville et sa population au temps de la Nouvelle France.* Quebec, 1991.

Greer, Allan. *Peasant, Lord, and Merchant: Rural Society in Three Quebec Parishes, 1740–1840.* Toronto, Ontario, 1985.

Henripin, Jacques. *La population canadienne au début du XVIIIe siècle: Nuptialité, fécondité, mortalité infantile.* Paris, 1954.

Jaenen, Cornelius J. *The Role of the Church in New France.* Toronto, Ontario, 1976.

Trudel, Marcel. *La population du Canada en 1663.* Montreal, 1973.

Jay Cassel

See also **Gender Relations** and **Marriage.**

THE SPANISH BORDERLANDS

In the Southwest, as the borderlands are now called, indigenous communities and Spanish, later Mexican, villages ritualized old age and death in practices that abided tradition, Native and European. Few Native Americans abandoned their old people. The Apache, Navajo, and Pueblo—groups who dominated the central borderlands—and indigenous communities elsewhere in the regions of the borderlands equated old age with wisdom. Elders were respected members of a community, entrusted to teach and correct the unmannerly or disorderly. It was untraditional among these groups to leave old or infirm people unattended. Unless the elderly and dying requested such treatment, the most common solution for those terminally ill or close to death was a cleansing ceremony followed by careful supervision by trusted family members. The curing ceremonies of the Navajo, and for men, the ritual bathings inside the Pueblo kivas (or ceremonial chambers) were full of regard for purification, but also for healing. Death was, despite what some anthropologists say, not necessarily feared, not always welcomed either, but incorporated instead into daily living. Anthropologists have suggested that some indigenous groups were so fearful of the dead that they avoided discussions of it, but they have overlooked the simple point that for many, death unleashed a new cycle of acknowledgment, cleansing, and grieving. No one part of the cycle was more important than any other.

The Spanish who entered the territories of the central borderlands and claimed for the Spanish Crown the lands of the Navajo, Apache, and Pueblo held similar notions about the regenerative quality of death, but used them for different purposes. Family scholars of the Spanish medieval period, for example, have focused attention on the importance of family, extended kin networks, and relational patterns among members of family groupings around death to describe the significance of inheritance, of consanguinity, essentially, to mark the beginning of a new cycle of the transfer of property. They argue that the Spanish similarly revered elders, long before the conditions for preindustrial capitalism had been set, and the demarcations of seniors over juniors also brought into play customs equating seniority with wisdom; at the base of the Spanish pyramid that organized some regions of their home country was community service, enacted by people considered "junior." At the top were the seniors: older, wiser, and more conservative.

Not all Spanish customs functioned smoothly, but when the social structure demanded them, or deemed respect and attention important, generally families and communities fell into line. These tendencies in social and cultural hierarchy were transferred to the New

World and existed in the colonial period throughout the regions of the Spanish Borderlands. The adaptations of customs by people of mixed inheritance, Native and Spanish, simply contributed to their longevity and suggest why they existed long after the colonial period ended.

THE ROLE OF THE CATHOLIC CHURCH

Catholicism particularly reinforced social and cultural mores. The organized church in the New World, and the Roman Catholic faith throughout Europe, considered old age and slow death blessings bestowed by the Holy Spirit on families and communities. Jesus Christ had shown his Father, God, the same respect he expected all elders to receive. Emulation was the cornerstone of these Catholic arrangements. The church bestowed honorific titles and commemorated its seniors, choosing its popes from the body of cardinals who were generally older; in the Americas and especially in the borderlands, priests were often sent out from the junior ranks, and elderly clerics frequently were persuaded, or ordered, to return to the capital cities, where it was thought that better care could be provided them in their old age.

It is difficult to know whether age and purity of conscience or morality were interrelated and equated in the same way during the colonial period in Spanish North America. Some evidence from the parishes and the missions suggests that the priests, old or young, were hardly paragons of godliness. As more researchers examine church records, here and in medieval Spain, the conclusion is inescapable that many priests were simply ordinary human beings, as driven by selfishness, brutish behavior, abusive personalities, and the like as their parishioners. This is not, however, to suggest that the societies and communities of New Spain did not strive to achieve some balance between purported church teachings about aging and dying and the actual circumstances of poor communities or remote villages that dotted the Spanish Borderlands. Still, this division between what was ascribed and prescribed, between what was said and what was practiced, is an important barometer of how well church doctrine was imparted or withstood modification (particularly in the arenas controlled as rigorously as Christian burials). The administration of the last rites, or extreme unction, adapted to the conditions Spanish colonizers encountered in the frontier regions of the empire, of necessity. These colonizers understood that the proper administration of sacraments prepared souls for heaven; failures or abstentions resulted in souls lost to purgatory.

Examples of adaptations in the borderlands abound. The church could be attentive to certain aspects of death, but not to all. For many families, death's warnings and messages were treated primarily as occasions to resurrect other traditions. Burials tended to be handled expeditiously, for preservation was always a problem. Where salt and vinegar, necessary for keeping the corpse from deteriorating, were scarce, burial occurred quickly and wakes followed the funerals. Grievers wailed for the lost soul, and women prayed often for days over the sins of the deceased. At the *velorio*, as the wake was called, rosaries were recited and special prayers were offered to assist the soul into heaven. The longer the ceremony, the older, more highly respected, or of higher status was the departed. By contrast, children's funerals occasioned fewer preparations, and were far more common than the ceremonies for adults. For one, infant mortality rates were high. From the earliest period of colonization until the mid nineteenth century, two out of every five children did not live past age three and thus tended not to receive, even in death, undue attention.

One conclusion to be drawn about aging and death in the borderlands is that they were linked in communal rituals as well as by Catholic church doctrines and practices. But the church could easily distend or alter circumstances to fit preconceived notions of proper behavior among the elderly, among seniors. Some parishioners were denied "proper" Catholic burials because they had been accused of witchcraft or of practicing heresies, including keeping alive indigenous traditions. Some allowances existed, deviations, for example, that remained confined to folkloric traditions. Midwifery and the sort of healing practiced by *curanderas* escaped the scrutiny of church officials, until something went wrong. Spells cast, or notations of procedures like those involving the glances of the evil eye, engendered verdicts of excommunication from the church or of banishment from a settlement.

In addition to these considerations, some Europeans of the colonial period equated aging and death with spiritual visitations, lending to these a supernatural meaning. Devout people, it was believed, would naturally place on a continuum a host of events, like death, famine, or pestilence. Philippe Ariès, discussing the subject of death and Europeans, suggested that before the nineteenth century, death acquired erotic meanings as well. As events, deaths and the wakes that followed them evoked passions, sorrows, and emotions and were even romanticized to such an extent that they symbolized excessiveness.

To understand the Spanish and Native handling of death in the colonial period, however, as mere display is to miss other important features of mortality and aging. Popular, folkloric conceptions of death suggest that both topics, the inevitability of death and the certainty of aging, were linked. Death, in fact, was celebrated in such national rituals as the Day of the Dead (2 November). Picnics, parties, and music accompanied the festive atmosphere that allowed mourners an opportunity to end one phase of their grieving. The popular Spanish adage, "How sad life would be if there were no death," draws the linkage clearly and strongly. It symbolized death's nature as eternal cycle. Deathbed testimonies, as Ariès found in pre-nineteenth-century Europe, and as scholars in the Americas have also discovered, were crucial in this regard. Regularly, prayers recited over the dying were interrupted by spontaneous testimonials to the afflicted's character or good will or devotion to family and friends. Children's deaths and diseases drew similar ceremonial attention. In the case of both adults and children, the longer the passions at the bedsides of the dying, the further removed the possibility that evil spirits, witches, or ghosts remained to take advantage of human frailties.

Medieval European and New World indigenous customs and attitudes were united powerfully in the *mestizo* populations of the Spanish Borderlands. Tradition and adaptation in the colonial period make up the legacy of that era. Long ago, borderland residents transcended through death worldliness; even in tragic circumstances, murders or accidents, the Spanish- and Native-speaking citizens of the New World linked old age and death with life and living. That was one of the important lessons their ceremonies imparted despite programs of colonization and colonialism that caused havoc and ensured suffering in the daily routines of so many. In rituals suggesting finality, they overcame some of the chaos and implanted institutional structures for handling their sorrows.

BIBLIOGRAPHY

Ariès, Philippe. *Centuries of Childhood: A Social History of Family Life.* Translated by Robert Baldick. New York, 1962.

———. *Western Attitudes Toward Death: From the Middle Ages to the Present.* Translated by Patricia M. Ranum. Baltimore, Md., 1974.

Austin, Alfredo López. *Textos de medicina nahuatl.* Mexico City, 1984.

Baytelman, Bernardo. *De enfermos y curanderos: Medicina tradicional en Morelos.* Mexico City, 1986.

Christensen, Bodil, and Samuel Martí. *Brujererías y papel precolombino/Witchcraft and Pre-Columbian Paper.* Mexico City, 1971; 3rd ed., 1979. Bilingual edition.

Coffin, Margaret. *Death in Early America: The History and Folklore of Customs and Superstitions of Early Medicine, Funerals, Burials, and Mourning.* Nashville, Tenn., 1976.

Kalish, Richard A., and David K. Reynolds. *Death and Ethnicity: A Psychocultural Study.* Los Angeles, Calif., 1976.

Lavrin, Asunción, ed. *Sexuality and Marriage in Colonial Latin America.* Lincoln, Nebr., 1989.

Montanos Ferrin, Emma. *La familia en la alta edad media española.* Pamplona, Spain, 1980.

Ochoa Zazueta, Jesús Ángel. *La muerte y los muertos: Culto, servicio, ofrenda y humor de una comunidad.* Mexico City, 1974.

Paxton, Frederick S. *Christianizing Death: The Creation of Ritual Process in Early Medieval Europe.* Ithaca, N.Y., 1990.

Sheehan, Michael M., ed. *Aging and the Aged in Medieval Europe.* Toronto, Ontario, 1990.

Torres, Eliseo. *The Folkhealer: The Mexican-American Tradition of Curanderismo.* Kingsville, Tex., 1983.

Viesca Trevino, Carlos. *Medicina prehispánica de México: El conocimiento médico de los nahuas.* Mexico City, 1986.

Deena J. González

See also **Gender Relations** and **Marriage**.

NATIVE AMERICAN FAMILIES AND LIFE CYCLES

THE CULTURES AND LANGUAGES of the several hundred Indian peoples Europeans encountered in the New World in the seventeenth and eighteenth centuries differed widely. Each people had a unique history and each adapted its culture to the environment in which it lived. Their various social institutions reflect these facts. Size of settlement, seasonal movement, and interpersonal relationships were dependent, to a considerable degree, on the nature of each group's means of subsistence. Other aspects of their cultures, those so different from ones familiar in Western civilization, were part of the complex Native heritage developed on the continent before European contact.

TYPES OF SUBSISTENCE

No group relied on a single source of food, but on some combination with a few species predominating. In areas where the growing season was sufficiently long and there was adequate summer rainfall for growing corn (maize), horticulture was practiced. The principal crops raised were corn, beans, and squash, which the Iroquois called "the three sisters" because like sisters they were found together in the fields. But even in those areas where horticulture was practiced, some or even substantial reliance was still placed on hunting, gathering, and fishing.

In the Arctic region, reliance was placed on hunting of sea mammals (especially seals, walruses, and whales) and caribou; in the Subarctic, on caribou, moose, and fish. In the cultures of the Northwest Coast, salmon were especially important, and that diet was supplemented by other fish, sea mammals, shellfish, berries, and roots. In the arid region west of the Rocky Mountains, an area including California, the Great Basin, and the American Southwest, the gathering of wild plants dominated. In California, acorns were a particularly important component of the peoples' diet, in the Great Basin, piñon nuts were a staple food; in the southwestern part of the Southwest, the seed pods of mesquite trees were harvested. Hunting of large game (especially deer) and small game (particularly rabbits) was secondary. Except along the coast, fish were of relatively little significance. In this western region, only in the Southwest was horticulture important: the Pueblo Indians particularly relied on it, others such as the Piman and River Yumans less so, and a few others, such as the Yavapai, not at all.

In the Plains region, buffalo hunting predominated, greatly facilitated by the introduction of the horse in the seventeenth century. Other animals were of some consequence, and wild plants were important to a somewhat lesser degree; fish were not eaten. A few groups on the

Prairie also relied on horticulture. East of the Mississippi, most groups practiced at least some horticulture, but throughout the region considerable reliance was also placed on hunting (especially deer), fishing, and gathering.

ALLOCATION OF TASKS

Division of labor by age, sex, and talent was universal among North American Indians as it was elsewhere in the world. Children in many instances were incapable of performing the tasks of adults, and the old generally did not have the vigor of the young; nor did the young have the knowledge and experience of the old. Although certain tasks customarily fell to men in some societies that in others were customarily allocated to women, everywhere the men hunted and the women gathered. In the cultural region of most intensive horticulture—that of the Pueblo—men did most of the horticultural work; in the East, where horticulture was of less importance, the women. Some activities, such as rabbit hunts, involved the cooperation of both sexes.

Where houses were relatively large and permanent, they were usually built by men; where they were relatively small and less permanent, they were most often constructed by the women. Men manufactured the tools they used and some of those used by women; women made the baskets and, where it was used, they made pottery. Women most often did the weaving. Men warred and traded; women made the clothing, prepared the food, and took care of children.

Although nowhere were individuals full-time craft specialists, those who had special talents and interests engaged more than others in the group in various of these activities. Other part-time specialists included political leaders, shamans and other religious leaders, and war chiefs.

COMMUNITY ORGANIZATION

Settlement location and size depended largely on availability of resources. Temporary camps were made at favored hunting, fishing, and gathering sites, and most often summer and winter villages were in different locations. Where reliance was placed on plants, both wild and cultivated, the winter settlements were larger than summer ones. Since winter was a time of leisure, the people gathered to spend their time at social activities. Where winter hunting was of importance, they dispersed. Where resources were relatively rich and the people were relatively more sedentary, the houses they built were multifamily homes.

Land generally belonged to those who used it; that is, an individual or group had rights to land for as long as they used it. Where heavy reliance was placed on particular resources, such as fishing sites in the Northwest, horticultural lands in the Pueblo Southwest, and beaver-trapping territories in the sub-Arctic in historic times, rights to these territories were more permanently controlled by individuals or groups. Tools, weapons, household articles, and the like used exclusively by an individual were generally regarded as the property of that individual. Incorporeal property—religious ritual including songs and dances, religious and political positions, and the like—might also be owned by individuals or groups who had exclusive rights to them.

Government rested on personal relations rather than as in Western society on territorial units (for example, township, county, and state). Those speaking the same language felt a special affinity and regarded themselves as a single people. Only exceptionally, however, were such groups united politically into a single unit. For most Indians, the important political unit was local. The village or the band council was the governing body and its chiefs were the political leaders. Council decisions had to be unanimous. If unanimity could not be achieved, a dissenting faction might simply move away, weakening the group. Hence, issues were apt to be discussed until a resolution was found, a procedure that could take considerable time. It was a system in which good orators and oratory were highly valued.

Except where population density was very low—and hence little organization was needed or possible—groups based on ascription or achievement (in a very broad sense of that word) or both were to be found within the society. Important among the latter were the so-called medicine societies, groups whose functions included but were not limited to curing. Important among the former were the clans, usually regarded as kin groups, but perhaps more accurately termed quasi-kin groups.

Throughout North America, polygyny was permitted. The principal exceptions were the Iroquoian-speaking peoples in the East and the Pueblo peoples of the Southwest. Divorce among these monogamous peoples was frequent, and an individual might have several spouses over the course of a lifetime.

Postnuptial residence varied considerably. Neolocal residence was rare; that is, rarely was it customary for a couple to establish a household separate from that of either the husband's or the wife's family. Most often, residence was patrilocal—the couple residing in or near the husband's father's house—or matrilocal—the couple dwelling in or near the wife's mother's house. In Northwest Coast cultures, there was some preference for avunculocal residence, the couple living with the husband's mother's brother. Initial residence might differ from that of a few years after marriage; for example, a couple might reside with the wife's family until their first child was born and subsequently go to live with the husband's family. It might vary with season, with the couple living part of the year with the wife's family and part with the husband's. In some societies, the residence rule did not vary; in others, there was considerable latitude as to whether couples would reside patrilocally or matrilocally. In certain societies, the couple was expected to move into the house of the parent; in certain others, they built a dwelling near that of the parent, but cooperated as a household.

Within this variation some trends are evident. Horticultural peoples and those who had in the recent past been horticulturalists were apt to be matrilocal; the principal exception to that rule was among the neolocal Rio Grande Pueblo. Groups relying heavily on fishing—such as some groups in the Northwest and the sub-Arctic—also tended to be matrilocal. Those who were more reliant on hunting and gathering were apt to be patrilocal or to exhibit no clear rule.

Among a number of North American Indians, particularly the larger and more sedentary groups in the East, the Southwest, and the North-

west Coast, clans were a leading, or even the most important, unit of social organization. Although variously termed clans, gentes, sibs, or even tribes, in many respects they were unlike those kinds of groups in Western society.

The names of the clans were those of animals or sometimes, though rarely, those of plants or natural phenomena. Although most often the name of the clan was that of an animal, there was no belief that the members of the clan were descended from the eponymous clan totem animal. Characteristically, the clans were exogamous; that is, marriage between a man and a woman belonging to the same clan was prohibited even if they could not trace an actual genealogical relationship between them. If two members of the same clan did marry, it was regarded as tantamount to incest. Characteristically also, clans were unilineal: in some societies every individual belonged to the clan of his or her mother (if so, the clan is said to be matrilineal); in others, every individual belonged to the clan of his or her father (if so, the clan is said to be patrilineal). In either case, clan affiliation did not change upon marriage. Nor did the members of a clan live together in a single community. Rather, almost universally members of a number of clans lived together in a village.

Members of a clan regarded each other as a kind of kin and called each other brother and sister; that is, by the terms used for one's own brother and sister. Commonly in North America an individual also called the children of one's mother's sister and father's brother by the terms used for one's own brother and sister. Furthermore, the words for brother and sister were used for those cousins in one's own generation who were descended from a sister of a female ancestor or from a brother of a male ancestor. Thus, an individual addressed and referred both to members of his or her clan and to certain of his or her cousins as brother and sister. This in addition to the fact that clans were exogamous and that clan membership was not an achieved status but an ascribed one has led a number of anthropologists to suggest that all members of a clan are in reality genealogically related, knowledge of the actual genealogical relationship between the lineages comprising the clan having been forgotten. Traditions of the Native Americans themselves, however, give little support to this idea.

Where they do exist, clans have a number of functions. In some Indian societies, they own personal names, each individual being given a name that belongs to the clan. In a number of groups, certain political and religious positions are owned by certain clans, and so may be passed only to members of the clan that possesses them. In some societies, religious ritual and paraphernalia were owned by the clans. Clan members were also expected to provide hospitality to other members visiting the village. When one of their number murdered a member of another clan, the clanspeople were also expected to provide compensation to the deceased's family.

In some Native American societies, the clans were grouped into moieties—that is, in two halves—and in some the moieties are exogamous. Moieties, however, are not necessarily groups of clans. Rather the term "moiety" has been used to refer to any division of the society into two groups regardless of how membership in the moiety is determined. As do the clans, moieties may have various functions. For example, they may form the basis of ceremonial groups or of sides in athletic contests. Commonly also they bury each other's dead.

RITES OF PASSAGE

Rituals marking transition from one stage of life to another were variously observed. Birth and marriage might be celebrated by rituals, but generally they were not elaborate. Rites after birth often included a naming ceremony. Marriage between young people often involved the exchange of gifts between the two families and perhaps a feast; marriages between older individuals were unaccompanied by ritual. Girls' puberty rites, which among other things announced a girl's eligibility for marriage, were common among those groups living west of the Rockies that relied on gathering and for whom resources were relatively rich. First menstruation provided the occasion for the rite. Boys were more frequently initiated as a group. Where such a celebration existed, a boy's puberty rite was often an initiation into a medicine society or other type of sodality. In some regions, notably the Plains, a vision quest undertaken by boys served as a puberty rite; the vision quest undertaken

by both boys and men was for the purpose of obtaining power from the supernatural. Everywhere the ghost was feared, and rites at death usually included some ceremonial component designed to keep the ghost away, to prevent it from bothering the living. Among some groups it was customary to hold a ceremony marking the anniversary of the death. Some groups held an annual ceremony for all the dead of the community.

Pregnant and menstruating women almost universally had to observe certain taboos; customarily, for example, menstruating women avoided contact with men about to go hunting lest they not be successful. Women about to give birth and menstruating women were often segregated in a separate part of the house or in a separate small house built for that purpose.

Most Indian groups used the cradle board, a flat board or framework to which the baby, wrapped in some soft material, was bound. The cradle board could be carried on the mother's back supported by a tumpline over the forehead, leaned up against the house or other support, or suspended from a tree.

Punishment of children was less frequent and less severe than the customary practices in Western society were. Discipline might be meted out by relatives—in matrilineal societies, for instance, by the mother's brother. Learning was most frequently by observation rather than by formal instruction, and as elsewhere children learned much through play. Children, particularly girls, often took care of their younger siblings. Parents and grandparents often gave moral instruction through somewhat formal addresses to a child.

EUROPEAN IMPACT ON NATIVE CULTURES

The effect of European contact varied with time and place. Everywhere, at one time or another, Indian populations were decimated by epidemics. In the Southeast some groups succumbed so severely that they died out before Europeans could record their customs, language, or even their very existence. Along the eastern seaboard, the colonists' desire for Native American land (obtained by purchase or otherwise) and wars between the Europeans and Indians left only a few scattered Native American communities, which adopted a number of the settlers' ways.

West of the Appalachian Mountains the situation was quite different. The fur trade, which was fueled by European desire for beaver fur out of which to make hats, affected all groups in the Northeast. Every Indian society in the area jockeyed for a share of this exchange; those favorably located, especially the Iroquois, rose to a position of great power. Farther west, on the Plains, the introduction of the horse in the late seventeenth century and in the eighteenth century made buffalo hunting easier and therefore more attractive, and a number of groups moved out onto the Plains. The exigencies of buffalo hunting and the contact between Plains peoples led to the development of a distinctive Plains Indian culture. On the Northwest Coast, the combined effects of epidemics introduced by whites (and thus uncertainty as to succession) and large quantities of European goods traded for furs, especially that of the sea otter, led to an efflorescence of the potlatch (the feast at which wealth was exhibited, titles were validated, and status confirmed) and other aspects of Northwest Indian culture in the nineteenth century.

In California, however, the aggregation of various parts of the Native American population into the Spanish missions, sometimes by force, led to a significant loss of traditional ways. Spanish missions among the Pueblo of the Southwest had some impact, but most other peoples of the Southwest had lesser contacts with the Spanish and their cultures were correspondingly less influenced by them.

BIBLIOGRAPHY

Driver, Harold Edson. *Indians of North America.* Chicago, 1961.

Hodge, Frederick Webb, ed. *Handbook of American Indians North of Mexico.* 2 vols. Washington, D.C., 1907–1910.

Martin, M. Marlene, and Timothy J. O'Leary. *Ethnographic Bibliography of North America: Supplement to the 1975 Edition.* 3 vols. New Haven, Conn., 1990.

Murdock, George Peter, and Timothy J. O'Leary. *Ethnographic Bibliography of North America.* 5 vols. 4th ed. New Haven, Conn., 1975.

Sturtevant, William C., ed. *Handbook of North American Indians.* Nine of projected twenty volumes published to date. Washington, D.C., 1978–.

Elisabeth Tooker

SEE ALSO **The First Americans; Native American Economies;** and **Native American Religions.**